THE ANALYTICAL GREEK LEXICON OF THE NEW TESTAMENT

THE ANALYTICAL GREEK LEXICON OF THE NEW TESTAMENT

GEORGE V. WIGRAM

EVERY WORD AND INFLECTION OF
THE GREEK NEW TESTAMENT
ARRANGED ALPHABETICALLY AND
WITH GRAMMATICAL ANALYSES

A Complete Series of Greek Paradigms,
With Grammatical Remarks and Explanations

HENDRICKSON PUBLISHERS, INC.
PEABODY, MASSACHUSETTS 01960

THE ANALYTICAL GREEK LEXICON
OF THE NEW TESTAMENT

Originally published by Samuel Bagster & Sons, Ltd., London, 1852.

First Printing October 1983

Printed in the United States of America

ISBN 0-913573-05-1

PREFACE.

THE ANALYTICAL GREEK LEXICON to the New Testament has been compiled for the purpose of affording the student of the original language of the Evangelists and Apostles of our Lord, the same assistance which is furnished by the Publishers' similar Lexicon to the Books of the Hebrew and Chaldee Scriptures.

The difficulties which have to be encountered in the study of the New Testament, though of a different kind from those which are presented by Shemitic languages, are nevertheless sufficiently considerable to call for an equally lucid and exhaustive explanation, especially in the case of students who, from whatever cause, have not gone through the entire curriculum of a Classical education, but who desire to obtain such knowledge of the Sacred Greek tongue as may be both interesting and instructive by studying for themselves.

These difficulties are in great part the result of the numerous tenses by which the Greek Verb is enriched with niceties of meaning not existing in Hebrew They are increased by the many Irregular and Defective Verbs of which the obsolete roots are not easily traced, and in some cases doubtful. To remove these and other impediments to the student's progress is the object of the present work. In addition to the ordinary contents of a Greek-English Lexicon, with the meanings classified according to their derivation, its distinguishing feature is, that every word of the New Testament, exactly as it stands in the original text, however inflected or declined, is here set down in precise Alphabetical order, with a complete grammatical Analysis and indication of its root, so that the entire elucidation of whatever difficulty may occur can instantly be found without any further search or trouble.

To enhance the critical value of the work, Various Readings of importance, with the authorities supporting them, are incorporated in their respective places; Concordantial References to the whereabouts of words are in great measure supplied; and an extensive grammatical Introduction, comprising Paradigms of the Nouns and Verbs, with full explanatory remarks, is prefixed. By comparison with these, the student, if so disposed, can readily verify the parsing of any word in the Lexicon.

ABBREVIATIONS.

absol.	absolutely, without case or adjunct.
acc.	accusative case
adj.	adjective
adv	adverb.
Æol.	Æolic dialect.
al.	*alibi*, in other texts.
al freq.	*alibi frequenter*, in many other texts.
aor.	aorist.
apoc.	apocope, cutting off the last syllable.
Aram.	Aramæan dialect.
Att.	Attic dialect.
bis	twice.
compar	comparative.
conj.	conjunction.
contr.	contraction, contracted.
dat.	dative case.
dimin.	diminutive.
enclit.	enclitic, throwing the accent on the preceding syllable.
&, et,	and.
&c., etc.	*et cætera*.
e. g.	*exempli gratia*, for example.
f., fem.	feminine.
f., fut.	future tense.
fr.	from.
gen	genitive case.
genr.	generally, in a general sense, not affected by adjuncts.
heb.	Hebrew, or the Hebrew idiom.
i. e.	*id est*, that is.
id., idem.	the same.
imp., imper., imperat.	imperative mood.

imperf.	imperfect tense.
impers.	impersonal.
impl.	implication.
ind.	indicative mood.
indec.	indeclinable.
inf., infin.	infinitive mood.
interj.	interjection.
interrog.	interrogation.
intrans.	intransitive.
Ion.	Ionic dialect.
i. q.	idem quod, the same as.
L. G.	later Greek.
lit.	literally.
LXX.	Septuagint.
m., masc.	masculine.
met.	metaphorically.
metath.	metathesis, the transposition of letters.
meton.	by metonymy.
mid.	middle voice
n., neut.	neuter.
N. T.	New Testament.
obsol.	obsolete.
O. T.	Old Testament.
om.	*omittit*, or *omittunt*.
opt., optat	optative mood.
part.	participle.
partic.	particle.
pass.	passive voice.
perf.	perfect tense.
p., pers.	person.
pl., plur	plural.
pluperf.	pluperfect tense.
pr.	properly, proper.
prep.	preposition.
pron.	pronoun.
q. d.	*quasi dicas*, as if, as it were.
q. v.	*quod vide*, which see.
sc.	*scilicet*, that is to say.

seq.	*sequente*, as seq. gen., *sequente genitivo*, with a genitive following.
s., sing.	singular. The figures placed before sing. or pl. denote the person.
spc.	specially, i. e. in a special and local meaning.
subj.	subjunctive mood.
subs.	substantive.
superl.	superlative.
sync.	syncope, contraction.
synec.	synecdoche.
ter	thrice.
trans.	transitively.
trop.	tropically, i. e. turned aside from its strict literal meaning.
v.	*vel*, or.
v. r.	a various reading to the common text.
viz.	*videlicet*, that is, namely.
voc.	vocative case.

ὁ attached to a word shows it to be masculine; ἡ, to be feminine; ὁ, ἡ, to be common, i. e. masculine or feminine; and τό, to be neuter.

§, tab., rem., refer to sections, tables, and remarks in the Tables of Paradigms.

AUTHORITIES REFERRED TO.

A. B. C. D.	Codices.
Rec.	*Textus Receptus*, the Received Text
Gb.	Griesbach.
Sch.	Scholz.
Ln.	Lachmann.
Tdf.	Tischendorf.
Elz.	Elzevir.
Ste.	Stephens

THE CONTENTS.

THE CONTENTS.

TABLES OF PARADIGMS

OF

GREEK DECLENSIONS AND CONJUGATIONS,

WITH

EXPLANATORY GRAMMATICAL REMARKS.

SECTION I.—THE ARTICLE.

TABLE A.

Singular.

	Masc.	*Fem.*	*Neut.*	
Nom.	ὁ,	ἡ,	τό,	*the.*
Gen.	τοῦ,	τῆς,	τοῦ,	*of the.*
Dat.	τῷ,	τῇ,	τῷ,	*to the.*
Acc.	τόν,	τήν,	τό,	*the.*

Plural.

	Masc.	*Fem.*	*Neut.*	
Nom.	οἱ,	αἱ,	τά,	*the.*
Gen.	τῶν,	τῶν,	τῶν,	*of the.*
Dat.	τοῖς,	ταῖς,	τοῖς,	*to the.*
Acc.	τούς,	τάς,	τά,	*the.*

Dual.

	Masc.	*Fem.*	*Neut.*	
Nom. Acc.	τώ,	τά,	τώ,	*the two.*
Gen. Dat.	τοῖν,	ταῖν,	τοῖν,	*of, to, the two.*

REMARKS.

1. The Article has no vocative. ὦ, which sometimes precedes a noun in the vocative, is an interjection.

2. The Article takes the consonant τ in every case, except in the nom. sing. masc. and fem. ὁ, ἡ, and in the nom. pl. masc. and fem. οἱ, αἱ, where the τ is superseded by the rough breathing (ʽ).*

3. To every declension the dative sing. ends in ι: but when ι unites, to form a diphthong, with a preceding *long* vowel, as is the case in the dative of the first and second declensions, it is, by a general rule of the language, *subscribed.* The same vowel also invariably enters into the termination of the dative plural.

4. The gen. pl., in all genders, ends in ων. This is the case also in every declension, without exception.

* The breathings, or aspirations, are two, the smooth and the rough. The former is not heard in pronunciation; the latter answers to our aspirated *h*. They are placed on initial vowels and diphthongs, e. g. ἐγώ, *I*, ἡμεῖς, *we*; αὐτός, *himself*, αὑτοῦ (for ἑαυτοῦ) *of himself.*

The vowel υ always receives the rough breathing; the other vowels the smooth or the rough, according to circumstances.

The consonant ρ is the only one which receives a breathing. This is invariably, when ρ is single, the rough; but when ρ is doubled, the first has the smooth, the second the rough breathing, e. g. ἀῤῥαβών, *an earnest.*

It may here be mentioned, that there are three accents, the acute (´), the grave (`), and the circumflex (῀); useful not merely as, to a certain extent, guides in pronunciation, but also as distinguishing words of the same orthography, but very different signification, according to the position of the accent; e. g. πατροκτόνος, *a parricide*, πατρόκτονος (in a passive sense), *killed by one's father.*

SECTION II.—NOUNS SUBSTANTIVE.

TABLE B.—FIRST DECLENSION

(a)	SINGULAR.		PLURAL.		DUAL.*
Nom.	ἡ κεφαλή, *the head.*	Nom.	αἱ κεφαλαί, *the heads.*	Nom. Acc. Voc.	τὰ κεφαλά, *the two heads*
Gen.	τῆς κεφαλῆς	Gen.	τῶν κεφαλῶν	Gen. Dat.	ταῖν κεφαλαῖν.
Dat.	τῇ κεφαλῇ	Dat.	ταῖς κεφαλαῖς		
Acc.	τὴν κεφαλήν	Acc.	τὰς κεφαλάς		
Voc.	κεφαλή.	Voc.	κεφαλαί.		

(b)	SINGULAR.		PLURAL.		DUAL.
Nom.	ἡ ἡμέρα, *the day.*	Nom.	αἱ ἡμέραι, *the days.*	Nom. Acc. Voc.	τὰ ἡμέρα, *the two days*
Gen.	τῆς ἡμέρας	Gen.	τῶν ἡμερῶν	Gen. Dat.	ταῖν ἡμέραιν.
Dat.	τῇ ἡμέρᾳ	Dat.	ταῖς ἡμέραις		
Acc.	τὴν ἡμέραν	Acc.	τὰς ἡμέρας		
Voc.	ἡμέρα.	Voc.	ἡμέραι.		

(c)	SINGULAR.		PLURAL.		DUAL.
Nom.	ὁ ποιητής, *the poet.*	Nom.	οἱ ποιηταί	Nom. Acc. Voc	τὼ ποιητα
Gen.	τοῦ ποιητοῦ	Gen.	τῶν ποιητῶν	Gen. Dat.	τοῖν ποιηταῖν.
Dat.	τῷ ποιητῇ	Dat.	τοῖς ποιηταῖς		
Acc.	τὸν ποιητήν	Acc.	τοὺς ποιητάς		
Voc.	ποιητά.	Voc.	ποιηταί.		

(d)	SINGULAR.		PLURAL.		DUAL.
Nom.	ὁ νεανίας, *the young man.*	Nom.	οἱ νεανίαι	Nom. Acc. Voc.	τὼ νεανία
Gen.	τοῦ νεανίου	Gen.	τῶν νεανιῶν	Gen. Dat.	τοῖν νεανίαιν.
Dat.	τῷ νεανίᾳ	Dat.	τοῖς νεανίαις		
Acc.	τὸν νεανίαν	Acc.	τοὺς νεανίας		
Voc.	νεανία.	Voc.	νεανίαι.		

REMARKS.

1. All nouns ending in η keep that vowel in every case of the singular, and are declined like κεφαλή.

2. All nouns ending in ρα and α *pure* (i.e. preceded by a vowel), as φιλία, *friendship*, keep α in every case, like ἡμέρα.

But in the New Testament the word σπεῖρα, *a band or troop*, has gen. σπείρης; Ac. 10. 1; 21. 31; 27. 1. This is according to the Ionic dialect.

3. All other nouns ending in α, preceded neither by a vowel nor ρ, form the gen. in ης, and the dat. in ῃ. In the acc. they resume α; e.g.

Nom. Voc.	δόξα, *glory.*	Dat.	δόξῃ.
Gen.	δόξης	Acc.	δόξαν.

The plural and dual are always terminated like those of the feminine article.

4. Nouns in ης and ας form the gen. sing. in ου, like the masc. article. In the other cases, those in ης retain η, as in κεφαλή; those in ας keep α, as in ἡμέρα.

The Doric termination α (contr. from αο) for ου, is found in Attic Greek, especially in the case of proper names: e.g. Καλλίας, gen. Καλλία; so also Θωμᾶς, *Thomas*, gen. Θωμᾶ, &c.

5. Such words as μνᾶ, gen. μνᾶς (contr. from μνάα, μνάας), *a mina or pound*, are declined like ἡμέρα.

Foreign names in ης sometimes form the gen. in η; e.g. Ἰωσῆς, *Joses*, gen. Ἰωσῆ.

6. The voc. sing. of nouns in ης and ας is formed by rejecting the σ of the nominative.

But most nouns in ης form the voc. in α *short*, especially those in της, as ποιητής, voc. ποιητά.

* In order to give a complete view of the Declensions, the Dual number is here inserted, although it does not appear that any instance of it occurs in the New Testament.

Those in πης, compounded of ὤψ, *an eye*, as κυνώπης, *shameless*, voc. κυνῶπα.

Compounds of μετρεω, *to measure*, as γεωμέτρης, *a geometer*, voc. γεωμέτρα.

Of πωλέω, *to sell*, as βιβλιοπώλης, *a bookseller*, voc. βιβλιοπῶλα.

Of τρίβω, *to wear*, hence *to exercise*, as παιδοτρίβης, *a trainer of boys*, voc. παιδοτρίβα.

SECTION III.

TABLE C.—SECOND DECLENSION.

(a) Singular.	Plural.	Dual.
Nom. ὁ λόγος, *the word.*	Nom. οἱ λόγοι	Nom. Acc. Voc. τὼ λόγω
Gen. τοῦ λόγου	Gen. τῶν λόγων	Gen. Dat. τοῖν λόγοιν.
Dat. τῷ λόγῳ	Dat. τοῖς λόγοις	
Acc. τὸν λόγον	Acc. τοὺς λόγους	
Voc. λόγε.	Voc. λόγοι.	

(b) Singular.	Plural.	Dual.
Nom. ἡ ὁδός, *the road.*	Nom. αἱ ὁδοί	Nom. Acc Voc. τὰ ὁδώ
Gen. τῆς ὁδοῦ	Gen. τῶν ὁδῶν	Gen. Dat. ταῖν ὁδοῖν.
Dat. τῇ ὁδῷ	Dat. ταῖς ὁδοῖς	
Acc. τὴν ὁδόν	Acc. τὰς ὁδούς	
Voc. ὁδέ.	Voc. ὁδοί.	

(c) Singular.	Plural	Dual.
Nom. τὸ δῶρον, *the gift.*	Nom. τὰ δῶρα	Nom. Acc. Voc. τὼ δώρω
Gen. τοῦ δώρου	Gen. τῶν δώρων	Gen. Dat. τοῖν δώροιν.
Dat. τῷ δώρῳ	Dat. τοῖς δώροις	
Acc. τὸ δῶρον	Acc. τὰ δῶρα	
Voc. δῶρον.	Voc. δῶρα.	

ATTIC DECLENSION.

(d) Singular.	Plural.	Dual.
Nom. ὁ λαγώς, *the hare.*	Nom. οἱ λαγῴ (ῳ for οι)	Nom. Acc. Voc. τὼ λαγώ
Gen. τοῦ λαγώ (ω for ου)	Gen. τῶν λαγῶν	Gen. Dat. τοῖν λαγῷν (ῳν for οιν).
Dat. τῷ λαγῷ	Dat. τοῖς λαγῷς (ῳς for οις)	
Acc. τὸν λαγών	Acc. τοὺς λαγώς (ως for ους)	
Voc. λαγώς.	Voc. λαγῷ (ῳ for οι).	

(e) Singular.	Plural.	Dual.
Nom. τὸ ἀνώγεων, *the dining-room.*	Nom. τὰ ἀνώγεω (ω for α)	Nom. Acc. Voc. τὼ ἀνώγεω
Gen. τοῦ ἀνώγεω (ω for ου)	Gen. τῶν ἀνώγεων	Gen. Dat. τοῖν ἀνώγεῳν (ῳν for οιν).
Dat. τῷ ἀνώγεῳ	Dat. τοῖς ἀνώγεῳς (ῳς for οις)	
Acc. τὸ ἀνώγεων	Acc. τὰ ἀνώγεω	
Voc. ἀνώγεων.	Voc. ἀνώγεω.	

REMARKS.

1. This declension comprises masc. and. fem. nouns in ος, which follow the terminations of the masc. article, and form the voc. in ε; also neuter nouns in ον, which follow the neuter article. The gen. sing. is in ου. The Attics often make the voc. like the nom.: ὁ Θεός, as well as Θεέ, occurs as the voc. of Θεός.

2. The neuters have the nom., acc., and voc. cases alike in the singular and plural, and in the plural these cases (except in the Attic declension) end in α.

3. Some nouns of this declension, the terminations of which are preceded by ε, ου, ο, are contracted in all cases; e. g.

Masculine.	*Neuter.*
N. νόος, νοῦς, *the mind.*	N. ὀστέον, ὀστοῦν, *a bone.*
G. νόου, νοῦ, &c.	G. ὀστέου, ὀστοῦ, &c.
No Plural.	Plural ὀστέα, ὀστᾶ, &c.

So πλόος, πλοῦς, *a voyage*, pl. πλόοι, πλοῖ; πλόων πλῶν; πλόοις. πλοῖς; πλόους, πλοῦς.

4. Attic form. The Attics change the termination ο into ω in all cases of this declension. Where an ι occurs it is *subscribed;* where an υ it is rejected. The vocative is always like the nominative. The three *corresponding* cases of the plural are in ω instead of α.

5. The Attics frequently omit the ν of the acc. sing.: e. g. λαγώ, for λαγών; Κῶ, the island *Cos*, for Κῶν; Ἀπολλώ, for Ἀπολλών, &c.

6. The two first declensions are termed *parisyllabic*, as having in each case the same number of syllables. The third declension is called *imparisyllabic*, because it has in the gen. and following cases one syllable more than in the nom. and voc. singular.

SECTION IV.

TABLE D.—THIRD DECLENSION.

(a) Singular.		Plural.		Dual.	
Nom.	ὁ Ἕλλην, *the Greek.*	Nom.	οἱ Ἕλληνες	Nom. Acc. Voc.	τὼ Ἕλληνε
Gen.	τοῦ Ἕλληνος	Gen.	τῶν Ἑλλήνων	Gen. Dat.	τοῖν Ἑλλήνοιν.
Dat.	τῷ Ἕλληνι	Dat.	τοῖς Ἕλλησι		
Acc.	τὸν Ἕλληνα	Acc.	τοὺς Ἕλληνας		
Voc.	Ἕλλην.	Voc.	Ἕλληνες.		
(b) Singular.		**Plural.**		**Dual.**	
Nom.	ἡ λαμπάς, *the lamp.*	Nom.	αἱ λαμπάδες	Nom. Acc. Voc.	τὰ λαμπάδε
Gen.	τῆς λαμπάδος	Gen.	τῶν λαμπάδων	Gen. Dat.	ταῖν λαμπάδοιν.
Dat.	τῇ λαμπάδι	Dat.	ταῖς λαμπάσι		
Acc.	τὴν λαμπάδα	Acc.	τὰς λαμπάδας		
Voc.	λαμπάς.	Voc.	λαμπάδες.		
(c) Singular.		**Plural.**		**Dual.**	
Nom.	τὸ σῶμα, *the body.*	Nom.	τὰ σώματα	Nom. Acc. Voc.	τὼ σώματε
Gen.	τοῦ σώμᾰτος	Gen.	τῶν σωμάτων	Gen. Dat.	τοῖν σωμάτοιν.
Dat.	τῷ σώματι	Dat.	τοῖς σώμασι		
Acc.	τὸ σῶμα	Acc.	τὰ σώματα		
Voc.	σῶμα.	Voc.	σώματα.		

REMARKS.

1. This declension contains nouns of all genders, and includes nine terminations: four vowels, α, ι, υ, ω, and five consonants, ν, ρ, σ, ξ, ψ.

The vocative is generally like the nominative. Exceptions will be indicated shortly

2. The gen. sing. is always in ος. The consonant which precedes this termination is found in all the following cases, except (generally) the dat. pl., rules for the formation of which will presently be given.

The nom. in this declension is not the *primitive form* of the noun. This is to be found in the gen. by throwing away the termination ος, according to the following rules —

(*a*) A mute of the first order* (π, β, φ) before the termination of the gen. indicates a nom. in ψ; e. g. gen. Ἄραβος, nom. Ἄραψ, *an Arabian;* ὠπός, nom. ὤψ, *an eye.*

(*b*) A mute of the second order (κ, γ, χ) indicates a nom. in ξ; e. g. gen. ἅρπαγος, nom. ἅρπαξ, *rapacious;* ὄνυχος, nom. ὄνυξ, *a nail, claw;* λάρυγγος, nom. λάρυγξ, *the throat.* But νύξ, *night*, makes νυκτός.

(*c*) A mute of the third order (τ, δ, θ) indicates a nom. in ς; e. g. gen. ἐλπίδος, nom. ἐλπίς, *hope;* γέλωτος, nom. γέλως, *laughter.* Except neuters in μα, gen. ματος, as σῶμα, σώματος; also ἧπαρ, ἥπατος, *the liver;* ὕδωρ, ὕδατος,

* The following Table of Mutes may be found useful:—

	First Order. *Labials.*	Second Order. *Gutturals.*	Third Order. *Dentals.*
Smooth	Π.	Κ.	Τ.
Middle	Β.	Γ.	Δ.
Aspirate	Φ.	Χ.	Θ.

The letters of each column are of the same nature, and are, in certain circumstances, interchanged.

If two mutes concur in the same syllable, *both* must be smooth, as ἑπτά, *seven;* middle, as ἕβδομος, *seventh;* or aspirate, as φθόνος, *envy.* Two successive syllables seldom commence with an aspirate: τρέχω, not θρέχω, *I run;* τριχός, not θριχός, from θρίξ, *a hair.*

water; φρέαρ, φρέατος, *a pit*; μέλι, μέλιτος, *honey*; and a few other neuters.

(*d*) ντ indicates ς or ν; e.g. gen. γίγαντος, nom. γίγας, *a giant*; ὀδόντος, nom. ὀδούς, *a tooth*; δράκοντος, nom. δράκων, *a dragon.*

(*e*) ν indicates ς or ν; e.g. μέλανος, nom. μέλας, *black*; φρενός, nom. φρήν, *the mind.*

(*f*) ρ indicates ρ; e.g. θηρός, nom. θήρ, *a wild beast*; πυρός, nom. πῦρ, *fire.*

(*g*) ος *pure* indicates ς; e.g. τριήρεος, nom. τριήρης, *a galley.*

3. (*a*) The dat. pl. always ends in σι. It is formed from the dat. sing. by inserting σ before ι; e.g. μάρτυρ, *a witness*, dat. sing. μάρτυρι, dat. pl. μάρτυρσι; (μάρτυσι, Ac. 10. 41;) ῥήτωρ, *an orator*, . . . ῥήτορι, . . . ῥήτορσι; κόραξ, *a raven*, . . . κόρακι, . . . κόραξι (for κόρακσι).

(*b*) If a mute of the third order (τ, δ, θ) occurs in the sing. it is rejected in the pl.; e.g. λαμπάς, λαμπάδι, λαμπάσι; σῶμα, σώματος, σώμασι; οὖς, ὠτός, ὠσί; πούς, ποδός, ποσί.

(*c*) ν is also rejected, whether alone, as Ἕλλην, Ἕλληνι, Ἕλλησι, or joined to a mute of the third order, as λύσας, *having loosed*, λύσαντι, λύσασι.

(*d*) If the dat. sing. ends in οντι, ντ being rejected, the ο is changed into ου; e.g. λέων, *a lion*, λέοντι, λέουσι.

(*e*) If the dat. sing. ends in εντι, ντ being rejected, the ε is changed into ει; e.g. λυθείς, *having been loosed*, λυθέντι, λυθεῖσι.

4. Some nouns in ις and υς (and a few in ους) take two terminations in the acc. sing., α and ν; e.g. ἔρις, ἔριδος, *strife*, acc. ἔριδα and ἔριν; (ἔριν in the New Test.;) pl. ἔριδες and ἔρεις; χάρις, χάριτος, *grace*, acc. χάριτα and χάριν; κλείς, κλειδός, *a key*, acc. κλεῖδα and κλεῖν.

Ὄρνις, ὄρνιθος, *a bird*, makes acc. sing. ὄρνιθα and ὄρνιν; acc. pl. ὄρνιθας and ὄρνις.

With the exception of κλείς, nouns which have this termination ν in the acc. (unless the gen. ends in ος *pure*) must have the nom. sing. *unaccented* on the last syllable; e.g. ἔρις, χάρις.

SECTION V.

TABLE E.—CONTRACTED NOUNS.

(*a*)

	Singular.		Plural.		Dual.
Nom.	ἡ τριήρης, *the galley.*	Nom.	αἱ τριήρεες, τριήρεις	Nom. Acc. Voc.	τὰ τριήρεε
Gen.	τῆς τριήρεος, τριήρους	Gen.	τῶν τριηρέων, τριηρῶν	Gen. Dat.	ταῖν τριηρέοιν, τριηροῖν
Dat.	τῇ τριήρεϊ, τριήρει	Dat.	ταῖς τριήρεσι		
Acc.	τὴν τριήρεα, τριήρη	Acc.	τὰς τριήρεας, τριήρεις		
Voc.	τρίηρες.	Voc.	τριήρεες, τριήρεις.		

(*b*)

	Singular.		Plural.		Dual.
Nom.	τὸ τεῖχος, *the wall.*	Nom.	τὰ τείχεα, τείχη	Nom. Acc. Voc.	τὼ τείχεε
Gen.	τοῦ τείχεος, τείχους	Gen.	τῶν τειχέων, τειχῶν	Gen. Dat.	τοῖν τειχέοιν, τειχοῖν.
Dat.	τῷ τείχεϊ, τείχει	Dat.	τοῖς τείχεσι		
Acc.	τὸ τεῖχος	Acc.	τὰ τείχεα, τείχη		
Voc.	τεῖχος.	Voc.	τείχεα, τείχη.		

(*c*)

	Singular. Ionic.	Attic.*		Plural. Ionic.	Attic.		Dual. Ionic.	Attic.
Nom.	ἡ πόλις, *the city.*		Nom.	αἱ πόλιες, πόλεες,	πόλεις	Nom. Acc. Voc.	πόλιε, πόλεε	
Gen.	τῆς πόλιος, πόλεος,	πόλεως	Gen.	τῶν πολίων, πολέων,	πόλεων	Gen. Dat.	πολίοιν, πολέοιν,	πόλεοιν.
Dat.	τῇ πόλι, πόλεϊ,	πόλει	Dat.	ταῖς πόλισι, πόλεσι				
Acc.	τὴν πόλιν		Acc.†	τὰς πόλιας, πόλεας,	πόλεις			
Voc.	πόλι.		Voc.	πόλιες, πόλεες,	πόλεις.			

(*d*)

	Singular.		Plural.		Dual.
Nom.	ὁ βασιλεύς, *the king.*	Nom.	οἱ βασιλέες, βασιλεῖς (& -λῆς)	Nom. Acc. Voc.	βασιλέε
Gen.	τοῦ βασιλέος, βασιλέως	Gen.	τῶν βασιλέων	Gen. Dat.	βασιλέοιν.
Dat.	τῷ βασιλέϊ, βασιλεῖ	Dat.	τοῖς βασιλεῦσι		
Acc.	τὸν βασιλέα, βασιλῆ (rarely)	Acc.	τοὺς βασιλέας, βασιλεῖς		
Voc.	βασιλεῦ.	Voc.	βασιλέες, βασιλεῖς.		

* The Attic form only of this word occurs in the New Testament.

† The acc. pl. is also sometimes contracted into ις, πόλιας, πόλις.

TABLE E.—CONTRACTED NOUNS.—(*Continued.*)

(*e*) SINGULAR.	PLURAL.	DUAL.
Nom. ὁ πέλεκυς, *the hatchet.*	Nom. οἱ πελέκεες, εις	Nom. Acc. Voc. πελέκεε
Gen. τοῦ πελέκεος, εως	Gen. τῶν πελεκέων	Gen. Dat. πελεκέοιν.
Dat. τῷ πελέκεϊ, ει	Dat. τοῖς πελέκεσι	
Acc. τὸν πέλεκυν	Acc. τοὺς πελέκεας, εις	
Voc. πέλεκυ.	Voc. πελέκεες, εις.	

(*f*) SINGULAR.	PLURAL.	DUAL.
Nom. τὸ ἄστυ, *the city.*	Nom. τὰ ἄστεα, ἄστη	Nom. Acc. Voc. ἄστεε
Gen. τοῦ ἄστεος, εως	Gen. τῶν ἀστέων	Gen. Dat. ἀστέοιν.
Dat. τῷ ἄστεϊ, ει	Dat. τοῖς ἄστεσι	
Acc. τὸ ἄστυ	Acc. τὰ ἄστεα, ἄστη	
Voc. ἄστυ.	Voc. ἄστεα, ἄστη.	

(*g*) SINGULAR.	PLURAL.	DUAL.
Nom. ὁ ἰχθύς, *the fish.*	Nom. οἱ ἰχθύες, ἰχθῦς	Nom. Acc. Voc. ἰχθύε
Gen. τοῦ ἰχθύος	Gen. τῶν ἰχθύων	Gen. Dat. ἰχθύοιν
Dat. τῷ ἰχθύϊ	Dat. τοῖς ἰχθύσι	
Acc. τὸν ἰχθύν	Acc. τοὺς ἰχθύας, ἰχθῦς	
Voc. ἰχθύ.	Voc. ἰχθύες, ἰχθῦς.	

(*h*) SINGULAR	(*i*) SINGULAR.
Nom. ἡ αἰδώς, *modesty*	Nom. ἡ ἠχώ, *the echo.*
Gen. τῆς αἰδόος, αἰδοῦς	Gen. τῆς ἠχόος, ἠχοῦς
Dat. τῇ αἰδόϊ, αἰδοῖ	Dat. τῇ ἠχόϊ, ἠχοῖ
Acc. τὴν αἰδόα, αἰδῶ	Acc. τὴν ἠχόα, ἠχώ
Voc. αἰδοῖ.	Voc. ἠχοῖ.

The plural and dual are declined like λόγοι, λόγων; e. g. *αἰδοί, αἰδῶν, αἰδοῖς, αἰδούς.*

(*j*) SINGULAR.	PLURAL.	DUAL.
Nom. τὸ κέρας, *the horn.*	Nom. τὰ κέρατα (κέραα), κέρα	Nom. Acc. Voc. κέρατε, κέραε, κέρα
Gen. τοῦ κέρᾱτος (κέραος), κέρως	Gen. τῶν κεράτων (κεράων), κερῶν	Gen. Dat. κεράτοιν, κεράοιν, κερῷν.
Dat. τῷ κέρατι (κέραϊ), κέρᾳ	Dat. τοῖς κέρασι	
Acc. τὸ κέρας	Acc. τὰ κέρατα (κέραα), κέρα	
Voc. κέρας.	Voc. κέρατα (κέραα), κέρα.	

REMARKS.

1. The above ten nouns present a model of all the varieties which can occur. (See rem. 4.) They are all of the third declension. The gen. sing. ends in ος *pure*, except nouns in ρας, in which the contraction is formed after throwing out the τ of the gen.; e. g. κέρατος, κέραος, κέρως.

2. The contracted nom. and acc. pl. are always alike. The termination ης is confined to proper names, and adjectives (such as ἀληθής), τριήρης itself being an adjective, at full length τριήρης ναῦς, *a vessel with three tiers of oars.*

3. The termination ος is limited to neuter nouns. The gen. pl. is often uncontracted: e. g. ἄνθεων, *of flowers* (from ἄνθος), not ἀνθῶν.

4. The termination ι is also confined to neuter, and mostly foreign, nouns: e. g. σίνηπι (σίναπι, New Test.), *mustard*, gen. σινήπιος, εος, εως; dat. σινήπιι, εϊ, ει; pl. σινήπια, σινήπεα; πέπερι, *pepper*; στίμμι, *antimony*, &c. The only true Greek word ending in ι seems to be μέλι, *honey*, declined like σῶμα, σώματος (μέλι, μέλιτος).

5. The termination ευς is found only in masculine nouns; e. g. βασιλεύς, *a king*, βραβεύς, *an umpire*, ἱερεύς, *a priest*, φονεύς, *a murderer*, &c.

Nouns in υς, gen. εος, are like βασιλεύς, except that the acc. sing. is in υν; e. g. πῆχυς, *a cubit*, gen. εος, εως, acc. πῆχυν.

6. Nouns in υς, gen. υος, are contracted in the plural in ῦς; e. g. nom. ἰχθύες, ἰχθῦς, acc. ἰχθύας, ἰχθῦς.

7. All nouns ending in ως, ω (αἰδώς, ἠχώ), are feminine. The last form in the above Table comprehends only

neuter nouns in ρας and ας *pure;* e. g. τέρας, *a wonder;* γῆρας, *old age;* κρέας, *flesh*, &c.

3. (*a*) The dat. pl. is never contracted, because its termination σι commences with a consonant. The gen. plur. is sometimes contracted, but only in nouns ending in ης, ος, and ας.

Ις and υς always form the acc. sing. in ν.

(*b*) Lastly, it may be observed, that as we have πόλεις, πόλιας, πόλις, so the contraction sometimes occurs even in nouns which have a consonant before the termination; e. g. acc. pl. ὄρνιθας, ὄρνις, *birds;* κλεῖδας, κλεῖς, from κλείς, κλειδός, *a key.*

SECTION VI.

IRREGULARITIES OF DECLENSION.

REMARKS.

1. Some nouns in ηρ, gen. ερος, in certain cases throw out the ε, though the termination be preceded by a consonant: they form the dat. pl. in ασι.

Singular.		Plural.	
Nom. ὁ πατήρ, *the father.*	Dat. τῷ (πατέρι) πατρί	Nom. πατέρες	Dat. πατράσι (ᾰ)
Gen. του (πατέρος) πατρός	Acc. τὸν πατέρα.	Gen. πατέρων	Acc. πατέρας.
Voc. πάτερ.			

2. So also μήτηρ, *mother*, and θυγάτηρ, *daughter.* Η γαστήρ, *the belly*, dat. pl. γαστῆρσι, rarely γαστράσι.

In ὁ ἀνήρ, *the man*, we find the vowel ε rejected in all cases, except the voc. sing., and supplied by δ, for the sake of euphony, or better pronunciation.

Singular.	Plural.	Dual.
Nom. ὁ ἀνήρ	Nom. οἱ (ἀνέρες) ἄνδρες	Nom. Acc. Voc. τὼ (ἀνέρε) ἄνδρε
Gen. τοῦ (ἀνέρος) ἀνδρός	Gen. τῶν (ἀνέρων) ἀνδρῶν	Gen. Dat. τοῖν (ἀνέροιν) ἀνδροῖν.
Dat. τῷ (ἀνέρι) ἀνδρί	Dat. τοῖς ἀνδράσι (ᾰ)	
Acc. τὸν (ἀνέρα) ἄνδρα	Acc. τοὺς (ἀνέρας) ἄνδρας	
Voc. ἄνερ.	Voc. (ἀνέρες) ἄνδρες.	

3. A very small number of nouns belong to the parisyllabic form of declension; e. g. nom. Ἰησοῦς, *Jesus*, gen. and dat. Ἰησοῦ, acc. Ἰησοῦν, voc. Ἰησοῦ.

4. Most belong to the imparisyllabic declension. A few are here given:—

(*a*) Nom. Ζεύς, *Jupiter*, gen. Διός, dat. Διί, acc. Δία, voc. Ζεῦ.

(*b*) Nom. γυνή, *a woman*, gen. γυναικός, and the rest of the cases as if from nom. γύναιξ, except voc. sing. γύναι. Nom. γάλα, *milk*, gen. γάλακτος, dat. γάλακτι, acc. γάλα.

(*c*) Nom. ἀστήρ, *a star*, gen. ἀστέρος: the irregularity is in the dat. pl. ἀστράσι.

(*d*) ἄρς (not used in nom.), *a lamb*, gen. ἀρνός, dat. ἀρνί, dat. pl. ἀρνάσι.

(*e*) Nom. κύων, *a dog*, gen. κυνός, dat. κυνί, acc. κύνα, voc. κύον. Pl. κύνες, κυνῶν, κυσί, κύνας.

(*f*) Nom. ἡ χείρ, *the hand*, gen. χειρός, dat. χειρί, acc. χεῖρα. Pl. χεῖρες, χειρῶν, χερσί, χεῖρας. Dual χεῖρε, χειροῖν, and χεροῖν.

(*g*) ἡ ναῦς, *the ship*, νεώς, νηΐ, ναῦν. Pl. νῆες, νεῶν, ναυσί, ναῦς. Attic form (the word occurs only once in the New Test.), τὴν ναῦν, Acts 27. 41.

(*h*) βοῦς, *an ox or cow*, gen. βοός, dat. βοΐ, acc. βοῦν Pl. βόες, gen. βοῶν, dat. βουσί, acc. βόας, βοῦς. (βόας in New Test.) The forms νοῦς, gen. νοός, dat. νοΐ, also occur; and πλοῦς, gen. πλοός, Acts 27. 9.

5. Defective nouns. Some of these are formed only in the plural; e. g. τὰ Διονύσια, *the festivals of Bacchus;* τὰ ἐγκαίνια, *the feast of dedication*, Jno. 10. 22.

Others only in the nom. and acc.; e. g. τὸ ὄναρ, *the dream:* others only in the nom.; e. g. τὸ ὄφελος, *the advantage.*

6. Indeclinable nouns, having one termination for all cases. These are (*a*) some foreign nouns; e. g. τὸ Πάσχα, *the Passover*, gen. τοῦ Πάσχα, dat. τῷ Πάσχα, &c., only in the singular.

(*b*) The cardinal numbers, from 5 to 100 inclusive.

(*c*) The names of *letters;* e. g. ἄλφα, βῆτα, &c.

7. A few nouns are of different genders in the sing. and pl.; e. g. ὁ δεσμός, *the bond*, pl. τὰ δεσμά; ὁ λύχνος, *the light*, τὰ λύχνα. But οἱ λύχνοι in New Test., Lu. 12. 35

8. The word σάββατον, ου, τό, forms, in the New Test., σάββασι, in the dat. pl., according to the third declension Mat. 12. 1, 5 et al.

SECTION VII.—DECLENSION OF ADJECTIVES

TABLE F.—CLASS I.—PARISYLLABIC.

(a)

SINGULAR.	Masc.	Fem.	Neut.
Nom.	ἀγαθός	ἀγαθή	ἀγαθόν, *good.*
Gen.	ἀγαθοῦ	ἀγαθῆς	ἀγαθοῦ
Dat.	ἀγαθῷ	ἀγαθῇ	ἀγαθῷ
Acc.	ἀγαθόν	ἀγαθήν	ἀγαθόν
Voc.	ἀγαθέ	ἀγαθή	ἀγαθόν.
PLURAL.			
Nom. Voc.	ἀγαθοί	ἀγαθαί	ἀγαθά
Gen.	ἀγαθῶν, for all genders		
Dat.	ἀγαθοῖς	ἀγαθαῖς	ἀγαθοῖς
Acc.	ἀγαθούς	ἀγαθάς	ἀγαθά.
DUAL.			
Nom. Acc. Voc.	ἀγαθώ	ἀγαθά	ἀγαθώ
Gen. Dat.	ἀγαθοῖν	ἀγαθαῖν	ἀγαθοῖν.

(b)

SINGULAR.	Masc. & Fem.	Neut.
Nom. Voc.	εὔγεως	εὔγεων, *fertile.*
Gen.	εὔγεω	} for all genders.
Dat.	εὔγεῳ	} for all genders.
Acc.	εὔγεων	} for all genders.
PLURAL.		
Nom. Voc.	εὔγεῳ	εὔγεω
Gen.	εὔγεων	} for all genders
Dat.	εὔγεῳς	} for all genders
Acc.	εὔγεως	εὔγεω.
DUAL.		
Nom. Acc. Voc.	εὔγεω	} for all genders.
Gen. Dat.	εὔγεῳν	} for all genders.

REMARKS.

1. The masc. of ἀγαθός is declined like λόγος, the fem. like κεφαλή, and the neut. like δῶρον. But if the fem. is in *a pure*, as ἅγιος, ἁγία, ἅγιον, *holy;* or in ρα, as ἱερός, ἱερά, ἱερόν, *sacred;* α is retained throughout.

2. Many adjectives (especially in Attic Greek, and those *compounded* or *derived*) have only two terminations, ος for masc. and fem., and ον for neut.; e. g. masc. and fem. ἔνδοξος, neut. ἔνδοξον, *illustrious;* ἄφθαρτος, ἄφθαρτον, *incorruptible;* βασίλειος, βασίλειον, *royal;* ἀΐδιος, ἀΐδιον, *eternal;* αἰώνιος, αἰώνιον, *everlasting.*

But αἰωνίαν, acc. sing. fem. occurs *twice* in the New Test., 2 Thes. 2. 16; Heb. 9. 12.

3. The masc. and fem. εὔγεως, is declined like λαγώς, the neut. like ἀνώγεων.

In the same way may be declined ἵλεως, neut. ἵλεων, *propitious.*

TABLE G.—CLASS II.—IMPARISYLLABIC.

(a)

SINGULAR.	Masc. & Fem.	Neut.
Nom.	εὐδαίμων	εὔδαιμον, *fortunate.*
Gen.	εὐδαίμονος	} for all genders
Dat.	εὐδαίμονι	} for all genders
Acc.	εὐδαίμονα	εὔδαιμον
Voc.	εὔδαιμον, for all genders.	
PLURAL.		
Nom. Voc.	εὐδαίμονες	εὐδαίμονα
Gen.	εὐδαιμόνων	} for all genders
Dat.	εὐδαίμοσι	} for all genders
Acc.	εὐδαίμονας	εὐδαίμονα.
DUAL.		
Nom. Acc. Voc.	εὐδαίμονε	} for all genders.
Gen. Dat.	εὐδαιμόνοιν	} for all genders.

(b)

SINGULAR.	Masc. & Fem.		Neut.
Nom.	ἀληθής		ἀληθές, *true.*
Gen.	ἀληθέος	ἀληθοῦς	} for all genders
Dat.	ἀληθέϊ	ἀληθεῖ	} for all genders
Acc.	ἀηλθέα	ἀληθῆ	
Voc.	ἀληθές, for all genders.		
PLURAL.			
Nom. Voc.	ἀληθέες,	ἀληθεῖς	ἀληθέα, ἀληθῆ
Gen.	ἀληθέων	ἀληθῶν	} for all genders
Dat.	ἀληθέσι		} for all genders
Acc.	ἀληθέας	ἀληθεῖς	ἀληθέα, ἀληθῆ
DUAL.			
Nom. Acc. Voc.	ἀληθέε	ἀληθῆ	
Gen. Dat.	ἀληθέοιν	ἀληθοῖν, for all genders.	

4. Like **εὐδαίμων** are declined σώφρων, *prudent*, ἄφρων, ***foolish*; ἐλεήμων**, *merciful*; ἄῤῥην, gen. ενος, ***male*; &c.**

5. (*a*) A large number are declined like ἀληθής; e. g. εὐγενής, ***nobly born, noble*;** πλήρης, ***full*;** ἀσθενής, *weak*; ἀκριβής, ***exact*; εὐσεβής**, *pious*; &c.

(*b*) A few are contracted in every case, and occur most frequently in the contracted form; e. g.—

Nom.	χρύσεος / χρυσοῦς	χρυσέη / χρυσῆ	χρυσέον / χρυσοῦν, ***of gold.***
Gen.	χρυσέου / χρυσοῦ	χρυσέης / χρυσῆς	χρυσέου / χρυσοῦ, &c.

So ἁπλόος, ἁπλοῦς, ***simple*;** διπλόος, διπλοῦς, ***double*;** τετραπλόος, οῦς, ***quadruple*;** &c.

(*c*) Nom. ἀργύρεος, ἀργυροῦς, ἀργυρέα, ἀργυρᾶ, ἀργύρεον, ἀργυροῦν, *of silver*. Gen. ἀργυρέου, ἀργυροῦ, ἀργυρέας, ἀργυρᾶς, ἀργυρέου, ἀργυροῦ. The fem. has α, because of ρ preceding.

TABLE H.—CLASS III.

(*a*)

SINGULAR.	*Masc.*	*Fem.*	*Neut.*
Nom.	μέλας	μέλαινα	μέλαν, *black.*
Gen.	μέλανος	μελαίνης	μέλανος
Dat.	μέλανι	μελαίνῃ	μέλανι
Acc.	μέλανα	μέλαιναν	μέλαν
Voc.	μέλαν	μέλαινα	μέλαν.
PLURAL.			
Nom. Voc.	μέλανες	μέλαιναι	μέλανα
Gen.	μελάνων	μελαινῶν	μελάνων
Dat.	μέλασι	μελαίναις	μέλασι
Acc.	μέλανας	μελαίνας	μέλανα
DUAL.			
Nom. Acc. Voc.	μέλανε	μελαίνα	μέλανε
Gen. Dat.	μελάνοιν	μελαίναιν	μελάνοιν

(*c*)

OTHER FORMS.	*Masc.*	*Fem.*	*Neut.*
Nom.	τέρην	τέρεινα	τέρεν, *tender.*
Gen.	τέρενος	τερείνης	τέρενος.
(*d*)			
Nom.	ἑκών	ἑκοῦσα	ἑκόν, *willing.*
Gen.	ἑκόντος	ἑκούσης	ἑκόντος.
(*e*)			
Nom.	χαρίεις	χαρίεσσα	χαρίεν, *graceful.*
Gen.	χαρίεντος	χαριέσσης	χαρίεντος.
(*f*)			
Nom.	τιμήεις	τιμήεσσα	τιμῆεν, *precious.*
contr.	τιμῆς	τιμῆσσα	τιμῆν
Gen.	τιμῆντος	τιμήσσης	τιμῆντος.

(*b*)

SINGULAR.	*Masc.*	*Fem.*	*Neut.*
Nom.	πᾶς	πᾶσα	πᾶν, *all.*
Gen.	παντός	πάσης	παντός
Dat.	παντί	πάσῃ	παντί
Acc.	πάντα	πᾶσαν	πᾶν.
PLURAL.			
Nom. Voc.	πάντες	πᾶσαι	πάντα
Gen.	πάντων	πασῶν	πάντων
Dat.	πᾶσι	πάσαις	πᾶσι
Acc.	πάντας	πάσας	πάντα.
DUAL.			
Nom. Acc. Voc.	πάντε	πάσα	πάντε
Gen. Dat.	πάντοιν	πάσαιν	πάντοιν.

(*g*)

SINGULAR.	*Masc.*	*Fem.*	*Neut.*
Nom.	ἡδύς	ἡδεῖα	ἡδύ, *sweet*
Gen.	ἡδέος	ἡδείας	ἡδέος
Dat.	ἡδέϊ, ἡδεῖ	ἡδείᾳ	ἡδέϊ, ἡδεῖ
Acc.	ἡδύν	ἡδεῖαν	ἡδύ
Voc.	ἡδύ	ἡδεῖα	ἡδύ.
PLURAL.			
Nom. Voc.	ἡδέες, ἡδεῖς	ἡδεῖαι	ἡδέα
Gen.	ἡδέων	ἡδειῶν	ἡδέων
Dat.	ἡδέσι	ἡδείαις	ἡδέσι
Acc.	ἡδέας, ἡδεῖς	ἡδείας	ἡδέα.
DUAL.			
Nom. Acc. Voc.	ἡδέε	ἡδεία	ἡδέε
Gen. Dat.	ἡδέοιν	ἡδείαιν	ἡδέοιν.

6. It will be seen that this class of adjectives follows the third declension in the masc. and neut., and the first in the fem.

Of those in υς, εια, υ, the masc. is like πέλεκυς, the fem. like ἡμέρα, and the neut. like ἄστυ.

7. Sometimes the termination εος of the gen. sing. is contracted into ους; e. g. ἥμισυς, *half*, gen. ἡμίσεος, contr. ἡμίσους. Mar. 6. 23.

8. The two adjectives, πολύς, ***much*,** and μέγας, ***great*,** belong to the third class as regards the nom. and acc. sing., and to the first as to all the other cases.

(a)	SINGULAR.			(b)	SINGULAR.		
	Masc.	*Fem.*	*Neut.*		*Masc.*	*Fem.*	*Neut.*
Nom.	πολύς	πολλή	πολύ	Nom.	μέγας	μεγάλη	μέγα
Gen.	πολλοῦ	πολλῆς	πολλοῦ	Gen.	μεγάλου	μεγάλης	μεγάλου
Dat.	πολλῷ	πολλῇ	πολλῷ	Dat.	μεγάλῳ	μεγάλῃ	μεγάλῳ
Acc.	πολύν	πολλήν	πολύ.	Acc.	μέγαν	μεγάλην	μέγα.

The PLURAL is declined like that of ἀγαθός:

πολλοί	πολλαί	πολλά.	μεγάλοι	μεγάλαι	μεγάλα.

So also the DUAL:

πολλώ	πολλά	πολλώ.	μεγάλω	μεγάλα	μεγάλω.

9. Of irregular adjectives, πρᾶος, *gentle*, may be noticed.

SINGULAR.—Nom.	πρᾶος, or πρᾷος	πραεῖα	πρᾷον	The fem. and pl. are formed from πραΰς, which is also found Mat. 21. 5.
Gen.	πρᾴου	πραείας	πρᾴου, &c.	
PLURAL.—Nom.	πραεῖς, or πρᾷοι	πραεῖαι	πραέα	
Gen.	πραέων	πραειῶν	πραέων, &c.	

SECTION VIII.—COMPARISON OF ADJECTIVES.

REMARKS.

1. Comparatives usually end in τερος, τερα, τερον; superlatives in τατος, τατη, τατον; e. g.

First Class.—σοφός, *wise*, σοφώτερος, σοφώτατος. ἅγιος, *holy*, ἁγιώτερος, ἁγιώτατος.

Second Class.—σώφρων, *prudent*, σωφρονέστερος, σωφρονέστατος. εὐσεβής, *pious*, εὐσεβέστερος, εὐσεβέστατος.

Third Class.—μέλας, *black*, μελάντερος, μελάντατος. εὐρύς, *broad*, εὐρύτερος, εὐρύτατος.

All these are declined like ἀγαθός, except that α appears in all cases of the fem. comparative, because the nom. sing. ends in ρα.

2. Many comparatives have ἰων, sometimes ων, for masc. and fem. terminations, their superlatives ιστος, ιστη, ιστον; e. g.

First Class.—κακός, *bad*, κακίων, κάκιστος. καλός, *beautiful*, καλλίων, κάλλιστος.

Third Class.—ἡδύς, *sweet*, ἡδίων, ἥδιστος. πολύς, *much many*, πλείων, πλεῖστος. μέγας, *great*, μείζων, μέγιστος μειζότερος is found in the New Test., 3 Jno. 4.

3. All comparatives in ιων and ων are declined as the following:—

	SINGULAR.			PLURAL.	
	Masc. & Fem.	*Neut.*		*Masc. & Fem.*	*Neut.*
Nom.	μείζων, *greater*	μεῖζον	Nom.	μείζονες, (μείζοες,) μείζους	μείζονα, (μείζοα,) μείζω
Gen.	μείζονος (for all genders)		Gen.	μειζόνων (for all genders)	
Dat.	μείζονι (for all genders)		Dat.	μείζοσι (for all genders)	
Acc.	μείζονα, (μείζοα,) μείζω	μεῖζον.	Acc.	μείζονας, (μείζοας,) μείζους	μείζονα, (μείζοα,) μείζω.

DUAL.

Nom. Acc. μείζονε. | Gen. Dat. μειζόνοιν, for all genders.

4. Adjectives in ος form the comparative in οτερος, if the syllable preceding ος has a diphthong, or a vowel long by nature or by position (followed by two consonants or a double letter); e. g. κοῦφος, *light*, κουφότερος, κουφότατος. ἔνδοξος, *illustrious*, ἐνδοξότερος, ἐνδοξότατος.

In ωτερος, if the vowel preceding ος is short; e. g. σοφός, *wise*, σοφώτερος, σοφώτατος.

Some change ος of the positive into εστερος; e. g. σπουδαῖος, *diligent*, σπουδαιέστερος (σπουδαιότερος in the New Test., 2 Cor. 8. 17, 22).

Contracted adjectives in οος—ους, take εστερος; e. g. ἁπλόος. ἁπλοῦς, ἁπλοέστερος contracted ἁπλούστερος. διπλόος, διπλοῦς, makes διπλότερος in the New Test., Mat. 23. 15.

5. The following offer some irregularity: ἐλαχύς, *small*, ἐλάσσων (for ἐλαχίων), ἐλάχιστος, from which a further comparative, ἐλαχιστότερος, is formed. Eph. 3. 8.

ταχύς, *swift*, θάσσων (for ταχίων), Att. θάττων, τάχιστος.

From the primitive word κρατυς, *strong*, are formed κρείσσων (κρείττων), κράτιστος.

From κακός, *bad*, χείρων, (also κακιων and κακώτερος) χείριστος.

From μικρός, *little*, μείων, (μικρότερος in the New. Test.). Also ἥσσων, (ἥττων) ἥκιστος.

From πολύς, *much*, *many*, πλείων, πλεῖστος, &c.

6. Some comparatives and superlatives are formed from prepositions; e g

πρό, *before*, πρότερος (πρότατος, contr. into) πρῶτος, *first*
ὑπέρ, *above*, ὑπέρτερος, ὑπέρτατος and ὕπατος, *supreme*.
ἐξ, *out of*, ἔσχατος, *extreme*, *last*.

The above appear to be a sufficient number of instances, though not comprehending *all* the varieties of comparison.

SECTION IX.—THE NUMERALS.

TABLE I.—CARDINAL NUMBERS.

(a)	*Masc.*	*Fem.*	*Neut.*
Nom.	εἷς	μία	ἕν, *one*.
Gen.	ἑνός	μιᾶς	ἑνός
Dat.	ἑνί	μιᾷ	ἑνί
Acc.	ἕνα	μίαν	ἕν.

(b)	
Nom. Acc.	δύο, or δύω, *two*, for all genders.
Gen. Dat.	δυοῖν
Also Dat.	δυσί.

(c)	*Masc. & Fem.*	*Neut.*
Nom. Acc.	τρεῖς *three*,	τρία
Gen.	τριῶν, } for all genders.	
Dat.	τρισί, }	

(d)	*Masc. & Fem.*	*Neut.*
Nom.	τέσσαρες, *four*,	τέσσαρα (τέτταρες, τέτταρα)
Gen.	τεσσάρων	
Dat.	τέσσαρσι	
Acc.	τέσσαρας	τέσσαρα.

(e) Indeclinable (from 5 to 100).

πέντε,	*five*,	εἴκοσι	*twenty*,
ἕξ,	*six*,	τριάκοντα,	*thirty*,
ἑπτά,	*seven*,	τεσσαράκοντα,	*forty*,
ὀκτώ,	*eight*,	πεντήκοντα,	*fifty*,
ἐννέα,	*nine*,	ἑξήκοντα,	*sixty*,
δέκα,	*ten*,	ἑβδομήκοντα,	*seventy*,
ἕνδεκα,	*eleven*,	ὀγδοήκοντα,	*eighty*,
δώδεκα,	*twelve*,	ἐννενήκοντα,	*ninety*,
		ἑκατόν,	*a hundred*.

Masc.	*Fem.*	*Neut.*	
διακόσιοι	διακόσιαι	διακόσια,	200,
τριακόσιοι	τριακόσιαι	τριακόσια,	300.
χίλιοι	χίλιαι	χίλια,	1000,
μύριοι	μύριαι	μύρια,	10,000.

Ordinals.

πρῶτος,	*first*,	εἰκοστός,	*twentieth*,
δεύτερος,	*second*,	τριακοστός,	*thirtieth*,
τρίτος,	*third*,	ἑκατοστός,	*hundredth*,
τέταρτος,	*fourth*,	διακοσιοστός,	*two hundredth*,
πέμπτος,	*fifth*, &c.	χιλιοστός,	*thousandth*, &c.

REMARK.

All the declinable ordinals are formed according to the first and second declensions; e. g. πρῶτος, η, ον, δεύτερος, ρα, ρον.

SECTION X.—PRONOMINAL ADJECTIVES.

TABLE J.

αὐτός, reflexive *self*.

(a)	Singular.		
Nom.	αὐτός	αὐτή	αὐτό
Gen.	αὐτοῦ	αὐτῆς	αὐτοῦ
Dat.	αὐτῷ	αὐτῇ	αὐτῷ
Acc.	αὐτόν	αὐτήν	αὐτό.

	Plural.		
Nom.	αὐτοί	αὐταί	αὐτά
Gen.	αὐτῶν, for all genders		
Dat.	αὐτοῖς	αὐταῖς	αὐτοῖς
Acc.	αὐτούς	αὐτάς	αὐτά.

	Dual.		
Nom. Acc.	αὐτώ	αὐτά	αὐτώ
Gen. Dat.	αὐτοῖν	αὐταῖν	αὐτοῖν

2

Demonstratives, ὅδε, οὗτος, ἐκεῖνος.

(b)

SINGULAR.			
Nom.	ὅδε	ἥδε	τόδε
Gen.	τοῦδε	τῆσδε	τοῦδε
Dat.	τῷδε	τῇδε	τῷδε
Acc.	τόνδε	τήνδε	τόδε.
PLURAL.			
Nom.	οἵδε	αἵδε	τάδε
Gen.	τῶνδε, for all genders		
Dat.	τοῖσδε	ταῖσδε	τοῖσδε
Acc.	τούσδε	τάσδε	τάδε.
DUAL.			
Nom. Acc.	τώδε	τάδε	τώδε
Gen. Dat	τοῖνδε	ταῖνδε	τοῖνδε.

(c)

SINGULAR.			
Nom.	οὗτος	αὕτη	τοῦτο
Gen.	τούτου	ταύτης	τούτου
Dat.	τούτῳ	ταύτῃ	τούτῳ
Acc.	τοῦτον	ταύτην	τοῦτο.
PLURAL.			
Nom.	οὗτοι	αὗται	ταῦτα
Gen.	τούτων, for all genders		
Dat.	τούτοις	ταύταις	τούτοις
Acc.	τούτους	ταύτας	ταῦτα.
DUAL.			
Nom. Acc.	τούτω	ταύτα	τούτω
Gen. Dat.	τούτοιν	ταύταιν	τούτοιν.

(d)

SINGULAR.			
Nom.	ἐκεῖνος	ἐκείνη	ἐκεῖνο
Gen.	ἐκείνου	ἐκείνης	ἐκείνου

The other cases, sing. and pl., like αὐτός.

τίς, interrogative, *who?*

(e)

SINGULAR.			
Nom.	τίς		τί
Gen.	τίνος,	for all genders	
Dat.	τίνι,		
Acc.	τίνα		τί.

PLURAL.			
Nom.	τίνες		τινα
Gen.	τίνων,	for all genders	
Dat.	τίσι,		
Acc.	τίνας		τίνα.

DUAL.		
Nom. Acc.	τίνε,	for all genders.
Gen. Dat.	τίνοιν,	

τις, indefinite.

(f)

SINGULAR.			
Nom.	τις		τι
Gen.	τινος,	for all genders	
Dat.	τινι,		
Acc.	τινα		τι.

PLURAL.			
Nom.	τινες		τινα
Gen.	τινων,	for all genders	
Dat.	τισι,		
Acc	τινας		τινα.

DUAL.		
Nom. Acc.	τινε,	for all genders.
Gen. Dat.	τινοιν,	

The Relative, ὅς, *who, which.*

(g)

SINGULAR.			
Nom.	ὅς	ἥ	ὅ
Gen.	οὗ	ἧς	οὗ
Dat.	ᾧ	ᾗ	ᾧ
Acc.	ὅν	ἥν	ὅ.

PLURAL.			
Nom.	οἵ	αἵ	ἅ
Gen.	ὧν, for all genders		
Dat.	οἷς	αἷς	οἷς
Acc	οὕς	ἅς	ἅ.

DUAL.			
Nom. Acc.	ὥ	ἅ	ὥ
Gen. Dat.	οἷν	αἷν	οἷν.

Relative, combined with τις.

(h)

SINGULAR.			
Nom.	ὅστις	ἥτις	ὅτι, *whoever, &c.*
Gen.	οὗτινος	ἧστινος	οὗτινος
Dat.	ᾧτινι	ᾗτινι	ᾧτινι
Acc.	ὅντινα	ἥντινα	ὅτι.

PLURAL.			
Nom.	οἵτινες	αἵτινες	ἅτινα
Gen.	ὧντινων, for all genders		
Dat.	οἷστισι	αἷστισι	οἷστισι
Acc.	οὕστινας	ἅστινας	ἅτινα.

DUAL.

apparently not in use.

The Attic form ὅτου occurs for οὗτινος.

REMARKS.

1. The article ὁ, ἡ, τό, may be considered as a demonstrative. Combined with the particle δε, ὅδε, ἥδε, τόδε, it is more precise in its signification, *this one, this here.*

2. Αὐτός is declined like ἀγαθός, except that ν is wanting in the neuter. It is always marked with the *smooth* breathing. If the article precedes αὐτός, it signifies *the same*; e. g. ὁ αὐτὸς βασιλεύς, *the same king.*

3. Οὗτος, αὕτη, τοῦτο, *this*, indicates present or near objects. Ἐκεῖνος, *that*, points to absent or distant objects.

4. The difference between τις, indefinite, *some one*, *any one*, and τίς, interrogative, *who?* will be easily perceived. The latter has the acute accent always on the first syllable of each case.*

5. Δεῖνα, or ὁ δεῖνα, *such an one*, is generally indeclinable, but is sometimes declined thus: Nom. δεῖνα, Gen. δεῖνος, Dat. δεῖνι, Acc. δεῖνα. Plural—Nom. δεῖνες, Gen. δείνων.

6. The following adjectives may be placed here:—

(*a*) ἄλλος, ἄλλη, ἄλλο, *other*. Declined like αὐτός

(*b*) ἕτερος, ἑτέρα, ἕτερον, *other*.

(*c*) μηδείς (μηδὲ εἷς), μηδεμία, μηδέν, } *none*, *no one*.
οὐδείς (οὐδὲ εἷς), οὐδεμία, οὐδέν, }
So οὐθείς.

(*d*) ἕκαστος, τη, τον, *each* of more than two.

(*e*) Nom. and Acc. ἄμφω, *both*, *two together:* Gen. and Dat. ἀμφοῖν. Ἀμφότερος, ρα, ρον, the same signification.

(*f*) PLURAL.

Gen.	ἀλλήλων, *of each other*			
Dat.	ἀλλήλοις,	ἀλλήλαις,	ἀλλήλοις,	*to each other*
Acc.	ἀλλήλους,	ἀλλήλας,	ἄλληλα,	*each other.*

DUAL.

Gen. & Dat.	ἀλλήλοιν,	ἀλλήλαιν,	ἀλλήλοιν
Acc.	ἀλλήλω,	ἀλλήλα,	ἀλλήλω. No Nom. case.

7. The following form a class.

DEMONSTRATIVES.	INTERROGATIVES.	CORRELATIVES.
(*a*) τοῖος, τοιοῦτος } *such.*	ποῖος, *of what kind?* (Relative, ὁποῖος, *of what kind.*)	οἷος, *such as*, or, *of what kind.*
(*b*) τόσος, τοσοῦτος } *so much.*	πόσος, *how great?* In pl. *how many?*	ὅσος, *how great*, *as great as.* In pl. *whosoever.*
(*c*) τηλίκος, τηλικοῦτος } *so great.*	πηλίκος, *how great?* or, *of what age?*	ἡλίκος, *how great*, referring to *age* or *size.*

8. Of these, τοιοῦτος, τοσοῦτος, and τηλικοῦτος are declined like οὗτος; but the Attic Greeks make the neuter τοιοῦτον and τοσοῦτον. In the New Test. we find neuter τοιοῦτον, Mat. 18. 5, and Acts 21. 25, τοσοῦτον, Heb. 12. 1. Τοῖος, τοιόσδε, οἷος, and ποῖος, are declined according to § VII., rem. 1.

SECTION XI.—THE PRONOUNS.

TABLE K.—PERSONAL PRONOUNS.

(*a*)	SINGULAR.	(*b*)	SINGULAR.	(*c*)	SINGULAR.
Nom.	ἐγώ, *I.*	Nom.	σύ, *thou.*		
Gen.	ἐμοῦ, μου	Gen.	σοῦ	Gen.	οὗ, *of himself, &c.*
Dat.	ἐμοί, μοι	Dat.	σοί	Dat.	οἷ
Acc.	ἐμέ, με.	Acc.	σέ.	Acc.	ἕ.
	PLURAL.		PLURAL.		PLURAL.
Nom.	ἡμεῖς	Nom.	ὑμεῖς		
Gen.	ἡμῶν	Gen.	ὑμῶν	Gen.	σφῶν
Dat.	ἡμῖν	Dat.	ὑμῖν	Dat.	σφίσι
Acc.	ἡμᾶς.	Acc.	ὑμᾶς.	Acc.	σφᾶς.
	DUAL.		DUAL.		DUAL.
Nom. Acc.	νῶϊ, νῷ	Nom. Acc.	σφῶϊ, σφῷ	Nom. Acc.	σφωέ, σφώ
Gen. Dat.	νῶϊν, νῷν.	Gen. Dat.	σφῶϊν, σφῷν.	Gen. Dat.	σφωΐν.

(*d*) COMPOUNDS.

1st Pers.	Gen.	ἐμαυτοῦ	ἐμαυτῆς	ἐμαυτοῦ, *of myself.*
	Dat.	ἐμαυτῷ	ἐμαυτῇ	ἐμαυτῷ
	Acc.	ἐμαυτόν	ἐμαυτήν	ἐμαυτό.
2nd Pers.	Gen.	σεαυτοῦ	σεαυτῆς	σεαυτοῦ, *of thyself.*
	Dat.	σεαυτῷ	σεαυτῇ	σεαυτῷ
	Acc.	σεαυτόν	σεαυτήν	σεαυτό.
3rd Pers. Singular	Gen.	ἑαυτοῦ	ἑαυτῆς	ἑαυτοῦ, *of himself.*
	Dat.	ἑαυτῷ	ἑαυτῇ	ἑαυτῷ
	Acc.	ἑαυτόν	ἑαυτήν	ἑαυτό.
Plural	Gen.	ἑαυτῶν, for all genders		
	Dat.	ἑαυτοῖς	ἑαυταῖς	ἑαυτοῖς
	Acc.	ἑαυτούς	ἑαυτάς	ἑαυτά.

* It may be noticed that in the Attic Greek τοῦ and τῷ are used for τίνος and τίνι, and του and τῳ, as enclitics, for τινος and τινι. In the New Testament an example of the latter usage occurs in the various reading, ὡσπερεί τῳ ἐκτρώματι, 1 Cor. 15. 8, where the common text has the article.

REMARKS.

1. The place of the 3rd personal pronoun is supplied in the oblique cases from αὐτός, αὐτή, αὐτό.

2. The compounds ἐμαυτοῦ and σεαυτοῦ have no plural. *Of ourselves* is expressed by ἡμῶν αὐτῶν; *to ourselves*, by ἡμῖν αὐτοῖς, &c.

3. σεαυτοῦ may be contracted into σαυτοῦ, and ἑαυτοῦ into αὑτοῦ, αὑτῆς, αὑτοῦ, &c.

4. The possessive pronominal adjectives are as follow: ἐμός, ἐμή, ἐμόν, *mine*; σός, σή, σόν, *thine*; ὅς (or ἑός), ἥ (or ἑή), ὅν (or ἑόν), *his*; ἡμέτερος, ρα, ρον, *ours*; ὑμέτερος, ρα, ρον, *yours*; σφέτερος, ρα, ρον, *theirs*; νωΐτερος, ρα, ρον, *ours* (dual); σφωΐτερος, ρα, ρον, *yours* (dual).

SECTION XII.

TABLE L.—THE VERB SUBSTANTIVE.

INDICATIVE.	IMPERATIVE.	SUBJUNCTIVE.	OPTATIVE.	INFIN.	PARTICIPLES.
Present. *I am*, &c.	*Be thou*, &c.	*That I may be*, &c.	*That I might be*, &c.	*To be.*	*Being.*
S. εἰμί, εἶς, or εἶ, ἐστι,	ἴσθι, ἔστω,	ὦ, ᾖς, ᾖ,	εἴην, εἴης, εἴη,	εἶναι.	M. ὤν, ὄντος,
P. ἐσμέν, ἐστέ, εἰσί,	ἔστε, ἔστωσαν,	ὦμεν, ἦτε, ὦσι,	εἴημεν, εἴητε, εἴησαν, or εἶεν,		F. οὖσα, οὔσης,
D. ἐστόν, ἐστόν.	ἔστον, ἔστων.	ἦτον, ἦτον.	εἰήτην, εἰήτην.		N. ὄν, ὄντος.
Imperfect. *I was*, &c.					
S. ἦν, ἦς, or ἦσθα, ἦ, or ἦν,					
P. ἦμεν, ἦτε, or ἦστε, ἦσαν,					
D. { ἤτην, ἤτην, or ἤστην, ἤστην.					
Future. *I shall be*, &c.			*That I may be about to be*, &c.	*To be about to be.*	*About to be.*
S. ἔσομαι, ἔσῃ, ἔσται,			ἐσοίμην, ἔσοιο, ἔσοιτο,	ἔσεσθαι.	M. ἐσόμενος, ου,
P. ἐσόμεθα, ἔσεσθε, ἔσονται,			ἐσοίμεθα, ἔσοισθε, ἔσοιντο,		F. ἐσομένη, ης,
D. ἐσόμεθον, ἔσεσθον, ἔσεσθον.			ἐσοίμεθον, ἐσοίσθην, ἐσοίσθην.		N. ἐσόμενον, ου.

Present Participle, the type of all participles in ων, without exception.

	SINGULAR.			PLURAL.			DUAL.		
	Masc.	*Fem.*	*Neut.*	*Masc.*	*Fem.*	*Neut.*		*Masc.*	*Fem.*	*Neut.*
Nom.	ὤν	οὖσα	ὄν	ὄντες	οὖσαι	ὄντα	Nom. Acc.	ὄντε	οὔσα	ὄντε
Gen.	ὄντος	οὔσης	ὄντος	ὄντων	οὐσῶν	ὄντων	Gen. Dat.	ὄντοιν	οὔσαιν	ὄντοιν.
Dat.	ὄντι	οὔσῃ	ὄντι	οὖσι	οὔσαις	οὖσι				
Acc.	ὄντα	οὖσαν	ὄν.	ὄντας	οὔσας	ὄντα.				

REMARKS.

1. In the present, the 2nd pers. εἶ is the ordinary form. ἔνι occurs for ἔνεστι.

2. In the imperfect the 2nd pers. is ordinarily ἦσθα, Mat. 26. 69. The 3rd pers. ἦν is more common than ἦ.

Another form of the imperfect occurs in the 1st pers. sing. and pl.; sing. ἤμην, pl. ἤμεθα. ἤμην, Mat. 25. 35. ἤμεθα, Mat. 23. 30. Acts 27. 37., where the common text has ἦμεν. ἤτω occurs, as 3rd pers. sing. of the imperative.

3. The future, in all its moods, is of the middle form. The 2nd pers. sing. is originally ἔσεσαι. By rejecting σ is formed ἔσεαι, and by contracting εα into η, and subscribing the ι, is formed ἔσῃ.

This remark applies to all 2nd pers. sing. in ῃ of passive and middle verbs, without exception.

4. The verb substantive has neither perfect, pluperfect, nor aorist. The imperfect supplies the place of these tenses.

SECTION XIII.—REGULAR VERB IN Ω.

TABLE M.—ACTIVE VOICE.

	INDICATIVE.	IMPERATIVE.	SUBJUNCTIVE.	OPTATIVE.	INFINITIVE.	PARTICIPLES.
Pres.	*I loose*, &c.					
Sing.	λύω		λύω	λύοιμι	λύειν	Masc. λύων
	λύεις	λύε	λύῃς	λύοις		λύοντος
	λύει	λυέτω	λύῃ	λύοι		Fem. λύουσα
Plur.	λύομεν		λύωμεν	λύοιμεν		λυούσης
	λύετε	λύετε	λύητε	λύοιτε		Neut. λύον
	λύουσι	λυέτωσαν	λύωσι	λύοιεν		λύοντος
Dual	λύετον	λύετον	λύητον	λυοίτην		
	λύετον	λυέτων	λύητον	λυοίτην		
Impf.						
Sing.	ἔλυον					
	ἔλυες					
	ἔλυε					
Plur.	ἐλύομεν					
	ἐλύετε					
	ἔλυον					
Dual	ἐλύετον					
	ελυέτην					
Fut.						
Sing.	λύσω			λύσοιμι	λύσειν	Masc. λύσων
	λύσεις			λύσοις		λύσοντος
	λύσει			λύσοι		Fem. λύσουσα
Plur.	λύσομεν			λύσοιμεν		λυσούσης
	λύσετε			λύσοιτε		Neut. λῦσον
	λύσουσι			λύσοιεν		λύσοντος
Dual	λύσετον			λυσοίτην		
	λύσετον			λυσοίτην		
Aor.						
Sing.	ἔλυσα		λύσω	λύσαιμι	λῦσαι	Masc. λύσας
	ἔλυσας	λῦσον	λύσῃς	λύσαις		λύσαντος
	ἔλυσε	λυσάτω (ᾰ)	λύσῃ	λύσαι		Fem. λύσᾱσα
Plur.	ἐλύσᾰμεν		λύσωμεν	λύσαιμεν		λυσάσης (ᾱ)
	ἐλύσᾰτε	λύσᾰτε	λύσητε	λύσαιτε		Neut. λῦσαν
	ἔλυσαν	λυσάτωσαν	λύσωσι	λύσαιεν		λύσαντος
Dual	ἐλύσατον (ᾰ)	λύσᾰτον	λύσητον	λυσαίτην		
	ἐλυσάτην (ᾰ)	λυσάτων (ᾰ)	λύσητον	λυσαίτην		
Perf.						
Sing.	λέλυκα		λελύκω	λελύκοιμι	λελυκέναι	Masc. λελυκώς
	λέλυκας	λέλυκε	λελύκῃς	λελύκοις		λελυκότος
	λέλυκε	λελυκέτω	λελύκῃ	λελύκοι		Fem. λελυκυῖα
Plur.	λελύκᾰμεν		λελύκωμεν	λελύκοιμεν		λελυκυίας
	λελύκᾰτε	λελύκετε	λελύκητε	λελύκοιτε		Neut. λελυκός
	λελύκᾱσι	λελυκέτωσαν	λελύκωσι	λελύκοιεν		λελυκότος
Dual	λελύκᾰτον	λελύκετον	λελύκητον	λελυκοίτην		
	λελύκᾰτον	λελυκέτων	λελύκητον	λελυκοίτην		

Pluperfect.

Singular.	ἐλελύκειν	Plural.	ἐλελύκειμεν	Dual.	ἐλελυκείτην
	ἐλελύκεις		ἐλελύκειτε		ἐλελυκείτην.
	ἐλελύκει.		ἐλελύκεισαν.		

REMARKS.

1. Syllabic augment, so called as adding a syllable to the tense. It occurs in the imperf., the first aorist (in the indic. mood), and pluperf.; e. g. ἔλυον, ἔλυσα, ἐλελύκειν.

Verbs commencing with ῥ double that consonant after the augment; e. g. ῥίπτω, *I cast*, ἔῤῥιπτον.

The Attic dialect gives η for ε in three verbs; viz., βούλομαι, *I wish*, ἠβουλόμην; δύναμαι, *I am able*, ἠδυνάμην; μέλλω, *I am about*, *I intend*, ἤμελλον.

2. Temporal augment, so called as increasing the *time*, or quantity, in pronunciation. It occurs when the verb begins with one of the vowels α, ε, or ο; α being changed into η, e. g. ἀνύτω, *I accomplish*, ἤνυτον; ε into η, ἐθέλω, *I wish*, ἤθελον; ο into ω, ὁρίζω, *I limit*, ὥριζον. Or with one of the diphthongs αι, οι, or αυ; αι into ῃ, αἰτέω, *I ask*, ᾔτεον; οι into ῳ, οἰκέω, *I inhabit*, ᾤκεον; αυ into ηυ, αὐξάνω, *I increase*, ηὔξανον.

3. The long vowels η, ω, and the three diphthongs ει, ευ, ου, are unchanged, and ι, υ, merely lengthened in quantity; e. g. ἠχέω, *I resound*, ἤχεον; ὤθω, *I push*, ὦθον; ἱκετεύω, *I supplicate*, ἱκέτευον (ῑ); ὑβρίζω, *I assault*, ὕβριζον (ῡ); εἰκάζω, *I imagine*, εἴκαζον; εὐθυνω, *I direct*, εὔθυνον; οὐτάζω, *I wound*, οὔταζον.

But the Attics often change ευ into ηυ; e. g. εὔχομαι, *I pray*, ηὐχόμην.

4. Several verbs commencing with ε receive the augment by inserting ι; e. g. ἔχω, *I have*, εἶχον; ἐργαζομαι, *I work*, εἰργαζόμην; ἐάω, *I permit*, εἴαον, contract. εἴων, etc. So ἔθω, perf. εἴωθα, *I am accustomed*, ω being interposed, and ἐθίζω, *I accustom*, perf. pass. εἴθισμαι.

The verb ὁράω, *I see*, receives both the syllabic and temporal augments, ε and ω; e. g. ὁράω, ἑώραον, contract. ἑώρων; perf. Attic ἑώρακα, for ὥρακα.

5. Reduplication. (*a*) This consists of ε added to the first consonant of the root, as in λέλυκα. All verbs commencing with a consonant have the reduplication in the perf., and retain it in all the moods.

(*b*) Verbs commencing with a vowel or a diphthong receive no reduplication, the first letter of the perf. being the same as that of the imperf.; e. g. ἀνύτω, imperf. ἤνυτον, perf. ἤνυκα. In such cases the temporal augment is retained through all the moods.

6. (*a*) If the first consonant of the present be an aspirate, it is replaced in the reduplication by the corresponding smooth consonant; e. g. φιλέω, *I love*, πεφίληκα; θύω *I sacrifice*, τέθυκα.

(*b*) Verbs which commence with ῥ, a double letter, or two consonants, want the reduplication; e. g. ῥάπτω, *I sew*, ἔῤῥαφα; ψάλλω, *I play on an instrument*, ἔψαλκα; σπείρω, *I sow*, ἔσπαρκα.

(*c*) As exceptions to this rule may be mentioned, verbs commencing with a mute and a liquid; e. g. γράφω, *I write*, γέγραφα; κλίνω, *I incline*, κέκλικα. Some commencing with πτ; e. g. πέπτωκα, from the old form πτόω, *I fall*.

7. (*a*) The Attics change the reduplications λε and με in the perf. into ει; e. g. λαμβάνω, *I take* (old form λήβω), εἴληφα, for λέληφα; μείρω, *I divide*, εἵμαρμαι, for μέμαρμαι.

(*b*) What is called the Attic reduplication occurs in some verbs commencing with a vowel. It consists in a repetition of the two first letters of the verb before the temporal augment; e. g. ὀρύττω, *I dig*, perf. ὤρυχα, Att. ὀρώρυχα; ἐλαύνω, *I drive*, perf. ἤλακα, Att. ἐλήλακα.

(*c*) If the third syllable, counting the reduplication, be long, it is shortened; e. g. ἀλέιφω, *I anoint*, ἤλειφα, Att. ἀλήλιφα; ἀκούω, *I hear*, ἤκουα, Att. ἀκήκοα.

(*d*) In the second aorist* this reduplication continues through the moods, but the temporal augment does not go beyond the indic.; e. g. from ἄγω, *I lead*, aor. 2, ἤγαγον (by transposition for ἄγηγον), but infin. ἀγαγεῖν.

8. Formation of the tenses of the Active Voice. Indicative mood.

(*a*) The present is formed of the root and the termination ω, εις, ει. Third pers. pl. ουσι, like the dat. pl. of the present participle.

(*b*) The imperfect is formed from the present by prefixing the augment, and changing ω into ον; λύω, ἔλυον. The 3rd pers. pl. is like the 1st pers. sing. in this tense.

(*c*) The future is the root, with the addition of the termination σω, σεις, σει, etc.

(*d*) The aorist is formed from the future by prefixing the augment, and changing σω into σα; λύσω, ἔλυσα. The 3rd pers. pl. is formed by adding ν to the 1st pers sing.; ἔλυσα, ἔλυσαν.

(*e*) The perfect is formed from the future by changing σω into κα, and prefixing the reduplication. Modifications of this termination will be hereafter noticed.

(*f*) The pluperfect is formed from the perfect by prefixing the augment ε, and changing the final α into ειν;

* It will be observed that in the Paradigm given above (λύω), the second aorist does not occur. This tense is regarded by Burnouf as only another form of what is usually called the first aorist, since it appears that if one aorist is used in a given verb, the other does not occur, at least in the same dialect. Buttmann (as quoted by Burnouf) lays it down, that no verb in which the second aorist is the same in form with the imperfect, or would differ only in the quantity of the penultimate syllable, can have this aorist, at any rate in the active voice.

Remarks on the second aorist will be found below, p. xxvi.

λέλυκα, ἐλελύκειν. Sometimes the augment is omitted; e. g. πεπιστεύκεισαν.

9. Imperative. (*a*) The present is formed by changing ω of the present indicative into ε; e. g. λύω, λύε, λυέτω, etc.

(*b*) The imperative aorist is in ον, ατω; e. g. λῦσον, λυσάτω.

(*c*) The perfect is the same in form as the 3rd pers. sing. of the perfect indicative; e. g. λέλυκε. All the 3rd persons, sing., pl., and dual, of the imperative have ω in the termination.

10. Subjunctive. (*a*) The present subjunctive is formed from the present indicative by changing the short vowels into long ones, and subscribing ι where it occurs; e. g. indic. λύω, λύεις, λύει; subj. λύω, λύῃς, λύῃ.

(*b*) The 2nd pers. pl., λύητε, and dual, λύητον, have no ι subscribed, there being none in the corresponding persons of the indicative.

11. Optative. (*a*) The present, future, and perfect optative are formed by changing the last letter of the same tenses of the indicative into οιμι; e. g. pres. λύω, optat. λύοιμι; fut. λύσω, optat. λύσοιμι; perf. λέλυκα, optat. λελύκοιμι.

*(*b*) The aorist optative rejects the augment, and changes α into αιμι; e. g. ἔλυσα, λύσαιμι.

12. Infinitive. All tenses terminating in ω in the indicative form the infinitive in ειν; the aorist forms it in αι, and the perfect in έναι.

13. Participles. Those tenses which have the infinitive in ειν form the participle in ων, ουσα, ον. The aorist participle ends in ας, ασα, αν; λύσας, λύσασα, λῦσαν, gen. λύσαντος, λυσάσης, λύσαντος, etc. The perfect participle ends in ως, υια, ος; λελυκώς, λελυκυῖα, λελυκός, gen. λελυκότος, λελυκυίας, λελυκότος, etc. They are all declined like adjectives of the third class.

SECTION XIV.—REGULAR VERB IN Ω.

TABLE N.—PASSIVE VOICE.

	INDICATIVE.	IMPERATIVE.	SUBJUNCTIVE.	OPTATIVE.	INFINITIVE.	PARTICIPLES.
Present	*I am loosed*, &c.					
Sing.	λύομαι		λύωμαι	λυοίμην	λύεσθαι	Masc. λυόμενος
	λύῃ	λύου	λύῃ	λύοιο		λυομένου
	λύεται	λυέσθω	λύηται	λύοιτο		
Plur.	λυόμεθα		λυώμεθα	λυοίμεθα		Fem. λυομένη
	λύεσθε	λύεσθε	λύησθε	λύοισθε		λυομένης
	λύονται	λυέσθωσαν	λύωνται	λύοιντο		
Dual	λυόμεθον		λυώμεθον	λυοίμεθον		Neut. λυόμενον
	λύεσθον	λύεσθον	λύησθον	λυοίσθην		λυομένου
	λύεσθον	λυέσθων	λύησθον	λυοίσθην		
Imperf.						
Sing.	ἐλυόμην					
	ἐλύου					
	ἐλύετο					
Plur.	ἐλυόμεθα					
	ἐλύεσθε					
	ἐλύοντο					
Dual	ἐλυόμεθον					
	ἐλυέσθην					
	ἐλυέσθην					

* Æolic aorist. λύσεια, λύσειας, λύσειε; pl. λυσείαμεν, λυσείατε, λύσειαν. The 2nd and 3rd pers. sing. and the 3rd pers. pl. are alone in use.

TABLE N.—PASSIVE VOICE.—*(Continued.)*

	INDICATIVE.	IMPERATIVE.	SUBJUNCTIVE.	OPTATIVE.	INFINITIVE.	PARTICIPLES.
Future Sing.	λυθήσομαι			λυθησοίμην	λυθήσεσθαι	Masc. λυθησόμενος
	λυθήσῃ			λυθήσοιο		λυθησομένου
	λυθήσεται			λυθήσοιτο		
Plur.	λυθησόμεθα			λυθησοίμεθα		Fem. λυθησομένη
	λυθήσεσθε			λυθήσοισθε		λυθησομένης
	λυθήσονται			λυθήσοιντο		
Dual	λυθησόμεθον			λυθησοίμεθον		Neut. λυθησόμενον
	λυθήσεσθον			λυθήσοισθον		λυθησομένου
	λυθήσεσθον			λυθησοίσθην		
Aorist Sing.	ἐλύθην		λυθῶ	λυθείην	λυθῆναι	Masc. λυθείς
	ἐλύθης	λύθητι	λυθῇς	λυθείης		λυθέντος
	ἐλύθη	λυθήτω	λυθῇ	λυθείη		
Plur.	ἐλύθημεν		λυθῶμεν	λυθείημεν		Fem. λυθεῖσα
	ἐλύθητε	λύθητε	λυθῆτε	λυθείητε		λυθείσης
	ἐλύθησαν	λυθήτωσαν	λυθῶσι	λυθείησαν		
Dual	ἐλύθητον	λύθητον	λυθῆτον	λυθειήτην		Neut. λυθέν
	ἐλυθήτην	λυθήτων	λυθῆτον	λυθειήτην		λυθέντος
Perfect Sing.	λέλυμαι		λελυμένος ὦ	λελυμένος εἴην	λελύσθαι	Masc. λελυμένος
	λέλυσαι	λέλυσο	λελυμένος ᾖς	λελυμένος εἴης		λελυμένου
	λέλυται	λελύσθω	λελυμένος ᾖ	λελυμένος εἴη		
Plur.	λελύμεθα		λελυμένοι ὦμεν	λελυμένοι εἴημεν		Fem. λελυμένη
	λέλυσθε	λέλυσθε	λελυμένοι ἦτε	λελυμένοι εἴητε		λελυμένης
	λέλυνται	λελύσθωσαν	λελυμένοι ὦσι	λελυμένοι εἴησαν		
Dual	λελύμεθον					Neut. λελυμένον
	λέλυσθον	λέλυσθον	λελυμένω ἦτον	λελυμένω εἰήτην		λελυμένου
	λέλυσθον	λελύσθων	λελυμένω ἦτον	λελυμένω εἰήτην		
Pluperf. Sing.	ἐλελύμην					
	ἐλέλυσο					
	ἐλέλυτο					
Plur.	ἐλελύμεθα					
	ἐλέλυσθε					
	ἐλέλυντο					
Dual	ἐλελύμεθον					
	ἐλελύσθην					
	ἐλελύσθην					
3rd Fut. Sing.	λελύσομαι			λελυσοίμην	λελύσεσθαι	Masc. λελυσόμενος
	λελύσῃ			λελύσοιο		λελυσομένου
	λελύσεται			λελύσοιτο		
Plur.	λελυσόμεθα			λελυσοίμεθα		Fem. λελυσομένη
	λελύσεσθε			λελύσοισθε		λελυσομένης
	λελύσονται			λελύσοιντο		
Dual	λελυσόμεθον			λελυσοίμεθον		Neut. λελυσόμενον
	λελύσεσθον			λελυσοίσθην		λελυσομένου
	λελύσεσθον			λελυσοίσθην		

REMARKS.

1. (*a*) The present indicative is formed from the present active by changing ω into ομαι; λύω, λύομαι.

(*b*) The imperfect from the imperfect active, by changing ον into ομην; ἔλυον, ἐλυόμην.

(*c*) The future, by adding the termination θησομαι to the root portion of the verb, especially as it appears in the future active and the perfect, and aspirating a preceding consonant; λύω, λυθήσομαι; σκοτίζω, σκοτίσω, σκοτισθήσομαι; ἄγω, ἄξω, ἀχθήσομαι. Some verbs have another form, termed the second future, which exhibits the same change of the root portion of the verb as the second aorist active, with the termination ησομαι; δέρω, δαρήσομαι; ἀλλάσσω, ἀλλαγήσομαι.

(*d*) The aorists of the first and second form have the termination ην in place of ησομαι in the futures, and prefix the augment; λύω, ἐλύθην; πέμπω, ἐπέμφθην; στρέφω, ἐστράφην; κρύπτω, ἐκρύβην.

(*e*) The termination of the perfect is μαι; λέλυκα, λέλυμαι; τετέλεκα, τετέλεσμαι; γέγραφα, γέγραμμαι.

(*f*) The pluperfect is formed from the perfect by changing μαι into μην, and prefixing the augment; λέλυμαι, ἐλελύμην. The augment is sometimes omitted; e. g. νενομοθέτητο, for ἐνενομοθέτητο.

(*g*) The third future, which mainly belongs to the passive voice, is formed from one of the perfects by substituting the termination σομαι; κέκραγα, (κεκράγσομαι) κεκράξομαι; γέγραπται, (γεγράπσομαι) γεγράψομαι.

2. (*a*) The imperative is formed from the indicative by the following changes:—

Pres. ind. 1 p. λύω, Imper. λύου, 3 p. λυέσθω.
Aor. ind. 3 p. ἐλύθη, Imper. λύθητι, 3 p. λυθήτω
Plup. ind. 2 p. ἐλέλυσο, Imper. λέλυσο, 3 p. λελύσθω.

(*b*) The 2nd person in ου of the imperfect is formed from εσο, by rejecting σ and contracting εο into ου; e. g. ἐλύεσο, ἐλύεο, ἐλύου.

3. (*a*) The present subjunctive is formed from the present indicative by changing the short vowels into long ones; e. g. λύομαι, λύωμαι. The 2nd pers. sing. is from ησαι, thus: ησαι, ηαι, ῃ.

(*b*) The aorist, from that of the indicative by rejecting the augment, and changing ην into ω; ἐλύθην, λυθῶ.

(*c*) The perfect, usually, by a combination of the perfect participle with the pres. subj. of the verb εἶναι, ὦ, ᾖς, ᾖ.

4. (*a*) The optative is formed by changing the termination of the indicative ομαι into οιμην; e. g. pres. indic. λύομαι, opt. λυοίμην; fut. λυθήσομαι, opt. λυθησοίμην, &c.

(*b*) The aorist rejects the augment, and changes ην into ειην; ἐλύθην, λυθείην. The plural is frequently contracted; e. g. λυθεῖμεν, λυθεῖτε, λυθεῖεν.

(*c*) The perfect is usually composed of the perfect participle and the optative of εἶναι; λελυμένος εἴην.

5. (*a*) The infinitive of the tenses ending in μαι is formed from the 3rd pers. of the indicative by changing ται into σθαι; e. g. pres. λύεται, infin. λύεσθαι; fut. λυθήσεται, infin. λυθήσεσθαι.

(*b*) The aorist infin. rejects the augment, and changes ην into ηναι; ἐλύθην, λυθῆναι; ἐκρύβην, κρυβῆναι.

6. (*a*) The participle of every tense in μαι ends in μενος; e. g. pres. λύομαι, part. λυόμενος; fut. λυθήσομαι, part. λυθησόμενος; third fut. λελύσομαι, part. λελυσόμενος, &c. All these are declined like ἀγαθός, ή, όν.

(*b*) The participle of the aorist rejects the augment, and changes ην into εις; ἐλύθην, λυθείς; ἐστράφην, στραφείς. It is declined like adjectives of the third class.

SECTION XV.—REGULAR VERB IN Ω.

TABLE O.—MIDDLE VOICE.

	INDICATIVE.	IMPERATIVE.	SUBJUNCTIVE.	OPTATIVE.	INFINITIVE.	PARTICIPLES.
Future	*I shall loose myself*, &c.					
Sing.	λύσομαι			λυσοίμην	λύσεσθαι	Masc. λυσόμενος
	λύσῃ			λύσοιο		λυσομένου
	λύσεται			λύσοιτο		
Plur.	λυσόμεθα			λυσοίμεθα		Fem. λυσομένη
	λύσεσθε			λύσοισθε		λυσομένης
	λύσονται			λύσοιντο		
Dual	λυσόμεθον			λυσοίμεθον		Neut. λυσόμενον
	λύσεσθον			λύσοισθον		λυσομένου
	λύσεσθον			λυσοίσθην		
Aorist						
Sing.	ἐλυσάμην		λύσωμαι	λυσαίμην	λύσασθαι	Masc. λυσάμενος
	ἐλύσω	λῦσαι	λύσῃ	λύσαιο		λυσαμένου
	ἐλύσατο	λυσάσθω	λύσηται	λύσαιτο		
Plur.	ἐλυσάμεθα		λυσώμεθα	λυσαίμεθα		Fem. λυσαμένη
	ἐλύσασθε	λύσασθε	λύσησθε	λύσαισθε		λυσαμένης
	ἐλύσαντο	λυσάσθωσαν	λύσωνται	λύσαιντο		
Dual	ἐλυσάμεθον		λυσώμεθον	λυσαίμεθον		Neut λυσάμενον
	ἐλυσάσθην	λύσασθον	λύσησθον	λύσαισθον		λυσαμένου
	ἐλυσάσθην	λυσάσθων	λύσησθον	λυσαίσθην		

REMARKS.

1. The middle voice has only two tenses peculiar to itself, the future and the aorist. As to the other tenses, the passive form is used to indicate reflexive action: thus the present, λύομαι, may mean *I am loosed* (passive), or, *I loose myself* (middle). The perfect, λέλυμαι, *I have been loosed*, or, *I have loosed myself*, &c.

2. The tense ending in α, e. g. κέκραγα, πέφευγα, commonly called the perfect middle, but which is, in fact, only a second form of the perfect active, will be noticed hereafter

3. (*a*) The future middle is formed from the future active by changing ω into ομαι; λύσω, λύσομαι.

(*b*) The aorist from the aorist active, by adding μην; ἔλυσα, ἐλυσάμην. The 2nd pers., ἐλύσω, from ἐλύσασο, by rejecting σ and contracting αο into ω.

SECTION XVI.—CONTRACTED VERB IN E'Ω.

TABLE P.—ACTIVE VOICE.

	INDICATIVE.	IMPERATIVE.	SUBJUNCTIVE.	OPTATIVE.	INFINITIVE.	PARTICIPLES.
Present	*I love*, &c.					
Sing.	φιλέω, ῶ		φιλέω, ῶ	φιλέοιμι, οῖμι	φιλέειν, εῖν	M. φιλέων, ῶν
	φιλέεις, εῖς	φίλεε, ει	φιλέῃς, ῇς	φιλέοις, οῖς		φιλέοντος, οῦντος
	φιλέει, εῖ	φιλεέτω, είτω	φιλέῃ, ῇ	φιλέοι, οῖ		
Plur.	φιλέομεν, οῦμεν		φιλέωμεν, ῶμεν	φιλέοιμεν, οῖμεν		F. φιλέουσα, οῦσα
	φιλέετε, εῖτε	φιλέετε, εῖτε	φιλέητε, ῆτε	φιλέοιτε, οῖτε		φιλεούσης, ούσης
	φιλέουσι, οῦσι	φιλεέτωσαν, είτωσαν	φιλέωσι, ῶσι	φιλέοιεν, οῖεν		
Dual	φιλέετον, εῖτον	φιλέετον, εῖτον	φιλέητον, ῆτον	φιλεοίτην, οίτην		N. φιλέον, οῦν
	φιλέετον, εῖτον	φιλεέτων, είτων	φιλέητον, ῆτον	φιλεοίτην, οίτην		φιλέοντος, οῦντος
Imperf.						
Sing.	ἐφίλεον, ουν					
	ἐφίλεες, εις					
	ἐφίλεε, ει					
Plur.	ἐφιλέομεν, οῦμεν					
	ἐφιλέετε, εῖτε					
	ἐφίλεον, ουν					
Dual	ἐφιλεέτην, είτην					
	ἐφιλεέτην, είτην					
Future	φιλήσω			φιλήσοιμι	φιλήσειν	φιλήσων, σοντος
Aorist	ἐφίλησα	φίλησον	φιλήσω	φιλήσαιμι	φιλῆσαι	φιλήσας, σαντος
Perfect	πεφίληκα	πεφίληκε	πεφιλήκω	πεφιλήκοιμι	πεφιληκέναι	πεφιληκώς, κότος
Pluperf.	ἐπεφιλήκειν					

REMARKS.

1. Rules of contraction: ε disappears before long vowels and diphthongs, εε is contracted into ει, εο into ου.

2. The contraction takes place only in the present and imperfect, because in these tenses alone the termination commences with a vowel.

3. In the future and perfect these verbs change often (not invariably) ε and α into η, and ο into ω, i. e. the short vowels of the root into their corresponding long ones; e. g. pres. φιλέω, fut. φιλήσω, perf. πεφίληκα. τιμάω, τιμήσω, τετίμηκα. δηλόω, δηλώσω, δεδήλωκα.

4. The uncontracted tenses being conjugated like **λύω**, the first persons only are given.

5. As regards the reduplication in the perfect, we find πεφίληκα, not φεφίληκα, because two successive syllables cannot commence with the same aspirate.

6. In place of the optative φιλοῖμι, the Attics wrote φιλοίην, φιλοίης, φιλοίη; but the 3rd pers. pl. is always φιλοῖεν (not φιλοίησαν). The 1st and 2nd pers. pl. φιλοίημεν, φιλοίητε, are scarcely used, on account of their length.

SECTION XVII.—CONTRACTED VERB IN ΕΩ.

TABLE Q.—PASSIVE VOICE.

	INDICATIVE.	IMPERATIVE.	SUBJUNCTIVE.	OPTATIVE.	INFINITIVE.	PARTICIPLES.
Present	*I am loved*, &c.					
Sing.	φιλέομαι, οῦμαι		φιλέωμαι, ῶμαι	φιλεοίμην, οίμην	φιλέεσθαι, εῖσθαι	Masc. φιλεόμενος, ούμενος
	φιλέῃ, ῇ	φιλέου, οῦ	φιλέῃ, ῇ	φιλέοιο, οῖο		φιλεομένου, ουμένου
	φιλέεται, εῖται	φιλεέσθω, είσθω	φιλέηται, ῆται	φιλέοιτο, οῖτο		
Plur.	φιλεόμεθα, ούμεθα		φιλεώμεθα, ώμεθα	φιλεοίμεθα, οίμεθα		Fem. φιλεομένη, ουμένη
	φιλέεσθε, εῖσθε	φιλέεσθε, εῖσθε	φιλέησθε, ῆσθε	φιλέοισθε, οῖσθε		φιλεομένης, ουμένης
	φιλέονται, οῦνται	φιλεέσθωσαν, είσθωσαν	φιλέωνται, ῶνται	φιλέοιντο, οῖντο		
Dual	φιλεόμεθον, ούμεθον		φιλεώμεθον, ώμεθον	φιλεοίμεθον, οίμεθον		Neut. φιλεόμενον, ούμενον
	φιλέεσθον, εῖσθον	φιλέεσθον, εῖσθον	φιλέησθον, ῆσθον	φιλεοίσθην, οίσθην		φιλεομένου, ουμένου
	φιλέεσθον, εῖσθον.	φιλεέσθων, είσθων	φιλέησθον, ῆσθον	φιλεοίσθην, οίσθην		
Imperf.						
Sing.	ἐφιλεόμην, ούμην					
	ἐφιλέου, οῦ					
	ἐφιλέετο, εῖτο					
Plur.	ἐφιλεόμεθα, ούμεθα					
	ἐφιλέεσθε, εῖσθε					
	ἐφιλέοντο, οῦντο					
Dual	ἐφιλεόμεθον, ούμεθον					
	ἐφιλεέσθην, είσθην					
	ἐφιλεέσθην, είσθην					
Future	φιληθήσομαι			φιληθησοίμην	φιληθήσεσθαι	φιληθησόμενος, ου
Aorist	ἐφιλήθην	φιλήθητι	φιληθῶ	φιληθείην	φιληθῆναι	φιληθείς, θέντος
Perfect	πεφίλημαι	πεφίλησο	πεφιλημένος ὦ	πεφιλημένος εἴην	πεφιλῆσθαι	πεφιλημένος, ου
Pluperf.	ἐπεφιλήμην					
3rd Fut.	πεφιλήσομαι			πεφιλησοίμην	πεφιλήσεσθαι	πεφιλησόμενος, ου

MIDDLE VOICE.

Future	φιλήσομαι			φιλησοίμην	φιλήσεσθαι	φιλησόμενος, ου
Aorist	ἐφιλησάμην	φίλησαι	φιλήσωμαι	φιλησαίμην	φιλήσασθαι	φιλησάμενος, ου

REMARKS.

1. The contraction takes place, as in the Active Voice, only in the present and imperfect; and, if φιλε be considered as the radical, the terminations are the same as in λύομαι.

2. Another form of the perfect, subjunctive, and optative, πεφιλῶμαι and πεφιλήμην, will be hereafter noticed.

SECTION XVIII.—CONTRACTED VERB IN Α Ω.

TABLE R.—ACTIVE VOICE.

	INDICATIVE.	IMPERATIVE.	SUBJUNCTIVE.	OPTATIVE.	INFINITIVE.	PARTICIPLES.
Present	*I honour*, &c.					
Sing.	τιμάω, ῶ		τιμάω, ῶ	τιμάοιμι, ῷμι	τιμάειν	M. τιμάων, ῶν
	τιμάεις, ᾷς	τίμαε, α	τιμάῃς, ᾷς	τιμάοις, ῷς		τιμάοντος, ῶντος
	τιμάει, ᾷ	τιμαέτω, άτω	τιμάῃ, ᾷ	τιμάοι, ῷ		
Plur.	τιμάομεν, ῶμεν		τιμάωμεν, ῶμεν	τιμάοιμεν, ῷμεν		F. τιμάουσα, ῶσα
	τιμάετε, ᾶτε	τιμάετε, ᾶτε	τιμάητε, ᾶτε	τιμάοιτε, ῷτε		τιμαούσης, ώσης
	τιμάουσι, ῶσι	τιμαέτωσαν, άτωσαν	τιμάωσι, ῶσι	τιμάοιεν, ῷεν		
Dual	τιμάετον, ᾶτον	τιμάετον, ᾶτον	τιμάητον, ᾶτον	τιμαοίτην, ῴτην		N. τιμάον, ῶν
	τιμάετον, ᾶτον	τιμαέτων, άτων	τιμάητον, ᾶτον	τιμαοίτην, ῴτην		τιμάοντος, ῶντος
Imperf.						
Sing.	ἐτίμαον, ων					
	ἐτίμαες, ας					
	ἐτίμαε, α					
Plur.	ἐτιμάομεν, ῶμεν					
	ἐτιμάετε, ᾶτε					
	ἐτίμαον, ων					
Dual	ἐτιμαέτην, άτην					
	ἐτιμαέτην, άτην					
Future	τιμήσω			τιμήσοιμι	τιμήσειν	τιμήσων, σοντος
Aorist	ἐτίμησα	τίμησον	τιμήσω	τιμήσαιμι	τιμῆσαι	τιμήσας, σαντος
Perfect	τετίμηκα	τετίμηκε	τετιμήκω	τετιμήκοιμι	τετιμηκέναι	τετιμηκώς, κότος
Pluperf.	ἐτετιμήκειν					

REMARKS.

1. Rules of contraction: 1st, αο, αω, αου into ω; 2nd, αοι into ῳ (ι subscript); 3rd, αε, αη, into α; 4th, αει, αῃ, into ᾳ (ι subscript).

2. For the optative, instead of τιμῷμι, the Attics wrote also τιμῴην, τιμῴης, τιμῴη, τιμῴημεν, τιμῴητε, τιμῷεν.

SECTION XIX.—CONTRACTED VERB IN Α'Ω.

TABLE S.—PASSIVE VOICE.

	INDICATIVE.	IMPERATIVE.	SUBJUNCTIVE.	OPTATIVE.	INFINITIVE.	PARTICIPLES.
Pres.	*I am honoured*, &c.					
Sing.	τιμάομαι, ῶμαι		τιμάωμαι, ῶμαι	τιμαοίμην, ῴμην	τιμάεσθαι, ᾶσθαι	M. τιμαόμενος, ώμενος τιμαομένου, ωμένου
	τιμάῃ, ᾷ	τιμάου, ῶ	τιμάῃ, ᾷ	τιμάοιο, ῷο		
	τιμάεται, ᾶται	τιμαέσθω άσθω	τιμάηται, ᾶται	τιμάοιτο, ῷτο		
Plur.	τιμαόμεθα, ώμεθα		τιμαώμεθα, ώμεθα	τιμαοίμεθα, ῴμεθα		F. τιμαομένη, ωμένη
	τιμάεσθε, ᾶσθε	τιμάεσθε, ᾶσθε	τιμάησθε, ᾶσθε	τιμάοισθε, ῷσθε		τιμαομένης, ωμένης
	τιμάονται, ῶνται	τιμαέσθωσαν, άσθωσαν	τιμάωνται, ῶνται	τιμάοιντο, ῷντο		
Dual	τιμαόμεθον, ώμεθον		τιμαώμεθον, ώμεθον	τιμαοίμεθον, ῴμεθον		N. τιμαόμενον, ώμενον
	τιμάεσθον, ᾶσθον	τιμαέσθον, άσθον	τιμάησθον, ᾶσθον	τιμαοίσθην, ῴσθην		τιμαομένου, ωμένου
	τιμάεσθον, ᾶσθον	τιμαέσθων, άσθων	τιμάησθον, ᾶσθον	τιμαοίσθην, ῴσθην		

TABLE S.—PASSIVE VOICE.—(*Continued.*)

	INDICATIVE.	IMPERATIVE.	SUBJUNCTIVE.	OPTATIVE.	INFINITIVE.	PARTICIPLES.
Impf.						
Sing.	ἐτιμαόμην, ώμην					
	ἐτιμάου, ῶ					
	ἐτιμάετο, ᾶτο					
Plur.	ἐτιμαόμεθα, ώμεθα					
	ἐτιμάεσθε, ᾶσθε					
	ἐτιμάοντο, ῶντο					
Dual	ἐτιμαόμεθον, ώμεθον					
	ἐτιμαέσθην, άσθην					
	ἐτιμαέσθην, άσθην					
Fut.	τιμηθήσομαι			τιμηθησοίμην	τιμηθήσεσθαι	τιμηθησόμενος, ου
Aor.	ἐτιμήθην	τιμήθητι	τιμηθῶ	τιμηθείην	τιμηθῆναι	τιμηθείς, θέντος
Perf.	τετίμημαι	τετίμησο	τετιμημένος ὦ	τετιμημένος εἴην	τετιμῆσθαι	τετιμημένος, ου
Plupf.	ἐτετιμήμην					
3d Fut.	τετιμήσομαι			τετιμησοίμην	τετιμήσεσθαι	τετιμησόμενος, ου

MIDDLE VOICE.

Fut.	τιμήσομαι			τιμησοίμην	τιμήσεσθαι	τιμησόμενος, ου
Aor.	ἐτιμησάμην	τίμησαι	τιμήσωμαι	τιμησαίμην	τιμήσασθαι	τιμησάμενος, ου

REMARKS.

1. The 3rd pers. sing. of the imperfect would originally be ἐτιμάεσο; by rejecting σ and contracting εο into ου, we have ἐτιμάου, then ἐτιμῶ.

2. The present subjunctive, after contraction, is the same as that of the indicative (as also in the active voice); because αε and αη are alike contracted in α.

SECTION XX.—CONTRACTED VERB IN O'Ω.

TABLE T.—ACTIVE VOICE.

	INDICATIVE.	IMPERATIVE.	SUBJUNCTIVE.	OPTATIVE.	INFINITIVE.	PARTICIPLES
Present	*I show*, &c.					
Sing.	δηλόω, ῶ		δηλόω, ῶ	δηλόοιμι, οῖμι	δηλόειν, οῦν	M. δηλόων, ῶν
	δηλόεις, οῖς	δήλοε, ου	δηλόῃς, οῖς	δηλόοις, οῖς		δηλόοντος, οῦντος
	δηλόει, οῖ	δηλοέτω, ούτω	δηλόῃ, οῖ	δηλόοι, οῖ		
Plur.	δηλόομεν, οῦμεν		δηλόωμεν, ῶμεν	δηλόοιμεν, οῖμεν		F. δηλόουσα, οῦσα
	δηλόετε, οῦτε	δηλόετε, οῦτε	δηλόητε, ῶτε	δηλόοιτε, οῖτε		δηλοούσης, ούσης
	δηλόουσι, οῦσι	δηλοέτωσαν, ούτωσαν	δηλόωσι, ῶσι	δηλόοιεν, οῖεν		
Dual	δηλόετον, οῦτον	δηλόετον, οῦτον	δηλόητον, ῶτον	δηλοοίτην, οίτην		N. δηλόον, οῦν
	δηλόετον, οῦτον	δηλοέτων, ούτων	δηλόητον, ῶτον	δηλοοίτην, οίτην		δηλόοντος, οῦντος
Imperf.						
Sing.	ἐδήλοον, ουν					
	ἐδήλοες, ους					
	ἐδήλοε, ου					
Plur.	ἐδηλόομεν, οῦμεν					
	ἐδηλόετε, οῦτε					
	ἐδήλοον, ουν					
Dual	ἐδηλοέτην, ούτην					
	ἐδηλοέτην, ούτην					
Future	δηλώσω			δηλώσοιμι	δηλώσειν	δηλώσων, σοντος
Aorist	ἐδήλωσα	δήλωσον	δηλώσω	δηλώσαιμι	δηλῶσαι	δηλώσας, σαντος
Perfect	δεδήλωκα	δεδήλωκε	δεδηλώκω	δεδηλώκοιμι	δεδηλωκέναι	δεδηλωκώς, κότος
Pluperf.	ἐδεδηλώκειν					

REMARKS.

1. Rules of contraction. 1st, οε, οο, οου, ου; 2nd, οη, οω, into ω; 3rd, οη, οει, οοι, into οι. In the infinitive, όειν is contracted into οῦν.

2. Instead of the form δηλοῖμι for the optative, the Attics also wrote δηλοίην, δηλοίης, δηλοίη, &c.

SECTION XXI.—CONTRACTED VERB IN Ο'Ω.

TABLE U.—PASSIVE VOICE.

	INDICATIVE.	IMPERATIVE.	SUBJUNCTIVE.	OPTATIVE.	INFINITIVE.	PARTICIPLES.
Present	*I am shown*, &c.					
Sing.	δηλόομαι, οῦμαι		δηλόωμαι, ῶμαι	δηλοοίμην, οίμην	δηλόεσθαι, οῦσθαι	M. δηλοόμενος, ούμενος
	δηλόῃ, οῖ	δηλόου, οῦ	δηλόῃ, οῖ	δηλόοιο, οῖο		δηλοομένου, ουμένου
	δηλόεται, οῦται	δηλοέσθω, ούσθω	δηλόηται, ῶται	δηλόοιτο, οῖτο		
Plur.	δηλοόμεθα, ούμεθα		δηλοώμεθα, ώμεθα	δηλοοίμεθα, οίμεθα		F. δηλοομένη, ουμένη
	δηλόεσθε, οῦσθε	δηλόεσθε, οῦσθε	δηλόησθε, ῶσθε	δηλόοισθε, οῖσθε		δηλοομένης, ουμένης
	δηλόονται, οῦνται	δηλοέσθωσαν, ούσθωσαν	δηλόωνται, ῶνται	δηλόοιντο, οῖντο		
Dual	δηλοόμεθον, ούμεθον		δηλοώμεθον, ώμεθον	δηλοοίμεθον, οίμεθον		N. δηλοόμενον, ούμενον
	δηλόεσθον, οῦσθον	δηλόεσθον, οῦσθον	δηλόησθον, ῶσθον	δηλοοίσθην, οίσθην		δηλοομένου ουμένου
	δηλόεσθον, οῦσθον	δηλοέσθων, ούσθων	δηλόησθον, ῶσθον	δηλοοίσθην, οίσθην		
Imperf.						
Sing.	ἐδηλοόμην, ούμην					
	ἐδηλόου, οῦ					
	ἐδηλόετο, οῦτο					
Plur.	ἐδηλοόμεθα, ούμεθα					
	ἐδηλόεσθε, οῦσθε					
	ἐδηλόοντο, οῦντο					
Dual	ἐδηλοόμεθον, ούμεθον					
	ἐδηλοέσθην, ούσθην					
	ἐδηλοέσθην, ούσθην					
Future	δηλωθήσομαι			δηλωθησοίμην	δηλωθήσεσθαι	δηλωθησόμενος, ου
Aorist	ἐδηλώθην	δηλώθητι	δηλωθῶ	δηλωθείην	δηλωθῆναι	δηλωθείς, θέντος
Perfect	δεδήλωμαι	δεδήλωσο	δεδηλωμενος ὦ	δεδηλωμένος εἴην	δεδηλῶσθαι	δεδηλωμένος, ου
Pluperf.	ἐδεδηλώμην					
3rd Fut.	δεδηλώσομαι			δεδηλωσοίμην	δεδηλώσεσθαι	δεδηλωσόμενος, ου

MIDDLE VOICE.

Future	δηλώσομαι			δηλωσοίμην	δηλώσεσθαι	δηλωσόμενος, ου
Aorist	ἐδηλωσάμην	δήλωσαι	δηλώσωμαι	δηλωσαίμην	δηλώσασθαι	δηλωσάμενος, ου

SECTION XXII.

REMARKS ON VERBS IN Ω PURE, I. E. PRECEDED BY A VOWEL.

1. Many verbs in έω make the future in έσω (not ήσω); e. g. τελέω, *I finish*, τελέσω; ἀρκέω, ἀρκέσω. Some have both forms; e. g. αἰνέω, *I praise*, αἰνέσω, and αἰνήσω; φορέω, *I bear*, φορέσω, and φορήσω.

2. Of verbs in άω, many keep α in the future. Those which have ε or ι before άω; e. g. ἐάω, *I permit*, ἐάσω; θεάομαι, *I behold*, θεάσομαι, perf. τεθέαμαι, aor. ἐθεάθην. Those in ραω; e. g. ὁράω, *I see*, ὁράσω (not used). Those

in λάω; e. g. γελάω, *I laugh*, γελάσω; κλάω, *I break*, κλάσω. Also κρεμάω, *I hang up*, κρεμάσω; σπάω, *I draw*, σπάσω. But χράω, *I lend*, has χρήσω; τλάω, *I bear*, τλήσω.

3. Of verbs in όω a very few keep ο in the future; e. g. ἀρόω, *I plough*, ἀρόσω. All others have ω, as δηλώσω.

4. Future and aorist passive. Many verbs have σ before θήσομαι in the future, and before θην in the aorist; e. g. χρίω, *I anoint*, χρίσω, χρισθήσομαι, ἐχρίσθην; τελέω, *I finish*, τελέσω, τελεσθήσομαι, ἐτελέσθην; κλείω, *I shut*, κλείσω, κλεισθήσομαι, ἐκλείσθην; ἀκούω, *I hear*, ἀκούσω, ἀκουσθήσομαι, ἠκούσθην. Indeed, almost all verbs which have a short vowel or a diphthong before the termination receive σ; καλέω, *I call*, καλέσω, makes κέκληκα, κέκλημαι, ἐκλήθην, as if from κλέω, κλήσω. But κέκληκα is for κεκάλεκα, by contraction.

5. Perfect passive. Generally, verbs which have σ in the future and aorist passive have it also in the perfect; e. g. τετέλεσμαι, κέχρισμαι, κέκλεισμαι, ἤκουσμαι.

But some have σ in the aorist, and not in the perfect; e. g. μνάομαι, *I remember*, ἐμνήσθην, but μέμνημαι; παύω, *I cause to cease*, ἐπαύσθην, but πέπαυμαι.

6. The perfect passive of verbs which have σ before μαι is conjugated as follows:—

	INDICATIVE.	PLUPERFECT.	IMPERATIVE.
Perfect. Sing.	ἤκουσμαι	ἠκούσμην	
	ἤκουσαι	ἤκουσο	ἤκουσο
	ἤκουσται	ἤκουστο	ἠκούσθω
Plur.	ἠκούσμεθα	ἠκούσμεθα	
	ἤκουσθε	ἤκουσθε	ἤκουσθε
	ἠκουσμένοι εἰσί	ἠκουσμένοι ἦσαν	ἠκούσθωσαι
Dual	ἠκούσμεθον	ἠκούσμεθον	
	ἤκουσθον	ἠκούσθην	ἤκουσθον
	ἤκουσθον	ἠκούσθην	ἠκούσθων

SUBJUNCTIVE.	ἠκουσμένος ὦ, ᾖς, ᾖ
OPTATIVE.	ἠκουσμένος εἴην, εἴης, εἴη
INFINITIVE.	ἠκοῦσθαι
PARTICIPLE.	ἠκουσμένος, μένη, μένον

7. According to the analogy of λέλυται, λέλυνται, the 3rd pers. pl. of ἤκουσμαι should be ἤκουσνται. The harshness of three consonants thus concurring is avoided by combining the 3rd pers. pl. indic. of εἶναι, *to be*, with the perf. part. ἠκουσμένοι εἰσί. The same remark applies to the pluperf., where the 3rd pers. plur. imperf. of εἶναι is used; ἠκουσμένοι ἦσαν

SECTION XXIII.

REMARKS ON VERBS WHICH HAVE A CONSONANT OR CONSONANTS BEFORE Ω.

1. Future and aorist active. (*a*) All verbs which have in the radical form a mute of the first order, Β, Π, Φ, form the future in ψω; e. g. τρίβω, *I bruise*, τρίψω; γράφω, *I write*, γράψω.

(*b*) Those which have a mute of the second order, Γ, Κ, Χ, form it in ξω; e. g. λέγω, *I say*, λέξω; βρέχω, *I wet*, βρέξω. So in the middle form, δέχομαι, fut. δέξομαι, &c.

(*c*) Those which have a mute of the third order, Δ, Τ, Θ, form it in σω; e. g. ᾄδω, *I sing*, ᾄσω; ἀνύτω, *I finish*, ἀνύσω; πλήθω, *I fill*, πλήσω

2. If the radical has τ before π, as in τύπτω, the τ is lost in the future; e. g. τύψω.

The aorists are in ψα, ξα, and σα; e. g. ἔτυψα, ἔλεξα, ἤνυσα.

3. Future and aorist passive. (*a*) Verbs which have in the radical a mute of the first order form the future pass. in φθήσομαι; e. g. τύπτω, τυφθήσομαι.

(*b*) Those with a mute of the second order form it in χθήσομαι; e. g. λέγω, λεχθήσομαι.

(*c*) Those with a mute of the third order, in σθήσομαι; e. g. ἀνύτω, ἀνυσθήσομαι.

4. Since the aorist pass. is formed from the future by changing θήσομαι into θην, the aorist will be, for the first order, φθην, ἐτύφθην; for the second, χθην, ελέχθην; for the third, σθην, ἠνύσθην.

5. Future and aorist middle. For the future, the ω of the future active is changed into ομαι; e. g. τύψω, τύψομαι; λέξω, λέξομαι; ἀνύσω, ἀνύσομαι.

For the aorist, μην is added to the aorist active; e. g. ἔτυψα, ἐτυψάμην; ἔλεξα, ἐλεξάμην; ἤνυσα, ἠνυσάμην.

6. Perfect and pluperfect active. Verbs which have the future in ψω, form the perfect in φα; e. g. τύψω, τέτυφα.

Those with the future in ξω, form the perfect in χα, with χ; e. g. πράξω, πέπραχα.

Those with the future in σω, form the perf. in κα, with κ; e. g. πείσω, πέπεικα.

The pluperfect is regularly formed by changing α into ειν, and prefixing the augment; e. g. τέτυφα, ἐτετύφειν, &c.

7. Perfect and pluperfect passive. Verbs which have the perf. act. in φα, form the perf. pass. in μμαι, with double μ; e. g. τέτυφα, τέτυμμαι (by assimilation for τέτυπμαι).

Those which have the perf. act. in χ, with χ, form the perf. pass. in γμαι; e. g. πέπραχα, πέπραγμαι.

Those with the perf. act. in κα, with κ, form the perf. pass. in σμαι; e. g. πέπεικα, πέπεισμαι.

The pluperfect is formed by changing μαι into μην, and prefixing the augment: ἐτετύμμην, ελελέγμην.

8 Example of perf. pass. in μμαι, from τύπτω, *I strike*:—

	INDICATIVE.	PLUPERFECT.	IMPERATIVE.		
Perfect. Sing.	τέτυμμαι	ἐτετύμμην		SUBJUNCTIVE.	τετυμμένος ὦ, ᾖς, ᾖ
	τέτυψαι	ἐτέτυψο	τέτυψο		
	τέτυπται	ἐτέτυπτο	τετύφθω	OPTATIVE.	τετυμμένος εἴην, εἴης, εἴη
Plur.	τετύμμεθα	ἐτετύμμεθα			
	τέτυφθε	ἐτέτυφθε	τέτυφθε	INFINITIVE.	τετύφθαι
	τετυμμένοι εἰσί	τετυμμένοι ἦσαν	τετύφθωσαν		
Dual	τετύμμεθον	ἐτετύμμεθον		PARTICIPLE.	τετυμμένος, μένη, μένον
	τέτυφθον	ἐτετύφθην	τέτυφθον		
	τέτυφθον	ἐτετύφθην	τετύφθων		

9. Perf. pass. in γμαι, from λέγω, *I say*.

	INDICATIVE.	PLUPERFECT.	IMPERATIVE.		
Perfect. Sing.	λέλεγμαι	ἐλελέγμην		SUBJUNCTIVE.	λελεγμένος ὦ, ᾖς, ᾖ
	λέλεξαι	ἐλέλεξο	λέλεξο		
	λέλεκται	ἐλέλεκτο	λελέχθω	OPTATIVE.	λελεγμένος εἴην, εἴης, εἴη
Plur.	λελέγμεθα	ἐλελέγμεθα			
	λέλεχθε	ἐλέλεχθε	λέλεχθε	INFINITIVE.	λελέχθαι
	λελεγμένοι εἰσί	λελεγμένοι ἦσαν	λελέχθωσαν		
Dual	λελέγμεθον	ἐλελέγμεθον		PARTICIPLE.	λελεγμένος, μένη, μένον
	λέλεχθον	ἐλελέχθην	λέλεχθον		
	λέλεχθον	ἐλελέχθην	λελέχθων		

Ἐλέγχω, *I convict*, forms the perf. ἐλήλεγμαι. But the γ of the radical re-appears in the 2nd and 3rd persons, ἐλήλεγξαι, ἐλήλεγκται; in the future, ἐλεγχθήσομαι, and in the aorist, ἠλέγχθην.

10. The conjugation of all perfects passive in σμαι accords with the example already given; § xxii. remark 6.

SECTION XXIV.

REMARKS ON THE SECOND AORIST AND SECOND FUTURE.

1. Very few verbs have both the 1st and 2nd aorist active. Both forms of the aorist have the same signification.

2. The active and middle voices have each only one form of the future: the passive has two, without difference of signification, though very few verbs exhibit both. The third future, already noticed, has a distinct meaning.

3. The radical portion of the second form of the future in the passive voice is the same as that of the second aorist active: the termination is ησομαι; e. g. ἔτυπον, τυπήσομαι, ήσῃ, ήσεται. Optat. τυπησοίμην, ήσοιο, ήσοιτο. Infin. τυπήσεσθαι. Part. τυπησόμενος.

4. The future middle is in many verbs used simply as the future of the active voice; e. g. ἀκούω, fut. ἀκούσομαι.

5. The second aorist active has the termination and augment of the imperfect. It is generally characterised by certain changes, in respect of the present, either in the final consonant of the root, or its vowel portion, or both. The penultimate syllable of this tense is mostly short in quantity. This form of the aorist has been supposed to be derived from an older and simpler form of the present It is conjugated like the imperf., but has all the moods; e. g. Indic. ἔτυπον, ες, ε. Imperat. τύπε, τυπέτω. Subjunct. τύπω, ῃς, ῃ. Optat. τύποιμι, οις, οι. Infin. τυπεῖν. Part. τυπών, όντος.

6. The second aorist passive is formed from the active, by changing ον into ην, and prefixing the augment; e. g. Indic. ἐτύπην, ης, η. Imperat. τύπηθι, ήτω. Subjunct. τυπῶ, ῇς, ῇ. Optat. τυπείην, είης, είη. Infin. τυπῆναι. Part. τυπείς, έντος. Very few verbs have both the active and passive second aorist.

7. The second aorist middle is formed from that of the active, by changing ον into όμην; e. g. Indic. ἐτυπόμην, ου, ετο. Imperat. τυποῦ, έσθω. Subjunct. τύπωμαι, ῃ, ηται. Optat. τυποίμην, οιο, οιτο. Infin. τυπέσθαι. Part. τυπόμενος.

8. Changes in the second aorist. (*a*) Several verbs change π of the pres. into β; e. g. κρύπτω, *I hide*, 2nd aor. pass. ἐκρύβην; βλάπτω, *I hurt*, ἐβλάβην, as if from primitives in βω.

(*b*) Others change π into φ; e. g. ῥίπτω, *I cast*, ἐῤῥίφην; βάπτω, *I dip*, ἐβάφην, as if from primitives in φω. So θάπτω, *I bury*, makes aor. pass. ἐτάφην.

(*c*) ψύχω, *I cool*, changes χ into γ; e. g. ψύχω, fut. ψύξω, 2nd aor. pass. ἐψύγην, 2nd fut. ψυγήσομαι.

9. If the termination of the pres. is preceded by η, it is changed in the 2nd aor. into α short; e. g. λήβω (primitive form of λαμβάνω, *I take*), ἔλαβον; λήθω, prim. of λανθάνω, *I am hidden*, ἔλαθον. But, πλήσσω, *I strike*. makes ἐπλήγην.

If the termination of the pres. is preceded by the dipththongs ει, ευ, they are shortened by rejecting the ι; e. g. λείπω, *I leave*, ἔλιπον; φεύγω, *I flee*, ἔφυγον.

10. Verbs of two syllables, with ε before the termination, preceded (or followed) by ρ or λ, change the ε into α in the 2nd aor.; e. g. τρέπω, *I turn*, ἔτραπον; τρέφω, *I nourish*, ἐτράφην.

11. Contracted verbs have no 2nd aor. or 2nd fut. So, generally, other verbs in ω pure. But a few have the 2nd aor. pass.; e. g. καίω, *I burn*, εκάην; φύω, *I produce*, ἐφύην.

SECTION XXV.

REMARKS ON THE SECOND OR MIDDLE PERFECT.

1. This form is properly a second perfect active, and is formed by adding α to the radical (τυπ), and prefixing the reduplication; e. g. τέτυπα.

Indic. perf. τετυπα, ας, ε. Pluperf. ἐτετυπειν, εις, ει. Imperat. τέτυπε, τετυπέτω. Subj. τετύπω, ῃς, ῃ. Optat. τετύποιμι, οις, οι. Infin. τετυπέναι. Part. τετυπώς, υῖα, ός; τετυπότος, υίας, ότος.

2. Very few verbs in ω pure have the 2nd perf.; contracted verbs never, because they all easily form the 1st perf. in κα.

3. In some verbs the 2nd perf. is alone used; e. g. φεύγω, *I flee*. πέφευγα.

4. In some verbs with both perfects, the 1st has an active, the 2nd a neuter or intransitive signification; e. g. πείθω, *I persuade*, 1st perf. πέπεικα, *I have persuaded*; 2nd perf. πέποιθα, *I trust*. So ἀνέῳχα τὴν θύραν, *I have opened the door*; ἀνέῳγεν ἡ θύρα, *the door is open*; ἐγήγερκα, *I have aroused*; ἐγρήγορα, *I am awake*; ὀλώλεκα, *I have lost*; ὄλωλα, *I am ruined*, &c.

5. Verbs which have αι in the pres. change it into η in the 2nd perf.; e. g. φαίνω, *I show*, πέφηνα. Those of two syllables which have ε in the pres. change it into ο; e. g. κτείνω, ἔκτονα. Lastly, ει of the pres. is changed into οι; e. g. λείπω, λέλοιπα; ἀμείβω, *I change*, ἤμοιβα; πείθω, πέποιθα.

SECTION XXVI.

REMARKS ON VERBS IN ΖΩ AND ΣΣΩ.

1. Most of these verbs come from primitives in ω pure, and therefore form the future in σω, and the perfect in κα. They take σ in the future, aorist, and perfect passive; e.g. ὁρίζω, *I limit*, ὁρίσω, ὥρισα, ὥρικα, ὥρισμαι, 1st aor. ὡρίσθην. The penultimate syllable of their futures in ασω and ισω is always short.

2. Several of them appear to come from primitives in γω, and form the future in ξω, and the perf. in χα; e.g. στίζω, *I puncture*, στίξω, ἔστιγμαι; κράζω, *I cry*, κράξω, 2nd perf. κέκραγα.

A few form the future both in σω and ξω; e.g. ἁρπάζω, *I carry off*, ἁρπάσω and ἁρπάξω.

3. The verbs in σσω seem also to come from primitives in γω, and form the future in ξω, and the perfect in χα; e.g. πράσσω, *I do*, πράξω, πέπραχα, πέπραγμαι; τάσσω, *I appoint*, fut. τάξω, makes 2nd aor. pass. ἐτάγην; σφάττω, *I slay*, σφάξω, ἐσφάγην; ἁρπάζω, *I carry off*, 2nd aor. pass. ἡρπάγην; ἀλλάττω, *I change*, ἀλλάξω, 2nd aor. pass. ἠλλάγην.

A very few come from primitives in ω pure, and form the future in σω; e.g. πλάσσω, *I form*, πλάσω, πέπλασμαι.

4. The verbs ending in ζω form the most numerous class in the language, next to those in ω pure. The Attic Greeks change the termination σσω into ττω; e.g. πράττω. for πράσσω, ἀλλάττω for ἀλλάσσω, &c.

SECTION XXVII.

REMARKS ON VERBS IN ΛΩ, ΜΩ, ΝΩ, ΡΩ.

1. Active voice. Future and first aorist. (*a*) These verbs do not take σ in the fut.,* which they form in ῶ, and conjugate like the contracted form of φιλέω; e.g. κρίνω, *I judge*, κρινῶ; νέμω, *I distribute*. νεμῶ; ἀμύνω, *I defend*, ἀμυνῶ.

(*b*) If the pres. has two consonants, one is rejected, in order to shorten the syllable which precedes the termination; e.g. ψάλλω, *I play on an instrument*, ψαλῶ; κάμνω, *I labour*, καμῶ; στέλλω, *I send*, στελῶ; ἀγγέλλω, *I announce*, ἀγγελῶ.

(*c*) If the diphthongs αι or ει precede the termination, they are shortened by rejecting the ι; e.g. φαίνω, *I show*, φανῶ; σημαίνω, *I signify*, σημανῶ; σπείρω, *I sow*, σπερῶ.

(*d*) But in the first aor. the ι occurs, even if wanting in the present: e.g. νέμω, fut. νεμῶ, aor. ἔνειμα; ἀγγέλλω, ἀγγελῶ, ἤγγειλα; σπείρω, σπερῶ, ἔσπειρα; στέλλω, στελῶ, ἔστειλα.

(*e*) The α of the fut. is changed into η in the aor., especially in Attic Greek; e.g. ψάλλω, ψαλῶ, ἔψηλα; φαίνω, φανῶ, ἔφηνα; σημαίνω, σημανῶ, ἐσήμηνα. The α, however, is often retained, and is long in quantity. It especially occurs when preceded by ρ; e.g. μαραίνω, *I wither*, μαρανῶ, ἐμάρανα.

(*f*) The vowel, then, which precedes the termination, is short in the fut., and long in the 1st aor.

2. Perfect. (*a*) This tense in these verbs is formed from the future, by changing ῶ into κα; e.g. ψάλλω. ψαλῶ, ἔψαλκα; ἀγγέλλω, ἀγγελῶ, ἤγγελκα. The consonant ν becomes γ before κ; e.g. φαίνω, φανῶ, πέφαγκα; πλατύνω, perf. act. πεπλάτυγκα, perf. pass. πεπλάτυμαι, 1st aor. pass. ἐπλατύνθην.

(*b*) Dissyllables in λω and ρω, which have ε in the fut., change it into α in the perf.; e.g. στέλλω, στελῶ, ἔσταλκα; σπείρω, σπερῶ, ἔσπαρκα; φθείρω, φθερῶ, ἔφθαρκα.

(*c*) Dissyllables in ίνω and ύνω reject the ν in the perf., which tense they form as if they came from ίω and ύω; e.g. κρίνω, κρινῶ, κέκρικα; πλύνω, *I wash*, πλυνῶ, πέπλυκα. κλίνω sometimes resumes the ν in the 1st aor. pass., ἐκλίνθην, for ἐκλίθην. Those in είνω form the perf. as if they came from άω; e.g. τείνω, *I stretch*, τενῶ, τέτακα, as if from the pres. τάω.

(*d*) Several verbs in μω and μνω form the perf. in ηκα, as if the fut. were in ήσω; e.g. νέμω, νεμῶ, νενέμηκα; κάμνω, καμῶ, καμοῦμαι, κέκμηκα (for κεκάμηκα), 2nd aor. ἔκαμον; τέμνω, τεμῶ, τέτμηκα (for τετάμηκα); μένω, μενῶ, μεμένηκα; &c. So βάλλω, βαλῶ, βέβληκα (for βεβάληκα), 2nd aor. ἔβαλον.

3. Passive voice. First future, first aorist, and perfect. These tenses are directly derived from the perf. act. by changing κα into μαι, θήσομαι, and θην; e.g. perf. act. βέβληκα, βέβλημαι, βληθήσομαι, ἐβλήθην; &c.: μιαίνω, fut. μιανῶ, makes perf. pass. μεμίασμαι 1st aor. pass. ἐμιάνθην.

4. Second aorist, active and passive, and second future passive. (*a*) Dissyllables change their vowel into α to form the 2nd aor.; e.g. σπείρω, σπερῶ, 2nd aor. pass. ἐσπάρην;

* Ἀποτίνω, *I repay*, makes fut. ἀποτίσω, but is, in fact, a compound of τίω.

φθείρω, φθερῶ, 2nd aor. pass. ἐφθάρην. But, ἀγγέλλω, 2nd aor. pass. ἠγγέλην.

(b) The 2nd aorist is formed in general as in other classes of verbs; e. g. κάμνω, 2nd aor. ἔκαμον; φαίνω, 2nd aor. pass. ἐφάνην; χαίρω, 2nd aor. pass. ἐχάρην.

(c) So in the case of the 2nd fut. pass.; e. g. φαίνω, 2nd fut. pass. φανήσομαι.

5. Second or middle perfect. All dissyllable verbs (of those in λω, μω, νω, ρω) which have ε in the future, take ο in the 2nd perf. (§ xxv. rem. 5); e. g. σπείρω, σπερῶ, ἔσπορα.

All those which have αι in the pres. and α in the fut. take η in the 2nd perf.; e.g. φαίνω, fut. φανῶ, 2nd perf. πέφηνα; θάλλω, *I flourish*, τέθηλα.

6. It should be observed that the fut. mid. of these verbs ends in ουμαι; e. g. αἰσχύνομαι, *I am ashamed*, αἰσχυνοῦμαι.

SECTION XXVIII.—VERBS IN MI.

REMARKS.

1. These are formed from primitives in εω, άω, όω, ύω, from which they differ as to conjugation in three tenses, the present, imperfect, and second aorist. The remaining tenses are regularly formed.

2. The primitive forms θέω, *I place*, στάω, *I set up*, δόω, *I give*, and δεικνύω, *I show*, may be taken as examples. To form a verb in μι from θέω, (1) the ω is changed into μι. (2) ε, the short vowel, becomes η; θημι. (3) ι with the reduplication is prefixed; τίθημι.

3. From στάω, (1) α is changed into η; στημι. (2) ι with the rough breathing is prefixed; ἵστημι. So when the root begins with πτ, ι aspirated is prefixed instead of the reduplication; e. g. πτάω, ἵπταμαι.

4. From δόω, ο being changed into ω, we have δωμι, and, with the reduplication, δίδωμι.

5. From δεικνύω, and all those which end in ύω, the change of the last letter ω into μι is sufficient; δεικνύω, δείκνυμι. In the Tables, the middle voice is given before the passive, to show more clearly the relation of the 2nd aor. middle with the 2nd aor. active.

TABLE V.—τίθημι, ACTIVE VOICE.

	INDICATIVE.	IMPERATIVE.	SUBJUNCTIVE.	OPTATIVE.	INFINITIVE.	PARTICIPLES.
Present	*I place, &c.*					
Sing.	τίθημι		τιθῶ	τιθείην	τιθέναι	M. τιθείς
	τίθης	τίθετε	τιθῇς	τιθείης		τιθέντος
	τίθησι	τιθέτω	τιθῇ	τιθείη		
Plur.	τίθεμεν		τιθῶμεν	τιθείημεν		F. τιθεῖσα
	τίθετε	τίθετε	τιθῆτε	τιθείητε		τιθείσης
	τιθεῖσι	τιθέτωσαν	τιθῶσι	τιθείησαν		
Dual	τίθετον	τίθετον	τιθῆτον	τιθειήτην		N. τιθέν
	τίθετον	τιθέτων	τιθῆτον	τιθειήτην		τιθέντος
Imperf.						
Sing.	ἐτίθην					
	ἐτίθης					
	ἐτίθη					
Plur.	ἐτίθεμεν					
	ἐτίθετε					
	ἐτίθεσαν					
Dual	ἐτιθέτην					
	ἐτιθέτην					

TABLE V.—τίθημι, ACTIVE VOICE.—(*Continued.*)

	INDICATIVE.	IMPERATIVE.	SUBJUNCTIVE.	OPTATIVE.	INFINITIVE.	PARTICIPLES.
2nd Aor. Sing.	ἔθην		θῶ	θείην	θεῖναι	M. θείς
	ἔθης	θές	θῇς	θείης		θέντος
	ἔθη	θέτω	θῇ	θείη		
Plur.	ἔθεμεν		θῶμεν	θείημεν		F. θεῖσα
	ἔθετε	θέτε	θῆτε	θείητε		θείσης
	ἔθεσαν	θέτωσαν	θῶσι	θείησαν		
Dual	ἐθέτην	θέτον	θῆτον	θειήτην		N. θέν
	ἐθέτην	θέτων	θῆτον	θειήτην		θέντος
Future	θήσω			θήσοιμι	θήσειν	M. θήσων, σοντος
1st Aor.	ἔθηκα					
Perfect	τέθεικα	τέθεικε	τεθείκω	τεθείκοιμι	τεθεικέναι	M. τεθεικώς, κότος
Pluperf.	ἐτεθείκειν					

TABLE W.—τίθημι, MIDDLE VOICE.

	INDICATIVE.	IMPERATIVE.	SUBJUNCTIVE.	OPTATIVE.	INFINITIVE.	PARTICIPLES.
Present Sing.	τίθεμαι		τιθῶμαι	τιθείμην	τίθεσθαι	M. τιθέμενος
	τίθεσαι	τίθεσο	τιθῇ	τιθεῖο		τιθεμένου
	τίθεται	τιθέσθω	τιθῆται	τιθεῖτο		
Plur.	τιθέμεθα		τιθώμεθα	τιθείμεθα		F. τιθεμένη
	τίθεσθε	τίθεσθε	τιθῆσθε	τιθεῖσθε		τιθεμένης
	τίθενται	τιθέσθωσαν	τιθῶνται	τιθεῖντο		
Dual	τιθέμεθον		τιθώμεθον	τιθείμεθον		N. τιθέμενον
	τίθεσθον	τίθεσθον	τιθῆσθον	τιθείσθην		τιθεμένου
	τίθεσθον	τιθέσθων	τιθῆσθον	τιθείσθην		
Imperf. Sing.	ἐτιθέμην					
	ἐτίθεσο					
	ἐτίθετο					
Plur.	ἐτιθέμεθα					
	ἐτίθεσθε					
	ἐτίθεντο					
Dual	ἐτιθέμεθον					
	ἐτιθέσθην					
	ἐτιθέσθην					
2nd Aor. Sing.	ἐθέμην		θῶμαι	θείμην	θέσθαι	M. θέμενος
	ἔθεσο	θέσο	θῇ	θεῖο		θεμένου
	ἔθετο	θέσθω	θῆται	θεῖτο		
Plur.	ἐθέμεθα		θώμεθα	θείμεθα		F. θεμένη
	ἔθεσθε	θέσθε	θῆσθε	θεῖσθε		θεμένης
	ἔθεντο	θέσθωσαν	θῶνται	θεῖντο		
Dual	ἐθέμεθον		θώμεθον	θείμεθον		N. θέμενον
	ἐθέσθην	θέσθον	θῆσθον	θείσθην		θεμένου
	ἐθέσθην	θέσθων	θῆσθον	θείσθην		
Future	θήσομαι			θησοίμην	θήσεσθαι	M. θησόμενος, ου
1st Aor.	ἐθηκάμην					M. θηκάμενος, ου

6. Present and imperfect active. For τιθεῖσι, the Attics wrote τιθέᾱσι.

The imperf. ἐτίθην, ης, η, is conjugated like the aor. pass. ἐλύθην; but, ἐτίθεμεν, &c., not ἐτίθημεν.

7. The second aorist is formed from the imperf. by rejecting the duplication τι; e. g. imperf. ἐτίθην, 2nd aor. ἔθην. It takes the long vowel in the sing., the short in the plur., ἔθην, ης, η; plur. ἔθεμεν, &c.

The imperat. θές, is an abbreviation for θέτι.

8. Middle voice. (*a*) The present middle (or passive) is formed by changing μι into μαι, and resuming the short vowel of the root: e. g. τίθημι, τίθεμαι. It is conjugated like the perf. pass. of λύω, the 2nd and 3rd pers. sing. being in the full, not the contracted form. But ἔθου occurs for ἔθεσο.

(*b*) The subjunctive is formed from the subjunctive active by adding μαι; e. g. τιθῶ, τιθῶμαι.

(*c*) The optative is regularly formed from the indicative by changing μαι into ίμην; e. g. τίθεμαι, τιθείμην.

(*d*) The second aorist is formed, like that of the active voice, from the imperf. by rejecting τι; e. g. ἐτιθέμην, ἐθέμην. In the imperat. the contracted form θοῦ for θέσο is found in παράθου; 2 Tim. ii. 2.

9. (*a*) The future is formed from the primitive θέω; e. g. fut. act. θήσω; mid. θήσομαι.

(*b*) The first aorist ends, not in σα, but in κα; ἔθηκα, κας, κε, &c. It is scarcely used, either in the act. or mid. except in certain persons of the indicative.

(*c*) There are two other aorists in κα; e. g. ἔδωκα from δίδωμι, and ἧκα from ἵημι.

(*d*) The perfect has the diphthong ει, as if from θείω; e. g. τέθεικα, pluperf. ἐτεθείκειν.

10. Passive voice. The following are the tenses in use: the pres. and imperf. are like those of the middle.

	INDICATIVE.	IMPERATIVE.	SUBJUNCTIVE.	OPTATIVE.	INFINITIVE.	PARTICIPLES.
1st Fut.	τεθήσομαι			τεθησοίμην	τεθήσεσθαι	τεθησόμενος
1st Aor.	ἐτέθην	τέθητι	τεθῶ	τεθείην	τεθῆναι	τεθείς
Perfect	τέθειμαι	τέθεισο	τεθειμένος ὦ	τεθειμένος εἴην	τεθεῖσθαι	τεθειμένος
Pluperf.	ἐτεθείμην					

SECTION XXIX.

TABLE X.—ἵστημι, ACTIVE VOICE.

	INDICATIVE.	IMPERATIVE.	SUBJUNCTIVE.	OPTATIVE.	INFINITIVE.	PARTICIPLES.
Present	*I set*, &c.					
Sing.	ἵστημι		ἱστῶ	ἱσταίην	ἱστάναι (ᾰ)	M. ἱστάς
	ἵστης	ἵστᾰθι	ἱστῇς	ἱσταίης		ἱστάντος
	ἵστησι	ἱστάτω	ἱστῇ	ἱσταίη		
Plur.	ἵστᾰμεν		ἱστῶμεν	ἱσταίημεν		F. ἱστᾶσα
	ἵστᾰτε	ἵστᾰτε	ἱστῆτε	ἱσταίητε		ἱστάσης
	ἱστᾶσι	ἱστάτωσαν	ἱστῶσι	ἱσταίησαν		
Dual	ἵστᾰτον	ἵστᾰτον	ἱστῆτον	ἱσταιήτην		N. ἱστάν
	ἵστᾰτον	ἱστάτων	ἱστῆτον	ἱσταιήτην		ἱστάντος
Imperf.						
Sing.	ἵστην					
	ἵστης					
	ἵστη					
Plur.	ἵστᾰμεν					
	ἵστᾰτε					
	ἵστᾰσαν					
Dual	ἱστάτην (ᾰ)					
	ἱστάτην					

TABLE X.—ἵστημι, ACTIVE VOICE.—(*Continued.*)

	INDICATIVE.	IMPERATIVE.	SUBJUNCTIVE.	OPTATIVE.	INFINITIVE.	PARTICIPLES.
2nd Aor.						
Sing.	ἔστην		στῶ	σταίην	στῆναι	M. στάς
	ἔστης	στῆθι	στῇς	σταίης		στάντος
	ἔστη	στήτω	στῇ	σταίη		
Plur	ἔστημεν		στῶμεν	σταίημεν		F. στᾶσα
	ἔστητε	στῆτε	στῆτε	σταίητε		στάσης
	ἔστησαν	στήτωσαν	στῶσι	σταίησαν		
Dual	ἐστήτην	στῆτον	στῆτον	σταιήτην		N. σταν
	ἐστήτην	στήτων	στῆτον	σταιήτην		στάντος
Future	στήσω			στήσοιμι	στήσειν	στήσων, σοντος
1st Aor.	ἔστησα	στῆσον	στήσω	στήσαιμι	στῆσαι	στήσας, σαντος
Perfect	ἕστηκα	ἕστηκε	ἑστήκω	ἑστήκοιμι	ἑστηκέναι	ἑστηκώς, κότος
Pluperf.	ἑστήκειν					

TABLE Y.—ἵστημι, MIDDLE VOICE.

	INDICATIVE.	IMPERATIVE.	SUBJUNCTIVE.	OPTATIVE.	INFINITIVE	PARTICIPLES.
Present						
Sing.	ἵστἄμαι		ἱστῶμαι	ἱσταίμην	ἵστασθαι	M. ἱστάμενος
	ἵστἄσαι	ἵστἄσο	ἱστῇ	ἱσταῖο		ἱσταμένου
	ἵστἄται	ἱστάσθω	ἱστῆται	ἱσταῖτο		
Plur.	ἱστάμεθα		ἱστώμεθα	ἱσταίμεθα		F. ἱσταμένη
	ἵστασθε	ἵστασθε	ἱστῆσθε	ἱσταῖσθε		ἱσταμένης
	ἵστανται	ἱστάσθωσαν	ἱστῶνται	ἱσταῖντο		
Dual	ἱστάμεθον		ἱστώμεθον	ἱσταίμεθον		N. ἱστάμενον
	ἵστασθον	ἵστασθον	ἱστῆσθον	ἱσταῖσθον		ἱσταμένου
	ἵστασθον	ἱστάσθων	ἱστῆσθον	ἱσταίσθην		
Imperf.						
Sing.	ἱστάμην (ᾰ)					
	ἵστἄσο					
	ἵστἄτο					
Plur.	ἱστάμεθα					
	ἵστασθε					
	ἵσταντο					
Dual	ἱστάμεθον					
	ἱστάσθην					
	ἱστάσθην					
2nd Aor.						
Sing.	ἐστάμην (ᾰ)		στῶμαι	σταίμην	στάσθαι	M. σταμενος
	ἔστἄσο	στάσο	στῇ	σταῖο		σταμενου
	ἔστἄτο	στάσθω	στῆται	σταῖτο		
Plur.	ἐστάμεθα		στώμεθα	σταίμεθα		F. σταμένη
	ἔστασθε	στάσθε	στῆσθε	σταῖσθε		σταμένης
	ἔσταντο	στάσθωσαν	στῶνται	σταῖντο		
Dual	ἐστάμεθον		στώμεθον	σταίμεθον		N. στάμενον
	ἐστάσθην	στάσθον	στῆσθον	σταίσθην		σταμένου
	ἐστάσθην	στάσθων	στῆσθον	σταίσθην		
Future	στήσομαι			στησοίμην	στήσεσθαι	στησόμενος, ου
1st Aor.	ἐστησάμην (ᾰ)	στῆσαι	στήσωμαι	στησαίμην	στήσασθαι	στησάμενος, ου.

REMARKS.

1. The 2nd aorist is formed by rejecting ι of the present, and prefixing the augment; ἔστην. This tense keeps the long vowel η in the plural and dual, as is the case with all verbs in μι which come from primitives in άω.

2. The imperative takes θι in the 2nd person, because the root has not an aspirated consonant, as is the case in τίθετι. It takes the short vowel in the pres., ἵσταθι; the long in the 2nd aor., στῆθι: ἀνάστα occurs for ἀνάστηθι.

3. The subjunctive present and 2nd aorist takes η, as in those of τίθημι; e.g. ἱστῶ, ῇς, ῇ; στῶ, στῇς, στῇ: so in the middle; ἱστῶμαι, ῇ, ῆται.

But also sometimes α; ἱστῶ, ᾷς, ᾷ, ἱστῶμαι, ᾷ, ᾶται; but these are formed from ἱστάω, not ἵστημι.

4. The perfect ἕστηκα is regularly formed from the future στήσω. Its augment ε has the rough breathing. This perf. has the sense of the Latin *stare*, *to stand*, and signifies *I am placed*, or, *I stand*, in a present sense. So the pluperf. ἑστήκειν (also εἱστήκειν), *I was standing*, *I stood*.

5. The pres. ἵστημι, imperf. ἵστην, fut. στήσω, 1st aor ἔστησα, part. ἱστάς, have all an active or transitive force; the perf. ἕστηκα, pluperf. ἑστήκειν, 2nd aor. ἔστην, 2nd aor. part. στάς, a neuter or intransitive signification.

6. Passive voice. The present and imperfect are like those of the middle.

	INDICATIVE.	IMPERATIVE.	SUBJUNCTIVE.	OPTATIVE.	INFINITIVE.	PARTICIPLES.
1st Fut.	σταθήσομαι			σταθησοίμην	σταθήσεσθαι	σταθησόμενος
1st Aor.	ἐστάθην (ᾰ)	στάθητι	σταθῶ	σταθείην	σταθῆναι	σταθείς
Perfect	ἕστᾰμαι	ἕστᾰσο	ἑσταμένος ὦ	ἑσταμένος εἴην	ἑστάσθαι	ἑσταμένος
Pluperf.	ἑστάμην					

SECTION XXX.

TABLE Z.—δίδωμι, ACTIVE VOICE.

	INDICATIVE.	IMPERATIVE.	SUBJUNCTIVE.	OPTATIVE.	INFINITIVE.	PARTICIPLES.
Present.	*I give*, &c.					
Sing.	δίδωμι		διδῶ	διδοίην	διδόναι	M. διδούς
	δίδως	δίδοθι	διδῷς	διδοίης		διδόντος
	δίδωσι	διδότω	διδῷ	διδοίη		
Plur.	δίδομεν		διδῶμεν	διδοίημεν		F. διδοῦσα
	δίδοτε	δίδοτε	διδῶτε	διδοίητε		διδούσης
	διδοῦσι	διδότωσαν	διδῶσι	διδοίησαν		N. διδόν
Dual	δίδοτον	δίδοτον	διδῶτον	διδοιήτην		διδόντος
	δίδοτον	διδότων	διδῶτον	διδοιήτην		
Imperf.						
Sing.	ἐδίδων					
	ἐδίδως					
	ἐδίδω					
Plur.	ἐδίδομεν					
	ἐδίδοτε					
	ἐδίδοσαν					
Dual	ἐδιδότην					
	ἐδιδότην					

TABLE Z.—δίδωμι, ACTIVE VOICE.—(*Continued.*)

	INDICATIVE.	IMPERATIVE.	SUBJUNCTIVE.	OPTATIVE.	INFINITIVE.	PARTICIPLES.
2nd Aor.						
Sing.	ἔδων		δῶ	δοίην	δοῦναι	M. δούς
	ἔδως	δός	δῷς	δοίης		δόντος
	ἔδω	δότω	δῷ	δοίη		
Plur.	ἔδομεν		δῶμεν	δοίημεν		F. δοῦσα
	ἔδοτε	δότε	δῶτε	δοίητε		δούσης
	ἔδοσαν	δότωσαν	δῶσι	δοίησαν		
Dual	ἐδότην	δότον	δῶτον	δοιήτην		N. δόν
	ἐδότην	δότων	δῶτον	δοιήτην		δόντος
Future	δώσω			δώσοιμι	δώσειν	δώσων, σοντος
1st Aor.	ἔδωκα					
Perfect	δέδωκα	δέδωκε	δεδώκω	δεδώκοιμι	δεδωκέναι	δεδωκώς, κότος
Pluperf.	ἐδεδώκειν					

TABLE A.A.—δίδωμι, MIDDLE VOICE.

	INDICATIVE.	IMPERATIVE.	SUBJUNCTIVE.	OPTATIVE.	INFINITIVE.	PARTICIPLES.
Present						
Sing.	δίδομαι		διδῶμαι	διδοίμην	δίδοσθαι	M. διδόμενος
	δίδοσαι	δίδοσο	διδῷ	διδοῖο		διδομένου
	δίδοται	διδόσθω	διδῶται	διδοῖτο		
Plur.	διδόμεθα		διδώμεθα	διδοίμεθα		F. διδομένη
	δίδοσθε	δίδοσθε	διδῶσθε	διδοῖσθε		διδομένης
	δίδονται	διδόσθωσαν	διδῶνται	διδοῖντο		
Dual	διδόμεθον		διδώμεθον	διδοίμεθον		N. διδόμενον
	δίδοσθον	δίδοσθον	διδῶσθον	διδοίσθην		διδομένου
	δίδοσθον	διδόσθων	διδῶσθον	διδοίσθην		
Imperf.						
Sing.	ἐδιδόμην					
	ἐδίδοσο					
	ἐδίδοτο					
Plur.	ἐδιδόμεθα					
	ἐδίδοσθε					
	ἐδίδοντο					
Dual	ἐδιδόμεθον					
	ἐδιδόσθην					
	ἐδιδόσθην					
2nd Aor.						
Sing.	ἐδόμην		δῶμαι	δοίμην	δόσθαι	M. δόμενος
	ἔδοσο	δόσο	δῷ	δοῖο		δομένου
	ἔδοτο	δόσθω	δῶται	δοῖτο		
Plur.	ἐδόμεθα		δώμεθα	δοίμεθα		F. δομένη
	ἔδοσθε	δόσθε	δῶσθε	δοῖσθε		δομένης
	ἔδοντο	δόσθωσαν	δῶνται	δοῖντο		
Dual	ἐδόμεθον		δώμεθον	δοίμεθον		N. δόμενον
	ἐδόσθην	δόσθον	δῶσθον	δοίσθην		δομένου
	ἐδόσθην	δόσθων	δῶσθον	δοίσθην		
Future	δώσομαι			δωσοίμην	δώσεσθαι	δωσόμενος, ου
1st Aor.	ἐδωκάμην (ᾰ)					

REMARKS.

1. δίδωμι takes (like τίθημι) σ in the 2nd aorist imperative; δός for δόθι, like θές for θέτι. It has a diphthong in the infinitive of the same tense, δοῦναι; and in the two participles, διδούς and δούς, like τιθείς and θείς.

2. The present and 2nd aorist subjunctive, active and middle, retain ω in all the persons: ι is subscribed in those persons in which verbs in όω have the diphthong οι; e.g. δηλῶ, οῖς, οῖ; διδῶ, ῷς, ῷ.

3. For διδοῦσι, 3rd pers. plur. present, the Attic Greeks write διδόᾱσι like τιθέασι.

4. Passive voice. The present and imperfect are like those of the middle.

	INDICATIVE.	IMPERATIVE.	SUBJUNCTIVE.	OPTATIVE.	INFINITIVE.	PARTICIPLES.
1st Fut.	δοθήσομαι			δοθησοίμην	δοθήσεσθαι	δοθησόμενος
1st Aor.	ἐδόθην	δόθητι	δοθῶ	δοθείην	δοθῆναι	δοθείς
Perfect	δέδομαι	δέδοσο	δεδομένος ὦ	δεδομένος εἴην	δεδόσθαι	δεδομένος
Pluperf.	ἐδεδόμην					

5. For δῶ, δῷς, δῷ, the forms δώω, δώῃς, δώῃ, also occur in the Ionic dialect.

SECTION XXXI.

TABLE B.B.—δείκνυμι, ACTIVE VOICE.

	INDICATIVE.	IMPERATIVE.	INFINITIVE.	PARTICIPLES.
Present	*I show*, &c.			
Sing.	δείκνῡμι		δεικνύναι (ῠ)	Masc. δεικνύς
	δείκνυς	δείκνῠθι		δεικνύντος
	δείκνῡσι	δεικνύτω (ῠ)		
Plur.	δείκνῠμεν			Fem. δεικνῦσα
	δείκνῠτε	δείκνῠτε		δεικνύσης
	δεικνῦσι-ύασι	δεικνύτωσαν		
Dual	δείκνῠτον	δείκνῠτον		Neut. δεικνύν
	δείκνῠτον	δεικνύτων (ῠ)		δεικνύντος
Imperf.				
Sing.	ἐδείκνυν			
	ἐδείκνυς			
	ἐδείκνυ			
Plur.	ἐδείκνῠμεν			
	ἐδείκνῠτε			
	ἐδείκνῠσαν			
Dual	ἐδείκνῠτον			
	ἐδεικνύτην (ῠ)			

TABLE B.B.—(*Continued.*)

δείκνυμι, PASSIVE AND MIDDLE VOICES.

	INDICATIVE.	IMPERATIVE.	INFINITIVE.	PARTICIPLES.
Present				
Sing.	δείκνῠμαι		δείκνυσθαι	Masc. δεικνύμενος
	δείκνῠσαι	δείκνῠσο		δεικνυμένου
	δείκνῠται	δεικνύσθω		
Plur.	δεικνύμεθα			Fem. δεικνυμένη
	δείκνυσθε	δείκνυσθε		δεικνυμένης
	δείκνυνται	δεικνύσθωσαν		
Dual	δεικνύμεθον			Neut. δεικνύμενον
	δείκνυσθον	δείκνυσθον		δεικνυμένου
	δείκνυσθον	δεικνύσθων		
Imperf.				
Sing.	ἐδεικνύμην (ῡ)			
	ἐδείκνῠσο			
	ἐδείκνῠτο			
Plur.	ἐδεικνύμεθα			
	ἐδείκνυσθε			
	ἐδείκνυντο			
Dual	ἐδεικνύμεθον			
	ἐδεικνύσθην			
	ἐδεικνύσθην			

REMARKS.

1. (*a*) The subjunctive and optative are formed from the verb in ύω; e. g. δεικνύω, ῃς, ῃ; δεικνύοιμι, οις, οι.

(*b*) The future and 1st aorist perfect and pluperfect come regularly from the primitive δείκω; e. g. δείξω, δέδειχα, δέδειγμαι, ἐδείχθην, &c.

(*c*) Verbs in μι, of more than two syllables, are without the 2nd aorist. But those of two syllables are generally only used in the 2nd aorist: e. g. ἔφυν, from φύω, *I produce;* ἔδυν, from δύνω, δύω, *I enter.*

(*d*) Several others are limited in their use to the 2nd aorist; e. g. τλάω, τλῆμι, *I bear*, ἔτλην; γνόω, γνῶμι, *I know*, ἔγνων; βάω, βῆμι *I walk*, ἔβην.

These keep the long vowel in the plural and dual. ἔβημεν, ἔγνωμεν. They take θι in the imperative; βῆθι, γνῶθι. But κατάβα occurs for κατάβηθι, and ἀνάβα for ἀνάβηθι.

2. The imperfect of verbs in μι, especially in the sing. is often conjugated like contracted verbs; e. g. ἐτίθεον, ουν; ἵσταον, ων; ἐδίδοον, ουν.

So in the imperative, τίθεε, τίθει; ἵσταε, ἵστη (for ἵστα); δίδοε, δίδου. In those in υμι, θι is sometimes rejected. δείκνυ for δείκνυθι.

3. In Attic Greek, the present and 2nd aorist middle optative are sometimes formed in οίμην, οιο, οιτο; e. g. τίθοιτο, as if from τίθομαι.

The optative present and 2nd aorist is sometimes contracted in the plural number; e. g. τιθεῖμεν, τιθεῖτε, τιθεῖεν; ἱσταῖμεν, ἱσταῖτε, ἱσταῖεν; διδοῖμεν, διδοῖτε, διδοῖεν; so θεῖμεν, θεῖτε, θεῖεν, &c.

SECTION XXXII.

TABLE C.C.—ἵημι, ACTIVE VOICE.

	INDICATIVE.	IMPERATIVE.	SUBJUNCTIVE.	OPTATIVE.	INFIN.	PARTICIPLES.
Present	*I send*, &c.					
Sing.	ἵημι, ἵης, ἵησι	ἵεθι, ἱέτω	ἱῶ, ἱῇς, ἱῇ	ἱείην, ἱείης, ἱείη	ἱέναι	M. ἱείς, ἱέντος
Plur.	ἵεμεν, ἵετε, ἱεῖσι	ἵετε, ἱέτωσαν	ἱῶμεν, ἱῆτε, ἱῶσι	ἱείημεν, ἱείητε, ἱείησαν		F. ἱεῖσα, ἱείσης
Dual	ἱέτην, ἵετον	ἵετον, ἱέτων	ἱῆτον, ἱῆτον	ἱειήτην, ἱειήτην		N. ἱέν, ἱέντος
Imperf.						
Sing.	ἵην, ἵης, ἵη					
Plur.	ἵεμεν, ἵετε, ἵεσαν					
Dual	ἱέτην, ἱέτην					
2nd Aor.						
Sing.	ἧν, ἧς, ἧ	ἕς, ἕτω	ὧ, ᾗς, ᾗ	εἵην, εἵης, εἵη	εἷναι	M. εἵς, ἕντος
Plur.	ἕμεν, ἕτε, ἕσαν	ἕτε, ἕτωσαν	ὧμεν, ἧτε, ὧσι	εἵημεν, εἵητε, εἵησαν		F. εἷσα, εἵσης
Dual	ἕτην, ἕτην	ἕτον, ἕτων	ἧτον, ἧτον	εἱήτην, εἱήτην		N. ἕν, ἕντος
Future	ἥσω, ἥσεις, ἥσει			ἥσοιμι, ἥσοις, ἥσοι	ἥσειν	ἥσων, ἥσοντος
Aorist	ἧκα, ἧκας, ἧκε					
Perfect	εἷκα, εἷκας, εἷκε				εἱκέναι	εἱκώς, εἱκότος
Pluperf.	εἵκειν, εἵκεις, εἵκει					

MIDDLE VOICE.

Present	ἵεμαι, ἵεσαι, ἵεται	ἵεσο, ἱέσθω	ἱῶμαι, ἱῇ, ἱῆται	ἱείμην, ἱεῖο, ἱεῖτο	ἵεσθαι	ἱέμενος, ου
Imperf.	ἱέμην, ἵεσο, ἵετο					
2nd Aor.	ἕμην, ἕσο, ἕτο	ἕσο, ἕσθω	ὧμαι, ᾗ, ἧται	εἵμην, εἷο, εἷτο	ἕσθαι	ἕμενος, ου
Future	ἥσομαι, ἥσῃ, ἥσεται			ἡσοίμην, οιο, οιτο	ἥσεσθαι	ἡσόμενος, ου
1st Aor.	ἡκάμην					

PASSIVE VOICE.

1st Fut.	ἑθήσομαι			ἑθησοίμην	ἑθήσεσθαι	ἑθησόμενος, ου
1st Aor.	ἕθην, or εἵθην	ἕθητι, ἑθήτω	ἑθῶ, ἑθῇς, ἑθῇ	ἑθείην	ἑθῆναι	ἑθείς, ἑθέντος
Perfect	εἷμαι. εἷσαι, εἷται	εἷσο, εἵσθω	εἱμένος ὦ	εἱμένος εἴην	εἷσθαι	εἱμένος, ου
Pluperf.	εἵμην, εἷσο, εἷτο					

REMARKS.

1. The simple form of this verb is rarely met with. The compound ἀνίημι occurs in the New Test., also ἀφίημι, very frequently.

2. The following are the principal forms of ἀφίημι, which present some irregularity: ἀφεῖς, 2nd pers. sing. pres. (as if from ἀφέω): ἤφιον, ες, ε, imperf. (as if from ἀφίω); ἀφέωνται, for ἀφεῖνται, 3rd pers. plur. perf. pass

SECTION XXXIII.

TABLE D.D.—φημί, ἴσημι, κεῖμαι.

INDICATIVE.	IMPER. φαθί, φάτω	INDICATIVE.	IMPERATIVE.
Present. *I say*, &c.	SUBJ. φῶ, φῇς, φῇ	Present. *I know*, &c.	ἴσθι, ἴστω
Sing. φημί, φής, φησι	OPTATIVE. φαίην, φαίης, φαίη	Sing. ἴσημι, ἴσης, ἴσησι	for ἴσαθι, ἰσάτω
Plur. φαμέν, φατέ, φασί	Plur. φαῖμεν (for φαίημεν), &c.	Plur. ἴσμεν, ἴστε } ἰσᾶσι	ἴστε, ἴστωσαν
Dual. φατόν, φατόν	INFIN. φάναι	for ἴσαμεν, ἴσατε }	ἴστον, ἴστων
Imperfect.	Participle. φάς, φᾶσα, φάν	Dual. ἴστον, ἴστον, for ἴσατον	
Sing. ἔφην, ἔφης, ἔφη	Future. φήσω. Aor. ἔφησα	Imperf. ἴσην, ἴσης, ἴση	INFIN. ἰσάναι
Plur. ἔφαμεν, ἔφατε, ἔφασαν	Aor. SUBJ. φήσω. OPT. φήσαιμι	Plur. ἴσαμεν, ἴσατε, ἴσασαν, or ἴσαν	Part. ἴσας, ἴσασα, ἴσαν
Dual. ἐφάτην, ἐφάτην	INFIN. φῆσαι. Part. φήσας	Dual. ἰσάτην, ἰσάτην.	

INDICATIVE.	IMPERFECT.	
Present. *I lie* (on the ground), &c.		IMPERATIVE. κεῖσο, κείσθω, &c.
Sing. κεῖμαι, κεῖσαι, κεῖται	ἐκείμην, ἔκεισο, ἔκειτο	INFINITIVE. κεῖσθαι
Plur. κείμεθα, κεῖσθε, κεῖνται	ἐκείμεθα, ἔκεισθε, ἔκειντο	Participle. κείμενος, η, ον.
Dual. κείμεθον, κεῖσθον, κεῖσθον	ἐκείμεθον, ἐκείσθην, ἐκείσθην	

REMARKS.

1. Of φημί, the 1st pers. sing. (φημί), 3rd pers. sing. (φησί), 3rd pers. pl. (φασί), of the present indicative, and the 3rd pers. sing. of the imperfect (ἔφη), are the only forms which occur in the New Test.

2. The verb ἴσημι is but little used (ἴσασι and ἴστε are found in the New Test.); it is perhaps connected with the obsolete εἴδω, fut. εἴσω, the forms of which will be hereafter noticed.

3. Ἐπίσταμαι, *I know*, of doubtful derivation, is conjugated like the middle voice of ἴστημι.

4. Of εἶμι, *I go* (prim. ἴω), a few tenses may be mentioned.

Pres. sing. εἶμι, εἶς or εἶ, εἶσι: pl. ἴμεν, ἴτε, ἴασι. Past tense, sing. ᾔειν, ᾔεις, ᾔει; pl. ᾔειμεν, ᾔειτε, ᾔεισαν and ᾔεσαν. Infin. ἰέναι. Part. ἰών, ἰοῦσα, ἰόν, ἰόντος, ἰούσης, ἰόντος, &c.

The following (compounded) forms occur in the New Testament: ἀπῄεσαν, εἰσίασιν, εἰσῄει, εἰσιέναι, ἐξῄεσαν, ἐξιέναι, ἐξιόντων, ἐπιούσῃ, pres. part. dat. sing. fem. of ἐπιέναι. συνιόντος, gen. sing. part. pres. of σύνειμι, Lu. 8. 4.

SECTION XXXIV.

REMARKS ON THE AUGMENT OF COMPOUNDED VERBS.

1. Verbs compounded with a preposition. (*a*) If the preposition changes the meaning of the verb, the augment and reduplication are placed after the preposition; e. g. προστάττω, *I enjoin*, προσέταττον; εἰσάγω, *I introduce*, εἰσῆγον.

(*b*) If the preposition end with a vowel, this is elided; e. g. διασπείρω, *I disperse*, διέσπειρον. But περί retains its ι; e. g. περιάγειν, περιέθηκε: and πρό (generally) its ο; e. g. προάγειν. The ο of πρό is often combined with the initial ε of a verb; e. g. προὔβην for προέβην; προὔβαλον for προέβαλον.

(*c*) If ἐν and σύν have lost or changed their ν because of the consonant following them, this ν re-appears before the augment; e. g. ἐμβλέπω, *I look upon*, ἐνέβλεπον; συλλέγω, *I collect*, συνέλεγον; συζητῶ, συνεζήτουν, &c.

(*d*) Some verbs take the augment both before and after the preposition; e. g. ἀνορθόω, *I correct*, ἠνώρθουν; ἀνέχομαι, *I sustain*, ἠνειχόμην.

2. If the preposition does not change the meaning of the verb, the augment usually comes before it; e. g. (ἵζω) καθίζω, *I sit down*, ἐκάθιζον; (εὕδω) καθεύδω, *I sleep*, ἐκάθευδον. But some take the augment after; e. g. προφητεύω, προεφήτευον; παρανομέω, παρηνόμησα.

3. Verbs compounded, but not with a preposition. (*a*) Those compounded with the privative particle α take the temporal augment η; e. g. ἀδικέω, *I act unjustly*, ἠδίκουν, &c.

(*b*) Those compounded with εὖ, if the verb begins with a vowel capable of augment, take η after εὐ; e. g. εὐεργετέω, *I benefit*, εὐηργέτουν.

(*c*) If the verb begins with a consonant or a long vowel, εὐ remains invariable, or else is changed into ηὐ, according to the Attic dialect; e. g. εὐδοκέω, ηὐδόκησα (also εὐδόκησα); εὐλογέω, ηὐλόγουν, ηὐλόγησα (also εὐλόγησα).

SECTION XXXV

REMARKS ON TENSES MORE OR LESS IRREGULAR.

1. Verbs in έω uncontracted. Dissyllables in έω are not usually contracted in the 1st pers. sing, or the 1st and 3rd pers. pl. of the present; e. g. πλέω, *I sail*, πλέομεν, πλέουσι; imperf. ἔπλεον. Nor are they contracted in the subjunctive and optative. The contracted form πνεῖ, however, occurs, John 3. 8.

2. In some verbs in άω, αε is contracted into η, instead of into α; e. g. ζάω, *I live*, ζῇς, ζῇ, infin. ζῆν; πεινάω, *I am hungry*, πεινῇς, ῇ, infin. πεινῆν. So διψάω, *I thirst;* and χράομαι, *I use*, χρῇ, χρῆται, infin. χρῆσθαι.

3. Futures in εύσω and αύσω, from verbs in έω and άω. A very few, as ῥέω, *I flow*, πλέω, *I sail*, πνέω, *I blow*, from the fut. in εύσω; e. g. ῥεύσω, πλεύσω (πλεύσομαι), πνεύσω. Two in αίω, κλαίω, *I weep*, and καίω, *I burn*, form it in αύσω; e. g. κλαύσω, καύσω. So perf. pass. κέκαυμαι, aor. 1, pass. ἐκαύθην..

4. Aspirated futures. Four verbs, ἔχω, τρέχω, τύφω, and τρέφω, take as the first letter of the future the aspirate which is in the second syllable of the present; e. g. ἕξω, θρέξομαι, θύψω, θρέψω.

5. Some verbs, though their termination is not preceded by a vowel, form the future in ήσω; e. g. θέλω, θελήσω; μέλλω, μελλήσω; αὐξάνω (αὔξω), αὐξήσω; βούλομαι, βουλήσομαι (aor. ἐβουλήθην). So μάχομαι, μαχέσομαι.

6. Three futures, though uncontracted, omit σ; e. g. πίομαι, *I shall drink*, from πίνω; ἔδομαι, φάγομαι, *I shall eat*, which serve as futures to ἐσθίω.

7. In the verb πίπτω, *I fall* (primitive πέτω), σ occurs in the 2nd aorist, ἔπεσον.

Besides ἔθηκα, ἧκα, and ἔδωκα, already cited, one or two others may be mentioned as wanting σ in the 1st aorist; e. g. ἤνεγκα (primitive ἐνέγκω), used as 1st aorist of φέρω; εἶπα, and 2nd aorist εἶπον (primitive ἔπω), which verb keeps the ι throughout the moods.

8. Perfects active without κ. One or two may be here given; e. g. τεθνηκέναι, *to have died*, by contraction, τεθνάναι, part. τεθνεώς for τεθνηκώς.

From ἵστημι, ἕστηκα, pl. ἑστήκαμεν, contr. ἕσταμεν, ἕστατε, ἑστᾶσι; pluperf. pl. ἕσταμεν, ἕστατε, ἕστασαν; imper. ἕσταθι, ἑστάτω, &c.; subj. ἑστῶ; opt. ἑσταίην; infin. ἑστάναι; part. ἑστώς, ἑστῶσα, ἑστός; gen. ἑστῶτος, ἑστώσης, ἑστῶτος, &c.

9. Perfect passive. τρέφω, στρέφω, and τρέπω, take α in this tense; τέθραμμαι, ἔστραμμαι, τέτραμμαι. In the 1st aorist passive ε re-appears; e. g. ἐθρέφθην, ἐστρέφθην.

10. Verbal adjectives in τέος may here be noticed. They are used to signify *necessity;* e. g. λυτέος, *that ought to be, or must be, loosed*, and are formed from the participle of the 1st aorist passive, by changing the termination θείς into τέος. One instance, at least, is fouud in the New Test., βλητέος from βληθείς, of βάλλω, *I cast.*

11. In Attic Greek, the termination of the 2nd pers. sing. passive or middle is usually ει, instead of ῃ: always in these three verbs; βούλομαι, *I will*, βούλει; οἴομαι, *I think*, οἴει; ὄψομαι, *I shall see*, ὄψει.

Futures in οῦμαι are also inflected by ει; e. g. ἀπολοῦμαι, *I shall perish*, ἀπολεῖ, ἀπολεῖται. So also, after the contraction of the active future (very frequent in verbs in ζω); e. g. from κομίζω, fut. κομίσω, Attic κομιῶ, fut. mid. κομιοῦμαι, κομιεῖ, κομιεῖται.

12. Occasionally such aorist forms as ἐξῆλθα, ἔπεσα, ἀνεῦρα, &c., are found, where the 2nd aorist would be more usual. These occur chiefly in various readings.

13. The termination ασι of the perfect active is sometimes shortened into αν; e. g. πέπτωκαν for πεπτώκασι, from πίπτω (var. reading). So γέγοναν for γεγόνασι, &c.

On the other hand (chiefly in the Alexandrian dialect), the termination ον is lengthened into οσαν; e. g. ἤλθοσαν for ἦλθον (var. reading). So ἐδολιοῦσαν for ἐδολίουν, imperf. of δολιόω

SECTION XXXVI.

REMARKS ON DEFECTIVE AND IRREGULAR VERBS.*

1. Those which borrow some tenses from verbs of similar signification, but different root:

αἱρέω, *I take*, fut. *αἱρήσω*, perf. *ᾕρηκα*, perf. pass. *ᾕρημαι*, aor. *ᾑρέθην*, fut. pass. *αἱρεθήσομαι*; (from *ἕλω*) 2nd aor. *εἷλον*, 2nd aor. mid. *εἱλόμην*.

εἰπεῖν, *to speak*, has only 2nd aor. and some persons of 1st aor. *εἶπα*. Its other tenses are, 1st (from *λέγω*); 2nd (from *εἴρω*), fut. *ἐρῶ*; 3rd (from *ῥέω*), perf. *εἴρηκα*, perf. pass. *εἴρημαι*, aor. *ἐῤῥέθην* or *ἐῤῥήθην*.

ἔρχομαι, *I come*, imperf. *ἠρχόμην*; (from *ἐλεύθω*) fut. *ἐλεύσομαι*, 2nd aor. *ἤλυθον*, *ἦλθον*, 2nd perf. *ἐλήλυθα*, pluperf. *ἐληλύθειν*.

ἐσθίω, *I eat*, perf. *ἐδήδοκα*, perf. pass. *ἐδήδομαι* and *ἐδήδεσμαι*: (from *φάγω*) 2nd aor. *ἔφαγον*, fut. *φάγομαι*

τρώγω, *I eat*, forms 2nd aor. *ἔτραγον*.

ὁράω, *I see*, imperf. *ἑώρων*, perf. *ἑώρακα*, perf. pass. *ἑώραμαι*, aor. 1, infin. pass. *ὁραθῆναι*; (from *εἴδω*), 2nd aor. *εἶδον*, *ἰδέ*, *ἴδω*, *ἴδοιμι*, *ἰδεῖν*, *ἰδών*; mid. *εἰδόμην*, &c.; (from *ὄπτω*, *ὄπτομαι*), fut. *ὄψομαι*, aor. *ὤφθην*, perf. *ὦμμαι*.

τρέχω, *I run*, fut. *θρέξομαι*, aor. *ἔθρεξα*, &c.; (from *δρέμω*, *δράμω*), fut. *δραμοῦμαι*, 2nd aor. *ἔδραμον*, perf. *δεδράμηκα*, 2nd perf. *δέδρομα*.

ῥέω, *I flow*, 2nd aor. *ἐῤῥύην*; hence *παραῤῥυῶμεν*, Heb. 2. 1, from *παραῤῥέω*.

χέω, *I pour*, fut. *χεύσω* and *χέω*, 1st aor. *ἔχευσα*, *ἔχευα* and *ἔχεα*, infin. *χέαι*.

φέρω, *I bear*, *carry*, imperf. *ἔφερον*; (from *οἴω*), fut. *οἴσω*, fut. pass. *οἰσθήσομαι*; (from *ἐνέγκω*) aor. *ἤνεγκα* and *ἤνεγκον*, perf. *ἐνήνοχα*, perf. pass. *ἐνήνεγμαι*, aor. *ἠνέχθην*, fut. *ἐνεχθήσομαι*.

2. Terminations *νω*, *άνω*. *αἰσθάνομαι*, *I perceive*, 2nd aor. *ᾐσθόμην*, fut. *αἰσθήσομαι*, perf. *ᾔσθημαι*.

ἁμαρτάνω, *I err*, *sin*, 2nd aor. *ἥμαρτον*, infin. *ἁμαρτεῖν*, fut. *ἁμαρτήσω*.

βλαστάνω, *I bud* (prim. *βλάστω*), 2nd aor. *ἔβλαστον*, infin. *βλαστεῖν*, fut. *βλαστήσω*.

δάκνω, *I bite* (prim. *δήκω*), 2nd aor. *ἔδακον*, fut. *δήξομαι*, perf. pass. *δέδηγμαι*.

θιγγάνω (*θίγω*), *I touch*, 2nd aor. *ἔθιγον*, fut. *θίξω* and *θίξομαι*.

ἱκάνω, *ἱκνέομαι*, *I come* (prim. *ἵκω*), 2nd aor. *ἱκόμην*, perf. *ἷγμαι*, with *ἀπό*, *ἀφῖγμαι*.

λαγχάνω, *I set by lot* (prim. *λήχω*), 2nd aor. *ἔλαχον*, fut. *λήξομαι*, perf. *εἴληχα*, 2nd perf. *λέλογχα*.

λαμβάνω, *I take* (prim. *λήβω*), 2nd aor. *ἔλαβον*, fut. *λήψομαι*, perf. *εἴληφα*, perf. pass. *εἴλημμαι*.

λανθάνω, *I am hidden* (prim. *λήθω*), fut. *λήσω*, 2nd aor. *ἔλαθον*, 2nd perf *λέληθα*. *λανθάνομαι*, *I forget*, 2nd aor. *ἐλαθόμην*, perf. *λέλησμαι*.

μανθάνω, *I learn* (prim. *μήθω* or *μαθω*), 2nd aor. *ἔμαθον*, infin. *μαθεῖν*, fut. *μαθήσω*, perf. *μεμάθηκα*.

ἐλαύνω, *I drive*, fut. *ἐλάσω*, 1st aor. *ἤλασα*, perf. *ἐλήλακα*, &c.

πυνθάνομαι, *I inquire* (prim. *πεύθομαι*), 2nd aor. *ἐπυθόμην*, fut. *πεύσομαι*, perf. *πέπυσμαι*.

τυγχάνω, *I obtain* (prim. *τεύχω*), fut. *τεύξομαι*, perf. *τετύχηκα*, 2nd aor. *ἔτυχον*.

3. Termination *σκω*, from *ω* pure. *ἀρέσκω*, *I please* (prim. *ἀρέω*), fut. *ἀρέσω*, 1st aor. *ἤρεσα*, 1st aor. pass *ἠρέσθην*.

βιβρώσκω, *I eat* (prim. *βρόω*), fut. *βρώσω*, *βρώσομαι*, perf. *βέβρωκα*, 2nd aor. *ἔβρων*.

μεθύσκω, *I inebriate* (*μεθύω*), fut. *μεθύσω*, &c.

γηράσκω, *I grow old* (prim. *γηράω*), fut. *γηράσομαι*, aor. infin. *γηράναι* or *γηρᾶναι*, part. *γήρας*, *γήραντος*.

γινώσκω, *I know* (prim. *γνόω*), fut. *γνώσομαι*, perf. *ἔγνωκα*, perf. pass. *ἔγνωσμαι*, 2nd aor. act. *ἔγνων*, *γνῶθι*, *γνῶ*, *γνοίην*, *γνῶναι*, part. *γνούς*, *γνόντες*: hence *ἀναγινώσκω*, *I read*, 1st aor. *ἀνέγνωσα*.

μιμνήσκω, *I call to mind* (prim. *μνάω*), perf. *μέμνημαι*. *I remember*, aor. *ἐμνήσθην*.

πιπράσκω, *I sell* (prim. *περάω*), fut. *περάσω*, perf. *πέπρακα* (for *πεπέρακα*), perf. pass. *πέπραμαι*, aor. *ἐπράθην*, 3rd fut *πεπράσομαι*.

ἀναλίσκω, *I consume* (prim. *ἁλόω*, *ἅλωμι*), fut. *ἀναλώσω*, perf. *ἀνήλωκα*, 1st aor. pass. *ἀνηλώθην*, &c.

4. Terminations *σκω* and *σχω*, from *ω* impure (not preceded by a vowel).

εὑρίσκω, *I find* (prim. *εὕρω*), 2nd aor. *εὗρον*, infin. *εὑρεῖν*, fut. *εὑρήσω*, perf. *εὕρηκα*, perf. pass. *εὕρημαι*, aor. *εὑρέθην*; also *εὕρησα* and *εὑράμην*, 1st aor. act. and mid.

θνήσκω, *I die* (prim. *θάνω*), 2nd aor. *ἔθανον*, fut. *θανοῦμαι*, perf. *τέθνηκα*.

πάσχω, *I suffer* (prim. *πάθω*), 2nd aor. *ἔπαθον*; (prim. *πένθω*), fut. *πείσομαι*, 2nd perf. *πέπονθα*.

ἔχω, *I have*, imperf. *εἶχον*, fut. *ἕξω*; (prim. *σχῶ*), 2nd aor. *ἔσχον*, *σχές*, *σχῶ*, *σχοίην*, *σχεῖν*, whence a new fut. *σχήσω*, and perf. *ἔσχηκα*. From *σχω* also comes *ἴσχω*, *I hold*, and the compound *ὑπισχνέομαι*, *I promise*, 2nd aor. *ὑπεσχόμην*, fut. *ὑποσχήσομαι*, perf. *ὑπέσχημαι*.

5. Termination *υμι*. *ἀμφιέννυμι*, *I clothe* (prim. *ἀμφιέω*), fut. *ἀμφιέσω*, *ἀμφιῶ*, perf. pass. *ἠμφίεσμαι*.

ζώννυμι, *I gird*, fut. *ζώσω*, 1st aor. mid. *ἐζωσάμην*, perf. pass. *ἔζωσμαι*.

κατάγνυμι, *I break in pieces*, fut. *κατεάξω*, 1st aor. *κατέαξα*, 2nd aor. pass. *κατεάγην*.

* A notice of those which occur in the New Test. may be found useful, though *not all* the forms here given appear in the Sacred Text.

κεράννυμι, *I mingle* (prim. κεράω), fut. κεράσω, perf. pass. κεκέρασμαι, aor. ἐκεράσθην, by syncope κέκραμαι, ἐκράθην.

κορέννυμι, *I satiate*, fut. κορέσω, perf. pass. κεκόρεσμαι, aor. ἐκορέσθην.

κρεμάννυμι, *I suspend* (prim. κρεμάω), fut. κρεμάσω, κρεμῶ, 1st aor. pass. ἐκρεμάσθην. Also κρέμαμαι, fut. κρεμήσομαι.

μίγνυμι, *I mix* (prim. μίσγω, μίγω), fut. μίξω, perf. pass. μέμιγμαι.

ὄλλυμι, *I destroy* (prim. ὄλω), fut. ὀλέσω, έω, ῶ, 1st aor. ὤλεσα, perf. ὀλώλεκα, fut. mid. ὀλοῦμαι, 2nd aor. mid. ὠλόμην, 2nd perf. ὄλωλα, part. ὀλωλώς, ὀλωλυῖα, ὀλωλός.

ὄμνυμι, *I swear* (prim. ὀμόω), 1st aor. ὤμοσα, perf. ὀμώμοκα, perf. pass. ὀμώμοσμαι; (prim. ὄμω), fut. ὀμοῦμαι, ὀμεῖ, ὀμεῖται, infin. ὀμεῖσθαι.

πετάννυμι, *I expand*, fut. πετάσω, 1st aor. ἐπέτασα, &c.

πήγνυμι, *I fix* (prim. πήγω), fut. πήξω, 1st aor. ἔπηξα, perf. pass. πέπηγμαι, aor. ἐπήχθην, 2nd aor. pass. ἐπάγην, 2nd perf. πέπηγα; the two last in a neuter sense.

ῥήγνυμι, ῥήσσω, *I break* (prim. ῥήγω), fut. ῥήξω, 1st aor. ἔῤῥηξα, 2nd aor. pass. ἐῤῥάγην, 2nd perf. ἔῤῥωγα, in a neuter sense.

ῥώννυμι, *I strengthen* (prim. ῥόω), fut. ῥώσω, perf. pass. ἔῤῥωμαι, aor. ἐῤῥώσθην, imp. perf. pass. ἔῤῥωσο, *farewell*.

σβέννυμι, *I extinguish* (prim. σβέω), fut. σβέσω, perf. pass. ἔσβεσμαι, 1st aor. pass. ἐσβέσθην; (prim. σβέω, σβῆμι) 2nd aor. ἔσβην, perf. ἔσβηκα.

στρώννυμι, *I strew*, fut. στρώσω, 1st aor. ἔστρωσα, perf. pass. ἔστρωμαι.

SECTION XXXVII.

REMARKS ON IRREGULAR VERBS CONTINUED.—VARIOUS TERMINATIONS.

1. ἅλλομαι, *I leap*, fut. ἁλοῦμαι, 1st aor. ἡλάμην.

(ἀνα, κατα) βαίνω (prim. βάω, βῆμι), fut. βήσομαι, perf. βέβηκα, 2nd aor. ἔβην; βήσω and ἔβησα in active sense.

ἀνοίγω, *I open*, imperf. ἀνέῳγον, 1st aor. ἀνέῳξα and ἤνοιξα, perf. ἀνέῳχα, perf. pass. ἀνέῳγμαι, ἠνέῳγμαι, 1st aor. pass. ἀνεῴχθην, ἠνεῴχθην, ἠνοίχθην, 2nd aor. pass. ἠνοίγην, 2nd fut. ἀνοιγήσομαι, 2nd perf. ἀνέῳγα, in neuter sense.

γίνομαι, *I become* (prim. γένω), 2nd aor. ἐγενόμην, 2nd perf. γέγονα, fut. γενήσομαι, perf. pass. γεγένημαι, aor. pass. ἐγενήθην.

δύναμαι, *I am able*, imperf. ἐδυνάμην and ἠδυνάμην, fut. δυνήσομαι, aor. ἐδυνήθην and ἠδυνήθην, perf. δεδύνημαι.

δέω, *I bind*, fut. δήσω, 1st aor. ἔδησα, perf. δέδεκα, perf. pass. δέδεμαι, aor. ἐδέθην.

δέω, *I want*, fut. δεήσω; impersonal δεῖ, *it is necessary*, fut. δεήσει, &c.; pass. δέομαι, *I pray*, also *I want*, fut. δεήσομαι, aor. ἐδεήθην.

ἐγείρω, *I arouse*, fut. ἐγερῶ, perf. Att. ἐγήγερκα; mid. ἐγείρομαι, *I awake*, 1st aor. ἠγειράμην, perf. pass. ἐγήγερμαι, fut. ἐγερθήσομαι, aor. ἠγέρθην, 2nd aor. mid. ἠγρόμην (for ἠγερόμην), 2nd perf. ἐγρήγορα, whence a new present, γρηγορέω, *I watch*.

εἴδω, *I see* (not used in the present), 2nd aor. εἶδον, infin. ἰδεῖν; 2nd perf. οἶδα, *I know*; pluperf. ᾔδειν, *I knew*. The forms are as follow: perf. indic. sing. οἶδα, οἶσθα, οἶδας, οἶδε, pl. (from ἴσημι) ἴσμεν, ἴστε, ἴσασι; imp. ἴσθι, ἴστω, &c.; pluperf. ᾔδειν, ᾔδεις, ᾔδει, pl. ᾔδειμεν, ᾔδειτε, ᾔδεισαν; subj. εἰδῶ; opt. εἰδείην; infin. εἰδέναι; part. εἰδώς, εἰδυῖα, εἰδός; fut. εἴσομαι, εἴσῃ, εἴσεται, &c.; also εἰδήσω, as if from εἰδέω, ῶ.

εἴκω, 2nd perf. ἔοικα, *I resemble*; part. ἐοικώς.

κτείνω, *I slay* (in New Test. ἀποκτείνω, and, in various readings, ἀποκτένω and ἀποκτέννω), fut. κτενῶ, 1st aor. ἔκτεινα, 1st aor. pass. ἐκτάνθην, infin. ἀποκτανθῆναι.

μαρτύρομαι, *I witness*, fut. μαρτυροῦμαι, 1st aor. ἐμαρτυράμην.

οἴομαι, *I think*, imperf. ᾠόμην (also οἶμαι, ᾤμην), fut. οἰήσομαι, aor. ᾠήθην, infin. οἰηθῆναι.

ὀνίνημι, *I help* (prim. ὀνάω), fut. mid. ὀνήσομαι, aor. ὠνησάμην, opt. ὀναίμην.

πίνω, *I drink*, fut. πίομαι, πίεσαι, also πιοῦμαι, 2nd aor. ἔπιον; (prim. πόω), perf. πέπωκα, perf. pass. πέπομαι, 1st aor. ἐπόθην (κατεπόθην).

πίπτω, *I fall* (prim. πέτω), fut. πεσοῦμαι, 1st aor. ἔπεσα, 2nd aor. ἔπεσον; (prim. πτόω), perf. πέπτωκα.

σπένδω, *I pour out*, fut. σπείσω, perf. ἔσπεικα, perf. pass. ἔσπεισμαι, aor. ἐσπείσθην.

σώζω, *I save*, perf. pass. σέσωμαι and σέσωσμαι, aor. ἐσώθην.

τίκτω, *I bring forth* (prim. τέκω), fut. τέξομαι, 2nd aor. ἔτεκον, 1st aor. pass. ἐτέχθην, 2nd perf. τέτοκα.

φθάνω, *I anticipate*, fut. φθάσω, 1st aor. ἔφθασα, perf. ἔφθακα; (prim. φθάω, φθῆμι), 2nd aor. ἔφθην, fut. φθήσομαι.

2. A few verbs in έω and άω form some tenses as if the verb terminated in ω impure.

γαμέω, *I marry* (prim. γάμω), 1st aor. ἔγημα and ἐγάμησα, perf. γεγάμηκα, regular.

δαμάω, *I tame* (prim. δάμνω), 2nd aor. ἔδαμον, 2nd aor. pass. ἐδάμην, perf. δέδμηκα (for δεδάμηκα).

δοκέω, *I appear* (prim. δόκω), fut. δόξω, 1st aor. ἔδοξα, perf. pass. δέδογμαι. Impersonally, δοκεῖ, *it seems good*, ἔδοξε, &c.

μυκάομαι, *I roar* (prim. μύκω), 2nd aor. ἔμυκον, 2nd perf. μέμυκα.

SECTION XXXVIII.

REMARKS ON SOME PERFECT TENSES EMPLOYED AS PRESENTS.

1. In a considerable number of verbs the perfect is used in a strictly present signification.

The explanation of this usage is simply derived from the complete idea conveyed by the perfect tense, as in the following examples.

2. ἔθω, *I accustom myself*, εἴωθα, *I have accustomed myself*; hence, *I am accustomed.*

εἴδω, *I see*, οἶδα, *I know*

ἔοικα, *I resemble.*

θνήσκω, *I die*, τέθνηκα, *I have suffered death*; hence, *I am dead.*

ἵστημι, *I place*, ἕστηκα (ἐμαυτόν), *I have placed myself*; hence, *I stand.*

κτάομαι, *I acquire*, κέκτημαι, *I have acquired and retain*; hence, *I possess.*

μνάομαι, *I call to mind*, μέμνημαι, *I have called to mind and retain*; hence, *I remember.*

So also in the perf. pass.; e. g. οἱ κεκλημένοι, *those who are in receipt of a call or invitation*; hence, *the invited ones, the guests.*

SECTION XXXIX.

THE USE OF THE TENSES.

The use of the present and future tenses is sufficiently explained by their names. But the present is sometimes used as a lively expression of a past action: as, ἄγουσιν αὐτὸν πρὸς τοὺς Φαρισαίους, Jno. 9. 13; and also of a certain futurity: as, μετὰ τρεῖς ἡμέρας ἐγείρομαι, Mat. 27. 63. The indicative of the future has occasionally the force of the imperative mood: as, ἔσεσθε οὖν ὑμεῖς τέλειοι, Mat. 5. 48.

The imperfect expresses a prolonged or recurrent action in past time.

The aorist is strictly the expression of a momentary or transient single action, being thus distinguished from the imperfect; and in the indicative mood it ordinarily signifies past time. It is, however, used of a prolonged action, if there is no positive need to make a direct expression of that circumstance. It is thus of constant use in the narrative of past transactions.

The perfect conveys the double notion of an action terminated in past time, and of its effect existing in the present: as, γυνὴ δέδεται, 1 Cor. 7. 39.

The pluperfect expresses the effect as past, as well as the action.

In the case of certain verbs, the latter part of the entire idea conveyed by these two tenses is so prominent, that they virtually become a present and imperfect respectively: as, οἶδα, *I know*, ᾔδειν, *I knew.*

SECTION XL.

THE USE OF THE INFINITIVE MOOD.

A verb in the infinitive mood, either alone or in combination with other words, mostly expresses either the subject of another verb: as, μακάριόν ἐστι διδόναι, Acts 20. 35; or the object of relation of the action or condition expressed by a verb, participle, or adjective: as, ἐπιποθῶ ἰδεῖν ὑμᾶς, Rom. 1. 11; δυνατὸς κωλῦσαι, Acts 11. 17; οὐκ ἔστιν ἐμὸν δοῦναι, Mat. 20. 23. The most usual grammatical situation of a verb in the infinitive is in immediate dependence on another verb.

A verb in the infinitive, with the neuter article (τό) prefixed becomes, by the inflexion of the article, admissible into the various grammatical positions of the substantive: as, γνώμη τοῦ ὑποστρέφειν, Acts 20. 3; διὰ παντὸς τοῦ ζῆν, He. 2. 15; ἐν τῷ ἱερατεύειν αὐτόν, Lu. 1. 8.

The infinitive is always a legitimate construction, though not the only one, after the particles πρίν and ὥστε: as, πρὶν γενέσθαι, Jno. 14. 29; ὥστε μὴ ἰσχύειν τινά, Mat. 8. 28.

A participle takes the place of an infinitive in dependence upon certain verbs: as, ἐπαύσατο λαλῶν, Lu. 5. 4; ὁρῶ σε ὄντα, Acts 8. 23.

SECTION XLI.

THE USE OF THE SUBJUNCTIVE MOOD.

In the principal verb of a sentence, the subjunctive mood is an expression of deliberative interrogation: as, δῶμεν, ἢ μὴ δῶμεν; Mar. 12. 15, *Should we pay, or should we not pay?* καὶ τί εἴπω; Jno. 12. 27, *And what should I say?* This is termed its deliberative use.

In the first person plural, it has also the suggestive force which is usually classed as an imperative: as, ἄγωμεν εἰς τὰς ἐχομένας κωμοπόλεις, Mar. 1. 38, *Let us go into the next towns.* This usage, if not actually identical with it, is nearly related to the preceding.

The aorist of this mood is used as an imperative with the particle μή: as, μὴ σαλπίσῃς, Mat. 6. 2.

The construction of the subjunctive with the combined particles οὐ μή, is a form of peremptory negation: as, οὐ μὴ νίψῃς, Jno. 13. 8. The future indicative is also used in the same construction.

In dependent clauses, the subjunctive is the ordinary mood after ἐάν, ἄν used hypothetically, and relative words when ἄν is subjoined to them: as, ὅταν (ὅτε ἄν), ὃς ἄν, &c., as also πρίν and ἕως with ἄν subjoined.

It is also the ordinary construction with the particles ἵνα, ὡς, ὅπως, when expressive of design: as, ἵνα πληρωθῇ, Mat. 2. 15. The same is the case when design is implied, though not expressed directly: as, τὸ κατάλυμα, ὅπου—φάγω, Mark 14. 14. The future indicative is also constructed with ὡς and ὅπως, and in the New Testament sometimes also with ἵνα.

SECTION XLII.

THE USE OF THE OPTATIVE MOOD.

In the principal verb, the optative mood is a simple form of wishing: as, τὸ ἀργύριον—εἴη εἰς ἀπώλειαν, Acts 8. 20.

In combination with the particle ἄν, it is an expression of a conditional futurity: as, πῶς ἂν δυναίμην; Acts 8. 31, *How should I be able?*

In dependent clauses, it is sometimes employed in oblique narration, that is, when the sentiments of a person are made a matter of narration, instead of being expressed in direct personal terms: as, ἐπυνθάνετο, τί εἴη ταῦτα, Lu. 15. 26.

The optative following the particle εἰ is one of the forms of a hypothetical clause, but of rare occurrence in the New Testament; as is also its use after particles expressive of design.

SECTION XLIII.

THE CONCORD OF THE VERB.

In Greek, as in language in general, the verb is ordinarily put in the same number and person as its subject, or nominative case. This is its agreement, or concord. There is, however, this special exception; that, when a word in the plural, expressive of the subject, is also in the neuter gender, the verb is usually in the singular: as, πάντα δι' αὐτοῦ ἐγένετο, John 1. 3.

A subject in the singular, when the idea conveyed by the word is that of plurality, may have its verb in the plural: as, ὄχλος ἔστρωσαν, Mat. 21. 8. This is termed a rational, as distinguished from a formal, concord.

When a verb is in the plural, as having several joint subjects, and these are of different persons, its concord will be with the first person in preference to the second, and with the second in preference to the third.

Since the verb, by its inflexion alone, always implies its pronominal subject in the first and second persons, these are, accordingly, not necessary to be expressed for the purpose of mere perspicuity: when, therefore, they are expressed, it is a mark of point or emphasis on the subject of the verb, of some kind or degree. And the same is the case to a certain extent with the third person

SECTION XLIV.

THE CONCORD OF THE ADJECTIVE, PARTICIPLE, AND PRONOUN.

The adjective, the participle, and the pronoun, agree with the substantive to which they have relation, in gender, number, and case. Rational concords are also admissible, as in the case of the verb.

An adjective, participle, or pronoun, in the masculine gender without any substantive expressed, has relation to persons; but in the neuter, to things: as, *μακάριοι οἱ πενθοῦντες*, Mat. 5. 4; *πάντα ταῦτα ἐφυλαξάμην*, Mat. 19. 20.

The relative pronoun, being either the subject of the verb in its own clause, or the object of government of some word in that clause, agrees with its antecedent in gender and number only: if it is in the nominative case, it is also reckoned of the same person with the antecedent.

SECTION XLV.

THE USE OF THE NOMINATIVE CASE.

A nominative case with the article prefixed is sometimes used for the vocative. as, *τὸ πνεῦμα τὸ ἄλαλον*, Mar. 9. 25.

A substantive or adjective which is attached to a neuter or passive verb, as a necessary supplement to the sense, is put in the same case with the subject of the verb; which, except in case of an infinitive, will be the nominative. as, *ἐγώ εἰμι ἡ ὁδός*, Jno. 14. 6; *ὁ λόγος σὰρξ ἐγένετο*, Jno. 1. 14; *αὐτοὶ υἱοὶ Θεοῦ κληθήσονται*, Mat. 5. 9; *πεπεισμένος ἐστὶν Ἰωάννην προφήτην εἶναι*, Lu. 20. 6.

If, instead of a verb, a participle is used, the case of the participle is continued in the supplemental word: as, *Φοίβην οὖσαν διάκονον*, Rom. 16. 1; *ἡμῖν Ῥωμαίοις οὖσι*, Acts 16. 21.

Of the same principle is the rule of apposition, namely, that two terms for the same thing, in the same grammatical clause, are put in the same case: as, *παραγίνεται Ἰωάννης ὁ βαπτιστής*, Mat. 3. 1; *ἐν ἡμέραις Ἡρώδου τοῦ βασιλέως*, Mat. 2. 1; *παραβάτην ἐμαυτὸν συνιστάνω*, Gal. 2. 18; *ὑμᾶς—ἔθετο ἐπισκόπους*, Acts 20. 28.

SECTION XLVI.

THE USE OF THE ACCUSATIVE CASE.

The accusative is the case of government of by far the greater number of transitive verbs, and may therefore be regarded as the ordinary case of the direct object of a verb.

The subject of a verb in the infinitive mood is ordinarily in the accusative case. as, *πάντας ἀνθρώπους θέλει σωθῆναι*, 1 Tim. 2. 4. But, if the subject of the verb in the infinitive is the same as that of the principal verb on which it depends, it is in the nominative: as, *δέομαι τὸ μὴ παρὼν θαῤῥῆσαι*, 2 Cor. 10. 2; *φάσκοντες εἶναι σοφοί*, Ro. 1. 22.

An object of relation, or in limitation, as distinguished from one which is direct, is also in the accusative; and in this way the case is found after adjectives, passive verbs, and a previous accusative in direct government: as, *σκηνοποιοὶ τὴν τέχνην*, Acts 18. 3; *δαρήσεται πολλάς*, Lu. 12. 47; *δεδεμένος τοὺς πόδας*, Jno. 11. 44; *γάλα ὑμᾶς ἐπότισα*, 1 Cor. 3. 2.

When the relative would, by its own proper government, be in the accusative, it sometimes exchanges this case for the genitive or dative of its antecedent. as, *ἐπὶ πᾶσιν οἷς ἤκουσαν*, Lu. 2. 20; *ἐκ τοῦ ὕδατος οὗ ἐγὼ δώσω*, Jno. 4. 14. This is termed attraction.

The accusative is employed in designations of space and time: as, *ἀπέχουσαν σταδίους ἑξήκοντα*, Lu. 24. 13; *ὡσεὶ ὥραν ἐννάτην*, Acts 10. 3.

SECTION XLVII.

THE USE OF THE GENITIVE CASE.

The most simple and ordinary use of the genitive, is to place a substantive in immediate construction with another substantive. This construction is an expression of some simple and obvious relation between the things signified by the two substantives; and thus the substantive in the genitive comes variously to signify a possessor, origin, cause, matter, object, &c.

In the New Testament, the genitive in construction has also the force of a qualifying adjective: as, *τὸν οἰκονόμον τῆς ἀδικίας*, Lu. 16. 8. This is a Hebraism.

An absolute participial clause, so termed, is one which has its subject distinct from the principal subject of the sentence of which it forms a part. Such clauses are distinguished by having their subject in the genitive case, hence termed the genitive absolute: as, *τοῦ δαιμονίου ἐξελθόντος, ἐλάλησεν ὁ κωφός*, Lu. 11. 14.

The genitive is used in designations of price: as, *ἐπράθη τριακοσίων δηναρίων*, Jno. 12. 5. Akin to this is the government of the genitive by the adjective *ἄξιος*.

It is also found in designations of time, Jno. 3. 2.

The genitive is constructed with words, that is, verbs and adjectives, implying—

(1) exclusive distinction: as, for instance, *διαφέρειν*, 1 Cor. 15. 41, and all comparatives: hence

(2) superiority, especially power and rule, Rom. 14. 9; 1 Tim. 2. 12.

(3) inclusive distinction: as, for instance, distributives and superlatives, Lu. 16. 5; 1 Cor. 15. 9.

(4) deprivation, Lu. 16. 4; abstinence, Acts 20. 29 and cessation, 1 Pet. 4. 1.

(5) fulness, and the opposite notions of emptiness, deficiency, need, Lu. 5. 12; Jno. 2. 7; 1 Tim. 1. 6; Ja. 1. 5.

(6) desire, objective pursuit, Mat. 5. 28.

(7) bodily perception, except sight, Mat. 2. 9.

(8) mental perception, as, for instance, memory, knowledge, Lu. 18. 32. But words of this class, as well as the preceding one, are also constructed with the accusative, Lu. 9. 45.

Certain verbs in the middle voice govern the genitive, as, *ἅπτομαι, ἔχομαι, γεύομαι, ὀρέγομαι, ἐπιλανθάνομαι*, Mat 8. 15; Heb. 6. 9; Mar. 9. 1; 1 Tim. 3. 1; Heb. 6. 10. Also certain verbs compounded of *κατά*, and conveying by their composition the idea of untoward action: as, *κατηγορῶ, καταμαρτυρῶ, καταδυναστεύω, κατακυριεύω, καταφρονῶ* Mat. 12. 10; Mar. 14. 60; Ja. 2. 6; Acts 19. 16; Mat 6. 24.

A criminal charge or sentence is expressed in the genitive, Mat. 26. 66.

The object of a partial action is in the genitive, Mar 2. 21; Acts 27. 36; Mar. 9. 27.

The construction of the genitive after verbs substantive is the same, in effect, with its immediate dependence upon a substantive, Mat. 19. 14; 1 Cor. 6. 19; Heb. 12. 11

SECTION XLVIII.

THE USE OF THE DATIVE CASE.

As a general principle, that to which anything is represented as accruing, is expressed in the dative case. It is thus constructed with words implying—

(1) address, Mat. 3. 7; Lu. 1. 19; Acts 26. 29.

(2) bestowal, Mat. 4. 9; Acts 3. 14.

(3) approach, Lu. 7. 12.

(4) gain or loss, advantage or disadvantage, Mat. 5. 44; Lu. 4. 22; Mat. 23. 31; Heb. 8. 8; Mat. 3. 16; Rom. 14. 6, 7.

(5) credence, reliance, Mat. 21. 25; 2 Cor. 10. 7.

(6) submission, subservience, Acts 5. 36; Lu. 2. 51; Acts 13. 36.

To these must be added, words signifying adaptation. likeness, equality, 2 Cor 2 6; Heb. 6. 7; Eph. 5. 3; Ja. 1. 6; Lu. 7. 32; Mat. 20. 12.

The dative is an expression of instrumentality, Mat 8. 16; Mar. 5. 3; as also causation, method, agency, and other kindred notions, Rom. 11. 20; Acts 15. 1; Phi 2. 7; 1 Cor. 14. 20.

The dative is used in designations of time, Lu. 12. 20; Acts 13. 20.

Certain verbs in the middle voice are followed by the dative: as, *χρῶμαι, διαλέγομαι, κρίνομαι*, Acts 27. 17; Heb. 12. 5; Mat. 5. 40.

The dative is frequently found in dependence upon a preposition involved in a compound verb, Mar. 3. 10; Acts 13. 43; 2 Pet. 1. 9; Mat. 26. 53.

SECTION XLIX.

PREPOSITIONS, ADVERBS, AND CONJUNCTIONS

The various governments of cases by the several prepositions are given at length in the Lexicon. Some prepositions are occasionally used as adverbs without a case in government, 2 Cor. 11. 23; and are also prefixed to adverbs, Mat. 4. 17; Acts 28. 23.

Certain adverbs may have a case in government, ordinarily the genitive, Mat. 10. 29; Jno. 6. 23; Mat. 13. 34.

The Greek language exhibits a peculiar usage in the repetition of a negative, Mat. 22. 16; Jno. 15. 5; Mar. 1. 44.

Words directly united by a simple conjunction, are ordinarily in the same grammatical construction.

ADDENDA.

P. 1. ἀγαθοποιεῖτε, 2 pers. plur. pres. imper. ἀγαθοποιέω.

P. 337. πορευόμενος, nom. sing. masc. part. pres. πορεύομαι.

P. 403. τηρήσατε, 2 pers. plur. aor. 1, imper. act. τηρέω.

THE ANALYTICAL

GREEK LEXICON.

A

Α, α, *Alpha,* the first letter of the Greek alphabet, and used for the *first,* Re. 1. 8, 11; 21. 6; 22. 13.
In composition it denotes *privation;* sometimes *augmentation* and *union.*

ἅ, nom. or acc. pl. neut. (§ 10. tab. J. g) . ὅς

Ἀαρών, ὁ, *Aaron,* pr. name, indecl.

Ἀβαδδών,[a] ὁ, *Abaddon,* pr. name, indecl.

ἀβαρῆ,[b] acc. sing. masc. . . . . ἀβαρής

ἀβᾰρής], έος, οῦς, ὁ, ἡ, τό, -ές. (ἀ & βάρος), *not burdensome, not chargeable,* (§ 7. tab. G. b).

Ἀββᾶ, indecl. Chald. or Syr. אַבָּא, *father,* Mar. 14. 36; Ro. 8. 15; Gal. 4. 6.

Ἀβέλ, ὁ, *Abel,* pr. name, indecl.

Ἀβιά, ὁ, *Abia,* pr. name, indecl.

Ἀβιάθαρ,[c] ὁ, *Abiathar,* pr. name, indecl.

Ἀβιληνή], ῆς, ἡ, (§ 2. tab. B. a) *Abilene,* a district of the Syrian Decapolis; from *Abila,* the chief town. Lat. 33. 35, long. 36. 5.

Ἀβιληνῆς,[d] gen. sing. . . . . . Ἀβιληνή

Ἀβιούδ, ὁ, *Abihud,* pr. name, indecl.

Ἀβραάμ, ὁ, *Abraham,* pr. name, indecl.

ἄβυσσον, acc. sing. (§ 3. tab. C. a) . ἄβυσσος

ἄβυσσος], ου, ἡ, pr. *bottomless; place of the dead, hell.*

ἀβύσσου, gen. sing. . . . . . ἄβυσσος

Ἄγαβος, ου, ὁ, *Agabus,* pr. name.

ἄγαγε, 2 pers. sing. aor. 2, imper.—A. Tdf. }
ἄγε, Rec. Gr. Sch. (2 Ti. 4. 11) } ἄγω

ἀγαγεῖν, aor. 2, inf. (§ 13. rem. 7 d) . id.

ἀγάγετε, 2 pers. pl. aor. 2, imper. . . ἄγω

ἀγάγῃ, 3 pers. sing. aor. 2, subj. . . id.

ἀγαγόντα, acc. sing. masc. part. aor. 2 . id.

ἀγαγόντες, nom. pl. masc. part. aor. 2 . id.

ἀγαγών, nom. sing. masc. part. aor. 2 . . id.

ἀγάγωσι, σιν, 3 pers. pl. aor. 2, subj. . id.

ἀγαθά, acc. pl. neut. (§ 7. tab. F. a) . . ἀγαθός

ἀγαθάς, acc. pl. fem. . . . . . id.

ἀγαθέ, voc. sing. masc. . . . . . id.

ἀγαθή, nom. sing. fem. . . . . id.

ἀγαθῇ, dat. sing. fem. . . . . . id.

ἀγαθήν, acc. sing. fem. . . . . id.

ἀγαθῆς, gen. sing. fem. . . . . . id.

ἀγαθοεργεῖν,[e] pres. infin. . . . ἀγαθοεργέω

ἀγαθοεργέω, ῶ], ἀγαθουργῶ, fut. ήσω, (§ 16. tab. P) (ἀγαθός & ἔργον), *to do good, confer benefits.* N.T.

ἀγαθοῖς, dat. plur. masc. and neut. . . ἀγαθός

ἀγαθόν, nom. and acc. sing. neut. & acc. m. id.

ἀγαθοποιέω, ῶ], fut. ήσω, (§ 16. tab. P) (ἀγαθός & ποιέω), *to do good, benefit, do well.* LXX.

ἀγαθοποιῆσαι, aor. 1, inf.—Rec. Gr. Sch. Tdf. }
τι ἀγαθὸν ποιῆσαι, D. (Mar. 3. 4) } ἀγαθοποιέω

ἀγαθοποιῆτε, 2 pers. pl. pres. subj . id.

ἀγαθοποιΐα], ας, ἡ, (§ 2. tab. B. b. and rem. 2), *well-doing, probity.* L.G.

ἀγαθοποιΐᾳ,[f] dat. sing.—Rec. Gr. Sch }
ἀγαθοποιΐαις, dat. pl.—A. Ln. Tdf. } ἀγαθοποιΐα

ἀγαθοποιός], οῦ, ὁ, ἡ, *a well-doer.* L.G.

ἀγαθοποιοῦντας, part. pres. masc. acc. pl. . ἀγαθοποιέω

---

a Re. 9. 11. b 2 Co. 11. 9. c Mar. 2. 26. d Lu. 3. 1. e 1 Ti. 6. 18. f 1 Pe. 4. 19.

ἀγαθοποιοῦντες, nom. pl. masc. part. pres. — ἀγαθοποιέω

ἀγαθοποιοῦσαι, nom. pl. fem. part. pres. — id.

ἀγαθοποιῶν, nom. sing. masc. part. pres. — id.

ἀγαθοποιῶν,[a] gen. pl. — ἀγαθοποιός

ἀγᾰθός, ή, όν, *good, profitable, generous, beneficent, upright, virtuous* (§ 7. tab. F. a): whence

ἀγαθωσύνη, ης, ἡ, *goodness, virtue, beneficence*. LXX.

ἀγαθοῦ, gen. sing. masc. and neut. — ἀγαθός

ἀγαθουργῶν,[b] nom. sing. part. pres.—Al. Ln. Tdf. } ἀγαθουργέω
ἀγαθοποιῶν, Rec. Gr. Sch. }

ἀγαθούς, acc. pl. masc. — ἀγαθός

ἀγαθῷ, dat. sing. neut. — id.

ἀγαθῶν, gen. pl. — id.

ἀγαθωσύνη, ης, ἡ, (§ 2. tab. B. a) — id.

ἀγαθωσύνῃ, dat. sing. — ἀγαθωσύνη

ἀγαθωσύνης, gen. sing — id.

ἀγαλλιάσει, dat. sing — ἀγαλλίασις

ἀγαλλιάσεως, gen. sing. — id.

ἀγαλλιᾶσθε, 2 pers. pl. pres. mid. (§ 19. tab. S) — ἀγαλλιάω

ἀγαλλιᾶσθε, 2 pers. pl. pres. imper. mid. — id.

ἀγαλλιασθῆναι, aor. 1, inf. pass.—Rec. } id.
ἀγαλλιαθῆναι, Gr. Sch. Tdf. (Jno. 5. 35) }

ἀγαλλίᾰσις, εως, ἡ, (§ 5. tab. E. c) *exultation, extreme joy*. LXX. from

ἀγαλλιάω, ῶ], fut. άσω, (§ 22. rem. 2) *to celebrate, praise*; also equivalent to ἀγαλλιάομαι, ῶμαι, *to exult, rejoice exceedingly; to desire ardently*, Jno. 8. 56. LXX.

ἀγαλλιώμεθα, 1 pers. pl. pres. subj. mid. — ἀγαλλιάω

ἀγαλλιῶμεν, 1 p. pl. pres. subj. act.—Al. Ln. Tdf. } id.
ἀγαλλιώμεθα, Rec. Gr. Sch. (Re. 19. 7) }

ἀγαλλιώμενοι, nom. pl. m. part. pres. mid. (§ 19. tab. S) — id.

ἀγάμοις, dat. pl. — ἄγαμος

ἄγᾰμος, ου, ὁ, ἡ, (§ 3. tab. C. a, b) (ἀ & γάμος), *unmarried*, 1 Co. 7. 8, 11, 32, 34.

ἀγανακτεῖν, pres. infin. — ἀγανακτέω

ἀγανακτέω, ῶ], fut. ήσω, (§ 16. tab. P) *to be pained; to be angry, vexed, indignant; to manifest indignation*: whence

ἀγανάκτησις], εως, ἡ, (§ 5. tab. E. c) *indignation*.

ἀγανάκτησιν,[c] acc. sing. — ἀγανάκτησις

ἀγανακτοῦντες, nom. pl. masc. part. pres. — ἀγανακτέω

ἀγανακτῶν, nom. sing. masc. part. pres. — id.

ἀγαπᾷ, 3 pers. sing. pres. indic. (§ 18. tab. R) — ἀγαπάω

ἀγαπᾷ, 3 pers. sing. pres. subj. — id.

ἀγάπαις, dat. plur. — ἀγάπη

ἀγαπᾶν, pres. infin. — ἀγαπάω

ἀγαπᾷς, 2 pers. sing. pres. indic. — id.

ἀγαπᾶτε, 2 pers. pl. pres. indic. — id.

ἀγαπᾶτε, 2 pers. pl. pres. imper. — id.

ἀγαπᾶτε, 2 pers. pl. pres. subj. — id.

ἀγαπάτω, 3 pers. sing. pres. imper. — id.

ἀγαπάω, ῶ, fut. ήσω, perf. ἠγάπηκα, (§ 18. tab. R) *to love, value, esteem, feel or manifest generous concern for, be faithful towards; to delight in; to set store upon*, Re. 12. 11: whence

ἀγάπη, ης, ἡ, (§ 2. tab. B. a) *love, generosity, kindly concern, devotedness*; pl. *love-feasts*, Jude 12. LXX.

ἀγαπητός, ή, όν, (§ 7. tab. F. a) *beloved, dear; worthy of love*.

ἀγάπῃ, dat. sing. — ἀγάπη

ἀγαπηθήσεται, 3 pers. sing. fut. 1, pass. (§ 19. tab. S) — ἀγαπάω

ἀγάπην, acc. sing. — ἀγάπη

ἀγάπης, gen. sing. — id.

ἀγαπήσαντι, dat. sing. masc. part. aor. 1 — ἀγαπάω

ἀγαπήσαντος, gen. sing. masc. part. aor. 1. — id.

ἀγαπήσας, nom. sing. masc. part. aor. 1 — id.

ἀγαπήσατε, 2 pers. pl. aor. 1, imper. — id.

ἀγαπήσει, 3 pers. sing. fut. (§ 16. rem. 3) — id.

ἀγαπήσεις, 2 pers. sing. fut. — id.

ἀγαπήσητε, 2 pers. pl. aor. 1, subj. — id.

ἀγαπήσω, 1 pers. sing. fut. — id.

ἀγαπητά, nom. and acc. pl. neut. — ἀγαπητός

ἀγαπητέ, voc. sing. masc. — id.

ἀγαπητῇ, dat. sing. fem. — id.

ἀγαπητήν, acc. sing. fem. — id.

ἀγαπητοί, nom. pl. masc. — id.

ἀγαπητοί, voc. pl. masc.—Rec. Gr. Sch. Tdf. } id.
ἀδελφοί, A. (Phi. 2. 12) }

ἀγαπητοῖς, dat. pl. masc. — id.

ἀγαπητόν, neut. and acc. sing. masc. — id.

ἀγαπητός, ή, όν, (§ 7. tab. F. a) — ἀγαπάω

ἀγαπητοῦ, gen. sing. masc. — ἀγαπητός

ἀγαπητῷ, dat. sing. masc. — id.

ἀγαπῶ, 1 pers. sing. pres. indic., contracted for — ἀγαπάω

ἀγαπῶμαι, 1 pers. sing. pres. indic. pass. — id.

ἀγαπῶμεν, 1 pers. pl. pres. indic. — id.

ἀγαπῶμεν, 1 pers. pl. pres. subj. — id.

ἀγαπῶν, nom. sing. masc. part. pres. — id.

ἀγαπῶντας, acc. pl. masc. part. pres. — id.

[a] 1 Pe. 2. 14. [b] Ac. 14. 17. [c] 2 Co. 7. 11.

ἀγαπῶντι, dat. s. m. part. pres.—Gr. Sch. Tdf. } ἀγαπάω
ἀγαπήσαντι, Rec. (Re. 1. 5)

ἀγαπώντων, gen. pl. masc. part. pres. . id.

ἀγαπῶσι, σιν, 3 pers. pl. pres. indic. . . id.

ἀγαπῶσι, σιν, dat. masc. pl. part. pres. . id.

Ἄγαρ, ἡ, *Agar*, pr. name, indecl.

ἀγγαρεύουσι, 3 pers. pl. pres. indic. . ἀγγαρεύω

ἀγγαρεύσει, 3 pers. sing. fut. . . . id.

ἀγγαρεύω], fut. εύσω, (§ 13. tab. M) (ἄγγαρος, a Persian courier, or messenger, who had authority to press into his service men, horses, etc.) *to press*, or *compel* another to go somewhere, or carry some burden.

ἀγγεῖα, acc. pl. (Mat. 13. 48) . . . ἀγγεῖον

ἀγγείοις, dat. pl. . . . . . . id.

ἀγγεῖον], ου, τό, (§ 3. tab. C. c) (ἄγγος, the same) *a vessel, utensil*, Mat. 25. 4.

ἀγγελία, ας, ἡ, (§ 2. tab. B. b, and rem. 2) ἄγγελος

ἀγγέλλουσα,[a] n. s. f. part. pres.—A. B. Ln. Tdf. } ἀγγέλλω
ἀπαγγέλλουσα, Rec. Gr. Sch. (Jno. 20. 18)

ἄγγελοι, nom. pl. . . . . ἄγγελος

ἀγγέλοις, dat. pl. . . . . . id.

ἄγγελον, acc. sing. . . . . . id.

ἄγγελος, ου, ὁ, ἡ, (§ 3. tab. C. a. b) *one sent, a messenger, angel*, (ἀγγέλλω, *to tell, to announce*.)

ἀγγελία, ας, ἡ, *a message, doctrine*, or *precept*, delivered in the name of any one, 1 Jno. 3. 4.

ἀγγέλου, gen. sing. . . . . . ἄγγελος

ἀγγέλους, acc. pl. . . . . . id.

ἀγγέλῳ, dat. sing. . . . . . id.

ἀγγέλων, gen. pl. . . . . . id.

ἄγε, a particle of exhortation, (pr. imperat. of ἄγω), *come, come now*, Ja. 4. 13; 5. 1.

ἄγε, 2 pers. sing. pres. imperat. . . . ἄγω

ἄγει, 3 pers. sing. pres. indic. . . . id.

ἄγειν, pres. infin. act. . . . . id.

ἄγεσθαι, pres. infin. pass. . . . id.

ἄγεσθε, 2 pers. pl. pres. indic. pass. . . id.

ἀγέλη, ης, ἡ, (§ 2. tab. B. a) . . . id.

ἀγέλην, acc. sing. . . . . . ἀγέλη

ἀγενεαλόγητος,[b] ου, ὁ, ἡ, (§ 7. rem. 2) (ἀ & γενεαλογέω) *not included in a pedigree; independent of pedigree*. N. T.

ἀγενῆ,[c] acc. pl. neut. . . . . ἀγενής

ἀγενής], έος, ὁ, ἡ, τό, -ές, (§ 7. tab. G. b) (ἀ & γένος) *ignoble, base*.

ἄγετε, 2 pers. pl. pres. imper.—B. C. Ln. Tdf. } ἄγω
ἀγάγετε, Rec. Gr. Sch. (Mat. 21. 2)

ἁγία, nom. sing. fem. . . . . ἅγιος

ἅγια, nom. pl. neut. (1 Co. 7. 14) . . id.

ἁγίᾳ, dat. sing. fem. . . . . id.

ἁγιάζει, 3 pers. sing. pres. indic. act. . ἁγιάζω

ἁγιάζεται, 3 pers. sing. pres. indic. pass. . id.

ἁγιαζόμενοι, nom. pl. masc. part. pres. pass. id.

ἁγιαζομένους, acc. pl. masc. part. pres. pass. . id.

ἁγιάζον, neut. sing. part. pres. act. . . id.

ἁγιάζω, fut. άσω, (§ 26. rem. 1) . . ἅγιος

ἁγιάζων, nom. sing. masc. part. pres. act. . ἁγιάζω

ἅγιαι, nom. pl. fem. . . . . ἅγιος

ἁγίαις, dat. pl. fem. . . . id.

ἁγίαν, acc. sing. fem. . . . . id.

ἁγίας, gen. sing. fem. . . . . id.

ἁγιάσαι, 3 pers. sing. aor. 1, opt. act. . . ἁγιάζω

ἁγιάσας, nom. s. m. part. aor. 1, act.—B. D. Ln. } id.
ἁγιάζων, Rec. Gr. Sch. Tdf. (Mat. 23. 17)

ἁγιάσατε, 2 pers. pl. aor. 1, imper. act. . id.

ἁγιάσῃ, 3 pers. sing. aor. 1, subj. act. . . id.

ἁγιασθήτω, 3 pers. sing. aor 1, imper. pass. id.

ἁγιασμόν, acc. sing. . . . . ἁγιασμός

ἁγιασμός, οῦ, ὁ, (§ 3. tab. C. a) . . ἅγιος

ἁγιασμῷ, dat. sing. . . . . ἁγιασμός

ἁγίασον, 2 pers. sing. aor. 1, imper. act. . ἁγιάζω

ἅγιε, voc. sing. masc. . . . . ἅγιος

ἅγιοι, nom. or voc. pl. masc. . . . id.

ἁγίοις, dat. pl. masc. . . . . id.

ἅγιον, acc. masc. and nom. or acc. neut. sing. id.

ἅγιος, ία, ιον, (§ 7. rem. 1) *separate from common condition and use; dedicated*, Lu. 2. 23; *hallowed*; used of things, τὰ ἅγια, *the sanctuary*; and of persons, *saints*, e. g. members of the first Christian communities; *pure, righteous*, ceremonially or morally; *holy*.

ἁγιότης, ητος, ἡ, (§ 4. rem. 2. c) *holiness, sanctity*, He. 12. 10. LXX.

ἁγιωσύνη, ης, ἡ, (§ 2. tab. B. a) *sanctification, sanctity, holiness*. LXX.

ἁγιάζω, fut. άσω, perf. pass. ἡγίασμαι, (§ 26. rem. 1) *to separate, consecrate; cleanse, purify, sanctify*; *regard* or *reverence as holy*. LXX.

ἁγιασμός, οῦ, ὁ, (§ 3. tab. C. a) *sanctification, moral purity, sanctity*. LXX.

[a] Jno. 20. 18. [b] He. 7. 3. [c] 1 Co. 1. 28.

ἁγιότης], ητος, ἡ, (§ 4. rem. 2 c) . . . ἅγιος

ἁγιότητι, dat. sing.—Al. Ln. Tdf. / ἁπλότητι, Rec. Gr. Sch. (2 Co. 1. 12) } ἁγιότης

ἁγιότητος,[a] gen. sing. . . . . . id.

ἁγίου, gen. sing. masc. and neut. . . ἅγιος

ἁγίους, acc. pl. masc. . . . . . id.

ἁγίῳ, dat. sing. masc. and neut. . . id.

ἁγίων, gen. pl. . . . . . . id.

ἁγιωσύνη, ης, ἡ, (§ 2. tab. B. a) . . id.

ἁγιωσύνῃ, dat. sing. . . . . . ἁγιωσύνη

ἁγιωσύνην, acc. sing. . . . . . id.

ἁγιωσύνης, gen. sing. . . . . . id.

ἁγιωτάτῃ, dat. sing. fem. superl. (§ 8. rem. 4) ἅγιος

ἀγκάλας,[b] acc. pl. . . . . ἀγκάλη

ἀγκάλη], ης, ἡ, (§ 2. tab. B. a) (ἀγκή, the same) *the arm*. (ᾰ).

ἄγκιστρον,[c] ου, τό, (§ 3. tab. C. c) *a hook, fish-hook*.

ἄγκῡρα], ας, ἡ, (§ 2. tab. B. b) *an anchor*, Ac. 27. 29, 30, 40.

ἄγκυραν, acc. sing. . . . . . ἄγκυρα

ἀγκύρας, acc. pl. . . . . . id.

ἁγνά, nom. pl. neut. . . . . ἁγνός

ἁγνάς, acc. pl. fem. . . . . . id.

ἄγνᾰφος], ου, ὁ, ἡ, (§ 7. rem. 2) (ἀ & γνάπτω, *to full, dress*) *unfulled, undressed; new*, Mat. 9. 16; Mar. 2. 21. N. T.

ἀγνάφου, gen. sing. neut. . . . . ἄγναφος

ἁγνεία], ας, ἡ, (§ 2. tab. B. b, and rem. 2) ἁγνός

ἁγνείᾳ, dat. sing. . . . . . ἁγνεία

ἁγνή, nom. sing. fem. . . . . ἁγνός

ἁγνήν, acc. sing. fem. . . . . . id.

ἁγνίζει, 3 pers. sing. pres. indic. act. . . ἁγνίζω

ἁγνίζω], fut. ἁγνίσω, (§ 26. rem. 1) . ἁγνός

ἁγνίσατε, 2 pers. pl. aor. 1, imper. act. . . ἁγνίζω

ἁγνισθείς, nom. s. m. part. aor. 1, pass. . id.

ἁγνίσθητι, 2 pers. sing. aor. 1, imper. pass. . id.

ἁγνισμός], οῦ, ὁ, (§ 3. tab. C. a) . . ἁγνός

ἁγνισμοῦ,[d] gen. sing. . . . . ἁγνισμός

ἁγνίσωσι, 3 pers. pl. aor. 1, subj. act. . ἁγνίζω

ἀγνοεῖ, 3 pers. sing. pres. indic. act. . . ἀγνοέω

ἀγνοεῖν, pres. infin. act. . . . . id.

ἀγνοεῖται, 3 pers. s. pres. ind. mid.—A. D. Ln. Tdf. / ἀγνοεῖ, Rec. Gr. Sch. (1 Co. 14. 38) } id.

ἀγνοεῖτε, 2 pers. pl. pres. indic. act. . . id.

ἀγνοείτω, 3 pers. sing. pres. imper. act. . id.

ἀγνοέω, ῶ], fut. ήσω, (§ 16. tab. P) *to be ignorant; not to understand; sin through ignorance*.

ἀγνόημα, ατος, τό, (§ 4. tab. D. c) *error, sin of ignorance*.

ἄγνοια, ας, ἡ, (§ 2. tab. B. b, and rem. 2) *ignorance*.

ἀγνόημα], ατος, τό . . . . . ἀγνοέω

ἀγνοημάτων,[e] gen. pl. . . . . ἀγνόημα

ἀγνοήσαντες, nom. pl. m. part. aor. 1, act. . ἀγνοέω

ἄγνοια], ας, ἡ . . . . . . id.

ἀγνοίᾳ, dat. sing. . . . . . ἄγνοια

ἄγνοιαν, acc. sing. . . . . . id.

ἀγνοίας, gen. sing. . . . . . id.

ἁγνόν, acc. sing. masc. . . . . ἁγνός

ἁγνός, ή, όν, (§ 7. tab. F. a) *pure, chaste, modest, innocent, blameless*.

ἁγνότης, τητος, ἡ, (§ 4. rem. 2. c) *purity, life of purity*.

ἁγνεία, ας, ἡ, (§ 2. tab. B. b, and rem. 2) *purity, chastity*, 1 Ti. 4. 12; 5. 2.

ἁγνίζω, fut. ίσω, (§ 26. rem. 1) *to purify; to purify morally, reform*. ἁγνίζομαι, perf. ἥγνισμαι, aor. 1, ἡγνίσθην, *to live like one under a vow of abstinence*, as the Nazarites.

ἁγνισμός, οῦ, ὁ, (§ 3. tab. C. a) *purification, abstinence*. L. G.

ἁγνῶς, adv. *purely, sincerely*.

ἀγνοοῦμεν, 1 pers. pl. pres. indic. act. . . ἀγνοέω

ἀγνοούμενοι, nom. pl. m. part. pres. pass. . id.

ἀγνοούμενος, nom. s. m. part. pres. pass. . id.

ἀγνοοῦντες, nom. pl. m. part. pres. act. . id.

ἀγνοοῦσι, 3 pers. pl. pres. indic. act. . . id.

ἀγνοοῦσι, dat. pl. masc. part. pres. act. . id.

ἁγνότης], ητος, ἡ, (§ 4. rem. 2, c) . . ἁγνός

ἁγνότητι, dat. sing. . . . . . ἁγνότης

ἁγνότητος, gen. sing.—Al. Ln. / Rec. Gr. Sch. Tdf. om. (2 Co. 11. 3) } id.

ἁγνότητι,[f] dat. sing. . . . . . id.

ἁγνούς, acc. pl. masc. . . . . . ἁγνός

ἀγνοῶν, nom. s. m. part. pres. act. . . ἀγνοέω

ἁγνῶς,[g] adv. . . . . ἁγνός

ἀγνωσία], ας, ἡ, (§ 2. tab. B. b, and rem. 2) (ἀ & γνῶσις) *ignorance*, 1 Co. 15. 34; 1 Pe. 2. 15.

ἀγνωσίαν, acc. sing. . . . . . ἀγνωσία

ἄγνωστος], ου, ὁ, ἡ, (§ 7. rem. 2) (ἀ & γνωστός) *unknown*.

ἀγνώστῳ,[h] dat. sing. masc. . . . ἄγνωστος

ἀγόμενα, acc. pl. neut. part. pres. pass. . ἄγω

[a] He. 12. 10. [b] Lu. 2. 28. [c] Mat. 17. 27. [d] Ac. 21. 26. [e] He. 9. 7. [f] 2 Co. 6. 6. [g] Phi. 1. 16. [h] Ac. 17. 23.

ἀγομένους, acc. pl. masc. part. pres. pass. . ἄγω
ἀγομένων, gen. pl. part. pres. pass. . . id.
ἄγονται, 3 pers. pl. pres. indic. pass. . id.
ἄγοντες, nom. pl. masc. part. pres. act. . id.
ἀγορά], ᾶς, ἡ, (§ 2. tab. B. b, and rem. 2) (ἀγείρω, *to gather together*) *a place of public concourse, forum, market-place; things sold in the market, provisions.*

ἀγοράζω, fut. άσω, (§ 26. rem. 1) perf. pass. ἠγόρασμαι, aor. 1, pass. ἠγοράσθην, *to buy; redeem, acquire* by a ransom or price paid.

ἀγοραῖος, ου, ὁ, ἡ, (§ 7. rem. 2) *one who visits the forum; a lounger, one who idles away his time in public places, a low fellow.*

ἀγόραιος, ου, ὁ, ἡ, (§ 7. rem. 2) *pertaining to the forum, judicial;* ἀγόραιοι, *court days.*

ἀγορᾷ, dat. sing. . . . . . . ἀγορά
ἀγοράζει, 3 pers. sing. pres. indic. act. . ἀγοράζω
ἀγοράζοντας, acc. pl. masc. part. pres. act. . id.
ἀγοράζοντες, nom. pl. masc. part. pres. act. id.
ἀγοράζω], fut. άσω, (§ 26. rem. 1) . . ἀγορά
ἀγόραιοι,[a] nom. pl. (ἡμέραι understood).—Gr. Sch. Tdf. . . . } ἀγόραιος
ἀγοραῖοι, Rec. (Ac. 19. 38) . . }
ἀγοραῖος], ου, ὁ, ἡ, (§ 7. rem. 2) . . ἀγορά
ἀγόραιος], ου, ὁ, ἡ . . . . . id.
ἀγοραῖς, dat. pl. . . . . . . id.
ἀγοραίων,[b] gen. pl. . . . . . ἀγοραῖος
ἀγοράν, acc. sing. . . . . . . ἀγορά
ἀγορᾶς, gen. sing. . . . . . id.
ἀγοράσαι, aor 1, infin. act. . . . ἀγοράζω
ἀγοράσαντα, acc. sing. masc. part. aor. 1, act. id.
ἀγοράσας, nom. sing. masc. part. aor. 1, act. id.
ἀγοράσατε, 2 pers. pl. aor. 1, imper. act. . id.
ἀγορασάτω, 3 pers. sing. aor. 1, imper act. . id.
ἀγοράσομεν, 1 pers. pl. fut. act. . id.
ἀγόρασον, 2 pers. sing. aor. 1, imper act. . id.
ἀγοράσωμεν, 1 pers. pl. aor. 1, subj. act. . id.
ἀγοράσωσι, 3 pers. pl. aor. 1, subj. act. . id.
ἄγουσι, 3 pers. pl. pres. indic. act. . ἄγω

ἄγρα], ας, ἡ, (§ 2. tab. B. b, and rem. 2) *a catching, thing taken, draught* of fishes, Lu. 5. 4, 9.

ἀγρεύω, fut. εύσω, (§ 13. tab. M) *to take in hunting, catch,* Mar. 12. 13.

ἄγρᾳ, dat. sing. . . . . . . ἄγρα
ἀγράμματοι,[c] nom. pl. masc. . . . ἀγράμματος
ἀγράμμᾰτος], ου, ὁ, ἡ, (§ 7. rem. 2) (ἀ & γράμμα) *illiterate, unlearned.*
ἄγραν, acc. sing. . . . . . . ἄγρα
ἀγραυλέω, ῶ], fut. ήσω, (§ 16. tab. P) (ἀγρός & αὐλή) *to remain in the open air,* especially *by night.*
ἀγραυλοῦντες,[d] nom. pl. masc. part. pres. . ἀγραυλέω
ἀγρεύσωσι,[e] 3 pers. pl. aor. 1, subj. act. . ἀγρεύω
ἀγρεύω], fut. εύσω . . . . . ἄγρα
ἄγρια, nom. pl. neut. . . . . . ἄγριος
ἀγριέλαιος, ου, ἡ, (§ 3. tab. C. b) (ἄγριος & ἐλαία) *a wild olive-tree, oleaster,* Ro. 11. 17, 24.
ἀγριελαίου, gen. sing. . . . . ἀγριέλαιος
ἄγριον, nom. and acc. neut. sing. . . ἄγριος
ἄγριος], ία, ιον, (§ 7. rem. 1) . . ἀγρός
Ἀγρίππα, gen. and voc. sing. . . . Ἀγρίππας
Ἀγρίππας, α, ὁ, (§ 2. rem. 4) *Agrippa,* pr. name.
ἀγρόν, acc. sing. . . . . . . ἀγρός

ἀγρός, οῦ, ὁ, (§ 3. tab. C. a) *a field,* especially *a cultivated field;* pl. *the country; lands, farms, villages.*

ἄγριος, ία, ιον, (§ 7. rem. 1) *belonging to the field, wild; fierce, raging.*

ἀγροῦ, gen. sing. . . . . . ἀγρός
ἀγρούς, acc. pl. . . . . . . id.
ἀγρυπνεῖτε, 2 pers. pl. pres. imper. . . ἀγρυπνέω
ἀγρυπνέω, ῶ], fut. ήσω, (§ 16. tab. P) *to be awake, watch; to be watchful, vigilant.*

ἀγρυπνία], ας, ἡ, (§ 2. tab. B. b, and rem. 2) *want of sleep, watching,* 2 Co. 6. 5; 11. 27.

ἀγρυπνία], ας, ἡ . . . . . ἀγρυπνέω
ἀγρυπνίαις, dat. pl. . . . . . ἀγρυπνία
ἀγρυπνοῦντες, nom. pl. masc. part. pres. . ἀγρυπνέω
ἀγρυπνοῦσι, 3 pers. pl. pres. indic. . id.
ἀγρῷ, dat. sing . . . . . ἀγρός

ἄγω, fut. ἄξω, (§ 23. rem. 1. b) perf. ἦχα & ἀγήοχα, (§ 23. rem. 6) aor. 2, ἤγαγον, (§ 13. rem. 7. d) fut. 1, pass. ἀχθήσομαι, (§ 23. rem. 3. b) aor. 1, pass. ἤχθην, (§ 23. rem. 4) perf. pass. ἦγμαι, (§ 23. rem. 7) *to lead, bring; lead away, drive off,* as a booty of cattle; *conduct, accompany; lead out, produce; conduct with force, drag, hurry away; guide, incite,*

[a] Ac. 19. 38. [b] Ac. 17. 5. [c] Ac. 4. 13. [d] Lu. 2. 8. [e] Mar. 12. 13.

entice; convey one's self, go, go away, pass or spend as time; *celebrate*

ἀγέλη, ης, ἡ, (§ 2. tab. B. a) *a drove, flock, herd.*

ἀγωγή, ης, ἡ, (§ 2. tab. B. a) *guidance, mode of instruction, discipline, course of life,* 2 Ti. 3. 10.

ἀγωγή], ης, ἡ . . . . ἄγω
ἀγωγῇ,[a] dat. sing. . . . . ἀγωγή
ἄγωμεν, 1 pers. pl. pres. subj. act. . . ἄγω

ἀγών], ῶνος, ὁ, (§ 4. rem. 2. e) *place of contest, racecourse, stadium; a contest, strife, contention; peril, toil.*

ἀγωνία, ας, ἡ, (§ 2. tab. B. b, and rem. 2) *contest, violent struggle; agony, anguish,* Lu. 22. 44.

ἀγωνίζομαι, fut. ίσομαι, perf. ἠγώνισμαι, (§ 26. rem. 1) *to be a combatant in the public games; to contend, fight, strive earnestly.*

ἀγῶνα, acc. sing. . . . ἀγών
ἀγῶνι, dat. sing. . . . id.
ἀγωνία], ας, ἡ . . . id.
ἀγωνίᾳ,[b] dat. sing. . . . ἀγωνία
ἀγωνίζεσθε, 2 pers. pl. pres. imper. . . ἀγωνίζομαι
ἀγωνίζομαι], (§ 26. rem. 1) . . . ἀγών
ἀγωνιζόμεθα, 1 pers. pl. pres.—A. C. Ln. } ἀγωνίζομαι
ὀνειδιζόμεθα, R. Gr. Sch. Tdf. (1 Ti. 4. 10) }
ἀγωνιζόμενος, nom. sing. masc. part. pres. id.
ἀγωνίζου, 2 pers. sing. pres. imper. . . id.
ἄγωσι, 3 pers. pl. aor. 2, subj. act. . . ἄγω
Ἀδάμ, ὁ, *Adam,* pr. name, indecl.
ἀδάπανον,[c] acc. sing. neut. . . . ἀδάπανος
ἀδάπᾰνος], ου, ὁ, ἡ, (§ 7. rem. 2) (ἀ & δαπάνη) *without expense, gratuitous.*
Ἀδδί,[d] ὁ, *Addi,* pr. name, indecl.
ἀδελφαί, nom. pl. . . . . ἀδελφή
ἀδελφάς, acc. pl. . . . . id.
ἀδελφέ, voc. sing. . . . . ἀδελφός
ἀδελφή, ῆς, ἡ, (§ 2. tab. B. a) . . . id.
ἀδελφῇ, dat. sing.—Al. Ln. Tdf. . . } ἀδελφή
ἀγαπητῇ, Rec. Gr. Sch. (Phile. 1) . }
ἀδελφήν, acc. sing. . . . . id.
ἀδελφῆς, gen. sing. . . . id.
ἀδελφοί, nom. pl. . . . . ἀδελφός
ἀδελφοί, voc. pl.—Rec. . . . } id.
ἀγαπητοί, Gr. Sch. Tdf. (1 Jno. 2. 7) }
ἀδελφοῖς, dat. pl. . . . . ἀδελφός
ἀδελφόν, acc. sing. . . . . id.

ἀδελφός, οῦ, ὁ, (§ 3. tab. C. a) (ἀ & δελφύς, *the womb*) *a brother; near kinsman or relative; one of the same nation or nature; one of equal rank and dignity; an associate, a member of the Christian community.*

ἀδελφή, ῆς, ἡ, (§ 2. tab. B. a) *a sister; near kinswoman, or female relative; a female member of the Christian community.*

ἀδελφότης, τητος, ἡ, *brotherhood, the body of the Christian brotherhood,* 1 Pe. 2. 17; 5. 9. LXX.

ἀδελφότης], τητος, ἡ, (§ 4. rem. 2. c) . . ἀδελφός
ἀδελφότητα, acc. sing. . . . . ἀδελφότης
ἀδελφότητι, dat. sing. . . id.
ἀδελφοῦ, gen. sing. . . ἀδελφός
ἀδελφούς, acc. pl. . . . . id.
ἀδελφῷ, dat. sing. . id.
ἀδελφῶν, gen. pl. . . . id.
ᾅδη, voc. sing. . . ᾅδης
ᾅδῃ, dat. sing. . . . . id.
ἄδηλα, nom. pl. neut. . . . . ἄδηλος
ἄδηλον, acc. sing. fem. . . . id.
ἄδηλος], ου, ὁ, ἡ, τό, -ον, (§ 7. rem. 2) (ἀ & δῆλος) *not apparent or obvious; uncertain, not distinct,* Lu. 11. 44; 1 Co. 14. 8.

ἀδηλότης, τητος, ἡ, *uncertainty, inconstancy,* 1 Ti. 6. 17. L.G.

ἀδήλως, adv. *not manifestly, uncertainly, dubiously,* 1 Co. 9. 26.

ἀδηλότης], τητος, ἡ, (§ 4. rem. 2. c) . ἄδηλος
ἀδηλότητι,[e] dat. sing. . . . ἀδηλότης
ἀδήλως,[f] adv. . . . . ἄδηλος
ἀδημονεῖν, pres. infin. . . . . ἀδημονέω
ἀδημονέω, ῶ], fut. ήσω, (§ 16. tab. P) *to be depressed or dejected, full of anguish or sorrow.*
ἀδημονῶν, nom. sing. part. pres. . ἀδημονέω

ᾅδης, ου, ὁ, (§ 2. tab. B. c) *the invisible abode or mansion of the dead; the place of punishment, hell; the lowest place or condition,* Mat. 11. 23; Lu. 10. 15.

ἀδιάκρῐτος,[g] ου, ὁ, ἡ, (§ 7. rem. 2) (ἀ & διακρίνω) *undistinguishing, impartial.*
ἀδιάλειπτον, acc. sing. fem. . . ἀδιάλειπτος

---

[a] 2 Ti. 3. 10. [b] Lu. 22. 44. [c] 1 Co. 9. 18. [d] Lu. 3. 28. [e] 1 Ti. 6. 17. [f] 1 Co. 9. 26. [g] Ja. 3. 17.

ἀδιάλειπτος, ου, ὁ, ἡ, (§ 7. rem. 2) (ἀ & διαλείπω) *unceasing, constant, settled,* Ro. 9. 2; 2 Ti. 1. 3.

ἀδιαλείπτως, adv. *unceasingly, by an unvarying practice.*

ἀδιαλείπτως adv. . . . . ἀδιάλειπτος

ἀδιαφθορία], ας, ἡ, (§ 2. tab. B. b, and rem. 2) (ἀ & διαφθορά) *incorruptness, genuineness, pureness.*

ἀδιαφθορίαν,[a] acc. sing. . . . ἀδιαφθορία

ἀδικεῖσθε, 2 pers. pl. pres. indic. pass. . . ἀδικέω

ἀδικεῖτε, 2 pers. pl. pres. indic. act. . . id.

ἀδικηθέντος, gen. sing. masc. part. aor. 1, act. id.

ἀδικηθῇ, 3 pers. sing. aor. 1, subj. pass. . id.

ἀδίκημα, ατος, τό, (§ 4. tab. D. c) . . id.

ἀδικήματα, plur. . . . . . ἀδίκημα

ἀδικῆσαι, aor. 1, infin. act. . . . ἀδικέω

ἀδικήσαντος, gen. sing. masc. part. aor. 1, pass. id.

ἀδικησάτω, 3 pers. sing. aor. 1, imper. act. . id.

ἀδικήσει, 3 pers. sing. fut. act. . . id.

ἀδικήσῃ, 3 pers. sing. aor. 1, subj. act.—Gr. Sch. } id.
ἀδικήσει, Rec. Ln. Tdf. (Lu. 10. 19) }

ἀδικήσῃς, 2 pers. sing. aor 1, subj. act. . . id.

ἀδικήσητε, 2 pers. pl. aor. 1, subj. act. . id.

ἀδικήσωσι, 3 pers. pl. aor. 1, subj. act. . id.

ἀδικία, ας, ἡ, (§ 2. tab. B. b, and rem. 2) . id.

ἀδικίᾳ, dat. sing. . . . . ἀδικία

ἀδικίαις, dat. pl. . . . . . id.

ἀδικίαν, acc. sing. . . . . . id.

ἀδικίας, gen. sing. . . . . . id.

ἄδικοι, nom. pl. masc. . . . . ἄδικος

ἄδικος, ου, ὁ, ἡ, τό, -ον, (ἀ & δίκη) (§ 7. rem. 2) *unjust, unrighteous, iniquitous, vicious; deceitful, fallacious.*

ἀδίκως, adv. *unjustly, undeservedly,* 1 Pe. 2. 19.

ἀδικέω, ῶ], fut. ήσω, perf. ηκα, (§ 16. tab. P) *to act unjustly; wrong; injure; violate a law.*

ἀδίκημα, ατος, τό, (§ 4. tab. D. c) *an act of injustice, crime.*

ἀδικία, ας, ἡ, (§ 2. tab. B. b, and rem. 2) *injustice, wrong; iniquity, falsehood, deceitfulness.*

ἀδικούμενον, acc. sing. masc. part. pres. pass. ἄδικος

ἀδίκους, acc. pl. masc. . . . . id.

ἀδικοῦσι, 3 pers. pl. pres. indic. act. . . ἀδικέω

ἀδίκῳ, dat. sing. masc. . . . . ἄδικος

ἀδικῶ, 1 pers. sing. pres. indic. act. . . ἀδικέω

ἀδίκων, gen. pl. . . . . . ἄδικος

ἀδικῶν, nom. sing. masc. part. pres. act. . ἀδικέω

ἀδίκως,[b] adv. . . . . . id.

ἀδόκιμοι, nom. pl. masc. . . . ἀδόκιμος

ἀδόκιμον, acc. sing. masc. . . . id.

ἀδόκιμος, ου, ὁ, ἡ, (§ 7. rem. 2) (ἀ & δόκιμος) *unable to stand test, rejected, refuse, worthless.*

ἄδολον,[c] acc. sing. neut. . . . ἄδολος

ἄδολος], ου, ὁ, ἡ, (§ 7. rem. 2) (ἀ & δόλος) *without deceit, sincere.*

ᾄδοντες, nom. pl. masc. part. pres. . ᾄδω

ᾅδου, gen. sing. . . . . . ᾅδης

ᾄδουσι, 3 pers. pl. pres. indic. . . ᾄδω

Ἀδραμυττηνός], ή, όν, (§ 7. tab. F. a) *of Adramyttium,* a Greek city on the coast of Æolia, in Asia Minor. Lat. 39. 35, long. 37. 1.

Ἀδραμυττηνῷ,[d] dat. sing. . . . Ἀδραμυττηνός

Ἀδρίᾳ,[e] dat. sing. . . . . . Ἀδρίας

Ἀδρίας], ου, ὁ, (§ 2. tab. B. d) *the Adriatic sea.*

ἀδρότης], τητος, ἡ, (§ 4. rem. 2. c) (ἁδρός, *mature, full*) *abundance.*

ἀδρότητι,[f] dat. sing. neut. . . . . ἀδρότης

ἀδύνατα, nom. pl. neut. . . . . ἀδύνατος

ἀδυνατέω, ῶ], fut. ήσω, (§ 16. tab. P) . . id.

ἀδυνατήσει, 3 pers. sing. fut. . . ἀδυνατέω

ἀδύνατον, nom. sing. neut . . . ἀδύνατος

ἀδύνατος, ου, ὁ, ἡ, τό, -ον, (§ 7. rem. 2) (ἀ & δύναμαι) *impotent, weak; impossible.*

ἀδυνατέω, ῶ, fut. ήσω, (§ 16. tab. P) *not to be able; to be impossible.*

ἀδυνάτων, gen. pl. . . . . ἀδύνατος

ᾄδω], (contr. from ἀείδω) fut. ᾄσω, & ᾄσομαι, (§ 23. rem. 1. c) *to sing.*

ἀεί, adv. *alway, for ever, aye.*

ἀέρα, acc. sing. . . . . . ἀήρ

ἀέρος, gen. sing. (§ 4. rem. 2. f) . . id.

ἀετοί, nom. pl . . . . . ἀετός

ἀετός], οὐ, ὁ, (§ 3. tab. C. a) *an eagle.*

ἀετοῦ, gen. sing. . . . . . ἀετός

ἀετοῦ, gen. sing.—Gr. Sch. Tdf. . } id.
ἀγγέλου, Rec. (Re. 8. 13) . . }

ἀετῷ, dat. sing. . . . . . id.

ἄζυμα, nom. pl. neut. . . . . ἄζυμος

ἄζυμοι, nom. pl. masc. . . . . id.

ἀζύμοις, dat. pl. neut. . . . . ἄζυμος

---

[a] Tit. 2. 7. [b] 1 Pe. 2. 19. [c] 1 Pe. 2. 2. [d] Ac. 27. 2. [e] Ac. 27. 27. [f] 2 Co. 8. 20.

ἄζῦμος], ου, ὁ, ἡ, (§ 7. rem. 2) (ἀ & ζύμη) *unleavened*; τὰ ἄζυμα, *the feast of unleavened bread*, metaph. *pure from foreign matter, unadulterated, genuine*; τὸ ἄζυμον, *genuineness*, 1 Co. 5. 7, 8.

ἀζύμων, gen. pl. . . . . . . ἄζυμος

Ἀζώρ, ὁ, *Azor*, pr. name, indecl.

Ἄζωτον,[a] acc. sing. . . . . . Ἄζωτος

Ἄζωτος], ου, ἡ, (§ 3. tab. C. b) *Azotus, Ashdod*, a seaport in Palestine. Lat. 31. 45, long. 34. 41.

ἀηδία], ας, ἡ, (§ 2. tab. B. b, and rem. 2) (ἀ & ἡδύς) *unpleasantness; dislike, hostility*.

ἀηδίᾳ,[b] dat. sing.—D. } ἀηδία
ἔχθρᾳ, Rec. Gr. Sch. Tdf. (Lu. 23. 12) }

ἀήρ, ἀέρος, ὁ, (§ 4. rem. 2. f) *air, atmosphere*.

ἀθανασία], ας, ἡ, (§ 2. tab. B. b, and rem. 2) (ἀ & θάνατος) *immortality*, 1 Co. 15. 53, 54; 1 Ti. 6. 16.

ἀθανασίαν, acc. sing. . . . . . ἀθανασία

ἀθεμίτοις, dat. pl. fem. . . . . ἀθέμιτος

ἀθέμιτον, ου, τό, nom. sing. neut. . . id.

ἀθέμιτος], ου, ὁ, ἡ, τό, -ον, (§ 7. rem. 2) (ἀ & θεμιτός, *lawful*) *unlawful, criminal, wicked*, Ac. 10. 28; 1 Pe. 4. 3.

ἄθεοι,[c] nom. pl. masc. . . . . ἄθεος

ἄθεος], ου, ὁ, ἡ, (§ 7. rem. 2) (ἀ & θεός) *an atheist; godless, estranged from the knowledge and worship of the true God*.

ἄθεσμος, ου, ὁ, ἡ, (§ 7. rem. 2) (ἀ & θεσμός, *law*) *lawless, unrestrained, licentious*, 2 Pe. 2. 7; 3. 17. L.G.

ἀθέσμων, gen. pl. . . . . . ἄθεσμος

ἀθετεῖ, 3 pers. sing. pres. indic. act. . . ἀθετέω

ἀθετεῖτε, 2 pers. pl. pres. indic. act. . . id.

ἀθετέω, ῶ], fut. ήσω, (§ 16. tab. P) (ἀ & τίθημι) pr. *to displace, set aside; to abrogate, annul, violate, swerve from; reject, contemn*. L.G.

ἀθέτησις, εως, ἡ, (§ 5. tab. E. c) *abrogation, annulling*, He. 7. 18; 9. 26.

ἀθετῆσαι, aor. 1, infin. act. . . . . ἀθετέω

ἀθετήσας, nom. sing. aor. 1, part. act. . id.

ἀθέτησιν, acc. sing. . . . . . ἀθέτησις

ἀθετήσω, 1 pers. sing. fut. act. . . . ἀθετέω

ἀθετοῦσι, 3 pers. pl. pres. indic. act. . id.

ἀθετῶ, 1 pers. sing. pres. indic. contr. . id.

ἀθετῶν, nom. sing. masc. part. pres. act. . id.

Ἀθῆναι], ῶν, αἱ, (§ 2. tab. B. a) *Athens*, one of the most important cities of Greece, called from Ἀθήνη, *Minerva*, to whom it was dedicated. Lat. 37. 58, long. 23. 44.

Ἀθηναῖος, αία, αῖον, (§ 7. rem. 1) *Athenian, inhabiting or belonging to Athens*.

Ἀθηναῖοι, nom. and voc. pl. masc. . . Ἀθηναῖος

Ἀθηναῖος], αία, αῖον . . . . . Ἀθῆναι

Ἀθήναις, dat. pl. . . . . . . id.

Ἀθηνῶν, gen. pl. . . . . . . id.

ἀθλέω, ῶ], fut. ήσω, perf. ἤθληκα, (§ 16. tab. P) (ἄεθλος, *strife, contest*) *to strive, contend, be a champion in the public games*, 2 Ti. 2. 5.

ἄθλησις, εως, ἡ, (§ 5. tab. E. c) *contest, combat, struggle, conflict*. L.G.

ἀθλῇ, 3 pers. sing. pres. subj. . . . ἀθλέω

ἀθλήσῃ, 3 pers. sing. aor. 1, subj. . . id.

ἄθλησιν,[d] acc. sing. . . . . . ἄθλησις

ἄθλησις], εως, ἡ, (§ 5. tab. E. c) . . . ἀθλέω

ἀθροίζω], fut. οίσω, perf. ἤθροικα, (§ 26. rem. 1) (ἀθρόος, *collected, crowded*) *to collect in a body*.

ἀθυμέω, ῶ], fut. ήσω, (§ 16. tab. P) (ἀ & θυμός) *to despond, be disheartened*.

ἀθυμῶσι,[e] 3 pers. pl. pres. subj. . . ἀθυμέω

ἀθῷον, acc. sing. neut. . . . . . ἀθῷος

ἀθῷος, ου, ὁ, ἡ, (§ 7. rem. 2) (ἀ & θωή, *a penalty*) *unpunished*; metaph. *innocent*, Mat. 27. 4, 24.

αἵ, nom. pl. fem. (§ 10. tab. J. g) . . ὅς

αἰγείοις,[f] dat. pl. neut. . . . . αἴγειος

αἴγειος], εία, ειον, (§ 7. rem. 1) (αἴξ, γός, *a goat*) *belonging to a goat*.

αἰγιαλόν, acc. sing. . . . . . αἰγιαλός

αἰγιαλός], ου, ὁ, (§ 3. tab. C. a) *seashore*.

Αἰγύπτιοι, nom. pl. . . . . . Αἰγύπτιος

Αἰγύπτιον, acc. sing. . . . . . id.

Αἰγύπτιος, ου, ὁ, *an Egyptian* . . . Αἴγυπτος

Αἰγυπτίων, gen. pl. . . . . . Αἰγύπτιος

Αἴγυπτον, acc. sing. . . . . . Αἴγυπτος

Αἴγυπτος, ου, ἡ, (§ 3. tab. C. b) *Egypt*.

Αἰγύπτου, gen. sing. . . . . . id.

Αἰγύπτῳ, dat. sing. . . . . . . id.

ἀϊδίοις, dat. pl. masc. . . . . . ἀΐδιος

ἀΐδιος, ου, ὁ, ἡ, (§ 7. rem. 2) (ἀεί) *always existing, eternal*, Ro. 1. 20; Jude 6.

αἰδοῦς, gen. sing. . . . . . αἰδώς

[a] Ac. 8. 40. [b] Lu. 23. 12. [c] Ep. 2. 12. [d] He. 10. 32. [e] Col. 3. 21. [f] He. 11. 37.

αἰδώς], όος, οῦς, ἡ, (§ 5. tab. E. h) *modesty, reverence,* 1 Ti. 2. 9; He. 12. 28.

Αἰθιόπων, gen. pl. . . . . . . Αἰθίοψ

Αἰθίοψ, οπος, ὁ, ἡ, (§ 4. rem. 2. a) *an Ethiopian.*

αἷμα, ατος, τό, (§ 4. tab. D. c) *blood; of the colour of blood; bloodshed; blood-guiltiness; natural descent.*

αἱματεκχυσία, ας, ἡ, (§ 2. tab. B. b, and rem. 2) (αἷμα & ἔκχυσις, from ἐκχέω) *an effusion or shedding of blood.* N.T.

αἱμοῤῥοέω, ῶ, fut. ήσω, (§ 16. tab. P) (αἷμα & ῥόος, from ῥέω) *to have a flux of blood.*

αἵματα, nom. pl.—Gr. Sch. Tdf. } αἷμα
αἷμα, Rec. Ln. (Re. 18. 24) }

αἱματεκχυσία], ας, ἡ . . . id.

αἱματεκχυσίας,[a] gen. sing. . αἱματεκχυσία

αἵματι, dat. sing. . . . αἷμα

αἵματος, gen. sing. . . . . . id.

αἱμάτων, gen. pl. . . . . . id.

αἱμοῤῥοέω, ῶ], fut. ησω, (§ 16. tab. P) . id.

αἱμοῤῥοοῦσα,[b] nom. sing. fem. part. pres. . αἱμοῤῥοέω

Αἰνέα, voc. sing. . . . . . Αἰνέας

Αἰνέαν, acc. sing. . . . . . id.

Αἰνέας], ου, ὁ, (§ 2. tab. B. d) *Æneas,* pr. name.

αἰνεῖν, pres. infin. . . . . . αἰνέω

αἰνεῖτε, 2 pers. pl. pres. imper. . id.

αἰνέσεως,[c] gen. sing. . . . . αἴνεσις

αἴνεσις], εως, ἡ, *praise,* (§ 5. tab. E. c) . αἶνος

αἰνέω, ῶ], fut. έσω, (§ 22. rem. 1) . . id.

αἴνιγμα], ατος, τό, (αἰνίσσω, *to intimate obscurely*) *an enigma, any thing obscurely expressed or intimated.*

αἰνίγματι,[d] dat. sing. . . . αἴνιγμα

αἶνον, acc. sing. . . . . . αἶνος

αἶνος], ου, ὁ, (§ 3. tab. C. a) *praise,* Mat. 21. 16; Lu. 18. 43.

αἰνέω, ῶ, fut. εσω, (§ 22. rem. 1) *to praise, celebrate.*

αἴνεσις, εως, ἡ, (§ 5. tab. E. c) *praise.* LXX.

αἰνοῦντα, acc. sing. masc. part. pres. . αἰνέω

αἰνοῦντες, nom. pl. masc. part. pres. . . id.

αἰνῶν, nom. sing. masc. part. pres. . . id.

Αἰνών,[e] ἡ, *Enon,* pr. n., indec. Lat. 32. 26, long. 35. 34.

αἶρε, 2 pers. sing. pres. imper. act. αἴρω

αἴρει, 3 pers. sing. pres. indic. act. . . αἴρω

αἴρεις, 2 pers. sing. pres. ind. act. . . id.

αἱρέσεις, nom. or acc. pl. . . . αἵρεσις

αἱρέσεως, gen. sing. . . . . . id.

αἵρεσιν, acc. sing. . . . . id.

αἵρεσις, εως, η, (§ 5. tab. E. c) . . . αἱρέομαι

αἴρεται, 3 pers. sing. pres. indic. pass. . αἴρω

αἴρετε, 2 pers. pl. imper. act. . . . id.

αἱρετίζω, fut. αἱρετίσω, (§ 26. rem. 1) . αἱρέω

αἱρετικόν,[f] acc. sing. . . . . αἱρετικός

αἱρετικός], ου, ὁ, (§ 3. tab. C. a) . . αἱρέω

αἱρέω, ῶ], fut. ήσω, perf. ᾕρηκα, perf. pass. ᾕρημαι, mid. αἱρέομαι, οῦμαι, aor. 2, εἱλόμην, (§ 36. rem. 1) *to take;* mid. *to choose.*

αἵρεσις, εως, ἡ, (§ 5. tab. E. c) strictly, *a choice or option;* hence, *a sect, faction;* by impl. *discord, contention.*

αἱρετίζω, fut. ίσω, aor 1, ᾑρέτισα. (§ 13. rem. 2) *to choose, choose with delight or love,* Mat. 12. 18.

αἱρετικός, ου, ὁ, (§ 3. tab. C. a) *one who creates or fosters factions.*

αἱρήσομαι, 1 pers. sing. fut. mid. . . αἱρέω

αἰρόμενον, acc. sing. masc. part. pres. pass. αἴρω

αἴροντος, gen. sing. masc. part. pres. act. . id.

αἴρω], fut. ἀρῶ, (§ 27. rem. 1. c) aor. 1, ἦρα, *to take up, lift, raise; bear, carry; take away, remove; destroy, kill.*

αἴρων, nom. sing. masc. part. pres. act. . . αἴρω

αἴρωσι, 3 pers. pl. pres. subj. act. . . id.

αἷς, dat. pl. fem. (§ 10. tab. J. g) . . ὅς

αἰσθάνομαι], fut. αἰσθήσομαι, aor. 2, ᾐσθόμην, (§ 36. rem. 2) *to perceive, understand.*

αἴσθησις, εως, ἡ, (§ 5. tab. E. c) *perception, understanding.*

αἰσθητήριον, ου, τό, (§ 3. tab. C. c) *an organ of perception; internal sense.*

αἰσθήσει,[g] dat. sing. . . . . αἴσθησις

αἴσθησις], εως, ἡ, (§ 5. tab. E. c) . . αἰσθάνομαι

αἰσθητήρια,[h] acc. pl. . . . . αἰσθητήριον

αἰσθητήριον], ου, τό, (§ 3. tab. C. c) . . αἰσθάνομαι

αἴσθωνται,[i] 3 pers. pl. aor. 2, subj. mid. . id.

αἰσχροκερδεῖς, acc. pl. masc. . . αἰσχροκερδής

αἰσχροκερδῆ, acc. sing. masc. . . . id.

[a] He. 9. 22. [b] Mat. 9. 20. [c] He. 13. 15. [d] 1 Co. 13. 12. [e] Jno. 3. 23. [f] Tit. 3. 10. [g] Phi. 1. 9. [h] He. 5. 14. [i] Lu. 9. 45.

αἰσχροκερδής], έος, οῦς, ὁ, ἡ, (§ 7. tab. G. b) (αἰσχρός & κέρδος) *eager for dishonourable gain, sordid*, 1 Ti. 3. 3, 8; Tit. 1. 7.

αἰσχροκερδῶς, adv. *for the sake of base gain, sordidly*. N.T.

αἰσχροκερδῶς,[a] adv. . . . . αἰσχροκερδής

αἰσχρολογία, ας, ἡ, (§ 2. tab. B. b, and rem. 2) (αἰσχρός & λόγος) *vile or obscene language, foul talk*.

αἰσχρολογίαν,[b] acc. sing. . . . . αἰσχρολογία

αἰσχρός], ά, όν, (§ 7. rem. 1) strictly, *deformed*, opposed to καλός: metaph. *indecorous, indecent, dishonourable, vile*.

αἰσχρότης, τητος, ἡ, (§ 4. rem. 2. c) *indecorum, indecency*.

αἰσχρότης,[c] τητος, ἡ . . . . αἰσχρός

αἰσχροῦ, gen. sing. neut. . . . id.

αἰσχύνας, acc. pl. . . . . . αἰσχύνη

αἰσχυνέσθω, 3 pers. sing. pres. imper. . αἰσχύνομαι

αἰσχύνη, ης, ἡ, (§ 2. tab. B. a) *shame, disgrace; cause of shame, dishonourable conduct*. (ῡ).

αἰσχύνομαι, fut. υνοῦμαι & υνθήσομαι, *to be ashamed, confounded*.

αἰσχύνῃ, dat. sing. . . . . . αἰσχύνη

αἰσχύνης, gen. sing. . . . . . id.

αἰσχυνθήσομαι, 1 pers. sing. fut. 1, pass. (§ 27. rem. 3) . . . . αἰσχύνομαι

αἰσχυνθῶμεν, 1 pers. pl. aor. 1, subj. pass. . id.

αἰσχύνομαι, fut. υνοῦμαι, (§ 27. rem. 6) αἰσχύνη

αἰτεῖν, pres. infin. act. . . . . . αἰτέω

αἰτεῖς, 2 pers. sing. pres. indic. act. . . id.

αἰτεῖσθαι, pres. infin. mid. (§ 17. tab. Q) . id.

αἰτεῖσθε, 2 pers. pl. pres. indic. mid. . . id.

αἰτεῖτε, 2 pers. pl. pres. imper. act. . . id.

αἰτείτω, 3 pers. sing. pres. imper. act. . . id.

αἰτέω, ῶ], fut. ήσω, aor. 1, ᾔτησα, (§ 16. tab. P) *to ask, request; demand; desire*, Ac. 7. 46.

αἴτημα, ατος, τό, (§ 4. tab. D. c) *a thing asked or sought for; petition, request*, Lu. 23. 24; 1 Jno. 5. 15.

αἴτημα, ατος, τό . . . . . αἰτέω

αἰτήματα, nom. and acc. pl. . . . αἴτημα

αἰτῆσαι, aor. 1, infin. act. . . . . αἰτέω

αἰτήσας, nom. sing. masc. part. aor. 1 . id.

αἰτήσασθε, 2 pers. pl. aor. 1, imper. mid.—A. B. D. Ln. Tdf. . . . } id.
αἰτήσεσθε, Rec. Gr. Sch. (1 Jno. 5. 15)

αἰτήσει, 3 pers. sing. fut. act. . . . αἰτέω

αἰτήσεσθε, 2 pers. pl. fut. mid. . . . id.

αἰτήσῃ, 3 pers. sing. aor. 1, subj. act. . id.

αἰτήσῃ, 2 pers. sing. aor. 1, subj. mid. . . id.

αἰτήσῃς, 2 pers. sing. aor. 1, subj. act. . id.

αἰτήσηται, 3 pers. sing. aor. 1, subj. mid. . id.

αἰτήσητε, 2 pers. pl. aor. 1, subj. act. . id.

αἰτήσομαι, 1 pers. sing. fut. mid. . . id.

αἴτησον, 2 pers. sing. aor. 1, imper. act. . id.

αἰτήσουσι, 3 pers. pl. fut. act. . . . id.

αἰτήσωμαι, 1 pers. sing. aor. 1, subj. mid.—Al. Ln. Tdf. . . . . . } id.
αἰτήσομαι, Rec. Gr. Sch. (Mar. 6. 24)

αἰτήσωμεν, 1 pers. pl. aor. 1, subj. act. . id.

αἰτήσωνται, 3 pers. pl. aor. 1, subj. mid. . id

αἰτῆτε, 2 pers. pl. pres. subj. act.—B. } id.
αἰτήσητε, Rec. Gr. Sch. Tdf. (Jno. 14. 13)

αἰτία, ας, ἡ, (§ 2. tab. B. b, and rem. 2) *cause, motive, incitement; accusation, crime, case*.

αἰτίαμα, ατος, τό, (§ 4. tab. D. c) *charge, accusation*.

αἰτιάομαι, ῶμαι, (§ 19. tab. S) *to charge, accuse*.

αἴτιος, ου, ὁ, ἡ, (§ 7. rem. 2) *causative*; αἴτιος, *an author or causer*, He. 5. 9; τὸ αἴτιον, equivalent to αἰτία.

αἰτίωμα, ατος, τό, (§ 4. tab. D. c) equivalent to αἰτίαμα. N.T.

αἰτίαμα], ατος, τό, (§ 4. tab. D. c) . αἰτία

αἰτιάματα,[d] acc. pl. . . . . . αἰτίαμα

αἰτιάομαι], ῶμαι, (§ 19. tab. S) . . αἰτία

αἰτίαν, acc. sing. . . . . . . id.

αἰτίας, gen. sing. . . . . . . id.

αἰτίας, acc. pl. . . . . . . id.

αἵτινες, nom. pl. fem. (§ 10. tab. J. h) . ὅστις

αἴτιον, acc. sing. neut. . . . . αἴτιος

αἴτιος,[e] ου, ὁ, ἡ, (§ 7. rem. 2) . . αἰτία

αἰτίου, gen. sing. neut. . . . . αἴτιος

αἰτίωμα], ατος, τό, *an accusation* . αἰτία

αἰτιώματα, acc. pl.—Gr. Sch. Tdf. . . } αἰτίωμα
αἰτιάματα, Rec. (Ac. 25. 7)

αἰτοῦμαι, 1 pers. sing. pres. indic. mid. αἰτέω

αἰτούμεθα, 1 pers. pl. pres. ind. mid. . id.

αἰτούμενοι, nom. pl. part. pres. mid. . id.

αἰτοῦντι, dat. sing. masc. part. pres. act. id.

αἰτοῦσα, nom. sing. fem. part. pres. act. . id.

αἰτοῦσι, 3 pers. pl. pres. indic. act. . . id.

[a] 1 Pe. 5. 2. [b] Col. 3. 8. [c] Ep. 5. 4. [d] Ac. 25. 7. [e] He. 5. 9.

αἰτοῦσι, dat. pl. masc. part. pres. act. . αἰτέω
αἰτώμεθα, 1 pers. pl. pres. subj. mid. . . id.
αἰτῶμεν, 1 pers. pl. pres. subj. act. . . id.
αἰτῶν, nom. sing. masc. part. pres. act. . . id.

αἰφνίδιος, ου, ὁ, ἡ, (§ 7. rem. 2) *unforeseen, unexpected, sudden*, Lu. 21. 34; 1 Thes. 5. 3.
αἰχμαλωσίαν, acc. sing. . . . αἰχμαλωσία
αἰχμαλωσία], ας, ἡ, (§ 2. tab. B. b, and rem. 2) αἰχμάλωτος
αἰχμαλωτεύοντες, nom. pl. masc. part. pres. αἰχμαλωτεύω
αἰχμαλωτεύω, fut. εύσω, (§ 13. tab. M) . αἰχμάλωτος
αἰχμαλωτίζοντα, acc. sing. masc. part. pres. αἰχμαλωτίζω
αἰχμαλωτίζοντες, nom. pl. masc. part. pres. . id.
αἰχμαλωτίζω], fut. ίσω, (§ 26. rem. 1) . αἰχμάλωτος
αἰχμαλωτισθήσονται, 3 pers. pl. fut. 1, pass. αἰχμαλωτίζω
αἰχμαλώτοις,[a] dat. pl. masc. . . αἰχμάλωτος
αἰχμάλωτος], ου, ὁ, ἡ, (§ 7. rem. 2) (αἰχμή, *a spear*, and ἁλίσκομαι, *to capture*) *a captive*.

αἰχμαλωσία, ας, ἡ, (§ 2. tab. B. b, and rem. 2) *captivity, state of captivity; captive multitude*, Ep.4.8; Re.13.10. L.G.

αἰχμαλωτεύω, fut. εύσω, *to lead captive*; met. *to captivate*, Ep.4.8; 2 Ti.3.6.

αἰχμαλωτίζω, fut. ίσω, *to lead captive*; by impl. *to subject*, Lu. 21. 24; Ro.7.23; 2 Co. 10. 5. L.G.

αἰών], ῶνος, ὁ, (§ 4. rem. 2. c) pr. *a period of time of significant character; life; an era; an age*: hence, *a state of things marking an age or era; the present order of nature; the natural condition of man, the world*; ὁ αἰών, *illimitable duration, eternity*; as also, οἱ αἰῶνες, ὁ αἰὼν τῶν αἰώνων, οἱ αἰῶνες τῶν αἰώνων; by an Aramaism οἱ αἰῶνες, *the material universe*, He. 1. 2.

αἰώνιος, ίου, ὁ, ἡ, & αἰώνιος, ία, ιον, (§ 7. rem. 2) *indeterminate as to duration, eternal, everlasting*.

αἰῶνα, acc. sing. . . . . . αἰών
αἰῶνας, acc. pl. . . . . id.
αἰῶνι, dat. sing. . . . . . id.
αἰώνια, nom. pl. neut. . . . . αἰώνιος
αἰωνίαν, acc. sing. fem. (§ 7. rem. 2) . id.
αἰωνίοις, dat. pl. . . . . . id.
αἰώνιον, nom. neut. and acc. sing. masc. and fem. id.
αἰώνιος, ου, ὁ, ἡ, & ία, ιον . . . αἰών
αἰωνίου, gen. sing. . . . . αἰώνιος
αἰωνίους, acc. pl. fem. . . . . id.
αἰωνίων, gen. pl. . . . . . id.
αἰῶνος, gen. sing. . . . . . αἰών
αἰώνων, gen. pl. . . . . . id.
αἰῶσι, dat. pl. . . . . . id.
ἀκαθαρσία, ας, ἡ, (§ 2. tab. B. b, and rem 2) (ἀ & καθαίρω) *uncleanness; lewdness; impurity* of motive, 1 Thes. 2. 3.
ἀκαθαρσίᾳ, dat. sing. . . . . ἀκαθαρσία
ἀκαθαρσίαν, acc. sing. . . . . id.
ἀκαθαρσίας, gen. sing. . . . id.
ἀκάθαρτα, nom. and acc. pl. neut. . ἀκάθαρτος
ἀκαθάρτης, τητος, ἡ, (§ 4. rem. 2. c) *impurity*. N.T.
ἀκαθάρτητος,[b] gen. sing. . . ἀκαθάρτης
ἀκαθάρτοις, dat. pl. . . . ἀκάθαρτος
ἀκάθαρτον, nom. and acc. sing. neut. . id.
ἀκάθαρτος, ου, ὁ, ἡ, (§ 7. rem. 2) *impure, unclean; lewd; foul*.
ἀκαθάρτου, gen. sing. neut. . . ἀκάθαρτος
ἀκαθάρτῳ, dat. sing. neut. . . id.
ἀκαθάρτων, gen. pl. . . . . id.
ἀκαιρέομαι, οῦμαι], fut. ήσομαι, (§ 17. tab. Q) (ἀ & καιρός) *to be without opportunity or occasion*, Phi. 4. 10. N.T.
ἀκαίρως,[c] adv. *unseasonably*.
ἄκακος, ου, ὁ, ἡ, (§ 7. rem. 2) (ἀ & κακός) *free from evil, innocent, blameless; artless, simple*, Ro. 16. 18; He. 7. 26.
ἀκάκων, gen. pl. . . . . ἄκακος

ἄκανθα], ης, ἡ, (§ 2. rem. 3) *a thorn, thorn-bush*, Mat. 7. 16.

ἀκάνθινος, ου, ὁ, ἡ, (§ 7. rem. 2) *thorny, made of thorns*, Mar. 15. 17; Jno. 19. 5.

ἄκανθαι, nom. pl. . . . . ἄκανθα
ἀκάνθας, acc. pl. . . . . id.
ἀκάνθινον, acc. sing. masc. . . ἀκάνθινος
ἀκάνθινος], ου, ὁ, ἡ . . . . ἄκανθα
ἀκανθῶν, gen. pl. . . . . . id.
ἄκαρπα, nom. pl. neut. . . . ἄκαρπος
ἄκαρποι, nom. pl. masc. . . . id.
ἀκάρποις, dat. pl. neut. . . . id.
ἄκαρπος, ου, ὁ, ἡ, τό, -ον, (§ 7. rem. 2) (ἀ & καρπός) *without fruit, unfruitful, barren*. by impl. *noxious*.
ἀκάρπους, acc. pl. masc. . . . ἄκαρπος

[a] Lu. 4. 18. [b] Re. 17. 4. [c] 2 Ti. 4. 2.

ἀκατάγνωστον,[a] acc. sing. masc. . . . ἀκατάγνωστος

ἀκατάγνωστος], ου, ὁ, ἡ, τό, -ον, (§ 7. rem. 2) (ἀ & καταγινώσκω) pr. *not worthy of condemnation* by a judge; hence, *irreprehensible.* LXX.

ἀκατακάλυπτον, acc. sing. fem. . . ἀκατακάλυπτος

ἀκατακάλυπτος], ου, ὁ, ἡ, (§ 7. rem. 2) (ἀ & κατακαλύπτω) *uncovered, unveiled,* 1 Co. 11. 5, 13. L.G.

ἀκατακαλύπτῳ, dat. sing. fem. . . . ἀκατακάλυπτος

ἀκατάκριτον, acc. sing. masc. . . . ἀκατάκριτος

ἀκατάκρῐτος], ου, ὁ, ἡ, (§ 7. rem. 2) (ἀ & κατακρίνω) *uncondemned* in a public trial, Ac. 16. 37; 22. 25. N.T.

ἀκατακρίτους, acc. pl. masc. . . ἀκατάκριτος

ἀκαταλύτου,[b] gen. sing. fem. . . . ἀκατάλυτος

ἀκατάλῠτος], ου, ὁ, ἡ, (§ 7. rem. 2) (ἀ & καταλύω) *incapable of dissolution, indissoluble;* hence, *enduring, everlasting.* L.G.

ἀκατάπαστος, ου, ὁ, ἡ, (§ 7. rem. 2) (ἀ & κατάπαστος, *filled, satiated,* which fr. πατέομαι, *to taste*) *unsatisfied, insatiable.*

ἀκαταπάστους,[c] acc. pl. masc.—B. Ln. }
ἀκαταπαύστους, Rec. Gr. Sch. Tdf. } ἀκατάπαστος
ἀκαταπαύστου, Const. . }

ἀκατάπαυστος, ου, ὁ, ἡ, (§ 7. rem. 2) (ἀ & καταπαύω) *which cannot be restrained* from a thing, *unceasing.* L.G.

ἀκαταπαύστους,[d] acc. pl. masc. . ἀκατάπαυστος

ἀκαταστασία, ας, ἡ, (§ 2. tab. B. b, and rem. 2) (ἀ & καθίσταμαι, *to be in a fixed and tranquil state*) pr. *instability:* hence, *an unsettled state; disorder, commotion, tumult, sedition,* Lu. 21. 9; 1 Co. 14. 33; 2 Co. 6. 5; 12. 20; Ja. 3. 16. L.G.

ἀκαταστασίαι, nom. pl. . . . ἀκαταστασία

ἀκαταστασίαις, dat. pl. . . . . id.

ἀκαταστασίας, gen. sing. . . . id.

ἀκαταστασίας, acc. pl. . . . . id.

ἀκατάστατον, nom. sing. neut.—A. B. Ln. Tdf. }
ἀκατάσχετον, Rec. Gr. Sch. (Ja. 3. 8) } ἀκατάστατος

ἀκατάστᾰτος,[e] ου, ὁ, ἡ, (§ 7. rem. 2) (ἀ & καθίσταμαι) *unstable, inconstant; unquiet, turbulent.*

ἀκατάσχετον,[f] nom. sing. neut. . . ἀκατάσχετος

ἀκατάσχετος], ου, ὁ, ἡ, (§ 7. rem. 2) (ἀ & κατέχω) *not coercible, irrestrainable, untameable, unruly.* L.G.

Ἀκέλδαμα,[g] τό, *Aceldama,* pr. name, indecl.—R. Gr. Sch.
Ἀχελαμάχ, A. B.
Ἀκελδαμάχ, D. Ln. Tdf.

ἀκέραιοι, nom. pl. masc. . . . . ἀκέραιος

ἀκέραιος, ου, ὁ, ἡ, (§ 7. rem. 2) (ἀ & κεράννυμι, *to mix*) pr. *unmixed:* hence, *without mixture of vice or deceit, sincere, artless, blameless,* Mat. 10. 16; Ro. 16. 19; Phil. 2. 15.

ἀκεραίους, acc. pl. masc. . . ἀκέραιος

ἀκλινῆ,[h] acc. sing. fem. . . . . ἀκλινής

ἀκλῐνής], εος, ὁ, ἡ, (§ 7. tab. G. b) (ἀ & κλίνω) *not declining, unwavering, steady.*

ἀκήκοα, 1 pers. sing. 2nd perf. Att. (§ 13. rem. 7. b. c) . . . . ἀκούω

ἀκηκόαμεν, 1 pers. pl. 2nd perf. Att. . id.

ἀκηκόασι, 3 pers. pl. 2nd perf. Att. . id.

ἀκηκόατε, 2 pers. pl. 2nd perf. Att. . . id.

ἀκηκοότας, acc. pl. masc. part. 2nd perf. Att. id.

ἀκμάζω, fut. άσω, (§ 26. rem. 1) . . ἀκμή

ἀκμή], ῆς, ἡ, (§ 2. tab. B. a) (ἀκή, idem) pr. *the point of a weapon; point of time:* ἀκμήν for κατ' ἀκμήν, adv. *yet, still, even now.*

ἀκμάζω, fut. άσω, (§ 26. rem. 1) *to flourish, ripen, be in one's prime,* Re. 14. 18.

ἀκμήν,[i] adv. . . . . . . ἀκμή

ἀκοαί, nom. pl. . . . . . ἀκοή

ἀκοαῖς, dat. pl. . . . . . id.

ἀκοάς, acc. pl. . . . . . id.

ἀκοή, ῆς, ἡ, (§ 2. tab. B. a) . . . ἀκούω

ἀκοῇ, dat. sing. . . . . . ἀκοή

ἀκοήν, acc. sing. . . . . . id.

ἀκοῆς, gen. sing. . . . . . id.

ἀκολουθεῖ, 3 pers. sing. pres. indic. . . ἀκολουθέω

ἀκολούθει, 2 pers. sing. pres. imper. . . id.

ἀκολουθεῖν, pres. infin. . . . . id.

ἀκολουθείτω, 3 pers. sing. pres. imper. . id.

ἀκολουθέω, ῶ], fut. ήσω, perf. ἠκολούθηκα, (§ 16. tab. P) *to follow; follow* as a disciple; *imitate.*

ἀκολουθῆσαι, aor 1, infin. . . . . ἀκολουθέω

ἀκολουθήσαντες, nom. pl. masc. part. aor. 1 id.

ἀκολουθησάντων, gen. pl. masc. part. aor. 1. id.

ἀκολουθήσατε, 2 pers. pl. aor. 1, imper. . id.

ἀκολουθήσεις, 2 pers. sing. fut. . . id.

ἀκολουθήσουσι, 3 p. pl. fut.—A. B. D. Ln. Tdf. }
ἀκολουθήσωσι, Rec. Gr. Sch. (Jno. 10. 5) } id.

ἀκολουθήσω, 1 pers. sing. fut. . . id.

[a] Tit. 2. 8. [b] He. 7. 16. [c] 2 Pe. 2. 14. [d] 2 Pe. 2. 14. [e] Ja. 1. 8. [f] Ja. 3. 8. [g] Ac. 1. 19. [h] He. 10. 23. [i] Mat. 15. 16.

ἀκολουθήσωσι, 3 pers. pl. aor. 1, subj. . ἀκολουθέω
ἀκολουθοῦντα, acc. sing. masc. part. pres. . id.
ἀκολουθοῦντας, acc. pl. masc. part. pres. . id.
ἀκολουθοῦντι, dat. sing. masc. part. pres. . id.
ἀκολουθούσης, gen. sing. fem. part. pres. id.
ἀκολουθοῦσι, dat. pl. masc. part. pres. . . id.
ἀκολουθοῦσι, 3 pers. pl. pres. indic. . id.
ἀκολουθῶν, nom. sing. masc. part. pres. . id.
ἄκουε, 2 pers. sing. pres. imper. act. . ἀκούω
ἀκούει, 3 pers. sing. pres. indic. act. . . id.
ἀκούειν, pres. infin. act. . . . id.
ἀκούεις, 2 pers. sing. pres. indic. act. . . id.
ἀκούεται, 3 p. sing. pres. ind. pass. (§ 14. tab. N) id.
ἀκούετε, 2 pers. pl. pres. indic. act. . . id.
ἀκούετε, 2 pers. pl. pres. imper. act. . id.
ἀκουέτω, 3 pers. sing. pres. imper. act. . id.
ἀκούομεν, 1 pers. pl. pres. indic. act. . . id.
ἀκούοντα, acc. sing. masc. and neut. pl. part. pres. id.
ἀκούοντας, acc. pl. masc. part. pres. act. . id.
ἀκούοντες, nom. pl. masc. part. pres. act. id.
ἀκούοντι, dat. sing. masc. part. pres. act. . id.
ἀκούοντος, gen. sing. masc. part. pres. act. id.
ἀκουόντων, gen. pl. masc. part. pres. act. . id.
ἀκούουσι, dat. pl. masc. part. pres. act. id.
ἀκούουσι, 3 pers. pl. pres. indic. act. . id.
ἀκοῦσαι, aor. 1, infin. act. . . id.
ἀκούσαντες, nom. pl. masc. part. aor. 1, act. . id.
ἀκουσάντων, gen. pl. masc. part. aor. 1, act. id.
ἀκούσας, nom. sing. masc. part. aor. 1, act. . id.
ἀκούσασα, nom. sing. fem. part. aor. 1, act. id.
ἀκούσασι, dat. pl. masc. part. aor. 1, act. . id.
ἀκούσατε, 2 pers. pl. aor. 1, imper. act. . id.
ἀκουσάτω, 3 pers. sing. aor. 1, imper. act. . id.
ἀκουσάτωσαν, 3 pers. pl. aor. 1, imper. act. . id.
ἀκούσει, 3 pers. sing. fut. act. . . id.
ἀκούσεσθε, 2 pers. pl. fut. mid. . . id.
ἀκούσετε, 2 pers. pl. fut. act. . . id.
ἀκούσῃ, 2 pers. sing. fut. mid. . . . id.
ἀκούσῃ, 3 pers. sing. aor. 1, subj. act. id.
ἀκούσητε, 2 pers. pl. aor. 1, subj. act. . . id.
ἀκουσθεῖσι, dat. pl. neut. part. aor. 1, pass. id.
ἀκουσθῇ, 3 pers. sing. aor. 1, subj. pass. . id.
ἀκουσθήσεται, 3 pers. sing. fut. pass. (§ 22. rem. 4) id.
ἀκουσόμεθα, 1 pers. pl. fut. mid. . . id.
ἀκούσονται, 3 pers. pl. fut. mid. . . id.
ἀκούσουσι, 3 pers. pl. fut. act. . . id.
ἀκούσω, 1 pers. sing. aor. 1, subj. act. . id.
ἀκούσωσι, 3 pers. pl. aor. 1, subj. act. . . id.

ἀκούω, fut. ούσομαι, and, later, ούσω, (§ 13. tab. M) perf. ἀκήκοα, (§ 13. rem. 7. b. c) perf. pass. ἤκουσμαι, (§ 22. rem. 6) aor. 1, pass. ἠκούσθην, *to hear; to hearken, listen to,* Mar. 4. 3; Lu. 19. 48; *to heed, obey,* Mat. 18. 15; Ac. 4. 19, et al.; *to understand,* 1 Co. 14. 2; *to take in or admit* to mental acceptance, Mar. 4. 33; Jno. 8. 43, 47.

ἀκοή, ῆς, ἡ, (§ 2. tab. B. a) *hearing, the act or sense of hearing,* 1 Co. 12. 17; 2 Pe. 2. 8, et al.; *the instrument of hearing, the ear,* Mar. 7. 35, et al.; *a thing heard;* announcement, *instruction, doctrine,* Jno. 12. 38; Ro. 10. 16; *report,* Mat. 4. 24, et al.

ἀκούω, 1 pers. sing. pres. subj. act. . . ἀκούω
ἀκούων, nom. sing. masc. part. pres. act. . id.
ἀκούωσι, 3 pers. pl. pres. subj. act. . . id.
ἀκρασία], ας, ἡ, (§ 2. tab. B. b, and rem. 2) . ἀκρατής
ἀκρασίαν, acc. sing. . . . . ἀκρασία
ἀκρασίας, gen. sing. . . . . id.
ἀκρατεῖς,[a] nom. pl. masc. . . . ἀκρατής
ἀκρᾰτής], έος, ὁ, ἡ, τό, -ές, (§ 7. tab. G. b) (ἀ & κράτος) *not master of one's self, intemperate,* 2 Ti. 3. 3.

ἀκρασία, ας, ἡ, (§ 2. tab. B. b, and rem. 2) *intemperance, incontinence,* Mat. 23. 25; *unruly appetite, lustfulness,* 1 Co. 7. 5.

ἄκρᾱτος], ου, ὁ, ἡ, τό, -ον, (§ 7. rem. 2) (ἀ & κεράννυμι) *unmixed, unmingled* wine.
ἀκράτου,[b] gen. sing. masc. . . . . ἄκρατος
ἀκρίβεια], ας, ἡ, (§ 2. tab. B. b, and rem. 2) ἀκριβής
ἀκρίβειαν,[c] acc. sing. . . . . ἀκρίβεια
ἀκριβεστάτην,[d] acc. sing. fem. superl. (§ 8. rem. 1) ἀκριβής
ἀκριβέστερον, neut. comp. adverbially . . id.

ἀκρῑβής], έος, ὁ, ἡ, τό, -ές, (§ 7. rem. 5. a) *accurate, exact,* Ac. 18. 26; 23. 15, 20; 24. 22; *precise, severe, rigorous,* Ac. 26. 5.

ἀκρίβεια, ας, ἡ, (§ 2. tab. B. b, and rem. 2) *accuracy, exactness; preciseness,* or, *rigour, severe discipline,* Ac. 22. 3.

ἀκριβόω, ῶ, fut. ώσω, perf. ἠκρίβωκα, (§ 20. tab. T) *to inquire accurately, or assiduously,* Mat. 2. 7, 16: comp. verse 8.

ἀκρῑβῶς, adv. *accurately, diligently,* Mat. 2. 8; Lu. 1. 3; Ac. 18. 25; *circum-*

[a] 2 Ti. 3. 3. [b] Re. 14. 10. [c] Ac. 22. 3. [d] Ac. 26. 5.

spectly, strictly, Ep. 5. 15; *precisely, distinctly,* 1 Thes. 5. 2.

ἀκριβόω, ῶ], fut. ώσω, (§ 20. tab. T) . ἀκριβής

ἀκριβῶς, adv. . . . . . . id.

ἀκρίδας, acc. pl. . . . . ἀκρίς

ἀκρίδες, nom. pl. . . . . . . id.

ἀκρίδων, gen. pl. . . . . id.

ἀκρίς], ίδος, ἡ, (§ 4. rem. 2. c) *a locust,* Mat 3. 4; Mar. 1. 6; Re. 9. 3, 7.

ἀκροατήριον,[a] **ου, τό,** (§ 3. tab. C. c) (**ἀκροάομαι,** *to hear*) *a place of audience.* L.G.

ἀκροαταί, nom. pl. . . . . . ἀκροατής

ἀκροατής, ου, ὁ, (§ 2. tab. B. c) *a hearer,* Ro. 2. 13; Ja. 1. 22, 23, 25.

ἀκροβυστία, ας, ἡ, (§ 2. tab. B. b, and rem. 2) (ἄκρον & βύω, *to cover*) *the prepuce, foreskin; uncircumcision, the state of being uncircumcised,* Ro. 4. 10, et al.; the abstract being put for the concrete, *uncircumcised men,* i. e. *Gentiles,* Ro. 4. 9, et al. LXX.

ἀκροβυστίᾳ, dat. sing. . . . . ἀκροβυστία

ἀκροβυστίαν, acc. sing. . . . . id.

ἀκροβυστίας, gen. sing. . . . . id.

ἀκρογωνιαῖον, acc. sing. masc. . . ἀκρογωνιαῖος

ἀκρογωνιαῖος], α, ον, (§ 7. rem. 1) (ἄκρος & γωνία) *corner-foundation* stone, Ep. 2. 20; 1 Pe. 2. 6. LXX.

ἀκρογωνιαίου, gen. sing. masc. . . ἀκρογωνιαῖος

ἀκροθίνιον], ου, τό, (§ 3. tab. C. c) (ἄκρος & θίν, *a heap*) *the first-fruits* of the produce of the ground, which were taken from the top of the heap and offered to the gods; *the best and choicest of the spoils* of war, usually collected in a heap.

ἀκροθινίων,[b] gen. pl. . . . . ἀκροθίνιον

ἄκρον, ου, τό, (§ 3. tab. C. c) . . . ἄκρος

ἄκρος], α, ον, (§ 7. rem. 1) (ἀκή, *a sharp point*) *pointed;* hence, *extreme,* Mat. 24. 31.

ἄκρον, ου, τό, *the top, tip, end, extremity,* Mar. 13. 27; Lu. 16. 24; He. 11. 21.

ἄκρου, gen. sing. neut. . . . . ἄκρος

ἄκρων, gen. pl. . . . . . ἄκρον

Ἀκύλαν, acc. sing. . . . . . Ἀκύλας

Ἀκύλας, α, ὁ, (§ 2. rem. 4) *Aquila,* pr. name.

ἀκυροῖ, 3 pers. sing. pres. indic. . . ἀκυρόω

ἀκυροῦντες, nom. pl. masc. part. pres. . . id.

ἀκυρόω, ῶ], fut. ώσω, (§ 20. tab. T) (ἀ & κυρόω) *to deprive of authority, annul, abrogate,* Mat. 15. 6 Mar. 7. 13; Gal. 3. 17. L.G.

ἀκωλύτως,[c] adv. (ἀ & κωλύω) *without hindrance, freely.* (ῡ).

ἄκων,[d] ουσα, ον, (for ἀέκων, from ἀ & ἑκών, *willing*) *unwilling,* (§ 7. tab. H. d).

ἅλα, ατος, τό, (same sign. as ἅλας).—A.B.D.Ln. } ἅλς
ἅλας, Rec. Gr. Sch. Tdf. (Mar. 9. 50) }

ἀλάβαστρον, ου, τό, (§ 3. tab. C. c) *alabaster; a vase to hold perfumed ointment,* properly made of alabaster, but also of other materials, Mat. 26. 7; Mar. 14. 3; Lu. 7. 37.

ἀλαζονεία, ας, ἡ, (§ 2. tab. B. b, and rem. 2) ἀλαζών

ἀλαζονείαις, dat. pl. . . . . ἀλαζονεία

ἀλαζόνας, acc. pl. masc. . . . . ἀλαζών

ἀλαζόνες, nom. pl. masc. . . . . id.

ἀλαζών, όνος, ὁ, ἡ, (§ 7. tab. G. a) *ostentatious, vain-glorious, arrogant, boasting,* Ro. 1. 30; 2 Ti. 3. 2.

ἀλαζονεία, ας, ἡ, *ostentation; presumptuous speech,* Ja. 4. 16; *haughtiness,* 1 Jno. 2. 16.

ἀλαλάζον, nom. sing. neut. part. pres. . . ἀλαλάζω

ἀλαλάζοντας, acc. pl. masc. part. pres. . id.

ἀλαλάζω], fut. άξω, άξομαι, (§ 26. rem. 2) pr. *to raise the war-cry,* ἀλαλά: hence, *to utter* other *loud sounds; to wail,* Mar. 5. 38; *to tinkle, ring,* 1 Co. 13. 1.

ἀλαλήτοις,[e] dat. pl. masc. . . . . ἀλάλητος

ἀλάλητος], ου, ὁ, ἡ, τό, -ον, (§ 7. rem. 2) (ἀ & λαλέω) *unutterable,* or, *unexpressed.* L.G.

ἄλαλον, nom. and. acc. neut. sing. . . ἄλαλος

ἄλᾰλος], ου, ὁ, ἡ, (§ 7. rem. 2) (ἀ & λαλέω) *unable to speak, dumb,* Mar. 7. 37.

ἅλας, ατος, τό, (§ 4. rem. 2. c) . . . ἅλς

Ἄλασσα, ης, ἡ, *Alassa,* pr. name.—A. Ln.
Λασαία, Rec. Gr. Sch.
Λασέα, Tdf. (Ac. 27. 8).

ἅλατι, dat. sing. . . . . . ἅλα

ἀλείφω], fut. ψω, (§ 23. rem. 1. a) *to anoint* with oil or ointment.

ἀλεῖψαι, 2 pers. sing. aor. 1, imper. mid. . ἀλείφω

ἀλείψαντες, nom. pl. masc. part. aor. 1, act. id.

ἀλείψασα, nom. sing. fem. part. aor. 1, act. id.

ἀλείψωσι, 3 pers. pl. aor. 1, subj. act. . id.

ἀλέκτορα, acc. sing. . . . . . ἀλέκτωρ

ἀλεκτοροφωνία], ας, ἡ, (§ 2. tab. B. b, and rem. 2) (ἀλέκτωρ & φωνή) *the cock-crowing, the*

[a] Ac. 25. 23. [b] He. 7. 4. [c] Ac. 28. 31. [d] 1 Co. 9. 17. [e] Ro. 8. 26.

third watch of the night, intermediate to midnight and daybreak, and termed *cock-crow.* L.G.

ἀλεκτοροφωνίας,[a] gen. sing. . . ἀλεκτοροφωνία

ἀλέκτωρ, ορος, ὁ, (§ 4 rem. 2. f) *a cock,* Mat. 26. 34; Mar 14. 30; Lu. 22. 34; Jno. 13. 38.

Ἀλεξανδρεύς, έως, ὁ, (§ 5. tab. E. d) *a native of Alexandria, an Alexandrine.*

Ἀλεξανδρέων, gen. pl. . . . . Ἀλεξανδρεύς

Ἀλεξανδρῖνον, acc. sing. neut. . . Ἀλεξανδρῖνος

Ἀλεξανδρῖνος], η, ον, (§ 7. tab. F. a) *Alexandrian.*

Ἀλεξανδρίνῳ, dat. sing. . . . Ἀλεξανδρῖνος

Ἀλέξανδρον, acc. sing. . . . Ἀλέξανδρος

Ἀλέξανδρος, ου, ὁ, (§ 3. tab. C. a) *Alexander,* pr. name.
I. *The High Priest's kinsman,* Ac. 4. 6.
II. *A Jew of Ephesus,* Ac. 19. 33.
III. *The coppersmith,* 1 Ti. 1. 20; 2 Ti. 4. 14.
IV. *Son of Simon of Cyrene,* Mar. 15. 21.

Ἀλεξάνδρου, gen. sing. . . . Ἀλέξανδρος

ἄλευρον], ου, τό, (§ 3. tab. C. c) (ἀλέω, *to grind*) *meal, flour,* Mat. 13. 33; Lu. 13. 21.

ἀλεύρου, gen. sing. . . . . . ἄλευρον

ἀλήθεια, ας, ἡ, (§ 2. tab. B. b, and rem. 2) ἀληθής

ἀληθείᾳ, dat. sing. . . . . ἀλήθεια

ἀλήθειαν, acc. sing. . . . . id.

ἀληθείας, gen. sing. . . . . id.

ἀληθεῖς, nom. pl. masc. . . . . ἀληθής

ἀληθές, nom. and acc. sing. neut. . . id.

ἀληθεύοντες, nom. pl. masc. part. pres. . ἀληθεύω

ἀληθεύω], fut. εύσω, (§ 13. tab. M) . . ἀληθής

ἀληθεύων, nom. sing. masc. part. pres. . ἀληθεύω

ἀληθῆ, acc. sing. fem. . . ἀληθής

ἀληθῆ, nom. and acc. pl. neut. . . . id.

ἀληθής, έος, ὁ, ἡ, τό, -ές, (§ 7. tab. G. b) *true,* Jno. 4. 18, et al.; *worthy of credit,* Jno. 5. 31; *truthful,* Jno. 7. 18, et al.

ἀλήθεια, ας, ἡ, (§ 2. tab. B. b, and rem. 2) *truth, verity,* Mar. 5. 33; *love of truth, veracity, sincerity,* 1 Co. 5. 8, et al.; divine *truth* revealed to man, Jno. 1. 17, et al.; *practice in accordance with* Gospel *truth,* Jno. 3. 21; 2 Jno. 4, et al.

ἀληθεύω, fut. εύσω, (§ 13. tab. M) *to speak or maintain the truth; to act truly or sincerely,* Ga. 4. 16; Ep. 4. 15.

ἀληθινός, ή, όν, (§ 7. tab. F. a) *sterling,* Lu 16. 11; *real,* Jno. 6. 32; 1 Thes. 1. 9, et al.; *unfeigned, trustworthy, true,* Jno. 19. 35, et al.

ἀληθῶς, adv. *truly, really,* Mat. 14. 33, et al.; *certainly, of a truth,* Jno. 17. 8; Ac. 12. 11; *truly, veraciously,* Jno. 4. 18, et al.

ἀληθιναι, nom. pl. fem. . . . ἀληθινός

ἀληθινή, nom. sing. fem. . . . . id.

ἀληθινῆς, gen. sing. fem. . . . id.

ἀληθινοί, nom. pl. masc. . . . id.

ἀληθινόν, acc. sing. masc. and nom. or acc. neut. id.

ἀληθινός, ή, όν, (§ 7. tab. F. a) . ἀληθής

ἀληθινῷ, dat. sing. masc. . . . . ἀληθινός

ἀληθινῶν, gen. pl. . . . . id.

ἀληθοῦς, gen. sing. . . . . . ἀληθής

ἀλήθουσαι, nom. pl. fem. part. pres. . ἀλήθω

ἀλήθω], fut. σω, (§ 23. rem. 1. c) (ἀλέω, idem) *to grind,* Mat. 24. 41; Lu. 17. 35.

ἀληθῶς, adv. . . . . . . ἀληθής

ἁλί,[b] dat. sing. . . . . ἅλς

ἁλιεῖς, nom. or acc. pl. . . . ἁλιεύς

ἁλιεύειν,[c] pres. infin. . . . ἁλιεύω

ἁλιεύς], έος, έως, (§ 5. tab. E. d) . . ἅλς

ἁλιεύω], fut. εύσω, (§ 13. tab. M) . . id.

ἁλίζω], fut. ίσω, (§ 26. rem. 1) . . . id.

ἀλίσγημα], ατος, τό, (§ 4. tab. D. c) (ἀλισγέω, *to pollute,* in the Sept.) *pollution, defilement.* N.T.

ἀλισγημάτων,[d] gen. pl. . . . . ἀλίσγημα

ἁλισθήσεται, 3 pers. sing. fut. pass. . . ἁλίζω

ἀλλά, conj. *but; however; but still more;* ἀλλάγε, *at all events;* ἀλλ' ἤ, *unless, except.* Ἀλλά also serves to introduce a sentence with keenness and emphasis, Ro. 6. 5; 7. 7; Phi. 3. 8; Jno. 16. 2.

ἄλλα, nom. pl. neut. . . . . ἄλλος

ἀλλαγησόμεθα, 1 pers. pl. fut. 2, pass. (§ 26. rem. 3) ἀλλάσσω

ἀλλαγήσονται, 3 pers. pl. fut. 2, pass. . . id.

ἄλλαι, nom. pl. fem. . . ἄλλος

ἀλλάξαι, aor. 1, inf. act. . . . ἀλλάσσω

ἀλλάξει, 3 pers. sing. fut. act. . . . id.

ἄλλας, acc. pl. fem. . . . . ἄλλος

ἀλλάσσω], fut. άξω, (§ 26. rem. 3) . . id.

ἀλλαχόθεν,[e] adv. (ἄλλος & θεν, denoting *from* a place) *from another place or elsewhere.* L.G.

---

[a] Mar. 13. 35. [b] Mar. 9. 49. [c] Jno. 21. 3. [d] Ac. 15. 20. [e] Jno. 10. 1.

ἄλλη, nom. sing. fem. . . . . . ἄλλος

ἀλληγορέω, ῶ], (§ 16. tab. P) (ἄλλος & ἀγορεύω, *to speak*) *to say what is either designed or fitted to convey a meaning other than the literal one, to allegorise*; ἀλληγορούμενος, *adapted to another meaning, otherwise significant*. L.G.

ἀλληγορούμενα,[a] nom. pl. neut. part. pres. pass. ἀλληγορέω

ἀλλήλοις, dat. pl. . . . . . ἀλλήλων

Ἀλληλούϊα, Heb. הַלְלוּ־יָהּ, *praise ye Jehovah*, Re. 19. 1, 3, 4, 6.

ἀλλήλους, acc. pl. . . . . . . ἀλλήλων

ἀλλήλων, gen. pl. (§ 10. rem. 6. f) . . ἄλλος

ἄλλην, acc. sing. fem. . . . . . id.

ἄλλης, gen. sing. fem. . . . . id.

ἄλλο, nom. sing. neut. . . . . . id.

ἀλλογενής,[b] έος, ὁ, ἡ, (§ 7. tab. G. b) (ἄλλος & γένος) *of another race or nation*, i.e. not a Jew; *a stranger, foreigner*. LXX.

ἄλλοι, nom. pl. masc. . . . . ἄλλος

ἄλλοις, dat. pl. masc. . . . . . id.

ἅλλομαι], fut. ἁλοῦμαι, aor. 1, ἡλάμην, (§ 37. rem. 1) *to leap, jump, leap up*, Ac. 3. 8; 14. 10; *to spring*, as water, Jno. 4. 14.

ἁλλόμενος, nom. sing. masc. part. pres. . ἅλλομαι

ἁλλομένου, gen. sing. neut. part. pres. . id.

ἄλλον, acc. sing. masc. . . . . . ἄλλος

ἄλλος, η, ο, (§ 10. rem. 6. a) *another, some other*; ὁ ἄλλος, *the other*; οἱ ἄλλοι, *the others, the rest*.

ἀλλάσσω, fut. άξω, aor. 1, pass. ἠλλάχθην, aor. 2, pass. ἠλλάγην, fut. ἀλλαγήσομαι, (§ 26. rem. 3) *to change, alter, transform*, Ac. 6. 14; Ro. 1. 23; 1 Co. 15. 51, 52; Gal. 4. 20; He. 1. 12.

ἀλλήλων, gen. pl., ἀλλήλοις, αις, οις, dat., ἀλλήλους, ας, α, acc., *one another, each other*.

ἀλλότριος, ία, ιον, (§ 7. rem. 1) *belonging to another*, Lu. 16. 12, et al.; *foreign*, Ac. 7. 6; He. 11. 9; *a foreigner, alien*, Mat. 17. 25.

ἄλλως, adv. *otherwise*, 1 Ti. 5. 25.

ἀλλοτρίᾳ, dat. sing. fem. . . . . ἀλλότριος

ἀλλοτρίαις, dat. pl. fem. . . . . . id.

ἀλλοτρίαν, acc. sing. fem. . . . . id.

ἀλλοτριοεπίσκοπος,[c] ου, ὁ, ἡ, (§ 3. tab. C. a. b) (ἀλλότριος & ἐπίσκοπος) pr. *one who meddles with the affairs of others, a busybody in other men's matters; factious*. N.T.

ἀλλοτρίοις, dat. pl. masc. . . . . . ἀλλότριος

ἀλλότριον, acc. sing. masc. . . . . id.

ἀλλότριος], α, ον, (§ 7. rem. 1) . . . ἄλλος

ἀλλοτρίῳ, dat. sing. masc. and neut. . ἀλλότριος

ἀλλοτρίων, gen. pl. . . . . . id.

ἄλλου, gen. sing. masc. . . . . ἄλλος

ἄλλους, acc. pl. masc. . . . . . id.

ἀλλόφῡλος], ου, ὁ, ἡ, (§ 7. rem. 2) (ἄλλος & φυλή) *of another race or nation*, i.e. not a Jew, *a foreigner*.

ἀλλοφύλῳ,[d] dat. sing. masc. . . . ἀλλόφυλος

ἄλλῳ, dat. sing. masc. . . . . . ἄλλος

ἄλλων, gen. pl. . . . . . . id.

ἄλλως,[e] adv. . . . . id.

ἀλοάω, ῶ], fut. ήσω, (§ 18. tab. R) and άσω, (§ 22. rem. 2) *to thresh*; *to tread, or thresh out*, 1 Co. 9. 9, 10; 1 Ti. 5. 18.

ἄλογα, nom. pl. neut. . . . . . ἄλογος

ἄλογον, nom. sing. neut. . . . . . id.

ἄλογος], ου, ὁ, ἡ, τό, -ον, (§ 7. rem. 2) (ἀ & λόγος) *without speech or reason, irrational, brute*, 2 Pe. 2. 12; Jude 10; *unreasonable, absurd*, Ac. 25. 27.

ἀλόη], ης, ἡ, (§ 2. tab. B. a) also termed ξυλαλόη, ἀγάλλοχον, *aloe, lign-aloe*, (excoecaria agallochon, Linn.), a tree which grows in India and Cochin-China, the wood of which is soft and bitter, though highly aromatic. It is used by the Orientals as a perfume; and employed for the purposes of embalming. L.G.

ἀλόης,[f] gen. sing. . . . . . ἀλόη

ἀλοῶν, nom. sing. masc. part. pres. . . ἀλοάω

ἀλοῶντα, acc. sing. masc. part. pres. . id.

ἅλς], ἁλός, ὁ, (§ 4. rem. 1, 2) *salt*, Mar. 9. 49.

ἁλιεύς, έως, ὁ, (§ 5. tab. E. d) *a fisherman*, Mat. 4. 18, 19; Mar. 1. 16, 17; Lu. 5. 2.

ἁλιεύω, fut. εύσω, (§ 13. tab. M) *to fish*, Jno. 21. 3.

ἁλίζω, fut. ίσω, (§ 26. rem. 1) *to salt, season with salt, preserve by salting*, Mat. 5. 13; Mar. 9. 49.

ἅλας, ατος, τό, (§ 4. rem. 2 c) *salt*, Mat. 9, 50, et al.; met. Mat. 5. 13; met.

a Gal. 4. 24. b Lu. 17. 18. c 1 Pe. 4. 15. d Ac. 10. 28. e 1 Ti. 5. 25. f Jno. 19. 39.

the salt of wisdom and prudence, Col. 4. 6. L.G.

ἅλα, ατος, τό, same signif. as ἅλας.

ἁλῠκός, ή, όν, (§ 7. tab. F. a) *brackish, bitter, salt.*

ἁλυκόν,[a] acc. sing. neut. . . . . . ἁλυκός

ἁλυκός], ή, όν . . . . . . ἅλς

ἄλῡπος], ου, ὁ, ἡ, (§ 7. rem. 2) (ἀ & λύπη) *free from grief or sorrow.*

ἀλυπότερος,[b] nom. sing. masc. comp. (§ 8. rem. 4) ἄλυπος

ἁλύσει, dat. sing. . . . . . . ἅλυσις

ἁλύσεις, nom. and acc. pl. . . . . id.

ἁλύσεσι, dat. pl. . . . . . . id.

ἅλυσιν, acc. sing. . . . . . id.

ἅλῠσις], εως, ἡ, (§ 5. tab. E. c) *a chain*, Mar. 5. 3, 4.

ἀλυσιτελές,[c] nom. sing. neut. . . . ἀλυσιτελής

ἀλυσιτελής], έος, ὁ, ἡ, (§ 7. tab. G. b) (ἀ & λυσιτελής, i.e. λύων τὰ τέλη) pr. *bringing in no revenue or profit*; hence, *unprofitable, useless; detrimental; ruinous, disastrous*, He. 13. 17.

Ἀλφαῖος], ου, ὁ, *Alphæus*, pr. name.

I. *Father of James the less.*

II. *Father of Levi*, (Matthew,) Mar. 2. 14.

Ἀλφαίου, gen. sing. . . . . Ἀλφαῖος

ἅλων], ωνος, ἡ, (§ 4. tab. D. a) (a later form of ἅλως, ω, ἡ) *a threshing-floor, a place where corn is trodden out*; meton. *the corn which is trodden out*, Mat. 3. 12; Lu. 3. 17.

ἅλωνα, acc. sing. . . . . . ἅλων

ἀλώπεκες, nom. pl. . . . . . . ἀλώπηξ

ἀλώπεκι, dat. sing. . . . . . id.

ἀλώπηξ], εκος, ἡ, (§ 4. rem. 2. b) *a fox*, Mat. 8. 20; Lu. 9. 58; met. *a fox-like, crafty man*, Lu. 13. 32.

ἅλωσιν,[d] acc. sing. . . . . . . ἅλωσις

ἅλωσις], εως, ἡ, (§ 5. tab. E. c) (ἁλίσκομαι, *to take*) *a taking, catching, capture.*

ἅμα, adv. *with, together with; at the same time.*

ἀμαθεῖς,[e] nom. pl. masc. . . . . ἀμαθής

ἀμᾰθής], έος, ὁ, ἡ, (§ 7. tab. G. b) (ἀ & μανθάνω) *unlearned, uninstructed, rude.*

ἀμαράντινον,[f] acc. sing. masc. . . . ἀμαράντινος

ἀμαράντινος], ου, ὁ, ἡ, (§ 7. rem. 2) (ἀ & μαραίνομαι) *unfading*; hence, *enduring.*

ἀμάραντον,[g] acc. sing. fem. . . . ἀμάραντος

ἀμάραντος], ου, ὁ, ἡ, same signif. and derivation as ἀμαράντινος. L.G.

ἁμάρτανε, 2 pers. sing. pres. imper. . . ἁμαρτάνω

ἁμαρτάνει, 3 pers. sing. pres. indic. . . id.

ἁμαρτάνειν, pres. infin. . . . id.

ἁμαρτάνετε, 2 pers. pl. pres. indic. . . id

ἁμαρτάνετε, 2 pers. pl. pres. imper. . . id.

ἁμαρτάνοντα, acc. sing. masc. part. pres. . id.

ἁμαρτάνοντας, acc. pl. masc. part. pres. . id.

ἁμαρτάνοντες, nom. pl. masc. part. pres. . id.

ἁμαρτανόντων, gen. pl. masc. part. pres. . id.

ἁμαρτάνουσι, dat. pl. masc. part. pres. . . id.

ἁμαρτάνω], fut. ἁμαρτήσομαι and, later, ἁμαρτήσω, aor. 1, ἡμάρτησα, aor. 2, ἥμαρτον, (§ 36. rem. 2) pr. *to miss a mark; to be in error*, 1 Co. 15. 34; Tit. 3. 11; *to sin*, Jno. 5. 14, et al.; *to be guilty of wrong*, Mat. 18. 15, et al.

ἁμάρτημα, ατος, τό, (§ 4. tab. D. c) *an error; sin, offence*, Mar. 3. 28; 4. 12, Ro. 3. 25; 1 Co. 6. 18.

ἁμαρτία, ας, ἡ, (§ 2. tab. B. b, and rem. 2) *error; offence, sin*, Mat. 1. 21, et al., *a principle or cause of sin*, Ro. 7. 7; *proneness to sin, sinful propensity*, Ro. 7. 17, 20; *guilt or imputation of sin*, Jno. 9. 41; He. 9. 26, et al.; *a guilty subject, sin-offering, expiatory victim*, 2 Co. 5. 21.

ἁμαρτωλός, οῦ, ὁ, ἡ, (§ 7. rem. 2) *one who deviates from the path of virtue, a sinner*, Mar. 2. 17, et al.; *depraved*, Mar. 8. 38; *sinful, detestable*, Ro. 7. 13. L.G.

ἁμαρτάνων, nom. sing. masc. part. pres. . ἁμαρτάνω

ἁμάρτῃ, 3 pers. sing. aor. 2, subj. . . id

ἁμάρτημα, ατος, τό, (§ 4. tab. D. c) . . id.

ἁμαρτήματα, nom. pl. . . . . ἁμάρτημα

ἁμαρτήματος, gen. sing.—Al. Ln. Tdf. . }
κρίσεως, Rec. Gr. Sch. (Mar. 3. 29) . } id.

ἁμαρτημάτων, gen. pl. . . . . id.

ἁμαρτήσαντας, acc. pl. masc. part. aor. 1. . ἁμαρτάνω

ἁμαρτήσαντος, gen. sing. masc. part. aor. 1. . id.

ἁμαρτησάντων, gen. pl. masc. part. aor 1. . id.

ἁμαρτήσασι, dat. pl. masc. part. aor. 1. . id.

ἁμαρτήσει, 3 pers. sing. fut. (§ 36. rem. 2) id.

ἁμαρτήσῃ, 3 pers. sing. aor. 1, subj. id.

ἁμαρτήσομεν, 1 pers. pl. fut. . . . id.

ἁμαρτήσωμεν, 1 p. pl. aor. 1, subj.—A.C.D.Ln.Tdf. }
ἁμαρτήσομεν, Rec. Gr. Sch. (Ro. 6. 15) } id.

ἁμάρτητε, 2 pers. pl. aor. 2, subj. . . id.

ἁμαρτία, ας, ἡ, (§ 2. tab. B. b, and rem. 2) id.

[a] Ja. 3. 12. [b] Phi. 2. 28. [c] He. 13. 17. [d] 2 Pe. 2. 12. [e] 2 Pe. 3. 16. [f] 1 Pe. 5. 4. [g] 1 Pe. 1. 4.

ἁμαρτίᾳ, dat. sing. . . . . ἁμαρτία
ἁμαρτίαι, nom. pl. . . . . . id.
ἁμαρτίαις, dat. pl. . . . . . id.
ἁμαρτίαν, acc. sing. . . . . . id.
ἁμαρτίας, gen. sing. . . . . . id.
ἁμαρτιῶν, gen. pl. . . . . . id.
ἀμάρτυρον,[a] acc. sing. masc. . . . ἀμάρτυρος
ἀμάρτῠρος], ου, ὁ, ἡ, (§ 7. rem. 2) (ἀ & μάρτυς) *without testimony or witness, without evidence.*
ἁμαρτωλοί, nom. and voc. pl. . . . ἁμαρτωλός
ἁμαρτωλοῖς, dat. pl. . . . . . id.
ἁμαρτωλόν, acc. sing. . . . . id.
ἁμαρτωλός, οῦ, ὁ, ἡ, (§ 7. rem. 2) . . ἁμαρτάνω
ἁμαρτωλούς, acc. pl. . . . . ἁμαρτωλός
ἁμαρτωλῷ, dat. sing. . . . . . id.
ἁμαρτωλῶν, gen. pl. . . . . . id.
ἄμαχον, acc. sing. masc. . . . . ἄμαχος
ἄμᾰχος], ου, ὁ, ἡ, (§ 7. rem. 2) (ἀ & μάχομαι) *not disposed to fight; not quarrelsome or contentious*, 1 Ti. 3. 3; Tit. 3. 2.
ἀμάχους, acc. pl. masc. . . . . ἄμαχος
ἀμάω, ῶ], fut. ήσω, (§ 18. tab. R) *to collect; to reap, mow, or cut down*, Ja. 5. 4.
ἀμέθυστος,[b] ου, ὁ, (§ 3. tab. C. a) (ἀ & μεθύω) *an amethyst*, a gem of a deep purple or violet colour, so called from its supposed efficacy in keeping off drunkenness.
ἀμέλει, 2 pers. sing. pres. imper. . . . ἀμελέω
ἀμελέω, ῶ], fut. ήσω, perf. ἠμέληκα, (§ 16. tab. P) (ἀμελής, ἀ & μέλει) *not to care for, to neglect, disregard*, Mat. 22. 5; 1 Ti. 4. 14, He. 2. 3; 8. 9; 2 Pe. 1. 12.
ἀμελήσαντες, nom. pl. masc. part. aor. 1. . ἀμελέω
ἀμελήσω, 1 pers. sing. fut. . . . . id.
ἄμεμπτοι, nom. pl. masc. . . . ἄμεμπτος
ἄμεμπτος, ου, ὁ, ἡ, (§ 7. rem. 2) (ἀ & μεμπτός, from μέμφομαι) *blameless, irreprehensible, without defect*, Lu. 1. 6; Phi. 2. 15; 3. 6; 1 Thes. 3. 13; He. 8. 7.
ἀμέμπτους, acc. pl. fem. . . . . ἄμεμπτος
ἀμέμπτως, adv. *blamelessly, unblamably, unexceptionably*, 1 Thes. 2. 10; 5. 23.
ἀμέριμνος], ου, ὁ, ἡ, (§ 7. rem. 2) (ἀ & μέριμνα) *free from care or solicitude*, Mat. 28. 14; 1 Co. 7. 32.
ἀμερίμνους, acc. pl. masc. . . . . ἀμέριμνος
ἀμετάθετον, acc. sing. neut. . . . . ἀμετάθετος
ἀμετάθετος], ου, ὁ, ἡ, (§ 7. rem. 2) (ἀ & μετατίθημι) *unchangeable*, He. 6. 17, 18. L.G.
ἀμεταθέτων, gen. pl. . . . . . ἀμετάθετος
ἀμετακίνητοι,[c] nom. pl. masc. . . . ἀμετακίνητος
ἀμετακίνητος], ου, ὁ, ἡ, (§ 7. rem. 2) (ἀ & μετακινέω) *immovable, firm.*
ἀμεταμέλητα, nom. pl. neut. . . . ἀμεταμέλητος
ἀμεταμέλητον, acc. sing. fem. . . . . id.
ἀμεταμέλητος], ου, ὁ, ἡ, (§ 7. rem. 2) (ἀ & μεταμέλομαι) *not to be repented of*; by impl *irrevocable, enduring*, Ro. 11. 29; 2 Co. 7. 10.
ἀμετανόητον,[d] acc. sing. fem. . . . ἀμετανόητος
ἀμετανόητος], ου, ὁ, ἡ, (§ 7. rem. 2) (ἀ & μετανοέω) *impenitent, obdurate.* L.G.
ἄμετρα, acc. pl. neut. . . . . . ἄμετρος
ἄμετρος], ου, ὁ, ἡ, (§ 7. rem. 2) (ἀ & μέτρον) *without or beyond measure, regardless of measure*, 2 Co. 10. 13, 15.
ἀμήν, (Heb. אָמֵן, *firm, faithful, true*) used as a particle both of affirmation and assent, *in truth, verily, most certainly; so be it*; ὁ ἀμήν, *the faithful and true one*, Re. 3. 14.
ἀμησάντων,[e] gen. pl. masc. part. aor 1. . ἀμάω
ἀμήτωρ,[f] ορος, ὁ, ἡ, (§ 7. tab. G. a) (ἀ & μήτηρ) pr. *without mother; independent of maternal descent.*
ἀμίαντον, acc. sing. fem. . . . . ἀμίαντος
ἀμίαντος, ου, ὁ, ἡ, (§ 7. rem. 2) (ἀ & μιαίνω) pr. *unstained, unsoiled*; met. *undefiled, chaste*, He. 13. 4; *pure, sincere*, Ja. 1. 27; *inviolate, unimpaired*, 1 Pe. 1. 4.
Ἀμιναδάβ, ὁ, *Aminadab*, pr. name, indecl.
ἄμμον, acc. sing. . . . . . . ἄμμος
ἄμμος, ου, ἡ, (§ 3. tab. C. b) *sand*, Mat. 7. 26, et al.
ἀμνός, οῦ, ὁ, (§ 3. tab. C. a) *a lamb*, Jno. 1. 29, 36; Ac. 8. 32; 1 Pe. 1. 19.
ἀμνοῦ, gen. sing. . . . . . . ἀμνός
ἀμοιβάς,[g] acc. pl. . . . . . ἀμοιβή
ἀμοιβή], ῆς, ἡ, (§ 2. tab. B. a) (ἀμείβω, ἀμείβομαι, *to requite*) *requital*; of kind offices, *recompense.*
ἄμπελον, acc. sing. . . . . . ἄμπελος
ἄμπελος, ου, ἡ, (§ 3. tab. C. b) *a vine, grape-vine.*
 ἀμπελών, ῶνος, ὁ, (§ 4. tab. D. a) *a vineyard.*
ἀμπέλου, gen. sing. . . . . . ἄμπελος
ἀμπελουργόν,[h] acc. sing. masc. . . . ἀμπελουργός

[a] Ac. 14. 17. [b] Re. 21. 20. [c] 1 Co. 15. 58. [d] Ro. 2. 5. [e] Ja. 5. 4. [f] He. 7. 3. [g] 1 Ti. 5. 4. [h] Lu. 13. 7.

ἀμπελουργός], οῦ, ὁ, ἡ (§ tab. C. a) (ἄμπελος & ἔργον) *a vine-dresser.*

ἀμπέλῳ, dat. sing. . . . . ἄμπελος

ἀμπελών], ῶνος, ὁ, (§ 4. tab. D. a) . id.

ἀμπελῶνα, acc. sing. . . . . ἀμπελών

ἀμπελῶνι, dat. sing. . . . id.

ἀμπελῶνος, gen. sing. . . . id.

Ἀμπλίαν,[a] acc. sing.—R. Gr. Sch. Tdf. } Ἀμπλίας
Αμπλιάτον, A. . . . . }

Ἀμπλίας], ου, ὁ, *Amplias*, pr. name, (§ 2. tab. B. d)

ἀμύνω], fut. υνῶ, (§ 27. rem. 1. a) aor. 1, ἤμυνα, *to ward off; to help, assist;* mid. ἀμύνομαι, *to repel from one's self, resist, make a defence; to assume the office of protector and avenger,* Ac. 7. 24.

ἀμφί], prep. *about, round about.* In the N.T. it only occurs in composition.

ἀμφιάζει, 3 pers. sing. pres. ind.—Al. Ln. Tdf. } ἀμφιάζω
ἀμφιέννυσι, Rec. Gr. Sch. (Lu. 12. 28) }

ἀμφιάζω], same signif. as ἀμφιέννυμι.

ἀμφιβάλλοντας,[b] acc. pl. masc. part. pres.— } ἀμφιβάλλω
Gr. Sch. Tdf. . . . . }
βάλλοντας, Rec. (Mar. 1. 16) . }

ἀμφιβάλλω], fut. βαλῶ, (§ 27. rem. 1. b) (ἀμφί & βάλλω) v. r. Mar. 1. 16, *to throw around; to cast* a net.

ἀμφίβληστρον, ου, τό, (§ 3. tab. C. c) pr. *what is thrown around,* e.g. a garment; *a large kind of fish-net, drag,* Mat. 4. 18; Mar. 1. 16.

ἀμφιέζει, 3 pers. sing. pres. indic.—D.D. } ἀμφιέζω
ἀμφιέννυσι, Rec. Gr. Sch. (Lu. 12. 28) }

ἀμφιέζω], same signif. as ἀμφιέννυμι.

ἀμφιέννυμι], fut. ἀμφιέσω, perf. pass. ἠμφίεσμαι, (§ 36. rem. 5) (ἀμφί & ἕννυμι, *to put on*) *to clothe, invest,* Mat. 6. 30; 11. 8; Lu. 7. 25; 12. 28.

ἀμφιέννυσι, 3 p. sing. pres. indic. (§ 31. tab. B.B) ἀμφιέννυμι

Ἀμφίπολιν,[c] acc. sing. . . . . Ἀμφίπολις

Ἀμφίπολις], εως, ἡ, (§ 5. tab. E. c) *Amphipolis,* a city of Thrace, on the river Strymon. Lat. 41, 10, long. 23, 41.

ἄμφοδον], ου, τό, (§ 3. tab. C. c) (equivalent to ἄμφοδος, ου, ἡ, from ἀμφί & ὁδός) pr. *a road leading round a town or village, the street of a village.*

ἀμφόδου,[d] gen. sing . . . . ἄμφοδον

ἀμφότερα, acc. pl. neut. . . . . ἀμφότερος

ἀμφότεροι, nom. pl. masc. . . id.

ἀμφοτέροις, dat. pl. masc. . . . id.

ἀμφότερος], α, ον, (§ 10. rem. 6. e) (ἄμφω, *both*) *both.* Only plural in the N.T.

ἀμφοτέρους, acc. pl. masc. . . . ἀμφότερος

ἀμφοτέρων, gen. pl.—Al. Ln. Tdf. . } id.
αὐτῶν, Rec. Gr. Sch. (Ac. 19. 16) . }

ἄμωμα, nom. pl. neut.—A. C. Ln. Tdf. . } ἄμωμος
ἀμώμητα, Rec. Gr. Sch. (Phi. 2. 15) }

ἀμώμητα, nom. pl. neut. . . . ἀμώμητος

ἀμώμητοι, nom. pl. masc. . . . id.

ἀμώμητος], ου, ὁ, ἡ, (§ 7. rem. 2) (ἀ & μῶμος) *blameless, irreprehensible,* Phi. 2. 15; 2 Pe. 3. 14.

ἄμωμοι, nom. pl. masc. . . . ἄμωμος

ἄμωμον, acc. sing. masc. . . . . id.

ἄμωμον,[e] ου, τό, (§ 3. tab. C. c) Gr. Sch. Tdf. (Rec. om.) *amomum,* an odoriferous shrub, from which a precious ointment was prepared.

ἄμωμος, ου, ὁ, ἡ, (§ 7. rem. 2) (ἀ & μῶμος) *blameless.*

ἀμώμου, gen. sing. masc. . . . ἄμωμος

ἀμώμους, acc. pl. masc. . . . . id.

Ἀμών, ὁ, *Amon,* pr. name, indecl.

Ἀμώς, ὁ, *Amos,* pr. name, indecl.

ἄν. The various constructions of this particle, and their significations, must be learnt from the grammars. Standing at the commencement of a clause, it is another form of ἐάν, *if,* Jno. 20. 23.

ἀνά, prep. used in the N.T. only in certain forms. ἀνὰ μέρος, *in turn;* ἀνὰ μέσον, *through the midst, between;* ἀνὰ δηνάριον, *at the rate of a denarius;* with numerals, ἀνὰ ἑκατόν, *in parties of a hundred.* In composition, *step by step, up, back, again.*

ἀνάβα, 2 pers. sing. aor. 2. imper. by apocope for ἀνάβηθι, (§ 31. rem. 1. d) . . ἀναβαίνω

ἀναβαθμός], οῦ, ὁ, (§ 3. tab. C. a) . . id.

ἀναβαθμούς, acc. pl. . . . . ἀναβαθμός

ἀναβαθμῶν, gen. pl. . . . . id.

ἀναβαίνει, 3 pers. sing. pres. indic. . . ἀναβαίνω

ἀναβαίνειν, pres. infin. . . . . id.

ἀναβαίνομεν, 1 pers. pl. pres. indic. . . id.

ἀναβαῖνον, nom. and acc. sing. neut. part. pres. id.

[a] Ro. 16. 8 [b] Mar. 1. 16. [c] Ac. 17. 1. [d] Mar. 11. 4. [e] Re. 18. 13.

ἀναβαίνοντα, acc. sing. masc. part. pres. . ἀναβαίνω
ἀναβαίνοντας, acc. pl. masc. part. pres. . id.
ἀναβαίνοντες, nom. pl. masc. part. pres. . id.
ἀναβαινόντων, gen. pl. masc. part. pres. . id.
ἀναβαίνουσι, 3 pers. pl. pres. indic. . . id.
ἀναβαίνω, fut. βήσομαι, perf. βέβηκα, aor. 2, ἀνέβην, (§ 37. rem. 1) (ἀνά & βαίνω) *to go up, ascend*, Mat. 5. 1, et al.; *to climb*, Lu. 19. 4; *to go on board*, Mar. 6. 51; *to rise, mount upwards*, as smoke, Re. 8. 4; *to grow or spring up*, as plants, Mat. 13. 7; *to spring up, arise*, as thoughts, Lu. 24. 38.

ἀναβαθμός, ου, ὁ, (§ 3. tab. C. a) *the act of ascending; means of ascent, steps, stairs*, Ac. 21. 35, 40.

ἀναβαίνων, nom. sing. masc. part. pres. . ἀναβαίνω
ἀναβάλλω], fut. βαλῶ, (§ 27. rem. 1. a. b) perf. βέβληκα, (§ 27. rem. 2. d) (ἀνά & βάλλω) *to throw back*; mid. *to put off, defer, adjourn*, Ac. 24. 22.

ἀναβολή, ῆς, ἡ, (§ 2. tab. B. a) *delay*, Ac. 25. 17.

ἀναβάντα, acc. sing. masc. part. aor. 2. . ἀναβαίνω
ἀναβάντες, nom. pl. masc. part. aor. 2. . . id.
ἀναβάντων, gen. pl. masc. part. aor. 2. . id.
ἀναβάς, ᾶσα, άν, nom. sing. part. aor. 2. . id.
ἀναβέβηκα, 1 pers. sing. perf. indic. . id.
ἀναβέβηκε, 3 pers. sing. perf. indic. . . id.
ἀνάβηθι, 2 pers. sing. aor. 2, imper.—Ln. . } id.
ἀνάβα, Rec. Gr. Sch. Tdf. (Re. 4. 1) }
ἀναβήσεται, 3 pers. sing. fut. . . . id.
ἀνάβητε, 2 pers. pl. aor. 2, imper. . . id.
ἀναβιβάζω], fut. άσω, aor. 1, ἀνεβίβασα, (§ 26. rem. 1) (ἀνά & βιβάζω) *to cause to come up or ascend, draw or bring up.*
ἀναβιβάσαντες,[a] nom. pl. masc. part. aor. 1. . ἀναβιβάζω
ἀναβλέπουσι, 3 pers. pl. pres. indic. . ἀναβλέπω
ἀναβλέπω], fut. ψω, (§ 23. rem. 1. a) (ἀνά & βλέπω) *to look upwards*, Mat. 14. 19, et al.; *to see again, recover sight*, Mat. 11. 5, et al.

ἀνάβλεψις, εως, ἡ, (§ 5. tab. E. c) *recovery of sight*, Lu. 4. 18.

ἀναβλέψαι, aor. 1, infin. . . . ἀναβλέπω
ἀναβλέψαντος, gen. sing. masc. part. aor. 1. id.
ἀναβλέψας, nom. sing. masc. part. aor. 1. . id.
ἀναβλέψασαι, nom. pl. fem. part. aor. 1. . id.
ἀναβλέψῃ, 3 pers. sing. aor. 1, subj. . id.
ἀναβλέψῃς, 2 pers. sing. aor. 1, subj. . . ἀναβλέπω
ἀνάβλεψιν,[b] acc. sing. . . . . ἀνάβλεψις
ἀνάβλεψις], εως, ἡ, (§ 5. tab. E. c) . . ἀναβλέπω
ἀνάβλεψον, 2 pers. sing. aor. 1, imper. . id.
ἀναβλέψω, 1 pers. sing. aor. 1, subj. . . id.
ἀναβοάω, ω], (§ 18. tab. R) fut. ήσομαι, aor. 1, ησα, (ἀνά & βοάω) *to cry out or aloud, exclaim*, Mat. 27. 46; Mar. 15. 8; Lu. 9. 38.
ἀναβοήσας, nom. sing. masc. part. aor. 1. . ἀναβοάω
ἀναβολή], ῆς, ἡ, (§ 2. tab. B. a) . . ἀναβάλλω
ἀναβολήν,[c] acc. sing. . . . . ἀναβολή
ἀναγαγεῖν, aor. 2, infin. (§ 13. rem. 7. d) . ἀνάγω
ἀνάγαιον, ου, τό, *an upper room*.—Gr. Sch. Tdf. ἀνώγεον, Rec. (Mar. 14. 15; Lu. 22. 12).
ἀναγαγών, nom. sing. masc. part. aor. 2. . ἀνάγω
ἀναγγεῖλαι, aor. 1, infin. (§ 27. rem. 1. d) . ἀναγγέλλω
ἀνάγγειλον, 2 pers. sing. aor. 1, imper. act. . id.
ἀναγγελεῖ, 3 pers. sing. fut. act. . . id.
ἀναγγέλλομεν, 1 pers. pl. pres. indic. act. . id.
ἀναγγέλλοντες, nom. pl. part. pres. act. . id.
ἀναγγέλλω], fut. γελῶ, aor. 1, ἀνήγγειλα, (§ 27. rem. 1. b. d) aor. 2, pass. ἀνηγγέλην, (§ 27. rem. 4. a) (ἀνά & ἀγγέλλω) *to bring back word, announce, report*, Mar. 5. 14, et al.; *to declare, set forth, teach* Jno. 5. 24, et al.
ἀναγγέλλων, nom. sing. masc. part. pres. act. ἀναγγέλλω
ἀναγγελῶ, 1 pers. sing. fut. act. . . . id.
ἀναγεννάω, ῶ], fut. ήσω, (§ 18. tab. R) perf. pass. ἀναγεγέννημαι, (ἀνά & γεννάω) *to beget or bring forth again; to regenerate*, 1 Pe. 1. 3, 23. N.T.
ἀναγεγεννημένοι, nom. pl. masc. part. p. pass. ἀναγεννάω
ἀναγεννήσας, nom. sing. masc. part. aor. 1, act. id.
ἀνάγεσθαι, pres. infin. mid. . . . ἀνάγω
ἀναγινώσκεις, 2 pers. sing. pres. ind. act. ἀναγινώσκω
ἀναγινώσκεται, 3 pers. sing. pres. ind. pass. id.
ἀναγινώσκετε, 2 pers. pl. pres. ind. act. . id.
ἀναγινώσκηται, [ἂν], 3 pers. sing. pres. subj. pass.—Al. Ln. Tdf. . . } id.
ἀναγινώσκεται, Rec. Gr. Sch. (2 Co. 3. 15) }
ἀναγινωσκομένας, acc. pl. fem. part. pres. pass. id.
ἀναγινωσκομένη, nom. sing. fem. part pr. pass. id.
ἀναγινωσκόμενος, nom. sing. masc. part. pr. pass. id.
ἀναγινώσκοντες, nom. pl. masc. part. pres. act. id.
ἀναγινώσκοντος, gen. sing. masc. part. pres. act. id.
ἀναγινώσκω], (§ 36. rem. 3) fut. γνώσομαι, aor. 2, ἀνέγνων, aor. 1, pass. ἀνεγνώσθην, (ἀνά

[a] Mat. 13. 48. [b] Lu. 4. 18. [c] Ac. 25. 17.

& γινώσκω) *to gather exact knowledge of, recognise, discern*; especially, *to read*.

ἀνάγνωσις, εως, ἡ, (§ 5. tab. E. c) *reading*, Ac. 13. 15; 2 Co. 3. 14; 1 Ti. 4. 13.

ἀναγινώσκων, nom. sing. masc. part. pres. . ἀναγινώσκω
ἀναγκάζεις, 2 pers. sing. pres. indic. . . ἀναγκάζω
ἀναγκάζουσι, 3 pers. pl. pres. indic. . id.
ἀναγκάζω], fut. άσω, (§ 26. rem. 1) . . ἀνάγκη
ἀναγκαῖα, nom. pl. neut. . . . ἀναγκαῖος
ἀναγκαίας, acc. pl. fem. . . . . id.
ἀναγκαῖον, nom. sing. neut. . . . id.
ἀναγκαῖος], α, ον, (§ 7. rem. 1) . . . ἀνάγκη
ἀναγκαιότερον, nom. s. neut. comparat. (§ 8. r. 4) ἀναγκαῖος
ἀναγκαίους, acc. pl. masc. . . . id.
ἀνάγκαις, dat. pl. . . . . . ἀνάγκη
ἀνάγκασον, 2 pers. sing. aor. 1, imper. . . ἀναγκάζω
ἀναγκαστῶς,[a] adv. . . . . . ἀνάγκη

ἀνάγκη, ης, ἡ, (§ 2. tab. B. a) (ἄγχω, *to compress*) *necessity*, Mat. 18. 7, et al.; *constraint, compulsion*, 2 Co. 9. 7, et al.; *obligation of duty*, moral or spiritual *necessity*, Ro. 13. 5, et al.; *distress, trial, affliction*, Lu. 21. 23; 1 Co. 7. 26; 2 Co. 6. 4; 12. 10; 1 Thes. 3. 7.

ἀναγκάζω, fut. άσω, (§ 26. rem. 1) *to force, compel*, Ac. 28. 19, et al.; *to constrain, urge*, Lu. 14. 23, et al.

ἀναγκαῖος, α, ον, (§ 7. rem. 1) *necessary, indispensable*, 1 Co. 12. 22; *necessary, needful, right, proper*, Ac. 13. 46; 2 Co. 9. 5; Phi. 1. 24; 2. 25; He. 8. 3; *near, intimate, closely connected*, as friends, Ac. 10. 24.

ἀναγκαστῶς, adv. *by constraint or compulsion, unwillingly*, opposite to ἑκουσίως, 1 Pe. 5. 2.

ἀνάγκῃ, dat. sing. . . . . ἀνάγκη
ἀνάγκην, acc. sing. . . . . . id.
ἀνάγκης, gen. sing. . . . . . . id.
ἀναγνόντες, nom. pl. masc. part. aor. 2. . ἀναγινώσκω
ἀναγνούς, nom. sing. masc. part. aor. 2. . id.
ἀναγνῶναι, aor. 2, infin. (§ 36. rem. 3) . id.
ἀναγνωρίζω], fut. ίσω, aor. 1, pass. ἀνεγνωρίσθην, (§ 26. rem. 1) (ἀνά & γνωρίζω) *to recognise*; pass. *to be made known, or to cause one's self to be recognised*, Ac. 7. 13.
ἀναγνώσει, dat. sing. . . . . . ἀνάγνωσις
ἀναγνωσθῇ 3 pers. sing. aor. 1, subj. pass. ἀναγινώσκω
ἀναγνωσθῆναι, aor. 1, inf. pass. . . ἀναγινώσκω
ἀνάγνωσιν, acc. sing. . . . . ἀνάγνωσις
ἀνάγνωσις], εως, ἡ, (§ 5. tab. E. c) . . ἀναγινώσκω
ἀναγνῶτε, 2 pers. pl. aor. 2, subj. act. . . id.
ἀναγομένοις, dat. pl. masc. part. pres. pass. ἀνάγω
ἀνάγω], fut. άξω, (§ 23. rem. 1. b) aor. 2, ἀνήγᾰγον, (§ 13. rem. 7. d) aor. 1, pass. ἀνήχθην, (ἀνά & ἄγω) *to conduct*; *to lead or convey* up from a lower place to a higher, Lu. 4. 5, et al.; *to offer up*, as a sacrifice, Ac. 7. 41; *to lead out, produce*, Ac. 12. 4; mid. ἀνάγομαι, aor. ἀνήχθην, as a nautical term, *to set sail, put to sea*, Lu. 8. 22, et al.
ἀναδείκνυμι, or νύω], fut. ξω, (§ 31. tab. B. B) (ἀνά & δείκνυμι) pr. *to show anything by raising it aloft*, as a torch; *to display, manifest, show plainly or openly*, Ac. 1. 24; *to mark out, constitute, appoint* by some outward sign, Lu. 10. 1.

ἀνάδειξις, εως, ἡ, (§ 5. tab. E. c) *a showing forth, manifestation; public entrance upon the duty or office to which one is consecrated*. L.G.

ἀναδείξεως,[b] gen. sing. . . ἀνάδειξις
ἀνάδειξις], εως, ἡ, (§ 5. tab. E. c) ἀναδείκνυμι
ἀνάδειξον, 2 pers. sing. aor. 1, imper. . id.
ἀναδεξάμενος, nom. sing. masc. part. aor. 1, mid. ἀναδέχομαι
ἀναδέχομαι], fut. ξομαι, (§ 23. rem. 1. b) (ἀνά & δέχομαι) *to receive*, as opposed to shunning or refusing, *to receive* with hospitality, Ac. 28. 7; *to embrace* a proffer or promise, He. 11. 17.
ἀναδίδωμι], fut. δώσω, aor. 2, ἀνέδων, (§ 30. tab. Z) (ἀνά & δίδωμι) *to give forth, up, or back*; *to deliver, present*, Ac. 23. 33.
ἀναδόντες,[c] nom. pl. masc. part. aor. 2. ἀναδίδωμι
ἀναζάω, ῶ], fut. ήσω, (§ 18. tab. R) (ἀνά & ζάω) *to live again, recover life*, Ro. 14. 9; Re. 20. 5; *to revive, recover activity*, Ro. 7. 9; met. *to live a new and reformed life*, Lu. 15. 24, 32. L.G.
ἀναζητέω, ῶ], fut. ήσω, (§ 16. tab. P) (ἀνά & ζητέω) *to track*; *to seek diligently, inquire after, search for*, Lu. 2. 44; Ac. 11. 25.
ἀναζητῆσαι, aor. 1, infin. . . ἀναζητέω
ἀναζητοῦντες, nom. pl. m. part. pres.—Al. Ln. Tdf. } id.
ζητοῦντες, Rec. Gr. Sch. (Lu. 2. 45) }

a 1 Pe. 5. 2. b Lu. 1. 80. c Ac. 23. 33.

ἀναζώννυμι], fut. ζώσω, (§ 31. tab. B.B) (ἀνά & ζώννυμι) *to gird* with a belt or girdle; mid. ἀναζώννυμαι, aor. 1, ἀνεζωσάμην, *to gird one's self*, 1 Pe. 1. 13. LXX.

ἀναζωπυρεῖν,[a] pres. infin. act. . . ἀναζωπυρέω

ἀναζωπῠρέω, ῶ], fut. ήσω, (§ 16. tab. P) (ἀνά & ζωπυρέω, *to revive a fire*, from ζωός & πῦρ) pr. *to kindle up a dormant fire*; met. *to revive, excite*; *to stir up, quicken* one's powers.

ἀναζωσάμενοι,[b] nom. pl. m. part. aor. 1, mid. ἀναζώννυμι

ἀναθάλλω], fut. θαλῶ, (§ 27. rem. 1. b) aor. 2, ἀνέθαλον, (ἀνά & θάλλω, *to thrive, flourish*) pr. *to recover verdure, flourish again*; met. *to receive, to recover activity*, Phi. 4. 10.

ἀνάθεμα, ατος, τό, (§ 4. tab. D. c) . . ἀνατίθημι

ἀναθέματι, dat. sing. . . . . ἀνάθεμα

ἀναθεματίζειν, pres. infin. . . . ἀναθεματίζω

ἀναθεματίζω], fut. ίσω, (§ 26. rem. 1) . . ἀνατίθημι

ἀναθεωρέω, ῶ], fut. ήσω, (§ 16. tab. P) (ἀνά & θεωρέω) *to view, behold attentively, contemplate*, Ac. 17. 23; He. 13. 7.

ἀναθεωροῦντες, nom. pl. masc. part. pres. . ἀναθεωρέω

ἀναθεωρῶν, nom. sing. masc. part. pres. . id.

ἀνάθημα], ατος, τό, (§ 4. tab. D. c) . ἀνατίθημι

ἀναθήμασι,[c] dat. pl. . . . . ἀνάθημα

ἀναίδεια,], ας, ἡ, (§ 2. tab. B. b, and rem. 2) (ἀ & αἰδώς) pr. *impudence*; hence, *importunate solicitation, pertinacious importunity*, without regard to time, place, or person.

ἀναίδειαν,[d] acc. sing. . . . . ἀναίδεια

ἀναιρεθῆναι, aor. 1, infin. pass. (§ 36. rem. 1) ἀναιρέω

ἀναιρεῖ, 3 pers. sing. pres. indic. act. . . id.

ἀναιρεῖν, pres. infin. act. . . . id.

ἀναιρεῖσθαι, pres. infin. pass. (§ 17. tab. Q) . id.

ἀναιρέσει, dat. sing. . . . . ἀναίρεσις

ἀναίρεσις], εως, ἡ, (§ 5. tab. E. c) . . ἀναιρέω

ἀναιρέω, ῶ], fut. ήσω, aor. 2, ἀνεῖλον, aor. 1, pass. ἀνῃρέθην, (§ 36. rem. 1) (ἀνά & αἱρέω) pr. *to take up, lift*, as from the ground; *to take off, put to death, kill, murder*, Mat. 2. 16, et al.; *to take away, abolish, abrogate*, He. 10. 9; mid. *to take up* infants in order to bring them up, Ac. 7. 21.

ἀναίρεσις, εως, ἡ, (§ 5. tab. E. c) *a taking up or away*; *a putting to death, murder*, Ac. 8. 1; 22. 20.

ἀναιρουμένων, gen. pl. part. pres. pass. . ἀναιρέω

ἀναιρούντων, gen. pl. masc. part. pres. act. . id.

ἀναίτιοι, nom. pl. masc. . . . ἀναίτιος

ἀναίτιος], ου, ὁ, ἡ, (§ 7. rem. 2) (ἀ & αἰτία) *guiltless, innocent*, Mat. 12. 5, 7.

ἀναιτίους, acc. pl. masc. . . . . ἀναίτιος

ἀνακαθίζω], fut. ίσω, (§ 26. rem. 1) (ἀνά & καθίζω) *to set up*; intrans. *to sit up*, Lu. 7. 15; Ac. 9. 40.

ἀνακαινίζειν,[e] pres. infin. act. . . . ἀνακαινίζω

ἀνακαινίζω], fut. ίσω, (§ 26. rem. 1) (ἀνά & καινίζω) *to renovate, renew*.

ἀνακαινούμενον, acc. sing. masc. part. pres. pass. ἀνακαινόω

ἀνακαινοῦται, 3 pers. sing. pres. indic. pass. (§ 21. tab. U) . . . . id.

ἀνακαινόω, ῶ], fut. ώσω, (§ 20. tab. T) (ἀνά & καινός) *to invigorate, renew*, 2 Co. 4. 16; Col. 3. 10. N.T.

ἀνακαίνωσις, εως, ἡ, (§ 5. tab. E. c) *renovation, renewal*, Ro. 12. 2; Tit. 3. 5.

ἀνακαίνωσις], εως, ἡ . . . . ἀνακαινόω

ἀνακαινώσει, dat. sing. . . . ἀνακαίνωσις

ἀνακαινώσεως, gen. sing. . . . id.

ἀνακαλυπτόμενον, nom. sing. neut. part. pr. p. ἀνακαλύπτω

ἀνακαλύπτω], fut. ψω, (§ 23. rem. 1. a) (ἀνά & καλύπτω) *to unveil, uncover*; pass. to be unveiled, 2 Co. 3. 18; met. *to be disclosed* in true character and condition, 2 Co. 3. 14.

ἀνακάμπτω], fut. ψω, (§ 23. rem. 1. a) (ἀνά & κάμπτω) pr. *to reflect, bend back*; hence, *to bend back* one's course, *return*, Mat. 2. 12; Lu. 10. 6; Ac. 18. 21; He. 11. 15.

ἀνακάμψαι, aor. 1, infin. act. . . . ἀνακάμπτω

ἀνακάμψει, 3 pers. sing. fut. act. . . id.

ἀνακάμψω, 1 pers. sing. fut. act. . . id.

ἀνάκειμαι], fut. είσομαι, (§ 33. tab. D.D) (ἀνά & κεῖμαι) *to be laid up*, as offerings; later, *to lie, be in a recumbent posture, recline* at table, Mat. 9. 10, et al.

ἀνακειμένοις, dat. pl. masc. part. pres. . . ἀνάκειμαι

ἀνακείμενον, nom. s. neut. part. pres.—Rec. Sch. Gr. Tdf. om. (Mar. 5. 40) . . } id.

ἀνακείμενος, nom. sing. masc. part. pres. . id.

ἀνακειμένου, gen. sing. masc. part. pres. . id.

ἀνακειμένους, acc. pl. masc. part. pres. . id.

ἀνακειμένων, gen. pl. masc. part. pres. . id.

ἀνάκειται, 3 pers. sing. pres. indic. . . id.

ἀνακεκαλυμμένῳ, dat. s. neut. part. perf. pass. ἀνακαλύπτω

---

[a] 2 Ti. 1. 6. [b] 1 Pe. 1. 13. [c] Lu. 21. 5. [d] Lu. 11. 8. [e] He. 6. 6.

ἀνακεφαλαιοῦται, 3 pers. sing. pres. indic. pass. (§ 21. tab. U) · ἀνακεφαλαιόω

ἀνακεφαλαιόω, ῶ], fut. ώσω, (§ 20. tab. T) (ἀνά & κεφάλαιον) *to bring together several things under one, reduce under one head; to comprise*, Ro. 13. 9; Ep. 1. 10. L.G.

ἀνακεφαλαιώσασθαι, aor. 1, inf. mid. · ἀνακεφαλαιόω

ἀνακλιθῆναι, aor. 1, infin. pass. · ἀνακλίνω

ἀνακλιθήσονται, 3 pers. pl. fut. pass. · id.

ἀνακλῖναι, aor. 1, infin. act. · id.

ἀνακλινεῖ, 3 pers. sing. fut. act. · id.

ἀνακλίνω], fut. ῐνῶ, (§ 27. rem. 1. a) (ἀνά & κλίνω) *to lay down*, Lu. 2. 7; *to cause to recline* at table, etc., Mar. 6. 39; Lu. 9. 15; 12. 37; mid. ἀνακλίνομαι, aor. 1, ἀνεκλίθην, (pass. form) (ῐ), f. ἀνακλιθήσομαι, (pass. form) *to recline at table*, Mat. 8. 11, et al.

ἀνακόπτω], fut. ψω, (§ 23. rem. 1. a) (ἀνά & κόπτω) pr. *to beat back*; hence, *to check, impede, hinder, restrain*, Gal. 5. 7.

ἀνακράζω], fut. ξομαι, (§ 26. rem. 2) aor. 1, ἀνέκραξα, in N.T. (ἀνά & κράζω) *to cry aloud, exclaim, shout*, Mar. 1. 23; 6. 49; Lu. 4. 33; 8. 28; 23. 18.

ἀνακράξας, nom. sing. masc. part. aor. 1. · ἀνακράζω

ἀνακρῐθῶ, 1 pers. sing. aor. 1, subj. pass. · ἀνακρίνω

ἀνακρίναντες, nom. pl. masc. part. aor. 1, act. · id.

ἀνακρίνας, nom. sing. masc. part. aor. 1, act. · id.

ἀνακρίνει, 3 pers. sing. pres. indic. act. · id.

ἀνακρίνεται, 3 pers. sing. pres. ind. pass. · id.

ἀνακρινόμεθα, 1 pers. pl. pres. ind. pass. · id.

ἀνακρίνοντες, nom. pl. masc. part. pres. act. · id.

ἀνακρίνουσι, dat. pl. masc. part. pres. act. · id.

ἀνακρίνω, fut. ῐνῶ, (§ 27. rem. 1. a) aor. 1, ἀνέκρῑνα, aor. 1, pass. ἀνεκρίθην, (ῐ), (ἀνά & κρίνω) *to sift; to examine closely*, Ac. 17. 11; *to scrutinise, scan*, 1 Co. 2. 14, 15; 9. 3; *to try* judicially, Lu. 23. 14, et al.; *to judge, give judgment upon*, 1 Co. 4. 3, 4; *to put questions, be inquisitive*, 1 Co. 10. 25, 27.

ἀνάκρῐσις, εως, ἡ, (§ 5. tab. E. c) *investigation, judicial examination, hearing of a cause.*

ἀνακρίνων, (ῑ), nom. sing. masc. part. pres. act. · ἀνακρίνω

ἀνακρίσεως,[a] gen. sing. · ἀνάκρισις

ἀνάκρισις], εως, ἡ, (§ 5. tab. E. c) · ἀνακρίνω

ἀνακύπτω], fut. ψω, (§ 23. rem. 1. a) (ἀνά & κύπτω) pr. *to raise up one's self, look up*, Lu. 13. 11; Jno. 8. 7, 10; met. *to look up* cheerily, *to be cheered*, Lu. 21. 28.

ἀνακύψαι, aor. 1, infin. · ἀνακύπτω

ἀνακύψας, nom. sing. masc. part. aor. 1 · id.

ἀνακύψατε, 2 pers. pl. aor. 1, imper. · id.

ἀναλάβετε, 2 pers. pl. aor. 2, imper. · ἀναλαμβάνω

ἀναλαβόντες, nom. pl. masc. part. aor. 2 · id.

ἀναλᾰβών, nom. sing. masc. part. aor. 2 · id.

ἀναλαμβάνειν, pres. infin. act. · id.

ἀναλαμβάνω], fut. λήψομαι, aor. 2, ἀνέλᾰβον, aor. 1, pass. ἀνελήφθην, (§ 36. rem. 2) *to take up, receive up*, Mar. 16. 19, et al.; *to take up, carry*, Ac. 7. 43; *to take on board*, Ac. 20. 13, 14; *to take* in company, Ac. 23. 31; 2 Ti. 4. 11.

ἀνάληψις, εως, ἡ, (§ 5. tab. E. c) *a taking up, receiving up*, Lu. 9. 51.

ἀναλημφθείς, nom. sing. masc. part. aor. 1, pass.—L. } ἀναλαμβάνω
ἀναληφθείς, R. Gr. Sch. Tdf. (Ac. 1. 11) }

ἀναληφθείς, nom. sing. masc. part. aor. 1, pass. · id.

ἀναλήψεως,[b] gen. sing. · ἀνάληψις

ἀνάληψις], εως, ἡ, (§ 5. tab. E. c) · ἀναλαμβάνω

ἀνᾱλίσκω], fut. λώσω, aor. 1, ἀνήλωσα & ἀνάλωσα, aor. 1, pass. ἀνηλώθην & ἀναλώθην, (§ 36. rem. 3) (ἀνά & ἁλίσκω) *to use up; to consume, destroy*, Lu. 9. 54; Gal. 5. 15; 2 Thes. 2. 8.

ἀναλογία], ας, ἡ, (§ 2. tab. B. b, and rem. 2) (ἀνά & λόγος) *analogy, ratio, proportion.*

ἀναλογίαν,[c] acc. sing. · ἀναλογία

ἀναλογίζομαι], fut. ίσομαι, (§ 26. rem. 1) (ἀνά & λογίζομαι) *to consider attentively.*

ἀναλογίσασθε,[d] 2 pers. pl. aor. 1, imper. mid. ἀναλογίζομαι

ἄναλον,[e] nom. sing. neut. · ἄναλος

ἄνᾰλος], ου, ὁ, ἡ, τό, -ον, (§ 7. rem. 2) (ἀ & ἅλς) *without saltness, without the taste and pungency of salt, insipid.*

ἀναλῦσαι, aor. 1, infin. act. · ἀναλύω

ἀναλύσει, 3 pers. sing. fut. act. · id.

ἀναλύσεως,[f] gen. sing. · ἀνάλυσις

ἀνάλυσις], εως, ἡ, (§ 5. tab. E. c) · ἀναλύω

ἀναλύω], fut. ύσω, (ῡ) (§ 13. tab. M) (ἀνά & λύω) pr. *to loose, dissolve*; intrans. *to loose* in order to departure; *to depart*, Lu. 12. 36; *to depart* from life, Phi. 1. 23.

ἀνάλῠσις, εως, ἡ, (§ 5. tab. E. c) pr. *dissolution*; met. *departure, death.*

[a] Ac. 25. 26. [b] Lu. 9. 51. [c] Ro. 12. 6. [d] He. 12. 3. [e] Mar. 9. 50. [f] 2 Ti. 4. 6.

ἀναλωθῆτε, 2 pers. pl. aor. 1, subj. pass. . ἀναλίσκω

ἀναλῶσαι, aor. 1, infin. act. . . . id.

ἀναλώσει, 3 pers. sing. fut. act. . . id.

ἀναμάρτητος,[a] ου, ὁ, ἡ, (§ 7. rem. 2) (ἀ & ἁμαρτάνω) *without sin, guiltless.*

ἀναμένειν,[b] pres. infin. . . . . ἀναμένω

ἀναμένω], fut. ενῶ, (§ 27. rem. 1. a) (ἀνά & μένω) *to await, wait for, expect.*

ἀναμιμνήσκεσθε, 2 pers. pl. pres. imper. mid. ἀναμιμνήσκω

ἀναμιμνησκομένου, gen. sing. masc. part. pr. mid. id.

ἀναμιμνήσκω, fut. μνήσω, (ἀνά & μιμνήσκω) *to remind, cause to remember,* 1 Co. 4. 17; *to exhort,* 2 Ti. 1. 6; mid. ἀναμιμνήσκομαι, aor. 1, (pass. form) ἀνεμνήσθην, *to call to mind, recollect, remember,* Mar. 14. 72; 2 Co. 7. 15; He. 10. 32.

ἀνάμνησις, εως, ἡ, (§ 5. tab. E. c) *remembrance; a commemoration, memorial,* Lu. 22. 19; 1 Co. 11. 24, 25; He. 10. 3.

ἀναμνήσει, 3 pers. sing. fut. act. . ἀναμιμνήσκω

ἀναμνησθείς, nom. sing. masc. part. aor. 1, pass. id.

ἀνάμνησιν, acc. sing. . . . . ἀνάμνησις

ἀνάμνησις, εως, ἡ, (§ 5. tab. E. c) . . ἀναμιμνήσκω

ἀνανεοῦσθαι,[c] pres. infin. pass. (§ 21. tab. U) ἀνανεόω

ἀνανεόω, ῶ], fut. ώσω, (§ 20. tab. T) *to renew;* pass. *to be renewed, be renovated,* by inward reformation.

ἀνανήφω], fut. ψω, (§ 23. rem. 1. a) (ἀνά & νήφω) *to become sober;* met. *to recover sobriety* of mind. L.G.

ἀνανήψωσι,[d] 3 pers. pl. aor. 1, subj. . ἀνανήφω

Ἀνανία, voc. sing. . . . . . Ἀνανίας

Ανανιαν, acc. sing. . . . . id.

Ἀνανίας, ου, ὁ, (§ 2. tab. B. d) *Ananias,* pr. name.

I. *A Christian of Jerusalem,* Ac. 5. 1, etc.

II. *A Christian of Damascus,* Ac. 9. 12, etc.

III. *High Priest,* Ac. 23. 2; 24. 1.

ἀναντίῤῥητος], ου, ὁ, ἡ, (§ 7. rem. 2) (ἀ & ἀντερῶ) *not to be contradicted, indisputable.* L.G.

ἀναντιῤῥήτως, adv., pr. *without contradiction or gainsaying; without hesitation, promptly.*

ἀναντιῤῥήτων,[e] gen. pl. . . . ἀναντίῤῥητος

ἀναντιῤῥήτως,[f] adv. . . . . id.

ἀνάξιοι,[g] nom. pl. masc. . . . ἀνάξιος

ἀνάξιος], ου, ὁ, ἡ, (§ 7. rem. 2) (ἀ & ἄξιος) *inadequate, unworthy.*

ἀναξίως, adv. *unworthily, in an improper manner,* 1 Co. 11. 27, 29.

ἀναξίως, adv. . . . . . ἀνάξιος

ἀναπαύεσθε, 2 pers. pl. pres. imper. mid. . ἀναπαύω

ἀναπαύεται, 3 pers. sing. pres. indic. mid. . id.

ἀναπαύου, 2 pers. sing. pres. imper. mid. . id.

ἀναπαύσασθε, 2 pers. pl. aor. 1, imper. mid. —A. B. C. Tdf. . . } id
ἀναπαύεσθε, Rec. Gr. Sch. Ln. (Mar. 6. 31)

ἀνάπαυσιν, acc. sing. . . . . ἀνάπαυσις

ἀνάπαυσις], εως, ἡ, (§ 5. tab. E. c) . . ἀναπαύω

ἀνάπαυσον, 2 pers. sing. aor. 1, imper. act. id.

ἀναπαύσω, 1 pers. sing. fut. act. . . id.

ἀναπαύσωνται, 3 pers. pl. aor. 1, subj. mid. . id.

ἀναπαύω], fut. αύσω, (§ 13. tab. M) (ἀνά & παύω) *to cause to rest,* to soothe, refresh, Mat. 11. 28, et al.; mid. *to take rest, repose, refreshment,* Mat. 26. 45, et al.; *to have a fixed place of rest, abide, dwell,* 1 Pe. 4. 14.

ἀνάπαυσις, εως, ἡ, (§ 5. tab. E. c) *rest, intermission,* Mat. 11. 29; Re. 4. 8; 14. 11; meton. *place of rest, fixed habitation,* Mat. 12. 43; Lu. 11. 24.

ἀναπείθει,[h] 3 pers. sing. pres. indic. act. . ἀναπείθω

ἀναπείθω], fut. είσω (§ 23. rem. 1. c) (ἀνά & πείθω) *to persuade* to a different opinion, *to seduce.*

ἀνάπειρος], ου, ὁ, ἡ, same signif. as ἀνάπηρος (?).

ἀναπείρους, acc. pl. masc.—B. D. Ln. . } ἀνάπειρος
ἀναπήρους, Rec. Gr. Sch. Tdf. (Lu. 14. 13, 21)

ἀναπέμπω], fut. ψω, (§ 23. rem. 1. a) (ἀνά & πέμπω) *to send back,* Phile. 11; *to send up, remit* to a tribunal, Lu. 23. 7, 11, 15.

ἀναπέμψω, 1 p. sing. aor. 1, subj.—A. Ln. Tdf. } ἀναπέμπω
πέμψω, Rec. Gr. Sch. (Ac. 25. 21) .

ἀναπέπαυται, 3 pers. sing. perf. ind. pass. ἀναπαυω

ἀνάπεσαι, 2 pers. sing. aor. 1, imper. mid. . ἀναπίπτω

ἀνάπεσε, 2 p. sing. aor. 2, imper.—A. Sch. Tdf. } id.
ἀνάπεσαι, Gr. ἀνάπεσον, Rec. (Lu. 14. 10)

ἀναπεσεῖν, aor. 2, infin. (§ 37. rem. 1) . id.

ἀνάπεσον, 2 pers. sing. aor. 1, imper. . . id.

ἀναπεσών, nom. sing. masc. part. aor. 2 . id.

ἀναπηδάω, ῶ], fut. ήσω, (§ 18. tab. R) (ἀνά & πηδάω) *to leap up.*

ἀναπηδήσας,[i] nom. sing. masc. part. aor. 1—B. D. Ln. Tdf. . . . } ἀναπηδάω
ἀναστάς, Rec. Gr. Sch. (Mar. 10. 50) .

ἀνάπηρος], ου, ὁ, ἡ, (§ 7. rem. 2) (ἀνά & πηρός,

[a] Jno. 8. 7. [b] 1 Thes. 1. 10. [c] Ep. 4. 23. [d] 2 Ti. 2. 26. [e] Ac. 19. 36. [f] Ac. 10. 29. [g] 1 Co. 6. 2. [h] Ac. 18. 13. [i] Mar. 10. 50.

maimed) *maimed, deprived of some member of the body, or at least of its use*, Lu. 14. 13, 21.

ἀναπήρους, acc. pl. masc. . . ἀνάπηρος

ἀναπίπτω], fut. πεσοῦμαι, aor. 2, ἀνέπεσον, (§ 37. rem. 1) (ἀνά & πίπτω) *to fall or recline backwards; to recline* at table, etc., Lu. 11. 37, et al.; *to throw one's self back*, Jno. 21. 20.

ἀναπληροῦται, 3 pers. sing. pres. ind. pass. (§ 21. tab. U) . . . . ἀναπληρόω

ἀναπληρόω, ῶ], fut. ώσω, (§ 20. tab. T) (ἀνά & πληρόω) *to fill up, complete*, 1 Thes. 2. 6; *to fulfil, confirm*, as a prophecy by the event, Mat. 13. 14; *to fill* the place of any one, 1 Co. 14. 16; *to supply, make good*, 1 Co. 16. 17; Phi. 2. 30; *to observe fully, keep*, the law, Ga. 6. 2.

ἀναπληρῶν, nom. sing. masc. part. pres. act. . ἀναπληρόω

ἀναπληρῶσαι, aor. 1, infin. act. . . id.

ἀναπληρώσατε, 2 pers. pl. aor. 1, imper. act. . id.

ἀναπληρώσετε, 2 p. pl. fut. act.—B. Ln. Tdf. ἀναπληρώσατε, Rec. Gr. Sch. (Gal. 6. 2) } id.

ἀναπληρώσῃ, 3 pers. sing. aor. 1, subj. act. id.

ἀναπολόγητος, ου, ὁ, ἡ, (§ 7. rem. 2) (ἀ & ἀπολογέομαι) *inexcusable*, Ro. 1. 20; 2. 1. L.G.

ἀναπολογήτους, acc. pl. masc. . . ἀναπολόγητος

ἀναπράττω], fut. ξω, *to exact, to demand*.

ἀνάπτει, 3 pers. sing. pres. ind. act. . . ἀνάπτω

ἀναπτύξας,[a] nom. sing. masc. part. aor. 1, act. ἀναπτύσσω

ἀναπτύσσω], fut. ξω, (§ 26. rem. 3) (ἀνά & πτύσσω) *to roll back, unrol, unfold*.

ἀνάπτω], fut. ψω, (§ 23. rem. 1. a) (ἀνά & ἅπτω) *to light, kindle, set on fire*, Lu. 12. 49; Ac. 28. 2; Ja. 3. 5.

ἀναρίθμητος,[b] ου, ὁ, ἡ, (§ 7. rem. 2) (ἀ & ἀριθμός) *innumerable*.

ἀνασείει, 3 pers. sing. pres. indic. act. ἀνασείω

ἀνασείω], fut. είσω, (§ 13. tab. M) (ἀνά & σείω) pr. *to shake up*; met. *to stir up, instigate*, Mar. 15. 11; Lu. 23. 5.

ἀνασκευάζοντες,[c] nom. pl. masc. part. pres. ἀνασκευάζω

ἀνασκευάζω], fut. άσω, (§ 26. rem. 1) (ἀνά & σκευάζω, from σκεῦος) pr. *to collect one's effects or baggage*, (σκεύη) in order to remove, *to lay waste by carrying off or destroying every thing*; met. *to unsettle, pervert, subvert*.

ἀνασπάσει, 3 pers. sing. fut. act. . . ἀνασπάω

ἀνασπάω, ῶ], fut. άσω, (ᾰ), (§ 22. rem. 2) (ἀνά & σπάω) *to draw up, to draw out*, Lu. 14. 5; Ac. 11. 10. (ᾰ).

ἀνάστα, 2 pers. sing. aor. 2, imper. by apocope for ἀνάστηθι, (§ 29. rem. 2) . . ἀνίστημι

ἀναστάν, nom. sing. neut. part. aor. 2 . . id.

ἀναστάντες, nom. pl. masc. part. aor. 2 . id.

ἀναστάς, nom. sing. masc. part. aor. 2 . . id.

ἀναστᾶσα, nom. sing. fem. part. aor. 2 . id.

ἀναστάσει, dat. sing. . . . ἀνάστασις

ἀναστάσεως, gen. sing. . . . id.

ἀνάστασιν, acc. sing. . . . . id.

ἀνάστᾰσις, εως, ἡ, (§ 5. tab. E. c) . . ἀνίστημι

ἀναστατοῦντες, nom. pl. masc. part. pres. . ἀναστατόω

ἀναστατόω, ῶ], fut. ώσω, (§ 20. tab. T) . ἀνίστημι

ἀναστατώσαντες, nom. pl. masc. part. aor. 1 ἀναστατόω

ἀναστατώσας, nom. sing. masc. part. aor. 1 . id.

ἀνασταυροῦντας,[d] acc. pl. masc. part. pres. ἀνασταυρόω

ἀνασταυρόω, ῶ], fut. ώσω, (§ 20. tab. T) (ἀνά & σταυρόω) pr. *to crucify*; met. *to crucify* by indignity.

ἀναστενάζω], fut. ξω, (§ 26. rem. 2) (ἀνά & στενάζω) *to sigh, groan deeply*.

ἀναστενάξας,[e] nom. sing. masc. part. aor. 1 ἀναστενάζω

ἀναστῇ, 3 pers. sing. aor. 2, subj. (§ 29. tab. X) ἀνίστημι

ἀνάστηθι, 2 pers. sing. aor. 2, imper. . id.

ἀναστῆναι, aor. 2, infin. . . . . id.

ἀναστήσας, nom. sing. masc. part. aor. 1, act. id.

ἀναστήσει, 3 pers. sing. fut. act. . . id.

ἀναστήσειν, fut. inf. act.—Rec. Sch. . Gr. Tdf. om. the words τὸ κατὰ σάρκα ἀναστήσειν τὸν Χρ. (Ac. 2. 30) } id.

ἀναστήσεται, 3 p. sing. fut. mid. (§ 29. tab. Y) id.

ἀναστήσονται, 3 pers. pl. fut. mid. . . id.

ἀναστήσω, 1 pers. sing. fut. act. . . id.

ἀναστράφητε, 2 pers. pl. aor. 2, imper. pass. (§ 24. rem. 10) . . . ἀναστρέφω

ἀναστρέφεσθαι, pres. infin. mid. . . id.

ἀναστρεφομένους, acc. pl. masc. part. pres. mid. id.

ἀναστρεφομένων, gen. pl. part. pres. mid. . id.

ἀναστρέφω], fut. ψω, (§ 23. rem. 1. a) (ἀνά & στρέφω) *to overturn, throw down*, Jno. 2. 15; *to turn back, return*, Ac. 5. 22; 15. 16; mid. ἀναστρέφομαι, aor. 2, (pass. form) ἀνεστράφην, *to abide, spend time*, Mat. 17. 22; *to live, to conduct one's self*, 2 Co. 1. 12; Ep.

[a] Lu. 4. 17. [b] He. 11. 12. [c] Ac. 15. 24. [d] He. 6. 6. [e] Mar. 8. 12.

2. 3; 1 Ti. 3. 15; He. 13. 18; 1 Pe. 1. 17, 2 Pe. 2. 18; *to gaze*, He. 10. 33.

ἀναστροφή, ῆς, ἡ, (§ 2. tab. B. a) *conversation, mode of life, conduct, deportment*, Ga. 1. 13, et al.

ἀναστρέψαντες, nom. pl. masc. part. aor. 1 . ἀναστρέφω

ἀναστρέψω, 1 pers. sing. fut. . . . id.

ἀναστροφαῖς, dat. pl. . . . . ἀναστροφή

ἀναστροφή], ῆς, ἡ, (§ 2. tab. B. a) . ἀναστρέφω

ἀναστροφῇ, dat. sing. . . . . ἀναστροφή

ἀναστροφήν, acc. sing. . . . . id.

ἀναστροφῆς, gen. sing. . . . . id.

ἀναστῶσι, 3 pers. pl. aor. 2, subj. (§ 29. tab. X) ἀνίστημι

ἀνατάξασθαι,[a] aor. 1, infin. . . ἀνατάσσομαι

ἀνατάσσομαι], fut. τάξομαι, (§ 23. rem. 7) (ἀνά & τάσσω) pr. *to arrange*; hence, *to compose*. L.G.

ἀνατεθραμμένος, nom. sing. masc. part. perf. pass. (§ 35. rem. 9) . . . ἀνατρέφω

ἀνατείλαντος, gen. sing. masc. part. aor. 1 . ἀνατέλλω

ἀνατείλῃ, 3 pers. sing. aor. 1, subj. . . id.

ἀνατέλλει, 3 pers. sing. pres. indic. . . id.

ἀνατέλλουσαν, acc. sing. fem. part. pres. . id.

ἀνατέλλω], fut. τελῶ, aor. 1, ἀνέτειλα, (§ 27. rem. 1. b. d) (ἀνά & τέλλω, *to make to rise*) *to cause to rise*, Mat. 5. 45; intrans. *to rise*, as the sun, stars, etc., Mat. 4. 16, et al.; *to spring* by birth, He. 7. 14.

ἀνατολή, ῆς, ἡ, (§ 2. tab. B. a) pr. *a rising* of the sun, etc.; *the place of rising, the east*, as also pl. ἀνατολαί, Mat. 2. 1, 2, et al.; met. *the dawn or day-spring*, Lu. 1. 78.

ἀνατέταλκε, 3 p. sing. perf. indic. (§ 27. rem. 2. b) ἀνατέλλω

ἀνατίθημι, mid. ἀνατίθεμαι], (§ 28. tab. V. W) aor. 2, ἀνεθέμην, (ἀνά & τίθημι) *to submit* to a person's *consideration a statement or report* of matters, Ac. 25. 14; Gal. 2. 2.

ἀνάθεμα, ατος, τό, (§ 4. tab. D. c) (a later equivalent to ἀνάθημα) *a devoted thing*, but ordinarily in a bad sense, *a person or thing accursed*, Ro. 9. 3; 1 Co. 12. 3; 16. 22; Gal. 1. 8, 9; *a curse, execration, anathema*, Ac. 23. 14.

ἀναθεματίζω, fut. ίσω, (§ 26. rem. 1) *to declare* any one *to be* ἀνάθεμα; *to curse, bind by a curse*, Mar. 14. 71; Ac. 23. 12, 14, 21. LXX.

ἀνάθημα, ατος, τό, (§ 4. tab. D. c) *a gift or offering consecrated to God*, Lu. 21. 5.

ἀνατολή, ῆς, ἡ, (§ 2. tab. B. a) . . ἀνατέλλω

ἀνατολῇ, dat. sing. . . . . . ἀνατολή

ἀνατολῆς, gen. sing. . . . . id.

ἀνατολῶν, gen. pl. . . . . . id.

ἀνατρέπουσι, 3 pers. pl. pres. indic. act. . ἀνατρέπω

ἀνατρέπω], fut. ψω, (§ 23. rem. 1. a) (ἀνά & τρέπω) pr. *to overturn, overthrow*; met. *to subvert, corrupt*, 2 Ti. 2. 18; Tit. 1. 11.

ἀνατρέφω], fut. θρέψω, (§ 35. rem. 4) perf. pass. ἀνατέθραμμαι, (§ 35. rem. 9) aor. 2, pass. ἀνετράφην, (ᾰ), (§ 24. rem. 10) (ἀνά & τρέφω) *to nurse*, as an infant, Ac. 7. 20; *to bring up, educate*, Ac. 7. 21; 22. 3.

ἀναφαίνεσθαι, pres. infin. pass. . . . ἀναφαίνω

ἀναφαίνω], fut. φανῶ, (§ 27. rem. 4. b) (ἀνά & φαίνω) *to bring to light, display*; mid. and pass. *to appear*, Lu. 19. 11; a nautical term, *to come in sight of*, Ac. 21. 3.

ἀναφανέντες, nom. pl. masc. part. aor. 2, pass. (§ 27. rem. 4. b) . . . ἀναφαίνω

ἀναφέρει, 3 pers. sing. pres. indic. act. . . ἀναφέρω

ἀναφέρειν, pres. infin. act. . . . . id.

ἀναφέρω], fut. ἀνοίσω, aor. 1, ἀνήνεγκα, aor. 2, ἀνήνεγκον, (§ 36. rem. 1) (ἀνά & φέρω) *to bear or carry upwards, lead up*, Mat. 17. 1, et al.; *to offer* sacrifices, He. 7. 27, et al.; *to bear aloft or sustain* a burden, as sins, 1 Pe. 2. 24; He. 9. 28.

ἀναφέρωμεν, 1 pers. pl. pres. subj. act. . . ἀναφέρω

ἀναφωνέω, ῶ], fut. ήσω, (§ 16. tab. P) (ἀνά & φωνέω) *to exclaim, cry out*, Lu. 1. 42.

ἀναχθέντες, nom. pl. masc. part. aor. 1, pass. ἀνάγω

ἀναχθῆναι, aor. 1, infin. pass. . . . id.

ἀνάχυσιν,[b] acc. sing. . . . . ἀνάχυσις

ἀνάχῠσις], εως, ἡ, (§ 5. tab. E. c) (ἀναχέω, *to pour out*) *a pouring out*; met. *excess*. L.G.

ἀναχωρεῖτε, 2 pers. pl. pres. imper. . . ἀναχωρέω

ἀναχωρέω, ῶ], fut. ήσω, (§ 16. tab. P) (ἀνά & χωρέω) *to go backward; to depart, go away*, Mat. 2. 12, et al.; *to withdraw, retire*, Mat. 9. 24; Ac. 23. 19; 26. 31.

ἀναχωρήσαντες, nom. pl. masc. part. aor. 1 . ἀναχωρέω

ἀναχωρησάντων, gen. pl. masc. part. aor. 1 id.

ἀναχωρήσας, nom. sing. masc. part. aor. 1 . id.

ἀνάψαντες, nom. pl. masc. part. aor. 1 . . ἀνάπτω

ἀναψύξεως,[c] gen. sing. . . . . ἀνάψυξις

[a] Lu. 1. 1. [b] 1 Pe. 4. 4. [c] Ac. 3. 19.

ἀνάψυξις], εως, ἡ, (§ 5. tab. E. c) . . ἀναψύχω
ἀναψύξω, 1 pers. sing. aor. 1, subj.—D. . } id.
συναναπαύσωμαι, Rec. Gr. Sch. . }
Tdf. om. (Ro. 15. 32) . }
ἀναψύχω], fut. ξω, (§ 23. rem. 1. b) (ἀνά & ψύχω) *to recreate by fresh air; to refresh, cheer*, 2 Ti. 1. 16. (ῡ).

ἀνάψυξις, εως, ἡ, (§ 5. tab. E. c) pr. *a refreshing coolness* after heat; met. *refreshing, recreation, rest*. L.G.

ἄνδρα, acc. sing. (§ 6. rem. 2) . . . ἀνήρ
ἀνδραποδισταῖς,[a] dat. pl. . . ἀνδραποδιστής
ἀνδραποδιστής], οῦ, ὁ, (§ 2. tab. B. c) (ἀνδράποδον, *a slave*) *a man-stealer, kidnapper*.
ἄνδρας, acc. pl. . . . . . . ἀνήρ
ἀνδράσι, dat. pl. . . . . . . id.
Ἀνδρέᾳ, dat. sing. . . . . . Ἀνδρέας
Ἀνδρέαν, acc. sing. . . . . . id.
Ἀνδρέας, ου, ὁ, (§ 2. tab. B. d) *Andrew*, pr. name.
Ἀνδρέου, gen. sing. . . . . . Ἀνδρέας
ἄνδρες, nom. and voc. pl. . . . ἀνήρ
ἀνδρί, dat. sing. . . . . . . id.
ἀνδρίζεσθε,[b] 2 pers. pl. pres. imper. mid. . ἀνδρίζω
ἀνδρίζω], fut. ίσω, (§ 26. rem. 1) . . ἀνήρ
Ἀνδρόνικον,[c] acc. sing. . . . . Ἀνδρόνικος
Ἀνδρόνῑκος], ου, ὁ, *Andronicus*, pr. name, (§ 3. tab. C. a).
ἀνδρός, gen. sing. . . . . . ἀνήρ
ἀνδροφόνοις,[d] dat. pl. . . . . ἀνδρόφονος
ἀνδροφόνος], ου, ὁ, (§ 3. tab. C. a) (ἀνήρ & φόνος) *a homicide, man-slayer, murderer*.
ἀνδρῶν, gen. pl. . . . . . . ἀνήρ
ἀνεβαίνομεν, 1 pers. pl. imperf. . . ἀναβαίνω
ἀνέβαινον, 3 pers. pl. imperf. . . . id.
ἀνεβάλετο,[e] 3 pers. sing. aor. 2, mid. . ἀναβάλλω
ἀνέβη, 3 pers. sing. aor. 2, (§ 31. rem. 1. d) . ἀναβαίνω
ἀνέβημεν, 2 pers. pl. aor. 2.—A. C. Tdf. . } id.
ἐπέβημεν, Rec. Gr. Sch. (Ac. 21. 6) }
ἀνέβην, 1 pers. sing. aor. 2, (§ 37. rem. 1) . id.
ἀνέβησαν, 3 pers. pl. aor. 2, ind. . . id.
ἀνέβλεψα, 1 pers. sing. aor. 1, ind. . . ἀναβλέπω
ἀνέβλεψαν, 3 pers. pl. aor. 1, ind. . . id.
ἀνέβλεψε, 3 pers. sing. aor. 1, ind. . . id.
ἀνεβόησε, 3 pers. sing. aor. 1, ind. . . ἀναβοάω
ἀνεγίνωσκε, 3 pers. sing. imperf. . ἀναγινώσκω
ἀνέγκλητοι, nom. pl. masc. . . . ἀνέγκλητος
ἀνέγκλητον, acc. sing. masc. . . . id.

ἀνέγκλητος, ου, ὁ, ἡ, (§ 7. rem. 2) (ἀ & ἐγκαλέω) *not arraigned; unblamable, irreproachable*, 1 Co. 1. 8; Col. 1. 22; 1 Ti. 3. 10; Tit. 1. 6, 7.
ἀνεγκλήτους, acc. pl. masc. . . ἀνέγκλητος
ἀνεγνωρίσθη,[f] 3 pers. sing. aor. 1, ind. pass. . ἀναγνωρίζω
ἀνέγνωσαν, 3 pers. pl. aor. 2, ind. (§ 31. rem. 1. d) ἀναγινώσκω
ἀνέγνωτε, 2 pers. pl. aor. 2, ind. (§ 36. rem. 3) id.
ἀνέδειξε, 3 pers. sing. aor. 1, ind. act. ἀναδείκνυμι
ἀνέζησαν, 3 pers. pl. aor. 1, ind. . ἀναζάω
ἀνέζησε, 3 pers. sing. aor. 1, ind. . . id.
ἀνεζήτουν, 3 pers. pl. imperf. . . ἀναζητέω
ἀνεθάλετε,[g] 2 p. pl. aor. 2, ind. (§ 27. rem. 3. b) ἀναθάλλω
ἀνεθεματίσαμεν, 1 pers. pl. aor. 1, ind. . ἀναθεματίζω
ἀνεθεμάτισαν, 3 pers. pl. aor. 1, ind. . . id.
ἀνεθέμην, 1 pers. sing. aor. 2, ind. mid. . ἀνατίθημι
ἀνέθετο, 3 pers. sing. aor. 2, mid. (§ 28. tab. W) id.
ἀνέθη, 3 p. sing. aor. 1, ind. pass. (§ 32. tab. C.C) ἀνίημι
ἀνεθρέψατο, 3 p. s. aor. 1, ind. mid. (§ 35. rem. 4) ἀνατρέφω
ἀνεῖλαν, 3 p. pl. aor. 1, (§ 35. rem. 12)—Al. Ln. Tdf. } ἀναιρέω
ἀνεῖλον, Rec. Gr. Sch. (Ac. 10. 39) }
ἀνείλατο, 3 pers. sing. aor. 1, mid.—Gr. Tdf. } id.
ἀνείλετο, Rec. Sch. (Ac. 7. 21) . }
ἀνεῖλε, 3 pers. sing. aor. 2, indic. (§ 36. rem. 1) id.
ἀνεῖλες, 2 pers. sing. aor. 2, ind. act. . id.
ἀνείλετε, 2 pers. pl. aor. 2, ind. act. . . id.
ἀνείλετο, 3 pers. sing. aor. 2, ind. mid. . id.
ἀνεῖλον, 3 pers. pl. aor. 2, ind. act. . . id.
ἀνείχεσθε, 2 pers. pl. imperf.—Gr. Sch. Tdf. } ἀνέχομαι
ἠνείχεσθε, Rec. ἀνέχεσθε, B. (2 Co. 11. 4) }
ἀνεκάθισε, 3 pers. sing. aor. 1, ind. . . ἀνακαθίζω
ἀνεκδιήγητος], ου, ὁ, ἡ, (§ 7. rem. 2) (ἀ & ἐκδιηγέομαι) *which cannot be related, inexpressible, unutterable*. L.G.
ἀνεκδιηγήτῳ,[h] dat. sing. fem. . . ἀνεκδιήγητος
ἀνεκλάλητος,] ου, ὁ, ἡ (§ 7. rem. 2) (ἀ & ἐκλαλέω) *unspeakable, ineffable*. L.G.
ἀνεκλαλήτῳ,[i] dat. sing. fem. . . . ἀνεκλάλητος
ἀνέκειτο, 3 pers. sing. imperf. . . ἀνάκειμαι
ἀνέκλειπτον,[k] acc. sing. masc. . . ἀνέκλειπτος
ἀνέκλειπτος], ου, ὁ, ἡ, (§ 7. rem. 2) (ἀ & ἐκλείπω) *unfailing, exhaustless*. L.G.
ἀνεκλίθη, 3 pers. sing. aor. 1, ind. pass. . ἀνακλίνω
ἀνέκλιναν, 3 pers. pl. aor. 1, ind. act. . id.
ἀνέκλινε, 3 pers. sing. aor. 1, ind. act. . . id.
ἀνέκοψε,[l] 3 pers. sing. aor. 1, ind. . . ἀνακόπτω
ἀνέκραγον, pers. pl. aor. 2, ind.—B. Tdf. } ἀνακράζω
ἀνέκραξαν, Rec. Gr. Sch. (Lu. 23. 18) }

a 1 Ti. 1. 10. b 1 Co. 16. 13. c Ro. 16. 7. d 1 Ti. 1. 9. e Ac. 24. 22. f Ac. 7. 13. g Phi. 4. 10.
h 2 Co. 9. 15. i 1 Pe. 1. 8. k Lu. 12. 33. l Gal. 5. 7.

ἀνέκραξαν, 3 pers. pl. aor. 1, ind. . . . ἀνακράζω
ἀνέκραξε, 3 pers. sing. aor. 1, ind. . . id.
ἀνεκτός], ή, όν, (§ 7. tab. F. a) . . ἀνέχομαι
ἀνεκτότερον, neut. sing. compar. (§ 8. rem. 4) ἀνεκτός
ἀνελάβετε, 2 pers. pl. aor. 2, ind. act. . ἀναλαμβάνω
ἀνελεήμονας,[a] acc. pl. masc. . . . ἀνελεήμων
ἀνελεήμων], ονος, ὁ, ἡ, (§ 7. tab. G. a, and rem. 4) (ἀ & ἐλεήμων) *unmerciful, uncompassionate, cruel.*
ἀνελεῖ, 3 pers. sing. fut.—Al. Ln. Tdf. } ἀναιρέω
ἀναλώσει, Rec. Gr. Sch. (2 Thes. 2. 8) }
ἀνελεῖν, aor. 2, infin. act. . . . . id.
ἀνέλεος,[b] ου, ὁ, ἡ, (§ 7. rem. 2) (ἀ & ἔλεος) *pitiless.*—Al. Ln. Tdf. (Ja. 2. 13).
ἀνίλεως, Rec. Gr. Sch. ἀνέλεως, B.
ἀνελήμφθη, 3 p. sing. aor. 1, ind. pass.—Ln. } ἀναλαμβάνω
ἀνελήφθη, Rec. Gr. Sch. Tdf. (Ac. 1. 2) }
ἀνελήφθη, 3 pers. sing. aor. 1, ind. pass. (§ 36. rem. 2) . . . id.
ἀνελύθη, (ῠ) 3 pers. sing. aor. 1, ind. pass.—D. } ἀναλύω
ἀνέθη, Rec. Gr. Sch. Tdf. (Ac. 16. 26) }
ἀνέλωσι, 3 p. pl. aor. 2, subj. act. (§ 36. rem. 1) ἀναιρέω
ἀνεμιζομένῳ,[c] dat. sing. masc. part. pres. pass. ἀνεμίζω
ἀνεμίζω], fut. ίσω, (§ 26. rem. 1) . . ἄνεμος
ἀνεμνήσθη, 3 pers. sing. aor. 1, ind. pass. . ἀναμιμνήσκω
ἄνεμοι, nom. pl. . . . . ἄνεμος
ἀνέμοις, dat. pl. . . . . . id.
ἄνεμον, acc. sing. . . . . . id.

ἄνεμος, ου, ὁ, (§ 3. tab. C. a) *the wind*; met. *a wind* of shifting doctrine, Ep. 4. 14.

ἀνεμίζω, fut. ίσω, (§ 26. rem. 1) *to agitate with the wind*; pass. *to be agitated or driven by the wind.* L.G.

ἀνέμου, gen. sing. . . . . ἄνεμος
ἀνέμους, acc. pl. . . . . . id.
ἀνέμῳ, dat. sing. . . . . . id.
ἀνέμων, gen. pl. . . . . . id.
ἀνένδεκτον,[d] nom. sing. neut. . . . ἀνένδεκτος
ἀνένδεκτος], ου, ὁ, ἡ, (§ 7. rem. 2) (ἀ & ἐνδέχεται, *it is possible*) *impossible, what cannot be.* N.T.
ἀνενέγκαι, aor. 1, infin. act. (§ 36. rem. 1) . ἀναφέρω
ἀνενέγκας, nom. sing. masc. part. aor. 1 . id.
ἀνέντες, nom. pl. masc. part. aor. 2, (§ 32. tab. C.C) ἀνίημι
ἀνενεγκεῖν, aor. 2, infin. act. . . ἀναφέρω
ἀνεξερεύνητα,[e] nom. pl. neut. . . ἀνεξερεύνητος
ἀνεξερεύνητος], ου, ὁ, ἡ, τό, -ον, (§ 7. rem. 2) (ἀ & ἐξερευνάω) *unsearchable, inscrutable.*

ἀνεξίκακον,[f] acc. sing. masc. . . . ἀνεξίκακος
ἀνεξίκᾰκος], ου, ὁ, ἡ, (§ 7. rem. 2) (ἀνέχομαι & κακός) *enduring or patient under evils and injuries.* L.G.
ἀνεξιχνίαστοι, nom. pl. fem. . . . ἀνεξιχνίαστος
ἀνεξιχνίαστος], ου, ὁ, ἡ, (§ 7. rem. 2) (ἀ & ἐξιχνιάζω), *to track out*, ἴχνος, *a track which cannot be explored, inscrutable, incomprehensible*, Ro. 11. 33; Ep. 3. 8. LXX.
ἀνεξιχνίαστον, acc. sing. masc. . . ἀνεξιχνίαστος
ἀνέξομαι, 1 pers. sing. fut. (§ 23. rem. 1. b) ἀνέχομαι
ἀνέξονται, 3 pers. pl. fut. . . . id.
ἀνεπαίσχυντον,[g] acc. sing. masc. . ἀνεπαίσχυντος
ἀνεπαίσχυντος], ου, ὁ, ἡ, (§ 7. rem. 2) (ἀ & ἐπαισχύνομαι) *without cause of shame, irreproachable.* N.T.
ἀνέπαυσαν, 3 pers. pl. aor. 1, ind. act. . . ἀναπαύω
ἀνέπεμψα, 1 pers. sing. aor. 1, ind. act. . ἀναπέμπω
ἀνέπεμψε, 3 pers. sing. aor. 1, ind. act. . . id.
ἀνέπεσαν, 3 pers. pl. aor. 1, ind. (§ 35. rem. 12) —B. Tdf. . . . . } ἀναπίπτω
ἀνέπεσον, Rec. Gr. Sch. (Mar. 6. 40) }
ἀνέπεσε, 3 pers. sing. aor. 2, indic. . . id.
ἀνέπεσον, 3 pers. pl. aor. 2, ind. . . id.
ἀνεπίληπτοι, nom. pl. masc. . . ἀνεπίληπτος
ἀνεπίληπτον, acc. sing. masc. and fem. . id.
ἀνεπίληπτος], ου, ὁ, ἡ, (§ 7. rem. 2) (ἀ & ἐπιλαμβάνω) pr. *not to be laid hold of*; met. *irreprehensible, unblamable*, 1 Ti. 3. 2; 5. 7; 6. 14.
ἀνεπλήρωσαν, 3 pers. pl. aor. 1, ind. act. . ἀναπληρόω
ἀνέπραξα, 1 pers. sing. aor. 1, indic.—A. . } ἀναπράττω
ἂν ἔπραξα, Rec. Gr. Sch. Tdf. (Lu. 19. 23) }
ἄνερ, voc. sing. (§ 6. rem. 2) . . . ἀνήρ
ἀνέρχομαι], fut. ἀνελεύσομαι, aor. 2, ἀνῆλθον, (§ 36. rem. 1) (ἀνά & ἔρχομαι) *to ascend, go up*, Jno. 6. 3; Gal. 1. 17, 18.
ἀνέσεισαν, 3 pers. pl. aor. 1, indic. act. . ἀνασείω
ἄνεσιν, acc. sing. . . . . ἄνεσις
ἄνεσις, εως, ἡ, (§ 5. tab. E. c) . . ἀνίημι
ἀνεσπάσθη, 3 pers. sing. aor. 1, ind. pass. . ἀνασπάω
ἀνέστη, 3 pers. sing. aor. 2, (§ 29. tab. X) . ἀνίστημι
ἀνέστησαν, 3 pers. pl. aor. 1, ind. . . id.
ἀνέστησε, 3 pers. sing. aor. 1, ind. . . id.
ἀνεστράφημεν, 1 p. pl. aor. 2, pass. (§ 24. rem. 10) ἀναστρέφω
ἀνέστρεψε, 3 pers. sing. aor. 1, ind. . . id.
ἀνεσχόμην, 1 p. sing. imperf.—A. B. Ln. Tdf. } ἀνέχομαι
ἠνεσχόμην, Rec. Gr. Sch. (Ac. 18. 14) }

[a] Ro. 1. 31. [b] Ja. 2. 13. [c] Ja. 1. 6. [d] Lu. 17. 1. [e] Ro. 11. 33. [f] 2 Ti. 2. 24. [g] 2 Ti. 2. 15

ἀνετάζειν, pres. infin. act. . . . ἀνετάζω
ἀνετάζεσθαι, pres. infin. pass. . . . id.
ἀνετάζω], fut. άσω, (§ 26. rem. 1) *to examine thoroughly; to examine* by torture, Ac. 22. 24, 29. LXX.
ἀνέτειλε, 3 pers. sing. aor. 1, ind. (§ 27. rem. 1. d) ἀνατέλλω
ἀνετράφη, 3 p. sing. aor. 2, pass. (§ 24. rem. 10) ἀνατρέφω
ἄνευ, prep. governing the gen., *without*, Mat. 10. 29; 1 Pe. 3. 1; 4. 9.
ἀνεύθετος], ου, ὁ, ἡ, (§ 7. rem. 2) (ἀ & εὔθετος) *not commodious, inconvenient.* N.T.
ἀνευθέτου,[a] gen. sing. masc. . . . ἀνεύθετος
ἀνεῦραν, 3 p. pl. aor. 1, (§ 35. rem. 12).—B. ἀνεῦρον, Rec. Gr. Sch. Tdf. (Lu. 2. 16) } ἀνευρίσκω
ἀνευρίσκω], fut. ρήσω, (§ 36. rem. 4) (ἀνά & εὑρίσκω) *to find by diligent search*, Lu. 2. 16; Ac. 21. 4.
ἀνεῦρον, 3 pers. pl. aor. 2, indic. . . . ἀνευρίσκω
ἀνευρόντες, nom. pl. masc. part. aor. 2 . id.
ἀνεφέρετο, 3 pers. sing. imperf. pass. . . ἀναφέρω
ἀνεφώνησε,[b] 3 pers. sing. aor. 1, ind. . ἀναφωνέω
ἀνέχεσθαι, pres. infin.—D. Ln. . . ἀνέχεσθε, Rec. Gr. Sch. Tdf. (He. 13. 22) } ἀνέχομαι
ἀνέχεσθε, 2 pers. pl. pres. ind. . . id.
ἀνέχεσθε, 2 pers. pl. pres. imper. . . id.
ἀνέχομαι], fut. έξομαι, imperf. ἀνειχόμην, ἠνειχόμην, ἠνεσχόμην, (§ 34. rem. 1. d) (ἀνά & ἔχω) *to endure patiently*, 1 Co. 4. 12; 2 Co. 11. 20; 2 Thes. 1. 4; *to bear with*, Mat. 17. 7, et al.; *to suffer, admit, permit*, Ac. 18. 14; 2 Co. 11. 4; 2 Ti. 4. 3; He. 13. 22.
  ἀνεκτός, ή, όν, (§ 7. tab. F. a) *tolerable, supportable*, Mat. 10. 15; 11. 22, 24; Mar. 6. 11; Lu. 10. 12, 14.
ἀνεχόμεθα, 1 pers. pl. pres. ind. . . ἀνέχομαι
ἀνεχόμενοι, nom. pl. masc. part. pres. . . id.
ἀνεχώρησαν, 3 pers. pl. aor. 1, ind. . . ἀναχωρέω
ἀνεχώρησε, 3 pers. sing. aor. 1, ind. . . id.
ἀνεψιός,[c] οῦ, ὁ, (§ 3. tab. C. a) *a nephew.*
ἀνέψυξε,[d] 3 pers. sing. aor. 1, ind. . . ἀναψύχω
ἀνέῳγε, 3 pers. sing. perf. 2 ind. (§ 25. rem. 4) ἀνοίγω
ἀνεῳγμένας, acc. pl. fem. part. perf. pass. (§ 37. rem. 1) . . . . . id.
ἀνεῳγμένη, nom. sing. fem. part. perf. pass.—Gr. Sch. . . . . . ἠνεῳγμένη, Rec. Tdf. (Re. 4. 1) . } id.
ἀνεῳγμένην, acc. sing. fem. part. perf. pass. id.
ἀνεῳγμένης, gen. sing. fem. part. perf. pass. ἀνοίγω
ἀνεῳγμένον, acc. sing. m. and neut. part. perf. pass. id.
ἀνεῳγμένος, nom. sing. masc. part. perf. pass. id.
ἀνεῳγμένους, acc. pl. masc. part. perf. pass. id.
ἀνεῳγμένων, gen. pl. part. perf. pass. . id.
ἀνεῳγότα, acc. sing. m. part. perf. 2 (§ 37. rem. 1) id.
ἀνέῳξε, 3 pers. sing. aor. 1, ind. . . . id.
ἀνεῴχθη, 3 p. sing. aor. 1, ind. pass. (§ 37. rem. 1) id.
ἀνεῳχθῆναι, aor. 1, infin. pass. . id.
ἀνεῴχθησαν, 3 pers. pl. aor. 1, ind. pass. id.
ἀνήγαγον, 3 p. pl. aor. 2, ind. Att. (§ 13. rem. 7. b. d) ἀνάγω
ἀνήγγειλαν, 3 p. pl. aor. 1, ind. (§ 27. rem. 1. d) ἀναγγέλλω
ἀνήγγειλε, 3 pers. sing. aor. 1, ind. act. . id.
ἀνηγγέλη, 3 p. s. aor. 2, ind. pass. (§ 27. rem. 4. b) id.
ἀνήγγελλον, 3 pers. pl. imperf. act.—B. Ln. Tdf. ἀνήγγειλαν, Rec. Gr. Sch. (Ac. 14. 27) } id.

ἄνηθον,[e] ου, τό, (§ 3. tab. C. c) *anethum, dill*, an aromatic plant.
ἀνῆκε, 3 pers. sing. perf. indic. . . . ἀνήκω
ἀνῆκον, acc. sing. neut. part. pres. . . id.
ἀνήκοντα, nom. pl. neut. part. pres. . . id.
ἀνήκω], (ἀνά & ἥκω) *to come up to, to pertain to;* ἀνήκει, impers. *it is fit, proper, becoming*, Col. 3. 18; Ep. 5. 4; Phile. 8.
ἀνῆλθε, 3 pers. sing. aor. 2, ind. (§ 36. rem. 1) ἀνέρχομαι
ἀνῆλθον, 1 pers. sing. aor. 2, ind. . . id.
ἀνήμεροι,[f] nom. pl. masc. . . . ἀνήμερος
ἀνήμερος], ου, ὁ, ἡ, (§ 7. rem. 2) (ἀ & ἥμερος, *gentle, mild*) *ungentle, fierce, ferocious.*
ἀνήνεγκε, 3 pers. sing. aor. 1, ind. (§ 36. rem. 1) ἀναφέρω

ἀνήρ, ἀνδρός, ὁ, (§ 6. rem. 2) *a male person of full age and stature*, as opposed to a child or female, 1 Co. 13. 11, et al.; *a husband*, Mat. 1. 16, et al.; *a man, human being, individual*, Lu. 11. 31, et al.; used also pleonastically with other nouns and adjectives, Lu. 5. 8; Ac. 1. 16, et al.
  ἀνδρίζω, fut. ίσω, (§ 26. rem. 1) *to render brave or manly*, mid. *to show or behave one's self like a man*, 1 Co. 16. 13.
ἀνῃρέθη, 3 p. sing. aor. 1, ind. pass. (§ 36. rem. 1) ἀναιρέω
ἀνήφθη, 3 p. sing. aor. 1, ind. pass. (§ 23. rem. 4) ἀνάπτω
ἀνήχθη, 3 pers. sing. aor. 1, ind. pass. ἀνάγω
ἀνήχθημεν, 1 pers. pl. aor. 1, ind. pass. . id.
ἀνήχθησαν, 3 pers. pl. aor. 1, ind. pass. . id.
ἀνθ', for ἀντί; ἀνθ' ὧν, *on which account, wherefore; because.*

[a] Ac. 27. 12. [b] Lu. 1. 42. [c] Col. 4. 10. [d] 2 Ti. 1. 16. [e] Mat. 23. 23. [f] 2 Ti. 3. 3.

ἀνθέξεται, 3 pers. sing. fut. mid. (§ 35. rem. 4) ἀντέχομαι

ἀνθέστηκε, 3 pers. sing. perf. ind. . . ἀνθίστημι

ἀνθεστηκότες, nom. pl. masc. part. perf. . id.

ἀνθίστανται, 3 p. pl. pres. ind. mid. (§ 29. tab. Y) id.

ἀνθίστατο, 3 pers. sing. imperf. mid. . . id.

ἀνθίστημι], fut. ἀντιστήσω, (ἀντί & ἵστημι) *to set in opposition*; intrans. aor. 2, ἀντέστην, perf. ἀνθέστηκα, (§ 29. tab. X) and mid., *to oppose, resist, stand out against.*

ἀνθομολογέομαι, οῦμαι], (§ 17. tab. Q) (ἀντί & ὁμολογέω) pr. *to come to an agreement*; hence, *to confess openly what is due*; *to confess, give thanks, render praise*, Lu. 2. 38.

ἄνθος, εος, ους, τό, (§ 5. tab. E. b) *a flower*, Ja. 1. 10, 11; 1 Pe. 1. 24, bis.

ἄνθρακας,[a] acc. pl. . . . . ἄνθραξ

ἀνθρακιά, ᾶς, ἡ, (§ 2. tab. B. b, and rem. 2) . id.

ἀνθρακιάν, acc. sing. . . . . ἀνθρακιά

ἄνθραξ], ἄκος, ὁ, (§ 4. rem. 2. b) *a coal, burning coal.*

ἀνθρακιά, ᾶς, ἡ, (§ 2. tab. B. b, and rem. 2) *a mass or heap of live coals*, Jno. 18. 18; 21. 9.

ἀνθρωπάρεσκοι, nom. pl. masc. . . ἀνθρωπάρεσκος

ἀνθρωπάρεσκος], ου, ὁ, ἡ, (§ 7. rem. 2) (ἄνθρωπος & ἀρέσκω) *desirous of pleasing men*, Ep. 6. 6; Col. 3. 22. LXX.

ἄνθρωπε, voc. sing. . . . . ἄνθρωπος

ἀνθρωπίνῃ, dat. sing. fem. . . . ἀνθρώπινος

ἀνθρωπίνης, gen. sing. fem. . . . id.

ἀνθρώπινον, acc. sing. neut. . id.

ἀνθρώπινος, η, ον, (§ 7. tab. F. a) . . ἄνθρωπος

ἀνθρωπίνων, gen. pl.—Al. Ln. Tdf. . } ἀνθρώπινος
ἀνθρώπων, Rec. Gr. Sch. (Ac. 17. 25) }

ἄνθρωποι, nom. pl. . . . . ἄνθρωπος

ἀνθρώποις, dat. pl. . . . . id.

ἀνθρωποκτόνος, ου, ὁ, ἡ, (§ 3. tab. C. a) (ἄνθρωπος & κτείνω) *a homicide, murderer*, Jno. 8. 44; 1 Jno. 3. 15.

ἄνθρωπον, acc. sing. . . . . ἄνθρωπος

ἄνθρωπος, ου, ὁ, ἡ, (§ 3. tab. C. a) *a human being*, Jno. 16. 21; Phi. 2. 7, et al.; *an individual*, Ro. 3. 28, et al. freq.; used also pleonastically with other words, Mat. 11. 19, et al., met. *the* spiritual frame of the inner *man*, Ro. 7. 22; Ep. 3. 16; 1 Pe. 3. 4.

ἀνθρώπινος, η, ον, (§ 7. tab. F. a) *human, belonging to man*, 1 Co. 2. 4, 13; 4. 3; 10. 13; Ja. 3. 7; 1 Pe. 2. 13; *suited to man*, Ro. 6. 19.

ἀνθρώπου, gen. sing. . . . . ἄνθρωπος

ἀνθρώπους, acc. pl. . . . . id.

ἀνθρώπῳ, dat. sing. . . . . id.

ἀνθρώπων, gen. pl. . . . . . id.

ἀνθυπατεύοντος,[b] gen. sing. masc. part. pres. —Rec. Gr. Sch. . . . } ἀνθυπατεύω
ἀνθυπάτου ὄντος, Al. Ln. Tdf. (Ac. 18. 12) }

ἀνθυπατεύω], fut. εύσω, (§ 13. tab. M) . ἀνθύπατος

ἀνθύπατοι, nom. pl. . . . . id.

ἀνθύπατον, acc. sing. . . . . id.

ἀνθύπατος, ου, ὁ, (§ 3. tab. C. a) (ἀντί & ὕπατος, *a consul*) *a proconsul*, Ac. 13. 7, 8, 12; 19. 38. L.G.

ἀνθυπατεύω, fut. εύσω, (§ 13. tab. M) *to be proconsul*, Ac. 18. 12.

ἀνθυπάτου, gen. sing.—Al. Ln. Tdf. . } ἀνθύπατος
ἀνθυπατεύοντος, Rec. Gr. Sch. (Ac. 18. 12) }

ἀνθυπάτῳ, dat. sing. . . . . id.

ἀνθωμολογεῖτο,[c] 3 pers. sing. imperf. (§ 34. rem. 1. a. b) . . ἀνθομολογέομαι

ἀνιέντες, nom. pl. masc. part. pres. . . ἀνίημι

ἀνίημι], fut. ἀνήσω, aor. 2, ἀνῆν, subj. ἀνῶ, aor. 1, pass. ἀνέθην, (§ 32. tab. CC) (ἀνά & ἵημι) *to loose, slacken*, Ac. 27. 40; *to unbind, unfasten*, Ac. 16. 26; *to omit, dispense with*, Ep. 6. 9; *to leave or neglect*, He. 13. 5.

ἄνεσις, εως, ἡ, (§ 5. tab. E. c) pr. *the relaxing* of a state of constraint; *relaxation* of rigour of confinement, Ac. 24. 23; met. *ease, rest, peace, tranquillity*, 2 Co. 2. 12; 7. 5; 8. 13; 2 Thes. 1. 7.

ἀνίλεως,[d] ω, ὁ, ἡ, (§ 7. tab. F. b, and rem. 3) (ἀ & ἵλεως) *uncompassionate, unmerciful, stern*. N.T.

ἀνίπτοις, dat. pl. fem. . . . . ἄνιπτος

ἄνιπτος], ου, ὁ, ἡ, (§ 7. rem. 2) (ἀ & νίπτω) *unwashed*, Mat. 15. 20; Mar. 7. 2, 5.

ἀνιστάμενος, nom. sing. masc. part. pres. mid. ἀνίστημι

ἀνίστασθαι, pres. infin. mid. (§ 29. tab. Y) . id.

ἀνίσταται, 3 pers. sing. pres. ind. mid. . id.

ἀνίστημι], fut. ἀναστήσω, aor. 1, ἀνέστησα, (§ 29. tab. X) trans. *to cause to stand up or rise*, Ac. 9. 41; *to raise up*, as the dead, Jno. 6. 39, et al.; *to raise up* into existence,

---

[a] Ro. 12. 20. [b] Ac. 18. 12. [c] Lu. 2. 38. [d] Ja. 2. 13.

Mat. 22. 24, et al.; intrans. aor. 2, ἀνέστην, imperat. ἀνάστηθι, ἀνάστα, and mid., *to rise up*, Mat. 9. 9, et al.; *to rise up* into existence, Ac. 7. 18; 20. 30.

ἀνάστᾰσις, εως, ἡ, (§ 5. tab. E. c) *a raising or rising up; resurrection*, Mat. 22. 23, et al.; meton. *the author of resurrection*, Jno. 11. 25; met. *an uprising* into a state of higher advancement and blessedness, Lu. 2. 34.

ἀναστατόω, ῶ, fut. ώσω, (§ 20. tab. T) i. e. ἀνάστατον ποιεῖν, *to lay waste, destroy; to disturb, throw into commotion*, Ac. 17. 6; *to excite to sedition and tumult*, Ac. 21. 38; *to disturb* the mind of any one by doubts, etc.; *to subvert, unsettle*, Gal. 5. 12. L.G.

Ἄννα,[a] ης, ἡ, (§ 2. rem. 3) *Anna*, pr. name.

Ἄννα, gen. sing. . . . . . . Ἄννας

Ἄνναν, acc. sing. . . . . . id.

Ἄννας, α, ὁ, (§ 2. rem. 4) *Annas*, pr. name.

ἀνόητοι, nom. and voc. pl. masc. . . ἀνόητος

ἀνοήτοις, dat. pl. masc. . . . id.

ἀνόητος, ου, ὁ, ἡ, (§ 7. rem. 2) (ἀ & νοέω) *inconsiderate, unintelligent, unwise*; Lu. 24. 25; Ro. 1. 14; Gal. 3. 1, 3; Tit. 3. 3; *brutish*, 1 Ti. 6. 9.

ἀνοήτους, acc. pl. fem. . . . . ἀνόητος

ἄνοια, ας, ἡ, (§ 2. tab. B. b, and rem. 2) (ἀ & νοῦς) *want of understanding; folly, rashness, madness*, Lu. 6. 11; 2 Ti. 3. 9.

ἀνοίας, gen. sing. . . . . ἄνοια

ἀνοίγει, 3 pers. sing. pres. ind. act. . . ἀνοίγω

ἀνοίγειν, pres. infin. act. . . . id.

ἀνοίγεται, 3 pers. sing. pres. ind. pass.—B. }
ἀνοιγήσεται, Rec. Gr. Sch. Tdf. (Mat. 7. 8) } id.

ἀνοιγήσεται, 3 pers. sing. fut. 2, pass. . . id.

ἀνοίγω], fut. ἀνοίξω, aor. 1, ἀνέῳξα, ἤνοιξα, perf. ἀνέῳχα, (§ 37. rem. 1) (ἀνά & οἴγω) trans. *to open*, Mat. 2. 11, et al.; intrans. perf. 2, ἀνέῳγα, perf. pass. ἀνέῳγμαι, ἠνέῳγμαι, aor. 1, pass. ἀνεῴχθην, ἠνεῴχθην, ἠνοίχθην, *to be opened, to be open*, Mat. 3. 16; Jno. 1. 52, et al.

ἄνοιξις, εως, ἡ, (§ 5. tab. E. c) *an opening, act of opening*, Ep. 6. 19.

ἀνοίγων, nom. sing. masc. part. pres. act. . ἀνοίγω

ἀνοιγῶσι, 3 pers. pl. aor. 2, subj. pass.—Al. Ln. }
ἀνοιχθῶσι, Rec. Gr. Sch. Tdf. (Mat. 20. 33) } id.

ἀνοικοδομέω, ῶ], fut. ήσω, (§ 16. tab. P) (ἀνά & οἰκοδομέω) *to rebuild*, Ac. 15. 16, bis.

ἀνοικοδομήσω, 1 pers. sing. fut. ind. . ἀνοικοδομέω

ἀνοῖξαι, aor. 1, infin. act. . . . ἀνοίγω

ἀνοίξαντες, nom. pl. masc. part. aor. 1 . . id.

ἀνοίξας, nom. sing. masc. part. aor. 1, act. . id.

ἀνοίξει,[b] dat. sing. . . . . . ἄνοιξις

ἀνοίξῃ, 3 pers. sing. aor. 1, subj. act. . ἀνοίγω

ἄνοιξις], εως, ἡ, (§ 5. tab. E. c) . . . id.

ἄνοιξον, 2 pers. sing. aor. 1, imper. act. . id.

ἀνοίξω, 1 pers. sing. fut. act. . . . id.

ἀνοίξωσι, 3 pers. pl. aor. 1, subj. act. . id.

ἀνοιχθήσεται, 3 p. sing. fut. 1, pass.—Const. Tdf. }
ἀνοιγήσεται, Rec. Gr. Sch. Ln. (Lu. 11. 9, 10) } id.

ἀνοιχθῶσι, 3 p. pl. aor. 1, subj. pass. (§ 37. rem. 1) id.

ἀνομία, ας, ἡ, (§ 2. tab. B. b, and rem. 2) . ἄνομος

ἀνομίᾳ, dat. sing. . . . . ἀνομία

ἀνομίαι, nom. pl. . . . . id.

ἀνομίαν, acc. sing. . . . . id.

ἀνομίας, gen. sing. . . . . . id.

ἀνομιῶν, gen. pl. . . . . . id.

ἀνόμοις, dat. pl. masc. . . . . ἄνομος

ἄνομος, ου, ὁ, ἡ, (§ 7. rem. 2) (ἀ & νόμος) *lawless, without law, not subject to law*, 1 Co. 9. 21; *lawless, violating law, wicked, impious*, Ac. 2. 23, et al.; *a transgressor*, Mar 15. 28; Lu. 22. 37.

ἀνομία, ας, ἡ, (§ 2. tab. B. b, and rem. 2) *lawlessness; violation of law*, 1 Jno. 3. 4; *iniquity, sin*, Mat. 7. 23, et al.

ἀνόμως, adv. *without* the intervention of *law*, Ro. 2. 12, bis.

ἀνόμους, acc. pl. masc. . . . ἄνομος

ἀνόμων, gen. pl. . . . . . id.

ἀνόμως, adv. . . . . . id.

ἀνορθόω, ῶ], fut. ώσω, (§ 20. tab. T) (ἀνά & ὀρθόω) *to restore to straightness or erectness*, Lu. 13. 13; *to re-invigorate*, He. 12. 12; *to re-erect*, Ac. 15. 16.

ἀνορθώσατε, 2 pers. pl. aor. 1, imper. . . ἀνορθόω

ἀνορθώσω, 1 pers. sing. fut. ind. . . id.

ἀνόσιοι, nom. pl. masc. . . . . ἀνόσιος

ἀνοσίοις, dat. pl. masc. . . . id.

ἀνόσιος], ου, ὁ, ἡ, (§ 7. rem. 2) (ἀ & ὅσιος, *pious*) *impious, unholy*, 1 Ti. 1. 9; 2 Ti. 3. 2.

ἀνοχή], ῆς, ἡ, (§ 2. tab. B. a) (ἀνέχομαι) *forbearance, patience*, Ro. 2. 4; 3. 26.

ἀνοχῇ, dat. sing. . . . . . ἀνοχή

[a] Lu. 2. 36.

[b] Ep. 6. 19.

ἀνοχῆς, gen. sing. . . . . . ἀνοχή

ἀνταγωνιζόμενοι,[a] nom. pl. masc. part. pres. ἀνταγωνίζομαι

ἀνταγωνίζομαι], fut. ίσομαι, (§ 26. rem. 1) (ἀντί & ἀγωνίζομαι) *to contend, strive against.*

ἀντάλλαγμα, ατος, τό, (§ 4. tab. D. c) (ἀνταλλάσσω, *to exchange*) *a price paid in exchange* for a thing; *compensation, equivalent ransom,* Mat. 16. 26; Mar. 8. 37.

ἀνταναπληρόω,[b] ῶ, fut. ώσω, (§ 20. tab. T) (ἀντί & ἀναπληρόω) *to fill up, complete, supply.*

ἀνταποδίδωμι], fut. δώσω, aor. 2, ἀνταπέδων, (§ 30. tab. Z) aor. 1, pass. ἀνταπεδόθην, (§ 30. rem. 4) (ἀντί & ἀποδίδωμι) *to repay, requite, recompense,* Lu. 14. 14, bis; Ro. 11. 35; 12. 19; 1 Thes. 3. 9; 2 Thes. 1. 6; He. 10. 30.

ἀνταπόδομα, ατος, τό, (§ 4. tab. D. c) *requital, recompense, retribution,* Lu. 14. 12; Ro. 11. 9. LXX.

ἀνταπόδοσις, εως, ἡ, (§ 5. tab. E. c) *recompense, reward,* Col. 3. 24.

ἀνταποδοθήσεται, 3 pers. sing. fut. 1, pass. ἀνταποδίδωμι

ἀνταπόδομα, τος, τό, (§ 4. tab. D. c) . . id.

ἀνταποδόσεως, gen. sing.—A. ⎫
ἀποκαλύψεως, Rec. Gr. Sch. Tdf. (Ro. 2. 5) ⎭ ἀνταπόδοσις

ἀνταπόδοσιν,[c] acc. sing. . . . . id.

ἀνταπόδοσις], εως, ἡ, (§ 5. tab. E. c) . ἀνταποδίδωμι

ἀνταποδοῦναι, aor. 2, infin. act. . . . id.

ἀνταποδώσω, 1 pers. sing. fut. ind. act. . id.

ἀνταποκριθῆναι, aor. 1, infin. . . ἀνταποκρίνομαι

ἀνταποκρίνομαι], aor. 1, (pass. form) ἀνταπεκρίθην, (ῐ) (§ 27. rem. 3) (ἀντί & ἀποκρίνομαι) *to answer, speak in answer,* Lu. 14. 6; *to reply against, contradict, dispute,* Ro. 9. 20. LXX.

ἀνταποκρινόμενος, nom. s. m. part. pres. ἀνταποκρίνομαι

ἀντειπεῖν, aor. 2, infin. (§ 36. rem. 1) . . ἀντιλέγω

ἀντεῖπον], infin. ἀντειπεῖν, see ἀντιλέγω.

ἀντελάβετο, 3 pers. sing. aor. 2, ind. ἀντιλαμβάνομαι

ἀντέλεγον, 3 pers. pl. imperf. . . . ἀντιλέγω

ἀντελοιδόρει,[d] 3. p. sing. imperf. (§ 34. rem. 1. a. b) ἀντιλοιδορέω

ἀντέστη, 3 pers. sing. aor. 2.—Al. Ln. Tdf. ⎫
ἀνθέστηκε, Rec. Gr. Sch. (2 Ti. 4. 15) ⎭ ἀνθίστημι

ἀντέστην, 1 pers. sing. aor. 2, ind. (§ 29. tab. X) id.

ἀντέστησαν, 3 pers. pl. aor. 2, ind. . . id.

ἀντέχεσθε, 2 pers. pl. pres. imper. . . ἀντέχομαι

ἀντέχομαι], fut. ἀνθέξομαι, (§ 35. rem. 4) (ἀντί & ἔχω) *to hold firmly, cling or adhere to; to be devoted to* any one, Lu. 16. 13; Tit. 1. 9; *to exercise a zealous care for* any one, 1 Thes. 5. 14.

ἀντεχόμενον, acc. sing. masc. part. pres. . ἀντέχομαι

ἀντί, pr. *over against;* hence, *in correspondence to, answering to,* Jno. 1. 16; *in place of,* Mat. 2. 22, et al.; *in retribution or return for,* Mat. 5. 38, et al.; *in consideration of,* He. 12. 2, 16; *on account of,* Mat. 17. 27; ἀνθ' ὧν, *because,* Lu. 1. 20, et al.

ἀντιβάλλετε,[e] 2 pers. pl. pres. ind. . . ἀντιβάλλω

ἀντιβάλλω], (ἀντί & βάλλω) pr. *to throw or toss from one to another;* met. *to agitate, to converse or discourse about.*

ἀντιδιαθεμένους, acc. pl. masc. part. aor. 2, mid. C. . . . . ⎫
ἀντιδιατιθεμένους, Rec. Gr. Sch. Tdf. (2 Ti. 2. 25) . . . ⎭ ἀντιδιατίθημι

ἀντιδιατιθεμένους,[f] acc. pl. m. part. pres. mid. id.

ἀντιδιατίθημι], (ἀντί & διατίθημι) *to set opposite;* mid. *to be of an opposite opinion, to be adverse,* part. ἀντιδιατιθέμενος, *opponent.* L.G.

ἀντίδικος, ου, ὁ, ἡ, (§ 3. tab. C. a) (ἀντί & δίκη) *an opponent in a lawsuit,* Mat. 5. 25, bis; Lu. 12. 58; 18. 3; *an adversary,* 1 Pe. 5. 8.

ἀντιδίκου, gen. sing. masc. . . . ἀντίδικος

ἀντιδίκῳ, dat. sing. masc. . . . . id.

ἀντιθέσεις,[g] acc. pl. . . . . . ἀντίθεσις

ἀντίθεσις], εως, ἡ, (§ 5. tab. E. c) (ἀντί & τίθημι) pr. *opposition;* hence, *a question proposed for dispute, disputation.*

ἀντικαθίστημι], fut. καταστήσω, (§ 29. tab. X) (ἀντί & καθίστημι) trans. *to set in opposition;* intrans. aor. 2, ἀντικατέστην, *to withstand, resist,* He. 12. 4.

ἀντικαλέσωσι,[h] 3 pers. pl. aor. 1, subj. act. ἀντικαλέω

ἀντικαλέω, ῶ], (ἀντί & καλέω) *to invite in return.*

ἀντικατέστητε,[i] 2 pers. pl. aor. 2, ind. . ἀντικαθίστημι

ἀντίκειμαι], fut. είσομαι, (§ 33. tab. D.D) (ἀντί & κεῖμαι) pr. *to occupy an opposite position;* met. *to oppose, be adverse to,* Ga. 5. 17; 1 Ti. 1. 10; part. ἀντικείμενος, *opponent, hostile,* Lu. 13. 7, et al.

ἀντικείμενοι, nom. pl. masc. part. pres. . ἀντίκειμαι

ἀντικείμενος, nom. sing. masc. part. pres. . id.

---

[a] He. 12. 4. [b] Col. 1. 24. [c] Col. 3. 24. [d] 1 Pe. 2. 23. [e] Lu. 24. 17. [f] 2 Ti. 2. 25. [g] 1 Ti. 6. 20. [h] Lu. 14. 12. [i] He. 12. 4.

ἀντικειμένῳ, dat. sing. masc. part. pres. . ἀντίκειμαι
ἀντικειμένων, gen. pl. part. pres. . . id.
ἀντίκειται, 3 pers. sing. pres. ind. . . id.
ἀντικρύ,[a] adv. *opposite to, over against.*—Rec. Gr. Sch.
ἀντικρύς, Al. Ln. Tdf.
ἀντιλαμβάνεσθαι, pres. infin. . . ἀντιλαμβάνομαι
ἀντιλαμβανόμενοι, nom. pl. masc. part. pres. id.
ἀντιλαμβάνομαι], fut. λήψομαι, (§ 36. rem. 2) (ἀντιλαμβάνω, *to take in turn*) *to aid, assist, help,* Lu. 1. 54; Ac. 20. 35; *to be a recipient,* 1 Ti. 6. 2.

ἀντίληψις, εως, ἡ, (§ 5. tab. E. c) *aid, assistance;* meton. *one who aids or assists, a help,* 1 Co. 12. 28.

ἀντιλέγει, 3 pers. sing. pres. ind. act. . . ἀντιλέγω
ἀντιλέγεται, 3 pers. sing. pres. ind. pass. . id.
ἀντιλεγόμενον, acc. sing. neut. part. pres. pass. id.
ἀντιλέγοντα, acc. sing. masc. part. pres. act. . id.
ἀντιλέγοντας, acc. pl. masc. part. pres. act. id.
ἀντιλέγοντες, nom. pl. masc. part. pres. act. id.
ἀντιλεγόντων, gen. pl. masc. part. pres. act. id.
ἀντιλέγω], fut. λέξω, (§ 23. rem. 1. b) aor. 2, ἀντεῖπον, (ἀντί & λέγω) *to speak against, contradict; to gainsay, deny,* Lu. 20. 27; *to oppose,* Jno. 19. 12; Ac. 13. 45; 28. 19; Ro. 10. 21; Tit. 1. 9; 2. 9; pass. *to be spoken against, decried,* Lu. 2. 34; Ac. 28. 22.

ἀντιλογία, ας, ἡ, (§ 2. tab. B. b, and rem. 2) *contradiction, question,* He. 6. 16; 7. 7; *opposition, rebellion,* Jude 11; *contumely,* He. 12. 3.

ἀντιλήψεις,[b] acc. pl. . . . . ἀντίληψις
ἀντίληψις], εως, ἡ, (§ 5. tab. E. c) . ἀντιλαμβάνομαι
ἀντιλογία], ας, ἡ, (§ 2. tab. B. b, and rem. 2) ἀντιλέγω
ἀντιλογίᾳ, dat. sing. . . . ἀντιλογία
ἀντιλογίαν, acc. sing. . . . . . id.
ἀντιλογίας, gen. sing. . . . . . id.
ἀντιλοιδορέω, ῶ], fut. ήσω, (§ 16. tab. P) (ἀντί & λοιδορέω) *to reproach or revile again or in return,* 1 Pe. 2. 23. L.G.
ἀντίλυτρον,[c] ου, τό, (§ 3. tab. C. c) (ἀντί & λύτρον) *a ransom.* N.T.
ἀντιμετρηθήσεται, 3 p. s. fut. 1, pass. (§ 17. tab. Q) ἀντιμετρέω
ἀντιμετρέω, ῶ], fut. ήσω, (§ 16. tab. P) (ἀντί & μετρέω) *to measure in return,* Lu. 6. 38; Mat. 7. 2. N.T.
ἀντιμισθίαν, acc. sing. . . . . ἀντιμισθία

ἀντιμισθία], ας, ἡ, (§ 2. tab. B. b, and rem. 2) (ἀντί & μισθός) *a retribution, recompense,* Ro. 1. 27; 2 Co. 6. 13. L.G.
Ἀντιοχέα,[d] acc. sing. . . . . Ἀντιοχεύς
Ἀντιόχεια], ας, ἡ, (§ 2. tab. B. b, and rem. 2).—I. *Antioch,* the metropolis of Syria, where the disciples first received the name of Christians.—II. *Antioch,* a city of Pisidia, Ac. 13. 14; 14. 19; 2 Ti. 3. 11.
Ἀντιοχείᾳ, dat. sing. . . . Ἀντιόχεια
Ἀντιόχειαν, acc. sing. . . . . . id.
Ἀντιοχείας, gen. sing. . . . . . id.
Ἀντιοχεύς], εως, ὁ, (§ 5. tab. E. d) *an inhabitant of Antioch.*
ἀντιπαρέρχομαι], fut. ελεύσομαι, aor. 2, ῆλθον, (§ 36. rem. 1) (ἀντί & παρέρχομαι) *to pass over against, to pass along* without noticing, Lu. 10. 31, 32. L.G.
ἀντιπαρῆλθε, 3 pers. sing. aor. 2, ind. ἀντιπαρέρχομαι
Ἀντίπας, α, ὁ, (§ 2. rem. 4) *Antipas,* pr. name.—Rec. Gr. Sch. Tdf.
Ἀντείπας, A. (Re. 2. 13).
Ἀντιπατρίδα,[e] acc. sing. . . . Ἀντιπατρίς
Ἀντιπατρίς], ίδος, ἡ, (§ 4. rem. 2. c) *Antipatris,* a city of Palestine.
ἀντιπέραν,[f] adv. *over against, on the opposite side.*—Rec. Gr. Sch.
ἀντιπέρα, A. D. Ln. Tdf. (Lu. 8. 26).
ἀντιπίπτετε,[g] 2 pers. pl. pres. ind. . . ἀντιπίπτω
ἀντιπίπτω], fut. πεσοῦμαι, (§ 37. rem. 1) (ἀντί & πίπτω) pr. *to fall upon, rush upon* any one; hence, *to resist by force, oppose, strive against.*
ἀντιστῆναι, aor. 2, infin. (§ 29. tab. X) ἀνθίστημι
ἀντίστητε, 2 pers. pl. aor. 2, imper. . . id.
ἀντιστρατευόμενον,[h] acc. sing. masc. part. pr. ἀντιστρατεύομαι
ἀντιστρατεύομαι], (§ 15. tab. O) (ἀντί & στρατεύω) *to war against; to contravene, oppose.*
ἀντιτάσσεται, 3 pers. sing. pres. ind. mid. . ἀντιτάσσω
ἀντιτασσόμενος, nom. sing. masc. part. pr. mid. id.
ἀντιτασσομένων, gen. pl. masc. part. pres. mid. id.
ἀντιτάσσω], fut. τάξω, (§ 26. rem. 3) (ἀντί & τάσσω) *to post in adverse array,* as an army; mid. *to set one's self in opposition, resist,* Ac. 18. 6; Ro. 13. 2; Ja. 5. 6; *to be averse,* Ja. 4. 6; 1 Pe. 5. 5.
ἀντίτυπα, acc. pl. neut. . ἀντίτυπος
ἀντίτυπον, nom. sing. neut. . . . id.

[a] Ac. 20. 15. [b] 1 Co. 12. 28. [c] 1 Ti. 2. 6. [d] Ac. 6. 5. [e] Ac. 23. 31. [f] Lu. 8. 26. [g] Ac. 7. 51. [h] Ro. 7. 23.

ἀντίτυπος], ου, ὁ, ἡ, (§ 7. rem. 2) (ἀντί & τύπος) *of correspondent stamp or form; corresponding, in correspondent fashion*, 1 Pe. 3. 21; τὸ ἀντίτυπον, *a copy, representation*, He. 9. 24.

ἀντίχριστοι, nom. pl. . . . ἀντίχριστος

ἀντίχριστος, ου, ὁ, (§ 3. tab. C. a) (ἀντί & Χριστός) *antichrist, an opposer of Christ*, 1 Jno. 2 18, 22; 4. 3; 2 Jno. 7.

ἀντιχρίστου, gen. sing. . . . ἀντίχριστος

ἀντλεῖν, pres. infin. act. . . . . ἀντλέω

ἀντλέω, ῶ], fut. ήσω, (§ 16. tab. P) (ἄντλος, *a sink*) *to draw*, e.g. wine, water, etc.; Jno. 2. 8, 9; 4. 7, 15.

ἄντλημα, ατος, τό, (§ 4. tab. D. c) pr. *that which is drawn; a bucket, vessel for drawing water*. L.G.

ἄντλημα,[a] ατος, τό, acc. sing. . . ἀντλέω

ἀντλῆσαι, aor. 1, infin. act. . . . id.

ἀντλήσατε, 2 pers. pl. aor. 1, imper. act. . id.

ἀντοφθαλμεῖν,[b] pres. infin. . . ἀντοφθαλμέω

ἀντοφθαλμέω, ῶ], fut. ήσω, (§ 16. tab. P) (ἀντί & ὀφθαλμός) pr. *to look in the face*, i. e. rectis oculis; met. a nautical term, *to bear up against* the wind. L.G.

ἄνυδροι, nom. pl. fem. . . . . ανυδρος

ἄνυδρος], ου, ὁ, ἡ, (§ 7. rem. 2) (ἀ & ὕδωρ) *without water, dry*, 2 Pe. 2. 17; Jude 12. τόποι ἄνυδροι, *dry places*, and therefore, in the East, *barren, desert*, Mat. 12. 43; Lu. 11. 24.

ἀνύδρων, gen. pl. . . . . . ἄνυδρος

ἀνυπόκριτον, acc. sing. fem. . . . ἀνυπόκριτος

ἀνυπόκριτος, ου, ὁ, ἡ, (§ 7. rem. 2) (ἀ & ὑποκρίνομαι) *unfeigned, real, sincere*, Ro. 12. 9, et al. L.G.

ἀνυποκρίτου, gen. sing. fem. . . ἀνυπόκριτος

ἀνυποκρίτῳ, dat. sing. fem. . . . id.

ἀνυπότακτα, acc. pl. neut. . . ἀτυπότακτος

ἀνυπότακτοι, nom. pl. masc. . . . id.

ἀνυποτάκτοις, dat. pl. masc. . . . id.

ἀνυπότακτον, acc. sing. neut. . . . id.

ἀνυπότακτος], ου, ὁ, ἡ, (§ 7. rem. 2) (ἀ & ὑποτάσσω) *not subjected, not made subordinate*, He. 2. 8; *insubordinate, refractory, disorderly, contumacious, lawless*, 1 Ti. 1. 9; Tit. 1. 6, 10. L.G.

ἄνω, adv. *above*, Ac. 2. 19; *up, upwards*, Jno. 11. 41; ὁ, ἡ, τό, ἄνω, *that which is above*, Jno. 8. 23, et al.; ἕως ἄνω, *to the top*, Jno. 2. 7.

ἄνωθεν, adv. of place, *from above, from a higher place*, Jno. 3. 31, et al.; of time, *from the first or beginning*, Ac. 26. 5; *from the source*, Lu. 1. 33; *again, anew*, Jno. 3. 3, 7; Ga. 4. 9; with a preposition, *the top, or upper part*, Mat. 27. 51.

ἀνωτερικός, ή, όν, (§ 7. tab. F. a) *upper, higher, inland*, Ac. 19. 1. N.T.

ἀνώτερος, α, ον, (§ 7. rem. 1) (compar. of ἄνω) *higher, superior; to a higher place*, Lu. 14. 10; *above, before*, He. 10. 8. L.G.

ἀνῶ, 1 pers. sing. aor. 2, subj. act. . . ἀνίημι

ἀνώγεων, or ἀνώγαιον, or ἀνώγεον, or ἀνάγειον, ου, τό, (§ 3. tab. C. e) (ἄνω & γῆ) *an upper room or chamber*, Mar. 14. 15; Lu. 22. 12.

ἄνωθεν, adv. . . . . . . ἄνω

ἀνωρθώθη, 3 p.s. aor. 1, ind. pass. (§ 34. rem. 1. d) ἀνορθόω

ἀνωτερικά,[c] acc. pl. neut. . . . ἀνωτερικός

ἀνωτερικός, ή, όν, (§ 7. tab. F. a) . . ἄνω

ἀνώτερον, neut. sing. used adverbially . . ἀνώτερος

ἀνωφελεῖς, nom. pl. fem. . . . ἀνωφελής

ἀνωφελές, acc. sing. neut. . . . id.

ἀνωφελής], έος, ὁ, ἡ, τό, -ές, (§ 7. tab. G. b) (ἀ & ὠφελέω) *useless, unprofitable*, Tit. 3. 9; He. 7. 18.

ἄξει, 3 pers. sing. fut. 1, ind. act. . . ἄγω

ἄξια, nom. or acc. pl. neut. . . . ἄξιος

ἀξία, nom. sing. fem. . . . . id.

ἀξίνη, ης, ἡ, (§ 2. tab. B. a) *an axe*, Mat. 3. 10; Lu. 3. 9. (ῑ).

ἄξιοι, nom. pl. masc. . . . . ἄξιος

ἄξιον, nom. sing. neut. or acc. sing. masc. and neut. id.

ἄξιος, ια, ιον, (§ 7. rem. 1) pr. *of equal value; worthy, estimable*, Mat. 10. 11, 13, et al.; *worthy of, deserving*, either good or evil, Mat. 10. 10, et al.; *correspondent to*, Mat. 3. 8; Lu. 3. 8; Ac. 26. 20; *comparable, countervailing*, Ro. 8. 18; *suitable, due*, Lu. 23. 41.

ἀξιόω, ῶ, fut. ώσω, (§ 20. tab. T) perf. pass. ἠξίωμαι, *to judge or esteem worthy or deserving; to deem fitting, to require*, Ac. 15. 38; 28. 22.

a Jno. 4. 11. b Ac. 27. 15. c Ac. 19. 1.

ἀξίως, adv. *worthily*, Col. 1. 10, et al.; *suitably, in a manner becoming*, Ro. 16. 2, et al.

ἀξιοῦμεν, 1 pers. pl. pres. ind. act. . . ἀξιόω

ἀξίους, acc. pl. masc. . . . . ἄξιος

ἀξιούσθωσαν, 3 p. pl. pres. imper. pass. (§ 21. tab. U) ἀξιόω

ἀξιόω, ῶ], fut. ώσω, (§ 20. tab. T) . . ἄξιος

ἀξιωθήσεται, 3 pers. sing. fut. 1, ind. pass. . ἀξιόω

ἀξίως, adv. . . . . . . ἄξιος

ἀξιώσῃ, 3 pers. sing. aor. 1, subj. act. . . ἀξιόω

ἄξων, nom. sing. masc. part. fut. act. . ἄγω

ἀόρατα, nom. pl. neut. . . . . ἀόρατος

ἀόρατον, acc. sing. masc. . . . id.

ἀόρᾱτος], ου, ὁ, ἡ, τό, -ον, (§ 7. rem. 2) (ἀ & ὁράω) *invisible*, Ro. 1. 20; Col. 1. 15, 16; 1 Ti. 1. 17; He. 11. 27.

ἀοράτου, gen. sing. masc. . . . . ἀόρατος

ἀοράτῳ, dat. sing. masc. . . . id.

ἀπ', by apostrophe for ἀπό.

ἀπάγᾰγε, 2 p. sing. aor. 2, imper. (§ 13. rem. 7. b. d) ἀπάγω

ἀπαγάγετε, 2 pers. pl. aor. 2, imper. act. . id.

ἀπαγᾰγών, nom. sing. masc. part. aor. 2 . id.

ἀπαγγεῖλαι, aor. 1, infin. act. (§ 27. rem. 1. d) ἀπαγγέλλω

ἀπαγγείλατε, 2 pers. pl. aor. 1, imper. act. . id.

ἀπαγγελεῖ, 3 pers. sing. fut. ind. act. . id.

ἀπαγγέλλομεν, 1 pers. pl. pres. ind. act. . id.

ἀπαγγέλλοντας, acc. pl. masc. part. pres. act. id.

ἀπαγγέλλοντες, nom. pl. masc. part. pres. act. id.

ἀπαγγέλλουσα, nom. sing. fem. part. pres. act. id.

ἀπαγγέλλουσι, 3 pers. pl. pres. ind. act. . id.

ἀπαγγέλλω], fut. γελῶ, (§ 27. rem. 1. b) aor. 1, ἀπήγγειλα, (§ 27. rem. 1. d) aor. 2, pass. ἀπηγγέλην, (§ 27. rem. 4. a) (ἀπό & ἀγγέλλω) *to enounce that with which a person is charged, or which is called for by circumstances; to carry back word*, Mat. 2. 8, et al.; *to report*, Mat. 8. 33, et al.; *to declare plainly*, He. 2. 12; *to announce* formally, 1 Jno. 1. 2, 3.

ἀπαγγέλλων, nom. sing. masc. part. pres. act. ἀπαγγέλλω

ἀπαγγελῶ, 1 pers. sing. fut. ind. act. . . id.

ἀπάγειν, pres. infin. act.—A. Ln. Tdf. . } ἀπάγω
ἄγειν, Rec. Gr. Sch. (Ac. 23. 10) . }

ἀπάγετε, 2 p. pl. pres. imper. act.—B. D. Ln. } id.
ἀπαγάγετε, Rec. Gr. Sch. Tdf. (Mar. 14. 44) }

ἀπαγόμενοι, nom. pl. masc. part. pres. pass. id.

ἀπαγομένους, acc. pl. masc. part. pres. pass.—B. D. Tdf. . . . . } id.
ἀγομένους, Rec. Gr. Sch. Ln. (Lu. 21. 12) }

ἀπάγουσα, nom. sing. fem. part. pres. act. ἀπάγω

ἀπάγχω], fut. άγξω, (§ 23. rem. 1. b) (ἀπό & ἄγχω, *to compress*) *to strangle*; mid. *to choke or strangle one's self, hang one's self*, Mat. 27. 5.

ἀπάγω], fut. ξω, (§ 23. rem. 1. b) aor. 2, ἀπήγᾰγον, (§ 13. rem. 7. b. d) aor. 1, pass. ἀπήχθην, (ἀπό & ἄγω) *to lead away*, Mat. 26. 57, et al.; *to conduct*, Mat. 7. 13, 14; pass. *to be led off* to execution, Ac. 12. 19; met. *to be led astray, seduced*, 1 Co. 12. 2.

ἀπαίδευτος], ου, ὁ, ἡ, (§ 7. rem. 2) (ἀ & παιδεύω) *uninstructed, ignorant; silly, unprofitable*.

ἀπαιδεύτους,[a] acc. pl. fem. . . . ἀπαίδευτος

ἀπαίρω], fut. αρῶ, (§ 27. rem. 1. c) aor. 1, pass. ἀπήρθην, (§ 27. rem. 3) subj. ἀπαρθῶ, (ἀπό & αἴρω) *to take away*; pass. *to be taken away; to be withdrawn*, Mat. 9. 15; Mar. 2. 20; Lu. 5. 35.

ἀπαίτει, 2 pers. sing. pres. imper. . . ἀπαιτέω

ἀπαιτέω, ῶ], fut. ήσω, (§ 16. tab. P) (ἀπό & αἰτέω) *to demand, require*, Lu. 12. 20; *to demand back*, Lu. 6. 30.

ἀπαιτήσουσι, 3 pers. pl. fut. ind.—D. . } ἀπαιτέω
αἰτήσουσι, Rec. Gr. Sch. Tdf. (Lu. 12. 48) }

ἀπαιτοῦσι, 3 pers. pl. pres. ind. . . . id.

ἀπαλγέω, ῶ], fut. ήσω, perf. ἀπήλγηκα, (§ 16. tab. P) (ἀπό & ἀλγέω, *to be in pain, grieve*) pr. *to desist from grief*; hence, *to become insensible or callous*, Ep. 4. 19.

ἀπαλλαγῆναι, aor. 2, inf. pass.—D. . . } ἀπαλλάσσω
ἀπηλλάχθαι, Rec. Gr. Sch. Tdf. (Lu. 12. 58) }

ἀπαλλάχθαι, perf. inf. pass.—A. . } id.
ἀπηλλάχθαι, Rec. Gr. Sch. Tdf. (Lu. 12. 58) }

ἀπαλλάξῃ, 3 pers. sing. aor. 1, subj. act. . id.

ἀπαλλάσσω], fut. ξω, aor. 1, pass. ἀπηλλάχθην, (§ 26. rem. 3, 4) perf. pass. ἀπήλλαγμαι, (§ 26. rem. 3) aor. 2, pass. ἀπηλλάγην, (§ 26. rem. 3) (ἀπό & ἀλλάσσω) *to set free, deliver, set at liberty*, He. 2. 15; *to rid* judicially, Lu. 12. 58; mid. *to depart, remove*, Ac. 19. 12.

ἀπαλλάσσεσθαι, pres. infin. pass. . ἀπαλλάσσω

ἀπαλλοτριόω, ῶ], fut. ώσω, (§ 20. tab. T) perf. pass. ἀπηλλοτρίωμαι, (§ 21. tab. U) (ἀπό & ἀλλοτριόω, *to alienate*) pass. *to be alienated from, be a stranger to*; perf. part. ἀπηλλοτριωμένος, *alien*, Ep. 2. 12; 4. 18; Col. 1. 21.

[a] 2 Ti. 2. 23.

ἀπαλός, ή, όν, (§ 7. tab. F. a) *soft, tender,* Mat. 24. 32; Mar. 13. 28.

ἅπαν, nom. sing. neut. (§ 7. tab. H. b) . ἅπας

ἅπαντα, acc. sing. masc. . . . . id.

ἅπαντα, nom. and acc. pl. neut. . . id.

ἅπαντας, acc. pl. masc. . . . id.

ἀπαντάω, ῶ], fut. ήσω, (§ 18. tab. R) (ἀπό & ἀντάω, *to meet) to meet,* Mat. 28. 9, et al. *to encounter,* Lu. 14. 31.

ἀπάντησις, εως, ἡ, (§ 5. tab. E. c) *a meeting, encounter;* εἰς ἀπάντησιν, *to meet,* Mat. 25. 1, 6; Ac. 28. 15; 1 Thes. 4. 17. L.G.

ἅπαντες, nom. pl. masc. . . ἅπας

ἀπαντῆσαι, aor. 1, infin. . . . ἀπαντάω

ἀπαντήσει, 3 pers. sing. fut. ind. . id.

ἀπάντησιν, acc. sing. . . . ἀπάντησις

ἀπάντησις], εως, ἡ, (§ 5. tab. E. c) ἀπαντάω

ἁπάντων, gen. pl. neut. . . . . ἅπας

ἅπαξ, adv. *once,* 2 Co. 11. 25, et al.; *once for all,* He. 6. 4; 9. 26, 28; 10. 2; 1 Pe. 3. 18, 20; Jude 3; εἰδὼς ἅπαξ, *knowing once for ever, unfailingly, constantly,* Jude 5.

ἀπαράβατον,[a] acc. sing. fem. . . . ἀπαράβατος

ἀπαράβᾰτος], ου, ὁ, ἡ, (§ 7. rem. 2) (ἀ & παραβαίνω) *not transient; not to be superseded, unchangeable.* L.G.

ἀπαρασκεύαστος], ου, ὁ, ἡ, (§ 7. rem. 2) (ἀ & παρασκευάζω) *unprepared.*

ἀπαρασκευάστους,[b] acc. pl. masc. . ἀπαρασκεύαστος

ἀπαρθῇ, 3 pers. sing. aor. 1, subj. pass. . . ἀπαίρω

ἀπαρνέομαι, οῦμαι], fut. ήσομαι, fut. 2, pass. ἀπαρνηθήσομαι, (§ 17. tab. Q) (ἀπό & ἀρνέομαι) *to deny, disown,* Mat. 26. 34, et al.; *to renounce, disregard,* Mat. 16. 24, et al.

ἀπαρνηθήσεται, 3 pers. sing. fut. 1, pass. . ἀπαρνέομαι

ἀπαρνησάσθω, 3 pers. sing. aor. 1, imper. mid. id.

ἀπαρνήσει, 2 pers. sing. fut.—Att. B.
ἀπαρνήσῃ, Rec. Gr. Sch. Tdf. (Mat. 26. 34) } id.

ἀπαρνήσῃ, 2 pers. sing. fut. mid. . . id.

ἀπαρνήσομαι, 1 pers. sing. fut. mid. . . id.

ἀπαρνήσωμαι, 1 pers. sing. aor. 1, subj. mid.—A.
ἀπαρνήσομαι, R. Gr. Sch. Tdf. (Mat. 26. 35) } id.

ἀπάρτι, or ἀπ' ἄρτι, *forthwith, at once,* Jno. 13. 19; 14. 7; *henceforward,* Mat. 26. 29; Re. 14. 13; *hereafter,* Mat. 26. 64; Jno. 1. 52. N.T.

ἀπαρτισμόν,[c] acc. sing. . . . ἀπαρτισμός

ἀπαρτισμός], ου, ὁ, (§ 3. tab. C. a) (ἀπαρτίζω, *to perfect,* from ἀπό & ἄρτιος) *completion, perfection.* L.G.

ἀπαρχή, ῆς, ἡ, (§ 2. tab. B. a) (ἀπό & ἀρχή) pr. *the first act of a sacrifice;* hence, *the first-fruits, first portion, firstling,* Ro. 8. 23, et al.

ἀπαρχήν, acc. sing. . . . . . ἀπαρχή

ἅπας, ασα, αν, (§ 7. tab. H. b) (a strengthened form of πᾶς) *all, the whole.*

ἅπασαν, acc. sing. fem. . . ἅπας

ἅπασι, dat. pl. masc. . . . . id.

ἀπασπάζομαι], fut. άσομαι, *to salute, greet,* v.r. Ac. 21. 6.

ἀπάταις, dat. pl. . . . . . ἀπάτη

ἀπατάτω, 3 pers. sing. pres. imper. act. . . ἀπατάω

ἀπάτη, ης, ἡ, (§ 2. tab. B. a) *deceit, deception, delusion.* (ᾰ).

ἀπατάω, ῶ], fut. ήσω, (§ 18. tab. R) aor. 1, pass. ἠπατήθην, *to deceive, seduce into error,* Ep. 5. 6; 1 Ti. 2. 14; Ja. 1. 26.

ἀπάτῃ, dat. sing. . . . . . ἀπάτη

ἀπατηθεῖσα, nom. sing. fem. part. aor. 1, pass. (§ 19. tab. S) . . . ἀπατάω

ἀπάτης, gen. sing. . . . . . ἀπάτη

ἀπατῶν, nom. sing. masc. part. pres. act. . ἀπατάω

ἀπάτωρ,[d] ορος, ὁ, ἡ, (§ 4. rem. 2. f) (ἀ & πατήρ) pr. *without a father, fatherless;* hence, *independent of paternal descent.* (ᾰ).

ἀπαύγασμα,[e] ατος, τό, (§ 4. tab. D. c) (ἀπό & αὐγάζω) *an effulgence.* L.G.

ἀπαχθῆναι, aor. 1, inf. pass. (§ 23. rem. 4) . ἀπάγω

ἀπέβησαν, 3 pers. pl. aor. 2, ind. (§ 37. rem. 1) ἀποβαίνω

ἀπέβλεπε,[f] 3 pers. sing. imperf. . . ἀποβλέπω

ἀπέδειξε, 3 pers. sing. aor. 1, ind. (§ 31. rem. 1. b) ἀποδείκνυμι

ἀπεδέξαντο, 3 p. pl. aor. 1, ind. mid.—Al. Ln. Tdf.
ἐδέξαντο, Rec. Gr. Sch. (Ac. 21. 17) } ἀποδέχομαι

ἀπεδέξατο, 3 pers. sing. aor. 1, ind. . id.

ἀπεδέχετο, 3 pers. sing. imperf. . . id.

ἀπεδέχθησαν, 3 p. pl. aor. 1, ind. pass. (§ 23. rem. 4) id.

ἀπεδήμησε, 3 pers. sing. aor. 1, ind. . . ἀποδημέω

ἀπεδίδουν, 3 pers. pl. imperf. (§ 31. rem. 2) ἀποδίδωμι

ἀπεδοκίμασαν, 3 pers. pl. aor. 1, ind. . ἀποδοκιμάζω

ἀπεδοκιμάσθη, 3 pers. sing. aor. 1, ind. pass. . id.

ἀπέδοντο, 3 p. pl. aor. 2, ind. mid. (§ 30. tab. A. A) ἀποδίδωμι

ἀπέδοσθε, 2 pers. pl. aor. 2, ind. mid. . id.

ἀπέδοτο, 3 pers. sing. aor. 2, ind. mid. . . id.

ἀπέδωκε, 3 p. sing. aor. 1, ind. act. (§ 30. tab. Z) id.

---

a He. 7. 24. b 2 Co. 9. 4. c Lu. 14. 28. d He. 7. 3. e He. 1. 3. f He. 11. 26.

ἀπέθανε, 3 pers. sing. aor. 2, ind. (§ 36. rem. 4) ἀποθνήσκω
ἀπεθάνετε, 2 pers. pl. aor. 2, ind. . . id.
ἀπεθάνομεν, 1 pers. pl. aor. 2, ind. . . id.
ἀπέθανον, 1 pers. sing. aor. 2, ind. . . id.
ἀπέθανον, 3 pers. pl. aor. 2, ind. . . id.
ἀπέθεντο, 3 p. pl. aor. 2, ind. mid. (§ 28. tab. W) ἀποτίθημι
ἀπέθετο, 3 pers. sing. aor. 2, ind. mid.—B. Ln. } id.
ἔθετο, Rec. Gr. Sch. Tdf. (Mat. 14. 3) }
ἀπέθνησκε, 3 pers. sing. imperf. . . ἀποθνήσκω
ἀπεῖδον, subj. ἀπίδω, (ῐ), see ἀφοράω.
ἀπείθεια], ας, ἡ, (§ 2. tab. B. b, and rem. 2) ἀπειθής
ἀπειθείᾳ, dat. sing. . . . . . ἀπείθεια
ἀπείθειαν, acc. sing. . . . . . id.
ἀπειθείας, gen. sing. . . . . . id.
ἀπειθεῖς, nom. and acc. pl. masc. . . ἀπειθής
ἀπειθέω, ῶ], fut. ήσω, (§ 16. tab. P) . id.
ἀπειθής, έος, οῦς, ὁ, ἡ, (§ 7. tab. G. b) (ἀ & πείθω) *who will not be persuaded, uncompliant; disobedient,* Ac. 26. 19; Ro. 1. 30; 2 Ti. 3. 2; *untoward, contumacious,* Lu. 1. 17; Tit. 1. 16; 3. 3.

ἀπείθεια, ας, ἡ, (§ 2. tab. B. b, and rem. 2) *an uncompliant disposition; obstinacy, contumacy, disobedience, unbelief,* Ro. 11. 30, 32; Ep. 2. 2; 5. 6; He. 4. 6, 11; Col. 3. 6.

ἀπειθέω, ῶ, fut. ήσω, (§ 16. tab. P) *to be uncompliant; to refuse belief, disbelieve,* Jno. 3. 36, et al.; *to refuse belief and obedience, be contumacious,* Ro. 10. 21; 1 Pe. 3. 20. et al.; *to refuse conformity,* Ro. 2. 8.

ἀπειθήσαντες, nom. pl. masc. part. aor. 1.— A. B. C. Ln. Tdf. . . . } ἀπειθέω
ἀπειθοῦντες, Rec. Gr. Sch. (Ac. 14. 2) }
ἀπειθήσασι, dat. pl. masc. part. aor. 1 . id.
ἀπειθοῦντα, acc. sing. masc. part. pres. . id.
ἀπειθοῦντες, nom. pl. masc. part. pres. . id.
ἀπειθούντων, gen. pl. masc. part. pres. . . id.
ἀπειθοῦσι, 3 pers. pl. pres. ind. . . id.
ἀπειθοῦσι, dat. pl. masc. part. pres. . . id.
ἀπειθῶν, nom. sing. masc. part. pres. . id.
ἀπειλάς, acc. pl. . . . . . . ἀπειλή
ἀπειλή, ῆς, ἡ, (§ 2. tab. B. a) *threat, commination,* Ac. 4. 17, 29; 9. 1; *harshness of language,* Ep. 6. 9.

ἀπειλέω, ῶ], and, later, also ἀπειλοῦμαι, fut. ήσω, aor. 1, ἠπείλησα, (§ 16. tab. P) *to threaten, menace, rebuke,* Ac. 4. 17; 1 Pe. 2. 23.

ἀπειλῇ, dat. sing. . . . . . . ἀπειλή
ἀπειλήν, acc. sing. . . . . . id.
ἀπειλῆς, gen. sing. . . . . . . id.
ἀπειλησώμεθα, 1 pers. pl. aor. 1, subj. mid. ἀπειλέω
ἄπειμι, fut. ἔσομαι, (ἀπό & εἰμί) *to be absent.*

ἀπουσία, ας, ἡ, (§ 2. tab. B. b, and rem. 2) *absence,* Phi. 2. 12.

ἄπειμι, imperf. ἀπῄειν, (§ 33. rem. 4) (ἀπό & εἶμι, *to go*) *to go away, depart,* Ac. 17. 10.
ἀπειπάμεθα,[a] 1 pers. pl. aor. 1, mid. (§ 13. rem. 4) ἀπεῖπον
ἀπεῖπον, aor. 2, act. *to tell out; to refuse, forbid;* mid., aor. 1, ἀπειπάμην, *to renounce, disclaim.*
ἀπείραστος,[b] ου, ὁ, ἡ, (§ 7. rem. 2) (ἀ & πειράζω) *not having tried, inexperienced,* or, *untried,* or, *incapable of being tried.* L.G.
ἄπειρος,[c] ου, ὁ, ἡ, (§ 7. rem. 2) (ἀ & πεῖρα) *inexperienced, unskilful, ignorant.*
ἀπεκαλύφθη, 3 pers. sing. aor. 1, ind. pass. ἀποκαλύπτω
ἀπεκάλυψας, 2 pers. sing. aor. 1, ind. act. . id.
ἀπεκάλυψε, 3 pers. sing. aor. 1, ind. act. . id.
ἀπεκατεστάθη, 3 pers. sing. aor. 1, ind. pass. —Gr. Sch. Tdf. . . . } ἀποκαθίστημι
ἀποκατεστάθη, Rec. (Mar. 3. 5) . }
ἀπεκδέχεται, 3 pers. sing. pres. ind. . ἀπεκδέχομαι
ἀπεκδέχομαι], fut. έξομαι, (§ 23. rem. 1. b) (ἀπό & ἐκδέχομαι) *to expect, wait or look for,* Ro. 8. 19, 23, 25; 1 Co. 1. 7; Gal. 5. 5; Phi. 3. 20; He. 9. 28. L.G.
ἀπεκδεχόμεθα, 1 pers. pl. pres. ind. . ἀπεκδέχομαι
ἀπεκδεχόμενοι, nom. pl. masc. part. pres. id.
ἀπεκδεχομένοις, dat. pl. masc. part. pres. . id.
ἀπεκδεχομένους, acc. pl. masc. part. pres. . id.
ἀπεκδύομαι], fut. ύσομαι, (§ 15. tab. O) (ἀπό & ἐκδύω) *to put off, renounce,* Col. 3. 9; *to despoil* a rival, Col. 2. 15. L.G.

ἀπέκδυσις, εως, ἡ, (§ 5. tab. E. c) *a putting or stripping off, renunciation.* N.T.

ἀπεκδυσάμενοι, nom. pl. masc. part. aor. 1 ἀπεκδύομαι
ἀπεκδυσάμενος, nom. sing. masc. part. aor. 1 id.
ἀπεκδύσει,[d] dat. sing. . . . . ἀπέκδυσις
ἀπέκδυσις], εως, ἡ, (§ 5. tab. E. c) . ἀπεκδύομαι
ἀπεκεφάλισα, 1 pers. sing. aor. 1, ind. act. ἀποκεφαλίζω
ἀπεκεφάλισε, 3 pers. sing. aor. 1, ind. act. . id.
ἀπέκοψαν, 3 pers. pl. aor. 1, ind. act. . . ἀποκόπτω
ἀπέκοψε, 3 p. sing. aor. 1, ind. act. (§ 23. rem. 1. a. & 2) id.

[a] 2 Co. 4. 2. [b] Ja. 1. 13. [c] He. 5. 13. [d] Col. 2. 11.

ἀπεκρίθη, 3 pers. sing. aor. 1, ind. pass. . ἀποκρίνομαι

ἀπεκρίθην, 1 p. sing. aor. 1, ind. pass. (§ 27. rem. 3) id.

ἀπεκρίθης, 2 pers. sing. aor. 1, ind. pass. . id.

ἀπεκρίθησαν, 3 pers. pl. aor. 1, ind. pass. . id.

ἀπεκρίνατο, 3 pers. sing. aor. 1, ind. mid. . id.

ἀπέκρυψας, 2 pers. sing. aor. 1, ind. act. . ἀποκρύπτω

ἀπέκρυψε, 3 pers. sing. aor. 1, ind. act. . id.

ἀπεκτάνθη, 3 p. sing. aor. 1, ind. pass. (§ 37. rem. 1) ἀποκτείνω

ἀπεκτάνθησαν, 3 pers. pl. aor. 1, ind. pass. id.

ἀπέκτειναν, 3 p. pl. aor. 1, ind. act. (§ 27. rem. 1. d) id.

ἀπεκτείνατε, 2 pers. pl. aor. 1, ind. act. . id.

ἀπέκτεινε, 3 pers. sing. aor. 1, ind. act. . id.

ἀπεκύησε, 3 pers. sing. aor. 1, ind. . . ἀποκυέω

ἀπεκύλισε, 3 pers. sing. aor. 1, ind. act. . ἀποκυλίω

ἀπέλαβε, 3 p. sing. aor. 2, ind. act. (§ 36. rem. 2) ἀπολαμβάνω

ἀπέλαβες, 2 pers. sing. aor. 2, ind. act. . id.

ἀπελαύνω], fut. ελάσω, aor. 1, ἀπήλἄσα, (§ 36. rem. 2) (ἀπό & ἐλαύνω) *to drive away*, Ac. 18. 16.

ἀπελεγμόν,[a] acc. sing. . . . . ἀπελεγμός

ἀπελεγμός], οῦ, ὁ, (§ 3. tab. C. a) (ἀπελέγχω, *to refute*, from ἀπό & ἐλέγχω) pr. *refutation*; by impl. *disesteem, contempt*. N.T.

ἀπέλειχον,[b] 3 pers. pl. imperf. . . ἀπολείχω

ἀπελεύθερος,[c] ου, ὁ, ἡ, (§ 3. tab. C. a) (ἀπό & ἐλεύθερος) *a freed-man*.

ἀπελεύσομαι, 1 pers. sing. fut. ind. (§ 36. rem. 1) ἀπέρχομαι

ἀπελευσόμεθα, 1 pers. pl. fut. ind. . . id.

ἀπελεύσονται, 3 pers. pl. fut. ind. . . id.

ἀπελήλυθε, 3 pers. sing. 2 perf. ind. . . id.

ἀπεληλύθεισαν, 3 pers. pl. pluperf. . . id.

ἀπελθεῖν, aor. 2, infin. . . . . id.

ἀπέλθῃ, 3 pers. sing. aor. 2, subj.—Al. Ln. }
βληθῇ, Rec. Gr. Sch. Tdf. (Mat. 5. 30) } id.

ἀπέλθητε, 2 pers. pl. aor. 2, subj. . . id.

ἀπελθόντες, nom. pl. masc. part. aor. 2 . id.

ἀπελθόντι, dat. sing. masc. part. aor. 2 . id.

ἀπελθόντων, gen. pl. masc. part. aor. 2 . id.

ἀπελθοῦσα, nom. sing. fem. part. aor. 2 . id.

ἀπελθοῦσαι, nom. pl. fem. part. aor. 2 . id.

ἀπέλθω, 1 pers. sing. aor. 2, subj. . . id.

ἀπελθών, nom. sing. masc. part. aor. 2 . id.

ἀπέλθωσι, 3 pers. pl. aor. 2, subj. . . id.

ἀπέλειπον, 1 pers. sing. imperf.—A. . }
ἀπέλιπον, Rec. Gr. Sch. Tdf. (2 Ti. 4. 13) } ἀπολείπω

ἀπέλιπον, 1 p. sing. aor. 2, ind. act. (§ 24. rem. 9) id.

Ἀπελλῆν,[d] acc. sing. . . . . Ἀπελλῆς

Ἀπελλῆς,] οῦ, ὁ, (§ 2. tab. B. c) *Apelles*, proper name

ἀπελογεῖτο, 3 pers. sing. imperf. . . ἀπολογέομαι

ἀπελούσασθε, 2 p. pl. aor. 1, ind. mid. (§ 15. tab. O) ἀπολούω

ἀπελπίζοντες,[e] nom. pl. masc. part pres. . ἀπελπίζω

ἀπελπίζω], fut. ίσω, (§ 26. rem. 1) (ἀπό & ἐλπίζω) *to lay aside hope, despond, despair*; also, *to hope for* something *in return*. L.G.

ἀπέλυε, 3 pers. sing. imperf. . . . ἀπολύω

ἀπελύθησαν, 3 p. pl. aor. 1, ind. pass. (§ 14. tab. N) id.

ἀπελύοντο, 3 pers. pl. imperf. pass. . . id.

ἀπέλῡσαν, 3 p. pl. aor. 1, ind. act. (§ 13. tab. M) id.

ἀπέλῡσε, 3 pers. sing. aor. 1, ind. act. . . id.

ἀπέναντι, adv. (ἀπό & ἔναντι) *opposite to, over against*, Mat. 21. 2; 27. 61; *contrary to, in opposition to, against*, Ac. 17. 7; *before, in the presence of*, Mat. 27. 24; Ac. 3. 16. L.G.

ἀπενεγκεῖν, aor. 2, infin. act. (§ 36. rem. 1) ἀποφέρω

ἀπενεχθῆναι, aor. 1, infin. pass. . . . id.

ἀπενίψατο,[f] 3 p. sing. aor. 1, mid. (§ 23. rem. 5) ἀπονίπτω

ἀπέπεσον,[g] 3 p. pl. aor. 2, ind. (§ 37. rem. 1) ἀποπίπτω

ἀπεξεδέχετο, 3 p. sing. imperf.—Gr. Sch. Tdf. }
ἅπαξ ἐξεδέχετο, Rec. (1 Pe. 3. 20) } ἀπεκδέχομαι

ἀπεπλανήθησαν, 3 pers. pl. aor. 1, ind. pass. (§ 19. tab. S) . . . ἀποπλανάω

ἀπέπλευσαν, 3 pers. pl. aor. 1, ind. . . ἀποπλέω

ἀπέπλυναν,[h] 3 pers. pl. aor. 1, ind. . . ἀποπλύνω

ἀπεπνίγη, 3 p. sing. aor. 2, ind. pass. (§ 24. rem. 6) ἀποπνίγω

ἀπέπνιξαν, 3 pers. pl. aor. 1, ind. act. . . id.

ἀπεράντοις,[i] dat. pl. fem. . . . ἀπέραντος

ἀπέραντος], ου, ὁ, ἡ, (§ 7. rem. 2) (ἀ & πέρας) *unlimited, interminable, endless*.

ἀπερισπάστως,[k] adv. (ἀ & περισπάω) *without distraction, without care or solicitude*. L.G.

ἀπερίτμητοι,[l] voc. pl. masc. . . ἀπερίτμητος

ἀπερίτμητος], ου, ὁ, ἡ, τό, -ον, (§ 7. rem. 2) (ἀ & περιτέμνω) pr. *uncircumcised*; met. *uncircumcised* in respect of untowardness and obduracy. L.G.

ἀπέρχεσθαι, pres. infin.—Al. Ln. Tdf. . }
πορεύεσθαι, Rec. Gr. Sch. (Ac. 23. 32) } ἀπέρχομαι

ἀπέρχῃ, 2 pers. sing. pres. subj. . . . id.

ἀπέρχομαι], fut. ελεύσομαι, aor. 2, ῆλθον, (§ 36 rem. 1) pass. ἀπελήλῠθα, (ἀπό & ἔρχομαι) *to go away, depart*, Mat. 8. 18, et al.; *to go forth, pervade*, as a rumour, Mat. 4. 24; *to arrive at* a destination, Lu.

[a] Ac. 19. 27. [b] Lu. 16. 21. [c] 1 Co. 7. 22. [d] Ro. 16. 10. [e] Lu. 6. 35. [f] Mat. 27. 24. [g] Ac. 8. 16. [h] Lu. 5. 2. [i] 1 Ti. 1. 4. [k] 1 Co. 7. 35. [l] Ac. 7. 51.

23.33; *to pass away, disappear*, Re. 21.4; in N.T. ἀπέρχομαι ὀπίσω, *to follow*, Mar. 1. 20, et al.

ἀπερχομένων, gen. pl. part. pres. . . ἀπέρχομαι
ἀπέσπᾰσε, 3 pers. sing. aor. 1, ind. act. . ἀποσπάω
ἀπεσπάσθη, 3 pers. sing. aor. 1, ind. pass. . id.
ἀπεστάθη, 3 pers. sing. aor. 1, ind. pass.—D. } ἀφίστημι
ἀπεσπάσθη, Rec. Gr. Sch. Tdf. (Lu. 22.41) }
ἀπεστάλη, 3 p. sing. aor. 2, ind. pass. (§ 27. rem. 4. b) ἀποστέλλω
ἀπεστάλην, 1 pers. sing. aor. 2, ind. pass. . id.
ἀπέσταλκα, 1 p. sing. perf. ind. act. (§ 27. rem. 2. b) id.
ἀπεστάλκαμεν, 1 pers. pl. perf. ind. act. . id.
ἀπεστάλκασι, 3 pers. pl. perf. ind. act. . id.
ἀπεστάλκατε, 2 pers. pl. perf. ind. act. . id.
ἀπέσταλκε, 3 pers. sing. perf. ind. act. . . id.
ἀπέσταλμαι, 1 pers. sing. perf. ind. pass. . id.
ἀπεσταλμένα, nom. pl. neut. part. perf. pass. id.
ἀπεσταλμένοι, nom. pl. masc. part. perf. pass. id.
ἀπεσταλμένος, nom. sing. masc. part. p. pass. id.
ἀπεσταλμένους, acc. pl. masc. part. perf. pass. id.
ἀπεστέγᾰσαν,[a] 3 pers. pl. aor. 1, ind. act. ἀποστεγάζω
ἀπέστειλα, 1 p. sing. aor. 1, ind. (§ 27. rem. 1. d) ἀποστέλλω
ἀπεστείλαμεν, 1 p. pl. aor. 1, ind.—B. D. Ln. } id.
ἐπεστείλαμεν, R. Gr. Sch. Tdf. (Ac. 21.25) }
ἀπέστειλαν, 3 pers. pl. aor. 1, ind. act. . id.
ἀπέστειλας, 2 pers. sing. aor. 1, ind. act. . id.
ἀπέστειλε, 3 pers. sing. aor. 1, ind. act. . id.
ἀπεστερημένος, nom. sing. masc. part. perf. pass. ἀποστερέω
ἀπεστερημένων, gen. pl. part. perf. pass. . id.
ἀπέστη, 3 pers. sing. aor. 2, ind. (§ 29. tab. X) ἀφίστημι
ἀπέστησαν, 3 pers. pl. aor. 2, ind. . . id.
ἀπέστησε, 3 pers. sing. aor. 1, ind. act. . id.
ἀπεστραμμένων, gen. pl. part. perf. pass.—D. } ἀποστρέφω
ἀπεστερημένων, Rec. Gr. Sch. Tdf. (1 Ti. 6.5) }
ἀπεστράφησαν, 3 pers. pl. aor. 2, ind. pass. (§ 24. rem. 10) . . . . id.
ἀπέστρεψε, 3 pers. sing. aor. 1, ind. (§ 23. rem. 2) id.
ἀπετάξατο, 3 pers. sing. aor. 1, ind. mid. (§ 26. rem. 3) . . . . ἀποτάσσομαι
ἀπεφθέγξατο, 3 pers. sing. aor. 1, ind. mid. (§ 23. rem. 1. b) . . ἀποφθέγγομαι
ἀπέχει, 3 pers. sing. pres. ind. . . . ἀπέχω
ἀπέχεσθαι, pres. infin. mid. . . . id.
ἀπέχεσθε, 2 pers. pl. pres. imper. mid. . . id.
ἀπέχετε, 2 pers. pl. pres. ind. act. . . id.
ἀπέχῃς, 2 pers. sing. pres. subj. act. . . id.
ἀπέχοντος, gen. sing. masc. part. pres. act. id.
ἀπέχουσαν, acc. sing. fem. part. pres. act. . id.
ἀπέχουσι, 3 pers. pl. pres. ind. act. . . ἀπέχω

ἀπέχω, fut. ἀφέξω, (§ 35. rem. 4) (ἀπό & ἔχω) trans. *to have in full* what is due or is sought, Mat. 6. 2, 5, 16; Lu. 6. 24; Phi. 4. 18; *to have altogether*, Phile. 15; hence, impers. ἀπέχει, *it is enough*, Mar. 14. 41; intrans. *to be distant*, Lu. 7. 6, et al.; *to be estranged*, Mat. 15. 8; Mar. 7. 6; mid. *to abstain from*, Ac. 15. 20, et al.

ἀπεχωρίσθη, 3 pers. sing. aor. 1, ind. pass. ἀποχωρίζω
ἀπήγαγε, 3 pers. sing. aor. 2, ind. (§ 13. rem. 7. d) ἀπάγω
ἀπήγαγον, 3 pers. pl. aor. 2, ind. act. . id.
ἀπήγγειλαν, 3 p. pl. aor. 1, ind. (§ 27. rem. 1. d) ἀπαγγέλλω
ἀπήγγειλε, 3 pers. sing. aor. 1, ind. act. . id.
ἀπηγγέλη, 3 p. sing. aor. 2, ind. pass. (§ 27. rem. 4. a) id.
ἀπήγγελλον, 1 pers. sing. imperf. act. . id.
ἀπήγξατο,[b] 3 p. sing. aor. 1, ind. mid. (§ 23. rem. 1. b) ἀπάγχω
ἀπῆγον, 3 pers. pl. aor. 2, ind. act.—B. } ἀπάγω
ἀπήγαγον, Rec. Gr. Sch. Tdf. (Lu. 23.26) }
ἀπῄεσαν,[c] 3 pers. pl. imperf. (§ 33. rem. 4) . ἄπειμι
ἀπήλασε,[d] 3 pers. sing. aor. 1, ind. (§ 36. rem. 2) ἀπελαύνω
ἀπηλγηκότες,[e] nom. pl. masc. part. perf. . ἀπαλγέω
ἀπῆλθα, 1 p. sing. aor. 1, (§ 35. rem. 12).—Ln. Tdf. } ἀπέρχομαι
ἀπῆλθον, Rec. Gr. Sch. (Re. 10. 9) }
ἀπῆλθαν, 3 pers. pl. aor. 1, ind.—B. D. Ln. Tdf. } id.
ἀπῆλθον, Rec. Gr. Sch. (Jno. 18. 6) }
ἀπῆλθε, 3 pers. sing. aor. 2, ind. (§ 36. rem. 1) id.
ἀπῆλθον, 1 pers. sing. and 3 pers. pl. aor. 2, ind. id.
ἀπηλλάχθαι, perf. inf. pass. (§ 26. rem. 3) ἀπαλλάττω
ἀπηλλοτριωμένοι, nom. pl. masc. part. perf. p. ἀπαλλοτριόω
ἀπηλλοτριωμένους, acc. pl. masc. part. perf. p. id.
ἀπηλπικότες, nom. pl. masc. part. perf.—D. } ἀπελπίζω
ἀπηλγηκότες, Rec. Gr. Sch. Tdf. (Ep. 4.19) }
ἀπήνεγκαν, 3 pers. pl. aor. 1, ind. (§ 36. rem. 1) ἀποφέρω
ἀπήνεγκε, 3 pers. sing. aor. 1, ind. . . id.
ἀπήντησαν, 3 pers. pl. aor. 1, ind. . . ἀπαντάω
ἀπήντησε, 3 pers. sing. aor. 1, ind. . . id.
ἀπησπασάμεθα, 1 p. pl. aor. 1, ind.—Al. Ln. Tdf. } ἀπασπάζομαι
ἀσπασάμενοι, Rec. Gr. Sch. (Ac. 21.6) }
ἀπίδω, 1 pers. sing. aor. 2, subj. (§ 36. rem. 1) ἀφοράω

ἄπιστος, ου, ὁ, ἡ, τό, -ον, (§ 7. rem. 2) (ἀ & πιστός) *unbelieving, without confidence* in any one, Mat. 17. 17, et al.; *violating one's faith, unfaithful, false, treacherous*, Lu. 12. 46; *an unbeliever, infidel, pagan*, 1 Co. 6. 6, et al.; pass. *incredible*, Ac. 26. 8.

ἀπιστέω, ῶ], fut. ήσω, (§ 16. tab. P) *to refuse belief, be incredulous, disbelieve*, Mar.

[a] Mar. 2. 4. [b] Mat. 27. 5. [c] Ac. 17. 10. [d] Ac. 18. 16. [e] Ep. 4. 19.

16. 11, 16; Lu. 24. 11, 41; Ac. 28. 24; *to prove false, violate one's faith, be unfaithful,* 2 Ti. 2. 13; Ro. 3. 3.

ἀπιστία, ας, ἡ, (§ 2. tab. B. b, and rem. 2) *unbelief, want of trust and confidence; a state of unbelief,* 1 Ti. 1. 13; *violation of faith, faithlessness,* Ro. 3. 3; He. 3. 12, 19.

ἀπιστήσας, nom. sing. masc. part. aor. 1 . ἀπιστέω

ἀπιστία, ας, ἡ, (§ 2. tab. B. b, and rem. 2) . ἄπιστος

ἀπιστίᾳ, dat. sing. . . . . ἀπιστία

ἀπιστίαν, acc. sing. . . . . id.

ἀπιστίας, gen. sing. . . . . id.

ἄπιστοι, nom. pl. masc. . . . . ἄπιστος

ἀπίστοις, dat. pl. masc. . . . . id.

ἄπιστον, nom. neut. and acc. sing. masc. and fem. id.

ἀπίστου, gen. sing. masc. . . . . id.

ἀπιστοῦμεν, 1 pers. pl. pres. ind. . . ἀπιστέω

ἀπιστούντων, gen. pl. masc. part. pres. . id.

ἀπιστοῦσι, dat. pl. masc. part. pres.—B. } id.
ἀπειθοῦσι, Rec. Gr. Sch. Tdf. (1 Pe. 2. 7) }

ἀπίστων, gen. pl. . . . . ἄπιστος

ἁπλόος, όη, όον, contr. οῦς, ῆ, οῦν, (§ 7. rem. 5. b) pr. *single;* hence, *simple, uncompounded; sound, perfect,* Mat. 6. 22; Lu. 11. 34.

ἁπλότης, ητος, ἡ, (§ 4. rem. 2. c) *simplicity, sincerity, purity or probity of mind,* Ro. 12. 8; 2 Co. 1. 12; 11. 3; Ep. 6. 5; Col. 3. 22; *liberality,* as arising from simplicity and frankness of character, 2 Co. 8. 2; 9. 11, 13.

ἁπλῶς, adv. *in simplicity; sincerely, really,* or, *liberally, bountifully,* Ja. 1. 5.

ἁπλότης], ητος, ἡ, (§ 4. rem. 2. c) . . ἁπλόος

ἁπλότητα, acc. sing. . . . . ἁπλότης

ἁπλότητι, dat. sing. . . . . id.

ἁπλότητος, gen. sing. . . . . id.

ἁπλῶς,[a] adv. . . . . ἁπλόος

ἀπό, prep., pr. *forth from, away from;* hence, it variously signifies *departure; distance of time or place; avoidance; riddance; derivation from a quarter, source, or material; origination from agency or instrumentality.*

ἀποβαίνω], fut. βήσομαι, aor. 2, ἀπέβην, (§ 37. rem. 1) (ἀπό & βαίνω) *to step off; to disembark* from a ship, Lu. 5. 2; Jno. 21. 9; *to become, result, happen,* Lu. 21. 13; Phi. 1. 19.

ἀποβάλητε, 2 pers. pl. aor. 2, subj. act. . ἀποβάλλω

ἀποβάλλω], fut. βαλῶ, aor. 2, ἀπέβᾰλον, (§ 27. rem. 2. d) (ἀπό & βάλλω) *to cast or throw off, cast aside,* Mar. 10. 50.

ἀπόβλητος, ου, ὁ, ἡ, τό, -ον, (§ 7 rem. 2) pr. *to be cast away;* met. *to be contemned, regarded as vile,* 1 Ti. 4. 4.

ἀποβολή, ῆς, ἡ, (§ 2. tab. B. a) *a casting off; rejection, reprobation,* Ro. 11. 15; *loss, deprivation,* of life, etc., Ac. 27. 22.

ἀποβαλώμεθα, 1 pers. pl. aor. 2, subj. mid.—D. } ἀποβάλλω
ἀποθώμεθα, Rec. Gr. Sch. Tdf. (Ro. 13. 12) }

ἀποβαλών, nom. sing. masc. part. aor. 2 . id.

ἀποβάντες, nom. pl. masc. part. aor. 2 . . ἀποβαίνω

ἀποβήσεται, 3 pers. sing. fut. ind. mid. . id.

ἀποβλέπω], fut. ψω, (§ 23. rem. 1. a) (ἀπό & βλέπω) pr. *to look off from all other objects and at a single one;* hence, *to turn a steady gaze, to look with fixed and earnest attention,* He. 11. 26.

ἀπόβλητον,[b] nom. sing. neut. . . . ἀπόβλητος

ἀπόβλητος], ου, ὁ, ἡ, (§ 7. rem. 2) . ἀποβάλλω

ἀποβολή, ῆς, ἡ, (§ 2. tab. B. a) . . id.

ἀπογεγραμμένων, gen. pl. part. perf. pass. . ἀπογράφω

ἀπογενόμενοι,[c] nom. pl. masc. part. aor. 2 . ἀπογίνομαι

ἀπογίνομαι], aor. 2, ἀπεγενόμην, (§ 37. rem. 1) (ἀπό & γίνομαι) *to be away from, unconnected with; to die;* met. *to die* to a thing by renouncing it.

ἀπογράφεσθαι, pres. infin. pass. and mid. . ἀπογράφω

ἀπογραφή, ῆς, ἡ, (§ 2. tab. B. a) . . id.

ἀπογραφῆς, gen. sing. . . . . ἀπογραφή

ἀπογράφω], fut. ψω, (§ 23. rem. 1. a) (ἀπό & γράφω) pr. *to copy;* hence, *to register, enrol,* Lu. 2. 1; He. 12. 23; mid. *to procure the registration of one's name, to give in one's name for registration,* Lu. 2. 3, 5.

ἀπογρᾰφή, ῆς, ἡ, (§ 2. tab. B. a) *a register, inventory; registration, enrolment,* Lu. 2. 2; Ac. 5. 37.

ἀπογράψασθαι, aor. 1, infin. mid. . . ἀπογράφω

ἀποδεδειγμένον, acc. sing. masc. part. perf. pass. (§ 31. rem. 1. b) . . . ἀποδείκνυμι

ἀποδεδοκιμασμένον, acc. sing. part. p. pass. ἀποδοκιμάζω

ἀποδείκνῡμι], fut. δείξω, (§ 31. tab. BB) *to point out, display; to prove, evince, demonstrate,* Ac. 25. 7; *to designate, proclaim, hold forth,*

[a] Ja. 1. 5. [b] 1 Ti. 4. 4. [c] 1 Pe. 2. 24.

2 Thes. 2. 4; *to constitute, appoint,* Ac. 2. 22; 1 Co. 4. 9; 2 Thes. 2. 4.

ἀπόδειξις, εως, ἡ, (§ 5. tab. E. c) *manifestation, demonstration, indubitable proof.*

ἀποδεικνύντα, acc. sing. masc. part. pres. — ἀποδείκνυμι

ἀποδεικνύοντα, acc. sing. masc. part. pres.—A. } ἀποδεικνύω
ἀποδεικνύντα, R. Gr. Sch. Tdf. (2 Thes. 2. 4) }

ἀποδεικνύω], same signif. as ἀποδείκνυμι. v. r.

ἀποδεῖξαι, aor. 1, infin. — ἀποδείκνυμι

ἀποδείξει,[a] dat. sing. — ἀπόδειξις

ἀπόδειξις], εως, ἡ, (§ 5. tab. E. c) — ἀποδείκνυμι

ἀποδεκταοῦν, pres. infin. — ἀποδεκατόω

ἀποδεκατοῦτε, 2 pers. pl. pres. ind. — id.

ἀποδεκατόω, ῶ, fut. ώσω, (§ 20. tab. T) (ἀπό & δεκατόω) *to pay or give tithes of,* Mat. 23. 23; Lu. 11. 42; 18. 12; *to tithe, levy tithes upon,* He. 7. 5. LXX.

ἀπόδεκτον, nom. sing. neut. — ἀπόδεκτος

ἀπόδεκτος], ου, ὁ, ἡ, (§ 7. rem. 2) — ἀποδέχομαι

ἀποδεξάμενοι, nom. pl. masc. part. aor. 1 — id.

ἀποδεξάμενος, nom. sing. masc. part. aor. 1. } id.
—Al. Ln. Tdf. }
δεξάμενος, Rec. Gr. Sch. (Lu. 9. 11) }

ἀποδέξασθαι, aor. 1, infin. — id.

ἀποδέχομαι], fut. δέξομαι, (§ 23. rem. 1. b) (ἀπό & δέχομαι) *to receive* kindly or heartily, *welcome,* Lu. 8. 40; Ac. 15. 4; 18. 27; 28. 30; *to receive* with hearty assent, *embrace,* Ac. 2. 41; *to accept* with satisfaction, Ac. 24. 3.

ἀπόδεκτος, ου, ὁ, ἡ, τό, -ον, (§ 7. rem. 2) *acceptable,* 1 Ti. 2. 3; 5. 4. L.G.

ἀποδοχή, ῆς, ἡ, (§ 2. tab. B. a) pr. *reception, welcome;* met. *reception* of hearty assent, 1 Ti. 1. 15; 4. 9.

ἀποδεχόμεθα, 1 pers. pl. pres. ind. — ἀποδέχομαι

ἀποδημέω, ῶ], fut. ήσω, (§ 16. tab. P) — ἀπόδημος

ἀπόδημος,[b] ου, ὁ, ἡ, (§ 7. rem. 2) (ἀπό & δῆμος) *absent* in foreign countries.

ἀποδημέω, ῶ, fut. ήσω, (§ 16. tab. P) *to be absent from one's home or country; to go on travel,* Mat. 21. 33; 25. 14, 15; Mar. 12. 1; Lu. 15. 13; 20. 9.

ἀποδημῶν, nom. sing. masc. part. pres. — ἀποδημέω

ἀποδιδόναι, pres. infin. act. — ἀποδίδωμι

ἀποδιδόντες, nom. pl. masc. part. pres. act. — id.

ἀποδιδότω, 3 pers. sing. pres. imper. act. — id.

ἀποδιδοῦν, neut. sing. part. pres. act. — ἀποδίδωμι

ἀποδιδούς, [ἕκαστος], nom. sing. part. pres. } id.
—Const. }
ἀποδιδοῦν, Rec. Gr. Sch. Tdf. (Re. 22. 2) }

ἀποδίδωμι, fut. ἀποδώσω, aor. 1, ἀπέδωκα, aor. 2, ἀπέδων, aor. 1, pass. ἀπεδόθην, (§ 30. tab. Z) (ἀπό & δίδωμι) *to give in answer to a claim or expectation; to render* a due, Mat. 12. 36; 16. 27; 21. 41; 22. 21, et al.; *to recompense,* Mat. 6. 4, 6, 18; *to discharge* an obligation, Mat. 5. 33; *to pay* a debt, Mat. 5. 26, et al.; *to render back, requite,* Ro. 12. 17, et al.; *to give back, restore,* Lu. 4. 20; 9. 42; *to refund,* Lu. 10. 35; 19. 8; mid., *to sell,* Ac. 5. 8; 7. 9; He. 12. 16; pass., *to be sold,* Mat. 18. 25; *to be given up* at a request, Mat. 27. 58.

ἀποδίδωσι, 3 pers. sing. pres. ind. act. — ἀποδίδωμι

ἀποδιορίζοντες,[c] nom. pl. masc. part. pres. — ἀποδιορίζω

ἀποδιορίζω], fut. ίσω, (§ 26. rem. 1) (ἀπό & διορίζω, *to set bounds*) pr. *to separate by intervening boundaries; to separate.* N.T.

ἀποδοθῆναι, aor. 1, infin. pass. (§ 30. rem. 4) — ἀποδίδωμι

ἀποδοκιμάζω], fut. άσω, (§ 26. rem. 1) (ἀπό & δοκιμάζω) *to reject upon trial; to reject,* Mat. 21. 42; Mar. 12. 10; Lu. 20. 17; 1 Pe. 2. 4, 7; pass., *to be disallowed* a claim, Lu. 9. 22; 17. 25; He. 12. 17.

ἀποδοκιμασθῆναι, aor. 1, inf. pass. — ἀποδοκιμάζω

ἀπόδος, 2 p. sing. aor. 2, imper. act. (§ 30. rem. 1) — ἀποδίδωμι

ἀπόδοτε, 2 pers. pl. aor. 2, imper. act. — id.

ἀποδοῦναι, aor. 2, infin. act. — id.

ἀποδούς, nom. sing. masc. part. aor. 2, act. — id.

ἀποδοχή], ῆς, ἡ, (§ 2. tab. B. a) — ἀποδέχομαι

ἀποδοχῆς, gen. sing. — ἀποδοχή

ἀποδῷ, 3 pers. sing. aor. 2, subj. act. — ἀποδίδωμι

ἀποδῴη, 3 pers. sing. aor. 2, opt. L.G. (§ 30. rem. 5) — id.

ἀποδῷς, 2 pers. sing. aor. 2, subj. act. — id.

ἀποδώσει, 3 pers. sing. fut. ind. act. — id.

ἀποδώσεις, 2 pers. sing. fut. ind. act. — id.

ἀποδώσοντες, nom. pl. masc. part. fut. act. — id.

ἀποδώσουσι, 3 pers. pl. fut. ind. act. — id.

ἀποδώσω, 1 pers. sing. fut. ind. act. — id.

ἀποθανεῖν, aor. 2, infin. (§ 36. rem. 4) — ἀποθνήσκω

ἀποθανεῖσθε, 2 pers. pl. fut. ind. mid. — id.

ἀποθανεῖται, 3 pers. sing. fut. ind. mid. — id.

ἀποθάνῃ, 3 pers. sing. aor. 2, subj. — id.

ἀποθανόντα, nom. pl. neut. part. aor. 2 — id.

---

[a] 1 Co. 2. 4. [b] Mar. 13. 34. [c] Jude 19.

ἀποθανόντες, nom. pl. masc. part. aor. 2,—Gr. Sch. Tdf.
ἀποθανόντος, Rec. (Ro. 7. 6) . . } ἀποθνήσκω
ἀποθανόντι, dat. sing. masc. part. aor. 2 . id.
ἀποθανόντος, gen. sing. masc. part. aor. 2 . id.
ἀποθανοῦνται, 3 pers. pl. fut. mid.—Const.
ἀπολοῦνται, R. Gr. Sch. Tdf. (Mat. 26. 52) } id.
ἀποθάνωμεν, 1 pers. pl. aor. 2, subj. . . id.
ἀποθανών, nom. sing. masc. part. aor. 2 . id.
ἀποθέμενοι, nom. pl. masc. part. aor. 2, mid. (§ 28. tab. W) . . . . ἀποτίθημι
ἀποθέσθαι, aor. 2, infin. mid. . . . id.
ἀπόθεσθε, 2 pers. pl. aor. 2, imper. mid. . id.
ἀπόθεσις, εως, ἡ, (§ 5. tab. E. c) . . id.
ἀποθήκας, acc. pl. . . . . . ἀποθήκη
ἀποθήκη, ης, ἡ, (§ 2. tab. B. a) . . ἀποτίθημι
ἀποθήκην, acc. sing. . . . . ἀποθήκη
ἀποθησαυρίζοντας,[a] acc. pl. masc. part. pr. ἀποθησαυρίζω
ἀποθησαυρίζω], fut. ίσω, (§ 26. rem. 1) (ἀπό & θησαυρίζω) pr. *to lay up in store, hoard*; met. *to treasure up, secure*. L.G.
ἀποθλίβουσι,[b] 3 pers. pl. pres. ind. act. . ἀποθλίβω
ἀποθλίβω], fut. ψω, (§ 23. rem. 1. a) (ἀπό & θλίβω) pr. *to press out; to press close, press upon, crowd*. (ῑ).
ἀποθνήσκει, 3 pers. sing. pres. ind. . . ἀποθνήσκω
ἀποθνήσκειν, pres. infin. . . . . id.
ἀποθνήσκομεν, 1 pers. pl. pres. ind. . . id.
ἀποθνήσκοντες, nom. pl. masc. part. pres. . id.
ἀποθνήσκουσα, nom. sing. fem. part. pres.—D.
ἀπέθνησκεν, Rec. Gr. Sch. Tdf. (Lu. 8. 42) } id.
ἀποθνήσκουσι, 3 pers. pl. pres. ind. . . id.
ἀποθνήσκω, fut. θανοῦμαι, aor. 2, ἀπέθᾰνον, (§ 36. rem. 4) (ἀπό & θνήσκω) *to die*, Mat. 8. 32, et al.; *to become putrescent, rot*, as seeds, Jno. 12. 24; 1 Co. 15. 36; *to wither, become dry*, as a tree, Jude 12; met. *to die* the death of final condemnation and misery, Jno. 6. 50; 8. 21, 24; *to die* to a thing by renunciation or utter separation, Ro. 6. 2; Gal. 2. 19; Col. 3. 3.
ἀποθνήσκωμεν, 1 pers. pl. pres. subj. . ἀποθνήσκω
ἀποθνήσκων, nom. sing. masc. part. pres. . id.
ἀποθώμεθα, 1 pers. pl. aor. 2, subj. mid. . ἀποτίθημι
ἀποκαθιστᾷ, 3 p. sing. pres. ind. (§ 31. rem. 2) ἀποκαθίστημι
ἀποκαθιστάνει, 3 pers. sing. pres. ind.—A. B. D. Ln. Tdf. . .
ἀποκαθιστᾷ, Rec. Gr. Sch. (Mar. 9. 12) } id.

ἀποκαθιστάνεις, 2 pers. sing. pres. ind. . ἀποκαθιστάνω
ἀποκαθίστημι], (or ἀποκαθιστάνω), fut. ἀποκαταστήσω, aor. 1, pass. ἀποκατεστάθην, (ᾰ), (§ 29. tab. X. and rem. 6) (ἀπό & καθίστημι) *to restore* a thing to its former place or state, Mat. 12. 13; 17. 11; Mar. 3. 5; 8. 25, et al.

ἀποκατάστᾰσις, εως, ἡ, (§ 5. tab. E. c) pr. *a restitution or restoration of* a thing to its former state; hence, *the renovation* of a new and better era, Ac. 3. 21.

ἀποκαλύπτεσθαι, pres. infin. pass. . . ἀποκαλύπτω
ἀποκαλύπτεται, 3 pers. sing. pres. ind. pass. . id.
ἀποκαλύπτω, fut. ψω, (ἀπό & καλύπτω) pr. *uncover; to reveal*, Mat. 11. 25, et al.; pass. *to be disclosed*, Lu. 2. 35; Eph. 3. 5; *to be plainly signified, distinctly declared*, Ro. 1. 17, 18; *to be set forth, announced*, Ga. 3. 23; *to be discovered* in true character, 1 Co. 3. 13; *to be manifested, appear*, Jno. 12. 38; Ro. 8. 18; 2 Thes. 2. 3, 6, 8; 1 Pe. 1. 5; 5. 1.

ἀποκάλυψις, εως, ἡ, *a disclosure, revelation*, Ro. 2. 5, et al.; *manifestation, appearance*, Ro. 8. 19; 1 Co. 1. 7; 2 Thes. 1. 7; 1 Pe. 1. 7, 13; 4. 13; met. spiritual *enlightenment*, Lu. 2. 32.

ἀποκαλυφθῇ, 3 pers. sing. aor. 1, subj. pass. (§ 23. rem. 4) . . . ἀποκαλύπτω
ἀποκαλυφθῆναι, aor. 1, infin. pass. . id.
ἀποκαλυφθήσεται, 3 pers. sing. fut. ind. pass. id.
ἀποκαλυφθῶσι, 3 pers. pl. aor. 1, subj. pass. . id.
ἀποκαλύψαι, aor. 1, infin. act. . . id.
ἀποκαλύψει, 3 pers. sing. fut. ind. act. . . id.
ἀποκαλύψει, dat. sing. . . . . ἀποκάλυψις
ἀποκαλύψεις, acc. pl. . . . . id.
ἀποκαλυψέων, gen. pl. . . . . id.
ἀποκαλύψεως, gen. sing. . . . . id.
ἀποκάλυψιν, acc. sing. . . . . id.
ἀποκάλυψις, εως, ἡ, (§ 5. tab. E. c) . ἀποκαλύπτω
ἀποκαρᾱδοκία, ας, ἡ, (§ 2. tab. B. b, and rem. 2) (ἀπό & καραδοκέω, *to watch with the head stretched out, to keep an eager look-out*; from κάρα, *the head*, and δοκεύω, *to watch*); *earnest expectation, eager hope*, Ro. 8. 19; Phi. 1. 20. N.T.
ἀποκαραδοκίαν, acc. sing. . . . ἀποκαραδοκία

[a] 1 Ti. 6. 19. [b] Lu. 8. 45.

ἀποκαταλλαγέντες, nom. pl. masc. part. aor. 2, pass.—D. . . ⎫
ἀποκατήλλαξεν, Rec. Gr. Sch. Tdf. (Col. 1. 21) . . . ⎭ ἀποκαταλλάσσω
ἀποκαταλλάξαι, aor. 1, infin. act. . . id.
ἀποκαταλλάξῃ, 3 pers. sing. aor. 1, subj. act. . id.
ἀποκαταλλάσσω], fut. ξω, (§ 26. rem. 3) (ἀπό & καταλλάσσω) *to transfer from a certain state to another which is quite different*; hence, *to reconcile, restore to favour*, Ep. 2. 16; Col. 1. 20, 21. N.T.
ἀποκαταστᾰθῶ, 1 pers. sing. aor. 1, subj. pass. (§ 29. rem. 6) . . . ἀποκαθίστημι
ἀποκαταστάσεως,[a] gen. sing. . . ἀποκατάστασις
ἀποκατάστασις], εως, ἡ, (§ 5. tab. E. c) . ἀποκαθίστημι
ἀποκαταστήσει, 3 pers. sing. fut. ind. act. . id.
ἀποκατεστάθη, 3 pers. sing. aor. 1, ind. pass. id.
ἀποκατέστη, 3 pers. sing. aor. 2, ind.—B. . ⎫
ἀποκατεστάθη, Rec. Gr. Sch. . ⎬ id.
ἀπεκατέστη, Tdf. (Mar. 8. 25) . ⎭
ἀποκατηλλάγητε, 2 pers. pl. aor. 2, ind. pass.—B. Ln. . . . ⎫
ἀποκατήλλαξεν, Rec. Gr. Sch. Tdf. (Col. 1. 21) . . . ⎭ ἀποκαταλλάσσω
ἀποκατήλλαξε, 3 p. sing. aor. 1, ind. act. . id.
ἀπόκειμαι], fut. είσομαι, (§ 33. tab. DD) (ἀπό & κεῖμαι) *to be laid up, preserved*, Lu. 19. 20; *to be in store, be reserved, await* any one; Col. 1. 5; 2 Ti. 4. 8; He. 9. 27.
ἀποκειμένην, acc. sing. fem. part. pres. . ἀπόκειμαι
ἀπόκειται, 3 pers. sing. pres. indic. . id.
ἀποκεκρυμμένην, acc. sing. fem. part. perf. pass. (§ 23. rem. 7) . . . ἀποκρύπτω
ἀποκεκρυμμένον, acc. sing. neut. part. p. pass. id.
ἀποκεκρυμμένου, gen. s. neut. part. perf. pass. id.
ἀποκεκυλισμένον, acc. s. masc. part. perf. pass. ἀποκυλίω
ἀποκεκύλισται, 3 pers. sing. perf. ind. pass. . id.
ἀποκεφαλίζω], fut. ίσω, (§ 26. rem. 1) (ἀπό & κεφαλή) *to behead*, Mat. 14. [illegible] Mar. 6. 16, 28; Lu. 9. 9.
ἀποκλείσῃ,[b] 3 pers. sing. aor. 1, subj. act. . ἀποκλείω
ἀποκλείω], fut. είσω, (§ 13. tab. M) (ἀπό & κλείω) *to close, shut up*.
ἀποκόπτω], fut. ψω, (§ 23. rem. 1. a) (ἀπό & κόπτω) *to cut off*, Mar. 9. 43, 45; Jno. 18. 10, 26; Ac. 27. 32; Gal. 5. 12.
ἀπόκοψον, 2 pers. sing. aor. 1, imper. act. . ἀποκόπτω
ἀποκόψονται, 3 pers. pl. fut. ind. mid. . id.

ἀποκριθείς, nom. sing. masc. part. aor. 1, p. ἀποκρίνομαι
ἀποκριθεῖσα, nom. sing. fem. part. aor. 1, pass. id.
ἀποκριθέν, nom. sing. neut. part. aor. 1, pass. . id.
ἀποκριθέντες, nom. pl. masc. pt. aor. 1, pass. id.
ἀποκριθῇ, 3 p. sing. aor. 1, subj. pass.—B. C. Tdf. ⎫
λαλήσῃ, Rec. Gr. Sch. Ln. (Mar. 9. 6) ⎭ id.
ἀποκριθῆναι, aor. 1, infin. pass. . . id.
ἀποκριθήσεται, 3 pers. sing. fut. ind. pass. . id.
ἀποκριθήσονται, 3 pers. pl. fut. ind. pass. . id.
ἀποκρίθητε, 2 pers. pl. aor. 1, imper. pass. . id.
ἀποκριθῆτε, 2 pers. pl. aor. 1, subj. pass. . id.
ἀποκριθῶσι, 3 pers. pl. aor. 1, subj. pass. . id.
ἀπόκρῐμα,[c] ατος, τό, (§ 4. tab. D. c) . id.
ἀποκρίνεσθαι, pres. infin. . . . . id.
ἀποκρίνεται, 3 pers. sing. pres. ind. . . id.
ἀποκρίνῃ, 2 pers. sing. pres. ind. . . id.
ἀποκρίνομαι], (§ 27. rem. 3) aor. 1, ἀπεκρινάμην and, later, also (pass. form) ἀπεκρίθην, (ῐ), fut. (pass. form) ἀποκριθήσομαι, (ἀποκρίνω, *to separate*, from ἀπό & κρίνω) *to answer*, Mat. 3. 15, et al.; in N.T. *to respond* to certain present circumstances, *to avow*, Mat. 11. 25, et al. (ῐ).

ἀπόκρῐμα, ατος, τό, (§ 4. tab. D. c) *a judicial sentence*. L.G.

ἀπόκρῐσις, εως, ἡ, (§ 5. tab. E. c) *an answer, reply*, Lu. 2. 47; 20. 26; Jno. 1. 22; 19. 9.

ἀποκρίσει, dat. sing. . . . . ἀπόκρισις
ἀποκρίσεσι, dat. pl. . . . . id.
ἀπόκρισιν, acc. sing. . . . . id.
ἀπόκρισις], εως, ἡ, (§ 5. tab. E. c) . ἀποκρίνομαι
ἀποκρύπτω], fut. ψω, (§ 23. rem. 1. a) (ἀπό & κρύπτω) *to hide away; to conceal, withhold from sight or knowledge*, Mat. 11. 25; 25. 18, et al.

ἀπόκρῠφος, ου, ὁ, ἡ, τό, -ον, (§ 7. rem. 2) *hidden away; concealed*, Mar. 4. 22; Lu. 8. 17; *stored up*, Col. 2. 3.

ἀπόκρυφοι, nom. pl. masc. . . . ἀπόκρυφος
ἀπόκρυφον, nom. sing. neut. . . . id.
ἀπόκρυφος], ου, ὁ, ἡ, (§ 7. rem. 2) . . ἀποκρύπτω
ἀποκταίνει, 3 pers. sing. pres. ind. act.—Ln. ⎫
ἀποκτείνει, Rec. Gr. Sch. (2 Co. 3. 6) ⎭ ἀποκταίνω
ἀποκταίνω], same signif. as ἀποκτείνω. v. r.
ἀποκτανθείς, nom. sing. masc. part. aor. 1, p. ἀποκτείνω
ἀποκτανθῆναι, aor. 1, inf. pass. (§ 37. rem. 1) id.
ἀποκτανθῶσι, 3 pers. pl. aor. 1, subj. pass. . id.

[a] Ac. 3. 21. [b] Lu. 13. 25. [c] 2 Co. 1. 9.

ἀποκτεῖναι, aor. 1, infin. act. . . . ἀποκτείνω
ἀποκτεινάντων, gen. pl. part. aor. 1, act. . id.
ἀποκτείνας, nom. sing. masc. part. aor. 1, act. id.
ἀποκτείνει, 3 pers. sing. pres. ind. act. . id.
ἀποκτείνεσθαι, pres. infin. pass. . . id.
ἀποκτείνοντες, nom. pl. masc. part. pres. act. . id.
ἀποκτεινόντων, gen. pl. masc. part. pres. act. id.
ἀποκτείνουσα, nom. sing. fem. part. pres. act. id.
ἀποκτείνω], fut. κτενῶ, aor. 1, pass. ἀπεκτάνθην, (§ 37. rem. 1) (ἀπό & κτείνω) *to kill*, Mat. 14. 5; *to destroy, annihilate*, Mat. 10. 28; *to destroy* a hostile principle, Eph. 2. 16; met. *to kill* by spiritual condemnation, Ro. 7. 11; 2 Co. 3. 6.
ἀποκτείνωμεν, 1 pers. pl. pres. subj. act. . ἀποκτείνω
ἀποκτείνωσι, 3 pers. pl. pres. subj. act. . id.
ἀποκτένει, 3 pers. sing. pres. ind. act.—A.C.D. } id.
ἀποκτείνει, Rec. Gr. Sch. (2 Co. 3. 6) }
ἀποκτενεῖ, 3 pers. sing. fut. ind. act. . id.
ἀποκτενεῖτε, 2 pers. pl. fut. ind. act. . . id.
ἀποκτέννει, 3 pers. sing. pres. ind. act.—Tdf. } ἀποκτέννω
ἀποκτείνει, Rec. Gr. Sch. (2 Co. 3. 6) }
ἀποκτέννεσθαι, pres. inf. pass.—Gr. Sch. Tdf. } id.
ἀποκτείνεσθαι, Rec. (Re. 6. 11) . }
ἀποκτέννοντες, nom. pl. masc. part. pres. act. Gr. Tdf. . . . } id.
ἀποκτείνοντες, Rec. Sch. (Mar. 12. 5) }
ἀποκτεννόντων, gen. pl. masc. part. pres.—C. D. Ln. Tdf. . . . }
ἀποκτεινόντων, Rec. . . } id.
ἀποκτενόντων, Gr. Sch. (Mat. 10. 28) }
ἀποκτέννουσα, nom. sing. fem. part. pres.—A. Tdf. . . . . } id.
ἀποκτείνουσα, Rec. Gr. Sch. (Mat. 23. 37) }
ἀποκτέννω], same signif. as ἀποκτείνω. v. r.
ἀποκτένουσα, nom. sing. fem. part. pres.—C. } ἀποκτένω
ἀποκτείνουσα, Rec. Gr. Sch. (Mat. 23. 37) }
ἀποκτενοῦσι, 3 pers. pl. fut. ind. act. . . ἀποκτείνω
ἀποκτενῶ, 1 pers. sing. fut. ind. act. . id.
ἀποκτένω], same signif. as ἀποκτείνω. v. r.
ἀποκυεῖ, 3 pers. sing. pres. ind. . . . . ἀποκυέω
ἀποκυέω, ῶ], fut. ήσω, (§ 16. tab. P) (ἀπό & κυέω) pr. *to bring forth*, as women; met. *to generate, produce*, Ja. 1. 15; *to generate* by spiritual birth, Ja. 1. 18. L.G.
ἀποκυλίσει, 3 pers. sing. fut. ind. act. . ἀποκυλίω
ἀποκυλίω], fut. ίσω, (§ 13. tab. M) (ἀπό & κυλίω) *to roll away*, Mat. 28. 2; Mar. 16. 3, 4; Lu. 24. 2. (ῑ). L.G.
ἀπολαβεῖν, aor. 2, infin. act. . . ἀπολαμβάνω

ἀπολάβῃ, 3 pers. sing. aor. 2, subj. act. . ἀπολαμβάνω
ἀπολάβητε, 2 p. pl. aor. 2, subj. act.—A.B.Ln.Tdf. } id.
ἀπολάβωμεν, Rec. Gr. Sch. (2 Jno. 8) }
ἀπολαβόμενος, nom. sing. masc. pt. aor. 2, mid. id.
ἀπολάβωμεν, 1 pers. pl. aor. 2, subj. act. . id.
ἀπολάβωσι, 3 pers. pl. aor. 2, subj. act. . id.
ἀπολαμβάνειν, pres. infin. act. . . . . id.
ἀπολαμβάνομεν, 1 pers. pl. pres. ind. act. . id.
ἀπολαμβάνοντες, nom. pl. masc. pt. pres. act. id.
ἀπολαμβάνω, fut. ἀπολήψομαι, aor. 2, ἀπέλᾰβον, (ἀπό & λαμβάνω) *to receive* what is due, sought, or needed, Lu. 23. 41; Ro. 1. 27; Ga. 4. 5; Col. 3. 24; 2 Jno. 8; *to receive in full*, Lu. 16. 25; *to receive back, recover*, Lu. 6. 34; 15. 27; 18. 30; *to receive* in hospitality, welcome, 3 Jno. 8; mid. *to take aside, lead away*, Mar. 7. 33.
ἀπόλαυσιν, acc. sing. . . . . ἀπόλαυσις
ἀπόλαυσις], εως, ἡ, (§ 5. tab. E. c) (ἀπολαύω, *to obtain a portion* of a thing, *enjoy*) *beneficial participation*, 1 Ti. 6. 17; *enjoyment, pleasure*, He. 11. 25.
ἀπολείπεται, 3 pers. sing. pres. ind. pass. . ἀπολείπω
ἀπολείπω], fut. ψω, (§ 23. rem. 1. a) (ἀπό & λείπω) *to leave, leave behind*; pass. *to be left, remain*, 2 Ti. 4. 13, 20; He. 4. 6, 9; 10. 26; *to relinquish, forsake, desert*, Jude 6.
ἀπολεῖσθε, 2 pers. pl. fut. ind. mid. . . ἀπόλλυμι
ἀπολεῖται, 3 p. s. fut. 2, ind. mid. (§ 35. rem. 11) id.
ἀπολείχω], fut. ξω, (§ 23. rem. 1. b) (ἀπό & λείχω, *to lick*) pr. *to lick off*; *to cleanse by licking, lick clean*, Lu. 16. 21. L.G.
ἀπολελυμένην, acc. sing. fem. part. perf. pass. (§ 14. tab. N) . . . ἀπολύω
ἀπολελυμένον, acc. sing. masc. part. perf. pass. id.
ἀπολέλῠσαι, 2 pers. sing. perf. ind. pass. . id.
ἀπολελύσθαι, perf. infin. pass. . . id.
ἀπολέσαι, aor. 1, infin. act. . . . ἀπόλλυμι
ἀπολέσας, nom. sing. masc. part. aor. 1, act. id.
ἀπολέσει, 3 pers. sing. fut. ind. act. . . id.
ἀπολέσῃ, 3 pers. sing. aor. 1, subj. act. . id.
ἀπολέσηται, 3 pers. sing. aor. 1, subj. mid.—B. } id.
ἀπολέσωμεν, Rec. Gr. Sch. (2 Jno. 8) }
ἀπολέσητε, 2 p. pl. aor. 1, subj. act.—A.Ln.Tdf. } id.
ἀπολέσωμεν, Rec. Gr. Sch. (2 Jno. 8) }
ἀπολέσθαι, aor. 2, infin. mid. . . . id.
ἀπολέσουσι, 3 pers. pl. fut. ind. act. . . id.
ἀπολέσω, 1 pers. sing. aor. 1, subj. act. . id.
ἀπολέσωμεν, 1 pers. pl. aor. 1, subj. act. . id.
ἀπολέσωσι, 3 pers. pl. aor. 1, subj. act. . id.

ἀπόληται, 3 pers. sing. aor. 2, subj. mid. . ἀπόλλυμι
ἀπολήψεσθε, 2 pers. pl. fut. ind. mid. . ἀπολαμβάνω
ἀπολιπόντας, acc. pl. masc. part. aor. 2, act. (§ 24. rem. 9) . . . . ἀπολείπω
ἀπόλλυε, 2 pers. sing. pres. imper. act. of ἀπολλύω, same signif. as . . ἀπόλλυμι
ἀπόλλυμαι, 1 pers. sing. pres. ind. pass. . id.
ἀπολλύμεθα, 1 pers. pl. pres. ind. pass. . id.
ἀπολλυμένην, acc. sing. fem. part. pres. pass. . id.
ἀπολλύμενοι, nom. pl. masc. part. pres. pass. id.
ἀπολλυμένοις, dat. pl. masc. part. pres. pass. id.
ἀπολλυμένου, gen. sing. neut. part. pres. pass. id.

ἀπόλλῡμι], fut. ολέσω & ολῶ, aor. 1, ἀπώλεσα, perf. ἀπολώλεκα, (ἀπό & ὄλλυμι) *to destroy utterly; to kill*, Mat. 2. 13, et al.; *to bring to nought, make void*, 1 Co. 1. 19; *to lose, be deprived of*, Mat. 10. 42, et al.; mid. ἀπόλλῠμαι, fut. ολοῦμαι, aor. 2, ἀπωλόμην, perf. 2, ἀπόλωλα, *to be destroyed, perish*, Mat. 9. 17, et al.; *to be put to death, to die*, Mat. 26. 52, et al.; *to be lost, to stray*, Mat. 10. 6, et al.

Ἀπολλύων, οντος, ὁ, (§ 7. tab. H. d) *Apollyon, Destroyer*, i. q. Ἀβαδδών, Re. 9. 11. N.T.

ἀπώλεια, ας, ἡ, (§ 2 tab. B. b, and rem. 2) *consumption, destruction; waste, profusion*, Mat. 26. 8; Mar. 14. 4; *destruction, state of being destroyed*, Ac. 25. 6; eternal *ruin, perdition*, Mat. 7. 13; Ac. 8. 20, et al.

ἀπόλλῠται, 3 pers. sing. pres. ind. pass.—A. B. D. Ln. Tdf. } ἀπόλλυμι
ἀπολεῖται, Rec. Gr. Sch. (1 Co. 8. 11) }
ἀπόλλυνται, 3 p. pl. pres. ind. pass.—B. Ln. } id.
ἀπολοῦνται, R. Gr. Sch. Tdf. (Mat. 9. 17) }
Ἀπολλύων,[a] οντος, ὁ, (§ 7. tab. H. d) . . id.
Ἀπολλῶ, gen. sing. . . . Ἀπολλῶς
Ἀπολλῶ, acc. sing. (§ 3. rem. 5) . . id.
Ἀπολλῶν, acc. sing.—B. Ln. . . . } id.
Ἀπολλῶ, Rec. Gr. Sch. Tdf. (1 Co. 4. 6) }

Ἀπολλωνία], ας, ἡ, (§ 2. tab. B. b, and rem. 2) *Apollonia*, a city of Macedonia.

Ἀπολλωνίαν,[b] acc. sing. . . . . Ἀπολλωνία

Ἀπολλῶς, λώ, ὁ, (§ 3. tab. C. d) *Apollos*, pr. name.

ἀπολογεῖσθαι, pres. infin. . . . ἀπολογέομαι

ἀπολογέομαι, οῦμαι], fut. ήσομαι, aor. 1, ἀπελογησάμην and, pass. form, ἀπελογήθην, (§ 17. tab. Q) (ἀπό & λόγος) *to defend one's self against a charge, to make a defence*, Lu. 12. 11; 21. 14, et al.

ἀπολογία, ας, ἡ, (§ 2. tab. B. b, and rem. 2) *a verbal defence*, Ac. 22. 1; 25. 16, et al.

ἀπολογηθῆναι, aor. 1, infin. pass. . . ἀπολογέομαι
ἀπολογήσησθε, 2 pers. pl. aor. 1, subj. . . id.
ἀπολογία, ας, ἡ, (§ 2. tab. B. b, and rem. 2) id.
ἀπολογίᾳ, dat. sing. . . . ἀπολογία
ἀπολογίαν, acc. sing. . . . . id.
ἀπολογίας, gen. sing. . . . . id.
ἀπολογοῦμαι, 1 pers. sing. pres. ind. contr. ἀπολογέομαι
ἀπολογούμεθα, 1 pers. pl. pres. ind. . . id.
ἀπολογουμένου, gen. sing. masc. part. pres. id.
ἀπολογουμένων, gen. pl. part. pres. . . id.
ἀπολομένου, gen. sing. masc. part. aor. 2, mid. ἀπόλλυμι
ἀπολοῦνται, 3 pers. pl. fut. mid. (§ 36 rem. 5) id.
ἀπόλουσαι, 2 pers. sing. aor. 1, imper. mid. . ἀπολούω

ἀπολούω], fut. ούσω, (§ 13. tab. M) (ἀπό & λούω) *to cleanse by bathing*; mid. *to cleanse one's self; to procure one's self to be cleansed*; met., of sin, Ac. 22. 16; 1 Co. 6. 11.

ἀπολύει, 3 pers. sing. pres. ind. act.—B. . } ἀπολύω
ἀπολέσει, Rec. Gr. Sch. Tdf. (Jno. 12. 25) }
ἀπολύειν, pres. infin. act. . . . . id.
ἀπολύεις, 2 pers. sing. pres. ind. act. . id.
ἀπολύετε, 2 pers. pl. pres. imper. act. . . id.
ἀπολυθέντες, nom. pl. masc. part. aor. 1, pass. id.
ἀπολυθήσεσθε, 2 pers. pl. fut. 1, ind. pass. id.
ἀπολυθῆτε, 2 pers. pl. aor. 1, subj. pass. . id
ἀπολῦσαι, aor. 1, infin. act. . . . id.
ἀπολύσας, nom. sing. masc. part. aor. 1, act. . id.
ἀπολύσῃ, 3 pers. sing. aor. 1, subj. act. . id.
ἀπολύσῃς, 2 pers. sing. aor. 1, subj. act. . id.
ἀπολύσητε, 2 pers. pl. aor. 1, subj. act. . id.
ἀπόλυσον, 2 pers. sing. aor. 1, imper. act. . id.
ἀπολύσω, 1 pers. sing. aor. 1, subj. act. . id.
ἀπολύσω, 1 pers. sing. fut. ind. act. . . id.
ἀπολυτρώσεως, gen. sing. . . . ἀπολύτρωσις
ἀπολύτρωσιν, acc. sing. . . . . id

ἀπολύτρωσις, εως, ἡ, (§ 5. tab. E. c) (ἀπολυτρόω, *to dismiss for a ransom paid*, from ἀπό & λυτρόω) *redemption, a deliverance procured by the payment of a ransom*; meton. the author of *redemption*, 1 Co. 1. 30; *deliverance*, simply, the idea of a ransom being excluded, Lu. 21. 28; He. 11. 35. N.T.

[a] Re. 9. 11. [b] Ac. 17. 1.

ἀπολύω], fut. ύσω, (§ 13. tab. M) (ἀπό & λύω) pr. *to loose; to release* from a tie or burden, Mat. 18. 27; *to divorce*, Mat. 1. 19, et al.; *to remit, forgive*, Lu. 6. 37; *to liberate, discharge*, Mat. 27. 15, et al.; *to dismiss*, Mat. 15. 23; Ac. 19. 40; *to allow to depart, to send away*, Mat. 14. 15, et al.; *to permit*, or, *signal departure* from life, Lu. 2. 29; mid. *to depart*, Ac. 28. 25; pass. *to be rid*, Lu. 13. 12. (ῡ).

ἀπολύων, nom. sing. masc. part. pres. act. . ἀπολύω

ἀπολῶ, 1 pers. sing. fut. ind. act. . . ἀπόλλυμι

ἀπολωλός, acc. sing. neut. part. perf. 2 . id.

ἀπολωλότα, acc. pl. neut. part. perf. 2 . id.

ἀπολωλώς, nom. sing. masc. part. perf. 2 . id.

ἀπόλωνται, 3 pers. pl. aor. 2, subj. mid. . id.

ἀπομασσόμεθα,[a] 1 pers. pl. pres. ind. mid. . ἀπομάσσω

ἀπομάσσω], fut. ξω, (§ 26. rem. 3) (ἀπό & μάσσω, *to wipe*) *to wipe off*; mid. *to wipe off one's self*.

ἀπονέμοντες,[b] nom. pl. masc. part. pres. act. ἀπονέμω

ἀπονέμω], fut. νεμῶ, (§ 27. rem. 1. a) (ἀπό & νέμω, *to allot*) *to portion off; to assign, bestow*.

ἀπονίπτω], fut. ψω, (§ 23. rem. 1. a) (ἀπό & νίπτω) *to cleanse* a part of the body *by washing*; mid., of one's self, Mat. 27. 24.

ἀπόντες, nom. pl. masc. part. pres. . . ἄπειμι

ἀποπίπτω], fut. πεσοῦμαι, aor. 2, ἀπέπεσον, (§ 37. rem. 1) (ἀπό & πίπτω) *to fall off*, or *from*, Ac. 9. 18.

ἀποπλανᾶν, pres. infin. act. . . ἀποπλανάω

ἀποπλᾰνάω, ῶ], fut. ήσω, (§ 18. tab. R) (ἀπό & πλανάω) *to cause to wander*; met. *to deceive, pervert, seduce*, Mar. 13. 22; pass. *to wander*; met. *to swerve from, apostatise*, 1 Ti. 6. 10.

ἀποπλεῖν, pres. infin. . . . . ἀποπλέω

ἀποπλεύσαντες, nom. pl. masc. part. aor. 1 id.

ἀποπλέω], fut. πλεύσομαι, aor. 1, ἀπέπλευσα, (§ 35. rem. 3) (ἀπό & πλέω) *to depart by ship, sail away*, Ac. 13. 4; 14. 26; 20. 15; 27. 1.

ἀποπλύνω], fut. υνῶ, (§ 27. rem. 1. a) (ἀπό & πλύνω) *to wash, rinse*, Lu. 5. 2. (ῡ).

ἀποπνίγω], fut. ξω, (§ 23. rem. 1. b) aor. 2, pass. ἀπεπνίγην, (ῐ), (ἀπό & πνίγω) *to choke, suffocate*, Mat. 13. 7; Lu. 8. 33; *to drown*, Lu. 8. 7. (ῑ).

ἀπορεῖσθαι, pres. inf. mid.—B. C. D. Ln. Tdf. / διαπορεῖσθαι, Rec. Gr. Sch. (Lu. 24. 4) } ἀπορέω

ἀπορέω, ῶ], fut. ήσω, (§ 16. tab. P) and ἀπορέομαι, οῦμαι, (§ 17. tab. Q) (ἀ & πόρος, *a way*) pr. *to be without means*; met. *to hesitate, be at a stand, be in doubt and perplexity*, Jno. 13. 22; Ac. 25. 20; 2 Co. 4. 8; Gal. 4. 20.

ἀπορία, ας, ἡ, (§ 2. tab. B. b, and rem. 2) *doubt, uncertainty, perplexity*.

ἀπορία], ας, ἡ, (§ 2. tab. B. b, and rem. 2) . ἀπορέω

ἀπορίᾳ,[c] dat. sing. . . . . ἀπορία

ἀποροῦμαι, 1 pers. sing. pres. ind. mid. . ἀπορέω

ἀπορούμενοι, nom. pl. masc. part. pres. mid. id.

ἀπορούμενος, nom. sing. masc. part. pres. mid. id.

ἀποῤῥίπτω], fut. ψω, (§ 23. rem. 1. a) (ἀπό & ῥίπτω) *to throw off*.

ἀποῤῥίψαντας,[d] acc. pl. masc. part. aor. 1, act. ἀποῤῥίπτω

ἀπορφανίζω], fut. ίσω, (§ 26. rem. 1) (ἀπό & ὄρφανος) *to deprive, bereave*.

ἀπορφανισθέντες,[e] nom. pl. m. part. aor. 1, pass. ἀπορφανίζω

ἀποσκευάζομαι], fut. άσομαι, (§ 26. rem. 1) (ἀποσκευάζω, *to pack up articles*, σκεύη, *for removal*) *to prepare for a journey, take one's departure*.

ἀποσκευασάμενοι,[f] nom. pl. m. part. aor. 1, m. ἀποσκευάζομαι

ἀποσκίασμα,[g] ατος, τό, (§ 4. tab. D. c) (ἀπό & σκιάζω, *to throw a shadow*, from σκιά) *a shadow cast*; met. *a shade, the slightest trace*. L.G.

ἀποσπᾶν, pres. infin. act. . . . ἀποσπάω

ἀποσπασθέντας, acc. pl. masc. part. aor. 1, pass. id.

ἀποσπάω, ῶ], fut. άσω, (§ 22. rem. 2) (ἀπό & σπάω) *to draw away from; to draw out* or *forth*, Mat. 26. 51; *to draw away, seduce*, Ac. 20. 30; mid., aor. 1, pass. form, ἀπεσπάσθην, *to separate one's self, to part*, Lu. 22. 41; Ac. 21. 1. (ᾰ).

ἀποσταλέντι, dat. sing. neut. part. aor. 2, pass. ἀποστέλλω

ἀποσταλῶσι, 3 pers. pl. aor. 2, subj. pass. (§ 27. rem. 4. a, b) . . . id.

ἀποστάντα, acc. sing. masc. part. aor. 2 . ἀφίστημι

ἀποστάς, nom. sing. masc. part. aor. 2 . . id.

ἀποστασία, ας, ἡ, (§ 2. tab. B. b, and rem. 2) id.

ἀποστασίαν, acc. sing. . . . . ἀποστασία

ἀποστάσιον, ου, τό, (§ 3. tab. C. c) . . ἀφίστημι

ἀποστασίου, gen. sing. . . . . ἀποστάσιον

ἀποστεγάζω], fut. άσω, (§ 26. rem. 1) (ἀπό &

[a] Lu. 10. 11. [b] 1 Pe. 3. 7. [c] Lu. 21. 25. [d] Ac. 27. 43. [e] 1 Thes. 2. 17. [f] Ac. 21. 15 [g] Ja. 1. 17.

στέγη) *to remove or break through a covering or roof* of a place, Mar. 2. 4.

ἀποστεῖλαι, aor. 1, infin. act. . . . ἀποστέλλω

ἀποστείλαντα, acc. sing. masc. part. aor. 1, act. id.

ἀποστείλαντας, acc. pl. masc. part. aor. 1.—Gr. Sch. Tdf. ἀποστόλους, Rec. (Ac. 15. 33) . . . id.

ἀποστείλαντες, nom. pl. masc. part. aor. 1, act. id.

ἀποστείλας, nom. sing. masc. part. aor. 1, act. id.

ἀποστείλῃ, 3 pers. sing. aor. 1, subj. act. . id.

ἀπόστειλον, 2 p. s. aor. 1, imper. act.—Gr. Tdf. ἐπίτρεψον ἡμῖν ἀπελθεῖν, Rec. Sch. (Mat. 8. 31) . . . id.

ἀποστελεῖ, 3 pers. sing. fut. ind. act. . id.

ἀποστέλλει, 3 pers. sing. pres. ind. act. . id.

ἀποστέλλειν, pres. infin. act. . . . id.

ἀποστέλλῃ, 3 pers. sing. pres. subj. act. . id.

ἀποστελλόμενα, nom. pl. neut. part. pres. pass. id.

ἀποστέλλουσι, 3 pers. pl. pres. ind. act. . id.

ἀποστέλλω, fut. στελῶ, (§ 27. rem. 1. b) aor. 1, ἀπέστειλα, (§ 27. rem. 1. d) perf. ἀπέσταλκα, (§ 27. rem. 2. b) perf. pass. ἀπέσταλμαι, (§ 27. rem. 3) aor. 2, pass. ἀπεστάλην, (ᾰ), (§ 27. rem. 4. b) (ἀπό & στέλλω) *to send forth* a messenger, agent, message, or command, Mat. 2. 16; 10. 5, et al.; *to put forth into action*, Mar. 4. 29; *to liberate, rid*, Lu. 4. 19; *to dismiss, send away*, Mar. 12. 3, et al.

ἀποστολή, ῆς, ἡ, (§ 2. tab. B. a) *a sending, expedition; office or duty of one sent as a messenger or agent; office of an apostle, apostleship*, Ac. 1. 25; Ro. 1. 5; 1 Co. 9. 2; Gal. 2. 8.

ἀπόστολος, ου, ὁ, (§ 3. tab. C. a) *one sent as a messenger or agent, the bearer of a commission, messenger*, Jno. 13. 16, et al.; *an apostle*, Mat. 10. 2, et al.

ἀποστελῶ, 1 pers. sing. fut. ind. act. . ἀποστέλλω

ἀποστερεῖσθε, 2 pers. pl. pres. ind. pass. . ἀποστερέω

ἀποστερεῖτε, 2 pers. pl. pres. ind. act. . id.

ἀποστερεῖτε, 2 pers. pl. pres. imper. act. . id.

ἀποστερέω, ῶ], fut. ήσω, (§ 16. tab. P) perf. pass. ἀπεστέρημαι, (§ 17. tab. Q) (ἀπό & στερέω, *to deprive*) *to deprive, detach; to debar*, 1 Co. 7. 5; *to deprive* in a bad sense, *defraud*, Mar. 10. 19; 1 Co. 6. 7; mid. *to suffer one's self to be deprived or defrauded*, 1 Co. 6. 8; pass. *to be destitute or devoid of*, 1 Ti 6. 5; *to be unjustly withheld*, Ja. 5. 4.

ἀποστερήσῃς, 2 pers. sing. aor. 1, subj. act. ἀποστερέω

ἀποστῇ, 3 pers. sing. aor. 2, subj. (§ 29. rem. 3) ἀφίστημι

ἀποστῆναι, aor. 2, infin. . . . id.

ἀποστήσονται, 3 pers. pl. fut. ind. mid. . id.

ἀπόστητε, 2 pers. pl. aor. 2, imper. . . id.

ἀποστήτω, 3 pers. sing. aor. 2, imper. . . id.

ἀποστολή], ῆς, ἡ, (§ 2, tab. B. a) . . ἀποστέλλω

ἀποστολήν, acc. sing. . . . ἀποστολή

ἀποστολῆς, gen. sing. . . . . id.

ἀπόστολοι, nom. pl. . . ἀπόστολος

ἀποστόλοις, dat. pl. . . . id.

ἀπόστολον, acc. sing. . . . . id.

ἀπόστολος, ου, ὁ, (§ 3. tab. C. a) . ἀποστέλλω

ἀποστόλου, gen. sing. . . . ἀπόστολος

ἀποστόλους, acc. pl. . . . . id.

ἀποστόλων, gen. pl. . . . . id.

ἀποστοματίζειν,[a] pres. infin. . . ἀποστοματίζω

ἀποστοματίζω], fut. ίσω, (§ 26. rem. 1) (ἀπό & στόμα) pr. *to speak or repeat off-hand*; also, *to require or lead* others *to speak without premeditation*, as by questions calculated to elicit unpremeditated answers, *to endeavour to entrap into unguarded language*.

ἀποστραφῇς, 2 pers. sing. aor. 2, pass. (with mid. sense) . . . ἀποστρέφω

ἀποστρέφειν, pres. infin. act. . . id.

ἀποστρεφόμενοι, nom. pl. masc. part. pr. mid. id.

ἀποστρεφομένων, gen. pl. part. pres. mid. . id.

ἀποστρέφοντα, acc. sing. masc. part. pres. act. id.

ἀποστρέφω], fut. ψω, (§ 23. rem. 1. a) (ἀπό & στρέφω) *to turn away; to remove*, Ac. 3. 26; Ro. 11. 26; 2 Ti. 4. 4; *to turn* a people from their allegiance to their sovereign, *pervert, incite to revolt*, Lu. 23. 14; *to replace, restore*, Mat. 26. 52; 27. 3; mid., aor. 2, pass. form, ἀπεστράφην, (ᾰ), (§ 24. rem. 10) *to turn away from* any one, *to slight, reject, repulse*, Mat. 5. 42; Tit. 1. 14; He. 12. 25; *to desert*, 2 Ti. 1. 15.

ἀποστρέψει, 3 pers. sing. fut. ind. act. ἀποστρέφω

ἀπόστρεψον, 2 pers. sing. aor. 1, imper. act. . id.

ἀποστρέψουσι, 3 pers. pl. fut. ind. act. . id.

ἀποστυγέω, ῶ], fut. ήσω, (§ 16. tab. P) (ἀπό & στυγέω, *to hate*) *to shrink from with abhorrence, detest*.

[a] Lu. 11. 53.

ἀποστυγοῦντες,[a] nom. pl. masc. part. pres. . ἀποστυγέω
ἀποσυνάγωγοι, nom. pl. masc. . ἀποσυνάγωγος
ἀποσυνάγωγος, ου, ὁ, ἡ, (§ 3. tab. C. a. b) (ἀπό & συναγωγή) *expelled or excluded from the synagogue, excommunicated, cut off from the rights and privileges of a Jew, and excluded from society,* Jno. 9. 22; 12. 42; 16. 2. N.T.
ἀποσυναγώγους, acc. pl. masc. . . . ἀποσυνάγωγος
ἀποταξάμενοι, nom. pl. m. part. aor. 1.—D. ἀποσκευασάμενοι, Rec. Gr. Sch. (Ac. 21. 15) . . . . } ἀποτάσσομαι
ἀποταξάμενος, nom. sing. masc. part. aor. 1 . id.
ἀποτάξασθαι, aor. 1, infin. . . . . id.
ἀποτάσσεται, 3 pers. sing. pres. ind. . . id.
ἀποτάσσομαι], fut. ξομαι, (§ 26. rem. 3) (ἀποτάσσω, *to set apart,* from ἀπό & τάσσω) *to take leave of, bid farewell to,* Lu. 9. 61; Ac. 18. 18, 21; 2 Co. 2. 13; *to dismiss, send away,* Mar. 6. 46; *to renounce, forsake,* Lu. 14. 33.
ἀποτελεσθεῖσα, nom. sing. fem. part. aor. 1, pass. ἀποτελέω
ἀποτελέω, ῶ], fut. έσω, (§ 22. rem. 1) aor. 1, pass. ἀπετελέσθην, (§ 22. rem. 4) (ἀπό & τελέω) *to complete;* pass. *to be perfected, to arrive at full stature or measure,* Ja. 1. 15.
ἀποτελοῦμαι, 1 pers. sing. pres. ind. mid.—D. ἀποτελῶ, B. Ln. Tdf. . . . ἐπιτελῶ, Rec. Gr. Sch. (Lu. 13. 32) } ἀποτελέω
ἀποτίθημι], fut. ἀποθήσω, (§ 28. tab. V) mid. ἀποτίθεμαι, aor. 2, ἀπεθέμην, (§ 28. tab. W) *to lay off, lay down or aside,* as garments, Ac. 7. 58; met. *to lay aside, put off, renounce,* Ro. 13. 12; Ep. 4. 22, 25; Col. 3. 8, et al.

ἀπόθεσις, εως, ἡ, (§ 5. tab. E. c) *a putting off or away, laying aside,* 1 Pe. 3. 21; 2 Pe. 1. 14.

ἀποθήκη, ης, ἡ, (§ 2. tab. B. a) *a place where anything is laid up for preservation, repository, granary, storehouse, barn,* Mat. 3. 12; 6. 26; 13. 30; Lu. 3. 17; 12. 18, 24.

ἀποτιναξάμενος, nom. sing. masc. part. aor. 1, mid.—A. Sch. Tdf. . . . ἀποτινάξας, Rec. Gr. Ln. (Ac. 28. 5) . } ἀποτινάσσω
ἀποτινάξας, nom. sing. masc. part. aor. 1, act. . id.
ἀποτινάξατε, 2 pers. pl. aor. 1, imper. act. . ἀποτινάσσω
ἀποτινάσσω], fut. ξω, (§ 26. rem. 3) (ἀπό & τινάσσω, *to shake*) *to shake off,* Lu. 9. 5; Ac. 28. 5.
ἀποτίνω], fut. ἀποτίσω, (ῑ), (§ 27. rem. 1, *note*) (ἀπό & τίνω) *to pay off* what is claimed or due; *to repay, refund, make good.*
ἀποτίσω,[b] 1 pers. sing. fut. ind. act. . . ἀποτίνω
ἀποτολμᾷ,[c] 3 pers. sing. pres. ind. . . ἀποτολμάω
ἀποτολμάω, ῶ], fut. ήσω, (§ 18. tab. R) (ἀπό & τολμάω) *to dare or risk outright; to speak outright, without reserve or restraint.*
ἀποτομία], ας, ἡ, (§ 2. tab. B. b, and rem. 2) (ἀπότομος, *cut off sheer,* from ἀποτέμνω, *to cut off,* from ἀπό & τέμνω) pr. *abruptness;* met. *summary severity, rigour,* Ro. 11. 22, bis. L.G.

ἀποτόμως, adv. *sharply, severely,* 2 Co. 13. 10; Tit. 1. 13.

ἀποτομίαν, acc. sing. . . . . . ἀποτομία
ἀποτόμως, adv. . . . . . . id.
ἀποτρέπου,[d] 2 pers. sing. pres. imper. mid. . ἀποτρέπω
ἀποτρέπω], fut. ψω, (§ 23. rem. 1. a) (ἀπό & τρέπω) *to turn* any one *away* from a thing; mid. *to turn one's self away* from any one; *to avoid, shun.*
ἀπουσίᾳ,[e] dat. sing. . . . . ἀπουσία
ἀπουσία], ας, ἡ, (§ 2. tab. B. b, and rem. 2) . ἄπειμι
ἀποφέρεσθαι, pres. inf. pass.—A. B. Ln. Tdf. ἐπιφέρεσθαι, Rec. Gr. Sch. (Ac. 19. 12) } ἀποφέρω
ἀποφέρω], fut. ἀποίσω, aor. 1, ἀπήνεγκα, aor. 2, ἀπήνεγκον, aor. 1, pass. ἀπηνέχθην, (§ 36. rem. 1) (ἀπό & φέρω) *to bear or carry away, conduct away,* Mar. 15. 1; Lu. 16. 22; 1 Co. 16. 3; Re. 17. 3; 21. 10.
ἀποφεύγοντας, acc. pl. m. part. pres.—Al. Tdf. ἀποφυγόντας, Rec. Gr. Sch. (2 Pe. 2. 18) } ἀποφεύγω
ἀποφεύγω], fut. ξομαι, (§ 23. rem. 1. b) aor. 2, ἀπέφῠγον, (§ 4. 2 rem. 9) (ἀπό & φεύγω) *to flee from, escape;* met. *to be rid, be freed from,* 2 Pe. 1. 4; 2. 18, 20.
ἀποφθέγγεσθαι, pres. infin. . . ἀποφθέγγομαι
ἀποφθέγγομαι, fut. έγξομαι, (§ 23. rem. 1. b) (ἀπό & φθέγγομαι) *to speak out, declare,* particularly solemn, weighty, or pithy sayings, Ac. 2. 4, 14; 26. 25. L.G.
ἀποφορτίζομαι], fut. ίσομαι, (§ 26. rem. 1) (ἀπό & φόρτος) *to unlade.* L.G.

---

a Ro. 12. 9. b Phile. 19. c Ro. 10. 20. d 2 Ti. 3. 5. e Phi. 2. 12.

ἀποφορτιζόμενον,[a] nom. sing. neut. pt. pres. ἀποφορτίζομαι

ἀποφυγόντας, acc. pl. masc. part. aor. 2 . ἀποφεύγω

ἀποφυγόντες, nom. pl. masc. part. aor. 2 . id.

ἀποχρήσει,[b] dat. sing. . . . . ἀπόχρησις

ἀπόχρησις], εως, ἡ, (§ 5. tab. E. c) (ἀποχράομαι, *to use up, consume by use*) *a using up*, or, *a discharge of an intended use*. L.G.

ἀποχωρεῖ, 3 pers. sing. pres. ind. . . ἀποχωρέω

ἀποχωρεῖτε, 2 pers. pl. pres. imper. . . id.

ἀποχωρέω, ῶ], fut. ήσω, (§ 16. tab. P) (ἀπό & χωρέω) *to go from or away, depart*, Mat. 7. 23; Lu. 9. 39; Ac. 13. 13.

ἀποχωρήσας, nom. sing. masc. part. aor. 1 . ἀποχωρεω

ἀποχωρίζω], fut. ίσω, aor. 1, pass. ἀπεχωρίσθην, (§ 26. rem. 1) (ἀπό & χωρίζω) *to separate*; pass. *to be swept aside*, Re. 6. 14; mid. *to part*, Ac. 15. 39.

ἀποχωρισθῆναι, aor. 1, infin. pass. . . ἀποχωρίζω

ἀποψυχόντων,[c] gen. pl. masc. part. pres. . ἀποψύχω

ἀποψύχω], fut. ξω, (§ 23. rem. 1. b) (ἀπό & ψύχω) pr. *to breathe out, faint away, die*; met. *to faint at heart, be dismayed*. (ῡ).

Ἀππίου φόρον], *the forum, or market-place, of Appius*; a village on the Appian road, near Rome.

Ἀππίου φόρου,[d] gen. sing. . . Ἀππίου φόρον

ἀπρόσιτον,[e] acc. sing. neut. . . . ἀπρόσιτος

ἀπρόσῐτος], ου, ὁ, ἡ, τό, -ον, 7. rem. 2) (ἀ & προσιτός, *accessible*, from πρόσειμι, *to approach*) *unapproached, unapproachable*. L.G.

ἀπρόσκοποι, nom. pl. masc. . . ἀπρόσκοπος

ἀπρόσκοπον, acc. sing. fem. . . . . id.

ἀπρόσκοπος], ου, ὁ, ἡ, (ἀ & προσκοπή) *not stumbling or jarring*; met. *not stumbling or jarring* against moral rule, *unblamable, clear*, Ac. 24. 16; Phi. 1. 10; *free from offensiveness*, 1 Co. 10. 32. N.T.

ἀπροσωπολήπτως,[f] adv. (ἀ & προσωποληπτέω) *without respect of persons, impartially*, N.T.

ἄπταιστος], ου, ὁ, ἡ, (ἀ & πταίω) *free from stumbling*; met. *free from* moral *stumbling or offence*; *irreprehensible*, Jude 24.

ἀπταίστους,[g] acc. pl. masc. . . . ἄπταιστος

ἅπτει, 3 pers. sing. pres. ind. act. . . ἅπτω

ἅπτεσθαι, pres. infin. mid. . . . id.

ἅπτεσθε, 2 pers. pl. pres. imper. mid. . id.

ἅπτεται, 3 pers. sing. pres. ind. mid. . . id.

ἅπτεται, 3 pers. sing. pres. ind. pass.—D. . } ἔρχεται, Rec. Gr. Sch. Tdf. (Mar. 4. 21) } ἅπτω

ἅπτηται, 3 pers. sing. pres. subj. mid. . . id.

ἅπτου, 2 pers. sing. pres. imper. mid. . id.

ἅπτω], fut. ψω, (§ 23. rem. 1. a) pr. *to bring in contact, fit, fasten; to light, kindle*, Mar. 4. 21; Lu. 8. 16, et al.; mid. ἅπτομαι, fut. ψομαι, aor. 1, ἡψάμην, *to touch*, Mat. 8. 3, et al.; *to meddle, venture to partake*, Col. 2. 21; *to have intercourse with, to know carnally*, 1 Co. 7. 1; by impl. *to harm*, 1 Jno. 5. 18.

Ἀπφία], ας, ἡ, *Appia*, pr. name.

Ἀπφίᾳ,[h] dat. sing. . . . . . Ἀπφία

ἀπωθεῖσθε, 2 pers. pl. pres. ind. mid. . ἀπωθέω

ἀπωθέω, ῶ], fut. ωθήσω & ώσω, and mid. ἀπωθέομαι, οῦμαι, aor. 1, ἀπωσάμην, (ἀπό & ὠθέω, *to thrust*) *to thrust away, repel from one's self, repulse*, Ac. 7. 27; *to refuse, reject, cast off*, Ac. 7. 39; 13. 46; Ro. 11. 1, 2; 1 Ti. 1. 19.

ἀπώλεια, ας, ἡ, (§ 2. tab. B. b, and rem. 2) . ἀπόλλυμι

ἀπωλείαις, dat. pl. . . . . ἀπώλεια

ἀπώλειαν, acc. sing. . . . . id.

ἀπωλείας, gen. sing. . . . . id.

ἀπώλεσα, 1 pers. sing. aor. 1, ind. act. . . ἀπόλλυμι

ἀπώλεσε, 3 pers. sing. aor. 1, ind. act. . id.

ἀπώλετο, 3 pers. sing. aor. 2, ind. mid. . . id.

ἀπώλλυντο, 3 pers. pl. imperf. mid.—B. Ln. } ἀπώλοντο, Rec. Gr. Sch. Tdf. (1 Co. 10. 9) } id.

ἀπώλοντο, 3 pers. pl. aor. 2, ind. mid. . id.

ἀπών, nom. sing. masc. part. pres. . . ἄπειμι

ἀπωσάμενοι, nom. pl. masc. part. aor. 1, mid. ἀπωθέω

ἀπώσαντο, 3 pers. pl. aor. 1, ind. mid. . id.

ἀπώσατο, 3 pers. sing. aor. 1, ind. mid. . id.

ἄρα. This particle denotes, first, transition from one thing to another by natural sequence; secondly, logical inference; in which case the premises are either expressed, Mat. 12. 28, or to be variously supplied. *Therefore, then, consequently; should it so result*, Ac. 17. 27.

ἆρα. A stronger form of the preceding, used mainly in interrogations, Lu. 18. 8; Ac. 8. 30; Gal. 2. 17.

ἀρά], ᾶς, ἡ, (§ 2. tab. B. b, and rem. 2) pr. *a prayer*; more commonly *a prayer for evil*; *curse, cursing, imprecation*.

[a] Ac. 21. 3. [b] Col. 2. 22. [c] Lu. 21. 26. [d] Ac. 28. 15. [e] 1 Ti. 6. 16. [f] 1 Pe. 1. 17. [g] Jude 24. [h] Phile. 2.

Ἄρᾰβες,[a] nom. pl. . . . . Ἄραψ
Ἀραβία], ας, ἡ, (§ 2. tab. B. b, and rem. 2) *Arabia.*
Ἀραβίᾳ, dat. sing. . . . . . Ἀραβία
Ἀραβίαν, acc. sing. . . . . id.
ἆραι, aor. 1, infin. act. . . . . αἴρω
Ἀράμ, ὁ, *Aram,* pr. name, indecl.
ἄραντες, nom. pl. masc. part. aor. 1, act. . id.
ἄρας, nom. sing. masc. part. aor. 1, act. . id.
ἀρᾶς,[b] gen. sing. . . . . . ἀρά
ἄρατε, 2 pers. pl. aor. 1, imper. act. . . αἴρω
ἀράτω, 3 pers. sing. aor. 1, imper. act. . . id.
Ἄραψ], αβος, ὁ, (§ 4. rem. 2. a) *an Arabian.*
ἀργαί, nom. pl. fem. . . . . . ἀργός
ἀργεῖ,[c] 3 pers. sing. pres. ind. . . . ἀργέω
ἀργέω, ῶ], fut. ήσω, (§ 16. tab. P) . . ἀργός
ἀργή, nom. sing. fem.—B. Ln. Tdf. . } id.
νεκρά Rec. Gr. Sch. (Ja. 2. 20) . . }
ἀργοί, nom. pl. masc. . . . . . id.
ἀργόν, nom. sing. neut. . . . . id.
ἀργός] ή, όν, (§ 7. tab. F. a) (ἀ & ἔργον) contr. from ἀεργός, pr. *inactive, unemployed,* Mat. 20. 3, 6: *idle, averse from labour,* 1 Ti. 5. 13; Tit. 1. 12; met. 2 Pe. 1. 8; *unprofitable, hollow,* or, by impl., *injurious,* Mat. 12. 36.

ἀργέω, ῶ, fut. ήσω, (§ 16. tab. P) pr. *to be unemployed; to be inoperative, to linger.*

ἀργούς, acc. pl. masc. . . . . . ἀργός
ἀργῠρᾶ, nom. and acc. pl. neut. contr. . ἀργύρεος
ἀργύρεος], έα, εον, contr. οῦς, ᾶ, οῦν . . ἄργυρος
ἀργύρια, acc. pl. . . . . . . ἀργύριον
ἀργύριον, ου, τό, (§ 3. tab. C. c) . . ἄργυρος
ἀργυρίου, gen. sing. . . . . . ἀργύριον
ἀργυρίῳ, dat. sing. . . . . . . id.
ἀργυροκόπος,[d] ου, ὁ, (§ 3. tab. C. a) (ἄργυρος & κόπτω) *a forger of silver, silversmith.* L.G.
ἄργυρον, acc. sing. . . . . . ἄργυρος

ἄργῠρος, ου, ὁ, (§ 3. tab. C. a) *silver;* meton. *anything made of silver; money.*

ἀργύρεος, έα, εον, contr. οῦς, ᾶ, οῦν, (§ 7. rem. 5. c) *made of silver,* Ac. 19. 24; 2 Ti. 2. 20; Re. 9. 20.

ἀργύριον, ου, τό, (§ 3. tab. C. c) *silver;* meton. *money;* spc. *a piece of silver money, a shekel.*

ἀργύρου, gen. sing. . . . . . ἄργυρος
ἀργῠροῦς, acc. pl. masc. contr. . . ἀργύρεος
ἀργύρῳ, dat. sing. . . . . . ἄργυρος
ἀρεῖ, 3 pers. sing. fut. ind. act.—B.D.Ln.Tdf. } αἴρω
αἴρει, Rec. Gr. Sch. (Jno. 16. 22) }
Ἄρειον πάγον, acc. sing. . . . Ἄρειος πάγος
Ἄρειος πάγος, ου, ὁ, *the Areopagus, or Hill of Mars,* in Athens.
Ἀρείου πάγου, gen. sing. . . . Ἄρειος πάγος
Ἀρεοπαγίτης,[e] ου, ὁ, (§ 2. tab. B. c) *a judge of the court of Areopagus.* (ῑ).
ἀρέσαι, aor. 1, infin. . . . . ἀρέσκω
ἀρεσάσης, gen. sing. fem. part. aor. 1 . . id.
ἀρέσει, 3 pers. sing. fut. ind. (§ 36. rem. 3) id.
ἀρέσῃ, 3 pers. sing. aor. 1, subj. . . . id.
ἀρέσκεια], ας, ἡ, (§ 2. tab. B. b, and rem. 2) . id.
ἀρέσκειαν,[f] acc. sing. . . . . ἀρέσκεια
ἀρέσκειν, pres. infin. . . . . ἀρέσκω
ἀρεσκέτω, 3 pers. sing. pres. imper. . . id.
ἀρέσκοντες, nom. pl. masc. part. pres. . . id.
ἀρεσκόντων, gen. pl. masc. part. pres. . id.

ἀρέσκω, fut. ἀρέσω, imperf. ἤρεσκον, aor. 1, ἤρεσα, *to please,* Mat. 14. 6, et al.; *to be pleasing, acceptable,* Ac. 6. 5; *to consult the pleasure of* any one, Ro. 15. 1, 2, 3; 1 Co. 10. 33; *to seek favour with,* Ga. 1. 10; 1 Thes. 2. 4.

ἀρέσκεια, ας, ἡ, (§ 2. tab. B. b, and rem. 2) *a pleasing, desire of pleasing,* Col. 1. 10.

ἀρεστός, ή, όν, (§ 7. tab. F. a) *pleasing, acceptable,* Jno. 3. 22; 8. 29; Ac. 12. 3; *deemed proper,* Ac. 6. 2.

ἀρεστά, acc. pl. neut. . . . . . ἀρεστός
ἀρεστόν, nom. sing. neut. . . . . id.
ἀρεστός], ή, όν, (§ 7. tab. F. a) . . ἀρέσκω
Ἀρέτα,[g] gen. sing. . . . . Ἀρέτας
Ἀρέτας], α, ὁ, (§ 2. rem. 4) *Aretas,* pr. name.
ἀρετάς, acc. pl. . . . . . . ἀρετή
ἀρετή, ῆς, ἡ, (§ 2. tab. B. a) *goodness, good quality* of any kind; *a gracious act* of God, 1 Pe. 2. 9; 2 Pe. 1. 3; *virtue, uprightness,* Phi. 4. 8; 2 Pe. 1. 5.
ἀρετῇ, dat. sing. . . . . . ἀρετή
ἀρετήν, acc. sing. . . . . . id.
ἀρετῆς, gen. sing. . . . . . id.
ἄρῃ, 3 pers. sing. aor. 1, subj. act. . . αἴρω

[a] Ac. 2. 11. [b] Ro. 3. 14. [c] 2 Pe. 2. 3. [d] Ac. 19. 24. [e] Ac. 17. 34. [f] Col. 1. 10. [g] 2 Co. 11. 32.

ἄρῃς, 2 pers. sing. aor. 1, subj. act. . . αἴρω
ἀρθῇ, 3 p. sing. aor. 1, subj. pass.—Gr. Sch. Tdf. } id.
ἐξαρθῇ, Rec. (1 Co. 5. 2) . }
ἀρθήσεται, 3 p. sing. fut. ind. pass. (§ 27. rem. 3) id.
ἄρθητι, 2 pers. sing. aor. 1, imper. pass. id.
ἀρθήτω, 3 pers. sing. aor. 1, imper. pass. . id.
ἀρθῶσι, 3 pers. pl. aor. 1, subj. pass. . id.
ἀριθμέω, ῶ], fut. ήσω, (§ 16. tab. P) . . ἀριθμός
ἀριθμῆσαι, aor. 1, infin. act. . . . ἀριθμέω
ἀριθμόν, acc. sing. . . . . . ἀριθμός
ἀριθμός, οῦ, ὁ, (§ 3. tab. C. a) *a number*, Lu. 22. 3; Jno. 6. 10; Ac. 4. 4; Re. 20. 8; 13. 18.

ἀριθμέω, ῶ, fut. ήσω, (§ 16. tab. P) aor. 1, ἠρίθμησα, perf. pass. ἠρίθμημαι, *to number*, Mat. 10. 30; Lu. 12. 7; Re. 7. 9.

ἀριθμοῦ, gen. sing. . . . . . ἀριθμός
ἀριθμῷ, dat. sing. . . . . . . id.
Ἀριμαθαία], ας, ἡ, (§ 2. tab. B. b, and rem. 2) *Arimathea*, a town of Palestine.
Ἀριμαθαίας, gen. sing. . . . . . Ἀριμαθαία
Ἀρίσταρχον, acc. sing. . . . . Ἀρίσταρχος
Ἀρίσταρχος, ου, ὁ, (§ 3. tab. C. a) *Aristarchus*, pr. name.
Ἀριστάρχου, gen. sing. . . . . . Ἀρίσταρχος
ἀριστάω, ῶ], fut. ήσω, (§ 18. tab. R) . . ἄριστον
ἀριστερά, nom. sing. fem. . . . . ἀριστερός
ἀριστερός], ά, όν, (§ 7. rem. 1) *the left*; ἀριστερά, sc. χείρ, *the left hand*, Mat. 6. 3; so ἐξ ἀριστερῶν, sc. μερῶν, Lu. 23. 33; 2 Co. 6. 7.
ἀριστερῶν, gen. pl. . . . . . . ἀριστερός
ἀριστήσατε, 2 pers. pl. aor. 1, imper. . ἀριστάω
ἀριστήσῃ, 3 pers. sing. aor. 1, subj. . . id.
Ἀριστόβουλος], ου, ὁ, (§ 3. tab. C. a) *Aristobulus*, pr. name.
Ἀριστοβούλου,[a] gen. sing. . . Ἀριστόβουλος

ἄριστον, ου, τό, (§ 3. tab. C. c) pr. *the first meal, breakfast*; afterwards extended to signify also *a slight mid-day meal, luncheon*, Mat. 22. 4.

ἀριστάω, ῶ, fut. ήσω, (§ 18. tab. R) aor. 1, ἠρίστησα, *to take the first meal, breakfast*, Jno. 21. 12, 15; also, *to take a mid-day meal*, Lu. 11. 37.

ἀρίστου, gen. sing. . . . . . . ἄριστον
ἀρκεῖ, 3 pers. sing. pres. ind. . . . . ἀρκέω
ἀρκεῖσθε, 2 pers. pl. pres. imper. pass. . . id.
ἀρκέσῃ, 3 pers. sing. aor. 1, subj. . . ἀρκέω
ἀρκεσθησόμεθα, 1 pers. pl. fut. pass. (§ 22. rem. 4) id.
ἀρκετόν, nom. sing. neut. . . . . . ἀρκετός
ἀρκετός, ή, όν, (§ 7. tab. F. a) . . ἀρκέω

ἀρκέω, ῶ], fut. έσω, (§ 22. rem. 1) aor. 1, ἤρκεσα, pr. *to ward off*; thence, *to be of service, avail*; *to suffice, be enough*, Mat. 25. 9, et al.; pass. *to be contented, satisfied*, Lu. 3. 14; 1 Ti. 6. 8; He. 13. 5; 3 Jno. 10.

ἀρκετός, ή, ον, (§ 7. tab. F. a) *sufficient, enough*, Mat. 6. 34; 10. 25; 1 Pe. 4. 3.

ἄρκος], ου, ὁ, same signif. as ἄρκτος. v.r.
ἄρκου, gen. sing.—Gr. Sch. Tdf. . . } ἄρκος
ἄρκτου, Rec. (Re. 13. 2) . . }
ἀρκούμενοι, nom. pl. masc. part. pres. mid. . ἀρκέω
ἀρκούμενος, nom. sing. masc. part. pres. mid. id.
ἀρκοῦσι, 3 pers. pl. pres. ind. . . . id.

ἄρκτος], ου, ὁ, ἡ, (§ 3. tab. C. a, b) *a bear*.

ἄρκτου,[b] gen. sing. . . . . . ἄρκτος
ἅρμα, ατος, τό, (§ 4. tab. D. c) *a chariot, vehicle*, Ac. 8. 28, 29, 38.
Ἀρμαγεδδών,[c] τό, *Armageddon*.—Rec.
Ἀρμαγεδών, Gr. Sch. Tdf.
ἅρματι, dat. sing. . . . . . ἅρμα
ἅρματος, gen. sing. . . . . . . id.
ἁρμάτων, gen. pl. . . . . . id.
ἁρμόζω], fut. όσω, (§ 26. rem. 1) *to fit together*; mid. ἁρμόζομαι, aor. 1, ἡρμοσάμην, *to join, unite* in marriage, *espouse, betroth*, 2 Co. 11. 2.
ἁρμός], οῦ, ὁ, (§ 3. tab. C. a) *a joint or articulation* of the bones.
ἁρμῶν,[d] gen. pl. . . . . . . ἁρμός
ἄρνας,[e] acc. pl. (§ 6. rem. 4. d) . . ἀρνός
ἀρνεῖσθαι, pres. infin.—Al. Ln. Tdf. . } ἀρνέομαι
ἀρνήσασθαι, Rec. Gr. Sch. (Ac. 4. 16) }

ἀρνέομαι, οῦμαι], fut. ήσομαι, (§ 17. tab. Q) perf. (pass. form) ἤρνημαι, aor. 1, ἠρνησάμην, *to deny, disclaim, disown*, Mat. 10. 33, et al.; *to renounce*, Tit. 2. 12, et al.; *to decline, refuse*, He. 11. 24; absol. *to deny, contradict*, Lu. 8. 15, et al.

ἀρνησάμενοι, nom. pl. masc. part. aor. 1 . ἀρνέομαι
ἀρνησάμενος, nom. sing. masc. part. aor. 1 . id.
ἀρνήσασθαι, aor. 1, infin. . . . . id.

[a] Ro. 16. 10. [b] Re. 13. 2. [c] Re. 16. 16. [d] He. 4. 12. [e] Lu. 10. 3.

ἀρνησάσθω, 3 pers. s. aor. 1, imper.—Gr. Tdf.
ἀπαρνησάσθω. Rec. Sch. (Lu. 9. 23) } ἀρνέομαι
ἀρνήσεται, 3 pers. sing. fut. ind. . . id.
ἀρνήσῃ, 2 pers. sing. fut. ind.—B. D. Ln. Tdf.
ἀπαρνήσῃ, Rec. Gr. Sch. (Jno. 13. 38) } id.
ἀρνήσηται, 3 pers. sing. aor. 1, subj. . id.
ἀρνήσομαι, 1 pers. sing. fut. ind. . . id.
ἀρνησόμεθα, 1 pers. pl. fut. ind.—A. Ln. Tdf.
ἀρνούμεθα, Rec. Gr. Sch. (2 Ti. 2. 12) } id.
ἀρνούμεθα, 1 pers. pl. pres. ind. . . id.
ἀρνούμενοι, nom. pl. masc. part. pres. . . id.
ἀρνούμενος, nom. sing. masc. part. pres. . id.
ἀρνουμένων, gen. pl. part. pres. . . . id.
ἀρνοῦνται, 3 pers. pl. pres. ind. . . id.
ἀρνία, acc. pl. . . . . . . ἀρνίον
ἀρνίον, ου, τό, (§ 3. tab. C. c) *a young lamb, lambkin, lamb*, Jno. 21. 15; Re. 5. 6, 8.
ἀρνίου, gen. sing. . . . . . ἀρνίον
ἀρνίῳ, dat. sing. . . . . . . id.
ἀρνός, (§ 6. rem. 4. d) a gen. without a nom. in use, its place being supplied by ἀμνός, *a lamb*.
ἀρξάμενοι, nom. pl. masc. part. aor. 1, mid. ἄρχω
ἀρξάμενον, acc. sing. neut. part. aor. 1, mid. id.
ἀρξάμενος, nom. sing. masc. part. aor. 1, mid. id.
ἀρξαμένου, gen. sing. masc. part. aor. 1, mid. id.
ἀρξαμένων, gen. pl. part. aor. 1, mid.—C. D.
ἀρξάμενον, Rec. Gr. Sch. . .
ἀρξάμενοι, Tdf. (Lu. 24. 47) . } id.
ἄρξασθαι, aor. 1, infin. mid. . . . id.
ἄρξεσθε, 2 pers. pl. fut. ind. mid. . . id.
ἄρξῃ, 2 pers. sing. aor. 1, subj. mid. . . id.
ἄρξησθε, 2 pers. pl. aor. 1, subj. mid. . . id.
ἄρξηται, 3 pers. sing. aor. 1, subj. mid. . id.
ἄρξονται, 3 pers. pl. fut. ind. mid. . . id.
ἄρξωνται, 3 pers. pl. aor. 1, subj. mid. . id.
ἆρον, 2 pers. sing. aor. 1, imper. act. . . αἴρω
ἀροτριᾶν, pres. infin. contr. . . . ἀροτριάω
ἀροτριάω, ῶ], fut. άσω, (§ 22. rem. 2. a) . ἄροτρον
ἀροτριῶν, nom. sing. masc. part. pres. . ἀροτριάω
ἀροτριῶντα, acc. sing. masc. part. pres. . id.
ἄροτρον, ου, τό, (§ 3. tab. C. c) (ἀρόω, *to plough*) *a plough*.

ἀροτριάω, ῶ, fut. άσω, (§ 22. rem. 2. a) *to plough*, Lu. 17. 7; 1 Co. 9. 10.

ἀροῦσι, 3 pers. pl. fut. ind. act. . . αἴρω
ἁρπαγέντα, acc. sing. masc. part. aor. 2, pass. . ἁρπάζω
ἅρπαγες, nom. pl. (§ 4. rem. 2. b) . . ἅρπαξ

ἁρπᾰγή], ῆς, ἡ, (§ 2. tab. B. a) . . . ἁρπάζω
ἁρπαγήν, acc. sing. . . . . . ἁρπαγή
ἁρπαγῆς, gen. sing. . . . . . . id.
ἁρπαγησόμεθα, 1 p. pl. 2 fut. pass. (§ 24. rem. 3) ἁρπάζω
ἁρπαγμόν,[a] acc. sing. . . . . . ἁρπαγμός
ἁρπαγμός], οῦ, ὁ, (§ 3. tab. C. a) ἁρπάζω
ἁρπάζει, 3 pers. sing. pres. ind. act. . . id.
ἁρπάζειν, pres. infin. act. . . . . id.
ἁρπάζοντες, nom. pl. masc. part. pres. act. id.
ἁρπάζουσι, 3 pers. pl. pres. ind. act. . id.

ἁρπάζω], fut. άσω & ξω, (§ 26. rem. 2) aor. 1, ἥρπασα, aor. 1, pass. ἡρπάσθην, aor. 2, pass. ἡρπάγην, (ᾰ), (§ 24. rem. 6) *to seize, as a wild beast*, Jno. 10. 12; *take away by force, snatch away*, Mat. 13. 19; Jno. 10. 28, 29; Ac. 23. 10; Jude 23; met. *to seize on with avidity, eagerly, appropriate*, Mat. 11. 12; *to convey away suddenly, transport hastily*, Jno. 6. 15, et al.

ἁρπᾰγή, ῆς, ἡ, (§ 2. tab. B. a) *plunder, pillage, rapine; the act of plundering*, He. 10. 34; *prey, spoil*, or, *rapacity*, Mat. 23. 25; Lu. 11. 39.

ἁρπαγμός, οῦ, ὁ, (§ 3. tab. C. a) *rapine, robbery, eager seizure*; in N.T., *a thing retained with an eager grasp, or eagerly claimed and conspicuously exercised*, Phi. 2. 6.

ἅρπαξ, ᾰγος, ὁ, ἡ, τό, (§ 4. rem. 2. b) pr. *ravenous, ravening*, as a wild beast, Mat. 7. 15; met. *rapacious, given to extortion and robbery, an extortioner*, Lu. 18. 11; 1 Co. 5. 10, 11; 6. 10.

ἅρπαξ, αγος, ὁ, ἡ, τό . . . . ἁρπάζω
ἅρπαξι, dat. pl. . . . . . . ἅρπαξ
ἁρπάσαι, aor. 1, infin. act. . . . ἁρπάζω
ἁρπάσει, 3 pers. sing. fut. ind. act. . . id.
ἀῤῥᾰβών, ῶνος, ὁ, (§ 4. rem. 2. e) (Heb. עֲרָבוֹן) *a pledge, earnest*, 2 Co. 1. 22; 5. 5; Ep. 1. 14.
ἀῤῥαβῶνα, acc. sing. . . . . . ἀῤῥαβών
ἄῤῥᾰφος,[b] ου, ὁ, ἡ, (§ 7. rem. 2) (ἀ & ῥάπτω, *to sew*) *not sewed, without seam*. N.T.
ἄῤῥενα, acc. sing. . . . . . ἄῤῥην
ἄῤῥενες, nom. pl. . . . . . . id.

ἄῤῥην], ἄῤῥεν, ενος, ὁ, τό, (§ 7. rem. 4) *male, of the male sex*, Ro. 1. 27; Re. 12. 5, 13.

ἄῤῥητα,[c] acc. pl. neut. . . . . ἄῤῥητος

---

a Phi. 2. 6. b Jno. 19. 23. c 2 Co. 12. 4.

ἄῤῥητος], ου, ὁ, ἡ, (§ 7. rem. 2) (ἀ & ῥητός) pr. *not spoken; what ought not to be spoken, secret; which cannot be spoken or uttered, ineffable.*

ἄῤῥωστοι, nom. pl. masc. . . . . . ἄῤῥωστος

ἄῤῥωστος], ου, ὁ, ἡ, (§ 7. rem. 2) (ἀ & ῥώννυμι) *infirm, sick, an invalid,* Mat. 14. 14; Mar. 6. 5. 13; 16. 18; 1 Co. 11. 30.

ἀῤῥώστοις, dat. pl. masc. . . . . ἄῤῥωστος

ἀῤῥώστους, acc. pl. masc. . . . . . id.

ἄρσεν, acc. sing. neut. . . . . . ἄρσην

ἄρσενες, nom. pl. masc. . . . . . id.

ἀρσενοκοῖται, nom. pl. . . . . ἀρσενοκοίτης

ἀρσενοκοίταις, dat. pl. . . . . . id.

ἀρσενοκοίτης], ου, ὁ, (§ 2. tab. B. c) (ἄρσην & κοίτη) *one who lies with a male, a sodomite,* 1 Co. 6. 9; 1 Ti. 1. 10. L.G.

ἄρσεσι, dat. pl. masc. . . . . . ἄρσην

ἄρσην], ἄρσεν, ενος, ὁ, τό, (§ 7. rem. 4) *male, of the male sex,* Mat. 19. 4; Mar. 10. 6; Lu. 2. 23; Ro. 1. 27; Gal. 3. 28.

Ἀρτεμᾶν,[a] acc. sing. . . . Ἀρτεμᾶς

Ἀρτεμᾶς, ᾶ, ὁ, (§ 2. rem. 4) *Artemas,* pr. name.

Ἀρτέμιδος, gen. sing. . . . . Ἄρτεμις

Ἄρτεμις, ῐδος, ἡ, (§ 4. rem. 2. c) *Artemis* or *Diana,* Ac. 19. 24, 27, 28, 34.

ἀρτέμονα,[b] acc. sing. (§ 4. rem. 2. e) . . ἀρτέμων

ἀρτέμων], ονος, ὁ, (ἀρτάω, *to suspend*) *a topsail, artemon, supparum;* or, according to others, *the dolon* of Pliny and Pollux, a small sail near the prow of the ship, which was hoisted when the wind was too strong to use larger sails. N.T.

ἄρτι, adv. of time, pr. *at the present moment, close upon it* either before or after; *now, at the present juncture,* Mat. 3. 15; *forthwith, presently; just now, recently,* 1 Thes. 3. 6; ἕως ἄρτι, *until now, hitherto,* Mat. 11. 12; Jno. 2. 10, et al.; ἀπ' ἄρτι, or ἀπάρτι, *from this time, henceforth,* Mat. 23. 39, et al.

ἀρτιγεννητα,[c] nom. pl. neut. . . . ἀρτιγέννητος

ἀρτιγέννητος], ου, ὁ, ἡ, (§ 7. rem. 2) (ἄρτι & γεννάω) *just born, new-born.* L.G.

ἄρτιος,[d] ου, ὁ, ἡ, (§ 7. rem. 2) (ἄρω, *to fit, adapt*) *entirely suited; complete* in accomplishment, *ready.*

ἄρτοι, nom. pl. . . . . . . ἄρτος

ἄρτοις, dat. pl. . . . . . . id.

ἄρτον, acc. sing. . . . . . . ἄρτος

ἄρτος, ου, ὁ, (§ 3. tab. C. a) *bread; a loaf or thin cake of bread,* Mat. 26. 26, et al.; *food,* Mat. 15. 2; Mar. 3. 20, et al.; *bread, maintenance, living, necessaries of life,* Mat. 6. 11; Lu. 11. 3; 2 Thes. 3. 8.

ἄρτου, gen. sing. . . . . . ἄρτος

ἄρτους, acc. pl. . . . . . . id.

ἄρτῳ, dat. sing. . . . . . . id.

ἄρτων, gen. pl. . . . . . . id.

ἀρτυθήσεται, 3 pers. sing. fut. 1, ind. pass. ἀρτύω

ἀρτύσεται, 3 pers. sing. fut. ind. mid.—A. D.
ἀρτύσετε, Rec. Gr. Sch. Tdf. (Mar. 9. 50) } id.

ἀρτύσετε, 2 pers. pl. fut. ind. act. . . . id

ἀρτύω], (or ἀρτύνω,) fut. ύσω, (§ 13. tab. M) fut. pass. ἀρτυθήσομαι, perf. pass. ἤρτυμαι, (ἄρω, *to fit*) pr. *to fit, prepare; to season, make savoury,* Mar. 9. 50; Lu. 14. 34; Col. 4. 6.

Ἀρφαξάδ,[e] ὁ, *Arphaxad,* pr. name, indecl.

ἀρχάγγελος, ου, ὁ, (§ 3. tab. C. a) (ἀρχή & ἄγγελος) *an archangel, chief angel,* 1 Thes. 4. 16; Jude 9. N.T.

ἀρχαγγέλου, gen. sing. . . . . ἀρχάγγελος

ἀρχαί, nom. pl. . . . . . . ἀρχή

ἀρχαῖα, nom. pl. neut. . . . . ἀρχαῖος

ἀρχαίοις, dat. pl. masc. . . . . id.

ἀρχαῖον, acc. sing. masc. . . . . id.

ἀρχαῖος, αία, αῖον, (§ 7. rem. 1) . . ἀρχή

ἀρχαίου, gen. sing. masc. . . . ἀρχαῖος

ἀρχαῖς, dat. pl. . . . . . . ἀρχή

ἀρχαίῳ, dat. sing. masc. . . . . ἀρχαῖος

ἀρχαίων, gen. pl. . . . . . . id.

ἀρχάς, acc. pl. . . . . . . ἀρχή

ἄρχειν, pres. infin. act. . . . . . ἄρχω

Ἀρχέλαος,[f] ου, ὁ, (§ 3. tab. C. a) *Archelaus,* pr. name.

ἀρχή, ῆς, ἡ, (§ 2. tab. B. a) *a beginning,* Mat. 24. 8, et al.; *an extremity, corner,* or, *an attached cord,* Ac. 10. 11; 11. 5; *first place, headship; high estate, eminence,* Jude 6; *authority,* Lu. 20. 20, et al.; *an authority, magistrate,* Lu. 12. 11; *a principality, prince,* of spiritual existence, Ep. 3. 10; 6. 12, et al.; ἀπ' ἀρχῆς, ἐξ ἀρχῆς, *from the first, originally,* Mat. 19. 4, 8; Lu. 1. 2; Jno. 6. 64; 2 Thes. 2. 13; 1 Jno. 1. 1; 2. 7, et al.; ἐν ἀρχῇ, κατ' ἀρχάς,

[a] Tit. 3. 12. [b] Ac. 27. 40. [c] 1 Pe. 2. 2. [d] 2 Ti. 3. 17. [e] Lu. 3. 36. [f] Mat. 2. 22.

in the beginning of things, Jno. 1. 1, 2; He. 1. 10; ἐν ἀρχῇ, *at the first*, Ac. 11. 15; τὴν ἀρχήν, used adverbially, *wholly, altogether*, Jno. 8. 25.

ἀρχαῖος, αία, αῖον, *old, ancient, of former age*, Mat. 5. 21, 27, 33, et al.; *of long standing, old, veteran*, Ac. 21. 16; ἀφ' ἡμερῶν ἀρχαίων, *from early days, from an early period*, of the Gospel, Ac. 15. 7.

ἄρχω, fut. ξω, (§ 23. rem. 1. b) pr. *to be first; to govern*, Mar. 10. 42; Ro. 15. 12; mid. *to begin*, Mat. 4. 17, et al.; *to take commencement*, Lu. 24. 47; 1 Pe. 4. 17.

ἄρχων, οντος, ὁ, (§ 4. rem. 2. d) *one invested with power and dignity, chief, ruler, prince, magistrate*, Mat. 9. 23; 20. 25, et al. freq.

ἀρχῇ, dat. sing. . . . . . . ἀρχή

ἀρχηγόν, acc. sing. . . . . . ἀρχηγός

ἀρχηγός], ου, ὁ, (§ 3. tab. C. a) (ἀρχή & ἄγω) *a chief, leader, prince*, Ac. 5. 31; *a prime author*, Ac. 3. 15; He. 2. 10; 12. 2.

ἀρχήν, acc. sing. . . . . . ἀρχή

ἀρχῆς, gen. sing. . . . . . id.

ἀρχιερατικός], ή, όν, (§ 7. tab. F. a) . . ἀρχιερεύς

ἀρχιερατικοῦ,[a] gen. sing. neut. . . ἀρχιερατικός

ἀρχιερέα, acc. sing. . . . . . ἀρχιερεύς

ἀρχιερεῖ, dat. sing. . . . . . id.

ἀρχιερεῖς, nom. and acc. pl. . . . . id.

ἀρχιερεύς, έως, ὁ, (§ 5. tab. E. d) (ἀρχι- & ἱερεύς) *a high-priest, chief-priest*.

ἀρχιερατικός, ή, όν, (§ 7. tab. F. a) *pontifical, belonging to or connected with the high-priest or his office*, Ac. 4. 6. N.T.

ἀρχιερεῦσι, dat. pl. . . . . . ἀρχιερεύς

ἀρχιερέων, gen. pl. . . . . . id.

ἀρχιερέως, gen. sing. . . . . . id.

ἀρχιποίμενος,[b] gen. sing. (§ 4. rem. 2. e) . ἀρχιποίμην

ἀρχιποίμην], ενος, ὁ, (ἀρχι- & ποιμήν) *chief shepherd*. N.T.

Ἄρχιππος], ου, ὁ, *Archippus*, pr. name.

Ἀρχίππῳ, dat. sing. . . . . . Ἄρχιππος

ἀρχισυνάγωγοι, nom. pl. . . . . ἀρχισυνάγωγος

ἀρχισυνάγωγον, acc. sing. . . . . id.

ἀρχισυνάγωγος, ου, ὁ, (§ 3. tab. C. a) (ἀρχι- & συναγωγή) *a president or moderating elder of a synagogue*, Mar. 5. 22, 35, 36, 38; Lu. 8. 49, et al. N.T.

ἀρχισυναγώγου, gen. sing. . . . ἀρχισυνάγωγ

ἀρχισυναγώγῳ, dat. sing. . . . . id.

ἀρχισυναγώγων, gen. pl. . . . . . id.

ἀρχιτέκτων,[c] ονος, ὁ, (§ 4. rem. 2. e) (ἀρχι- & τέκτων) *architect, head or master-builder*.

ἀρχιτελώνης,[d] ου, ὁ, (§ 2. tab. B. d) (ἀρχι- & τελώνης) *a chief publican, chief collector of the customs or taxes*. N.T.

ἀρχιτρίκλῖνος, ου, ὁ, (§ 3. tab. C. a) (ἀρχι- & τρίκλινος, *triclinium, a dining-room in which three couches were placed round the table*, etc.) *director of a feast*, Jno. 2. 8, 9. N.T.

ἀρχιτρικλίνῳ, dat. sing. . . . . ἀρχιτρίκλινος

ἀρχόμεθα, 1 pers. pl. pres. ind. mid. . . ἄρχω

ἀρχόμενος, nom. sing. masc. part. pres. mid. id.

ἀρχομένων, gen. pl. part. pres. mid. . . id.

ἄρχοντα, acc. sing. . . . . . . ἄρχων

ἄρχοντας, acc. pl. . . . . . id.

ἄρχοντες, nom. and voc. pl. . . . . id.

ἄρχοντι, dat. sing. . . . . . id.

ἄρχοντος, gen. sing. . . . . . id.

ἀρχόντων, gen. pl. . . . . . id.

ἄρχουσι, dat. pl. . . . . . . id.

ἄρχω], fut. ξω, (§ 23. rem. 1. b) . . ἀρχή

ἄρχων, οντος, ὁ, (§ 4. rem. 2. d) . . id

ἀρῶ, 1 pers. sing. fut. ind. (§ 27. rem. 1. c) αἴρω

ἄρωμα], ατος, τό, (§ 4. tab. D. c) *an aromatic substance, spice*, etc., Mar. 16. 1; Lu. 23. 56; 24. 1; Jno. 19. 40.

ἀρώματα, acc. pl. . . . . . . ἄρωμα

ἀρωμάτων, gen. pl. . . . . . . id.

Ἀσά, ὁ, *Asa*, pr. name, indecl.

ἀσάλευτον, acc. sing. fem. . . . . ἀσάλευτος

ἀσάλευτος, ου, ὁ, ἡ, τό, -ον, (§ 7. rem. 2) (ἀ & σαλεύω) *unshaken, immovable*, Ac. 27. 41; met. *firm, stable, enduring*, He. 12. 28.

ἄσβεστον, acc. sing. neut. . . . . ἄσβεστος

ἄσβεστος], ου, ὁ, ἡ, τό, -ον, (§ 7. rem. 2) (ἀ & σβέννυμι) *unquenched; inextinguishable, unquenchable*, Mat. 3. 12; Mar. 9. 43, 45; Lu. 3. 17.

ἀσβέστῳ, dat. sing. neut. . . . . ἄσβεστος

ἀσέβεια], ας, ἡ, (§ 2. tab. B. b, and rem. 2) ἀσεβής

ἀσέβειαν, acc. sing. . . . . . ἀσέβεια

ἀσεβείας, gen. sing. . . . . . id.

ἀσεβείας, acc. pl. . . . . . . id.

[a] Ac. 4. 6. [b] 1 Pe. 5. 4. [c] 1 Co. 3. 10. [d] Lu. 19. 2.

ἀσεβειῶν, gen. pl. . . . . ἀσέβεια

ἀσεβεῖν, pres. infin. . . . . ἀσεβέω

ἀσεβέω, ῶ], fut. ήσω, (§ 16. tab. P) ἀσεβής

ἀσεβεῖς, nom. and acc. pl. masc. . . id.

ἀσεβέσι, dat. pl. masc. . . . id.

ἀσεβῆ, acc. sing. masc. . . . . id.

ἀσεβής, έος, οῦς, ὁ, ἡ, τό, -ές, (§ 7. tab. G. b) (ἀ & σέβομαι) *impious, ungodly; wicked, sinful,* Ro. 4. 5; 5. 6, et al.

ἀσέβεια, ας, ἡ, (§ 2. tab. B. b, and rem. 2) *impiety, ungodliness; improbity, wickedness,* Ro. 1. 18; 11. 26; 2 Ti. 2. 16. Tit. 2. 12; Jude 15, 18.

ἀσεβέω, ῶ, fut. ήσω, (§ 16. tab. P) perf. ἠσέβηκα, aor. 1, ἠσέβησα, *to be impious, to act impiously or wickedly, live an impious life,* 2 Pe. 2. 6; Jude 15.

ἀσεβῶν, gen. pl. . . . . ἀσεβής

ἀσέλγεια, ας, ἡ, (§ 2. tab. B. b, and rem. 2) (ἀσελγής, *outrageous*) *intemperance; licentiousness, lasciviousness,* Ro. 13. 13, et al.; *insolence, outrageous behaviour,* Mar. 7. 22.

ἀσελγείᾳ, dat. sing. . . . . ἀσέλγεια

ἀσελγείαις, dat. pl. . . . . id.

ἀσέλγειαν, acc. sing. . . . . id.

ἀσήμου,[a] gen. sing. fem. . . . ἄσημος

ἄσημος], ου, ὁ, ἡ, (§ 7. rem. 2) (ἀ & σῆμα) pr. *not marked;* met. *not noted, not remarkable, unknown to fame, ignoble, mean, inconsiderable.*

Ἀσήρ, ὁ, *Aser,* pr. name, indecl.

ἀσθενεῖ, 3 pers. sing. pres. indic. . . ἀσθενέω

ἀσθένεια, ας, ἡ, (§ 2. tab. B. b, and rem. 2) ἀσθενής

ἀσθενείᾳ, dat. sing. . . . . ἀσθένεια

ἀσθενείαις, dat. pl. . . . . . id.

ἀσθένειαν, acc. sing. . . . . id.

ἀσθενείας, gen. sing. . . . . id.

ἀσθενείας, acc. pl. . . . . id.

ἀσθενεῖς, nom. and acc. pl. masc. . . ἀσθενής

ἀσθενειῶν, gen. pl. . . . . ἀσθένεια

ἀσθενές, nom. and acc. sing. neut. . . ἀσθενής

ἀσθενέσι, dat. pl. masc. . . . id.

ἀσθενέστερα, nom. pl. neut. compar. (§ 8. rem. 1) id.

ἀσθενεστέρῳ, dat. sing. neut. compar. . . id.

ἀσθενέω, ῶ], fut. ήσω, (§ 16. tab. P) . id.

ἀσθενῆ, acc. sing. masc. and pl. neut. . . id.

ἀσθένημα], ατος, τό, (§ 4. tab. D. c) . id.

ἀσθενήματα,[b] acc. pl. . . ἀσθένημα

ἀσθενής, έος, οῦς, ὁ, ἡ, τό, -ές, (§ 7. rem. 5. a) (ἀ & σθένος, *strength*) *without strength, weak, infirm,* Mat. 26. 41; Mar. 14. 38; 1 Pe. 3. 7; *helpless,* Ro. 5. 6; *imperfect, inefficient,* Gal. 4. 9; *feeble, without energy,* 2 Co. 10. 10; *infirm* in body, *sick, sickly,* Mat. 25. 39, 43, 44, et al.; *weak,* mentally or spiritually, *dubious, hesitating,* 1 Co. 8. 7, 10; 9. 22; 1 Thes. 5. 14; *afflicted, distressed, oppressed with calamities,* 1 Co. 4. 10.

ἀσθένεια, ας, ἡ, (§ 2. tab. B. b, and rem. 2) *want of strength, weakness, feebleness,* 1 Co. 15. 43; bodily *infirmity, state of ill health, sickness,* Mat. 8. 17; Lu. 5. 15, et al.; met. *infirmity, frailty, imperfection,* intellectual and moral, Ro. 6. 19; 1 Co. 2. 3; He. 5. 2; 7. 28; *suffering, affliction distress, calamity,* Ro. 8. 26, et al.

ἀσθενέω, ῶ, fut. ήσω, (§ 16. tab. P) aor. 1, ἠσθένησα, *to be weak, infirm, deficient in strength; to be inefficient,* Ro. 8. 3; 2 Co. 13. 3; *to be sick,* Mat. 25. 36, et al.; met. *to be weak* in faith, *to doubt, hesitate, be unsettled, timid,* Ro. 14. 1; 1 Co. 8. 9, 11, 12; 2 Co. 11. 29; *to be deficient in authority, dignity, or power, be contemptible,* 2 Co. 11. 21; 13. 3, 9; *to be afflicted, distressed, needy,* Ac. 20. 35; 2 Co. 12. 10; 13. 4, 9.

ἀσθένημα, ατος, τό, (§ 4. tab. D. c) pr. *weakness, infirmity,* met. *doubt, scruple, hesitation,* Ro. 15. 1. N.T.

ἀσθενήσας, nom. sing. masc. part. aor. 1 . ἀσθενέω

ἀσθενήσασαν, acc. sing. fem. part. aor. 1 . id.

ἀσθενοῦμεν, 1 pers. pl. pres. ind. . . id.

ἀσθενοῦντα, acc. sing. masc. part. pres. . id.

ἀσθενοῦντας, acc. pl. masc. part. pres. . id.

ἀσθενούντων, gen. pl. masc. part. pres. . . id.

ἀσθενοῦς, gen. sing. masc. . . . ἀσθενής

ἀσθενοῦσαν, acc. sing. fem. part. pres. . . ἀσθενέω

ἀσθενοῦσι, dat. pl. masc. part. pres. . . id.

ἀσθενῶ, 1 pers. sing. pres. subj. . . . id.

ἀσθενῶμεν, 1 pers. pl. pres. subj. . . id.

ἀσθενῶν, nom. sing. masc. part. pres. . . id.

ἀσθενῶν, gen. pl. . . . . ἀσθενής

Ἀσία, ας, ἡ, (§ 2. tab. B. b, and rem. 2) [unless it

[a] Ac. 21. 39. [b] Ro. 15. 1.

be the fem. adj. γῆ being understood] *Asia*, the Roman province.

Ἀσιανός, οῦ, ὁ, ἡ, *belonging to the Roman province of Asia.*

Ἀσίᾳ, dat. sing. . . . . . Ἀσία

Ἀσίαν, acc. sing. . . . . . id.

Ἀσιανοί,[a] nom. pl. masc. . . . Ἀσιανός

Ἀσιανός], οῦ, ὁ, ἡ, (§ 7. rem. 2) . . Ἀσία

Ἀσιάρχης], ου, ὁ, (§ 2. tab. B. c) (Ἀσία & ἀρχή) *an Asiarch*, an officer in the province of Asia, as in other eastern provinces of the Roman empire, selected, with others, from the more opulent citizens, to preside over the things pertaining to religious worship, and to exhibit annual public games at their own expense in honour of the gods, in the manner of the ædiles at Rome. L.G.

Ἀσιαρχῶν,[b] gen. pl. . . . . Ἀσιάρχης

Ἀσίας, gen. sing. . . . . . Ἀσία

ἀσιτία], ας, ἡ, (§ 2. tab. B. b, and rem. 2) . ἄσιτος

ἀσιτίας,[c] gen. sing. . . . . ἀσιτία

ἄσιτοι,[d] nom. pl. masc. . . . . ἄσιτος

ἄσῖτος], ου, ὁ, ἡ, (§ 7. rem. 2) (ἀ & σῖτος) *abstaining from food, fasting.*

ἀσιτία, ας, ἡ, (§ 2. tab. B. b, and rem. 2) *abstinence from food, fasting.*

ἀσκέω, ῶ, fut. ήσω, (§ 16. tab. P) pr. *to work* materials; absol. *to train or exert one's self, make endeavour*, Ac. 24. 16.

ἀσκοί, nom. pl. . . . . . ἀσκός

ἀσκός], οῦ, ὁ, (§ 3. tab. C. a) *a leathern bag or bottle, bottle of skin*, Mat. 9. 17; Mar. 2. 22; Lu. 5. 37, 38.

ἀσκούς, acc. pl. . . . . . ἀσκός

ἀσκῶ,[e] 1 pers. sing. pres. ind. contr. . ἀσκέω

ἀσμένως, adv. *gladly, joyfully*, Ac. 2. 41; 21. 17.

ἄσοφοι,[f] nom. pl. masc. . . . . ἄσοφος

ἄσοφος], ου, ὁ, ἡ, (§ 7. rem. 2) (ἀ & σοφός) *unwise; destitute of* Christian *wisdom.*

ἀσπάζεσθαι, pres. infin. . . . . ἀσπάζομαι

ἀσπάζεται, 3 pers. sing. pres. ind. . . . id.

ἀσπάζομαι, fut. σομαι, (§ 26. rem. 1) aor. 1, ἠσπασάμην, perf. ἤσπασμαι, *to salute, greet, welcome, express good wishes, pay respects*, Mat. 10. 12; Mar. 9. 15, et al. freq.; *to bid farewell*, Ac. 20. 1; 21. 6; *to treat with affection*, Mat. 5. 47; met. *to embrace* mentally, *welcome* to the heart or understanding, He. 11. 13.

ἀσπασμός, οῦ, ὁ, (§ 3. tab. C. a) *salutation, greeting*, Mat. 23. 7; Mar. 12. 38, et al.

ἀσπάζονται, 3 pers. pl. pres. ind. . ἀσπάζομαι

ἀσπάζου, 2 pers. sing. pres. imper. . . id.

ἄσπασαι, 2 pers. sing. aor. 1, imper. . id.

ἀσπασάμενοι, nom. pl. masc. part. aor. 1 . id.

ἀσπασάμενος, nom. sing. masc. part. aor. 1 id.

ἀσπάσασθε, 2 pers. pl. aor. 1, imper. . id.

ἀσπάσησθε, 2 pers. pl. aor. 1, subj. . . id.

ἀσπασμόν, acc. sing. . . . . ἀσπασμός

ἀσπασμός, οῦ, ὁ, (§ 3. tab. C. a) . ἀσπάζομαι

ἀσπασμοῦ, gen. sing. . . . . ἀσπασμός

ἀσπασμούς, acc. pl. . . . . . id.

ἀσπασόμενοι, nom. pl. masc. part. fut. . ἀσπάζομαι

ἀσπίδων,[g] gen. pl. (§ 4. rem. 2. c) . . ἀσπίς

ἄσπιλοι, nom. pl. masc. . . . . ἄσπιλος

ἄσπιλον, acc. sing. masc. and fem. . . id.

ἄσπῐλος], ου, ὁ, ἡ, (§ 7. rem. 2) (ἀ & σπίλος) *spotless, unblemished, pure*, 1 Ti. 6. 14; Ja. 1. 27; 1 Pe. 1. 19; 2 Pe. 3. 14. L.G.

ἀσπίς], ίδος, ἡ, *an asp*, a species of serpent of the most deadly venom.

ἄσπονδοι, nom. pl. masc. . . . . ἄσπονδος

ἄσπονδος], ου, ὁ, ἡ, (§ 7. rem. 2) (ἀ & σπονδή, *a libation* usually conjoined with the making of a treaty) pr. *unwilling to make a treaty*; hence, *implacable, irreconcilable*, Ro. 1. 31; 2 Ti. 3. 3.

ἀσπόνδους, acc. pl. masc. . . . . ἄσπονδος

ἀσσάριον], ου, τό, (§ 3. tab. C. c) dimin. of the Latin *as*, a Roman brass coin of the value of one-tenth of a denarius, or δραχμή, and equal to three and one-tenth farthings of our money, used to convey the idea of a very trifling sum, like the English term *a doit*, Mat. 10. 29; Lu. 12. 6. N.T.

ἀσσαρίου, gen. sing. . . . . . ἀσσάριον

ἀσσαρίων, gen. pl. . . . . . id.

ἆσσον,[h] adv. *nearer; very nigh, close*; used as the compar. of ἄγχι.

Ἄσσον, acc. sing. . . . . . Ἄσσος

Ἄσσος], ου, ἡ, (§ 3. tab. C. b) *Assos*, a maritime city of Mysia, in Asia Minor.

a Ac. 20. 4. b Ac. 19. 31. c Ac. 27. 21. d Ac. 27. 33. e Ac. 24. 16. f Ep. 5. 15. g Ro. 3. 13. h Ac. 27. 13.

ἀστατέω, ῶ], fut. ήσω, (§ 16. tab. P) (ἄστατος, *unfixed, unstable,* from ἀ & ἵστημι) *to be unsettled, to be a wanderer, be homeless.* L.G.

ἀστατοῦμεν,[a] 1 pers. pl. pres. ind. . . . ἀστατέω

ἀστεῖον, acc. sing. neut. . . . . ἀστεῖος

ἀστεῖος, ου, ὁ, ἡ, (§ 7. rem. 2) (ἄστυ, *a city*) pr. *belonging to a city; well bred, polite, polished;* hence, *elegant, fair, comely, beautiful,* Ac. 7. 20; He. 11. 23.

ἀστέρα, acc. sing. . . . . . . ἀστήρ

ἀστέρας, acc. pl. . . . . . . id.

ἀστέρες, nom. pl. . . . . . . id.

ἀστέρος, gen. sing. (§ 4. rem. 2. f) . . id.

ἀστέρων, gen. pl. . . . . . . id.

ἀστήρ, έρος, ὁ, (§ 6. rem. 4. c) *a star, luminous body like a star, luminary,* Mat. 2. 2, 7, 9, 10; Re. 1. 16, et al.

ἀστήρικτοι, nom. pl. masc. . . . ἀστήρικτος

ἀστήρικτος], ου, ὁ, ἡ, (§ 7. rem. 2) (ἀ & στηρίζω) *not made firm; unsettled, unstable, unsteady,* 2 Pe. 2. 14; 3. 16. L.G.

ἀστηρίκτους, acc. pl. fem. . . . ἀστήρικτος

ἄστοργοι, nom. pl. masc. . . . ἄστοργος

ἄστοργος], ου, ὁ, ἡ, (§ 7. rem. 2) (ἀ & στοργή, *natural or instinctive affection*) *devoid of natural or instinctive affection, without affection to kindred,* Ro. 1. 31; 2 Ti. 3. 3.

ἀστόργους, acc. pl. masc. . . . . ἄστοργος

ἀστοχέω, ῶ], fut. ήσω, (§ 16. tab. P) aor. 1, ἠστόχησα, (ἀ & στόχος, *a mark*) pr. *to miss the mark;* met. *to err, deviate, swerve from,* 1 Ti. 1. 6, 21; 2 Ti. 2. 18. L.G.

ἀστοχήσαντες, nom. pl. masc. part. aor. 1 . ἀστοχέω

ἄστρα, nom. pl. . . . . . . ἄστρον

ἀστραπαί, nom. pl. . . . . . ἀστραπή

ἀστρᾰπή, ῆς, ἡ, (§ 2. tab. B. a) . . . ἀστράπτω

ἀστραπῇ, dat. sing. . . . . . ἀστραπή

ἀστραπήν, acc. sing. . . . . . id.

ἀστράπτουσα, nom. sing. fem. part. pres. . ἀστράπτω

ἀστραπτούσαις, dat. pl. fem. part. pres. . id.

ἀστράπτω], fut. ψω, (§ 23. rem. 1. a) *to lighten, flash as lightning,* Lu. 17. 24; *to be bright, shining,* Lu. 24. 4.

ἀστρᾰπή, ῆς, ἡ, (§ 2. tab. B. a) *lightning,* Mat. 24. 27; *brightness, lustre,* Lu. 11. 36.

ἄστροις, dat. pl. . . . . . . ἄστρον

ἄστρον, ου, τό, (§ 3. tab. C. c) *a constellation; a star,* Lu. 21. 25; Ac. 7. 43; 27. 20; He. 11. 12.

ἄστρων, gen. pl. . . . . . . ἄστρον

Ἀσύγκριτον,[b] acc. sing. . . . . Ἀσύγκριτος

Ἀσύγκρῐτος], ου, ὁ, *Asyncritus,* pr. name.

ἀσύμφωνοι,[c] nom. pl. masc. . . . ἀσύμφωνος

ἀσύμφωνος], ου, ὁ, ἡ, (§ 7. rem. 2) (ἀ & σύμφωνος) *discordant in sound;* met. *discordant, at difference.*

ἀσύνετοι, nom. pl. masc. . . . . ἀσύνετος

ἀσύνετος, ου, ὁ, ἡ, (§ 7. rem. 2) (ἀ & συνετός from συνίημι) *unintelligent, dull,* Mat. 15. 16; Mar. 7. 18; *reckless, perverse,* Ro. 1. 21, 31; *unenlightened, heathenish,* Ro. 10. 19.

ἀσυνέτους, acc. pl. masc. . . . . ἀσύνετος

ἀσυνέτῳ, dat. sing. neut. . . . . id.

ἀσύνθετος], ου, ὁ, ἡ, (§ 7. rem. 2) (ἀ & συντίθεμαι, *to make a covenant*) *regardless of covenants, perfidious.*

ἀσυνθέτους,[d] acc. pl. masc. . . . ἀσύνθετος

ἀσφάλεια, ας, ἡ, (§ 2. tab. B. b, and rem. 2) ἀσφαλής

ἀσφαλείᾳ, dat. sing. . . . . . ἀσφάλεια

ἀσφάλειαν, acc. sing. . . . . . id.

ἀσφαλές, nom. and acc. sing. neut. . . ἀσφαλής

ἀσφαλῆ, acc. sing. fem. . . . . . id.

ἀσφαλῆν, acc. sing.—Al. Ln. . . . } id.
ἀσφαλῆ, Rec. Gr. Sch. Tdf. (He. 6. 19) }

ἀσφᾰλής], έος, οῦς, ὁ, ἡ, τό, -ές, (§ 7. tab. G. b) (ἀ & σφάλλομαι, *to stumble, fall*) pr. *firm, secure from falling; firm, sure, steady, immovable,* He. 6. 19; met. *certain, sure,* Ac. 21. 34; 22. 30; 25. 26; *safe, making secure,* Phi. 3. 1.

ἀσφάλεια, ας, ἡ, (§ 2. tab. B. b, and rem. 2) pr. *state of security from falling, firmness; safety, security,* 1 Thes. 5. 3; *certainty, truth,* Lu. 1. 4; *means of security,* Ac. 5. 23.

ἀσφαλίζω, fut. ίσω, (§ 26. rem. 1) *to make fast, safe, or secure,* Mat. 27. 64, 65, 66; Ac. 16. 24. L.G.

ἀσφαλῶς, adv. *securely, safely; without fail, safely,* Mar. 14. 44; Ac. 16. 23; *certainly, assuredly,* Ac. 2. 36.

ἀσφαλίζω], fut. ίσω, (§ 26. rem. 1) . . ἀσφαλής.

[a] 1 Co. 4. 11. [b] Ro. 16. 14. [c] Ac. 28. 25. [d] Ro. 1. 31.

ἀσφαλίσασθε, 2 pers. pl. aor. 1, imper. mid. . ἀσφαλίζω
ἀσφαλισθῆναι, aor. 1, infin. pass. . . id.
ἀσφαλῶς, adv. . . . . . . ἀσφαλής
ἀσχήμονα,[a] nom. pl. neut. . . ἀσχήμων
ἀσχημονεῖ, 3 pers. sing. pres. ind. . . ἀσχημονέω
ἀσχημονεῖν, pres. infin. . . . id.
ἀσχημονέω, ῶ], fut. ήσω, (§ 16. tab. P) . ἀσχήμων
ἀσχημοσύνη], ης, ἡ, (§ 2. tab. B. a) . id.
ἀσχημοσύνην, acc. sing. . . . ἀσχημοσύνη

ἀσχήμων], ονος, ὁ, ἡ, τό, -ον, (§ 7. tab. G. a) (ἀ & σχῆμα) *indecorous, uncomely, indecent.*

ἀσχημονέω, ῶ, fut. ήσω, (§ 16. tab. P) *to behave in an unbecoming manner, or indecorously,* 1 Co. 13. 5; *to behave in a manner open to censure,* 1 Co. 7. 36.

ἀσχημοσύνη, ης, ἡ, (§ 2. tab. B. a) pr. *external indecorum; nakedness, shame, pudenda,* Re. 16. 15; *indecency, infamous lust, or lewdness,* Ro. 1. 27.

ἀσωτία, ας, ἡ, (§ 2. tab. B. b, and rem. 2) (pr. *the disposition and life of one who is* **ἄσωτος,** *abandoned, recklessly debauched) profligacy, dissoluteness, debauchery,* Ep. 5. 18; Tit. 1. 6; 1 Pe. 4. 4.

ἀσώτως, adv. *dissolutely, profligately.*

ἀσωτίας, gen. sing. . . . . ἀσωτία
ἀσώτως,[b] adv. . . . . . . id.
ἀτακτέω, ῶ], fut. ήσω, (§ 16. tab. P) . ἄτακτος

ἄτακτος], ου, ὁ, ἡ, (§ 7. rem. 2) (ἀ & τάσσω) pr. used of soldiers, *disorderly;* met. *irregular* in conduct, *disorderly.*

ἀτακτέω, ῶ, fut. ήσω, (§ 16. tab. P) pr. *to infringe* military *order;* met. *to be irregular, behave disorderly,* 2 Thes. 3. 7.

ἀτάκτως, adv. *disorderly,* 2 Thes. 3. 6, 11.

ἀτάκτους,[c] acc. pl. masc. . . . . ἄτακτος
ἀτάκτως, adv. . . . . . . id.

ἄτεκνος, ου, ὁ, ἡ, (§ 7. rem. 2) (ἀ & τέκνον) *childless,* Lu. 20. 28, 29, 30.

ἀτενίζετε, 2 pers. pl. pers. ind. . . . ἀτενίζω
ἀτενίζοντες, nom. pl. masc. part. pres. . id.

ἀτενίζω], fut. ίσω, aor. 1, ἠτένισα, (§ 26. rem. 1) (ἀτενής, *intent*) *to fix one's eyes upon, to look steadily, gaze intently,* Lu. 4. 20, et al.

ἀτενίσαι, aor. 1, infin. . . . . ἀτενίζω
ἀτενίσαντες, nom. pl. masc. part. aor. 1 . id.
ἀτενίσας, nom. sing. masc. part. aor. 1 . . id.
ἀτενίσασα, nom. sing. fem. part. aor. 1 . id.

ἄτερ, *without,* Lu. 22. 6, 35.

ἀτιμάζεις, 2 pers. sing. pres. ind. act. . . ἀτιμάζω
ἀτιμάζεσθαι, pres. infin. pass. . . id.
ἀτιμάζετε, 2 pers. pl. pres. ind. act. . . id.
ἀτιμάζω], fut. άσω, (§ 26. rem. 1) . . ἄτιμος
ἀτιμάσαντες, nom. pl. masc. part. aor. 1, act. . ἀτιμάζω
ἀτιμασθῆναι, aor. 1, infin. pass. . . id.
ἀτιμάω, ῶ], fut. ήσω, (§ 18. tab. R) v.r. . ἄτιμος
ἀτιμία, ας, ἡ, (§ 2. tab. B. b, and rem. 2) . id.
ἀτιμίᾳ, dat. sing. . . . . ἀτιμία
ἀτιμίαν, acc. sing. . . . id.
ἀτιμίας, gen. sing. . . . . . id.
ἄτιμοι, nom. pl. masc. . . . . ἄτιμος

ἄτῑμος, ου, ὁ, ἡ, (§ 7. rem. 2) (ἀ & τιμή) *unhonoured, without honour,* Mat. 13. 57; Mar. 6. 4; *ignoble,* 1 Co. 4. 10; 12. 23.

ἀτῑμάζω, fut. άσω, (§ 26. rem. 1) aor. 1, ἠτίμασα, aor. 1, pass. ἠτιμάσθην, *to dishonour, slight,* Jno. 8. 49; Ro. 2. 23; Ja. 2. 6; *to treat with contumely or indignity,* Lu. 20. 11; Ac. 5. 41; *to abuse, debase,* Ro. 1. 24.

ἀτῑμάω, ῶ, fut. ήσω, *to dishonour.* v.r.

ἀτῑμία, ας, ἡ, (§ 2. tab. B. b, and rem. 2) *dishonour, infamy,* Ro. 1. 26; *indecorum,* 1 Co. 11. 14; *meanness, vileness,* 1 Co. 15. 43; 2 Co. 6. 8; *a mean use,* Ro. 9. 21; 2 Ti. 2. 20; κατὰ ἀτιμίαν, *slightingly, disparagingly,* 2 Co. 11. 21.

ἀτῑμόω, ῶ, (§ 20. tab. T) perf. pass. ἠτίμωμαι, *to dishonour; to outrage,* Mar. 12. 4.

ἄτινα, nom. pl. neut. . . . . ὅστις
ἀτμίδα, acc. sing. . . . . . ἀτμίς

ἀτμίς, ίδος, ἡ, (§ 4. rem. 2. d) *an exhalation, vapour, smoke,* Ac. 2. 19; Ja. 4. 14.

ἄτομος], ου, ὁ, ἡ, (§ 7. rem. 2) (ἀ & τέμνω) *indivisible,* and by impl. *exceedingly minute;* ἐν ἀτόμῳ, sc. χρόνῳ, *in an indivisible point of time, in an instant or moment.*

ἀτόμῳ,[d] dat. sing. neut. . . . . ἄτομος
ἄτοπον, nom. and acc. sing. neut. . . ἄτοπος

ἄτοπος], ου, ὁ, ἡ, (§ 7. rem. 2) (ἀ & τόπος) pr. *out of place; inopportune, unsuitable, absurd; new, unusual, strange;* in N.T. *improper, amiss, wicked,* Lu. 23. 41; 2 Thes. 3. 2; *noxious, harmful,* Ac. 28. 6.

a 1 Co. 12. 23. b Lu. 15. 13. c 1 Thes. 5. 14. d 1 Co. 15. 52.

ἀτόπων, gen. pl. . . . . . . ἄτοπος

Ἀττάλεια], ας, ἡ, (§ 2. tab. B. b, and rem. 2) *Attalia*, a city of Pamphylia.

Ἀττάλειαν,[a] acc. sing. . . . . Ἀττάλεια

αὐγάζω], fut. άσω, (§ 26. rem. 1) . . αὐγή

αὐγάσαι,[b] aor. 1, infin. . . αὐγάζω

αὐγή], ῆς, η, (§ 2. tab. B. a) *radiance; daybreak*.

αὐγάζω, fut. άσω, (§ 26. rem. 1) *to see distinctly, discern*, or, intrans., *to shine, give light*.

αὐγῆς,[c] gen. sing. . . . . . . αὐγή

Αὔγουστος], ου, ὁ, Καῖσαρ, *Cæsar Augustus*.

Αὐγούστου,[d] gen. sing. . . . . Αὔγουστος

αὐθάδεις, nom. pl. masc. . . αὐθάδης

αὐθαδῆ, acc. sing. masc. . . id.

αὐθάδης], εος, οῦς, ὁ, ἡ, (§ 7. tab. G. b) (αὐτός & ἥδομαι) *one who pleases himself, wilful, obstinate; arrogant, imperious*, Tit. 1. 7; 2 Pe. 2. 10. (ᾰ).

αὐθαίρετοι, nom. pl. masc. . . . αὐθαίρετος

αὐθαίρετος, ου, ὁ, ἡ, (§ 7. rem. 2) (αὐτός & αἱρέομαι) pr. *one who chooses his own course of action; acting spontaneously, of one's own accord*, 2 Co. 8. 3, 17.

αὐθεντεῖν,[e] pres. infin. . . . . αὐθεντέω

αὐθεντέω, ῶ], fut. ήσω, (§ 16. tab. P) (*to be* αὐθέντης, *one acting by his own authority or power*, contr. from αὐτοέντης, *one who executes with his own hand*) *to have authority over, domineer*. N.T.

αὐλέω, ῶ], fut. ήσω, (§ 16. tab. P) . . αὐλός

αὐλή], ῆς, ἡ, (§ 2. tab. B. a) pr. *an unroofed enclosure; court-yard; sheepfold*, Jno. 10. 1. 16; *an exterior court*, i.q. προαύλιον, an enclosed place between the door and the street, Re. 11. 2; *an interior court, quadrangle*, the open court in the middle of Oriental houses, which are commonly built in the form of a square enclosing this court, Mat. 26. 58, 69, et al.; by synecd. *a house, mansion, palace*, Mat. 26. 3; Lu. 11. 21.

αὐλίζομαι, fut. ίσομαι, (§ 26. rem. 1) aor. 1, (pass. form) ηὐλίσθην, pr. *to pass the time in a court-yard; to lodge, bivouac*; hence, *to pass the night* in any place, *to lodge at night, pass or remain through the night*, Mat. 21. 17; Lu. 21. 37.

αὐλῇ, dat. sing. . . . . . . αὐλή

αὐλήν, acc. sing. . . . . . . id.

αὐλῆς, gen. sing. . . . . . id.

αὐλητάς, acc. pl. . . . . . αὐλητής

αὐλητής], οῦ, ὁ, (§ 2. tab. B. c) . . αὐλός

αὐλητῶν, gen. pl. . . . . . αὐλητής

αὐλίζομαι], fut. ίσομαι, (§ 26. rem. 1) . αὐλή

αὐλός,[f] οῦ, ὁ, (§ 3. tab. C. a) *a pipe* or *flute*.

αὐλέω, ῶ, fut. ήσω, (§ 16. tab. P) aor. 1, ηὔλησα, *to play on a pipe or flute, pipe*, Mat. 11. 17; Lu. 7. 32; 1 Co. 14. 7.

αὐλητής, ου, ὁ, (§ 2. tab. B. c) *a player on a pipe or flute*, Mat. 9. 23; Re. 18. 22.

αὐλούμενον, nom. sing. neut. part. pres. pass. . αὐλέω

αὐξάνει, 3 pers. sing. pres. indic. . . αὐξάνω

αὐξάνειν, pres. infin. . . . id.

αὐξάνετε, 2 pers. pl. pres. imper. . . id.

αὐξανομένης, gen. sing. fem. part. pres. pass. . id.

αὐξανόμενοι, nom. pl. masc. part. pres. pass. id.

αὐξανόμενον, nom. sing. neut. pt. pr. pass.—Gr. Sch. Tdf. . . . } Rec. om. (Col. 1. 6) . . } id.

αὐξανόμενον, acc. sing. masc. pt. pr. pass.—Al. Ln. Tdf. . . . } αὐξάνοντα, Rec. Gr. Sch. (Mar. 4. 8) } id.

αὐξάνοντα, acc. sing. masc. part. pres. . . id.

αὐξάνω (ᾰ) or **αὔξω**], fut. ήσω, (§ 35. rem. 5) aor. 1, ηὔξησα, aor. 1, pass. ηὐξήθην, trans. *to cause to grow or increase*; pass. *to be increased, enlarged*, Mat. 13. 32; 1 Co. 3. 6, 7, et al.; intrans. *to increase, grow*, Mat. 6. 28; Mar. 4. 8, et al.

αὔξησις, εως, ἡ, (§ 5. tab. E. c) *increase, growth*, Ep. 4. 16; Col. 2. 19.

αὐξάνων, nom. sing. masc. part. pres. . αὐξάνω

αὔξει, 3 pers. sing. pres. ind. . . . αὔξω

αὐξηθῇ, 3 pers. sing. aor. 1, subj. pass . αὐξάνω

αὐξηθῆτε, 2 pers. pl. aor. 1, subj. pass. . id.

αὐξήσαι, 3 pers. sing. aor. 1, optat. . . id.

αὐξήσει, 3 pers. sing. fut. ind.—Gr. Sch. Tdf. } αὐξήσαι, Rec. (2 Co. 9. 10) . } id.

αὔξησιν, acc. sing. . . . . . αὔξησις

αὔξησις], εως, ἡ, (§ 5. tab. E. c) . . αὐξάνω

[a] Ac. 14. 25. [b] 2 Co. 4. 4. [c] Ac. 20. 11. [d] Lu. 2. 1. [e] 1 Ti. 2. 12. [f] 1 Co. 14. 7.

αὐξήσωμεν, 1 pers. pl. aor. 1, subj. . . αὐξάνω

αὔριον, adv. *to-morrow*, Mat. 6. 30, et al.; ἡ αὔριον, sc. ἡμέρα, *the morrow, the next day*, Mat. 6. 34, et al.

αὐστηρός, ά, όν, (§ 7. rem. 1) pr. *harsh, sour in flavour*; met. *harsh, rigid, ungenerous*, Lu. 19. 21, 22.

αὐτά, nom. and acc. pl. neut. . . . αὐτός

αὗται, nom. pl. fem. . . . . οὗτος

αὐταῖς, dat. pl. fem. . . . . αὐτός

αὐτάρκεια], ας, ἡ, (§ 2. tab. B. b, and rem. 2) αὐτάρκης

αὐτάρκειαν, acc. sing. . . . . αὐτάρκεια

αὐταρκείας, gen. sing. . . . . id.

αὐτάρκης,[a] εος, ους, ὁ, ἡ, (§ 7. tab. G. b) (αὐτός & ἀρκέω) pr. *sufficient or adequate in one's self; contented with one's lot.*

αὐτάρκεια, ας, ἡ, (§ 2. tab. B. b, and rem. 2) *a competence of the necessaries of life*, 2 Co. 9. 8; *a frame of mind viewing one's lot as sufficient, contentedness*, 1 Ti. 6. 6.

αὐτάς, acc. pl. fem. . . . . αὐτός

αὐτή, nom. sing. fem. . . . . id.

αὕτη, nom. sing. fem. . . . . οὗτος

αὐτῇ, dat. sing. fem. . . . . αὐτός

αὐτήν, acc. sing. fem. . . . . id.

αὑτήν, acc. sing. fem. (§ 11. rem. 3) . αὑτοῦ

αὐτῆς, gen. sing. fem. . . . . αὐτός

αὑτῆς, gen. sing. fem. . . . . αὑτοῦ

αὐτό, nom. and acc. sing. neut. . . . αὐτός

αὐτοί, nom. pl. masc. . . . . id.

αὐτοῖς, dat. pl. masc. . . . . id.

αὑτοῖς, dat. pl. masc. . . . . αὑτοῦ

αὐτοκατάκρῐτος,[b] ου, ὁ, ἡ, (§ 7. rem. 2) (αὐτός & κατακρίνω) *self-condemned*. N.T.

αὐτομάτη, nom. sing. fem. . . . αὐτόματος

αὐτόμᾰτος], η, ον, (§ 7. tab. F. a) (αὐτός & μέμαα, *to be excited*) *self-excited, acting spontaneously, spontaneous, of his own accord*, Mar. 4. 8; Ac. 12. 10.

αὐτόν, acc. sing. masc. . . . αὐτός

αὑτόν, acc. sing. masc. . . . . αὑτοῦ

αὐτόπται,[c] nom. pl. . . . . αὐτόπτης

αὐτόπτης], ου, ὁ, ἡ, (§ 2. tab. B. c) (αὐτός & ὄψομαι) *an eye-witness.*

αὐτός, ή, ό, (§ 10. tab. J. b, and rem. 2) a reflexive pron. *self, very; alone*, Mar. 6. 31; 2 Co 12. 13; *of one's self, of one's own motion*, Jno. 16. 27; used also in the oblique cases independently as a personal pron. of the third person; ὁ αὐτός, *the same; unchangeable*, He. 1. 12; κατὰ τὸ αὐτό, *at the same time, together*, Ac. 14. 1; ἐπὶ τὸ αὐτό, *in one and the same place*, Mat. 22. 34; *at the same time, together*, Ac. 3. 1. But for a full account of the uses of αὐτός, see the grammars.

αὐτοῦ, gen. sing. masc. and neut. . . αὐτός

αὑτοῦ, ῆς, οῦ, (§ 11. rem. 3) recip. pron. contr. from ἑαυτοῦ, ῆς, οῦ, *himself, herself, itself*, Mat. 1. 21, et al. freq.; for σεαυτοῦ, ῆς, οῦ, *thyself*, Mat. 23. 37.

αὐτοῦ, adv. of place, pr. *in the very place; here, there, in this, or that place*, Mat. 26. 36; Ac. 15. 34; 18. 19; 21. 4.

αὐτούς, acc. pl. masc. . . . . αὐτός

αὑτούς, acc. pl. masc. . . . . αὑτοῦ

αὐτόχειρ], ρος, ὁ, ἡ, (§ 4. rem. 2. f) (αὐτός & χείρ) *acting or doing anything with one's own hands.*

αὐτόχειρες,[d] nom. pl. masc. . . . αὐτόχειρ

αὐτῷ, dat. sing. masc. and neut. . . αὐτός

αὑτῷ, dat. sing. masc. . . . . αὑτοῦ

αὐτῶν, gen. pl. . . . . αὐτός

αὑτῶν, gen. pl. . . . . αὑτοῦ

αὐχμηρός], ά, όν, (§ 7. rem. 1) (αὐχμέω, *to be dry, squalid, filthy*) *squalid, filthy*; by impl. *dark, obscure, murky.*

αὐχμηρῷ,[e] dat. sing. masc. . . . αὐχμηρός

ἀφαιρεθήσεται, 3 pers. sing. fut. pass. . . ἀφαιρέω

ἀφαιρεῖν, pres. infin. act. . . . id.

ἀφαιρεῖται, 3 pers. sing. pres. mid. (§ 17. tab. Q) id.

ἀφαιρέω, ῶ], fut. ήσω, aor. 2, ἀφεῖλον, (§ 36. rem. 1) aor. 1, pass. ἀφαιρεθήσομαι (ἀπό & αἱρέω) *to take away, remove*, Lu. 1. 25; 10. 42, et al.; *to take off, cut off, remove by cutting off*, Mat. 26. 15; Mar. 14. 47; Lu. 22. 50.

ἀφαιρῇ, 3 pers. sing. pres. subj. act. . . ἀφαιρέω

ἀφαιρήσει, 3 pers. sing. fut. ind. act. . id.

ἀφᾰνής,[f] έος, οῦς, ὁ, ἡ, τό, -ές, (§ 7. tab. G. b) (ἀ & φαίνω) *out of sight; not manifest, hidden, concealed.*

ἀφανίζω, fut. ίσω, (§ 26. rem. 1) *to*

[a] Phi. 4. 11. [b] Tit. 3. 11. [c] Lu. 1. 2. [d] Ac. 27. 19. [e] 2 Pe. 1. 19. [f] He. 4. 13.

remove out of sight, cause to disappear; pass. *to disappear, vanish,* Ja. 4. 14; by impl. *to destroy, consume,* so that nothing shall be left visible, Mat. 6. 19, 20; met. *to spoil, deform, disfigure,* Mat. 6. 16.

ἀφανισμός, οῦ, ὁ, (§ 3. tab. C. a) *a disappearing, vanishing away;* met. *destruction, abolition, abrogation.* L.G.

ἀφανίζει, 3 pers. sing. pres. ind. act. . ἀφανίζω
ἀφανιζομένη, nom. sing. fem. part. pr. pass. id.
ἀφανίζουσι, 3 pers. pl. pres. ind. act. id.
ἀφανίζω], fut. ίσω, (§ 26. rem. 1) . . ἀφανής
ἀφανίσθητε, 2 pers. pl. aor. 1, imper. pass. ἀφανίζω
ἀφανισμός], οῦ, ὁ, (§ 3. tab. C. a) . . ἀφανής
ἀφανισμοῦ,[a] gen. sing. . . ἀφανισμός
ἄφαντος,[b] ου, ὁ, ἡ, (§ 7. rem. 2) (ἀ & φαίνω) *not appearing, not seen, invisible;* hence, ἄφαντος γενέσθαι, *to disappear, vanish.*
ἀφεδρῶνα, acc. sing. . . . . ἀφεδρών
ἀφεδρών], ῶνος, ὁ, (§ 4. rem. 2. e) (ἀπό & ἕδρα, *a seat*) *a privy,* Mat. 15. 17; Mar. 7. 19. L.G.
ἀφεθῇ, 3 pers. sing. aor. 1, subj. pass. (§ 32. tab. C.C) ἀφίημι
ἀφέθησαν, 3 pers. pl. aor. 1, ind. pass. . id.
ἀφεθήσεται, 3 pers. sing. fut. ind. pass. . id.
ἀφειδία], ας, ἡ, (§ 2. tab. B. b, and rem. 2) (ἀ & φείδομαι) pr. *the disposition of one who is* ἀφειδής, *unsparing;* hence, in N.T. *unsparingness* in the way of rigorous treatment, *non-indulgence.*
ἀφειδίᾳ,[c] dat. sing. . . . . ἀφειδία
ἀφεῖλε, 3 pers. sing. aor. 2, ind. act. (§ 36. rem. 1) ἀφαιρέω
ἀφεῖς, 2 pers. sing. pres. ind. of ἀφέω, ῶ, an irregular form of ἀφίημι, (§ 32. rem. 2) Gr. Sch. Tdf. ἐᾷς, Rec. (Re. 2. 20)
ἀφείς, nom. sing. masc. part. aor. 2 . . ἀφίημι
ἀφελεῖ, 3 pers. sing. fut. 2, ind.—Gr. Sch. Tdf. } ἀφαιρέω
ἀφαιρήσει, Rec. (Re. 22. 19) . . }
ἀφελεῖν, aor. 2, infin. act. . . . . id.
ἀφέλῃ, 3 pers. sing. aor. 2, subj. act.—Gr. Sch. Tdf. } id.
ἀφαιρῇ, Rec. (Re. 22. 19) . . }
ἀφελότης], τητος, ἡ, (§ 4. rem. 2. c) (ἀφελής, *not rough, plain,* met. *simple, sincere,* from ἀ & φελλεύς, *a rough, stony region*) *sincerity, simplicity.* N.T.
ἀφελότητι,[d] dat. sing. . . . . ἀφελότης
ἀφέλωμαι, 1 pers. sing. aor. 2, subj. mid. . ἀφαιρέω
ἀφέντες, nom. pl. masc. part. aor. 2 . . ἀφίημι

ἄφες, 2 pr. s. aor. 2, imper. (§ 32. tab. C.C) ἀφίημι
ἀφέσει, dat. sing. . . . . ἄφεσις
ἄφεσιν, acc. sing. . . . . . id.
ἄφεσις, εως, ἡ, (§ 5. tab. E. c) . . ἀφίημι
ἄφετε, 2 pers. pl. aor. 2, imper. act. . . id.
ἀφέωνται, 3 pers. pl. perf. ind. pass. (§ 32. rem. 2) id.
ἀφῇ, 3 pers. sing. aor. 2, subj. act. . . id.
ἁφή], ῆς, ἡ, (§ 2. tab. B. a) (ἅπτω, *to fasten*) *a fastening; a ligature,* by which the different members are connected, *commissure, joint,* Ep. 4. 16; Col. 2. 19.
ἀφῆκα, 1 pers. sing. aor. 1, ind. act. (§ 28. rem. 9. c) ἀφίημι
ἀφήκαμεν, 1 pers. pl. aor. 1, ind. act. . . id.
ἀφῆκαν, 3 pers. pl. aor. 1, ind. act. . . id.
ἀφῆκας, 2 pers. sing. aor. 1, ind. act. . . id.
ἀφήκατε, 2 pers. pl. aor. 1, ind. act. . id.
ἀφῆκε, 3 pers. sing. aor. 1, ind. act. . . id.
ἁφῆς, gen. sing. . . . . . ἁφή
ἀφήσει, 3 pers. sing. fut. ind. act. . . ἀφίημι
ἀφήσεις, 2 pers. sing. fut. ind. act. . . id.
ἀφήσουσι, 3 pers. pl. fut. ind. act. . . id.
ἀφήσω, 1 pers. sing. fut. ind. act. . . id.
ἀφῆτε, 2 pers. pl. aor. 2, subj. act. . . id.
ἀφθαρσίᾳ, dat. sing. . . . . ἀφθαρσία
ἀφθαρσίαν, acc. sing. . . . . id.
ἄφθαρτοι, nom. pl. masc. . . . ἄφθαρτος
ἄφθαρτον, acc. sing. masc. and fem. . . id.
ἄφθαρτος, ου, ὁ, ἡ, (§ 7. rem. 2) (ἀ & φθείρω) *incorruptible, immortal, imperishable, undying, enduring,* Ro. 1. 23; 1 Co. 9. 25; 15. 52, et al.

ἀφθαρσία], ας, ἡ, (§ 2. tab. B. b, and rem. 2) *incorruptibility,* 1 Co. 15. 42, 53, 54; *immortality,* Ro. 2. 7; 2 Ti. 1. 10; *soundness, purity;* ἐν ἀφθαρσίᾳ, *purely, sincerely,* or, *constantly, unfailingly,* Ep. 6. 24. L.G.

ἀφθορία, ας, ἡ, (§ 2. tab. B. b, and rem. 2) v. r., Tit. 2. 7, pr. *incapability of decay;* met. *incorruptness, integrity, genuineness, purity.* N.T.

ἀφθάρτου, gen. sing. masc. and fem. . . ἀφθάρτος
ἀφθάρτῳ, dat. sing. masc. . . . id.
ἀφθορία], ας, ἡ, (§ 2. tab. B. b, and rem. 2) . ἀφθαρσία
ἀφθορίαν,[e] acc. sing.—A. C. D. Ln. Tdf. . } ἀφθορία
ἀδιαφθορίαν, Rec. Gr. Sch. (Tit. 2. 7) }
ἀφίδω, 1 pers. sing. aor. 2, subj.—Al. Ln. } ἀφοράω
ἀπίδω, Rec. Gr. Sch. Tdf. (Phi. 2. 23) }
ἀφίεμεν, 1 pers. pl. pres. ind. act. . . ἀφίημι

[a] He. 8. 13. [b] Lu. 24. 31. [c] Col. 2. 23. [d] Ac. 2. 46. [e] Tit. 2. 7.

ἀφιέναι, pres. infin. act. . . ἀφίημι
ἀφίενται, 3 pers. pl. pres. ind. pass. . . id.
ἀφίεται, 3 pers. sing. pres. ind. pass. . id.
ἀφίετε, 2 pers. pl. pres. ind. act. . . . id.
ἀφίετε, 2 pers. pl. pres. imper. act. . . id.
ἀφιέτω, 3 pers. sing. pres. imper. act. . . id.

ἀφίημι, (§ 32. tab. C.C) fut. ἀφήσω, aor. 1, ἀφῆκα, aor. 1, pass. ἀφείθην & ἀφέθην, fut. pass. ἀφεθήσομαι, imperf. 3 pers. sing. ἤφιε, Mar. 1. 34; 11. 16; perf. pass. 3 pers. pl. ἀφέωνται, pres. 2 pers. sing. ἀφεῖς, v.r., Re. 2. 20, (ἀπό & ἵημι) *to send away, dismiss, suffer to depart; to emit, send forth;* τὴν φωνήν, *the voice, to cry out, utter an exclamation,* Mar. 15. 37; τὸ πνεῦμα, *the spirit, to expire,* Mat. 27. 50; *to omit, pass over or by; to let alone, care not for,* Mat. 15. 14; 23. 23; He. 6. 1; *to permit, suffer, let, forbid not; to give up, yield, resign,* Mat. 5. 40; *to remit, forgive, pardon; to relax, suffer to become less intense,* Re. 2. 4; *to leave, depart from; to desert, forsake; to leave remaining or alone; to leave behind,* sc. at one's death, Mar. 12. 19, 20, 21, 22; Jno. 14. 27.

ἄφεσις, εως, ἡ, (§ 5. tab. E. c) *dismission, deliverance* from captivity, Lu. 4. 18, bis; *remission, forgiveness, pardon,* Mat. 26. 28, et al.

ἀφίησι, 3 pers. sing. pres. ind. act. . . ἀφίημι
ἀφίκετο,[a] 3 pers. sing. aor. 2, ind. . . ἀφικνέομαι

ἀφικνέομαι, οῦμαι], fut. ἵξομαι, aor. 2, ἀφῑκόμην, (§ 36. rem. 2) (ἀπό & ἱκνέομαι, *to come, arrive*) *to come, arrive at; to reach* as a report.

ἄφιξις, εως, ἡ, (§ 5. tab. E. c) *arrival; departure,* Ac. 20. 29.

ἀφιλάγαθοι,[b] nom. pl. masc. . . . ἀφιλάγαθος

ἀφιλάγᾰθος], ου, ὁ, ἡ, (§ 7. rem. 2) (ἀ, φίλος & ἀγαθός) *not a lover of, inimical to, good and good men.* N.T.

ἀφιλάργυρον, acc. sing. masc. . . ἀφιλάργυρος

ἀφιλάργῠρος, ου, ὁ, ἡ, (§ 7. rem. 2) (ἀ, φίλος, & ἄργυρος) *not fond of money, not covetous, liberal, generous,* 1 Ti. 3. 3; He. 13. 5. N.T.

ἄφιξιν,[c] acc. sing. . . . . ἄφιξις
ἄφιξις], εως, ἡ, (§ 5. tab. E. c) . . . ἀφικνέομαι

ἀφίστανται, 3 pers. pl. pres. mid. (§ 29. tab. Y) ἀφίστημι
ἀφίστασο, 2 pers. sing. pres. imper. mid. . id.
ἀφίστατο, 3 pers. sing. imperf. mid. . . id.

ἀφίστημι], (§ 29. tab. X) fut. ἀποστήσω, aor. 1, ἀπέστησα, (ἀπό & ἵστημι) trans. *to put away, separate; to draw off or away, withdraw, induce to revolt,* Ac. 5. 37; intrans., perf. ἀφέστηκα, aor. 2, ἀπέστην, and mid., *to depart, go away from,* Lu. 2. 37, et al.; met. *to desist or refrain from, let alone,* Ac. 5, 38; 22. 29; 2 Co. 12. 8; *to make defection, fall away, apostatise,* Lu. 8. 13; 1 Ti. 4. 1; He. 3. 12; *to withdraw from, have no intercourse with,* 1 Ti 6. 5; *to abstain from,* 2 Ti. 2. 19.

ἀποστασία, ας, ἡ, (§ 2. tab. B. b, and rem. 2) *a defection, apostasy,* Ac. 21. 21; 2 Thes. 2. 3. L.G.

ἀποστάσιον, ου, τό, (§ 3. tab. C. c) *defection, desertion,* as of a freedman from a patron; in N.T. *the act of putting away a wife, repudiation, divorce,* Mat. 19. 7; Mar. 10. 4; meton. *a bill of repudiation, deed of divorce,* Mat. 5. 31.

ἄφνω, adv. *suddenly, unexpectedly,* Ac. 2. 2; 16. 26; 28. 6.

ἀφόβως, adv. (ἄφοβος, *fearless,* from ἀ & φόβος) *fearlessly, boldly, intrepidly,* Phi. 1. 14; *securely, peacefully, tranquilly,* Lu. 1. 74; 1 Co. 16. 10; *impudently, shamelessly,* Jude 12.

ἀφομοιόω, ῶ], fut. ώσω, (§ 20. tab. T) (ἀπό & ὁμοιόω) *to assimilate, cause to resemble,* He. 7. 3.

ἀφοράω, ῶ], fut. ἀπόψομαι, aor. 2, ἀπεῖδον, (§ 36. rem. 1) (ἀπό & ὁράω) *to view with undivided attention* by looking away from every other object; *to regard fixedly and earnestly,* He. 12. 2; *to see distinctly,* Phi. 2. 23.

ἀφοριεῖ, 3 pers. sing. fut. Att. (§ 35. rem. 11) ἀφορίζω
ἀφορίζει, 3 pers. sing. pres. ind. act. . id.

ἀφορίζω], fut. ίσω & ἀφοριῶ, perf. pass. ἀφώρισμαι, (§ 26. rem. 1) (ἀπό & ὁρίζω) *to limit off; to separate, sever* from the rest, Mat. 13. 49, et al.; *to separate* from society, *cut off from all intercourse, excommunicate,* Lu. 6. 22; *to set apart, select,* Ac. 13. 2; Ro. 1. 1; Gal. 1. 15.

[a] Ro. 16. 19. [b] 2 Ti. 3. 3. [c] Ac. 20. 29.

ἀφοριοῦσι, 3 pers. pl. fut. Att. (§ 35. rem. 11) ἀφορίζω
ἀφορίσας, nom. sing. masc. part. aor. 1 . id.
ἀφορίσατε, 2 pers. pl. aor. 1, imper. act. . id.
ἀφορίσθητε, 2 pers. pl. aor. 1, imper. pass. . id.
ἀφορίσωσι, 3 pers. pl. aor. 1, subj. act. . id.
ἀφορμή], ῆς, ἡ, (§ 2. tab. B. a) (ἀπό & ὁρμή) pr. *a starting point; means* to accomplish an object; *occasion, opportunity,* Ro. 7. 8, 11, et al.
ἀφορμήν, acc. sing. . . . . . ἀφορμή
ἀφορῶντες, nom. pl. masc. part. pres. . ἀφοράω
ἀφρίζει, 3 pers. sing. pres. ind. . . . ἀφρίζω
ἀφρίζω], fut. ίσω, (§ 26. rem. 1) . . ἀφρός
ἀφρίζων, nom. sing. masc. part. pres. . . ἀφρίζω
ἄφρον, voc. sing. masc. . . . . ἄφρων
ἄφρονα, acc. sing. masc. . . . . id.
ἄφρονες, nom. and voc. pl. masc. . . id.
ἀφρόνων, gen. pl. . . . . . . id.

ἀφρός], οῦ, ὁ, (§ 3. tab. C. a) *froth, foam.*
ἀφρίζω, fut. ίσω, (§ 26. rem. 1) *to froth, foam,* Mar. 9. 18, 20.

ἀφροσύνη, ης, ἡ, (§ 2. tab. B. a) . . ἄφρων
ἀφροσύνῃ, dat. sing. . . . . ἀφροσύνη
ἀφροσύνης, gen. sing. . . . . id.
ἀφροῦ,[a] gen. sing. . . . . . ἀφρός
ἄφρων, ονος, ὁ, ἡ, (§ 7. tab. G. a, and rem. 4) (ἀ & φρήν) *unwise, inconsiderate, simple, foolish,* Lu. 11. 40; 12. 20; 1 Co. 15. 36; *ignorant,* religiously *unenlightened,* Ro. 2. 20; Ep. 5. 17; 1 Pe. 2. 15; boastfully *foolish, vain,* 2 Co. 11. 16, 19; 12. 6, 11.
ἀφροσύνη, ης, ἡ, (§ 2. tab. B. a) *inconsiderateness, folly;* boastful *folly,* 2 Co. 11. 1, 17, 21; in N.T. *foolishness, levity, wickedness, impiety,* Mar. 7. 22. (ῠ).

ἀφυπνόω, ῶ], fut. ώσω, (§ 20. tab. T) (ἀπό & ὕπνος) *to awake from sleep;* in N.T. *to go off into sleep, fall asleep.*
ἀφύπνωσε,[b] 3 pers. sing. aor. 1, ind. . ἀφυπνόω
ἀφῶμεν, 1 pers. pl. aor. 2, subj. act. . . ἀφίημι
ἀφωμοιωμένος,[c] nom. sing. masc. pt. p. pass. ἀφομοιόω
ἀφῶν, gen. pl. . . . . . . ἀφή
ἄφωνα, acc. pl. neut. . . . . ἄφωνος
ἄφωνον, nom. sing. neut. . . . . id.
ἄφωνος, ου, ὁ, ἡ, (§ 7. rem. 2) (ἀ & φωνή) *dumb, destitute of the power of speech,* 1 Co. 12. 2; 2 Pe. 2. 16; *silent, mute, uttering no voice,* Ac. 8. 32; *inarticulate, consisting of inarticulat sounds, unmeaning,* 1 Co. 14. 10.
ἀφώριζε, 3 pers. sing. imperf. . . . ἀφορίζω
ἀφώρισε, 3 pers. sing. aor. 1, ind. act. . id.
ἀφωρισμένος, nom. sing. masc. pt. perf. pass. id.
Ἀχάζ, ὁ, *Achaz,* pr. name, indecl.
Ἀχαΐα, ας, ἡ, (§ 2. tab. B. b, and rem. 2) *Achaia,* the Roman province, comprehending all Greece to the south of Thessaly.
Ἀχαΐᾳ, dat. sing. . . . Ἀχαΐα
Ἀχαΐαν, acc. sing. . . . . . id.
Ἀχαΐας, gen. sing. . . . . . id.
Ἀχαϊκός], οῦ, ὁ, *Achaicus,* pr. name.
Ἀχαϊκοῦ,[d] gen. sing. . . . . Ἀχαϊκός
ἀχάριστοι, nom. pl. masc. . . . ἀχάριστος
ἀχάριστος], ου, ὁ, ἡ, (§ 7. rem. 2) (ἀ & χάρις) *unthankful, ungrateful,* Lu. 6. 35; 2 Ti. 3. 2.
ἀχαρίστους, acc. pl. masc. . . . ἀχάριστος
Ἀχείμ, ὁ, *Achim,* pr. name, indecl.
ἀχειροποίητον, acc. sing. masc. and fem. ἀχειροποίητος
ἀχειροποίητος], ου, ὁ, ἡ, (§ 7. rem. 2) (ἀ & χειροποίητος) *not made with hands,* Mar. 14. 58; 2 Co. 5. 1; Col. 2. 11. N.T.
ἀχειροποιήτῳ, dat. sing. fem. . . ἀχειροποίητος
ἀχθῆναι, aor. 1, infin. pass. (§ 23. rem. 4) . ἄγω
ἀχθήσεσθε, 2 pers. pl. fut. ind. pass. . . id.

ἀχλύς,[e] υος, ἡ, (§ 5. tab. E. g) *a mist; darkening, dimness,* of the sight.

ἀχρεῖοι, nom. pl. masc. . . . ἀχρεῖος
ἀχρεῖον, acc. sing. masc. . . . . id.
ἀχρεῖος], α, ον, (§ 7. rem. 1) (ἀ & χρεία) *useless, unprofitable, worthless,* Mat. 25. 30; *unmeritorious,* Lu. 17. 10.
ἀχρειόω, ῶ, fut. ώσω, (§ 20. tab. T) aor. 1, pass. ἠχρειώθην, *to render useless;* met. pass. *to become corrupt, depraved,* Ro. 3. 12. L.G.
ἀχρειόω, ῶ], fut. ωσω . . . . ἀχρεῖος
ἄχρηστον,[f] acc. sing. masc. . . . ἄχρηστος
ἄχρηστος], ου, ὁ, ἡ, (§ 7. rem. 2) (ἀ & χρηστός) *unuseful, useless, unprofitable,* and by impl. *detrimental, causing loss.*
ἄχρι, or ἄχρις, originally an adv. of place, used as a prep., with respect to place, *as far as;* to time, *until, during;* as a conj. *until.*

ἄχυρον, ου, τό, (§ 3. tab. C. c) *chaff, straw broken up* by treading out the grain, Mat. 3. 12; Lu. 3. 17.

---

[a] Lu. 9. 39. [b] Lu. 8. 23. [c] He. 7. 3. [d] 1 Co. 16. 17. [e] Ac. 13. 11. [f] Phile. 11.

ἁψάμενος, nom. sing. masc. part. aor. 1, mid. ἅπτω
ἅψαντες, nom. pl. masc. part. aor. 1, act.—A. B. Ln. } id.
ἀνάψαντες, Rec. Gr. Sch. Tdf. (Ac. 28. 2)
ἁψάντων, gen. pl. masc. part. aor. 1, act. id.
ἅψας, nom. sing. masc. part. aor. 1, act. id.

ἀψευδής,[a] έος, οῦς, ὁ, ἡ, (§ 7. tab. G. b) (ἀ & ψευδής) *free from falsehood; incapable of falsehood.*

ἅψῃ, 2 pers. sing. aor. 1, subj. mid. ἅπτω
ἅψηται, 3 pers. sing. aor. 1, subj. mid. id.
ἄψινθον, acc. sing. ἄψινθος

ἄψινθος, ου, ἡ, (§ 3. tab. C. a) *wormwood*, Re. 8. 11; where, as a proper name, it is masculine, according to the various reading, ὁ Ἄψινθος, Gr. Sch. Tdf. Rec. om. ὁ.

ἄψυχα,[b] nom. pl. neut. ἄψυχος
ἄψῡχος], ου, ὁ, ἡ, τό, -ον, (§ 7. rem. 2) (ἀ & ψυχή) *void of life or sense, inanimate.*

ἅψωμαι, 1 pers. sing. aor. 1, subj. mid. ἅπτω
ἅψωνται, 3 pers. pl. aor. 1, subj. mid. id.

Β.

Βάαλ,[c] ὁ, *Baal*, pr. name, indecl. (Heb. בַּעַל).
Βαβυλών, ῶνος, ἡ, (§ 4. rem. 2. e) *Babylon.*
Βαβυλῶνι, dat. sing. Βαβυλών
Βαβυλῶνος, gen. sing. id.
βαθέα, acc. pl. neut.—Gr. Sch. Tdf. } βαθύς
βάθη, Rec. (Re. 2. 24)
βαθεῖ, dat. sing. masc. id.
βαθέος, gen. sing. masc. id.
βαθέως, adv.—A. C. D. Ln. Tdf. } βάθος
βαθέος, Rec. Gr. Sch. (Lu. 24. 1) } βαθύς
βάθη, acc. pl. βάθος
βαθμόν,[d] acc. sing. βαθμός
βαθμός], οῦ, ὁ, (§ 3. tab. C. a) (βαίνω, *to walk, go*) pr. *a step, stair*; met. *grade* of dignity, *degree, rank, standing.*
βαθύ, nom. sing. neut. βαθύς
βαθύνω], fut. ὑνῶ, (§ 27. rem. 1. a) βάθος

βαθύς, εῖα, ύ, (§ 7. tab. H. g) *deep*, Jno. 4. 11; met. *deep, profound*, Ac. 20. 9; ὄρθρου βαθέος, lit. *at deep morning twilight, at the earliest dawn*, Lu. 24. 1.

βαθέως, adv. *deeply*. v.r.

βάθος, εος, ους, τό, (§ 5. tab. E. b) *depth*; τὸ βάθος, *deep water*, Lu. 5. 4; Mat. 13. 5, et al.; met. *fulness, abundance, immensity*, Ro. 11. 33; *an extreme degree*, 2 Co. 8. 2; pl. *profundities, deep-laid plans*, 1 Co. 2. 10; Re. 2. 24.

βαθύνω, fut. ὑνῶ, (§ 27. rem. 1. a) *to deepen, excavate*, Lu. 6. 48.

βάϊα,[e] acc. pl. βαΐον

βάϊον, or βαΐον], ου, τό, *a palm branch.* LXX.

Βαλαάμ, ὁ, *Balaam*, pr. name, indecl.
Βαλάκ,[f] ὁ, *Balac*, pr. name, indecl.
βαλάντια, acc. pl. βαλάντιον

βαλάντιον, ου, τό, (§ 3. tab. C. c) *a bag, purse*, Lu. 10. 4; 12. 33; 22. 35, 36.

βαλαντίου, gen. sing. βαλάντιον
βάλε, 2 pers. sing. aor. 2, imper. act. βάλλω
βαλεῖ, 3 pers. sing. fut. act.—B. D. Ln. Tdf. } id.
βάλῃ, Gr. Sch.
βάλλῃ, Rec. (Lu. 12. 58)
βαλεῖν, aor. 2, infin. act. id.
βάλετε, 2 pers. pl. aor. 2, imper. act. id.
βαλέτω, 3 pers. sing. aor. 2, imper. act. id.
βάλῃ, 3 pers. sing. aor. 2, subj. act. id.
βάλητε, 2 pers. pl. aor. 2, subj. act. id.
βαλλάντια, acc. pl.—A. D. Ln. Tdf. } βαλλάντιον
βαλάντια, Rec. Gr. Sch. (Lu. 12. 33)
βαλλάντιον, ου, τό.—A. D. Ln. Tdf.
βαλάντιον, Rec. Gr. Sch. (Lu. 10. 4)
βαλλαντίου, gen. sing.—A. B. D. Ln. Tdf. } id.
βαλαντίου, Rec. Gr. Sch. (Lu. 22. 35)
βάλλει, 3 pers. sing. pres. ind. act. βάλλω
βάλλειν, pres. infin. act.—Al. Ln. Sch. Tdf. } id.
βαλεῖν, Rec. Gr. (Re. 2. 10)
βάλλεται, 3 pers. sing. pres. ind. pass. id.
βάλλῃ, 3 pers. sing. pres. subj. act. id.
βάλλομεν, 1 pers. pl. pres. ind. act. id.
βαλλόμενα, nom. pl. neut. part. pres. pass. id.
βαλλόμενον, acc. sing. masc. part. pres. pass. id.
βάλλοντας, acc. pl. masc. part. pres. act. id.
βάλλοντες, nom. pl. masc. part. pres. act. id.
βαλλόντων, gen. pl. masc. part. pres. act. id.
βάλλουσαν, acc. sing. fem. part. pres. act. id.
βάλλουσι, 3 pers. pl. pres. ind. act. id.

βάλλω, fut. βαλῶ, (§ 27. rem. 1. b) aor. 2, ἔβαλον, (§ 27. rem. 2. d) perf. βέβληκα, perf. pass. βέβλημαι, aor. 1, pass. ἐβλήθην, fut. pass. βληθήσομαι, (§ 27. rem. 3)

[a] Tit. 1. 2. [b] 1 Co. 14. 7. [c] Ro. 11. 4. [d] 1 Ti. 3. 13. [e] Jno. 12. 13. [f] Re. 2. 14.

to throw, cast; *to lay*, Re. 2. 22; Mat. 8. 6, 14, et al.; *to put, place*, Ja. 3. 3; *to place, deposit*, Mat. 27. 6; Mar. 12. 41–44; Lu. 21. 1–4; Jno. 12. 6; *to pour*, Jno. 13. 5; *to thrust*, Jno. 18. 11; 20. 27; Mar. 7. 33; Re. 14. 19; *to send forth*, Mat. 10. 34; *to assault, strike*, Mar. 14. 65; met. *to suggest*, Jno. 13. 2; intrans. *to rush, beat*, as the wind, Ac. 27. 14.

βλητέος, α, ον, verbal adj. (§ 35. rem. 10) *requiring to be cast or put*, Mar. 2. 22; Lu. 5. 38. N.T.

βολή, ῆς, ἡ, (§ 2. tab. B. a) *a cast, a throw; the distance to which a thing can be thrown*, Lu. 22. 41.

βολίζω, fut. ίσω, aor. 1, ἐβόλισα, (§ 26. rem. 1) *to heave the lead, sound*, Ac. 27. 28. L.G.

βολίς, ίδος, ἡ, (§ 4. rem. 2. c) *a missile weapon, dart, javelin*, He. 12. 20; also, *a plummet, lead for sounding*. L.G.

βαλόντες, nom. pl. masc. part. aor. 2, act.—A. D. Ln. Tdf. } βάλλω
βάλλοντες, Rec. Gr. Sch. (Mat. 27. 35) }

βαλόντων, gen. pl. masc. part. aor. 2, act. . id.
βαλοῦσα, nom. sing. fem. part. aor. 2, act. . id.
βαλοῦσι, 3 pers. pl. fut. ind. act. . . id.
βαλῶ, 1 pers. sing. fut. ind. act. . . . id.
βαλῶ, 1 pers. sing. aor. 2, subj. act. . . id.
βαλῶσι, 3 pers. pl. aor. 2, subj. act. . . id.
βαπτίζει, 3 pers. sing. pres. ind. act. . βαπτίζω
βαπτίζειν, pres. infin. act. . . . id.
βαπτίζεις, 2 pers. sing. pres. ind. act. . id.
βαπτίζομαι, 1 pers. sing. pres. ind. pass. . id.
βαπτιζόμενοι, nom. pl. masc. pt. pres. pass. id.
βαπτίζονται, 3 pers. pl. pres. ind. pass. . id.
βαπτίζοντες, nom. pl. masc. pt. pres. act. . id.
βαπτίζω, fut. ίσω, (§ 26. rem. 1) . . βάπτω
βαπτίζων, nom. sing. masc. pt. pres. act. . βαπτίζω
βάπτισαι, 2 pers. sing. aor. 1, imper. mid. . id.

βαπτίσαντες, nom. pl. masc. pt. aor. 1, act.—B. D. } id.
βαπτίζοντες, R. Gr. Sch. Tdf. (Mat. 28. 19) }

βαπτίσει, 3 pers. sing. fut. ind. act. . . id.
βαπτισθείς, nom. sing. masc. part. aor. 1, pass. id.
βαπτισθέντες, nom. pl. masc. part. aor. 1, pass. id.
βαπτισθέντος, gen. sing. masc. part. aor. 1, pass. id.
βαπτισθῆναι, aor. 1, infin. pass. . . id.
βαπτισθήσεσθε, 2 pers. pl. fut. ind. pass. . id.

βαπτισθήτω, 3 pers. sing. aor. 1, imper. pass. βαπτίζ
βάπτισμα, ατος, τό, (§ 4. tab. D. c) . βάπτω
βαπτίσματος, gen. sing. . . . . βάπτισμα
βαπτίσματι, dat. sing. . . . id.
βαπτισμοῖς, dat. pl. . . . . βαπτισμός
βαπτισμός], οῦ, ὁ, (§ 3. tab. C. a) . . βάπτω
βαπτισμούς, acc. pl. . . . . βαπτισμός

βαπτισμῷ, dat. sing.—B. D. . . } id.
βαπτίσματι, R. Gr. Sch. Tdf. (Col. 2. 12) }

βαπτισμῶν, gen. pl. . . . . id.
βαπτιστήν, acc. sing. . . . βαπτιστής
βαπτιστής, οῦ, ὁ, (§ 2. tab. B. c) . . βάπτω
βαπτιστοῦ, gen. sing. . . . . βαπτιστής
βαπτίσωνται, 3 pers. pl. aor. 1, subj. mid. . βαπτίζω

βάπτω], fut. ψω, (§ 23. rem. 1. a) aor. 1, ἔβαψα, perf. pass. βέβαμμαι, (§ 23. rem. 7) *to dip*, Jno. 13. 26; Lu. 16. 24; *to dye*, Re. 19. 13.

βαπτίζω, fut. ίσω, aor. 1, ἐβάπτισα, perf. pass. βεβάπτισμαι, aor. 1, pass. ἐβαπτίσθην, (§ 26. rem. 1) pr. *to dip, immerse; to cleanse or purify by washing; to administer the rite of baptism, to baptize*; met. with various reference to the ideas associated with Christian baptism as an act of dedication, e.g. marked designation, devotion, trial, etc.; mid. *to procure baptism for one's self, to undergo baptism*, Ac. 22. 16.

βάπτισμα, ατος, τό, (§ 4. tab. D. c) pr. *immersion, baptism, ordinance of baptism*, Mat. 3. 7; Ro. 6. 4, et al.; met. *baptism* in the trial of suffering, Mat. 20. 22, 23; Mar. 10. 38, 39. N.T.

βαπτισμός, οῦ, ὁ, (§ 3. tab. C. a) pr. *an act of dipping or immersion; a baptism*, He. 6. 2; *an ablution*, Mar. 7. 4, 8; He. 9. 10. N.T.

βαπτιστής, οῦ, ὁ, (§ 2. tab. B. c) *one who baptizes, a baptist*, Mat. 3. 1; 11. 11, 12, et al. N.T.

βάρ, indecl. ὁ, (בַּר, Chald. or Syr.) *a son*, Mat. 16. 17.
Βαραββᾶν, acc. sing. . . . . Βαραββᾶς
Βαραββᾶς, ᾶ, ὁ, (§ 2. rem. 4) *Barabbas*, pr. name.
Βαράκ,[a] ὁ, *Barak*, pr. name, indecl.
Βαραχίας], ου, ὁ, (§ 2. tab. B. d) *Barachias*, pr. name.
Βαραχίου,[b] gen. sing. . . . . Βαραχίας
βάρβαροι, nom. pl. . . . . βάρβαρος

[a] He. 11. 32. [b] Mat. 23. 35.

βάρβᾰρος, ου, ὁ, (§ 3. tab. C. a) pr. *one to whom a pure Greek dialect is not native; one who is not a proper Greek, a barbarian*, Ro. 1. 14; Col. 3. 11; Ac. 28. 2, 4; *a foreigner speaking a strange language*, 1 Co. 14. 11.

βαρέα, acc. pl. neut. . . . . . βαρύς

βάρει, dat. sing. . . . . . βάρος

βαρεῖαι, nom. pl. fem. . . . . βαρύς

βαρεῖς, nom. pl. masc. . . . . id.

βαρείσθω, 3 pers. sing. pres. imper. pass. . βαρέω

βαρέω, ῶ], fut. ήσω, (§ 16. tab. P) . βάρος

βαρέως, adv. . . . . id.

βάρη, acc. pl. . . . . . id.

βαρηθῶσι, 3 pers. pl. aor. 1, subj. pass.—Gr. Sch. Tdf. . . . } βαρέω
βαρυνθῶσι, Rec. (Lu. 21. 34) . . }

Βαρθολομαῖον, acc. sing. . . . Βαρθολομαῖος

Βαρθολομαῖος, ου, ὁ, (§ 3. tab. C. a) *Bartholomew*, pr. name.

Βαριησοῦς, οῦ, ὁ, (§ 6. rem. 3) *Bar-jesus*, pr. name, (Ac. 13. 6) Rec. Gr. Sch. Tdf.

βαριησοῦν, A. D.

βαριησοῦ, C.

Βὰρ Ἰωνᾶ, *Bar-jona*, pr. name.—Rec. Gr. Sch. Tdf.

Βαριωνᾶ, Ln. (Mat. 16. 17).

Βαρνάβᾳ, dat. sing. . . . . Βαρνάβας

Βαρνάβα, gen. sing. . . . . id.

Βαρνάβαν, acc. sing. . . . . id.

Βαρνάβας, α, ὁ, (§ 2. rem. 4) *Barnabas*, pr. name.

βαρούμενοι, nom. pl. masc. part. pres. pass. . βαρέω

Βαρσαβᾶν, acc. sing. . . . . Βαρσαβᾶς

Βαρσαβᾶς], ᾶ, ὁ, (§ 2. rem. 4) *Barsabas*, pr. name.
I. *Joseph, surnamed Justus*, Ac. 1. 23.
II. *Judas*, Ac. 15. 22.

Βαρσαββᾶν, acc. sing.—A. B. Ln. Tdf.

Βαρσαβᾶν, Rec. Gr. Sch. (Ac. 1. 23; 15. 22).

Βαρτίμαιος,[a] ου, ὁ, *Bartimæus*, pr. name.

βαρυνθῶσι, 3 pers. pl. aor. 1, subj. pass. . βαρύνω

βαρύνω], fut. υνῶ, (§ 27. rem. 1. a) . βάρος

βαρύς, εῖα, ύ, (§ 7. tab. H. g) *heavy*; met. *burdensome, oppressive, or difficult of observance*, as precepts, Mat. 23. 4; 1 Jno. 5. 3; *weighty, important, momentous*, Mat. 23. 23; Ac. 25. 7; *grievous, oppressive, afflictive, violent, rapacious*, Ac. 20. 29; *authoritative, strict, stern, severe*, 2 Co. 10. 10.

βάρος, εος, τό, (§ 5. tab. E. b) *weight, heaviness; a burden, anything grievous and hard to be borne*, Mat. 20. 12; Ac. 15. 28; Re. 2. 24; *burden, charge*, or, *weight, influence, dignity, honour*, 1 Thes. 2. 6; with another noun in government, *fulness, abundance, excellence*, 2 Co. 4. 17.

βαρέω, ῶ, fut. ήσω, (§ 16. tab. P) perf. pass. βεβάρημαι *to be heavy upon, weigh down, burden, oppress*, as sleep, Mat. 26. 43; Mar. 14. 40; Lu. 9. 32; *surfeiting*, v.r. Lu. 21. 34; *calamities*, 2 Co. 1. 8; 5. 4; or, *trouble, care, expense*, etc. 1 Ti. 5. 16.

βαρέως, adv. *heavily*; met. *with difficulty, dully, stupidly*, Mat. 13. 15; Ac. 28. 27.

βαρύνω, fut. υνῶ, (§ 27. rem. 1. a) aor. 1, pass. ἐβαρύνθην, see βαρέω, Lu. 21. 34. (ῡ).

βαρύτερα, acc. pl. neut. comp. (§ 8. rem. 1) βαρύς

βαρυτίμου,[b] gen. sing. neut. . . . βαρύτιμος

βαρύτῑμος], ου, ὁ, ἡ, (§ 7. rem. 2) (βαρύς & τιμή) *of great price, precious*.

βασανιζομένη, nom. sing. fem. part. pr. pass. βασανίζω

βασανιζόμενον, nom. sing. neut. part. pr. pass. id.

βασανιζόμενος, nom. sing. masc. part. pr. pass. id.

βασανιζομένους, acc. pl. masc. part. pr. pass. id.

βασανίζω], fut. ίσω, (§ 26. rem. 1) . . βάσανος

βασανίσαι, aor. 1, infin. act. . . . βασανίζω

βασανίσῃς, 2 pers. sing. aor. 1, subj. act. . id.

βασανισθήσεται, 3 pers. sing. fut. ind. pass. id.

βασανισθήσονται, 3 pers. pl. fut. ind. pass. id.

βασανισθῶσι, 3 pers. pl. aor. 1, subj. pass. id.

βασανισμόν, acc. sing. . . . . βασανισμός

βασανισμός, οῦ, ὁ, (§ 3. tab. C. a) . . βάσανος

βασανισμοῦ, gen. sing. . . . βασανισμός

βασανισταῖς,[c] dat. pl. . . . βασανιστής

βασανιστής], οῦ, ὁ, (§ 2. tab. B. c) βάσανος

βασάνοις, dat. pl. . . . . . id.

βάσᾰνος], ου, ἡ, (§ 3. tab. C. b) pr. *lapis Lydius*, a species of stone from Lydia, which being applied to metals was thought to indicate any alloy which might be mixed with them, and therefore used in the trial of metals; hence, *examination* of a person, especially by torture; in N.T. *torture, torment, severe pain*, Mat. 4. 24; Lu. 16. 23, 28.

[a] Mar. 10. 46. [b] Mat. 26. 7. [c] Mat. 18. 34.

βασανίζω, fut. ίσω, (§ 26. rem. 1) aor. 1, pass. ἐβασανίσθην, pr. *to apply the lapis Lydius or touchstone*; met. *to examine, scrutinise, try*, either by words or torture; in N.T. *to afflict, torment*; pass. *to be afflicted, tormented, pained*, by diseases, Mat. 8. 6, 29, et al.; *to be tossed, agitated*, as by the waves, Mat. 14. 24.

βασανισμός, οῦ, ὁ, (§ 3. tab. C. a) pr. *examination by the lapis Lydius or by torture; torment, torture*, Re. 9. 5; 14. 11; 18. 7, 10, 15.

βασανιστής, οῦ, ὁ, (§ 2. tab. B. c) pr. *an inquisitor, tormentor*; in N.T. *a keeper of a prison, gaoler*, Mat. 18. 34.

βασάνου,	gen. sing.	βάσανος
βάσεις,[a]	nom. pl.	βάσις
βασιλέα,	acc. sing.	βασιλεύς
βασιλεῖ,	dat. sing.	id.
βασιλεία, ας, ἡ,	(§ 2. tab. B. b, and rem. 2)	id.
βασιλείᾳ,	dat. sing.	βασιλεία
βασιλεῖαι,	nom. pl.—Rec. βασιλεία, Gr. Sch. Tdf. (Re. 11. 15)	id.
βασιλείαν,	acc. sing.	id.
βασιλείας,	gen. sing.	id.
βασιλείας,	acc. pl.	id.
βασιλείοις,	dat. pl.	βασίλειος
βασίλειον,	nom. sing. neut.	id.
βασίλειος], ου, ὁ, ἡ,	(§ 7. rem. 2)	βασιλεύς
βασιλεῖς,	nom. and acc. pl.	id.
βασιλειῶν,	gen. pl.—Sch. βασιλέων, Rec. Gr. Tdf. (Mat. 11. 8)	βασίλειος
βασιλεῦ,	voc. sing.	βασιλεύς
βασιλεύει,	3 pers. sing. pres. ind.	βασιλεύω
βασιλεύειν,	pres. infin.	id.
βασιλευέτω,	3 pers. sing. pres. imper.	id.
βασιλευόντων,	gen. pl. masc. part. pres.	id.

βασιλεύς, έως, ὁ, (§ 5. tab. E. d) *a king, monarch, one possessing regal authority.*

βασιλεία, ας, ἡ, (§ 2. tab. B. b, and rem. 2) *a kingdom, realm*, the region or country governed by a king; *kingly power, authority, dominion, reign*; *royal dignity, the title and honour of king*; ἡ βασιλεία, Mat. 9. 35, ἡ βασιλεία τοῦ Θεοῦ,—τοῦ Χριστοῦ,—τοῦ οὐρανοῦ,—τῶν οὐρανῶν, *the reign or kingdom of the Messiah*, both in a false and true conception of it; used also, with various limitation, of its administration and coming history, as in the parables; its distinctive nature, Ro. 14. 17; its requirements, privileges, rewards, consummation.

βασίλειος, ου, ὁ, ἡ, (§ 7. rem. 2) *royal, regal*; met. *possessed of high prerogatives and distinction*, 1 Pe. 2. 9; τὰ βασίλεια, sc. δώματα, *regal mansions, palaces*, Lu. 7. 25.

βασιλεύω, fut. εύσω, (§ 13. tab. M) *to possess regal authority, be a king, reign*; *to rule, govern*, Mat. 2. 22; met. *to be in force, predominate, prevail*, Ro. 5. 14, 17, 21; met. *to be in kingly case, fare royally*, 1 Co. 4. 8.

βασιλικός, ή, όν, (§ 7. tab. F. a) *royal, regal*, Ac. 12. 20, 21; βασιλικός, used as a subst. *a person attached to the king, courtier*; met. *royal, of the highest excellence*, Ja. 2. 8.

βασίλισσα, ης, ἡ, (§ 2. tab. B. a) (a later form of βασιλίς) *a queen*, Mat. 12. 42; Lu. 11. 31; Ac. 8. 27; Re. 18. 7.

βασιλεῦσαι,	aor. 1, infin. (§ 13. rem. 12)	βασιλεύω
βασιλεύσει,	3 pers. sing. fut. ind.	id.
βασιλεύσῃ,	3 pers. sing. aor. 1, subj.	id.
βασιλεύσομεν,	1 pers. pl. fut. ind.	id.
βασιλεύσουσι,	3 pers. pl. fut. ind.	id.
βασιλεύω],	fut. εύσω, (§ 13. tab. M)	βασιλεύς
βασιλέων,	gen. pl.	id.
βασιλέως,	gen. sing.	id.
βασιλικήν,	acc. sing. fem.	βασιλικός
βασιλικῆς,	gen. sing. fem.	id.
βασιλικόν,	acc. sing. masc.	id.
βασιλικός, ή, όν,	(§ 7. tab. F. a)	βασιλεύς
βασιλίσκος, ου, ὁ,	*a prince, regulus*.—D. βασιλικός, Rec. Gr. Sch. Tdf. (Jno. 4. 46, 49)	
βασίλισσα, ης, ἡ,	(§ 2. tab. B. a)	βασιλεύς
βασιλίσσης,	gen. sing.	βασίλισσα

βάσις], εως, ἡ, (§ 5. tab. E. c) (βαίνω) pr. *a step*; *the foot*, Ac. 3. 7.

βασκαίνω], fut. ανῶ, aor. 1, ἐβάσκηνα & ἐβάσκᾱνα, (§ 27. rem. 1. c. e) pr. *to slander*; thence, *to bewitch* by spells, or by any other means; *to delude*, Gal. 3. 1.

[a] Ac. 3. 7.

βαστάζει, 3 pers. sing. pres. ind. act. . βαστάζω
βαστάζειν, pres. infin. act. . . . id.
βαστάζεις, 2 pers. sing. pres. ind. act. . id.
βαστάζεσθαι, pres. infin. pass. . . . id.
βαστάζετε, 2 pers. pl. pres. imper. act. . id.
βαστάζοντες, nom. pl. masc. part. pres. act. . id.
βαστάζοντος, gen. sing. neut. part. pres. act. id.

βαστάζω, fut. άσω, aor. 1, ἐβάστασα, (§ 26. rem. 1) pr. *to lift, raise, bear aloft; to bear, carry*, in the hands or about the person; *carry* as a message, Ac. 9. 15; *to take away, remove*, Mat. 8. 17; Jno. 20. 15; *to take up*, Jno. 10. 31; Lu. 14. 27; *to bear* as a burden, *endure, suffer; to sustain*, Ro. 11. 18; *to bear with, tolerate; to sustain* mentally, *comprehend*, Jno. 16. 12.

βαστάζων, nom. sing. masc. part. pr. act. . βαστάζω
βαστάσαι, aor. 1, infin. act. . . . id.
βαστάσασα, nom. sing. fem. part. aor. 1, act. id.
βαστάσασι, dat. pl. masc. part. aor. 1, act. id.
βαστάσει, 3 pers. sing. fut. ind. act. . id.

βάτος], ου, ὁ, & ἡ, (§ 3. tab. C. a. b) *a bush, bramble*, Mar. 12. 26, et al.

βάτος], ου, ὁ, (Heb. בַּת) *a bath*, a measure for liquids, which is stated by Josephus (Ant. l. viii. c. 2. 9) to contain seventy-two sextarii, or about thirteen and a half gallons. Others make it about nine gallons; and others, seven and a half gallons.

βάτου, gen. sing. . . . . βάτος
βάτῳ, dat. sing. . . . . . id.
βάτους,[a] acc. pl. (בַּת) . . . id.
βάτραχοι,[b] nom. pl.—Gr. Sch. Tdf. . . } βάτραχος
[ὅμοια] βατράχοις, Rec. . . }

βάτρᾰχος], ου, ὁ, (§ 3. tab. C. a) *a frog*.

βαττολογήσητε,[c] 2 pers. pl. aor. 1, subj.— Rec. Gr. Sch. Tdf. . . . } βαττολογέω
βατταλογήσητε, B. D. . . . }

βαττολογέω, ῶ], fut. ήσω, (§ 16. tab. P) (*βάττος, a stammerer*) pr. *to stammer*; hence, *to babble; to use vain repetitions*. L.G.

βάψας, nom. sing. masc. part. aor. 1, act. . βάπτω
βάψῃ, 3 pers. sing. aor. 1, subj. act. . . id.
βάψω, 1 pers. sing. fut. ind. act.—B. C. Tdf. } id.
βάψας, Rec. Gr. Sch. (Jno. 13. 26) . }
βδέλυγμα, ατος, τό, (§ 4. tab. D. c) . βδελύσσομαι
βδελυγμάτων, gen. pl. . . . . βδέλυγμα
βδελυκτοί,[d] nom. pl. masc. . . . βδελυκτός
βδελυκτός], ή, όν, (§ 7. tab. F. a) . . βδελύσσομαι

βδελύσσομαι], fut. ξομαι, perf. ἐβδέλυγμαι, (§ 26. rem. 3) *to abominate, loathe, detest, abhor*, Ro. 2. 22; pass. *to be abominable, detestable*, Re. 21. 8.

βδέλυγμα, ατος, τό, (§ 4. tab. D. c) *an abomination, an abominable thing*, Mat. 24. 15; Mar. 13. 14, et al.; *idolatry with all its pollutions*, Re. 17. 4, 5; 21. 7. LXX.

βδελυκτός, ή, όν, (§ 7. tab. F. a) *abominable, detestable*, Tit. 1. 16. LXX.

βδελυσσόμενος, nom. sing. masc. part. pres. βδελύσσομαι
βεβαία, nom. sing. fem. . . . . βέβαιος
βεβαίαν, acc. sing. fem. . . . id.

βέβαιος, αία, ον, (§ 7. rem. 1) (*βέβαα*, perf. of *βαίνω*) *firm, stable, steadfast*, He. 3. 6, 14; 6. 19; *sure, certain, established*, Ro. 4. 16, et al.

βεβαιόω, ῶ, fut. ώσω, aor. 1, ἐβεβαίωσα, (§ 20. tab. T) *to confirm, establish; to render constant and unwavering*, 1 Co. 1. 8, et al.; *to strengthen or establish* by arguments or proofs, *ratify*, Mar. 16. 20; *to verify*, as promises, Ro. 15. 8.

βεβαίωσις, εως, ἡ, (§ 5. tab. E. c) *confirmation, firm establishment*, Phi. 1. 7; He. 6. 16.

βεβαιότερον, acc. sing. masc. comp. (§ 8. rem. 4) βέβαιος
βεβαιούμενοι, nom. pl. masc. part. pres. pass. βεβαιόω
βεβαιοῦντος, gen. sing. masc. part. pres. act. . id.
βεβαιοῦσθαι, pres. infin. pass. (§ 21. tab. U) id.
βεβαιόω, ῶ], fut. ώσω, (§ 20. tab. T) . βέβαιος
βεβαιῶν, nom. sing. masc. part. pres. act. . βεβαιόω
βεβαιῶσαι, aor. 1, infin. act. . . . . id.
βεβαιώσει, 3 pers. sing. fut. ind. act. . . id.
βεβαιώσει, dat. sing. . . . . . βεβαίωσις
βεβαμμένον, acc. sing. neut. part. perf. pass. . βάπτω
βεβάπτικα, 1 pers. sing. perf. ind. act.—D. } βαπτίζω
ἐβάπτισα, Rec. Gr. Sch. Tdf. (1 Co. 1. 16) }
βεβαπτισμένοι, nom. pl. masc. pt. perf. pass. id.
βεβαρημένοι, nom. pl. masc. pt. perf. pass. βαρέω
βεβήλοις, dat. pl. masc. . . . . βέβηλος

βέβηλος, ου, ὁ, ἡ, (§ 7. rem. 2) (*βαίνω, to tread*, and *βηλός, a threshold*) pr. *what is open and accessible to all*; hence, *profane, not religious, not connected with religion; un-*

[a] Lu. 16. 6. [b] Re. 16. 13. [c] Mat. 6. 7. [d] Tit. 1. 16.

holy; a despiser, scorner, 1 Ti. 1. 9; 4. 7, et al.

βεβηλόω, ῶ, fut. ώσω, aor. 1, ἐβεβήλωσα, (§ 20. tab. T) *to profane, pollute, violate,* Mat. 12. 5; Ac. 24. 6. L.G.

βεβήλους, acc. pl. masc. . . . . . βέβηλος
βεβηλοῦσι, 3 pers. pl. pres. ind. act. . . βεβηλόω
βεβηλόω, ῶ], fut. ώσω, (§ 20. tab. T) . . βέβηλος
βεβηλῶσαι, aor. 1, infin. act. . . . βεβηλόω
βέβληκε, 3 p. sing. perf. ind. act. (§ 27. rem. 2. d) βάλλω
βεβληκότος, gen. sing. masc. part. perf. act. . id.
βεβλημένην, acc. sing. fem. part. perf. pass. id.
βεβλημένον, acc. sing. masc. part. perf. pass. id.
βεβλημένος, nom. sing. masc. part. perf. pass. id.
βέβληται, 3 pers. sing. perf. ind. pass. . id.
βεβρωκόσι,[a] dat. pl. masc. part. perf. (§ 36. rem. 3) βιβρώσκω
Βεελζεβούλ, ὁ, *Beelzeboul,* pr. name, indecl.
βέλη,[b] acc. pl. . . . . . . βέλος
Βελίαλ, ὁ, *Belial,* pr. name, indecl.—Rec. Ln.
Βελίαρ, Gr. Sch. Tdf. (2 Co. 6. 15).

βέλος], εος, τό, (§ 5. tab. E. c) *a missile weapon, dart, arrow.*

βελόνη, ης, ἡ, (§ 2. tab. B. a) v.r. pr. *the point of a spear; a needle.*

βελόνη], ης, ἡ . . . . . . βέλος
βελόνης,[c] gen. sing.—B. D. Ln. Tdf. ⎫ βελόνη
ῥαφίδος, Rec. Gr. Sch. ⎭
βέλτιον,[d] neut. sing. used adverbially . . βελτίων
βελτίων], ονος, ὁ, ἡ, τό, -ον, compar. of ἀγαθός) (§ 8. rem. 3) *better;* βέλτῖον, as an adv. *very well, too well to need informing,* 2 Ti. 1. 18.
Βενιαμίν, ὁ, *Benjamin,* pr. name, indecl.
Βερνίκη, ης, ἡ, (ῑ), (§ 2. tab. B. a) *Bernice,* pr. name.
Βερνίκης, gen. sing. . . . . . Βερνίκη
Βέροια], ας, ἡ, (§ 2. tab. B. b, and rem. 2) *Beræa,* a town of Macedonia.
Βεροίᾳ, dat. sing. . . . . . Βέροια
Βέροιαν, acc. sing. . . . . . id.
Βεροιαῖος,[e] α, ον, (§ 7. rem. 1) *belonging to Beræa.*
Βηθαβαρά], ᾶς, ἡ, (§ 2. tab. B. b, and rem. 2) *Bethabara,* a town of Palestine.
Βηθαβαρᾷ,[f] dat. sing.—Rec. ⎫ Βηθαβαρά
Βηθανίᾳ, Gr. Sch. Tdf. (Jno. 1. 28) ⎭
Βηθανία, ας, ἡ, (§ 2. tab. B. b, and rem. 2) *Bethany.*
I. A village near Jerusalem, at the Mount of Olives, Mat. 21. 17; Mar. 11. 1, et al.
II. A village beyond the Jordan, Jno. 1. 28
Βηθανίᾳ, dat. sing. . . . . . Βηθανία
Βηθανίαν, acc. sing. . . . . . id.
Βηθανίας, gen. sing. . . . . . id.
Βηθεσδά, ἡ, *Bethesda,* indecl., a pool in Jerusalem.
Βηθλεέμ, ἡ, *Bethlehem,* indecl., a town in Palestine.
Βηθσαϊδά, and Βηθσαϊδάν, ἡ, *Bethsaida,* indecl.
I. A city of Galilee, Mat. 11. 21; Mar. 6. 45, et al.
II. A city of Lower Gaulanitis, near the Lake of Gennesareth, Lu. 9. 10.
Βηθφαγή, ἡ, *Bethphage,* indecl., a part of the Mount of Olives.—Rec. Gr. Sch. Tdf.
Βηθσφαγή, B. D. Ln. (Mat. 21. 1; Mar. 11. 1; Lu. 19. 29).
βῆμα, ατος, τό, (§ 4. tab. D. c) (βαίνω) *a step, footstep, foot-breadth, space to set the foot on,* Ac. 7. 5; *an elevated place ascended by steps, tribunal, throne,* Mat. 27. 19; Ac. 12. 21, et al.
βήματος, gen. sing. . . . . . βῆμα
βήματι, dat. sing. . . . . . id.
βήρυλλος,[g] ου, ὁ, ἡ, (§ 3. tab. C. a. b) *a beryl,* a precious stone of a sea-green colour, found chiefly in India. L.G.

βία], ας, ἡ, (§ 2. tab. B. b, and rem. 2) *force, impetus, violence,* Ac. 5. 26; 21. 35, et al.

βιάζω, fut. άσω, (§ 26. rem. 1) and mid. βιάζομαι, *to urge, constrain, overpower by force; to press earnestly forward, to rush,* Lu. 16. 16; pass. *to be an object of an impetuous movement,* Mat. 11. 12.

βίαιος, α, ον, (§ 7. rem. 1) *violent, vehement,* Ac. 2. 2.

βιαστής, οῦ, ὁ, (§ 2. tab. B. c) *one who uses violence, or is impetuous; one who is forceful* in eager pursuit, Mat. 11. 12. L.G.

βιάζεται, 3 pers. sing. pres. ind. pass. and mid. βιάζω
βιάζω], fut. άσω, (§ 26. rem. 1) . . βία
βιαίας,[h] gen. sing. fem. . . . . βίαιος
βίαιος], α, ον, (§ 7. rem. 1) . . . βία
βίαν, acc. sing. . . . . . . id.
βίας, gen. sing. . . . . . . id.
βιασταί,[i] nom. pl. . . . . . βιαστής
βιαστής], οῦ, ὁ, (§ 2. tab. B. c) . . βία

[a] Jno. 6. 13. [b] Ep. 6. 16. [c] Lu. 18. 25. [d] 2 Ti. 1. 18. [e] Ac. 20. 4. [f] Jno. 1. 28. [g] Re. 21. 20. [h] Ac. 2. 2. [i] Mat. 11. 12

βιβλαρίδιον, ου, τό, (§ 3. tab. C. c).—Rec. Gr. Sch. Tdf. } βίβλος
βιβλιδάριον, C. (Re. 10. 2) } βίβλος

βιβλία, nom. and acc. pl. . . . βιβλίον

βιβλίοις, dat. pl. . . . . id.

βιβλίον, ου, τό, (§ 3. tab. C. c) . . . βίβλος

βιβλίου, gen. sing. . . . . βιβλίον

βιβλίῳ, dat. sing. . . . . . id.

βίβλος, ου, ἡ, (§ 3. tab. C. b) pr. *the inner bark or rind of the papyrus,* which was anciently used instead of paper; hence, *a written volume, or roll, book, catalogue, account,* Mat. 1. 1; Mar. 12. 26, et al.

βιβλαρίδιον, ου, τό, (§ 3. tab. C. c) (dimin. of βιβλάριον, *a roll*) *a small volume or scroll, a little book,* Re. 10. 2, 8, 9, 10. L.G.

βιβλίον, ου, τό, (§ 3. tab. C. c) (pr. dimin. of βίβλος) *a written volume or roll, book,* Lu. 4. 17, 20, et al.; *a scroll, bill, billet,* Mat. 19. 7; Mar. 10. 4.

βίβλου, gen. sing. . . . . βίβλος

βίβλους, acc. pl. . . . . . id.

βίβλῳ, dat. sing. . . . . id.

βιβρώσκω], fut. βρώσομαι, perf. βέβρωκα, (§ 36. rem. 3) *to eat.*

βρῶμα, ατος, τό, (§ 4. tab. D. c) *food,* Mat. 14. 15; Mar. 7. 19, et al.; *solid food,* 1 Co. 3. 2.

βρώσῐμος, ου, ὁ, ἡ, (§ 7. rem. 2) *eatable, that may be eaten,* Lu. 24. 41.

βρῶσις, εως, ἡ, (§ 5. tab. E. c) *eating, the act of eating,* Ro. 14. 17; 1 Co. 8. 4, et al.; *meat, food,* Jno. 6. 27; He. 12. 16; *a canker or rust, ærugo,* Mat. 6. 19, 20.

Βιθυνία], ας, ἡ, (§ 2. tab. B. b, and rem. 2) *Bithynia,* a province of Asia Minor.

Βιθυνίαν, acc. sing. . . . . . Βιθυνία

Βιθυνίας, gen. sing. . . . . id.

βίον, acc. sing. . . . . . βίος

βίος], ου, ὁ, (§ 3. tab. C. a) *life; means of living; sustenance, maintenance, substance, goods,* Mar. 12. 44, et al.

βιόω, ῶ, (§ 20. tab. T) fut. ώσω, aor. 1, ἐβίωσα, *to live,* 1 Pe. 4. 2.

βίωσις, εως, ἡ, (§ 5. tab. E. c) *manner of life,* Ac. 26. 4. LXX.

βιωτῐκός, ή, όν, (§ 7. tab. F. a) *pertaining to this life, or the things of this life,* Lu. 21. 34; 1 Co. 6. 3, 4.

βίου, gen. sing. . . . . . βίος

βιόω, ῶ], fut. ώσω, (§ 20. tab. T) . . id.

βιῶσαι,[a] aor. 1, infin. . . . . βιόω

βίωσιν,[b] acc. sing. . . . . βίωσις

βίωσις], εως, ἡ, (§ 5. tab. E. c) . . βίος

βιωτικά, acc. pl. neut. . . . . βιωτικός

βιωτικαῖς, dat. pl. fem. . . . id.

βιωτικός], ή, όν, (§ 7. tab. F. a) . . βίος

βλαβεράς,[c] acc. pl. fem. . . . βλαβερός

βλαβερός], ά, όν, (§ 7. rem. 1) . . . βλάπτω

βλάπτω], fut. ψω, aor. 1, ἔβλαψα, (§ 23. rem. 1. a, and rem. 2) pr. *to weaken, hinder, disable; to hurt, harm, injure,* Mar. 16. 18; Lu. 4. 35.

βλαβερός, ά, όν, (§ 7. rem. 1) *hurtful,* 1 Ti. 6. 9.

βλαστᾷ, 3 pers. sing. pres. subj. (as if from βλαστάω).—B. D. } βλαστάνω
βλαστάνῃ, R. Gr. Sch. Tdf. (Mar. 4. 27) } βλαστάνω

βλαστάνῃ, 3 pers. sing. pres. subj. . . id.

βλαστάνω], fut. ήσω, aor. 1, ἐβλάστησα, aor. 2, ἔβλαστον, (§ 36. rem. 2) intrans. *to germinate, bud, sprout, spring up,* Mat. 13. 26; Mar. 4. 27; He. 9. 4; trans. and causat. *to cause to shoot, to produce, yield,* Ja. 5. 18.

βλαστήσασα, nom. sing. fem. part. aor. 1 . βλαστάνω

Βλάστον,[d] acc. sing. . . . . Βλάστος

Βλάστος], ου, ὁ, (§ 3. tab. C. a) *Blastus,* pr. name.

βλάσφημα, acc. pl. neut. . . . βλάσφημος

βλασφημεῖ, 3 pers. sing. pres. ind. act. βλασφημέω

βλασφημεῖν, pres. infin. act. . . . id.

βλασφημεῖς, 2 pers. sing. pres. ind. act. . id.

βλασφημείσθω, 3 pers. sing. pres. imper. pass. id.

βλασφημεῖται, 3 p. sing. pres. pass. (§ 17. tab. Q) id.

βλάσφημος, ου, ὁ, ἡ, (§ 7. rem. 2) *calumnious, railing, reproachful,* 2 Ti. 3. 2; 2 Pe. 2. 11; *blasphemous,* Ac. 6. 11, 13; 1 Ti. 1. 13.

βλασφημέω, ῶ], fut. ήσω, (§ 16. tab. P) perf. βεβλασφήμηκα, aor. 1, ἐβλασφήμησα, *to calumniate, revile, treat with calumny and contumely,* Mat.

---

[a] 1 Pe. 4. 2. [b] Ac. 26. 4. [c] 1 Ti. 6. 9. [d] Ac. 12. 20.

27.39, et al.; *to speak of God or divine things in terms of impious irreverence, to blaspheme,* Mat.9.3; 26.65, et al.

βλασφημία, ας, ἡ, (§ 2. tab. B. b, and rem. 2) *calumny, railing, reproach,* Mat.15.19; Mar.7.22, et al.; *blasphemy,* Mat. 12.31; 26.65, et al.

βλασφημηθήσεται, 3 pers. sing. fut. ind. pass. . . βλασφημέω
βλασφημῆσαι, aor. 1, infin. act. . . . id.
βλασφημήσαντι, dat. sing. masc. part. aor. 1, act. . id.
βλασφημήσῃ, 3 pers. sing. aor. 1, subj. act. . id.
βλασφημήσωσι, 3 pers. pl. aor. 1, subj. act. . id.
βλασφημῆται, 3 pers. sing. pres. subj. pass. . id.
βλασφημία, ας, ἡ, (§ 2. tab. B. b, and rem. 2) id.
βλασφημίαι, nom. pl. . . . . . βλασφημία
βλασφημίαν, acc. sing. . . . . . id.
βλασφημίας, gen. sing. . . . . id.
βλασφημίας, acc. pl. . . . . . id.
βλάσφημοι, nom. pl. masc. . . . . βλάσφημος
βλάσφημον, acc. sing. masc. and fem. . . id.
βλασφημοῦμαι, 1 pers. sing. pres. ind. pass. βλασφημέω
βλασφημούμεθα, 1 pers. pl. pres. ind. pass. id.
βλασφημούμενοι, nom. pl. masc. pt. pr. pass. id.
βλασφημοῦντας, acc. pl. masc. pt. pres. act. id.
βλασφημοῦντες, nom. pl. masc. pt. pres. act. id.
βλασφημούντων, gen. pl. masc. pt. pres. act. id.
βλασφημοῦσι, 3 pers. pl. pres. ind. act. . id.
βλάψαν, nom. sing. neut. part. aor. 1, act. . βλάπτω
βλάψει, 3 pers. sing. fut. ind. act. . . id.
βλέμμα], ατος, τό, (§ 4. tab. D. c) . . βλέπω
βλέμματι,[a] dat. sing. . . . . . βλέμμα
βλέπε, 2 pers. sing. pres. imper. act. . . βλέπω
βλέπει, 3 pers. sing. pres. ind. act. . . id.
βλέπειν, pres. infin. act. . . . . . id.
βλέπεις, 2 pers. sing. pres. ind. act. . . id.
βλέπετε, 2 pers. pl. pres. ind. act. . . id.
βλέπετε, 2 pers. pl. pres. imper. act. . id.
βλεπέτω, 3 pers. sing. pres. imper. act. . id.
βλέπῃ, 3 pers. sing. pres. subj. act. . . id.
βλέπῃς, 2 pers. sing. pres. subj. act. . . id.
βλέπομεν, 1 pers. pl. pres. ind. act. . id.
βλεπόμενα, nom. and acc. pl. neut. pt. pres. pass. id.
βλεπομένη, nom. sing. fem. part. pres. pass. . id.
βλεπόμενον, acc. sing. neut. part. pres. pass.—Al. Ln. Tdf. . . . . } id.
βλεπόμενα, Rec. Gr. Sch. (He. 11. 3) }
βλεπομένων, gen. pl. part. pres. pass. . . id.
βλέποντα, acc. sing. masc. part. pres. act. . id.
βλέποντας, acc. pl. masc. part. pres. act. . βλέπω
βλέποντες, nom. pl. masc. part. pres. act. . id.
βλεπόντων, gen. pl. masc. part. pres. act. . id.
βλέπουσι, 3 pers. pl. pres. ind. act. . id.

βλέπω, fut. ψω, aor. 1, ἔβλεψα, (§ 23. rem. 1. a, and rem. 2) *to have the faculty of sight, to see,* Mat. 12. 22, et al.; *to exercise sight, to see,* Mat. 6. 4, et al.; *to look* towards or at, Mat. 22. 16, et al.; *to face,* Ac. 27. 12; *to take heed,* Mat. 24. 4, et al.; in N.T., βλέπειν ἀπό, *to beware of, shun,* Mar. 8.15; trans., *to cast a look on,* Mat. 5.28; *to see, behold,* Mat. 13. 17, et al.; *to observe,* Mat. 7. 3, et al.; *to have an eye to, see to,* Mar. 13.9; Col. 4.17; 2 Jno. 8; *to discern* mentally, *perceive,* Ro. 7. 23; 2 Co. 7. 8; Ja. 2. 22; *to guard against,* Phi. 3. 2; pass., *to be an object of sight, be visible,* Ro. 8. 24, et al.

βλέμμα, ατος, τό, (§ 4. tab. D. c) *a look; the act of seeing, sight,* 2 Pe. 2. 8.

βλέπων, nom. sing. masc. part. pres. act. . βλέπω
βλέπωσι, 3 pers. pl. pres. subj. act. . id.
βλέψετε, 2 pers. pl. fut. ind. act. . . id.
βλέψον, 2 pers. sing. aor. 1, imper. act. . id.
βληθείς, nom. sing. part. aor. 1, pass.—B. Tdf. } βάλλω
βεβλημένος, Rec. Gr. Sch. (Lu. 23. 19) }
βληθείσῃ, dat. sing. fem. part. aor. 1, pass. . id.
βληθέν, nom. sing. neut. part. aor. 1, pass.—B. L. } id.
βληθῆναι, Rec. Gr. Sch. Tdf. (Mat. 5. 13) }
βλήθῃ, 3 pers. sing. aor. 1, subj. pass. . id.
βληθῆναι, aor. 1, infin. pass. . . . . id.
βληθήσεται, 3 p. sing. fut. ind. pass. (§ 27. rem. 3) id.
βληθήσῃ, 2 pers. sing. fut. ind. pass. . id.
βλήθητι, 2 pers. sing. aor. 1, imper. pass. . id.
βλητέον, nom. sing. neut. . . . . βλητέος
βλητέος], α, ον, (§ 35. rem. 10) . . βάλλω
βοαί,[b] nom. pl. . . . . . . βοή
βόας, acc. pl. (§ 6. rem. 4. h) . . . βοῦς
Βοανεργές,[c] *Boanerges,* pr. name, indecl.—Rec. Gr. Sch. Tdf.

Βοανηργές, Ln.

βοάω, ῶ], fut. ήσω, (§ 18. tab. R) . . βοή

βοή], ῆς, ἡ, (§ 2. tab. B. b, and rem. 2) *a cry, outcry, exclamation.*

βοάω, ῶ, fut. ήσω, aor. 1, ἐβόησα, (§ 18. tab. R) *to cry out; to exclaim,*

[a] 2 Pe. 2. 8. [b] Ja. 5. 4. [c] Mar. 3. 17.

proclaim, Mat. 3. 3; 15. 34; Ac. 8. 7, et al.; πρός τινα, *to invoke, implore the aid of any one*, Lu. 18. 7.

βοήθει, 2 pers. sing. pres. imper. act. . . . βοηθέω

βοήθεια], ας, ἡ, (§ 2. tab. B. b, and rem. 2) id.

βοηθείαις, dat. pl. . . . . . βοήθεια

βοήθειαν, acc. sing. . . . . . id.

βοηθεῖτε, 2 pers. pl. pres. imper. act. . βοηθέω

βοηθέω, ῶ], fut. ήσω, aor. 1, ἐβοήθησα, (§ 16. tab. P) (βοή, & θέω, *to run*) pr. *to run to the aid of those who cry for help; to advance to the assistance of any one, help, aid, succour*, Mat. 15. 25; Mar. 9. 22, 24, et al.

βοήθεια, ας, ἡ, (§ 2. tab. B. b, and rem. 2) *help, succour*, He. 4. 16; meton. pl. *helps, contrivances for relief and safety*, Ac. 27. 17.

βοηθός, οῦ, ὁ, (§ 3. tab. C. a) *a helper*.

βοηθῆσαι, aor. 1, infin. act. . . . βοηθέω

βοήθησον, 2 pers. sing. aor. 1, imper. act. . id.

βοηθός,[a] οῦ, ὁ, (§ 3. tab. C. a) . . . id.

βόησον, 2 pers. sing. aor. 1, imper. . βοάω

βόθυνον, acc. sing. . . . . . βόθυνος

βόθυνος], ου, ὁ, (§ 3. tab. C. a) *a pit, well, or cistern*, Mat. 12. 11; 15. 14; Lu. 6. 39.

βολή], ῆς, ἡ, (§ 2. tab. B. a) . . . βάλλω

βολήν,[b] acc. sing. . . . . . βολή

βολίδι,[c] dat. sing.—Rec. Gr. Sch. Tdf. om. } βολίς

βολίζω], fut. ίσω, (§ 26. rem. 1) . . βάλλω

βολίς], ίδος, ἡ, (§ 4. rem. 2. c) . . . id.

βολίσαντες, nom. pl. masc. part. aor. 1 . βολίζω

Βοόζ, ὁ, *Booz*, pr. name, indecl.—Rec. Gr. Sch. Βοός, Al. Ln. Tdf. (Lu. 3. 32).

βόρβορος], ου, ὁ, (§ 3. tab. C. a) *mud, mire, dung, filth*.

βορβόρου,[d] gen. sing. . . . . βόρβορος

βορρᾶ, gen. sing. . . . . . βορρᾶς

βορρᾶς], ᾶ, ὁ, (§ 2. rem. 4) i. q. βορέας, pr. *the north, or N.N.E. wind*; meton. *the north*, Lu. 13. 29; Re. 21. 13.

βόσκε, 2 pers. sing. pres. imper. act. . . βόσκω

βόσκειν, pres. infin. act. . . . . id.

βοσκομένη, nom. sing. fem. part. pres. mid. id.

βοσκομένων, gen. pl. part. pres. mid. . . id.

βόσκοντες, nom. pl. masc. part. pres. act. . id.

βόσκω], fut. βοσκήσω, (§ 35. rem. 5) aor. 1, ἐβόσκησα *to feed, pasture, tend while grazing*; βόσκομαι, *to feed, be feeding*, Mat. 8. 30, 33; Lu. 8. 32, 34, et al.

βοτάνη, ης, ἡ, (§ 2. tab. B. a) *herb, herbage, produce of the earth*. (ᾰ).

Βοσόρ,[e] ὁ, *Bosor*, pr. name, indecl.—Rec. Gr. Sch. Tdf. Βεώρ, B.

βοτάνη], ης, ἡ, (§ 2. tab. B. a) . . . βόσκω

βοτάνην,[f] acc. sing. . . . . βοτάνη

βότρυας,[g] acc. pl. . . . . . βότρυς

βότρυς], υος, ὁ, (§ 5. tab. E. g) *a bunch or cluster of grapes*.

βουλάς, acc. pl. . . . . . βουλή

βούλει, 2 pers. sing. pres. ind. Att. (§ 35. rem. 11) βούλομαι

βούλεσθε, 2 pers. pl. pres. ind. . . . id.

βούλεται, 3 pers. sing. pres. ind. . . id.

βουλεύεται, 3 pers. sing. pres. ind. mid. . βουλεύω

βουλεύομαι, 1 pers. sing. pres. ind. mid. . id.

βουλευόμενος, nom. sing. masc. pt. pres. mid. id.

βουλευτής, οῦ, ὁ, (§ 2. tab. B. c) . . βούλομαι

βουλεύω], fut. εύσω, (§ 13. tab. M) . . id.

βουλή, ῆς, ἡ, (§ 2. tab. B. a) . . . id.

βουλῇ, dat. sing. . . . . . βουλή

βουλήθῃ, 3 pers. sing. aor. 1, subj. pass. . βούλομαι

βουληθείς, nom. sing. masc. pt. aor. 1, pass. id.

βούλημα, ατος, τό,—A. C. Ln. Tdf. . θέλημα, Rec. Gr. Sch. (1 Pe. 4. 3) . } id.

βουλήματι, dat. sing. . . . . βούλημα

βουλήματος, gen. sing. . . . . id.

βουλήν, acc. sing. . . . . . βουλή

βουλῆς, gen. sing. . . . . . id.

βούληται, 3 pers. sing. pres. subj. . . βούλομαι

βούλοιτο, 3 pers. sing. pres. optat. . . id.

βούλομαι, fut. βουλήσομαι, (§ 35. rem. 5) imperf. ἐβουλόμην and Att. ἠβουλόμην, aor. 1, (pass. form) ἐβουλήθην & ἠβουλήθην, perf. (pass. form) βεβούλημαι, *to be willing, disposed*, Mar. 15. 15; Ac. 25. 20; 28. 18, et al.; *to intend*, Mat. 1. 19; Ac. 5. 28; 12. 4; 2 Co. 1. 15; *to desire*, 1 Ti. 6. 9; *to choose, be pleased*, Jno. 18. 39; Ac. 18. 15; Ja. 3. 4; *to will, decree, appoint*, Lu. 22. 42; Ja. 1. 18; 1 Co. 12. 11; 1 Ti. 2. 8; 5. 14, et al.; ἐβουλόμην, *I could wish*, Ac. 25. 22.

βούλημα, ατος, τό, (§ 4. tab. D. c)

---

[a] He. 13. 6. [b] Lu. 22. 41. [c] He. 12. 20. [d] 2 Pe. 2. 22. [e] 2 Pe. 2. 15. [f] He. 6. 7. [g] Re. 14. 18.

purpose, will, determination, Ac. 27. 43; Ro. 9. 19.

βουλή, ῆς, ἡ, (§ 2. tab. B. a) *counsel, purpose, design, determination, decree*, Lu. 7. 30; 23. 51, et al. freq.; by impl. *secret thoughts, cogitations* of the mind, 1 Co. 4. 5.

βουλεύω, fut. εύσω, (§ 13. tab. M) *to give counsel, to deliberate*; mid. βουλεύομαι, *to deliberate*, Lu. 14. 31; Jno. 12. 10; Ac. 5. 33; *to purpose, determine*, Ac. 15. 37; 27. 39; 2 Co. 1. 17.

βουλευτής, οῦ, ὁ, (§ 2. tab. B. c) *a counsellor, senator; member of the Sanhedrim*, Mar. 15. 43; Lu. 23. 50.

βουλόμεθα, 1 pers. pl. pres. ind. . . βούλομαι
βουλόμενοι, nom. pl. masc. part. pres. . id.
βουλόμενος, nom. sing. masc. part. pres. . id.
βουλομένου, gen. sing. masc. part. pres. . id.
βουλομένους, acc. pl. masc. part. pres. . . id.
βούλονται, 3 pers. pl. pres. ind.—A. C. . } θέλουσιν, Rec. Gr. Sch. Tdf. (Gal. 6. 13) } id.
βοῦν, acc. sing. . . . . . . βοῦς
βουνοῖς, dat. pl. . . . . . βουνός

βουνός, οῦ, ὁ, (§ 3. tab. C. a) *a hill, hillock, rising ground*, Lu. 3. 5; 23. 30.

βοῦς, βοός, ὁ, ἡ, (§ 6. rem. 4. h) *an ox, a bull, or cow*, an animal of the ox kind, Lu. 13. 15, et al.

βοῶν, gen. pl. . . . . . . βοῦς
βοῶντα, nom. pl. neut. part. pres. . . βοάω
βοῶντες, nom. pl. masc. part. pres. . . id.
βοῶντος, gen. sing. masc. part. pres. . id.
βοώντων, gen. pl. masc. part. pres. . . id.
βραβεῖον, ου, τό, (§ 3. tab. C. c) (βραβεύς, *a judge or arbiter in the public games*) *a prize* bestowed on victors in the public games, such as a crown, wreath, chaplet, garland, etc. 1 Co. 9. 24; Phi. 3. 14. L.G.

βραβεύω, fut. εύσω, (§ 13. tab. M) pr. *to be a director or arbiter in the public games*; in N.T. *to preside, direct, rule, govern, be predominant*, Col. 3. 15.

βραβευέτω,[a] 3 pers. sing. pres. imper. . βραβεύω
βραβεύω], fut. εύσω, (§ 13. tab. M) . . βραβεῖον
βραδεῖς, nom. pl. masc. . . . βραδύς
βραδύνει, 3 pers. sing. pres. ind. . . βραδύνω
βραδύνω], fut. υνῶ, (§ 27. rem. 1. a) . βραδύς
βραδύνω, 1 pers. sing. pres. subj. . . βραδύνω
βραδυπλοέω, ῶ], fut. ήσω, (§ 16. tab. P) (βραδύς & πλέω) *to sail slowly*. L.G.
βραδυπλοοῦντες,[b] nom. pl. masc. pt. pr. . βραδυπλοέω

βραδύς, εῖα, ύ, (§ 7. tab. H. g) *slow, not hasty*, Ja. 1. 19; *slow* of understanding, *heavy, stupid*, Lu. 24. 25.

βραδύνω, fut. υνῶ, (§ 27. rem. 1. a) *to be slow, to delay*, 1 Ti. 3. 15; *to be behindhand*, 2 Pe. 3. 9.

βραδύτής, τῆτος, ἡ, (§ 4. rem. 2. c) *slowness, tardiness, delay*.

βραδυτής], τῆτος, ἡ . . . . . βραδύς
βραδύτητα,[c] acc. sing. . . . . βραδυτής
βραχέων, gen. pl. neut. . . . . βραχύς
βραχίονι, dat. sing. . . . . βραχίων
βραχίονος, gen. sing. . . . . . id.
βραχίων, ονος, ὁ, (§ 4. rem. 2. e) . . βραχύς
βραχύ, acc. sing. neut. . . . . . id.

βραχύς], εῖα, ύ, (§ 7. tab. H. g) *short, brief; few, small*, Lu. 22. 58; Jno. 6. 7, et al.

βραχίων, ονος, ὁ, (§ 4. rem. 2. e) *the arm*; *the arm* as a symbol of power, Lu. 1. 51; Jno. 12. 38; Ac. 13. 17. (ῑ).

βρέξαι, aor. 1, infin. . . . . βρέχω
βρέφη, nom. and. acc. pl. . . . . βρέφος

βρέφος, εος, τό, (§ 5. tab. E. b) *a child*; whether unborn, *an embryo, fœtus*, Lu. 1. 41, 44; or just born, *an infant*, Lu. 2. 12, 16; Ac. 7. 19; or partly grown, Lu. 18. 15; 2 Ti. 3. 15; met. *a babe* in simplicity of faith, 1 Pe. 2. 2.

βρέφους, gen. sing. . . . . βρέφος
βρέχει, 3 pers. sing. pres. ind. . . βρέχω
βρέχειν, pres. infin. . . . . . id.
βρέχῃ, 3 pers. sing. pres. subj. . . . id.

βρέχω], fut. ξω, aor. 1, ἔβρεξα, (§ 23. rem. 1. b, and rem. 2) *to wet, moisten*, Lu. 7. 38; *to rain, cause or send rain*, Mat. 5. 45; Lu. 17. 29, et al.

βροχή, ῆς, ἡ, (§ 2. tab. B. a) *rain*, Mat. 7. 25, 27. L.G.

βρονταί, nom. pl. . . . . . βροντή
βροντή], ῆς, ἡ, (§ 2. tab. B. a) *thunder*, Mar. 3. 17; Jno. 12. 29, et al.

[a] Col. 3. 15. [b] Ac. 27. 7. [c] 2 Pe. 3. 9.

βροντήν, acc. sing. . . . . . . βροντή
βροντῆς, gen. sing . . . . . id.
βροντῶν, gen. pl. . . . . . . id.
βροχή, ῆς, ἡ, (§ 2. tab. B. a) . . . βρέχω
βρόχον,[a] acc. sing. . . . . . βρόχος

βρόχος], ου, ὁ, (§ 3. tab. C. a) *a cord, noose.*

βρυγμός, οῦ, ὁ, (§ 3. tab. C. a) . . βρύχω
βρύει,[b] 3 pers. sing. pres. ind. . . . βρύω

βρύχω], fut. ξω, (§ 23. rem. 1. b) *to grate or gnash* the teeth, Ac. 7. 54. (ῡ).

βρύω], pr. *to be full, to swell* with anything; *to emit, send forth,* Ja. 3. 11.

βρῶμα, ατος, τό, (§ 4. tab. D. c) . . βιβρώσκω
βρώμασι, dat. pl. . . . . . . βρῶμα
βρώματα, nom. and acc. pl. . . . . id.
βρώματι, dat. sing. . . . . . id.
βρώματος, gen. sing. . . . . . id.
βρωμάτων, gen. pl. . . . . . id.
βρώσει, dat. sing. . . . . . βρῶσις
βρώσεως, gen. sing. . . . . . id.
βρώσιμον,[c] acc. sing. neut. . . . βρώσιμος
βρώσῐμος], ου, ὁ, ἡ, (§ 7. rem. 2) . . βιβρώσκω
βρῶσιν, acc. sing. . . . . . βρῶσις
βρῶσις, εως, ἡ, (§ 5. tab. E. c) . . . βιβρώσκω
βυθίζεσθαι, pres. infin. pass. . . . βυθίζω
βυθίζουσι, 3 pers. pl. pres. ind. act. . . id.
βυθίζω], fut. ίσω, (§ 26. rem. 1) . . βυθός

βυθός], οῦ, ὁ, (§ 3. tab. C. a) *the bottom, lowest part; the deep, sea.*

βυθίζω, fut. ίσω, aor. 1, ἐβύθισα, (§ 26. rem. 1) *to immerse, submerge, cause to sink,* Lu. 5. 7; *to plunge deep, drown,* 1 Ti. 6. 9.

βυθῷ,[d] dat. sing. . . . . . βυθός
βυρσεῖ, dat. sing. . . . . . βυρσεύς
βυρσεύς], έως, ὁ, (§ 5. tab. E. d) (βύρσα, *a hide*) *a tanner, leather-dresser,* Ac. 9. 43; 10. 6, 32. L.G.

βύσσινον, nom. and acc. sing. neut. . . βύσσινος
βύσσῐνος], η, ον, (§ 7. tab. F. a) . . βύσσος
βυσσίνου, gen. sing. neut.—Gr. Sch. Tdf. } βύσσινος
βύσσου, Rec. (Re. 18. 12) . . }
βύσσον, acc. sing. . . . . . βύσσος

βύσσος], ου, ἡ, (§ 3. tab. C. b) *byssus,* a species of fine cotton highly prized by the ancients, Lu. 16. 19, v.r.; Re. 18. 12.

βύσσῐνος, η, ον, (§ 7. tab. F. a) *made of byssus or fine cotton,* Re. 18. 16.

βύσσου, gen. sing. . . . . . βύσσος
βωμόν,[e] acc. sing. . . . . . βωμός

βωμός], οῦ, ὁ, (§ 3. tab. C. a) pr. *a slightly-elevated spot, base, pedestal;* hence, *an altar.*

Γ.

Γαββαθᾶ,[f] *Gabbutha,* pr. name, indecl.
Γαβριήλ, ὁ, *Gabriel,* pr. name, indecl.
γάγγραινα,[g] ης, ἡ, (§ 2. rem. 3) (γράω, γραίνω, *to eat, gnaw*) *gangrene, mortification.*
Γάδ,[h] ὁ, *Gad,* pr. name, indecl.
Γαδαρηνός], οῦ, ὁ, (§ 3. tab. C. a) *an inhabitant of Gadara,* the chief city of Peræa.
Γαδαρηνῶν, gen. pl. . . . . . Γαδαρηνός
Γάζα], ης, ἡ, (§ 2. rem. 3) *Gaza,* a strong city of Palestine.

γάζα], ης, ἡ, *a treasure, treasury.*

Γάζαν,[i] acc. sing. . . . . . Γάζα
γάζης,[k] gen. sing. . . . . . . γάζα
γαζοφυλάκιον, ου, τό, (§ 3. tab. C. c) (γάζα & φυλακή) *a treasury; the sacred treasury,* Mar. 12. 41, 43; Lu. 21. 1; Jno. 8. 20. L.G.
γαζοφυλακίου, gen. sing. . . . γαζοφυλάκιον
γαζοφυλακίῳ, dat. sing. . . . . id.
Γάϊον, acc. sing. . . . . . . Γάϊος
Γάϊος, ου, ὁ, (§ 3. tab. C. a) *Gaius,* pr. name.

I. *Of Macedonia,* Ac. 19. 29.
II. *Of Corinth,* 1 Co. 1. 14.
III. *Of Derbe,* Ac. 20. 4.
IV. *A Christian to whom John addressed his third Epistle,* 3 Jno. 1.

Γαΐῳ, dat. sing. . . . . . . Γάϊος
γάλα, γάλακτος, τό, (§ 6. rem. 4. b) *milk,* 1 Co. 9. 7; met. spiritual *milk,* consisting in the elements of Christian instruction, 1 Co. 3. 2; He. 5. 12, 13; spiritual *nutriment,* 1 Pe. 2. 2.
γάλακτος, gen. sing. . . . . . γάλα
Γαλάται,[l] ῶν, *the inhabitants of Galatia.* (ᾰ).
Γαλατία], ας, ἡ, (§ 2 tab. B. b, and rem. 2) *Galatia, or Gallo-Græcia,* a province of Asia Minor.
Γαλατίαν, acc. sing. . . . . . Γαλατια
Γαλατίας, gen. sing. . . . . . id.
Γαλατικήν, acc. sing. fem. . . . Γαλατικός

---

[a] Co. 7. 35. [b] Ja. 3. 11. [c] Lu. 24. 41. [d] 2 Co. 11. 25. [e] Ac. 17. 23. [f] Jno. 19. 13. [g] 2 Ti. 2. 17.
[h] Re. 7. 5. [i] Ac. 8. 26. [k] Ac. 8. 27. [l] Gal. 3. 1.

Γαλατικός], ή, όν, (§ 7. tab. F. a) *Galatian.*

γαλήνη, ης, ἡ, (§ 2. tab. B. a) *tranquillity of the sea, a calm,* Mat. 8. 26; Mar. 4. 39; Lu. 8. 24.

Γαλιλαία, ας, ἡ, (§ 2. tab. B. b, and rem. 2) *Galilee,* a district of Palestine north of Samaria.

Γαλιλαίᾳ, dat. sing. . . . . . **Γαλιλαία**

Γαλιλαίαν, acc. sing. . . . . . id.

Γαλιλαίας, gen. sing. . . . . . id.

Γαλιλαῖοι, nom. and voc. pl. . . . **Γαλιλαῖος**

Γαλιλαῖος, ου, ὁ, (§ 3. tab. C. a) *a native of Galilee.*

Γαλιλαίου, gen. sing. . . . . . **Γαλιλαῖος**

Γαλιλαίους, acc. pl. . . . . . id.

Γαλιλαίων, gen. pl. . . . . . id.

Γαλλίων, ωνος, ὁ, (§ 4. rem. 2. e) *Gallio,* pr. name.

Γαλλίωνι, dat. sing. . . . . . **Γαλλίων**

Γαλλίωνος, gen. sing. . . . . . id.

Γαμαλιήλ, ὁ, *Gamaliel,* pr. name, indecl.

γαμεῖν, pres. infin. act. . . . . . γαμέω

γαμείτωσαν, 3 pers. pl. pres. imper. act. . id.

γαμέω, ῶ], fut. ῶ, and, later, ήσω, perf. γεγάμηκα, aor. 1, ἔγημα & ἐγάμησα, aor. 1, pass. ἐγαμήθην, (§ 37. rem. 2) *to marry,* Mat. 5. 32, et al.; absol. *to marry, enter the marriage state,* Mat. 19. 10, et al.; mid. *to marry, be married,* Mar. 10. 12; 1 Co. 7. 39.

γαμίζω, fut. ίσω, (§ 26. rem. 1) *to give in marriage, permit to marry,* v.r. 1 Co. 7. 38. N.T.

γαμίσκω, *to give in marriage,* v.r. Mat. 24. 38.

γαμίσκομαι, pass. *to be given in marriage,* Mar. 12. 25. L.G.

γάμος, ου, ὁ, (§ 3. tab. C. a) *a wedding; nuptial festivities, a marriage festival,* Mat. 22. 2; 25. 10; Jno. 2. 1, 2; Re. 19. 7, 9; any *feast or banquet,* Lu. 12. 36; 14. 8; *the marriage state,* He. 13. 4.

γαμηθῇ, 3 pers. sing. aor. 1, subj. pass. . γαμέω

γαμηθῆναι, aor. 1, infin. pass. . . id.

γαμῆσαι, aor. 1, infin. act. . . . id.

γαμήσας, nom. sing. masc. part. aor. 1, act. id.

γαμήσασα, nom. sing. fem. part. aor. 1, act. . id.

γαμησάτωσαν, 3 pers. pl. aor. 1, imper. act. id.

γαμήσῃ, 3 pers. sing. aor. 1, subj. act. . id.

γαμήσῃς, 2 pers. sing. aor. 1, subj. act.—A. B. Ln. Tdf. . . . } id.
γήμῃς, Rec. Gr. Sch. (1 Co. 7. 28) . }

γαμίζονται, 3 pers. pl. pres. ind. mid.—B. C. Ln. Tdf. . . . . } γαμίζω
γαμίσκονται, Rec. Gr. Sch. (Mar. 12. 25) }

γαμίζω], fut. ίσω, (§ 26. rem. 1) v.r. . γαμέω

γαμίζων, nom. sing. masc. part. pres.—A. Ln. Sch. Tdf. . . . } γαμίζω
ἐκγαμίζων, Rec. Gr. (1 Co. 7. 38) . }

γαμίσκονται, 3 pers. pl. pres. ind. mid. . γαμίσκω

γαμίσκοντες, nom. pl. masc. part. pres.—B. Ln. } id.
ἐκγαμίζοντες, R. Gr. Sch. Tdf. (Mat. 24. 38) }

γαμίσκω], fut. ίσω, v.r. . . . γαμέω

γάμον, acc. sing. . . . . . . γάμος

γάμος, ου, ὁ, (§ 3. tab. C. a) . . . γαμέω

γαμοῦντες, nom. pl. masc. part. pres. act. . id.

γάμους, acc. pl. . . . . . γάμος

γαμοῦσι, 3 pers. pl. pres. ind. act. . . γαμέω

γάμων, gen. pl. . . . . . γάμος

γαμῶν, nom. sing. masc. part. pres. act. . γαμέω

γάρ, a causal particle or conjunction, *for;* it is, however, frequently used with an ellipsis of the clause to which it has reference, and its force must then be variously expressed: Mat. 15. 27; 27. 23, et al.: it is also sometimes epexegetic, or introductory of an intimated detail of circumstances, *now, then, to wit,* Mat. 1. 18.

γαστέρες, nom. pl. . . . . . γαστήρ

γαστήρ], τέρος, τρός, ἡ, (§ 6. rem. 2) *the belly, stomach; the womb,* Lu. 1. 31; ἐν γαστρὶ ἔχειν, *to be with child,* Mat. 1. 18, 23; 24. 19, et al.; γαστέρες, *paunches, gluttons,* Tit. 1. 12.

γαστρί, dat. sing. . . . . . γαστήρ

γε, an enclitic particle imparting emphasis; indicating that a particular regard is to be had to the term to which it is attached. Its force is to be conveyed, when this is possible, by various expressions; *at least, indeed, even,* etc.

γεγαμηκόσι, dat. pl. masc. part. perf. act. . γαμέω

γεγενημένον, acc. sing. neut. part. perf. pass. (§ 37. rem. 1) . . . . γίνομαι

γεγενημένους, acc. pl. masc. pt. perf. pass.—A. } id.
γεγονότας, Rec. Gr. Sch. Tdf. (Ja. 3. 9) }

γεγενῆσθαι, perf. infin. pass. . . . id.

γεγένησθε, 2 pers. pl. perf. ind. pass. . . id.

γεγέννηκα, 1 pers. sing. perf. ind. act. . γεννάω

γεγέννημαι, 1 pers. sing. perf. ind. pass. . id.

γεγεννήμεθα, 1 pers. pl. perf. ind. pass. . id

γεγεννημένα, nom. pl. neut. pt. perf. pass.—Rec. Gr. Tdf. γεγενημένα, A. Sch. (2 Pe. 2. 12) . } γεννάω
γεγεννημένον, nom. neut. and acc. sing. masc. and neut. part. perf. pass. . . id.
γεγεννημένος, nom. sing. masc. part. perf. pass. id.
γεγεννημένου, gen. sing. masc. part. perf. pass. id.
γεγέννηται, 3 pers. sing. perf. ind. pass. . id.
γέγονα, 1 pers. sing. perf. 2, ind. . . γίνομαι
γεγόναμεν, 1 pers. pl. perf. 2, ind. . . id.
γέγοναν, 3 pers. pl. contr. perf. 2, (§ 35. rem. 13).—Ln. Tdf. . . γεγόνασιν, Rec. Gr. Sch. (Ro. 16. 7) . } id.
γέγονας, 2 pers. sing. perf. 2, ind. . . id.
γεγόνασι, 3 pers. pl. perf. 2, ind. . . id.
γεγόνατε, 2 pers. pl. perf. 2, ind. . . id.
γέγονε, 3 pers. sing. perf. 2, ind. . . id.
γεγονέναι, perf. 2, infin. . . . . id.
γεγονός, nom. and acc. sing. neut. part. perf. 2 id.
γεγονότας, acc. pl. masc. part. perf. 2 . id.
γεγονότες, nom. pl. masc. part. perf. 2 . . id.
γεγονότι, dat. sing. neut. part. perf. 2 . id.
γεγονυῖα, nom. sing. fem. part. perf. 2 . . id.
γεγονώς, nom. sing. masc. part. perf. 2 . id.
γεγραμμένα, nom. and acc. pl. neut. part. perf. pass. (§ 13. rem. 6. c) . . γράφω
γεγραμμένας, acc. pl. fem. part. perf. pass. id.
γεγραμμένη, nom. sing. fem. part. perf. pass. id.
γεγραμμένην, acc. sing. fem. part. perf. pass. id.
γεγραμμένοι, nom. pl. masc. part. perf. pass. id.
γεγραμμένοις, dat. pl. part. perf. pass. . id.
γεγραμμένον, nom. and acc. sing. neut. pt. p. pass. id.
γεγραμμένος, nom. sing. masc. part. perf. pass. id.
γεγραμμένων, gen. pl. part. perf. pass. . id.
γέγραπται, 3 pers. s. perf. ind. pass. (§ 23. rem. 8) id.
γέγραφα, 1 pers. sing. perf. ind. act. (§ 13. rem. 6. c) id.
γεγυμνασμένα, acc. pl. neut. part. perf. pass. γυμνάζω
γεγυμνασμένην, acc. sing. fem. part. perf. pass. id.
γεγυμνασμένοις, dat. pl. masc. part. perf. pass. id.
Γεδεών,[a] ὁ, *Gedeon*, pr. name, indecl.
Γέεννα, ης, ἡ, (§ 2. rem. 3) (Heb. גֵּיא הִנֹּם) *Gehenna*, pr. *the valley of Hinnom*, south of Jerusalem, once celebrated for the horrid worship of Moloch, and afterwards polluted with every species of filth, as well as the carcases of animals, and dead bodies of malefactors; to consume which, in order to avert the pestilence which such a mass of corruption would occasion, constant fires were kept burning; hence, *hell, the fires of Tartarus, the place of punishment in Hades*, Mat. 5. 22, 29, 30; 10. 28; 18. 9, et al. N.T.
γέενναν, acc. sing. . . . . . γέεννα
γεέννῃ, dat. sing. . . . . . id.
γεέννης, gen. sing. . . . . . id.
Γεθσημανῆ, *Gethsemane*, pr. name, indecl. (Mat. 26. 36).—Rec. Gr.
Γεθσημανεί, Sch.
Γεθσημανεῖ, Al. Ln. Tdf.
γείτονας, acc. pl. masc. and fem. . . γείτων
γείτονες, nom. pl. masc. . . . . id.

γείτων], ονος, ὁ, ἡ, (§ 4. rem. 2. e) *a neighbour*, Lu. 14. 12; 15. 6, 9; Jno. 9. 8.

γελάσετε, 2 pers. pl. fut. ind. . . . γελάω

γελάω, ῶ], fut. άσομαι, and, later, άσω, (§ 22. rem. 2. c) aor. 1, ἐγέλασα, *to laugh, smile*; by impl. *to be merry, happy, to rejoice*, Lu. 6. 21, 25. (ᾰ).

γέλως, ωτος, ὁ, (§ 4. rem. 2. c) *laughter*; by impl. *mirth, joy, rejoicing*.

γελῶντες, nom. pl. masc. part. pres. . . γελάω
γέλως,[b] ωτος, ὁ . . . . . id.
γέμει, 3 pers. sing. pres. ind. . . . γέμω
γεμίζεσθαι, pres. infin. pass. . . . γεμίζω
γεμίζω], fut. ίσω, (§ 26. rem. 1) . . γέμω
γεμίσαι, aor. 1, inf. act. . . . γεμίζω
γεμίσας, nom. sing. masc. part. aor. 1, act. . id.
γεμίσατε, 2 pers. pl. aor. 1, imper. act. . id
γεμισθῇ, 3 pers. sing. aor. 1, subj. pass. . id.
γέμον, acc. sing. neut. part. pres. . . γέμω
γέμοντα, nom. pl. neut. part. pres. . . id.
γεμούσας, acc. pl. fem. part. pres. . . id
γέμουσι, 3 pers. pl. pres. ind. . . . id.

γέμω], fut. γεμῶ, (§ 27. rem. 1. a) *to be full*, Mat. 23. 27; Lu. 11. 39, et al.

γεμίζω, fut. ίσω, (§ 26. rem. 1) aor. 1, ἐγέμισα, aor. 1, pass. ἐγεμίσθην, *to fill*, Mat. 4. 37; 15. 36, et al.

γόμος, ου, ὁ, (§ 3. tab. C. a) *the lading* of a ship, Ac. 21. 3; by impl. *merchandise*, Re. 18. 11, 12.

γενεά, ᾶς, ἡ, (§ 2. tab. B. b, and rem. 2) . γίνομαι
γενεά, voc. sing. . . . . . γενεά
γενεᾷ, dat. sing. . . . . . id.

[a] He. 11. 32.
[b] Ja. 4. 9.

γενεαί, nom. pl. . . . . . . γενεά
γενεαῖς, dat. pl. . . . . . id.
γενεαλογέω, ῶ], fut. ήσω, (§ 16. tab. P) (γενεά & λέγω) *to reckon one's descent, derive one's origin*, He. 7. 6.
γενεαλογία], ας, ἡ, (§ 2. tab. B. b, and rem. 2) *genealogy, catalogue of ancestors, history of descent*, 1 Ti. 1. 4; Tit. 3. 9.
γενεαλογίαις, dat. pl. . . . . . γενεαλογία
γενεαλογίας, acc. pl. . . . . . id.
γενεαλογούμενος,[a] nom. sing. m. part. pres. pass. γενεαλογέω
γενεάν, acc. sing. . . . . . γενεά
γενεᾶς, gen. sing. . . . . . . id.
γενεάς, acc. pl. . . . . . . id.
γένει, dat. sing. . . . . . . γένος
γενέσει, dat. sing.—Gr. Sch. Tdf. . . } γένεσις
  γεννήσει, Rec. (Lu. 1. 14) . }
γενέσεως, gen. sing. . . . . . id.
γενέσθαι, aor. 2, infin. . . . . . γίνομαι
γένεσθε, 2 pers. pl. aor. 2, imper. . . id.
γενέσθω, 3 pers. sing. aor. 2, imper. . . id.
γενέσια], ων, τά, (§ 3. tab. C. c) . . id.
γενεσίοις, dat. pl. . . . . . . γενέσια
γένεσις, εως, ἡ, (§ 5. tab. E. c) . . γίνομαι
γενεσίων, gen. pl. . . . . . . γενέσια
γενετή], ῆς, ἡ, (§ 2. tab. B. a) . . γίνομαι
γενετῆς,[b] gen. sing. . . . . . . γενετή
γενεῶν, gen. pl. . . . . . . γενεά
γένη, nom. and acc. pl. . . . . γένος
γενηθέντας, acc. pl. masc. part. aor. 1, pass. γίνομαι
γενηθέντες, nom. pl. masc. part. aor. 1, pass. id.
γενηθέντων, gen. pl. neut. part. aor. 1, pass. id.
γενηθῆναι, aor. 1, infin. pass. . . . . id.
γενήθητε, 2 pers. pl. aor. 1, imper. pass. . id.
γενηθήτω, 3 pers. sing. aor. 1, imper. pass. . id.
γενηθῶμεν, 1 pers. pl. aor. 1, subj. pass.—A. C. Ln. Tdf. . . . } id.
  γενώμεθα, Rec. Gr. Sch. (Tit. 3. 7) . }
γένημα], ατος, τό, v.r. same signif. as γέννημα.
γενήματα, acc. pl.—Gr. Sch. . . } γένημα
  γεννήματα, R. Tdf. (Lu. 12. 18; 2 Co. 9. 10) }
γενήματος, gen. sing.—A. D. Ln. . } id.
  γεννήματος, R. Gr. Sch. Tdf. (Mat. 26. 29) }
γενήσεσθε, 2 pers. pl. fut. ind. . . . γίνομαι
γένησθε, 2 pers. pl. aor. 2, subj. . . . id.
γενησόμενον, acc. sing. neut. part. fut. . id.
γενήσονται, 3 pers. pl. fut. ind.—B. D. . } id.
  γενήσεται, Rec. Gr. Sch. Tdf. (Jno. 10. 16) }

γένηται, 3 pers. sing. aor. 2, subj. . . γίνομαι
γεννᾶται, 3 pers. sing. pres. ind. pass. (§ 19. tab. S) γεννάω
γεννάω, ῶ], fut. ήσω, (§ 18. tab. R) . γίνομαι
γεννηθείς, nom. sing. masc. part. aor. 1, pass. . γεννάω
γεννηθέν, nom. sing. neut. part. aor. 1, pass. id.
γεννηθέντος, gen. sing. masc. part. aor. 1, pass. id.
γεννηθέντων, gen. pl. masc. part. aor. 1, pass. id.
γεννηθῇ, 3 pers. sing. aor. 1, subj. pass. . id.
γεννηθῆναι, aor. 1, infin. pass. . . . id.
γέννημα], ατος, τό, (§ 4. tab. D. c) . . γίνομαι
γεννήματα, nom. acc. and voc. pl. . . γέννημα
γεννήματος, gen. sing. . . . . id.
γεννήσαντα, acc. sing. masc. part. aor. 1, act. . γεννάω
Γεννησαρέτ, ἡ, *Gennesaret*, a lake of Palestine, called also the *Sea of Tiberias*.—R. Gr. Sch. Tdf.
  Γεννησαρέθ, Ln.
  Γεννησάρ, D. (Mat. 14. 34).
γεννήσει, 3 pers. sing. fut. ind. act. . . γεννάω
γεννήσει, dat. sing. . . . . γέννησις
γεννήσῃ, 3 pers. sing. aor. 1, subj. act. . γεννάω
γέννησις, εως, ἡ, (§ 5. tab. E. c) . . γίνομαι
γεννητοῖς, dat. pl. masc. . . . γεννητός
γεννητός], ή, όν, (§ 7. tab. F. a) . . γίνομαι
γεννώμενον, nom. sing. neut. part. pres. pass. γεννάω
γεννῶσα, nom. sing. fem. part. pres. act. . id.
γεννῶσι, 3 pers. pl. pres. ind. act. . . id.
γένοιτο, 3 pers. sing. aor. 2, optat. . . γίνομαι
γενόμενα, acc. pl. neut. part. aor. 2 . . id.
γενόμεναι, nom. pl. fem. part. aor. 2 . id.
γενομένην, acc. sing. fem. part. aor. 2 . id.
γενομένης, gen. sing. fem. part. aor. 2 . id.
γενόμενοι, nom. pl. masc. part. aor. 2 . id.
γενομένοις, dat. pl. neut. part. aor. 2 . id.
γενόμενον, acc. sing. masc. and neut. part. aor. 2 id.
γενόμενος, nom. sing. masc. part. aor. 2 . id.
γενομένου, gen. sing. masc. part. aor. 2 . id.
γενομένων, gen. pl. part. aor. 2 . id.
γένος, εος, ους, τό, (§ 5. tab. E. b) . id.
γένους, gen. sing. . . . . γένος
γένωμαι, 1 pers. sing. aor. 2, subj. . . γίνομαι
γενώμεθα, 1 pers. pl. aor. 2, subj. . . id.
γένωνται, 3 pers. pl. aor. 2, subj. . . id.
Γεργεσηνός], οῦ, ὁ, (§ 3. tab. C. a) *a Gergesene, an inhabitant of Gergasa*, a city in Peræa.
Γεργεσηνῶν, gen. pl.—Rec. Gr. . . } Γεργεσηνός
  Γερασηνῶν, Ln. . . . . }
  Γαδαρηνῶν, B. C. Sch. Tdf. (Mat. 8. 28) . . . . }

[a] He. 7. 6. [b] Jno. 9. 1.

γερουσία], ας, ἡ, (§ 2. tab. B. b, and rem. 2) γέρων
γερουσίαν,[a] acc. sing. . . . . γερουσία

γέρων,[b] οντος, ὁ, (§ 4. rem. 2. d) *an old man.*

γερουσία, ας, ἡ, *a senate, assembly of elders; the elders* of Israel collectively.

γεύομαι], fut. γεύσομαι, aor. 1, ἐγευσάμην, (§ 15. tab. O) (mid. of γεύω, *to cause to taste*) *to taste,* Mat. 27. 34; Jno. 2. 9; absol. *to take food,* Ac. 10. 10, et al.; met. *to have perception of, experience,* He. 6. 4, 5; 1 Pe. 2. 3; θανάτου γεύεσθαι, *to experience death, to die,* Mat. 16. 28, et al.

γευσάμενος, nom. sing. masc. part. aor. 1 . γεύομαι
γευσαμένους, acc. pl. masc. part. aor. 1 . id.
γεύσασθαι, aor. 1, infin. . . . id.
γεύσεται, 3 pers. sing. fut. ind. . . . id.
γεύσῃ, 2 pers. sing. aor. 1, subj. . . id.
γεύσηται, 3 pers. sing. aor. 1, subj. . . id.
γεύσονται, 3 pers. pl. fut. ind. . . id.
γεύσωνται, 3 pers. pl. aor. 1, subj. . . id.
γεωργεῖται,[c] 3 pers. sing. pres. ind. pass. . γεωργέω
γεωργέω, ῶ], fut. ήσω, (§ 16. tab. P) . . γεωργός
γεώργιον,[d] ου, τό, (§ 3. tab. C. c) . . id.
γεωργοί, nom. pl. . . . . . id.
γεωργοῖς, dat. pl. . . . . id.
γεωργόν, acc. sing. . . . . . id.
γεωργός, οῦ, ὁ, (§ 3. tab. C. a) (γῆ & ἔργον) *a husbandman, one who tills the earth,* 2 Ti. 2. 6; Ja. 5. 7; in N.T. spc. *a vine-dresser, keeper of a vineyard,* i.q. ἀμπελουργός, Mat. 21. 33, 34, et al.

γεωργέω, ῶ, fut. ήσω, (§ 16. tab. P) *to cultivate, till the earth,* He. 6. 7.

γεώργιον, ου, τό, (§ 3. tab. C. c) *cultivated field or ground, a farm,* 1 Co. 3. 9.

γεωργούς, acc. pl. . . . . γεωργός
γεωργῶν, gen. pl. . . . . . id.

γῆ, γῆς, ἡ, (§ 2. tab. B. a) (contr. from γέα) *earth, soil,* Mat. 13. 5; Mar. 4. 8, et al.; *the ground, surface of the earth,* Mat. 10. 29; Lu. 6. 49, et al.; *the land,* as opposed to the sea or a lake, Lu. 5. 11; Jno. 21. 8, 9, 11; *the earth, world,* Mat. 5. 18, 35, et al.; by synecd. *the inhabitants of the earth,* Mat. 5. 13; 6. 10; 10. 34; *a land, region, tract, country, territory,* Mat. 2. 20; 14. 34; by way of eminence, *the chosen land,* Mat. 5. 5; 24. 30; 27. 45; Ep 6. 3; *the inhabitants of a region or country,* Mat. 10. 15; 11. 24, et al.

γῇ, dat. sing. . . . . . . γῆ
γήμας, nom. sing. masc. part. aor. 1.—B. Ln. } γαμέω
γαμήσας, Rec. Gr. Sch. Tdf. (Mat. 22. 25) }
γήμῃ, 3 pers. sing. aor. 1, subj. (§ 37. rem. 2) id.
γήμῃς, 2 pers. sing. aor. 1, subj. . . . id.
γῆν, acc. sing. . . . . . . γῆ
γήρᾳ,[e] dat. sing. . . . . . γῆρας
γῆρας], αος, ως, τό, (§ 5. tab. E. j) dat. γήραϊ, γήρᾳ, also γήρει, *old age.*

γηράσκω, or γηράω, ῶ, fut. άσομαι, aor. 1, ἐγήρᾱσα & ἐγήρᾱνα, *to be or become old,* Jno. 21. 18; He. 8. 13.

γήρει, dat. sing.—Gr. Sch. Tdf. . . } γῆρας
γήρᾳ, Rec. (Lu. 1. 36) . . }
γῆς, gen. sing. . . . . . . γῆ
γίνεσθαι, pres. infin. . . . . γίνομαι
γίνεσθε, 2 pers. pl. pres. imper. . . id.
γινέσθω, 3 pers. sing. pres. imper. . . id.
γίνεται, 3 pers. sing. pres. ind. . . id.

γίνομαι], (§ 37. rem. 1) (a later form of γίγνομαι) fut. γενήσομαι, perf. γέγονα and γεγένημαι, aor. 1, ἐγενήθην, aor. 2, ἐγενόμην, *to come into existence; to be created, exist by creation,* Jno. 1. 3, 10; He. 11. 3; Ja. 3. 9; *to be born, produced, grow,* Mat. 21. 19; Jno. 8. 58, et al.; *to arise, come on, occur,* as the phenomena of nature, etc.; Mat. 8. 24, 26; 9. 16, et al.; *to come, approach,* as morning or evening, Mat. 8. 16; 14. 15, 23; *to be appointed, constituted, established,* Mar. 2. 27; Gal. 3. 17 et al.; *to take place, come to pass, happen, occur,* Mat. 1. 22; 24. 6, 20, 21, 34, et al. freq.; *to be done, performed, effected,* Mat. 21. 42, et al.; *to be fulfilled, satisfied,* Mat. 6. 10; 26. 42, et al.; *to come into a particular state or condition; to become, assume the character and appearance* of anything, Mat. 5. 45; 12. 45, et al. *to become or be made* anything, *be changed or converted,* Mat. 4. 3; 21. 42; Mar. 1. 17, et al.; *to be, esse,* Mat. 11. 26; 19. 8; γίνεσθαι ὑπό τινα, *to be subject to,* Gal. 4. 4; γίνεσθαι ἐν ἑαυτῷ, *to come to one's self, to recover*

[a] Ac. 5. 21. [b] Jno. 3. 4. [c] He. 6. 7. [d] 1 Co. 3. 9. [e] Lu. 1. 36.

from a trance or surprise, Ac. 12. 11; μὴ γένοιτο, *let it not be, far be it from, God forbid*, Lu. 20. 16; Ro. 3. 4, 31, et al.; *to be kept, celebrated, solemnised*, as festivals, Mat. 26.2, et al.; *to be finished, completed*, He. 4. 3.

γενεά, ᾶς, ἡ, (§ 2. tab. B. b, and rem. 2) pr. *birth*; hence, *progeny*; *a generation* of mankind, Mat. 11. 16; 23. 36, et al.; *a generation*, a step in a genealogy, Mat. 1. 17; *a generation*, an interval of time, *an age*; in N.T. *course of life*, in respect of its events, interests, or character, Lu. 16. 8; Ac. 13. 36.

γενέσια, ων, τά, pr. *a day observed in memory of the dead*; in N.T. equivalent to γενέθλια, *celebration of one's birthday, birthday-festival*, Mat. 14. 6; Mar. 6. 21.

γένεσις, εως, ἡ, (§ 5. tab. E. c) *birth, nativity*, Mat. 1. 18; Lu. 1. 14; Ja. 1. 23; *successive generation, descent, lineage*, Mat. 1. 1; meton. *life*, Ja. 3. 6.

γενετή, ῆς, ἡ, (§ 2. tab. B. a) *birth*, Jno. 9. 1.

γένημα, ατος, τό, (§ 4. tab. D. c) v.r. Lu. 12. 18; 2 Co. 9. 10, *natural produce, fruit, increase*. N.T.

γεννάω, ῶ, fut. ήσω, (§ 18. tab. R) perf. γεγέννηκα, aor. 1, ἐγέννησα, perf. pass. γεγέννημαι, aor. 1, pass. ἐγεννήθην, used of men, *to beget, generate*, Mat. 1. 2–16, et al.; of women, *to bring forth, bear, give birth to*, Lu. 1. 13, 57, et al.; pass. *to be born, produced*, Mat. 2. 1, 4, et al.; met. *to produce, excite, give occasion to, effect*, 2 Ti. 2. 23; from the Heb. *to constitute as son, to constitute as king, or as the representative or vicegerent of God*, Ac. 13. 33; He. 1. 5; 5. 5; by impl. *to be a parent to* any one; pass. *to be a son or child to* any one, Jno. 1. 13; 1 Co. 4. 15, et al.

γέννημα, ατος, τό, (§ 4. tab. D. c) *what is born or produced, offspring, progeny, brood*, Mat. 3. 7; 12. 34, et al.; *fruit, produce*, Mat. 26. 29; Mar. 14. 25, et al.; *fruit, increase*, Lu. 12. 18; 2 Co. 9. 10.

γέννησις, εως, ἡ, (§ 5. tab. E. c) *birth, nativity*, Mat. 1. 18; Lu. 1. 14.

γεννητός, ή, όν, (§ 7. tab. F. a) *born, or produced of*, Mat. 11. 11; Lu. 7. 28.

γένος, εος, τό, (§ 5. tab. E. b) *offspring, progeny*, Ac. 17. 28, 29; *family, kindred, lineage*, Ac. 7. 13, et al.; *race, nation, people*, Mar. 7. 26; Ac. 4. 36, et al.; *kind, sort, species*, Mat. 13. 47, et al.

γνήσιος, ου, ὁ, ἡ, (§ 7. rem. 2) *lawful, legitimate*, as children; *genuine*, in faith, etc.; 1 Ti. 1. 2; Tit. 1. 4; *true, sincere*, 2 Co. 8. 8; Phi. 4. 3.

γνησίως, adv. *genuinely, sincerely*, Phi. 2. 20.

γονεύς, εως, ὁ, (§ 5. tab. E. d) *a father*; pl. *parents*, Mat. 10. 21; Lu. 2. 27, 41; 2 Co. 12. 14.

γινόμενα, acc. pl. neut. part. pres. . . . γίνομαι
γινομένη, nom. sing. fem. part. pres. . . . id.
γινομένῃ, dat. sing. fem. part. pres. . . . id.
γινομένης, gen. sing. fem. part. pres.—A. C. }
γενομένης, Rec. Gr. Sch. Tdf. (Jno. 21. 4) } id.
γινόμενοι, nom. pl. masc. part. pres. . . . id.
γινόμενον, acc. sing. masc. and nom. and acc. sing. neut. part. pres. . . . id.
γινομένων, gen. pl. part. pres. . . . id.
γίνονται, 3 pers. pl. pres. ind. . . . id.
γίνου, 2 pers. sing. pres. imper. . . . id.
γινώμεθα, 1 pers. pl. pres. subj. . . . id.
γίνωνται, 3 pers. pl. pres. subj. . . . id.
γίνωσκε, 2 pers. sing. pres. imper. act. . . γινώσκω
γινώσκει, 3 pers. sing. pres. ind. act. . . id.
γινώσκειν, pres. infin. act. . . . id.
γινώσκεις, 2 pers. sing. pres. ind. act. . . id.
γινώσκεται, 3 pers. sing. pres. ind. pass. . . id.
γινώσκετε, 2 pers. pl. pres. ind. act. . . id.
γινώσκετε, 2 pers. pl. pres. imper. act. . . id.
γινωσκέτω, 3 pers. sing. pres. imper. act. . . id.
γινώσκῃ, 3 pers. sing. pres. subj. act. . . id.
γινώσκητε, 2 pers. pl. pres. subj. act.—B. Ln. Tdf. }
πιστεύσητε, Rec. Gr. Sch. (Jno. 10. 38) } id.
γινώσκομαι, 1 pers. sing. pres. ind. pass. . . id.
γινώσκομεν, 1 pers. pl. pres. ind. act. . . id.
γινωσκομένη, nom. sing. fem. part. pres. pass. id.
γινώσκοντες, nom. pl. masc. part. pres. act. id.
γινώσκουσι, 3 p. pl. pres. ind. act.—B. D. Ln. Tdf. }
γινώσκομαι, [ὑπὸ τῶν ἐμῶν], Rec. Gr. Sch. (Jno. 10. 14) . . . } id.
γινώσκουσι, dat. pl. masc. part. pres. act. . id.

γῑνώσκω, (§ 36. rem. 3) (a later form of γιγνώσκω) fut. γνώσομαι, perf. ἔγνωκα, aor. 2, ἔγνων, perf. pass. ἔγνωσμαι, aor. 1, pass.

ἐγνώσθην, *to know*, whether the action be inceptive or complete and settled; *to perceive*, Mat. 22. 18; Mar. 5. 29; 8. 17; 12. 12; Lu. 8. 46; *to mark, discern*, Mat. 25. 24; Lu. 19. 44; *to ascertain by examination*, Mar. 6. 38; Jno. 7. 51; Ac. 23. 28; *to understand*, Mar. 4. 13; Lu. 18. 34; Jno. 12. 16; 13. 7; Ac. 8. 30; 1 Co. 14. 7, 9; *to acknowledge*, Mat. 7. 23; 2 Co. 3. 2; *to resolve, conclude*, Lu. 16. 4; Jno. 7. 26; 17. 8; *to be assured*, Lu. 21. 20; Jno. 6. 69; 8. 52; 2 Pe. 1. 20; *to be skilled, to be master of* a thing, Mat. 16. 3; Ac. 21. 37; *to know* carnally, Mat. 1. 25; Lu. 1. 34; from the Heb. *to view with favour*, 1 Co. 8. 3; Gal. 4. 9.

γνώμη, ης, ἡ, (§ 2. tab. B. a) *the mind*, as the means of knowing and judging; *assent*, Phile. 14; *purpose, resolution*, Ac. 20. 3; *opinion, judgment*, 1 Co. 1. 10; 7. 40; *suggestion, suggested advice*, as distinguished from positive injunction, 1 Co. 7. 25; 2 Co. 8. 10.

γνωρίζω, fut. ίσω, (§ 26. rem. 1) Att. ιῶ, (§ 35. rem. 11) aor. 1, ἐγνώρισα, aor. 1, pass. ἐγνωρίσθην, *to make known, reveal, declare*, Jno. 15. 15; 17. 26, et al.; *to know*, Phi. 1. 22.

γνῶσις, εως, ἡ, (§ 5. tab. E. c) *knowledge*, Lu. 1. 77; *knowledge* of an especial kind and relatively high character, Lu. 11. 52; Ro. 2. 20; 1 Ti. 6. 20; more particularly in respect of Christian enlightenment, Ro. 15. 14; 1 Co. 8. 10; 12. 8; 2 Co. 11. 6, et al.

γνώστης, ου, ὁ, (§ 2. tab. B. c) *one acquainted with* a thing, *knowing, skilful*, Ac. 26. 3. L.G.

γνωστός, ή, όν, (§ 7. tab. F. a) *known*, Jno. 18. 15, 16, et al.; *certain, incontrovertible*, Ac. 4. 16; τὸ γνωστόν, *that which is known or is cognisable, the unquestionable attributes*, Ro. 1. 19; subst. *an acquaintance*, Lu. 2. 44; 23. 49.

γινώσκωμεν, 1 pers. pl. pres. subj. act. . γινώσκω

γινώσκων, nom. sing. masc. part. pres. act. id.

γινώσκωσι, 3 pers. pl. pres. subj. act. . id.

γλεῦκος], εος, τό, (§ 7. tab. E. b) . . γλυκύς

γλεύκους,[a] gen. sing. . . . . γλεῦκος

γλυκύ, nom. and acc. sing. neut. . . . γλυκύς

γλυκύς], εῖα, ύ, (§ 7. tab. H. g) *sweet*, Ja. 3. 11, 12; Re. 10. 9, 10.

γλεῦκος, εος, ους, τό, (§ 5. tab. E. b) pr. *the unfermented juice of grapes, must*; hence, *sweet new wine*, Ac. 2. 13.

γλῶσσα, ης, ἡ, (§ 2. rem. 3) *the tongue*, Mar. 7. 33, 35, et al.; meton. *speech, talk*, 1 Jno. 3. 18; *a tongue, language*, Ac. 2. 11; 1 Co. 13. 1, et al.; meton. *a language not proper to a speaker, a gift or faculty of such language*, Mar. 16. 17; 1 Co. 14. 13, 14, 26, et al.; from Heb. *a nation*, as defined by its language, Re. 5. 9, et al.; met. *a tongue-shaped flame*, Ac. 2. 3.

γλῶσσαι, nom. pl. . . . . γλῶσσα

γλώσσαις, dat. pl. . . . . id.

γλῶσσαν, acc. sing. . . . . id.

γλώσσας, acc. pl. . . . . id.

γλώσσῃ, dat. sing. . . . . id.

γλώσσης, gen. sing. . . . . id.

γλωσσῶν, gen. pl. . . . . id.

γλωσσόκομον, ου, τό, (§ 3. tab. C. c) (γλῶσσα & κομέω, *to keep, preserve*) pr. *a box for keeping the tongues, mouth-pieces, or reeds, of musical instruments*; hence, genr. *any box or receptacle*; in N.T. *a purse, money-bag*, Jno. 12. 6; 13. 29. L.G.

γναφεύς,[b] έως, ὁ, (§ 5. tab. E. d) (γνάφος, *a teasel, or thistle*) *a fuller*, part of whose business it was to raise a nap by means of teasels, etc.

γνήσιε, voc. sing. masc. . . . . γνήσιος

γνήσιον, acc. sing. neut. . . . id.

γνήσιος], ου, ὁ, ἡ, (§ 7. rem. 2) . . γίνομαι

γνησίῳ, dat. sing. neut. . . . γνήσιος

γνησίως,[c] adv. . . . . . γίνομαι

γνοῖ, 3 pers. sing. aor. 2, subj. act. (§ 30. rem. 5) —Al. Ln. Tdf. . . . } γινώσκω
γνῷ, Rec. Gr. Sch. (Mar. 5. 43) . }

γνόντα, acc. sing. masc. part. aor. 2, act. . id.

γνόντες, nom. pl. masc. part. aor. 2, act. . id.

γνούς, nom. sing. masc. pt. aor. 2, (§ 36. rem. 3) id

γνόφος], ου, ὁ, (§ 3. tab. C. a) *a thick cloud, darkness*.

[a] Ac. 2. 13. [b] Mar. 9. 3. [c] Phi. 2. 20.

γνόφῳ,[a] dat. sing. . . . . . γνόφος
γνῶ, 1 pers. sing. aor. 2, subj. act. . . γινώσκω
γνῷ, 3 pers. sing. aor. 2, subj. act. . . id.
γνῶθι, 2 pers. sing. aor. 2, imper. act. . . id.
γνώμη, ης, ἡ, (§ 2. tab. B. a) . . id.
γνώμῃ, dat. sing. . . . . . γνώμη
γνώμην, acc. sing. . . . . id.
γνώμης, gen. sing. . . . . . id.
γνῶναι, aor. 2, infin. act. . . . γινώσκω
γνωριζέσθω, 3 pers. sing. pres. imper. pass. . γνωρίζω
γνωρίζομεν, 1 pers. pl. pres. ind. act. . id.
γνωρίζω, fut. ίσω, (§ 26. rem. 1) . . γινώσκω
γνωριοῦσι, 3 pers. pl. fut. Att. (§ 35. rem. 11) γνωρίζω
γνωρίσαι, aor. 1, infin. act. . . id.
γνωρίσας, nom. sing. masc. part. aor. 1, act. . id.
γνωρίσει, 3 pers. sing. fut. ind. act. . . id.
γνωρίσῃ, 3 pers. sing. aor. 1, subj. act. . . id.
γνωρισθέντος, gen. sing. neut. pt. aor. 1, pass. id.
γνωρισθῇ, 3 pers. sing. aor. 1, subj. pass. . id.
γνωρίσουσι, 3 pers. pl. fut. ind. act.—B. D. Ln.
γνωριοῦσι, Rec. Gr. Sch. Tdf. (Col. 4. 9) } id.
γνωρίσω, 1 pers. sing. fut. ind. act. . . id.
γνῷς, 2 pers. sing. aor. 2, subj. act. . . γινώσκω
γνώσει, dat. sing. . . . . . γνῶσις
γνώσεσθε, 2 pers. pl. fut. ind. mid. . γινώσκω
γνώσεται, 3 pers. sing. fut. ind. mid. . . id.
γνώσεως, gen. sing. . . . . γνῶσις
γνώσῃ, 2 pers. sing. fut. ind. mid. . . γινώσκω
γνωσθέντες, nom. pl. masc. pt. aor. 1, pass. id.
γνώσθῃ, 3 pers. s. aor. 1, subj. pass.—B. Ln. Tdf.
γνωσθήσεται, Rec. Gr. Sch. (Lu. 8. 17.) } id.
γνωσθήσεται, 3 pers. sing. fut. 1, ind. pass. id.
γνωσθήτω, 3 pers. sing. aor. 1, imper. pass. . id.
γνῶσι, 3 pers. pl. aor. 2, subj. act. . . id.
γνῶσιν, acc. sing. . . . . . γνῶσις
γνῶσις, εως, ἡ, (§ 5. tab. E. c) . . γινώσκω
γνώσομαι, 1 pers. sing. fut. ind. mid. . . id.
γνώσονται, 3 pers. pl. fut. ind. mid. . id.
γνωστά, nom. pl. neut. . . . . γνωστός
γνώστην,[b] acc. sing. . . . . γνώστης
γνώστης], ου, ὁ, (§ 2. tab. B. c) . . . γινώσκω
γνωστοί, nom. pl. masc. . . . γνωστός
γνωστοῖς, dat. pl. masc. . . . . id.
γνωστόν, nom. sing. neut. . . . id.
γνωστός, ή, όν, (§ 7. tab. F. a) . . . γινώσκω
γνῶτε, 2 pers. pl. aor. 2, imper. act. . . id.
γνῶτε, 2 pers. pl. aor. 2, subj. act. . . id.
γνώτω, 3 pers. sing. aor. 2. imper. act. . id.

γογγύζετε, 2 pers. pl. pres. imper. . . γογγύζω
γογγύζοντος, gen. sing. masc. part. pres. . id.
γογγύζουσι, 3 pers. pl. pres. ind. . . id.

γογγύζω], fut. ύσω, aor. 1, ἐγόγγυσα, (§ 26. rem. 1) *to speak privately and in a low voice, mutter*, Jno. 7. 32; *to utter secret and sullen discontent, express indignant complaint, murmur, grumble*, Mat. 20. 11; Lu. 5. 30; Jno. 6. 41, 43, 61. L.G.

γογγυσμός, οῦ, ὁ, (§ 3. tab. C. a) *a muttering, murmuring, low and suppressed discourse*, Jno. 7. 12; *the expression of secret and sullen discontent, murmuring, complaint*, Ac. 6. 1; Phi. 2. 14, 1 Pe. 4. 9. L.G.

γογγυστής, οῦ, ὁ, (§ 2. tab. B. c) *a murmurer*, Jude 16. L.G.

γογγυσμός, οῦ, ὁ . . . . . γογγύζω
γογγυσμοῦ, gen. sing.—A. B. Ln. Tdf. .
γογγυσμῶν, Rec. Gr. Sch. (1 Pe. 4. 9) } γογγυσμός
γογγυσμῶν, gen. pl. . . . . . id.
γογγυσταί,[c] nom. pl. . . . . γογγυστής
γογγυστής], οῦ, ὁ . . . . . γογγύζω

γόης], ητος, ὁ, (§ 4. rem. 2. c) *a juggler, diviner*; hence, by impl. *an impostor, cheat*.

γόητες,[d] nom. pl. . . . . γόης
Γολγοθᾶ, *Golgotha*, pr. name, indecl.
γόμον, acc. sing. . . . . γόμος
Γόμοῤῥα, ας, ἡ, and Γόμοῤῥα, ων, τά, *Gomorrha*, pr. name.
Γομόῤῥας, gen. sing. . . . . Γόμοῤῥα
Γομόῤῥοις, dat. pl. . . . . . id.
Γομόῤῥων, gen. pl. . . . . . . id.
γόμος], ου, ὁ, (§ 3. tab. C. a) . . γέμω
γόνασι, dat. pl. . . . . . γόνυ
γόνατα, acc. pl. . . . . . . id.
γονεῖς, nom. and acc. pl. . . . . γονεύς
γονεύς], εως, ὁ, (§ 5. tab. E. d) . . γίνομαι
γονεῦσι, dat. pl. . . . . . γονεύς

γόνυ, ἄτος, τό, *the knee*, Lu. 22. 41; He. 12. 12, et al.

γονυπετέω, ῶ], fut. ήσω, aor. 1, ἐγονυπέτησα, (§ 16. tab. P) (γόνυ & πίπτω) *to fall upon one's knees, to kneel before*, Mat. 17. 14; 27. 29; Mar. 1. 40; 10. 17.

γονυπετήσαντες, nom. pl. masc. part. aor. 1 γονυπετέω

[a] He. 12. 18. [b] Ac. 26. 3. [c] Jude 16. [d] 2 Ti. 3. 13.

γονυπετήσας, nom. sing. masc. part. aor. 1 — γονυπετέω
γονυπετῶν, nom. sing. masc. part. pres. — id.
γράμμα, ατος, τό, (§ 4. tab. D. c) — γράφω
γράμμασι, dat. pl. — γράμμα
γράμματα, nom. and acc. pl. — id.
γραμματεῖς, nom. acc. and voc. pl. — γραμματεύς
γραμμᾰτεύς, εως, ὁ, (§ 5. tab. E. d) — γράφω
γραμματεῦσι, dat. pl. — γραμματεύς
γραμματέων, gen. pl. — id.
γράμματι, dat. sing. — γράμμα
γράμματος, gen. sing. — id.
γραπτόν,[a] acc. sing. neut. — γραπτός
γραπτός], ή, όν, (§ 7. tab. F. a — γράφω
γραφαί, nom. pl. — γραφή
γραφαῖς, dat. pl. — id.
γραφάς, acc. pl. — id.
γράφε, 2 pers. sing. pres. imper. act. — γράφω
γράφει, 3 pers. sing. pres. ind. act. — id.
γράφειν, pres. infin. act. — id.
γράφεσθαι, pres. infin. pass. — id.
γραφή, ῆς, ή, (§ 2. tab. B. a) — id.
γραφῇ, dat. sing. — γραφή
γραφήν, acc. sing. — id.
γραφῆς, gen. sing. — id.
γράφηται, 3 pers. sing. pres. subj. pass. — γράφω
γράφομεν, 1 pers. pl. pres. ind. act. — id.
γραφόμενα, acc. pl. neut. part. pres. pass. — id.

γράφω, fut. ψω, aor. 1, ἔγραψα, (§ 23. rem. 1. a, and rem. 2) perf. γέγραφα, (§ 23. rem. 6) *to engrave, write*, according to the ancient method of writing on plates of metal, waxed tables, etc., Jno. 8. 6, 8; *to write* on parchment, paper, etc., generally, Mat. 27. 37, et al.; *to write* letters to another, Ac. 23. 25; 2 Co. 2. 9; 13. 10, et al.; *to describe in writing*, Jno. 1. 46; Ro. 10. 5; *to inscribe* in a catalogue, etc., Lu. 10. 20; Re. 13. 8; 17. 8, et al.; *to write* a law, *command or enact in writing*, Mar. 10. 5; 12. 19; Lu. 2. 23, et al.

γράμμα, ατος, τό, (§ 4. tab. D. c) pr. *that which is written or drawn; a letter, character of the alphabet*, Lu. 23. 38; *a writing, book*, Jno. 5. 47; *an acknowledgment of debt, an account, a bill, note*, Lu. 16. 6, 7; *an epistle, letter*, Ac. 28. 21; Gal. 6. 11; ἱερὰ γράμματα, *Holy writ, the sacred books of the Old Testament, the Jewish Scriptures*, 2 Ti. 3. 15; spc. *the letter* of the law of Moses, *the bare literal sense*, Ro. 2. 27, 29; 2 Co. 3. 6, 7; pl. *letters, learning*, Jno. 7. 15; Ac. 26. 24.

γραμμᾰτεύς, εως, ὁ, (§ 5. tab. E. d) *a scribe; a clerk, town-clerk, registrar, recorder*, Ac. 19. 35; *one skilled in the Jewish law, a teacher or interpreter of the law*, Mat. 2. 4; 5. 20, et al. freq.; genr. *a religious teacher*, Mat. 13. 52; by synecd. *any one distinguished for learning or wisdom*, 1 Co. 1. 20.

γραπτός, ή, όν, (§ 7. tab. F. a) *written*, Ro. 2. 15.

γραφή, ῆς, ή, (§ 2. tab. B. a) *a writing*; in N.T. *the Holy Scriptures, the Jewish Scriptures, or Books of the Old Testament*, Mat. 21. 42; Jno. 5. 39, et al.; by synecd. *doctrines, declarations, oracles, or promises* contained in the sacred books, Mat. 22. 29; Mar. 12. 24, et al.; spc. *a prophecy*, Mat. 26. 54; Mar. 14. 49; Lu. 4. 21; 24. 27, 32; with the addition of προφητική, Ro. 16. 26; of τῶν προφητῶν, Mat. 26. 56.

γράφων, nom. sing. masc. part. pres. act. — γράφω
γραφῶν, gen. pl. — γραφή
γράψαι, aor. 1, infin. act. — γράφω
γράψαντες, nom. pl. masc. pt. aor. 1, act. — id.
γράψας, nom. sing. masc. part. aor. 1, act. — id.
γράψῃς, 2 pers. sing. aor. 1, subj. act. — id.
γράψον, 2 pers. sing. aor. 1, imper. act. — id.
γραώδεις,[b] acc. pl. masc. — γραώδης
γραώδης], εος, ὁ, ή, τό, -ες, (§ 7. tab. G. b) (γραῦς, *an old woman*) *old-womanish*; by impl. *silly, absurd*. L.G.
γρηγορεῖτε, 2 pers. pl. pres. imper. — γρηγορέω
γρηγορέω, ῶ], fut. ήσω, (§ 16. tab. P) aor. 1, ἐγρηγόρησα, (a later form from the pref. ἐγρήγορα) *to be awake, to watch*, Mat. 26. 38, 40, 41; Mar. 14. 34, 37, 38; *to be alive*, 1 Thes. 5. 10; met. *to be watchful, attentive, vigilant, circumspect*, Mat. 25. 13; Mar. 13. 35, et al.
γρηγορῇ, 3 pers. sing. pres. subj. — γρηγορέω
γρηγορῆσαι, aor. 1, infin. — id.
γρηγορήσατε, 2 pers. pl. aor. 1, imper. — id.

[a] Ro. 2. 15.
[b] 1 Ti. 4. 7.

γρηγορήσῃς, 2 pers. sing. aor. 1, subj. . . γρηγορέω
γρηγοροῦντας, acc. pl. masc. part. pres. . id.
γρηγοροῦντες, nom. pl. masc. part. pres. . id.
γρηγορῶμεν, 1 pers. pl. pres. subj. . . id.
γρηγορῶν, nom. sing. masc. part. pres. . id.
γύμναζε, 2 pers. sing. pres. imper. act. . γυμνάζω
γυμνάζω], fut. άσω, (§ 26. rem. 1) . . γυμνός
γυμνασία,[a] ας, ἡ, (§ 2. tab. B. b, and rem. 2) id.
γυμνητεύομεν,[b] 1 pers. pl. pres. ind. . . γυμνητεύω
γυμνητεύω], fut. εύσω, (§ 13. tab. M) . γυμνός
γυμνά, nom. pl. neut. . . . id.
γυμνήν, acc. sing. fem. . . . id.
γυμνοί, nom. pl. masc. . . . id.
γυμνόν, acc. sing. masc. . . . id.

γυμνός, ή, όν, (§ 7. tab. F. a) *naked, without clothing*, Mar. 14. 51, 52; *without the upper garment, and clad only with an inner garment or tunic*, Jno. 21. 7; *poorly or meanly clad, destitute of proper and sufficient clothing*, Mat. 25. 36, 38, 43, 44; Ac. 19. 16; Ja. 2. 15; met. *unclothed* with a body, 2 Co. 5. 3; *not covered, uncovered, open, manifest*, He. 4. 13; *bare, mere*, 1 Co. 15. 37; *naked of* spiritual *clothing*, Re. 3. 17; 16. 15; 17. 16.

γυμνάζω, fut. άσω, (§ 26. rem. 1) perf. pass. γεγύμνασμαι, pr. *to train in gymnastic discipline*: hence, *to exercise* in anything, *train to use, discipline*, 1 Ti. 4. 7; He. 5. 14; 12. 11; 2 Pe. 2. 14.

γυμνασία, ας, ἡ, (§ 2. tab. B. b, and rem. 2) pr. *gymnastic exercise*; hence, *bodily discipline* of any kind, 1 Ti. 4. 8.

γυμνητεύω, fut. εύσω, (§ 13. tab. M) *to be naked*; by synecd. *to be poorly clad, or destitute of proper and sufficient clothing*, 1 Co. 4. 11. L.G.

γυμνότης, τητος, ἡ, (§ 4. rem. 2. c) *nakedness*; *want of proper and sufficient clothing*, Ro. 8. 35; 2 Co. 11. 27; spiritual *nakedness, being destitute of* spiritual *clothing*, Re. 3. 18. LXX.

γυμνοῦ, gen. sing. neut. . . . γυμνός
γυμνούς, acc. pl. masc. . . . id.
γυμνότης, τητος, ἡ, (§ 4. rem. 2. c) . . id.
γυμνότητι, dat. sing. . . . γυμνότης
γυμνότητος, gen. sing. . . . id.

γύναι, voc. sing. (§ 6. rem. 4. b) . . γυνή
γυναῖκα, acc. sing. . . . . . id.
γυναικάρια,[c] acc. pl. . . . . γυναικάριον
γυναικάριον], ου, τό, (§ 3. tab. C. c) . . γυνή
γυναῖκας, acc. pl. . . . . id.
γυναικεῖος], εία, εῖον, (§ 7. rem. 1) . . id.
γυναικείῳ,[d] dat. sing. neut. . . γυναικεῖος
γυναῖκες, nom. pl. . . . . γυνή
γυναικί, dat. sing. . . . . id.
γυναικός, gen. sing. . . . . id.
γυναικῶν, gen. pl. . . . . id.
γυναιξί, dat. pl. . . . . id.

γυνή, γυναικός, ἡ, (§ 6. rem. 4. b) *a woman*, Mat. 5. 28, et al.; *a* married *woman, wife*, Mat. 5. 31, 32; 14. 3, et al.; in the voc. ὦ γύναι, *O woman!* an ordinary mode of addressing females under every circumstance; met. used of the Church, as united to Christ, Re. 19. 7; 21. 9.

γυναικάριον, ου, τό, (§ 3. tab. C. c) (dimin. of γυνή) *a little woman, muliercula, a trifling, weak, silly woman*, 2 Ti. 3. 6. L.G.

γυναικεῖος, εία, εῖον, (§ 7. rem. 1) *pertaining to women, female*, 1 Pe. 3. 7.

Γώγ,[e] ὁ, *Gog*, pr. name of a nation, indecl.

γωνία], ας, ἡ, (§ 2. tab. B. b, and rem. 2) *an* exterior *angle, projecting corner*, Mat. 6. 5; 21. 42, et al.; *an* interior *angle*; by impl. *a* dark *corner, obscure place*, Ac. 26. 26; *corner, extremity, or quarter* of the earth, Re. 7. 1; 20. 8.

γωνίᾳ, dat. sing. . . . . γωνία
γωνίαις, dat. pl. . . . . . id.
γωνίας, gen. sing. . . . . id.
γωνίας, acc. pl. . . . . . id.

Δ.

Δαβίδ, ὁ, *David*, pr. name, indecl.—Rec.
Δαυΐδ, Gr. Sch. Tdf. passim.

δαίμονες, nom. pl. . . . . δαίμων
δαιμόνια, nom. and acc. pl. . . . δαιμόνιον
δαιμονίζεται, 3 pers. sing. pres. ind. . δαιμονίζομαι
δαιμονίζομαι], fut. ίσομαι, (§ 26. rem. 1) δαίμων
δαιμονιζόμενοι, nom. pl. masc. part. pres. . δαιμονίζομαι
δαιμονιζόμενον, acc. sing. masc. part. pres. . id.

a 1 Ti. 4. 8. b 1 Co. 4. 11. c 2 Ti. 3. 6. d 1 Pe. 3. 7. e Re. 20. 8.

δαιμονιζόμενος, nom. sing. masc. part. pres. δαιμονίζομαι
δαιμονιζομένου, gen. sing. masc. part. pres. id.
δαιμονιζομένους, acc. pl. masc. part. pres. . id.
δαιμονιζομένῳ, dat. sing. masc. part. pres. . id.
δαιμονιζομένων, gen. pl. part. pres. . . id.
δαιμονίοις, dat. pl. . . . . . δαιμόνιον
δαιμόνιον, ου, τό, (§ 3. tab. C. c) . . δαίμων
δαιμονίου, gen. sing. . . . . δαιμόνιον
δαιμονισθείς, nom. sing. masc. part. aor. 1 δαιμονίζομαι
δαιμονιώδης,[a] εος, ὁ, ἡ, (§ 7. tab. G. b) . δαίμων
δαιμονίων, gen. pl. . . . . . δαιμόνιον
δαίμονος, gen. sing. . . . . δαίμων
δαιμόνων, gen. pl. . . . . . id.

δαίμων], ονος, ὁ, ἡ, (§ 4. rem. 2. e) *a god, a superior power*; in N.T. *a malignant demon, evil angel*, Mat. 8. 31; Mar. 5. 12; Lu. 8. 29; Re. 16. 14; 18. 2.

δαιμονίζομαι, fut. ίσομαι, aor. 1, pass. ἐδαιμονίσθην, (§ 26. rem. 1) in N.T. *to be possessed, afflicted, vexed, by a demon, or evil spirit*, i.q. δαιμόνιον ἔχειν, Mat. 4. 24; 8. 16, 28, 33, et al.

δαιμόνιον, ου, τό, (§ 3. tab. C. c) *a heathen god, deity*, Ac. 17. 18; 1 Co. 10. 20, 21; Re. 9. 20; in N.T., *a demon, evil spirit*, Mat. 7. 22; 9. 33, 34; 10. 8; 12, 24, et al.

δαιμονιώδης, εος, ὁ, ἡ, (§ 7. tab. G. b) *pertaining to or proceeding from demons; demoniacal, devilish*, Ja. 3. 15. L.G.

δάκνετε,[b] 2 pers. pl. pres. ind. act. . . δάκνω
δάκνω], fut. δήξομαι, aor. 2, ἔδακον, perf. δέδηχα, (§ 36. rem. 2) *to bite, sting*; met. *to molest, vex, injure*.

δάκρυ], υος, τό, (§ 4. rem. 1) *a tear*.
δάκρυον, ου, τό, (§ 3. tab. C. c) *a tear*.

δακρύω, fut. ύσω, aor. 1, ἐδάκρυσα, (§ 13. tab. M) *to shed tears, weep*, Jno. 11. 35. (ῡ).

δάκρυσι, dat. pl. . . . . . δάκρυ
δακρύω], fut. ύσω, (§ 13. tab. M) . . id.
δακρύων, gen. pl. . . . . . δάκρυον
δακτύλιον,[c] acc. sing. . . . . δακτύλιος
δακτύλιος], ου, ὁ, (§ 3. tab. C. a) . . δάκτυλος
δάκτυλον, acc. sing. . . . . id.

δάκτῠλος], ου, ὁ, (§ 3. tab. C. a) *a finger*, Mat. 23. 4; Mar. 7. 33, et al.; from Heb. *power*, Lu. 11. 20.

δακτύλιος, ου, ὁ, *a ring for the finger*, Lu. 15. 22.

δακτύλου, gen. sing. . . . . δάκτυλος
δακτύλους, acc. pl. . . . . . id.
δακτύλῳ, dat. sing. . . . . . id.
δακτύλων, gen. pl. . . . . id.
Δαλμανουθά,[d] ἡ, *Dalmanutha*, indecl., a small town on the shore of the Sea of Tiberias.
Δαλματία], ας, ἡ, (§ 2. tab. B. b, and rem. 2) *Dalmatia*.
Δαλματίαν,[e] acc. sing. . . . . Δαλματία
δαμάζεται, 3 pers. sing. pres. ind. pass. . δαμάζω
δαμάζω], fut. άσω, (§ 26. rem. 1) aor. 1, ἐδάμασα, perf. pass. δεδάμασμαι, (δαμάω, the same) *to subdue, tame*, Mar. 5. 4; Ja. 3. 7; met. *to restrain within proper limits*, Ja. 3. 8. (μᾰ).
δαμάλεως,[f] gen. sing. . . . . δάμαλις

δάμᾰλις], εως, ἡ, (§ 5. tab. E. c) *a heifer*.

Δάμαρις,[g] ιδος, ἡ, (§ 4. rem. 2. c) *Damaris*, pr. name.
δαμάσαι, aor. 1, infin. act. . . . δαμάζω
Δαμασκηνός], οῦ, ὁ, (§ 3. tab. C. a) *a Damascene, a native of Damascus*.
Δαμασκηνῶν,[h] gen. pl. . . . Δαμασκηνός
Δαμασκόν, acc. sing. . . . . Δαμασκός
Δαμασκός], οῦ, ἡ, (§ 3. tab. C. b) *Damascus*, the capital city of Syria.
Δαμασκῷ, dat. sing. . . . . Δαμασκός
δανείζετε, 2 pers. pl. pres. imper. . . δανείζω
δανείζητε, 2 pers. pl. pres. subj. . . id.
δανείζουσι, 3 pers. pl. pres. ind. . . id.
δανείζω], fut. είσω, (§ 26. rem. 1) . . δάνειον
δανείσασθαι, aor. 1, infin. mid. . . δανείζω
δάνειον,[i] ου, τό, (§ 3. tab. C. c) (δάνος, *a gift, loan*) *a loan, debt*.

δανείζω, fut. είσω, aor. 1, ἐδάνεισα, (§ 26. rem. 1) *to lend money*, Lu. 6. 34, 35; mid. *to borrow money*, Mat. 5. 42.

δανειστής, οῦ, ὁ, (§ 2. tab. B. c) *a lender, creditor*. L.G.

δανειστῇ,[k] dat. sing. . . . . δανειστής
δανειστής], οῦ, ὁ, (§ 2. tab. B. c) . . δάνειον
Δανιήλ, ὁ, *Daniel*, pr. name, indecl.
δαπανάω, ῶ], fut. ήσω, (§ 18. tab. R) . . δαπάνη

δαπάνη], ης, ἡ, (§ 2. tab. B. a) *expense, cost*. (πᾰ).

[a] Ja. 3. 15. [b] Gal. 5. 15. [c] Lu. 15. 22. [d] Mar. 8. 10. [e] 2 Ti. 4. 10. [f] He. 9. 13. [g] Ac. 17. 34. [h] 2 Co. 11. 32. [i] Mat. 18. 27. [k] Lu. 7. 41.

δαπανάω, ῶ, fut. ήσω, aor. 1, ἐδαπάνησα, (§ 18. tab. R) *to expend, be at expense,* Mar. 5. 26; Ac. 21. 24; 2 Co. 12. 15; *to spend, waste, consume by extravagance,* Lu. 15. 14; Ja. 4. 3.

δαπάνην,[a] acc. sing. . . . . . δαπάνη
δαπανήσαντος, gen. sing. masc. part. aor. 1 . δαπανάω
δαπανήσασα, nom. sing. fem. part. aor. 1 . id.
δαπανήσητε, 2 pers. pl. aor. 1, subj. . . id.
δαπάνησον, 2 pers. sing. aor. 1, imper. . id.
δαπανήσω, 1 pers. sing. fut. ind. . . id.
δαρήσεσθε, 2 pers. pl. fut. 2, pass. . . δέρω
δαρήσεται, 3 pers. sing. fut. 2, pass. (§ 24. rem. 3) id.
Δαυίδ, ὁ, *David,* Gr. Sch. Tdf. passim, for Δαβίδ.
δέ, a conjunctive particle, marking the superaddition of a clause, whether in opposition or in continuation, to what has preceded, and it may be variously rendered *but, on the other hand, and, also, now,* etc.; καὶ δέ, when there is a special superaddition in continuation, *too, yea,* etc. It sometimes is found at the commencement of the apodosis of a sentence, Ac. 11. 17. It serves also to mark the resumption of an interrupted discourse, 2 Co. 2. 10; Gal. 2. 6.
δεδάμασται, 3 pers. sing. perf. ind. pass. δαμάζω
δεδεκάτωκε, 3 pers. sing. perf. ind. act. . δεκατόω
δεδεκάτωται, 3 pers. sing. perf. ind. pass. id.
δέδεκται, 3 pers. sing. perf. ind. (§ 23. rem. 7) δέχομαι
δεδεκώς, nom. sing. masc. pt. perf. act. (§ 37. rem. 1) δέω
δέδεμαι, 1 pers. sing. perf. ind. pass. . id.
δεδεμένα, nom. pl. neut. part. perf. pass. . id.
δεδεμένην, acc. sing. fem. pt. perf. pass. . id.
δεδεμένον, nom. neut. and acc. s. masc. pt. p. pass. id.
δεδεμένος, nom. sing. masc. part. perf. pass. . id.
δεδεμένους, acc. pl. masc. part. perf. pass. . id.
δέδεσαι, 2 pers. sing. perf. ind. pass. . . id.
δεδέσθαι, perf. infin. pass. . . id.
δέδεται, 3 pers. sing. perf. ind. pass. . . id.
δεδικαίωμαι, 1 pers. s. perf. pass. (§ 21. tab. U) δικαιόω
δεδικαιωμένος, nom. sing. masc. pt. perf. pass. id.
δεδικαίωται, 3 pers. sing. perf. ind. pass. . id.
δεδιωγμένοι, nom. pl. masc. part. perf. pass. . διώκω
δεδοκιμάσμεθα, 1 pers. pl. perf. ind. pass. . δοκιμάζω
δεδομένην, acc. s. f. part. perf. pass. (§ 30. rem. 4) δίδωμι
δεδομένον, nom. sing. neut. part. perf. pass. id.
δεδόξασμαι, 1 pers. sing. perf. ind. pass. . δοξάζω
δεδοξασμένῃ, dat. sing. fem. pt. perf. pass. . id.
δεδοξασμένον, nom. sing. neut. pt. perf. pass. δοξάζω
δεδόξασται, 3 pers. sing. perf. ind. pass. . id.
δέδοται, 3 pers. sing. perf. ind. pass. (§ 30. rem. 4) δίδωμι
δεδουλεύκαμεν, 1 pers. pl. perf. ind. act. . δουλεύω
δεδουλωμένας, acc. pl. fem. pt. perf. pass. . δουλόω
δεδουλωμένοι, nom. pl. masc. pt. perf. pass. . id.
δεδούλωται, 3 pers. sing. perf. ind. pass. . id.
δέδωκα, 1 pers. sing. perf. ind. act. (§ 30. tab. Z) δίδωμι
δέδωκας, 2 pers. sing. perf. ind. act. . . id.
δέδωκε, 3 pers. sing. perf. ind. act. . . id.
δεδώκει, Att. for ἐδεδώκει, 3 pers. s. pluperf. act. id.
δεδώκεισαν, Att. for ἐδεδώκεισαν, 3 pers. pl. pluperf. ind. . . . . id.
δεδωκώς, nom. sing. masc. part. perf. act.—D. (ὁ δεδωκώς) . . . . } id.
ὃς δέδωκε, Rec. Gr. Sch. Tdf. (Jno. 10. 29)
δεδωρημένης, gen. sing. fem. part. perf. pass. . δωρέομαι
δεδώρηται, 3 pers. sing. perf. ind. pass. . id.
δέῃ, subj. of δεῖ . . . . . . δέω
δεηθέντων, gen. pl. masc. pt. aor. 1, pass. . δέω, δέομαι
δεήθητε, 2 pers. pl. aor. 1, imper. pass. . id.
δεήθητι, 2 pers. sing. aor. 1, imper. pass. . id.
δεήσει, dat. sing. . . . . δέησις
δεήσεις, acc. pl. . . . . id.
δεήσεσι, dat. pl. . . . . id.
δεήσεως, gen. sing. . . . . id.
δέησιν, acc. sing. . . . . id.
δέησις, εως, ἡ, (§ 5. tab. E. c) δέω, δέομαι
δεθῆναι, aor. 1, infin. pass. . . δέω
δεῖ, 3 pers. sing. pres. impers. . . id.
δεῖγμα,[b] ατος, τό, (§ 4. tab. D. c) . . δείκνυμι
δειγματίζω], fut. ίσω, (§ 26. rem. 1) . id.
δειγματίσαι, aor. 1, infin. act.—B. Ln. Tdf. } δειγματίζω
παραδειγματίσαι, R. Gr. Sch. (Mat. 1. 19)
δεικνύειν, pres. infin. act. . . . . δεικνύω
δεικνύεις, 2 pers. sing. pres. ind. act. . id.
δεικνύοντος, gen. sing. masc. part. pres. act. . id.
δείκνυσι, 3 pers. sing. pres. ind. act. . . δείκνυμι

δεικνύω, (ῠ) or δείκνυμι, fut. δείξω, aor. 1, ἔδειξα, aor. 1, pass. ἐδείχθην, (§ 31. tab. BB) *to show, point out, present to the sight,* Mat. 4. 8; 8. 4, et al.; *to exhibit, permit to see, cause to be seen,* Jno. 2. 18; 10. 32; 1 Ti. 6. 15; *to demonstrate, prove,* Ja. 2. 18; 3. 13; met. *to teach, make known, declare, announce,* Mat. 16. 21; Jno. 5. 20; Ac. 10. 28, et al.

[a] Lu. 14. 28.
[b] Jude 7.

δεῖγμα, ατος, τό, (§ 4. tab. D. c) pr. *that which is shown, a specimen, sample*; met. *an example* by way of warning, Jude 7.

δειγματίζω, fut. ίσω, aor. 1, ἐδειγμάτισα, (§ 26. rem. 1) *to make a public show or spectacle of*, Col. 2. 15. N.T.

δειλία], ας, ἡ, (§ 2. tab. B. b, and rem. 2) . δειλός

δειλίας,[a] gen. sing. . . . . δειλία

δειλιάτω,[b] 3 pers. sing. pres. imper. . . δειλιάω

δειλιάω, ῶ], fut. άσω, (§ 22. rem. 2) . δειλός

δειλοί, nom. pl. masc. . . . . id.

δειλοῖς, dat. pl. masc. . . . . id.

δειλός], ή, όν, (§ 7. tab. F. a) *timid, fearful, pusillanimous, cowardly*, Mat. 8. 26; Mar. 4. 40; Re. 21. 8.

δειλία, ας, ἡ, (§ 2. tab. B. b, and rem. 2) *timidity*, 2 Ti. 1. 7.

δειλιάω, ῶ, fut. άσω, (§ 22. rem. 2) *to be timid, be in fear*, Jno. 14. 27. L.G.

δεῖν, infin. of δεῖ . . . . . δέω

δεῖνα,[c] ὁ, ἡ, τό, gen. δεῖνος, acc. δεῖνα, (§ 10. rem. 5) *such a one, a certain one.*

δεινῶς, adv. (δεινός, *terrible, vehement*) *dreadfully, grievously, greatly, vehemently*, Mat. 8. 6; Lu. 11. 53.

δεῖξαι, aor. 1, infin. act. . . . δείκνυμι

δείξατε, 2 pers. pl. aor. 1, imper. act. —Gr. Sch. Tdf. . . . } id.
ἐπιδείξατε, Rec. (Lu. 20. 24) . . }

δειξάτω, 3 pers. sing. aor. 1, imper. act. . id.

δείξει, 3 pers. sing. fut. ind. act. . . id.

δεῖξον, 2 pers. sing. aor. 1, imper. act. . . id.

δείξω, 1 pers. sing. fut. ind. act. . . id.

δείξω, 1 pers. sing. aor. 1, subj. act. . . id.

δειπνέω, ῶ], fut. ήσω, (§ 16. tab. P) . δεῖπνον

δειπνῆσαι, aor. 1, infin. . . . . δειπνέω

δειπνήσω, 1 pers. sing. fut. ind. . . id.

δειπνήσω, 1 pers. sing. aor. 1, subj. . . id.

δείπνοις, dat. pl. . . . . δεῖπνον

δεῖπνον, ου, τό, (§ 3. tab. C. c) pr. *a meal; supper, the principal meal taken in the evening*, Lu. 14. 12; Jno. 13. 2, 4, et al.; meton. *food*, 1 Co. 11. 21; *a feast, banquet*, Mat. 23. 6; Mar. 6. 21; 12. 39, et al.

δειπνέω, ῶ, fut. ήσω & ήσομαι, aor. 1, ἐδείπνησα, (§ 16. tab. P) *to sup*, Lu. 17. 8; 22. 20; 1 Co. 11. 25; Re. 3. 20.

δείπνου, gen. sing. . . . . . δεῖπνον

δείπνῳ, dat. sing. . . . . id.

δείραντες, nom. pl. masc. pt. aor. 1, (§ 27. rem. 1. d) δέρω

δεισιδαιμονεστέρους,[d] acc. pl. masc. compar. (§ 8. rem. 1) . . . δεισιδαίμων

δεισιδαιμονία], ας, ἡ, (§ 2. tab. B. b, and rem. 2) id.

δεισιδαιμονίας,[e] gen. sing. . . . δεισιδαιμονία

δεισιδαίμων], ονος, ὁ, ἡ, (§ 7. tab. G. a) (δείδω, *to fear*, and δαίμων) *reverencing the gods and divine things, religious*; in a bad sense, *superstitious*; in N.T. *careful and precise in the discharge of religious services*, Ac. 17. 22.

δεισιδαιμονία, ας, ἡ, (§ 2. tab. B. b, and rem. 2) *fear of the gods*; in a bad sense, *superstition*; *a form of religious belief*, Ac. 25. 19. L.G.

δειχθέντα, acc. sing. masc. part. aor. 1, pass. (§ 31. rem. 1. b) . . . δείκνυμι

δέκα, οἱ, αἱ, τά, indecl. *ten*, Mat. 20. 24; 25. 1, et al.; ἡμερῶν δέκα, *ten days, a few days, a short time*, Re. 2. 10.

δέκατος, η, ον, (§ 7. tab. F. a) *tenth*, Jno. 1. 40; Re. 11. 13; 21. 20; δεκάτη, sc. μερίς, *a tenth part, tithe*, He. 7. 2, 4, 8, 9.

δεκατόω, ῶ, fut. ώσω, perf. δεδεκάτωκα, (§ 20. tab. T) *to cause to pay tithes*; pass. *to be tithed, pay tithes*, He. 7. 6, 9. N.T.

δεκαδύο, οἱ, αἱ, τά, indecl. (δέκα & δύο) i.q. δώδεκα, *twelve*, Ac. 19. 7; 24. 11.

δεκαπέντε, οἱ, αἱ, τά, indecl. (δέκα & πέντε) *fifteen*, Jno. 11. 18; Ac. 27. 28; Gal. 1. 18.

Δεκαπόλει, dat. sing. . . . . Δεκάπολις

Δεκαπόλεως, gen. sing. . . . . id.

Δεκάπολις], εως, ἡ, (§ 5. tab. E. c) *Decapolis*, a district of Palestine beyond Jordan.

δεκάτας, acc. pl. fem. . . . . δέκατος

δεκατέσσαρες, οἱ, αἱ, & τὰ δεκατέσσαρα, (δέκα & τέσσαρες) *fourteen*, Mat. 1. 17; 2 Co. 12. 2; Gal. 2. 1.

δεκατεσσάρων, gen. pl. . . . δεκατέσσαρες

δεκάτη, nom. sing. fem. . . . . δέκατος

δεκάτην, acc. sing. fem. . . . . id.

δέκατον, nom. sing. neut. . . . . id.

δέκατος, η, ον, (§ 7. tab. F. a) . . . δέκα

δεκατόω, ῶ], fut. ώσω, (§ 20. tab. T) . id.

δεκτήν, acc. sing. fem. . . . . δεκτός

δεκτόν, acc. sing. masc. . . . . id.

[a] 2 Ti. 1. 7. [b] Jno. 14. 27. [c] Mat. 26. 18. [d] Ac. 17. 22. [e] Ac. 25. 19.

δεκτός, ή, όν, (§ 7. tab. F. a) . . . δέχομαι

δεκτῷ, dat. sing. masc. . . . . δεκτός

δελεαζόμενος, nom. sing. masc. part. pr. pass. δελεάζω

δελεάζοντες, nom. pl. masc. part. pres. act. . id.

δελεάζουσι, 3 pers. pl. pres. ind. act. . id.

δελεάζω], fut. άσω, (§ 26. rem. 1) (δέλεαρ, *a bait*) pr. *to entrap take or catch* with a bait; met. *allure, entice, delude,* Ja. 1. 14; 2 Pe. 2. 14, 18.

δένδρα, nom. and acc. pl. . . . . δένδρον

δένδρον, ου, τό, (§ 3. tab. C. c) *a tree,* Mat. 3. 10; 7. 17; 13. 32.

δένδρων, gen. pl. . . . . δένδρον

δέξαι, 2 pers. sing. aor. 1, imper. . . δεχομαι

δεξαμένη, nom. sing. fem. part. aor. 1 . id.

δεξάμενοι, nom. pl. masc. part. aor. 1 . . id.

δεξάμενος, nom. sing. masc. part. aor. 1 . id.

δέξασθαι, aor. 1, infin. . . . . id.

δέξασθε, 2 pers. pl. aor. 1, imper. . . id.

δέξηται, 3 pers. sing. aor. 1, subj. . . id.

δεξιά, nom. sing. fem. . . . . δεξιός

δεξιά, acc. pl. neut. . . . . . id.

δεξιᾷ, dat. sing. fem. . . . . id.

δεξιάν, acc. sing. fem. . . . . id.

δεξιᾶς, gen. sing. fem. . . . . id.

δεξιάς, acc. pl. fem. . . . . id.

δεξιοβόλος], ου, ὁ, (δεξιά & βολή, *a cast,* which from βάλλω) *a javelin-man,* v.r.

δεξιοβόλους, acc. pl.—A. Ln. . . } δεξιοβόλος
δεξιολάβους, R. Gr. Sch. Tdf. (Ac. 23. 23) }

δεξιολάβος], ου, ὁ, (§ 3. tab. C. a) (δεξιός & λαμβάνω) *one posted on the right hand; a flank guard; a light armed spearman,* (ᾰ). N.T.

δεξιολάβους,[a] acc. pl. . . . . δεξιολάβος

δεξιόν, acc. sing. masc. and neut. . . δεξιός

δεξιοῖς, dat. pl. neut. . . . . id.

δεξιός, ά, όν, (§ 7. rem. 1) *right,* as opposed to left, Mat. 5. 29, 30; Lu. 6. 6, et al.; ἡ δεξιά, sc. χείρ, *the right hand,* Mat. 6. 3; 27. 29, et al.; τὰ δεξιά, sc. μέρη, *the parts towards the right hand, the right hand side;* καθίζειν, or, καθῆσθαι, or, ἑστάναι, ἐκ δεξιῶν (μερῶν) τινος, *to sit or stand at the right hand of any one,* as a mark of the highest honour and dignity which he can bestow, Mat. 20. 21; 26. 64, et al.; εἶναι ἐκ δεξιῶν (μερῶν) τινος, *to be at one's right hand,* as a helper, Ac. 2. 25; δεξιὰς (χεῖρας) διδόναι, *to give the right hand* to any one, as a pledge of sincerity in one's promises, Gal. 2. 9.

δεξιῶν, gen. pl. . . . . . δεξιός

δέξωνται, 3 pers. pl. aor. 1, subj. . . δέχομαι

δέομαι, 1 pers. sing. pres. ind. mid. . . δέω, δέομαι

δεόμεθα, 1 pers. pl. pres. ind. mid. . . id.

δεόμενοι, nom. pl. masc. part. pres. mid. . id.

δεόμενος, nom. sing. masc. part. pres. mid. . id.

δέον, οντος, τό, (§ 37. rem. 1) . . δέω

δέος], δέους, τό, (δείδω, *to fear*) *fear.* v.r.

δέους, gen. s.—Al. Ln. Tdf. εὐλαβείας καὶ δέους. }
αἰδοῦς καὶ εὐλαβείας, Re. Gr. Sch. } δέος
(He. 12. 28) . . . }

Δερβαῖος,[b] ου, ὁ, *an inhabitant of Derbe.*

Δέρβη], ης, ἡ, (§ 2. tab. B. a) *Derbe,* a city of Lycaonia.

Δέρβην, acc. sing. . . . . Δέρβη

δέρει, 3 pers. sing. pres. ind. act. . . δέρω

δέρεις, 2 pers. sing. pres. ind. act. . . id.

δέρμα], ᾰτος, τό, (§ 4. tab. D. c) . . id.

δέρμασι,[c] dat. pl. . . . . δέρμα

δερματίνην, acc. sing. fem. . . . δερμάτινος

δερμάτινος], η, ον, (§ 7. tab. F. a) . . δέρω

δέροντες, nom. pl. masc. part. pres. act. . id.

δέρω], fut. δερῶ, (§ 27. rem. 1. a) aor. 1, ἔδειρα, (§ 27. rem. 1. d) fut. 2, pass. δαρήσομαι, (§ 27. rem. 4. c) *to skin, flay;* hence, *to beat, scourge,* Mat. 21. 35; Mar. 12. 3, 5; 13. 9, et al.

δέρμα, ᾰτος, τό, (§ 4. tab. D. c) *the skin* of an animal, He. 11. 37.

δερμάτῐνος, η, ον, (§ 7. tab. F. a) *made of skin, leathern,* Mat. 3. 4; Mar. 1. 6.

δέρων, nom. sing. masc. part. pres. act. . δέρω

δεσμά, nom. and acc. pl. (§ 6. rem. 7) . δεσμός

δεσμάς,[d] acc. pl. . . . . δεσμή

δεσμεύουσι, 3 pers. pl. pres. ind. act. . . δεσμεύω

δεσμεύω], fut. εύσω, (§ 13. tab. M) . . δέω

δεσμεύων, nom. sing. masc. part. pres. act. . δεσμεύω

δεσμέω, ῶ], fut. ήσω, (§ 16. tab. P) . δέω

δεσμή], ῆς, ἡ, (§ 2. tab. B. a) . . id.

δέσμιοι, nom. pl. . . . . δέσμιος

δεσμίοις, dat. pl.—Gr. Sch. Tdf. . . } id.
δεσμοῖς μου, Rec. (He. 10. 34) . }

a Ac. 23. 23. b Ac. 20. 4. c He. 11. 37. d Mat. 13. 30.

δέσμιον, acc. sing. . . . . . δέσμιος

δέσμιος, ου, ὁ, (§ 3. tab. C. a) . . δέω

δεσμίους, acc. pl. . . . . . δέσμιος

δεσμίων, gen. pl. . . . . . id.

δεσμοῖς, dat. pl. . . . . . δεσμός

δεσμός, οῦ, ὁ, (§ 6. rem. 7) . . . δέω

δεσμοῦ, gen. sing. . . . . . δεσμός

δεσμούς, acc. pl. . . . . . id.

δεσμοφύλακι, dat. sing. . . . . δεσμοφύλαξ

δεσμοφύλαξ, ἄκος, ὁ, (§ 4. rem. 2. b) (δεσμός & φυλάσσω) *a keeper of a prison, jailer,* Ac. 16. 23, 27, 36. (ῠ). L.G.

δεσμῶν, gen. pl. . . . . . δεσμός

δεσμώτας, acc. pl. . . . . . δεσμώτης

δεσμωτήριον, ου, τό, (§ 3. tab. C. c) (δεσμόω, *to bind*) *a prison,* Mat. 11. 2; Ac. 5. 21, 23; 16. 26.

δεσμωτηρίου, gen. sing. . . . . δεσμωτήριον

δεσμωτηρίῳ, dat. sing. . . . . . id.

δεσμώτης], ου, ὁ, (§ 2. tab. B. c) (δεσμόω) *a prisoner,* i.q. δέσμιος, Ac. 27. 1, 42.

δέσποτα, voc. sing. (§ 2. rem. 6) . . δεσπότης

δεσπόταις, dat. pl. . . . . . id.

δεσπότας, acc. pl. . . . . . id.

δεσπότῃ, dat. sing. . . . . . id.

δεσπότην, acc. sing. . . . . . id.

δεσπότης,

ου, ὁ, (§ 2. tab. B. c) *a lord, master,* especially of slaves, 1 Ti. 6. 1, 2; 2 Ti. 2. 21; Tit. 2. 9; 1 Pe. 2. 18; by impl. as denoting the possession of supreme authority, *Lord, sovereign,* used of God, Lu. 2. 29; Ac. 4. 24; Re. 6. 10; and of Christ, 2 Pe. 2. 1; Jude 4.

δεῦρο, adv. *hither, here;* used also as a sort of imperative, *come, come hither!* Mat. 19. 21; Mar. 10. 21, et al.; used of time, ἄχρι τοῦ δεῦρο, sc. χρόνου, *to the present time,* Ro. 1. 13.

δεῦτε, i.e. δεῦρ' ἴτε, an exclamation in the plural, of which the singular form is δεῦρο, *come,* Mat. 4. 19; 11. 28, et al.; as a particle of exhortation, incitement, etc., and followed by an imperative, *come now,* etc. Mat. 21. 38; 28. 6, et al.

δευτέρα, nom. sing. fem. . . . . δεύτερος

δευτέρᾳ, dat. sing. fem. . . . . . id.

δευτεραῖοι,[a] nom. pl. masc. . . . . δευτεραῖος

δευτεραῖος], αία, αῖον, (§ 7. rem. 1) . **δύο**

δευτέραν, acc. sing. fem. . . . . **δεύτερος**

δευτέρας, gen. sing. fem. . . . . **id.**

δεύτερον, nom. and acc. sing. neut. . . . **id.**

δεύτερον, neut. used adverbially . . . **id.**

δευτερόπρωτος], ου, ὁ, ἡ, (§ 7. rem. 2) (δεύτερος & πρῶτος) *second-first,* an epithet of uncertain meaning, but probably appropriated to the Sabbath following the first day of unleavened bread. N.T.

δευτεροπρώτῳ,[b] dat. sing. neut. . . **δευτερόπρωτος**

δεύτερος, α, ον, (§ 7. rem. 1) . . . δύο

δευτέρου, gen. sing. masc. and neut. . . **δεύτερος**

δευτέρῳ, dat. sing. masc. and neut. . . **id.**

δέχεται, 3 pers. sing. pres. ind. . . . **δέχομαι**

δέχομαι],

fut. ξομαι, perf. (pass. form) δέδεγμαι, (§ 23. rem. 1. b, and rem. 7) aor. 1, ἐδεξάμην, *to take* into one's hands, etc. Lu. 2. 28; 16. 6, 7, et al.; *to receive,* Ac. 22. 5; 28. 21; Phil. 4. 18; *to receive into and retain, contain,* Ac. 3. 21; met. *to receive* by the hearing, *learn, acquire a knowledge of,* 2 Co. 11. 4; Ja. 1. 21; *to receive, admit, grant access to, receive kindly, welcome,* Mat. 10. 40, 41; 18. 5, et al.; *to receive* in hospitality, *entertain,* Lu. 9. 53; He. 11. 31; *to bear with, bear patiently,* 2 Co. 11. 16; met. *to receive, approve, assent to,* Mat. 11. 14; Lu. 8. 13; Ac. 8. 14; 11. 1, et al.; *to admit,* and by impl. *to embrace, follow,* 1 Co. 2. 14; 2 Co. 8. 17, et al.

δεκτός, ή, όν, (§ 7. tab. F. a) *accepted, acceptable, agreeable, approved,* Lu. 4. 24; Ac. 10. 35; Phil. 4. 18; by impl. when used of a certain time, *marked by* divine *acceptance, propitious,* Lu. 4. 19; 2 Co. 6. 2. LXX.

δοχή, ῆς, ἡ, (§ 2. tab. B. a) pr. *reception* of guests; in N.T. *a banquet, feast,* Lu. 5. 29; 14. 13.

δεχόμενος, nom. sing. masc. part. pres. . **δέχομαι**

δέχονται, 3 pers. pl. pres. ind. . . . **id.**

δέχωνται, 3 pers. pl. pres. subj. . . **id.**

δέω],

fut. δήσω, perf. δέδεκα, aor. 1, ἔδησα, perf. pass. δέδεμαι, aor. 1, pass. ἐδέθην, (§ 37. rem. 1) *to bind, tie,* Mat. 13. 30; 21. 2,

[a] Ac. 28. 13.

[b] Lu. 6. 1.

et al.; *to bind, confine*, Mat. 27. 2; 14. 3, et al.; *to impede, hinder*, 2 Ti. 2. 9; *to bind* with infirmity, Lu. 13. 16; *to bind* by a legal or moral tie, as marriage, Ro. 7. 2; 1 Co. 7. 27, 39; by impl. *to impel, compel*, Ac. 20. 22; in N.T. *to pronounce or declare to be binding or obligatory*, or, *to declare to be prohibited and unlawful*, Mat. 16. 19; 18. 18.

δεῖ, imperson. fut. δεήσει, aor. 1, ἐδέησε, imperf. ἔδει, subj. δέῃ, infin. δεῖν, part. δέον, *it is binding, it is necessary, it behoveth, it is proper; it is inevitable*, Ac. 21. 22.

δέον, οντος, τό, (part. of δεῖ) *necessary*, 1 Pe. 1. 6; *proper, right*, Ac. 19. 36; 1 Ti. 5. 13.

δεσμή, ῆς, ἡ, (§ 2. tab. B. a) *a bundle*, as of tares, Mat. 13. 20.

δεσμός, οῦ, ὁ, (§ 3. tab. C. a) pl. τά δεσμά, & οἱ δεσμοί, (§ 6. rem. 7) *a bond, anything by which one is bound, a cord, chain, fetters*, etc.; and by meton. *imprisonment*, Lu. 8. 29; Ac. 16. 26; 20. 23, et al.; *a string or ligament*, as of the tongue, Mar. 7. 35; met. *an impediment, infirmity*, Lu. 13. 16.

δέσμιος, ίου, ὁ, (§ 3. tab. C. a) *one bound, a prisoner*, Mat. 27. 15, 16; Mar. 15. 6, et al.

δεσμέω, ῶ, fut. ήσω, (§ 16. tab. P) *to bind, confine*, i.q. δεσμεύω, Lu. 8. 29. L.G.

δεσμεύω, fut. εύσω, (§ 13. tab. M) *to bind, bind up*, as a bundle, Mat. 23. 4; *to bind, confine*, Ac. 22. 4.

δεω], fut. δεήσω, aor. 1, ἐδέησα, *to lack, fall short of*, (§ 37. rem. 1) mid.

δέομαι, fut. δεήσομαι, aor. 1, (pass. form) ἐδεήθην, *to be in want, to need; to ask, request*, Mat. 9. 38; Lu. 5. 12; 8. 28, 38, et al.; in N.T. absol. *to pray, offer prayer, beseech, supplicate*, Lu. 21. 36; 22. 32; Ac. 4. 31; 8. 22, 24, et al.

δέησις, εως, ἡ, (§ 5. tab. E. c) *want, entreaty; prayer, supplication*, Lu. 1. 13; 2. 37; 5. 33, et al.

δή, a particle serving to add an intensity of expression to a term or clause. Its simplest and most ordinary uses are when it gives impressiveness to an affirmation, *indeed, really, doubtless*, Mat. 13. 23; 2 Co. 12. 1; or earnestness to a call, injunction, or entreaty, Lu. 2. 15; Ac. 13. 2; 15. 36; 1 Co. 6. 20.

δηλοῖ, 3 pers. sing. pres. ind. act. . . δηλόω

δῆλον, nom. sing. neut. and acc. sing. masc. δῆλος

δῆλος], η, ον, pr. *clearly visible; plain, manifest, evident*, Mat. 26. 73; 1 Co. 15. 27; Gal. 3. 11; 1 Ti. 6. 7.

δηλόω, ῶ, fut. ώσω, aor. 1, ἐδήλωσα, (§ 20. tab. T) *to render manifest or evident; to make known, to tell, relate, declare*, 1 Co. 1. 11; Col. 1. 8; *to show, point out, bring to light*, 1 Co. 3. 13; *to intimate, signify*, He. 8. 9; 12. 27; 1 Pe. 1. 11.

δηλοῦντος, gen. sing. neut. part. pres. act. . δηλόω

δηλόω, ῶ], fut. ώσω, (§ 20. tab. T) . . δῆλος

δηλώσας, nom. sing. masc. part. aor. 1, act. δηλόω

δηλώσει, 3 pers. sing. fut. ind. act. . . id.

Δημᾶς, ᾶ, ὁ, (§ 2. rem. 4) *Demas*, pr. name.

δημηγορέω, ῶ], fut. ήσω, (§ 16. tab. P) (δῆμος & ἀγορεύω) *to address a public assembly, to deliver an harangue or public oration*, Ac. 12. 21.

Δημήτριος, ου, ὁ, (§ 3. tab. C. a) *Demetrius*, pr. name.

I. *The Ephesian silversmith*, Ac. 19. 24, 38.

II. *A certain Christian*, 3 Jno. 12.

Δημητρίῳ, dat. sing. . . . . Δημήτριος

δημιουργός,[a] ου, ὁ, (§ 3. tab. C. a) (δῆμος & ἔργον) pr. *one who labours for the public*, or, *exercises some public calling; an architect*, especially, the Divine *Architect* of the universe.

δῆμον, acc. sing. . . . δῆμος

δῆμος, ου, ὁ, (§ 3. tab. C. a) *the people*, Ac. 12. 22; 17. 5; 19. 30, 33.

δημόσιος, ία, ον, (§ 7. rem. 1) *public, belonging to the public*, Ac. 5. 18; δημοσίᾳ, *publicly*, Ac. 16. 37; 18. 28; 20. 20.

δημοσίᾳ, dat. sing. fem. . . . . δημόσιος

δημοσίᾳ, dat. sing. fem. used adverbially . id.

δημόσιος], α, ον, (§ 7. rem. 1) . . . δῆμος

δήμῳ, dat. sing. . . . . . id.

[a] He. 11. 10.

δηνάρια, acc. pl. . . . . . . δηνάριον

δηνάριον, ίου, τό, (§ 3. tab. C. c) Lat. *denarius*, a Roman silver coin. The silver denarius was at first equivalent to about eightpence halfpenny of English money, declining, under the empire, to about sevenpence halfpenny; and was therefore somewhat less than the Greek δραχμή. The name originally imported *ten asses*.

δηναρίου, gen. sing. . . . . . δηνάριον

δηναρίων, gen. pl. . . . . . . id.

δήποτε,[a] an intensive combination of the particle δή with ποτε, which see; as an intensive, Jno. 5. 4.—Rec. Gr. Sch.

Tdf. om.

δηποτοῦν, A.

οἱῳδηποτοῦν, Ln.

δήπου,[b] see που.

δῆσαι, aor. 1, infin. act. . . . . δέω

δήσαντες, nom. pl. masc. part. aor. 1, act. . id.

δήσατε, 2 pers. pl. aor. 1, imper. act. . id.

δήσῃ, 3 pers. sing. aor. 1, subj. act. . . id.

δήσῃς, 2 pers. sing. aor. 1, subj. act. . id.

δήσητε, 2 pers. pl. aor. 1, subj. act. . . id.

δήσουσι, 3 pers. pl. fut. ind. act. . . id.

δι', by apostrophe for διά.

διά, prep. with a genitive, *through*, used of place or medium, Mat. 7. 13; Lu. 6. 1; 2 Co. 11. 33, et al.; *through*, of time, *during*, *in the course of*, He. 2. 15; Ac. 5. 19, et al.; *through*, of immediate agency, causation, instrumentality, *by means of*, *by*, Jno. 1. 3; Ac. 3. 18, et al.; of means or manner, *through*, *by*, *with*, Lu. 8. 4; 2 Co. 5. 7; 8. 8, et al.; of state or condition, *in a state of*, Ro. 4. 11, et al.; with an accusative, used of causation which is not direct and immediate in the production of a result, *on account of*, *because of*, *for the sake of*, *with a view to*, Mar. 2. 27; Jno. 1. 31, et al.; rarely, *through*, *while subject to* a state of untoward circumstances, Gal. 4. 13.

Δία, acc. sing. (§ 6. rem. 4. a) . . . . Ζεύς

διαβαίνω], fut. βήσομαι, aor. 2, διέβην, (§ 37. rem. 1) (διά & βαίνω) *to pass through or over*, Lu. 16. 26; Ac. 16. 9; He. 11. 29.

διαβάλλω], fut. βαλῶ, (§ 27. rem. 1. b) (διά & βάλλω) *to throw or convey through or over; to thrust through; to defame, inform against*, Lu. 16. 1.

διάβολος, ου, ὁ, ἡ, (§ 3. tab. C. a. b) *a calumniator, slanderer*, 1 Ti. 3. 11; 2 Ti. 3. 3; Tit. 2. 3; *a treacherous informer, traitor*, Jno. 6. 70; ὁ διάβολος, *the devil*.

διαβάς, nom. sing. masc. part. aor. 2 . διαβαίνω

διαβεβαιόομαι, οῦμαι], (§ 21. tab. U) (διά & βεβαιόω) *to assert strongly, asseverate*, 1 Ti. 1. 7; Tit. 3. 8.

διαβεβαιοῦνται, 3 pers. pl. pres. ind. . διαβεβαιόομαι

διαβεβαιοῦσθαι, pres. infin. . . . id.

διαβῆναι, aor. 2, infin. . . . . διαβαίνω

διαβλέπω], fut. ψω, (§ 23. rem. 1. a) (διά & βλέπω) *to look through; to view steadily; to see clearly or steadily*, Mat. 7. 5; Lu. 6. 42.

διαβλέψεις, 2 pers. sing. fut. ind. . . διαβλέπω

διάβολοι, nom. pl. masc. . . . . διάβολος

διάβολον, acc. sing. masc. . . . id.

διάβολος, ου, ὁ, ἡ, (§ 3. tab. C. a. b) . . διαβάλλω

διαβόλου, gen. sing. masc. . . . διάβολος

διαβόλους, acc. pl. fem. . . . . id.

διαβόλῳ, dat. sing. masc. . . . id.

διαγγελῇ, 3 pers. sing. aor. 2, subj. pass. . διαγγέλλω

διαγγέλλω], fut. γελῶ, aor. 1, διήγγειλα, (§ 27. rem. 1. b. d) aor. 2, pass. διηγγέλην, (§ 27. rem. 4. a) (διά & ἀγγέλλω) *to publish abroad*, Lu. 9. 60; Ro. 9. 17; *to certify* to the public, Ac. 21. 26; *to tell, announce, give notice of, divulge, publish abroad*, Ac. 21. 26; *to declare, promulgate, teach*, Lu. 9. 60; from the Heb. *to celebrate, praise*, Ro. 9. 17.

διαγγέλλων, nom. sing. masc. part. pres. act. διαγγέλλω

διαγενομένου, gen. sing. masc. and neut. pt. aor 2 διαγίνομαι

διαγενομένων, gen. pl. part. aor. 2 . . id.

διαγίνομαι], fut. γενήσομαι, aor. 2, διεγενόμην, (§ 37. rem. 1) (διά & γίνομαι) *to continue through: to intervene, elapse*, Mar. 16. 1; Ac. 25. 13; 27. 9.

διαγινώσκειν, pres. infin. . . . διαγινώσκω

διαγινώσκω], fut. γνώσομαι, (§ 36. rem. 3) (διά & γινώσκω) pr. *to distinguish; to resolve determinately; to examine, inquire into*, judicially, Ac. 23. 15; 24. 22.

[a] Jno. 5. 4.

[b] He. 2. 16.

διάγνωσις, εως, ἡ, (§ 5. tab. E. c) pr. *an act of distinguishing or discernment; a determination; examination* judicially, *hearing, trial*, Ac. 25. 21.

διαγνωρίζω], fut. ίσω, (§ 26. rem. 1) (διά & γνωρίζω) *to tell abroad, publish*, Lu. 2. 17. N.T.

διάγνωσιν,[a] acc. sing. . . . . διάγνωσις

διάγνωσις], εως, ἡ, (§ 5. tab. E. c) . διαγινώσκω

διαγνώσομαι, 1 pers. sing. fut. ind. . . id.

διαγογγύζω], fut. ύσω, (§ 26. rem. 1) (διά & γογγύζω) *to murmur, mutter*, Lu. 15. 2; 19. 7. L.G.

διάγοντες, nom. pl. masc. part. pres. . διάγω

διαγρηγορέω, ῶ], fut. ήσω, (§ 16. tab. P) (διά & γρηγορέω) *to remain awake; to wake thoroughly*. L.G.

διαγρηγορήσαντες,[b] nom. pl. masc. pt. aor. 1 διαγρηγορέω

διάγω], fut. ξω, (§ 23. rem. 1. b) (διά & ἄγω) *to conduct or carry through or over; to pass or spend* time, *live*, 1 Ti. 2. 2; Tit. 3. 3.

διάγωμεν, 1 pers. pl. pres. subj. . . διάγω

διαδεξάμενοι,[c] nom. pl. masc. part. aor. 1 . διαδέχομαι

διαδέχομαι], fut. δέξομαι, (§ 23. rem. 1. b) (διά & δέχομαι) *to receive by transmission; to receive by succession.*

διάδοχος, ου, ὁ, ἡ, (§ 3. tab. C. a. b) *a successor*, Ac. 24. 27.

διάδημα], ατος, τό, (§ 4. tab. D. c) (διαδέω, διά & δέω) pr. *a band or fillet; a diadem*, the badge of a sovereign, Re. 12. 3; 13. 1; 19. 12.

διαδήματα, nom. and acc. pl. . . . διάδημα

διαδίδωμι], fut. δώσω, aor. 1, διέδωκα, (§ 30. tab. Z) (διά & δίδωμι) *to deliver from hand to hand; to distribute, divide*, Lu. 11. 22; 18. 22; Jno. 6. 11; Ac. 4. 35.

διαδίδωσι, 3 pers. sing. pres. ind. act. . . διαδίδωμι

διαδιδώσουσι, 3 pers. pl. fut. ind. act. irreg. for διαδώσουσι . . . . . id.

διάδος, 2 pers. sing. aor. 2, imper. (§ 30. rem. 1) id.

διάδοχον,[d] acc. sing. masc. . . . διάδοχος

διάδοχος], ου, ὁ, ἡ, (§ 3. tab. C. a. b) . διαδέχομαι

διαζώννυμι], or, ζωννύω, fut. ζώσω, (§ 31. tab. B. B) perf. pass. διέζωσμαι, (διά & ζώννυμι) *to gird firmly round*, Jno. 13. 4, 5; mid. *to gird round one's self*, Jno. 21. 7.

διαθέμενος, nom. sing. masc. part. aor. 2, mid. (§ 28. tab. W) . . . . διατίθημι

διαθεμένου, gen. sing. masc. part. aor. 2, mid. διατίθημι

διαθῆκαι, nom. pl. . . . διαθήκη

διαθήκη, ης, ἡ, (§ 2. tab. B. a) . . διατίθημι

διαθήκῃ, dat. sing. . . . . διαθήκη

διαθήκην, acc. sing. . . . . id.

διαθήκης, gen. sing. . . . . id.

διαθηκῶν, gen. pl. . . . . . id.

διαθήσομαι, 1 pers. sing. fut. ind. mid. . διατίθημι

διαιρέσεις, nom. pl. . . . . . διαίρεσις

διαίρεσις], εως, ἡ, (§ 5. tab. E. c) . . διαιρέω

διαιρέω, ῶ], fut. ήσω, aor. 2, διεῖλον, (§ 36. rem. 1) (διά & αἱρέω) *to divide, to divide out, distribute*, Lu. 15. 12; 1 Co. 12. 11.

διαίρεσις, εως, ἡ, (§ 5. tab. E. c) *a division; a distinction, difference, diversity*, 1 Co. 12. 4, 5, 6.

διαιροῦν, nom. sing. neut. part. pres. act. . διαιρέω

διακαθαριεῖ, 3 pers. sing. fut. ind. act. Att. (§ 35. rem. 11) . . . διακαθαρίζω

διακαθαρίζω], fut. ιῶ, (διά & καθαρίζω) *to cleanse thoroughly*, Mat. 3. 12; Lu. 3. 17. N.T.

διακατελέγχομαι], fut. έγξομαι, (§ 23. rem. 1. b) (διά, κατά, & ἐλέγχομαι) *to maintain discussion strenuously and thoroughly.* N.T.

διακατηλέγχετο,[e] 3 pers. sing. imperf. . διακατελέγχομαι

διακόνει, 2 pers. sing. pres. imper. . . διακονέω

διακονεῖ, 3 pers. sing. pres. ind. . . . id.

διακονεῖν, pres. infin. . . . . id.

διακονείτωσαν, 3 pers. pl. pres. imper. . id.

διακονέω, ῶ], fut. ήσω, (§ 16. tab. P) . διάκονος

διακονῇ, 3 pers. sing. pres. subj. . . . διακονέω

διακονηθεῖσα, nom. sing. fem. pt. aor. 1, pass. id.

διακονηθῆναι, aor. 1, infin. pass. (§ 17. tab. Q) id.

διακονῆσαι, aor. 1, infin. . . . id.

διακονήσαντες, nom. pl. masc. part. aor. 1 . id.

διακονήσει, 3 pers. sing. fut. ind. . . id.

διακονία, ας, ἡ, (§ 2. tab. B. b, and rem. 2) . διάκονος

διακονίᾳ, dat. sing. . . . διακονία

διακονίαν, acc. sing. . . . . id.

διακονίας, gen. sing. . . . . id.

διακονιῶν, gen. pl. . . . . . id.

διάκονοι, nom. pl. masc. . . . διάκονος

διακόνοις, dat. pl. masc. . . . . id.

διάκονον, acc. sing. masc. and fem. . . id.

διάκονος, ου, ὁ, ἡ, (§ 3. tab. C. a. b) *one who renders service* to another; *an attendant, servant*, Mat. 20. 26; 22. 13; Jno. 2. 5, 9, et al.; *one who executes a commission, a deputy*, Ro.

[a] Ac. 25. 21. [b] Lu. 9. 32. [c] Ac. 7. 45. [d] Ac. 24. 27. [e] Ac. 18. 28.

13.4; Χριστοῦ, Θεοῦ, ἐν κυρίῳ, etc., *a commissioned minister or preacher* of the Gospel, 1 Co. 3. 5; 2 Co. 6. 4, et al.; *a minister* charged with an announcement or sentence, 2 Co. 3. 6; Gal. 2. 17; Col. 1. 23; *a minister* charged with a significant characteristic, Ro. 15. 8; *a servitor, devoted follower*, Jno. 12. 26; *a deacon or deaconess*, whose official duty was to superintend the alms of the Church, with other kindred services, Ro. 16. 1; Phi. 1. 1; 1 Ti. 3. 8, 12. (ᾱ).

διᾱκονέω, ῶ, fut. ήσω, (§ 16. tab. P) imperf. ἐδιακόνουν, aor. 1, ἐδιακόνησα, perf. δεδιακόνηκα, but later, διηκόνουν, διηκόνησα, δεδιηκόνηκα, *to wait, attend upon, serve*, Mat. 8. 15; Mar. 1. 31; Lu. 4. 39, et al.; *to be an attendant or assistant*, Ac. 19. 22; *to minister to, relieve, assist, or supply with the necessaries of life, provide the means of living*, Mat. 4. 11; 27. 55; Mar. 1. 13; 15. 41; Lu. 8. 3, et al.; *to fill the office of* διάκονος, *deacon, perform the duties of deacon*, 1 Ti. 3. 10, 13; 1 Pe. 4. 11; *to convey in charge, administer*, 2 Co. 3. 3; 8. 19, 20; 1 Pe. 1. 12; 4. 10; pass. *to receive service*, Mat. 20. 28; Mar. 10. 45.

διακονία, ας, ἡ, (§ 2. tab. B. b, and rem. 2) *serving, service, waiting, attendance, the act of rendering friendly offices*, Lu. 10. 40; 2 Ti. 4. 11; He. 1. 14; *relief, aid*, Ac. 6. 1; 11. 29; 2 Co. 8. 4; 9. 1, 12, 13; *a commission*, Ac. 12. 25; Ro. 15. 31; *a commission or ministry* in the service of the Gospel, Ac. 1. 17, 25; 20. 24; Ro. 11. 13; 2 Co. 4. 1; 5. 18; 1 Ti. 1. 12; *service* in the Gospel, Ac. 6. 4; 21. 19; 1 Co. 16. 15; 2 Co. 6. 3; 11. 8; Ep. 4. 12; Re. 2. 19; *a function, ministry, or office* in the Church, Ro. 12. 7; 1 Co. 12. 5; Col. 4. 17; 2 Ti. 4. 5; *a ministering* in the conveyance of a revelation from God, 2 Co. 3. 7, 8, 9.

διακόνους, acc. pl. masc. . . . . . διάκονος
διακονουμένῃ, dat. sing. fem. part. pres. pass. διακονέω
διακονοῦντες, nom. pl. masc. part. pres. . id.
διακονούντων, gen. pl. masc. part. pres. . id.
διακονοῦσαι, nom. pl. fem. part. pres. . id.
διακονῶν, nom. sing. masc. part. pres. . . διακονέω
διακόσιαι, nom. pl. fem. . . . διακόσιοι
διακοσίας, acc. pl. fem. . . . . id.

διᾱκόσιοι], αι, α, (§ 9. tab. I. e) *two hundred*, Mar. 6. 37; Jno. 6. 7, et al.

διακοσίους, acc. pl. masc. . . . διακόσιοι
διακοσίων, gen. pl. . . . . . id.
διακούσομαι,[a] 1 pers. sing. fut. ind. mid. . διακούω

διακούω], fut. ούσομαι, (διά & ἀκούω) *to hear a thing through; to hear* judicially.

διακρῐθῇ, 3 pers. sing. aor. 1, subj. pass. . διακρίνω
διακριθῆτε, 2 pers. pl. aor. 1, subj. pass. . id.
διακρῖναι, aor. 1, infin. act. . . . id.
διακρίναντα, acc. sing. m. part. aor. 1.—A. B. Ln. } διακρινόμενον, Rec. Gr. Sch. . . } Tdf. om. (Ac. 11. 12) . . } id.
διακρίνει, 3 pers. sing. pres. ind. act. . id.
διακρίνειν, pres. infin. act. . . . id.
διακρινέτωσαν, 3 pers. pl. pres. imper. act. id
διακρινόμενοι, nom. pl. masc. part. pres. mid. id
διακρινόμενον, acc. sing. masc. part. pres. mid. id
διακρινόμενος, nom. sing. masc. part. pres. mid. id.
διακρινομένους, acc. pl. masc. part. pres. mid. } —A. C. Ln. Tdf. . . . } διακρινόμενοι, Rec. Gr. Sch. (Jude 22) } id.

διακρίνω, fut. ἵνῶ, (§ 27. rem. 1. a) (διά & κρίνω) *to separate, sever; to make a distinction or difference*, Ac. 15. 9; 1 Co. 11. 29; *to make to differ, distinguish, prefer, confer a superiority*, 1 Co. 4. 7; *to examine, scrutinise, estimate*, 1 Co. 11. 31; 14. 29; *to discern, discriminate*, Mat. 16. 3; *to judge, to decide a cause*, 1 Co. 6. 5; mid. διακρίνομαι, aor. 1, (pass. form) διεκρίθην, (ῐ), *to dispute, contend*, Ac. 11. 2; Jude 9; *to make a distinction* mentally Ja. 2. 4; Jude 22; in N.T. *to hesitate, be in doubt, doubt*, Mat. 21. 21; Mar. 11. 23, et al. (ῑ).

διάκρῐσις, εως, ἡ, (§ 5. tab. E. c) *a separation; a distinction*, or, *doubt*, Ro. 14. 1; *a discerning, the act of discerning or distinguishing*, He. 5. 14; *the faculty of distinguishing and estimating*, 1 Co. 12. 10.

διακρίνων, nom. sing. masc. part. pres. act. . διακρίνω
διακρίσεις, nom. and acc. pl. . . διάκρισις
διάκρισιν, acc. sing. . . . . id.
διάκρισις], εως, ἡ, (§ 5. tab. E. c) . . διακρίνω

διακωλύω], fut. ύσω, (§ 13. tab. M) (διά &

[a] Ac. 23. 35.

κωλύω) *to hinder, restrain, prohibit*, Mat. 3. 14. (ῡ).

διαλαλέω, ῶ], fut. ήσω, (§ 16. tab. P) (διά & λαλέω) *to talk with*; by impl. *to consult, deliberate*, Lu. 6. 11; *to divulge, publish, spread by rumour*, Lu. 1. 65.

διαλέγεται, 3 pers. sing. pres. ind. . . διαλέγομαι

διαλέγομαι], fut. λέξομαι, aor. 1, (pass. form) διελέχθην, (§ 23. rem. 4) (διά & λέγω) *to discourse, argue, reason*, Ac. 17. 2, 17; 24. 12, et al.; *to address, speak to*, He. 12. 5; *to contend, dispute*, Mar. 9. 34; Jude 9.

διάλεκτος, ου, ἡ, (§ 3. tab. C. b) *speech; manner of speaking; peculiar language* of a nation, *dialect, vernacular idiom*, Ac. 1. 19; 2. 6, 8; 21. 40; 22. 2; 26. 14.

διαλεγόμενον, acc. sing. masc. part. pres. . διαλέγομαι

διαλεγόμενος, nom. sing. masc. part. pres. id.

διαλεγομένου, gen. sing. masc. part. pres. . id.

διαλείπω], fut. ψω, (§ 23. rem. 1. a) aor. 2, διέλῐπον, (§ 24. rem. 9) (διά & λείπω) *to leave an interval; to intermit, cease*, Lu. 7. 45.

διάλεκτος], ου, ἡ . . . . . διαλέγομαι

διαλέκτῳ, dat. sing. . . . . διάλεκτος

διαλλάγηθι,[a] 2 pers. sing. aor. 2, imper. pass. . διαλλάσσω

διαλλάσσω], (διά & ἀλλάσσω) *to change, exchange*; pass. διαλλάσσομαι, aor. 2, διηλλάγην, (§ 26. rem. 3) *to be reconciled* to another.

διαλογίζεσθαι, pres. infin. . . διαλογίζομαι

διαλογίζεσθε, 2 pers. pl. pres. ind. . . id.

διαλογίζομαι], fut. ίσομαι, (§ 26. rem. 1) (διά & λογίζομαι) pr. *to make a settlement of accounts; to reason, deliberate, ponder, consider*, Mat. 16. 7, 8; Mar. 2. 6, 8; Jno. 11. 50, et al.; *to dispute, contend*, Mar. 9. 33.

διαλογισμός, οῦ, ὁ, (§ 3. tab. C. a) *reasoning, ratiocination, thought, cogitation, purpose*, Mat. 15. 19; Mar. 7. 21, et al.; *discourse, dispute, disputation, contention*, Lu. 9. 46, et al.; *doubt, hesitation, scruple*, Lu. 24. 38.

διαλογιζόμενοι, nom. pl. masc. part. pres. διαλογίζομαι

διαλογιζομένων, gen. pl. masc. part. pres. . id.

διαλογίζονται, 3 pers. pl. pres. ind. . . id.

διαλογισμοί, nom. pl. . . . διαλογισμός

διαλογισμοῖς, dat. pl. . . . . διαλογισμός

διαλογισμόν, acc. sing. . . . id.

διαλογισμός, οῦ, ὁ, (§ 3. tab. C. a) . . διαλογίζομαι

διαλογισμοῦ, gen. sing. . . . διαλογισμός

διαλογισμούς, acc. pl. . . . . id.

διαλογισμῶν, gen. pl. . . . . id.

διαλύω], fut. ύσω, (§ 13. tab. M) (διά & λύω) *to dissolve, dissipate, disperse*, Ac. 5. 36.

διαμαρτυράμενοι, nom. pl. masc. part. aor. 1 διαμαρτύρομαι

διαμαρτύρασθαι, aor. 1, infin. . . id.

διαμαρτύρεται, 3 pers. sing. pres. ind. . . id.

διαμαρτύρηται, 3 pers. sing. pres. subj. . id.

διαμαρτύρομαι, fut. ροῦμαι, aor. 1, διεμαρτυράμην, (§ 37. rem. 1) (διά & μαρτύρομαι) *to make solemn affirmation, protest; to make a solemn and earnest charge*, Lu. 16. 28; Ac. 2. 40, et al.; *to declare solemnly and earnestly*, Ac. 8. 25; 18. 5, et al. (ῡ).

διαμαρτυρόμενος, nom. sing. masc. pt. pres. διαμαρτύρομαι

διαμάχομαι], fut. χέσομαι, contr. χοῦμαι, (διά & μάχομαι) *to fight out, to fight resolutely*; met. *to contend vehemently, insist*, Ac. 23. 9.

διαμείνῃ, 3 pers. sing. aor. 1, subj. . . διαμένω

διαμεμενηκότες, nom. pl. masc. part. perf. (§ 27. rem. 2. d) . . . id.

διαμεμερισμένοι, nom. pl. masc. part. p. pass. διαμερίζω

διαμένει, 3 pers. sing. pres. ind. . . διαμένω

διαμένεις, 2 pers. sing. pres. ind. . . id.

διαμένω], fut. ενῶ, aor. 1, διέμεινα, (§ 27. rem. 1. a. d) perf. διαμεμένηκα, (διά & μένω) *to continue throughout; to continue, be permanent or unchanged*, Lu. 1. 22; Gal. 2. 5; He. 1. 11; 2 Pe. 3. 4; *to continue, remain constant*, Lu. 22. 28.

διαμεριζόμεναι, nom. pl. fem. part. pres. pass. διαμερίζω

διαμεριζόμενοι, nom. pl. masc. part. pres. mid. id.

διαμερίζονται, 3 pers. pl. pres. ind. mid.—Gr. Sch. Tdf. . . . . } id.
διεμέριζον, Rec. (Mar. 15. 24) . }

διαμερίζω], fut. ίσω, (§ 26. rem. 1) (διά & μερίζω) *to divide into parts and distribute*, Mat. 27. 35; Mar. 15. 24; Ac. 2. 3, et al.; pass. in N.T. *to be in a state of dissension*, Lu. 11. 17, 18; 12. 52, 53.

διαμερισμός, οῦ, ὁ, (§ 3. tab. C. a) *division*; met. in N.T. *disunion, dissension*, Lu. 12. 51. L.G.

διαμερίσατε, 2 pers. pl. aor. 1, imper. act. . διαμερίζω

[a] Mat. 5. 24.

διαμερισθεῖσα, nom. sing. fem. pt. aor. 1, pass. διαμερίζω
διαμερισθήσεται, 3 pers. sing. fut. 1, ind. pass. id.
διαμερισμόν,[a] acc. sing. . . . διαμερισμός
διαμερισμός], οῦ, ὁ, (§ 3. tab. C. a) . . διαμερίζω
διανεμηθῇ,[b] 3 pers. sing. aor. 1, subj. pass. . διανέμω
διανέμω], fut. νεμῶ, (§ 27. rem. 1. a) aor. 1, pass. διενεμήθην, (διά & νέμω) *to distribute, to divulge, spread abroad.*
διανεύω], fut. εύσω, (§ 13. tab. M) (διά & νεύω) *to signify by a nod, beckon, make signs.* L.G.
διανεύων,[c] nom. sing. masc. part. pres. . . διανεύω
διανόημα], ατος, τό, (§ 4. tab. D. c) (διανοέομαι, *to turn over in the mind, think,* from διά & νοέω) *thought.*
διανοήματα,[d] acc. pl. . . . . διανόημα
διάνοια, ας, ἡ, (§ 2. tab. B. b, and rem. 2) (διά & νοέω) pr. *thought, intention; the mind, intellect, understanding,* Mat. 22. 37; Mar. 12. 30; Lu. 10. 27, et al.; *an operation of the understanding, thought, imagination,* Lu. 1. 51; *insight, comprehension,* 1 Jno. 5. 20; *mode of thinking and feeling, disposition of mind and heart, the affections,* Ep. 2. 3; Col. 1. 21.
διανοίᾳ, dat. sing. . . . . . διάνοια
διάνοιαν, acc. sing. . . . . id.
διανοίας, gen. sing. . . . . . id.
διανοῖγον, nom. sing. neut. part. pres. act. . διανοίγω
διανοίγω], fut. οίξω, (§ 37. rem. 1) (διά & ἀνοίγω) *to open,* Mar. 7. 34, 35; Lu. 2. 23; 24. 31; met. *to open* the sense of a thing, *explain, expound,* Lu. 24. 32; Ac. 17. 3; διανοίγειν τὸν νοῦν, τὴν καρδίαν, *to open the mind, the heart,* so as to understand and receive, Lu. 24. 45; Ac. 16. 14.
διανοίγων, nom. sing. masc. part. pres. act. διανοίγω
διανοίχθητι, 2 pers. sing. aor. 1, imper. pass. id.
διανοιῶν, gen. pl. . . . . διάνοια
διανυκτερεύω], fut. εύσω, (§ 13. tab. M) (διά & νύξ) *to pass the night, spend the whole night.*
διανυκτερεύων,[e] nom. sing. masc. part. pres. διανυκτερεύω
διανύσαντες,[f] nom. pl. masc. part. aor. 1, act. διανύω
διανύω], fut. ύσω, (§ 13. tab. M) (διά & ἀνύω, *to accomplish*) *to complete, finish.* (ῠ).
διαπαντός, (i. e. διά παντός) *through all time; throughout; always,* Mar. 5. 5, et al.; *continually* by stated routine, Lu. 24. 53; He. 9. 6.
διαπαρατριβαί,[g] nom. pl.—Gr. Sch. Tdf. παραδιατριβαί, Rec. (1 Ti. 6. 5) . } διαπαρατριβη
διαπαρατρῐβή], ῆς, ἡ, (§ 2. tab. B. a) (διά & παρατριβή, *collision, altercation,* from παρατρίβω, *to rub against,* παρά & τρίβω) *pertinacious disputation,* v.r. N.T.
διαπεράσαντες, nom. pl. masc. part. aor. 1 . διαπεράω
διαπεράσαντος, gen. sing. masc. part. aor. 1 id.
διαπεράω, ῶ], fut. άσω, (§ 22. rem. 2) (διά & περάω) *to pass through or over,* Mat. 9. 1; 14. 34; Mar. 5. 21, et al. (ᾱ).
διαπερῶν, acc. sing. neut. part. pres. . διαπεράω
διαπερῶσι, 3 pers. pl. pres. subj. (§ 18. tab. R) id.
διαπλεύσαντες,[h] nom. pl. masc. part. aor. 1 . διαπλέω
διαπλέω], fut. εύσομαι, (§ 35. rem. 3) aor. 1 διέπλευσα, (διά & πλέω) *to sail through or over.*
διαπονέομαι, οῦμαι], (§ 17. tab. Q) fut. ήσομαι, aor. 1, διεπονήθην, (διαπονέω, *to elaborate,* from διά & πονέω) pr. *to be thoroughly exercised with labour; to be wearied; to be vexed,* Ac. 4. 2; 16. 18.
διαπονηθείς, nom. sing. masc. part. aor. 1 . διαπονέομαι
διαπονούμενοι, nom. pl. masc. part. pres. . id.
διαπορεῖσθαι, pres. infin. pass. . . διαπορέω
διαπορεύεσθαι, pres. infin. . . διαπορεύομαι
διαπορεύομαι], fut. εύσομαι, (§ 14. tab. N) (διά & πορεύομαι) *to go or pass through,* Lu. 6. 1; 13. 22; Ac. 16. 4; *to pass by,* Lu. 18. 36, i.q. παρέρχομαι, ver. 37.
διαπορευόμενος, nom. sing. masc. part. pres. διαπορεύομαι
διαπορευομένου, gen. sing. masc. part. pres. . id.
διαπορέω, ῶ], fut. ήσω, (§ 16. tab. P) (διά & ἀπορέω) *to be utterly at a loss; to be in doubt and perplexity,* Lu. 9. 7; 24. 4, et al.
διαπραγματεύομαι], fut. εύσομαι, (§ 15. tab. O) (διά & πραγματεύομαι) *to despatch a matter thoroughly; to make profit in business, gain in trade,* Lu. 19. 15.
διαπρίω], fut. ίσω, (§ 13. tab. M) (διά & πρίω) *to divide with a saw, saw asunder; to grate* the teeth in a rage; pass. met. *to be cut* to the heart, *to be enraged,* Ac. 5. 33; 7. 54. (ῑ).
διαρπάζω], fut. άσω, (§ 26. rem. 2) (διά & ἁρπάζω) *to plunder, spoil, pillage,* Mat. 12. 29, bis.; Mar. 3. 27, bis.

[a] Lu. 12. 51. [b] Ac. 4. 17. [c] Lu. 1. 22. [d] Lu. 11. 17. [e] Lu. 6. 12. [f] Ac. 21. 7. [g] 1 Ti. 6. 5. [h] Ac. 27. 5.

διαρπάσαι, aor. 1, infin. act. . . . διαρπάζω
διαρπάσει, 3 pers. sing. fut. ind. act. . . id.
διαρπάσῃ, 3 pers. sing. aor. 1, subj. act.—Const. } id.
 διαρπάσει, Rec. Gr. Sch. Tdf. (Mar. 3. 27) }
διαῤῥήγνυμι and διαῤῥήσσω], fut. ήξω, (§ 36. rem. 5) (διά & ῥήγνυμι) *to break asunder, rend, tear, burst*, Mat. 26. 65, et al.
διαῤῥήξαντες, nom. pl. masc. part. aor. 1 . διαῤῥήγνυμι
διαῤῥήξας, nom. sing. masc. part. aor. 1 . id.
διαῤῥήσσων, nom. sing. masc. pt. pres. . διαῤῥήσσω
διασαφέω, ῶ], fut. ήσω, (§ 16. tab. P) aor. 1, διεσάφησα, (διά & σαφής, *manifest*) *to make known, declare, tell plainly, or fully*, Mat. 18. 31.
διασάφησον, 2 pers. sing. aor. 1, imper.—B. Ln. } διασαφέω
 φράσον, R. Gr. Sch. Tdf. (Mat. 13. 36) }
διασείσητε,[a] 2 pers. pl. aor. 1, subj. act. . διασείω
διασείω], fut. σω, (§ 13. tab. M) (διά & σείω) pr. *to shake thoroughly or violently; to harass, intimidate, extort from.*
διασκορπίζω], fut. ίσω, (§ 26. rem. 1) (διά & σκορπίζω) *to disperse, scatter*, Mat. 26. 31; Mar. 14. 27, et al.; *to dissipate, waste*, Lu. 15. 13; 16. 1; *to winnow*, or, *to strew*, Mat. 25. 24, 26. L.G.
διασκορπίζων, nom. sing. masc. part. pres. . διασκορπίζω
διασκορπισθήσεται, 3 pers. sing. fut. 1, pass. . id.
διασκορπισθήσονται, 3 pers. pl. fut. 1, pass. —Al. Ln. Tdf. . . . } id.
 διασκορπισθήσεται, Rec. Gr. Sch. (Mat. 26. 31) . . . . }
διασπαρέντες, nom. pl. masc part. aor. 2, pass. (§ 27. rem. 4. b) . . . διασπείρω
διασπασθῇ, 3 pers. sing. aor. 1, subj. pass. . διασπάω
διασπάω, ῶ], fut. άσομαι, (§ 22. rem. 2) perf. pass. διέσπασμαι, aor. 1, pass. διεσπάσθην, (διά & σπάω) *to pull or tear asunder or in pieces, burst*, Mar. 5. 4; Ac. 23. 10. (ᾰ).
διασπείρω], fut. ερῶ, (§ 27. rem. 1. c) aor. 2, pass. διεσπάρην, (§ 27. rem. 4. a) (διά & σπείρω) *to scatter abroad or in every direction*, as seed; *to disperse*, Ac. 8. 1, 4; 11. 19.

 διασπορά, ᾶς, ἡ, (§ 2. tab. B. b, and rem. 2) pr. *a scattering*, as of seed; *dispersion*; in N.T. meton. *the dispersed portion* of the Jews, specially termed *the dispersion*, Jno. 7. 35; Ja. 1. 1; 1 Pe. 1. 1. L.G.

διασπορά], ᾶς, ἡ . . . . . διασπείρω
διασπορᾷ, dat. sing. . . . . διασπορά
διασποράν, acc. sing. . . . . id.
διασπορᾶς, gen. sing. . . . . id.
διαστάσης, gen. sing. fem. part. aor. 2, (§ 29. tab. X) . . . . διΐστημι
διαστελλόμενον, acc. sing. neut. part. pres. pass. διαστέλλω
διαστέλλω], (διά & στέλλω) *to separate, distinguish*; mid. διαστέλλομαι, aor. 1, διεστειλάμην, (§ 27. rem. 1. d) *to determine, issue a decision; to state or explain distinctly and accurately*; hence, *to admonish, direct, charge, command*, Ac. 15. 24; He. 12. 20; when followed by a negative clause, *to interdict, prohibit*, Mat. 16. 20; Mar. 5. 43, et al.

 διαστολή, ῆς, ἡ, (§ 2. tab. B. a) *distinction, difference*, Ro. 3. 22; 10. 12; 1 Co. 14. 7. L.G.

διάστημα,[b] ατος, τό, (§ 4. tab. D. c) . . διΐστημι
διαστήσαντες, nom. pl. masc. part. aor. 1 . id.
διαστολή, ῆς, ἡ, (§ 2. tab. B. a) . . διαστέλλω
διαστολήν, acc. sing. . . . . διαστολή
διαστρέφοντα, acc. sing. masc. part. pres. act. διαστρέφω
διαστρέφω], fut. ψω, (§ 23. rem. 1. a) perf. pass. διέστραμμαι, (§ 23. rem. 7. 8) (διά & στρέφω) *to distort, turn away*; met. *to pervert, corrupt*, Mat. 17. 17; Lu. 9. 41, et al.; *to turn out of the way, cause to make defection*, Lu. 23. 2; Ac. 13. 8; διεστραμμένος, *perverse, corrupt, erroneous.*
διαστρέφων, nom. sing. masc. part. pres. act. . διαστρέφω
διαστρέψαι, aor. 1, infin. act. . . . id.
διασώζω], fut. σώσω, aor. 1, pass. διεσώθην, (§ 26. rem. 1) (διά & σώζω) *to bring safe through; to convey in safety*, Ac. 23. 24; pass. *to reach a place or state of safety*, Ac. 27. 44; 28. 1, 4; 1 Pe. 3. 20; *to heal, to restore to health*, Mat. 14. 36; Lu. 7. 3.
διασωθέντα, acc. sing. masc. part. aor. 1, pass. διασώζω
διασωθέντες, nom. pl. masc. part. aor. 1, pass. id.
διασωθῆναι, aor. 1, infin. pass. . . . id.
διασῶσαι, aor. 1, infin. act. . . . id.
διασώσῃ, 3 pers. sing. aor. 1, subj. act. . . id.
διασώσωσι, 3 pers. pl. aor. 1, subj. act. . id.

[a] Lu. 3. 14.

[b] Ac. 5. 7.

διαταγάς, acc. pl. . . . . . . διαταγή

διαταγείς, nom. sing. masc. part. aor. 2, pass. (§ 26. rem. 3) . . . διατάσσω

διαταγῇ, dat. sing. . . . . . διαταγή

διαταγή], ῆς, ἡ, (§ 2. tab. B. a) . . διατάσσω

διάταγμα,[a] ατος, τό, (§ 4. tab. D. c) . . id.

διαταράσσω], fut. ξω, (§ 26. rem. 3) (διά & ταράσσω) *to throw into a state of perturbation, to move or trouble greatly*, Lu. 1. 29.

διαταξάμενος, nom. sing. masc. part. aor. 1, mid. διατάσσω

διατάξομαι, 1 pers. sing. fut. ind. mid. . id.

διατάξωμαι, 1 pers. sing. aor. 1, subj. mid.—A. D. } id.
διατάξομαι, R. Gr. Sch. Tdf. (1 Co. 11. 34) }

διατάσσομαι, 1 pers. sing. pres. ind. mid. . id.

διατάσσω], fut. ξω, (§ 26. rem. 3) and mid. διατάσσομαι, (διά & τάσσω) pr. *to arrange, make a precise arrangement; to prescribe*, 1 Co. 11. 34; 16. 1; Tit. 1. 5; *to direct*, Lu. 8. 55; Ac. 20. 13; *to charge*, Mat. 11. 1; *to command*, Ac. 18. 2, et al.; *to ordain*, Gal. 3. 19.

διατᾰγή, ῆς, ἡ, (§ 2. tab. B. a) *an injunction, institute, ordinance*, Ro. 13. 2, Ac. 7. 53. L.G.

διάταγμα, ατος, τό, (§ 4. tab. D. c) *a mandate, commandment, ordinance*, He. 11. 23. L.G.

διατάσσων, nom. sing. masc. part. pres. act. διατάσσω

διαταχθέντα, acc. pl. neut. part. aor. 1, pass. id.

διατελεῖτε,[b] 2 pers. pl. pres. ind. . . διατελέω

διατελέω, ῶ], fut. έσω, (§ 22. rem. 1) (διά & τελέω) *to complete, finish*; intrans. *to continue, persevere*, in a certain state or course of action.

διατεταγμένον, acc. sing. neut. part. perf. pass. διατάσσω

διατεταγμένος, nom. sing. masc. part. perf. pass. id.

διατεταχέναι, perf. infin. act. . . . id.

διατηροῦντες, nom. pl. masc. part. pres. . διατηρέω

διατηρέω, ῶ], fut. ήσω, (§ 16. tab. P) (διά & τηρέω) *to watch carefully, guard with vigilance; to treasure up*, Lu. 2. 51; ἑαυτὸν ἐκ, *to keep one's self from, to abstain wholly from*, Ac. 15. 29.

διατί, i.e. διὰ τί, interrog. *for what? why? wherefore?* Mat. 9. 14; 13. 10; Lu. 19. 23, 31.

διατίθεμαι, pres. ind. mid. (§ 28. tab. W) . διατίθημι

διατίθημι], (§ 28. tab. V) (διά & τίθημι) *to arrange*; mid. διατίθεμαι, fut. θήσομαι, aor. 2, διεθέμην, *to arrange according to one's own mind; to make a disposition, to make a will; to settle the terms of a covenant, to ratify*, Ac. 3. 25; He. 8. 10; 10. 16; *to assign*, Lu. 22. 29.

διαθήκη, ης, ἡ, (§ 2. tab. B. a) *a testamentary disposition, will; a covenant*, He. 9. 16, 17; Gal. 3. 15; in N.T., *a covenant of God with men*, Gal. 3. 17; 4. 24; He. 9. 4; Mat. 26. 28, et al.; *the writings of the old covenant*, 2 Co. 3. 14.

διατρίβοντες, nom. pl. masc. part. pres. . διατρίβω

διατριβόντων [αὐτῶν], gen. pl. masc. part. pres.—C. D. Ln. . . } id.
Rec. Gr. Sch. Tdf. om. (Ac. 14. 18) . }

διατρίβω], fut. ψω, (§ 23. rem. 1. a) (διά & τρίβω) pr. *to rub, wear away by friction*; met. *to pass or spend time, to remain, stay, tarry, continue*, Jno. 3. 22; 11. 54; Ac. 12. 19; 14. 3, 28, et al. (ῑ).

διατρίψας, nom. sing. masc. part. aor. 1 . διατρίβω

διατροφάς,[c] acc. pl. . . . . . διατροφή

διατροφή], ῆς, ἡ, (§ 2. tab. B. a) (διατρέφω, *to nourish*) *food, sustenance*.

διατροφήν, acc. sing.—D. . . } διατροφή
διατροφάς, Rec. Gr. Sch. Tdf. (1 Ti. 6. 8) }

διαυγάζω], fut. άσω, (§ 26. rem. 1) (διά & αὐγάζω) *to shine through, shine out, dawn*. L.G.

διαυγάσαι, aor. 1, infin.—A. . . . } διαυγάζω
αὐγάσαι, Rec. Gr. Sch. Tdf. (2 Co. 4. 4) }

διαυγάσῃ,[d] 3 pers. sing. aor. 1, subj. . . id.

διαυγής, εος, οῦς, ὁ, ἡ, (§ 7. tab. G. b) (διά & αὐγή) *translucent, transparent, pellucid*.—Gr. Sch. Tdf.

διαφανής, Rec. (Re. 21. 21).

διαφᾰνής,[e] εος, οῦς, ὁ, ἡ, (§ 7. tab. G. b) (διαφαίνω *to show through*) *transparent, pellucid*.

διαφέρει, 3 pers. sing. pres. ind. . . διαφέρω

διαφέρετε, 2 pers. pl. pres. ind. . . id.

διαφερομένων, gen. pl. part. pres. pass. . id.

διαφέροντα, acc. pl. neut. part. pres. . . id.

διαφέρω], fut. διοίσω, aor. 1, διήνεγκα, aor. 2, διήνεγκον, (§ 36. rem. 1) (διά & φέρω) *to convey through, across*, Mar. 11. 16; *to carry different ways or into different parts, separate*; pass. *to be borne, driven, or tossed hither and thither*, Ac. 27. 27; *to be promulgated, proclaimed, published*, Ac. 13. 49; intrans.

[a] He. 11. 23. [b] Ac. 27. 33. [c] 1 Ti. 6. 8. [d] 2 Pe. 1. 19. [e] Re. 21. 21.

met. *to differ*, 1 Co. 15. 41; *to excel, be better or of greater value, be superior*, Mat. 6. 26; 10. 31, et al.; impers. διαφέρει, *it makes a difference, it is of consequence*; with οὐδέν, *it makes no difference, it is nothing*, Gal. 2. 6.

διάφορος, ου, ὁ, ἡ, (§ 7. rem. 2) *different, diverse, of different kinds*, Ro. 12. 6; He. 9. 10; *excellent, superior*, He. 1. 4; 8. 6.

διαφεύγω], fut. ξομαι, aor. 2, διέφυγον, (§ 24. rem. 5) (διά & φεύγω) *to flee through, escape by flight*, Ac. 27. 42.

διαφημίζειν, pres. infin. act. . . . διαφημίζω

διαφημίζω], fut. ίσω, (§ 26. rem. 1) διεφήμισα, (διά & φημή) *to report, proclaim, publish, spread abroad*, Mat. 9. 31; 28. 15; Mar. 1. 45.

διαφθεῖραι, aor. 1, infin. act. . . . διαφθείρω

διαφθείρει, 3 pers. sing. pres. ind. act. . id.

διαφθείρεται, 3 pers. sing. pres. ind. pass. . id.

διαφθείροντας, acc. pl. masc. part. pres. act. id.

διαφθείρω], fut. φθερῶ, aor. 1, διέφθειρα, perf. διέφθαρκα, (§ 27. rem. 1. c. d, and rem. 2. b) aor. 2, pass. διεφθάρην, perf. pass. διέφθαρμαι, (§ 27. rem. 3 and 4. a) (διά & φθείρω) *to corrupt or destroy utterly; to waste, bring to decay*, Lu. 12. 33; 2 Co. 4. 16; *to destroy*, Re. 8. 9; 11. 18, met. *to corrupt, pervert utterly*, 1 Ti. 6. 5.

διαφθορά, ᾶς, ἡ, (§ 2. tab. B. b, and rem. 2) *corruption, dissolution*, Ac. 2. 27, 31; 13. 34, 35, 36, 37.

διαφθορά], ᾶς, ἡ . . . διαφθείρω

διαφθοράν, acc. sing. . . . διαφθορά

διάφορα, acc. pl. neut. . . . . διάφορος

διαφόροις, dat. pl. masc. . . . . id.

διάφορος], ου, ὁ, ἡ, (§ 7. rem. 2) . διαφέρω

διαφορωτέρας, gen. sing. fem. comparat. (§ 8. rem. 1 and 4) . . . . διάφορος

διαφορώτερον, acc. sing. neut. compar. . id.

διαφύγῃ, 3 pers. sing. aor. 2, subj.—Gr. Sch. Tdf. } διαφεύγω
διαφύγοι, Rec. (Ac. 27. 42) . . }

διαφύγοι,[a] 3 pers. sing. aor. 2, opt. (§ 24. rem. 9) id.

διαφυλάξαι,[b] aor. 1, infin. act. . . διαφυλάσσω

διαφυλάσσω], fut. ξω, (§ 26. rem. 3) (διά & φυλάσσω) *to keep or guard carefully or with vigilance; to guard, protect.*

διαχειρίζω and διαχειρίζομαι], (§ 26. rem. 1) (διά & χείρ) pr. *to have in the hands, to manage*; mid. later, *to kill*, Ac. 5. 30; 26. 21.

διαχειρίσασθαι, aor. 1, infin. mid. . . διαχειρίζω

διαχλευάζοντες, nom. pl. masc. part. pres.— } διαχλευάζω
Gr. Sch. Tdf. . . . }
χλευάζοντες, Rec. (Ac. 2. 13) . }

διαχλευάζω], fut. άσω, (§ 26. rem. 1) (διά & χλευάζω) *to jeer outright, deride*, v. r. Ac. 2. 13.

διαχωρίζεσθαι,[c] pres. infin. . . διαχωρίζομαι

διαχωρίζομαι], fut. ίσομαι, (mid. of διαχωρίζω, *to separate*, from διά & χωρίζω) *to depart, go away.*

διδακτικόν, acc. sing. masc. . διδακτικός

διδακτικός], ή, όν, (§ 7. tab. F. a) . . διδάσκω

διδακτοί, nom. pl. masc. . . . διδακτός

διδακτοῖς, dat. pl. masc. . . . . id.

διδακτός], ή, όν, (§ 7. tab. F. a) . διδάσκω

διδάξαι, aor. 1, infin. act. . . . . id.

διδάξει, 3 pers. sing. fut. ind. act. . . id.

διδάξῃ, 3 pers. sing. aor. 1, subj. act. . id.

δίδαξον, 2 pers. sing. aor. 1, imper. act. . id.

διδάξωσι, 3 pers. pl. aor. 1, subj. act. . . id.

διδάσκαλε, voc. sing. . . . . διδάσκαλος

διδασκαλία, ας, ἡ, (§ 2. tab. B. b, and rem. 2) διδάσκω

διδασκαλίᾳ, dat. sing. . . . . διδασκαλία

διδασκαλίαις, dat. pl. . . . . id.

διδασκαλίαν, acc. sing. . . . . id.

διδασκαλίας, gen. sing. and acc. pl. . . id.

διδάσκαλοι, nom. pl. . . . . διδάσκαλος

διδάσκαλον, acc. sing. . . . . id.

διδάσκαλος, ου, ὁ, (§ 3. tab. C. a) . . διδάσκω

διδασκάλους, acc. pl. . . . . διδάσκαλος

διδασκάλων, gen. pl. . . . . id.

δίδασκε, 2 pers. sing. pres. imper. act. . διδάσκω

διδάσκει, 3 pers. sing. pres. ind. act. . . id.

διδάσκειν, pres. infin. act. . . . id.

διδάσκεις, 2 pers. sing. pres. ind. act. . . id.

διδάσκῃ, 3 pers. sing. pres. subj. act. . id.

διδάσκοντες, nom. pl. masc. part. pres. act. . id.

διδάσκοντι, dat. sing. masc. pt. pres. act. . id.

διδάσκοντος, gen. sing. masc. part. pres. act. . id.

διδασκόντων, gen. pl. masc. part. pres. act.— }
C. D. Ln. . . . . . }
διατριβόντων αὐτῶν καὶ διδασκόντων, } id.
(Ac. 14. 18) . . }
Rec. Gr. Sch. Tdf. omit this clause. }

---

[a] Ac. 27. 42. [b] Lu. 4. 10. [c] Lu. 9. 33.

διδάσκω, fut. διδάξω, perf. δεδίδαχα, (§ 23. rem. a. b, and rem. 6) aor. 1, ἐδίδαξα, aor. 1, pass. ἐδιδάχθην, (§ 23. rem. 2 & 4) *to teach*, Mat. 4. 23; 22. 16, et al.; *to teach or speak in a public assembly*, 1 Ti. 2. 12; *to direct, admonish*, Mat. 28. 15; Ro. 2. 21, et al.

διδακτός, ή, όν, (§ 7. tab. F. a) pr. *taught, teachable*, of things; in N.T. *taught*, of persons, Jno. 6. 45; 1 Co. 2. 13.

διδακτῐκός, ή, όν, (§ 7. tab. F. a) *apt or qualified to teach*, 1 Ti. 3. 2; 2 Ti. 2. 24. N.T.

διδάσκᾰλος, ου, ὁ, (§ 3. tab. C. a) *a teacher, master*, Ro. 2. 20, et al.; in N.T. as an equivalent to ῥαββί, Jno. 1. 39, et al.

διδασκαλία, ας, ἡ, (§ 2. tab. B. b, and rem. 2) *the act or occupation of teaching*, Ro. 12. 7; 1 Ti. 4. 13, et al.; *information, instruction*, Ro. 15. 4; 2 Ti. 3. 16; *matter taught, precept, doctrine*, Mat. 15. 9; 1 Ti. 1. 10, et al.

διδᾰχή, ῆς, ἡ, (§ 2. tab. B. a) *instruction, the giving of instruction, teaching*, Mar. 4. 2; 12. 38, et al.; *instruction, what is taught, doctrine*, Mat. 16. 12; Jno. 7. 16, 17, et al.; meton. *mode of teaching and kind of doctrine taught*, Mat. 7. 28; Mar. 1. 27.

διδάσκων, nom. sing. masc. part. pres. act. . . διδάσκω
διδαχαῖς, dat. pl. . . . . . . διδαχή
διδαχή, ῆς, ἡ, (§ 2. tab. B. a) . . διδάσκω
διδαχῇ, dat. sing. . . . . . διδαχή
διδαχήν, acc. sing. . . . . . id.
διδαχῆς, gen. sing. . . . . . . id.
διδόᾱσι, 3 pers. pl. pres. ind. act. for διδοῦσι, (§ 30. rem. 3).—Gr. Sch. Tdf. . διαδιδώσουσι, Rec. (Re. 17. 13) . } δίδωμι
διδόμενον, nom. sing. neut. part. pres. pass. id.
διδόναι, pres. infin. act. . . . . id.
διδόντα, nom. pl. neut. part. pres. act. . . id.
διδόντες, nom. pl. masc. part. pres. act. . id.
διδόντι, dat. sing. masc. part. pres. act. . id.
διδόντος, gen. sing. masc. part. pres. act. . id.
δίδοται, 3 pers. sing. pres. ind. pass. . . id.
δίδοτε, 2 pers. pl. pres. imper. act. . . id.
δίδου, 2 pers. sing. pres. imper. act. (§ 31. rem. 2) id.
διδούς, nom. sing. masc. part. pres. act. . id.
δίδραχμα, acc. pl. . . . . δίδραχμον

δίδραχμον], ου, τό, (§ 3. tab. C. c) (δίς & δραχμή) *a didrachmon, or double drachm*, a silver coin equal to the drachm of Alexandria, to two Attic drachms, to two Roman denarii, and to the half-shekel of the Jews, in value about fifteen-pence halfpenny of our money, Mat. 17. 24, bis.

δίδυμος, ου, ὁ, ἡ, (§ 7. rem. 2) . . . δύο

δίδωμι, fut. δώσω, perf. δέδωκα, aor. 1, ἔδωκα, aor. 2, ἔδων, perf. pass. δέδομαι, aor. 1, pass. ἐδόθην, *to give, bestow, present*, Mat. 4. 9; 6. 11; Jno. 3. 16; 17. 2, et al. freq.; *to give, cast, throw*, Mat. 7. 6; *to supply, suggest*, Mat. 10. 19; Mar. 13. 11; *to distribute* alms, Mat. 19. 21; Lu. 11. 41, et al.; *to pay* tribute, etc., Mat. 22. 17; Mar. 12. 14; Lu. 20. 22; *to be the author or source* of a thing, Lu. 12. 51; Ro. 11. 8, et al.; *to grant, permit, allow*, Ac. 2. 27; 13. 35; Mat. 13. 11; 19. 11, et al.; *to deliver to, intrust, commit to the charge* of any one, Mat. 25. 15; Mar. 12. 9, et al.; *to give or deliver up*, Lu. 22. 19; Jno. 6. 51, et al.; *to reveal, teach*, Ac. 7. 38; *to appoint, constitute*, Ep. 1. 22; 4. 11; *to consecrate, devote, offer in sacrifice*, 2 Co. 8. 5; Gal. 1. 4; Re. 8. 3, et al.; *to present, expose* one's self in a place, Ac. 19. 31; *to recompense*, Re. 2. 23; *to attribute, ascribe*, Jno. 9. 24; Re. 11. 13; from the Heb. *to place, put, fix, inscribe*, He. 8. 10; 10. 16, et al.; *to infix, impress*, 2 Co. 12. 7, Re. 13. 16; *to inflict*, Jno. 18. 22; 19. 3; 2 Thes. 1. 8; *to give in charge, assign*, Jno. 5. 36; 17. 4; Re. 9. 5; *to exhibit, put forth*, Mat. 24. 24; Ac. 2. 19; *to yield, bear* fruit, Mat. 13. 8; διδόναι ἐργασίαν, *to endeavour, strive*, Lu. 12. 58; διδόναι ἀπόκρισιν, *to answer, reply*, Jno. 1. 22; διδόναι τόπον, *to give place, yield*, Lu 14. 9; Ro. 12. 19.

δόμα, ατος, τό, (§ 4. tab. D. c) *a gift, present*, Mat. 7. 11, et al. L.G.

δόσις, εως, ἡ, (§ 5. tab. E. c) pr. *giving, outlay*; Phi. 4. 15; *a donation, gift*, Ja. 1. 17.

δότης, ου, ὁ, (§ 2. tab. B. c) *a giver*, 2 Co. 9. 7. LXX.

δῶρον, ου, τό, (§ 3. tab. C. c) *a gift, present*, Mat. 2. 11; Ep. 2. 8; Re. 11. 10, *an offering, sacrifice,* Mat. 5. 23, 24; 8. 4, et al.; δῶρον, sc. ἐστι, *it is consecrated to God,* Mat. 15. 5; Mar. 7. 11; *contribution* to the temple, Lu. 21. 1, 4.

δωρέομαι, οῦμαι, (§ 17. tab. Q) fut. ήσομαι, perf. δεδώρημαι, *to give freely, grant,* Mar. 15. 45; 2 Pe. 1. 3, 4.

δώρημα, ατος, τό, (§ 4. tab. D. c) *a gift, free gift,* Ro. 5. 16; Ja. 1. 17.

δωρεά, ᾶς, ἡ, (§ 2. tab. B. b, and rem. 2) *a gift, free gift, benefit,* Jno. 4. 10; Ac. 2. 38, et al.

δωρεάν, accus. of δωρεά, adv. *gratis, gratuitously, freely,* Mat. 10. 8; Ro. 3. 24, et al.; in N.T. *undeservedly, without cause,* Jno. 15. 25; *in vain,* Gal. 2. 21.

δίδωσι, 3 pers. sing. pres. ind. act. (§ 30. tab. Z) — δίδωμι

διέβησαν, 3 pers. pl. aor. 2, ind. (§ 37. rem. 1) — διαβαίνω

διέβλεψε, 3 pers. s. aor. 1, ind.—B. (Mar. 8. 25) ἐποίησεν, αὐτὸν ἀναβλέψαι, Rec. Gr. Sch. Tdf. — διαβλέπω

διεβλήθη,[a] 3 pers. sing. aor. 1, ind. pass. — διαβάλλω

διεγείρειν, pres. infin. act. — διεγείρω

διεγείρουσι, 3 pers. pl. pres. ind. act. — id.

διεγείρω, fut. διεγερῶ, aor. 1, pass. διηγέρθην, (§ 37. rem. 1) (διά & ἐγείρω) *to arouse or awake thoroughly,* Mat. 1. 24; Mar. 4. 38, 39; Lu. 8. 24; pass. *to be raised, excited, agitated,* as a sea, Jno. 6. 18; met. *to stir up, arouse, animate,* 2 Pe. 1. 13; 3. 1.

διεγερθείς, nom. sing. masc. part. aor. 1, pass. — διεγείρω

διεγνώρισαν,[b] 3 pers. pl. aor. 1, ind. act. — διαγνωρίζω

διεγόγγυζον, 3 pers. pl. imperf. — διαγογγύζω

διεδίδοτο, 3 pers. sing. imperf. (§ 30. rem. 4) — διαδίδωμι

διέδωκε, 3 pers. sing. aor. 1, ind. act. — id.

διεζώσατο, 3 pers. sing. aor. 1, ind. mid. (§ 31. tab. B.B) — διαζώννυμι

διέζωσε, 3 pers. sing. aor. 1, ind. act. — id.

διεζωσμένος, nom. sing. masc. part. perf. pass. — id.

διέθετο, 3 pers. sing. aor. 2, ind. mid. (§ 30. tab. A.A) — διατίθημι

διεῖλε, 3 pers. sing. aor. 2, ind. act. (§ 36. rem. 1) — διαιρέω

διεκρίθη, 3 pers. sing. aor. 1, ind. pass. (§ 27. rem. 3) — διακρίνω

διεκρίθητε, 2 pers. pl. aor. 1, ind. pass. — id.

διέκρινε, 3 pers. sing. aor. 1, ind. act. — id.

διεκρίνομεν, 1 pers. pl. imperf. act. — id.

διεκρίνοντο, 3 pers. pl. imperf. mid. — id.

διεκώλυε,[c] 3 pers. sing. imperf. act. — διακωλύω

διελαλεῖτο, 3 pers. sing. imperf. pass. (§ 17. tab. Q) — διαλαλέω

διελάλουν, 3 pers. pl. imperf. act. — id.

διελέγετο, 3 pers. sing. imperf. — διαλέγομαι

διελεύσεται, 3 pers. sing. fut. ind. (§ 36. rem. 1) — διέρχομαι

διελέχθη, 3 pers. sing. aor. 1, ind. (§ 23. rem. 4) — διαλέγομαι

διελέχθησαν, 3 pers. pl. aor. 1, ind. — id.

διεληλυθότα, acc. sing. masc. part. perf. 2 — διέρχομαι

διελθεῖν, aor. 2, infin. — id.

διελθόντα, acc. sing. masc. part. aor. 2 — id.

διελθόντες, nom. pl. masc. part. aor. 2 — id.

διέλθω, 1 pers. sing. aor. 2, subj. — id.

διέλθωμεν, 1 pers. pl. aor. 2, subj. — id.

διελθών, nom. sing. masc. part. aor. 2 — id.

διέλιπε,[d] 3 pers. sing. aor. 2, ind. (§ 24. rem. 9) — διαλείπω

διελογίζεσθε, 2 pers. pl. imperf. — διαλογίζομαι

διελογίζετο, 3 pers. sing. imperf. — id.

διελογίζοντο, 3 pers. pl. imperf. — id.

διελύθησαν,[e] 3 pers. pl. aor. 1, pass. (§ 14. tab. N) — διαλύω

διεμαρτυράμεθα, 1 pers. pl. aor. 1, ind. — διαμαρτύρομαι

διεμαρτύρατο, 3 pers. sing. aor. 1, (§ 37. rem. 1) — id.

διεμαρτύρετο, 3 pers. sing. imperf. — id.

διεμαρτύρω, 2 pers. sing. aor. 1, ind. — id.

διεμάχοντο,[f] 3 pers. pl. imperf. — διαμάχομαι

διέμενε, 3 pers. sing. imperf. — διαμένω

διεμέριζον, 3 pers. pl. imperf. — διαμερίζω

διεμερίσαντο, 3 pers. pl. aor. 1, ind. mid. — id.

διεμερίσθη, 3 pers. sing. aor. 1, ind. pass. — id.

διενέγκῃ, 3 pers. sing. aor. 2, subj. (§ 36. rem. 1) — διαφέρω

διενθυμέομαι, οῦμαι], (διά & ἐνθυμέομαι) *to revolve thoroughly in the mind, consider carefully,* v.r. L.G.

διενθυμουμένου, gen. sing. masc. part. pres. —Gr. Sch. Tdf. ἐνθυμουμένου, Rec. (Ac. 10. 19) — διενθυμέομαι

διεξελθοῦσα, nom. sing. fem. part. aor. 2, —A. Sch. Tdf. ἐξελθοῦσα, Rec. Gr. (Ac. 28. 3) — διεξέρχομαι

διεξέρχομαι], fut. διεξελεύσομαι, (διά & ἐξέρχομαι) *to come out through* anything, *find one's way out.* v.r.

διέξοδος], ου, ἡ, (§ 3. tab. C. b) (διά & ἔξοδος) *a passage throughout ; a line of road, a thoroughfare.*

διεξόδους,[g] acc. pl. — διέξοδος

διεπέρασε, 3 pers. sing. aor. 1, ind. act. — διαπεράω

διεπορεύετο, 3 pers. sing. imperf. — διαπορεύομαι

διεπορεύοντο, 3 pers. pl. imperf. — id.

διεπραγματεύσατο,[h] 3 pers. s. aor. 1, ind. — διαπραγματεύομαι

---

[a] Lu. 16. 1. [b] Lu. 2. 17. [c] Mat. 3. 14. [d] Lu. 7. 45. [e] Ac. 5. 36. [f] Ac. 23. 9. [g] Mat. 22. 9. [h] Lu. 19. 15.

διεπρίοντο, 3 pers. pl. imperf. pass. . . διαπρίω

διερμηνευέτω, 3 pers. sing. pres. imper. act. διερμηνεύω

διερμηνεύῃ, 3 pers. sing. pres. subj. act. . id.

διερμηνευομένη, nom. sing. fem. pt. pres. pass. id.

διερμηνεύουσι, 3 pers. pl. pres. ind. act. . id.

διερμηνευτής,[a] οῦ, ὁ . . . . id.

διερμηνεύω], fut. εύσω, (§ 13. tab. M) a late compound used as an equivalent to the simple ἑρμηνεύω, *to explain, interpret, translate,* Lu. 24. 27; Ac. 9. 36; 1 Co. 14. 5, 13, 27; *to be able to interpret,* 1 Co. 12. 30.

διερμηνευτής, οῦ, ὁ, (§ 2. tab. B. c) *an interpreter.* L.G.

διεῤῥήγνυτο, 3 pers. sing. imperf. pass. . διαῤῥήγνυμι

διέῤῥηξε, 3 pers. sing. aor. 1, ind. act. id.

διέῤῥησσε, 3 pers. sing. imperf. act.—B. } διαῤῥήσσω
διεῤῥήγνυτο, Rec. Gr. Sch. Tdf. (Lu. 5. 6) }

διέρχεσθαι, pres. infin. . . . . διέρχομαι

διέρχεται, 3 pers. sing. pres. ind. . . id.

διέρχομαι, fut. ελεύσομαι, aor. 2, διῆλθον, (§ 36. rem. 1) (διά & ἔρχομαι) *to pass through,* Mar. 10. 25; Lu. 4. 30, et al.; *to pass over, cross,* Mar. 4. 35; Lu. 8. 22; *to pass along,* Lu. 19. 4; *to proceed,* Lu. 2. 15; Ac. 9. 38, et al.; *to travel through or over a country, wander about,* Mat. 12. 43; Lu. 9. 6, et al.; *to transfix, pierce,* Lu. 2. 35; *to spread abroad, be prevalent,* as a rumour, Lu. 5. 15; met. *to extend to,* Ro. 5. 12.

διερχόμενον, acc. sing. masc. part. pres. . διέρχομαι

διερχόμενος, nom. sing. masc. part. pres. . id.

διερωτάω, ῶ], fut. ήσω, (§ 18. tab. R) (διά & ἐρωτάω) *to sift by questioning,* of persons; in N.T., of things, *to ascertain by inquiry,* Ac. 10. 17.

διερωτήσαντες,[b] nom. pl. masc. part. aor. 1 . διερωτάω

διεσάφησαν, 3 pers. pl. aor. 1, ind. act. . διασαφέω

διεσκόρπισα, 1 pers. sing. aor. 1, ind. act. διασκορπίζω

διεσκόρπισας, 2 pers. sing. aor. 1, ind. act. . id.

διεσκόρπισε, 3 pers. sing. aor. 1, ind. act. . id.

διεσκορπίσθησαν, 3 pers. pl. aor. 1, ind. pass. id.

διεσκορπισμένα, acc. pl. neut. part. perf. pass. id.

διεσπάρησαν, 3 pers. pl. aor. 1, ind. pass. (§ 27. rem. 4. a. b) . . . . διασπείρω

διεσπᾶσθαι, perf. infin. pass. . διασπάω

διεστειλάμεθα, 1 pers. pl. aor. 1, ind. mid. . διαστέλλω

διεστείλατο, 3 pers. s. aor. 1, mid. (§ 27. rem. 1. d) id.

διεστέλλετο, 3 pers. sing. imperf. mid. . διαστέλλω

διέστη, 3 pers. sing. aor. 2. ind. . . . διΐστημι

διεστραμμένα, acc. pl. neut. part. perf. pass. (§ 35. rem. 9) . . . διαστρέφω

διεστραμμένη, nom. sing. fem. part. perf. pass. id.

διεστραμμένης, gen. sing. fem. part. perf. pass. id.

διεσώθησαν, 3 pers. pl. aor. 1, pass. (§ 37. rem. 1) διασώζω

διεταράχθη,[c] 3 pers. sing. aor. 1, ind. pass. διαταράσσω

διέταξα, 1 pers. sing. aor. 1, ind. act. . . διατάσσω

διεταξάμην, 1 pers. sing. aor. 1, ind. mid. . id.

διετάξατο, 3 pers. sing. aor. 1, ind. mid. . id.

διέταξε, 3 pers. sing. aor. 1, ind. act. . id.

διετήρει, 3 pers. sing. imperf. act. . . διατηρέω

διετής], έος, οῦς, ὁ, ἡ, τό, -ές, (§ 7. tab. G. b) (δίς & ἔτος) *of two years; of the age of two years,* Mat. 2. 16.

διετία, ας, ἡ, (§ 2. tab. B. b, and rem. 2) *the space of two years,* Ac. 24. 27; 28. 30. N.T.

διετία], ας, ἡ . . . διετής

διετίαν, acc. sing. . . . διετία

διετίας, gen. sing. . . . . id.

διετοῦς,[d] gen. sing. neut. . . . . διετής

διέτριβε, 3 pers. sing. aor. 2, ind. act. . διατρίβω

διέτριβον, 3 pers. pl. aor. 2, ind. act. . . id.

διετρίψαμεν, 1 pers. pl. aor. 1, ind. act. . id.

διέτριψαν, 3 pers. pl. aor. 1, ind. act. . . id.

διεφέρετο, 3 pers. sing. imperf. pass. . διαφέρω

διεφήμισαν, 3 pers. pl. aor. 1, ind. act. . διαφημίζω

διεφημίσθη, 3 pers. sing. aor. 1, ind. pass. . id.

διεφθάρη, 3 pers. sing. aor. 2, pass. (§ 27. rem. 4. a. b) . . . . διαφθείρω

διεφθάρησαν, 3 pers. pl. aor. 2, pass.—A. Const. Tdf. . . . . } id.
διεφθάρη, Rec. Gr. Sch. (Re. 8. 9) . }

διεφθαρμένων, gen. pl. part. perf. pass. . id.

διέφθειρε, 3 pers. s. imperf. act.—Const. Tdf. } id.
ἔφθειρε, Rec. Gr. Sch. (Re. 19. 2) . }

διεχειρίσασθε, 2 pers. pl. aor. 1, ind. mid. . διαχειρίζω

διήγειραν, 3 pers. pl. aor. 1, ind. act. . . διεγείρω

διηγείρετο, 3 pers. sing. imperf. pass. . id.

διηγέομαι, οῦμαι], fut. ήσομαι, (§ 17. tab. Q) (διά & ἡγέομαι) pr. *to lead throughout; to declare thoroughly, detail, recount, relate, tell,* Mar. 5. 16; 9. 9; Lu. 8. 39; Ac. 8. 33; He. 11. 32, et al.

διήγησις, εως, ἡ, (§ 5. tab. E. c) *a narration, relation, history,* Lu. 1. 1.

---

[a] 1 Co. 14. 28. [b] Ac. 10. 17. [c] Lu. 1. 29. [d] Mat. 2. 16.

διηγήσαντο, 3 pers. pl. aor. 1, ind. . . διηγέομαι
διηγήσατο, 3 pers. sing. aor. 1, ind. . id.
διηγήσεται, 3 pers. sing. fut. ind. . . id.
διήγησιν,[a] acc. sing. . . . . διήγησις
διήγησις], εως, ἡ, (§ 5. tab. E. c) . . διηγέομαι
διηγήσωνται, 3 pers. pl. aor. 1, subj. . id.
διηγοῦ, 2 pers. sing. pres. imper. . . id.
διηγούμενον, acc. sing. masc. part. pres. . id.
διηκόνει, 3 pers. sing. imper. act. . . διακονέω
διηκονήσαμεν, 1 pers. pl. aor. 1, ind. act. . id.
διηκόνησε, 3 pers. sing. aor. 1, ind. act. . id.
διηκόνουν, 3 pers. pl. imperf. act. . . id.
διῆλθε, 3 pers. sing. aor. 2, ind. (§ 36. rem. 1) διέρχομαι
διῆλθον, 1 pers. sing. and 3 pers. pl. aor. 2, ind. id.
διηνεκές, acc. sing. neut. . . . . διηνεκής
διηνεκής], έος, οῦς, ὁ, ἡ, τό, -ές, (§ 7. tab. G. b) (διά & ἠνεκής, *extended, prolonged*) *continuous, uninterrupted*; εἰς τὸ διηνεκές, *perpetually*, He. 7. 3; 10. 1, 12, 14.
διήνοιγε, 3 pers. sing. imperf. act. (§ 37. rem. 1) διανοίγω
διηνοιγμένους, acc. pl. masc. part. perf. pass. A. B. C. Ln. Tdf. . . . } id.
ἀνεῳγμένους, Rec. Gr. Sch. (Ac. 7. 56)
διήνοιξε, 3 pers. sing. aor. 1, ind. act. . . id.
διηνοίχθησαν, 3 pers. pl. aor. 1, ind. pass. . id.
διηπόρει, 3 pers. sing. imperf. . . . διαπορέω
διηπόρουν, 3 pers. pl. imperf. . . id.
διηποροῦντο, 3 pers. pl. imperf. mid.—B. Tdf. } id.
διηπόρουν, Rec. Gr. Sch. (Ac. 2. 12)
διηρμήνευε, 3 pers. sing. imperf. act. . . διερμηνεύω
διηρμήνευσε, 3 pers. sing. aor. 1, ind. act.—B. } id.
διηρμήνευε, Rec. Gr. Sch. . . .
διερμήνευσε, Tdf. (Lu. 24. 27)
διήρχετο, 3 pers. sing. imperf. . . . διέρχομαι
διήρχοντο, 3 pers. pl. imperf. . . id.
διθάλασσον,[b] acc. sing. masc. . . . διθάλασσος
διθάλασσος], ου, ὁ, ἡ, (§ 7. rem. 2) (δίς & θάλασσα) *washed on both sides by the sea*; τόπος διθάλασσος, *a shoal or sand-bank formed by the confluence of opposite currents*. L.G.
διϊκνέομαι, οῦμαι], fut. ίξομαι, (§ 36. rem. 2) (διά & ἱκνέομαι) *to go or pass through*; *to penetrate*.
διϊκνούμενος,[c] nom. sing. masc. part. pres. . διϊκνέομαι
διΐστημι], fut. διαστήσω, (§ 29. tab. X) (διά & ἵστημι) *to set at an interval, apart*; *to station at an interval* from a former position, Ac. 27. 28; intrans. aor. 2, διέστην, *to stand apart*; *to depart, be parted*, Lu. 24. 51; of time, *to intervene, be interposed*, Lu. 22. 59.

διάστημα, ατος, τό, (§ 4. tab. D. c) *interval, space, distance*, Ac. 5. 7.

διϊσχυρίζετο, 3 pers. sing. imperf. . διϊσχυρίζομαι
διϊσχυρίζομαι], fut. ίσομαι, (διά & ἰσχυρίζομαι, from ἰσχυρός) *to feel or express reliance*; *to affirm confidently, asseverate*, Lu. 22. 59; Ac. 12. 15.
δικαία, nom. sing. fem. . . δίκαιος
δίκαια, nom. pl. neut. . . . id.
δίκαιαι, nom. pl. fem. . . id.
δικαίαν, acc. sing. fem. . . id.
δικαίας, gen. sing. fem. . . id.
δίκαιε, voc. sing. masc. . . id.
δίκαιοι, nom. pl. masc. . . id.
δικαιοῖ, 3 pers. sing. pres. ind. act. . δικαιόω
δικαίοις, dat. pl. masc. . . . . δίκαιος
δικαιοκρισία], ας, ἡ, (§ 2. tab. B. b, and rem. 2) (δίκαιος & κρίσις) *just or righteous judgment*. LXX.
δικαιοκρισίας,[d] gen. sing. . . . δικαιοκρισία
δίκαιον, acc. sing. masc. . . . δίκαιος
δίκαιον, nom. and acc. sing. neut. . . id.
δίκαιος, αία, αιον, (§ 7. rem. 1) . . δίκη
δικαιοσύνη, ης, ἡ, (§ 2. tab. B. a) . id.
δικαιοσύνῃ, dat. sing. . . . δικαιοσύνη
δικαιοσύνην, acc. sing. . . . id.
δικαιοσύνης, gen. sing. . . id.
δικαίου, gen. sing. masc. . . . . δίκαιος
δικαιούμενοι, nom. pl. masc. part. pres. pass. δικαιόω
δικαιοῦν, pres. infin. act. . . . id.
δικαιοῦντα, acc. sing. masc. part. pres. act. . id.
δικαιοῦντες, nom. pl. masc. part. pres. act. . id.
δικαίους, acc. pl. masc. . . . . δίκαιος
δικαιοῦσθαι, pres. infin. pass. (§ 21. tab. U) δικαιόω
δικαιοῦσθε, 2 pers. pl. pres. ind. pass. . id.
δικαιοῦται, 3 pers. sing. pres. ind. pass. . id.
δικαιόω, ῶ], fut. ώσω, (§ 20. tab. T) . δίκη
δικαίῳ, dat. sing. masc. . . . . δίκαιος
δικαιωθέντες, nom. pl. masc. part. aor. 1, pass. δικαιόω
δικαιωθῆναι, aor. 1, infin. pass. . . id.
δικαιωθῇς, 2 pers. sing. aor. 1, subj. pass. . id.
δικαιωθήσεται, 3 pers. sing. fut. 1, ind. pass. id.
δικαιωθήσῃ, 2 pers. sing. fut. 1, ind. pass. . id.
δικαιωθήσονται, 3 pers. pl. fut. 1, ind. pass. id.

[a] Lu. 1. 1. [b] Ac. 27. 41. [c] He. 4. 12. [d] Ro. 2. 5.

δικαιωθήτω, 3 pers. sing. aor. 1, imper. pass. . δικαιόω
δικαιωθῶμεν, 1 pers. pl. aor. 1, subj. pass. . id.
δικαίωμα, ατος, τό, (§ 4. tab. D. c) . δίκη
δικαιώμασι, dat. pl. . . . . δικαίωμα
δικαιώματα, nom. and acc. pl. . . id.
δικαιώματος, gen. sing. . . . . id.
δικαιῶν, nom. sing. masc. part. pres. act. . δικαιόω
δικαίων, gen. pl. . . . . . δίκαιος
δικαίως, adv. . . . . . . δίκη
δικαιῶσαι, aor. 1, infin. act.—B. C. D. Ln. Tdf. δικαιοῦν, Rec. Gr. Sch. (Lu. 10. 29) } δικαιόω
δικαιώσει, 3 pers. sing. fut. ind. act. . . id.
δικαίωσιν, acc. sing. . . . . δικαίωσις
δικαίωσις], εως, ἡ, (§ 5. tab. E. c) . . δίκη
δικαστήν, acc. sing. . . . δικαστής
δικαστής], οῦ, ὁ, (§ 2. tab. B. c) . . δίκη

δίκη, ης, ἡ, (§ 2. tab. B. a) *right, justice;* in N.T. *judicial punishment, vengeance,* 2 Thes. 1. 9; Jude 7; *sentence of punishment, judgment,* Ac. 25. 15; personified, *the goddess of justice or vengeance, Nemesis, Pœna,* Ac. 28. 4.

δίκαιος, αία, αιον, (§ 7. rem. 1) used of things, *just, equitable, fair,* Mat. 20. 4; Lu. 12. 57; Jno. 5. 30, Col. 4. 1, et al.; of persons, *just, righteous,* absolutely, Jno. 17. 25; Ro. 3. 10, 26; 2 Ti. 4. 8; 1 Pe. 3. 18; 1 Jno. 1. 9; 2. 1, 29; Re. 16. 5; *righteous* by account and acceptance, Ro. 2. 13; 5. 19, et al.; in ordinary usage, *just, upright, innocent, pious,* Mat. 5. 45; 9. 13, et al. freq.; ὁ δίκαιος, *the Just One,* one of the distinctive titles of the Messiah, Ac. 3. 14; 7. 52; 22. 14.

δικαίως, adv. *justly, with strict justice,* 1 Pe. 2. 23; *deservedly,* Lu. 23. 41; *as it is right, fit or proper,* 1 Co. 15. 34; *uprightly, honestly, piously, religiously,* 1 Thes. 2. 10; Tit. 2. 12.

δικαιοσύνη, ης, ἡ, (§ 2. tab. B. a) *fair and equitable dealing, justice,* Ac. 17. 31; He. 11. 33; Ro. 9. 28; *rectitude, virtue,* Lu. 1. 75; Ep. 5. 9; in N.T. *generosity, alms,* 2 Co. 9. 10, v.r.; Mat. 6. 1; *piety, godliness,* Ro. 6. 13, et al.; *investiture with the attribute of righteousness, acceptance as righteous, justification,* Ro. 4. 11; 10. 4, et al. freq.; *a provision or means for justification,* Ro. 1. 17; 2 Co. 3. 9, et al.; *an instance of justification,* 2 Co. 5. 21. (ῡ).

δικαιόω, ῶ, fut. ώσομαι & ώσω, aor. 1, ἐδικαίωσα, perf. pass. δεδικαίωμαι, aor. 1, pass. ἐδικαιώθην, (§ 20. tab. T; § 21 tab. U) pr. *to make or render right or just;* mid. *to act with justice,* Re. 22. 11; *to avouch to be good and true, to vindicate,* Mat. 11. 19; Lu. 7. 29, et al.; *to set forth as good and just,* Lu. 10. 29; 16. 15; in N.T. *to hold as guiltless, to accept as righteous, to justify,* Ro. 3. 26, 30; 4. 5; 8. 30, 33, et al.; pass. *to be held acquitted, to be cleared,* Ac. 13. 39; Ro. 3. 24; 6. 7; *to be approved, to stand approved, to stand accepted,* Ro. 2. 13; 3. 20, 28, et al.

δικαίωμα, ατος, τό, (§ 4. tab. D. c) pr. *a rightful act, act of justice, equity; a sentence,* of condemnation, Re. 15. 4; in N.T., of acquittal, *justification,* Ro. 5. 16; *a decree, law, ordinance,* Lu. 1. 6; Ro. 1. 32; 2. 26; 8. 4; He. 9. 1, 10; *a meritorious act, an instance of perfect righteousness,* Ro. 5. 18; *state of righteousness,* Re. 19. 8.

δικαίωσις, εως, ἡ, (§ 5. tab. E. c) pr. *a making right or just; a declaration of right or justice; a judicial sentence;* in N.T., *acquittal, acceptance, justification,* Ro. 4. 25; 5. 18.

δικαστής, οῦ, ὁ, (§ 2. tab. B. c) δικάζω, *to judge*) *a judge,* Lu. 12. 14; Ac. 7. 27, 35.

δίκην, acc. sing. . . . . . δίκη
δίκτυα, acc. pl. . . . . . δίκτυον

δίκτυον, ου, τό, (§ 3. tab. C. c) *a net, fishing-net,* Mat. 4. 20, 21, et al.

δίλογος], ου, ὁ, ἡ, (§ 7. rem. 2) (δίς & λόγος) pr. *saying the same thing twice;* in N.T. *double-tongued, speaking one thing and meaning another, deceitful in words.* N.T.

διλόγους,[a] acc. pl. masc. . . . δίλογος
διό, (i.e. δι' ὅ) *on which account, wherefore, therefore,* Mat. 27. 8; 1 Co. 12. 3, et al.
διοδεύσαντες, nom. pl. masc. part. aor. 1 . διοδεύω

[a] 1 Ti. 3. 8.

διοδεύω], fut. εύσω, (§ 13. tab. M) (διά & ὁδεύω) *to travel through* a place, *traverse*, Lu. 8. 1; Ac. 17. 1. L.G.

Διονύσιος,[a] ου, ὁ, *Dionysius*, pr. name.

διόπερ, conj. strengthened from διό, *on this very account, for this very reason, wherefore*, 1 Co. 8. 13; 10. 14; 14. 13.

Διοπετής], έος, οῦς, ὁ, ἡ, τό, -ές, (§ 7. tab. G. b) (Ζεύς, Διός, & πίπτω) *which fell from Jupiter, or heaven*; τοῦ Διοπετοῦς, sc. ἀγάλματος, Ac. 19. 35.

Διοπετοῦς,[b] gen. sing. . . . . Διοπετής

διόρθωμα], ατος, τό, (§ 4. tab. D. c) (διορθόω, *to correct*, from διά & ὀρθόω, *to make straight*, from ὀρθός) *correction, emendation, reformation*, v.r.

διορθωμάτων,[c] gen. pl.—A. B. Ln. Tdf. . } διόρθωμα
κατορθωμάτων, Rec. Gr. Sch. (Ac. 24. 3) }

διορθώσεως,[d] gen. sing. . . . διόρθωσις

διόρθωσις], εως, ἡ, (§ 5. tab. E. c) (διορθόω, *to correct*) *a complete rectification, reformation.*

διορυγῆναι, aor. 2, infin. pass. (§ 26. rem. 3) . διορύσσω

διορύσσουσι, 3 pers. pl. pres. ind. act. . id.

διορύσσω], fut. ξω, (διά & ὀρύσσω) *to dig or break through*, Mat. 6. 19, 20; 24. 43; Lu. 12. 39.

Διός, gen. sing. (§ 6. rem. 4. a) . . Ζεύς

Διόσκουροι, or Διόσκοροι], ων, οἱ, (§ 3. tab. C. a) (Ζεύς, Διός, & κοῦρος, *a youth*) *the Dioscuri, Castor and Pollux*, sons of Jupiter by Leda, and patrons of sailors.

Διοσκούροις,[e] dat. pl. . . . . Διόσκουροι

διότι, conj. (διά, ὅτι) *on the account that, because*, Lu. 2. 7; 21. 28; *in as much as*, Lu. 1. 13; Ac. 18. 10, et al.

Διοτρεφής,[f] έος, οῦς, ὁ, (§ 5. tab. E. a) *Diotrephes*, pr. name.

διπλᾶ, acc. pl. neut. . . . . διπλόος

διπλῆς, gen. sing. fem. . . . id.

διπλόος, οῦς], όη, ῆ, όον, οῦν, (§ 7. rem. 5. b) *double*, Mat. 23. 15; 1 Ti. 5. 17; Re. 18. 6.

διπλόω, ῶ, fut. ώσω, aor. 1, ἐδίπλωσα, (§ 20. tab. T) *to double; to render back double*, Re. 18. 6.

διπλότερον, acc. sing. masc. comp. (§ 8. rem. 4) διπλόος

διπλοῦν, acc. sing. neut. . . . . id.

διπλόω, ῶ], fut. ώσω, (§ 20. tab. T) . id.

διπλώσατε,[g] 2 pers. pl. aor. 1, imper. . . διπλόω

δίς, adv. . . . . . . δύο

διστάζω], fut. άσω, (§ 26. rem. 1) . . id.

δίστομον, acc. sing. fem. . . . δίστομος

δίστομος, ου, ὁ, ἡ, (§ 7. rem. 2) (δίς & στόμα) pr. *having two mouths; two-edged*, He. 4. 12; Re. 1. 16; 2. 12.

δισχίλιοι,[h] αι, α, (δίς & χίλιοι) *two thousand*. (ῐ).

διυλίζοντες,[i] nom. pl. masc. part. pres. . . διυλίζω

διυλίζω], fut. ίσω, (§ 26. rem. 1) (διά & ὑλίζω, *to strain, filter*) *to strain, filter thoroughly; to strain out or off.*

διχάσαι,[k] aor. 1, infin. act. . . . διχάζω

διχάζω], fut. άσω, (§ 26. rem. 1) (δίχα, *apart*) *to cut asunder, disunite*; met. *to cause to disagree, set at variance.*

διχοστασία], ας, ἡ, (§ 2. tab. B. b, and rem. 2 (δίχα & στάσις) *a standing apart; a division, dissension*, Ro. 16. 17; 1 Co. 3. 3; Gal. 5. 20.

διχοστασίαι, nom. pl. . . . . διχοστασία

διχοστασίας, acc. pl. . . . . . id.

διχοτομέω, ῶ], fut. ήσω, (§ 16. tab. P) (δίχα & τέμνω) pr. *to cut into two parts, cut asunder*; in N.T. *to inflict a punishment of extreme severity*, Mat. 24. 51; Lu. 12. 46.

διχοτομήσει, 3 pers. sing. fut. ind. act. . διχοτομέω

διψᾷ, 3 pers. sing. pres. subj. . . . διψάω

διψάω, ῶ, fut. ήσω, (§ 18. tab. R) aor. 1, ἐδίψησα, (δίψα, *thirst*) *to thirst, be thirsty*, Mat. 25. 35, 37, 42, 44, et al.; met. *to thirst after* in spirit, *to desire or long for ardently*, Mat. 5. 6; Jno. 4. 14; 6. 35, et al.

δίψει,[l] dat. sing. . . . . . δίψος

διψήσει, 3 pers. sing. fut. ind. . . διψάω

διψήσῃ, 3 pers. sing. aor. 1, subj. . . id.

διψήσουσι, 3 pers. pl. fut. ind. . . id.

δίψος], εος, τό, (§ 5. tab. E. b) *thirst.*

δίψυχοι, nom. pl. masc. . . . . δίψυχος

δίψῡχος, ου, ὁ, ἡ, (§ 7. rem. 2) (δίς & ψυχή) *double-minded, inconstant, fickle*, Ja. 1. 8; 4. 8. L.G.

διψῶ, 1 pers. sing. pres. ind. contr. . διψάω

διψῶ, 1 pers. sing. pres. subj. . . . id.

διψῶμεν, 1 pers. pl. pres. subj. . . id.

διψῶν, nom. sing. masc. part. pres. . . id.

[a] Ac. 17. 34. [b] Ac. 19. 35. [c] Ac. 24. 3. [d] He. 9. 10. [e] Ac. 28. 11. [f] 3 Jno. 9. [g] Re. 18. 6. [h] Mar. 5. 13. [i] Mat. 23. 24. [k] Mat. 10. 35. [l] 2 Co. 11. 27.

διψῶντα, acc. sing. masc. part. pres. . διψάω
διψῶντες, nom. pl. masc. part. pres. . . id.
διψῶντι, dat. sing. masc. part. pres. . . id.
διωγμοῖς, dat. pl. . . . . . διωγμός
διωγμόν, acc. sing. . . . . . id.
διωγμός, οῦ, ὁ, (§ 3. tab. C. a) . . . διώκω
διωγμοῦ, gen. sing. . . . διωγμός
διωγμούς, acc. pl. . . . . . id.
διωγμῶν, gen. pl. . . . . id.
διώδευε, 3 pers. sing. imperf. . . . διοδεύω
δίωκε, 2 pers. sing. pres. imper. act. . . διώκω
διώκεις, 2 pers. sing. pres. ind. act. . . id.
διώκετε, 2 pers. pl. pres. imper. act. . . id.
διώκομαι, 1 pers. sing. pres. ind. pass. . . id.
διωκόμενοι, nom. pl. masc. part. pres. pass. id.
διώκοντα, nom. pl. neut. part. pres. act. . id.
διώκοντας, acc. pl. masc. part. pres. act. . id.
διώκοντες, nom. pl. masc. part. pres. act. . id.
διωκόντων, gen. pl. masc. part. pres. act. . id.
διώκτην,[a] acc. sing. . . . . διώκτης
διώκτης], ου, ὁ, (§ 2. tab. B. c) . . . διώκω

διώκω, fut. ώξω, aor. 1, ἐδίωξα, (§ 23. rem. 1. b, and rem. 2) perf. pass. δεδίωγμαι, aor. 1, pass. ἐδιώχθην, (§ 23. rem. 7 & 4) *to put in rapid motion; to pursue; to follow, pursue the direction of*, Lu. 17. 23; *to follow eagerly, endeavour earnestly to acquire*, Ro. 9. 30, 31; 12. 13, et al.; *to press forwards*, Phi. 3. 12, 14; *to pursue* with malignity, *persecute*, Mat. 5. 10, 11, 12, 44, et al.

διωγμός, οῦ, ὁ, (§ 3. tab. C. a) pr. *chase, pursuit; persecution*, Mat. 13. 21, Mar. 4. 17; 10. 30, et al.

διώκτης, ου, ὁ, (§ 2. tab. B. c) *a persecutor*, 1 Ti. 1. 13. L.G.

διώκωμεν, 1 pers. pl. pres. subj. act. . . διώκω
διώκων, nom. sing. masc. part. pres. act. . . id.
διώκωνται, 3 pers. pl. pres. subj. pass. . id.
διώκωσι, 3 pers. pl. pres. subj. act. . . id.
διωξάτω, 3 pers. sing. aor. 1, imper. act. . id.
διώξετε, 2 pers. pl. fut. ind. act. . . . id.
διώξητε, 2 pers. pl. aor. 1, subj. act. . . id.
διώξουσι, 3 pers. pl. fut. ind. act. . . id.
διωχθήσονται, 3 pers. pl. fut. 1, ind. pass. . id.
δόγμα, ατος, τό, (§ 4. tab. D. c) . . . δοκέω
δόγμασι, dat. pl. . . . . . . δόγμα

δόγματα, acc. pl. . . . . . . δόγμα
δογμάτων, gen. pl. . . . . . id.
δογματίζεσθε,[b] 2 pers. pl. pres. ind. mid. . δογματίζω
δογματίζω], fut. ίσω, (§ 26. rem. 1) . δοκέω
δοθείη, 3 pers. sing. aor. 1, opt. pass. (§ 30. rem. 4) δίδωμι
δοθεῖσα, nom. sing. fem. part. aor. 1, pass. . id.
δοθεῖσαν, acc. sing. fem. part. aor. 1, pass. . id.
δοθείσῃ, dat. sing. fem. part. aor. 1, pass. . id.
δοθείσης, gen. sing. fem. part. aor. 1, pass. . id.
δοθέντος, gen. sing. neut. part. aor. 1, pass. . id.
δοθῇ, 3 pers. sing. aor. 1, subj. pass. . . id.
δοθῆναι, aor. 1, infin. pass. (§ 30. rem. 4) . id.
δοθήσεται, 3 pers. sing. fut. 1, ind. pass. . id.
δοῖ, 3 pers. sing. aor. 2, subj. (for δῷ, § 30. rem. 5).—B. . . . . } id.
δώσει, Rec. Gr. Sch. Tdf. (Mar. 8. 37) }
δοκεῖ, 3 pers. sing. pres. ind. (§ 37. rem. 2) δοκέω
δοκεῖν, pres. infin. . . . . . . id.
δοκεῖς, 2 pers. sing. pres. ind. . . id.
δοκεῖτε, 2 pers. pl. pres. ind. . . . id.
δοκεῖτε, 2 pers. pl. pres. imper. . . id.

δοκέω, ῶ], fut. δόξω, aor. 1, ἔδοξα, (§ 37. rem. 2) *to think, imagine, suppose, presume*, Mat. 3. 9; 6. 7, et al.; *to seem, appear*, Lu. 10. 36; Ac. 17. 18, et al.; impers. δοκεῖ, *it seems; it seems good, best, or right, it pleases*, Lu. 1. 3; Ac. 15. 22, 25, et al.

δόγμα, ατος, τό, (§ 4. tab. D. c) *a decree, statute, ordinance*, Lu. 2. 1; Ac. 16. 4; 17. 7; Ep. 2. 15; Col. 2. 14.

δογματίζω, fut. ίσω, (§ 26. rem. 1) *to decree, prescribe an ordinance*; mid. *to suffer laws to be imposed on one's self, to submit to, bind one's self by, ordinances*, Col. 2. 20. L.G.

δόξα, ης, ἡ, (§ 2. rem. 3) pr. *a seeming; appearance; a notion, imagination, opinion; the opinion which obtains respecting one; reputation, credit, honour, glory*; in N.T. *honourable consideration*, Lu. 14. 10; *praise, glorification, honour*, Jno. 5. 41, 44; Ro. 4. 20; 15. 7, et al.; *dignity, majesty*, Ro. 1. 23; 2 Co. 3. 7, et al.; *a glorious manifestation, glorious working*, Jno. 11. 40; 2 Pe. 1. 3, et al.; pl. *dignitaries*, 2 Pe. 2. 10; Jude 8; *glorification* in a future state of bliss, 2 Co. 4. 17; 2 Ti.

[a] 1 Ti. 1. 13. [b] Col. 2. 20.

2. 10, et al.; *pride, ornament*, 1 Co. 11. 15; 1 Thes. 2. 20; *splendid array, pomp, magnificence*, Mat. 6. 29; 19. 28, et al.; *radiance, dazzling lustre*, Lu. 2. 9; Ac. 22. 11, et al.

δοξάζω, fut. άσω, (§ 26. rem. 1) aor. 1, ἐδόξασα, perf. pass. δεδόξασμαι, aor. 1, pass. ἐδοξάσθην, according to the various significations of δόξα, *to think, suppose, judge*; *to extol, magnify*, Mat. 6. 2; Lu. 4. 15, et al.; in N.T. *to adore, worship*, Ro. 1. 21, et al.; *to invest with dignity, or majesty*, 2 Co. 3. 10; He. 5. 5, et al.; *to signalise with a manifestation of dignity, excellence, or majesty*, Jno. 12. 28; 13. 32, et al.; *to glorify* by admission to a state of bliss, *to beatify*, Ro. 8. 30, et al.

δοκῇ, 3 pers. sing. pres. subj. . . . δοκέω

δοκιμάζει, 3 pers. sing. pres. ind. act. . δοκιμάζω

δοκιμάζειν, pres. infin. act. . . . id.

δοκιμάζεις, 2 pers. sing. pres. ind. act. . id.

δοκιμαζέσθωσαν, 3 pers. pl. pres. imper. pass. id.

δοκιμάζετε, 2 pers. pl. pres. ind. act. . . id.

δοκιμάζετε, 2 pers. pl. pres. imper. act. . id.

δοκιμαζέτω, 3 pers. sing. pres. imper. act. . id.

δοκιμαζομένου, gen. sing. neut. part. pres. pass. id.

δοκιμάζοντες, nom. pl. masc. part. pres. act. id.

δοκιμάζοντι, dat. sing. masc. part. pres. act. id.

δοκιμάζω], fut. άσω, (§ 26. rem. 1) . . δόκιμος

δοκιμάζων, nom. sing. masc. part. pres. act. δοκιμάζω

δοκιμάσαι, aor. 1, infin. act. . . . id.

δοκιμάσει, 3 pers. sing. fut. ind. act. . . id.

δοκιμάσητε, 2 pers. pl. aor. 1, subj. act. . id.

δοκιμασία], ας, ἡ, (§ 2. tab. B. b, and rem. 2) v.r. δόκιμος

δοκιμασίᾳ, dat. sing.—Al. Ln. Tdf. ἐνδοκιμασίᾳ. ἐδοκίμασάν με, Rec. Gr. Sch. (He. 3. 9)

δοκιμή, ῆς, ἡ, (§ 2. tab. B. a) . . . δόκιμος

δοκιμῇ, dat. sing. . . . . . δοκιμή

δοκιμήν, acc. sing. . . . . . id.

δοκιμῆς, gen. sing. . . . . . id.

δοκίμιον, ου, τό, (§ 3. tab. C. c) . . δόκιμος

δόκιμοι, nom. pl. masc. . . . . id.

δόκιμον, acc. sing. masc. . . . . id.

δόκῐμος, ου, ὁ, ἡ, (§ 7. rem. 2) *proved, tried*; *approved* after examination and trial, Ro. 16. 10; Ja. 1. 12, et al.; by impl. *acceptable*, Ro. 14. 18.

δοκιμάζω, fut. άσω, (§ 26. rem. 1) aor. 1, ἐδοκίμασα, perf. pass. δεδοκίμασμαι, *to prove* by trial; *to test, assay* metals, 1 Pe. 1. 7; *to prove, try, examine, scrutinise*, Lu. 14. 19; Ro. 12. 2, et al.; *to put to the proof, tempt*, He. 3. 9; *to approve* after trial, *judge worthy, choose*, Ro. 14. 22; 1 Co. 16. 3; 2 Co. 8. 22, et al.; *to decide upon* after examination, *judge of, distinguish, discern*, Lu. 12. 56; Ro. 2. 18, Phi. 1. 10.

δοκιμασία, ας, ἡ, (§ 2. tab. B. b, and rem. 2) *proof, probation*, v.r. He. 3. 9.

δοκίμιον, ου, τό, (§ 3. tab. C. c) *that by means of which anything is tried, proof, criterion, test*; *trial, the act of trying or putting to proof*, Ja. 1. 3; *approved character*, 1 Pe. 1. 7.

δοκῐμή, ῆς, ἡ, (§ 2. tab. B. a) *trial, proof by trial*, 2 Co. 8. 2; *the state or disposition of that which has been tried and approved, approved character or temper*, Ro. 5. 4; 2 Co. 2. 9, et al.; *proof, document, evidence*, 2 Co. 13. 3. L.G.

δοκόν, acc. sing. . . . . . . δοκός

δοκός, οῦ, ἡ & ὁ, (§ 3. tab. C. a. b) *a beam or spar* of timber, Mat. 7. 3, 4, 5; Lu. 6. 41, 42.

δοκοῦμεν, 1 pers. pl. pres. ind. . . δοκέω

δοκοῦν, acc. sing. neut. part. pres. . . id.

δοκοῦντα, nom. pl. neut. part. pres. . . id.

δοκοῦντες, nom. pl. masc. part. pres. . . id.

δοκούντων, gen. pl. masc. part. pres. . id.

δοκοῦσα, nom. sing. fem. part. pres. . . id.

δοκοῦσι, 3 pers. pl. pres. ind. . . . id.

δοκοῦσι, dat. pl. masc. part. pres. . . id.

δοκῶ, 1 pers. sing. pres. ind. contr. . . id.

δοκῶν, nom. sing. masc. part. pres. . . id.

δόλιοι,[a] nom. pl. masc. . . . . δόλιος

δόλιος], ία, ιον, (§ 7. rem. 1) . . . δόλος

δολιόω, ῶ], fut. ώσω, (§ 20. tab. T) . . id.

δολοῖ, 3 pers. sing. pres. ind. act.—D. ζυμοῖ, Rec. Gr. Sch. Tdf. (1 Co. 5. 6) } δολιόω

δόλον, acc. sing. . . . . . δόλος

δόλος, ου, ὁ, (§ 3. tab. C. a) pr. *a bait or contrivance for entrapping*; *fraud, deceit, insidious artifice, guile*, Mat. 26. 4; Mar. 7. 22; 14. 1, et al.

δόλιος, ία, ιον, (§ 7. rem. 1) and ος,

[a] 2 Co. 11. 13.

ον, (§ 7. rem. 2) *fraudulent, deceitful,* 2 Co. 11. 13.

δολιόω, ῶ, fut. ώσω, (§ 20. tab. T) *to deceive, use fraud or deceit,* Ro. 3. 13. LXX.

δολόω, ῶ, fut. ώσω, (§ 20. tab. T) pr. *to entrap, beguile; to adulterate, corrupt, falsify,* 2 Co. 4. 2.

δόλου, gen. sing. . . . δόλος
δολοῦντες,[a] nom. pl. masc. part. pres. act. . δολόω
δολόω, ῶ], fut. ώσω, (§ 20. tab. T) . . δόλος
δόλῳ, dat. sing. . . . . . . id.
δόμα, ατος, τό, (§ 4. tab. D. c) . . . δίδωμι
δόματα, acc. pl. . . . . . . δόμα
δόντα, acc. sing. masc. part. aor. 2, (§ 30. tab. Z) δίδωμι
δόντι, dat. sing. masc. part. aor. 2.—D. . } id.
διδόντι, Rec. Gr. Sch. Tdf. (1 Co. 15. 57) }
δόντος, gen. sing. masc. part. aor. 2, act. . id.
δόξα, ης, ἡ, (§ 2. rem. 3) . . . . δοκέω
δοξάζειν, pres. infin. act. . . . δοξάζω
δοξάζεται, 3 pers. sing. pres. ind. pass. . . id.
δοξαζέτω, 3 pers. sing. pres. imper. act. . id.
δοξάζηται, 3 pers. sing. pres. subj. pass. . id.
δοξάζητε, 2 pers. pl. pres. subj. act. . . id.
δοξαζόμενος, nom. sing. masc. part. pres. pass. id.
δοξάζοντες, nom. pl. masc. part. pres. act. . id.
δοξάζω, fut. άσω, (§ 26. rem. 1) . . δοκέω
δοξάζων, nom. sing. masc. part. pres. act. . δοξάζω
δόξαν, acc. sing. . . . . . δόξα
δόξαντες, nom. pl. masc. part. aor. 1 . . δοκέω
δόξας, acc. pl. . . . . . . δόξα
δοξάσαι, aor. 1, infin. act. . . . . δοξάζω
δοξάσατε, 2 pers. pl. aor. 1, imper. act. . id.
δοξάσει, 3 pers. sing. fut. ind. act. . . id.
δοξάσῃ, 3 pers. sing. aor. 1, subj. act. . id.
δοξασθῇ, 3 pers. sing. aor. 1, subj. pass. . id.
δοξασθῶσι, 3 pers. pl. aor. 1, subj. pass. . id.
δόξασον, 2 pers. sing. aor. 1, imper. act. . id.
δοξάσω, 1 pers. sing. fut. ind. act. . . id.
δοξάσωσι, 3 pers. pl. aor. 1, subj. act. . . id.
δόξῃ, 3 pers. sing. aor. 1, subj. . . δοκέω
δόξῃ, dat. sing. . . . . . . δόξα
δόξης, gen. sing. . . . . . . id.
δόξητε, 2 pers. pl. aor. 1, subj. . . . δοκέω
δόξω, 1 pers. sing. aor. 1, subj. . id.
Δορκάς, άδος, ἡ, (§ 4. rem. 2. c) *Dorcas,* pr. name, signifying *a gazelle or antelope,* Ac. 9. 36, 39.
δός, 2 pers. sing. aor. 2, imper. act. (§ 30. rem. 1) δίδωμι

δόσεως, gen. sing. . . . . . δόσις
δόσις, εως, ἡ, (§ 5. tab. E. c) . . δίδωμι
δότε, 2 pers. pl. aor. 2, imper. act. . . id.
δότην,[b] acc. sing. . . . . . δότης
δότης], ου, ὁ, (§ 2. tab. B. c) . . . δίδωμι
δότω, 3 pers. sing. aor. 2, imper. act. . id.
δοῦλα, acc. pl. neut. . . . . . δοῦλος
δουλαγωγέω,[c] ῶ, fut. ήσω, (§ 16. tab. P) (δοῦλος & ἄγω) pr. *to bring into slavery; to treat as a slave; to discipline into subjection.* L.G.
δούλας, acc. pl. fem. . . . . . δοῦλος
δοῦλε, voc. sing. masc. . . . . id.
δουλεία], ας, ἡ, (§ 2. tab. B. b, and rem. 2) id.
δουλείαν, acc. sing. . . . . . δουλεία
δουλείας, gen. sing. . . . . . id.
δουλεύει, 3 pers. sing. pres. ind. . . δουλεύω
δουλεύειν, pres. infin. . . . id.
δουλεύετε, 2 pers. pl. pres. ind. . . id.
δουλεύετε, 2 pers. pl. pres. imper. . . id.
δουλευέτωσαν, 3 pers. pl. pres. imper. . id.
δουλεύοντες, nom. pl. masc. part. pres. . . id.
δουλεύουσι. 3 pers. pl. pres. ind. . . id.
δουλεύσει, 3 pers. sing. fut. ind. . . id.
δουλεύσωσι. 3 pers. pl. aor. 1, subj. . . id.
δουλεύω, fut. εύσω, (§ 13. tab. M) . . δοῦλος
δουλεύων, nom. sing. masc. part. pres. . δουλεύω
δούλη, nom. sing. fem. . . . . δοῦλος
δούλης, gen. sing. fem. . . . . id.
δοῦλοι, nom. pl. masc. . . . . id.
δούλοις, dat. pl. masc. . . . . id.
δοῦλον, acc. sing. masc. . . . . id.

δοῦλος, η, ον, adj. *enslaved, enthralled, subservient,* Ro. 6. 19; as a subst. δοῦλος, *a male slave, or servant,* of various degrees, Mat. 8. 9, et al. freq.; *a servitor, person of mean condition,* Phi. 2. 7; fem. δούλη, *a female slave; a handmaiden,* Lu. 1. 38, 48; Ac. 2. 18; δοῦλος, used figuratively, in a bad sense, *one involved in* moral or spiritual *thraldom,* Jno. 8. 34; Ro. 6. 17, 20; 1 Co. 7. 23; 2 Pe. 2. 19; in a good sense, *a* devoted *servant or minister,* Ac. 16. 17; Ro. 1. 1, et al.; *one pledged or bound to serve,* 1 Co. 7. 22; 2 Co. 4. 5.

δουλεία, ας, ἡ, (§ 2. tab. B. b, and rem. 2) *slavery, bondage, servile condition;* in N.T. met. with reference to degrada-

[a] 2 Co. 4. 2. [b] 2 Co. 9. 7. [c] 1 Co. 9. 27.

tion and unhappiness, *thraldom* spiritual or moral, Ro. 8. 15, 21; Gal. 4. 24; 5. 1; He. 2. 15.

δουλεύω, fut. εύσω, perf. δεδούλευκα, aor. 1, ἐδούλευσα, (§ 13. tab. M) *to be a slave or servant; to be in slavery or subjection*, Jno. 8. 33; Ac. 7. 7; Ro. 9. 12; *to discharge the duties of a slave or servant*, Ep. 6. 7; 1 Ti. 6. 2; *to serve, be occupied in the service of, be devoted, subservient*, Mat. 6. 24; Lu. 15. 29; Ac. 20. 19; Ro. 14. 18; 16. 18, et al.; met. *to be enthralled, involved in a slavish service*, spiritually or morally, Gal. 4. 9, 25; Tit. 3. 3.

δουλόω, ῶ, fut. ώσω, (§ 20. tab. T) aor. 1, ἐδούλωσα, perf. pass. δεδούλωμαι aor. 1, pass. ἐδουλώθην, *to reduce to servitude, enslave, oppress by retaining in servitude*, Ac. 7. 6; 2 Pe. 2. 19; met. *to render subservient*, 1 Co. 9. 19; pass. *to be under restraint*, 1 Co. 7. 15; *to be in bondage*, spiritually or morally, Gal. 4. 3; Tit. 2. 3; *to become devoted to the service of*, Ro. 6. 18, 22.

δούλου, gen. sing. masc. . . . . δοῦλος
δούλους, acc. pl. masc. . . . . id.
δουλόω, ῶ], fut. ώσω, (§ 20. tab. T) . id.
δούλῳ, dat. sing. masc. . . . . id.
δουλωθέντες, nom. pl. masc. part. aor. 1, pass. δουλόω
δουλώσουσι, 3 pers. pl. fut. ind. act. id.
δούλων, gen. pl. masc. . . . . δοῦλος
δοῦναι, aor. 2, infin. (§ 30. tab. Z) . . δίδωμι
δούς, nom. sing. masc. part. aor. 2, act. . . id.
δοχή], ῆς, ἡ, (§ 2. tab. B. a) . . . δέχομαι
δοχήν, acc. sing. . . . . . δοχή
δράκοντα, acc. sing. . . . . δράκων
δράκοντι, dat. sing.—Gr. Sch. Tdf. } id.
δράκοντα, Rec. (Re. 13. 4) }
δράκοντος, gen. sing. . . . . id.

δράκων, οντος, ὁ, (§ 4. rem. 2. d) *a dragon or large serpent*; met. *the devil or Satan*, Re. 12. 3, 4, 7, 9, 13, 16, 17; 13. 2, 4, 11; 16. 13; 20. 2.

δραμών, nom. s. masc. part. aor. 2, (§ 36. rem. 1) τρέχω

δράσσομαι], (§ 26. rem. 3) (δράξ, *the fist*) pr. *to grasp with the hand, clutch; to lay hold of, seize, take, catch.*

δραχμή, ῆς, ἡ, (§ 2. tab. B. a) *a drachm*, an Attic silver coin of nearly the same value as the Roman *denarius*, about seven-pence three-farthings of our money, Lu. 15. 8, 9.

δρασσόμενος,[a] nom sing. masc. part. pres. . δράσσομαι
δραχμάς, acc. pl. . . . . . δραχμή
δραχμή], ῆς, ἡ, (§ 2. tab. B. a) . . δράσσομαι
δραχμήν, acc. sing. . . . . . δραχμή

δρέπανον, ου, τό, (§ 3. tab. C. c) (δρέπω, *to crop, cut off*) *an instrument with a curved blade*, as *a sickle*, Mar. 4. 29; Re. 14. 14, 15, 16, 17, 18, 19.

δρόμον, acc. sing. . . . . . δρόμος
δρόμος], ου, ὁ, (§ 3. tab. C. a) . . τρέχω
Δρούσιλλα], ης, ἡ, (§ 2. rem. 3) *Drusilla*, pr. name.
Δρουσίλλῃ,[b] dat. sing. . . . . Δρούσιλλα
δυναίμην, 1 pers. sing. pres. optat. . . δύναμαι
δύναιντο, 3 pers. pl. pres. optat. . . id.

δύνᾰμαι, fut. δυνήσομαι, imperf. ἐδυνάμην & ἠδυνάμην, aor. 1, ἐδυνησάμην & (pass. form) ἐδυνάσθην, ἐδυνήθην, ἠδυνήθην, (§ 37. rem. 1) *to be able*, either intrinsically and absolutely, which is the ordinary signification; or, for specific reasons, Mat. 9. 15; Lu. 16. 2.

δύνᾰμις, εως, ἡ, (§ 5. tab. E. c) *power; strength, ability*, Mat. 25. 15; He. 11. 11; *efficacy*, 1 Co. 4. 19, 20; Phi. 3. 10; 1 Thes. 1. 5; 2 Ti. 3. 5; *energy*, Col. 1. 29; 2 Ti. 1. 7; *meaning, purport* of language, 1 Co. 14. 11; *authority*, Lu. 4. 36; 9. 1; *might, power, majesty*, Mat. 22. 29; 24. 30; Ac. 3. 12; Ro. 9. 17; 2 Thes. 1. 7; 2 Pe. 1. 16; in N.T. *a manifestation or instance of power, mighty means*, Ac. 8. 10; Ro. 1. 16; 1 Co. 1. 18, 24; ἡ δύναμις, *omnipotence*, Mat. 26. 64; Lu. 22. 69; Mat. 14. 62; pl. *authorities*, Ro. 8. 38; Ep. 1. 21; 1 Pe. 3. 22; *miraculous power*, Mar. 5. 30; Lu. 1. 35; 5. 17; 6. 19; 8. 46; 24. 49; 1 Co. 2. 4; *a miracle*, Mat. 11. 20, 21, et al. freq.; *a worker of miracles*, 1 Co. 12. 28, 29; from the Heb. αἱ δυνάμεις τῶν οὐρανῶν, *the heavenly luminaries*, Mat. 24. 29; Mar. 13. 25; Lu. 21. 26; αἱ δυνάμεις, *the spiritual powers*, Mat. 14. 2; Mar. 6. 14.

[a] 1 Co. 3. 19.

[b] Ac. 24. 24.

δυναμόω, ῶ, fut. ώσω, (§ 20. tab. T) *to strengthen, confirm*, Col. 1. 11. L.G.

δυνάστης, ου, ὁ, (§ 2. tab. B. c) *a potentate, sovereign, prince*, Lu. 1. 52; 1 Ti. 6. 15; *a person of rank and authority, a grandee*, Ac. 8. 27.

δυνᾰτός, ή, όν, (§ 7. tab. F. a) *able, having power, powerful, mighty*; δυνατὸς εἶναι, *to be able*, i.q. δύνασθαι, Lu. 14. 31; Ac. 11. 17, et al.; ὁ δυνατός, *the Mighty One, God*, Lu. 1. 49; τὸ δυνατόν, *power*, i.q. δύναμις, Ro. 9. 22; *valid, powerful, efficacious*, 2 Co. 10. 4; *distinguished for rank, authority, or influence*, Ac. 25. 5; 1 Co. 1. 26; *distinguished for skill or excellence*, Lu. 24. 19; Ac. 7. 22; Ro. 15. 1; δυνατόν & δυνατά, *possible, capable of being done*, Mat. 19. 26; 24. 24, et al.

δυνᾰτέω, ῶ, fut. ήσω, (§ 16. tab. P) *to be powerful, mighty, to show one's self powerful*, 2 Co. 13. 3, v.r. Ro. 14. 4. N.T.

δυνάμεθα, 1 pers. pl. pres. ind. . . . δύναμαι
δυνάμει, dat. sing. . . . . . δύναμις
δυνάμεις, nom. and acc. pl. . . . id.
δυνάμενα, acc. pl. neut. part. pres. . . δύναμαι
δυνάμεναι, nom. pl. fem. part. pres. . . id.
δυναμένη, nom. sing. fem. part. pres. . . id.
δυνάμενοι, nom. pl. masc. part. pres. . id.
δυνάμενον, acc. sing. masc. part. pres. . . id.
δυνάμενος, nom. sing. masc. part. pres. . id.
δυναμένου, gen. sing. masc. part. pres. . . id.
δυναμένους, acc. pl. masc. part. pres. . id.
δυναμένῳ, dat. sing. masc. part. pres. . . id.
δυναμένων, gen. pl. part. pres. . . id.
δυνάμεσι, dat. pl. . . . . δύναμις
δυναμέων, gen. pl. . . . . . id.
δυνάμεως, gen. sing . . . . id.
δύναμιν, acc. sing. . . . . . id.
δύναμις, εως, ἡ, (§ 5. tab. E. c) . . . δύναμαι
δυναμούμενοι,[a] nom. pl. masc. part. pres. pass. δυναμόω
δυναμόω, ῶ], fut. ώσω, (§ 20. tab. T) . δύναμαι
δύνανται, 3 pers. pl. pres. ind. . . . id.
δύνασαι, 2 pers. sing. pres. ind. . . id.
δύνασθαι, pres. infin. . . . . id.
δύνασθε, 2 pers. pl. pres. ind. . . . id
δυνάστας, acc. pl. . . . . . δυνάστης
δυνάστης, ου, ὁ, (§ 2. tab. B. c) . . δύναμαι
δυνατά, nom. pl. neut. . . . . δυνατός

δύναται, 3 pers. sing. pres. ind. . . δύναμαι
δυνατεῖ, 3 pers. sing. pres. ind. . . . δυνατέω
δυνατέω, ῶ], fut. ήσω, (§ 16. tab. P) . δύναμαι
δυνατοί, nom. pl. masc. . . . . δυνατός
δυνατόν, nom. and acc. sing. neut. . . id.
δυνατός, ή, όν, (§ 7. tab. F. a) . . . δύναμαι
δύνῃ, 2 pers. sing. pres. ind. contr. for δύνασαι id.
δυνηθῆτε, 2 pers. pl. aor. 1, subj. (§ 37. rem. 1) id.
δυνήσεσθε, 2 pers. pl. fut. ind. . . id.
δυνήσεται, 3 pers. sing. fut. ind. . . . id.
δυνήσῃ, 2 pers. sing. fut. ind. . . id.
δυνησόμεθα, 1 pers. pl. fut. ind. . . id.
δυνήσονται, 3 pers. pl. fut. ind. . . id.
δύνηται, 3 pers. sing. pres. subj. . . . id.
δύνοντος, gen. sing. masc. part. pres. . δύνω

δύνω], aor. 2, ἔδυν, (§ 31. rem. 1. c) *to sink, go down, set* as the sun, Mar. 1. 32; Lu. 4. 40.

δυσμή, ῆς, ἡ, (§ 2. tab. B. a) *a sinking or setting*; pl. δυσμαί, *the setting of the sun*; hence, *the west*, Mat. 8. 11; 24. 27, et al.

δύνωνται, 3 pers. pl. pres. subj. . . . δύναμαι

δύο, (§ 9. tab. I. b) both indecl. and also with gen. and dat. δυοῖν, in N.T., both indecl. and also with later dat. δυσί, *two*, Mat. 6. 24; 21. 28, 31, et al. freq.; οἱ δύο, *both*, Jno. 20. 4; δύο ἢ τρεῖς, *two or three, some, a few*, Mat. 18. 20; from the Heb. δύο δύο, *two and two*, Mar. 6. 7, i.q. ἀνὰ δύο, Lu. 10. 1, and κατὰ δύο, 1 Co. 14. 27.

δεύτερος, α, ον, (§ 7. rem. 1) *second*, Mat. 22. 26, et al.; τὸ δεύτερον, *again, the second time, another time*, Jude 5; so ἐκ δευτέρου, Mat. 26. 42, et al.; and ἐν τῷ δευτέρῳ, Ac. 7. 13.

δεύτερον, neut. of δεύτερος, used as an adv. *the second time, again*, Jno. 3. 4; 21. 16, et al.

δευτεραῖος, αία, αῖον, (§ 7. rem. 1) *on the second day* of a certain state or process, and used as an epithet of the subject or agent, Ac. 28. 13.

δίδῠμος, ου, ὁ, ἡ, (§ 7. rem. 2) *a twin*; the Greek equivalent to the name Thomas, Jno. 11. 16; 20. 24; 21. 2.

δίς, adv. *twice*, Mar. 14. 30, 72, et al.;

[a] Col. 1. 11.

in the sense of *entirely, utterly*, Jude 12; ἅπαξ καὶ δίς, *once and again, repeatedly*, Phi. 4. 16.

δισтάζω, fut. άσω, (§ 26. rem. 1) aor. 1, ἐδίσтασα, *to doubt, waver, hesitate*, Mat. 14. 31; 28. 17.

δυς-, an inseparable particle, conveying the notion of untowardness, as *hard, ill, unlucky, dangerous*, like the English *un-, mis-*; opp. to εὖ.

δύσαντος, gen. sing. masc. part. aor. 1.—D. } δύνω
δύνοντος, Rec. Gr. Sch. Tdf. (Lu. 4. 40) }

δυσβάστακτα, acc. pl. neut. . . . δυσβάστακτος

δυσβάστακτος], ου, ὁ, ἡ, (§ 7. rem. 2) (δυς & βαστάζω) *difficult or grievous to be borne, oppressive*, Mat. 23. 4; Lu. 11. 46. L.G.

δυσεντερία], ας, ἡ, (§ 2. tab. B. b, and rem. 2) (δυς & ἔντερον, *an intestine*) *a dysentery*.

δυσεντερίᾳ,[a] dat. sing.—Rec. Gr. Sch. . } δυσεντερία
δυσεντερίῳ, Al. Ln. Tdf. (Ac. 28. 8) . }

δυσερμήνευτος,[b] ου, ὁ, ἡ, (§ 7. rem. 2) (δυς & ἑρμηνεύω) *difficult to be explained, hard to be understood*. L.G.

δυσί, dat. pl. . . . . . . δύο

δύσκολον,[c] nom. sing. neut. . . . δύσκολος

δύσκολος], ου, ὁ, ἡ, (§ 7. rem. 2) (δυς & κόλον, *food*) pr. *peevish about food; hard to please, disagreeable*; in N.T. *difficult*.

δυσκόλως, adv. *with difficulty, hardly*, Mat. 19. 23; Mar. 10. 23, et al.

δυσκόλως, adv. . . . . . . δύσκολος

δυσμή], ῆς, ἡ, (§ 2. tab. B. a) . . δύνω

δυσμῶν, gen. pl. . . . . . δυσμή

δυσνόητα,[d] nom. pl. neut. . . . δυσνόητος

δυσνόητος], ου, ὁ, ἡ, (§ 7. rem. 2) (δυς & νοητός, from νοέω) *hard to be understood*. L.G.

δυσφημέω, ῶ], fut. ήσω, (§ 16. tab. P) . δυσφημία

δυσφημία], ας, ἡ, (§ 2. tab. B. b, and rem. 2) (δυς & φήμη) *ill words; words of ill omen; reproach, contumely*.

δυσφημέω, ῶ, fut. ήσω, (§ 16. tab. P) pr. *to use ill words; to reproach, revile*, v.r. 1 Co. 4. 13.

δυσφημίας,[e] gen. sing. . . . δυσφημία

δυσφημούμενοι, nom. pl. masc. part. pres. } δυσφημέω
pass.—A. Tdf. . . . }
βλασφημούμενοι, R. Gr. Sch. (1 Co. 4. 13) }

δῷ, 3 pers. sing. aor. 2, subj. act. . . δίδωμι

δώδεκα, οἱ, αἱ, τά, (δύο & δέκα) *twelve*, Mat. 9. 20; 10. 1, et al.; οἱ δώδεκα, *the twelve* apostles, Mat. 26. 14, 20, et al.

δωδέκατος, η, ον, (§ 7. tab. F. a) *the twelfth*.

δωδέκατος,[f] η, ον . . . . . . δώδεκα

δωδεκάφυλον,[g] ου, τό, (§ 3. tab. C. c) (δώδεκα & φυλή) *twelve tribes*. N.T.

δῴη, 3 pers. sing. aor. 2, opt. act. (§ 30. rem. 5) δίδωμι

δῶμα, ατος, τό, (§ 4. tab. D. c) pr. *a house*; synecd. *a roof*, Mat. 10. 27; 24. 17, et al.

δώματος, gen. sing. . . . . . δῶμα

δωμάτων, gen. pl. . . . . . . id.

δῶμεν, 1 pers. pl. aor. 2, subj. act. (§ 30. tab. Z) δίδωμι

δῶρα, nom. and acc. pl. . . . . δῶρον

δωρεά, ᾶς, ἡ, (§ 2. tab. B. b, and rem. 2) . δίδωμι

δωρεᾷ, dat. sing. . . . . . . δωρεά

δωρεάν, acc. sing. . . . . . . id.

δωρεάν, adv. . . . . . . δίδωμι

δωρεᾶς, gen. sing. . . . . . . δωρεά

δωρέομαι, οῦμαι], fut. ήσομαι, (§ 17. tab. Q) δίδωμι

δώρημα, ατος, τό, (§ 4. tab. D. c) . . id.

δώροις, dat. pl. . . . . . . δῶρον

δῶρον, ου, τό, (§ 3. tab. C. c) . . δίδωμι

δωροφορία, ας ἡ, (§ 2. tab. B. b, and rem. 2) (δῶρον & φέρω) *an offering of gifts*.—B. D. Ln. Tdf.

διακονία, Rec. Gr. Sch. (Ro. 15. 31).

δώρῳ, dat. sing. . . . . . . δῶρον

δῷς, 2 pers. sing. aor. 2, subj. act. (§ 30. tab. Z) δίδωμι

δώσει, 3 pers. sing. fut. ind. act. . . id.

δώσεις, 2 pers. sing. fut. ind. act. . . id.

δώσῃ, 3 pers. sing. aor. 1, subj. act. (as if from ἔδωσα for the usual aor. ἔδωκα).

δῶσι, 3 pers. pl. aor. 2, subj. act. . . id

δώσομεν, 1 pers. pl. fut. ind. act.—Al. Ln. Tdf. } id
δῶμεν, Rec. Gr. Sch. (Mar. 6. 37) . }

δώσουσι, 3 pers. pl. fut. ind. act. . . id.

δώσω, 1 pers. sing. fut. ind. act. . . id.

δῶτε, 2 pers. pl. aor. 2, subj. act. . . id.

E.

ἔα, interj. *ha!* an expression of surprise or displeasure, Mar. 1. 24; Lu. 4. 34.

ἐάν, conj. *if*. The particulars of the use of ἐάν must be learnt from the grammars. Ἐὰν μή, *except, unless*; also equivalent

[a] Ac. 28. 8. [b] He. 5. 11. [c] Mar. 10. 24. [d] 2 Pe. 3. 16. [e] 2 Co. 6. 8. [f] Re. 21. 20. [g] Ac. 26. 7.

to ἀλλά, Gal. 2. 16. Ἐάν, in N.T. as in the later Greek, is substituted for ἄν after relative words, Mat. 5. 19, et al. freq.

ἐάνπερ, a strengthening of ἐάν, by the enclitic particle περ, *if it be that, if at all events*, He. 3. 6, 14; 6. 3.

ἐᾷς, 2 pers. sing. pres. ind. . . . ἐάω
ἐάσαντες, nom. pl. masc. part. aor. 1 . id.
ἐάσατε, 2 pers. pl. aor. 1, imper. . . id.
ἐάσει, 3 pers. sing. fut. ind. . . . id.
ἐᾶτε, 2 pers. pl. pres. imper. . . . id.
ἑαυταῖς, dat. pl. fem. . . . . ἑαυτοῦ
ἑαυτάς, acc. pl. fem. . . . . id.
ἑαυτῇ, dat. sing. fem. . . . . id.
ἑαυτήν, acc. sing. fem. . . . id.
ἑαυτῆς, gen. sing. fem. . . . id.
ἑαυτό, acc. sing. neut. . . . id.
ἑαυτοῖς, dat. pl. masc. . . . . id.
ἑαυτόν, acc. sing. masc. . . . . id.

ἑαυτοῦ, ῆς, οῦ, contr. αὑτοῦ, ῆς, οῦ, pl. ἑαυτῶν, (§ 11. tab. K. d) a reflexive pronoun of the third person, *himself, herself, itself*, Mat. 8. 22; 12. 26; 9. 21, et al.; also used for the first and second persons, Ro. 8. 23; Mat. 23. 31; also equivalent to ἀλλήλων, Mar. 10. 26; Jno. 12. 19; ἀφ' ἑαυτοῦ, ἀφ' ἑαυτῶν, *of himself, themselves, voluntarily, spontaneously*, Lu. 12. 47; 21. 30, et al.; *of one's own will merely*, Jno. 5. 19; δι' ἑαυτοῦ, *of itself, in its own nature*, Ro. 14. 14; ἐξ ἑαυτῶν, *of one's own self merely*, 2 Co. 3. 5; καθ' ἑαυτόν, *by one's self, alone*, Ac. 28. 16; Ja. 2. 17; παρ' ἑαυτῷ, *with one's self, at home*, 1 Co. 16. 2; πρὸς ἑαυτόν, *to one's self, to one's home*, Lu. 24. 12; Jno. 20. 10; or, *with one's self*, Lu. 18. 11.

ἑαυτούς, acc. pl. masc. . . . ἑαυτοῦ
ἑαυτῷ, dat. sing. masc. . . . . id.
ἑαυτῶν, gen. pl. . . . . . id.

ἐάω, ῶ], fut. άσω, (ᾱ) (§ 22. rem. 2) imperf. εἴων, aor. 1, εἴᾱσα, (§ 13. rem. 4) *to let, allow, permit, suffer to be done*, Mat. 24. 43; Lu. 4. 41, et al.; *to let be, let alone, desist from*, Lu. 22. 51; Ac. 5. 38; *to commit* a ship to the sea, *let* her *drive*, Ac. 27. 40.

ἐβάθυνε,[a] 3 pers. sing. aor. 1, ind. act. . . βαθύνω
ἔβαλε, 3 pers. sing. aor. 2, ind. act. (§ 27. rem. 4. b) βάλλω
ἔβαλλον, 3 pers. pl. imperf. act. . . id.
ἔβαλον, 3 pers. pl. aor. 2, ind. act. . . id.
ἐβάπτιζε, 3 pers. sing. imperf. act. . . βαπτίζω
ἐβαπτίζοντο, 3 pers. pl. imperf. pass. . . id.
ἐβάπτισα, 1 pers. sing. aor. 1, ind. act. . id.
ἐβαπτίσαντο, 3 pers. pl. aor. 1, ind. mid. . id.
ἐβάπτισε, 3 pers. sing. aor. 1, ind. act. . id.
ἐβαπτίσθη, 3 pers. sing. aor. 1, pass. (§ 26. rem. 1) id.
ἐβαπτίσθημεν, 1 pers. pl. aor. 1, ind. pass. . id.
ἐβαπτίσθησαν, 3 pers. pl. aor. 1, ind. pass. id.
ἐβαπτίσθητε, 2 pers. pl. aor. 1, ind. pass. . id.
ἐβαρήθημεν, 1 pers. pl. aor. 1, ind. pass. . βαρέω
ἐβασάνιζε, 3 pers. sing. imperf. act. . . βασανίζω
ἐβασάνισαν, 3 pers. pl. aor. 1, ind. act. . id.
ἐβασίλευσαν, 3 pers. pl. aor. 1, ind. (§ 13. rem. 8. d) βασιλεύω
ἐβασίλευσας, 2 pers. sing. aor. 1, ind. . id.
ἐβασιλεύσατε, 2 pers. pl. aor. 1, ind. . . id.
ἐβασίλευσε, 3 pers. sing. aor. 1, ind. . id.
ἐβάσκανε,[b] 3 pers. sing. aor. 1, ind. act. . βασκαίνω
ἐβάσταζε, 3 pers. sing. imperf. act. . . βαστάζω
ἐβαστάζετο, 3 pers. sing. imperf. pass. . . id.
ἐβάστασαν, 3 pers. pl. aor. 1, ind. act. . id.
ἐβάστασας, 2 pers. sing. aor. 1, ind. act. . id.
ἐβάστασε, 3 pers. sing. aor. 1, ind. act. . id.
ἐβδελυγμένοις, dat. pl. masc. part. perf. pass. (§ 26. rem. 3) . . . βδελύσσομαι
ἑβδόμῃ, dat. sing. fem. . . . ἕβδομος
ἑβδομήκοντα, οἱ, αἱ, τά . . . ἑπτά
ἑβδομηκοντάκις,[c] adv. . . . . id.
ἑβδόμην, acc. sing. fem. . . . . ἕβδομος
ἑβδόμης, gen. sing. fem. . . . . id.
ἕβδομος, η, ον, (§ 7. tab. F. a) . . . ἑπτά
ἑβδόμου, gen. sing. masc. . . . ἕβδομος
ἐβεβαιώθη, 3 pers. sing. aor. 1, ind. pass. . βεβαιόω
ἐβέβλητο, 3 pers. s. pluperf. pass. (§ 13. rem. 8. f) βάλλω
Ἔβερ,[d] ὁ, *Heber*, pr. name, indecl.—Rec.
Ἐβέρ, Gr. Sch.
Ἔβερ, Ln. Tdf. (Lu. 3. 35)
ἐβλάστησε, 3 sing. aor. 1, ind. (§ 36. rem. 2) βλαστάνω
ἐβλασφήμει, 3 pers. sing. imperf. act. . βλασφημέω
ἐβλασφήμησαν, 3 pers. pl. aor. 1, ind. act. . id.
ἐβλασφήμησε, 3 pers. sing. aor. 1, ind. act. id.
ἐβλασφήμουν, 3 pers. pl. imperf. act. . id.
ἔβλεπε, 3 pers. sing. imperf. act. . βλέπω
ἔβλεπον, 3 pers. pl. imperf. act. . . id.
ἔβλεψα, 1 pers. sing. aor. 1, ind. act. . . id.

[a] Lu. 6. 48. [b] Gal. 3. 1. [c] Mat. 18. 22. [d] Lu. 3. 35.

ἐβλήθη, 3 pers. s. aor. 1, ind. pass. (§ 27. rem. 3) βάλλω
ἐβλήθησαν, 3 pers. pl. aor. 1, ind. pass. id.
ἐβοήθησα, 1 pers. sing. aor. 1, ind. βοηθέω
ἐβοήθησε, 3 pers. sing. aor. 1, ind. id.
ἐβόησε, 3 pers. sing. aor. 1, ind. βοάω
ἐβούλετο, 3 pers. sing. imperf.—A.B.C.Ln.Tdf. } βούλομαι
ἐβουλεύσατο, Rec. Gr. Sch. (Ac. 15. 37) }
ἐβουλεύοντο, 3 pers. pl. imperf. mid. βουλεύω
ἐβουλεύσατο, 3 pers. sing. aor. 1, ind. mid. id.
ἐβουλεύσαντο, 3 pers. pl. aor. 1, ind. mid. id.
ἐβουλήθη, 3 pers. sing. aor. 1, ind. βούλομαι
ἐβουλόμην, 1 pers. sing. imperf. id.
ἐβούλοντο, 3 pers. pl. imperf. id.
ἐβόων, 3 pers. pl. imperf. βοάω
Ἑβραΐδι, dat. sing. (§ 4. rem. 2. c) Ἑβραΐς
Ἑβραϊκοῖς,[a] dat. pl. neut. Ἑβραϊκός
Ἑβραϊκός], ή, όν, (§ 7. tab. F. a) Ἑβραῖος
Ἑβραῖοι, nom. pl. masc. id.
Ἑβραῖος, αία, αῖον, (§ 7. rem. 1) or ου, ὁ, *a Hebrew, one descended from Abraham the Hebrew*, 2 Co. 11. 22; Phi. 3. 5; in N.T., *a Jew of Palestine*, opp. to Ἑλληνιστής, Ac. 6. 1.

Ἑβραϊκός, ή, όν, *Hebrew*, Lu. 23. 38.

Ἑβραΐς, ΐδος, ἡ, sc. διάλεκτος, *the Hebrew* dialect, i.e. the Hebræo-Aramæan dialect of Palestine, Ac. 21. 40, et al.

Ἑβραϊστί, adv. *in Hebrew*, Jno. 5. 2; 19. 13, et al.

Ἑβραίους, acc. pl. masc. Ἑβραῖος
Ἑβραΐς, ΐδος, ἡ, (§ 4. rem. 2. c) id.
Ἑβραϊστί, adv. id.
Ἑβραίων, gen. pl. masc. id.
ἔβρεξε, 3 pers. sing. aor. 1, ind. βρέχω
ἔβρυχον,[b] 3 pers. pl. imperf. βρύχω
ἐγάμησε, 3 pers. sing. aor. 1, ind. γαμέω
ἐγαμίζοντο, 3 p. pl. imperf. pass.—B.D.Ln.Tdf. } γαμίζω
ἐξεγαμίζοντο, Rec. Gr. Sch. (Lu. 17. 27) }
ἐγγεγραμμένη, nom. sing. fem. part. perf. pass. (§ 23. rem. 7) ἐγγράφω
ἐγγέγραπται, 3 pers. s. perf. ind. pass.—B. Tdf. } id.
ἐγράφη, Rec. Gr. Ln. Sch. (Lu. 10. 20) }
ἐγγιεῖ, 3 pers. sing. fut. Att. (§ 35. rem. 11) ἐγγίζω
ἐγγίζει, 3 pers. sing. pres. ind. id.
ἐγγίζειν, pres. infin. id.
ἐγγίζομεν, 1 pers. pl. pres. ind. id.
ἐγγίζοντες, nom. pl. masc. part. pres. id.
ἐγγίζοντι, dat. sing. masc. part. pres. id.
ἐγγίζοντος, gen. sing. masc. part. pres. ἐγγίζω
ἐγγιζόντων, gen. pl. masc. part. pres. id.
ἐγγίζουσαν, acc. sing. fem. part. pres. id.
ἐγγίζουσι, 3 pers. pl. pres. ind. id.
ἐγγίζω], fut. ίσω, (§ 26. rem. 1) ἐγγύς
ἐγγίζωμεν, 1 pers. pl. pres. subj.—A. } ἐγγίζω
ἐγγίζομεν, Rec. Gr. Sch. Tdf. (He. 7. 19) }
ἐγγίσαι, aor. 1, infin. id.
ἐγγίσαντος, gen. sing. masc. part. aor. 1 id.
ἐγγίσας, nom. sing. masc. part. aor. 1 id.
ἐγγίσατε, 2 pers. pl. aor. 1, imper. id.
ἐγγράφω], fut. ψω, (§ 23. rem. 1. a) perf. pass. ἐγγέγραμμαι, (§ 23. rem. 7) (ἐν & γράφω) *to engrave, inscribe*; met. ἐγγεγραμμένος, *imprinted*, 2 Co. 3. 2, 3.
ἔγγυος,[c] ου, ὁ, ἡ, (§ 3. tab. C. a. b) (from ἐγγύη, *a pledge*) *a surety, sponsor*.

ἐγγύς, adv. *near*, as to place, Lu. 19. 11, et al.; *close at hand*, Ro. 10. 8; *near*, in respect of ready interposition, Phi. 4. 5; *near*, as to time, Mat. 24. 32, 33, et al.; *near* to God, as being in covenant with him, Ep. 2. 13; οἱ ἐγγύς, *the people near* to God, the Jews, Ep. 2. 17.

ἐγγίζω, fut. ίσω, Att. ιῶ, perf. ἤγγικα, aor. 1, ἤγγισα, (§ 26. rem. 1) pr. *to cause to approach*; in N.T. intrans. *to approach, draw near*, Mat. 21. 1; Lu. 18. 35, et al.; met. *to be at hand, impend*, Mat. 3. 2; 4. 17, et al.; μέχρι θανάτου ἐγγίζειν, *to be at the point of death*, Phi. 2. 30; from Heb. *to draw near* to God, *to offer* him *reverence and worship*, Mat. 15. 8; He. 7. 19; Ja. 4. 8; used of God, *to draw near* to men, *assist* them, *bestow favours* on them, Ja. 4. 8. L.G.

ἐγγύτερον, adv. (pr. neut. of ἐγγύτερος, compar. of ἐγγύς) *nearer*, Ro. 13. 11.

ἐγγύτερον,[d] adv. ἐγγύς
ἐγεγόνει, 3 pers. sing. pluperf. mid. (§ 13. rem. 8. f) γίνομαι
ἔγειραι, 2 pers. sing. aor. 1, imper. mid. ἐγείρω
ἐγεῖραι, aor. 1, infin. act. id.
ἐγείραντα, acc. sing. masc. part. aor. 1, act. id.
ἐγείραντος, gen. sing. masc. part. aor. 1, act id.
ἐγείρας, nom. sing. masc. part. aor. 1, act. id.
ἔγειρε, 2 pers. s. pres. imper.—A.C.D.Gr.Sch.Tdf. } id.
ἔγειραι, Rec. Ln. (Mar. 2. 9, 11) }

[a] Lu. 23. 38. [b] Ac. 7. 54. [c] He. 7. 22. [d] Ro. 13. 11.

ἐγείρει, 3 pers. sing. pres. ind. act. . . ἐγείρω
ἐγείρειν, pres. infin. act. . . . . id.
ἐγείρεσθε, 2 pers. pl. pres. imper. mid. . id.
ἐγείρεται, 3 pers. sing. pres. ind. mid. . . id.
ἐγείρετε, 2 pers. pl. pres. imper. act. . id.
ἐγείρηται, 3 pers. sing. pres. subj. mid. . id.
ἐγείρομαι, 1 pers. sing. pres. ind. mid. . id.
ἐγείρονται, 3 pers. pl. pres. ind. mid. . . id.
ἐγείροντι, dat. sing. masc. part. pres. act. . id.
ἐγείρου, 2 pers. sing. pres. imper. mid. . . id.

ἐγείρω], (§ 37. rem. 1) fut. ἐγερῶ, perf. ἐγήγερκα, aor. 1, ἤγειρα, perf. pass. ἐγήγερμαι, aor. 1, pass. ἠγέρθην, *to excite, arouse, awaken*, Mat. 8. 25, et al.; mid. *to awake*, Mat. 2. 13, 20, 21, et al.; met. mid. *to rouse one's self* to a better course of conduct, Ro. 13. 11; Ep. 5. 14; *to raise* from the dead, Jno. 12. 1, et al.; and mid. *to rise* from the dead, Mat. 27. 52; Jno. 5. 21, et al.; met. *to raise* as it were from the dead, 2 Co. 4. 14; *to raise up, cause to rise up* from a recumbent posture, Ac. 3. 7; and mid. *to rise up*, Mat. 17. 7, et al.; *to restore to health*, Ja. 5. 15; met. et seq. ἐπί, *to excite* to war; mid. *to rise up against*, Mat. 24. 7, et al.; *to raise up again, rebuild*, Jno. 2. 19, 20; *to raise up* from a lower place, *to draw up or out of* a ditch, Mat. 12. 11; from Heb. *to raise up, to cause to arise or exist*, Ac. 13. 22, 23; mid. *to arise, exist, appear*, Mat. 3. 9; 11. 11, et al.

ἔγερσις, εως, ἡ, (§ 5. tab. E. c) pr. *the act of waking or rising up; resurrection, resuscitation*, Mat. 27. 53.

ἐγέμισαν, 3 pers. pl. aor. 1, ind. act. . γεμίζω
ἐγέμισε, 3 pers. sing. aor. 1, ind. act. . . id.
ἐγεμίσθη, 3 pers. sing. aor. 1, ind. pass. . id.
ἐγένεσθε, 2 pers. pl. aor. 2, ind. mid. . . γίνομαι
ἐγένετο, 3 pers. sing. aor. 2, ind. (§ 37. rem. 1) id.
ἐγενήθη, 3 pers. sing. aor. 1, ind. pass. . id.
ἐγενήθημεν, 1 pers. pl. aor. 1, ind. pass. . id.
ἐγενήθησαν, 3 pers. pl. aor. 1, ind. pass. . id.
ἐγενήθητε, 2 pers. pl. aor. 1, ind. pass. . . id.
ἐγεννήθη, 3 pers. sing. aor. 1, ind. pass. . γεννάω
ἐγεννήθημεν, 1 pers. pl. aor. 1, ind. pass. . id.
ἐγεννήθης, 2 pers. sing. aor. 1, ind. pass. . id.
ἐγεννήθησαν, 3 pers. pl. aor. 1, ind. pass. . γεννάω
ἐγέννησα, 1 pers. sing. aor. 1, ind. act. . id.
ἐγέννησαν, 3 pers. pl. aor. 1, ind. act. . . id
ἐγέννησε, 3 pers. sing. aor. 1, ind. act. . id.
ἐγενόμην, 1 pers. sing. aor. 2, ind. mid. . γίνομαι
ἐγένοντο, 3 pers. pl. aor. 2, ind. mid. . id.
ἐγένου, 2 pers. sing. aor. 2, ind. mid. . . id.
ἐγερεῖ, 3 pers. sing. fut. ind. act. (§ 37. rem. 1) ἐγείρω
ἐγερεῖς, 2 pers. sing. fut. ind. act. . . id.
ἐγερθείς, nom. sing. masc. part. aor. 1, pass. . id.
ἐγερθέντι, dat. sing. masc. part. aor. 1, pass. id.
ἐγερθῇ, 3 pers. sing. aor. 1, subj. pass. . id.
ἐγερθῆναι, aor. 1, infin. pass. . . . id.
ἐγερθήσεται, 3 pers. sing. fut. 1, ind. pass. . id.
ἐγερθήσονται, 3 pers. pl. fut. 1, ind. pass. . id.
ἐγέρθητε, 2 pers. pl. aor. 1, imper. pass. . id.
ἐγέρθητι, 2 pers. sing. aor. 1, imper. pass. . id.
ἔγερσιν,[a] acc. sing. . . . . ἔγερσις
ἔγερσις], εως, ἡ, (§ 5. tab. E. c) . . ἐγείρω
ἐγερῶ, 1 pers. sing. fut. ind. act. . . id.
ἐγεύσασθε, 2 pers. pl. aor. 1, ind. . . γεύομαι
ἐγεύσατο, 3 pers. sing. aor. 1, ind. (§ 15. tab. O) id.
ἐγηγερμένον, acc. sing. masc. part. perf. pass. ἐγείρω
ἐγήγερται, 3 pers. sing. perf. ind. pass. . id.
ἔγημα, 1 pers. sing. aor. 1, ind. (§ 37. rem. 2) γαμέω
ἐγίνετο, 3 pers. sing. imperf. . . . γίνομαι
ἐγίνωσκε, 3 pers. sing. imperf. act. . . γινώσκω
ἐγίνωσκον, 3 pers. pl. imperf. act. . . id.
ἐγκάθετος], ου, ὁ, ἡ, (§ 7. rem. 2) (ἐν & καθίημι) *suborned*.
ἐγκαθέτους,[b] acc. pl. masc. . . . ἐγκάθετος
ἐγκαίνια,[c] ίων, τά, (§ 6. rem. 5) (ἐν & καινός) *initiation, consecration*; in N.T. *the feast of dedication*, an annual festival of eight days in the month Kisleu.
ἐγκαινίζω], fut. ίσω, (§ 26. rem. 1) aor. 1, ἐνεκαίνισα, perf. pass. ἐγκεκαίνισμαι, *to handsel, initiate, consecrate, dedicate, renovate*; *to institute*, He. 9. 18; 10. 20. LXX.
ἐγκακεῖν, pres. infin.—Al. Ln. Tdf. . } ἐγκακέω
ἐκκακεῖν, Rec. Gr. Sch. (Lu. 18. 1) . }
ἐγκᾰκέω, ῶ], fut. ήσω, v.r. probably the same in signification as ἐκκακέω, *to despond, be faint-hearted, be remiss*.
ἐγκακήσητε, 2 pers. pl. aor. 1, subj.—B. Ln. Tdf. } ἐγκακέω
ἐκκακήσητε, Rec. Gr. Sch. (2 Thes. 3. 13) }
ἐγκακοῦμεν, 1 pers. pl. pres. ind.—A. D. Ln. Tdf. } id.
ἐκκακοῦμεν, Rec. Gr. Sch. (2 Co. 4. 1) }

[a] Mat. 27. 53. [b] Lu. 20. 20. [c] Jno. 10. 22.

ἐγκακῶμεν, 1 pers. pl. pres. subj.—Al. Ln. Tdf. } ἐγκακέω
ἐκκακῶμεν, Rec. Gr. Sch. (Gal. 6. 9)

ἐγκαλεῖσθαι, pres. infin. pass. . . . ἐγκαλέω

ἐγκαλείτωσαν, 3 pers. pl. pres. imper. act. . id.

ἐγκαλέσει, 3 pers. sing. fut. ind. act. . . id.

ἐγκαλέω, ῶ], fut. έσω, (§ 22. rem. 1) (ἐν & καλέω) *to bring a charge against, accuse; to institute judicial proceedings*, Ac. 19. 38, 40; 23. 28, 29; 26. 2, 7; Ro. 8. 33.

ἔγκλημα, ατος, τό, (§ 4. tab. D. c) *an accusation, charge, crimination*, Ac. 23. 29; 25. 16.

ἐγκαλοῦμαι, 1 pers. s. pres. ind. pass. (§ 17. tab. Q) ἐγκαλέω

ἐγκαλούμενον, acc. sing. masc. part. pres. pass. id.

ἐγκαταλειπόμενοι, nom. pl. masc. pt. pres. pass. ἐγκαταλείπω

ἐγκαταλείποντες, nom. pl. masc. part. pres. act. id.

ἐγκαταλείψεις, 2 pers. sing. fut. ind. act. . id.

ἐγκαταλείπω], fut. ψω, (§ 23. rem. 1. a) aor. 2, ἐγκατέλῐπον, (§ 24. rem. 9) (ἐν & καταλείπω) *to leave* in a place or situation, Ac. 2. 27; *to leave behind; to forsake, abandon*, Mat. 27. 46, et al.; *to leave*, as a remnant from destruction, Ro. 9. 29.

ἐγκαταλίπω, 1 pers. sing. aor. 2, subj. act. ἐγκαταλείπω

ἐγκατελείφθη, 3 pers. s. aor. 1, pass.—Al. Ln. Tdf. } id.
κατελείφθη, Rec. Gr. Sch. (Ac. 2. 31)

ἐγκατέλιπε, 3 pers. sing. aor. 2, ind. act. . id.

ἐγκατέλιπες, 2 pers. sing. aor. 2, ind. act. . id.

ἐγκατέλιπον, 3 pers. pl. aor. 2, ind. act. . id.

ἐγκατοικέω, ῶ], fut. ήσω, (§ 16. tab. P) (ἐν & κατοικέω) *to dwell in, or among*.

ἐγκατοικῶν,[a] nom. sing. masc. part. pres. . ἐγκατοικέω

ἐγκαυχάομαι, ῶμαι], fut. ήσομαι, (ἐν & καυχάομαι) *to boast in, or of*, v.r.

ἐγκαυχᾶσθαι, pres. infin.—A. B. Ln. Tdf. } ἐγκαυχάομαι
καυχᾶσθαι, Rec. Gr. Sch. (2 Thes. 1. 4)

ἐγκεκαίνισται, 3 pers. sing. perf. ind. pass. . ἐγκαινίζω

ἐγκεντρίζω], fut. ίσω, (§ 26. rem. 1) (ἐν & κεντρίζω, *to prick*) *to ingraft*; met. Ro. 11. 17, 19, 23, 24.

ἐγκεντρίσαι, aor. 1, infin. act. . . . ἐγκεντρίζω

ἐγκεντρισθήσονται, 3 pers. pl. fut. 1, ind. pass. id.

ἐγκεντρισθῶ, 1 pers. sing. aor. 1, subj. pass. id.

ἔγκλημα, ατος, τό, (§ 4. tab. D. c) . . ἐγκαλέω

ἐγκλήματος, gen. sing. . . . . ἔγκλημα

ἐγκομβόομαι, οῦμαι], fut. ώσομαι, (§ 21. tab. U) (κόμβος, *a string, band*; whence ἐγκόμβωμα, *a garment which is fastened by tying*) pr. *to put on a garment which is to be tied*, in N.T. *to put on, clothe one's self with*; met. 1 Pe. 5. 5.

ἐγκομβώσασθε,[b] 2 pers. pl. aor. 1, imper. . ἐγκομβόομαι

ἐγκοπή], ῆς, ἡ, (§ 2. tab. B. a) . . . ἐγκόπτω

ἐγκοπήν,[c] acc. sing. . . . . ἐγκοπή

ἐγκόπτεσθαι, pres. infin. pass.—Gr. Sch. Tdf. } ἐγκόπτω
ἐκκόπτεσθαι, Rec. (1 Pe. 3. 7)

ἐγκόπτω], fut. ψω, (§ 23. rem. 1. a) (ἐν & κόπτω) pr. *to cut or strike in*; hence, *to impede, interrupt, hinder*, Ro. 15. 22; 1 Thes. 2. 18. 1 Pe. 3. 7; Gal. 5. 7.

ἐγκοπή, ῆς, ἡ, (§ 2. tab. B. a) pr. *an incision*, e.g. a trench, etc., cut in the way of an enemy; *an impediment, hindrance*, 1 Co. 9. 12. L.G.

ἐγκόπτω, 1 pers. sing. pres. subj. act. ἐγκόπτω

ἐγκράτεια, ας, ἡ, (§ 2. tab. B. b, and rem. 2) . ἐγκρατής

ἐγκρατείᾳ, dat. sing. . . . . ἐγκράτεια

ἐγκράτειαν, acc. sing. . . . . id.

ἐγκρατείας, gen. sing. . . . . id.

ἐγκρατεύεται, 3 pers. sing. pres. ind. . ἐγκρατεύομαι

ἐγκρατεύομαι], fut. εύσομαι, (§ 14. tab. N) ἐγκρατής

ἐγκρατεύονται, 3 pers. pl. pres. ind. . . ἐγκρατεύομαι

ἐγκρατῆ,[d] acc. sing. masc. . . . . ἐγκρατής

ἐγκρᾰτής], έος, οῦς, ὁ, ἡ, (§ 7. tab. G. b) (κράτος) *strong, stout; possessed of mastery; master of self*.

ἐγκράτεια, ας, ἡ, (§ 2. tab. B. b, and rem. 2) *self-control, continence, temperance*, Ac. 24. 25, et al.

ἐγκρατεύομαι, fut. εύσομαι, (§ 14. tab. N) *to possess the power of self-control or continence*, 1 Co. 7. 9; *to practise abstinence*, 1 Co. 9. 25. N.T.

ἐγκρῖναι,[e] aor. 1, infin. act. . . . ἐγκρίνω

ἐγκρίνω], fut. ινῶ, (§ 27. rem. 1. a) (ἐν & κρίνω) *to judge or reckon among, consider as belonging to, adjudge to the number of, class with, place in the same rank*. (ῑ).

ἐγκρύπτω], fut. ψω, (§ 23. rem. 1. a) (ἐν & κρύπτω) *to conceal in* anything; *to mix, intermix*, Mat. 13. 33; Lu. 13. 21.

ἔγκῠος], ου, ἡ, (§ 3. tab. C. b) (ἐν & κύω) *with child, pregnant*.

ἐγκύῳ,[f] dat. sing. fem. . . . . ἔγκυος

ἔγνω, 3 pers. sing. aor. 2, ind. act. (§ 36. rem. 3) γινώσ

ἔγνωκα, 1 pers. sing. perf. ind. act. . . id.

ἐγνώκαμεν, 1 pers. pl. perf. ind. act. . . id.

---

[a] 2 Pe. 2. 8. [b] 1 Pe. 5. 5. [c] 1 Co. 9. 12. [d] Tit. 1. 8. [e] 2 Co. 10. 12. [f] Lu. 2. 5.

ἔγνωκαν, 3 pers. pl. perf. ind. act.—Alex. . . γινώσκω
ἔγνωκας, 2 pers. sing. perf. ind. act. . . id.
ἐγνώκατε, 2 pers. pl. perf. ind. act. . . id.
ἔγνωκε, 3 pers. sing. perf. ind. act. . . id.
ἐγνώκειτε, 2 pers. pl. pluperf. act. . . id.
ἐγνωκέναι, perf. infin. act.—Al. Ln. Tdf.
 εἰδέναι, Rec. Gr. Sch. (1 Co. 8. 2) . } id.
ἐγνωκότες, nom. pl. masc. part. perf. act. . id.
ἔγνων, 1 pers. sing. aor. 2, ind. act. . . id.
ἐγνώρισα, 1 pers. sing. aor. 1, ind. act. . γνωρίζω
ἐγνωρίσαμεν, 1 pers. pl. aor. 1, ind. act. . id.
ἐγνώρισαν, 3 pers. pl. aor. 1, ind. act.—B.D.Ln.
 διεγνώρισαν, R. Gr. Sch. Tdf. (Lu. 2. 17) } id.
ἐγνώρισας, 2 pers. sing. aor. 1, ind. act. . id.
ἐγνώρισε, 3 pers. sing. aor. 1, ind. act. . . id.
ἐγνωρίσθη, 3 pers. sing. aor. 1, ind. pass. . id.
ἔγνως, 2 pers. sing. aor. 2, ind. act. . . γινώσκω
ἔγνωσαν, 3 pers. pl. aor. 2, ind. act. . id.
ἐγνώσθη, 3 pers. s. aor. 1, ind. pass. (§ 36. rem. 3) id.
ἔγνωσται, 3 pers. sing. perf. ind. pass. . . id.
ἐγόγγυζον, 3 pers. pl. imperf. . . . γογγύζω
ἐγόγγυσαν, 3 pers. pl. aor. 1, ind. . . id.
ἔγραφε, 3 pers. sing. imperf. act. . . γράφω
ἐγράφη, 3 pers. sing. aor. 2, ind. pass. (§ 24. rem. 6) id.
ἔγραψα, 1 pers. sing. aor. 1, ind. act. . . id.
ἔγραψαν, 3 pers. pl. aor. 1, ind. act. . id.
ἐγράψατε, 2 pers. pl. aor. 1, ind. act. . . id.
ἔγραψε, 3 pers. sing. aor. 1, ind. act. . id.
ἐγρηγόρησε, 3 pers. sing. aor. 1, ind. . . γρηγορέω
ἐγχρῖσαι, aor. 1, infin. act.—Gr. Sch. .
 ἔγχρισον, Rec. . . . .
 ἐγχρῖσαι, Tdf. (Re. 3. 18) . } ἐγχρίω
ἔγχρισον,[a] 2 pers. sing. aor. 1, imper. act. . id.
ἐγχρίω], fut. ίσω, (§ 13. tab. M) (ἐν & χρίω) *to rub in, anoint.* (ῑ).

ἐγώ, gen. ἐμοῦ & μου, (§ 11. tab. K. a) *I.*
ἐδάκρυσε,[b] 3 pers. sing. aor. 1, ind. . . δακρύω
ἐδαφίζω], fut. ίσω, (§ 26. rem. 1) . . ἔδαφος
ἐδαφιοῦσι,[c] 3 pers. pl. fut. Att. (§ 35. rem. 11) ἐδαφίζω
ἔδἄφος,[d] εος, τό, (§ 5. tab. E. b) pr. *a bottom, base;* hence, *the ground.*

ἐδαφίζω, fut. ίσω, Att. ιῶ, pr. *to form a level and firm surface; to level with the ground, overthrow, raze, destroy.*

ἐδέετο, 3 pers. sing. imperf. . . . . δέω, δέομαι
ἐδεήθη, 3 pers. s. aor. 1, ind. pass. (§ 37. rem. 1) id.
ἐδεήθην, 1 pers. sing. aor. 1, ind. pass. . . id.

ἔδει, 3 pers. s. imperf. of δεῖ, impers. (§ 37. rem. 1) δέω
ἐδειγμάτισε,[e] 3 pers. sing. aor. 1, ind. act. . δειγματίζω
ἔδειξα, 1 pers. sing. aor. 1, ind. act. . . δείκνυμι
ἔδειξε, 3 pers. sing. aor. 1, ind. act. (§ 31. tab. B. B) id.
ἔδειραν, 3 pers. pl. aor. 1, ind. act. (§ 27. rem. 1. d) δέρω
ἐδεῖτο, 3 pers. sing. imperf.—Tdf. (Lu. 8. 38)
 ἐδέετο, Rec. Gr. Sch. . . .
 ἐδεεῖτο, A. Ln. . . . } δέω, δέομαι
ἐδεξάμεθα, 1 pers. pl. aor. 1, ind. . . δέχομαι
ἐδέξαντο, 3 pers. pl. aor. 1, ind. . . . id.
ἐδέξασθε, 2 pers. pl. aor. 1, ind. . . id.
ἐδέξατο, 3 pers. sing. aor. 1, ind. . . id.
ἐδεσμεῖτο,[f] 3 pers. s. imperf. pass. (§ 17. tab. Q) δεσμέω
ἐδήλου, 3 pers. sing. imperf. act. . . δηλόω
ἐδηλώθη, 3 pers. s. aor. 1, ind. pass. (§ 21. tab. U) id.
ἐδήλωσε, 3 pers. sing. aor. 1, ind. act. . . id.
ἐδημηγόρει,[g] 3 pers. sing. imperf. . . δημηγορέω
ἔδησαν, 3 pers. pl. aor. 1, ind. act. . . δέω
ἔδησε, 3 pers. sing. aor. 1, ind. act. . . id.
ἐδίδαξα, 1 pers. sing. aor. 1, ind. act. . . διδάσκω
ἐδίδαξαν, 3 pers. pl. aor. 1, ind. act. . . id.
ἐδίδαξας, 2 pers. sing. aor. 1, ind. act. . . id.
ἐδίδαξε, 3 pers. sing. aor. 1, ind. act. . id.
ἐδίδασκε, 3 pers. sing. imperf. act. . . id.
ἐδίδασκον, 3 pers. pl. imperf. act. . . id.
ἐδιδάχθην, 1 pers. sing. aor. 1, ind. pass. . id.
ἐδιδάχθησαν, 3 p. pl. aor. 1, ind. pass. (§ 23. rem. 4) id.
ἐδιδάχθητε, 2 pers. pl. aor. 1, ind. pass. . id.
ἐδίδου, 3 pers. sing. imperf. act. . . . δίδωμι
ἐδίδουν, 3 pers. pl. imperf. act. (§ 31. rem. 2) id.
ἐδικαιώθη, 3 pers. sing. aor. 1, ind. pass. δικαιόω
ἐδικαιώθητε, 2 pers. pl. aor. 1, ind. pass. . id.
ἐδικαίωσαν, 3 pers. pl. aor. 1, ind. act. . id.
ἐδικαίωσε, 3 pers. sing. aor. 1, ind. act. . id.
ἐδίστασαν, 3 pers. pl. aor. 1, ind. . . διστάζω
ἐδίστασας, 2 pers. sing. aor. 1, ind. . . id.
ἐδίψησα, 1 pers. sing. aor. 1, ind. . . διψάω
ἐδίωκε, 3 pers. sing. imperf. act. . . . διώκω
ἐδίωκον, 1 pers. sing. and 3 pers. pl. imperf. act. id.
ἐδίωξα, 1 pers. sing. aor. 1, ind. act. . . id.
ἐδίωξαν, 3 pers. pl. aor. 1, ind. act. . . id.
ἐδίωξε, 3 pers. sing. aor. 1, ind. act. . . id.
ἐδόθη, 3 pers. sing. aor. 1, ind. pass. (§ 30. rem. 4) δίδωμι
ἐδόθησαν, 3 pers. pl. aor. 1, ind. pass. . id.
ἐδόκει, 3 pers. sing. imperf. . . . δοκέω
ἐδοκιμάσαμεν, 1 pers. pl. aor. 1, ind. act. . δοκιμάζω
ἐδοκίμασαν, 3 pers. pl. aor. 1, ind. act. . id.
ἐδόκουν, 3 pers. pl. imperf. . . . δοκέω

a Re. 3. 18. b Jno. 11. 35. c Lu. 19. 44. d Ac. 22. 7. e Col. 2. 15. f Lu. 8. 29. g Ac. 12. 21.

ἐδολιοῦσαν,[a] 3 p. pl. imp. Alex. (§ 35. rem. 13) δολιόω
ἔδοξα, 1 pers. sing. aor. 1, ind. (§ 37. rem. 2) δοκέω
ἐδόξαζε, 3 pers. sing. imperf. act. . . δοξάζω
ἐδόξαζον, 3 pers. pl. imperf. act. . . id.
ἔδοξαν, 3 pers. pl. aor. 1, ind. . . . δοκέω
ἐδόξασα, 1 pers. sing. aor. 1, ind. act. . δοξάζω
ἐδόξασαν, 3 pers. pl. aor. 1, ind. act. . . id.
ἐδόξασε, 3 pers. sing. aor. 1, ind. act. . id.
ἐδοξάσθη, 3 pers. sing. aor. 1, ind. pass. . id.
ἔδοξε, 3 pers. sing. aor. 1, ind. . . δοκέω
ἐδουλεύσατε, 2 pers. pl. aor. 1, ind. . . δουλεύω
ἐδούλευσε, 3 pers. sing. aor. 1, ind. . . id.
ἐδουλώθητε, 2 pers. pl. aor. 1, ind. pass. . δουλόω
ἐδούλωσα, 1 pers. sing. aor. 1, ind. act. . id.
ἑδραῖοι, nom. pl. masc. . . . . ἑδραῖος
ἑδραῖος, αία, αῖον, (§ 7. rem. 1) (ἕδρα, *a seat*) *sedentary*; met. *settled, steady, firm, steadfast, constant*, 1 Co. 7. 37; 15. 58; Col. 1. 23.

ἑδραίωμα, ατος, τό, (§ 4. tab. D. c) (ἑδραιόω, *to settle*, from preceding) *a basis, foundation* N.T.

ἑδραίωμα,[b] ατος, τό . . . . ἑδραῖος
ἔδραμε, 3 pers. sing. aor. 2, ind. (§ 36. rem. 1) τρέχω
ἔδραμον, 1 pers. sing. and 3 pers. pl. aor. 2, ind. id.
ἔδυ, 3 pers. sing. aor. 2, ind. (§ 31. rem. 1. c) δύνω
ἐδυναμώθησαν, 3 pers. pl. aor. 1, pass.—A. D. Ln. } ἐνεδυναμώθησαν, Rec. Gr. Sch. Tdf. } (He. 11. 34) . . . } δυναμόω
ἐδύναντο, 3 pers. pl. imperf.—A. D. Ln. Tdf. } ἠδύναντο, Rec. Gr. Sch. (Mar. 4. 33) . } δύναμαι
ἐδύνασθε, 2 pers. pl. imperf.—Gr. Sch. Tdf. } ἠδύνασθε, Rec. (1 Co. 3. 2) . } id.
ἐδύνατο, 3 pers. sing. imperf. . . . id.
ἔδυσε, 3 pers. sing. aor. 1, ind.—B. D. Ln. Tdf. } ἔδυ, Rec. Gr. Sch. (Mar. 1. 32) . } δύνω
ἔδωκα, 1 pers. sing. aor. 1, ind. act. (§ 29. rem. 9. c) . . . δίδωμι
ἐδώκαμεν, 1 pers. pl. aor. 1, ind act . id.
ἔδωκαν, 3 pers. pl. aor. 1, ind. act. . . id.
ἔδωκας, 2 pers. sing. aor. 1, ind. act. . id.
ἐδώκατε, 2 pers. pl. aor. 1, ind. act. . . id.
ἔδωκε, 3 pers. sing. aor. 1, ind. act. . . id.
ἐδωρήσατο, 3 pers. sing. aor. 1, ind. . . δωρέομαι
Ἐζεκίαν, acc. sing. . . . . Ἐζεκίας
Ἐζεκίας, ου, ὁ, (§ 2. tab. B. d) *Ezekias*, pr. name.
ἐζημιώθην, 1 pers. sing. aor. 1, ind. pass. . ζημιόω
ἔζησα, 1 pers. sing. aor. 1, ind. . ζάω
ἔζησαν, 3 pers. pl. aor. 1, ind. . . . ζάω
ἔζησε, 3 pers. sing. aor. 1, mid. . . id.
ἐζῆτε, 2 pers. pl. imperf. (§ 35. rem. 2) . id.
ἐζήτει, 3 pers. sing. imperf. act. . . ζητέω
ἐζητεῖτε, 2 pers. pl. imperf. act. . . . id.
ἐζητεῖτο, 3 pers. sing. imperf. pass. . . id.
ἐζητήσαμεν, 1 pers. pl. aor. 1, ind. act. . id.
ἐζήτησαν, 3 pers. pl. aor. 1, ind. act. . id.
ἐζήτησε, 3 pers. sing. aor. 1, ind. act. . . id.
ἐζητοῦμεν, 1 pers. pl. imperf. act. . . id.
ἐζήτουν, 3 pers. pl. imperf. act. . . . id.
ἐζυμώθη, 3 pers. sing. aor. 1, ind. pass. . ζυμόω
ἐζωγρημένοι, nom. pl. masc. part. perf. pass. . ζωγρέω
ἔζων, 1 pers. sing. imperf. . ζάω
ἐζώννυες, 2 pers. sing. imperf. act. . . ζωννύω
ἐθαμβήθησαν, 3 pers. pl. aor. 1, ind. pass. . θαμβέω
ἐθαμβοῦντο, 3 pers. pl. imperf. pass. . . id.
ἐθανατώθητε, 2 pers. pl. aor. 1, ind. pass. . θανατόω
ἐθαύμαζε, 3 pers. sing. imperf. act. . . θαυμάζω
ἐθαύμαζον, 3 pers. pl. imperf. act. . . id.
ἐθαύμασα, 1 pers. sing. aor. 1, ind. act. . id.
ἐθαύμασαν, 3 pers. pl. aor. 1, ind. act. . id.
ἐθαύμασας, 2 pers. sing. aor. 1, ind. act. . id.
ἐθαύμασε, 3 pers. sing. aor. 1, ind. act. . id.
ἐθαυμάσθη, 3 pers. sing. aor. 1, ind. pass. . id.
ἔθαψαν, 3 pers. pl. aor. 1, ind. act. . . θάπτω
ἐθεάθη, 3 pers. sing. aor. 1, ind. pass. . . θεάομαι
ἐθεασάμεθα, 1 pers. pl. aor. 1, ind. . . id.
ἐθεάσαντο, 3 pers. pl. aor. 1, ind. . . id.
ἐθεάσασθε, 2 pers. pl. aor. 1, ind. . . id.
ἐθεάσατο, 3 pers. sing. aor. 1, ind. . . id.
ἔθει, dat. sing. . . . . . . ἔθος
ἐθελοθρησκεία], ας, ἡ, (§ 2. tab. B. b, and rem. 2) (ἐθέλω & θρησκεία) *self-devised worship, supererogatory worship, will-worship.*
ἐθελοθρησκείᾳ,[c] dat. sing. . . . ἐθελοθρησκεία
ἐθέλω, see θέλω.
ἐθεμελίωσας, 2 pers. sing. aor. 1, ind. act. . θεμελιόω
ἔθεντο, 3 pers. pl. aor. 2, ind. mid. (§ 28. tab. W) τίθημι
ἐθεραπεύθη, 3 pers. sing. aor. 1, ind. pass. . θεραπεύω
ἐθεραπεύθησαν, 3 pers. pl. aor. 1, ind. pass. id.
ἐθεράπευον, 3 pers. pl. imperf. act. . . id.
ἐθεραπεύοντο, 3 pers. pl. imperf. pass. . id.
ἐθεράπευσε, 3 pers. sing. aor. 1, ind. act. . id.
ἐθερίσθη, 3 pers. sing. aor. 1, ind. pass. . θερίζω
ἐθερμαίνοντο, 3 pers. pl. imperf. mid. . θερμαίνω
ἔθεσθε, 2 pers. pl. aor. 2, ind. mid. . . τίθημι
ἔθεσι, dat. pl. . . . . . ἔθος

[a] Ro. 3. 13. [b] 1 Ti. 3. 15. [c] Col. 2. 23.

ἔθετο, 3 pers. s. aor. 2, ind. mid. (§ 28. rem. 8. d) τίθημι
ἐθεώρει, 3 pers. sing. imperf. act. . . θεωρέω
ἐθεώρησαν, 3 pers. pl. aor. 1, ind. act. . id.
ἐθεώρουν, 1 pers. sing. and 3 pers. pl. imperf. act. id.
ἔθη, acc. pl. . . . . ἔθος
ἔθηκα, 1 pers. s. aor. 1, ind. act. (§ 28. rem. 9. b) τίθημι
ἔθηκαν, 3 pers. pl. aor. 1, ind. act. . . id.
ἔθηκας, 2 pers. sing. aor. 1, ind. act. . . id.
ἔθηκε, 3 pers. sing. aor. 1, ind. act. . . id.
ἐθήλασαν, 3 pers. pl. aor. 1, ind. act. . . θηλάζω
ἐθήλασας, 2 pers. sing. aor. 1, ind. act. . id.
ἐθηριομάχησα,[a] 1 pers. sing. aor. 1, ind. θηριομαχέω
ἐθησαυρίσατε, 2 pers. pl. aor. 1, ind. act. . θησαυρίζω
ἐθίζω], fut. ίσω . . . . . ἔθος
ἐθνάρχης,[b] ου, ὁ, (§ 2. tab. B. c) (ἔθνος & ἄρχω) *a governor, chief, or head of any tribe or nation, prefect.* L.G.
ἔθνει, dat. sing. . . . . ἔθνος
ἔθνεσι, dat. pl. . . . . id.
ἔθνη, nom. and acc. pl. . . . id.
ἐθνικοί, nom. pl. masc. . . . ἐθνικός
ἐθνικός, ή, όν, (§ 7. tab. F. a) . . . ἔθνος
ἐθνικῶν, gen. pl.—Al. Ln. Tdf. . } ἐθνικός
ἐθνῶν, Rec. Gr. Sch. (3 Jno. 7) . }
ἐθνικῶς,[c] adv. . . . . . . ἔθνος

ἔθνος, εος, τό, (§ 5. tab. E. b) *a multitude, company,* Ac. 17. 26; 1 Pe. 2. 9; Re. 21. 24; *a nation, people,* Mat. 20. 25; 21. 43, et al.; pl. ἔθνη, from the Heb., *nations or people as distinguished from the Jews, the heathen, gentiles,* Mat. 4. 15; 10. 5; Lu. 2. 32, et al.

ἐθνῐκός, ή, όν, (§ 7. tab. F. a) *national;* in N.T. *gentile, heathen, not Israelitish,* Mat. 6. 7; 18. 17. L.G.

ἐθνῐκῶς, adv. *after the manner of the gentiles, heathenishly.* N.T.

ἔθνους, gen. sing. . . . . . ἔθνος
ἐθνῶν, gen. pl. . . . . . id.
ἐθορύβουν, 3 pers. pl. imperf. act. . . θορυβέω

ἔθος, εος, τό, (§ 5. tab. E. b) *a custom, usage,* Lu. 2. 42; 22. 39, et al.; *an institute, rite,* Lu. 1. 9; Ac. 6. 14; 15. 1, et al.

ἐθίζω, fut. ίσω, perf. pass. εἴθισμαι, (§ 13. rem. 4) *to accustom;* pass. *to be customary,* Lu. 2. 27.

εἴωθα, perf. 2, from an old pres. ἔθω, with a present signification, (§ 38. rem. 2) pluperf. εἰώθειν, part. εἰωθώς, *to be accustomed, to be usual,* Mat. 27. 15, et al.

ἔθου, 2 pers. sing. aor. 2, ind. mid. (§ 28. rem. 8. a) τίθημι
ἐθρέψαμεν, 1 pers. pl. aor. 1, ind. act. . τρέφω
ἔθρεψαν, 3 pers. pl. aor. 1, ind. act.—B. Ln. Tdf. } id.
ἐθήλασαν, Rec. Gr. Sch. (Lu. 23. 29) }
ἐθρέψατε, 2 pers. pl. aor. 1, ind. act. . . id.
ἐθρηνήσαμεν, 1 pers. pl. aor. 1, ind. act. . θρηνέω
ἐθρήνουν, 3 pers. pl. imperf. act. . . id.
ἐθύθη, 3 pers. sing. aor. 1, ind. pass. . θύω
ἐθυμώθη,[d] 3 pers. sing. aor. 1, ind. pass. . θυμόω
ἔθυον, 3 pers. pl. imperf. act. . . θύω
ἔθυσας, 2 pers. sing. aor. 1, ind. act. . . id.
ἔθυσε, 3 pers. sing. aor. 1, ind. act. . . id.
ἐθῶν, gen. pl. . . . . ἔθος

εἰ, conj. *if,* Mat. 4. 3, 6; 12. 7; Ac. 27. 39, et al. freq.; *since,* Ac. 4. 9, et al., *whether,* Mar. 9. 23; Ac. 17. 11, et al.; *that,* in certain expressions, Ac. 26. 8, 23; He. 7. 15; by a suppression of the apodosis of a sentence, εἰ serves to express a wish; *O if! O that!* Lu. 19. 42; 22. 42; also a strong negation, Mar. 8. 12; He. 3. 11; 4. 3; εἰ καί, *if even, though, although,* Lu. 18. 4, et al.; εἰ μή, *unless, except,* Mat. 11. 27, et al.; also equivalent to ἀλλά, *but,* Mat. 12. 4; Mar. 13. 32; Lu. 4. 26, 27; εἰ μήτι, *unless perhaps, unless it be,* Lu. 9. 13, et al.; εἴ τις, εἴ τι, pr. *if any one; whosoever, whatsoever,* Mat. 18. 28, et al. The syntax of this particle must be learnt from the grammars. As an interrogative particle, *whether,* Ac. 17. 11, et al.; in N.T. as a mere note of interrogation, Lu. 22. 49, et al.

εἶ, 2 pers. sing. pres. ind. (§ 12. rem. 1) . εἰμί
εἴα, 3 pers. sing. imperf. (§ 13. rem. 4) ἐάω
εἴᾱσαν, 3 pers. pl. aor. 1, ind. . . id.
εἴᾱσε, 3 pers. sing. aor. 1, ind. . . id.
εἶδαν, 3 pers. pl. for εἶδον, (§ 35. rem. 12). —B. C. Tdf. . . . } ὁράω
εἶδον, Rec. Gr. Sch. (Lu. 10. 24) . }
εἶδε, 3 pers. sing. aor. 2, ind. act. (§ 36. rem. 1) id.
εἴδει, dat. sing. . . . . . εἶδος
εἰδέναι, perf. infin. (§ 37. rem. 1) . . οἶδα
εἶδες, 2 pers. sing. aor. 2, ind. act. . . ὁράω
εἴδετε, 2 pers. pl. aor. 2, ind. act . id.

a 1 Co. 15. 32. b 2 Co. 11. 32. c Gal. 2. 14. d Mat. 2. 16.

εἰδῇς, 2 pers. sing. subj. (§ 37. rem. 1) — οἶδα
εἰδήσουσι, 3 pers. pl. fut. ind. — id.
εἰδῆτε, 2 pers. pl. subj. — id.
εἴδομεν, 1 pers. pl. aor. 2, ind. act. — ὁράω
εἶδον, imperat. ἰδέ & ἴδε, optat. ἴδοιμι, subj. ἴδω, infin. ἰδεῖν, part. ἰδών, (§ 36. rem. 1). See ὁράω.
εἶδος, εος, τό, (§ 5. tab. E. b) (εἴδω, a form not in use, *to see*) *form, external appearance*, Lu. 3. 22; 9. 29; Jno. 5. 37; *kind, species*, 1 Thes. 5. 22; *sight, perception*, 2 Co. 5. 7.

εἴδωλον, ου, τό, (§ 3. tab. C. c) pr. *a form, shape, figure; image or statue*; hence, *an idol, image of a god*, Ac. 7. 41, et al.; meton. *a heathen god*, 1 Co. 8. 4, 7, et al.; for εἰδωλόθυτον, *the flesh of victims sacrificed to idols*, Ac. 15. 20.

εἰδωλεῖον, ου, τό, (§ 3. tab. C. c) *a heathen temple*, 1 Co. 8. 10. LXX.

εἴδοσαν, 3 p. pl. for εἶδον, (§ 35. rem. 13).—D.
εἶδον, Rec. Gr. Sch. Tdf. (Mar. 9. 9) } ὁράω
εἰδόσι, dat. pl. masc. part. (§ 37. rem. 1) — οἶδα
εἰδότα, nom. pl. neut. part. — id.
εἰδότας, acc. pl. masc. part. — id.
εἰδότες, nom. pl. masc. part. — id.
εἰδότι, dat. sing. masc. part. — id.
εἴδους, gen. sing. — εἶδος
εἰδυῖα, nom. sing. fem. part. perf. — οἶδα
εἰδῶ, εἰδέναι, εἰδώς. See οἶδα.
εἴδωλα, acc. pl. — εἴδωλον
εἰδωλεῖον], ου, τό, (§ 3. tab. C. c) — εἶδος
εἰδωλείῳ,[a] dat. sing. — εἰδωλεῖον
εἰδωλόθυτα, acc. pl. neut. — εἰδωλόθυτος
εἰδωλόθυτον, nom. and acc. sing. neut. — id.
εἰδωλόθῦτος], ου, ὁ, ἡ, τό, -ον, (§ 7. rem. 2) (εἴδωλον & θύω) pr. *sacrificed to an idol*; meton. *the remains of victims sacrificed to idols*, reserved for eating, Ac. 15. 29; 21. 25, et al. N.T.
εἰδωλοθύτων, gen. pl. — εἰδωλόθυτος
εἰδωλολάτραι, nom. pl. — εἰδωλολάτρης
εἰδωλολάτραις, dat. pl. — id.
εἰδωλολατρεία, ας, ἡ, (§ 2. tab. B. b, and rem. 2) (εἴδωλον & λατρεία) *idolatry, worship of idols*, 1 Co. 10. 14; Gal. 5. 23, et al. N.T.
εἰδωλολατρείαις, dat. pl. — εἰδωλολατρεία
εἰδωλολατρείας, gen. sing. — id.
εἰδωλολάτρης, ου, ὁ, (§ 2. tab. B. c) (εἴδωλον & λάτρις, *a servant, worshipper*) *an idolater, worshipper of idols*, 1 Co. 5. 10, 11; 6. 9; 10. 7, et al. N.T. (ᾰ).
εἴδωλον, ου, τό, (§ 3. tab. C. c) — εἶδος
εἰδώλου, gen. sing. — εἴδωλον
εἰδώλῳ, dat. sing. — id.
εἰδώλων, gen. pl. — id.
εἰδῶμεν, 1 pers. pl. subj. — οἶδα
εἰδώς, nom. sing. masc. part. — id.
εἴη, 3 pers. sing. pres. optat. — εἰμί
εἴης, 2 pers. sing. pres. optat. — id.
εἰθισμένον, acc. sing. neut. part. perf. pass. (§ 13. rem. 4) — ἐθίζω
εἰκῆ, adv. *without plan or system; without cause, lightly, rashly*, Mat. 5. 22; Col. 2. 18; *to no purpose, in vain*, Ro. 13. 4; 1 Co. 15. 2; Gal. 3. 4; 4. 11.
εἰκόνα, acc. sing. — εἰκών
εἰκόνι, dat. sing. — id.
εἰκόνος, gen. sing. — id.

εἴκοσι, οἱ, αἱ, τά, *twenty*, Lu. 14. 31, et al.
εἰκοσιπέντε,[b] (εἴκοσι & πέντε) *twenty-five*.
εἰκοσιτέσσαρες, (εἴκοσι & τέσσαρες) *twenty-four*, Re. 5. 8, 14.
εἰκοσιτρεῖς,[c] (εἴκοσι & τρεῖς) *twenty-three*.
εἴκω], fut. ξω, *to yield, give place, submit*, Gal. 2. 5.
εἰκών, ονος, ἡ, (§ 4. tab. D. a) (εἴκω, an obsolete form, *to be like*) *a material image, likeness, effigy*, Mat. 22. 20; Mar. 12. 16, et al.; *a similitude, representation, exact image*, 1 Co. 11. 7, et al.; *resemblance*, Ro. 8. 29, et al.

εἵλατο, 3 pers. sing. aor. 1, mid. (§ 35. rem. 12). —Al. Ln. Tdf.
εἵλετο, Rec. Gr. Sch. (2 Thes. 2. 13) } αἱρέω
εἵλετο, 3 pers. sing. aor. 2, ind. mid. (§ 36. rem. 1) — id.
εἰλημμένην, acc. sing. fem. part. perf. pass.—D.
κατειλημμένην, R. Gr. Sch. Tdf. (Jno. 8. 3) } λαμβάνω
εἴληφα, 1 pers. sing. perf. ind. act. (§ 13. rem. 7. a) — id.
εἴληφας, 2 pers. sing. perf. ind. act. — id.
εἴληφε, 3 pers. sing. perf. ind. act. — id.
εἰληφώς, nom. sing. masc. part. perf. act. — id.
εἰλικρινῆ, acc. sing. fem. — εἰλικρινής
εἰλικρινείᾳ, dat. sing. — εἰλικρινεία
εἰλικρινεία], ας, ἡ, (§ 2. tab. B. b, and rem. 2) — εἰλικρινής
εἰλικρινείας, gen. sing. — εἰλικρινεία
εἰλικρινεῖς, nom. pl. masc. — εἰλικρινής

---

[a] 1 Co. 8. 10. [b] Jno. 6. 19. [c] 1 Co. 10. 8.

εἰλικρῐνής], εος, ὁ, ἡ, (§ 7. tab. G. b) (εἵλη, *sunshine*, and κρίνω) pr. *that which being viewed in the sunshine is found clear and pure;* met. *spotless, sincere, ingenuous*, Phi. 1. 10; 2 Pe. 3. 1.

εἰλικρινεία, ας, ἡ, (§ 2. tab. B. b, and rem. 2) *clearness, purity;* met. *sincerity, integrity, ingenuousness*, 1 Co. 5. 8, et al.

εἱλισσόμενον,[a] nom. sing. neut. part. pres. pass. — εἱλίσσω

εἱλίσσω], fut. ξω, (§ 26. rem. 2) (properly Ionic for ἑλίσσω) (εἰλέω, *to roll*) *to roll up.*

εἷλκον, 3 pers. pl. imperf. (§ 13. rem. 4) — ἕλκω

εἵλκῠσαν, 3 pers. pl. aor. 1, ind. act. — ἑλκύω

εἵλκῠσε, 3 pers. sing. aor. 1, ind. act. — id.

εἱλκωμένος, nom. sing. masc. part. perf. pass.—A. B. D. Ln. Tdf. ἡλκωμένος, Rec. Gr. Sch. (Lu. 16. 20) — ἑλκόω

εἰμί, (§ 12. tab. L) imperf. ἦν & ἤμην, fut. ἔσομαι imperat. ἴσθι, ἔστω & ἤτω, subj. ὦ, infin. εἶναι, part. ὤν, a verb of existence, *to be, to exist*, Jno. 1. 1; 17. 5; Mat. 6. 30; Lu. 4. 25, et al. freq.; ἐστί, *it is possible, proper*, He. 9. 5; a simple copula to the subject and predicate, and therefore in itself affecting the force of the sentence only by its tense, mood, etc., Jno. 1. 1; 15. 1, et al. freq.; it also forms a frequent circumlocution with the participles of the present and perfect of other verbs, Mat. 19. 22; Mar. 2. 6, et al.

ὄντως, adv. (ὤν, ὄντος, pres. part. of εἰμί) *really, in truth, truly*, Mar. 11. 32; Lu. 23. 47, et al.

οὐσία, ας, ἡ, (§ 2. tab. B. b, and rem. 2) (ὤν, οὖσα, ὄν, part. of εἰμί) *substance, property, goods, fortune*, Lu. 15. 12, 13.

εἶμι, *to go, come*, but generally with a future signification, v.r. Jno. 7. 34, 36.

εἶναι, pres. infin. — εἰμί

εἵνεκεν, equivalent to ἕνεκα, *on account of*, 2 Co. 7. 12, ter.

εἴξαμεν,[b] 1 pers. pl. aor. 1, ind. — εἴκω

εἶπα, (§ 35. rem. 7) Mat. 26. 25, et al., imperat. εἶπον or εἰπόν, v.r. Ac. 28. 26. See λέγω.

εἶπαν, 3 pers. pl.—Ln. Tdf. εἶπον, Rec. Gr. Sch. (Mar. 10. 4) — εἶπα

εἶπας, 2 pers. sing. — id.

εἴπας, nom. sing. masc.—B. Tdf. εἰπών, Rec. Gr. Sch. (Ac. 22. 24) — εἶπα

εἴπατε, 2 pers. pl. ind. — id.

εἴπατε, 2 pers. pl. imper. — id.

εἰπάτω, 3 pers. sing. imper. — id.

εἰπάτωσαν, 3 pers. pl. imper. — id.

εἶπε, 3 pers. sing. ind. — εἶπον

εἰπέ, 2 pers. sing. imper. — id.

εἰπεῖν, infin. — id.

εἴπερ, a strengthening of εἰ by the enclitic particle περ, *if indeed, if it be so that*, Ro. 8. 9; 1 Co. 15. 15; *since indeed, since*, 2 Thes. 1. 6; 1 Pe. 2. 3; *although indeed*, 1 Co. 8. 5.

εἴπῃ, 3 pers. sing. subj. — εἶπον

εἴπῃς, 2 pers. sing. subj. — id.

εἴπητε, 2 pers. pl. subj. — id.

εἰπόν, 2 pers. sing. imper.—Gr. Sch. Tdf. εἰπέ, Rec. (Ac. 28. 26) — εἶπα

εἶπον, imperat. εἰπέ, subj. εἴπω, optat. εἴποιμι, infin. εἰπεῖν, part. εἰπών. See λέγω.

εἰπόντα, acc. sing. masc. part. — εἶπον

εἰπόντες, nom. pl. masc. part. — id.

εἰπόντι, dat. sing. masc. part. — id.

εἰπόντας, gen. sing. masc. part. — id.

εἰποῦσα, nom. sing. fem. part. — id.

εἴπω, 1 pers. sing. subj. — id.

εἴπωμεν, 1 pers. pl. subj. — id.

εἰπών, nom. sing. masc. part. — id.

εἴπως, (εἰ & πως) *if by any means, if possibly*, Ac. 27. 12, et al.

εἴπωσι, 3 pers. pl. subj. — εἶπον

εἰργάζετο, 3 pers. sing. imperf. (§ 13. rem. 4) — ἐργάζομαι

εἰργασάμεθα, 1 pers. pl. aor. 1, ind. — id.

εἰργάσαντο, 3 pers. pl. aor. 1, ind. — id.

εἰργάσασθε, 2 pers. pl. aor. 1, ind.—A. Ln. Tdf. εἰργασάμεθα, Rec. Gr. Sch. (2 Jno. 8) — id.

εἰργάσατο, 3 pers. sing. aor. 1, ind. — id.

εἰργασμένα, nom. pl. neut. part. perf. pass. — id.

εἴρηκα, 1 pers. sing. perf. Att. (§ 36. rem. 1) — ῥέω

εἴρηκαν, 3 pers. pl. perf. ind. (§ 35. rem. 13) — id.

εἴρηκας, 2 pers. sing. perf. ind. Att. — id.

εἰρήκασι, 3 pers. pl. perf. ind. Att. — id.

εἰρήκατε, 2 pers. pl. perf. ind. Att. — id.

εἴρηκε, 3 pers. sing. perf. ind. Att. — id.

εἰρήκει, 3 pers. sing. pluperf. Att. — id.

εἰρηκέναι, perf. infin.—Al. Ln. Tdf. προειρηκέναι, Rec. Gr. Sch. (He. 10. 15) — id.

εἰρηκότος, gen. sing. masc. part. perf. Att. — id

[a] Re. 6. 14. [b] Gal. 2. 5.

εἰρημένον, nom. and acc. s. neut. pt. perf. pass. Att. ῥέω
εἰρηνεύετε, 2 pers. pl. pres. imper. . . εἰρηνεύω
εἰρηνεύοντες, nom. pl. masc. part. pres. . id.
εἰρηνεύω], fut. εύσω, (§ 13. tab. M) . . εἰρήνη

εἰρήνη, ης, ἡ, (§ 2. tab. B. a) *peace,* Lu. 14. 32; Ac. 12. 20, et al.; *tranquillity,* Lu. 11. 21; Jno. 16. 33; 1 Thes. 5. 3; *concord, unity, love of peace,* Mat. 10. 34; Lu. 12. 51, et al.; meton. *the author of peace or concord,* Ep. 2. 14; from the Heb. *felicity, every kind of blessing and good,* Lu. 1. 79; 2. 14, 29, et al.; meton. *a salutation expressive of good wishes, a benediction, blessing,* Mat. 10. 13, et al.

εἰρηνεύω, fut. εύσω, (§ 13. tab. M) *to be at peace; to cultivate peace, concord, or harmony,* Mat. 9. 50; Ro. 12. 18, et al.

εἰρηνικός, ή, όν, (§ 7. tab. F. a) *pertaining to peace; peaceable, disposed to peace and concord,* Ja. 3. 17; from the Heb. *profitable, blissful,* He. 12. 11.

εἰρήνῃ, dat. sing. . . . . εἰρήνη
εἰρήνην, acc. sing. . . . . id.
εἰρήνης, gen. sing. . . . . . id.
εἰρηνική, nom. sing. fem. . . . εἰρηνικός
εἰρηνικόν, acc. sing. masc. . . . id.
εἰρηνικός], ή, όν, (§ 7. tab. F. a) . εἰρήνη
εἰρηνοποιέω, ῶ], fut. ήσω, (§ 16. tab. P) (εἰρήνη & ποιέω) *to make peace, restore concord.* L.G.
εἰρηνοποιήσας,[a] nom. sing. masc. part. aor. 1 εἰρηνοποιέω
εἰρηνοποιοί,[b] nom. pl. masc. . . εἰρηνοποιός
εἰρηνοποιός], οῦ, ὁ, ἡ, *a peace-maker, one who cultivates peace and concord.*
εἴρηται, 3 pers. sing. perf. ind. pass. (§ 36. rem. 1) ῥέω
εἴρω], an almost obsolete pres., fut. ἐρῶ, (§ 36 rem. 1) *to say, speak,* etc., joined in usage with the forms λέγω, εἶπον, & εἴρηκα.

εἰς, *into,* Mat. 2. 11, et al.; *to, as far as, to the extent of,* Mat. 2. 23; 4. 24, et al.; *until,* Jno. 13. 1, et al.; *against,* Mat. 18. 15; Lu. 12. 10; *before, in the presence of,* Ac. 22. 30, et al.; *in order to, for, with a view to,* Mar. 1. 38, et al.; *for the use or service of,* Jno. 6. 9; Lu. 9. 13; 1 Co. 16. 1; *with reference to,* 2 Co. 10. 13, 16; *in accordance with,* Mat. 12. 41; Lu. 11. 32; 2 Ti. 2. 26; also equivalent to ἐν, Jno. 1. 18, et al.; *by,* in forms of swearing, Mat. 5. 35, et al.; from the Heb. εἶναι, γίνεσθαι εἰς—, *to become, result in, amount to,* Mat. 19. 5; 1 Co. 4. 3, et al.; εἰς τί, *why, wherefore,* Mat. 26. 8.

εἷς, μία, ἕν, gen. ἑνός, μιᾶς, ἑνός, (§ 9. tab. I. a) *one,* Mat. 10. 29, et al. freq.; *only,* Mar. 12. 6; *one* virtually by union, Mat. 19. 5, 6; Jno. 10. 30; *one and the same,* Lu. 12. 52; Ro. 3. 30, et al.; *one* in respect of office and standing, 1 Co. 3. 8; equivalent to τις, *a certain one,* Mat. 8. 19; 16. 14, et al.; *a, an,* Mat. 21. 19; Ja. 4. 13, et al.; εἷς ἕκαστος, *each one, every one,* Lu. 4. 40; Ac. 2. 3, et al.; εἷς τὸν ἕνα, *one another,* 1 Thes. 5. 11; εἷς—καὶ εἷς, *the one—and the other,* Mat. 20. 21, et al.; εἷς καθ' εἷς & ὁ δὲ καθ' εἷς, *one by one, one after another, in succession,* Mar. 14. 19; Jno. 8. 9, et al.; from the Heb. as an ordinal, *first,* Mat. 28. 1, et al.

ἑνότης, τητος, ἡ, (§ 4. rem. 2. c) *oneness, unity,* Ep. 4. 3, 13.

εἰσάγαγε, 2 pers. s. aor. 2, imper. (§ 13. rem. 7. d) εἰσάγω
εἰσαγαγεῖν, aor. 2, infin. act. . . . id.
εἰσαγάγῃ, 3 pers. sing. aor. 2, subj. act. . id.
εἰσάγειν, pres. infin. act.—Ln. Tdf. } id.
εἰσαγαγεῖν, Rec. Gr. Sch. (Lu. 2. 27) . }
εἰσάγεσθαι, pres. infin. pass. . . . id.
εἰσάγω], fut. ξω, (§ 23. rem. 1. b) (εἰς & ἄγω) *to lead or bring in, introduce, conduct or usher in or to* a place or person, Lu. 2. 27; 14. 21; 22. 54, et al.
εἰσακουσθείς, nom. sing. masc. part. aor. 1, pass. εἰσακούω
εἰσακουσθήσονται, 3 pers. pl. fut. 1, ind. pass. id.
εἰσακούσονται, 3 pers. pl. fut. ind. mid. . id.
εἰσακούω], fut. ούσομαι, (εἰς & ἀκούω) *to hear or hearken to; to heed,* 1 Co. 14. 21; *to listen to* the prayers of any one, *accept one's petition,* Mat. 6. 7; Lu. 1. 13; Ac. 10. 31; He. 5. 7.
εἰσδέξομαι,[c] 1 pers. sing. fut. ind. . . εἰσδέχομαι
εἰσδέχομαι], fut. δέξομαι, (§ 23. rem. 1. b) (εἰς & δέχομαι) *to admit; to receive into* favour, *receive kindly, accept with favour.*
εἰσδραμοῦσα,[d] nom. s. f. part. aor. 2, (§ 36. rem. 1) εἰστρέχω

[a] Col. 1. 20. [b] Mat. 5. 9. [c] 2 Co. 6. 17. [d] Ac. 12. 14.

εἴσειμι], (§ 33. rem. 4) (εἰς & εἶμι, *to go*) imperf. εἰσῄειν, *to go in, enter*, Ac. 3. 3; 21. 18, 26; He. 9. 6.

εἰσελεύσεσθαι, fut. infin. (§ 36. rem. 1) . εἰσέρχομαι
εἰσελεύσεται, 3 pers. sing. fut. ind. . . id.
εἰσελεύσομαι, 1 pers. sing. fut. ind. . id.
εἰσελεύσονται, 3 pers. pl. fut. ind. . . id.
εἰσελήλυθαν, 3 pers. pl. perf. 2, (§ 35. rem. 13). —B. Ln. Tdf. . . . . } id.
εἰσεληλύθασιν, Rec. Gr. Sch. (Ja. 5. 4)
εἰσεληλύθασι, 3 pers. pl. perf. 2 . . . id.
εἰσεληλύθατε, 2 pers. pl. perf. 2 . . id.
εἰσέλθατε, 2 pers. pl. aor. 1, imper. (§ 35. rem. 12).—B. Ln. . . . } id.
εἰσέλθετε, Rec. Gr. Sch. Tdf. (Mat. 7. 13)
εἰσελθάτω, 3 pers. sing. aor. 1, imper. (§ 35. rem. 12).—A. D. Ln. Tdf. . . } id.
εἰσελθέτω, Rec. Gr. Sch. (Mar. 13. 15)
εἴσελθε, 2 pers. sing. aor. 2, imper. . . id.
εἰσελθεῖν, aor. 2, infin. . . . . . id.
εἰσέλθετε, 2 pers. pl. aor. 2, imper. . . id.
εἰσελθέτω, 3 pers. sing. aor. 2, imper. . id.
εἰσέλθῃ, 3 pers. sing. aor. 2, subj. . . id.
εἰσέλθῃς, 2 pers. sing. aor. 2, subj. . . id.
εἰσέλθητε, 2 pers. pl. aor. 2, subj. . . id.
εἰσελθόντα, acc. sing. masc. part. aor. 2 . id.
εἰσελθόντα, nom. pl. neut. part. aor. 2 . id.
εἰσελθόντες, nom. pl. masc. part. aor. 2 . id.
εἰσελθόντι, dat. sing. masc. part. aor. 2 . id.
εἰσελθόντος, gen. sing. masc. part. aor. 2 . id.
εἰσελθόντων, gen. pl. masc. part. aor. 2 . id.
εἰσελθοῦσα, nom. sing. fem. part. aor. 2 . id.
εἰσελθοῦσαι, nom. pl. fem. part. aor. 2 . id.
εἰσελθούσης, gen. sing. fem. part. aor. 2 . id.
εἰσέλθωμεν, 1 pers. pl. aor. 2, subj. . . id.
εἰσελθών, nom. sing. masc. part. aor. 2 . id.
εἰσέλθωσι, 3 pers. pl. aor. 2, subj. . . id.
εἰσενέγκῃς, 2 pers. sing. aor. 1, subj. (§ 36. rem. 1) . . . . εἰσφέρω
εἰσενεγκεῖν, aor. 2, infin. act. . . . id.
εἰσενέγκωσι, 3 pers. pl. aor. 2, subj. act. . id.
εἰσεπήδησαν, 3 pers. pl. aor. 1, ind. . . εἰσπηδάω
εἰσεπήδησε, 3 pers. sing. aor. 1, ind. . . id.
εἰσεπορεύετο, 3 pers. sing. imperf. . . εἰσπορεύομαι
εἰσέρχεσθε, 2 pers. pl. pres. ind. . . εἰσέρχομαι
εἰσερχέσθωσαν, 3 pers. pl. pres. imper. . id.
εἰσέρχεται, 3 pers. sing. pres. ind. . . id.
εἰσέρχησθε, 2 pers. pl. pres. subj. . . id.

εἰσέρχομαι], (§ 36. rem. 1) fut. εἰσελεύσομαι, aor. 2, εἰσῆλθον, (εἰς & ἔρχομαι) *to go or come in, enter*, Mat. 7. 13; 8. 5, 8, et al.; spc. *to enter* by force, *break in*, Mar. 3. 27; Ac. 20. 29; met. with εἰς κόσμον, *to begin to exist, come into existence*, Ro. 5. 12; 2 Jno. 7, or, *to make one's appearance on earth*, He. 10. 5; *to enter into or take possession of*, Lu. 22. 3; Jno. 13. 27; *to enter into, enjoy, partake of*, Mat. 19. 23, 24, et al.; *to enter into* any one's labour, *be* his *successor*, Jno. 4. 38; *to fall into, be placed in* certain circumstances, Mat. 26. 41, et al.; *to be put into*, Mat. 15. 11; Ac. 11. 8; *to present one's self before*, Ac. 19. 30; met. *to arise, spring up*, Lu. 9. 46; from the Heb. εἰσέρχεσθαι καὶ ἐξέρχεσθαι, *to go in and out, to live, discharge the ordinary functions of life*, Ac. 1. 21.

εἰσερχόμεθα, 1 pers. pl. pres. ind. . . εἰσέρχομαι
εἰσερχομένην, acc. sing. fem. part. pres. . id.
εἰσερχόμενοι, nom. pl. masc. part. pres. . id.
εἰσερχόμενον, nom. sing. neut. part. pres. . id.
εἰσερχόμενος, nom. sing. masc. part. pres. . id.
εἰσερχομένου, gen. sing. masc. part. pres. . id.
εἰσερχομένους, acc. pl. masc. part. pres. . id.
εἰσερχώμεθα, 1 pers. pl. pres. subj.—A. C. . } id.
εἰσερχόμεθα, R. Gr. Sch. Tdf. (He. 4. 3)
εἰσήγαγε, 3 pers. sing. aor. 2, act. (§ 34. rem. 1. a) εἰσάγω
εἰσήγαγον, 3 pers. pl. aor. 2, act. (§ 13. rem. 7. b. d) . . . . id.
εἰσῄει, 3 pers. sing. pluperf. (§ 33. rem. 4) εἴσειμι
εἰσηκούσθη, 3 pers. sing. aor. 1, ind. pass. (§ 22. rem. 4) . . . . . εἰσακούω
εἰσήλθατε, 2 pers. pl. aor. 1, ind. (§ 35. rem. 12).—Al. Tdf. . . } εἰσέρχομαι
εἰσήλθετε, Rec. Gr. Sch. (Lu. 11. 52)
εἰσῆλθε, 3 pers. sing. aor. 2, ind. . . id.
εἰσῆλθες, 2 pers. sing. aor. 2, ind. . . id.
εἰσήλθετε, 2 pers. pl. aor. 2, ind. . . id.
εἰσήλθομεν, 1 pers. pl. aor. 2, ind. . . id.
εἰσῆλθον, 1 pers. sing. and 3 pers. pl. aor. 2, ind. id.
εἰσηνέγκαμεν, 1 pers. pl. aor. 1, ind. (§ 36. rem. 1) εἰσφέρω
εἰσί, 3 pers. pl. pres. ind. (§ 12. tab. L) . εἰμί
εἰσίασι, 3 pers. pl. pres. for εἴσεισι, (§ 33. rem. 4) εἴσειμι
εἰσιέναι, pres. infin. . . . . . id.
εἰσκαλεσάμενος,[a] nom. sing. masc. pt. aor. 1, mid. εἰσκαλέω

[a] Ac. 10. 23.

εἰσκαλέω, ῶ], fut. έσω, and mid. εἰσκαλέομαι, οῦμαι, (§ 17. tab. Q) (εἰς & καλέω) *to call in; to invite in.*

εἴσοδον, acc. sing. . . . . . εἴσοδος

εἴσοδος, ου, ἡ, (§ 3. tab. C. b) (εἰς & ὁδός) *a place of entrance; the act of entrance,* He. 10. 19; *admission, reception,* 1 Thes. 1. 9; 2 Pe. 1. 11; *a coming, approach, access,* 1 Thes. 2. 1; *entrance* upon office, *commencement* of ministry, Ac. 13. 24.

εἰσόδου, gen. sing. . . . . . εἴσοδος

εἰσπηδάω, ῶ], fut. ήσω, (§ 18. tab. R) (εἰς & πηδάω, *to leap*) *to leap or spring in, rush in eagerly,* Ac. 14. 14; 16. 29.

εἰσπορεύεται, 3 pers. sing. pres. ind. . εἰσπορεύομαι

εἰσπορεύομαι], fut. εύσομαι, (§ 14. tab. N) (εἰς & πορεύομαι) *to go or come in, enter,* Mar. 1. 21; 5. 40, et al.; *to come to, visit,* Ac. 28. 30; *to be put in,* Mat. 15. 17; Mar. 7. 15, 18, 19; *to intervene,* Mar. 4. 19; from the Heb. εἰσπορεύεσθαι καὶ ἐκπορεύεσθαι equivalent to εἰσέρχεσθαι καὶ ἐξέρχεσθαι, above, Ac. 9. 28.

εἰσπορευόμεναι, nom. pl. fem. part. pres. εἰσπορεύομαι

εἰσπορευόμενοι, nom. pl. masc. part. pres. . id.

εἰσπορευόμενον, nom. sing. neut. part. pres. id.

εἰσπορευόμενος, nom. sing. masc. part. pres. id.

εἰσπορευομένους, acc. sing. masc. part. pres. id.

εἰσπορευομένων, gen. pl. part. pres. . . id.

εἰσπορεύονται, 3 pers. pl. pres. ind. . . id.

εἱστήκει, 3 pers. sing. pluperf. (§ 29. rem. 4) ἵστημι

εἱστήκεισαν, 3 pers. pl. pluperf. . . id.

εἰστρέχω], aor. 2, εἰσέδρᾰμον, (§ 36. rem. 1) (εἰς & τρέχω) *to run in,* Ac. 12. 14.

εἰσφέρεις, 2 pers. sing. pres. ind. act. . . εἰσφέρω

εἰσφέρεται, 3 pers. sing. pres. ind. pass. . id.

εἰσφέρω], fut. εἰσοίσω, aor. 1, εἰσήνεγκα, aor. 2, εἰσήνεγκον, (§ 36. rem. 1) (εἰς & φέρω) *to bring in, to, or into,* Lu. 5. 18, 19; 1 Ti. 6. 7; He. 13. 11; *to bring to* the ears of any one, *to announce,* Ac. 17. 20; *to lead into,* Mat. 6. 13; Lu. 11. 4.

εἰσφέρωσι, 3 pers. pl. pres. subj. act.—B. Tdf.
προσφέρωσι, Rec. Gr. Sch. (Lu. 12. 11) } εἰσφέρω

εἶτα, adv. *then, afterwards, thereupon,* Mar. 4. 17, 28; Lu. 8. 12, et al.; *in the next place,* 1 Co. 12. 28; *besides,* He. 12. 9.

εἶχαν, 3 pers. pl. for εἶχον, (§ 35. rem. 12).—D.
εἶχον, Rec. Gr. Sch. (§ 15. rem. 15) } ἔχω

εἶχε, 3 pers. sing. imperf. (§ 13. rem. 4) . ἔχω

εἶχες, 2 pers. sing. imperf. . . . id.

εἴχετε, 2 pers. pl. imperf. . . . . id.

εἴχομεν, 1 pers. pl. imperf. . . . id.

εἶχον, 1 pers. sing. and 3 pers. pl. imperf. . id.

εἴχοσαν, 3 pers. pl. for εἶχον, (§ 35. rem. 13).
—B. Ln. Tdf. . . .
εἶχον, Rec. Gr. Sch. (Jno. 15. 22) . } id.

εἴωθα], perf. 2, of ἔθω, obsolete. . . ἔθος

εἰώθει, 3 pers. sing. pluperf. (§ 38. rem. 2) . εἴωθα

εἰωθός, acc. sing. neut. part. . . . id.

εἴων, 3 pers. pl. imperf. act. (§ 13. rem. 4) . ἐάω

ἐκ, before a consonant, **ἐξ**, before a vowel, prep. *from, out of,* a place, Mat. 2. 15; 3. 17; *of, from, out of,* denoting origin or source, Mat. 1. 3; 21. 19; *of, from* some material, Mat. 3. 9; Ro. 9. 21; *of, from, among,* partitively, Mat. 6. 27; 21. 31; Mar. 9. 17, *from,* denoting cause, Re. 8. 11; 17. 6; means or instrument, Mat. 12. 33, 37; *by, through,* denoting the author or efficient cause, Mat. 1. 18; Jno. 10. 32; *of,* denoting the distinguishing mark of a class, Ro. 2. 8; Gal. 3. 7, et al.; of time, *after,* 2 Co. 4. 6; Re. 17. 11; *from, after, since,* Mat. 19. 12; Lu. 8. 27; *for, with,* denoting a rate of payment, price, Mat. 20. 2; 27. 7; *at,* denoting position, Mat. 20. 21, 23; after passive verbs, *by, of, from,* marking the agent, Mat. 15. 5; Mar. 7. 11; forming with certain words a periphrasis for an abverb, Mat. 26, 42, 44; Mar. 6. 51; Lu. 23. 8; put after words of freeing, Ro. 7. 24; 2 Co. 1. 10; used partitively after verbs of eating, drinking, etc., Jno. 6. 26; 1 Co. 9. 7.

ἐκαθάρισε, 3 pers. sing. aor. 1, ind. act. . καθαρίζω

ἐκαθαρίσθη, 3 pers. sing. aor. 1, ind. pass. (§ 26. rem. 1) . . . . . id.

ἐκαθαρίσθησαν, 3 pers. pl. aor. 1, ind. pass. . id.

ἐκαθέζετο, 3 pers. sing. imperf. (§ 34. rem. 2) καθέζομαι

ἐκαθεζόμην, 1 pers. sing. imperf. . . id.

ἐκάθευδε, 3 pers. sing. imperf. (§ 34. rem. 2) . καθεύδω

ἐκάθευδον, 3 pers. pl. imperf. . . . id.

ἐκάθητο, 3 pers. sing. imperf. . . . κάθημαι

ἐκάθισα, 1 pers. sing. aor. 1, ind. (§ 34. rem. 2) καθίζω

ἐκάθισαν, 3 pers. pl. aor. 1, ind. . . id.

ἐκάθισε, 3 pers. sing. aor. 1, ind. . . id.

ἐκάκωσαν, 3 pers. pl. aor. 1, ind. act. . κακόω

ἐκάκωσε, 3 pers. sing. aor. 1, ind. act. . . κακόω
ἐκάλεσα, 1 pers. sing. aor. 1, ind. act. . καλέω
ἐκάλεσε, 3 pers. sing. aor. 1, ind. act. . . id.
ἐκάλουν, 3 pers. pl. imperf. act. . . id.
ἐκάμμῠσαν, 3 pers. pl. aor. 1, ind. . . καμμύω
ἔκαμψαν, 3 pers. pl. aor. 1, ind. act. . κάμπτω
ἐκαρτέρησε,[a] 3 pers. sing. aor. 1, ind. . . καρτερέω
ἑκάστη, nom. sing. fem. . . ἕκαστος
ἑκάστην, acc. sing. fem. . . . . id.
ἑκάστοις, dat. pl. masc. . . . id.
ἕκαστον, acc. sing. masc. . . . . id.
ἕκαστον, nom. and acc. sing. neut. . . id.
ἕκαστος, η, ον, (§ 10. rem. 6. d) *each one, every one separately,* Mat. 16. 27; Lu. 13. 15, et al.

ἑκάστοτε, adv. *always.*

ἑκάστοτε,[b] adv . . ἕκαστος
ἑκάστου, gen sing. masc. and neut. . id.
ἑκάστῳ, dat. sing. masc. . . . . id.

ἑκατόν, οἱ, αἱ, τά, indecl., *one hundred,* Mat. 13. 8; Mar. 4. 8, et al.

ἑκατονταετής,[c] εος, ὁ, ἡ, (§ 5. tab. E. a) (ἑκατόν & ἔτος) *a hundred years old.*
ἑκατονταπλασίονα, acc. s. m. and pl. neut. ἑκατονταπλασίων
ἑκατονταπλασίων], ονος, ὁ, ἡ, (§ 8. rem. 3) *a hundredfold, centuple,* Mat. 19. 29, et al.
ἑκατοντάρχῃ, dat. sing. . . . ἑκατοντάρχης
ἑκατοντάρχης, ου, ὁ, (§ 2. tab. B. c) and
ἑκατόνταρχος, ου, ὁ, (§ 3. tab. C. a) (ἑκατόν & ἄρχος) *commander of a hundred men, a centurion,* Mat. 8. 5, 8, 13; Lu. 7. 2, 6, et al.
ἑκατόνταρχον, acc. sing. . . . ἑκατόνταρχος
ἑκατοντάρχου, gen. sing. . . id.
ἑκατοντάρχους, acc. pl. . . . . id.
ἑκατοντάρχῳ, dat. sing. . . . id.
ἑκατοντάρχων, gen. pl. . . . . id.
ἐκαυματίσθη, 3 pers. s. aor. 1, pass. (§ 26. rem. 1) καυματίζω
ἐκαυματίσθησαν, 3 pers. pl. aor. 1, ind. pass. id.
ἐκβαίνω], fut. βήσομαι, aor. 2, ἐξέβην, (§ 37. rem. 1) (ἐκ & βαίνω) *to go forth, go out of.* v.r.
ἔκβᾰλε, 2 pers. sing. aor. 2, imper. act. . ἐκβάλλω
ἐκβᾰλεῖν, aor. 2, infin. act. . . . id.
ἐκβάλετε, 2 pers. pl. aor. 2, imper. act. . id.
ἐκβάλῃ, 3 pers. sing. aor. 2, subj. act. . . id.
ἐκβάλλει, 3 pers. sing. pres. ind. act. . id.
ἐκβάλλειν, pres. infin. act. . . . id.
ἐκβάλλεις, 2 pers. sing. pres. ind. act. . id.

ἐκβάλλεται, 3 pers. sing. pres. ind. pass. . ἐκβάλλω
ἐκβάλλετε, 2 pers. pl. pres. imper. act. . id.
ἐκβάλλῃ, 3 pers. sing. pres. subj. act. . . id.
ἐκβαλλόμενοι, nom. pl. masc. part. pres. mid. id.
ἐκβαλλομένους, acc. pl. masc. part. pres. pass. id.
ἐκβάλλοντα, acc. sing. masc. part. pres. act. id.
ἐκβάλλουσι, 3 pers. pl. pres. ind. act. . id.
ἐκβάλλω, fut. βαλῶ, (§ 27. rem. 1. b) aor. 2, ἐξέβᾰλον, (§ 27. rem. 2. d) (ἐκ & βάλλω) *to cast out, eject by force,* Mat. 15. 17; Ac. 27. 38; *to expel, force away,* Lu. 4. 29; Ac. 7. 58; *to refuse,* Jno. 6. 37; *to extract,* Mat. 7. 4; *to reject with contempt, despise, contemn,* Lu. 6. 22; in N.T. *to send forth, send out,* Mat. 9. 38; Lu. 10. 2; *to send away, dismiss,* Mat. 9. 25; Mar. 1. 12; met. *to spread abroad,* Mat. 12. 20; *to bring out, produce,* Mat. 12. 35; 13. 52, et al.

ἐκβολή, ῆς, ἡ, (§ 2. tab. B. a) *a casting out;* especially, *a throwing overboard* of a cargo, Ac. 27. 18.

ἐκβάλλων, nom. sing. masc. part. pres. act. . ἐκβάλλω
ἐκβάλλωσι, 3 pers. pl. pres. subj. act. . id.
ἐκβαλόντες, nom. pl masc. part. aor. 2, act. . id.
ἐκβαλοῦσα, nom. sing. fem. part. aor. 2, act. id.
ἐκβαλοῦσι, 3 pers. pl. fut. ind. act. . . id.
ἐκβάλω, 1 pers. sing. aor. 2, subj. act. . . id.
ἐκβᾰλών, nom. sing. masc. part. aor. 2, act. id.
ἐκβάλωσι, 3 pers. pl. aor. 2, subj. act. . id.
ἔκβασιν, acc. sing. . . . . . ἔκβασις
ἔκβᾰσις], εως, ἡ, (§ 5. tab. E. c) (ἐκβαίνω) *way out, egress;* hence, *result, issue,* He. 13. 7; *means of clearance or successful endurance,* 1 Co. 10. 13.
ἐκβεβλήκει, 3 pers. s. pluperf. act. (§ 13. rem. 8. f) ἐκβάλλω
ἐκβληθέντος, gen. sing. neut. part. aor. 1, pass. id.
ἐκβληθήσεται, 3 pers. s. fut. 1, pass. (§ 27. rem. 3) id.
ἐκβληθήσονται, 3 pers. pl. fut. 1, ind. pass. id.
ἐκβολή], ῆς, ἡ, (§ 2. tab. B. a) . . . id.
ἐκβολήν,[d] acc. sing. . . . . ἐκβολή
ἐκγαμίζονται, 3 pers. pl. pres. ind. pass. . ἐκγαμίζω
ἐκγαμίζοντες, nom. pl. masc. part. pres. act. id.
ἐκγαμίζω], fut. ίσω, (§ 26. rem. 1) (ἐκ & γαμίζω) *to give in marriage,* Mat. 22. 30; 24. 38; Lu. 17. 27; v.r. 1 Co. 7. 38. L.G.
ἐκγαμίζων, nom. sing. masc. part. pres. act. ἐκγαμίζω
ἐκγαμίσκονται, 3 pers. pl. pres. ind. pass. . ἐκγαμίσκω

[a] He. 11. 27. [b] 2 Pe. 1. 15. [c] Ro. 4. 19. [d] Ac. 27. 18.

ἐκγαμίσκω], (ἐκ & γαμίσκω) i.q. ἐκγαμίζω, Lu. 20. 34, 35. L.G.

ἔκγονα,[a] acc. pl. neut. . . . . . ἔκγονος

ἔκγονος], ου, ὁ, ἡ, (§ 7. rem. 2) (ἐκγίνομαι, *to be born*) *born of, descended from; ἔκγονα, descendants, grandchildren.*

ἐκδαπανάω, ῶ], fut. ήσω, (§ 18. tab. R) (ἐκ & δαπανάω) *to expend, consume, exhaust.* L.G.

ἐκδαπανηθήσομαι,[b] 1 pers. s. fut. 1, ind. pass. ἐκδαπανάω

ἐκδέχεσθε, 2 pers. pl. pres. imper. . . ἐκδέχομαι

ἐκδέχεται, 3 pers. sing. pres. ind. . . id.

ἐκδέχομαι, fut. ξομαι, (§ 23. rem. 1. b) (ἐκ & δέχομαι) pr. *to receive from* another; *to expect, look for,* Ac. 17. 16, et al.; *to wait for, to wait,* 1 Co. 11. 33; 1 Pe. 3. 20, et al.

ἐκδοχή, ῆς, ἡ, (§ 2. tab. B. a) in N.T. *a looking for, expectation,* He. 10. 27.

ἐκδεχόμενος, nom. sing. masc. part. pres. . ἐκδέχομαι

ἐκδεχομένου, gen. sing. masc. part. pres. . id.

ἐκδεχομένων, gen. pl. part. pres. . . id.

ἔκδηλος,[c] ου, ὁ, ἡ, (§ 7. rem. 2) (ἐκ & δῆλος) *clearly manifest, evident.*

ἐκδημέω, ῶ], fut. ήσω, (§ 16. tab. P) (ἐκ & δῆμος) pr. *to be absent from home, go abroad, travel;* hence, *to be absent from* any place or person, 2 Co. 5. 6, 8, 9.

ἐκδημῆσαι, aor. 1, infin. . . . ἐκδημέω

ἐκδημοῦμεν, 1 pers. pl. pres. ind. . . id.

ἐκδημοῦντες, nom. pl. masc. part. pres. . id.

ἐκδίδωμι], fut. ἐκδώσω, (§ 30. tab. Z) aor. 2, mid. ἐξεδόμην, (ἐκ & δίδωμι) *to give out, to give up; to put out* at interest; in N.T. *to let out* to tenants, Mat. 21. 33, 41, et al.

ἔκδοτος, ου, ὁ, ἡ, (§ 7. rem. 2) *delivered up,* Ac. 2. 23.

ἐκδιηγέομαι, οῦμαι], fut. ήσομαι, (§ 17. tab. Q) (ἐκ & διηγέομαι) *to narrate fully, detail,* Ac. 13. 14; 15. 3. L.G.

ἐκδιηγῆται, 3 pers. sing. pres. subj. . ἐκδιηγέομαι

ἐκδιηγούμενοι, nom. pl. masc. part. pres. . id.

ἐκδικεῖς, 2 pers. sing. pres. ind. act. . . ἐκδικέω

ἐκδικῆσαι, aor. 1, infin. act. . . . id.

ἐκδικήσεως, gen. sing. . . . . ἐκδίκησις

ἐκδίκησιν, acc. sing. . . . . id.

ἐκδίκησις, εως, ἡ, (§ 5. tab. E. c) . . ἐκδικέω

ἐκδίκησον, 2 pers. sing. aor. 1, imper. act. . id.

ἐκδικήσω, 1 pers. sing. fut. ind. act. . ἐκδικέω

ἔκδικος, ου, ὁ, ἡ, (§ 7. rem. 2) (ἐκ & δίκη) *maintaining right; an avenger, one who inflicts punishment,* Ro. 13. 4; 1 Thes. 4. 6.

ἐκδικέω, ῶ], fut. ήσω, (§ 16. tab. P) pr. *to execute right and justice; to punish,* 2 Co. 10. 6; in N.T. *to right, avenge* a person, Lu. 18. 3, 5, et al. L.G.

ἐκδίκησις, εως, ἡ, (§ 5. tab. E. c) *satisfaction; vengeance, punishment, retributive justice,* Lu. 21. 22; Ro. 12. 19, et al.; ἐκδίκησιν ποιεῖν, *to vindicate, avenge,* Lu. 18. 7, 8, et al.; διδόναι ἐκδ. *to inflict vengeance,* 2 Thes. 1. 8.

ἐκδικοῦντες, nom. pl. masc. part. pres. act. . ἐκδικέω

ἐκδιώκω], fut. ώξω, (§ 23. rem. 1. b) (ἐκ & διώκω) pr. *to chase away, drive out;* in N.T. *to persecute, vex, harass,* Lu. 11. 49; 1 Thes. 2. 15.

ἐκδιωξάντων, gen. pl. masc. part. aor. 1 . ἐκδιώκω

ἐκδιώξουσι, 3 pers. pl. fut. ind. . . id.

ἐκδόσεται, 3 pers. sing. fut. mid. (§ 30. tab. AA) ἐκδίδωμι

ἔκδοτον,[d] acc. sing. masc. . . . ἔκδοτος

ἔκδοτος], ου, ὁ, ἡ, (§ 7. rem. 2) . . . ἐκδίδωμι

ἐκδοχή,[e] ῆς, ἡ, (§ 2. tab. B. a) . . ἐκδέχομαι

ἐκδυσάμενοι, nom. pl. masc. part. aor. 1, mid.—D. . . . . . }
ἐνδυσάμενοι, Rec. Gr. Sch. Tdf. (2 Co. 5. 3) } ἐκδύω

ἐκδύσαντες, nom. pl. masc. part. aor. 1, act. . id.

ἐκδύσασθαι, aor. 1, infin. mid. . . id.

ἐκδύω], or δύνω, fut. ύσω, (§ 13. tab. M) (ἐκ & δύνω) pr. *to go out from; to take off, strip, unclothe,* Mat. 27. 28, 31, et al.; mid. *to lay aside, to put off,* 2 Co. 5. 4. (ῡω, ῡνω, ῡσω).

ἐκδώσεται, 3 pers. sing. fut. ind. mid.—Gr. Tdf. }
ἐκδόσεται, Rec. Sch. (Mat. 21. 41) } ἐκδίδωμι

ἐκεῖ, adv. *there, in that place,* Mat. 2. 13, 15, et al.; *thither,* Mat. 2. 22; 17. 20, et al.

ἐκεῖθεν, adv. *from there, thence,* Mat. 4. 21; 5. 26, et al.

ἐκεῖνος, η, ο, (§ 10. tab. J, and rem. 3) a demonstrative pronoun, used with reference to a thing previously mentioned or implied, or already familiar; *that, this, he,* etc., Mat. 17. 27; 10. 14; 2 Ti. 4. 8, et al.; in contrast with οὗτος, referring

[a] 1 Ti. 5. 4. [b] 2 Co. 12. 15. [c] 2 Ti. 3. 9. [d] Ac. 2. 23. [e] He. 10. 27.

to the former of two things previously mentioned, Lu. 18. 14, et al.

ἐκεῖσε, adv. *thither, there,* Ac. 21. 3; 22. 5.

ἐκεῖθεν, adv. . . . . . . ἐκεῖ

ἐκεῖνα, nom. and acc. pl. neut. . . ἐκεῖνος

ἐκεῖναι, nom. pl. fem. . . . . id.

ἐκείναις, dat. pl. fem. . . . id.

ἐκείνας, acc. pl. fem. . . . id.

ἐκείνη, nom. sing. fem. . . . . id.

ἐκείνῃ, dat. sing. fem. . . . . id.

ἐκείνην, acc. sing. fem. . . . . id.

ἐκείνης, gen. sing. fem. . . . . id.

ἐκεῖνο, nom. and acc. sing. neut. . . id.

ἐκεῖνοι, nom. pl. masc. . . . . id.

ἐκείνοις, dat. pl. masc. . . . id.

ἐκεῖνον, acc. sing. masc. . . . . id.

ἐκεῖνος, η, ο, (§ 10. tab. J. and rem. 3) . ἐκεῖ

ἐκείνου, gen. sing. masc. and neut. . ἐκεῖνος

ἐκείνους, acc. pl. masc. . . id.

ἐκείνῳ, dat. sing. masc. . . . . id.

ἐκείνων, gen. pl. . . . . id.

ἐκεῖσε, adv. . . . . . . ἐκεῖ

ἔκειτο, 3 pers. sing. imperf. . . . κεῖμαι

ἐκέλευον, 3 pers. pl. imperf. . . . κελεύω

ἐκέλευσα, 1 pers. sing. aor. 1, ind. . . id.

ἐκέλευσε, 3 pers. sing. aor. 1, ind. . . id.

ἐκένωσε, 3 pers. sing. aor. 1, ind. act. . κενόω

ἐκέρἄσε, 3 pers. sing. aor. 1, ind. (§ 36. rem. 5) κεράννυμι

ἐκέρδησα, 1 pers. sing. aor. 1, ind. act. . . κερδαίνω

ἐκέρδησας, 2 pers. sing. aor. 1, ind. act. . id.

ἐκέρδησε, 3 pers. sing. aor. 1, ind. act. . . id.

ἐκεφαλαίωσαν,[a] 3 pers. pl. aor. 1, ind. . κεφαλαιόω

ἐκζητέω, ῶ], fut. ήσω, (§ 16. tab. P) (ἐκ & ζητέω) *to seek out, investigate diligently, scrutinise,* 1 Pe. 1. 10; *to ask for, beseech earnestly,* He. 12. 17; *to seek diligently or earnestly after,* Ac. 15. 17; Ro. 3. 11; He. 11. 6; from the Heb. *to require, exact, demand,* Lu. 11. 50, 51. L.G.

ἐκζητηθῇ, 3 pers. sing. aor. 1, subj. pass. . ἐκζητέω

ἐκζητηθήσεται, 3 pers. sing. fut. 1, ind. pass. id.

ἐκζητήσας, nom. sing. masc. part. aor. 1, act. . id.

ἐκζητήσωσι, 3 pers. pl. aor. 1, subj. act. . id.

ἐκζητοῦσι, dat. pl. masc. part. pres. act. . id.

ἐκζητῶν, nom. sing. masc. part. pres. act. . id.

ἐκηρύξαμεν, 1 pers. pl. aor. 1, ind. act. . κηρύσσω

ἐκήρυξαν, 3 pers. pl. aor. 1, ind. act. . id.

ἐκήρυξε, 3 pers. sing. aor. 1, ind. act. . . id.

ἐκήρυσσε, 3 pers. sing. imperf. act. . . κηρύσσω

ἐκήρυσσον, 3 pers. pl. imperf. act. . . id.

ἐκηρύχθη, 3 pers. s. aor. 1, ind. pass. (§ 26. rem. 3) id.

ἐκθαμβεῖσθαι, pres. infin. . . . ἐκθαμβέομαι

ἐκθαμβεῖσθε, 2 pers. pl. pres. imper. . . id.

ἐκθαμβέομαι, οῦμαι] . . . ἔκθαμβος

ἔκθαμβοι,[b] nom. pl. masc. . . . id.

ἔκθαμβος], ου, ὁ, ἡ, (§ 7. rem. 2) (ἐκ & θάμβος) *amazed, awe-struck.* L.G.

ἐκθαμβέομαι, οῦμαι, (§ 17. tab. Q) *to be amazed, astonished, awe-struck,* Mar. 9. 15; 14. 33; 16. 5, 6.

ἔκθετα,[c] acc. pl. neut. . . . . ἔκθετος

ἔκθετος], ου, ὁ, ἡ, (§ 7. rem. 2) . . . ἐκτίθημι

ἐκινδύνευον, 3 pers. pl. imperf. . . κινδυνεύω

ἐκινήθη, 3 pers. sing. aor. 1, ind. pass. . . κινέω

ἐκινήθησαν, 3 pers. pl. aor. 1, ind. pass. . id.

ἐκκαθαίρω], fut. αρῶ, aor. 1, ἐξεκάθηρα, and, later, ᾱρα, (§ 27. rem. 1. c, and e) (ἐκ & καθαίρω) *to cleanse thoroughly, purify,* 2 Ti. 2. 21; *to purge out, eliminate,* 1 Co. 5. 7.

ἐκκαθάρατε, 2 pers. pl. aor. 1, imper. act. . ἐκκαθαίρω

ἐκκαθάρῃ, 3 pers. sing. aor. 1, subj. act. . id.

ἐκκαίομαι], aor. 1, pass. ἐξεκαύθην, (§ 35. rem. 3) (ἐκκαίω, *to kindle up,* ἐκ & καίω) *to blaze out; to be inflamed,* Ro. 1. 27.

ἐκκακεῖν, pres. infin. . . . . ἐκκακέω

ἐκκᾰκέω, ῶ], fut. ήσω, (§ 16. tab. P) (ἐκ & κακός) *to lose spirits, to be faint-hearted, despond,* Ep. 3. 13; *to faint, to flag, be remiss, indolent, slothful,* Lu. 18. 1; Gal. 6. 9; 2 Co. 4. 1, 16; 2 Thes. 3. 13. L.G.

ἐκκακήσητε, 2 pers. pl. aor. 1, subj. . ἐκκακέω

ἐκκακοῦμεν, 1 pers. pl. pres. ind. . id.

ἐκκακῶμεν, 1 pers. pl. pres. subj. . id.

ἐκκεντέω, ῶ], fut. ήσω, (§ 16. tab. P) (ἐκ & κεντέω) *to stab, pierce deeply, transfix,* Jno. 19. 37; Re. 1. 7. L.G

ἐκκέχῠται, 3 pers. sing. perf. ind. pass. ἐκχέω

ἐκκλάω], fut. άσω, (§ 22. rem. 2) aor. 1, pass. ἐξεκλάσθην, (ἐκ & κλάω) *to break off,* Ro. 11. 17, 19, 20.

ἐκκλεῖσαι, aor. 1, infin. act. . . . ἐκκλείω

ἐκκλείω], fut. είσω, (§ 22. rem. 4) (ἐκ & κλείω) *to shut out, exclude; to shut off, separate, insulate;* Gal. 4. 17; *to leave no place for, eliminate,* Ro. 3. 27.

ἐκκλησία, ας, ἡ, (§ 2. tab. B. b. and rem. 2)

[a] Mar. 12. 4. [b] Ac. 3. 11. [c] Ac. 7. 19.

(ἐκκαλέω, *to summon forth*) *a popular assembly*, Ac. 19. 32, 39, 41; in N.T. *the congregation* of the children of Israel, Ac. 7. 38; transferred to the Christian body, of which the congregation of Israel was a figure, *the Church*, 1 Co. 12. 28; Col. 1. 18, et al.; a local portion of the Church, *a local church*, Ro. 16. 1, et al.; *a Christian congregation*, 1 Co. 14. 4, et al.

ἐκκλησίᾳ, dat. sing. . . . . . ἐκκλησία
ἐκκλησίαι, nom. pl. . . . . id.
ἐκκλησίαις, dat. pl. . . . . . id.
ἐκκλησίαν, acc. sing. . . . id.
ἐκκλησίας, gen. sing. . . . . id.
ἐκκλησίας, acc. pl. . . . . id.
ἐκκλησιῶν, gen. pl. . . . . id.
ἐκκλίνατε, 2 pers. pl. aor. 1, imper. . . ἐκκλίνω
ἐκκλινάτω, 3 pers. sing. aor. 1, imper. . . id.
ἐκκλίνετε, 2 pers. pl. pres. imper.—B. C. . } id.
ἐκκλίνατε, Rec. Gr. Sch. Tdf. (Ro. 16. 17) }

ἐκκλίνω], fut. ινῶ, (§ 27. rem. 1. a) (ἐκ & κλίνω) *to deflect, deviate*, Ro. 3. 12; *to decline or turn away from, avoid*, Ro. 16. 17; 1 Pe. 3. 11.

ἐκκολυμβάω, ῶ], fut. ήσω, (§ 18. tab. R) (ἐκ & κολυμβάω) *to swim out* to land.

ἐκκολυμβήσας,[a] nom. sing. masc. part. aor. 1 ἐκκολυμβάω

ἐκκομίζω], fut. ίσω, (§ 26. rem. 1) (ἐκ & κομίζω) *to carry out, bring out*; especially, *to carry out* a corpse for burial, Lu. 7. 12.

ἐκκοπήσῃ, 2 pers. sing. fut. 2, pass. (§ 24. rem. 6) ἐκκόπτω
ἐκκόπτεσθαι, pres. infin. pass. . . . id.
ἐκκόπτεται, 3 pers. sing. pres. ind. pass. . id.

ἐκκόπτω], fut. ψω, (§ 23. rem. 1. a) (ἐκ & κόπτω) *to cut out; to cut off*, Mat. 3. 10; 5. 30, et al.; met. *to cut off* occasion, *remove, prevent*, 2 Co. 11. 12; *to render ineffectual*, 1 Pe. 3. 7.

ἐκκόψεις, 2 pers. sing. fut. ind. act. . . ἐκκόπτω
ἔκκοψον, 2 pers. sing. aor. 1, imper. act. . id.
ἐκκόψω, 1 pers. sing. aor. 1, subj. act. . . id.

ἐκκρέμᾰμαι], (§ 36. rem. 5) (ἐκ & κρέμαμαι) *to hang upon* a speaker, *fondly listen to, be earnestly attentive*, Lu. 19. 48.

ἔκλαιε, 3 pers. sing. imperf. . . . κλαίω
ἔκλαιον, 1 pers. sing. and 3 pers. pl. imperf. . id.

ἐκλαλέω, ῶ], fut. ήσω, (§ 16. tab. P) (ἐκ & λαλέω) *to speak out; to tell, utter, divulge*.

ἐκλαλῆσαι,[b] aor. 1, infin. . . . . ἐκλαλέω

ἐκλάμπω], fut. ψω, (§ 23. rem. 1. a) (ἐκ & λάμπω) *to shine out or forth, be resplendent*.

ἐκλάμψουσι,[c] 3 pers. pl. fut. ind. . . ἐκλάμπω

ἐκλανθάνω], (§ 36. rem. 2) (ἐκ & λανθάνω) *to make to forget quite*; mid. ἐκλανθάνομαι, perf. (pass. form) ἐκλέλησμαι, *to forget entirely*, He. 12. 5.

ἔκλᾰσα, 1 pers. sing. aor. 1, ind. act. . κλάω
ἔκλᾰσε, 3 pers. sing. aor. 1, ind. act. . . id.
ἐκλαύσατε, 2 pers. pl. aor. 1, ind. (§ 35. rem. 3) κλαίω
ἔκλαυσε, 3 pers. sing. aor. 1, ind. . . id.

ἐκλέγω], fut. ξω, (§ 23. rem. 1. b) *to pick out*; in N.T. mid. ἐκλέγομαι, aor. 1, ἐξελεξάμην, *to choose, select*, Lu. 6. 13; 10. 42, et al.; in N.T. *to choose out* as the recipients of special favour and privilege, Ac. 13. 17; 1 Co. 1. 27, et al.

ἐκλεκτός, ή, όν, (§ 7. tab. F. a) *chosen out, selected*; in N.T. *chosen* as a recipient of special privilege, *elect*, Col. 3. 12, et al., *specially beloved*, Lu. 23. 35; *possessed of prime excellence, exalted*, 1 Ti. 5. 21; *choice, precious*, 1 Pe. 2. 4, 6.

ἐκλογή, ῆς, ἡ, (§ 2. tab. B. a) *the act of choosing out, election*; in N.T. *election* to privilege by divine grace, Ro. 11. 5, et al.; ἡ ἐκλογή, *the aggregate of those who are chosen, the elect*, Ro. 11. 7, ἐκλογῆς, equivalent to ἐκλεκτόν, by Hebraism, Ac. 9. 15.

ἐκλείπῃ, 3 pers. sing. pres. subj. . . . ἐκλείπω
ἐκλείπητε, 2 pers. pl. pres. subj.—B. . } id.
ἐκλίπητε, Rec. Gr. Tdf. (Lu. 16. 9) }

ἐκλείπω], fut. ψω, (§ 23. rem. 1. a) (ἐκ & λείπω) intrans. *to fail*, Lu. 22. 32; *to come to an end*, He. 1. 12; *to be defunct*, Lu. 16. 9.

ἔκλεισε, 3 pers. sing. aor. 1, ind. act. . . κλείω
ἐκλείσθη, 3 pers. s. aor. 1, ind. pass. (§ 22. rem. 4) id.
ἐκλείσθησαν, 3 pers. pl. aor. 1, ind. pass. . id.
ἐκλείψουσι, 3 pers. pl. fut. ind. . . . ἐκλείπω
ἐκλεκτῇ, dat. sing. fem. . . . ἐκλεκτός
ἐκλεκτῆς, gen. sing. fem. . . . id.
ἐκλεκτοί, nom. pl. masc. . . . id.
ἐκλεκτοῖς, dat. pl. masc. . . . . id.
ἐκλεκτόν, acc. sing. masc. and nom. neut. . id.
ἐκλεκτός, ή, όν, (§ 7. tab. F. a) . . ἐκλέγω
ἐκλεκτούς, acc. pl. masc. . . . ἐκλεκτος

[a] Ac. 27. 43. [b] Ac. 23. 22. [c] Mat. 13. 43.

ἐκλεκτῶν, gen. pl. . . . . . ἐκλεκτός

ἐκλελεγμένος, nom. sing. masc. part. perf. pass.—B. Tdf. . . . . }
ἀγαπητός, Rec. Gr. Sch. Ln. (Lu. 9. 35) } ἐκλέγω

ἐκλέλησθε,[a] 2 pers. pl. perf. ind. pass. (§ 36. rem. 2) ἐκλανθάνω

ἐκλελυμένοι, nom. pl. masc. part. perf. pass. . ἐκλύω

ἐκλεξάμενος, nom. sing. masc. part. aor. 1, mid. ἐκλέγω

ἐκλεξαμένους, acc. pl. masc. part. aor. 1, mid. id.

ἔκλεψαν, 3 pers. pl. aor. 1, ind. act. . . κλέπτω

ἐκλήθη, 3 pers. s. aor. 1, ind. pass. (§ 22. rem. 4) καλέω

ἐκλήθημεν, 1 pers. pl. aor. 1, ind. pass.—A. D. Ln. }
ἐκληρώθημεν, R. Gr. Sch. Tdf. (Ep. 1. 11) } id.

ἐκλήθητε, 2 pers. pl. aor. 1, ind. pass. . . id.

ἐκληρώθημεν,[b] 1 pers. pl. aor. 1, ind. pass. . κληρόω

ἔκλιναν, 3 pers. pl. aor. 1, ind. act. . . κλίνω

ἐκλίπῃ, 3 pers. s. aor. 2, subj. act.—A. D. Ln. Sch. }
ἐκλίπητε, Rec. Gr. Tdf. (Lu. 16. 9) . } ἐκλείπω

ἐκλίπητε, 2 pers. pl. aor. 2, subj. (§ 24. rem. 9) id.

ἐκλογή, ῆς, ἡ, (§ 2. tab. B. a) . . . ἐκλέγω

ἐκλογήν, acc. sing. . . . . ἐκλογή

ἐκλογῆς, gen. sing. . . . . . id.

ἐκλυθήσονται, 3 pers. pl. fut. 1, ind. pass. . ἐκλύομαι

ἐκλυθῶσι, 3 pers. pl. aor. 1, subj. pass. . . id.

ἐκλύομαι], (§ 14. tab. N) (ἐκλύω, *to loosen, debilitate*, ἐκ & λύω) *to be weary, exhausted, faint*, Mat. 9. 36; 15. 32; Mar. 8. 3; Gal. 6. 9; *to faint, despond*, He. 12. 3, 5.

ἐκλυόμενοι, nom. pl. masc. part. pres. . ἐκλύομαι

ἐκλύου, 2 pers. sing. pres. imper. . . id.

ἐκμάξασα, nom. sing. fem. part. aor. 1, act. ἐκμάσσω

ἐκμάσσειν, pres. infin. act. . . . id.

ἐκμάσσω], fut. ξω, (§ 26. rem. 3) (ἐκ & μάσσω) *to wipe off; to wipe dry*, Lu. 7. 38, 44; Jno. 11. 2; 12. 3; 13. 5.

ἐκμυκτηρίζω], fut. ίσω, (§ 26. rem. 1) (ἐκ & μυκτηρίζω, from μυκτήρ, *the nose*) *to mock, deride, scoff at*, Lu. 16. 14; 23. 35.

ἐκνέω], fut. ἐκνεύσομαι, (§ 35. rem. 3) aor. 1, ἐξένευσα, pr. *to swim out, to escape by swimming*; hence, generally, *to escape, get clear of* a place, Jno. 5. 13; though ἐκνεύσας, in this place, may be referred to ἐκνεύω, *to deviate, withdraw*.

ἐκνήφω], fut. ψω, (§ 23. rem. 1. a) (ἐκ & νήφω) pr. *to awake sober after intoxication*; met. *to shake off mental bewilderment, to wake up* from delusion and folly.

ἐκνήψατε,[c] 2 pers. pl. aor. 1, imper. . . ἐκνήφω

ἐκοιμήθη, 3 pers. sing. aor. 1, ind. pass. κοιμάω

ἐκοιμήθησαν, 3 pers. pl. aor. 1, ind. pass. . id.

ἐκοινώνησαν, 3 pers. pl. aor. 1, ind. . κοινωνέω

ἐκοινώνησε, 3 pers. sing. aor. 1, ind. . id.

ἐκολάφισαν, 3 pers. pl. aor. 1, ind. act. . κολαφίζω

ἐκολλήθη, 3 pers. sing. aor. 1, ind. pass. . κολλάω

ἐκολλήθησαν, 3 pers. pl. aor. 1, ind. pass.—Gr. Sch. Tdf. . . . }
ἠκολούθησαν, Rec. (Re. 18. 5) . } id.

ἐκολοβώθησαν, 3 pers. pl. aor. 1, ind. pass. κολοβόω

ἐκολόβωσε, 3 pers. sing. aor. 1, ind. act. . id.

ἐκομισάμην, 1 pers. sing. aor. 1, ind. mid. κομίζω

ἐκομίσαντο, 3 pers. pl. aor. 1, ind. mid. . id.

ἐκομίσατο, 3 pers. sing. aor. 1, ind. mid. id.

ἐκόπασε, 3 pers. sing. aor. 1, ind. κοπάζω

ἐκοπίασα, 1 pers. sing. aor. 1, ind. . κοπιάω

ἐκοπίασας, 2 pers. s. aor. 1, ind.—Gr. Sch. Tdf. }
κεκοπίακας, Rec. (Re. 2. 3) . } id.

ἐκοπίασε, 3 pers. sing. aor. 1, ind. . . id.

ἔκοπτον, 3 pers. pl. imperf. act. . . κόπτω

ἐκόπτοντο, 3 pers. pl. imperf. mid. . id.

ἐκόσμησαν, 3 pers. pl. aor. 1, ind. act. . κοσμέω

ἐκόσμουν, 3 pers. pl. imperf. act. . . id.

ἑκοῦσα, nom. sing. fem. (§ 7. tab. H. d) . ἑκών

ἑκούσιον,[d] acc. sing. neut. . . ἑκούσιος

ἑκούσιος], α, ον, and ου, ὁ, ἡ . ἑκών

ἑκουσίως, adv. . . . . . id.

ἐκούφιζον,[e] 3 pers. pl. imperf. act. . . κουφίζω

ἐκόψασθε, 2 pers. pl. aor. 1, ind. mid. . . κόπτω

ἔκπαλαι, adv. (ἐκ & πάλαι) *of old, long since*, 2 Pe. 2. 3; 3. 5. L.G.

ἐκπειράζοντες, nom. pl. masc. part. pres.—D. }
πειράζοντες, R. Gr. Sch. Tdf. (Jno. 8. 6) } ἐκπειράζω

ἐκπειράζω], fut. άσω, (§ 26. rem. 1) (ἐκ & πειράζω) *to tempt, put to the proof*, Mat. 4. 7; Lu. 4. 12; 1 Co. 10. 9; *to try, sound*, Lu. 10. 25. L.G.

ἐκπειράζωμεν, 1 pers. pl. pres. subj. act. ἐκπειράζω

ἐκπειράζων, nom. sing. masc. part. pres. act. . id.

ἐκπειράσεις, 2 pers. sing. fut. ind. act. . id.

ἐκπέμπω], fut. ψω, (§ 23. rem. 1. a) (ἐκ & πέμπω) *to send out, or away*, Ac. 13. 4; 17. 10.

ἐκπεμφθέντες, nom. pl. masc. part. aor. 1, pass. ἐκπέμπω

ἐκπεπλήρωκε,[f] 3 pers. sing. perf. ind. act. . ἐκπληρόω

ἐκπέπτωκας, 2 pers. sing. perf. ind. (§ 37. rem. 1) ἐκπίπτω

ἐκπέπτωκε, 3 pers. sing. perf. ind. . . id.

[a] He. 12. 5. [b] Ep. 1. 11. [c] 1 Co. 15. 34. [d] Phile 14. [e] Ac. 27. 38. [f] Ac. 13. 33.

ἐκπερισσῶς,[a] adv. (strengthened from περισσῶς) *exceedingly, vehemently.*—Al. Ln. Tdf.
ἐκ περισσοῦ, Rec. Gr. Sch. (Mar. 14. 31).

ἐκπεσεῖν, aor. 2, infin. (§ 37. rem. 1) . . **ἐκπίπτω**

ἐκπέσητε, 2 pers. pl. aor. 2, subj. . . id.

ἐκπέσωμεν, 1 pers. pl. aor. 2, subj. . . id.

ἐκπέσωσι, 3 pers. pl. aor. 2, subj. . . id.

ἐκπετάννῡμι], fut. άσω, (§ 36. rem. 5) (ἐκ & πετάννυμι) *to stretch forth, expand, extend,* Ro. 10. 21. (ᾰ).

ἐκπεφευγέναι, perf. 2, infin. (§ 25. rem. 3) . **ἐκφεύγω**

ἐκπηδάω, ῶ], fut. ήσω, (§ 18. tab. R) (ἐκ & πηδάω, *to leap, spring*) *to leap forth, rush out,* v.r. Ac. 14. 14.

ἐκπίπτει, 3 pers. sing. pres. ind. . . **ἐκπίπτω**

ἐκπίπτοντες, nom. pl. masc. part. pres. . id.

ἐκπίπτω], fut. πεσοῦμαι, perf. πέπτωκα, aor. 1, ἐξέπεσα, aor. 2, ἐξέπεσον, (§ 37. rem. 1) *to fall off or from,* Mar. 13. 25; Ac. 12. 7; 27. 32, et al.; met. *to fall from, forfeit, lose,* Gal. 5. 4; 2 Pe. 3. 17; Re. 2. 5; *to be cast ashore,* Ac. 27. 17, 26, 29; *to fall to the ground, be fruitless, ineffectual,* Ro. 9. 6; *to cease, come to an end,* 1 Co. 13. 8.

ἐκπλεῦσαι, aor. 1, infin. (§ 35. rem. 3) . **ἐκπλέω**

ἐκπλέω], fut. εύσομαι, aor. 1, ἐξέπλευσα, (ἐκ & πλέω) *to sail out of or from* a place, Ac. 15. 39; 18. 18; 20. 6.

ἐκπληρόω, ῶ], fut. ώσω, (§ 20. tab. T) (ἐκ & πληρόω) *to fill out, complete, fill up;* met. *to fulfil, perform, accomplish,* Ac. 13. 32.
ἐκπλήρωσις, εως, ἡ, (§ 5. tab. E. c) pr. *a filling up, completion;* hence, *a fulfilling, accomplishment.* L.G.

ἐκπλήρωσιν,[b] acc. sing. . . . **ἐκπλήρωσις**

ἐκπλήρωσις], εως, ἡ . . . . **ἐκπληρόω**

ἐκπλησσόμενος, nom. sing. masc. pt. pres. pass. **ἐκπλήσσω**

ἐκπλήσσω, or ττω], fut. ξω, (§ 26. rem. 3) aor. 2, pass. ἐξεπλάγην, (§ 24. rem. 9) (ἐκ & πλήσσω) pr. *to strike out of;* hence, *to strike out of* one's wits, *to astound, amaze;* pass. Mat. 7. 28; 13. 54, et al.

ἐκπλήττεσθαι, pres. infin. pass.—Rec. Gr. Sch. } **ἐκπλήσσω**
ἐκπλήσσεσθαι, B. C. D. Ln. Tdf. (Mat. 13. 54) . . . . }

ἐκπνέω], fut. εύσω and εύσομαι, (§ 35. rem. 3) (ἐκ & πνέω) *to breathe out; to expire, die,* Mar. 15. 37, 39; Lu. 23. 46.

ἐκπορεύεσθαι, pres. infin. . . . **ἐκπορεύομαι**

ἐκπορευέσθω, 3 pers. sing. pres. imper. . id.

ἐκπορεύεται, 3 pers. sing. pres. ind. . id.

ἐκπορεύομαι], fut. εύσομαι, (§ 14. tab. N) (ἐκ & πορεύομαι) *to go from or out of* a place, *depart from,* Mar. 11. 19; 13. 1, et al.; *to be voided,* Mar. 7. 19; *to be cast out,* Mat. 17. 21; *to proceed from, be spoken,* Mat. 4. 4; 15. 11, et al.; *to burst forth,* Re. 4. 5; *to be spread abroad,* Lu. 4. 37; *to flow out,* Re. 22. 1; from the Heb. ἐκπορ. & εἰσπορ. See εἰσέρχομαι, Ac. 9. 28.

ἐκπορευόμενα, nom. pl. neut. part. pres. **ἐκπορεύομαι**

ἐκπορευομένη, nom. sing. fem. part. pres. . id.

ἐκπορευομένῃ, dat. sing. fem. part. pres. . id.

ἐκπορευόμενοι, nom. pl. masc. part. pres. . id.

ἐκπορευομένοις, dat. pl. masc. part. pres. . id.

ἐκπορευόμενον, nom. s. neut. & acc. masc. pt. pres. id.

ἐκπορευόμενος, nom. sing. masc. part. pres. . id.

ἐκπορευομένου, gen. sing. masc. and neut. pt. pres. id.

ἐκπορευομένῳ, dat. sing. neut. part. pres. . id.

ἐκπορευομένων, gen. pl. part. pres. . . id.

ἐκπορεύονται, 3 pers. pl. pres. ind. . . id.

ἐκπορεύσονται, 3 pers. pl. fut. ind. . . id.

ἐκπορνεύσασαι,[c] nom. pl. fem. part. aor. 1 . **ἐκπορνεύω**

ἐκπορνεύω], fut. εύσω, (§ 13. tab. M) (ἐκ & πορνεύω) *to be given to fornication.* L.G.

ἐκπτύω], fut. ύσω & ύσομαι, (§ 13. tab. M) (ἐκ & πτύω) *to spit out;* met. *to reject,* Gal. 4. 14. (ῠ).

ἔκραζε, 3 pers. sing. imperf. . . . **κράζω**

ἔκραζον, 3 pers. pl. imperf. . . . id.

ἔκραξα, 1 pers. sing. aor. 1, ind. . . id.

ἔκραξαν, 3 pers. pl. aor. 1, ind. . . id.

ἔκραξε, 3 pers. sing. aor. 1, ind. . . id.

ἐκραταιοῦτο, 3 pers. sing. imperf. pass. . **κραταιόω**

ἐκρατήσαμεν, 1 pers. pl. aor. 1, ind. act. . **κρατέω**

ἐκράτησαν, 3 pers. pl. aor. 1, ind. act. . . id.

ἐκρατήσατε, 2 pers. pl. aor. 1, ind. act. . id.

ἐκράτησε, 3 pers. sing. aor. 1, ind. act. . id.

ἐκρατοῦντο, 3 pers. pl. imperf. pass. . id.

ἐκραύγαζον, 3 pers. pl. imperf.—B. D. Ln. Tdf. } **κραυγάζω**
ἔκραζον, Rec. Gr. Sch. (Jno. 12. 13) }

ἐκραύγασαν, 3 pers. pl. aor. 1, ind. . . id.

ἐκραύγασε, 3 pers. sing. aor. 1, ind. . id.

ἐκριζόω, ῶ], fut. ώσω, (§ 20. tab. T) (ἐκ & ῥιζόω. ῥίζα) *to root up, eradicate,* Mat. 13. 29; 15. 13; Lu. 17. 6; Jude 12. L.G.

---

[a] Mar. 14. 31. [b] Ac. 21. 26. [c] Jude 7.

ἐκριζωθέντα, nom. pl. neut. part. aor. 1, pass. . ἐκριζόω

ἐκριζωθήσεται, 3 pers. sing. fut. 1, ind. pass. id.

ἐκριζώθητι, 2 pers. sing. aor. 1, imper. pass. . id.

ἐκριζώσητε, 2 pers. pl. aor. 1, subj. act. . id.

ἐκρίθη, 3 pers. sing. aor. 1, ind. pass. (§ 27. rem. 3) κρίνω

ἐκρίθησαν, 3 pers. pl. aor. 1, ind. pass. . . id.

ἔκρινα, 1 pers. sing. aor. 1, ind. act. . . id.

ἔκρινας, 2 pers. sing. aor. 1, ind. act. . . id.

ἔκρινε, 3 pers. sing. aor. 1, ind. act. . . id.

ἐκρινόμεθα, 1 pers. pl. imperf. pass. . . id.

ἐκρύβη, 3 pers. s. aor. 2, ind. pass. (§ 24. rem. 8. a) κρύπτω

ἔκρυψα, 1 pers. sing. aor. 1, ind. act. . id.

ἔκρυψαν, 3 pers. pl. aor. 1, ind. act. . . id.

ἔκρυψας, 2 pers. sing. aor. 1, ind. act.—B.D.Ln. } id.
ἀπέκρυψας, R. Gr. Sch. Tdf. (Mat. 11. 25) }

ἔκρυψε, 3 pers. sing. aor. 1, ind. act. . id.

ἐκστάσει, dat. sing. . . . . ἔκστασις

ἐκστάσεως, gen. sing. . . . . id.

ἔκστασις, εως, ἡ, (§ 5. tab. E. c) . . ἐξίστημι

ἐκστρέφω], fut. ψω, perf. pass. ἐξέστραμμαι, (§ 35. rem. 9) (ἐκ & στρέφω) pr. *to turn out of, to turn inside out*; hence, *to change entirely*; in N.T. pass. *to be perverted*, Tit. 3. 11.

ἐκταράσσουσι,[a] 3 pers. pl. pres. ind. act. . ἐκταράσσω

ἐκταράσσω], fut. ξω, (§ 26. rem. 3) (ἐκ & ταράσσω) *to disturb, disquiet, throw into confusion*.

ἐκτεθέντα, acc. sing. masc. part. aor. 1, pass. . ἐκτίθημι

ἐκτεθέντος, gen. sing. masc. part. aor. 1, pass. } id.
—Al. Ln. Tdf. . . . }
ἐκτεθέντα, Rec. Gr. Sch. (Ac. 7. 21) }

ἐκτείνας, nom. sing. masc. part. aor. 1, act. . ἐκτείνω

ἐκτείνειν, pres. infin. act. . . . id.

ἔκτεινον, 2 pers. sing. aor. 1, imper. act. . id.

ἐκτείνω], fut. τενῶ, (§ 27. rem. 1. c) (ἐκ & τείνω) *to stretch out*, Mat. 8. 3; 12. 13, et al.; *to lay* hands on any one, Lu. 22. 53; *to exert* power and energy, Ac. 4. 30; *to cast out, let down* an anchor, Ac. 27. 30.

ἐκτενής, έος, ὁ, ἡ, το, -ές, (§ 7. tab. G. b) pr. *extended*; met. *intense, earnest, fervent*, Ac. 12. 5; 1 Pe. 4. 8.

ἐκτενῶς, adv. *intensely, fervently, earnestly*, 1 Pe. 1. 22.

ἐκτένεια, ας, ἡ, (§ 2. tab. B. b, and rem. 2) pr. *extension*; in N.T. *intenseness, intentness*; ἐν ἐκτενείᾳ, *intently, assiduously*, Ac. 26. 7. L.G.

ἐκτενέστερον, adv. *very earnestly*, Lu. 22. 44 pr. neut. compar. of ἐκτενής.

ἐκτελέσαι, aor. 1, infin. act. . . . . ἐκτελέω

ἐκτελέω, ῶ], fut. έσω, (§ 22. rem. 1) (ἐκ & τελέω) *to bring quite to an end, to finish, complete*, Lu. 14. 29, 30.

ἐκτένεια], ας, ἡ, (§ 2. tab. B. b, and rem. 2) . ἐκτείνω

ἐκτενείᾳ,[b] dat. sing. . . . . . ἐκτένεια

ἐκτενεῖς, 2 pers. sing. fut. ind. act. . . ἐκτείνω

ἐκτενέστερον,[c] adv. . . . . . id.

ἐκτενῆ, acc. sing. fem. . . . . ἐκτενής

ἐκτενής, έος, οῦς, ὁ, ἡ, (§ 7. tab. G. b) . ἐκτείνω

ἐκτενῶς,[d] adv. . . . . ἐκτενής

ἕκτη, nom. sing. fem. . . . . ἕκτος

ἕκτην, acc. sing. fem. . . . . id.

ἕκτης, gen. sing. fem. . . . . id.

ἐκτησάμην, 1 pers. sing. aor. 1, ind. . . κτάομαι

ἐκτήσατο, 3 pers. sing. aor. 1, ind. . . id.

ἐκτίθημι], fut. ἐκθήσω, (§ 28. tab. V) (ἐκ & τίθημι) pr. *to place outside, put forth*; *to expose* an infant, Ac. 7. 21; met. *to set forth, declare, explain*, Ac. 11. 4; 18. 26; 28. 23.

ἔκθετος, ου, ὁ, ἡ, τό, -ον, (§ 7. rem. 2) *exposed, cast out, abandoned*, Ac. 7. 19.

ἐκτιναξάμενοι, nom. pl. masc. part. aor. 1, mid. ἐκτινάσσω

ἐκτιναξάμενος, nom. sing. masc. part. aor. 1, mid. id.

ἐκτινάξατε, 2 pers. pl. aor. 1, imper. act. . id.

ἐκτινάσσω], fut. ξω, (§ 26. rem. 3) (ἐκ & τινάσσω, *to shake*) *to shake out, shake off*, Mat. 10. 14; Mar. 6. 11, et al.

ἔκτισας, 2 pers. sing. aor. 1, ind. act. . κτίζω

ἔκτισε, 3 pers. sing. aor. 1, ind. act. . . id.

ἐκτίσθη, 3 pers. sing. aor. 1, ind. pass. . id.

ἐκτίσθησαν, 3 pers. pl. aor. 1, ind. pass. . id.

ἔκτισται, 3 pers. sing. perf. ind. pass. . id.

ἕκτος, η, ον, (§ 7. tab. F. a) . . . ἕξ

ἐκτός, adv. (ἐκ) *without, on the outside*; τὸ ἐκτός, *the exterior, outside*, Mat. 23. 26; met. *besides*, Ac. 26. 22; 1 Co. 15. 27; ἐκτὸς εἰ μή, *unless, except*, 1 Co. 14. 5, et al.

ἐκτραπῇ, 3 pers. s. aor. 2, subj. pass. (§ 24. rem. 10) ἐκτρέπω

ἐκτραπήσονται, 3 pers. pl. fut. 2, ind. pass. id.

ἐκτρεπόμενος, nom. sing. masc. part. pres. mid. id.

ἐκτρέπω], fut. ψω, (§ 23. rem. 1. a) (ἐκ & τρέπω) *to turn out or aside*, He. 12. 13; mid., aor. 2, (pass. form) ἐξετράπην, *to turn aside or away, swerve*, 1 Ti.

[a] Ac. 16. 20. [b] Ac. 26. 7. [c] Lu. 22. 44. [d] 1 Pe. 1. 22.

1. 6; 5. 15; 2 Ti. 4. 4; *to turn from, avoid*, 1 Ti. 6. 20.

ἐκτρέφει, 3 pers. sing. pres. ind. act. . ἐκτρέφω

ἐκτρέφετε, 2 pers. pl. pres. imper. act. . . id.

ἐκτρέφω], fut. ἐκθρέψω, (§ 35. rem. 4) (ἐκ & τρέφω) *to nourish, promote health and strength*, Ep. 5. 29; *to bring up, educate*, Ep. 6. 4.

ἔκτρωμα], ατος, τό, (§ 4. tab. D. c) (ἐκτιτρώσκω, *to cause abortion*) *an abortion, fœtus prematurely born; a puny birth.*

ἐκτρώματι,[a] dat. sing. . . . ἔκτρωμα

ἔκτῳ, dat. sing. masc. . . . . . ἔκτος

ἐκύκλευσαν, 3 p. pl. aor. 1, ind. act.—A. Ln. Tdf.
ἐκύκλωσαν, Rec. Gr. Sch. (Re. 20. 9) } κυκλεύω

ἐκύκλωσαν, 3 pers. pl. aor. 1, ind. act. . κυκλόω

ἐκυλίετο,[b] 3 pers. sing. imperf. mid. . . κυλίω

ἐκφέρειν, pres. infin. act. . . . ἐκφέρω

ἐκφέρουσα, nom. sing. fem. part. pres. act. . id.

ἐκφέρω], fut. ἐξοίσω, aor. 1, ἐξήνεγκα, aor. 2, ἐξήνεγκον, (§ 36. rem. 1) (ἐκ & φέρω) *to bring forth, carry out*, Lu. 15. 22; Ac. 5. 15; 1 Ti. 6. 7; *to carry out* for burial, Ac. 5. 6, 9, 10; *to produce, yield*, He. 6. 8.

ἐκφεύγω], fut. ξομαι, aor. 2, ἐξέφῠγον, (§ 25. rem. 3) perf. 2, ἐκπέφευγα, (§ 24. rem. 9) (ἐκ & φεύγω) intrans. *to flee out, to make an escape*, Ac. 16. 27; 19. 16; trans. *to escape, avoid*, Lu. 21. 36; Ro. 2. 3, et al.

ἐκφεύξῃ, 2 pers. sing. fut. ind. mid. . ἐκφεύγω

ἐκφευξόμεθα, 1 pers. pl. fut. ind. mid. . id.

ἐκφοβεῖν,[c] pres. infin. act. . . . ἐκφοβέω

ἐκφοβέω, ῶ], fut. ήσω, (§ 16. tab. P) (ἐκ & φοβέω) *to terrify.*

ἔκφοβοι, nom. pl. masc. . . . . . ἔκφοβος

ἔκφοβος, ου, ὁ, ἡ, (§ 7. rem. 2) (ἐκ & φόβος) *affrighted*, Mar. 9. 6; He. 12. 21.

ἐκφυγεῖν, aor. 2, infin. . . . . ἐκφεύγω

ἐκφύγωσι, 3 pers. pl. aor. 2, subj. . . id.

ἐκφύῃ, 3 pers. sing. pres. subj. . . ἐκφύω

ἐκφύω], fut. ύσω, (§ 13. tab. M) (ἐκ & φύω) *to generate; to put forth, shoot*, Mat. 24. 32; Mar. 13. 28. (ῠ, ῡσ—).

ἐκχέαι, aor. 1, infin. act. (§ 36. rem. 1) . ἐκχέω

ἐκχέατε, 2 pers. pl. aor. 1, imper. act. . id.

ἐκχεῖται, 3 pers. sing. pres. ind. pass. . id.

ἐκχέω], fut. ἐκχεῶ, or ἐκχέω, aor. 1, ἐξέχεα, perf. ἐκκέχῠκα, perf. pass. ἐκκέχῠμαι, aor. 1, ἐξεχύθην, (ῠ), (§ 36. rem. 1) *to pour out*, Re. 16. 1, 2, 3, et al.; *to shed* blood, Mat. 26. 28; Mar. 14. 24, et al.; pass. *to gush out*, Ac. 1. 18; *to spill, scatter*, Mat. 9. 17; Jno. 2. 15; met. *to give largely, bestow liberally*, Ac. 2. 17, 18, 33; 10. 45, et al.; pass. *to rush headlong* into anything, *be abandoned to*, Jude 11.

ἐκχεῶ, 1 pers. sing. fut. ind. act. . . ἐκχέω

ἐκχυθήσεται, 3 pers. sing. fut. 1, ind. pass. . id.

ἐκχυνόμενον, nom. sing. neut. part. pres. pass. id.

ἐκχύνω], a later form equivalent to ἐκχέω, Mat. 23. 35, et al.

ἐκχωρείτωσαν,[d] 3 pers. pl. pres. imper. . ἐκχωρέω

ἐκχωρέω, ῶ], fut. ήσω, (§ 16. tab. P) (ἐκ & χωρέω) *to go out, depart from, flee.*

ἐκψύχω], fut. ξω, (§ 23. rem. 1. b) *to expire, give up the ghost*, Ac. 5. 5, 10; 12. 23. (ῡ).

ἐκωλύθην, 1 pers. sing. aor. 1, ind. pass. . κωλύω

ἐκωλύομεν, 1 pers. pl. imperf. act.—B. D. Tdf.
ἐκωλύσαμεν, Rec. Gr. Sch. (Mar. 9. 38) } id.

ἐκωλύσαμεν, 1 pers. pl. aor. 1, ind. act. . id.

ἐκωλύσατε, 2 pers. pl. aor. 1, ind. act. . . id.

ἐκώλυσε, 3 pers. sing. aor. 1, ind. act. . id.

ἑκών, οῦσα, όν, (§ 7. tab. H. d) *willing, voluntary*, Ro. 8. 20; 1 Co. 9. 17.

ἑκούσιος, α, ον, and ου, ὁ, ἡ, *voluntary, spontaneous*, Phile. 14.

ἑκουσίως, adv. *voluntarily, spontaneously*, He. 10. 26; 1 Pe. 5. 2.

ἔλαβε, 3 pers. sing. aor. 2, ind. act. (§ 34. rem. 9) λαμβάνω

ἔλαβες, 2 pers. sing. aor. 2, ind. act. . . id.

ἐλάβετε, 2 pers. pl. aor. 2, ind. act. . . id.

ἐλάβομεν, 1 pers. pl. aor. 2, ind. act. . . id.

ἔλαβον, 1 pers. s. and 3 pers. pl. aor. 2, ind. act. id.

ἔλαθε, 3 pers. sing. aor. 2, ind. (§ 24. rem. 9) λανθάνω

ἔλαθον, 3 pers. pl. aor. 2, ind. . . id.

ἐλαία], ας, ἡ, (§ 2. tab. B. b, and rem. 2) *an olive tree*, Mat. 21. 1; 24. 3, et al.; *an olive, fruit of the olive tree*, Ja. 3. 12.

ἔλαιον, ου, τό, (§ 3. tab. C. c) *olive oil, oil*, Mat. 25. 3, 4, 8; Mar. 6. 13, et al.

ἐλαιών, ῶνος, ὁ, (§ 4. rem. 2. e) *an olive garden*; in N.T. the mount *Olivet*, Ac. 1. 12.

---

[a] 1 Co. 15. 8. [b] Mar. 9. 20. [c] 2 Co. 10. 9. [d] Lu. 21. 21.

ἐλαίᾳ, dat. sing. . . . ἐλαία
ἐλαῖαι, nom. pl. . . . id.
ἐλαίας, gen. sing. and acc. pl. . . . id.
ἔλαιον, ου, τό, (§ 3. tab. C. c) . . . id.
ἐλαίου, gen. sing. . . . ἔλαιον
ἐλαίῳ, dat. sing. . . . id.
ἐλαιῶν, gen. pl. . . . ἐλαία
ἐλαιών], ῶνος, ὁ, (§ 4. rem. 2. e) . . . id.
ἐλαιῶνος,[a] gen. sing. . . . ἐλαιών
ἐλάκησε,[b] 3 pers. sing. aor. 1, ind. . . . λάσκω
ἐλάλει, 3 pers. sing. imperf. act. . . . λαλέω
ἐλαλήθη, 3 pers. sing. aor. 1, ind. pass. . . . id.
ἐλάλησα, 1 pers. sing. aor. 1, ind. act. . . . id.
ἐλαλήσαμεν, 1 pers. pl. aor. 1, ind. act. . . . id.
ἐλάλησαν, 3 pers. pl. aor. 1, ind. act. . . . id.
ἐλαλήσατε, 2 pers. pl. aor. 1, ind. act. . . . id.
ἐλάλησε, 3 pers. sing. aor. 1, ind. act. . . . id.
ἐλαλοῦμεν, 1 pers. pl. imperf. act. . . . id.
ἐλάλουν, 1 pers. sing. and 3 pers. pl. imperf. act. . . . id.
ἐλάμβἄνον, 3 pers. pl. imperf. act. . . . λαμβάνω
Ἐλαμῖται,[c] nom. pl. . . . Ἐλαμίτης

Ἐλαμίτης], ου, ὁ, (§ 2. tab. B. c) *an Elamite; an inhabitant of Elam*, a province of Persia.

ἔλαμψε, 3 pers. sing. aor. 1, ind. . . . λάμπω
ἐλάσσονι, dat. sing. masc. . . . ἐλάσσων
ἐλάσσω, acc. sing. contr. masc. . . . id.

ἐλάσσων, or ττων], ονος, ὁ, ἡ, τό, -ον, (§ 8. rem. 5) (compar. of the old word ἐλαχύς) *less; less* in age, *younger*, Ro. 9. 12; *less* in dignity, *inferior*, He. 7. 7; *less* in quality, *inferior, worse*, Jno. 2. 10.

ἔλαττον, adv. (pr. neut. of preced.) *less*, 1 Ti. 5. 9.

ἐλαττονέω, ῶ, fut. ήσω, aor. 1, ἠλαττόνησα, (§ 16. tab. P) trans. *to make less*; intrans. *to be less, inferior; to have too little, want, lack*, 2 Co. 8. 15. L.G.

ἐλαττόω, ῶ, fut. ώσω, perf. pass. ἠλάττωμαι, (§ 20. tab. T; § 21. tab. U) *to make less or inferior*, He. 2. 7; pass. *to be made less or inferior*, He. 2. 9; *to decline* in importance, Jno. 3. 30.

ἐλάχιστος, η, ον, (§ 8. rem. 5) (superl. of μικρός, from ἐλαχύς) *smallest, least*, Mat. 2. 6; 5. 19, et al.

ἐλαχιστότερος, α, ον, (§ 8. rem. 5) (compar. of preced.) *far less, far inferior*, Ep. 3. 8. L.G.

ἐλατόμησε, 3 pers. sing. aor. 1, ind. act. . . . λατομέω
ἐλάτρευσαν, 3 pers. pl. aor. 1, ind. . . . λατρεύω
ἔλαττον, nom. sing. neut. . . . ἐλάττων
ἔλαττον,[d] adv. . . . id.
ἐλαττονέω, ῶ], fut. ήσω, (§ 16. tab. P) . . . id.
ἐλαττοῦσθαι, pres. infin. pass. (§ 21. tab. U) . . . ἐλαττόω
ἐλαττόω, ῶ], fut. ώσω, (§ 20. tab. T) . . . ἐλάττων
ἐλαύνειν, pres. infin. act. . . . ἐλαύνω
ἐλαυνόμενα, nom. pl. neut. part. pres. pass. . . . id.
ἐλαυνόμεναι, nom. pl. fem. part. pres. pass. . . . id.

ἐλαύνω], fut. ἐλάσω, perf. ἐλήλακα, (§ 36. rem. 2) *to drive, urge forward, spur on*, Lu. 8. 29; Ja. 3. 4; 2 Pe. 2. 17; *to impel* a vessel by oars, *to row*, Mar. 6. 48; Jno. 6. 19.

ἐλαφρία], ας, ἡ, (§ 2. tab. B. b, and rem. 2) . . . ἐλαφρός
ἐλαφρίᾳ,[e] dat. sing. . . . ἐλαφρία
ἐλαφρόν, nom. sing. neut. . . . ἐλαφρός

ἐλαφρός], ά, όν, (§ 7. rem. 1) *light, not heavy*, Mat. 11. 30; 2 Co. 4. 17.

ἐλαφρία, ας, ἡ, (§ 2. tab. B. b, and rem. 2) *lightness* in weight; hence, *lightness of mind, levity*. L.G.

ἔλαχε, 3 pers. sing. aor. 2, ind. (§ 36. rem. 2) . . . λαγχάνω
ἐλαχίστη, nom. sing. fem. . . . ἐλάχιστος
ἐλάχιστον, acc. sing. neut. . . . id.
ἐλάχιστος, η, ον, (§ 8. rem. 5) . . . ἐλάσσων
ἐλαχιστότερος], α, ον, (§ 8. rem. 5) . . . id.
ἐλαχιστοτέρῳ,[f] dat. sing. masc. . . . ἐλαχιστότερος
ἐλαχίστου, gen. sing. neut. . . . ἐλάχιστος
ἐλαχίστῳ, dat. sing. neut. . . . id.
ἐλαχίστων, gen. pl. . . . id.
ἐλεᾷ, 3 pers. sing. pres. ind. act.—D. / ἐλεεῖ, Rec. Gr. Sch. Tdf. (Ro. 9. 18) } ἐλεάω
Ἐλεάζαρ, ὁ, *Eleazar*, pr. name, indecl.
ἐλεᾶτε, 2 pers. pl. pres. imper. act.—B. Tdf. / ἐλεεῖτε, Rec. Gr. Sch. (Jude 23) } id.
ἐλεάω, ῶ], same signif. as ἐλεέω, ῶ. v.r.
ἔλεγε, 3 pers. sing. imperf. act. . . . λέγω
ἐλέγετε, 2 pers. pl. imperf. or aor. 2, act. . . . id.
ἐλεγμόν, acc. sing.—A. Ln. Tdf. / ἔλεγχον, Rec. Gr. Sch. (2 Ti. 3. 16) } ἐλεγμός
ἐλεγμός], οῦ, ὁ, (§ 3. tab. C. a) . . . ἐλέγχω
ἐλέγξαι, aor. 1, infin. act.—A. B. Ln. Tdf. / ἐξελέγξαι, Rec. Gr. Sch. (Jude 15) } id.
ἐλέγξει, 3 pers. sing. fut. ind. act. . . . id.
ἔλεγξιν,[g] acc. sing. . . . ἔλεγξις

[a] Ac. 1. 12. [b] Ac. 1. 18. [c] Ac. 2. 9. [d] 1 Ti. 5. 9. [e] 2 Co. 1. 17. [f] Ep. 3. 8. [g] 2 Pe. 2. 16.

ἔλεγξις], εως, ἡ, (§ 5. tab. E. c) . . . ἐλέγχω
ἔλεγξον, 2 pers. sing. aor. 1, imper. act. . id.
ἔλεγον, 1 pers. sing. and 3 pers. pl. aor. 2, ind. act. λέγω
ἔλεγχε, 2 pers. sing. pres. imper. act. . . ἐλέγχω
ἐλέγχει, 3 pers. sing. pres. ind. act. . . id.
ἐλέγχειν, pres. infin. act. . . . . id.
ἐλέγχεται, 3 pers. sing. pres. ind. pass. . id.
ἐλέγχετε, 2 pers. pl. pres. imper. act. . . id.
ἐλεγχθῇ, 3 pers. sing. aor. 1, subj. pass. (§ 23. rem. 9) id.
ἐλεγχόμενα, nom. pl. neut. part. pres. pass. id.
ἐλεγχόμενοι, nom. pl. masc. part. pres. pass. id.
ἐλεγχόμενος, nom. sing. masc. part. pres. pass. id.
ἔλεγχον, acc. sing. . . . . ἔλεγχος
ἔλεγχος, ου, ὁ, (§ 3. tab. C. a) . . . ἐλέγχω

ἐλέγχω, fut. γξω, aor. 1, ἤλεγξα, aor. 1, pass. ἠλέγχθην, (§ 23. rem. 9) *to put to proof, to test; to convict*, Jno. 8. 46; Ja. 2. 9; *to refute, confute*, 1 Co. 14. 24; Tit. 1. 9; *to detect, lay bare, expose*, Jno. 3. 20; Ep. 5. 11, 13; *to reprove, rebuke*, Mat. 18. 15; Lu. 3. 19; 1 Ti. 5. 20, et al.; *to discipline, chastise*, He. 12. 5; Re. 3. 19; pass., *to experience conviction*, Jno. 8. 9; 1 Co. 14. 24.

ἐλεγμός, οῦ, ὁ, (§ 3. tab. C. a) v.r. 2 Ti. 3. 16, a later equivalent to ἔλεγχος.

ἔλεγξις, εως, ἡ, (§ 5. tab. E. c) (a later form for ἔλεγχος) *reproof, confutation*, 2 Pe. 2. 16.

ἔλεγχος, ου, ὁ, (§ 3. tab. C. a) pr. *a trial in order to proof, a proof*; meton. *a certain persuasion*, He. 11. 1; *reproof, refutation*, 2 Ti. 3. 16.

ἐλέει, dat. sing. . . . . . ἔλεος
ἐλεεῖ, 3 pers. sing. pres. ind. act. . . ἐλεέω
ἐλεεινός, ή, όν, (§ 7. tab. F. a) . . ἔλεος
ἐλεεινότεροι, nom. pl. masc. comp. (§ 8. rem. 4) ἐλεεινός
ἐλεεῖτε, 2 pers. pl. pres. imper. act. . . ἐλεέω
ἐλεέω, ῶ], fut. ήσω, (§ 16. tab. P) . ἔλεος
ἐλεηθέντες, nom. pl. masc. part. aor. 1, pass. . ἐλεέω
ἐλεηθήσονται, 3 pers. pl. fut. 1, ind. pass. . id.
ἐλεηθῶσι, 3 pers. pl. aor. 1, subj. pass. . id.
ἐλεήμονες, nom. pl. masc. . . ἐλεήμων
ἐλεημοσύναι, nom. pl. . . . ἐλεημοσύνη
ἐλεημοσύνας, acc. pl. . . . . id.
ἐλεημοσύνη, ης, ἡ, (§ 2. tab. B. a) . . ἔλεος
ἐλεημοσύνην, acc. sing. . . ἐλεημοσύνη
ἐλεημοσυνῶν, gen. pl. . . . id.
ἐλεήμων, ονος, ὁ, ἡ, (§ 7. tab. G. a) ἔλεος

ἐλεῆσαι, aor. 1, infin. act. . . . . ἐλεέω
ἐλεήσῃ, 3 pers. sing. aor. 1, subj. act. . id.
ἐλέησον, 2 pers. sing. aor. 1, imper. act. . id.
ἐλεήσω, 1 pers. sing. fut. ind. act. . . id.
ἔλειχον, 3 pers. pl. imperf. act.—D. (Lu. 16. 21)
ἀπέλειχον, Rec. Gr. Sch. . } λείχω
ἐπέλειχον, A. B. Ln. Tdf. .
ἔλεον, acc. sing. . . . . . . ἔλεος

ἔλεος, ου, ὁ, and in N.T. έους, τό, (§ 5. tab. E. b) *pity, mercy, compassion*, Mat. 9. 13; 12. 7; Lu. 1. 50, 78, et al.; meton. *benefit* which results from compassion, *kindness, mercies, blessings*, Lu. 1. 54, 58, 72; 10. 37; Ro. 9. 23, et al.

ἐλεεινός, ή, όν, (§ 7. tab. F. a) *pitiable, wretched, miserable*, 1 Co. 15. 19; Re. 3. 17.

ἐλεέω, ῶ, fut. ήσω, aor. 1, ἠλέησα, (§ 16. tab. P) perf. pass. ἠλέημαι, aor. 1, pass. ἠλεήθην, (§ 17. tab. Q) *to pity, commiserate, have compassion on*; pass. *to receive pity, experience compassion*, Mat. 5. 7; 9. 27; 15. 22, et al.; *to be gracious to* any one, *show gracious favour and saving mercy towards*; pass. *to be an object of gracious favour and saving mercy*, Ro. 9. 15, 16, 18; 11. 30, 31, 32, et al.; spc. *to obtain pardon and forgiveness*, 1 Ti. 1. 13, 16.

ἐλεάω, ῶ, fut. ήσω, v.r., same signification as ἐλεέω, Ro. 9. 16, 18; Jude 23.

ἐλεήμων, ονος, ὁ, ἡ, (§ 7. tab. G. a, and rem. 4) *merciful, pitiful, compassionate*, Mat. 5. 7; He. 2. 17.

ἐλεημοσύνη, ης, ἡ, (§ 2. tab. B. a) *pity, compassion*; in N.T. *alms, almsgiving*, Mat. 6. 2, 3, 4; Lu. 11. 41, et al. (ῠ).

ἐλεοῦντος, gen. sing. masc. part. pres. act. . ἐλεέω
ἐλέους, gen. sing. . . . . . ἔλεος
ἐλευθέρα, nom. sing. fem. . . . ἐλεύθερος
ἐλευθέρας, gen. sing. fem. . . . id.
ἐλευθερία, ας, ἡ, (§ 2. tab. B. b, and rem. 2) id.
ἐλευθερίᾳ, dat. sing. . . . ἐλευθερία
ἐλευθερίαν, acc. sing. . . . id.
ἐλευθερίας, gen. sing. . . . . id.
ἐλεύθεροι, nom. pl. masc. . . . ἐλεύθερος

ἐλεύθερος, α, ον, (§ 7. rem. 1) *free, in a state of freedom* as opposed to slavery, 1 Co. 12. 13; Gal. 3. 28, et al.; *free, exempt*, Mat. 17. 26; 1 Co. 7. 39, et al.; *unrestricted*, unfettered, 1 Co. 9. 1; *free* from the dominion of sin, etc., Jno. 8. 36; Ro. 6. 20; *free* in the possession of Gospel privileges, 1 Pe. 2. 16.

ἐλευθερία, ας, ἡ, (§ 2. tab. B. b, and rem. 2) *liberty, freedom,* 1 Co. 10. 29; Gal. 2. 4, et al.

ἐλευθερόω, ῶ, fut. ώσω, (§ 20. tab. T) *to free, set free,* Jno. 8. 32, 36; Ro. 6. 18. 22, et al.

ἐλευθέρους, acc. pl. masc. . . . ἐλεύθερος
ἐλευθερόω, ῶ], fut. ώσω . . . . id.
ἐλευθερωθέντες, nom. pl. masc. part. aor. 1, pass. (§ 21. tab. U) . . . ἐλευθερόω
ἐλευθερωθήσεται, 3 pers. sing. fut. 1, ind. pass. id.
ἐλευθέρων, gen. pl. . . . . ἐλεύθερος
ἐλευθερώσει, 3 pers. sing. fut. ind. act. . ἐλευθερόω
ἐλευθερώσῃ, 3 pers. sing. aor. 1, subj. act. . id.
ἐλεύκᾶναν, 3 pers. pl. aor. 1, ind. (§ 27. rem. 1. e) λευκαίνω
ἐλεύσεται, 3 pers. sing. fut. ind. (§ 36. rem. 1) ἔρχομαι
ἐλεύσεως,[a] gen. sing. . . . . ἔλευσις
ἔλευσις, εως, ἡ, (§ 5. tab. E. c) (obsol. ἐλεύθω) *a coming, advent.* L.G.
ἐλεύσομαι, 1 pers. sing. fut. (§ 36. rem. 1) ἔρχομαι
ἐλευσόμεθα, 1 pers. sing. fut. ind. . . id.
ἐλεύσονται, 3 pers. pl. fut. ind. . . . id.
ἐλεφάντινον,[b] acc. sing. neut. . . ἐλεφάντινος
ἐλεφάντῐνος], η, ον, (§ 7. tab. F. a) (ἐλέφας, *ivory*) *ivory, made of ivory.*
ἐλεῶ, 1 pers. sing. pres. subj. act. . . ἐλεέω
ἐλεῶν, nom. sing. masc. part. pres. act. . id.
ἐλεῶντος, gen. s. masc. part. pres.—Al. Ln. Tdf. } ἐλεάω
ἐλεοῦντος, Rec. Gr. Sch. (Ro. 9. 16) }
ἐληλακότες, nom. pl. masc. part. perf. Att. for ἠλακότες, (§ 13. rem. 7. b) . ἐλαύνω
ἐλήλυθα, 1 pers. sing. perf. 2, (§ 36. rem. 1) ἔρχομαι
ἐλήλυθας, 2 pers. sing. perf. 2 . . id.
ἐλήλυθε, 3 pers. sing. perf. 2 . . . id.
ἐληλύθει, 3 pers. sing. pluperf. . . id.
ἐληλύθεισαν, 3 pers. pl. pluperf. . . . id.
ἐληλυθότα, acc. sing. masc. part. perf. 2 . id.
ἐληλυθότες, nom. pl. masc. part. perf. 2 . id.
ἐληλυθυῖαν, acc. sing. fem. part. perf. 2 . id.
ἐλθάτω, 3 pers. sing. aor. 1, imper. (§ 35. rem. 12).—C. Tdf. . . } id.
ἐλθέτω, Rec. Gr. Sch. (Mat. 10. 13) . }
ἐλθέ, 2 pers. sing. aor. 2, imper. . . . id.
ἐλθεῖν, aor. 2, infin. . . . . . id.

ἐλθέτω, 3 pers. sing. aor. 2, imper. . . ἔρχομαι
ἔλθῃ, 3 pers. sing. aor. 2, subj. . . id.
ἔλθῃς, 2 pers. sing. aor. 2, subj. . . . id.
ἐλθόν, nom. sing. neut. part. aor. 2 . id.
ἐλθόντα, acc. sing. masc. part. aor. 2 . id.
ἐλθόντας, acc. pl. masc. part. aor. 2 . . id.
ἐλθόντες, nom. pl. masc. part. aor. 2 . . id.
ἐλθόντι, dat. sing. masc. part. aor. 2 . . id.
ἐλθόντος, gen. sing. masc. part. aor. 2 . . id.
ἐλθόντων, gen. pl. masc. part. aor. 2 id.
ἐλθοῦσα, nom. sing. fem. part. aor. 2 id.
ἐλθοῦσαι, nom. pl. fem. part. aor. 2 . id.
ἐλθούσης, gen. sing. fem. part. aor. 2 . . id.
ἔλθω, 1 pers. sing. aor. 2, subj. . . id.
ἔλθωσι, 3 pers. pl. aor. 2, subj. . . . id.
Ἐλιακείμ, ὁ, *Eliakim,* pr. name, indecl.
Ἐλιέζερ,[c] ὁ, *Eliezer,* pr. name, indecl.
ἐλιθάσθην, 1 pers. s. aor. 1, ind. pass. (§ 26. rem. 1) λιθάζω
ἐλιθάσθησαν, 3 pers. pl. aor. 1, ind. pass. . id.
ἐλιθοβόλησαν, 3 pers. pl. aor. 1, ind. pass. . λιθοβολέω
ἐλιθοβόλουν, 3 pers. pl. imperf. act. . id.
ἑλίξεις,[d] 2 pers. sing. fut. ind. act. . . ἑλίσσω
Ἐλιούδ, ὁ, *Eliud,* pr. name, indecl.
Ἐλισαβέτ, ἡ, *Elisabeth,* pr. name, indecl.
Ἐλισσαῖος], ου, ὁ, (§ 3. tab. C. a) *Elisæus,* pr. name; in O.T. *Elisha.*
Ἐλισσαίου,[e] gen. sing.—Rec. Gr. Sch. . } Ἐλισσαῖος
Ἐλισαίου, Tdf. . . . }
ἑλίσσω], fut. ξω, (§ 26. rem. 3) *to roll, fold up,* as garments, He. 1. 12.
ἕλκη, acc. pl. . . . . ἕλκος
ἕλκος, εος, τό, (§ 5. tab. E. b) pr. *a wound;* hence, *an ulcer, sore,* Lu. 16. 21; Re. 16. 2, 11.

ἑλκόω, ῶ, fut. ώσω, (§ 20. tab. T) *to ulcerate, exulcerate;* pass. *to be afflicted with ulcers,* Lu. 16. 20.

ἕλκουσι, 3 pers. pl. pres. ind. act. . . ἕλκω
ἑλκόω, ῶ], fut. ώσω . . . . . ἕλκος
ἑλκῦσαι, or, **ἑλκύσαι,** aor. 1, infin. act. . . ἑλκύω
ἑλκύσῃ, 3 pers. sing. aor. 1, subj. act. . id.
ἑλκύσω, 1 pers. sing. fut. ind. act. . . id.

ἕλκω, and L.G. **ἑλκύω],** imperf. εἷλκον, fut. ύσω, aor. 1, εἵλκῠσα, (§ 13. rem. 4) *to draw, drag,* Jno. 21. 6, 11; Ac. 16. 19; 21. 30; Ja. 2. 6; *to draw* a sword, *unsheath,* Jno. 18. 10; met. *to draw* mentally and morally, Jno. 6. 44; 12. 32.

[a] Ac. 7. 52. [b] Re. 18. 12. [c] Lu. 3. 29. [d] He. 1. 12. [e] Lu. 4. 27.

ἑλκῶν, gen. pl. . . . ἕλκος
Ἑλλάδα,[a] acc. sing. . . Ἑλλάς

Ἑλλάς], άδος, (ᾰ) (§ 4. tab. D. b) *Hellas, Greece;* in N.T. *the southern portion of Greece* as distinguished from Macedonia.

Ἕλλην, ηνος, ὁ, (§ 4. tab. D. a) *a Greek,* Ac. 18. 17; Ro. 1. 14; *one not a Jew, a Gentile,* Ac. 14. 1; 16. 1, 3, et al.

Ἑλληνῐκός, ή, όν, (§ 7. tab. F. a) *Greek, Grecian,* Lu. 23. 28; Re. 9. 11.

Ἑλληνίς, ίδος, (ῐ) ἡ, (§ 4. rem. 2. c) *a female Greek,* Mar. 7. 26; Ac. 17. 12.

Ἑλληνιστής, οῦ, ὁ, (§ 2. tab. B. c) (ἑλληνίζω, *to imitate the Greeks*) pr. *one who uses the language and follows the customs of the Greeks;* in N.T. *a Jew by blood, but a native of a Greek-speaking country, Hellenist,* Ac. 6. 1; 9. 29.

Ἑλληνιστί, adv. *in the Greek language,* Jno. 19. 20; Ac. 21. 37.

Ἕλλην, ηνος, ὁ, (§ 4. tab. D. a) . Ἑλλάς
Ἕλληνας, acc. pl. . . . Ἕλλην
Ἕλληνες, nom. pl. . . . id.
Ἕλληνι, dat. sing. . . . id.
Ἑλληνίδων, gen. pl. . . . Ἑλληνίς
Ἑλληνικῇ, dat. sing. fem. . . Ἑλληνικός
Ἑλληνικοῖς, dat. pl. neut. . . id.
Ἑλληνικός], ή, όν, (§ 7. tab. F. a) . Ἑλλάς
Ἑλληνίς, ίδος, ἡ, (§ 4. rem. 2. c) . id.
Ἑλληνιστάς, acc. pl. . . . Ἑλληνιστής
Ἑλληνιστής], οῦ, ὁ, (§ 2. tab. B. c) . Ἑλλάς
Ἑλληνιστί, adv. . . . id.
Ἑλληνιστῶν, gen. pl. . . . Ἑλληνιστής
Ἕλληνος, gen. sing. . . . Ἕλλην
Ἑλλήνων, gen. pl. . . . id.
Ἕλλησι, dat. pl. . . . id.
ἐλλόγα, 2 pers. sing. pres. imper. act.—Al. Ln. Tdf. } ἐλλογάω
ἐλλόγει, Rec. Gr. Sch. (Phile. 18) }
ἐλλογᾶτο, 3 pers. sing. pres. imper. pass.—A. } id.
ἐλλογεῖται, R. Gr. Sch. Tdf. (Ro. 5. 13) }
ἐλλογάω, ῶ], fut. ήσω, same signif. as ἐλλογέω. v.r.
ἐλλόγει, 2 pers. sing. pres. imper. act. . ἐλλογέω
ἐλλογεῖται, 3 pers. sing. pres. ind. pass. . id.
ἐλλογέω, ῶ], fut. ήσω, (§ 16. tab. P) (ἐν & λόγος) *to enter in an account, to put to one's account,* Phile. 18; in N.T. *to impute,* Ro. 5. 13.

Ἐλμωδάμ,[b] ὁ, *Elmodam,* pr. name, indecl.
ἐλογιζόμην, 1 pers. sing. imperf. . λογίζομαι
ἐλογίζοντο, 3 pers. pl. imperf. . . id.
ἐλογίσθη, 3 pers. sing. aor. 1, ind. pass. . id.
ἐλογίσθημεν, 1 pers. pl. aor. 1, ind. pass. . id.
ἐλοιδόρησαν, 3 pers. pl. aor. 1, ind. act. . λοιδορέω
ἑλόμενος, nom. sing. masc. part. aor. 2, mid. . αἱρέω
ἔλουσε, 3 pers. sing. aor. 1, ind. act. . λούω
ἐλπίδα, acc. sing. . . . ἐλπίς
ἐλπίδι, dat. sing. . . . id.
ἐλπίδος, gen. sing. . . . id.
ἐλπίζει, 3 pers. sing. pres. ind. act. . ἐλπίζω
ἐλπίζετε, 2 pers. pl. pres. ind. act. . id.
ἐλπίζομεν, 1 pers. pl. pres. ind. act. . id.
ἐλπιζομένων, gen. pl. part. pres. pass. . id.
ἐλπίζουσαι, nom. pl. fem. part. pres. act. . id.
ἐλπίζω, fut. ίσω, (§ 26. rem. 1) . . ἐλπίς
ἐλπίζων, nom. sing. masc. part. pres. act. . ἐλπίζω
ἐλπιοῦσι, 3 pers. pl. fut. ind. Att. (§ 35. rem. 11) id.

ἐλπίς, ίδος, (ῐ), ἡ, (§ 4. rem. 2. c) pr. *expectation; hope,* Ac. 24. 15; Ro. 5. 4, et al.; meton. *the object of hope, thing hoped for,* Ro. 8. 24; Gal. 5. 5, et al.; *the author or source of hope,* Col. 1. 27; 1 Ti. 1. 1, et al.; *trust, confidence,* 1 Pe. 1. 21; ἐπ' ἐλπίδι, *in security, with a guarantee,* Ac. 2. 26; Ro. 8. 20.

ἐλπίζω, fut. ίσω, Att. ιῶ, (§ 35. rem. 11) perf. ἤλπῐκα, aor. 1, ἤλπισα, *to hope, expect,* Lu. 23. 8; 24. 21, et al.; *to repose hope and confidence in, trust, confide,* Mat. 12. 21; Jno. 5. 45, et al.

ἐλπίσατε, 2 pers. pl. aor. 1, imper. act . ἐλπίζω
ἔλυε, 3 pers. sing. imperf. act. . . λύω
ἐλύετο, 3 pers. sing. imperf. pass. . . id.
ἐλύθη, 3 pers. s. aor. 1, ind. pass. (§ 14. rem. 1. d) id.
ἐλύθησαν, 3 pers. pl. aor. 1, ind. pass. . id.
ἐλυμαίνετο,[c] 3 pers. sing. imperf. . λυμαίνομαι
Ἐλύμας,[d] α, ὁ, (§ 2. rem. 4) *Elymas,* pr. name.
ἐλυπήθη, 3 pers. s. aor. 1, ind. pass. (§ 17. tab. Q) λυπέω
ἐλυπήθησαν, 3 pers. pl. aor. 1, ind. pass. . id.
ἐλυπήθητε, 2 pers. pl. aor. 1, ind. pass. . id.
ἐλύπησα, 1 pers. sing. aor. 1, ind. act. . id.
ἐλύπησε, 3 pers. sing. aor. 1, ind. act. . id.
ἔλυσε, 3 pers. sing. aor. 1, ind. act. . λύω
ἐλυτρώθητε, 2 pers. pl. aor. 1, ind. pass. . λυτρόω
Ἐλωΐ, (Aram. אֱלָהִי) *my God,* Mar. 15. 34.

a Ac. 20. 2. b Lu. 3. 28. c Ac. 8. 3. d Ac. 13. 8.

ἐμά, nom. and acc. pl. neut. . . . ἐμός
ἔμαθε, 3 pers. sing. aor. 2, ind. act. (§ 24. rem. 5) μανθάνω
ἔμαθες, 2 pers. sing. aor. 2, ind. act. . id.
ἐμάθετε, 2 pers. pl. aor. 2, ind. act. . . id.
ἐμαθητεύθη, 3 pers. sing. aor. 1, ind. pass.—C. D. Ln. . . . } μαθητεύω
ἐμαθήτευσε, R. Gr. Sch. Tdf. (Mat. 27. 57) }
ἐμαθήτευσε, 3 pers. sing. aor. 1, ind. act. . id.
ἔμαθον, 1 pers. sing. aor. 2, ind. act. . . μανθάνω
ἐμαρτύρει, 3 pers. sing. imperf. act. . . μαρτυρέω
ἐμαρτυρεῖτο, 3 pers. sing. imperf. pass. . . id.
ἐμαρτυρήθη, 3 pers. sing. aor. 1, ind. pass. . id.
ἐμαρτυρήθησαν, 3 pers. pl. aor. 1, ind. pass. . id.
ἐμαρτυρήσαμεν, 1 pers. pl. aor. 1, ind. act. id.
ἐμαρτύρησαν, 3 pers. pl. aor. 1, ind. act. . id.
ἐμαρτύρησε, 3 pers. sing. aor. 1, ind. act . id.
ἐμαρτύρουν, 3 pers. pl. imperf. act. . . id.
ἐμάς, acc. pl. fem. . . . . ἐμός
ἐμασσῶντο,[a] 3 pers. pl. imperf. . . μασσάομαι
ἐμαστίγωσε, 3 pers. sing. aor. 1, ind. act. . μαστιγόω
ἐματαιώθησαν,[b] 3 pers. pl. aor. 1, ind. pass. . ματαιόω
ἐμαυτόν, acc. masc. . . . . ἐμαυτοῦ
ἐμαυτοῦ, ῆς, οῦ, (§ 11. tab. K. d) reflexive pron. (ἐμοῦ & αὐτοῦ) *myself*, Lu. 7. 7; Jno. 5. 31, et al.
ἐμαυτῷ, dat. masc. . . . . ἐμαυτοῦ
ἐμάχοντο, 3 pers. pl. imperf. . . . μάχομαι
ἐμβαίνοντος, gen. s. mas. pt. pres.—Al. Ln. Tdf. } ἐμβαίνω
ἐμβάντος, Rec. Gr. Sch. (Mar. 5. 18) }
ἐμβαίνω], fut. ἐμβήσομαι, aor. 2, ἐνέβην, (§ 37. rem. 1) (ἐν & βαίνω) *to step in; to go on board* a ship, *embark*, Mat. 8. 23; 9. 1; 13. 2, et al.
ἐμβαλεῖν,[c] aor. 2, infin. act. . . . ἐμβάλλω
ἐμβάλλω], fut. βαλῶ, aor. 2, ἐνέβἄλον, (§ 27. rem. 1. b, and 2. d) (ἐν & βάλλω) *to cast into*.
ἐμβάντα, acc. sing. masc. part. aor. 2 . ἐμβαίνω
ἐμβάντες, nom. pl. masc. part. aor. 2 . . id.
ἐμβάντι, dat. sing. masc. part. aor. 2 . id.
ἐμβάντος, gen. sing. masc. part. aor. 2 . id.
ἐμβάντων, gen. pl. masc. part. aor. 2 . id.
ἐμβαπτόμενος, nom. sing. masc. pt. pres. mid. ἐμβάπτω
ἐμβάπτω], fut. ψω, (§ 23. rem. 1. a) (ἐν & βάπτω) *to dip in*, Mat. 26. 23; Jno. 13. 26; mid. ἐμβάπτομαι, *to dip* for food in a dish, Mar. 14. 20.
ἐμβάς, nom. sing. masc. part. aor. 2 . . ἐμβαίνω

ἐμβατεύω], fut. εύσω, (§ 13. tab. M) (ἐν & βαίνω) pr. *to step into or upon; met. to search into, investigate; to pry into intrusively*.
ἐμβατεύων,[d] nom. sing. masc. part. pres. . ἐμβατεύω
ἐμβάψας, nom. sing. masc. part. aor. 1, act. ἐμβάπτω
ἐμβῆναι, aor. 2, infin. (§ 37. rem. 1) . . ἐμβαίνω
ἐμβιβάζω], fut. άσω, (§ 26. rem. 1) (ἐν & βιβάζω) *to cause to step into or upon; to set in or upon;* especially, *to put on board*, Ac. 27. 6.
ἐμβλέποντες, nom. pl. masc. part. pres. . ἐμβλέπω
ἐμβλέπω], fut. ψω, (§ 23. rem. 1. a) (ἐν & βλέπω) *to look attentively, gaze earnestly*, at an object, followed by εἰς, Mar. 6. 26; Ac. 1. 11; *to direct a glance, to look searchingly or significantly*, at a person, followed by the dat., Mar. 10. 21; 14. 67; Lu. 22. 61, et al.; absol. *to see clearly*, Mar. 8. 25; Ac. 22. 11.
ἐμβλέψας, nom. sing. masc. part. aor. 1 ἐμβλέπω
ἐμβλέψασα, nom. sing. fem. part. aor. 1 . id.
ἐμβλέψατε, 2 pers. pl. aor. 1, imper. . . id.
ἐμβριμάομαι, ῶμαι], fut. ήσομαι, (§ 19. tab. S) (ἐν & βριμάομαι, *to snort*) *to be greatly fretted or agitated*, Jno. 11. 33; *to charge or forbid sternly or vehemently*, Mat. 9. 30; Mar. 1. 43; *to express indignation, to censure*, Mar. 14. 5.
ἐμβριμησάμενος, nom. sing. masc. part. aor. 1 ἐμβριμάομαι
ἐμβριμώμενος, nom. sing. masc. part. pres. id.
ἐμέ, acc. sing. (§ 11 tab. K. a) . . . ἐγώ
ἐμεγάλυνε, 3 pers. sing. imperf. act. . μεγαλύνω
ἐμεγαλύνετο, 3 pers. sing. imperf. pass. . . id.
ἐμεθύσθησαν, 3 pers. pl. aor. 1, ind. pass. (§ 22. rem. 4) . . . . . μεθύω
ἐμείναμεν, 1 pers. pl. aor. 1, ind. (§ 27. rem. 1. d) μένω
ἔμειναν, 3 pers. pl. aor. 1, ind. . . . id.
ἔμεινε, 3 pers. sing. aor. 1, ind. . . id.
ἔμελε, 3 pers. sing. imperf. . . μέλει
ἐμελέτησαν, 3 pers. pl. aor. 1, ind. . μελετάω
ἔμελλε, 3 pers. sing. imperf. . . μέλλω
ἔμελλον, 1 pers. sing. and 3 pers. pl. imperf. id.
ἐμέμψαντο, 3 pers. pl. aor. 1, ind. (§ 23. rem. 5) μέμφομαι
ἔμενε, 3 pers. sing. imperf. . . μένω
ἔμενον, 3 pers. pl. imperf. . . . id.
ἐμέρισε, 3 pers. sing. aor. 1, ind. act. . . μερίζω
ἐμερίσθη, 3 pers. sing. aor. 1, ind. pass. . id.
ἐμέσαι,[e] aor. 1, infin. . . . . ἐμέω

[a] Re. 16. 10. [b] Ro. 1. 21. [c] Lu. 12. 5. [d] Col. 2. 18. [e] Re. 3. 16.

ἐμεσίτευσε,[a] 3 pers. sing. aor. 1, ind. . μεσιτεύω
ἐμέτρησε, 3 pers. sing. aor. 1, ind. act. . . μετρέω
ἐμέω, ῶ], fut. έσω, (§ 22. rem. 1) *to vomit,* Rev. 3. 16.
ἐμή, nom. sing. fem. . ἐμός
ἐμῇ, dat. sing. fem. . . . . . id.
ἐμήν, acc. sing. fem. . . . . . id.
ἐμήνυσε, 3 pers. sing. aor. 1, ind. act. . . μηνύω
ἐμῆς, gen. sing. fem. . . . . . ἐμός
ἔμιξε, 3 pers. sing. aor. 1, ind. (§ 36. rem. 5) μίγνυμι
ἐμίσησα, 1 pers. sing. aor. 1, ind. act. . . μισέω
ἐμίσησαν, 3 pers. pl. aor. 1, ind. act. . id.
ἐμίσησε, 3 pers. sing. aor. 1, ind. act. . . id.
ἐμισθώσατο, 3 pers. sing. aor. 1, ind. mid. . μισθόω
ἐμίσουν, 3 pers. pl. imperf. act. . . . μισέω
ἐμμαίνομαι], fut. ανοῦμαι, (§ 24. rem. 4) (ἐν & μαίνομαι) *to be mad against, be furious towards.* L.G.
ἐμμαινόμενος,[b] nom. sing. masc. part. pr. . ἐμμαίνομαι
Ἐμμανουήλ,[c] ὁ, *Emmanuel,* pr. name, indecl.
Ἐμμαούς,[d] ὁ, *Emmaus,* pr. name, indecl., of a village near Jerusalem.
ἐμμένει, 3 pers. sing. pres. ind. . . . ἐμμένω
ἐμμένειν, pres. infin. . . . . . id.
ἐμμένω], fut. ενῶ, (§ 27. rem. 1. a) (ἐν & μένω) pr. *to remain in* a place; met. *to abide by, to continue firm in, persevere in,* Acts 14. 22; Gal. 3. 10; He. 8. 9.
Ἐμμόρ,[e] ὁ, *Emmor,* pr. name, indecl. Rec. Gr. Sch.
Ἐμμώρ, Al. Ln. Tdf.
ἐμνημόνευον, 3 pers. pl. imperf. . . . μνημονεύω
ἐμνημόνευσε, 3 pers. sing. aor. 1, ind. . id.
ἐμνήσθη, 3 pers. s. aor. 1, ind. pass. (§ 36. rem. 3) μιμνήσκω
ἐμνήσθημεν, 1 pers. pl. aor. 1, ind. pass. . id.
ἐμνήσθην, 1 pers. sing. aor. 1, ind. pass. . id.
ἐμνήσθησαν, 3 pers. pl. aor. 1, ind. pass. . id.
ἐμνηστευμένῃ, dat. sing. fem. part. perf. pass.—A. B. D. Ln. Tdf. . . . μνηστεύω
μεμνηστευμένῃ, Rec. Gr. Sch. (Lu. 2. 5)
ἐμνηστευμένην, acc. sing. fem. part. pres. pass.—A. B. Ln. Tdf. . . . id.
μεμνηστευμένην, Rec. Gr. Sch. (Lu. 1. 27)
ἐμοί, dat. sing. . . . . . . ἐγώ
ἐμοί, nom. pl. masc. . . . ἐμός
ἐμοῖς, dat. pl. neut. . . . . . . id.
ἐμοίχευσε, 3 pers. sing. aor. 1, ind. act. . μοιχεύω
ἐμόλυναν, 3 pers. pl. aor. 1, ind. act. . . μολύνω
ἐμολύνθησαν, 3 pers. pl. aor. 1, ind. pass. . id.

ἐμόν, acc. masc. and nom. and acc. neut. sing. ἐμός
ἐμός, ή, όν, (§ 11. rem. 4) possessive adj. of the first pers. *my, mine,* Jno. 7. 16; 8. 37. et al.
ἐμοσχοποίησαν,[f] 3 pers. pl. aor. 1, ind. μοσχοποιέω
ἐμοῦ, gen. sing. . . . . . . ἐγώ
ἐμοῦ, gen. sing. neut. . . . . ἐμός
ἐμούς, acc. pl. masc. . . . . . . id.
ἐμπαιγμονή], ῆς, ἡ, (§ 2. tab. B. a) . ἐμπαίζω
ἐμπαιγμονῇ, dat. sing.—Gr. Sch. Tdf. . } ἐμπαιγμονή
Rec. om. (2 Pe. 3. 3) . .
ἐμπαιγμός], οῦ, ὁ, (§ 3. tab. C. a) . . ἐμπαίζω
ἐμπαιγμῶν,[g] gen. pl. . . . . ἐμπαιγμός
ἐμπαίζειν, pres. infin. . . . . ἐμπαίζω
ἐμπαίζοντες, nom. pl. masc. part. pres. . id.
ἐμπαίζω], fut. αίξω, (§ 26. rem. 2) (ἐν & παίζω) *to play upon, deride, mock, treat with scorn and contumely,* Mat. 20. 19; 27. 29, et al.; by impl. *to illude, delude, deceive,* Mat. 2. 16.

ἐμπαιγμονή, ῆς, ἡ, *mocking, scoffing, derision,* v. r. 2 Pe. 3. 3. N.T.

ἐμπαιγμός, οῦ, ὁ, (§ 3. tab. C. a) *mocking, scoffing, scorn,* He. 11. 36. L.G.

ἐμπαίκτης, ου, ὁ, (§ 2. tab. B. c) *a mocker, derider, scoffer,* 2 Pe. 3. 3; Jude 18. L.G.

ἐμπαῖκται, nom. pl. . . . ἐμπαίκτης
ἐμπαίκτης], ου, ὁ . . . . ἐμπαίζω
ἐμπαῖξαι, aor. 1, infin. act. . . . id.
ἐμπαίξουσι, 3 pers. pl. fut. ind. act. . . id.
ἐμπαιχθήσεται, 3 pers. sing. fut. 1, ind. pass. id.
ἐμπεπλησμένοι, nom. pl. masc. part. perf. pass. ἐμπίπλημι
ἐμπεριπατέω, ῶ], fut. ήσω, (§ 16. tab. P.) (ἐν & περιπατέω) pr. *to walk about in* a place; met. in N.T. *to live among, be conversant with.*
ἐμπεριπατήσω,[h] 1 pers. sing. fut. ind. . ἐμπεριπατέω
ἐμπεσεῖν, aor. 2, infin. (§ 37. rem. 1) . . ἐμπίπτω
ἐμπεσεῖται, 3 pers. sing. fut. ind. . . id.
ἐμπέσῃ, 3 pers. sing. aor. 2, subj. . . id.
ἐμπεσόντος, gen. sing. masc. part. aor. 2 . id.
ἐμπεσοῦνται, 3 pers. pl. fut. ind.—B.D.Ln.Tdf. } id.
πεσοῦνται, Rec. Gr. Sch. (Lu. 6. 39)
ἐμπίπλημι, and ἐμπιπλάω, ῶ], fut. ἐμπλήσω, aor. 1, pass. ἐνεπλήσθην, (ἐν & πίμπλημι) *to fill,* Ac. 14. 17; pass. *to be satisfied, satiated, full,* Lu. 1. 53; 6. 25; Jno. 6. 12;

[a] He. 8. 17. [b] Ac. 26. 11. [c] Mat. 1. 23. [d] Lu. 24. 13. [e] Ac. 7. 16. [f] Ac. 7. 41. [g] He. 11. 36. [h] 2 Co. 6. 16.

met. *to have the full enjoyment of,* Ro. 15. 24.

ἐμπιπλῶν, nom. sing. masc. part. pres. act. . ἐμπιπλάω

ἐμπίπτουσι, 3 pers. pl. pres. ind. . . ἐμπίπτω

ἐμπίπτω], fut. πεσοῦμαι, aor. 2, ἐνέπεσον, (§ 37. rem. 1) (ἐν & πίπτω) *to fall into,* Mat. 12. 11; Lu. 14. 5; *to encounter,* Lu. 10. 36; *to be involved in,* 1 Ti. 3. 6, 7; 6. 9; εἰς χεῖρας, *to fall under the chastisement of,* He. 10. 31.

ἐμπλακέντες, nom. pl. masc. part. aor. 2, pass. (§ 24. rem. 10) . . . . ἐμπλέκω

ἐμπλέκεται, 3 pers. sing. pres. ind. pass. . id.

ἐμπλέκω], fut. ξω, (§ 23. rem. 1. b) (ἐν & πλέκω) pr. *to intertwine;* met. *to implicate, entangle, involve;* pass. *to be implicated, involved, or to entangle one's self in,* 2 Ti. 2. 4; 2 Pe. 2. 20.

ἐμπλοκή, ῆς, ἡ, (§ 2. tab. B. a) *braiding or plaiting* of hair. L.G.

ἐμπλησθῶ, 1 pers. sing. aor. 1, subj. pass. . ἐμπίπλημι

ἐμπλοκή], ῆς, ἡ, ... ἐμπλέκω

ἐμπλοκῆς,[a] gen. sing. . . . . ἐμπλοκή

ἐμπνέω], fut. εύσω, (§ 35. rem. 3) (ἐν & πνέω) *to breathe into or upon; to respire, breathe;* met. *to breathe of, be animated with the spirit of.*

ἐμπνέων,[b] nom. sing. masc. part. pres. . ἐμπνέω

ἐμπορεύομαι], fut. εύσομαι, (§ 15. tab. O) (ἐν & πορεύομαι) *to travel; to travel for business' sake; to trade, traffic,* Jas. 4. 13; by impl., trans., *to make a gain of, deceive for one's own advantage,* 2 Pe. 2. 3.

ἐμπορεύσονται, 3 pers. pl. fut. ind. . ἐμπορεύομαι

ἐμπορευσώμεθα, 1 pers. pl. aor. 1, subj. . id.

ἐμπορία], ας, η, (§ 2. tab. B. b, and rem. 2) id.

ἐμπορίαν,[c] acc. sing. . . . . ἐμπορία

ἐμπόριον], ου, τό, (§ 3. tab. C. c) . ἐμπορεύομαι

ἐμπορίου,[d] gen. sing. . . . . ἐμπόριον

ἔμποροι, nom. pl. . . . . . ἔμπορος

ἔμπορος, ου, ὁ, (§ 3. tab. C. a) (ἐν & πόρος) pr. *a passenger by sea; a traveller; one who travels about for traffic, a merchant,* Mat. 13. 45; Re. 18. 3, 11, 15, 23.

ἐμπορία, ας, ἡ, (§ 2. tab. B. b, and rem. 2) *traffic, trade,* Mat. 22. 5.

ἐμπόριον, ου, τό, (§ 3. tab. C. c) *a mart, market-place, emporium;* meton. *traffic,* Jno. 2. 16.

ἐμπόρῳ, dat. sing. . . . . . ἔμπορος

ἐμπρήθω], fut. πρήσω, (§ 23. rem. 1. c) *to set on fire, to burn,* Mat. 22. 7.

ἔμπροσθεν, adv. used also as a prep. *before, in front of,* Lu. 19. 4; Phi. 3. 14; *before, in the presence of, in the face of,* Mat. 5. 24; 23. 14; *before, previous to,* Jno. 1. 15, 27, 30; from the Heb. *in the sight or estimation of,* Mat. 11. 26; 18. 14, et al.

ἐμπτύειν, pres. infin. . . . . . ἐμπτύω

ἐμπτύσαντες, nom. pl. masc. part. aor. 1 . id.

ἐμπτυσθήσεται, 3 pers. sing. fut. 1, ind. pass. id.

ἐμπτύσουσι, 3 pers. pl. fut. ind. . . id.

ἐμπτύω], fut. ύσω, (§ 13. tab. M) (ἐν & πτύω) *to spit upon,* Mat. 26. 67; 27. 30, et al. (ῡω, ὕσω). L.G.

ἐμφανῆ, acc. sing. masc. . . . . ἐμφανής

ἐμφᾰνής, έος, οῦς, ὁ, ἡ, τό, -ές, (§ 7. tab. G. b) (ἐν & φαίνω) *apparent, conspicuous, obvious to the sight,* Ac. 10. 40; met. *manifest, known, comprehended,* Ro. 10. 20.

ἐμφανίζω, fut. ίσω, aor. 1, ἐνεφάνισα, (§ 26. rem. 1) *to cause to appear clearly; to communicate, report,* Ac. 23. 15, 22; *to lay an information,* Ac. 24. 1; 25. 2, 15; *to manifest, intimate plainly,* He. 11. 14; *to reveal, make known,* Jno. 14. 21, 22; pass. *to appear, be visible,* Mat. 27. 53; *to present one's self,* He. 9. 24.

ἐμφανίζειν, pres. infin. act. . . . ἐμφανίζω

ἐμφανίζουσι, 3 pers. pl. pres. ind. act. . . id.

ἐμφανίζω], fut. ίσω, (§ 26. rem. 1) . ἐμφανής

ἐμφανίσατε, 2 pers. pl. aor. 1, imper. act. . ἐμφανίζω

ἐμφανισθῆναι, aor. 1, infin. pass. . . id.

ἐμφανίσω, 1 pers. sing. fut. ind. act. . . id.

ἔμφοβοι, nom. pl. masc. . . . ἔμφοβος

ἔμφοβος, ου, ὁ, ἡ, (§ 7. rem. 2) ἐν & φόβος) *terrible;* in N.T. *terrified, affrighted,* Lu. 24. 5, 37; Ac. 10. 4; 22. 9, et al.

ἐμφόβων, gen. pl. . . . . . ἔμφοβος

ἐμφῡσάω, ῶ], fut. ήσω, (§ 18. tab. R) (ἐν & φυσάω, *to breathe*) *to blow or breathe into, inflate;* in N.T. *to breathe upon,* Jno. 20. 22.

ἔμφυτον,[e] acc. sing. masc. . . . ἔμφυτος

ἔμφῠτος], ου, ὁ, ἡ, (§ 7. rem. 2) (ἐν & φύω) *implanted, ingrafted, infixed.*

ἐμῷ, dat. sing. masc. and neut. . . . ἐμός

[a] 1 Pe. 3. 3. [b] Ac. 9. 1. [c] Mat. 22. 5. [d] Jno. 2. 16. [e] Ja. 1. 21.

ἐμῶν, gen. pl. . . . . . . ἐμός

ἐμώρᾶνε, 3 pers. sing. aor. 1, ind. act. . . μωραίνω

ἐμωράνθησαν, 3 pers. pl. aor. 1, ind. pass. . id.

ἐν, prep. pr. referring to place, *in,* Mat. 8. 6; Mar. 12. 26; Re. 6. 6, et al. freq.; *upon,* Lu. 8. 32, et al.; *among,* Mat. 11. 11, et al.; *before, in the presence of,* Mar. 8. 38, et al.; *in the sight, estimation of,* 1 Co. 14. 11, et al.; *before,* judicially, 1 Co. 6. 2; *in,* of state, occupation, habit, Mat. 21. 22; Lu. 7. 25; Ro. 4. 10, et al.; *in the case of,* Mat. 17. 12, et al.; *in respect of,* Lu. 1. 7; 1 Co. 1. 7, et al.; *on occasion of, on the ground of,* Mat. 6. 7; Lu. 1. 21, et al.; used of the thing by which an oath is made, Mat. 5. 34, et al.; of the instrument, means, efficient cause, Ro. 12. 21; Ac. 4. 12, et al.; *equipped with, furnished with,* 1 Co. 4. 21; He. 9. 25, et al.; *arrayed with, accompanied by,* Lu. 14. 31; Jude 14, et al., of time, *during, in the course of,* Mat. 2. 1, et al.; in N.T. of demoniacal possession, *possessed by,* Mar. 5. 2, et al.

ἔνθεν, adv. *hence, from this place,* v.r. Lu. 16. 26.

ἐντός, adv. *inside, within,* Lu. 17. 21; τὸ ἐντός, *the interior, inside,* Mat. 23. 26.

ἕν, nom. and acc. sing. neut. . . . . εἷς

ἕνα, acc. sing. masc. . . . . . id.

ἐναγκαλίζομαι], fut. ίσομαι, (§ 26. rem. 1) (ἐν & ἀγκάλη) *to take into or embrace in one's arms,* Mar. 9. 36; 10. 16. L.G.

ἐναγκαλισάμενος, nom. s. masc. part. aor. 1 ἐναγκαλίζομαι

ἐνάλιος], ία, ιον, and ου, ὁ, ἡ, (§ 7. rem. 1, and rem. 2) (ἐν & ἅλς) *marine, living in the sea.*

ἐναλίων,[a] gen. pl. . . . . . . ἐνάλιος

ἔναντι,[b] adv. (ἐν & ἀντί) *over against, in the presence of.* L.G.

ἐναντίον, adv. (pr. neut. of ἐναντίος) *before, in the presence of,* Mar. 2. 12; Lu. 20. 26; Ac. 8. 32; from the Heb. *in the sight or estimation of,* Ac. 7. 10; with τοῦ θεοῦ, an intensive expression, Lu. 24. 19.

ἐναντίος, α, ον, (§ 7. rem. 1) *opposite to, over against,* Mar. 15. 39; *contrary,* as the wind, Mat. 14. 24; Ac. 26. 9; 28. 17 ὁ ἐξ ἐναντίας, *an adverse party, enemy,* Tit. 2. 8; *adverse, hostile, counter,* 1 Thes. 2. 15.

ἐναντία, acc. pl. neut. . . . . ἐναντίος

ἐναντίας, gen. sing. fem. . . . . id.

ἐναντίον, acc. sing. neut. . . . . id.

ἐναντίον, adv. . . . . . ἔναντι

ἐναντίος, ία, ιον, and ου, ὁ, ἡ . . id.

ἐναντίους, acc. pl. masc. . . . . ἐναντίος

ἐναντίων, gen. pl. . . . . . id.

ἐναρξάμενοι, nom. pl. masc. part. aor. 1 . ἐνάρχομαι

ἐναρξάμενος, nom. sing. masc. part. aor. 1 . id.

ἐνάρχομαι], fut. ξομαι, (§ 23. rem. 1. b) (ἐν & ἄρχομαι) *to begin, commence,* Gal. 3. 3; Phi. 1. 6.

ἔνατος, η, ον, *the ninth,* in Lachmann's text, for ἔννατος

ἐναυάγησα, 1 pers. sing. aor. 1, ind. . . ναυαγέω

ἐναυάγησαν, 3 pers. pl. aor. 1, ind. . id.

ἐνδεδυμένοι, nom. pl. masc. part. perf. pass. . ἐνδύω

ἐνδεδυμένον, acc. sing. masc. part. perf. pass. id.

ἐνδεδυμένος, nom. sing. masc. part. perf. pass. id.

ἐνδεής,[c] έος, οῦς, ὁ, ἡ, (§ 7. tab. G. b) (ἐνδέω) *indigent, poor, needy.*

ἔνδειγμα,[d] ατος, τό, (§ 4. tab. D. c) ἐνδείκνυμαι

ἐνδείκνῦμαι] fut. δείξομαι, (§ 31. tab. B.B) (mid. of ἐνδείκνῦμι, *to point out*) *to manifest, display,* Ro. 9. 17, 22; He. 6. 10, et al; *to give outward proof of,* Ro. 2. 15; *to display* a certain bearing towards a person; hence, *to perpetrate openly,* 2 Ti. 4. 14.

ἔνδειγμα, ατος, τό, (§ 4. tab. D. c) *a token, evidence, proof,* 2 Thes. 1. 5.

ἔνδειξις, εως, ἡ, (§ 5. tab. E. c) *a pointing out;* met. *manifestation, public declaration,* Ro. 3. 25, 26; *a token, sign, proof,* i.q. ἔνδειγμα, 2 Co. 8. 24; Phi. 1. 28.

ἐνδεικνύμενοι, nom. pl. m. pt. pres.—B. D. Ln. Tdf. ἐνδείξασθε, Rec. Gr. Sch. (2 Co. 8. 24) . . . . . } ἐνδείκνυμαι

ἐνδεικνυμένους, acc. pl. masc. part. pres. . id.

ἐνδείκνυνται, 3 pers. pl. pres. ind. . id.

ἐνδείξασθαι, aor. 1, infin. . . . . id.

ἐνδείξασθε, 2 pers. pl. aor. 1, imper. . id

ἐνδείξηται, 3 pers. sing. aor. 1, subj. . . id.

ἔνδειξιν, acc. sing. . . . . . ἔνδειξις

ἔνδειξις, εως, ἡ, (§ 5. tab. E. c) . . . ἐνδείκνυμαι

[a] Ja. 3. 7. [b] Lu. 1. 8. [c] Ac. 4. 34. [d] 2 Thes. 1. 5.

ἐνδείξωμαι, 1 pers. sing. aor. 1, subj. . ἐνδείκνυμαι

ἕνδεκα, οἱ, αἱ, τά, (εἷς, ἕν, & δέκα) *eleven*, Mat. 28. 16; Mar. 16. 14, et al.

ἑνδέκᾰτος, η, ον, (§ 7. tab. F. a) *eleventh*, Mat. 20. 6, 9; Re. 21. 20.

ἑνδεκάτην, acc. sing. fem. . . . . ἑνδέκατος

ἑνδέκατος, η, ον . . . . . . ἕνδεκα

ἐνδέχεται,[a] impers. (ἐνδέχομαι, *to admit*) *it is possible.*

ἐνδημέω, ῶ], fut. ήσω, (§ 16. tab. P) (ἐν & δῆμος) *to dwell in a place, be at home*, 2 Cor. 5. 6, 8, 9.

ἐνδημῆσαι, aor. 1. infin. . . . . ἐνδημέω

ἐνδημοῦντες, nom. pl. masc. part. pres. . id.

ἐνδιδύσκουσι, 3 pers. pl. pres. ind. act.—B. C. D. Ln. Tdf. } ἐνδιδύσκω
ἐνδύουσι, Rec. Gr. Sch. (Mar. 15. 17) }

ἐνδιδύσκω] . . . . ἐνδύω

ἔνδικον, nom. neut. and acc. fem. sing. . ἔνδικος

ἔνδῐκος], ου, ὁ, ἡ, (§ 7. rem. 2) (ἐν & δίκη) *fair, just*, Ro. 3. 8; He. 2. 2.

ἐνδόμησις,[b] εως, ἡ, (§ 5. tab. E. c) (ἐνδομέω) pr. *a thing built in*; in N.T. *a building, structure.* L.G.

ἐνδοξάζω], fut. άσω, (§ 26. rem. 1) (ἐν & δοξάζω) *to invest with glory*; pass. *to be glorified, to be made a subject of glorification*, 2 Thes. 1. 10, 12. LXX.

ἐνδοξασθῇ, 3 pers. sing. aor. 1, subj. pass. ἐνδοξάζω

ἐνδοξασθῆναι, aor. 1, infin. pass. . . id.

ἔνδοξοι, nom. pl. masc. . . . . ἔνδοξος

ἐνδόξοις, dat. pl. neut. . . . . . id.

ἔνδοξον, acc. sing. fem. . . . . . id.

ἔνδοξος], ου, ὁ, ἡ, (§ 7. rem. 2) (ἐν & δόξα) *honoured*, 1 Co. 4. 10; *notable, memorable*, Lu. 13. 17; *splendid, gorgeous*, Lu. 7. 25; *in unsullied array*, Ep. 5. 27.

ἐνδόξῳ, dat. sing. masc.. . . . . ἔνδοξος

ἔνδῠμα, ατος, τό, (§ 4. tab. D. c) . . ἐνδύω

ἐνδύμασι, dat. pl. . . . . . ἔνδυμα

ἐνδύματος, gen. sing. . . . . . id.

ἐνδυναμοῦ, 2 pers. s. pres. imper. mid. (§ 21. tab. U) ἐνδυναμόω

ἐνδυναμοῦντι, dat. sing. masc. part. pres. act. id.

ἐνδυναμοῦσθε, 2 pers. pl. pres. imper. mid. id.

ἐνδυνᾰμόω, ῶ], fut. ώσω, (§ 20. tab. T) (ἐν & δύναμις) *to empower, invigorate*, Phi. 4. 13, 1 Ti. 1. 12; 2 Ti. 4. 17; mid. *to summon up vigour, put forth energy*, Ep. 6. 10, 2 Ti. 2. 1; pass. *to acquire strength, be invigorated, be strong*, Ac. 9. 22; Ro. 4. 20; He. 11. 34. N.T.

ἐνδυναμώσαντι, dat. sing. masc. part. aor. 1, act. ἐνδυναμόω

ἐνδύνοντες, nom. pl. masc. part. pres. . ἐνδύνω

ἐνδύουσι, 3 pers. pl. pres. ind. act. . . ἐνδύω

ἐνδυσάμενοι, nom. pl. masc. part. aor. 1, mid. id.

ἐνδυσάμενος, nom. sing. masc. part. aor. 1, mid. id.

ἐνδύσασθαι, aor. 1, infin. mid. . . id.

ἐνδύσασθε, 2 pers. pl. aor. 1, imper. mid. . id.

ἐνδύσατε, 2 pers. pl. aor. 1, imper. act . id.

ἐνδύσεως,[c] gen. sing. . . . ἔνδυσις

ἐνδύσησθε, 2 pers. pl. aor. 1, subj. mid. . ἐνδύω

ἐνδύσηται, 3 pers. sing. aor. 1, subj. mid. . id.

ἔνδῠσις], εως, ἡ, (§ 5. tab. E. c) . . id.

ἐνδυσώμεθα, 1 pers. pl. aor. 1, subj. mid. . id.

ἐνδύω and ἐνδύνω], fut. ύσω, (§ 13. tab. M) (ἐν & δύω) *to enter*, 2 Ti. 3. 6; *to put on, clothe, invest, array*, Mat. 27. 31; Mar. 15. 17, 20; mid. *clothe one's self, be clothed or invested*, Mat. 22. 11; 27, 31, et al.; trop. *to be invested* with spiritual gifts, graces, or character, Lu. 24. 49; Ro. 13. 14, et al. (ῡω, ῠνω, ῡσω).

ἐνδιδύσκω, a later form, equivalent to ἐνδύω, Lu. 8. 27; 16. 19; and v.r. Mar. 15. 17.

ἔνδῠμα, ατος, τό, (§ 4. tab. D. c) *clothing, a garment*, Mat. 6. 25, 28; 22. 11, 12, et al.; in particular, *an outer garment, cloak, mantle*, Mat. 3. 4. L.G.

ἔνδῠσις, εως, ἡ, (§ 5. tab. E. c) *a putting on, or wearing* of clothes, 1 Pe. 3. 3.

ἐνέβη, 3 pers. sing. aor. 2, (§ 37. rem. 1) . ἐμβαίνω

ἐνέβημεν, 1 pers. pl. aor. 2, ind.—B. Ln. } id.
ἐπέβημεν, Rec. Gr. Sch. . . }
ἀνέβημεν, Tdf. (Ac. 21. 6) . }

ἐνέβησαν, 3 pers. pl. aor. 2, ind. . . . id.

ἐνεβίβασε, 3 pers. sing. aor. 1, ind. act. . ἐμβιβάζω

ἐνέβλεπε, 3 pers. sing. imperf.—B. Ln. Tdf. } ἐμβλέπω
ἐνέβλεψε, Rec. Gr. Sch. (Mar. 8. 25) . }

ἐνέβλεπον, 3 pers. pl. imperf. (§ 34. rem. 1 c) id.

ἐνέβλεψε, 3 pers. sing. aor. 1, ind. . . id.

ἐνεβριμήθη, 3 pers. s. aor. 1, ind. pass.—B. Ln. } ἐμβριμάομαι
ἐνεβριμήσατο, Rec. Gr. Sch. Tdf. (Mat. 9. 30) . . . }

ἐνεβριμήσατο, 3 pers. sing. aor. 1, ind. . . id.

ἐνεβριμῶντο, 3 pers. pl. imperf. . . id.

[a] Lu. 13. 33   [b] Re. 21. 18.   [c] 1 Pe. 3. 3

ἐνέγκαντες, nom. pl. masc. pt. aor. 1, (§ 36. rem. 1) — φέρω

ἐνέγκας, nom. sing. masc. part. aor. 1, act. — id.

ἐνέγκατε, 2 pers. pl. aor. 1, imper. act. — id.

ἐνεδείξασθε, 2 pers. pl. aor. 1, ind. — ἐνδείκνυμαι

ἐνεδείξατο, 3 pers. sing. aor. 1, ind. — id.

ἐνεδιδύσκετο, 3 pers. sing. imperf. mid. — ἐνδιδύσκω

ἐνέδρα], ας, ἡ, (§ 2. tab. B. b, and rem. 2) (ἐν & ἕδρα) pr. *a sitting in or on a spot; an ambush, ambuscade, or lying in wait*, Ac. 23. 16; 25. 3.

ἐνεδρεύω, fut. εύσω, (§ 13. tab. M) *to lie in wait or ambush for*, Ac. 23. 21; *to endeavour to entrap*, Lu. 11 54.

ἔνεδρον, ου, τό, (§ 3. tab. C. c) i.q. ἐνέδρα, Ac. 23. 16. N.T.

ἐνέδραν, acc. sing. — ἐνέδρα

ἐνεδρεύοντες, nom. pl. masc. part. pres. — ἐνεδρεύω

ἐνεδρεύουσι, 3 pers. pl. pres. ind. — id.

ἐνεδρεύω], fut. εύσω, (§ 13. tab. M) — ἐνέδρα

ἔνεδρον,[a] ου, τό, B. Sch. Tdf. } id.
ἐνέδραν, Rec. Gr. (Ac. 23. 16) }

ἐνεδυναμοῦτο, 3 pers. sing. imperf. pass. — ἐνδυναμόω

ἐνεδυναμώθη, 3 pers. sing. aor. 1, ind. pass. — id.

ἐνεδυναμώθησαν, 3 pers. pl. aor. 1, ind. pass. — id.

ἐνεδυνάμωσε, 3 pers. sing. aor. 1, ind. act. — id.

ἐνέδῡσαν, 3 pers. pl. aor. 1, ind. act. — ἐνδύω

ἐνεδύσασθε, 2 pers. pl. aor. 1, ind. mid. — id.

ἐνειλέω, ῶ], fut. ήσω, (§ 16. tab. P) (ἐν & εἰλέω) *to inwrap, envelope.*

ἐνείλησε,[b] 3 pers. sing. aor. 1, ind. act. — ἐνειλέω

ἔνειμι], (§ 12. tab. L) (ἐν & εἰμί) *to be in or within*; τὰ ἐνόντα, *those things which are within*, Lu. 11. 41.

ἔνι, (§ 12. rem. 1) (for ἔνεστι) *there is in, there is contained, there exists*, Gal. 3. 28, ter, Col. 3. 11; Ja. 1. 17.

ἐνεῖχε, 3 pers. sing. imperf. (§ 13. rem. 4) — ἐνέχω

ἕνεκα, or ἕνεκεν, or εἵνεκεν, adv. *on account of, for the sake of, by reason of*, Mat. 5. 10, 11; 10. 18, 39, et al.

ἐνεκαίνισε, 3 pers. sing. aor. 1, ind. act. — ἐγκαινίζω

ἐνεκάλουν, 3 pers. pl. imperf. act. — ἐγκαλέω

ἕνεκεν, adv. — ἕνεκα

ἐνεκεντρίσθης, 2 pers. sing. aor. 1, ind. pass. — ἐγκεντρίζω

ἐνεκοπτόμην, 1 pers. sing. imperf. pass. — ἐγκόπτω

ἐνέκοψε, 3 pers. sing. aor. 1, ind. act. — id.

ἐνέκρυψε, 2 pers. sing. aor. 1, ind. act. — ἐγκρύπτω

ἐνέμειναν, 3 pers. pl. aor. 1, ind. (§ 34. rem. 1. c) — ἐμμένω

ἐνένευον,[c] 3 pers. pl. imperf. — ἐννεύω

ἐνέπαιζον, 3 pers. pl. imperf. act. — ἐμπαίζω

ἐνέπαιξαν, 3 pers. pl. aor. 1, ind. act. — id.

ἐνεπαίχθη, 3 pers. sing. aor. 1, ind. pass. — id.

ἐνέπλησε, 3 pers. sing. aor. 1, ind. act. — ἐμπίπλημι

ἐνεπλήσθησαν, 3 pers. pl. aor. 1, ind. pass. — id.

ἐνέπρησε,[d] 3 pers. sing. aor. 1, ind. act. — ἐμπρήθω

ἐνέπτυον, 3 pers. pl. imperf. — ἐμπτύω

ἐνέπτῠσαν, 3 pers. pl. aor. 1, ind. — id.

ἐνεργεῖ, 3 pers. sing. pres. ind. — ἐνεργέω

ἐνέργεια], ας, ἡ, (§ 2. tab. B. b, and rem. 2) — ἐνεργής

ἐνέργειαν, acc. sing. — ἐνέργεια

ἐνεργείας, gen. sing. — id.

ἐνεργεῖν, pres. infin. — ἐνεργέω

ἐνεργεῖται, 3 pers. sing. pres. ind. mid. (§ 17. tab. Q) — id.

ἐνεργέω, ῶ], fut. ήσω, (§ 16. tab. P) — ἐνεργής

ἐνέργημα], ατος, τό, (§ 4. tab. D. c) — id.

ἐνεργήματα, nom. pl. — ἐνέργημα

ἐνεργημάτων, gen. pl. — id.

ἐνεργής, έος, οῦς, ὁ, ἡ, (§ 7. tab. G. b) (ἐν & ἔργον) *active*, Phile. 6; *efficient, energetic*, Heb. 4. 12; *adapted to accomplish* a thing, *effectual*, 1 Co. 16. 9.

ἐνέργεια, ας, ἡ, (§ 2. tab. B. b, and rem. 2) *energy, efficacy, power*, Phi. 3. 21; Col. 2. 12; *active energy, operation*, Ep. 4. 16; Col. 1. 29, et al.

ἐνεργέω, ῶ, fut. ήσω, aor. 1, ἐνήργησα, *to effect*, 1 Co. 12. 6, 11; Gal. 3. 5; Ep. 1. 11; Phi. 2. 13; *to put into operation*, Ep. 1. 20; absol. *to be active*, Mat. 14. 2; Mar. 6. 14; Ep. 2. 2; in N.T. *to communicate energy and efficiency*, Gal. 2. 8; pass. or mid. *to come into activity, be actively developed; to be active, be in operation*, towards a result, 2 Co. 4. 12; 2 Thes. 2. 7; *to be an active power or principle*, Ro. 7. 5; 1 Thes. 2. 12; part. ἐνεργούμενος, *instinct with activity; in action, operative*, 2 Co. 1 6; Gal. 5. 6; Ep. 3. 20; Col. 1. 29; *earnest*, Ja. 5. 16.

ἐνέργημα, ατος, τό, (§ 4. tab. D. c) *an effect, thing effected*, 1 Co. 12. 6; *operation, working*, 1 Co. 12. 10. L.G.

ἐνεργήσας, nom. sing. masc. part. aor. 1. — ἐνεργέω

ἐνεργουμένη, nom. sing. fem. part. pres. mid. — id.

ἐνεργουμένην, acc. sing. fem. part. pres. mid. — id.

---

[a] Ac. 23. 16. [b] Mar. 15. 46. [c] Lu. 1. 62. [d] Mat. 22. 7.

ἐνεργουμένης, gen. sing. fem. part. pres. mid. — ἐνεργέω
ἐνεργοῦντος, gen. sing. masc. and neut. part. pres. — id.
ἐνεργοῦσι, 3 pers. pl. pres. ind. — id.
ἐνεργῶν, nom. sing. masc. part. pres. — id.
ἐνέστηκε, 3 pers. sing. perf. ind. (§ 29. tab. X) — ἐνίστημι
ἐνεστηκότα, acc. sing. masc. part. perf. — id.
ἐνεστῶσαν, acc. sing. fem. part. perf. (§ 35. rem. 8) — id.
ἐνεστῶτα, nom. pl. neut. part. perf. — id.
ἐνεστῶτος, gen. sing. masc. part. perf. — id.
ἐνετειλάμην, 1 pers. sing. aor. 1, ind. — ἐντέλλομαι
ἐνετείλατο, 3 pers. s. aor. 1, ind. (§ 27. rem. 1. d) — id.
ἐνετρεπόμεθα, 1 pers. pl. imperf. mid. — ἐντρέπω
ἐνετύλιξε, 3 pers. sing. aor. 1, ind. act. — ἐντυλίσσω
ἐνέτυχον, 3 pers. pl. aor. 2, ind. — ἐντυγχάνω
ἐνευλογέω, ῶ], fut. ήσω, (§ 16. tab. P) (ἐν & εὐλογέω) *to bless in respect of, or by means of*, Ac. 3. 25; Gal. 3. 8. LXX.
ἐνευλογηθήσονται, 3 pers. pl. fut. 1, ind. pass. — ἐνευλογέω
ἐνεφάνισαν, 3 pers. pl. aor. 1, ind. act. — ἐμφανίζω
ἐνεφάνισας, 2 pers. sing. aor. 1, ind. act. — id.
ἐνεφανίσθησαν, 3 pers. pl. aor. 1, ind. pass. — id.
ἐνεφύσησε,[a] 3 pers. sing. aor. 1, ind. — ἐμφυσάω
ἐνέχειν, pres. infin. — ἐνέχω
ἐνέχεσθε, 2 pers. pl. pres. imper. pass. — id.
ἐνεχθεῖσαν, acc. sing. fem. part. aor. 1, pass. (§ 36. rem. 1) — φέρω
ἐνεχθείσης, gen. sing. fem. part. aor. 1, pass. — id.
ἐνεχθῆναι, aor. 1, infin. pass. — id.
ἐνέχω], fut. ξω, imperf. ἐνεῖχον, (§ 13. rem. 4) (ἐν & ἔχω) *to hold within; to fix upon;* in N.T. intrans. (scil. χόλον) *to entertain a grudge against*, Mar. 6. 19; *to be exasperated against*, Lu. 11. 53; pass. *to be entangled, held fast in*, Gal. 5. 1.

ἔνοχος, ου, ὁ, ἡ, (§ 7. rem. 2) *held in or by; subjected to*, He. 2. 15; *obnoxious, liable to*, Mat. 5. 21, 22; 26. 66; Mar. 3. 29; 14. 64; *an offender against*, 1 Co. 11. 27; Ja. 2. 10.

ἐνηργεῖτο, 3 pers. sing. imperf. mid. — ἐνεργέω
ἐνήργηκε, 3 pers. sing. perf. ind.—A. B. Ln. Tdf. } id.
ἐνήργησε, Rec. Gr. Sch. (Ep. 1. 20) }
ἐνήργησε, 3 pers. sing. aor. 1, ind. — id.
ἐνήρξατο, 3 pers. sing. aor. 1, ind.—B. Ln. } ἐνάρχομαι
προενήρξατο, R. Gr. Sch. Tdf. (2 Co. 8. 6) }
ἐνθάδε, adv. (ἔνθα, *here*, & δε, an enclitic particle) pr. *hither, to this place*, Jno. 4. 15, 16, et al.; also, *here, in this place*, Lu. 24. 41, et al.

ἔνθεν, adv.—Gr. Sch. } ἐν
ἐντεῦθεν, Rec. }
Tdf. om. (Lu. 16. 26) }
ἐνθυμεῖσθε, 2 pers. pl. pres. ind. — ἐνθυμέομαι
ἐνθυμέομαι, οῦμαι], fut. ήσομαι, aor. 1, (pass. form) ἐνεθυμήθην, (§ 17. tab. Q) (ἐν & θυμός) *to ponder in one's mind, think of, meditate on*, Mat. 1. 20; 9. 4; Ac. 10. 19.

ἐνθύμησις, εως, ἡ, (§ 5. tab. E. c) *the act of thought, cogitation, reflection*, Mat. 9. 4; 12. 25; He. 4. 12; *the result of thought, invention, device*, Ac. 17. 29.

ἐνθυμηθέντος, gen. sing. masc. part. aor. 1, pass. — ἐνθυμέομαι
ἐνθυμήσεις, acc. pl. — ἐνθύμησις
ἐνθυμησέων, gen. pl. — id.
ἐνθυμήσεως, gen. sing. — id.
ἐνθύμησις], εως, ἡ, (§ 5. tab. E. c) — ἐνθυμέομαι
ἐνθυμουμένου, gen. sing. masc. part. pres. — id.
ἐνί, dat. sing. masc. and neut. — εἷς
ἔνι, for ἔνεστι, (§ 12. rem. 1) — ἔνειμι
ἐνιαυτόν, acc. sing. — ἐνιαυτός
ἐνιαυτός], οῦ, ὁ, (§ 3. tab. C. a) (ἔνος) *a year*, more particularly as being a cycle of seasons, and in respect of its revolution, Jno. 11. 49, 51; 18. 13, et al.; in N.T. *an era*, Lu. 4. 19.
ἐνιαυτοῦ, gen. sing. — ἐνιαυτός
ἐνιαυτούς, acc. pl. — id.
ἐνίκησα, 1 pers. sing. aor. 1, ind. act. — νικάω
ἐνίκησαν, 3 pers. pl. aor. 1, ind. act. — id.
ἐνίκησε, 3 pers. sing. aor. 1, ind. act. — id.
ἐνίοτε, adv. *sometimes*, (ἔνι, for ἔνεστι, and ὅτε, *when*) (Mat. 17. 15)—D. Ln.
πολλάκις, Rec. Gr. Sch. Tdf.
ἐνίστημι], fut. ἐνστήσω, (§ 29. tab. X.) (ἐν & ἵστημι) *to place in or upon;* intrans., perf. ἐνέστηκα, part. ἐνεστηκώς and ἐνεστώς, fut. mid. ἐνστήσομαι, *to stand close upon; to be at hand, impend, to be present*, Ro. 8. 38; 2 Thes. 2. 2, et al.
ἐνίσχυσε, 3 pers. sing. aor. 1, ind. — ἐνισχύω
ἐνισχύω], fut. ύσω, (§ 13. tab. M) (ἐν & ἰσχύω) *to strengthen, impart strength and vigour*, Lu. 22. 43; intrans. *to gain, acquire, or recover strength and vigour, be strengthened*, Ac. 9. 19. (ῦσ).
ἐνισχύων, nom. sing. masc. part. pres. — ἐνισχύω
ἔνιψα, 1 pers. sing. aor. 1, ind. act. — νίπτω

[a] Jno. 20. 22.

ἐνιψάμην, 1 pers. sing. aor. 1, ind. mid. . νίπτω
ἐνίψατο, 3 pers. sing. aor. 1, ind. mid. . id.
ἔνιψε, 3 pers. sing. aor. 1, ind. act. . . id.
ἐννάτῃ, dat. sing. fem. . . . . ἔννατος
ἐννάτην, acc. sing. fem. . . . . id.
ἔννατος, η, ον, (§ 7. tab. F. a) . . ἐννέα

ἐννέα,[a] οἱ, αἱ τά, *nine*, Lu. 17. 17.

ἔννᾰτος, or ἔνᾰτος, άτη, ον, *ninth*, Mat. 20. 5; Re. 21. 20, et al.

ἐννενήκοντα, οἱ, αἱ, τά, *ninety*.

ἐννενηκονταεννέα, οἱ, αἱ, τά, *ninety-nine*, Mat. 18. 12, 13; Lu. 15. 4, 7.

ἐννενηκοντα,] οἱ, αἱ, τά . . . . ἐννέα
ἐννενηκονταεννέα, οἱ, αἱ, τά, Rec. Gr. Sch. } id.
ἐνενήκοντα ἐννέα, Ln. . . . }
ἐννεοί,[b] nom. pl. masc.—Rec. Gr. Sch. . } ἐννεός
ἐνεοί, A. B. Ln. Tdf. (Ac. 9. 7) . . }

ἐννεός], ου, ὁ, ἡ, and ἐνεός, (§ 7. rem. 2) *stupid; dumb; struck dumb with amazement, bewildered, stupified.*

ἐννεύω], fut. εύσω, (§ 13. tab. M) (ἐν & νεύω) *to nod at, signify by a nod; to make signs; to intimate by signs*, Lu. 1. 62.

ἔννοια], ας, ἡ, (§ 2. tab. B. b, and rem. 2) (ἐν & νοέω, νοῦς) *notion, idea; thought, purpose, intention*, He. 4. 12; 1 Pe. 4. 1.

ἔννοιαν, acc. sing. . . . . . ἔννοια
ἐννοιῶν, gen. pl. . . . . . . id.

ἔννομος, ου, ὁ, ἡ, (§ 7. rem. 2) (ἐν & νόμος) *within law; lawful, legal*, Ac. 19. 39; in N.T. *subject or under a law, obedient to a law*, 1 Co. 9. 21.

ἐννόμῳ, dat. sing. fem. . . . . ἔννομος
ἔννυχον,[c] adv.—Rec. Gr. Sch. . . . } ἔννυχος
ἔννυχα,—Al. Ln. Tdf. (Mar. 1. 35) }

ἔννῠχος], ου, ὁ, ἡ, (§ 7. rem. 2) (ἐν & νύξ) *nocturnal*; neut. ἔννυχον, as an adv. *by night*.

ἐνοικέω, ῶ], fut. ήσω, (§ 16. tab. P) (ἐν & οἰκέω) *to dwell in, inhabit*; in N.T. met. *to be indwelling* spiritually, Ro. 8. 11; Col. 3. 16; 2 Ti. 1. 14; *to be infixed* mentally, 2 Ti. 1. 5; of the Deity, *to indwell*, by special presence, 2 Co. 6. 16.

ἐνοικείτω, 3 pers. sing. pres. imper. . . ἐνοικέω
ἐνοικήσω, 1 pers. sing. fut. ind. . . id.
ἐνοικοδομεῖσθε, 2 pers. pl. pres. ind. pass.—C. } ἐνοικοδομέω
οἰκοδομεῖσθε, R. Gr. Sch. Tdf. (1 Pe. 2. 5) }

ἐνοικοδομέω, ῶ], fut. ήσω, (§ 16. tab. P) (ἐν & οἰκοδομέω) *to build in, or together*. v.r.

ἐνοικοῦν, acc. sing. neut. part. pres. . . ἐνοικέω
ἐνοικοῦντος, gen. sing. neut. part. pres. . id.
ἐνοικοῦσαν, acc. sing. fem. part. pres.—A. } id.
μένουσαν, Rec. Gr. Sch. Tdf. (2 Jno. 2) }
ἐνόμιζε, 3 pers. sing. imperf. act. . . νομίζω
ἐνομίζετο, 3 pers. sing. imperf. pass. . . id.
ἐνόμιζον, 3 pers. pl. imperf. act. . . id.
ἐνόμισαν, 3 pers. pl. aor. 1, ind. act. . id.
ἐνόμισας, 2 pers. sing. aor. 1, ind. act. . . id.
ἐνόντα,[d] acc. pl. neut. part. pres. . . ἔνειμι

ἐνορκίζω, fut. ίσω, (ἐν & ὁρκίζω) *to adjure*. —Al. Ln. Tdf.

ὁρκίζω, Rec. Gr. Sch. (1 Thes. 5. 27).

ἑνός, gen. sing. masc. and neut. . : . εἷς
ἐνοσφίσατο, 3 pers. sing. aor. 1, ind. mid. . νοσφίζω
ἑνότης], ητος, ἡ, (§ 4. rem. 2. c) . . εἷς
ἑνότητα, acc. sing. . . . . . ἑνότης

ἐνοχλέω, ῶ], fut. ήσω, (§ 16. tab. P) (ἐν & ὀχλέω) *to trouble, annoy; to be a trouble*, He. 12. 15.

ἐνοχλῇ,[e] 3 pers. sing. pres. subj. act. . . ἐνοχλέω
ἐνοχλούμενοι, nom. pl. masc. part. pres. pass. } id.
—A. B. Tdf. . . . . }
ὀχλούμενοι, Rec. Gr. Sch. Ln. (Lu. 6. 18) }
ἔνοχοι, nom. pl. masc. . . . . . ἔνοχος
ἔνοχον, acc. sing. masc. . . . . . id.
ἔνοχος, ου, ὁ, ἡ, (§ 7. rem. 2) . . . ἐνέχω
ἐνστήσονται, 3 pers. pl. fut. ind. mid. (§ 29. tab. Y) ἐνίστημι
ἔνταλμα], ατος, τό, (§ 4. tab. D. c) . ἐντέλλομαι
ἐντάλματα, acc. pl. . . . . . . ἔνταλμα
ἐνταφιάζειν, pres. infin. . . . ἐνταφιάζω

ἐνταφιάζω], fut. άσω, (§ 26. rem. 1) (ἐντάφιος, θάπτω) *to prepare* a body *for burial*, Mat. 26. 12; absol. *to make the ordinary preparations for burial*, Jno. 19. 40. L.G.

ἐνταφιασμός, οῦ, ὁ, (§ 3. tab. C. a) *preparation* of a corpse *for burial*, Mar. 14. 8; Jno. 12. 7. N.T.

ἐνταφιάσαι, aor. 1, infin. act. . . ἐνταφιάζω
ἐνταφιασμόν, acc. sing. . . . ἐνταφιασμός
ἐνταφιασμός], οῦ, ὁ, (§ 3. tab. C. a) . ἐνταφιάζω
ἐνταφιασμοῦ, gen. sing. . . . ἐνταφιασμός
ἐντειλάμενος, nom. sing. masc. part. aor. 1 ἐντέλλομαι
ἐντελεῖται, 3 pers. sing. fut. ind. (§ 35. rem. 11) id.

ἐντέλλομαι, fut. τελοῦμαι, aor. 1, ἐνετειλάμην, (§ 27. rem. 1. d) perf. ἐντέταλμαι, (§ 27.

[a] Lu. 17. 17. [b] Ac. 9. 7. [c] Mar. 1. 35. [d] Lu. 11. 41. [e] He. 12. 15.

rem. 2. b) *to enjoin, charge, command,* Mat. 4. 6; 15. 4; 17. 9, et al.; *to direct,* Mat. 19. 7; Mar. 10. 3.

ἔνταλμα, ατος, τό, (§ 4. tab. D. c) equivalent to ἐντολή, *a precept, commandment, ordinance,* Mat. 15. 9; Mar. 7. 7; Col. 2. 22. LXX.

ἐντολή, ῆς, ἡ, (§ 2. tab. B. a) *an injunction; a precept, commandment,* Mat. 5. 19; 15. 3, 6, et al.; *an order, direction,* Ac. 17. 15; *an edict,* Jno. 11. 57; *a direction,* Mar. 10. 5; *a commission,* Jno. 10. 18, *a charge* of matters to be proclaimed or received, Jno. 12. 49, 50; 1 Ti. 6. 14; 2 Pe. 2. 21, et al.

ἐντέταλται, 3 pers. sing. perf. ind. pass. . ἐντέλλομαι

ἐντετυλιγμένον, acc. sing. neut. part. perf. pass. ἐντυλίσσω

ἐντετυπωμένη,[a] nom. sing. fem. part. perf. pass. ἐντυπόω

ἐντεῦθεν, adv. *hence, from this place,* Mat. 17. 20; Lu. 4. 9, et al.; ἐντεῦθεν καὶ ἐντεῦθεν, *hence and hence, on each side,* Re. 22. 2; *hence, from this cause,* Ja. 4. 1.

ἐντεύξεις, acc. pl. . . . . . ἔντευξις

ἐντεύξεως, gen. sing. . . . . . id.

ἔντευξις], εως, ἡ, (§ 5. tab. E. c) . . ἐντυγχάνω

ἔντιμον, acc. sing. masc. . . . . ἔντιμος

ἐντιμότερος, nom. sing. masc. comp. (§ 8. rem. 4) id.

ἐντίμους, acc. pl. masc. . . . . id.

ἔντῑμος, ου, ὁ, ἡ, (§ 7. rem. 2) (ἐν & τιμή) *honoured, estimable, dear,* Lu. 7. 2; 14. 8; Phi. 2. 29; *highly-valued, precious, costly,* 1 Pe. 2. 4, 6.

ἐντολαί, nom. pl. . . . . . ἐντολή

ἐντολαῖς, dat. pl. . . . . . id.

ἐντολάς, acc. pl. . . . . . . id.

ἐντολή, ῆς, ἡ, (§ 2. tab. B. a) . . ἐντέλλομαι

ἐντολήν, acc. sing. . . . . . ἐντολή

ἐντολῆς, gen. sing. . . . . . id.

ἐντολῶν, gen. pl. . . . . . . id.

ἐντόπιοι,[b] nom. pl. masc. . . . . ἐντόπιος

ἐντόπιος], ου, ὁ, ἡ, (§ 7. rem. 2) (ἐν & τόπος) i.q. ἔντοπος, *in or of a place; an inhabitant, citizen.*

ἐντός, adv. . . . . ἐν

ἐντράπῃ, 3 pers. s. aor. 2, subj. pass. (§ 24. rem. 10) ἐντρέπω

ἐντραπήσονται, 3 pers. pl. fut. 2, ind. pass. . id.

ἐντρέπομαι, 1 pers. sing. pres. ind. mid. . id.

ἐντρεπόμενος, nom. sing. masc. part. pres. mid. id.

ἐντρέπω], fut. ψω, (§ 23. rem 1. a) (ἐν & τρέπω) pr. *to turn* one *back upon himself;* hence, *to put to shame, make ashamed;* mid. ἐντρέπομαι, fut. (pass. form) ἐντραπήσομαι, aor. 2, (pass. form) ἐνετράπην, (§ 24. rem. 10) *to revere, reverence, regard,* Mat. 21. 37, Mar. 12. 6, et al.; absol. *to feel shame, be put to shame,* 2 Thes. 3. 14; Tit. 2. 8.

ἐντροπή, ῆς, ἡ, (§ 2. tab. B. a) *reverence;* in N.T. *shame,* 1 Co. 6. 5; 15. 34.

ἐντρέπων, nom. sing. masc. part. pres. act. . ἐντρέπω

ἐντρεφόμενος,[c] nom. sing. masc. part. pres. pass. ἐντρέφω

ἐντρέφω], fut. ἐνθρέψω, (§ 35. rem. 4) (ἐν & τρέφω) *to nourish in, bring up or educate in;* pass. *to be imbued.*

ἔντρομος, ου, ὁ, ἡ, (§ 7. rem. 2) (ἐν & τρόμος) *trembling, terrified,* Ac. 7. 32; 16. 29; He. 12. 21. L.G.

ἐντροπή], ῆς, ἡ, (§ 2. tab. B. a) . . ἐντρέπω

ἐντροπήν, acc. sing. . . . . . . ἐντροπή

ἐντρυφάω, ῶ], fut. ήσω, (§ 18. tab. R) (ἐν & τρυφάω) *to live luxuriously, riot, revel.*

ἐντρυφῶντες, nom. pl. masc. part. pres. . ἐντρυφάω

ἐντυγχάνει, 3 pers. sing. pres. ind. . . ἐντυγχάνω

ἐντυγχάνειν, pres. infin. . . . . id.

ἐντυγχάνω], fut. τεύξομαι, aor. 2, ἐνέτῠχον, (§ 36. rem. 2) (ἐν & τυγχάνω) *to fall in with, meet; to have converse with, address; to address or apply to* any one, Ac. 25. 24; ὑπέρ τινος, *to intercede for any one, plead the cause of,* Ro. 8. 27, 34; He. 7. 25; κατά τινος, *to address a representation or suit against any one, to accuse, complain of,* Ro. 11. 2. (ᾰ).

ἔντευξις, εως, ἡ, (§ 5. tab. E. c) pr. *a meeting with;* hence, *converse, address; prayer, supplication, intercession,* 1 Ti. 2. 1; 4. 5.

ἐντυλίσσω], fut. ξω, perf. pass. ἐντετύλιγμαι, (§ 26. rem. 3) (ἐν & τυλίσσω) *to wrap up in, inwrap, envelope,* Mat. 27. 59; Lu. 23. 53; *to wrap up, roll or fold together,* Jno. 20. 7.

ἐντυπόω, ῶ], fut. ώσω, (§ 20. tab. T) (ἐν & τυπόω, from τύπος, *an impress*) *to impress a figure, instamp, engrave,* 2 Co. 3. 7.

ἐνυβρίζω], fut. ίσω, (§ 26. rem. 1) (ἐν & ὕβρις) *to insult, outrage, contemn.*

[a] 2 Co. 3. 7. [b] Ac. 21. 12. [c] 1 Ti. 4. 6.

ἐνυβρίσας,[a] nom. sing. masc. part. aor. 1 . ἐνυβρίζω
ἔνυξε,[b] 3 pers. sing. aor. 1, ind. act. . . νύσσω
ἐνύπνια,[c] acc. pl. . . . . . ἐνύπνιον
ἐνυπνιαζόμενοι, nom. pl. masc. part. pres. mid. ἐνυπνιάζω
ἐνυπνιάζω], fut. άσω, (§ 26. rem. 1) . ἐνύπνιον
ἐνυπνιασθήσονται, 3 pers. pl. fut. 1, ind. pass. ἐνυπνιάζω
ἐνυπνίοις, dat. pl.—Gr. Sch. Tdf. . . } ἐνύπνιον
ἐνύπνια, Rec. (Ac. 2. 17) . . }

ἐνύπνιον, ου, τό, (§ 3. tab. C. c) (pr. neut. of ἐνύπνιος, *presented during sleep,* from ἐν & ὕπνος) *a dream;* in N.T. *a supernatural suggestion or impression received during sleep, a sleep-vision.*

ἐνυπνιάζω, fut. άσω, (§ 26. rem. 1) and ἐνυπνιάζομαι, fut. (pass. form) ἐνυπνιασθήσομαι, *to dream;* in N.T. *to dream* under supernatural impression, Ac. 2. 17; *to dream* delusion, Jude 8.

ἐνύσταξαν, 3 pers. pl. aor. 1, ind. . . . νυστάζω
ἐνῴκησε, 3 pers. sing. aor. 1, ind. (§ 13. rem. 2) ἐνοικέω

ἐνώπιον, adv. (pr. neut. of ἐνώπιος, *in sight or front*) *before, in the presence of,* Lu. 5. 25; 8. 47; *in front of,* Re. 4. 5, 6; *immediately preceding* as a forerunner, Lu. 1. 17; Re. 16. 19; from the Heb. *in the presence of,* metaphysically, *i.e.* in the sphere of sensation or thought, Lu. 12. 9; 15. 10; Ac. 10. 31; *in the eyes of, in the judgment of,* Lu. 16. 15; 24. 11; Ac. 4. 19, et al. L.G.

Ἐνώς,[d] ὁ, *Enos,* pr. name, indecl.

ἐνωτίζομαι], fut. ίσομαι, aor. ἐνωτισάμην, (§ 26. rem. 1) (ἐν & οὖς) *to give ear, listen, hearken to.* L.G.

ἐνωτίσασθε,[e] 2 pers. pl. aor. 1, imper. . ἐνωτίζομαι

Ἐνώχ, ὁ, *Enoch,* pr. name, indecl.

ἐξ. See ἐκ.

ἕξ, οἱ, αἱ, τά, *six,* Mat. 17. 1; Mar. 9. 2, et al.

ἕκτος, η, ον, (§ 7. tab. F. a) *sixth,* Mat. 20. 5; 27. 45, et al.

ἑξήκοντα, οἱ, αἱ, τά, *sixty,* Mat. 13. 8. 23, et al.

ἐξαγαγεῖν, aor. 2, infin. (§ 13. rem. 7. b. d) . ἐξάγω
ἐξαγαγέτωσαν, 3 pers. pl. aor. 2, imper. act. id.
ἐξαγαγόντες, nom. pl. masc. part. aor. 2, act. . id.
ἐξαγαγών, nom. sing. masc. part. aor. 2, act. id.
ἐξαγγείλητε,[f] 2 pers. pl. aor. 1, subj. (§ 27. rem. 1. d) ἐξαγγέλλω

ἐξαγγέλλω, fut. γελῶ, (§ 27. rem. 1. b) (ἐξ & ἀγγέλλω) *to tell forth, divulge, publish; to declare abroad, celebrate.*

ἐξάγει, 3 pers. sing. pres. ind. act. . . ἐξάγω
ἐξαγοραζόμενοι, nom. pl. masc. pt. pres. mid. ἐξαγοράζω

ἐξαγοράζω], fut. άσω, (§ 26. rem. 1) (ἐξ & ἀγοράζω) *to buy out* of the hands of a person; *to redeem, set free,* Gal. 3. 13; mid. *to redeem, buy off, to secure for one's self or one's own use; to rescue* from loss or misapplication, Ep. 5. 16; Col. 4. 5. L.G.

ἐξαγοράσῃ, 3 pers. sing. aor. 1, subj. act. . ἐξαγοράζω
ἐξάγουσι, 3 pers. pl. pres. ind. act. . . ἐξάγω

ἐξάγω], fut ξω, (§ 23. rem. 1. b) aor. 2, ἐξήγἄγον, (§ 13. rem. 7. b. d) (ἐξ & ἄγω) *to bring or lead forth, conduct out of,* Mar. 8. 23; 15. 20; Lu. 24. 50, et al. (ᾰ).

ἐξαιρέω, ῶ], fut. ήσω, aor. 2, ἐξεῖλον, (§ 36. rem. 1) (ἐξ & αἱρέω) *to take out of; to pluck out, tear out,* Mat. 5. 29; 18. 9; mid. *to take out of, select, choose,* Ac. 26. 17; *to rescue, deliver,* Ac. 7. 10, 34; 12. 11; 23. 27; Gal. 1. 4.

ἐξαιρούμενος, nom. sing. masc. part. pres. mid. ἐξαιρέω

ἐξαίρω, fut. αρῶ, (§ 27. rem. 1. c) (ἐξ & αἴρω) pr. *to lift up out of;* in N.T. *to remove, eject,* 1 Co. 5. 2, 13.

ἐξαιτέω, ῶ], fut. ήσω, (§ 16. tab. P) (ἐξ & αἰτέω) *to ask for from; to demand;* mid. *to demand for one's self,* Lu. 22. 31; also, *to obtain by asking.*

ἐξαίφνης, adv. (ἐξ & αἴφνης) *suddenly, unexpectedly,* Mar. 13. 36, et al.

ἐξακολουθέω, ῶ], fut. ήσω, (§ 16. tab. P) (ἐξ & ἀκολουθέω) *to follow out; to imitate,* 2 Pe. 2. 2, 15; *to observe as a guide,* 2 Pe. 1. 16. L.G.

ἐξακολουθήσαντες, nom. pl. masc. pt. aor. 1 ἐξακολουθέω
ἐξακολουθήσουσι, 3 pers. pl. fut. ind. . id.

ἑξακόσιοι, αι, α, (ἕξ & ἑκατόν) *six hundred,* Re. 13. 18; 14. 20.

ἑξακοσίων, gen. pl. . . . . . ἑξακόσιοι
ἐξαλειφθῆναι, aor. 1, infin. pass. . . ἐξαλείφω

ἐξαλείφω], fut. ψω, (§ 23. rem. 1. a) (ἐξ & ἀλείφω) pr. *to anoint or smear over;* hence, *to wipe off or away,* Re. 7. 17; 21. 4; *to blot out, obliterate, expunge,*

[a] He. 10. 29. [b] Jno. 19. 34. [c] Ac. 2. 17. [d] Lu. 3. 38. [e] Ac. 2. 14. [f] 1 Pe. 2. 9.

Col. 2. 14; Re. 3. 5; met. *to wipe out* guilt, Ac. 3. 19.

ἐξαλείψας, nom. sing. masc. part. aor. 1, act. . ἐξαλείφω

ἐξαλείψει, 3 pers. sing. fut. ind. act. . id.

ἐξαλείψω, 1 pers. sing. fut. ind. act. . . id.

ἐξάλλομαι], fut. αλοῦμαι, (§ 37. rem. 1) (ἐξ & ἄλλομαι) *to leap or spring up or forth.*

ἐξαλλόμενος,[a] nom. sing. masc. part. pres. . ἐξάλλομαι

ἐξανάστασιν,[b] acc. sing. . . . ἐξανάστασις

ἐξανάστᾰσις], εως, ἡ, (§ 5. tab. E. c) (ἐξ & ἀνάστασις) *a raising up; a dislodgment, a rising up; a resurrection* from the dead.

ἐξαναστήσῃ, 3 pers. sing. aor. 1, subj. act. ἐξανίστημι

ἐξανατέλλω], fut. τελῶ, (§ 27. rem. 1. b) (ἐξ & ἀνατέλλω) *to raise up, make to spring up;* intrans. *to rise up, sprout, spring up or forth,* Mat. 13. 5; Mar. 4. 5.

ἐξανέστησαν, 3 pers. pl. aor. 2, ind. . ἐξανίστημι

ἐξανέτειλε, 3 pers. s. aor. 1, ind. (§ 27. rem. 1. d) ἐξανατέλλω

ἐξανίστημι], fut. ἐξαναστήσω, (§ 29. tab. X) (ἐξ & ἀνίστημι) *to cause to rise up, raise up;* from the Heb. *to raise up* into existence, Mar. 12. 19; Lu. 20. 28; intrans. aor. 2, ἀνέστην, *to rise up from, stand forth,* Ac. 15. 5.

ἐξαπατάω, ῶ], fut. ήσω, (§ 18. tab. R) (ἐξ & ἀπατάω) pr. *to deceive thoroughly; to deceive, delude, beguile,* Ro. 7. 11, 16. 8; 1 Co. 3. 18, et al.

ἐξαπατάτω, 3 pers. sing. pres. imper. act. . ἐξαπατάω

ἐξαπατηθεῖσα, nom. sing. fem. part. aor. 1, p. —Al. Ln. Tdf. . . } id.
ἀπατηθεῖσα, Rec. Gr. Sch. (1 Ti. 2. 14)

ἐξαπατήσῃ, 3 pers. sing. aor. 1, subj. act. . id.

ἐξαπατῶσι, 3 pers. pl. pres. ind. act. . id.

ἐξαπεστάλη, 3 pers. sing. aor. 2, ind. pass.—A. B. D. Ln. Tdf. . } ἐξαποστέλλω
ἀπεστάλη, Rec. Gr. Sch. (Ac. 13. 26)

ἐξαπέστειλαν, 3 pers. pl. aor. 1, ind. act. . id.

ἐξαπέστειλε, 3 pers. sing. aor. 1, ind. act. (§ 27. rem. 1. d) . . . . id.

ἐξάπῐνα,[c] adv. a later form for ἐξαπίνης, *suddenly, immediately, unexpectedly.*

ἐξαπορέω, ῶ, and ἐξαπορέομαι, οῦμαι], fut. ήσομαι, (ἐξ & ἀπορέω) *to be in the utmost perplexity or despair,* 2 Co. 1. 8; 4. 8. L.G.

ἐξαπορηθῆναι, aor. 1, infin. pass. . . ἐξαπορέω

ἐξαπορούμενοι, nom. pl. masc. part. pres. mid. id.

ἐξαποστέλλω], fut. στελῶ, (§ 27. rem. 1. b) (ἐξ & ἀποστέλλω) *to send out or forth; to send away, dismiss,* Lu. 1. 53, et al.; *to despatch* on a service or agency, Ac. 7. 12, et al.; *to send forth* as a pervading influence, Gal. 4. 6.

ἐξαποστελῶ, 1 pers. sing. fut. ind. act. . ἐξαποστέλλω

ἐξάρατε, 2 pers. pl. aor. 1, imperf. act.—Gr. Tdf. } ἐξαίρω
ἐξαρεῖτε, Rec. Sch. (1 Co. 5. 13) .

ἐξαρεῖτε, 2 pers. pl. fut. ind. act. . . ἐξαίρω

ἐξαρθῇ, 3 pers. s. aor. 1, subj. pass. (§ 27. rem. 3) id.

ἐξαρτίζω], fut. ίσω, perf. pass. ἐξήρτισμαι, (§ 26 rem. 1) (ἐξ & ἄρτιος) *to equip or furnish completely,* 2 Ti. 3. 17; *to complete* time, Ac. 21. 5. L.G.

ἐξαρτίσαι, aor. 1, infin. act. . . . ἐξαρτίζω

ἐξαστράπτω], fut. ψω, (§ 23. rem. 1. a) (ἐξ & ἀστράπτω) pr. *to flash forth;* hence, *to glisten.*

ἐξαστράπτων,[d] nom. sing. masc. part. pres. . ἐξαστράπτω

ἐξαυτῆς, adv. (ἐξ αὐτῆς, sc. τῆς ὥρας) lit. *at the very time; presently, instantly, immediately,* Mar. 6. 25; Ac. 10. 33; 11. 11, et al.

ἐξέβαλε, 3 pers. s. aor. 2, ind. act. (§ 27. rem. 2. d) ἐκβάλλω

ἐξέβαλλον, 3 pers. pl. imperf. act. . . id.

ἐξεβάλομεν, 1 pers. pl. aor. 2, ind. act. . id.

ἐξέβαλον, 3 pers. pl. aor. 2, ind. act. . . id.

ἐξέβησαν, 3 pers. pl. aor. 2.—Al. Ln. Tdf. } ἐκβαίνω
ἐξῆλθον, Rec. Gr. Sch. (He. 11. 15)

ἐξεβλήθη, 3 pers. sing. aor. 1, pass. (§ 27. rem. 3) ἐκβάλλω

ἐξεγαμίζοντο, 3 pers. pl. imperf. pass. . ἐκγαμίζω

ἐξεγείρει, 3 pers. sing. pres. ind. act.—Ln. Tdf. } ἐξεγείρω
ἐξεγερεῖ, Rec. Gr. Sch. (1 Co. 6. 14)

ἐξεγερεῖ, 3 pers. sing. fut. ind. act. . . id.

ἐξεγείρω], fut. γερῶ, (§ 27. rem. 1. c) (ἐξ & ἐγείρω) *to excite, arouse* from sleep; *to raise up* from the dead, 1 Co. 6. 14; *to raise up* into existence, or into a certain condition, Ro. 9. 17.

ἐξεδέχετο, 3 pers. sing. imperf. . . ἐκδέχομαι

ἐξεδίκησε, 3 pers. sing. aor. 1, ind. act. . . ἐκδικέω

ἐξέδοτο, 3 pers. s. aor. 2, ind. mid. (§ 30. tab. A. A) ἐκδίδωμι

ἐξέδυσαν, 3 pers. pl. aor. 1, ind. act. ἐκδύω

ἐξεζήτησαν, 3 pers. pl. aor. 1, ind. act. . ἐκζητέω

ἐξεθαμβήθη, 3 pers. sing. aor. 1, ind. pass. ἐκθαμβέομαι

ἐξεθαμβήθησαν, 3 pers. pl. aor. 1, ind. pass. id.

ἐξέθεντο, 3 pers. pl. aor. 2, ind. mid. (§ 28. tab. W) ἐκτίθημι

[a] Ac. 3. 8. [b] Phi. 3. 11. [c] Mar. 9. 8. [d] Lu. 9. 29.

ἐξέθρεψαν, 3 pers. pl. aor. 1, ind. act.—D. ἐθήλασαν, Rec. Gr. Sch. ἔθρεψαν, Tdf. (Lu. 23. 29) . . . ἐκτρέφω
ἔξει, 3 pers. sing. fut. ind. (§ 35. rem. 4) . . . ἔχω
ἐξείλατο, 3 pers. sing. aor. 1, ind. mid. (§ 35. rem. 12).—Gr. Tdf. ἐξείλετο, Rec. Sch. (Ac. 7. 10) . . . ἐξαιρέω
ἐξείλετο, 3 pers. sing. aor. 2, ind. mid. (§ 36. rem. 1) . . . id.
ἐξειλόμην, 1 pers. sing. aor. 2, ind. mid. . . . id.
ἔξειμι], (ἐξ & εἶμι) (§ 33. rem. 4) imperf. ἐξῄειν, inf. ἐξιέναι, part. ἐξιών, *to go out or forth*, Ac. 13. 42; *to depart*, Ac. 17. 15; 20. 7; ἐπὶ τὴν γῆν, *to get to land*, from the water, Ac. 27. 43.
ἔξεις, 2 pers. sing. fut. ind. act. . . . ἔχω
ἐξεκαύθησαν,[a] 3 pers. pl. aor. 1, ind. pass. (§ 35. rem. 3) . . . ἐκκαίομαι
ἐξεκέντησαν, 2 pers. pl. aor. 1, ind. act. . . . ἐκκεντέω
ἐξεκλάσθησαν, 3 pers. pl. aor. 1, ind. pass. (§ 22. rem. 4) . . . ἐκκλάω
ἐξεκλείσθη, 3 pers. sing. aor. 1, ind. pass. . . . ἐκκλείω
ἐξέκλιναν, 3 pers. pl. aor. 1, ind. . . . ἐκκλίνω
ἐξεκομίζετο,[b] 3 pers. sing. imperf. pass. . . . ἐκκομίζω
ἐξεκόπης, 2 pers. sing. aor. 2, pass. (§ 24. rem. 6) . . . ἐκκόπτω
ἐξεκρέματο,[c] 3 pers. sing. imperf. . . . ἐκκρέμαμαι
ἔξελε, 2 pers. sing. aor. 2, imper. act. . . . ἐξαιρέω
ἐξελέγξαι,[d] aor. 1, infin. act. . . . ἐξελέγχω
ἐξελέγοντο, 3 pers. pl. imperf. mid. . . . ἐκλέγω
ἐξελέγχω], fut. ξω, (§ 23. rem. 1. b) (ἐξ & ἐλέγχω) *to search thoroughly, to test; to convict, condemn*, Jude 15.
ἐξελεξάμην, 1 pers. sing. aor. 1, ind. mid. . . . ἐκλέγω
ἐξελέξαντο, 3 pers. pl. aor. 1, ind. mid. . . . id.
ἐξελέξασθε, 2 pers. pl. aor. 1, ind. mid. . . . id.
ἐξελέξατο, 3 pers. sing. aor. 1, ind. mid. . . . id.
ἐξελέξω, 2 pers. sing. aor. 1, ind. mid. . . . id.
ἐξελέσθαι, aor. 2, infin. mid. (§ 36. rem. 1) . . . ἐξαιρέω
ἐξελεύσεται, 3 pers. sing. fut. ind. (§ 36. rem. 1) . . . ἐξέρχομαι
ἐξελεύσονται, 3 pers. pl. fut. ind. . . . id.
ἐξελήλυθα, 1 pers. sing. perf. ind. . . . id.
ἐξεληλύθασι, 3 pers. pl. perf. ind. . . . id.
ἐξεληλύθατε, 2 pers. pl. perf. ind. . . . id.
ἐξελήλυθε, 3 pers. sing. perf. ind. . . . id.
ἐξεληλύθει, 3 pers. sing. pluperf. . . . id.
ἐξεληλυθός, acc. sing, neut. part. perf. . . . id.
ἐξεληλυθότας, acc. pl. masc. part. perf. . . . id.
ἐξέληται, 3 pers. sing. aor. 2, subj. mid. . . . ἐξαιρέω

ἐξέλθατε, 2 pers. pl. aor. 1, imper. (§ 35. rem. 12)—B. C. Ln. Tdf. ἐξέλθετε, Rec. Gr. Sch. (2 Co. 6. 17) . . . ἐξέρχομαι
ἔξελθε, 2 pers. sing. aor. 2, imper. . . . id.
ἐξελθεῖν, aor. 2, infin. . . . id.
ἐξέλθετε, 2 pers. pl. aor. 2, imper. . . . id.
ἐξέλθῃ, 3 pers. sing. aor. 2, subj. . . . id.
ἐξέλθῃς, 2 pers. sing. aor. 2, subj. . . . id.
ἐξέλθητε, 2 pers. pl. aor. 2, subj. . . . id.
ἐξελθόντα, acc. s. masc. and nom. pl. neut. pt. aor. 2 . . . id.
ἐξελθόντες, nom. pl. masc. part. aor. 2 . . . id.
ἐξελθόντι, dat. sing. masc. part. aor. 2 . . . id.
ἐξελθόντος, gen. sing. neut. part. aor. 2 . . . id.
ἐξελθόντων, gen. pl. masc. part. aor. 2 . . . id.
ἐξελθοῦσα, nom. sing. fem. part. aor. 2 . . . id.
ἐξελθοῦσαι, nom. pl. fem. part. aor. 2 . . . id.
ἐξελθοῦσαν, acc. sing. fem. part. aor. 2 . . . id.
ἐξελθούσῃ, dat. sing. fem. part. aor. 2.—Gr. Sch. Tdf. ἐκπορευομένῃ, Rec. (Re. 19. 21) . . . id.
ἐξελθών, nom. sing. masc. part. aor. 2 . . . id.
ἐξελκόμενος,[e] nom. sing. masc. part. pres. pass. . . . ἐξέλκω
ἐξέλκω], fut. ξω, (§ 23. rem. 1. b) (ἐξ & ἕλκω) *to draw or drag out; met. to withdraw, allure, hurry away*.
ἐξέμαξε, 3 pers. sing. aor. 1, ind. act. . . . ἐκμάσσω
ἐξέμασσε, 3 pers. sing. imperf. act. . . . id.
ἐξεμυκτήριζον, 2 pers. pl. imperf. act. . . . ἐκμυκτηρίζω
ἐξενέγκαντες, nom. pl. masc. pt. aor. 1 (§ 36. rem. 1) . . . ἐκφέρω
ἐξενέγκατε, 2 pers. pl. aor. 1, imper. . . . id.
ἐξενεγκεῖν, aor. 2, infin. . . . id.
ἐξένευσε,[f] 3 pers. sing. aor. 1, ind. . . . ἐκνεύω
ἐξένισε, 3 pers. sing. aor. 1, ind. act. . . . ξενίζω
ἐξενοδόχησε,[g] 3 pers. sing. aor. 1, ind. act. . . . ξενοδοχέω
ἐξεπείρασαν, 3 pers. pl. aor. 1, ind. act.—D. ἐπείρασαν, Rec. Gr. Sch. Tdf. (1 Co. 10. 9) . . . ἐκπειράζω
ἐξέπεμψαν, 3 pers. pl. aor. 1, ind. act. . . . ἐκπέμπω
ἐξέπεσαν, 3 pers. pl. aor. 1, ind. (§ 37. rem. 1).—Ln. Tdf. ἐξέπεσον, Rec. Gr. Sch. (Ac. 12. 7) . . . ἐκπίπτω
ἐξεπέσατε, 2 pers. pl. aor. 1, ind. . . . id.
ἐξέπεσε, 3 pers. sing. aor. 2, ind. . . . id.
ἐξέπεσον, 3 pers. pl. aor. 2, ind. . . . id.
ἐξεπέτασα,[h] 1 pers. sing. aor. 1, ind. act. . . . ἐκπετάννυμι
ἐξεπήδησαν, 3 pers. pl. aor. 1, ind.—Gr. Sch. Tdf. εἰσεπήδησαν, Rec. (Ac. 14. 14) . . . ἐκπηδάω
ἐξεπλάγησαν, 3 pers. pl. aor. 2, pass. (§ 24. rem. 9) . . . ἐκπλήσσω
ἐξέπλει, 3 pers. sing. imperf. . . . ἐκπλέω

[a] Ro. 1. 27. [b] Lu. 7. 12. [c] Lu. 19. 48. [d] Jude 15. [e] Ja. 1. 14. [f] Jno. 5. 13. [g] 1 Ti. 5. 10. [h] Ro. 10. 21.

ἐξεπλεύσαμεν, 1 pers. pl. aor. 1, ind. (§ 35. rem. 3) ἐκπλέω
ἐξεπλήσσετο, 3 pers. sing. imperf. pass. . ἐκπλήσσω
ἐξεπλήσσοντο, 3 pers. pl. imperf. pass. . id.
ἐξέπνευσε, 3 pers. sing. aor. 1, ind. (§ 35. rem. 3) ἐκπνέω
ἐξεπορεύετο, 3 pers. sing. imperf. . ἐκπορεύομαι
ἐξεπορεύοντο, 3 pers. pl. imperf.—Const. . } id.
  ἐξεπορεύετο, Rec. Gr. Sch. Tdf. (Mar. 1. 5) }
ἐξεπτύσατε,[a] 2 pers. pl. aor. 1, ind. act. . ἐκπτύω
ἐξέρᾶμα,[b] ατος, τό, (§ 4. tab. D. c) (ἐξεράω, *to vomit*) *vomit*. L.G.
ἐξερευνάω, ῶ], fut. ήσω, (§ 18. tab. K) (ἐξ & ἐρευνάω) *to search out, to examine closely*, 1 Pe. 1. 10.
ἐξέρχεσθαι, pres. infin. . . . ἐξέρχομαι
ἐξέρχεσθε, 2 pers. pl. pres. imper. . id.
ἐξέρχεται, 3 pers. sing. pres. ind. . . id.
ἐξέρχομαι, (§ 36. rem. 1) fut. ἐξελεύσομαι, aor. 2, ἐξῆλθον, perf. ἐξελήλῠθα, (ἐξ & ἔρχομαι) *to go or come out of; to come out*, Mat. 5. 26; 8. 34, et al.; *to proceed, emanate, take rise from*, Mat. 2. 6; 15. 18; 1 Co. 14. 36, et al.; *to come abroad*, 1 Jno. 4. 1, et al.; *to go forth, go away, depart*, Mat. 9. 31; Lu. 5. 8, et al.; *to escape*, Jno. 10. 39; *to pass away, come to an end*, Ac. 16. 19.
ἐξερχόμενοι, nom. pl. masc. part. pres. . ἐξέρχομαι
ἐξερχόμενος, nom. sing. masc. part. pres. . id.
ἐξερχομένων, gen. pl. part. pres. . . id.
ἐξέρχονται, 3 pers. pl. pres. ind. . id.
ἐξερχώμεθα, 1 pers. pl. pres. subj. . . id.
ἐξεστακέναι, perf. infin. . . . ἐξίστημι
ἐξέστη, 3 pers. sing. aor. 2, (§ 29. tab. X) . id.
ἐξέστημεν, 1 pers. pl. aor. 2, ind. . . id.
ἐξέστησαν, 3 pers pl. aor. 2, ind. . . id.
ἔξεστι, impers. part. ἐξόν, *it is possible; it is permitted, it is lawful*, Mat. 12. 2, 4, et al.

ἐξουσία, ας, ἡ, (§ 2. tab. B. b, and rem. 2) *power, ability, faculty*, Mat. 9. 8; 10. 1, et al.; *efficiency, energy*, Lu. 4. 32, et al.; *liberty, licence*, Jno. 10. 18; Ac. 5. 4; *authority, rule, dominion, jurisdiction*, Mat. 8. 9; 28. 18; meton. pl. *authorities, potentates, powers*, Lu. 12. 11; 1 Co. 15. 24; Ep. 1. 21; *right, authority, full power*, Mat. 9. 6; 21. 23; *privilege, prerogative*, Jno. 1. 12; perhaps, *a veil*, 1 Co. 11. 10.

ἐξουσιάζω, fut. άσω, (§ 26. rem. 1) *to have or exercise power or authority over* any one, Lu. 22. 25; *to possess independent control over*, 1 Co. 7. 4, bis; pass. *to be subject to, under the power or influence of*, 1 Co. 6. 12. L.G.

ἐξέστραπται,[c] 3 pers. s. perf. ind. pass. (§ 35. rem. 9) ἐκστρέφω
ἐξετάζω], fut. άσω, (§ 26. rem. 1) (ἐξ & ἐτάζω, *to inquire, examine*) *to search out; to inquire by interrogation, examine strictly*, Mat. 2. 8; 10. 11; *to interrogate*, Jno. 21. 12.
ἐξετάσαι, aor. 1, infin. act. . . . ἐξετάζω
ἐξετάσατε, 2 pers. pl. aor. 1, imper. act. . id.
ἕξετε, 2 pers. pl. fut. ind. (§ 35. rem. 4) . ἔχω
ἐξετείνατε, 2 pers. pl. aor. 1, ind. act. . . ἐκτείνω
ἐξέτεινε, 3 pers. s. aor. 1, ind. act. (§ 27. rem. 1. d) id.
ἐξετίθετο, 3 pers. sing. imperf. mid. . ἐκτίθημι
ἐξετράπησαν, 3 p. pl. aor. 2, pass. (§ 24. rem. 10) ἐκτρέπω
ἐξέφῠγον, 1 pers. sing. and 3 pers. pl. aor. 2, ind. ἐκφεύγω
ἐξέχεαν, 3 pers. pl. aor. 1, ind. (§ 36. rem. 1) ἐκχέω
ἐξέχεε, 3 pers. sing. aor. 1, ind. act. . . id.
ἐξεχεῖτο, 3 pers. sing. imperf. pass. . . id.
ἐξεχύθη, 3 pers. sing. aor. 1, ind. pass. . . id.
ἐξεχύθησαν, 3 pers. pl. aor. 1, ind. pass. . id.
ἐξεχύνετο, 3 pers. s. imperf. pass.—A.B. Ln. Tdf. } ἐκχύνω
  ἐξεχεῖτο, Rec. Gr. Sch. (Ac. 22. 20) . }
ἐξέψυξε, 3 pers. sing. aor. 1, ind. (§ 23. rem. 3) ἐκψύχω
ἐξήγᾰγε, 3 pers. s. aor. 2, ind. act. (§ 13. rem. 7. b. d) ἐξάγω
ἐξήγειρα, 1 pers. s. aor. 1, ind. act. (§ 27. rem. 1. d) ἐξεγείρω
ἐξηγεῖτο, 3 pers. sing. imperf. . . . ἐξηγέομαι
ἐξηγέομαι, οῦμαι], fut. ήσομαι, (§ 17. tab. Q) (ἐξ & ἡγέομαι) *to be a leader; to detail, to set forth in language; to tell, narrate, recount*, Lu. 24. 35; Ac. 10. 8, et al.; *to make known, reveal*, Jno. 1. 18.
ἐξηγησάμενος, nom. sing. masc. part. aor. 1 . ἐξηγέομαι
ἐξηγήσατο, 3 pers. sing. aor. 1, ind. . . id.
ἐξηγόρασε, 3 pers. sing. aor. 1, ind. act. . ἐξαγοράζω
ἐξηγουμένων, gen. pl. part. pres. . . ἐξηγέομαι
ἐξηγοῦντο, 3 pers. pl. imperf. . . . id.
ἐξῄεσαν, 3 pers. pl. imperf. (§ 33. rem. 4) . ἔξειμι
ἑξήκοντα, οἱ, αἱ, τά . . . . . ἕξ
ἐξήλθατε, 2 pers. pl. aor. 1, ind.—Al. Ln. Tdf. } ἐξέρχομαι
  ἐξήλθετε, Rec. Gr. Sch. (Mat. 11. 7, 8, 9) }
ἐξῆλθε, 3 pers. sing. aor. 2, ind. (§ 36. rem. 1) id.
ἐξῆλθες, 2 pers. sing. aor. 2, ind. . . . id.
ἐξήλθετε, 2 pers. pl. aor. 2, ind. . . . id.
ἐξήλθομεν, 1 pers. pl. aor. 2, ind. . id.

[a] Gal. 4. 14. [b] 2 Pe. 2. 22. [c] Tit. 3. 11.

ἐξῆλθον, 1 pers. sing. and 3 pers. pl. aor. 2, ind. ἐξέρχομαι
ἐξηπάτησε, 3 pers. sing. aor. 1, ind. act. . ἐξαπατάω
ἐξηραμμένην, acc. sing. fem. part. perf. pass. (§ 27. rem. 2. a, and rem. 3) . ξηραίνω
ἐξήρᾶνε, 3 pers. sing. aor. 1, ind. act. (§ 27. rem. 1. e) id.
ἐξηράνθη, 3 pers. sing. aor. 1, ind. pass. . id.
ἐξήρανται, 3 pers. sing. perf. ind. pass. . id.
ἐξηρεύνησαν,[a] 3 pers. pl. aor. 1, ind. . . ἐξερευνάω
ἐξηρτισμένος, nom. sing. masc. part. perf. pass. ἐξαρτίζω
ἐξήρχετο, 3 pers. sing. imperf. . . ἐξέρχομαι
ἐξήρχοντο, 3 pers. pl. imperf. . . . id.
ἑξῆς, adv. *successively, in order*; in N.T. with the art. ὁ, ἡ, τό ἑξῆς, *next*, Lu. 7. 11; 9. 37, et al.
ἐξητήσατο,[b] 3 pers. s. aor. 1, ind. mid. (§ 13. rem. 2) ἐξαιτέω
ἐξηχέω, ῶ], fut. ήσω, (§ 16. tab. P) perf. pass. ἐξήχημαι, (ἐξ & ἠχέω) *to make to sound forth or abroad*; pass. *to sound forth, to come abroad*. L.G.
ἐξήχηται,[c] 3 pers. sing. perf. ind. pass. . ἐξηχέω
ἐξιέναι, pres. infin. (§ 33. rem. 4) . . ἔξειμι
ἕξιν,[d] acc. sing. . . . . . . ἕξις
ἐξιόντων, gen. pl. m. part. aor. 2, (§ 33. rem. 4) ἔξειμι
ἕξις], εως, ἡ, (§ 5. tab. E. c) . . . ἔχω
ἐξίσταντο, 3 pers. pl. imperf. mid. (§ 29. tab. Y) ἐξίστημι
ἐξιστάνω], same signif. as ἐξίστημι, v.r. (ᾰ).
ἐξιστάνων, nom. sing. masc. part. pres.—A. B. C. Ln. Tdf. . . } ἐξιστάνω
ἐξιστῶν, Rec. Gr. Sch. (Ac. 8. 9) . }
ἐξίστασθαι, pres. infin. mid. . . . ἐξίστημι
ἐξίστατο, 3 pers. sing. imperf. mid. . . id.
ἐξίστημι, and ἐξιστάω, ῶ], fut. ἐκστήσω, aor. 1, ἐξέστησα, later perf. ἐξέστακα, (§ 29. tab. X) (ἐξ & ἵστημι) trans. pr. *to put out of its place; to astonish, amaze*, Lu. 24. 22; Ac. 8. 9, 11; intrans. aor. 2, ἐξέστην, and mid. ἐξίσταμαι, *to be astonished*, Mat. 12. 23, et al.; *to be beside one's self*, Mar. 3. 21; 2 Co. 5. 13.

ἐξιστάνω, same signif. as ἐξίστημι, v.r.; Ac. 8. 9.

ἔκστᾰσις, εως, ἡ, (§ 5. tab. E. c) pr. *a displacement; hence, a displacement of the mind from its ordinary state and self-possession; amazement, astonishment*, Mar. 5. 42; *excess of fear; fear, terror*, Mar. 16. 8; Lu. 5. 26; Ac. 3. 10; in N.T. *an ecstasy, a trance*, Ac. 10. 10; 11. 5; 22. 17.

ἐξιστῶν, nom. sing. masc. part. pres. . . ἐξιστάω
ἐξισχύσητε,[e] 2 pers. pl. aor. 1, subj. . ἐξισχύω
ἐξισχύω], fut. ύσω, (§ 13. tab. M) (ἐξ & ἰσχύω) *to be fully able*. L.G.
ἔξοδον, acc. sing. . . . . . ἔξοδος
ἔξοδος], ου, ἡ, (§ 3. tab. C. b) (ἐξ & ὁδός) *a way out, a going out; a going out, departure*, He. 11. 22; met. *a departure* from life, *decease, death*, Lu. 9. 31; 2 Pe. 1. 15.
ἐξόδου, gen. sing. . . . . . . ἔξοδος
ἐξοίσουσι, 3 pers. pl. fut. ind. (§ 36. rem. 1) ἐκφέρω
ἐξολοθρευθήσεται,[f] 3 pers. sing. fut. 1, ind. pass. ἐξολοθρεύω
ἐξολοθρεύω], fut. εύσω, (§ 13. tab. M) (ἐξ & ὀλοθρεύω) *to destroy utterly, exterminate*. L.G.
ἐξομολογεῖσθε, 2 pers. pl. pres. imper. mid. ἐξομολογέω
ἐξομολογέω, ῶ], fut. ήσω, (§ 16. tab. P) (ἐξ & ὁμολογέω) *to agree, bind one's self, promise*, Lu. 22. 6; mid. *to confess*, Mat. 3. 6; *to profess openly*, Phi. 2. 11; Re. 3. 5; *to make open avowal* of benefits; *to praise, celebrate*, Mat. 11. 25; Lu. 10. 21, et al. L.G.
ἐξομολογήσεται, 3 pers. sing. fut. ind. mid. ἐξομολογέω
ἐξομολογήσηται, 3 pers. sing. aor. 1, subj. mid. id.
ἐξομολογήσομαι, 1 pers. sing. fut. ind. mid. . id.
ἐξομολογοῦμαι, 1 pers. s. pres. mid. (§ 17. tab. Q.) id.
ἐξομολογούμενοι, nom. pl. masc. part. pres. mid. id.
ἐξόν, nom. sing. neut. part. pres. (impers.) ἔξεστι
ἐξορκίζω,[g] fut. ίσω, (§ 26. rem. 1) (ἐξ & ὁρκίζω) *to put an oath* to a person, *to adjure*.

ἐξορκιστής, οῦ, ὁ, (§ 2. tab. B. c) pr. *one who puts an oath*; in N.T. *an exorcist, one who by various kinds of incantations, etc., pretended to expel demons*.

ἐξορκιστῶν,[h] gen. pl. . . . . . ἐξορκιστής
ἐξορύξαντες, nom. pl. masc. part. aor. 1, act. . ἐξορύσσω
ἐξορύσσω], fut. ξω, (§ 26. rem. 3) (ἐξ & ὀρύσσω) *to dig out or through, force up*, Mar. 2. 4; *to pluck out* the eyes, Gal. 4. 15.
ἐξουδενέω, ῶ], fut. ήσω, same signif. as ἐξουδενόω.
ἐξουδενηθῇ, 3 pers. sing. aor. 1, subj. pass.—B. D. Ln. Tdf. . . . } ἐξουδενέω
ἐξουδενωθῇ, Rec. Gr. Sch. (Mar. 9. 12) }
ἐξουδενημένος, nom. sing. masc. pt. perf. pass.—B. Ln. . . . . . } ἐξουδενέω
ἐξουθενημένος, Rec. Gr. Sch. Tdf. (2 Co. 10. 10) . . . . }

[a] 1 Pe. 1. 10. [b] Lu 22. 31. [c] 1 Thes. 1. 8. [d] He. 5. 14. [e] Ep. 3. 18. [f] Ac. 3. 23. [g] Mat. 26. 63. [h] Ac. 19 13.

ἐξουδενόω, ῶ], fut. ώσω, (§ 20. tab. T) equivalent to ἐξουθενέω. N.T.

ἐξουδενωθῇ,[a] 3 pers. sing. aor. 1, subj. pass. . ἐξουδενόω

ἐξουθενεῖς, 2 pers. sing. pres. ind. act. . . ἐξουθενέω

ἐξουθενεῖτε, 2 pers. pl. pres. imper. act. . id.

ἐξουθενείτω, 3 pers. sing. pres. imper. act. . id.

ἐξουθενέω, ῶ], fut. ήσω, (§ 16. tab. P) (ἐξ & οὐθέν, a later form of οὐδέν) *to make light of, set at nought, despise, contemn, treat with contempt and scorn*, Lu. 18. 9, et al.; *to neglect, disregard*, 1 Thes. 5. 20; ἐξουθενημένος, *paltry, contemptible*, 2 Co. 10. 10; *of small account*, 1 Co. 1. 28; 6. 4; by impl. *to reject with contempt*, Ac. 4. 11. LXX.

ἐξουθενηθείς, nom. sing. masc. part. aor. 1, pass. ἐξουθενέω

ἐξουθενημένα, acc. pl. neut. part. perf. pass. id.

ἐξουθενημένος, nom. sing. masc. part. perf. pass. id.

ἐξουθενημένους, acc. pl. masc. part. perf. pass. id.

ἐξουθενήσας, nom. sing. masc. part. aor. 1, act. id.

ἐξουθενήσατε, 2 pers. pl. aor. 1, ind. act. . id.

ἐξουθενήσῃ, 3 pers. sing. aor. 1, subj. act. . id.

ἐξουθενοῦντας, acc. pl. masc. part. pres. act. . id.

ἐξουσία, ας, ἡ, (§ 2. tab. B. b, and rem. 2) ἔξεστι

ἐξουσίᾳ, dat. sing. . . . . . ἐξουσία

ἐξουσιάζει, 3 pers. sing. pres. ind. . . ἐξουσιάζω

ἐξουσιάζοντες, nom. pl. masc. part. pres. . id.

ἐξουσιάζω], fut. άσω, (§ 26. rem. 1) . ἔξεστι

ἐξουσίαι, nom. pl. . . . . . ἐξουσία

ἐξουσίαις, dat. pl. . . . . id.

ἐξουσίαν, acc. sing. . . . . . id.

ἐξουσίας, gen. sing. and acc. pl. . . id.

ἐξουσιασθήσομαι, 1 pers. sing. fut. 1, ind. pass. ἐξουσιάζω

ἕξουσι, 3 pers. pl. fut. ind. (§ 35. rem. 4) . ἔχω

ἐξουσιῶν, gen. pl. . . . . ἐξουσία

ἐξοχή], ῆς, ἡ, (§ 2. tab. B. a) (ἐξέχω, *to be prominent*) pr. *prominency, anything prominent*; in N.T. *eminence, distinction*.

ἐξοχήν,[b] acc. sing. . . . . . ἐξοχή

ἐξυπνίζω], fut. ίσω, (§ 26. rem. 1) . . ἔξυπνος

ἐξυπνίσω,[c] 1 pers. sing. aor. 1, subj. act. . ἐξυπνίζω

ἔξυπνος,[d] ον, ὁ, ἡ, (§ 7. rem. 2) (ἐξ & ὕπνος) *awake, aroused from sleep*. L.G.

ἐξυπνίζω, fut. ίσω, *to awake, arouse from sleep*, Jno. 11. 11. L.G.

ἐξυρημένῃ, dat. s. fem. pt. perf. pass. (§ 19. tab. S) ξυράω

ἔξω, adv. (ἐξ) *without, out of doors*; Mat. 12. 46, 47; ὁ, ἡ, τὸ ἔξω, *outer, external, foreign*, Ac. 26. 11; 2 Co. 4. 16; met. *not belonging to one's community*, Mar. 4. 11; 1 Co. 5. 12, 13; *out, away*, from a place or person, Mat. 5. 13; 13. 48; as a prep. *out of*, Mar. 5. 10, et al.

ἔξωθεν, adv. *outwardly, externally*, Mat. 23. 27, 28; Mar. 7. 15; ὁ, ἡ, τὸ ἔξωθεν, *outer, external*, Mat. 23. 25; Lu. 11. 39; τὸ ἔξωθεν, *the exterior*, Lu. 11. 40. οἱ ἔξωθεν, *those who are without* the Christian community, 1 Ti. 3. 7, et al.

ἐξώτερος, α, ον (§ 7. rem. 1) (compar. of ἔξω) *outer, exterior, external*, Mat. 8. 12; 23. 13; 25. 30. LXX.

ἔξωθεν, adv. . . . . . ἔξω

ἐξωθέω, ῶ], fut. θήσω, and ἐξώσω, aor. 1, ἐξέωσα, in N.T. ἔξωσα, (ἐξ & ὠθέω) *to expel, drive out*, Ac. 7. 45; *to propel, urge forward*, Ac. 27. 39.

ἐξωμολόγησε, 3 pers. s. aor. 1, ind. (§ 13. rem. 2) ἐξομολογέω

ἐξῶσαι, aor. 1, infin. act. . . . . ἐξωθέω

ἔξωσε, 3 pers. sing. aor. 1, ind. act. . . id.

ἐξώτερον, acc. sing. neut. . . . . ἐξώτερος

ἐξώτερος], α, ον, (§ 7. rem. 1) . . ἔξω

ἔοικα], perf. with pres. signif. (§ 38. rem. 2) from obsolete εἴκω, *to be like*, Jas. 1. 6, 23.

ἔοικε, 3 pers. sing. (§ 37. rem. 1) . . ἔοικα

ἑορτάζω], fut. άσω, (§ 26. rem. 1) . . ἑορτή

ἑορτάζωμεν,[e] 1 pers. pl. pres. subj. . . ἑορτάζω

ἑορτή, ῆς, ἡ, (§ 2. tab. B. a) *a solemn feast, public festival*, Lu. 2. 41; 22. 1; Jno. 13. 1; spc. used of *the passover*, Mat. 26. 5; 27. 15, et al.

ἑορτάζω, fut. άσω, (§ 26. rem. 1) *to keep a feast, celebrate a festival*, 1 Co. 5. 8.

ἑορτῇ, dat. sing. . . . . . ἑορτή

ἑορτήν, acc. sing. . . . . . id.

ἑορτῆς, gen. sing. . . . . id.

ἐπ', by apostrophe for ἐπί.

ἐπαγαγεῖν, aor. 2, infin. act. (§ 13. rem. 7. d) ἐπάγω

ἐπαγγειλάμενον, acc. s. masc. part. aor. 1, mid. ἐπαγγέλλω

ἐπαγγειλάμενος, nom. s. masc. part. aor. 1, mid. id.

ἐπαγγελία, ας, ἡ, (§ 2. tab. B. b, and rem. 2) id.

ἐπαγγελίᾳ, dat. sing. . . . . ἐπαγγελία

ἐπαγγελίαι, nom. pl. . . . . id.

ἐπαγγελίαις, dat. pl. . . . id.

ἐπαγγελίαν, acc. sing. . . . id.

ἐπαγγελίας, gen. sing. and acc. pl. id.

ἐπαγγελιῶν, gen. pl. . . . . id.

ἐπαγγελλομέναις, dat. pl. fem. part. pres. mid. ἐπαγγέλλω

---

[a] Mar. 9. 12. [b] Ac. 25. 23. [c] Jno. 11. 11. [d] Ac. 16. 27. [e] 1 Co. 5. 8.

ἐπαγγελλόμενοι, nom. pl. masc. part. pres. mid. **ἐπαγγέλλω**

ἐπαγγέλλω], fut. ελῶ, (§ 27. rem. 1. b) (ἐπί & ἀγγέλλω) *to declare, announce*; mid. *to promise, undertake*, Mar. 14. 11; Ro. 4. 21, et al.; *to profess*, 1 Ti. 2. 10.

ἐπαγγελία, ας, ἡ, (§ 2. tab. B. b, and rem. 2) *annunciation*, 2 Ti. 1. 1; *a promise, act of promising*, Ac. 13. 23, 32; 23. 21; meton. *the thing promised, promised favour and blessing*, Lu. 24. 49; Ac. 1. 4, et al.

ἐπάγγελμα, ατος, τό, (§ 4. tab. D. c) *a promise*, 2 Pe. 3. 13; meton. *promised favour or blessing*, 2 Pe. 1. 4.

ἐπάγγελμα, ατος, τό . . . ἐπαγγέλλω

ἐπαγγέλματα, nom. pl. . . . ἐπάγγελμα

ἐπάγοντες, nom. pl. masc. part. pres. act. ἐπάγω

ἐπάγω], fut. άξω, (§ 23. rem. 1. b) aor. 2, ἐπήγᾰγον, (§ 13. rem. 7. b. d) (ἐπί & ἄγω) *to bring upon, cause to come upon*, 2 Pe. 2. 1, 5; met. *to cause to be imputed or attributed to, to bring* guilt *upon*, Ac. 5. 28.

ἐπαγωνίζεσθαι,[a] pres. infin. . . ἐπαγωνίζομαι

ἐπαγωνίζομαι], fut. ίσομαι, (§ 26. rem. 1) (ἐπί & ἀγωνίζομαι) *to contend strenuously in defence of*. L.G.

ἔπαθε, 3 pers. sing. aor. 2, ind. (§ 36. rem. 4) πάσχω

ἐπάθετε, 2 pers. pl. aor. 2, ind. . . id.

ἔπαθον, 1 pers. sing. aor. 2, ind. . . . id.

ἐπαθροιζομένων,[b] gen. pl. part. pres. pass. ἐπαθροίζω

ἐπαθροίζω], fut. οίσω, (§ 26. rem. 1) (ἐπί & ἀθροίζω, *to gather together, to collect close upon, or beside*; mid. *to crowd upon*.

ἐπαιδεύθη, 3 pers. sing. aor. 1, ind. pass. . παιδεύω

ἐπαίδευον, 3 pers. pl. imper. ind. act. . . id.

ἐπαινέσατε, 2 pers. pl. aor. 1, imper. act. . ἐπαινέω

ἐπαινεσάτωσαν, 3 pers. pl. aor. 1, imperf. act.—A. B. Ln. Tdf. . . } id.
ἐπαινέσατε, Rec. Gr. Sch. (Ro. 15. 11)

ἐπαινέσω, 1 pers. sing. fut. ind. act. . . id.

Ἐπαίνετον,[c] acc. sing. . . . . Ἐπαίνετος

Ἐπαίνετος], ου, ὁ, (§ 3. tab. C. a) *Epænetus*, pr. name.

ἐπαινέω, ῶ], fut. έσω and έσομαι, (§ 22. rem. 1) aor. 1, ἐπήνεσα, (ἐπί & αἰνέω) *to praise, commend, applaud*, Lu. 16. 8; Ro. 15. 11; 1 Co. 11. 2, 17, 22, bis.

ἔπαινον, acc. sing. . . . . ἔπαινος

ἔπαινος, ου, ὁ, (§ 3. tab. C. a) (ἐπί & αἶνος) *praise applause, honour paid*, Ro. 2. 29; 2 Co. 8. 18, et al.; meton. *ground or reason of praise or commendation*, Phi. 4. 8; *approval*, Ro. 13. 3; 1 Pe. 2. 14; 1 Co. 4. 5.

ἐπαινῶ, 1 pers. sing. pres. ind. act. . . ἐπαινέω

ἐπαινῶν, nom. sing. masc. part. pres. act.—A. C. Ln. Tdf. . . } id.
ἐπαινῶ, Rec. Gr. Sch. (1 Co. 11. 17)

ἐπαίρεται, 3 pers. sing. pres. ind. mid. . . ἐπαίρω

ἐπαιρόμενον, acc. sing. neut. part. pres. mid. id.

ἐπαίροντας, acc. pl. masc. part. pres. act. . id.

ἐπαίρω], fut. αρῶ, aor. 1 ἐπῆρα, (§ 27. rem. 1. c. e) aor. 1, pass. ἐπήρθην, *to lift up, raise, elevate; to hoist*, Ac. 27. 40; τὴν φωνήν, *to lift up the voice, to speak in a loud voice*, Lu. 11. 27; τὰς χεῖρας, *to lift up the hands* in prayer, Lu. 24. 50; 1 Ti. 2. 8; τοὺς ὀφθαλμούς, *to lift up the eyes, to look*, Mat. 17. 8; τὴν κεφαλήν, *to lift up the head, to be encouraged, animated*, Lu. 21. 28; τὴν πτέρναν, *to lift up the heel, to attack, assault*; or, *to seek one's overthrow or destruction*, Jno. 13. 18; pass. *to be borne upwards*, Ac. 1. 9; met. mid. *to exalt one's self, assume consequence, be elated*, 2 Co. 10. 5, et al.

ἔπαισε, 3 pers. sing. aor. 1, ind. act. . . παίω

ἐπαισχύνεσθε, 2 pers. pl. pres. ind. . . ἐπαισχύνομαι

ἐπαισχύνεται, 3 pers. sing. pres. ind. . . id.

ἐπαισχύνθη, 3 pers. sing. aor. 1, ind. pass.—A. D. Ln. . . . . } id.
ἐπῃσχύνθη, Rec. Gr. Sch. Tdf. (2 Ti. 1. 16)

ἐπαισχυνθῇ, 3 pers. sing. aor. 1, subj. pass. . id.

ἐπαισχυνθῇς, 3 pers. sing. aor. 1, subj. pass. id.

ἐπαισχυνθήσεται, 3 pers. sing. fut. ind. pass. id.

ἐπαισχύνομαι, aor. 1, ἐπῃσχύνθην, (§ 13. rem. 2) fut. ἐπαισχυνθήσομαι, (ἐπί & αἰσχύνομαι) *to be ashamed of*, Mat. 8. 38; Lu. 9. 26, et al.

ἐπαιτεῖν,[d] pres. infin. . . . ἐπαιτέω

ἐπαιτέω, ῶ], fut. ήσω, (§ 16. tab. P) (ἐπί & αἰτέω) *to prefer a suit or request in respect of certain circumstances; to ask alms, beg*.

ἐπαιτῶν, nom. s. masc. part. pres.—B. D. Ln. Tdf. } ἐπαιτέω
προσαιτῶν, Rec. Gr. Sch. (Lu. 18. 35)

ἐπακολουθέω, ῶ], fut. ήσω, (§ 16. tab. P) (ἐπί & ἀκολουθέω) *to follow upon; to accom-*

---

[a] Jude 3. [b] Lu. 11. 29. [c] Ro. 16. 5. [d] Lu. 16. 3

pany, be attendant, Mar. 16. 20; *to appear in the sequel,* 1 Ti. 5. 24; met. *to follow* one's steps, *to imitate,* 1 Pe. 2. 21; *to follow* a work, *pursue, prosecute, be studious of, devoted to,* 1 Ti. 5. 10.

ἐπακολουθήσητε, 2 pers. pl. aor. 1, subj. . . ἐπακολουθέω

ἐπακολουθούντων, gen. pl. neut. part. pres. . . id.

ἐπακολουθοῦσι, 3 pers. pl. pres. ind. . . id.

ἐπακούω], fut. ούσομαι, (ἐπί & ἀκούω) *to listen or hearken to; to hear with favour,* 2 Co. 6. 2.

ἐπακροάομαι, ῶμαι], (§ 19. tab. S) (ἐπί & ἀκροάομαι, *to hear*) *to hear, hearken, listen to,* Ac. 16. 25.

ἐπάν, conj. (ἐπεί & ἄν) *whenever, as soon as,* Mat. 2. 8; Lu. 11. 22, 34.

ἐπανάγἄγε, 2 pers. pl. aor. 2, imper. act. . . ἐπανάγω

ἐπαναγἄγεῖν, aor. 2, infin. act. (§ 13. rem. 7. d) . . id.

ἐπάναγκες,[a] adv. (ἐπί & ἀνάγκη) *of necessity, necessarily;* τὰ ἐπάναγκες, *necessary things.*

ἐπανάγω], fut. ξω, (§ 23. rem. 1. b) aor. 2, ἐπανήγἄγον, (ἐπί & ἀνάγω) *to bring up or back;* intrans. *to return,* Mat. 21. 18; a nautical term, *to put off from shore,* Lu. 5. 3, 4.

ἐπανάγων, nom. sing. masc. part. pres. . . ἐπανάγω

ἐπαναμιμνήσκω], fut. ἐπαναμνήσω, (§ 36. rem. 3) (ἐπί & ἀναμιμνήσκω) *to remind, put in remembrance.*

ἐπαναμιμνήσκων,[b] nom. s. masc. part. pres. . ἐπαναμιμνήσκω

ἐπαναπαύῃ, 2 pers. sing. pres. ind. mid. . . ἐπαναπαύω

ἐπαναπαύσεται, 3 pers. sing. fut. ind. mid. . . id.

ἐπαναπαύω], fut. αύσω, (§ 13. tab. M) (ἐπί & ἀναπαύω) pr. *to make to rest upon;* mid. *to rest upon; to abide with,* Lu. 10. 6; *to rely on, confide in, abide by confidingly,* Ro. 2. 17. L.G.

ἐπαναστήσονται, 3 pers. pl. fut. mid. (§ 29. tab. Y) . . . . ἐπανίστημι

ἐπανελθεῖν, aor. 2, infin. . . . ἐπανέρχομαι

ἐπανέρχεσθαι, pres. infin. . . . id.

ἐπανέρχομαι], aor. 2, ἐπανῆλθον, (§ 36. rem. 1) (ἐπί & ἀνέρχομαι) *to come back, return,* Lu. 10. 35; 19. 15.

ἐπανίστημι], (§ 29. tab. X) (ἐπί & ἀνίστημι) *to raise up against;* mid. *to rise up against,* Mat. 10. 21; Mar. 13. 12.

ἐπανόρθωσιν,[c] acc. sing. . . . ἐπανόρθωσις

ἐπανόρθωσις], εως, ἡ, (§ 5. tab. E. c) (ἐπανορθόω, *to set upright again; to set to rights;* ἐπί & ἀνορθόω) *correction, reformation.*

ἐπάνω, adv. (ἐπί & ἄνω) *above, over, upon,* of place, Mat. 2. 9; 5. 14; *over,* of authority, Lu. 19. 17, 19; *above, more than,* Mar. 14. 5, et al. (ᾰ).

ἐπάξας, nom. sing. masc. part. aor. 1, act. . . ἐπάγω

ἐπᾶραι, aor. 1 infin. act. (§ 27. rem. 1. f) . . ἐπαίρω

ἐπάραντες, nom. pl. masc. part. aor. 1, act. . . id.

ἐπάρας, om. sing. masc. part. aor. 1, act. (ᾱ) . . id.

ἐπάρασα, nom. sing. fem. part. aor. 1, act. . . id.

ἐπάρατε, 2 pers. pl. aor. 1, imper. act. . . id.

ἐπάρατοι, nom. pl. masc.—B. Ln. Tdf. } ἐπάρατος
ἐπικατάρατοι, Rec. Gr. Sch. (Jno. 7. 49) }

ἐπάρᾱτος], ου, ὁ, ἡ, (§ 7. rem. 2) same signif. as ἐπικατάρατος, *accursed.* v.r.

ἐπαρκείτω, 3 pers. sing. pres. imper. . . ἐπαρκέω

ἐπαρκέσῃ, 3 pers. sing. aor. 1, subj. . . id.

ἐπαρκέω, ῶ], fut. έσω, (§ 22. rem. 1) (ἐπί & ἀρκέω) pr. *to ward off; to assist, relieve, succour;* 1 Ti. 5. 10, 16, bis.

ἐπαῤῥησιάζετο, 3 pers. sing. imperf. . . παῤῥησιάζομαι

ἐπαῤῥησιασάμεθα, 1 pers. pl. aor. 1, ind. . . id.

ἐπαῤῥησιάσατο, 3 pers. sing. aor. 1, ind. . . id.

ἐπαρχία], ας, ἡ, (§ 2. tab. B. b, and rem. 2) (ἔπαρχος, *a prefect,* etc.) *a prefecture, province,* Ac. 23. 34; 25. 1. L.G.

ἐπαρχίᾳ, dat. sing. . . . . ἐπαρχία

ἐπαρχίας, gen. sing. . . . . id.

ἐπάταξε, 3 pers. sing. aor. 1, ind. act. . . πατάσσω

ἐπατήθη, 3 pers. sing. aor. 1, ind. pass. . . πατέω

ἔπαυλις,[d] εως, ἡ, (§ 5. tab. E. c) (ἐπί & αὐλίζομαι) pr. *a place to pass the night in; a cottage;* in N.T. *a dwelling, habitation.*

ἐπαύριον, adv. (ἐπί & αὔριον) *to-morrow;* ἡ ἐπαύριον, sc. ἡμέρα, *the next or following day,* Mat. 27. 62; Mar. 11. 12, et al.

ἐπαύοντο, 3 pers. pl. imperf. mid. . . παύω

ἐπαυσάμην, 1 pers. sing. aor. 1, ind. mid. . . id.

ἐπαύσαντο, 3 pers. pl. aor. 1, ind. mid. . . id.

ἐπαύσατο, 3 pers. sing. aor. 1, ind. mid. . . id.

ἐπαυτοφώρῳ,[e] adv. (ἐπί & αὐτόφωρος, from αὐτός & φώρ, *a thief*) pr. *in the very theft;* in N.T. *in the very act.*

Ἐπαφρᾶ, gen. sing. (§ 2. rem. 4) . . Ἐπαφρᾶς

Ἐπαφρᾶς, ᾶ, ὁ, *Epaphras,* pr. name.

ἐπαφρίζοντα,[f] nom. pl. neut. part. pres. . . ἐπαφρίζω

ἐπαφρίζω], fut. ίσω, (§ 26. rem. 1) (ἐπί & ἀφρίζω)

a Ac. 15. 28. b Ro. 15. 15. c 2 Ti. 3. 16. d Ac. 1. 20. e Jno. 8. 4. f Jude 13.

to foam out; to pour out like foam, vomit forth.

Ἐπαφρόδιτον, acc. sing. . . . Ἐπαφρόδιτος

Ἐπαφρόδῖτος, ου, ὁ, (§ 3. tab. C. a) *Epaphroditus,* pr. name.

Ἐπαφροδίτου, gen. sing. . . . . Ἐπαφρόδιτος

ἐπαχύνθη, 3 pers. sing. aor. 1, ind. pass. . παχύνω

ἐπέβᾰλε, 3 pers. sing. aor. 2, ind. act. . ἐπιβάλλω

ἐπέβαλλε, 3 pers. sing. imperf. act. . . id.

ἐπέβᾰλον, 3 pers. pl. aor. 2, ind. act. . . id.

ἐπέβημεν, 1 pers. pl. aor. 2, ind. (§ 37. rem. 1) ἐπιβαίνω

ἐπέβην, 1 pers. sing. aor. 2, ind. . . id.

ἐπεβίβασαν, 3 pers. pl. aor. 1, ind. act. . ἐπιβιβάζω

ἐπέβλεψε, 3 pers. sing. aor. 1, ind. act. . ἐπιβλέπω

ἐπεγέγραπτο, 3 pers. sing. pluperf. pass. (§ 23. rem. 8) . . . . . ἐπιγράφω

ἐπεγείρω], fut. γερῶ, (§ 27. rem. 1. c) (ἐπί & ἐγείρω) *to raise or stir up against, excite or instigate against,* Ac. 13. 50; 14. 2.

ἐπεγένετο, 3 pers. s. aor. 2, ind.—A. Ln. Tdf.
ἐγένετο, Rec. Gr. Sch. (Ac. 27. 27) . } ἐπιγίνομαι

ἐπεγίνωσκε, 3 pers. sing. imperf. ind. act.—A.
ἐγίνωσκε, Rec. Gr. Sch. Tdf. (Mar. 14. 10) } ἐπιγινώσκω

ἐπεγίνωσκον, 3 pers. pl. imperf. act. . . id.

ἐπεγνωκέναι, perf. infin. act. . . . id.

ἐπεγνωκόσι, dat. pl. masc. perf. act. . . id.

ἐπέγνωμεν, 1 pers. pl. aor. 2, ind. act.—Al. Ln. Tdf. . . . .
ἐπέγνωσαν, Rec. Gr. Sch. (Ac. 28. 1) } id.

ἐπέγνωσαν, 3 pers. pl. aor. 2, ind. act. . . id.

ἐπεγνώσθην, 1 pers. sing. aor. 1, ind. pass. id.

ἐπέγνωτε, 2 pers. pl. aor. 2, ind. act. . id.

ἐπέδειξε, 3 pers. sing. aor. 1, ind. act. . ἐπιδείκνυμι

ἐπεδίδου, 3 pers. sing. imperf. act. (§ 31. rem. 2) ἐπιδίδωμι

ἐπεδόθη, 3 pers. s. aor. 1, ind. pass. (§ 30. rem. 4) id.

ἐπέδωκαν, 3 pers. pl. aor. 1, ind. act. . id.

ἐπεζήτησε, 3 pers. sing. aor. 1, ind. act. . ἐπιζητέω

ἐπεζήτουν, 3 pers. pl. imperf. act.—Gr. Sch. Tdf.
ἐζήτουν, Rec. (Lu. 4. 42) . . } id.

ἐπέθεντο, 3 pers. pl. aor. 2, ind. mid. (§ 28. tab. W) ἐπιτίθημι

ἐπέθηκαν, 3 pers. pl. aor. 1, ind. act. (§ 28. tab. U) id.

ἐπέθηκε, 3 pers. sing. aor. 1, ind. act. . . id.

ἐπεθύμει, 3 pers. sing. imperf. . . ἐπιθυμέω

ἐπεθύμησα, 1 pers. sing. aor. 1, ind. . . id.

ἐπεθύμησαν, 3 pers. pl. aor. 1, ind. . . id.

ἐπεί, conj. *when, after, as soon as,* Lu. 7. 1; *since, because, in as much as,* Mat. 18. 32; 27. 6; *for, for then, for else, since in that case,* Ro. 3. 6; 11. 6, et al.

ἐπεῖδε, 3 pers. sing. . . . . . . ἐπεῖδον

ἐπειδή, conj. (ἐπεί & δή) *since, because, in as much as,* Mat. 21. 46; Lu. 11. 6; Ac. 13. 46, et al.

ἐπειδήπερ,[a] conj. (ἐπειδή & περ) *since now, since indeed, considering that.*

ἐπεῖδον], aor. 2, of ἐφοράω, (§ 36. rem. 1) imperat. ἔπῐδε, *to look upon, regard;* in N.T. *to look upon* with favour, Lu. 1. 25; *to mark* with disfavour, Ac. 4. 29.

ἔπειθε, 3 pers. sing. imperf. act. . . πείθω

ἐπείθετο, 3 pers. sing. imperf. mid. . . id.

ἔπειθον, 3 pers. pl. imperf. act. . . id.

ἐπείθοντο, 3 pers. pl. imperf. mid. . . id.

ἔπειμι], (§ 33. rem. 4) (ἐπί & εἶμι) part. ἐπιών, *to come upon; to come after; to succeed immediately,* Ac. 7. 26; 16. 11; 20. 15; 21. 18; 23. 11.

ἐπείνᾱσα, 1 pers. sing. aor. 1, ind. . . πεινάω

ἐπείνᾱσαν, 3 pers. pl. aor. 1, ind. . . id.

ἐπείνᾱσε, 3 pers. sing. aor. 1, ind. . . id.

ἐπείπερ,[b] conj. (ἐπεί & περ) *since indeed, seeing that.*

ἐπείραζον, 3 pers. pl. imperf. act. . . πειράζω

ἐπείρᾰσαν, 3 pers. pl. aor. 1, ind. act. . id.

ἐπείρᾰσας, 2 pers. sing. aor. 1, ind. act.—Gr. Sch. Tdf. . . .
ἐπειράσω, Rec. (Re. 2. 2) . . } id.

ἐπείρᾰσε, 3 pers. sing. aor. 1, ind. act. . . id.

ἐπειράσθησαν, 3 pers. pl. aor. 1, ind. pass. id.

ἐπειράσω, 2 pers. sing. aor. 1, ind. mid. (§ 15. tab. O) πειράομαι

ἐπειρᾶτο, 3 pers. sing. imperf. . . id.

ἐπειρῶντο, 3 pers. pl. imperf. . . . id.

ἐπεισαγωγή,[c] ῆς, ἡ, (§ 2. tab. B. a) (ἐπί & εἰσάγω) *a superinduction, a further introduction,* whether by way of addition or substitution.

ἔπεισαν, 3 pers. pl. aor. 1, ind. act. . πείθω

ἐπεισελεύσεται, 3 pers. sing. fut. ind.—B. D. Ln. Tdf. . . .
ἐπελεύσεται, Rec. Gr. Sch. (Lu. 21. 35) } ἐπεισέρχομαι

ἐπεισέρχομαι], fut. ελεύσομαι, (§ 36. rem. 1) (ἐπί & εἰσέρχομαι) *to come in upon, invade, surprise.* v.r.

ἐπείσθησαν, 3 pers. pl. aor. 1, ind. pass. (§ 23. rem. 4) . . . . . πείθω

ἔπειτα, adv. (ἐπί & εἶτα) *thereupon, then, after that, in the next place, afterwards,* Mar. 7. 5; Lu. 16. 7, et al.

ἐπεῖχε, 3 pers. sing. imperf. (§ 13. rem. 4) . ἐπέχω

[a] Lu. 1. 1. [b] Ro. 3. 30. [c] He. 7. 19.

ἐπεκάθισαν,[a] 3 pers. pl. aor. 1, ind. act. . ἐπικαθίζω
ἐπεκάθισε, 3 pers. sing. aor. 1, ind.—Gr. Sch. Tdf. . . . } id.
ἐπεκάθισαν, Rec. (Mat. 21. 7) . }
ἐπεκάλεσαν, 3 pers. pl. aor. 1, ind. act.—Gr. Sch. Tdf. . . . } ἐπικαλέω
ἐκάλεσαν, Rec. (Mat. 10. 25) . . }
ἐπεκαλύφθησαν,[b] 3 pers. pl. aor. 1, ind. pass. ἐπικαλύπτω
ἐπέκειλαν, 3 pers. pl. aor. 1, ind.—A.C.Ln.Tdf. } ἐπικέλλω
ἐπώκειλαν, Rec. Gr. Sch. (Ac. 27. 41) }
ἐπέκεινα,[c] adv. (i.e. ἐπ' ἐκεῖνα) *on yonder side, beyond.*
ἐπέκειντο, 3 pers. pl. imperf. . . . ἐπίκειμαι
ἐπέκειτο, 3 pers. sing. imperf. . . id.
ἐπεκέκλητο, 3 pers. sing. pluperf. pass. . . ἐπικαλέω
ἐπεκλήθη, 3 pers. s. aor. 1, ind. pass. (§ 22. rem. 4) id.
ἐπέκρῖνε,[d] 3 pers. sing. aor. 1, ind. . . ἐπικρίνω
ἐπεκτεινόμενος,[e] nom. sing. masc. part. pres. mid. ἐπεκτείνω
ἐπεκτείνω], fut. ενῶ, (§ 27. rem. 1. c) (ἐπί & ἐκτείνω) pr. *to stretch out farther*; in N.T. mid. *to reach out towards, strain for.*
ἐπελάβετο, 3 pers. sing. aor. 2, ind. mid. (§ 36. rem. 2) . . . . ἐπιλαμβάνω
ἐπελάθετο, 3 pers. s. aor. 2, ind. (§ 36. rem. 2) ἐπιλανθάνομαι
ἐπελάθοντο, 3 pers. pl. aor. 2, ind. . . id.
ἐπέλειχον, 3 pers. pl. imperf. act.—A.B.Ln.Tdf. } ἐπιλείχω
ἀπέλειχον, Rec. Gr. Sch. (Lu. 16. 21) }
ἐπελεύσεται, 3 pers. sing. fut. ind. (§ 36. rem. 1) ἐπέρχομαι
ἐπέλθῃ, 3 pers. sing. aor. 2, subj. . . id.
ἐπελθόντος, gen. sing. neut. part. aor. 2 . id.
ἐπελθών, nom. sing. masc. part. aor. 2 . . id.
ἐπέλυε, 3 pers. sing. imperf. act. . . ἐπιλύω
ἐπέμεινα, 1 pers. s. aor. 1, ind. (§ 27. rem. 1. d) ἐπιμένω
ἐπεμείναμεν, 1 pers. pl. aor. 1, ind. . . id.
ἐπεμελήθη, 3 pers. sing. aor. 1, ind. ἐπιμελέομαι
ἐπέμενε, 3 pers. sing. imperf. . . ἐπιμένω
ἐπέμενον, 3 pers. pl. imperf. . . . id.
ἐπέμφθη, 3 pers. s. aor. 1, ind. pass. (§ 23. rem. 4) πέμπω
ἔπεμψα, 1 pers. sing. aor. 1, ind. act. . id.
ἐπέμψαμεν, 1 pers. pl. aor. 1, ind. act. . id.
ἐπέμψατε, 2 pers. pl. aor. 1, ind. act. . . id.
ἔπεμψε, 3 pers. sing. aor. 1, ind. act. . id.
ἐπενδύσασθαι, aor. 1, infin. mid. . . ἐπενδύω
ἐπενδύτην,[f] acc. sing. . . . . ἐπενδύτης
ἐπενδύτης], ου, ὁ, (§ 2. tab. B. c) . . ἐπενδύω
ἐπενδύω], fut. ύσω, (§ 13. tab. M) (ἐπί & ἐνδύω) *to put on over or in addition to*; mid. *to put on one's self in addition; to be further invested,* 2 Co. 5. 2, 4.

ἐπενδύτης, ου, ὁ, *the outer or upper tunic,* worn between the inner tunic and the external garments. (ῠ).

ἐπενεγκεῖν, aor. 2, infin. act. (§ 36. rem. 1) ἐπιφέρω
ἐπένευσε,[g] 3 pers. sing. aor. 1, ind. . . ἐπινεύω
ἐπενθήσατε, 2 pers. pl. aor. 1, ind. . πενθέω
ἐπέπεσαν, 3 pers. pl. aor. 1, ind.—A.D. (Ac. 12. 7) . . . . . } ἐπιπίπτω
ἐξέπεσον, Rec. Gr. Sch. . . }
ἐξέπεσαν, Tdf. . . . }
ἐπέπεσε, 3 pers sing. aor. 2, ind. (§ 37. rem. 1) id.
ἐπέπεσον, 3 pers. pl. aor. 2, ind. . . . id.
ἐπέπνιξαν, 3 pers. pl. aor. 1, ind. act.—Schmidt. } ἐπιπνίγω
ἀπέπνιξαν, Rec. Gr. Sch. Tdf., with most copies (Lu. 8. 7) . . . }
ἐπεποίθει, 3 pers. sing. pluperf. 2 (§ 25. rem. 5) πείθω
ἐπερίσσευον, 3 pers. pl. imperf. . . περισσεύω
ἐπερίσσευσαν, 3 pers. pl. aor. 1. ind.—B. D. Ln. Tdf. . . . } id.
ἐπερίσσευσεν, Rec. Gr. Sch. (Jno. 6. 13) }
ἐπερίσσευσε, 3 pers. sing. aor. 1, ind. . . id.
ἐπέρχομαι], fut. ελεύσομαι, (§ 36. rem. 1) aor. 2. ἐπῆλθον, (ἐπί & ἔρχομαι) *to come to,* Ac. 14. 19; *to come upon,* Lu. 1. 35; 21. 26; Ac. 1. 8; Jas. 5. 1; *to come upon* unexpectedly, *overtake,* Lu. 21. 35; *to be coming on, to succeed,* Ep. 2. 7; *to occur, happen to,* Ac. 8. 24; 13. 40; *to come against, attack,* Lu. 11. 22.
ἐπερχομέναις, dat. pl. fem. part. pres. . ἐπέρχομαι
ἐπερχομένοις, dat. pl. masc. part. pres. . . id.
ἐπερχομένων, gen. pl. part. pres. . . id.
ἐπερωτᾶν, pres. infin. act. . . . . ἐπερωτάω
ἐπερωτᾷς, 2 pers. sing. pres. ind. act. . id.
ἐπερωτάτωσαν, 3 pers. pl. pres. imper. act. . id.
ἐπερωτάω, ῶ], fut. ήσω, (§ 18. tab. R) (ἐπί & ἐρωτάω) *to interrogate, question, ask,* Mat. 12. 10; 17. 10, et al.; in N.T. *to request, require,* Mat. 16. 1; from the Heb. ἐπερωτᾶν τὸν Θεόν, *to seek after, desire an acquaintance with God,* Ro. 10. 20.

ἐπερώτημα, ατος, τό, (§ 4. tab. D. c) pr. *an interrogation, question*; in N.T. *profession, pledge,* 1 Pe. 3. 21.

ἐπερωτηθείς, nom. sing. masc. part. aor. 1, pass. ἐπερωτάω
ἐπερώτημα,[h] ατος, τό, (§ 4. tab. D. c) . id.

[a] Mat. 21. 7. [b] Ro. 4. 7. [c] Ac. 7. 43. [d] Lu. 23. 24. [e] Phi. 3. 14. [f] Jno. 21. 7. [g] Ac. 18. 20. [h] 1 Pe. 3. 21.

ἐπερωτῆσαι, aor. 1, infin. act. — ἐπερωτάω
ἐπερωτήσας, nom. sing. masc. part. aor. 1, act. — id.
ἐπερώτησον, 2 pers. sing. aor. 1, imper. act. — id.
ἐπερωτήσω, 1 pers. sing. fut. ind. act. — id.
ἐπερωτῶ, 1 pers. sing. pres. ind. act.—B. Tdf. } id.
ἐπερωτήσω, Rec. Gr. Sch. Ln. (Lu. 6. 9) }
ἐπερωτῶντα, acc. sing. masc. part. pres. act. — id.
ἐπερωτῶσι, dat. pl. masc. part. pres. act. — id.
ἐπερωτῶσι, 3 pers. pl. pres. ind. act. — id.
ἔπεσα, 1 pers. sing. aor. 1, ind. (§ 35. rem. 12) — πίπτω
ἔπεσαν, 3 pers. pl. aor. 1, ind. — id.
ἔπεσε, 3 pers. sing. aor. 2, ind. (§ 35. rem. 7) — id.
ἐπεσκέψασθε, 2 pers. pl. aor. 1, ind. — ἐπισκέπτομαι
ἐπεσκέψατο, 3 pers. sing. aor. 1, ind. — id.
ἐπεσκίασε, 3 pers. sing. aor. 1, ind. — ἐπισκιάζω
ἔπεσον, 1 pers. s. and 3 pers. pl. aor. 2 (§ 37. rem. 1) — πίπτω
ἐπέσπειρε, 3 pers. sing. imperf. act.—B. Ln. Tdf. } ἐπισπείρω
ἔσπειρε, Rec. Gr. Sch. (Mat. 13. 25) }
ἐπέστειλα, 1 pers. sing. aor. 1, ind. act. (§ 27. rem. 1. d) — ἐπιστέλλω
ἐπεστείλαμεν, 1 pers. pl. aor. 1, ind. act. — id.
ἐπέστη, 3 pers. sing. aor. 2, ind. (§ 29. tab. X) — ἐφίστημι
ἐπεστήριξαν, 3 pers. pl. aor. 1, ind. act. — ἐπιστηρίζω
ἐπέστησαν, 3 pers. pl. aor. 2, ind. — ἐφίστημι
ἐπεστράφητε, 2 pers. pl. aor. 2, ind. pass. (§ 24. rem. 10) — ἐπιστρέφω
ἐπέστρεψα, 1 pers. sing. aor. 1, ind. act. — id.
ἐπέστρεψαν, 3 pers. pl. aor. 1, ind. act. — id.
ἐπεστρέψατε, 2 pers. pl. aor. 1, ind. act. — id.
ἐπέστρεψε, 3 pers. sing. aor. 1, ind. act. — id.
ἐπέσχε, 3 pers. sing. aor. 2, ind. (§ 36. rem. 4) — ἐπέχω
ἐπέταξας, 2 pers. sing. aor. 1, ind. — ἐπιτάσσω
ἐπέταξε, 3 pers. sing. aor. 1, ind. — id.
ἐπετίθεσαν, 3 pers. pl. imperf. act.—A. C. D. Ln. Tdf. } ἐπιτίθημι
ἐπετίθουν, Rec. Gr. Sch. (Ac. 8. 17) }
ἐπετίθουν, 3 pers. pl. imperf. act. (§ 31. rem. 2) — id.
ἐπετίμα, 3 pers. sing. imperf. — ἐπιτιμάω
ἐπετίμησαν, 3 pers. pl. aor. 1, ind. — id.
ἐπετίμησε, 3 pers. sing. aor. 1, ind. — id.
ἐπετίμων, 3 pers. pl. imperf. (§ 18. tab. R) — id.
ἐπετράπη, 3 pers. s. aor. 1, ind. pass. (§ 24. rem. 10) — ἐπιτρέπω
ἐπέτρεψε, 3 pers. sing. aor. 1, ind. act. — id.
ἐπέτυχε, 3 pers. sing. aor. 2, ind. (§ 36. rem. 2) — ἐπιτυγχάνω
ἐπετύχον, 2 pers. pl. aor. 2, ind. — id.
ἐπεφάνη, 3 pers. s. aor. 2, ind. pass. (§ 27. rem. 4. b) — ἐπιφαίνω
ἐπιφέρον, 2 pers. pl. imperf. act. — ἐπιφέρω
ἐπεφώνει, 3 pers. sing. imperf. — ἐπιφωνέω
ἐπεφώνουν, 3 pers. pl. imperf. — ἐπιφωνέω
ἐπέφωσκε, 3 pers. sing. imperf. — ἐπιφώσκω
ἔπεχε, 2 pers. sing. pres. imper. — ἐπέχω
ἐπεχείρησαν, 3 pers. pl. aor. 1, ind. — ἐπιχειρέω
ἐπεχείρουν, 3 pers. pl. imperf. — id.
ἐπέχοντες, nom. pl. masc. part. pres. — ἐπέχω
ἐπέχρισε, 3 pers. sing. aor. 1, ind. act. — ἐπιχρίω

ἐπέχω], fut. ἐφέξω, imperf. ἐπεῖχον, aor. 2, ἐπέσχον, (§ 36. rem. 4.) (ἐπί & ἔχω) trans. *to hold out, present, exhibit, display*, Phi. 2. 16; intrans. *to observe, take heed to, attend to*, Lu. 14. 7; Ac. 3. 5; 1 Ti. 4. 16; *to stay, delay*, Ac. 19. 22.

ἐπέχων, nom. sing. masc. part. pres. — ἐπέχω
ἐπηγγείλαντο, 3 pers. pl. aor. 1, ind. mid. (§ 27. rem. 1. d) — ἐπαγγέλλω
ἐπηγγείλατο, 3 pers. sing. aor. 1, ind. mid. — id.
ἐπήγγελται, 3 pers. s. perf. ind. pass. (§ 27. rem. 3) — id.
ἐπήγειραν, 3 pers. pl. aor. 1, ind. act. — ἐπεγείρω
ἐπηκολούθησε, 3 pers. sing. aor. 1, ind. — ἐπακολουθέω
ἐπήκουσα,[a] 1 pers. sing. aor. 1, ind. — ἐπακούω
ἐπηκροῶντο,[b] 3 pers. pl. imperf. — ἐπακροάομαι
ἐπῆλθαν, 3 pers. pl. aor. 1, (§ 35. rem. 12).—Ln. Tdf. } ἐπέρχομαι
ἐπῆλθον, Rec. Gr. Sch. (Ac. 14. 19) }
ἐπῆλθον, 3 pers. pl. aor. 2, ind. — id.
ἐπῄνεσε, 3 pers. s. aor. 1, ind. act. (§ 13. rem. 2) — ἐπαινέω
ἔπηξε,[c] 3 pers. sing. aor. 1, ind. act. (§ 36. rem. 5) — πήγνυμι
ἐπῆραν, 3 pers. pl. aor. 1, ind. act. — ἐπαίρω
ἐπῆρε, 3 pers. sing. aor. 1, ind. act. — id.
ἐπηρεάζοντες, nom. pl. masc. part. pres. — ἐπηρεάζω
ἐπηρεαζόντων, gen. pl. masc. part. pres. — id.

ἐπηρεάζω], fut. άσω, (§ 26. rem. 1) *to harass, insult*, Mat. 5. 44; Lu. 6. 28; *to traduce, calumniate*, 1 Pe. 3. 16.

ἐπήρθη, 3 pers. s. aor. 1, ind. pass. (§ 27. rem. 3) — ἐπαίρω
ἐπήρκεσε, 3 pers. sing. aor. 1. ind. — ἐπαρκέω
ἐπηρώτα, 3 pers. sing. imperf. act. — ἐπερωτάω
ἐπηρώτησαν, 3 pers. pl. aor. 1, ind. act. — id.
ἐπηρώτησε, 3 pers. sing. aor. 1, ind. act. — id.
ἐπηρώτων, 3 pers. pl. imperf. act. — id.
ἐπῃσχύνθη, 3 pers. sing. aor. 1, ind. (§ 13. rem. 2) — ἐπαισχύνομαι

ἐπί, prep. with the gen., *upon, on*, Mat. 4. 6; 9. 2; 27. 19, et al.; *in*, of locality, Mar. 8. 4, et al.; *near upon, by, at*, Mat. 21. 19; Jno. 21. 1, et al.; *upon, over*, of authority, Mat.

a 2 Co. 6. 2. b Ac. 16. 25. c He. 8. 2.

2. 22; Ac. 8. 27, et al.; *in the presence of*, especially in a judicial sense, 2 Cor. 7. 14; Ac. 25. 9, et al.; *in the case of, in respect of*, Jno. 6. 2; Gal. 3. 16; *in the time of, at the time of*, Ac. 11. 28; Ro. 1. 10, et al.; ἐπ' ἀληθείας, *really, bona fide*, Mar. 12. 32, et al.; with the dat., *upon, on*, Mat. 14. 8; Mar. 2. 21; Lu. 12. 44, et al.; *close upon, by*, Mat. 24. 33; Jno. 4. 6, et al.; *in the neighbourhood or society of*, Ac. 28. 14; *over*, of authority, Mat. 24. 47, et al.; *to*, of addition, *besides*, Mat. 25. 20; Ep. 6. 16; Col. 3. 14, et al.; supervening *upon, after*, 2 Co. 1. 4; 7. 4; *immediately upon*, Jno. 4. 27; *upon*, of the object of an act, *towards, to*, Mar. 5. 33; Lu. 18. 7; Ac. 5. 35, et al.; *against*, of hostile posture or disposition, Lu. 12. 52, et al.; *in dependance upon*, Mat. 4. 4; Lu. 5. 5; Ac. 14. 3, et al.; *upon the ground of*, Mat. 19. 9; Lu. 1. 59; Phi. 1. 3; He. 7. 11, 8. 6; 9. 17, et al.; *with a view to*, Gal. 5. 13; 1 Thes. 4. 7, et al.; with the acc., *upon*, with the idea of previous or present motion, Mat. 4. 5; 14. 19, 26, et al.; *towards*, of place, *to*, Mat. 3. 13; 22. 34, et al.; *towards*, of the object of an action, Lu. 6. 35; 9. 38, et al.; *against*, of hostile movement, Mat. 10. 21, et al.; *over*, of authority, Lu. 1. 33, et al.; *to the extent of*, both of place and time, Re. 21. 16; Ro. 7. 1, et al.; *near, by*, Mat. 9. 9, et al.; *about, at*, of time, Ac. 3. 1, et al.; *in order to, with a view to, for the purpose of*, Mat. 3. 7; Lu. 7. 44, et al.

ἐπίασαν, 3 pers. pl. aor. 1, ind. act. . . πιάζω

ἐπιάσατε, 2 pers. pl. aor. 1, ind. act. . id.

ἐπίασε, 3 pers. sing. aor. 1, ind. act. . . id.

ἐπιάσθη, 3 pers. s. aor. 1, ind. pass. (§ 26. rem. 1) id.

ἐπιβαίνειν, pres. infin.—A. C. Ln. Tdf. } ἐπιβαίνω
ἀναβαίνειν, Rec. Gr. Sch. (Ac. 21. 4) }

ἐπιβαίνω], fut. βήσομαι, perf. βέβηκα, aor. 2, ἐπέβην, (§ 37. rem. 1) (ἐπί & βαίνω) pr. *to step upon; to mount*, Mat. 21. 5; *to go on board*, Ac. 21. 2; 27. 2; *to enter*, Ac. 20. 18; *to enter upon*, Ac. 25. 1.

ἐπιβἄλεῖν, aor. 2, infin. act. . . . . ἐπιβάλλω

ἐπιβάλλει, 3 pers. sing. pres. ind. act. . id.

ἐπιβάλλον, acc. sing. neut. part. pres. . . ἐπιβάλλω

ἐπιβάλλουσι, 3 pers. pl. pres. ind. act.—Al. Gr. Tdf. . . . . } ἐπιβάλλω
ἐπέβαλον, Rec. Sch. (Mar. 11. 7) . }

ἐπιβάλλω], fut. βαλῶ, aor. 2, ἐπέβἄλον, (§ 27. rem. 1. b, and rem. 2. d) (ἐπί & βάλλω) *to cast or throw upon*, Mar. 11. 7; 1 Co. 7. 35; *to lay on, apply to*, Lu. 9. 62; *to put on, sew on*, Mat. 9. 16; Lu. 5. 36; τὰς χεῖρας, *to lay hands on, offer violence to, seize*, Mat. 26. 50, et al.; also, *to lay hand to, undertake, commence*, Ac. 12. 1; intrans. *to rush, dash, beat into*, Mar. 4. 37, *to ponder, reflect on*, Mar. 14. 72; *to fall to one's share, pertain to*, Lu. 15. 12.

ἐπίβλημα, ατος, τό, (§ 4. tab. D. c) *that which is put over or upon*; in N.T. *a patch*, Mat. 9. 16; Mar. 2. 21; Lu. 5. 36, bis. L.G.

ἐπιβαλοῦσι, 3 pers. pl. fut. ind. act. . ἐπιβάλλω

ἐπιβάλω, 1 pers. sing. aor 2, subj. act. . id.

ἐπιβἄλών, nom. sing. masc. part. aor. 2 . id.

ἐπιβάντες, nom. sing. masc. part. aor. 2 . ἐπιβαίνω

ἐπιβἄρέω, ῶ], fut. ήσω, (§ 16. tab. P) (ἐπί & βαρέω) *to burden*; met. *to be burdensome, chargeable to*, 1 Thes. 2. 9; 2 Thes. 3. 8; *to bear hard upon, overcharge, overcensure*, 2 Co. 2. 5. L.G.

ἐπιβαρῆσαι, aor. 1, infin. . . . . ἐπιβαρέω

ἐπιβαρῶ, 1 pers. sing. pres. subj. . . id.

ἐπιβάς, nom. sing. masc. part. aor. 2 . ἐπιβαίνω

ἐπιβεβηκώς, nom. sing. masc. part. perf. . id.

ἐπιβιβάζω], fut. άσω, (§ 26. rem. 1) (ἐπί & βιβάζω) *to cause to ascend or mount, to set upon*, Lu. 10. 34; 19. 35; Ac. 23. 24.

ἐπιβιβάσαντες, nom. pl. masc. part. aor. 1 ἐπιβιβάζω

ἐπιβιβάσας, nom. sing. masc. part. aor. 1 . id.

ἐπιβλέπω], fut. ψω, (§ 23. rem. 1 a) (ἐπί & βλέπω) *to look upon*; *to regard* with partiality, Ja. 2. 3; *to regard* with kindness and favour, *to compassionate*, Lu. 1. 48; 9. 38.

ἐπίβλεψαι, 2 pers. sing. aor. 1, imper. mid.—Gr. Sch. Tdf. . . . } ἐπιβλέπω
ἐπίβλεψον, Rec. Ln. (Lu. 9. 38) . }

ἐπιβλέψητε, 2 pers. pl. aor. 1, subj. act. . id.

ἐπίβλεψον, 2 pers. sing. aor. 1, imper. act. . id.

ἐπίβλημα, ατος, τό, (§ 4. tab. D. c) . ἐπιβάλλω

ἐπιβοάω, ῶ], fut. ήσω, (§ 18. tab. R) (ἐπί & βοάω) *to cry out to or against, to vociferate*, Ac. 25. 24.

ἐπιβουλαῖς, dat. pl. . . . . . ἐπιβουλή

ἐπιβουλή, ῆς, ἡ, (§ 2. tab. B. a) (ἐπί & βουλή) *a purpose or design against* any one; *conspiracy, plot*, Ac. 9. 24; 20. 3, 19; 23. 30.

ἐπιβουλῆς, gen. sing. . . . . ἐπιβουλή

ἐπιβοῶντες,[a] nom. pl. masc. part. pres. . ἐπιβοάω

ἐπιγαμβρεύσει,[b] 3 pers. sing. fut. ind. . ἐπιγαμβρεύω

ἐπιγαμβρεύω], fut. εύσω, (§ 13. tab. M) (ἐπί & γαμβρεύω, *to marry*) *to marry* a wife *by the law of affinity*. LXX.

ἐπιγεγραμμένα, acc. pl. neut. part. perf. pass. . ἐπιγράφω

ἐπιγεγραμμένη, nom. sing. fem. part. perf. pass. id.

ἐπίγεια, nom. and acc. pl. neut. . . ἐπίγειος

ἐπίγειος, ου, ὁ, ἡ, τό, -ον, (§ 7. rem. 2) (ἐπί & γῆ) pr. *on the earth*, Phi. 2. 10; *earthly, terrestrial*, Jno. 3. 12; 1 Co. 15. 40; 2 Co. 5. 1; Phi. 3. 19; *earthly, low, grovelling*, Ja. 3. 15.

ἐπιγείων, gen. pl. . . . . . ἐπίγειος

ἐπιγενομένου,[c] gen. sing. masc. part. aor. 2 ἐπιγίνομαι

ἐπιγίνομαι], (§ 37. rem. 1) (ἐπί & γίνομαι) *to come on, spring up*, as the wind.

ἐπιγινώσκει, 3 pers. sing. pres. ind. act. . ἐπιγινώσκω

ἐπιγινώσκεις, 2 pers. sing. pres. ind. act. . id.

ἐπιγινώσκετε, 2 pers. pl. pres. ind. act. . id.

ἐπιγινώσκετε, 2 pers. pl. pres. imper. act. . id.

ἐπιγινωσκέτω, 3 pers. sing. pres. imper. act. id.

ἐπιγινωσκόμενοι, nom. pl. masc. part. pres. pass. id.

ἐπιγινώσκω], fut. γνώσομαι, aor. 1, pass. ἐπεγνώσθην, (§ 36. rem. 3) (ἐπί & γινώσκω) pr. *to make* a thing *a subject of observation*; hence, *to arrive at knowledge from preliminaries; to attain to a knowledge of*, Mat. 11. 27, et al.; *to ascertain*, Lu. 7. 37, 23. 7, et. al.; *to perceive*, Mar. 2. 8; 5. 30, et al.; *to discern, detect*, Mat. 7. 16, 20, et al.; *to recognise*, Mar. 6. 33; Lu. 24. 16, 31; Ac. 3. 10, et al.; *to acknowledge, admit*, 1 Co. 14. 37; 1 Ti. 4. 3, et al.; pass. *to have one's character discerned and acknowledged*, 2 Co. 6. 9; from the Heb. *to regard* with favour and kindness, 1 Co. 16. 18.

ἐπίγνωσις, εως, ἡ, (§ 5. tab. E. c) *the coming at the knowledge* of a thing, *ascertainment*, Ro. 3. 20; *a distinct perception or impression, acknowledgment*, Col. 2. 2, et al.

ἐπιγνόντες, nom. pl. masc. part. aor. 2, act. ἐπιγινώσκω

ἐπιγνόντων, gen. pl. masc. part. aor. 2, act. . id.

ἐπιγνούς, nom. sing. masc. part. aor. 2, act. id.

ἐπιγνοῦσα, nom. sing. fem. part. aor. 2, act. id.

ἐπιγνοῦσι, dat. pl. masc. part. aor. 2, act. . id.

ἐπιγνῷ, 3 pers. sing. aor. 2, subj. act. . . id.

ἐπιγνῶναι, aor. 2, infin. act. . . . id.

ἐπιγνῷς, 2 pers. sing. aor. 2, subj. act. . . id.

ἐπιγνώσει, dat. sing. . . . . ἐπίγνωσις

ἐπιγνώσεσθε, 2 pers. pl. fut. ind. mid. . ἐπιγινώσκω

ἐπιγνώσεως, gen. sing. . . . . ἐπίγνωσις

ἐπίγνωσιν, acc. sing. . . . . id.

ἐπίγνωσις, εως, ἡ, (§ 5. tab. E. c) . . ἐπιγινώσκω

ἐπιγνώσομαι, 1 pers. sing. fut. ind. mid. . id.

ἐπιγρᾰφή, ῆς, ἡ, (§ 2. tab. B. a) . . ἐπιγράφω

ἐπιγραφήν, acc. sing. . . . . ἐπιγραφή

ἐπιγράφω], fut. ψω, (§ 23. rem 1. a) (ἐπί & γράφω) *to imprint a mark on; to inscribe, engrave, write on*, Mar. 15. 26; Ac. 17. 23; Re. 21. 12; met. *to imprint, impress deeply on*, He. 8. 10; 10. 16. (ᾰ).

ἐπιγρᾰφή, ῆς, ἡ, (§ 2. tab. B. a) *an inscription; a legend* of a coin, Mat. 22. 20; Mar. 12. 16; Lu. 20. 24; *a label* of a criminal's name and offence, Mar. 15. 26; Lu. 23. 38.

ἐπιγράψω, 1 pers. sing. fut. ind. act. ἐπιγράφω

ἔπῐδε, 2 pers. sing. imperat. . . . ἐπεῖδον

ἐπιδεικνύμεναι, nom. pl. fem. part. pres. mid. ἐπιδείκνυμι

ἐπιδείκνῡμι], or νύω, and mid. ἐπιδείκνῡμαι, fut. δείξω, (§ 31. tab. BB) (ἐπί & δείκνυμι) *to exhibit*, Mat. 16. 1; Ac. 9. 39; *to show*, Mat. 22. 19; Lu. 17. 14; 20. 24; 24. 40; *to point out*, Mat. 24. 1; *to demonstrate, prove*, Ac. 18. 28; He. 6. 17.

ἐπιδεικνύς, nom. sing. masc. part. pres. . ἐπιδείκνυμι

ἐπιδεῖξαι, aor. 1, infin. . . . . id.

ἐπιδείξατε, 2 pers. pl. aor. 1, imper. . id.

ἐπιδέχεται, 3 pers. sing. pres. ind. . ἐπιδέχομαι

ἐπιδέχομαι], fut. δέξομαι, (§ 23. rem. 1. b) (ἐπί & δέχομαι) *to admit; to receive kindly, welcome, entertain*, 3 Jno. 10; met. *to admit, approve, assent to*, 3 Jno. 9.

ἐπιδημέω, ῶ], fut. ήσω, (§ 16. tab. P) (ἐπί & δῆμος) *to dwell among a people; to be at home among one's own people*; and in N.T. *to sojourn as a stranger among another people*, Ac. 2. 10; 17. 21.

[a] Ac. 25. 24. [b] Mat. 22. 24. [c] Ac. 28. 13.

ἐπιδημοῦντες, nom. pl. masc. part. pres. — ἐπιδημέω

ἐπιδιατάσσεται,[a] 3 pers. sing. pres. ind. — ἐπιδιατάσσομαι

ἐπιδιατάσσομαι], fut. ξομαι, (§ 26. rem. 3) (ἐπί & διατάσσω) *to enjoin anything additional, superadd an injunction*, etc. N.T.

ἐπιδίδωμι], fut. δώσω, (§ 30. tab. Z) (ἐπί & δίδωμι) *to give in addition; also, to give to, deliver to, give into one's hands*, Mat. 7. 9, 10; Lu. 4. 17; 24. 30, 42, et al.; intrans. probably a nautical term, *to commit a ship to the wind, let her drive*, Ac. 27. 15.

ἐπιδιορθόω, ῶ], fut. ώσω, (§ 20. tab. T) (ἐπί & διορθόω) *to set further to rights, to carry on an amendment*.

ἐπιδιορθώσῃ,[b] 2 pers. sing. aor. 1, subj. mid. — ἐπιδιορθόω

ἐπιδιορθώσῃς, 2 pers. sing. aor. 1, subj. act. —A. D. Ln. Sch. Tdf. } id.
ἐπιδιορθώσῃ, Rec. Gr. (Tit. 1. 5)

ἐπιδόντες, nom. pl. masc. part. aor. 2. — ἐπιδίδωμι

ἐπιδυέτω,[c] 3 pers. sing. pres. imper. — ἐπιδύω

ἐπιδύω], fut. δύσω, (ἐπί & δύω) of the sun, *to set upon, to set during*.

ἐπιδώσει, 3 pers. sing. fut. ind. act. — ἐπιδίδωμι

ἐπιδώσω, 1 pers. sing. fut. ind. act. — id.

ἔπιε, 3 pers. sing. aor. 2, ind. act. (§ 37. rem. 1) — πίνω

ἐπιείκεια], ας, ἡ, (§ 2. tab. B. b, and rem. 2) — ἐπιεικής

ἐπιεικείᾳ, dat. sing. — ἐπιείκεια

ἐπιεικείας, gen. sing. — id.

ἐπιεικεῖς, acc. pl. masc. — ἐπιεικής

ἐπιεικές, nom. sing. neut. — id.

ἐπιεικέσι, dat. pl. masc. — id.

ἐπιεικῆ, acc. sing. masc. — id.

ἐπιεικής, έος, οῦς, ὁ, ἡ, (§ 7. tab. G. b) (ἐπί & εἰκός) pr. *suitable; fair, reasonable; gentle, mild, patient*, 1 Ti. 3. 3; Tit. 3. 2; Ja. 3. 17; 1 Pe. 2. 18; τὸ ἐπιεικές, *mildness, gentleness, probity*, Phi. 4. 5.

ἐπιείκεια, ας, ἡ, (§ 2. tab. B. b, and rem. 2) *reasonableness, equity*; in N.T. *gentleness, mildness*, 2 Co. 10. 1; *lenity, clemency*, Ac. 24. 4.

ἐπιζητεῖ, 3 pers. sing. pres. ind. act. — ἐπιζητέω

ἐπιζητεῖτε, 3 pers. pl. pres. ind. act. — id

ἐπιζητέω, ῶ], fut. ήσω, (§ 16. tab. P) (ἐπί & ζητέω) *to seek for, make search for*, Ac. 12. 19; *to require, demand*, Mat. 12. 39, 16. 4; Ac. 19. 39; *to desire, endeavour to obtain*, Ro. 11. 7; He. 11. 14, et al.; *to seek with care and anxiety*, Mat. 6. 32.

ἐπιζητήσας, nom. sing. masc. part. aor. 1, act. — ἐπιζητέω

ἐπιζητοῦμεν, 1 pers. pl. pres. ind. act. — id.

ἐπιζητοῦσι, 3 pers. pl. pres. ind. act. — id.

ἐπιζητῶ, 1 pers. sing. pres. ind. act. — id.

ἐπιθανάτιος], ου, ὁ, ἡ, (§ 7. rem. 2) (ἐπί & θάνατος) *condemned to death, under sentence of death*. L.G.

ἐπιθανατίους,[d] acc. pl. masc. — ἐπιθανάτιος

ἐπιθεῖναι, aor. 2, infin. act. (§ 28. tab. U) — ἐπιτίθημι

ἐπιθείς, nom. sing. masc. part. aor. 2, act. — id.

ἐπιθέντα, acc. sing. masc. part. aor. 2, act. — id.

ἐπιθέντες, nom. pl. masc. part. aor. 2, act. — id.

ἐπιθέντος, gen. sing. masc. part. aor. 2, act. — id.

ἐπίθες, 2 pers. sing. aor. 2, imper. act. — id.

ἐπιθέσεως, gen. sing. — ἐπίθεσις

ἐπίθεσις], εως, ἡ, (§ 5. tab. E. c) — ἐπιτίθημι

ἐπιθῇ, 3 pers. sing. aor. 2, subj. act. — id.

ἐπιθῇς, 2 pers. sing. aor. 2, subj. act. — id.

ἐπιθήσει, 3 pers. sing. fut. ind. act. — id.

ἐπιθήσεται, 3 pers. s. fut. ind. mid. (§ 28. tab. W) — id.

ἐπιθήσουσι, 3 pers. pl. fut. ind. act. — id.

ἐπιθυμεῖ, 3 pers. sing. pres. ind. — ἐπιθυμέω

ἐπιθυμεῖτε, 2 pers. pl. pres. ind. — id.

ἐπιθυμέω, ῶ], fut. ήσω, (§ 16. tab. P) (ἐπί & θυμός) *to set the heart upon; to desire, long for, have earnest desire*, Mat. 13. 17; Lu. 15. 16, et al.; *to lust after*, Mat. 5. 28. et al.; spc. *to covet*, Ro. 13. 9, et al.

ἐπιθυμητής, οῦ, ὁ, (§ 2. tab. B. c) *one who has an ardent desire for* anything, 1 Co. 10. 6.

ἐπιθυμία, ας, ἡ, (§ 2. tab. B. b, and rem. 2) *earnest desire*, Lu. 22. 15, et al.: *irregular or violent desire, cupidity*, Mar. 4. 19, et al.; spc. impure *desire, lust*, Ro. 1. 24, et al.; met. *the object of desire, what enkindles desire*, 1 Jno. 2. 16, 17.

ἐπιθυμῆσαι, aor. 1, infin. — ἐπιθυμέω

ἐπιθυμήσεις, 2 pers. sing. fut. ind. — id.

ἐπιθυμήσετε, 2 pers. pl. fut. ind. — id.

ἐπιθυμήσουσι, 3 pers. pl. fut. ind. — id.

ἐπιθυμητάς,[e] acc. pl. — ἐπιθυμητής

ἐπιθυμητής], οῦ, ὁ, (§ 2. tab. B. c) — ἐπιθυμέω

ἐπιθυμία, ας, ἡ, (§ 2. tab. B. b, and rem. 2) — id.

ἐπιθυμίᾳ, dat. sing. — id.

ἐπιθυμίαι, nom. pl. — id.

[a] Gal. 3. 15 [b] Tit. 1. 5. [c] Ep. 4. 26. [d] 1 Co. 4. 9. [e] 1 Co. 10. 6.

ἐπιθυμίαις, dat. pl. . . . . . ἐπιθυμία
ἐπιθυμίαν, acc. sing. . . . . . id.
ἐπιθυμίας, gen. sing. and acc. pl. . . id.
ἐπιθυμιῶν, gen. pl. . . . . . . id.
ἐπιθυμοῦμεν, 1 pers. pl. pres. ind. . . ἐπιθυμέω
ἐπιθυμοῦσι, 3 pers. pl. pres. ind. . . id.
ἐπιθυμῶν, nom. sing. masc. part. pres. . id.
ἐπιθῶ, 1 pers. sing. aor. 2, subj. act. (§ 28. tab. U) . . . . . . ἐπιτίθημι

ἐπικαθίζω], fut. ίσω, (§ 26. rem. 1) (ἐπί & καθίζω) *to cause to sit upon, seat upon*, Mat. 21. 7; or, according to the v.r., ἐπεκάθισεν, intrans. *to sit upon.*

ἐπικαλεῖσθαι, pres. infin. pass. . . . ἐπικαλέω
ἐπικαλεῖσθε, 2 pers. pl. pres. ind. mid. . id.
ἐπικαλεῖται, 3 pers. sing. pres. ind. pass. . id.
ἐπικαλεσάμενος, nom. s. masc. part. aor. 1, mid. id.
ἐπικαλεσαμένου, gen. s. masc. part. aor. 1, mid. id.
ἐπικαλέσασθαι, aor. 1, infin. mid. . . id.
ἐπικαλέσηται, 3 pers. sing. aor. 1, subj. mid. id.
ἐπικαλέσονται, 3 pers. pl. fut. ind. mid. . id.
ἐπικαλέσωνται, 3 pers. pl. aor. 1, subj. mid.—A. D. Ln. Tdf. . . . } id.
ἐπικαλέσονται, Rec. Gr. Sch. (Ro. 10. 14)

ἐπικαλέω, ῶ], fut. έσω, perf. pass. ἐπικέκληται, aor. 1, pass. ἐπεκλήθην, (§ 22. rem. 1. and 4) (ἐπί & καλέω) *to call on; to attach or connect a name*, Ac. 15. 17; Ja. 2. 7; *to attach an additional name, to surname*, Mat. 10. 3, et al.; pass. to *receive an appellation or surname*, He. 11. 16; mid. *to call upon, invoke*, 2 Co. 1. 23, et al.; *to appeal to*, Ac. 25. 11, 12, 21.

ἐπικαλοῦμαι, 1 pers. sing. pres. ind. mid. . ἐπικαλέω
ἐπικαλουμένοις, dat. pl. masc. part. pres. mid. id.
ἐπικαλούμενον, acc. sing. masc. part. pres. pass. and mid. . . . . . id.
ἐπικαλούμενος, nom. sing. masc. part. pres. pass. id.
ἐπικαλουμένου, gen. sing. masc. part. pres. pass. id.
ἐπικαλουμένους, acc. pl. masc. part. pres. mid. id.
ἐπικαλουμένων, gen. pl. part. pres. mid. . id.
ἐπικάλυμμα,[a] ατος, τό, (§ 4. tab. D. c) . ἐπικαλύπτω

ἐπικαλύπτω], fut. ψω, (§ 23. rem. 1. a) (ἐπί & καλύπτω) *to cover over*; met. *to cover or veil* by a pardon, Ro. 4. 7.

ἐπικάλυμμα, ατος, τό, (§ 4. tab. D. c) *a covering, veil*; met. *a cloak*, 1 Pe. 2. 16.

ἐπικατάρατοι, nom. pl. masc. . . ἐπικατάρατος

ἐπικατάρᾱτος, ου, ὁ, ἡ, (§ 7. rem. 2) (ἐπί & κατάρατος) *cursed, accursed; obnoxious to the curse* of condemnation, Gal. 3. 10; *infamous*, Gal. 3. 13; *outcast, vile*, Jno. 7. 49.

ἐπίκειμαι], fut. κείσομαι, (§ 33. tab. DD) (ἐπί & κεῖμαι) *to lie upon, be placed upon*, Jno. 11. 38; 21. 9; *to press, urge upon*, Lu. 5. 1; Ac. 27. 20; *be urgent, importunate upon*, Lu. 23. 23; *to be imposed upon, be imposed* by law, He. 9. 10; by necessity, 1 Co. 9. 16.

ἐπικείμενα, nom. pl. neut. part. pres. . . ἐπίκειμαι
ἐπικείμενον, acc. sing. neut. part. pres. . id.
ἐπικειμένου, gen. sing. masc. part. pres. . id.
ἐπικεῖσθαι, pres. infin. . . . . id.
ἐπίκειται, 3 pers. sing. pres. ind. . . . id.
ἐπικέκλησαι, 2 pers. sing. perf. ind. pass. . ἐπικαλέω
ἐπικέκληται, 3 pers. sing. perf. ind. pass. . id.

ἐπικέλλω], equivalent to ἐποκέλλω, *to push* a ship *to shore*, v.r. Ac. 27. 41.

ἐπικληθείς, nom. sing. masc. part. aor. 1, pass. ἐπικαλέω
ἐπικληθέν, acc. sing. neut. part. aor. 1, pass. id.
ἐπικληθέντα, acc. sing. masc. part. aor. 1, pass. id.

Ἐπικούρειος], ου, ὁ, *an Epicurean, follower of the philosophy of Epicurus.*

Ἐπικουρείων,[b] gen. pl. . . . . Ἐπικούρειος

ἐπικουρία], ας, ἡ, (§ 2. tab. B. b, and rem. 2) (ἐπίκουρος, *a helper*) *help, assistance.*

ἐπικουρίας,[c] gen. sing. . . . ἐπικουρία
ἐπικράνθη, 3 pers. sing. aor. 1, ind. pass. (§ 27. rem. 3) . . . . πικραίνω
ἐπικράνθησαν, 3 pers. pl. aor. 1, ind. pass. . id.

ἐπικρίνω], fut. ινῶ, (§ 27. rem. 1. a) (ἐπί & κρίνω) *to decide; to decree*, Lu. 23. 24. (ῑ).

ἐπιλαβέσθαι, aor. 2, infin. mid. . ἐπιλαμβάνω
ἐπιλαβόμενοι, nom. pl. masc. part. aor. 2, mid. id.
ἐπιλαβόμενος, nom. sing. masc. part. aor. 2, mid. id.
ἐπιλαβομένου, gen. sing. masc. part. aor. 2, mid. id.
ἐπιλᾰβοῦ, 2 pers. sing. aor. 2, imper. mid. id.
ἐπιλάβωνται, 3 pers. pl. aor. 2, subj. mid. . id.
ἐπιλαθέσθαι, aor. 2, infin. (§ 36. rem. 2) ἐπιλανθάνομαι
ἐπιλαμβάνεται, 3 pers. sing. pres. ind. mid. ἐπιλαμβάνω

ἐπιλαμβάνω], fut. λήψομαι, (§ 36. rem. 2) and mid. ἐπιλαμβάνομαι, (ἐπί & λαμβάνω) *to take hold of*, Mat. 14. 31; Mar. 8. 23;

[a] 1 Pe. 2. 16. [b] Ac. 17. 18. [c] Ac. 26. 22.

to lay hold of, seize, Lu. 23. 26; Ac. 16. 19, et al.; met. *to seize on* as a ground of accusation, Lu. 20. 20, 26; *to grasp, obtain* as if by seizure, 1 Ti. 6. 12, 19; *to assume a portion of, to assume the nature of,* or, *to attach or ally one's self to,* He. 2. 16.

ἐπιλανθάνεσθε, 2 pers. pl. pres. imper. ἐπιλανθάνομαι

ἐπιλανθάνομαι], fut. λήσομαι, aor. 2, ἐπελαθόμην, (§ 36. rem. 2) (ἐπί & λανθάνω) *to forget,* Mat. 16. 5, et al.; *to be forgetful, neglectful of, to disregard,* Phi. 3. 14; He. 6. 10, et al.; perf. pass. part. ἐπιλελησμένος, in N.T. in a passive sense, *forgotten,* Lu. 12. 6.

ἐπιλησμονή, ῆς, ἡ, (§ 2. tab. B. a) *forgetfulness, oblivion,* Ja. 1. 25. LXX.

ἐπιλανθανόμενος, nom. s. masc. part. pres. ἐπιλανθάνομαι

ἐπιλεγομένη, nom. s. fem. part. pres. pass. . ἐπιλέγω

ἐπιλέγω], fut. ξω, (§ 23. rem. 1. b) (ἐπί & λέγω) *to call, denominate,* Jno. 5. 2; mid. *to select for one's self, choose,* Ac. 15. 40.

ἐπιλείπω], fut. ψω, (§ 23. rem. 1. a) (ἐπί & λείπω) *to be insufficient, to run short, to fail,* He. 11. 32.

ἐπίλοιπος, ου, ὁ, ἡ, (§ 7. rem. 2) *remaining, still left,* 1 Pe. 4. 2.

ἐπιλείχω], fut. ξω, (ἐπί & λείχω) *to lick,* v.r. Lu. 16. 21.

ἐπιλείψει,[a] 3 pers. sing. fut. ind. act. . ἐπιλείπω

ἐπιλελησμένον, nom. s. neut. part. p. pass. ἐπιλανθάνομαι

ἐπιλεξάμενος, nom. sing. masc. part. aor. 1, mid. ἐπιλέγω

ἐπιλησμονή], ῆς, ἡ, (§ 2. tab. B. a) . ἐπιλανθάνομαι

ἐπιλησμονῆς,[b] gen. sing. . . . ἐπιλησμονή

ἐπίλοιπον,[c] acc. sing. masc. . . . ἐπίλοιπος

ἐπίλοιπος], ου, ὁ, ἡ, (§ 7. rem. 2) . . ἐπιλείπω

ἐπιλυθήσεται, 3 pers. sing. fut. 1, ind. pass. ἐπιλύω

ἐπιλύσεως,[d] gen. sing. . . . . ἐπίλυσις

ἐπίλυσις], εως, ἡ, (§ 5. tab. E. c) . . ἐπιλύω

ἐπιλύω], fut. ύσω, (§ 13. tab. M) (ἐπί & λύω) *to loose* what has previously been fastened or entangled, as a knot; met. *to solve, to explain,* what is enigmatical, as a parable, Mar. 4. 34; *to settle, put an end to* a matter of debate, Ac. 19. 39.

ἐπίλυσις, εως, ἡ, (§ 5. tab. E. c) *a loosing, liberation;* met. *interpretation* of what is enigmatical and obscure, 2 Pe. 1. 20.

ἐπιμαρτυρέω, ῶ], fut. ήσω, (§ 16. tab. P) (ἐπί & μαρτυρέω) *to bear testimony to; to testify solemnly.*

ἐπιμαρτυρῶν,[e] nom. sing. masc. part. pres. ἐπιμαρτυρέω

ἐπιμεῖναι, aor. 1, infin. (§ 27. rem. 1. d) . ἐπιμένω

ἐπιμείνῃς, 3 pers. sing. aor. 1, subj. . . id.

ἐπιμείνωσι, 3 pers. pl. aor. 1, subj. . . id.

ἐπιμέλεια], ας, ἡ, (§ 2. tab. B. b, and rem. 2) (ἐπιμελής, *careful*) *care, attention,* Ac. 27. 3.

ἐπιμελείας,[f] gen. sing. . . . . ἐπιμέλεια

ἐπιμέλομαι, v. ἐπιμελέομαι, οῦμαι], fut. (pass. form) ἐπιμεληθήσομαι, and, later, ἐπιμελήσομαι, aor. 1, (pass. form) ἐπεμελήθην, (§ 17. tab. Q) (ἐπί & μέλομαι) *to take care of,* Lu. 10. 34, 35; 1 Ti. 3. 5.

ἐπιμελήθητι, 2 pers. sing. aor. 1, imper. pass. ἐπιμελέομαι

ἐπιμελήσεται, 3 pers. sing. fut. ind. . ἐπιμέλομαι

ἐπιμελῶς,[g] adv. (ἐπιμελής, *careful*) *carefully, diligently,* Lu. 15. 8.

ἐπίμενε, 2 pers. sing. pres. imper. . . ἐπιμένω

ἐπιμένειν, pres. infin. . . . . id.

ἐπιμένετε, 2 pers. pl. pres. ind. . . . id.

ἐπιμενόντων, gen. pl. masc. part. pres. . id.

ἐπιμενοῦμεν, 1 pers. pl. fut. ind. . . id.

ἐπιμένω], fut. νῶ, (§ 27. rem. 1. a) (ἐπί & μένω) *to stay longer, prolong a stay, remain on,* Ac. 10. 48; 15. 34, et. al.; *to continue, persevere,* Jno. 8. 7; Ac. 12. 16; *to adhere to, continue to embrace,* Ac. 13. 43; Ro. 11. 22; *to persist in,* Ro. 6. 1, et al.

ἐπιμενῶ, 1 pers. sing. fut. ind. . . . ἐπιμένω

ἐπιμένωμεν, 1 pers. pl. pres. subj.—A. B. C. D. Gr. Tdf. . . . . } id.
ἐπιμενοῦμεν, Rec. Sch. (Ro. 6. 1) .

ἐπινεύω], fut. εύσω, (§ 13. tab. M) (ἐπί & νεύω) *to nod to;* met. *to assent to, consent,* Ac. 18. 20.

ἐπίνοια,[h] ας, ἡ, (§ 2 tab. B. b, and rem. 2) (ἐπί & νοῦς) *cogitation, purpose, device.*

ἐπίομεν, 1 pers. pl. aor. 2, ind. act. (§ 37. rem. 1) πίνω

ἔπινον, 3 pers. pl. imperf. act. . . . id.

ἔπιον, 3 pers. pl. aor. 2, ind. act. . . id.

ἐπιορκέω, ῶ], fut. ήσω, (§ 16. tab. P) . ἐπίορκος

ἐπίορκος, ου, ὁ, ἡ, (§ 7. rem. 2) (ἐπί & ὅρκος) *one who violates his oath, perjured.*

ἐπιορκέω, ῶ], fut. ήσω, (§ 16. tab. P)

[a] He. 11. 32. [b] Ja. 1. 25. [c] 1 Pe. 4. 2. [d] 2 Pe. 1. 20. [e] 1 Pe. 5. 12. [f] Ac. 27. 3. [g] Lu. 15. 8. [h] Ac. 8. 22.

to forswear one's self, to fail of observing one's oath.

ἐπιορκήσεις,[a] 2 pers. sing. fut. ind. . . . ἐπιορκέω

ἐπιόρκοις,[b] dat. pl. masc. . . . ἐπίορκος

ἐπίορκος], ου, ὁ, ἡ, (§ 7. rem. 2) . . ἐπιορκέω

ἐπιούσῃ, dat. sing. fem. part. pres. (§ 33. rem. 4) ἔπειμι

ἐπιούσιον, acc. sing. masc. . . . ἐπιούσιος

ἐπιούσιος], ίου, ὁ, ἡ, (§ 7. rem. 2) *supplied with the coming day* (ἡ ἐπιοῦσα), *daily*, or *sufficient*, Mat. 6. 11; Lu. 11. 3. N.T.

ἐπιπεπτωκός, nom. sing. neut. part. perf. . ἐπιπίπτω

ἐπιπεσόντες, nom. pl. masc. part. aor. 2 . id.

ἐπιπεσών, nom. sing. masc. part. aor. 2 . id.

ἐπιπίπτειν, pres. infin. . . . id.

ἐπιπίπτω], fut. πεσοῦμαι, aor. 2, ἐπέπεσον, (§ 37. rem. 1) (ἐπί & πίπτω) *to fall upon; to throw one's self upon*, Lu. 15. 20; Jno. 13. 25; Ac. 20. 10, 37; *to press, urge upon*, Mar. 3. 10; *to light upon*, Ro. 15. 3; *to come over*, Ac. 13. 11; *to come upon, fall upon* mentally or spiritually, Lu. 1. 12; Ac. 8. 16; 10. 10, 44; 11. 15; 19. 17.

ἐπιπλήξῃς,[c] 2 pers. sing. aor. 1, subj. act. ἐπιπλήσσω

ἐπιπλήσσω, or ττω], fut. ξω, (§ 26. rem. 3) (ἐπί & πλήσσω) pr. *to inflict blows upon*; met. *to chide, reprove*.

ἐπιπνίγω], fut. ξω, (§ 23. rem. 1. b) (ἐπί & πνίγω) pr. *to suffocate*; met. *to choke, obstruct the growth of*, v.r. Lu. 8. 7. N.T.

ἐπιποθεῖ, 3 pers. sing. pres. ind. . . . ἐπιποθέω

ἐπιποθέω, ῶ], fut. ήσω, (§ 19. tab. P) (ἐπί & ποθέω) *to desire besides*; also, *to desire earnestly, long for*, 2 Co. 5. 2; *to have a strong bent*, Ja. 4. 5; by impl. *to love, have affection for*, 2 Co. 9. 14, et al.

ἐπιπόθησις, εως, ἡ, (§ 5. tab. E. c) *earnest desire, strong affection*, 2 Co. 7. 7, 11.

ἐπιπόθητος, ου, ὁ, ἡ, τό, -ον, (§ 7. rem. 2) *earnestly desired, longed for*, Phi. 4. 1. L.G.

ἐπιποθία, ας, ἡ, (§ 2. tab. B. b, and rem. 2) *earnest desire*, Ro. 15. 23. N.T.

ἐπιποθήσατε, 2 pers. pl. aor. 1, imper. . ἐπιποθέω

ἐπιπόθησιν, acc. sing. . . . ἐπιπόθησις

ἐπιπόθησις], εως, ἡ, (§ 5. tab. E. c) . ἐπιποθέω

ἐπιπόθητοι,[d] nom. pl. masc. . ἐπιπόθητος

ἐπιπόθητος], ου, ὁ, ἡ, (§ 7. rem. 2) . . ἐπιποθέω

ἐπιποθία], ας, ἡ, (§ 2. tab. B. b, and rem. 2) id.

ἐπιποθίαν,[e] acc. sing. . . . . ἐπιποθία

ἐπιποθοῦντες, nom. pl. masc. part. pres. . ἐπιποθέω

ἐπιποθούντων, gen. pl. masc. part. pres. . id.

ἐπιποθῶ, 1 pers. sing. pres. ind. . . id.

ἐπιποθῶν, nom. sing. masc. part. pres. . id.

ἐπιπορεύομαι], fut. εύσομαι, (§ 14. tab. N) (ἐπί & πορεύομαι) *to travel to; to come to*.

ἐπιπορευομένων,[f] gen. pl. part. pres. . ἐπιπορεύομαι

ἐπίπρασκον, 3 pers. pl. imperf. act. . . πιπράσκω

ἐπιῤῥάπτει,[g] 3 pers. sing. pres. ind. . ἐπιῤῥάπτω

ἐπιῤῥάπτω], fut. ψω (§ 23. rem. 1. a) (ἐπί & ῥάπτω) *to sew upon*. N.T.

ἐπιῤῥίπτω], fut. ψω, (ἐπί & ῥίπτω) *to throw or cast upon*, Lu. 19. 35; met. *to devolve upon, commit to*, in confidence, 1 Pe. 5. 7.

ἐπιῤῥίψαντες, nom. pl. masc. part. aor. 1 . ἐπιῤῥίπτω

ἐπίσημοι, nom. pl. masc. . . . ἐπίσημος

ἐπίσημον, acc. sing. masc. . . . id.

ἐπίσημος], ου, ὁ, ἡ, (§ 7. rem. 2) (ἐπί & σῆμα) pr. *bearing a distinctive mark or device; noted, eminent*, Ro. 16. 7; *notorious*, Mat. 27. 16.

ἐπισιτισμόν,[h] acc. sing. . . . ἐπισιτισμός

ἐπισιτισμός], οῦ, ὁ, (§ 3. tab. C. a) (ἐπισιτίζομαι, *to provision*, fr. ἐπί & σιτίζω, *to feed*, fr. σῖτος) *supply of food, provisions*.

ἐπισκέπτεσθαι, pres. infin. . . ἐπισκέπτομαι

ἐπισκέπτῃ, 2 pers. sing. pres. ind. . . id.

ἐπισκέπτομαι], fut. ψομαι, (§ 23. rem. 1. a) (ἐπί & σκέπτομαι) *to look at observantly, to inspect; to look out, select*, Ac. 6. 3; *to go to see, visit*, Ac. 7. 23; 15. 36; *to visit* for the purpose of comfort and relief, Mat. 25. 36, 43; Ja. 1. 27; from the Heb., of God, *to visit*, with gracious interposition, Lu. 1. 68, 78, et al.

ἐπισκευάζομαι], fut άσομαι, (§ 26. rem. 1) (ἐπισκευάζω, *to put in readiness*) *to prepare for a journey*, v.r. Ac. 21. 15.

ἐπισκευασάμενοι, nom. pl. masc. part. aor. 1 —A. B. Ln. Tdf. . . } ἐπισκευάζομαι
ἀποσκευασάμενοι, Rec. Gr. Sch. . (Ac. 21. 15) . . }

ἐπισκέψασθαι, aor. 1, infin. . . ἐπισκέπτομαι

ἐπισκέψασθε, 2 pers. pl. aor. 1, imper. . id.

---

[a] Mat. 5. 33. [b] 1 Ti. 1. 10. [c] 1 Ti. 5. 1. [d] Phi. 4. 1. [e] Ro. 15. 23. [f] Lu. 8. 4. [g] Mar. 2. 21. [h] Lu. 9. 12.

ἐπισκεψώμεθα, 1 pers. pl. aor. 1, subj. . ἐπισκέπτομαι

ἐπισκηνόω, ῶ], fut. ώσω, (§ 20. tab. T) (ἐπί & σκηνή, *a tent*) *to quarter in or at*; met. *to abide upon.* L.G.

ἐπισκηνώσῃ,[a] 3 pers. sing. aor. 1, subj. . ἐπισκηνόω

ἐπισκιάζουσα, nom. sing. fem. part. pres. ἐπισκιάζω

ἐπισκιάζω], fut. άσω, (§ 26. rem. 1) (ἐπί & σκιάζω, *to shade*, fr. σκιά) *to overshadow*, Mat. 17. 5, et al.; met. *to overshadow, to shed influence upon*, Lu. 1. 35.

ἐπισκιάσει, 3 pers. sing. fut. ind. . . ἐπισκιάζω

ἐπισκιάσῃ, 3 pers. sing. aor. 1, subj. . id.

ἐπισκοπέω, ῶ], fut. ήσω, (§ 16. tab. P) (ἐπί & σκοπέω) *to look at, inspect*; met. *to be circumspect, heedful*, He. 12. 15; *to oversee, to exercise the office of* ἐπίσκοπος, 1 Pe. 5. 2.

ἐπισκοπή], ῆς, ἡ, (§ 2. tab. B. a) . ἐπισκοπος

ἐπισκοπήν, acc. sing. . . . . ἐπισκοπή

ἐπισκοπῆς, gen. sing. . . . . id.

ἐπισκόποις, dat. pl. . . . . ἐπίσκοπος

ἐπίσκοπον, acc. sing. . . . . id.

ἐπίσκοπος, ου, ὁ, (§ 3. tab. C. a) (ἐπί & σκοπός) pr. *an inspector, overseer; a watcher, guardian*, 1 Pe. 2. 25; in N.T. *an* ecclesiastical *overseer*, Ac 20. 28; Phi. 1. 1; 1 Ti. 3. 2; Tit. 1. 7.

ἐπισκοπή, ῆς, ἡ, (§ 2. tab. B. a) *inspection, oversight, visitation*; of God, *visitation, interposition*, whether in mercy or judgment, Lu. 19, 44; 1 Pe. 2. 12; *the office of an ecclesiastical overseer*, 1 Ti. 3. 1; from the Heb. *charge, function*, Ac. 1. 20. LXX.

ἐπισκοποῦντες, nom. pl. masc. part. pres. . ἐπίσκοπος

ἐπισκόπους, acc. pl. . . . . id.

ἐπισπάσθω,[b] 3 pers. sing. pres. imper. mid. . ἐπισπάω

ἐπισπάω, ῶ], fut. άσω, (§ 18. tab. R) (ἐπί & σπάω) *to draw upon or after*; in N.T. mid. *to obliterate circumcision* by artificial extension of the foreskin.

ἐπισπείρω], fut. ερῶ, (ἐπί & σπείρω) *to sow in or among*, v.r. Mat. 13. 25.

ἐπίσταμαι, σαι, ται, (§ 33. rem. 3) *to be versed in, to be master of*, 1 Ti. 6. 4; *to be acquainted with*, Ac. 18. 25; 19. 15; Jude 10; *to know*, Ac. 10. 28, et al.; *to remember, comprehend*, Mar. 14. 68

ἐπιστήμων, ονος, ὁ, ἡ, (§ 7. tab. G. a) *knowing, discreet*, Ja. 3. 13.

ἐπιστάμενος, nom. sing. masc. part. pres. . ἐπίσταμαι

ἐπίστανται, 3 pers. pl. pres. ind. . . id.

ἐπιστάντες, nom. pl. masc. part. aor. 2 . . ἐφίστημι

ἐπιστάς, nom. s. masc. part. aor. 2 (§ 29. tab. X) id.

ἐπιστᾶσα, nom. sing. fem. part. aor. 2 . id.

ἐπίστασθε, 2 pers. pl. pres. ind. . . ἐπίσταμαι

ἐπίστασιν, acc. sing.—A. B. Ln. Tdf. } ἐπίστασις
ἐπισύστασιν, Rec. Gr. Sch. (Ac. 24. 12) }

ἐπίστασις, εως, ἡ, (§ 5. tab. E. c) pr. *care of, attention to.*—B. Ln. Tdf. (2 Co. 11. 28)

ἐπισύστασις, Rec. Gr. Sch.

Also, *insurrection, tumult*, as if fr. ἐπί & στάσις, Ac. 24. 12. v.r.

ἐπιστάτα, voc. sing. (§ 2. rem. 6) . . ἐπιστάτης

ἐπίσταται, 3 pers. sing. pres. ind. . . ἐπίσταμαι

ἐπιστάτης], ου, ὁ, (§ 2. tab. B. c) . . ἐφίστημι

ἐπιστεῖλαι, aor. 1, infin. act. (§ 27. rem. 1. d) ἐπιστέλλω

ἐπιστέλλω], fut. ελῶ, (§ 27. rem. 1. b) (ἐπί & στέλλω) *to send word to, to send injunctions*, Ac. 15. 20; 21. 25; *to write to, write* a letter, He. 13. 22.

ἐπιστολή, ῆς, ἡ, (§ 2. tab. B. a) *word sent; an order, command; an epistle, letter*, Ac. 9. 2; 15. 30, et al.

ἐπίστευε, 3 pers. sing. imperf. . . πιστεύω

ἐπιστεύετε, 2 pers. pl. imperf . . id.

ἐπιστεύθη, 3 pers. sing. aor. 1, ind. pass. . id.

ἐπιστεύθην, 1 pers. sing. aor. 1, ind. pass. . id.

ἐπιστεύθησαν, 3 pers. pl. aor. 1, ind. pass. id.

ἐπίστευον, 3 pers. pl. imperf. . . . id.

ἐπίστευσα, 1 pers. sing. aor. 1, ind. . . id.

ἐπιστεύσαμεν, 1 pers. pl. aor. 1, ind. . id.

ἐπίστευσαν, 3 pers. pl. aor. 1, ind. . . id.

ἐπίστευσας, 2 pers. sing. aor. 1, ind. . id.

ἐπιστεύσατε, 2 pers. pl. aor. 1, ind. . . id.

ἐπίστευσε, 3 pers. sing. aor. 1, ind. . . id.

ἐπιστῇ, 3 pers. sing. aor. 2, subj. (§ 29. rem. 3) ἐφίστημι

ἐπίστηθι, 2 pers. sing. aor. 2, imper. . . id.

ἐπιστήμων,[c] ονος, ὁ, ἡ, (§ 7. tab. G. a) . ἐπίσταμαι

ἐπιστηρίζοντες, nom. pl. masc. part. pres. ἐπιστηρίζω

ἐπιστηρίζω], fut. ίξω, (§ 26. rem. 2) (ἐπί & στηρίζω) pr. *to cause to rest or lean on, to settle upon*; met. *to confirm, strengthen, establish*, Ac. 14. 22; 15. 32, 41; 18. 23.

ἐπιστηρίζων, nom. sing. masc. part. pres. ἐπιστηρίζω

ἐπιστολαί. nom. pl. . . . . ἐπιστολή

a 2 Co. 12. 9. b 1 Co. 7. 18. c Ja. 3. 13.

ἐπιστολαῖς, dat. pl. . . . . . ἐπιστολή
ἐπιστολάς, acc. pl. . . . . . id.
ἐπιστολή, ῆς, ἡ, (§ 2. tab. B. a) . . ἐπιστέλλω
ἐπιστολῇ, dat. sing. . . . . . ἐπιστολή
ἐπιστολήν, acc. sing. . . . . id.
ἐπιστολῆς, gen. sing. . . . . . id.
ἐπιστολῶν, gen. pl. . . . . . id.
ἐπιστομίζειν,[a] pres. infin. . . ἐπιστομίζω
ἐπιστομίζω], fut. ίσω, (§ 26. rem. 1) (ἐπί & στόμα) *to apply a curb or muzzle*; met. *to put to silence*.
ἐπιστραφείς, nom. sing. masc. part. aor. 2, pass. (§ 24. rem. 10) . . . ἐπιστρέφω
ἐπιστραφήτω, 3 pers. sing. aor. 2, imper. pass. id.
ἐπιστραφῶσι, 3 pers. pl. aor. 2, subj. pass. . id.
ἐπιστρέφειν, pres. infin. act. . . . . id.
ἐπιστρέφετε, 2 pers. pl. pres. ind. act. . id.
ἐπιστρέφουσι, dat. pl. masc. part. pres. act. id.
ἐπιστρέφω], fut. ψω, aor. 2, pass. ἐπεστράφην, (ᾰ), (§ 24. rem. 10) (ἐπί & στρέφω) trans. *to turn towards; to turn round; to bring back, convert*, Lu. 1. 16, 17; Ja. 5. 19, 20; intrans. and mid. *to turn one's self upon or towards*, Ac. 9. 40; Re. 1. 12; *to turn about*, Mat. 9. 22, et al.; *to turn back, return*, Mat. 12. 44, et al.; met. *to be converted*, Ac. 28. 27, et al.

ἐπιστροφή, ῆς, ἡ, (§ 2. tab. B. a) *a turning towards, a turning about*; in N.T. met. *conversion*, Ac. 15. 3.

ἐπιστρέψαι, aor. 1, infin. act. . . . . ἐπιστρέφω
ἐπιστρέψαντες, nom. pl. masc. pt. aor. 1, act. id.
ἐπιστρέψας, nom. sing. masc. part. aor. 1, act. id.
ἐπιστρέψατε, 2 pers. pl. aor. 1, imper. . id.
ἐπιστρεψάτω, 3 pers. sing. aor. 1, imper. . id.
ἐπιστρέψει, 3 pers. sing. fut. ind. . . id.
ἐπιστρέψῃ, 3 pers. sing. aor. 1, subj. . . id.
ἐπιστρέψω, 1 pers. sing. fut. ind. . . id.
ἐπιστρέψωσι, 3 pers. pl. aor 1, subj. . . id.
ἐπιστροφή], ῆς, ἡ, (§ 2. tab. B. a) . . id.
ἐπιστροφήν,[b] acc. sing. . . . ἐπιστροφή
ἐπιστώθης,[c] 3 pers. s. aor. 1, pass. (§ 21. tab. U) πιστόω
ἐπισυναγαγεῖν, aor. 2, infin. (§ 13. rem. 7. d) ἐπισυνάγω
ἐπισυνάγει, 3 pers. sing. pres. ind. act. . id.
ἐπισυνάγω] fut. ξω, (§ 23. rem. 1. b) (ἐπί & συνάγω) *to gather to* a place; *to gather together, assemble, convene*, Mat. 23. 37; 24. 31, et al. (ᾰ). L.G.

ἐπισυναγωγή, ῆς, ἡ, (§ 2. tab. B. a) *the act of being gathered together or assembled*, 2 Thes. 2. 1; *an assembling together*, He. 10. 25. LXX.

ἐπισυναγωγή], ῆς, ἡ . . . . ἐπισυνάγω
ἐπισυναγωγήν, acc. sing. . . . ἐπισυναγωγή
ἐπισυναγωγῆς, gen. sing. . . . . id.
ἐπισυνάξαι, aor. 1, infin. act. . . ἐπισυνάγω
ἐπισυνάξει, 3 pers. sing. fut. ind. act. . . id.
ἐπισυνάξουσι, 3 pers. pl. fut. ind. act. . id.
ἐπισυναχθεισῶν, gen. pl. fem. part. aor. 1, pass. id.
ἐπισυνηγμένη, nom. sing. fem. part. perf. pass. id.
ἐπισυντρέχει,[d] 3 pers. sing. pres. ind. . ἐπισυντρέχω
ἐπισυντρέχω], (ἐπί & συντρέχω) *to run together* to a place. L.G.
ἐπισύστασιν, acc. sing. . . . ἐπισύστασις
ἐπισύστᾰσις, εως, ἡ, (§ 5. tab. E. c) (ἐπισυνίσταμαι) *a gathering, concourse, tumult*, Ac. 24. 12; *a crowding* of calls upon the attention and thoughts, 2 Co. 11. 28.
ἐπισφᾰλής], έος, οῦς, ὁ, ἡ, τό, -ές, (§ 7. tab. G. b) (ἐπί & σφάλλω, *to supplant*) *on the verge of falling, unsteady*; met. *insecure, hazardous, dangerous*.
ἐπισφαλοῦς,[e] gen. sing. masc. . . ἐπισφαλής
ἐπίσχυον,[f] 3 pers. pl. imperf. . . . ἐπισχύω
ἐπισχύω], fut. ύσω, (§ 13. tab. M) (ἐπί & ἰσχύω) *to strengthen*; intrans. *to gather strength*; met. *to be urgent, to press on* a point.
ἐπισωρεύσουσι,[g] 3 pers. pl. fut. ind. . ἐπισωρεύω
ἐπισωρεύω], fut. εύσω, (ἐπί & σωρεύω, fr. σωρός, *a heap*) *to heap up, accumulate largely*; met. *to procure in abundance*. L.G.
ἐπιταγή], ῆς, ἡ, (§ 2. tab. B. a) . . ἐπιτάσσω
ἐπιταγήν, acc. sing. . . . . ἐπιταγή
ἐπιταγῆς, gen. sing. . . . . . id.
ἐπιτάξῃ, 3 pers. sing. aor. 1, subj. . . ἐπιτάσσω
ἐπιτάσσει, 3 pers. sing. pres. ind. . . id.
ἐπιτάσσειν, pres. infin. . . . . id.
ἐπιτάσσω, fut. ξω, (§ 26. rem. 3) (ἐπί & τάσσω) *to set over or upon; to enjoin, charge*, Mar. 1. 27; 6. 39; Lu. 4. 36, et al.

ἐπιτᾰγή, ῆς, ἡ, (§ 2. tab. B. a) (a later form for ἐπίταξις or ἐπίταγμα) *injunction*, 1 Co. 7. 6, 25; 2 Co. 8. 8; *a decree*, Ro. 16. 26; 1 Ti. 1. 1; Tit. 1. 3; *authoritativeness, strictness*, Tit. 2. 15.

ἐπιτεθῇ, 3 pers. s. aor. 1, subj. pass. (§ 28. rem. 10) ἐπιτίθημι

a Tit. 1. 11. b Ac. 15. 3. c 2 Ti. 3. 14. d Mar. 9. 25. e Ac. 27. 9. f Lu. 23. 5. g 2 Ti. 4. 3

ἐπιτελεῖν, pres. infin. act. . . . ἐπιτελέω
ἐπιτελεῖσθαι, pres. infin. pass. . . . id.
ἐπιτελεῖσθε, 2 pers. pl. pres. ind. mid. . id.
ἐπιτελέσαι, aor. 1, infin. act. . . . id.
ἐπιτελέσας, nom. sing. masc. part. aor. 1, act. id.
ἐπιτελέσατε, 2 pers. pl. aor. 1, imper. act. . id.
ἐπιτελέσει, 3 pers. sing. fut. ind. act. (§ 22. rem. 1) id.
ἐπιτελέσῃ, 3 pers. sing. aor. 1, subj. act. . id.
ἐπιτελέω, ῶ], fut. έσω, (§ 22. rem. 1) (ἐπί & τελέω) *to bring to an end; to finish, complete, perfect,* Ro. 15. 28; 2 Co. 8. 6, 11; *to perform,* Lu. 13. 32; *to carry into practice, to realise,* 2 Co. 7. 1; *to discharge,* He. 9. 6; *to execute,* He. 8. 5; *to carry out to completion,* Phi. 1. 6; mid. *to end, make an end,* Gal. 3. 3; pass. *to be fully undergone, endured,* 1 Pe. 5. 9.
ἐπιτελοῦντες, nom. pl. masc. part. pres. act. ἐπιτελέω
ἐπιτελῶ, 1 pers. sing. pres. ind. act. . . id.
ἐπιτέτραπται, 3 pers. s. perf. pass. (§ 35. rem. 9) ἐπιτρέπω
ἐπιτήδεια,[a] acc. pl. neut. . . . . ἐπιτήδειος
ἐπιτήδειος], εία, ειον, (§ 7. rem. 1) (ἐπιτηδές, *fit*) *fit, suitable, necessary.*
ἐπιτιθέασι, 3 pers. pl. pres. ind. act. Att. for ἐπιτιθεῖσι, (§ 28. rem. 6) . ἐπιτίθημι
ἐπιτίθει, 2 pers. sing. pres. imper. (§ 31. rem. 2) id.
ἐπιτιθείς, nom. sing. masc. part. pres. act.—B. D. Ln. Tdf. . . } id.
ἐπιθείς, Rec. Gr. Sch. (Lu. 4. 40) . }
ἐπιτίθεσθαι, pres. infin. mid. . . . id.
ἐπιτιθῇ, 3 pers. sing. pres. subj. act. . id.
ἐπιτίθημι], fut. ἐπιθήσω, (§ 28. tab. V) (ἐπί & τίθημι) *to put, place, or lay upon,* Mat. 9. 18; Lu. 4. 40, et al.; *to impose* a name, Mar. 3. 16, 17; *to inflict,* Ac. 16. 23; Lu. 10. 30; Re. 22. 18; mid. *to impose* with authority, Ac. 15. 28; *to lade,* Ac. 28. 10; *to set or fall upon, assail, assault, attack,* Ac. 18. 10.

ἐπίθεσις, εως, ἡ, (§ 5. tab. E. c) *the act of placing upon, imposition* of hands, Ac. 8. 18, et al.

ἐπιτίθησι, 3 pers. sing. pres. ind. act. . . ἐπιτίθημι
ἐπιτιμᾶν, pres. infin. act. . . . ἐπιτιμάω
ἐπιτῑμάω, ῶ], fut. ήσω, (§ 18. tab. R) (ἐπί & τιμάω) pr. *to set a value upon; to assess a penalty; to allege as a crimination;* hence, *to reprove, chide, censure, rebuke, reprimand,* Mat. 19. 13; Lu. 23. 40, et al.; in N.T *to admonish strongly, enjoin strictly,* Mat. 12. 16; Lu. 17. 3.

ἐπιτιμία, ας, ἡ, (§ 2. tab. B. b, and rem. 2) used in N.T. in the sense of ἐπιτίμημα or ἐπιτίμησις, *a punishment, penalty,* 2 Co. 2. 6.

ἐπιτιμῆσαι, 3 pers. sing. aor. 1, optat. ἐπιτιμάω
ἐπιτιμήσας, nom. sing. masc. part. aor. 1 . id.
ἐπιτίμησον, 2 pers. sing. aor. 1, imper. . id.
ἐπιτιμία,[b] ας, ἡ, (§ 2. tab. B. b, and rem. 2) id.
ἐπιτιμῶν, nom. sing. masc. part. pres. . . id.
ἐπιτρέπεται, 3 pers. sing. pres. ind. pass. . ἐπιτρέπω
ἐπιτρέπῃ, 3 pers. sing. pres. subj. act. . . id.
ἐπιτρέπω, fut. ψω, (§ 23. rem. 1. a) aor. 2, pass. ἐπετράπην, (ᾰ) (§ 24. rem. 10) perf. ἐπιτέτραμμαι, (§ 35. rem. 9) (ἐπί & τρέπω) *to give over, to leave to the entire trust or management of* any one; hence, *to permit, allow, suffer,* Mat. 8. 21; Mar. 5. 13, et al.

ἐπιτροπή, ῆς, ἡ, (§ 2. tab. B. a) *a trust; a commission,* Ac. 26. 12.

ἐπίτροπος, ου, ὁ, (§ 3. tab. C. a) *one to whose charge or control a thing is left; a steward, bailiff, agent, manager,* Mat. 20. 8; *steward or overseer* of the revenue, *treasurer,* Lu. 8. 3; *a guardian* of children, Gal. 4. 2.

ἐπιτρέψαντος, gen. sing. masc. part. aor. 1 . ἐπιτρέπω
ἐπιτρέψῃ, 3 pers. sing. aor. 1, subj. . . id.
ἐπίτρεψον, 2 pers. sing. aor. 1, imper. . id.
ἐπιτροπή], ῆς, ἡ, (§ 2. tab. B. a) . . id.
ἐπιτροπῆς,[c] gen. sing. . . . ἐπιτροπή
ἐπίτροπος], ου, ὁ, (§ 3. tab. C. a) . . ἐπιτρέπω
ἐπιτρόπου, gen. sing. . . . . ἐπίτροπος
ἐπιτρόπους, acc. pl. . . . . id.
ἐπιτρόπῳ, dat. sing. . . . . id.
ἐπιτυγχάνω], aor. 2, ἐπέτῠχον, (§ 36. rem. 2) ἐπί & τυγχάνω) *to light upon, find; to hit, reach; to acquire, obtain, attain,* Ro. 11. 7; He. 6. 15; 11. 33; Ja. 4. 2.
ἐπιτῠχεῖν, aor. 2, infin. . . . ἐπιτυγχάνω
ἐπιφαινόντων, gen. pl. neut. part. pres. . ἐπιφαίνω
ἐπιφαίνω], fut. φανῶ, aor. 1, ἐπέφηνα, later and in N.T. ἐπέφᾱνα, (§ 27. rem. 1. c. e) aor. 2, pass. ἐπεφάνην, (ᾰ) (§ 27. rem. 4. b) (ἐπί & φαίνω) *to make to appear, to display;* pass. *to be manifested, revealed,*

[a] Ja. 2. 16. [b] 2 Co. 2. 6. [c] Ac. 26. 12.

Tit. 2. 11; 3. 4; intrans. *to give light, shine,* Lu. 1. 79; Ac. 27. 20.

ἐπιφᾰνής, έος, οῦς, ὁ, ἡ, (§ 7. tab. G. b) pr. *in full and clear view; splendid, glorious, illustrious,* Ac. 2. 20.

ἐπιφάνεια, ας, ἡ, (§ 2 tab. B. b, and rem. 2) *appearance, manifestation,* 1 Ti. 6. 14; 2 Ti. 1. 10, et al.; *glorious display,* 2 Thes. 2. 8.

ἐπιφᾶναι, aor. 1, infin. (§ 27. rem. 1. f) . ἐπιφαίνω

ἐπιφάνεια], ας, ἡ, (§ 2. tab. B. b, and rem. 2) id.

ἐπιφανείᾳ, dat. sing. . . . . ἐπιφάνεια

ἐπιφάνειαν, acc. sing. . . . . id.

ἐπιφανείας, gen. sing. . . . . id.

ἐπιφανῆ,[a] acc. sing. fem. . . . . ἐπιφανής

ἐπιφανής], έος, οῦς, ὁ, ἡ, (§ 7. tab. G. b) ἐπιφαίνω

ἐπιφαύσει,[b] 3 pers. sing. fut. ind. . . ἐπιφαύσκω

ἐπιφαύσκω], in N.T. fut. αύσω, (φῶς) *to shine upon, give light to, enlighten*

ἐπιφέρειν, pres. inf. act. . . . ἐπιφέρω

ἐπιφέρεσθαι, pres. inf. pass. . . . id.

ἐπιφέρω], fut. ἐποίσω, aor. 2, ἐπήνεγκον, (§ 36. rem. 1) (ἐπί & φέρω) *to bring upon or against,* Ac. 25. 18; Jude 9; *to inflict,* Ro. 3. 5; *to bring to, apply to,* Ac. 19. 12; *to bring in addition, add, superadd,* Phi. 1. 16.

ἐπιφέρων, nom. sing. masc. part. pres. . ἐπιφέρω

ἐπιφωνέω, ῶ], fut. ήσω, (§ 16. tab. P) (ἐπι & φωνέω) *to cry aloud, raise a shout* at a speaker, whether applaudingly, Ac. 12. 22, or the contrary, *to clamour at,* Lu. 23. 21; Ac. 22. 24.

ἐπιφωσκούσῃ, dat. sing. fem. part. pres. . ἐπιφώσκω

ἐπιφώσκω], a varied form of ἐπιφαύσκω, *to dawn,* Mat. 28. 1; hence, used of the reckoned commencement of the day, *to be near commencing, to dawn on,* Lu. 23. 54.

ἐπιχειρέω, ῶ], fut. ήσω, (§ 16. tab. P) (ἐπί & χείρ) *to put hand to* a thing; *to undertake, attempt,* Lu. 1. 1; Ac. 9. 29; 19. 13.

ἐπιχέω], fut. εύσω, (§ 36. rem. 1) (ἐπί & χέω) *to pour upon.*

ἐπιχέων,[c] nom. sing. masc. part. pres. ἐπιχέω

ἐπιχορηγέω, ῶ], fut. ήσω, (§ 16. tab. P) (ἐπί & χορηγέω) *to supply further; to superadd,* 2 Pe. 1. 5; *to supply, furnish, give,* 2 Co. 9. 10; Gal. 3. 5; 2 Pe. 1. 11; pass. *to gather vigour,* Col. 2. 19.

ἐπιχορηγία, ας, ἡ, (§ 2. tab. B. b, and rem. 2) *supply, aid,* Ep. 4. 16; Phi. 1. 19. L.G.

ἐπιχορηγηθήσεται, 3 pers. sing. fut. 1, pass. ἐπιχορηγέω

ἐπιχορηγήσατε, 2 pers. pl. aor. 1, imper. act. id.

ἐπιχορηγία], ας, ἡ, (§ 2. tab. B. b, and rem. 2) id.

ἐπιχορηγίας, gen. sing. . . . ἐπιχορηγία

ἐπιχορηγούμενον, nom. s. neut. part. pres. pass. ἐπιχορηγέω

ἐπιχορηγῶν, nom. sing. masc. part. pres. act. . id.

ἐπιχρίω], fut. ίσω, (§ 22. rem 4) (ἐπί & χρίω) *to smear upon, to anoint,* Jno. 9. 6, 11. (ῑ).

ἐπλανήθησαν, 3 pers. pl. aor. 1, ind. pass. πλανάω

ἐπλάνησε, 3 pers. sing. aor. 1, ind. act. . id.

ἐπλάσθη, 3 pers. sing. aor. 1, ind. pass. . πλάσσω

ἐπλέομεν, 1 pers. pl. imperf. (§ 35. rem. 1) πλέω

ἐπλεόνασε, 3 pers. sing. aor. 1, ind. . πλεονάζω

ἐπλεονέκτησα, 1 pers. sing. aor. 1, ind. πλεονεκτέω

ἐπλεονεκτήσαμεν, 1 pers. pl. aor. 1, ind. . id.

ἐπλεονέκτησε, 3 pers. sing. aor. 1, ind. . id.

ἐπλήγη,[d] 3 pers. s. aor. 2, ind. pass. (§ 24. rem. 9) πλήσσω

ἐπληθύνετο, 3 pers. sing. imperf. pass. . . πληθύνω

ἐπληθύνθη, 3 pers. sing. aor. 1, ind. pass. . id.

ἐπληθύνοντο, 3 pers. pl. imperf. pass. . . id.

ἐπλήρου, 3 pers. sing. imperf. act. . . πληρόω

ἐπληροῦντο, 3 pers. pl. imperf. pass. . . id.

ἐπληροῦτο, 3 pers. sing. imperf. pass. . id.

ἐπληρώθη, 3 pers. sing. aor. 1, ind. pass. . id.

ἐπλήρωσαν, 3 pers. pl. aor. 1, ind. act. . id.

ἐπλήρωσε, 3 pers. sing. aor. 1, ind. act. . id.

ἔπλησαν, 3 pers. pl. aor. 1, ind act. . . πλήθω

ἐπλήσθη, 3 pers. sing. aor. 1, pass. (§ 23. rem. 4) id.

ἐπλήσθησαν, 3 pers. pl. aor. 1, ind. pass. . id.

ἐπλουτήσατε, 2 pers. pl. aor. 1, ind. . πλουτέω

ἐπλούτησαν, 3 pers. pl. aor. 1, ind. . . id.

ἐπλουτίσθητε, 2 pers. pl. aor. 1, pass. (§ 26. rem. 1) . . . . . πλουτίζω

ἔπλυναν, 3 pers. pl. aor. 1, ind. act. . . πλύνω

ἔπλυνον, pers. pl. imperf. act.—D. Ln. } id.
ἀπέπλυναν, Rec. Gr. Sch. Tdf. (Lu. 5. 2) }

ἔπνευσαν, 3 pers. pl. aor. 1, ind. (§ 35. rem. 3) πνέω

ἔπνιγε, 3 pers. sing. imperf. act. . . . πνίγω

ἐπνίγοντο, 3 pers. pl. imperf. pass. . . id.

ἐποίει, 3 pers. sing. imperf. act. . . . ποιέω

ἐποιεῖτε, 2 pers. pl. imperf. act. . . id.

ἐποίησα, 1 pers. sing. aor. 1, ind. act. . . id.

ἐποιήσαμεν, 1 pers. pl. aor. 1, ind. act. . id.

ἐποιησάμην, 1 pers. sing. aor. 1, ind. mid. . id.

ἐποίησαν, 3 pers. pl. aor. 1, ind. act. . id.

ἐποιήσαντο, 3 pers. pl. aor. 1, ind. mid. . id.

[a] Ac. 2. 20. [b] Ep. 5. 14. [c] Lu. 10. 34. [d] Re. 8. 12.

ἐποίησας, 2 pers. sing. aor. 1, ind. act. . . ποιέω
ἐποιήσατε, 2 pers. pl. aor. 1, ind. act. . id.
ἐποίησε, 3 pers. sing. aor. 1, ind. act. . . id.
ἐποικοδομεῖ, 3 pers. sing. pres. ind. act. . ἐποικοδομέω
ἐποικοδομέω, ῶ], fut. ήσω, (§ 16. tab. P) (ἐπί & οἰκοδομέω) met. *to build upon,* 1 Co. 3. 10, 12, 14; pass. met. *to be built upon* as parts of a spiritual structure, Ep. 2. 20; *to build up, carry up a building;* met. *to build up* in spiritual advancement, Ac. 20. 32, et al.
ἐποικοδομηθέντες, nom. pl. masc. pt. aor. 1, p. ἐποικοδομέω
ἐποικοδομῆσαι, aor. 1, inf. act. . . id.
ἐποικοδομούμενοι, nom. pl. masc. pt. pres. pass. id.
ἐποικοδομοῦντες, nom. pl. masc. part. pres. act. id.
ἐποίουν, 3 pers. pl. imperf. act. . . . ποιέω
ἐποιοῦντο, 3 pers. pl. imperf. pass. . . id.
ἐποκέλλω], aor. 1, ἐπώκειλα, (§ 27. rem. 1. d) (ἐπί & ὀκέλλω, idem) *to run* a ship *aground,* Ac. 27. 41.
ἐπολέμησαν, 3 pers. pl. aor. 1, ind. . . πολεμέω
ἐπολέμησε, 3 pers. sing. aor. 1, ind. . id.
ἐπονομάζῃ,[a] 2 pers. sing. pres. ind. pass. ἐπονομάζω
ἐπονομάζω], fut. άσω, (§ 26. rem. 1) (ἐπί & ὀνομάζω) *to attach a name to;* pass. *to be named, to be styled.*
ἐπόπται,[b] nom. pl. . . . . . . ἐπόπτης
ἐποπτεύοντες, nom. pl. masc. part. pr.—B. Ln. } ἐποπτεύω
ἐποπτεύσαντες, Rec. Gr. Sch. Tdf. (1 Pe. 2. 12) . . .
ἐποπτεύσαντες, nom. fut. masc. pt. aor. 1 . id.
ἐποπτεύω], fut. εύσω . . . . . ἐπόπτης
ἐπόπτης], ου, ὁ, (§ 2. tab. B. c) (ἐπί & ὄψομαι) *a looker-on, eye-witness,* 2 Pe. 1. 16.

ἐποπτεύω, fut. εύσω, (§ 13. tab. M) *to look upon, observe, watch; to witness, be an eye-witness of,* 1 Pe. 2. 12; 3. 2.

ἐπορεύετο, 3 pers. sing. imperf. . . . πορεύομαι
ἐπορεύθη, 3 pers. sing. aor. 1, ind. . . id.
ἐπορεύθησαν, 3 pers. pl. aor. 1, ind. . . id.
ἐπορευόμεθα, 1 pers. pl. imperf. . . id.
ἐπορευόμην, 1 pers. sing. imperf. . . id.
ἐπορεύοντο, 3 pers. pl. imperf. . . id.
ἐπόρθει, 3 pers. sing. imperf. act. . . πορθέω
ἐπόρθουν, 1 pers. sing. imperf. act. . . id.
ἐπόρνευσαν, 3 pers. pl. aor. 1, ind. . . πορνεύω
ἔπος,[c] εος, τό, (§ 5. tab. E. b) (εἶπον) *a word, that which is expressed by words;* ὡς ἔπος εἰπεῖν, *so to say, if the expression may be allowed*
ἐπότιζε, 3 pers. sing. imperf. act. . . ποτίζω
ἐπότιζον, 3 pers. pl. imperf. act. . . id.
ἐπότισα, 1 pers. sing. aor. 1, ind. act. . id.
ἐποτίσαμεν, 1 pers. pl. aor. 1, ind. act. . id.
ἐποτίσατε, 2 pers. pl. aor. 1, ind. act. . id.
ἐπότισε, 3 pers. sing. aor. 1, ind. act. . id.
ἐποτίσθημεν, 1 pers. pl. aor. 1, pass. (§ 26. rem. 1) id.
ἐπουράνια, nom. and acc. pl. neut. . . ἐπουράνιος
ἐπουράνιοι, nom. pl. masc. . . . id.
ἐπουρανίοις, dat. pl. neut. . . . id.
ἐπουράνιον, acc. sing. fem. . . . id.
ἐπουράνιος, ου, ὁ, ἡ, (§ 7. rem. 2) (ἐπί & οὐρανός) *heavenly,* in respect of locality, Ep. 1. 20; Phi. 2. 10, et al.; τὰ ἐπουράνια, *the upper regions* of the air, Ep. 6. 12; *heavenly,* in respect of essence and character, *unearthly,* 1 Co. 15. 48, 49, et al.; met. *divine, spiritual,* Jno. 3. 12, et al.
ἐπουρανίου, gen. sing. masc. and fem. . ἐπουράνιος
ἐπουρανίῳ, dat. sing. fem. . . . id.
ἐπουρανίων, gen. pl. . . . . id.
ἐπράθη, 3 pers. sing. aor. 1, pass. (§ 36. rem. 3) πιπράσκω
ἔπραξα, 1 pers. sing. aor. 1, ind. act. . πράσσω
ἐπράξαμεν, 1 pers. pl. aor. 1, ind. . . id.
ἔπραξαν, 3 pers. pl. aor. 1, ind. . . id.
ἐπράξατε, 2 pers. pl. aor. 1, ind. . . . id.
ἔπραξε, 3 pers. sing. aor. 1, ind. (§ 26. rem. 8) id.
ἔπρεπε, 3 pers. sing. imperf. . . . πρέπει
ἐπρίσθησαν,[d] 3 pers. pl. aor. 1, pass. (§ 22. rem. 4) πρίζω
ἐπροφήτευον, 3 pers. pl. imperf.—B. Ln. Tdf. } προφητεύω
προεφήτευον, Rec. Gr. Sch. (Ac. 19. 6)
ἐπροφητεύσαμεν, 1 pers. pl. aor. 1, ind.—C. Ln. Tdf. . . . } id.
προεφητεύσαμεν, R. Gr. Sch. (Mat. 7. 22)
ἐπροφήτευσαν, 3 pers. pl. aor. 1, ind.—Ln. Tdf. } id.
προεφήτευσαν, R. Gr. Sch. (Mat. 11. 13)
ἐπροφήτευσε, 3 pers. sing. aor. 1, ind.—C. D. Ln. Tdf. . . . } id.
προεφήτευσε, Rec. Gr. Sch. (Mat. 15. 7)

ἑπτά, οἱ, αἱ, τά, *seven,* Mat. 15. 34, 37, et al.; by Jewish usage for a round number, Mat. 12. 45; Lu. 11. 26.

ἑπτάκις, adv. *seven times,* Mat. 18. 21, 22; Lu. 17. 4, bis. (ᾰ).

ἕβδομος, η, ον, (§ 7. tab. F. a) *seventh,* Jno. 4. 52; He. 4. 4, et al.

[a] Ro. 2. 17. [b] 2 Pe. 1. 16. [c] He. 7. 9. [d] He. 11. 37.

ἑβδομήκοντα, οἱ, αἱ, τά, *seventy*, Ac. 7. 14, et al.; οἱ ἑβδομ. *the seventy* disciples, Lu. 10. 1, 17.

ἑβδομηκοντάκις, adv. *seventy times*, Mat. 18. 22. (ă).

ἔπταισαν, 3 pers. pl. aor. 1, ind. . . . πταίω

ἑπτάκις, adv. . . . . . . ἑπτά

ἑπτακισχίλιοι], αι, α, (ἑπτάκις & χίλιοι), *seven thousand*.

ἑπτακισχιλίους,[a] acc. pl. masc. . . ἑπτακισχίλιοι

ἔπτυσε, 3 pers. sing. aor. 1, ind. . . πτύω

ἐπτώχευσε,[b] 3 pers. sing. aor. 1, ind. . . πτωχεύω

ἐπύθετο, 3 pers. sing. aor. 2, ind. (§ 36. rem. 2) πυνθάνομαι

ἐπυνθάνετο, 3 pers. sing. imperf. . . id.

ἐπυνθάνοντο, 3 pers. pl. imperf. . . . id.

ἐπώκειλαν,[c] 3 pers. pl. aor. 1, ind. . . ἐποκέλλω

ἐπῳκοδόμησε, 3 pers. sing. aor. 1, ind. act. (§ 13. rem. 2) . . . ἐποικοδομέω

ἐπώλησε, 3 pers. sing. aor. 1, ind. act. . πωλέω

ἐπώλουν, 3 pers. pl. imperf. act. . . id.

ἐπωρώθη, 3 pers. sing. aor. 1, ind. pass. . πωρόω

ἐπωρώθησαν, 3 pers. pl. aor. 1, ind. pass. . id.

Ἔραστον, acc. sing. . . . . Ἔραστος

Ἔραστος, ου, ὁ, (§ 3. tab. C. a) *Erastus*, pr. name.

ἔργα, nom. and acc. pl. . . . . ἔργον

ἐργάζεσθαι, pres. infin. . . . . ἐργάζομαι

ἐργάζεσθε, 2 pers. pl. pres. ind. . . . id.

ἐργάζεσθε, 2 pers. pl. pres. imper. . . . id.

ἐργάζεται, 3 pers. sing. pres. ind. . . . id.

ἐργάζῃ, 2 pers. sing. pres. ind. . . . id.

ἐργάζομαι, fut. άσομαι . . . . ἔργον

ἐργαζόμεθα, 1 pers. pl. pres. ind.—A. Ln. ἐργαζώμεθα, R. Gr. Sch. Tdf. (Gal. 6. 10) } ἐργάζομαι

ἐργαζόμενοι, nom. pl. masc. part. pres. . id.

ἐργαζόμενος, nom. sing. masc. part. pres. . id.

ἐργαζομένους, acc. pl. masc. part. pres. id.

ἐργαζομένῳ, dat. sing. masc. part. pres. . id.

ἐργάζονται, 3 pers. pl. pres. ind. . . id.

ἐργάζου, 2 pers. sing. pres. imper. . . id.

ἐργαζώμεθα, 1 pers. pl. pres. subj. . . id.

ἐργάσῃ, 2 pers. sing. aor. 1, subj. . . . id.

ἐργασία], ας, ἡ, (§ 2. tab. B. b, and rem. 2) . ἔργον

ἐργασίαν, acc. sing. . . . . ἐργασία

ἐργασίας, gen. sing. . . . . id.

ἐργάται, nom. pl. . . . . ἐργάτης

ἐργάτας, acc. pl. . . . . id.

ἐργάτην, acc. sing. . . . . id.

ἐργάτης, ου, ὁ, (§ 2. tab. B. c) . . . ἔργον

ἐργατῶν, gen. pl. . . . . . ἐργάτης

ἔργοις, dat. pl . . . . ἔργον

ἔργον, ου, τό, (§ 3. tab. C. c) *anything done or to be done; a deed, work, action*, Jno. 3. 21; Ep. 2. 10; 2 Co. 9. 8, et al. freq.; *duty enjoined, office, charge, business*, Mar. 13. 34; Jno. 4. 34, et al. freq.; *a process, course of action*, Ja. 1. 4; *a work, product of an action or process*, Ac. 7. 41; He. 1. 10, et al.; *substance in effect*, Ro. 2. 15.

ἐργάζομαι, fut. άσομαι, aor. 1, εἰργασάμην, perf. εἴργασμαι, (§ 13. rem. 4) intrans. *to work, labour*, Mat. 21. 28; Lu. 13. 14; *to trade, traffic, do business*, Mat. 25. 16; Re. 18. 17; *to act, exert one's power, be active*, Jno. 5. 17; trans. *to do, perform, commit*, Mat. 26. 10; Jno. 6. 28; *to be engaged in, occupied upon*, 1 Co. 9. 13; Re. 18. 17; *to acquire, gain by one's labour*, Jno. 6. 27, et al.

ἐργᾰσία, ας, ἡ, (§ 2. tab. B. b, and rem. 2) *work, labour*; in N.T. ἐργασίαν διδόναι, *operam dare, to endeavour, strive*, Lu. 12. 58; *performance, practice*, Ep. 4. 19; *a trade, business, craft*, Ac. 19. 25; *gain* acquired by labour or trade, *profit*, Ac. 16. 16, 19; 19. 24, 25.

ἐργάτης, ου, ὁ, (§ 2. tab. B. c) *a workman, labourer*, Mat. 9. 37, 38; 20. 1, 2, 8; met. *a* spiritual *workman or labourer*, 2 Co. 11. 13, et al.; *an artisan, artificer*, Ac. 19. 25; *a worker, practiser*, Lu. 13. 27. (ă).

ἔργου, gen. sing. . . . . . ἔργον

ἔργῳ, dat. sing. . . . . . . id.

ἔργων, gen. pl. . . . . . . id.

ἐρεθίζετε, 2 pers. pl. pres. imper. . . ἐρεθίζω

ἐρεθίζω], fut. ίσω, aor. 1, ἠρέθισα, (§ 26. rem. 1) (ἐρέθω, idem, fr. ἔρις) *to provoke, to irritate, exasperate*, Col. 3. 21; *to incite, stimulate*, 2 Co. 9. 2.

ἐρεῖ, 3 pers. sing. fut. ind. . . . . εἴρω

ἐρείδω], fut. είσω, aor. 1, ἤρεισα, (§ 23. rem. 1. c) *to make to lean upon; to fix firmly*, intrans. *to become firmly fixed, stick fast*, Ac. 27. 41.

ἔρεις, nom. and acc. pl. (§ 4. rem. 4) . ἔρις

[a] Ro. 11. 4. [b] 2 Co. 8. 9. [c] Ac. 27. 41

ἐρεῖς, 2 pers. sing. fut. ind. . . . εἴρω
ἐρείσασα,[a] nom. sing. fem. part. aor. 1 . ἐρείδω
ἐρεῖτε, 2 pers. pl. fut. ind. . . . . εἴρω
ἐρεύγομαι], fut. ξομαι, (§ 23. rem. 1. b) *to vomit, disgorge;* met. *to utter, declare openly,* Mat. 13. 35.
ἐρευνᾷ, 3 pers. sing. pres. ind. . . ἐρευνάω
ἐρευνᾶτε, 2 pers. pl. pres. imper. . . id.
ἐρευνάω, ῶ], fut. ήσω, (§ 18. tab. R) *to search, trace, investigate, explore,* Jno. 5. 39; 7. 52, et al.
ἐρεύνησον, 2 pers. sing. aor. 1, imper. . ἐρευνάω
ἐρευνῶν, nom. sing. masc. part. pres. . id.
ἐρευνῶντες, nom. pl. masc. part. pres. . id.
ἐρεύξομαι,[b] 1 pers. sing. fut. ind. . . ἐρεύγομαι
ἐρημία], ας, ἡ, (§ 2. tab. B. b, and rem. 2) ἔρημος
ἐρημίᾳ, dat. sing. . . . . ἐρημία
ἐρημίαις, dat. pl. . . . . . id.
ἐρημίας, gen. sing. . . . . id.
ἐρήμοις, dat. pl. . . . . ἔρημος
ἔρημον, acc. sing. . . . . id.

ἔρημος, ου, ὁ, ἡ, & η, ον, (§ 7. rem. 2. and tab. F. a) *lone, desert, waste, uninhabited,* Mat. 14. 13, 15; Mar. 6. 31, 32, 35; *lone, abandoned* to ruin, Mat. 23. 38; Lu. 13. 35; met. *lone, unmarried,* Gal. 4. 27; as a subs. *a desert, uninhabited region, waste,* Mat. 3. 1; 24. 26; Ac. 7. 36, et al.

ἐρημία, ας, ἡ, *a solitude, uninhabited region, waste, desert,* Mat. 15. 33, et al.

ἐρημόω, ῶ, fut. ώσω, perf. pass. ἠρήμωμαι, aor. 1, pass. ἠρημώθην, (§§ 20. tab. T. 21. tab. U) *to lay waste, make desolate, bring to ruin,* Mat. 12. 25; Lu 11. 17; Re. 17. 16; 18. 16, 19.

ἐρήμωσις, εως, ἡ, ((§ 5. tab. E. c) *desolation, devastation,* Mat. 24. 15; Mar. 13. 14, et al. L.G

ἐρήμου, gen. sing. . . . . . ἔρημος
ἐρήμους, acc. pl. . . . . . id.
ἐρημοῦται, 3 pers. sing. pres. ind. pass. . ἐρημόω
ἐρημόω, ῶ], fut. ώσω, (§ 20. tab. T) . ἔρημος
ἐρήμῳ, dat. sing. . . . . . id.
ἐρημώσεως, gen. sing. . . . . ἐρήμωσις
ἐρήμωσις, εως, ἡ, (§ 5. tab. E. c) . . ἔρημος
ἔριδες, nom. pl. . . . . . ἔρις
ἔριδι, dat. sing. . . . . . id.
ἔριδος, gen. sing. . . . . . ἔρις
ἐρίζω], fut. ίσω, (§ 26. rem. 1) . . . id.
ἐρῑθεία, ας, ἡ, (§ 2. tab. B. b, and rem. 2) (ἐριθεύομαι, *to serve for hire, to serve a party,* fr. ἔρῑθος, *a hired labourer*) *the service of a party, party spirit; feud, faction,* 2 Co. 12. 20; *contentious disposition,* Ja. 3. 14, et al.; by impl. *untowardness, disobedience,* Ro. 2. 8.
ἐριθεῖαι, nom. pl. . . . . ἐριθεία
ἐριθείαν, acc. sing. . . . . . id.
ἐριθείας, gen. sing. . . . . id.
ἔριν, acc. sing. (§ 4. rem. 4) . . . ἔρις
ἔριον, ου, τό, (§ 3. tab. C. c) (ἔρος, εἶρος, idem) *wool,* He. 9. 19; Re. 1. 14.
ἐρίου, gen. sing. . . . . ἔριον

ἔρις, ῐδος, ἡ, (§ 4. rem. 2. c) *altercation, strife,* Ro. 13. 13; *contentious disposition,* Ro. 1. 29; Phi. 1. 15, et al.

ἐρίζω, fut. ίσω, (§ 26. rem. 1) *to quarrel; to wrangle; to use the harsh tone of a wrangler or brawler, to grate.*

ἐρίσει,[c] 3 pers. sing. fut. ind. . . . ἐρίζω
ἐρίφια,[d] acc. pl. . . . . . ἐρίφιον
ἐρίφιον], ου, τό, (§ 3. tab. C. a) . . . ἔριφος
ἔριφον, acc. sing. . . . . id.
ἔρῐφος], ου, ὁ, ἡ, ((§ 3. tab. C. a. b) *a goat, kid,* Mat. 25. 32; Lu. 15. 29.

ἐρίφιον, ου, τό, *a goat, kid,* Mat. 25. 33.

ἐρίφων, gen. pl. . . . . . ἔριφος
Ἑρμᾶν,[e] acc. sing.—Rec. Sch. . . } Ἑρμᾶς,
Ἑρμῆν, Gr. Tdf. . . . }
Ἑρμᾶς], ᾶ, ὁ, (§ 2. rem. 4) *Hermas,* pr. name.
Ἑρμῆν,[f] acc. sing. . . . . Ἑρμῆς
ἑρμηνεία, ας, ἡ, (§ 2. tab. B. b, and rem. 2) . ἑρμηνεύω
ἑρμηνείαν, acc. sing. . . . . ἑρμηνεία
ἑρμηνεύεται, 3 pers. sing. pres. ind. pass. . ἑρμηνεύω
ἑρμηνευόμενον, nom. s. neut. part. pres. pass. id.
ἑρμηνευόμενος, nom. s. masc. part. pres. pass. id.
ἑρμηνευτής, οῦ, ὁ, (§ 2. tab. B. c)—B. Ln. } id.
διερμηνευτής, R. Gr. Sch. Tdf. (1 Co. 14. 28) }
ἑρμηνεύω], fut. εύσω, (§ 13. tab. M) (ἑρμηνεύς, *an interpreter*) *to explain, interpret, translate,* Jno. 1. 39, 43; 9. 7; He. 7. 2.

ἑρμηνεία, ας, ἡ, (§ 2. tab. B. b, and rem. 2) *interpretation, explanation,* 1 Co.

[a] Ac. 27. 41. [b] Mat. 13. 35. [c] Mat. 12. 19. [d] Mat. 25. 33. [e] Ro. 16. 14. [f] Ac. 14. 12.

14. 26; meton. *the power or faculty of interpreting*, 1 Co. 12. 10.

ἑρμηνευτής, οῦ, ὁ, (§ 2. tab. B. c) *an interpreter*, v.r. 1 Co. 14. 28.

Ἑρμῆς], οῦ, ὁ, (§ 2. tab. B. c) *Hermes* or *Mercury*, son of Jupiter and Maia, the messenger and interpreter of the gods, and the patron of eloquence, learning, etc., Ac. 14. 12.

Ἑρμογένης,[a] εος, ους, ὁ, (§ 5. tab. E. a) *Hermogenes*, pr. name.

ἐροῦμεν, 1 pers. pl. fut. ind. . . . εἴρω
ἐροῦσι, 3 pers. pl. fut. ind. . . . id.
ἑρπετά, nom. and acc. pl. . . . ἑρπετόν

ἑρπετόν], οῦ, τό, (§ 3. tab. C. c) (ἕρπω, *to creep*) *a creeping animal, a reptile*, Ac. 10. 12, et al.

ἑρπετῶν, gen. pl. . . . ἑρπετόν
ἐῤῥαβδίσθην, 1 pers. sing. aor. 1, ind. pass. . ῥαβδίζω
ἐῤῥάντισε, 3 pers. sing. aor. 1, ind. act. . ῥαντίζω
ἐῤῥαντισμένοι, nom. pl. masc. part. perf. pass. id.
ἐῤῥάπισαν, 3 pers. pl. aor. 1, ind. act. . . ῥαπίζω
ἐῤῥέθη, 3 pers. sing. aor. 1, ind. pass. . ῥέω
ἐῤῥέθησαν, 3 pers. pl. aor. 1, ind. pass.—A. C. D. Ln. Tdf. . . }
ἐῤῥήθησαν, Rec. Gr. Sch. (Gal. 3. 16) } id.
ἐῤῥήθη, 3 pers. sing. aor. 1, ind. pass. . id.
ἐῤῥήθησαν, 3 pers. pl. aor. 1, ind. pass. . id.
ἔῤῥηξε, 3 pers. sing. aor. 1, ind. (§ 36. rem. 5) ῥήγνυμι
ἐῤῥιζωμένοι, nom. pl. masc. part. perf. pass. ῥιζόω
ἐῤῥιμμένοι, nom. pl. masc. part. perf. pass. ῥίπτω
ἔῤῥιπται, 3 pers. sing. perf. pass. (§ 13. rem. 6. b) id.
ἐῤῥίψαμεν, 1 pers. pl. aor. 1, ind. act. . id.
ἔῤῥιψαν, 3 pers. pl. aor. 1, ind. act. . . id.
ἐῤῥύσατο, 3 pers. sing. aor. 1, ind. mid. . ῥύω
ἐῤῥύσθην, 1 pers. sing. aor. 1, ind. pass. . id.
ἔῤῥωσθε, 2 pers. pl. perf. imper. pass. . ῥώννυμι
ἔῤῥωσο, 2 pers. sing. perf. imper. p. (§ 36. rem. 5) id.
ἐρυθρᾷ, dat. sing. fem. . . . . ἐρυθρός
ἐρυθράν, acc. sing. fem. . . . id.

ἐρυθρός], ά, όν, (§ 7. rem. 1) *red*, Ac. 7. 36; He. 11. 29.

ἔρχεσθαι, pres. infin. . . . . ἔρχομαι
ἔρχεσθε, 2 pers. pl. pres. imper. . . id.
ἐρχέσθω, 3 pers. sing. pres. imper. . . id.
ἔρχεται, 3 pers. sing. pres. ind. . . id.
ἔρχῃ, 2 pers. sing. pres. ind. . . . id.
ἔρχηται, 3 pers. sing. pres. subj. . . id.

ἔρχομαι, fut. ἐλεύσομαι, aor. 2, ἤλυθον, by sync. ἦλθον, perf. ἐλήλυθα, (§ 36. rem. 1) *to come, to go, to pass*. By the combination of this verb with other terms, a variety of meaning results, which, however, is due, not to a change of meaning in the verb, but to the adjuncts. Ὁ ἐρχόμενος, *He who is coming, the expected Messiah*, Mat. 11. 3, et al.

ἐρχόμεθα, 1 pers. pl. pres. ind. . . . ἔρχομαι
ἐρχόμενα, acc. pl. neut. part. pres. . id.
ἐρχομένη, nom. sing. fem. part. pres. . . id.
ἐρχομένην, acc. sing. fem. part. pres. . id.
ἐρχομένης, gen. sing. fem. part. pres. . . id.
ἐρχόμενοι, nom. pl. masc. part. pres. . id.
ἐρχόμενον, acc. sing. masc. and neut. part. pres. id.
ἐρχόμενος, nom. sing. masc. part. pres. . id.
ἐρχομένου, gen. sing. masc. part. pres. id.
ἐρχομένους, acc. pl. masc. part. pres. . . id.
ἐρχομένῳ, dat. sing. masc. and neut. part. pres. id.
ἐρχομένων, gen. pl. part. pres. . . id.
ἔρχονται, 3 pers. pl. pres. ind. . . . id.
ἔρχου, 2 pers. sing. pres. imper. . . id.
ἔρχωμαι, 1 pers. sing. pres. subj. . . id.
ἐρῶ, 1 pers. sing. fut. ind. . . εἴρω
ἐρωτᾷ, 3 pers. sing. pres. ind. . . . ἐρωτάω
ἐρωτᾷ, 3 pers. sing. pres. subj. . . id.
ἐρωτᾶν, pres. infin. . . . . . . id.
ἐρωτᾷς, 2 pers. sing. pres. ind.—A. B. C. Ln. Tdf. }
ἐπερωτᾷς, Rec. Gr. Sch. (Jno. 18. 21) } id.

ἐρωτάω, ῶ], fut. ήσω, (§ 18. tab. R) *to ask, interrogate, inquire of*, Mat. 21. 24; Lu. 20. 3; in N.T. *to ask, request, beg, beseech*, Mat. 15. 23; Lu. 4. 38; Jno. 14. 16, et al.

ἐρωτῆσαι, aor. 1, infin. . . . . ἐρωτάω
ἐρωτήσατε, 2 pers. pl. aor. 1, imper. . id.
ἐρωτήσετε, 2 pers. pl. fut. ind. . . . id.
ἐρωτήσῃ, 3 pers. sing. aor. 1, subj. . . id.
ἐρώτησον, 2 pers. sing. aor. 1, imper.—B. C. Ln. Tdf. . . . }
ἐπερώτησον, Rec. Gr. Sch. (Jno. 18. 21) } id.
ἐρωτήσω, 1 pers. sing. fut. ind. . . id.
ἐρωτήσω, 1 pers. sing. aor. 1, subj. . . id.
ἐρωτήσωσι, 3 pers. pl. aor. 1, subj. . . id.
ἐρωτῶ, 1 pers. sing. pres. ind. . . . id.
ἐρωτῶμεν, 1 pers. pl. pres. ind. . . id.
ἐρωτῶν, nom. sing. masc. part. pres. . . id.
ἐρωτῶντες, nom. pl. masc. part. pres. . id.

[a] 2 Ti. 1. 15.

ἐρωτώντων, gen. pl. masc. part. pres. . . ἐρωτάω

ἐσαλεύθη, 3 pers. sing. aor. 1, pass. (§ 14. tab. N) σαλεύω

ἐσάλευσε, 3 pers. sing. aor. 1, ind. act. . id.

ἐσάλπισε, 3 pers. sing. aor. 1, ind. . . σαλπίζω

ἔσβεσαν, 3 pers. pl. aor. 1, ind. (§ 36. rem. 5) σβέννυμι

ἐσεβάσθησαν,[a] 3 pers. pl. aor. 1, ind. (§ 26. rem. 1) σεβάζομαι

ἐσείσθη, 3 pers. sing. aor. 1, ind. pass. . σειω

ἐσείσθησαν, 3 pers. pl. aor. 1, pass. (§ 22. rem. 4) id.

ἔσεσθαι, fut. infin. . . . . . . εἰμί

ἔσεσθε, 2 pers. pl. fut. ind. . . . id.

ἔσῃ, 2 pers. sing. fut. ind. . . id.

ἐσήμᾶνε, 3 pers. sing. aor. 1, ind. (§ 27. rem. 1. e) σημαίνω

ἐσθήσεσι,[b] dat. pl. . . . ἔσθησις

ἐσθής], ῆτος, ἡ, (§ 4. rem. 2. c) (ἕννυμι, *to clothe*) *a robe, vestment, raiment,* Lu. 23. 11; Ac. 1. 10, et al.

ἔσθησις], εως, ἡ, (§ 5. tab. E. c) *a garment, robe, raiment.* L.G.

ἐσθῆτα, acc. sing. . . . . . . ἐσθής

ἔσθητε, 2 pers. pl. pres. subj.—B. D. Ln. Tdf.; ἐσθίητε, Rec. Gr. Sch. (Lu. 22. 30) } ἔσθω

ἐσθῆτι, dat. sing. . . . . . ἐσθής

ἐσθίει, 2 pers. sing. pres. ind. . . . ἐσθίω

ἐσθίειν, pres. infin. . . . . . id.

ἐσθίετε, 2 pers. pl. pres. imper. . . . id.

ἐσθιέτω, 3 pers. sing. pres. imper. . . id.

ἐσθίῃ, 3 pers. sing. pres. subj. . . . id.

ἐσθίητε, 2 pers. pl. pres. subj. . . . id.

ἐσθίοντα, acc. sing. masc. part. pres. . . id.

ἐσθίοντας, acc. pl. masc. part. pres. . id.

ἐσθίοντες, nom. pl. masc. part. pres. . . id.

ἐσθίοντι, dat. sing. masc. part. pres. . id.

ἐσθιόντων, gen. pl. masc. part. pres. . . id.

ἐσθίουσι, 3 pers. pl. pres. ind. . . id.

ἐσθίω], fut. ἔδομαι, and in N.T. φάγομαι, εσαι, aor. 2, ἔφᾰγον, (§ 36. rem. 1) (ἔδω) *to eat,* Mat. 12. 1; 15. 27; ἐσθίειν καὶ πίνειν, *to eat and drink, to eat and drink* in the usual manner, *follow the common mode of living,* Mat. 11. 18; also with the associated notion of supposed security, Lu. 17. 27; *to feast, banquet,* Mat. 24. 49; met. *to devour, consume,* He. 10. 27; Ja. 5. 3; from the Heb. ἄρτον ἐσθίειν, *to eat bread, to take food, take the usual meals,* Mat. 15. 2, et al.

ἐσθίων, nom. sing. masc. part. pres. . . ἐσθίω

ἐσθίωσι, 3 pers. pl. pres. subj. . . . id.

ἔσθοντες, nom. pl. masc. part. pres.—B. D. Ln. Tdf. . . . . ; ἐσθίοντες, Rec. Gr. Sch. (Lu. 10. 7) } ἔσθω

ἔσθω], equivalent to ἐσθίω. v.r.

ἔσθων, nom. sing. masc. part. pres.—B. D. Ln. Tdf. . . . . ; ἐσθίων, Rec. Gr. Sch. (Lu. 7. 33) . } ἔσθω

ἐσίγησαν, 3 pers. pl. aor. 1, ind. . . . σιγάω

ἐσίγησε, 3 pers. sing. aor. 1, ind. . . id.

ἐσιώπα, 3 pers. sing. imperf. . . . σιωπάω

ἐσιώπων, 3 pers. pl. imperf. . . . id.

ἐσκανδαλίζοντο, 3 pers. pl. imperf. pass. σκανδαλίζω

ἐσκανδαλίσθησαν, 3 pers. pl. aor. 1, pass. . id.

ἔσκαψε, 3 pers. sing. aor. 1, ind. . . σκάπτω

ἐσκήνωσε, 3 pers. sing. aor. 1, ind. . . σκηνόω

ἐσκίρτησε, 3 pers. sing. aor. 1, ind. . . σκιρτάω

ἐσκληρύνοντο, 3 pers. pl. imperf. pass. . σκληρύνω

ἐσκόρπισε, 3 pers. sing. aor. 1, ind. . σκορπίζω

ἐσκοτίσθη, 3 pers. sing. aor. 1, ind. pass. . σκοτίζω

ἐσκοτισμένοι, nom. pl. masc. part. perf. pass. id.

ἐσκοτωμένη,[c] nom. sing. fem. part. perf. pass. σκοτόω

ἐσκοτωμένοι, nom. pl. masc. part. perf. pass.—A. Ln. Tdf. . . . . ; ἐσκοτισμένοι, Rec. Gr. Sch. (Ep. 4. 18) } id.

ἐσκυλμένοι, nom. pl. masc. part. perf. pass.—Gr. Sch. Tdf. . . . ; ἐκλελυμένοι, Rec. (Mat. 9. 36) . } σκύλλω

Ἐσλί,[d] ὁ, *Esli,* pr. name, indecl.

ἐσμέν, 1 pers. pl. pres. ind. . . . εἰμί

ἐσμυρνισμένον,[e] acc. sing. masc. part. perf. pass. σμυρνίζω

ἔσομαι, 1 pers. sing. fut. ind. . . εἰμί

ἐσόμεθα, 1 pers. pl. fut. ind. . . . id.

ἐσόμενον, acc. sing. neut. part. fut. . id.

ἔσονται, 3 pers. pl. fut. ind. . . id.

ἔσοπτρον], ου, τό, (§ 3. tab. C. c) (ὄψομαι) *a mirror, speculum,* Ja. 1. 23; 1 Co. 13. 12.

ἐσόπτρου, gen. sing. . . . . ἔσοπτρον

ἐσόπτρῳ, dat. sing. . . . . . id.

ἐσπάραξε, 3 pers. sing. aor. 1, ind. (§ 26. rem. 3) σπαράσσω

ἐσπαργανωμένον, acc. sing. neut. part. perf. pass. σπαργανόω

ἐσπαργάνωσε, 3 pers. sing. aor. 1, ind. act. . id.

ἐσπαρμένον, acc. sing. neut. part. perf. pass. (§ 27. rem. 3) . . . . σπείρω

ἐσπαταλήσατε, 2 pers. pl. aor. 1, ind. . . σπαταλάω

ἔσπειρα, 1 pers. sing. aor. 1, ind. act. . σπείρω

ἐσπείραμεν, 1 pers. pl. aor. 1, ind. act. . . id.

ἔσπειρας, 2 pers. sing. aor. 1, ind. act. . id.

ἔσπειρε, 3 pers. sing. aor. 1, ind. act. . . id.

[a] Ro. 1. 25. [b] Lu. 24. 4. [c] Re. 16. 10. [d] Lu. 3. 25. [e] Mar. 15. 23.

ἔσπειρες, 2 pers. sing. imperf. act.—C. D.
ἔσπειρας, Rec. Gr. Sch. Tdf. (Mat. 13. 27) } σπείρω

ἑσπέρα, ας, ἡ, (§ 2. tab. B. b, and rem. 2) (fem. of ἕσπερος) *evening,* Lu. 24. 29; Ac. 4. 3; 28. 23.

ἑσπέραν, acc. sing. ἑσπέρα

ἑσπέρας, gen. sing. id.

ἔσπευδε, 3 pers. sing. imperf. σπεύδω

ἐσπιλωμένον, acc. sing. masc. part. perf. pass. (§ 21. tab. U) σπιλόω

ἐσπλαγχνίσθη, 3 pers. s. aor. 1, ind. pass. σπλαγχνίζομαι

ἐσπούδασα, 1 pers. sing. aor. 1, ind. σπουδάζω

ἐσπουδάσαμεν, 1 pers. pl. aor. 1, ind. id.

Ἐσρώμ, ὁ, *Esrom,* pr. name, indecl.

ἐστάθη, 3 pers. s. aor. 1, ind. pass. (§ 29. rem. 6) ἵστημι

ἐστάθην, 1 pers. sing. aor. 1, ind. pass. id.

ἔσται, 3 pers. sing. fut. ind. (§ 12. tab. L) εἰμί

ἑστάναι, perf. infin. (§ 35. rem. 8) ἵστημι

ἐσταυρώθη, 3 pers. sing. aor. 1, ind. pass. σταυρόω

ἐσταυρωμένον, acc. sing. masc. part. perf. pass. id.

ἐσταυρωμένος, nom. sing. masc. part. perf. pass. id.

ἐσταύρωσαν, 3 pers. pl. aor. 1, ind. act. id.

ἐσταυρώσατε, 2 pers. pl. aor. 1, ind. act. id.

ἐσταύρωται, 3 pers. sing. perf. ind. pass. id.

ἐστέ, 2 pers. pl. pres. ind. (§ 12. tab. L) εἰμί

ἐστέναξε, 3 pers. sing. aor. 1, ind. στενάζω

ἐστερεοῦντο, 3 pers. pl. imperf. pass. (§ 21. tab. U) στερεόω

ἐστερεώθησαν, 3 pers. pl. aor. 1, ind. pass. id.

ἐστερέωσε, 3 pers. sing. aor. 1, ind. act. id.

ἐστεφανωμένον, acc. sing. masc. part. perf. pass. στεφανόω

ἐστεφάνωσας, 2 pers. sing. aor. 1, ind. act. id.

ἔστη, 3 pers. sing. aor. 2, ind. (§ 29. rem. 1. 5) ἵστημι

ἕστηκα, 1 pers. sing. perf. ind. (§ 38. rem. 2) id.

ἑστήκαμεν, 1 pers. pl. perf. ind. (§ 29. rem. 4. 5) id.

ἕστηκας, 2 pers. sing. perf. ind. id.

ἑστήκασι, 3 pers. pl. perf. ind. id.

ἕστηκε, 3 pers. sing. perf. ind. id.

ἑστήκεσαν, 3 pers. pl. pluperf. Att. for εἱστήκεισαν, (§ 29. rem. 4. 5) id.

ἑστηκός, nom. sing. neut. part. perf. id.

ἑστηκότες, nom. pl. masc. part. perf. id.

ἑστηκότων, gen. pl. masc. part. perf. id.

ἑστηκώς, nom. sing. masc. part. perf. id.

ἐστηριγμένους, acc. pl. masc. part. perf. pass. στηρίζω

ἐστήρικται, 3 pers. sing. perf. pass. (§ 26. rem. 2) id.

ἐστήριξε, 3 pers. sing. aor. 1, ind. act. id.

ἔστησαν, 3 pers. pl. aor. 1, ind. (§ 29. rem. 5) ἵστημι

ἔστησαν, 3 pers. pl. aor. 2, ind. ἵστημι

ἔστησε, 3 pers. sing. aor. 1, ind. id.

ἐστί, 3 pers. sing. pres. ind. εἰμί

ἑστός, acc. sing. neut. part. perf.—B. Ln. Tdf.
ἑστώς, Rec. Gr. Sch. (Mat. 24. 15) } ἵστημι

ἐστράφη, 3 pers. s. aor. 2, pass. (§ 24. rem. 10) στρέφω

ἐστράφησαν, 3 pers. pl. aor. 2, ind. pass. id.

ἔστρεψε, 3 pers. sing. aor. 1, ind. act. id.

ἐστρηνίασε, 3 pers. sing. aor. 1, ind. στρηνιάω

ἐστρωμένον, acc. sing. neut. part. perf. pass. (§ 36. rem. 5) στρώννυμι

ἐστρώννυον, 3 pers. pl. imperf. act. στρωννύω

ἔστρωσαν, 3 pers. pl. aor. 1, ind. act. id.

ἔστω, 3 pers. sing. pres. imper. (§ 12. tab. L) εἰμί

ἑστώς, nom. sing. masc. and acc. neut. part. perf. (§ 35. rem. 8) ἵστημι

ἑστῶσα, nom. sing. fem. part. perf. id.

ἑστῶσαι, nom. pl. fem. part. perf. id.

ἔστωσαν, 3 pers. pl. pres. imper. (§ 12. tab. L) εἰμί

ἑστῶτα, acc. sing. masc. and pl. neut. part. perf. ἵστημι

ἑστῶτας, acc. pl. masc. part. perf. id.

ἑστῶτες, nom. pl. masc. part. perf. id.

ἑστῶτος, gen. sing. masc. part. perf. id.

ἑστώτων, gen. pl. masc. part. perf. id.

ἐσυκοφάντησα, 1 pers. sing. aor. 1, ind. συκοφαντέω

ἐσύλησα,[a] 1 pers. sing. aor. 1, ind. (§ 18. tab. R) συλάω

ἔσυρον, 3 pers. pl. imperf. σύρω

ἐσφάγης, 2 pers. sing. aor. 2, pass. (§ 26. rem. 3) σφάζω σφάττω

ἐσφαγμένην, acc. sing. fem. part. perf. pass. id.

ἐσφαγμένον, nom. sing. neut. part. perf. pass. id.

ἐσφαγμένου, gen. sing. neut. part. perf. pass. id.

ἐσφαγμένων, gen. pl. part. perf. pass. id.

ἔσφαξε, 3 pers. sing. aor. 1, ind. act. id.

ἐσφράγισε, 3 pers. sing. aor. 1, ind. act. σφραγίζω

ἐσφραγίσθητε, 2 pers. pl. aor. 1, ind. pass. id.

ἐσφραγισμένοι, nom. pl. masc. part. perf. pass. id.

ἐσφραγισμένων, gen. pl. part. p. pass. (§ 26. rem. 1) id.

ἔσχατα, nom. and acc. pl. neut. ἔσχατος

ἐσχάταις, dat. pl. fem. id.

ἐσχάτας, acc. pl. fem. id.

ἐσχάτη, nom. sing. fem. id.

ἐσχάτῃ, dat. sing. fem. id.

ἔσχατοι, nom. pl. masc. id.

ἔσχατον, acc. sing. masc. and nom. neut. id.

ἔσχατος, η, ον, (§ 8. rem. 6) *farthest; last, latest,*

[a] 2 Co. 11. 8.

Mat. 12. 45; Mar. 12. 6; *lowest*, Mat. 19. 30; 20. 16, et al.; *in the lowest plight*, 1 Co. 4. 9.

ἐσχατως, adv. *extremely*; ἐσχάτως ἔχειν, *to be in the last extremity*, Mar. 5. 23.

ἐσχάτου, gen. sing. neut. . . . . ἔσχατος

ἐσχάτους, acc. pl. masc. . . . . id.

ἐσχάτῳ, dat. sing. masc. . . . id.

ἐσχάτων, gen. pl. . . . . . id.

ἐσχάτως,[a] adv. . . . . . id.

ἔσχε, 3 pers. sing. aor. 2, ind. (§ 36. rem. 4) . ἔχω

ἔσχες, 2 pers. sing. aor. 2, ind. . . id.

ἔσχηκα, 1 pers. sing. perf. ind. . . . id.

ἐσχήκαμεν, 1 pers. pl. perf. ind. . . id.

ἔσχηκε, 3 pers. sing. perf. ind. . . . id.

ἐσχηκότα, acc. sing. masc. part. perf. . . id.

ἐσχίσθη, 3 pers. sing. aor. 1, pass. (§ 26. rem. 1) σχίζω

ἐσχίσθησαν, 3 pers. pl. aor. 1, ind. pass. . id.

ἔσχομεν, 1 pers. pl. aor. 2, ind. . . . ἔχω

ἔσχον, 1 pers. sing. or 3 pers. pl. aor. 2, ind. id.

ἔσω, adv. for the more usual form εἴσω, *in, within, in the interior of*, Mat. 26. 58, Jno. 20. 26, et al.; ὁ, ἡ, τό ἔσω, *inner, interior, internal*; met. *within* the pale of community, 1 Co. 5. 12; ὁ ἔσω ἄνθρωπος, *the inner man, the mind, soul*, Ro. 7. 22.

ἔσωθεν, adv. *from within, from the interior*, Mar. 7. 21, 23; *within, in the internal parts*, Mat. 7. 15, et al.; ὁ, ἡ, τό ἔσωθεν, *interior, internal*, Lu. 11. 39, 40; ὁ ἔσωθεν ἄνθρωπος, *the mind, soul*, 2 Co. 4. 16.

ἐσώτερος, α, ον, (§ 7. rem. 1) *inner, interior*, Ac. 16. 24; He. 6. 19.

ἐσώζοντο, 3 pers. pl. imperf. pass. . . σώζω

ἔσωθεν, adv. . . . . ἔσω

ἐσώθη, 3 pers. sing. aor. 1, ind. pass. (§ 37. rem. 1) σώζω

ἐσώθημεν, 1 pers. pl. aor. 1, ind. pass. . id.

ἔσωσε, 3 pers. sing. aor. 1, ind. act. . . id.

ἐσωτέραν, acc. sing. fem. . . . ἐσώτερος

ἐσώτερον, acc. sing. neut. . . . . id.

ἐσώτερος], α, ον, (§ 7. rem. 1) . . ἔσω

ἑταῖρε, voc. sing. . . . . . ἑταῖρος

ἑταίροις, dat. pl. . . . . . id.

ἑταῖρος], ου, ὁ, (§ 3. tab. C. a) *a companion, associate, fellow-comrade, friend*, Mat. 11. 16; 20. 13; 22. 12; 26. 50.

ἔταξαν, 3 pers. pl. aor. 1, ind. act. . . τάσσω

ἐτάξατο, 3 pers. sing. aor. 1, ind. mid. . τάσσω

ἐταπείνωσε, 3 pers. sing. aor. 1, ind. act. . ταπεινόω

ἐτάραξαν, 3 pers. pl. aor. 1, ind. act. . ταράσσω

ἐτάραξε, 3 pers. sing. aor. 1, ind. act. . . id.

ἐτάρασσε, 3 pers. sing. imperf. act. . id.

ἐταράχθη, 3 pers. sing. aor. 1, ind. pass. . id.

ἐταράχθησαν, 3 pers. pl. aor. 1, ind. pass. . id.

ἐτάφη, 3 pers. sing. aor. 2, pass. (§ 24. rem. 8. b) θάπτω

ἐτέθη, 3 pers. sing. aor. 1, pass. (§ 28. rem. 10) τίθημι

ἐτέθην, 1 pers. sing. aor. 1, ind. pass. . . id.

ἐτέθησαν, 3 pers. pl. aor. 1, ind. pass. . id.

ἐτεθνήκει, 3 pers. sing. pluperf. (§ 36. rem. 4) θνήσκω

ἔτει, dat. sing. . . . . . . ἔτος

ἔτεκε, 3 pers. sing. aor. 2, ind. (§ 37. rem. 1) . τίκτω

ἐτεκνοτρόφησε,[b] 3 pers. sing. aor. 1, ind. τεκνοτροφέω

ἐτελειώθη, 3 pers. sing. aor. 1, pass. (§ 21. tab. U) τελειόω

ἐτελείωσα, 1 pers. sing. aor. 1, act. (§ 20. tab. T) id.

ἐτελείωσε, 3 pers. sing. aor. 1, ind. act. . id.

ἐτέλεσαν, 3 pers. pl. aor. 1, ind. act. . τελέω

ἐτέλεσε, 3 pers. sing. aor. 1, ind. act. . . id.

ἐτελέσθη, 3 pers. sing. aor. 1, pass. (§ 22. rem. 4) id.

ἐτελεύτησε, 3 pers. sing. aor. 1, ind. . τελευτάω

ἑτέρα, nom. sing. fem. . . . . . ἕτερος

ἑτέρᾳ, dat. sing. fem. . . . . id.

ἕτερα, nom. or acc. pl. neut. . . . id.

ἕτεραι, nom. pl. fem. . . . . id.

ἑτέραις, dat. pl. fem. . . . . id.

ἑτέραν, acc. sing. fem. . . . . id.

ἑτέρας, gen. sing. fem. . . . . id.

ἑτερογλώσσοις,[c] dat. pl. . . ἑτερόγλωσσος

ἑτερόγλωσσος], ου, ὁ, ἡ, (§ 7. rem. 2) (ἕτερος & γλῶσσα) *one who speaks another or foreign language*. L.G.

ἑτεροδιδασκαλεῖ, 3 pers. sing. pres. ind. ἑτεροδιδασκαλέω

ἑτεροδιδασκαλεῖν, pres. infin. . . . id.

ἑτεροδιδασκᾰλέω, ῶ], fut. ήσω, (§ 16. tab. P) ἕτερος & διδασκαλία) *to teach other or different doctrine*, and spc. *what is foreign to the Christian religion*, 1 Ti. 1. 3; 6. 3. N.T.

ἑτεροζυγέω, ῶ], (ἕτερος & ζυγέω) *to be unequally yoked or matched*.

ἑτεροζῠγοῦντες,[d] nom. pl. masc. part. pres. ἑτεροζυγέω

ἕτεροι, nom. pl. masc. . . . . ἕτερος

ἑτέροις, dat. pl. masc. and. neut. . . id.

ἕτερον, nom. neut. and acc. masc. sing. . id.

ἕτερος, α, ον, (§ 10. rem. 6. b) *other*, Mat.

a Mar. 5. 23. b 1 Ti. 5. 10. c 1 Co. 14. 21. d 2 Co. 6. 14.

12. 45, et al.; *another, some other,* Mat. 8. 21, et al.; *besides,* Lu. 23. 32; ὁ ἕτερος, *the other* of two, Mat. 6. 24; τῇ ἑτέρᾳ, *on the next* day, Ac. 20. 15; 27. 3; ὁ ἕτερος, *one's neighbour,* Ro. 13. 8, et al.; *different,* Lu. 9. 29, et al.; *foreign, strange,* Ac. 2. 4; 1 Co. 14. 21; *illicit,* Jude 7.

ἑτέρως, adv. *otherwise, differently,* Phi. 3. 15.

ἑτέρου, gen. sing. masc. . . . . . ἕτερος
ἑτέρους, acc. pl. masc. . . . . . id.
ἑτέρῳ, dat. sing. masc. and neut. . . id.
ἑτέρων, gen. pl. . . . . . id.
ἑτέρως,[a] adv. . . . . id.
ἔτεσι, dat. pl. . . . . . . ἔτος
ἐτέχθη, 3 pers. sing. aor. 1, pass. (§ 37. rem. 1) τίκτω
ἔτη, nom. and acc. pl. . . . . . ἔτος
ἐτηρεῖτο, 3 pers. sing. imperf. pass. (§ 17. tab. Q) τηρέω
ἐτήρησα, 1 pers. sing. aor. 1, ind. act. . id.
ἐτήρησαν, 3 pers. pl. aor. 1, ind. act. . . id.
ἐτήρησας, 2 pers. sing. aor. 1, ind. act. . id.
ἐτήρουν, 1 pers. sing. or 3 pers. pl. imperf. act. id.

ἔτι, adv. *yet, still,* Mat. 12. 46; *still, further, longer,* Lu. 16. 2; *further, besides, in addition,* Mat. 18. 16; with a compar. *yet, still,* Phi. 1. 9.

ἐτίθει, (ῐ), 3 pers. sing. imperf. act. (§ 31. rem. 2) τίθημι
ἐτίθουν, (ῐ), 3 pers. pl. imperf. act. . . id.
ἔτιλλον, 3 pers. pl. imperf. act. . . τίλλω
ἐτίμησαν, 3 pers. pl. aor. 1, ind. act. . . τιμάω
ἐτιμήσαντο, 3 pers. pl. aor. 1, ind. mid. . id.
ἕτοιμα, nom. and acc. pl. neut. . . . ἕτοιμος
ἑτοίμαζε, 2 pers. sing. pres. imper. act. . ἑτοιμάζω
ἑτοιμάζω], fut. άσω, (§ 26. rem. 1) . . ἕτοιμος
ἑτοιμάσαι, aor. 1, infin. act. . . . ἑτοιμάζω
ἑτοιμάσας, nom. sing. masc. part. aor. 1, act. id.
ἑτοιμάσατε, 2 pers. pl. aor. 1, imper. act. . id.
ἑτοιμασθῇ, 3 pers. sing. aor. 1, subj. pass. . id.
ἑτοιμασία], ας, ἡ, (§ 2. tab. B. b, and rem. 2) ἕτοιμος
ἑτοιμασίᾳ,[b] dat. sing. . . . . . ἑτοιμασία
ἑτοιμάσομεν, 1 pers. pl. fut. ind. act.—D. ἑτοιμάσωμεν, Rec. Gr. Sch. Tdf. (Mat. 26. 17) . . . ἑτοιμάζω
ἑτοίμασον, 2 pers. sing. aor. 1, imper. act. . id.
ἑτοιμάσω, 1 pers. sing. aor. 1, subj. act. . id.
ἑτοιμάσωμεν, 1 pers. pl. aor. 1, subj. act. . id.
ἑτοίμην, acc. sing. fem. . . . ἕτοιμος
ἕτοιμοι, nom. pl. masc. and fem. . . . id.

ἕτοιμον, acc. sing. neut. . . . . ἕτοιμος

ἕτοιμος, η, ον, also ἑτοῖμος, ου, ὁ, ἡ, *ready, prepared,* Mat. 22. 4, 8; Mar. 14. 15, et al.

ἑτοιμάζω, fut. άσω, (§ 26. rem. 1) *to make ready, prepare,* Mat. 22. 4; 26. 17, et al.

ἑτοιμασία, ας, ἡ, (§ 2. tab. B. b, and rem. 2) *preparation; preparedness, readiness, alacrity,* Ep. 6. 15.

ἑτοίμως, adv. *in readiness, preparedly.* Ac. 21. 13, et al.

ἑτοίμους, acc. pl. masc. . . . . ἕτοιμος
ἑτοίμῳ, dat. sing. neut. . . . . id.
ἑτοίμως, adv. . . . . . . id.
ἐτόλμα, 3 pers. sing. imperf. (§ 18. tab. R) τολμάω
ἐτόλμησε, 3 pers. sing. aor. 1, ind. . . id.
ἐτόλμων, 3 pers. pl. imperf. . . . id.

ἔτος, εος, ους, τό, (§ 5. tab. E. b) *a year,* Lu. 2. 41; 3. 23, et al.

ἐτρέχετε, 2 pers. pl. imperf. . . . τρέχω
ἔτρεχον, 3 pers. pl. imperf. . . . id.
ἐτροποφόρησε,[c] 3 pers. sing. aor. 1, ind. . τροποφορέω
ἐτροφοφόρησε, 3 pers. sing. aor. 1, ind.—A. C. Gr. Sch. Tdf. ἐτροποφόρησε, Rec. (Ac. 13. 18) τροφοφορέω
ἐτρύγησε, 3 pers. sing. aor. 1, ind. . . τρυγάω
ἐτρυφήσατε,[d] 2 pers. pl. aor. 1, ind. . τρυφάω
ἐτύθη, 3 pers. sing. aor. 1, ind. pass. (§ 14. tab. N) θύω
ἐτυμπανίσθησαν,[e] 3 pers. pl. aor. 1, ind. pass. τυμπανίζω
ἔτυπτε, 3 pers. sing. imperf. act. . . . τύπτω
ἔτυπτον, 2 pers. pl. imperf. act. . . id.
ἐτύφλωσε, 3 pers. sing. aor. 1, ind. act. . τυφλόω
ἐτῶν, gen. pl. . . . . . . ἔτος

εὖ, adv. *well, good, happily, rightly,* Mar. 14. 7; Ac. 15. 29; *well! well done!* Mat. 25. 21, 23, et al.

Εὖα, ας, ἡ, *Eva, Eve,* pr. name.
εὐαγγελίζεσθαι, pres. infin. mid. εὐαγγελίζω
εὐαγγελίζεται, 3 pers. sing. pres. ind. p. and mid. id.
εὐαγγελίζηται, 3 pers. sing. pres. subj. mid. id.
εὐαγγελίζομαι, 1 pers. sing. pres. ind. mid. id.
εὐαγγελιζόμεθα, 1 pers. pl. pres. ind. mid. id.
εὐαγγελιζόμενοι, nom. pl. masc. part. pr. mid. id.
εὐαγγελιζόμενος, nom. sing. masc. part. pr. mid. id.
εὐαγγελιζομένου, gen. sing. masc. part. pres. mid. id.
εὐαγγελιζομένῳ, dat. sing. masc. part. pres. mid. id.

a Phi. 3. 15. b Ep. 6. 15. c Ac. 13. 18. d Ja. 5. 5. e He. 11. 35.

εὐαγγελιζομένων, gen. pl. part. pres. mid. — εὐαγγελίζω
εὐαγγελίζονται, 3 pers. pl. pres. ind. pass. — id.
εὐαγγελίζω], fut. ίσω, (§ 26. rem. 1) . — εὐαγγέλιον
εὐαγγελίζωμαι, 1 pers. sing. pres. subj. mid. — εὐαγγελίζω
εὐαγγέλιον, ου, τό, (§ 3. tab. C. c) (εὖ & ἄγγελος) *glad tidings, good or joyful news,* Mat. 4. 23; 9. 35; *the Gospel, doctrines of the Gospel,* Mat. 26. 13; Mar. 8. 35; meton. *the preaching of, or instruction in, the Gospel,* 1 Co. 4. 15; 9. 14, et al.

εὐαγγελίζω, fut. ίσω, (§ 26. rem. 1) *to address with good tidings,* Re. 10. 7; 14. 6; but elsewhere mid. εὐαγγελίζομαι, *to proclaim as good tidings, to announce good tidings of,* Lu. 1. 19, et al.; *to address with good tidings,* Ac. 13. 32; 14. 15; *to address with Gospel teaching, evangelise,* Ac. 16. 10; Gal. 1. 9; absol. *to announce the good tidings* of the Gospel, Lu. 4. 18; 9. 6, et al.; pass. *to be announced as good tidings,* Lu. 16. 16; *to be addressed with good tidings,* Mat. 11. 5; Lu. 7. 22; He. 4. 2.

εὐαγγελιστής, οῦ, ὁ, (§ 2. tab. B. c) pr. *one who announces glad tidings; an evangelist, preacher of the Gospel, teacher of the Christian religion,* Ac. 21. 8; Ep. 4. 11; 2 Ti. 4. 5. N.T.

εὐαγγελίου, gen. sing. . . . . — εὐαγγέλιον
εὐαγγελίσαι, aor. 1, infin. act. . . — εὐαγγελίζω
εὐαγγελισαμένου, gen. s. masc. part. aor. 1, mid. — id.
εὐαγγελισαμένων, gen. pl. part. aor. 1, mid. — id.
εὐαγγελίσασθαι, aor. 1, infin. mid. . . — id.
εὐαγγελισθέν, nom. or acc. sing. neut. part. aor. 1, pass. . . . . — id.
εὐαγγελισθέντες, nom. pl. masc. part. aor. 1, pass. — id.
εὐαγγελιστάς, acc. pl. . . . — εὐαγγελιστής
εὐαγγελιστής], οῦ, ὁ, (§ 2. tab. B. c) . — εὐαγγελίζω
εὐαγγελιστοῦ, gen. sing. . . . — εὐαγγελιστής
εὐαγγελίῳ, dat. sing. . . . — εὐαγγέλιον
Εὖαν, acc. sing. . . . . . — Εὖα
εὐαρεστεῖται, 3 pers. sing. pres. pass. (§ 17. tab. Q) — εὐαρεστέω
εὐαρεστέω, ῶ], fut. ήσω, (§ 16. tab. P) . — εὐάρεστος
εὐαρεστηκέναι, perf. infin.—A. Ln. Tdf. . } εὐηρεστηκέναι, Rec. Gr. Sch. (He. 11. 5) } — εὐαρεστέω
εὐαρεστῆσαι, aor. 1, infin. . . . — id.
εὐάρεστοι, nom. pl. masc. . . . — εὐάρεστος
εὐάρεστον, nom. or acc. s. neut. and acc. s. fem. — id.
εὐάρεστος, ου, ὁ, ἡ, τό, -ον, (§ 7. rem. 2) (εὖ & ἀρεστός fr. ἀρέσκω) *well-pleasing, acceptable, grateful,* Ro. 12. 1, 2, et al.

εὐαρεστέω, ῶ, fut. ήσω, perf. εὐηρέστηκα, (§ 16. tab. P) *to please well,* He. 11. 5, 6; pass. *to take pleasure in, be well pleased with,* He. 13. 6. L.G.

εὐαρέστως, adv. *acceptably,* He. 12. 28.

εὐαρέστους, acc. pl. masc. . . . — εὐάρεστος
εὐαρέστως,[a] adv. . . . . . — id.
Εὔβουλος,[b] ου, ὁ, (§ 3. tab. C. a) *Eubulus,* pr. name.
εὖγε, adv. *well done!*—B. D. Ln. Tdf.
εὖ, Rec. Gr. Sch. (Lu. 19. 17)
εὐγενεῖς, nom. pl. masc. . . . — εὐγενής
εὐγενέστεροι, nom. pl. masc. compar. (§ 8. rem. 1) — id.
εὐγενής, έος, οῦς, ὁ, ἡ, (§ 7. rem. 5. a) (εὖ & γένος) *well-born, of high rank, honourable,* Lu. 19. 12; 1 Co. 1. 26; *generous, ingenuous, candid,* Ac. 17. 11.
εὐδία,[c] ας, ἡ, (§ 2. tab. B. b, and rem. 2) (εὖ & Ζεύς, Διός, *Jupiter,* lord of the air and heavens) *serenity of the heavens, a cloudless sky, fair or fine weather.*
εὐδοκεῖ, 3 pers. sing. pres. ind. . . . — εὐδοκέω
εὐδοκέω, ῶ], fut. ήσω, (§ 16. tab. P) (εὖ & δοκέω) *to think well, approve, acquiesce, take delight or pleasure,* Mat. 3. 17; 17. 5; Mar. 1. 11; Lu. 3. 22; 12. 32, et al. L.G.

εὐδοκία, ας, ἡ, (§ 2. tab. B. b, and rem. 2) *approbation; good will, favour,* Lu. 2. 14; *good pleasure, purpose, intention,* Mat. 11. 26; Lu. 10. 21; Ep. 1. 5. 9; Phi. 2. 13; by impl. *desire,* Ro. 10. 1.

εὐδόκησα, 1 pers. sing. aor. 1, (§ 34. rem. 3. c) — εὐδοκέω
εὐδοκήσαμεν, 1 pers. pl. aor. 1, ind. . — id.
εὐδόκησαν, 3 pers. pl. aor. 1, ind. . . — id.
εὐδοκήσαντες, nom. pl. masc. part. aor. 1 . — id.
εὐδόκησας, 2 pers. sing. aor. 1, ind. . . — id.
εὐδόκησε, 3 pers. sing. aor. 1, ind. . . — id.
εὐδοκία, ας, ἡ, (§ 2. tab. B. b, and rem. 2) . — id.
εὐδοκίαν, acc. sing. . . . . — εὐδοκία
εὐδοκίας, gen. sing. . . . . — id.
εὐδοκοῦμεν, 1 pers. pl. pres. ind. . . — εὐδοκέω
εὐδοκῶ, 1 pers. sing. pres. ind. . . . — id.
εὐεργεσία], ας, ἡ, (§ 2. tab. B. b, and rem. 2) — εὐεργέτης
εὐεργεσίᾳ, dat. sing. . . . . — εὐεργεσία
εὐεργεσίας, gen. sing. . . . . — id.
εὐεργέται,[d] nom. pl. . . . . — εὐεργέτης
εὐεργετέω, ῶ], fut. ήσω, (§ 16. tab. P) . — id.

[a] He. 12. 28. [b] 2 Ti. 4. 21. [c] Mat. 16. 2. [d] Lu. 22. 25.

εὐεργέτης], ου, ὁ, (§ 2. tab. B. c) (εὖ & ἔργον) *a well-doer; a benefactor*, Lu. 22. 25.

εὐεργεσία, ας, ἡ, (§ 2. tab. B. b, and rem. 2) *well-doing; a good deed, benefit conferred*, Ac. 4. 9; *duty, good offices*, 1 Ti. 6. 2.

εὐεργετέω, ῶ, fut. ήσω, (§ 16. tab. P) *to do good, exercise beneficence.*

εὐεργετῶν,[a] nom. sing. masc. part. pres. . εὐεργετέω
εὐηγγελίζετο, 3 pers. sing. imperf. mid. . εὐαγγελίζω
εὐηγγελίζοντο, 3 pers. pl. imperf. mid.—Al. Ln. Tdf. . . . id.
εὐηγγελίσαντο, Rec. Gr. Sch. (Ac. 8. 25)
εὐηγγελισάμεθα, 1 pers. pl. aor. 1, ind. mid. id.
εὐηγγελισάμην, 1 pers. sing. aor. 1, ind. mid. id.
εὐηγγελίσαντο, 3 pers. pl. aor. 1, ind. mid. . id.
εὐηγγελίσατο, 3 pers. sing. aor. 1, ind. mid. id.
εὐηγγέλισε, 3 pers. sing. aor. 1, ind. act. . id.
εὐηγγελίσθη, 3 pers. sing. aor. 1, ind. pass. . id.
εὐηγγελισμένοι, nom. pl. masc. part. p. pass. (§ 26. rem. 1) . . . id.
εὐηρεστηκέναι, perf. infin. (§ 34. rem. 3. b) εὐαρεστέω
εὐθεῖα, nom. sing. fem. . . . . . εὐθύς
εὐθεῖαν, acc. sing. fem. . . . . id.
εὐθείας, acc. pl. fem. . . . . . id.
εὔθετον, nom. neut. and acc. sing. fem. . εὔθετος

εὔθετος, ου, ὁ, ἡ, (§ 7. rem. 2) (εὖ & τίθημι) pr. *well arranged, rightly disposed; fit, proper, adapted*, Lu. 9. 62; 14. 35; *useful*, He. 6. 7.

εὐθέως, adv. . . . . . . εὐθύς

εὐθυδρομέω, ῶ], fut. ήσω, (§ 16. tab. P) (εὐθύς & δρόμος) *to run on a straight course; to sail on a direct course*, Ac. 16. 11; 21. 1. L.G.

εὐθυδρομήσαμεν, 1 pers. pl. aor. 1, ind. . εὐθυδρομέω
εὐθυδρομήσαντες, nom. pl. masc. part. aor. 1 id.
εὐθυμεῖ, 3 pers. sing. pres. ind. . . εὐθυμέω
εὐθυμεῖν, pres. infin. . . . . id.
εὐθυμεῖτε, 2 pers. pl. pres. imper. . . id.
εὐθυμέω, ῶ], fut. ήσω, (§ 16. tab. P) . εὔθυμος
εὔθυμοι,[b] nom. pl. masc. . . . id.

εὔθυμος], ου, ὁ, ἡ, (§ 7. rem. 2) (εὖ & θυμός) *of good cheer or courage, cheerful.*

εὐθυμέω, ῶ, fut. ήσω, (§ 16. tab. P) *to be cheerful, be in good spirits, take courage*, Ac. 27. 22, 25; Ja. 5. 13.

εὐθυμότερον, adv. (pr. neut. compar. of preced.) *more cheerfully*, Ac. 24. 10.

εὐθύμως, adv. *cheerfully*, v.r. Ac. 24. 10.

εὐθυμότερον,[c] adv. (§ 8. rem. 4) . . εὔθυμος
εὐθύμως, adv.—A. B. Ln. Tdf. . . id.
εὐθυμότερον, Rec. Gr. Sch. (Ac. 24. 10)
εὐθύνατε, 2 pers. pl. aor. 1, imper. (§ 13. rem. 3) εὐθύνω
εὐθύνοντος, gen. sing. masc. part. pres. . . id.
εὐθύνω], fut. υνῶ, (§ 27. rem. 1. a) . . εὐθύς

εὐθύς], εῖα, ύ, ((§ 7. tab. H. g) *straight*, Mat. 3. 3; Mar. 1. 3; met. *right, upright, true*, Ac. 8. 21, et al.

εὐθύς, adv. *straight forwards; directly, immediately, instantly, forthwith*, Mat. 3. 16; 13, 20, 21, et al.

εὐθέως, adv. *immediately, forthwith, instantly, at once*, Mat. 8. 3; 13. 5, et al.

εὐθύνω, fut. υνῶ, aor. 1, ῡνα, (§ 27. rem. 1. a. f) *to guide straight; to direct, guide, steer* a ship, Ja. 3. 4; *to make straight*, Jno. 1. 23.

εὐθύτης, τητος, ἡ, (§ 4. rem. 2. c) *rectitude, righteousness, equity*, He. 1. 8. (ῠ).

εὐθύς, adv. . . . . εὐθύς
εὐθύτης], τητος, ἡ . . . . . id.
εὐθύτητος,[d] gen. sing. . . . . . εὐθύτης
εὐκαιρέω, ῶ], fut. ήσω, (§ 16. tab. P) . εὔκαιρος
εὐκαιρήσῃ, 3 pers. sing. aor. 1, subj. . . εὐκαιρέω
εὐκαιρία], ας, ἡ, (§ 2. tab. B. b, and rem. 2) εὔκαιρος
εὐκαιρίαν, acc. sing. . . . . . εὐκαιρία
εὔκαιρον, acc. sing. fem. . . . . εὔκαιρος

εὔκαιρος], ου, ὁ, ἡ, (§ 7. rem. 2) (εὖ & καιρός) *timely, opportune, seasonable, convenient*, Mar. 6. 21; He. 4. 16.

εὐκαιρέω, ῶ, fut. ήσω, (§ 16. tab. P) aor. 1, ηὐκαίρησα, *to have convenient time or opportunity, have leisure*, Mar. 6. 31; 1 Co. 16. 12; *to be at leisure* for a thing, *to be disposed to attend, to give time*, Ac. 17. 21. L.G.

εὐκαιρία, ας, ἡ, (§ 2. tab. B. b, and rem. 2) *convenient opportunity, favourable occasion*, Mat. 26. 16; Lu. 22. 6.

εὐκαίρως, adv. *opportunely, seasonably, conveniently*, Mar. 14. 11; 2 Ti. 4. 2.

εὐκαίρου, gen. sing. fem. . . . . εὔκαιρος
εὐκαίρουν, 3 pers. pl. imperf. . . . εὐκαιρέω
εὐκαίρως, adv. . . . . . . εὔκαιρος
εὐκοπώτερον, nom. sing. neut. . . εὐκοπώτερος

a Ac. 10. 38. b Ac. 27. 36. c Ac. 24. 10. d He. 1. 8.

εὐκοπώτερος], α, ον, compar. of εὔκοπος, *easy*, (fr. εὖ & κόπος) (§ 8. rem. 4) *easier, more feasible*, Mat. 9. 5; 19. 24; Mar. 2. 9, et al. L.G.

εὐλάβεια], ας, ἡ, (§ 2. tab. B. b, and rem. 2) . εὐλαβής

εὐλαβείας, gen. sing. . . . . εὐλάβεια

εὐλαβεῖς, nom. pl. masc. . . . . εὐλαβής

εὐλαβέομαι, οῦμαι], fut. ήσομαι, (§ 17. tab. Q) id.

εὐλαβηθείς, nom. s. masc. part. aor. 1, pass. εὐλαβέομαι

εὐλαβής, έος, οῦς, ὁ, ἡ, (§ 7. tab. G. b) (εὖ & λαμβάνω) pr. *taking hold of well*, i.e. *warily*; hence, *cautious, circumspect; full of reverence* towards God, *devout, pious, religious*, Lu. 2. 25; Ac. 2. 5; 8. 2.

εὐλάβεια, ας, ἡ, (§ 2. tab. B. b, and rem. 2) *the disposition of one who is* εὐλαβής, *caution, circumspection*; in N.T. *reverence* to God, *piety*, He. 5. 7; 12. 28.

εὐλαβέομαι, οῦμαι, fut. ήσομαι, aor. 1, (pass. form) ηὐλαβήθην, (§ 17. tab. Q) *to be cautious or circumspect; to fear, be afraid or apprehensive*, Ac. 23. 10; in N.T. absol. *to reverence* God, *to be influenced by pious awe*, He. 11. 7.

εὐλόγει, 3 pers. sing. imperf.—A. C. D. Sch. Ln.
ηὐλόγει, Rec. Gr. . . . } εὐλογέω
κατηυλόγει, Tdf. (Mar. 10. 16) .

εὐλογεῖν, pres. infin. act. . . . . εὐλογέω

εὐλογεῖται, 3 pers. s. pres. ind. pass. (§ 17. tab. Q) id.

εὐλογεῖτε, 2 pers. pl. pres. imper. act. . id.

εὐλογέω, ῶ], fut. ήσω, perf. ηκα, (§ 16. tab. P) (εὖ & λόγος) pr. *to speak well of*; in N.T. *to bless, ascribe praise and glorification*, Lu. 1. 64, et al.; *to bless, invoke a blessing upon*, Mat. 5. 44, et al.; *to bless, confer a favour or blessing upon*, Ep. 1. 3; He. 6. 14; pass. *to be blessed, to be an object of favour or blessing*, Lu. 1. 28, et al.

εὐλογητός, οῦ, ὁ, ἡ, (§ 7. rem. 2) *worthy of praise or blessing, blessed*, Mar. 14. 61; Lu. 1. 68, et al. LXX.

εὐλογία, ας, ἡ, (§ 2. tab. B. b, and rem. 2) pr. *good speaking; fair speech, flattery*, Ro. 16. 18; in N.T. *blessing, praise, celebration*, 1 Co. 10. 16; Re. 5. 12, 13; *invocation of good, benediction*, Ja. 3. 10; *a divine blessing or boon*, Ro. 15. 29, et al.; *a gift, benevolence*, 2 Co. 9. 5; *a frank gift*, as opposed to πλεονεξία, 2 Co. 9. 5; ἐπ' εὐλογίαις, *liberally*, 2 Co. 9. 6

εὐλογηθήσονται, 3 pers. pl. fut. 1, ind. pass. . εὐλογέω

εὐλόγηκε, 3 pers. sing. perf. ind. act. . id.

εὐλογημένη, nom. sing. fem. part. perf. pass. . id.

εὐλογημένοι, nom. pl. masc. part. perf. pass. id.

εὐλογημένος, nom. sing. masc. part. perf. pass. id.

εὐλογῇς, 2 pers. sing. pres. subj. act.—A. B. D.
Ln. Tdf. . . . . } id.
εὐλογήσῃς, Rec. Gr. Sch. (1 Co. 14. 16)

εὐλογήσας, nom. sing. masc. part. aor. 1, act. id.

εὐλόγησε, 3 pers. sing. aor. 1, ind. act. . id.

εὐλογήσῃς, 2 pers. sing. aor. 1, subj. act. id.

εὐλογήσω, 1 pers. sing. fut. ind. act. . . id.

εὐλογητός], ου, ὁ, ἡ, (§ 7. rem. 2) . . id.

εὐλογητοῦ, gen. sing. masc. . . . εὐλογητός

εὐλογία], ας, ἡ, (§ 2. tab. B. b, and rem. 2) εὐλογέω

εὐλογίᾳ, dat. sing. . . . . εὐλογία

εὐλογίαις, dat. pl. . . . . id.

εὐλογίαν, acc. sing. . . . . id.

εὐλογίας, gen. sing. . . . . id.

εὐλογοῦμεν, 1 pers. pl. pres. ind. act. . . εὐλογέω

εὐλογοῦντα, acc. sing. masc. part. pres. act. id.

εὐλογοῦνται, 3 pers. pl. pres. ind. pass. . id.

εὐλογοῦντες, nom. pl. masc. part. pres. act. . id.

εὐλογῶν, nom. sing. masc. part. pres. act. . id.

εὐμετάδοτος], ου, ὁ, ἡ, (§ 7. rem. 2) (εὖ & μεταδίδωμι) *ready in imparting, liberal, bountiful*. L.G.

εὐμεταδότους,[a] acc. pl. masc. . . εὐμετάδοτος

Εὐνίκη], ης, ἡ, (§ 2. tab. B. a) *Eunice*, pr. name. (ῐ).

Εὐνίκῃ,[b] dat. sing. . . . . Εὐνίκη

εὐνοέω, ῶ], fut. ήσω, (§ 16. tab. P) (εὔνοος, εὖ & νόος, νοῦς) *to have kind thoughts, be well affected or kindly disposed* towards, Mat. 5. 25.

εὔνοια], ας ἡ, (§ 2. tab. B. b, and rem. 2) (εὔνοος) *good will, kindliness; heartiness*, Ep. 6. 7; *conjugal duty*, 1 Co. 7. 3.

εὔνοιαν, acc. sing. . . . . . εὔνοια

εὐνοίας, gen. sing. . . . . id.

εὐνουχίζω], fut. ίσω, (§ 26. rem. 1) . . εὐνοῦχος

εὐνούχισαν, 3 pers. pl. aor. 1, ind. act. . εὐνουχίζω

εὐνουχίσθησαν, 3 pers. pl. aor. 1, ind. pass. id.

εὐνοῦχοι, nom. pl. . . . . . εὐνοῦχος

εὐνοῦχος, ου, ὁ, (§ 3. tab. C. a) (εὐνή, *a bed*, & ἔχω) pr. *one who has charge of the bedchamber*; hence, *a eunuch, one emasculated*, Mat. 19. 12; as eunuchs in the East often rose to places of power and

[a] 1 Ti. 6. 18. [b] 2 Ti. 1. 5.

trust, hence, *a minister of a court*, Ac. 8. 27, 34.

εὐνουχίζω, fut. ίσω, (§ 26. rem. 1) aor. 1, εὐνούχισα, *to emasculate, make a eunuch; to impose chaste abstinence on, to bind to a practical emasculation*, Mat. 19. 12. L.G.

εὐνοῶν,[a] nom. sing. masc. part. pres. . εὐνοέω

εὐξαίμην, 1 pers. s. aor. 1, optat. (§ 23. rem. 1. b) εὔχομαι

Εὐοδία], ας, ἡ, (§ 2. tab. B. b, and rem. 2) *Euodia*, pr. name.

Εὐοδίαν,[b] acc. sing. . . . . . Εὐοδία

εὐοδοῦσθαι, pres. infin. pass. . . . εὐοδόω

εὐοδοῦται, 3 pers. sing. pres. ind. pass. . id.

εὐοδόω, ῶ], fut. ώσω, (§ 20. tab. T) (εὖ & ὁδός) *to give a prosperous journey; cause to prosper or be successful*; pass. *to have a prosperous journey, to succeed in a journey*, Ro. 1. 10; met. *to be furthered, to prosper*, temporally or spiritually, 1 Co. 16. 2; 3 Jno. 2, bis.

εὐοδωθῇ, 3 pers. sing. aor. 1, subj. pass.—A. C. }
εὐοδῶται, Rec. Gr. Sch. Tdf. (1 Co. 16. 2) } εὐοδόω

εὐοδωθήσομαι, 1 pers. sing. fut. 1, ind. pass. . id.

εὐοδῶται, 3 pers. sing. pres. subj. pass. . id.

εὐπάρεδρον, acc. sing. neut.—Gr. Sch. Tdf. }
εὐπρόσεδρον, Rec. (1 Co. 7. 35) . } εὐπάρεδρος

εὐπάρεδρος], ου, ὁ, ἡ, (§ 7. rem. 2) (εὖ & πάρεδρος, *one who sits by, an assistant, assessor*, fr. παρά & ἕδρα, *a seat*) *constantly attending; assiduous, devoted to*; τὸ εὐπάρεδρον, *assiduity, devotedness*, v.r. 1 Co. 7. 35. L.G.

εὐπειθής,[c] έος, οῦς, (§ 7. tab. G. b) (εὖ & πείθω) *easily persuaded, pliant.*

εὐπερίστατον,[d] acc. sing. fem. . . εὐπερίστατος

εὐπερίστᾰτος], ου, ὁ, ἡ, (§ 7. rem. 2) (εὖ & περιΐσταμαι) *easily or constantly environing or besetting*. N.T.

εὐποιΐα], ας, ἡ, (§ 2. tab. B. b, and rem. 2) (εὖ & ποιέω) *doing good, beneficence*. L.G.

εὐποιΐας,[e] gen. sing. . . . . . εὐποιΐα

εὐπορέομαι, οῦμαι], fut. ήσομαι, (§ 17. tab. Q) (εὐπορέω, *to supply*, fr. εὔπορος, *easy, abounding, in easy circumstances*) *to be in prosperous circumstances, enjoy plenty*, Ac. 11. 29.

εὐπορία,[f] ας, ἡ, (§ 2. tab. B. b, and rem. 2) (εὔπορος) *wealth, abundance.*

εὐπρέπεια,[g] ας, ἡ, (εὐπρεπής, *well-looking*, fr. εὖ & πρέπει) *grace, beauty.*

εὐπρόσδεκτος, ου, ὁ, ἡ, (§ 7. rem. 2) (εὖ & προσδέχομαι) *acceptable, grateful, pleasing*, Ro. 15. 16, 31; 2 Co. 8. 12; 1 Pe. 2. 5; in N.T. *gracious*, 2 Co. 6. 2. L.G.

εὐπροσδέκτους, acc. pl. fem. . . . εὐπρόσδεκτος

εὐπρόσεδρον,[h] acc. sing. neut. . . εὐπρόσεδρος

εὐπρόσεδρος], ου, ὁ, ἡ, (§ 7. rem. 2) (εὖ & πρόσεδρος, *an assessor*) *constantly attending, assiduous, devoted to*, 1 Co. 7. 35; equivalent to εὐπάρεδρος.

εὐπροσωπέω, ῶ], fut. ήσω, (§ 16. tab. P) (εὐπρόσωπος, *of a fair countenance*, fr. εὖ & πρόσωπον) *to carry or make a fair appearance, to be specious*. N.T.

εὐπροσωπῆσαι,[i] aor. 1, infin. . . εὐπροσωπέω

εὐρακύλων, ωνος, ὁ, *the north-east wind*, from the Latin words Eurus and Aquilo. —A. B. Ln. Tdf. (Ac. 27. 14) (ῠ).
εὐροκλύδων, Rec. Sch.
εὐρυκλύδων, Gr.

εὑράμενος, nom. sing. masc. part. aor. 1, mid. (§ 36. rem. 4) . . . εὑρίσκω

εὗρε, 3 pers. sing. aor. 2, ind. act. . . id.

εὑρεθείς, nom. sing. masc. part. aor. 1, pass. id.

εὑρέθη, 3 pers. sing. aor. 1, ind. pass. . id.

εὑρεθῇ, 3 pers. sing. aor. 1, subj. pass. . . id.

εὑρέθημεν, 1 pers. pl. aor. 1, ind. pass. . id.

εὑρέθην, 1 pers. sing. aor. 1, ind. pass. . id.

εὑρεθῆναι, aor. 1, infin. pass. . . . id.

εὑρέθησαν, 3 pers. pl. aor. 1, ind. pass. . id.

εὑρεθησόμεθα, 1 pers. pl. fut. 1, ind. pass. id.

εὑρεθῆτε, 2 pers. pl. aor. 1, subj. pass. . id.

εὑρεθῶ, 1 pers. sing. aor. 1, subj. pass. . id.

εὑρεθῶσι, 3 pers. pl. aor. 1, subj. pass. . id.

εὑρεῖν, aor. 2, infin. act. . . . id.

εὗρε, 3 pers. sing. aor. 2, ind. act. . . id.

εὗρες, 2 pers. sing. aor. 2, ind. act. . . id.

εὕρῃ, 3 pers. sing. aor. 2, subj. act. . . id.

εὕρηκα, 1 pers. sing. perf. act. (§ 36. rem. 4) id.

εὑρήκαμεν, 1 pers. pl. perf. ind. act. . id.

εὑρηκέναι, perf. infin. act. . . . id.

εὑρήσει, 3 pers. sing. fut. ind. act. . . id.

εὑρήσεις, 2 pers. sing. fut. ind. act. . . id.

εὑρήσετε, 2 pers. pl. fut. ind. act. . . id.

εὑρήσῃς, 2 pers. sing. aor. 1, subj. act. . id.

εὑρήσομεν, 1 pers. pl. fut. ind. act. . . id.

[a] Mat. 5. 25. [b] Phi. 4. 2. [c] Ja. 3. 17. [d] He. 12. 1. [e] He. 13. 16. [f] Ac. 19. 25. [g] Ja. 1. 11. [h] 1 Co. 7. 35 [i] Gal. 6. 12.

εὑρήσουσι, 3 pers. pl. fut. ind. act. . εὑρίσκω
εὕρητε, 2 pers. pl. aor. 2, subj. act. . . id.
εὑρίσκει, 3 pers. sing. pres. ind. act. . id.
εὑρίσκετο, 3 pers. sing. imperf. pass. . . id.
εὑρισκόμεθα, 1 pers. pl. pres. ind. pass. . id.
εὑρίσκομεν, 1 pers. pl. pres. ind. act. . . id.
εὕρισκον, 3 pers. pl. imperf. act. . . id.
εὑρίσκον, nom. sing. neut. part. pres. act. . id.
εὑρίσκοντες, nom. pl. masc. part. pres. act. id.

εὑρίσκω, (§ 36. rem. 4) fut. εὑρήσω, perf. εὕρηκα, aor. 2, εὗρον, aor. 1, pass. εὑρέθην, later aor. 1, εὕρησα, and aor. 1, mid. εὑράμην, He. 9. 12; *to find, to meet with, light upon*, Mat. 18. 28; 20. 6; *to find out, to detect, discover*, Lu. 23. 2, 4, 14; *to acquire, obtain, win, gain*, Lu. 1. 30; 9. 12; *to find* mentally, *to comprehend, recognise*, Ac. 17. 27; Ro. 7. 21; *to find* by experience, *observe, gather*, Ro. 7. 18; *to devise* as feasible, Lu. 5. 19; 19. 48.

εὕροιεν, 3 pers. pl. aor. 2, optat. act. . . εὑρίσκω
Εὐροκλύδων,[a] ονος, ὁ, (§ 4. tab. D. a) (εὖρος, *the east wind*, κλύδων, *a wave*) *Euroclydon*, the name of a tempestuous wind, Ac. 27. 14. There are, however, two various readings, εὐρυκλύδων, (εὐρύς), and εὐρακύλων, *Euroaquilo*. (ῠ). N.T.
εὕρομεν, 1 pers. pl. aor. 2, ind. act. . εὑρίσκω
εὗρον, 1 pers. sing. and 3 pers. pl. aor. 2, ind. act. id.
εὑρόντες, nom. pl. masc. part. aor. 2, act. . id.
εὑροῦσα, nom. sing. fem. part. aor. 2, act. . id.
εὑροῦσαι, nom. pl. fem. part. aor. 2, act. . id.
εὐρύχωρος,[b] ου, ὁ, ἡ, (§ 7. rem. 2) (εὐρύς, *broad*, & χώρα) *spacious; broad, wide.*
εὕρω, 1 pers. sing. aor. 2, subj. act. . εὑρίσκω
εὕρωμεν, 1 pers. pl. aor. 2, subj. act. . . id.
εὑρών, nom. sing. masc. part. aor. 2, act. . id.
εὕρωσι, 3 pers. pl. aor. 2, subj. act. . . id.
εὐσέβεια], ας, ἡ, (§ 2. tab. B. b, and rem. 2) εὐσεβής
εὐσεβείᾳ, dat. sing. . . . . . εὐσέβεια
εὐσεβείαις, dat. pl. . . . . . id.
εὐσέβειαν, acc. sing. . . . . . id.
εὐσεβείας, gen. sing. . . . . . id.
εὐσεβεῖν, pres. infin. . . . . εὐσεβέω
εὐσεβεῖς, acc. pl. masc. . . . . εὐσεβής
εὐσεβεῖτε, 2 pers. pl. pres. ind. . . . εὐσεβέω
εὐσεβέω, ῶ], fut. ήσω, (§ 16. tab. P) . εὐσεβής

εὐσεβῆ, acc. sing. masc. . . . . . εὐσεβής
εὐσεβής, έος, οῦς, ὁ, ἡ, (§ 7. tab. G. b) (εὖ & σέβομαι) *reverent; pious, devout, religious*, Ac. 10. 2, 7; 22. 12; 2 Pe. 2. 9.

εὐσέβεια, ας, ἡ, (§ 2. tab. B. b, and rem. 2) *reverential feeling; piety, devotion, godliness*, Ac. 3. 12; 1 Ti. 2. 2; 4. 7, 8, et al.; *religion, the* Christian *religion*, 1 Ti. 3. 16.

εὐσεβέω, fut. ήσω, (§ 16. tab. P) *to exercise piety*; towards a deity, *to worship*, Ac. 17. 23; towards relatives, *to be dutiful towards*, 1 Ti. 5. 4.

εὐσεβῶς, adv. *piously, religiously*, 2 Ti. 3. 12; Tit. 2. 12.

εὐσεβῶς, adv. . . . . . . εὐσεβής
εὔσημον,[c] acc. sing. masc. . . . . εὔσημος
εὔσημος], ου, ὁ, ἡ, (§ 7. rem. 2) (εὖ & σῆμα) pr. *well marked, strongly marked*; met. *significant, intelligible, perspicuous.*
εὔσπλαγχνοι, nom. pl. masc. . . . εὔσπλαγχνος
εὔσπλαγχνος], ου, ὁ, ἡ, (§ 7. rem. 2) (εὖ & σπλάγχνον) in N.T. *tender-hearted, compassionate*, Ep. 4. 32; 2 Pe. 3. 8.
εὔσχημον, acc. sing. neut. . . . εὐσχήμων
εὐσχήμονα, nom. pl. neut. . . . . id.
εὐσχήμονας, acc. pl. masc. . . . . id.
εὐσχημόνων, gen. pl. . . . . . id.
εὐσχημόνως, adv. . . . . . . id.
εὐσχημοσύνη], ης, ἡ, (§ 2. tab. B. a) . id.
εὐσχημοσύνην,[d] acc. sing. . . εὐσχημοσύνη
εὐσχήμων, ονος, ὁ, ἡ, (§ 7. tab. G. a) (εὖ & σχῆμα) *of good appearance, pleasing to look upon, comely*, 1 Co. 12. 24; met. *becoming, decent*, τὸ εὔσχημον, *decorum, propriety*, 1 Co. 7. 35; *honourable, reputable, of high standing and influence*, Mar. 15. 43; Ac. 13. 50; 17. 12.

εὐσχημόνως, adv. *in a becoming manner, with propriety, decently, gracefully*, Ro. 13. 13; 1 Co. 14. 40; 1 Thes. 4. 12.

εὐσχημοσύνη, ης, ἡ, (§ 2. tab. B. a) *comeliness, gracefulness*; artificial *comeliness, ornamental array, embellishment*, 1 Co. 12. 23. (ῠ).

εὐτόνως, adv. (εὔτονος, *on the stretch*, fr. εὖ & τείνω) *intensely, vehemently, strenuously*, Lu. 23. 10; Ac. 18. 28.

[a] Ac. 27. 14. [b] Mat. 7. 13. [c] 1 Co. 14. 9. [d] 1 Co. 12. 23.

εὐτραπελία,[a] ας, ἡ, (§ 2. tab. B. b, and rem. 2) (εὐτράπελος, *ready, witty*, fr. εὖ & τρεπω) *facetiousness, pleasantry*; hence, *buffoonery, ribaldry*.

Εὔτυχος,[b] ου, ὁ, (§ 3. tab. C. a) *Eutychus*, pr. name.

εὔφημα,[c] nom. pl. neut. . . . . εὔφημος

εὐφημία], ας, ἡ, (§ 2. tab. B. b, and rem. 2) id.

εὐφημίας,[d] gen. sing. . . . εὐφημία

εὔφημος], ου, ὁ, ἡ, (§ 7. rem. 2) (εὖ & φήμη) pr. *of good omen, auspicious*; hence, *of good report, commendable, laudable, reputable*.

εὐφημία, ας, ἡ, (§ 2. tab. B. b, and rem. 2) pr. *use of words of good omen*; hence, *favourable expression, praise, commendation*.

εὐφορέω, ῶ], fut. ήσω, (§ 16. tab. P) (εὔφορος, εὖ & φέρω) *to bear or bring forth well or plentifully, yield abundantly*.

εὐφόρησε,[e] 3 pers. sing. aor. 1, ind. . εὐφορέω

εὐφραίνεσθαι, pres. infin. mid. . . . εὐφραίνω

εὐφραίνεσθε, 2 pers. pl. pres. imper. mid. . id.

εὐφραινόμενος, nom. sing. masc. pt. pres. mid. id.

εὐφραίνοντο, 3 pers. pl. imperf. mid. . . id.

εὐφραίνου, 2 pers. sing. pres. imper. pass. . id.

εὐφραίνω], fut. ανῶ, aor. 1, εὔφρηνα & εὔφρᾶνα, (§ 27. rem. 1. c. e) (εὔφρων, εὖ & φρήν) *to gladden*, 2 Co. 2. 2; pass. *to be glad, exult, rejoice*, Lu. 12. 19; Ac. 2. 26; mid. *to feast in token of joy, keep a day of rejoicing*, Lu. 15. 23, 24, 29, 32, et al.

εὐφραίνων, nom. sing. masc. part. pres. act. εὐφραίνω

εὐφράνθη, 3 pers. sing. aor. 1, ind. pass. . id.

εὐφρανθῆναι, aor. 1, infin. pass. . . id.

εὐφρανθήσονται, 3 pers. pl. fut. 1, ind. pass. id.

εὐφράνθητε, 2 pers. pl. aor. 1, imper. pass. id.

εὐφράνθητι, 2 pers. sing. aor. 1, imper. pass. id.

εὐφρανθῶ, 1 pers. sing. aor. 1, subj. pass. . id.

εὐφρανθῶμεν, 1 pers. pl. aor. 1, subj. pass. . id.

Εὐφράτῃ, dat. sing. . . . . Εὐφράτης

Εὐφράτην, acc. sing. . . . . . id.

Εὐφράτης], ου, ὁ, (§ 2. tab. B. c) the river *Euphrates*.

εὐφροσύνη], ης, ἡ, (§ 2 tab. B. a) (εὔφρων) *joy, gladness, rejoicing*, Ac. 2. 28; 14. 17. (ῠ).

εὐφροσύνης, gen. sing. . . . εὐφροσύνη

εὐχαριστεῖ, 3 pers. sing. pres. ind. . εὐχαριστέω

εὐχαριστεῖν, pres. infin. . . . . id.

εὐχαριστεῖς, 2 pers. sing. pres. ind. . id.

εὐχαριστεῖτε, 2 pers. pl. pres. imper. . id.

εὐχαριστέω, ῶ], fut. ήσω, (§ 16. tab. P) εὐχάριστος

εὐχαριστηθῇ, 3 pers. sing. aor. 1, subj. pass. εὐχαριστέω

εὐχαρίστησαν, 3 pers. pl. aor. 1, ind. . id.

εὐχαριστήσαντος, gen. sing. masc. part. aor. 1 id.

εὐχαριστήσας, nom. sing. masc. part. aor. 1 . id.

εὐχαρίστησε, 3 pers. sing. aor. 1, ind. id.

εὐχαριστία], ας, ἡ, (§ 2. tab. B. b, and rem. 2) εὐχάριστος

εὐχαριστίᾳ, dat. sing. . . . εὐχαριστία

εὐχαριστίαν, acc. sing. . . . id.

εὐχαριστίας, gen. sing. and acc. pl. . . id.

εὐχαριστιῶν, gen. pl. . . . . . id.

εὐχάριστοι,[f] nom. pl. masc. . . εὐχάριστος

εὐχάριστος], ου, ὁ, ἡ, (§ 7. rem. 2) (εὖ & χάρις) *grateful, pleasing; grateful, mindful of benefits, thankful*.

εὐχαριστία, ας, ἡ, (§ 2. tab. B. b, and rem. 2) *gratitude, thankfulness*, Ac 24. 3; *thanks, the act of giving thanks, thanksgiving*, 1 Co. 14. 16, et al.; *conversation marked by the gentle cheerfulness of a grateful heart*, as contrasted with the unseemly mirth of εὐτραπελία, Ep. 5. 4.

εὐχαριστέω, ῶ, fut. ήσω, (§ 16. tab. P) aor. 1, ησα, *to thank*, Lu. 17. 16, et al.; absol. *to give thanks*, Mat. 15. 36; 26. 27, et al., pass. *to be made a matter of thankfulness*, 2 Co. 1. 11.

εὐχαριστοῦμεν, 1 pers. pl. pres. ind. . εὐχαριστέω

εὐχαριστοῦντες, nom. pl. masc. part. pres. . id.

εὐχαριστῶ, 1 pers. sing. pres. ind. . . id.

εὐχαριστῶν, nom. sing. masc. part. pres. . id.

εὔχεσθε, 2 pers. pl. pres. imper. . . εὔχομαι

εὐχή, ῆς, ἡ, (§ 2. tab. B. a) *a wish, prayer*, Ja. 5. 15; *a vow*, Ac. 21. 23.

εὔχομαι, fut. ξομαι, aor. 1, ηὐξάμην, (§ 23. rem. 1. c) *to pray, offer prayer*, Ac. 26. 29; 2 Co. 13. 7, 9; Ja. 5. 16; *to wish, desire*, Ac. 27. 29; Ro. 9. 3; 3 Jno. 2.

εὐχήν, acc. sing. . . . . . . εὐχή

εὔχομαι], fut. ξομαι . . . . id.

εὐχόμεθα, 1 pers. pl. pres. ind. . . . εὔχομαι

εὔχρηστον, nom. neut. and acc. sing. masc. εὔχρηστος

εὔχρηστος, ου, ὁ, ἡ, (§ 7. rem. 2) (εὖ & χρηστός) *highly useful, very profitable*, 2 Ti. 2. 21; 4. 11; Phile. 11.

εὐψυχέω, ῶ], fut. ήσω, (§ 16. tab. P) (εὔψῦχος, *of good courage*, εὖ & ψυχή) *to be animated, encouraged, in good spirits*.

[a] Ep. 5. 4. [b] Ac. 20. 9. [c] Phi. 4. 8. [d] 2 Co. 6. 8. [e] Lu. 12. 16. [f] Col. 3. 15.

εὐψυχῶ,[a] 1 pers. sing. pres. subj. . . . εὐψυχέω
εὐωδία, ας, ἡ, (§ 2. tab. B. b, and rem. 2) (εὐώδης, εὖ & ὄδωδα, perf. fr. ὄζω) *a sweet smell, grateful odour, fragrance*, 2 Co. 2. 15; Ep. 5. 2; Phi. 4. 18.
εὐωδίας, gen. sing. . . . . . . εὐωδία
εὐώνυμον, acc. sing. masc. and fem. . . εὐώνυμος
εὐώνυμος], ου, ὁ, ἡ, (§ 7. rem. 2) (εὖ & ὄνομα) *of good name or omen*; used also as an euphemism by the Greeks instead of ἀριστερός, which was a word of bad import, as all omens on the left denoted misfortune; *the left*, Mat. 20. 21, 23; 25. 33, 41, et al.
ευωνύμων, gen. pl. . . . . . . εὐώνυμος
ἐφ', for ἐπί, before an aspirated vowel.
ἔφαγε, 3 pers. sing. aor. 2, ind. (§ 36. rem. 1) ἐσθίω
ἐφάγετε, 2 pers. pl. aor. 2, ind. act. . id.
ἐφάγομεν, 1 pers. pl. aor. 2, ind. act. . . id.
ἔφαγον, 1 pers. s. and 3 pers. pl. aor. 2, ind. act. id.
ἐφάλλομαι], fut. αλοῦμαι, (§ 24. rem. 4) (ἐπί & ἅλλομαι) *to leap or spring upon, assault*.
ἐφαλλόμενος,[b] nom. sing. masc. part. pres. Rec. Gr. Sch. . . . } ἐφάλλομαι
ἐφαλόμενος, Ln. Tdf. (Ac. 19. 16) }
ἐφανερώθη, 3 pers. sing. aor. 1, ind. pass. . φανερόω
ἐφανερώθησαν, 3 pers. pl. aor. 1, ind. pass. id.
ἐφανέρωσα, 1 pers. sing. aor. 1, ind. act. . id.
ἐφανέρωσε, 3 pers. sing. aor. 1, ind. act. . id.
ἐφάνη, 3 pers. sing. aor. 2, ind. pass. (§ 27. rem. 4. b) . . . . . φαίνω
ἐφάνησαν, 3 pers. pl. aor. 2, ind. pass. . . id.
ἐφάπαξ, adv. (ἐπί & ἅπαξ) *once for all*, Ro. 6. 10; *at once*, 1 Co. 15. 6. (ἄ).
ἔφασκε, 3 pers. sing. imperf. . . . . φάσκω
ἐφείσατο, 3 pers. sing. aor. 1, ind. act. (§ 23. rem. 5) . . . . . φείδομαι
ἔφερε, 3 pers. sing. imperf. act. . . . φέρω
ἐφερόμεθα, 1 pers. pl. imperf. pass. . id.
ἔφερον, 3 pers. pl. imperf. act. . . . id.
ἐφέροντο, 3 pers. pl. imperf. pass. . . . id.
Ἐφεσίνης,[c] gen. sing. fem. . . . . Ἐφεσῖνος
Ἐφεσῖνος], η, ον, (§ 27. tab. F. a) . . . Ἔφεσος
Ἐφέσιοι, nom. pl. masc. . . . . . Ἐφέσιος
Ἐφέσιον, acc. sing. masc. . . . . . id.
Ἐφέσιος], α, ον, (§ 7. rem. 1) . . . . Ἔφεσος
Ἐφεσίων, gen. pl. . . . . . . Ἐφέσιος
Ἔφεσον, acc. . . . . Ἔφεσος

Ἔφεσος], ου, ἡ, (§ 3. tab. C. b) *Ephesus*, a celebrated city of Asia Minor.

Ἐφεσῖνος, η, ον, (§ 7. tab. F. a) *Ephesian*, Re. 2. 1.

Ἐφέσιος, ία, ιον, (§ 7. rem. 1) *Ephesian*, belonging to Ephesus, Ac. 19. 28, 34, 35; 21. 29.

Ἐφέσου, gen. . . . . Ἔφεσος
Ἐφέσῳ, dat. . . . . id.
ἐφέστηκε, 3 pers. sing. perf. ind. (§ 29. tab. X) ἐφίστημι
ἐφεστώς, nom. sing. masc. part. perf. (§ 35. rem. 8) id.
ἐφεστῶτα, acc. sing. masc. part. perf. . . id.
ἐφευρετάς,[d] acc. pl. . . . . . ἐφευρετής
ἐφευρετής], οῦ, ὁ, (§ 2. tab. B. c) (ἐφευρίσκω, *to come upon, find, discover*, fr. ἐπί & εὑρίσκω) *an inventor, deviser*.
ἔφη, 3 pers. sing. aor. 2, ind. (§ 33. rem. 1) φημί
ἐφημερία], ας, ἡ, (§ 2. tab. B. b, and rem. 2) ἐφήμερος
ἐφημερίας, gen. sing. . . . . . ἐφημερία
ἐφήμερος], ου, ὁ, ἡ, (§ 7. rem. 2) (ἐπί & ἡμέρα) *lasting for a day; daily; sufficient for a day, necessary for every day*.

ἐφημερία, ας, ἡ, pr. *daily course*; *the daily service* of the temple; *a course* of priests to which the daily service for a week was allotted in rotation, Lu. 1. 5, 8. L.G.

ἐφημέρου,[e] gen. sing. fem. . . . . ἐφήμερος
ἔφθακε, 3 pers. sing. perf. ind.—B. Ln. . } φθάνω
ἔφθασε, Rec. Gr. Sch. Tdf. (1 Thes. 2. 16) }
ἐφθάσαμεν, 1 pers. pl. aor. 1, ind. . . id.
ἔφθασε, 3 pers. sing. aor. 1, ind. . . id.
ἐφθείραμεν, 1 pers. pl. aor. 1, ind. act. . φθείρω
ἔφθειρε, 3 pers. sing. imperf. act. . . id.
ἐφικέσθαι, aor. 2, infin. . . . . ἐφικνέομαι
ἐφικνέομαι, οῦμαι], fut. ἵξομαι, aor. 2, ἐφικόμην, (§ 36. rem. 2) (ἐπί & ἱκνέομαι, *to come*) *to come or reach to, to reach* a certain point or end; *to reach, arrive at*, 2 Co. 10. 13, 14.
ἐφικνούμενοι, nom. pl. masc. part. pres. . ἐφικνέομαι
ἐφίλει, 3 pers. sing. imperf. act. . . φιλέω
ἐφιμώθη, 3 pers. sing. aor. 1, ind. pass. . φιμόω
ἐφίμωσε, 3 pers. sing. aor. 1, ind. act. . id.
ἐφίσταται, 3 pers. sing. pres. mid. (§ 29. tab. Y) ἐφίστημι
ἐφίστημι], fut. ἐπιστήσω, (§ 29. tab. X) (ἐπί & ἵστημι) trans. *to place upon, over, close by*; intrans., perf. ἐφέστηκα, part. ἐφεστώς, aor. 2, ἐπέστην, mid. ἐφίσταμαι, *to stand by or near*, Lu. 2. 38; 4. 39;

[a] Phi. 2. 19. [b] Ac. 19. 16. [c] Re. 2. 1. [d] Ro. 1. 30. [e] Ja. 2. 15.

to come suddenly upon, Lu. 2. 9; 24. 4; to come upon, assault, Ac. 6. 12; 17. 5; to come near, approach, Lu. 10. 40; to impend, be instant, to be at hand, 1 Thes. 5. 3; to be present, Ac. 28. 2; to be pressing, urgent, earnest, 2 Ti. 4. 2.

ἐπιστάτης, ου, ὁ, (§ 2. tab. B. c) pr. one who stands by; one who is set over; in N.T., in voc., equivalent to διδάσκαλε, or ῥαββί, master, doctor, Lu. 5. 5; 8. 24, 45, et al. (ᾰ).

ἐφοβεῖτο, 3 pers. s. imperf. mid. (§ 17. tab. Q) φοβέω
ἐφοβήθη, 3 pers. sing. aor. 1, ind. pass. id.
ἐφοβήθησαν, 3 pers. pl. aor. 1, ind. pass. id.
ἐφοβούμην, 1 pers. sing. imperf. mid. id.
ἐφοβοῦντο, 3 pers. pl. imperf. mid. id.
ἐφονεύσατε, 2 pers. pl. aor. 1, ind. act. φονεύω
ἐφορέσαμεν, 1 pers. pl. aor. 1, ind. act. φορέω
Ἐφραΐμ,[a] ὁ, Ephraim, pr. name, indecl.
ἔφραξαν, 3 pers. pl. aor. 1, ind. act. φράσσω
ἐφρονεῖτε, 2 pers. pl. imperf. φρονέω
ἐφρόνουν, 1 pers. sing. imperf. id.
ἐφρούρει, 3 pers. sing. imperf. act. φρουρέω
ἐφρουρούμεθα, 1 pers. pl. imperf. pass. id.
ἐφρύαξαν,[b] 3 pers. pl. aor. 1, ind. φρυάσσω
ἔφυγε, 3 pers. sing. aor. 2, ind. (§ 24. rem. 9) φεύγω
ἔφυγον, 3 pers. pl. aor. 2, ind. id.
ἐφύλαξα, 1 pers. sing. aor. 1, ind. act. φυλάσσω
ἐφυλαξάμην, 1 pers. sing. aor. 1, ind. mid. id.
ἐφυλάξατε, 2 pers. pl. aor. 1, ind. act. id.
ἐφύλαξε, 3 pers. sing. aor. 1, ind. act. id.
ἐφυσιώθησαν, 3 pers. pl. aor. 1, pass. (§ 21. tab. U) φυσιόω
ἐφύτευον, 3 pers. pl. imperf. act. φυτεύω
ἐφύτευσα, 1 pers. sing. aor. 1, ind. act. id.
ἐφύτευσε, 3 pers. sing. aor. 1, ind. act. id.
ἐφφαθά,[c] (Aramaean, אֶתְפְּתַח) be thou opened.
ἐφώνει, 3 pers. sing. imperf. act. φωνέω
ἐφώνησαν, 3 pers. pl. aor. 1, ind. act. id.
ἐφώνησε, 3 pers. sing. aor. 1, ind. act. id.
ἐφώτισε, 3 pers. sing. aor. 1, ind. act. φωτίζω
ἐφωτίσθη, 3 pers. sing. aor. 1, ind. pass. id.
ἔχαιρε, 3 pers. sing. imperf. χαίρω
ἔχαιρον, 3 pers. pl. imperf. id.
ἐχαλάσθην, 1 pers. s. aor. 1, pass. (§ 22. rem. 4) χαλάω
ἐχάρη, 3 pers. s. aor. 2, ind. pass. (§ 27. rem. 4. b) χαίρω
ἐχάρημεν, 1 pers. pl. aor. 2, ind. pass. id.
ἐχάρην, 1 pers. sing. aor. 2, ind. pass. id.
ἐχάρησαν, 3 pers. pl. aor. 2, ind. pass. id.
ἐχάρητε, 2 pers. pl. aor. 2, ind. pass. χαίρω
ἐχαρίσατο, 3 pers. sing. aor. 1, ind. χαρίζομαι
ἐχαρίσθη, 3 pers. sing. aor. 1, ind. pass. id.
ἐχαρίτωσε, 3 pers. sing. aor. 1, ind. act. χαριτόω
ἔχε, 2 pers. sing. pres. imper. ἔχω
ἔχει, 3 pers. sing. pres. ind. id.
ἔχειν, pres. infin. id.
ἔχεις, 2 pers. sing. pres. ind. id.
ἔχετε, 2 pers. pl. pres. ind. id.
ἔχετε, 3 pers. pl. pres. imper. id.
ἐχέτω, 3 pers. sing. pres. imper. id.
ἔχῃ, 3 pers. sing. pres. subj. id.
ἔχητε, 2 pers. pl. pres. subj. id.
ἐχθές, adv. yesterday.—A. C. D. Ln. Tdf.
χθές, Rec. Gr. Sch. (Jno. 4. 52)
ἔχθρα], ας, ἡ, (§ 2 tab. B. b, and rem. 2) ἐχθρός
ἔχθρᾳ, dat. sing. ἔχθρα
ἔχθραι, nom. pl. id.
ἔχθραν, acc. sing. id.
ἐχθρέ, voc. sing. masc. ἐχθρός
ἐχθροί, nom. pl. masc. id.
ἐχθρόν, acc. sing. masc. id
ἐχθρός, ά, όν, (§ 7. rem. 1) hated, under disfavour, Ro. 11. 28; inimical, hostile, Mat. 13. 28; Col. 1. 21; as a subst., an enemy, adversary, Mat. 5. 43, 44; 10. 36; Lu. 27. 35, et al.

ἔχθρα, ας, ἡ, (§ 2. tab. B. b, and rem. 2) enmity, discord, feud, Lu. 23. 12; Gal. 5. 20; alienation, Ep. 2. 15, 16; a principle or state of enmity, Ro. 8. 7.

ἐχθροῦ, gen. sing. masc. ἐχθρός
ἐχθρούς, acc. pl. masc. id.
ἐχθρῶν, gen. pl. id.
ἔχιδνα, ης, ἡ, (§ 2. tab. B. and rem. 3) (ἔχις) a viper, poisonous serpent, Ac. 28. 3; used also fig. of persons, Mat. 3. 7.

ἐχιδνῶν, gen. pl. ἔχιδνα
ἐχλεύαζον, 3 pers. pl. imperf. χλευάζω
ἔχοι, 3 pers. sing. pres. optat. act. ἔχω
ἔχοιεν, 3 pers. pl. pres. optat. id.
ἔχομεν, 1 pers. pl. pres. ind. id.
ἐχόμενα, acc. pl. neut. part. pres. pass. id.
ἐχομένας, acc. pl. fem. part. pres. pass. id.
ἐχομένῃ, dat. sing. fem. part. pres. pass. id.
ἐχομένῳ, dat. sing. neut. part. pres. pass.—Gr. Sch. Tdf. } id.
ἐρχομένῳ, B. D. Rec. (Ac. 13. 44)

[a] Jno. 11. 54. [b] Ac. 4. 25. [c] Mar. 7. 34.

ἔχον, nom. and acc. sing. neut. part. pres. act. ἔχω
ἔχοντα, acc. s. masc. and nom. pl. neut. part. pres. id.
ἔχοντας, acc. pl. masc. part. pres. id.
ἔχοντες, nom. pl. masc. part. pres. id.
ἔχοντι, dat. sing. masc. part. pres. id.
ἔχοντος, gen. sing. masc. part. pres. id.
ἐχόντων, gen. pl. masc. part. pres. id.
ἐχορτάσθησαν, 3 pers. pl. aor. 1, pass. (§ 26. rem. 1) χορτάζω
ἐχορτάσθητε, 2 pers. pl. aor. 1, ind. pass. id.
ἔχουσα, nom. sing. fem. part. pres. act. ἔχω
ἔχουσαι, nom. pl. fem. part. pres. id.
ἐχούσαις, dat. pl. fem. part. pres. id.
ἔχουσαν, acc. sing. fem. part. pres. id.
ἐχούσῃ, dat. sing. fem. part. pres. id.
ἐχούσης, gen. sing. fem. part. pres. id.
ἔχουσι, 3 pers. pl. pres. ind. act. id.
ἐχρηματίσθη, 3 pers. sing. aor. 1, ind. pass. χρηματίζω
ἐχρησάμεθα, 1 pers. pl. aor. 1, ind. mid. (§ 19. tab. S) χράομαι
ἐχρησάμην, 1 pers. sing. aor. 1, ind. mid. id.
ἔχρισας, 2 pers. sing. aor. 1, ind. act. χρίω
ἔχρισε, 3 pers. sing. aor. 1, ind. id.
ἐχρῶντο, 3 pers. pl. imperf. mid. χράομαι

ἔχω, (§ 36. rem. 4) fut. ἕξω, imperf. εἶχον, aor. 2, ἔσχον, perf. ἔσχηκα, *to hold*, Re. 1. 16, et al.; *to seize, possess* a person, Mar. 16. 8; *to have, possess*, Mat. 7. 29, et al. freq.; *to have, have ready, be furnished with*, Mat. 5. 23; Jno. 5. 36; 6. 68, et al.; *to have* as a matter of crimination, Mat. 5. 23; Mar. 11. 25, et al.; *to have* at command, Mat. 27. 65; *to have* the power, *be able*, Mat. 18. 25; Lu. 14. 14; Ac. 4. 14, et al.; *to have* in marriage, Mat. 14. 4, et al.; *to have, be affected by, subjected to*, Mat. 3. 14; 12. 10; Mar. 3. 10; Jno. 12. 48; 15. 22, 24; 16. 21, 22; Ac. 23. 29; 1 Ti. 5. 12; He. 7. 28; 1 Jno. 1. 8; 4. 18; χάριν ἔχειν, *to feel gratitude, be thankful*, 1 Ti. 1. 12; 2 Ti. 1. 3; Phile. 7; *to hold, esteem, regard*, Mat. 14. 5; Lu. 14. 18, 19, et al.; *to have or hold* as an object of knowledge, faith, or practice, Jno. 5. 38, 42; 14. 21; 1 Jno. 5. 12; 2 Jno. 9; *to hold on* in entire possession, *to retain*, Ro. 15. 4; 2 Ti. 1. 13; He. 12. 28; intrans. with adverbs or adverbial expressions, *to be, to fare*, Mat. 9. 12; Mar. 2. 17; 5. 23; Lu. 5. 31; Jno. 4. 52; Ac. 7. 1; 12. 15; 15. 36; 21. 13, 2 Co. 10. 6; 12. 14; 1 Ti. 5. 25; 1 Pe. 4. 5; τὸ νῦν ἔχον, *for the present*; in N.T. ἔχειν ἐν γαστρί, *to be pregnant*, Mat. 1. 18, et al.; as also ἔχειν κοίτην, Ro. 9. 10; ἔχειν δαιμόνιον, *to be possessed*, Mat. 11. 18, et al.; of time, *to have continued, to have lived*, Jno. 5. 5, 6; 8. 57; of space, *to embrace, be distant*, Ac. 1. 12; mid. pr. *to hold by, cling to*; hence, *to border upon, be next*, Mar. 1. 38; Lu. 13. 33; Ac. 20. 15; 21. 26; *to tend immediately to*, He. 6. 9.

ἕξις, εως, ἡ, (§ 5. tab. E. c) *a condition of body or mind*, strictly, as resulting from practice; *habitude*, He. 5. 14.

ἔχω, 1 pers. sing. pres. subj. act. ἔχω
ἔχωμεν, 1 pers. pl. pres. subj. id.
ἔχων, nom. sing. masc. part. pres. id.
ἐχωρίσθη, 3 pers. sing. aor. 1, ind. pass. χωρίζω
ἔχωσι, 3 pers. pl. pres. subj. ἔχω
ἐψευδομαρτύρουν, 3 pers. pl. imperf. ψευδομαρτυρέω
ἐψεύσω, 2 pers. s. aor. 1, ind. mid. (§ 23. rem. 5) ψεύδω
ἐψηλάφησαν, 3 pers. pl. aor. 1, ind. ψηλαφάω
ἑώρακα, 1 pers. sing. perf. ind. Att. for ὤρακα, (§ 13. rem. 4) ὁράω
ἑωράκαμεν, 1 pers. pl. perf. Att. id.
ἑώρακαν, 3 pers. pl. (§ 35. rem. 13)—A. B. D. Ln. Tdf. } id.
ἑωράκασι, Rec. Gr. Sch. (Col. 2. 1)
ἑώρακας, 2 pers. sing. perf. Att. (§ 13. rem. 4) id.
ἑωράκασι, 3 pers. pl. perf. Att. id.
ἑωράκατε, 2 pers. pl. perf. Att. id.
ἑώρακε, 3 pers. sing. perf. Att. id.
ἑωράκει, 3 pers. sing. pluperf. Att. id.
ἑωρακέναι, perf. infin. Att. id.
ἑωρακότες, nom. pl. masc. part. perf. Att. id.
ἑωρακώς, nom. sing. masc. part. perf. Att. id.
ἑώρων, 3 pers. pl. imperf. Att. (§ 36. rem. 1) id.

ἕως, conjunc., of time, *while, as long as*, Jno. 9. 4; *until*, Mat. 2. 9; Lu. 15. 4; as also in N.T. ἕως οὗ, ἕως ὅτου, Mat. 5. 18, 26; ἕως ἄρτι, *until now*, Mat. 11. 12; ἕως πότε, *until when, how long*, Mat. 17. 17; ἕως σήμερον, *until this day, to this time*, 2 Co. 3. 15; as a prep., of time, *until*, Mat. 24. 21; of place, *unto, even to*, Mat. 11. 23; Lu. 2. 15; ἕως ἄνω, *to the brim*, Jno. 2. 7; ἕως εἰς, *even to, as far as*, Lu. 24. 50; ἕως κάτω, *to the bottom*; ἕως ὧδε, *to this place*, Lu. 23. 5; of state, *unto, even to*

Mat. 26. 38; of number, *even, so much as*, Ro. 3. 12, et al. freq.

Z.

Ζαβουλών, ὁ, *Zabulon*, pr. name, indecl.

Ζακχαῖε, voc. . . . . . . Ζακχαῖος

Ζακχαῖος, ου, ὁ, (§ 3. tab. C. a) *Zacchæus*, pr. name.

Ζαρά,[a] ὁ, *Zara*, pr. name, indecl.

Ζαχαρία, voc. . . . . . . Ζαχαρίας

Ζαχαρίαν, acc. . . . . . . id.

Ζαχαρίας, ου, ὁ, (§ 2. tab. B. d) *Zacharias*, pr. name. I. *Son of Barachias*, Mat. 23. 35; Lu. 11. 51. II. *Father of John the Baptist*, Lu. 1. 5, et al.

Ζαχαρίου, gen. . . . . . . Ζαχαρίας

ζάω, ζῶ, ζῇς, ζῇ, (§ 35. rem. 2) fut. ζήσω & ζήσομαι, aor. 1, ἔζησα, perf. ἔζηκα, *to live, to be possessed of vitality, to exercise the functions of life*, Mat. 27. 63; Ac. 17. 28, et al.; τὸ ζῆν, *life*, He. 2. 15; *to have means of subsistence*, 1 Co. 9. 14; *to live, to pass existence* in a specific manner, Lu. 2. 36; 15. 13, et al.; *to be instinct with life and vigour*; hence, ζῶν, *living*, an epithet of God, in a sense peculiar to Himself; ἐλπὶς ζῶσα, *a living hope* in respect of vigour and constancy, 1 Pe. 1. 3; ὕδωρ ζῶν, *living water* in respect of a full and unfailing flow, Jno. 4. 10, 11; *to be alive* with cheered and hopeful feelings, 1 Thes. 3. 8; *to be alive* in a state of salvation from spiritual death, 1 Jno. 4. 9, et al.

ζωή, ῆς, ἡ, (§ 2. tab. B. a) *life, living existence*, Lu. 16. 25; Ac. 17. 25; in N.T. spiritual *life* of deliverance from the proper penalty of sin, which is expressed by θάνατος, Jno. 6. 51; Ro. 5. 18; 6. 4, et al.; the final *life* of the redeemed, Mat. 25. 46, et al.; *life, source of* spiritual *life*, Jno. 5. 39; 11. 25; Col. 3. 4.

ζῶον, ου, τό, (§ 3. tab. C. c) *a living creature, animal*, He. 13. 11; 2 Pe. 2. 12, et al.

Ζεβεδαῖον, acc. . . . . . . Ζεβεδαῖος

Ζεβεδαῖος], ου, ὁ, (§ 3. tab. C. a) *Zebedee*, pr. name.

Ζεβεδαίου, gen. . . . . . . Ζεβεδαῖος

ζέοντες, nom. pl. masc. part. pres. (§ 35. rem. 1) ζέω

ζεστός, ή, όν], (§ 7. tab. F. a) . . ζέω

ζεύγη, acc. pl. . . . . . . ζεῦγος

ζεῦγος, εος, ους, τό, (§ 5. tab. E. b) *a yoke* of animals; *a pair, couple*, Lu. 2. 24; 14. 19.

ζευκτηρία], ας, ἡ, (§ 2. tab. B. b, and rem. 2) (pr. fem. of ζευκτήριος, fr. ζεύγνυμι, *to yoke, join*) *a fastening, band*.

ζευκτηρίας,[b] acc. pl. . . . . . ζευκτηρία

Ζεύς], Διός, ὁ, (§ 6. rem. 4. a) the supreme God of the Greeks, answering to the *Jupiter* of the Romans, Ac. 14. 12, 13.

ζέω], fut. ζέσω, (§ 22. rem. 1) *to boil, to be hot*; in N.T. met. *to be fervent, ardent, zealous*, Ac. 18. 25; Ro. 12. 11.

ζεστός, ή, όν, (§ 7. tab. F. a) pr. *boiled; boiling, boiling hot*; met. *glowing with zeal, fervent*, Re. 3. 15, 16.

ζῆλος, ου, ὁ, (§ 3. tab. C. a) in a good sense, *generous rivalry; noble aspiration*; in N.T., *zeal, ardour in behalf of, ardent affection*, Jno. 2. 17; Ro. 10. 2; in a bad sense, *jealousy, envy, malice*, Ac. 13. 45; Ro. 13. 13; *indignation, wrath*, Ac. 5. 17, et al.

ζηλόω, ῶ, fut. ώσω, (§ 20. tab. T) *to have strong affection towards, be ardently devoted to*, 2 Co. 11. 2; *to make a show of affection and devotion towards*, Gal. 4. 17; *to desire earnestly, aspire eagerly after*, 1 Co. 12. 31; 14. 1, 39; absol. *to be fervent, to be zealous*, Re. 3. 19; *to be jealous, envious, spiteful*, Ac. 7. 9; 17. 5; 1 Co. 13. 4; Ja. 4. 2; pass. *to be an object of warm regard and devotion*, Gal. 4. 18.

ζηλωτής, οῦ, ὁ, (§ 2. tab. B. c) pr. *a generous rival, an imitator*; in N.T. *an aspirant*, 1 Co. 14. 12; Tit. 2. 14; *a devoted adherent, a zealot*, Ac. 21. 20; 22. 3; Gal. 1. 14.

ζέων, nom. sing. masc. part. pres. (§ 35. rem. 1) ζέω

ζῇ, 3 pers. sing. pres. ind. (§ 35. rem. 2) . ζάω

ζήλευε, 2 pers. s. pres. imper.—A. C. Ln. Tdf. } ζηλεύω
ζήλωσον, Rec. Gr. Sch. (Re. 3. 19) }

ζηλεύω], fut. εύσω, i. q. ζηλόω, v.r.

ζῆλοι, nom. pl. . . . . . . ζῆλος

ζηλοῖ, 3 pers. sing. pres. ind. . . . ζηλόω

ζῆλον, acc. sing. . . . . . ζῆλος

[a] Mat. 1. 3.

[b] Ac. 27. 40.

ζῆλος, ου, ὁ, (§ 3. tab. C. a) . . . ζέω
ζήλου, gen. sing. . . . . . ζῆλος
ζηλοῦσθαι, pres. infin. pass. (§ 21. tab. U) . ζηλόω
ζηλοῦσι, 3 pers. pl. pres. ind. act. . . id.
ζηλοῦτε, 2 pers. pl. pres. ind. . . id.
ζηλοῦτε, 2 pers. pl. pres. imper. . . id.
ζηλοῦτε, 2 pers. pl. pres. subj. . . . id.
ζηλόω, ῶ], fut. ώσω, (§ 20. tab. T) . . ζέω
ζήλῳ, dat. sing. . . . . . ζῆλος
ζηλῶ, 1 pers. sing. pres. ind. . . . ζηλόω
ζηλώσαντες, nom. pl. masc. part. aor. 1 . id.
ζήλωσον, 2 pers. sing. aor. 1, imper. . id.
ζηλωταί, nom. pl. . . . . . ζηλωτής
ζηλωτήν, acc. sing. . . . . id.
ζηλωτής, οῦ, ὁ, (§ 2. tab. B. c) . . . ζέω

ζημία], ας, ἡ, (§ 2. tab. B. b, and rem. 2) *damage, loss, detriment*, Ac. 27. 10, 21; Phi. 3. 7, 8.

ζημιόω, ῶ, fut. ώσω, (§ 20. tab. T) *to visit with loss or harm*; pass. *to suffer loss or detriment*, 1 Co. 3. 15; 2 Co. 7. 9; *to lose, to forfeit*, Mat. 16. 26; Mar. 8. 36; Phi. 3. 8.

ζημίαν, acc. sing. . . . . ζημία
ζημίας, gen. sing. . . . . . id.
ζημιόω, ῶ], fut. ώσω, (§ 20. tab. T) . id.
ζημιωθείς, nom. sing. masc. part. aor. 1, pass. . . . . . ζημιόω
ζημιωθῇ, 3 pers. sing. aor. 1, subj. pass. . id.
ζημιωθήσεται, 3 pers. sing. fut. 1, ind. pass. . id.
ζημιωθῆτε, 2 pers. pl. aor. 1, subj. pass. . id.
ζῆν, pres. infin. (§ 35. rem. 2) . . . ζάω
Ζηνᾶν,[a] acc. . . . . . Ζηνᾶς
Ζηνᾶς], ᾶ, ὁ, (§ 2. rem. 4) *Zenas*, pr. name.
ζῇς, 2 pers. sing. pres. ind. . . . ζάω
ζήσασα, nom. sing. fem. part. aor. 1 . id.
ζήσεσθε, 2 pers. pl. fut. ind. mid. . id.
ζήσεται, 3 pers. sing. fut. ind. mid. . id.
ζήσῃ, 2 pers. sing. fut. ind. mid. . . id.
ζήσῃ, 3 pers. sing. aor. 1, subj.—Al. Ln. Tdf. } ζήσεται, Rec. Gr. Sch. (Mar. 5. 23) . } id.
ζησόμεθα, 1 pers. pl. fut. ind. mid. . id.
ζήσομεν, 1 pers. pl. fut. ind. . . . id.
ζήσονται, 3 pers. pl. fut. ind. mid. . . id.
ζήσουσι, 3 pers. pl. fut. ind.—B. D. Ln. Tdf. . . . . . } ζήσονται, Rec. Gr. Sch. (Jno. 5. 25) } id.

ζήσω, 1 pers. sing. aor. 1, subj. . . ζάω
ζήσωμεν, 1 pers. pl. aor. 1, subj. . . . id.
ζῆτε, 2 pers. pl. pres. ind. . . . id.
ζητεῖ, 3 pers. sing. pres. ind. act. ζητέω
ζήτει, 2 pers. sing. pres. imper. act. id.
ζητεῖν, pres. infin. act. . . . id.
ζητεῖς, 2 pers. sing. pres. ind. act. . . id.
ζητεῖται, 3 pers. sing. pres. ind. pass. id.
ζητεῖτε, 2 pers. pl. pres. ind. act. . id.
ζητεῖτε, 2 pers. pl. pres. imper. act. . . id.
ζητείτω, 3 pers. sing. pres. imper. act. . ζητέω
ζητέω, ῶ, fut. ήσω (§ 16. tab. P) *to seek, look for*, Mat. 18. 12; Lu. 2. 48, 49; *to search after*, Mat. 13. 45; *to be on the watch for*, Mat. 26. 16; *to pursue, endeavour to obtain*, Ro. 2. 7; 1 Pe. 3. 11, et al.; *to desire, wish, want*, Mat. 12. 47; *to seek, strive for*, Mat. 6. 33; *to endeavour*, Mat. 21. 46; *to require, demand, ask for*, Mar. 8. 11; Lu. 11. 16; 12. 48; *to inquire or ask questions, question*, Jno. 16. 19; *to deliberate*, Mar. 11. 18; Lu. 12. 29; in N.T. fr. Heb. ζητεῖν τὴν ψυχήν, *to seek the life* of any one, *to seek to kill*, Mat. 2. 20.

ζήτημα, ατος, τό, (§ 4. tab. D. c) *a question; a subject of debate or controversy*, Ac. 15. 2; 18. 15; 23. 29, et al.

ζήτησις, εως, ἡ, (§ 5. tab. E. c) *a seeking; an inquiry, a question; a dispute, debate, discussion*, Jno. 3. 25; 1 Ti. 1. 4; *a subject of dispute or controversy*, Ac. 25. 20, et al.

ζητηθήσεται, 3 pers. sing. fut. 1, pass. (§ 17. tab. Q) . . . . ζητέω
ζήτημα, ατος, τό, (§ 4. tab. D. c) . . id.
ζητήματα, acc. pl. . . . . ζήτημα
ζητήματος, gen. sing. . . . . id.
ζητημάτων, gen. pl. . . . . id.
ζητῆσαι, aor. 1, infin. act. . . . ζητέω
ζητησάτω, 3 pers. sing. aor. 1, imper. act. . id.
ζητήσεις, acc. pl. . . . . . ζήτησις
ζητήσετε, 2 pers. pl. fut. ind. act. . . ζητέω
ζητήσεως, gen. sing.—A. B. C. D. Gr. Sch. Tdf. } συζητήσεως, Rec. (Ac. 15. 2) } ζήτησις
ζητήσῃ, 3 pers. sing. aor. 1, subj. act. . ζητέω
ζήτησιν, acc. sing. . . . ζήτησις
ζήτησις, εως, ἡ, (§ 5. tab. E. c) . . ζητέω

[a] Tit. 3. 13.

ζήτησον, 2 pers. sing. aor. 1, imper. act. . ζητέω
ζητήσουσι, 3 pers. pl. fut. ind. act. . . id.
ζητοῦν, nom. sing. neut. part. pres. act. . id.
ζητοῦντες, nom. pl. masc. part. pres. act. . id.
ζητοῦντι, dat. sing. masc. part. pres. act. . id.
ζητούντων, gen. pl. masc. part. pres. act. . id.
ζητοῦσι, dat. pl. masc. part. pres. act. . id.
ζητοῦσι, 3 pers. pl. pres. ind. act. . . id.
ζητῶ, 1 pers. sing. pres. ind. act. . . id.
ζητῶν, nom. sing. masc. part. pres. act. . id.
ζιζάνια, nom. and acc. pl. . . . ζιζάνιον

ζιζάνιον], ου, τό, (§ 3. tab. C. c) *zizanium, darnel, spurious wheat*, a plant found in Palestine, which resembles wheat both in its stalk and grain, but is worthless and deleterious, Mat. 13. 26, 27, 29, 30, 36, 38, 40. L.G.

ζιζανίων, gen. pl. . . . . ζιζάνιον
Ζοροβάβελ, ὁ, *Zorobabel*, pr. name, indecl.
ζόφον, acc. sing. . . ζόφος

ζόφος, ου, ὁ, (§ 3. tab. C. a) *gloom, thick darkness*, 2 Pe. 2. 4, 17; Jude 6, 13.

ζόφου, gen. sing. . . . . . ζόφος
ζόφῳ, dat. sing.—Al. Ln. Tdf. . . } id.
σκότῳ, Rec. Gr. Sch. (He. 12. 18) }
ζυγόν, acc. sing. . . . . ζυγός

ζυγός, οῦ, ὁ, (§ 3. tab. C. a) a collateral form of ζυγόν, (ζεύγνυμι) pr. *a cross bar or band; a yoke;* met. *a yoke* of servile condition, 1 Ti. 6. 1; *a yoke* of service or obligation, Mat. 11. 29, 30; Ac. 15. 10; Gal. 5. 1; *the beam* of a balance; *a balance*, Re. 6. 5.

ζυγῷ, dat. sing. . . . . . ζυγός

ζύμη, ης, ἡ, (§ 2. tab. B. a) *leaven*, Mat. 16. 12; 13. 33; met. *leaven* of the mind and conduct, by a system of doctrine or morals, used in a bad sense, Mat. 16. 6, 11; 1 Co. 5. 6, et al.

ζυμόω, ῶ, fut. ώσω, (§ 20. tab. T) *to leaven, cause to ferment*, Mat. 13. 33; Lu. 13. 21; 1 Co. 5. 6; Gal. 5. 9.

ζύμῃ, dat. sing. . . . . . ζύμη
ζύμην, acc. sing. . . . . . id.
ζύμης, gen. sing. . . . . . id.
ζυμοῖ, 3 pers. sing. pres. ind. act. . . ζυμόω
ζυμόω, ῶ], fut. ώσω, (§ 20. tab. T) . . ζύμη
ζῶ, 1 pers. sing. pres. ind. . . . ζάω
ζῶα, nom. pl. . . . ζῶον

ζωγρέω, ῶ], fut. ήσω, perf. ἐζώγρηκα, (§ 16. tab. P) (ζωός, *alive*, & ἀγρεύω) pr. *to take alive, take prisoner in war* instead of killing; *to take captive, enthral*, 2 Ti. 2. 26; also, *to catch* animals, as fish; in which sense it is used figuratively, Lu. 5. 10.

ζωγρῶν, nom. sing. masc. part. pres. . ζωγρέω
ζωή, ῆς, ἡ, (§ 2. tab. B. a) . . . ζάω
ζωῇ, dat. sing. . . . . . ζωή
ζωήν, acc. sing. . . . . . id.
ζωῆς, gen. sing. . . . . . id.
ζῶμεν, 1 pers. pl. pres. ind. . . . ζάω
ζῶμεν, 1 pers. pl. pres. subj. . . . id.
ζῶν, nom. masc. and acc. neut. sing. part. pres. id.
ζώνας, acc. pl. . . . . . ζώνη

ζώνη, ης, ἡ, (§ 2. tab. B. a) *a zone, belt, girdle*, Mat. 3. 4; 10. 9, et al.

ζώννῡμι, and in N.T. ζωννύω, (ῠ) fut. ζώσω, (§ 31. tab. B. B) *to gird, gird on, put on one's girdle*, Jno. 21. 18, bis.

ζώνην, acc. sing. . . . . ζώνη
ζώννῡμι, and ζωννύω], fut. ζώσω, (§ 31. tab. B. B) . . . . id.
ζῶντα, acc. sing. masc. and pl. neut. part. pres. ζάω
ζῶντας, acc. pl. masc. part. pres. . . id.
ζῶντες, nom. pl. masc. part. pres. . . id.
ζῶντι, dat. sing. masc. part. pres. . . id.
ζῶντος, gen. sing. masc. and neut. part. pres. id.
ζώντων, gen. pl. masc. part. pres. . . id.
ζωογονεῖσθαι, pres. infin. pass. (§ 17. tab. Q) ζωογονέω

ζωογονέω, ῶ], fut. ήσω, (§ 16. tab. P) (ζωός & γόνος) pr. *to bring forth living creatures;* in N.T. *to preserve alive, save*, Lu. 17. 33; Ac. 7. 19.

ζωογονήσει, 3 pers. sing. fut. ind. act. . ζωογονέω
ζωογονοῦντος, gen. sing. masc. part. pres.— } id.
Al. Ln. Tdf. . . . }
ζωοποιοῦντος, Rec. Gr. Sch. (1 Ti. 6. 13) }
ζῶον, ου, τό, (§ 3. tab. C. c) . . . ζάω
ζωοποιεῖ, 3 pers. sing. pres. ind. act. . ζωοποιέω
ζωοποιεῖται, 3 pers. sing. pres. ind. pass. . id.

ζωοποιέω, ῶ], fut. ήσω, (§ 16. tab. P) (ζωός & ποιέω) pr. *to engender living creatures; to quicken, make alive, vivify*, Ro. 4. 17; 8. 11; 1 Co. 15. 36; in N.T. met. *to quicken* with the life of salvation, Jno. 6. 63; 2 Co. 3. 6, et al.

ζωοποιηθείς, nom. sing. masc. part. aor. 1, pass. ζωοποιέω
ζωοποιηθήσονται, 3 pers. pl. fut. 1, ind. pass. id.

ζωοποιῆσαι, aor. 1, infin. act. . . ζωοποιέω
ζωοποιήσει, 3 pers. sing. fut. ind. act. . id.
ζωοποιοῦν, nom. and acc. s. neut. part. pres. act. id.
ζωοποιοῦντος, gen. sing. masc. part. pres. act. id.
ζώου, gen. sing. . . . . . ζῶον
ζῶσα, nom. sing. fem. part. pres. . . ζάω
ζῶσαι, 2 pers. sing. aor. 1, imper. mid.—A. B. D. Ln. Tdf. . . . . } ζώννυμι
περίζωσαι, Rec. Gr. Sch. (Ac. 12. 8) }
ζῶσαν, acc. sing. fem. part. pres. . . ζάω
ζώσας, acc. pl. fem. part. pres. . . id.
ζώσει, 3 pers. sing. fut. ind. . . . ζώννυμι
ζῶσι, 3 pers. pl. pres. ind. . . . ζάω
ζῶσι, 3 pers. pl. pres. subj. . . . id.
ζώων, gen. pl. . . . . . ζῶον

Η.

ἤ, *either, or*, Mat. 6. 24, et al.; after comparatives, and ἄλλος, ἕτερος, expressed or implied, *than*, Mat. 10. 15; 18. 8; Ac. 17. 21; 24. 21; intensive after ἀλλά & πρίν, Lu. 12. 51; Mat. 1. 18; it also serves to point an interrogation, Ro. 3. 29, et al.

ἦ, a particle occurring in the N.T. only in the combination ἦ μήν, introductory to the terms of an oath, He. 6. 14.

ᾖ, 3 pers. sing. pres. subj. (§ 12. tab. L) . εἰμί
ᾗ, dat. sing. fem. . . . . . ὅς
ἠβουλήθην, 1 pers. sing. aor. 1, ind. (§ 13. rem. 1) . . . . . βούλομαι
ἤγαγε, 3 pers. sing. aor. 2, (§ 13. rem. 7. d) . ἄγω
ἠγάγετε, 2 pers. pl. aor. 2, ind. act. . id.
ἤγαγον, 3 pers. pl. aor. 2, ind. act. . . id.
ἠγαλλιάσατο, 3 pers. sing. aor. 1, ind. mid. ἀγαλλιάω
ἠγαλλίασε, 3 pers. sing. aor. 1, ind. . id.
ἠγανάκτησαν, 3 pers. pl. aor. 1, ind. . . ἀγανακτέω
ἠγανάκτησε, 3 pers. sing. aor. 1, ind. . id.
ἠγάπα, 3 pers. sing. imperf. act. . . ἀγαπάω
ἠγαπᾶτε, 2 pers. pl. imperf. act. . . id.
ἠγαπηκόσι, dat. pl. masc. part. perf. act. (§ 16. rem. 3) . . . . . . id.
ἠγαπημένην, acc. sing. fem. part. perf. pass. id.
ἠγαπημένοι, nom. pl. masc. part. perf. pass. id.
ἠγαπημένοις, dat. pl. masc. part. perf. pass.—Al. Ln. Tdf. . . . . } id.
ἡγιασμένοις, Rec. Gr. Sch. (Jude 1) }
ἠγαπημένῳ, dat. sing. masc. part. perf. pass. id.

ἠγάπησα, 1 pers. sing. aor. 1, ind. act. . ἀγαπάω
ἠγαπήσαμεν, 1 pers. pl. aor. 1, ind. act. . id.
ἠγάπησαν, 3 pers. pl. aor. 1, ind. act. . id.
ἠγάπησας, 2 pers. sing. aor. 1, ind. act. . id.
ἠγάπησε, 3 pers. sing. aor. 1, ind. act. . id.
ἠγγάρευσαν, 3 pers. pl. aor. 1, ind. act. . ἀγγαρεύω
ἤγγιζε, 3 pers. sing. imperf. . . . ἐγγίζω
ἤγγικε, 3 pers. sing. perf. ind. . . id.
ἤγγισαν, 3 pers. pl. aor. 1, ind. . . . id.
ἤγγισε, 3 pers. sing. aor. 1, ind. . . id.
ἦγε, 3 pers. sing. aor. 2, ind. act.—Ln. Tdf. } ἄγω
ἤγαγε, Rec. Gr. Sch. (Ac. 5. 26) . }
ἤγειραν, 3 pers. pl. aor. 1, ind. act. . . ἐγείρω
ἤγειρε, 3 pers. sing. aor. 1, ind. act. (§ 27. rem. 1. d) id.
ἡγεῖσθαι, pres. infin. (§ 17. tab. Q) . . ἡγέομαι
ἡγεῖσθε, 2 pers. pl. pres. imper. . . id.
ἡγείσθωσαν, 3 pers. pl. pres. imper. . . id.
ἡγεμόνα, acc. sing. . . . . ἡγεμών
ἡγεμόνας, acc. pl. . . . . . id.
ἡγεμονεύοντος, gen. sing. masc. part. pres. ἡγεμονεύω
ἡγεμονεύω], fut. εύσω, (§ 13. tab. M) . ἡγέομαι
ἡγεμόνι, dat. sing. . . . . . ἡγεμών
ἡγεμονία], ας, ἡ, (§ 2. tab. B. b, and rem. 2) ἡγέομαι
ἡγεμονίας,[a] gen. sing. . . . . ἡγεμονία
ἡγεμόνος, gen. sing. . . . . ἡγεμών
ἡγεμόνων, gen. pl. . . . . id.
ἡγεμόσι, dat. pl. . . . . id
ἡγεμών, όνος, ὁ, (§ 4. rem. 2. e) . . ἡγέομαι

ἡγέομαι, οῦμαι, fut. ἡγήσομαι, (§ 17. tab. Q) *to lead the way; to take the lead*, Ac. 14. 12; *to be chief, to preside, govern, rule*, Mat. 2. 6; Ac. 7. 10; ἡγούμενος, *a chief officer* in the church, He. 13. 7, 17, 24; also, with perf. ἥγημαι, *to think, consider, count, esteem, regard*, Ac. 26. 2; 2 Co. 9. 5, et al.

ἡγεμών, όνος, ὁ, (§ 4. rem. 2. e) *a guide; a leader; a chieftain, prince*, Mat. 2. 6; *a Roman provincial governor*, under whatever title, Mat. 27. 2, et al.

ἡγεμονία, ας, ἡ, (§ 2. tab. B. b, and rem. 2) *leadership, sovereignty*; in N.T. *a reign*, Lu. 3. 1.

ἡγεμονεύω, fut. εύσω, (§ 13. tab. M) *to be a guide, leader, chief*; in N.T. *to hold the office of a Roman provincial governor*, Lu. 2. 2; 3. 1.

[a] Lu. 3. 1.

ἠγέρθη, 3 pers. sing. aor. 1, pass. (§ 37. rem. 1) . . . ἐγείρω
ἠγέρθησαν, 3 pers. pl. aor. 1, ind. pass. . . . id.
ἤγεσθε, 2 pers. pl. imperf. pass. . . . ἄγω
ἤγετο, 3 pers. sing. imperf. pass. . . . id.
ἥγημαι, 1 pers. sing. perf. ind. pass. . . . ἡγέομαι
ἡγησάμενος, nom. sing. masc. part. aor. 1 . . . id.
ἡγησάμην, 1 pers. sing. aor. 1, ind. . . . id.
ἡγήσασθε, 2 pers. pl. aor. 1, ind. . . . id.
ἡγήσατο, 3 pers. sing. aor. 1, ind. . . . id.
ἡγίασε, 3 pers. sing. aor. 1, ind. act. . . . ἁγιάζω
ἡγιάσθη, 3 pers. sing. aor. 1, ind. pass. . . . id.
ἡγιάσθητε, 2 pers. pl. aor. 1, ind. pass. . . . id.
ἡγιασμένη, nom. sing. fem. part. perf. pass. . . . id.
ἡγιασμένοι, nom. pl. masc. part. perf. pass. . . . id.
ἡγιασμένοις, dat. pl. masc. part. perf. pass. . . . id.
ἡγιασμένον, nom. sing. neut. part. perf. pass. . . . id.
ἡγίασται, 3 pers. sing. perf. ind. pass. . . . id.
ἡγνικότες, nom. pl. masc. part. perf. act. . . . ἁγνίζω
ἡγνισμένον, acc. sing. masc. part. perf. pass. . . . id.
ἠγνόουν, 3 pers. pl. imperf. . . . ἀγνοέω
ἤγοντο, 3 pers. pl. imperf. pass. . . . ἄγω
ἠγόραζον, 3 pers. pl. imperf. act. . . . ἀγοράζω
ἠγόρασα, 1 pers. sing. aor. 1, ind. act. . . . id.
ἠγόρασαν, 3 pers. pl. aor. 1, ind. act. . . . id.
ἠγόρασας, 2 pers. sing. aor. 1, ind. act. . . . id.
ἠγόρασε, 3 pers. sing. aor. 1, ind. act. . . . id.
ἠγοράσθησαν, 3 pers. pl. aor. 1, ind. pass. . . . id.
ἠγοράσθητε, 2 pers. pl. aor. 1, ind. pass. . . . id.
ἠγορασμένοι, nom. pl. masc. part. perf. pass. . . . id.
ἡγοῦμαι, 1 pers. sing. pres. ind. . . . ἡγέομαι
ἡγούμενον, acc. sing. masc. part. pres. . . . id.
ἡγούμενοι, nom. pl. masc. part. pres. . . . id.
ἡγουμένοις, dat. pl. masc. part. pres. . . . id.
ἡγούμενος, nom. sing. masc. part. pres. . . . id.
ἡγουμένους, acc. pl. masc. part. pres. . . . id.
ἡγουμένων, gen. pl. part. pres. . . . id.
ἡγοῦνται, 3 pers. pl. pres. ind. (§ 17. tab. Q) . . . id.
ἠγωνίζοντο, 3 pers. pl. imperf. . . . ἀγωνίζομαι
ἠγώνισμαι, 1 pers. sing. perf. ind. (§ 26. rem. 1) . . . id.
ᾔδει, 3 pers. sing. pluperf. (§ 37. rem. 1) . . . οἶδα
ᾔδειν, 1 pers. sing. pluperf. . . . id.
ᾔδεις, 2 pers. sing. pluperf. . . . id.
ᾔδεισαν, 3 pers. pl. pluperf. . . . id.
ᾔδειτε, 2 pers. pl. pluperf. . . . id.
ἡδέως, adv. (ἡδύς, *sweet*) *with pleasure, gladly, willingly*, Mar. 6. 20; 12. 37; 2 Co. 11. 19.
ἤδη, adv. *before now, now, already*, Mat. 3. 10; 5. 28, et al.; ἤδη ποτέ, *at length*, Ro. 1. 10; Phi. 4. 10.
ἠδίκησα, 1 pers. s. aor. 1, ind. (§ 34. rem. 3. a) . . . ἀδικέω
ἠδικήσαμεν, 1 pers. pl. aor. 1, ind. . . . id.
ἠδικήσατε, 2 pers. pl. aor. 1, ind. . . . id.
ἠδίκησε, 3 pers. sing. aor. 1, ind. . . . id.
ἥδιστα, adv. (pr. neut. pl. superlat. of ἡδύς) *with the greatest pleasure, most gladly*, 2 Co. 12. 9, 15.
ἡδοναῖς, dat. pl. . . . ἡδονή
ἡδονή], ῆς, ἡ, (§ 2. tab. B. a) (ἧδος) *pleasure, gratification*; esp. *sensual pleasure*, Lu. 8. 14, Tit. 3. 3; Ja. 4. 3; 2 Pe. 2. 13; *a passion*, Ja. 4. 1.
ἡδονήν, acc. sing. . . . ἡδονή
ἡδονῶν, gen. pl. . . . id.
ἠδύναντο, 3 pers. pl. imperf. Att. for ἐδύναντο, (§ 37. rem. 1) . . . δύναμαι
ἠδύνασθε, 2 pers. pl. imperf. Att. (§ 13. rem. 1) . . . id.
ἠδύνατο, 3 pers. sing. imperf. Att. . . . id.
ἠδυνήθη, 3 pers. sing. aor. 1, ind. Att. . . . id.
ἠδυνήθημεν, 1 pers. pl. aor. 1, ind. Att. . . . id.
ἠδυνήθην, 1 pers. sing. aor. 1, ind. Att. . . . id.
ἠδυνήθησαν, 3 pers. pl. aor. 1, ind. Att. . . . id.
ἠδυνήθητε, 2 pers. pl. aor. 1, ind. Att. . . . id.
ἡδύοσμον, ου, τό, (§ 3. tab. C. c) (ἡδύς & ὀσμή) *garden mint*, Mat. 23. 23; Lu. 11. 42.
ἤθελε, 3 pers. sing. imperf. . . . ἐθέλω
ἤθελες, 2 pers. sing. imperf. . . . id.
ἠθέλησα, 1 pers. sing. aor. 1, ind. . . . id.
ἠθελήσαμεν, 1 pers. pl. aor. 1, ind. . . . id.
ἠθέλησαν, 3 pers. pl. aor. 1, ind. . . . id.
ἠθέλησας, 2 pers. sing. aor. 1, ind. . . . id
ἠθελήσατε, 2 pers. pl. aor. 1, ind. . . . id.
ἠθέλησε, 3 pers. sing. aor. 1, ind. . . . id.
ἤθελον, 3 pers. sing. and 3 pers. pl. imperf. . . . id.
ἠθέτησαν, 3 pers. pl. aor. 1, ind. . . . ἀθετέω
ἤθη,[a] acc. pl. . . . ἦθος
ἦθος], εος, τό, (§ 5. tab. E. b) pr. *a place of customary resort, a haunt*; hence, *a settled habit of mind and manners*.
ἠθροισμένους, acc. pl. masc. part. perf. pass.—B. D. Ln. Tdf. } ἀθροίζω
συνηθροισμένους, R. Gr. Sch. (Lu. 24. 33) }
ἠκαιρεῖσθε,[b] 2 pers. pl. imperf. . . . ἀκαιρέομαι
ἥκασι, 3 pers. pl. perf. ind—A. D. Ln. }
ἥκουσι, Rec. Gr. Sch. } ἥκω
εἰσί, Tdf. (Mar. 8. 3) }
ἥκει, 3 pers. sing. pres. ind. . . . id.

[a] 1 Co. 15. 33.
[b] Phi. 4. 10.

ἤκμασαν,[a] 3 pers. pl. aor. 1, ind. . . . ἀκμάζω
ἠκολούθει, 3 pers. sing. imperf. . . ἀκολουθέω
ἠκολουθήσαμεν, 1 pers. pl. aor. 1, ind. . id.
ἠκολούθησαν, 3 pers. pl. aor. 1, ind. . id.
ἠκολούθησε, 3 pers. sing. aor. 1, ind. . . id.
ἠκολούθουν, 3 pers. pl. imperf. . . id.
ἧκον, 3 pers. pl. imperf. . . . ἥκω
ἤκουε, 3 pers. sing. imperf. act. . . ἀκούω
ἤκουον, 3 pers. pl. imperf. act. . . . id.
ἤκουσα, 1 pers. sing. aor. 1, ind. act. . id.
ἠκούσαμεν, 1 pers. pl. aor. 1, ind. act. . . id.
ἤκουσαν, 3 pers. pl. aor. 1, ind. act. . id.
ἤκουσας, 2 pers. sing. aor. 1, ind. act. . . id.
ἠκούσατε, 2 pers. pl. aor. 1, ind. act. . id.
ἤκουσε, 3 pers. sing. aor. 1, ind. act. . . id.
ἠκούσθη, 3 pers. sing. aor. 1, pass. (§ 22. rem. 4) id.
ἥκουσι, 3 pers. pl. pres. ind. . . . ἥκω
ἠκρίβωσε, 3 pers. sing. aor. 1, ind. . . ἀκριβόω
ἠκυρώσατε, 2 pers. pl. aor. 1, ind. act. . ἀκυρόω

ἥκω, fut. ἥξω, imperf. ἧκον, later, perf. ἧκα, *to be come, have arrived*, Lu. 15. 27, et al.

ἥλατο, 3 pers. sing. aor. 1, ind.—Gr. Sch. Tdf. } ἅλλομαι
ἥλλετο, Rec. (Ac. 14. 10) . . }
ἠλαττόνησε, 3 pers. sing. aor. 1, ind. . ἐλαττονέω
ἠλαττωμένον, acc. sing. masc. part. perf. pass. ἐλαττόω
ἠλάττωσας, 2 pers. sing. aor. 1, ind. act. . id.
ἠλαύνετο, 3 pers. sing. imperf. pass. . ἐλαύνω
ἠλεήθημεν, 1 pers. pl. aor. 1, ind. pass. . ἐλεέω
ἠλεήθην, 1 pers. sing. aor. 1, ind. pass. . id.
ἠλεήθητε, 2 pers. pl. aor. 1, ind. pass. . . id.
ἠλεημένοι, nom. pl. masc. part. perf. pass. id.
ἠλεημένος, nom. sing. masc. part. perf. pass. id.
ἠλέησα, 1 pers. sing. aor. 1, ind. act. . id.
ἠλέησε, 3 pers. sing. aor. 1, ind. act. . . id.
ἤλειφε, 3 pers. sing. imperf. act. . . ἀλείφω
ἤλειφον, 3 pers. pl. imperf. act. . . id.
ἤλειψας, 2 pers. sing. aor. 1, ind. (§ 23. rem. 2) id.
ἤλειψε, 3 pers. sing. aor. 1, ind. . . id.
ἠλευθέρωσε, 3 pers. sing. aor. 1, ind. . ἐλευθερόω
ἤλθατε, 2 pers. pl. aor. 1.—Al. Ln. Tdf. (§ 35. rem. 12) . . . . } ἔρχομαι
ἤλθετε, Rec. Gr. Sch. (Mat. 25. 36) }
ἦλθε, 3 pers. sing. aor. 2, ind. (§ 36. rem. 1) . id.
ἦλθες, 2 pers. sing. aor. 2, ind. . . id.
ἤλθετε, 2 pers. pl. aor. 2, ind. . . . id.
ἤλθομεν, 1 pers. pl. aor. 2, ind. . . id.
ἦλθον, 1 pers. sing. and 3 pers. pl. aor. 2, ind. id.

ἤλθοσαν, 3 pers. pl. Alex. for ἦλθον,—B. D. Ln. (§ 35. rem. 13) . . } ἔρχομαι
ἦλθεν, Rec. Gr. Sch. . . . }
ἦλθον, Tdf. (Mar. 9. 33) . . }
Ἠλί,[b] (Heb. אֵלִי *my God!*) Rec. Gr. Sch. Tdf.
ἠλεί, D.
ἐλωεί, B.
ἠλί, Ln. (Mat. 27. 46)
Ἠλί,[c] ὁ, *Eli*, pr. name, indecl.
Ἠλίᾳ, dat. sing. . . . . . . Ἠλίας
Ἠλίαν, acc. sing. . . . . . id
Ἠλίας, ου, ὁ, (§ 2. tab. B. d) *Elias*, pr. name.
ἡλίκην, acc. sing. fem. . . . . ἡλίκος
ἡλικία], ας, ἡ, (§ 2. tab. B. b, and rem. 2) (ἧλιξ) *a particular period of life; the period fitted for a particular function, prime*, He. 11. 11; *full age, years of discretion*, Jno. 9. 21, 23; perhaps, *the whole duration of life*, Mat. 6. 27; Lu. 12. 25; otherwise, *stature*, Lu. 19. 3; Ep. 4. 13.
ἡλικίᾳ, dat. sing. . . . . . ἡλικία
ἡλικίαν, acc. sing. . . . . . . id.
ἡλικίας, gen. sing. . . . . . id.
ἡλίκον, nom. sing. neut.—A. B. C. Ln. Tdf. } id.
ὀλίγον, Rec. Gr. Sch. (Ja. 3. 5) . }
ἡλίκον, acc. sing. masc. . . . . id.
ἡλίκος], η, ον, (§ 10. rem. 7. c) *as great as; how great*, Col. 2. 1; Ja. 3. 5. (ῐ).
ἥλιον, acc. sing. . . . . . ἥλιος

ἥλιος, ου, ὁ, (§ 3. tab. C. a) *the sun*, Mat. 13. 43; 17. 2; Mar. 1. 32, et al.; meton. *light of the sun, light*, Ac. 13. 11.

Ἠλίου, gen. sing. . . . . Ἠλίας
ἡλίου, gen. sing. . . . . . ἥλιος
ἡλίῳ, dat. sing. . . . . . . id.
ἡλκωμένος,[d] nom. sing. masc. part. perf. pass. (§ 21. tab. U) . . . . ἑλκόω
ἤλλαξαν, 3 pers. pl. aor. 1, ind. act. . . ἀλλάσσω
ἥλλετο, 3 pers. sing. imperf. . . . ἅλλομαι

ἧλος], ου, ὁ, (§ 3. tab. C. a) *a nail*, Jno. 20. 25, bis.

ἤλπιζε, 3 pers. sing. imperf. . . . ἐλπίζω
ἠλπίζομεν, 1 pers. pl. imperf. . . . id.
ἠλπίκαμεν, 1 pers. pl. perf. ind. (§ 13. rem. 5. b) id.
ἠλπίκατε, 2 pers. pl. perf. ind. . . id.
ἤλπικε, 3 pers. sing. perf. ind. . . . id.

[a] Re. 14. 18. [b] Mat. 27 46. [c] Lu. 3. 23. [d] Lu. 16. 20.

ἠλπικέναι, perf. infin. . . . . . ἐλπίζω
ἠλπικότες, nom. pl. masc. part. perf. . id.
ἠλπίσαμεν, 1 pers. pl. aor. 1, ind. . . id.
ἥλων, gen. pl. . . . . . . ἧλος
ἥμαρτε, 3 pers. sing. aor. 2, ind. (§ 36. rem. 2) ἁμαρτάνω
ἥμαρτες, 2 pers. sing. aor. 2, ind. . . id.
ἡμαρτήκαμεν, 1 pers. pl. perf. ind. . . id.
ἥμαρτον, 1 pers. sing. or 3 pers. pl. aor. 2, ind. id.
ἡμᾶς, acc. pl. . . . . . . ἐγώ
ἤμεθα, 1 pers. pl. imperf. (§ 12. rem. 2) Gr. Sch. Tdf. . . . } εἰμί
ἦμεν, Rec. (Mat. 23. 30) . . }
ἡμεῖς, nom. pl. (§ 11. tab. K. a) . . ἐγώ
ἠμέλησα, 1 pers. pl. aor. 1, ind. . . . ἀμελέω
ἤμελλε, 3 pers. sing. imperf. Att. (§ 13. rem. 1) μελλω
ἤμελλον, 1 pers. sing. imperf.—Ln. Tdf. . } id.
ἔμελλον, Rec. Gr. Sch. (Re. 10. 4) }
ἤμελλον, 3 pers. pl. imperf. Const. . } id.
ἔμελλον, Rec. Gr. Sch. Tdf. (Jno. 7. 39.) }
ἦμεν, 1 pers. pl. imperf. (§ 12. tab. L) . εἰμί

ἡμέρα, ας, ἡ, (§ 2. tab. B. b, and rem. 2) *day, a day, the interval from sunrise to sunset,* opp. to νύξ, Mat. 4. 2; 12. 40; Lu. 2. 44; *the interval of twenty-four hours,* comprehending day and night, Mat. 6. 34: 15. 32; from the Heb. ἡμέρᾳ καὶ ἡμέρᾳ, *day by day, every day,* 2 Co. 4. 16; ἡμέραν ἐξ ἡμέρας, *from day to day, continually,* 2 Pe. 2. 8; καθ' ἡμέραν, *every day, daily,* Ac. 17. 17; He. 3. 13; *a point or period of time,* Lu. 19. 42; Ac. 15. 7; Ep. 6. 13, et al.; *a judgment, trial,* 1 Co. 4. 3.

ἡμέρᾳ, dat. sing. . . . . . . ἡμέρα
ἡμέραι, nom. pl. . . . . . id.
ἡμέραις, dat. pl. . . . . . id.
ἡμέραν, acc. sing. . . . . . id.
ἡμέρας, gen. sing. or acc. pl. . . . . id.
ἡμερῶν, gen. pl. . . . . id.
ἡμετέρα, nom. sing. fem. . . . . ἡμέτερος
ἡμετέραις, dat. pl. fem. . . . . id.
ἡμετέραν, acc. sing. fem. . . . . id.
ἡμετέρας, gen. sing. fem. . . . . id.
ἡμέτεροι, nom. pl. masc. . . . . id.
ἡμετέροις, dat. pl. masc. . . id.
ἡμέτερον, acc. sing. masc. . . . id.
ἡμέτερος], α, ον, (§ 11. rem. 4) *our,* Ac. 2. 11; 24. 6, et al.

ἡμετέρων, gen. pl. . . . . . ἡμέτερος
ἤμην, 1 pers. sing. imperf. (§ 12. rem. 2) εἰμί
ἡμιθανῆ,[a] acc. sing. masc. . . ἡμιθανής
ἡμιθανής], έος, οῦς, ὁ, ἡ, (§ 7. tab. G. b) (ἡμι- & θνήσκω) *half dead.*
ἡμῖν, dat. pl. . . . . . . ἐγώ
ἡμίση, acc. pl. neut. . . . . . ἥμισυς
ἡμίσους, gen. sing. neut. (§ 7. rem. 7) . . id.
ἥμισυ, acc. sing. neut. . . . . . id.
ἥμισυς, σεια, συ, ((§ 7. tab. H. g) *half,* Mar. 6. 23; Lu. 19. 8; Re. 11. 11; 12. 14.
ἡμιώριον,[b] ου, τό, (§ 3. tab. C. c) (ἡμι- & ὥρα) *half an hour.* L.G.
ἠμύνατο,[c] 3 pers. s. aor. 1, ind. mid. (§ 13. rem. 2) ἀμύνω
ἠμφιεσμένον, acc. sing. masc. part. perf. pass. (§ 36. rem. 5) . . . αμφιέννυμι
ἡμῶν, gen. pl. . . . . . . ἐγώ
ἦν, 3 pers. sing. imperf. (§ 12. rem. 2) . εἰμί
ἥν, acc. sing. fem. . . . . . ὅς
ἠνάγκαζον, 1 pers. sing. imperf. act. . . ἀναγκάζω
ἠναγκάσατε, 2 pers. pl. aor. 1, ind. act. . id.
ἠνάγκασε, 3 pers. sing. aor. 1, ind. act. . id.
ἠναγκάσθη, 3 pers. sing. aor. 1, ind. pass. (§ 26. rem. 1) . . . . . id.
ἠναγκάσθην, 1 pers. sing. aor. 1, ind. pass. . id.
ἤνεγκα, 1 pers. sing. aor. 1, ind. (§ 35. rem. 7) φέρω
ἤνεγκαν, 3 pers. pl. aor. 1, ind. . . id
ἤνεγκε, 3 pers. sing. aor. 1, ind. . . . id.
ἠνείχεσθε, 2 pers. pl. imperf. (§ 34. rem. 1. d) ἀνέχομαι
ἠνεσχόμην, 1 pers. sing. aor. 2, ind. . . id.
ἠνέχθη, 3 pers. sing. aor. 1, pass. (§ 36. rem. 1) φέρω
ἠνεῳγμένη, nom. sing. fem. part. perf. pass. (§ 37. rem. 1) . . . . ἀνοίγω
ἠνεῳγμένον, acc. sing. neut. part. perf. pass. id.
ἠνεῴχθη, 3 pers. sing. aor. 1, ind. pass. . id.
ἠνεῴχθησαν, 3 pers. pl. aor. 1, ind. pass. . id.
ἡνίκα], adv. *when,* 2 Co. 3. 15, 16. (ῐ).
ἠνοίγη, 3 pers. sing. aor. 2, pass. (§ 37. rem. 1) ἀνοίγω
ἠνοίγησαν, 3 pers. pl. aor. 2, pass.—B. D. Ln. Tdf. . . . . } id.
διηνοίχθησαν, Rec. Gr. Sch. (Mar. 7. 35) }
ἤνοιξε, 3 pers. sing. aor. 1, ind. act. . id.
ἠνοίχθη, 3 pers. s. aor. 1, ind. pass. (§ 23. rem. 4) id.
ἠνοίχθησαν, 3 pers. pl. aor. 1, ind. pass.— Gr. Sch. Tdf. . . . } id.
ἠνεῴχθησαν, Rec. (Re. 20. 12) . }
ἠντληκότες, nom. pl. masc. part. perf. . ἀντλέω
ἥξει, 3 pers. sing. fut. ind. . . . ἥκω

[a] Lu. 10. 30 [b] Re. 8. 1. [c] Ac. 7. 24.

ἥξῃ, 3 pers. sing. aor. 1, subj. . . ἥκω
ἠξίου, 3 pers. sing. imperf. . . . ἀξιόω
ἠξίωσα, 1 pers. sing. aor. 1, ind. . . id.
ἠξίωται, 3 pers. sing. perf. pass. (§ 21. tab. U) id.
ἥξουσι, 3 pers. pl. fut. ind. . . . ἥκω
ἥξω, 1 pers. sing. fut. ind. . . . id.
ἥξω, 1 pers. sing. aor. 1, subj. . . . id.
ἥξωσι, 3 pers. pl. aor. 1, subj. . . id.
ἠπατήθη, 3 pers. sing. aor. 1, ind. pass. . ἀπατάω
ἠπείθησαν, 3 pers. pl. aor. 1, ind. . . ἀπειθέω
ἠπειθήσατε, 2 pers. pl. aor. 1, ind. . . id.
ἠπείθουν, 3 pers. pl. imperf. (§ 16. tab. P) id.
ἠπείλει, 3 pers. sing. imperf. . . . ἀπειλέω
ἤπερ,[a] (ἤ & περ) an emphatic form of ἤ, *than*.
ἤπιον, acc. sing. masc. . . . . ἤπιος
ἤπιοι, nom. pl. masc. . . . . id.

ἤπιος], ου, ὁ, ἡ, (§ 7. rem. 2) *mild, gentle, kind*, 1 Thes. 2. 7; 2 Ti. 2. 24.

ἠπίστησαν, 3 pers. pl. aor. 1, ind. . . ἀπιστέω
ἠπίστουν, 3 pers. pl. imperf. . . . id.
ἥπτοντο, 3 pers. pl. imperf. mid. . . ἅπτω
Ἤρ,[b] ὁ, *Er*, pr. name, indecl.—R. Gr. Sch. Tdf.
Ἤρ, Ln. (Lu. 3. 28)
ἦραν, 3 pers. pl. aor. 1, ind. act. . . αἴρω
ἤρατε, 2 pers. pl. aor. 1, ind. act. . . id.
ἦρε, 3 pers. sing. aor. 1, ind. act. . . id.
ἠρέθισε, 3 pers. sing. aor. 1, ind. . . ἐρεθίζω
ἤρεμον,[c] acc. sing. masc. . . . ἤρεμος
ἤρεμος], ου, ὁ, ἡ, (§ 7. rem. 2) equivalent to the ordinary form ἠρεμαῖος, *tranquil, quiet*, N.T.
ἤρεσε, 3 pers. sing. aor. 1, ind. (§ 36. rem. 3) ἀρέσκω
ἤρεσκον, 1 pers. sing. imperf. . . . id.
ἡρέτισα,[d] 1 pers. sing. aor. 1, ind. (§ 13. rem. 2) αἱρετίζω
ἠρημωμένην, acc. sing. fem. part. perf. pass. ἐρημόω
ἠρημώθη, 3 pers. s. aor. 1, ind. pass. (§ 21. tab. U) id.
ἤρθη, 3 pers. sing. aor. 1 ind. pass. (§ 27. rem. 3) αἴρω
ἠριθμημέναι, nom. pl. fem. part. perf. pass. ἀριθμέω
ἠρίθμηνται, 3 pers. pl. perf. pass. (§ 17. tab. Q) id.
ἠρίστησαν, 3 pers. pl. aor. 1, ind. . . ἀριστάω
ἦρκε, 3 pers. sing. perf. ind. act. (§ 27. rem. 2. a) αἴρω
ἠρμένον, acc. sing. masc. part. perf. pass. . id.
ἡρμοσάμην,[e] 1 pers. sing. aor. 1, ind. mid. ἁρμόζω
ἠρνεῖτο, 3 pers. sing. imperf. . . . ἀρνέομαι
ἠρνημένοι, nom. pl. masc. part. perf. pass. . id.
ἠρνήσαντο, 3 pers. pl. aor. 1, ind. . . id.
ἠρνήσασθε, 2 pers. pl. aor. 1, ind. . . id.
ἠρνήσατο, 3 pers. sing. aor. 1, ind. . . ἀρνέομαι
ἠρνήσω, 2 pers. sing. aor. 1, ind. . . id.
ἤρνηται, 3 pers. sing. perf. ind. . . id.
ἤρξαντο, 3 pers. pl. aor. 1, ind. mid. (§ 23. rem. 5) ἄρχω
ἤρξατο, 3 pers. sing. aor. 1, ind. mid. . . id.
ἡρπάγη, 3 pers. s. aor. 2, ind. pass. (§ 26. rem. 3) ἁρπάζω
ἥρπασε, 3 pers. sing. aor. 1, ind. act. . id.
ἡρπάσθη, 3 pers. s. aor. 1, ind. pass. (§ 26. rem. 1) id.
ἠρτυμένος, nom. sing. masc. part. perf. pass. . ἀρτύω
ἤρχετο, 3 pers. sing. imperf. . . . ἔρχομαι
ἤρχοντο, 3 pers. pl. imperf. . . . id.
ἤρχου, 2 pers. sing. imperf. . . . id.
Ἡρώδῃ, dat. sing. . . . . . Ἡρώδης
Ἡρώδην, acc. sing. . . . . . id.
Ἡρώδης, ου, ὁ, (§ 2. tab. B. c) *Herod*, pr. name.
I. *Herod the Great*, Mat. 2. 1, et al.
II. *Herod Antipas*, tetrarch of Galilee and Peræa, Mat. 14. 1, et al.
III. *Herod Agrippa*, Ac. 12. 1, et al.
Ἡρωδιάδα, acc. sing. . . . . . Ἡρωδιάς
Ἡρωδιάδος, gen. sing. . . . . id.
Ἡρωδιανοί], ων, οἱ, *Herodians*, partisans of Ἡρώδης, *Herod Antipas*, Mat. 22. 16; Mar. 3. 6; 12. 13.
Ἡρωδιανῶν, gen. pl. . . . . Ἡρωδιανοί
Ἡρωδιάς], άδος, ἡ, (§ 4. tab. D. b) *Herodias*, pr. name.
Ἡρωδίων], ωνος, ὁ, (§ 4. rem. 2. e) *Herodian*, pr. name.
Ἡρωδίωνα,[f] acc. sing. . . . . Ἡρωδίων
Ἡρώδου, gen. sing. . . . . . Ἡρώδης
ἠρώτα, 3 pers. sing. imperf. (§ 18. tab. R) . ἐρωτάω
ἠρώτησαν, 3 pers. pl. aor. 1, ind. . . id.
ἠρώτησε, 3 pers. sing. aor. 1, ind. . . id.
ἠρώτων, 3 pers. pl. imperf. . . . id.
ἦς, 2 pers. sing. imperf. (§ 12. tab. L) . . εἰμί
ᾖς, 2 pers. sing. pres. subj. . . . id.
ἧς, gen. sing. fem. . . . . . ὅς
Ἡσαΐᾳ, dat. sing.—B. D. Gr. Sch. Tdf. ἐν τοῖς προφήταις, Rec. (Mar. 1. 2) } Ἡσαΐας
Ἡσαΐαν, acc. sing. . . . . . id.
Ἡσαΐας, ου, ὁ, (§ 2. tab. B. d) *Esaias*, pr. name. Rec.
Ἡσαΐας, Gr. Sch. Tdf.
Ἡσαΐου, gen. sing. . . . . Ἡσαΐας
ἦσαν, 3 pers. pl. imperf. (§ 12. tab. L) . εἰμί
Ἡσαῦ, ὁ, *Esau*, pr. name, indecl.
ἠσέβησαν, 3 pers. pl. aor. 1, ind. . . ἀσεβέω

[a] Jno. 12. 43. [b] Lu. 3. 28. [c] 1 Ti. 2. 2. [d] Mat. 12. 18. [e] 2 Co. 11. 2. [f] Ro. 16. 11.

ἦσθα, 2 pers. sing. imperf. for ἦς, (§ 12. rem. 2) εἰμί

ἠσθένει, 3 pers. sing. imperf. (§ 16. tab. P) . ἀσθενέω

ἠσθενήκαμεν, 1 pers. pl. perf. ind.—B. Ln.
ἠσθενήσαμεν, Rec. Gr. Sch. Tdf. . } id.
(2 Co. 11. 21) . . .

ἠσθένησα, 1 pers. sing. aor. 1, ind. . . id.

ἠσθενήσαμεν, 1 pers. pl. aor. 1, ind. . . id.

ἠσθένησε, 3 pers. sing. aor. 1, ind. . . id.

ἤσθιον, 3 pers. pl. imperf. . . . . ἐσθίω

ἠσπάζοντο, 3 pers. pl. imperf. . . ἀσπάζομαι

ἠσπάσατο, 3 pers. sing. aor. 1, ind. . . id.

ἡσσώθητε, 2 pers. pl. aor. 1, pass. (as if from
ἡσσόομαι, οῦμαι, equivalent to } ἡττάομαι
ἡττάομαι)—B. D. Ln. Tdf. .
ἡττήθητε, Rec. Gr. Sch. (2 Co. 12. 13)

ἠστόχησαν, 3 pers. pl. aor. 1, (§ 16. tab. P) . ἀστοχέω

ἡσυχάζειν, pres. infin. . . . . ἡσυχάζω

ἡσυχάζω], fut. άσω, (§ 26. rem. 1) (ἥσυχος, *quiet*) *to be still, at rest; to live peaceably, be quiet*, 1 Thes. 4. 11; *to rest* from labour, Lu. 23. 56; *to be silent or quiet, acquiesce, to desist* from discussion, Lu. 14. 4; Ac. 11. 18; 21. 14.

ἡσυχάσαμεν, 1 pers. pl. aor. 1, ind. . . ἡσυχάζω

ἡσύχασαν, 3 pers. pl. aor. 1, ind. . . id.

ἡσυχία], ας, ἡ, (§ 2. tab. B. b, and rem. 2) *rest, quiet, tranquillity; a quiet, tranquil life*, 2 Thes. 3. 12; *silence, silent attention*, Ac. 22. 2; 1 Ti. 2. 11, 12.

ἡσυχίᾳ, dat. sing. . . . . . ἡσυχία

ἡσυχίαν, acc. sing. . . . . . id.

ἡσυχίας, gen. sing. . . . . . id.

ἡσύχιον, acc. sing. masc. . . . ἡσύχιος

ἡσύχιος], ου, ὁ, ἡ, (§ 7. rem. 2) equivalent to ἥσυχος, *quiet, tranquil, peaceful*, 1 Ti. 2. 2; 1 Pe. 3. 4.

ἡσυχίου, gen. sing. neut. . . . . ἡσύχιος

ἠσφαλίσατο, 3 pers. sing. aor. 1, ind. mid. ἀσφαλίζω

ἠσφαλίσαντο, 3 pers. pl. aor. 1, ind. mid. id.

ἠτακτήσαμεν,[a] 1 pers. pl. aor. 1, ind. . ἀτακτέω

ἦτε, 2 pers. pl. imperf. or pres. subj. (§ 12. tab. L) εἰμί

ᾐτήκαμεν, 1 pers. pl. perf. ind. (§ 13. rem. 2) αἰτέω

ᾐτήσαντα, 3 pers. pl. aor. 1, ind. mid. . . id.

ᾔτησας, 2 pers. sing. aor. 1, ind. act. . id.

ᾐτήσασθε, 2 pers. pl. aor. 1, ind. mid. . . id.

ᾐτήσατε, 2 pers. pl. aor. 1, ind. act. . id.

ᾐτήσατο, 3 pers. sing. aor. 1, ind. act. . . id.

ἠτιμάσατε, 2 pers. pl. aor. 1, ind. act. . ἀτιμάζω

ἠτίμησαν, 3 pers. pl. aor. 1, ind. act.—B. D.
Ln. Tdf. . . . . . } ἀτιμάζω
ἀπέστειλαν ἠτιμωμένον, Rec. Gr. Sch.
(Mar. 12. 4) . . .

ἠτιμωμένον,[b] acc. sing. masc. part. perf. pass. ἀτιμόω

ἥτις, nom. sing. fem. (§ 10. tab. J. h) . ὅστις

ἤτοι,[c] conj. (ἤ & τοι) in N.T. only in the usage, ἤτοι—ἤ, *whether*, with an elevated tone.

ἡτοίμακα, 1 pers. sing. perf. ind. act.—B. C. D.
Ln. Tdf. . . . . } ἑτοιμάζω
ἡτοίμασα, Rec. Gr. Sch. (Mat. 22. 4)

ἡτοίμασα, 1 pers. sing. aor. 1, ind. act. . id.

ἡτοίμασαν, 3 pers. pl. aor. 1, ind. act. . id.

ἡτοίμασας, 2 pers. sing. aor. 1, ind. act. . id.

ἡτοίμασε, 3 pers. sing. aor. 1, ind. act. . id.

ἡτοιμασμένην, acc. sing. fem. part. perf. pass. id.

ἡτοιμασμένον, nom. and acc. sing. neut. and acc. masc. part. perf. pass. . id.

ἡτοιμασμένοι, nom. pl. masc. part. perf. pass. (§ 26. rem. 1) . . . . id.

ἡτοιμασμένοις, dat. pl. masc. part. perf. pass. id.

ἡτοίμασται, 3 pers. sing. perf. ind. pass. . id.

ᾐτοῦντο, 3 pers. pl. imperf. mid. (§ 13. rem. 2) αἰτέω

ἡττάομαι, ῶμαι], (§ 19. tab. S) . . . ἥττων

ἡττήθητε, 2 pers. pl. aor. 1, ind. pass. . ἡττάομαι

ἥττημα], ατος, τό, (§ 4. tab. D. c) . . ἥττων

ἥττηται, 3 pers. sing. perf. ind. pass. . ἡττάομαι

ἧττον,[d] acc. sing. neut.—Rec. Gr. Sch. . } ἧττον
ἥσσων, Al. Ln. Tdf. (1 Co. 11. 17) .

ἧττον,[e] adv. *less*.—Rec. Gr. Sch.
ἧσσον, B. Ln. Tdf. (2 Co. 12. 15)

ἥττων, Att. for ἥσσων, ονος, ὁ, ἡ, (§ 8. rem. 5) *less*.

ἡττάομαι, ῶμαι, fut. ἡττηθήσομαι, & ἡττήσομαι, perf. ἥττημαι, *to be less, inferior to; to fare worse, to be in a less favoured condition*, 2 Co. 12. 13; by impl. *to be overcome, vanquished*, 2 Pe. 2. 19, 20.

ἥττημα, ατος, τό, (§ 4. tab. D. c) *an inferiority*, to a particular standard; *default, failure, shortcoming*, Ro. 11. 12; 1 Co. 6. 7. LXX.

ἡττῶνται, 3 pers. pl. pres. ind. . . . ἡττάομαι

ἤτω, 3 pers. sing. pres. imper. (§ 12. rem. 2) εἰμί

ηὐδόκησα, 1 pers. sing. aor. 1, ind. (§ 34. rem. 3. c) . . . . . εὐδοκέω

ηὐδόκησας, 2 pers. sing. aor. 1, ind.—Ln. Tdf. } id.
εὐδόκησας, Rec. Gr. Sch. (He. 10. 6, 8)

[a] 2 Thes. 3. 7. [b] Mar. 12. 4. [c] Ro. 6. 16. [d] 1 Co. 11. 17. [e] 2 Co. 12. 15.

ηὐδόκησε, 3 pers. sing. aor. 1, ind.—B. Ln. Tdf. } εὐδοκέω
εὐδόκησε, Rec. Gr. Sch. (1 Co. 10. 5) }

ηὐκαίρουν, 3 pers. pl. imperf. (§ 34. rem. 3. c) . εὐκαιρέω

ηὐλήσαμεν, 1 pers. pl. aor. 1, ind. . . αὐλέω

ηὐλίζετο, 3 pers. sing. imperf. . . . αὐλίζομαι

ηὐλίσθη, 2 pers. sing. aor. 1, ind. . . id.

ηὐλόγει, 3 pers. sing. imperf. (§ 34. rem. 3. c) εὐλογέω

ηὐλόγηκε, 3 pers. sing. perf. ind. act.—Ln. } id.
εὐλόγηκε, Rec. Gr. Sch. Tdf. (He. 7. 6) }

ηὐλόγησε, 3 pers. s. aor. 1, ind. act.—Ln. Tdf. } id.
εὐλόγησε, Rec. Gr. Sch. (He. 11. 21) }

ηὔξανε, 3 pers. sing. imperf. act. (§ 13. rem. 2) αὐξάνω

ηὔξησε, 3 pers. sing. aor. 1, ind. . . id.

ηὐπορεῖτο,[a] 3 pers. sing. imperf. mid. . εὐπορέω

ηὕρισκον, 3 pers. pl. imperf. act.—B. D. Ln. Tdf. . . . . . } εὑρίσκω
εὕρισκον, Rec. Gr. Sch. (Mar. 14. 55) }

ηὐφράνθη, 3 pers. sing. aor. 1, pass.—Al. Ln. Tdf. . . . . . } εὐφραίνω
εὐφράνθη, Rec. Gr. Sch. (Ac. 2. 26) }

ηὐφόρησε, 3 pers. sing. aor. 1, ind.—A. D. Ln. } εὐφορέω
εὐφόρησε, R. Gr. Sch. Tdf. (Lu. 12. 16) }

ηὐχαρίστησαν, 3 pers. pl. aor. 1, ind.—Gr. Sch. Tdf. . . . . . } εὐχαριστέω
εὐχαρίστησαν, Rec. (Ro. 1. 21) . }

ηὐχόμην, 1 pers. sing. imperf. (§ 34. rem. 3. c) εὔχομαι

ηὔχοντο, 3 pers. pl. imperf. . . . id.

ἤφιε, 3 pers. sing. imperf. act. (§ 32. rem. 2) . ἀφίημι

ἠχέω, ῶ], fut. ήσω, (§ 16. tab. P) (ἠχή) *to sound, ring*, 1 Co. 13. 1; *to roar*, as the sea, Lu. 21. 25.

ἤχθη, 3 pers. sing. aor. 1, pass. (§ 23. rem. 4) ἄγω

ᾐχμαλώτευσε, 3 pers. sing. aor. 1, ind. (§ 13. rem. 2) . . . αἰχμαλωτεύω

ἦχος, ου, ὁ, (§ 3. tab. C. a) equivalent to ἠχή, *sound, noise*, Ac. 2. 2; He. 12. 19; met. *report, fame, rumour*, Lu. 4. 37.

ἦχος], εος, τό, (§ 5. tab. E. b) *sound*. v.r.

ἤχους, gen. sing.—A. B. Gr. Tdf. . . } [τὸ] ἦχος
ἠχούσης, Rec. Sch. (Lu. 21. 25) . }

ἠχούσης, gen. sing. fem. part. pres. . ἠχέω

ἠχρειώθησαν,[b] 3 pers. pl. aor. 1, ind. pass. (§ 21. tab. U) . . . ἀχρειόω

ἤχῳ, dat. sing. . . . . . ἦχος

ἠχῶν, nom. sing. masc. part. pres. . . ἠχέω

ἥψαντο, 3 pers. pl. aor. 1, ind. mid. . . ἅπτω

ἥψατο, 3 pers. sing. aor. 1, ind. mid. (§ 23. rem. 5) . . . . id.

Θ.

Θαδδαῖον, acc. . . . . Θαδδαῖος

Θαδδαῖος, ου, ὁ, (§ 3. tab. C. a) *Thaddæus*, pr. name.

θάλασσα, ης, ἡ, (§ 2. rem. 3) *the sea*, Mat. 23. 15; Mar. 9. 42; *a sea*, Ac. 7. 36; *an inland sea, lake*, Mat. 8. 24, et al.

θάλασσαν, acc. sing. . . . . . θάλασσα

θαλάσσῃ, dat. sing. . . . . . id.

θαλάσσης, gen. sing. . . . . . id.

θάλπει, 3 pers. sing. pres. ind. act. . . θάλπω

θάλπῃ, 3 pers. sing. pres. subj. . . id.

θάλπω, fut. ψω, (§ 23. rem. 1. a) *to impart warmth*; met. *to cherish, nurse, foster*, Ep. 5. 29; 1 Thes. 2. 7.

Θάμαρ,[c] ἡ, *Thamar*, pr. name, indecl.

θαμβέω, ῶ], fut. ήσω, (§ 16. tab. P) . . θάμβος

θάμβος, εος, τό, (§ 5. tab. E. b) *astonishment, amazement, awe*, Lu. 4. 36, et al.

θαμβέω, ῶ, fut. ησω, aor. 1, ἐθάμβησα, *to be astonished, amazed*, Ac. 9. 6; later, pass. *to be astonished, amazed, awe-struck*, Mar. 1. 27; 10. 24, 32.

θάμβους, gen. sing. . . . . θάμβος

θαμβῶν, nom. sing. masc. part. pres. . . θαμβέω

θανάσιμον,[d] acc. sing. neut. . . . θανάσιμος

θανάσιμος], ου, ὁ, ἡ, (§ 7. rem. 2) . . θνήσκω

θάνατε, voc. sing. . . . . . θάνατος

θανατηφόρου,[e] gen. sing. masc. . . θανατηφόρος

θανατηφόρος], ου, ὁ, ἡ, (§ 7. rem. 2) (θάνατος & φέρω) *mortiferous, bringing or causing death, deadly, fatal*.

θανάτοις, dat. pl. . . . . . θάνατος

θάνατον, acc. sing. . . . . . id.

θάνατος], ου, ὁ, (§ 3. tab. C. a) . . θνήσκω

θανάτου, gen. sing. . . . . . θάνατος

θανατούμεθα, 1 pers. pl. pres. pass. (§ 21. tab. U) . . . . θανατόω

θανατούμενοι, nom. pl. masc. part. p. pass. id.

θανατοῦτε, 2 pers. pl. pres. ind. act. . id.

θανατόω, ῶ], fut. ώσω, (§ 20. tab. T) . . θνήσκω

θανάτῳ, dat. sing. . . . . . θάνατος

θανατωθείς, nom. sing. masc. part. perf. pass. θανατόω

θανατῶσαι, aor. 1, infin. act. . . . id.

θανατώσουσι, 3 pers. pl. fut. ind. act. . id.

θανατώσωσι, 3 pers. pl. aor. 1, subj. act. . id.

---

[a] Ac. 11. 29. [b] Ro. 3. 12. [c] Mat. 1. 3. [d] Mar. 16. 18. [e] Ja. 3. 8.

θάπτω], fut. ψω, (§ 23. rem. 1. a) perf. τέτᾰφα, aor. 1, ἔθαψα, aor. 2, pass. ἐτάφην, (ᾰ) (§ 24. rem. 8. b) *to bury, inter*, Mat. 8. 21, 22; 14. 12. et al.

ταφή, ῆς, ἡ, (§ 2. tab. B. a) *burial, the act of burying, sepulture*, Mat. 27. 7.

τάφος, ου, ὁ, (§ 3. tab. C. a) *a sepulchre*, Mat. 23. 27, 29; 27. 61, 64, 66; 28. 1; met. Ro. 3. 13.

Θάρα,[a] ὁ, Thara, pr. name, indecl.

θαῤῥῆσαι, aor. 1, infin. . . . . θαῤῥέω

θαῤῥοῦμεν, 1 pers. pl. pres. ind. . . id.

θαῤῥοῦντας, acc. pl. masc. part. pres. . . id.

θαῤῥοῦντες, nom. pl. masc. part. pres. . id.

θαῤῥῶ, 1 pers. sing. pres. ind. contr. . . id.

θάρσει, 2 pers. sing. pres. imper. . . θαρσέω

θαρσεῖτε, 2 pers. pl. pres. imper. . . id.

θαρσέω, ῶ, and, new Attic, θαῤῥέω, ῶ] . θάρσος

θάρσος,[b] εος, τό, (§ 5. tab. E. b) *courage, confidence.*

θαρσέω, ῶ, and, new Attic, θαῤῥέω, ῶ, fut. ήσω, (§ 16. tab. P) imperat. θάρσει, *to be of good courage, be of good cheer*, Mat. 9. 2, et al.; *to be confident, hopeful*, 2 Co. 7. 16, et al.; *to be bold, maintain a bold bearing*, 2 Co. 10. 1, 2.

θαῦμα,[c] ατος, τό, (§ 4. tab. D. c) *a wonder; wonder, admiration, astonishment.*

θαυμάζω, fut. άσω, and άσομαι, perf. τεθαύμακα, aor. 1, ἐθαύμασα, (§ 26. rem. 1) *to admire, regard with admiration, wonder at*, Lu. 7. 9; Ac. 7. 31; *to reverence, adore*, 2 Thes. 1. 10; absol. *to wonder, be filled with wonder, admiration, or astonishment*, Mat. 8. 10; Lu. 4. 22, et al.

θαυμάσιος, α, ον, (§ 7. rem. 1) *wonderful, admirable, marvellous*; τὸ θαυμάσιον, *a wonder, wonderful work*, Mat. 21. 15.

θαυμαστός, ή, όν, (§ 7. tab. F. a) *wondrous, glorious*, 1 Pe. 2. 9; Re. 15. 1; *marvellous, strange, uncommon*, Mat. 21. 42; Mar. 12. 11.

θαυμάζειν, pres. infin. . . . θαυμάζω

θαυμάζετε, 2 pers. pl. pres. ind. . . id.

θαυμάζετε, 2 pers. pl. pres. imper. . . id.

θαυμάζητε, 2 pers. pl. pres. subj. . . id.

θαυμάζοντες, nom. pl. masc. part. pres. . θαυμάζω

θαυμαζόντων, gen. pl. masc. part. pres. . id.

θαυμάζω, fut. άσω, (§ 26. rem. 1) . . θαῦμα

θαυμάζων, nom. sing. masc. part. pres. . θαυμάζω

θαυμάσαι, aor. 1, infin. . . . . id.

θαυμάσαντες, nom. pl. masc. part. aor. 1 . id.

θαυμάσατε, 2 pers. pl. aor. 1, imper. . . id.

θαυμάσῃς, 2 pers. sing. aor. 1, subj. . id.

θαυμασθῆναι, aor. 1, infin. pass. . . id.

θαυμάσια,[d] acc. pl. neut. . . . θαυμάσιος

θαυμάσιος], α, ον, (§ 7. rem. 1) . . θαῦμα

θαυμάσονται, 3 pers. pl. fut. ind. mid. . θαυμάζω

θαυμαστά, nom. pl. neut. . . θαυμαστός

θαυμαστή, nom. sing. fem. . . . id.

θαυμαστόν, nom. and acc. sing. neut. . . id.

θαυμαστός], ή, όν, (§ 7. tab. F. a) . θαῦμα

θάψαι, aor. 1, infin. act. . . . . θάπτω

θαψάντων, gen. pl. masc. part. aor. 1, act. . id.

θεά], ᾶς, ἡ, (§ 2. tab. B. b, and rem. 2) . θεός

θεαθῆναι, aor. 1, infin. pass. (§ 22. rem. 2) θεάομαι

θεάν, acc. sing. . . . . . θεά

θεάομαι, ῶμαι], fut. άσομαι, perf. (pass. form) τεθέᾱμαι, aor. 1, pass. ἐθεάθην, (ᾱ) (§ 19. tab. S) *to gaze upon*, Mat. 6. 1; 23. 5; Lu. 7. 24; *to see, discern with the eyes*, Mar. 16. 11, 14; Lu. 5. 27; Jno. 1. 14, 32, 38, et al.; *to see, visit*, Ro. 15. 24.

θέᾱτρον, ου, τό, (§ 3. tab. C. c) *a theatre, a place where public games and spectacles are exhibited*, Ac. 19. 29, 31; meton. *a show, gazing-stock*, 1 Co. 4. 9.

θεατρίζομαι, *to be exposed as in a theatre, to be made a gazing-stock, object of scorn*, He. 10. 33. N.T.

θεᾶς, gen. sing. . . . . . θεά

θεασάμενοι, nom. pl. masc. part. aor. 1 . θεάομαι

θεασαμένοις, dat. pl. masc. part. aor. 1 . id.

θεασάμενος, nom. sing. masc. part. aor. 1 id.

θεάσασθαι, aor. 1, infin. . . . id.

θεάσασθε, 2 pers. pl. aor. 1, imper. . . id.

θεατρίζομαι], fut. ίσομαι . . . id.

θεατριζόμενοι,[e] nom. pl. masc. part. press. p. θεατρίζομαι

θέατρον, ου, τό, (§ 3. tab. C. c) . . θεάομαι

θεέ, voc. sing. (§ 3. rem. 1) . . . θεός

θείας, gen. sing. fem. . . . . θεῖος

θεῖναι, aor. 2, infin. act. (§ 28. tab. V) . τίθημι

θεῖος], α, ον, (§ 7. rem. 1) . . . θεός

[a] Lu. 3. 34. [b] Ac. 28. 15. [c] Re. 17. 6. [d] Mat. 21. 15. [e] He. 10. 33.

θεῖον, ου, τό, (§ 3. tab. C. c) *brimstone, sulphur,* Lu. 17. 29; Re. 9. 17, 18, et al.

θειώδης, εος, ους, ὁ, ἡ, (§ 7. tab. G. b) *of brimstone, sulphurous,* Re. 9. 17. L.G.

θειότης,[a] τητος, ἡ, (§ 4. rem. 2. c) . . θεός
θείς, nom. s. masc. part. aor. 2, act. (§ 28. tab. U) τίθημι
θείου, gen. sing. . . . . . θεῖον
θείῳ, dat. sing. . . . . . id.
θειώδεις,[b] acc. pl. masc. . . . . θειώδης
θειώδης], εος, ους, ὁ, ἡ, (§ 7. tab. G. b) . θεῖον
θέλει, 3 pers. sing. pres. ind. . . . θέλω
θέλειν, pres. infin. . . . . id.
θέλεις, 2 pers. sing. pres. ind. . . . id.
θέλετε, 2 pers. pl. pres. ind. . . . id.
θέλῃ, 3 pers. sing. pres. subj. . . . id.
θέλημα, ατος, τό, (§ 4. tab. D. c) . . id.
θελήματα, acc. pl. . . . . . θέλημα
θελήματι, dat. sing. . . . . id.
θελήματος, gen. sing. . . . . id.
θέλῃς, 2 pers. sing. pres. subj. . . . θέλω
θελήσαντας acc. pl. masc. part. aor. 1 . . id.
θελήσῃ, 3 pers. sing. aor. 1, subj. . . id.
θέλησιν,[c] acc. sing. . . . . . θέλησις
θέλησις], εως, ἡ, (§ 5. tab. E. c) . . θέλω
θελήσω, 1 pers. sing. aor. 1, subj. . . id.
θελήσωσι, 3 pers. pl. aor. 1, subj. . . id.
θέλητε, 2 pers. pl. pres. subj. . . . id.
θέλοι, 3 pers. sing. pres. optat. . . id.
θέλομεν, 1 pers. pl. pres. ind. . . . id.
θέλοντα, acc. sing. masc. part. pres. . . id.
θέλοντας, acc. pl. masc. part. pres. . . id.
θέλοντες, nom. sing. masc. part. pres. . . id.
θέλοντι, dat. sing. masc. part. pres. . . id.
θέλοντος, gen. sing. masc. part. pres. . . id.
θελόντων, gen. pl. masc. part. pres. . . id.
θέλουσι, 3 pers. pl. pres. ind. . . . id.

θέλω, and ἐθέλω, the former being the form in the present in N.T., fut. θελήσω & ἐθελήσω, imperf. ἤθελον, aor. 1, ἠθέλησα, (§ 35. rem. 5) *to exercise the will,* properly by an unimpassioned operation; *to be willing,* Mat. 17. 4, et al.; *to be inclined, disposed,* Ro. 13. 3, et al.; *to choose,* Lu. 1. 62; *to intend, design,* Lu. 14. 28, et al.; *to will,* Jno. 5. 21; 21. 22, et al.; ἤθελον, *I could wish,* Gal. 4. 20.

θέλημα, ατος, τό, (§ 4. tab. D. c) *will, bent, inclination,* 1 Co. 16. 12; Ep. 2. 3; 1 Pe. 4. 3; *resolve,* 1 Co. 7. 37; *will, purpose, design,* 2 Ti. 2. 26; 2 Pe. 1. 21; *will, sovereign pleasure, behest,* Mat. 18. 14; Lu. 12. 47; Ac. 13. 22, et al. freq.; ἐν τῷ θελήματι Θεοῦ, *Deo permittente, if God please or permit,* Ro. 1. 10. LXX.

θέλησις, εως, ἡ, (§ 5. tab. E. c) *will, pleasure,* He. 2. 4. L.G.

θέλω, 1 pers. sing. pres. subj. . . . θέλω
θέλων, nom. sing. masc. part. pres. . . id.
θέλωσι, 3 pers. pl. pres. subj. . . . id.
θεμέλια, acc. pl. . . . . θεμέλιον
θεμέλιοι, nom. pl. . . . . . θεμέλιος
θεμέλιον, acc. sing. . . . . . id.
θεμέλιον, ου, τό, and θεμέλιος, ου, ὁ . . τίθημι
θεμελίου, gen. sing. . . . . θεμέλιος
θεμελίους, acc. sing. . . . . id.
θεμελίῳ, dat. sing. . . . . . id.
θεμελιόω, ῶ], fut. ώσω, (§ 20. tab. T) . . τίθημι
θεμελιώσαι, 3 pers. sing. aor. 1, optat. act. θεμελιόω
θεμελιώσει, 3 pers. sing. fut. act—Gr. Sch. } id.
θεμελιώσαι, Rec. . . . }
Tdf. om. (1 Pe. 5. 10) . . }
θέμενος, nom. sing. masc. part. aor. 2, mid. (§ 28. tab. W.) . . . τίθημι
θέντες, nom. pl. masc. part. aor. 2, act. (§ 28. tab. U) . . . . . id.
θέντος, gen. sing. masc. part. aor. 2, act. . id.
θεοδίδακτοι,[d] nom. pl. masc. . . . θεοδίδακτος
θεοδίδακτος], ου, ὁ, ἡ, (§ 7. rem. 2) (θεός & διδακτός) *taught of God, divinely instructed.* N.T.
θεοί, nom. pl. . . . . . θεός
θεοῖς, dat. pl. . . . . . id.
θεομαχέω, ῶ], fut. ήσω, (§ 16. tab. P) (θεός & μάχομαι) *to fight or contend against God, to seek to counteract the divine will,* Ac. 23. 9.

θεομάχος, ου, ὁ, (§ 3. tab C. a) *fighting against God, in conflict with God,* Ac. 5. 39. (ᾰ).

θεομάχοι,[e] nom. pl. . . . . θεομάχος
θεομάχος], ου, ὁ, (§ 3. tab. C. a) . . θεομαχέω
θεομαχῶμεν,[f] 1 pers. pl. pres. subj.—Rec. } id.
Gr. Sch. Tdf. om. . . . }
θεόν, acc. sing. . . . . . θεός

[a] Ro. 1. 20. [b] Re. 9. 17. [c] He. 2. 4. [d] 1 Thes. 4. 9. [e] Ac. 5. 39. [f] Ac. 23. 9.

θεόν, acc. sing. of ἡ θεός, *a goddess.*—Gr. Sch. Tdf.
θεάν, Rec. (Ac. 19. 37)

θεόπνευστος,[a] ου, ὁ, ἡ, (§ 7. rem. 2) (θεός & πνέω) *divinely inspired.* L.G.

θεός, οῦ, ὁ, & ἡ, (§ 3. rem. 1) *a deity,* Ac. 7. 43; 1 Co. 8. 5; *an idol,* Ac. 7. 40; *God, the true God,* Mat. 3. 9, et al. freq.; *God, possessed of true godhead,* Jno. 1. 1; Ro. 9. 5; from the Heb. applied to potentates, Jno. 10. 34, 35; τῷ θεῷ, an intensive term, from the Heb., *exceedingly,* Ac. 7. 20, and, perhaps, 2 Co. 10. 4.

θεά, ᾶς, ἡ, (§ 2. tab. B. b, and rem. 2) *a goddess,* Ac. 19. 27, 35, 37.

θεῖος, α, ον, (§ 7. rem. 1) *divine, pertaining to God,* 2 Pe. 1. 3, 4; τὸ θεῖον, *the divine nature, divinity,* Ac. 17. 29.

θειότης, τητος, ἡ, (§ 4. rem. 2. c) *divinity, deity, godhead, divine majesty,* Ro. 1. 20. L.G.

θεότης, τητος, ἡ, (§ 4. rem. 2. c) *divinity, deity, godhead,* Col. 2. 9. L.G.

θεοσέβεια], ας, ἡ, (§ 2. tab. B. b, and rem. 2) — θεοσεβής
θεοσέβειαν,[b] acc. sing. — θεοσέβεια
θεοσεβής,[c] έος, οῦς, ὁ, ἡ, (§ 7. tab. G. b) (θεός & σέβομαι) *reverencing God, pious, godly, devout, a sincere worshipper of God.*

θεοσέβεια, ας, ἡ, (§ 2. tab. B. b, and rem. 2) *worshipping of God, reverence towards God, piety.*

θεοστυγεῖς,[d] acc. pl. masc. — θεοστυγής
θεοστῠγής], έος, οῦς, ὁ, ἡ, (§ 7. tab. G. b) (θεός & στυγέω, *to hate*) *God-hated;* in N.T. *a hater and contemner of God.*
θεότης], τητος, ἡ, (§ 4. rem. 2. c) — θεός
θεότητος,[e] gen. sing. — θεότης
θεοῦ, gen. sing. — θεός
θεούς, acc. pl. — id.
Θεόφιλε, voc. — Θεόφιλος
Θεόφιλος], ου, ὁ, (§ 3. tab. C. a) *Theophilus,* pr. name.
θεραπεία, ας, ἡ, (§ 2. tab. B. b, and rem. 2) — θεράπων
θεραπείαν, acc. sing. — θεραπεία
θεραπείας, gen. sing. — id.
θεραπεύει, 3 pers. sing. pres. ind.—A. D. Ln. Tdf. / θεραπεύσει, Rec. Gr. Sch. (Lu. 6. 7) — θεραπεύω
θεραπεύειν, pres. infin. act. — id.
θεραπεύεσθαι, pres. infin. pass. (§ 14. tab. N) — θεραπεύω
θεραπεύεσθε, 2 pers. pl. pres. imper. pass. — id.
θεραπεύεται, 3 pers. sing. pres. ind. pass. — id.
θεραπεύετε, 2 pers. pl. pres. imper. act. — id.
θεραπεύοντες, nom. pl. masc. part. pres. act. — id.
θεραπεῦσαι, aor. 1, infin. act. — id.
θεραπεύσει, 3 pers. sing. fut. ind. act. — id.
θεραπευθῆναι, aor. 1, infin. pass. — id.
θεράπευσον, 2 pers. sing. aor. 1, imper. act. — id.
θεραπεύσω, 1 pers. sing. fut. ind. act. — id.
θεραπεύω], fut. εύσω, (§ 13. tab. M) — θεράπων
θεραπεύων, nom. sing. masc. part. pres. act. — θεραπεύω

θεράπων,[f] οντος, ὁ, (§ 4. rem. 2. d) *an attendant, a servant; a minister.*

θεραπεία, ας, ἡ, (§ 2. tab. B. b, and rem. 2) *service, attendance; healing, cure,* Lu. 9. 11; Re. 22. 2; meton. *those who render service, servants, domestics, family household,* Mat. 24. 45; Lu. 12. 42.

θεραπεύω, fut. εύσω, aor. 1, ἐθεράπευσα, (§ 13. tab. M) *to serve, minister to, render service and attendance; to render* divine *service, worship,* Ac. 17. 25; *to heal, cure,* Mat. 4. 23, 24; 8. 16, et al.; pass. *to receive service,* Ac. 17. 25.

θερίζειν, pres. infin. act. — θερίζω
θερίζεις, 2 pers. sing. pres. ind. act. — id.
θερίζουσι, 3 pers. pl. pres. ind. act. — id.
θερίζω, fut. ίσω, (§ 26. rem. 1) — θέρος
θερίζων, nom. sing. masc. part. pres. act. — θερίζω
θερίσαι, aor. 1, infin. act. — id.
θερισάντων, gen. pl. masc. part. aor. 1, act. — id.
θερίσει, 3 pers. sing. fut. ind. act. — id.
θερισμόν, acc. sing. — θερισμός
θερισμός, οῦ, ὁ, (§ 3. tab. C. a) — θέρος
θερισμοῦ, gen. sing. — θερισμός
θερίσομεν, 1 pers. pl. fut. ind. act. — θερίζω
θέρισον, 2 pers. sing. aor. 1, imper. act. — id.
θερισταί, nom. pl. — θεριστής
θερισταῖς, dat. pl. — id.
θεριστής], οῦ, ὁ, (§ 2. tab. B. c) — θέρος
θερμαίνεσθε, 2 pers. pl. pres. imper. mid. — θερμαίνω
θερμαινόμενον, acc. sing. masc. part. pres. mid. — id.
θερμαινόμενος, nom. sing. masc. part. pres. mid. — id.
θερμαίνω], fut. ανῶ, (§ 27. rem. 1. c) — θέρμη
θέρμη], ης, ἡ, (§ 2. tab. B. a) (θερμός, θέρω) *heat, warmth,* Ac. 28. 3.

[a] 2 Ti. 3. 16. [b] 1 Ti. 2. 10. [c] Jno. 9. 31. [d] Ro. 1. 30. [e] Col. 2. 9. [f] He. 3. 5.

θερμαίνω, fut. ανῶ, (§ 27. rem. 1. c) *to warm;* mid. *to warm one's self,* Mar. 14. 54, 67; Jno. 18. 18, 25; Ja. 2. 16.

θέρμης,[a] gen. sing. . . . . . θέρμη

θέρος, εος, τό, (§ 5. tab. E. b) *the warm season of the year, summer,* Mat. 24. 32; Mar. 13. 38; Lu. 21. 30.

θερίζω, fut. ίσω, aor. 1, ἐθέρισα, (§ 26. rem. 1) *to gather in harvest, reap,* Mat. 6. 26; 25. 24, 26; met. *to reap* the reward of labour, 1 Co. 9. 11; 2 Co. 9. 6, *to reap* the harvest of vengeance, Re. 14. 15, 16.

θερισμός, οῦ, ὁ, (§ 3. tab. C. a) *harvest, the act of gathering in the harvest, reaping,* Jno. 4. 35, et al.; met. *the harvest* of the Gospel, Mat. 9. 37, 38; Lu. 10. 2; *a crop;* met. *the crop* of vengeance, Re. 14. 15.

θεριστής, οῦ, ὁ, (§ 2. tab. B. c) *one who gathers in the harvest, a reaper,* Mat. 13. 30, 39.

θέσθε, 2 pers. pl. aor. 2, imper. mid. . . τίθημι

Θεσσαλονικεύς], έως, ὁ, (§ 5. tab. E. d) *Thessalonian, of Thessalonica.*

Θεσσαλονικέων, gen. pl. . . . Θεσσαλονικεύς

Θεσσαλονικέως, gen. sing. . . . . id.

Θεσσαλονίκη], ης, ἡ, (§ 2. tab. B. a) *Thessalonica,* a city of Macedonia.

Θεσσαλονίκῃ, dat. sing. . . . Θεσσαλονίκη

Θεσσαλονίκης, gen. sing. . . . . id.

θέτε, 2 pers. pl. aor. 2, imper. act.—A. D. Ln. Tdf. . . . . } τίθημι
θέσθε, Rec. Gr. Sch. (Lu. 21. 14) . }

Θευδᾶς,[b] ᾶ, ὁ, (§ 2. rem. 4) *Theudas,* pr. name.

θεῷ, dat. sing. . . . . . θεός

θεωρεῖ, 3 pers. sing. pres. ind. . . . θεωρέω

θεωρεῖν, pres. infin. . . . . id.

θεωρεῖς, 2 pers. sing. pres. ind. . . id.

θεωρεῖτε, 2 pers. pl. pres. ind. . . id.

θεωρεῖτε, 2 pers. pl. pres. imper. . . id.

θεωρέω, ῶ], fut. ήσω, (§ 16. tab. P) *to be a spectator, to gaze on, contemplate; to behold, view* with interest and attention, Mat. 27. 55; 28. 1, et al.; *to contemplate* mentally, *consider,* He. 7. 4; in N.T. *to see, perceive,* Mar. 3. 11, et al.; *to come to a knowledge of,* Jno. 6. 40; from the Heb., *to experience, undergo,* Jno. 8. 51, et al.

θεωρία, ας, ἡ, (§ 2. tab. B. b, and rem. 2) *a beholding; a sight, spectacle,* Lu. 23. 48.

θεωρῇ, 3 pers. sing. pres. subj. . . θεωρέω

θεωρῆσαι, aor. 1, infin. . . . . id.

θεωρήσαντες, nom. pl. masc. part. aor. 1—B. C. D. Ln. Tdf. . . . } id.
θεωροῦντες, Rec. Gr. Sch. (Lu. 23. 48) }

θεωρήσῃ, 3 pers. sing. aor. 1, subj. . . id.

θεωρήσωσι, 3 pers. pl. aor. 1, subj. . . id.

θεωρῆτε, 2 pers. pl. pres. subj. . . . id.

θεωρία], ας, ἡ, (§ 2. tab. B. b, and rem. 2) id.

θεωρίαν,[c] acc. sing. . . . . θεωρία

θεωροῦντας, acc. pl. masc. part. pres. . . θεωρέω

θεωροῦντες, nom. pl. masc. part. pres. . id.

θεωροῦντι, dat. sing. masc. part. pres. . . id.

θεωροῦντος, gen. sing. masc. part. pres.—A. B. Ln. Tdf. . . . } id.
θεωροῦντι, Rec. Gr. Sch. (Ac. 17. 16) }

θεωρούντων, gen. pl. masc. part. pres. . . id.

θεωροῦσαι, nom. pl. fem. part. pres. . id.

θεωροῦσι, 3 pers. pl. pres. ind. . . . id.

θεωρῶ, 1 pers. sing. pres. ind. . . id.

θεωρῶν, nom. sing. masc. part. pres. . . id.

θεωρῶσι, 3 pers. pl. pres. subj. . . id.

θῇ, 3 pers. sing. aor. 2, subj. act. (§ 28. tab. V) τίθημι

θήκη], ης, ἡ, (§ 2. tab. B. a) . . . id.

θήκην,[d] acc. sing. . . . . θήκη

θηλαζόντων, gen. pl. masc. part. pres. . . θηλάζω

θηλαζούσαις, dat. pl. fem. part. pres. . id.

θηλάζω], fut. άσω, aor. 1, ἐθήλασα, (§ 26. rem. 1) (θηλή, *a nipple*) *to suckle, give suck,* Mat. 24. 19; Mar. 13. 17., Lu. 21. 23; 23. 29; *to suck,* Mat. 21. 16; Lu. 11. 27.

θήλειαι, nom. pl. fem. . . . . θῆλυς

θηλείας, gen. sing. fem. . . . id.

θῆλυ, nom. and acc. sing. neut. . . . id.

θῆλυς], θήλεια, θῆλυ, (§ 7. tab. H. g) *female;* τὸ θῆλυ, sc. γένος, *a female,* Mat. 19. 4; Mar. 10. 6; Gal. 3. 28; ἡ θήλεια, *woman,* Ro. 1. 26, 27.

θήρα], ας, ἡ, (§ 2. tab. B. b) (θήρ, *a wild beast*) *hunting, the chase;* met. *means of capture, a cause of destruction,* Ro. 11. 9.

θηρεύω, fut. εύσω, (§ 13. tab. M)

[a] Ac. 28. 3. [b] Ac. 5. 36. [c] Lu. 23. 48. [d] Jno. 18. 11.

to hunt, catch; met. *to seize on, lay hold of.*

θήραν,[a] acc. sing. . . . . . θήρα

θηρεῦσαι,[b] aor. 1, infin. . . . θηρεύω

θηρεύω], fut. εύσω . . . . θήρα

θηρία, nom. and acc. pl. . . . θηρίον

θηριομαχέω, ῶ], fut. ήσω, aor. 1, ἐθηριομάχησα, (§ 16. tab. P) θηρίον & μάχομαι) *to fight with wild beasts*; met. *to be exposed to furious hostility*, 1 Co. 15. 32. L.G.

θηρίον, ου, τό, (§ 3. tab. C. c) (equivalent to θήρ, but pr. a dimin. from it) *a beast, wild animal*, Mar. 1. 13; Ac. 10. 12, et al.; met. *a brute, brutish man*, Ti. 1. 12.

θηρίου, gen. sing. . . . . . θηρίον

θηρίῳ, dat. sing. . . . . id.

θηρίων, gen. pl. . . . . . id.

θησαυρίζειν, pres. infin. act. . . . θησαυρίζω

θησαυρίζεις, 2 pers. sing. pres. ind. . . id.

θησαυρίζετε, 2 pers. pl. pres. imper. . id.

θησαυρίζω], fut. ίσω, (§ 26. rem. 1) . . θησαυρός

θησαυρίζων, nom. sing. masc. part. pres. . θησαυρίζω

θησαυροί, nom. pl. . . . . θησαυρός

θησαυρόν, acc. sing. . . . . id.

θησαυρός, οῦ, ὁ, (§ 3. tab. C. a) *a treasury, a store, treasure, precious deposit*, Mat. 6. 19, 20, 21, et al.; *a receptacle in which precious articles are kept, a casket*, Mat. 2. 11; *a storehouse*, Mat. 12. 35.

θησαυρίζω, fut. ίσω, aor. 1, ἐθησαύρισα, (§ 26. rem. 1) *to collect and lay up stores or wealth, treasure up*, Mat. 6. 19, 20; *to heap up, accumulate*, Ro. 2. 5; 1 Co. 16. 2; *to reserve, keep in store*, 2 Pe. 3. 7.

θησαυροῦ, gen. sing. . . . . θησαυρός

θησαυρούς, acc. pl. . . . id.

θησαυρῷ, dat. sing. . . . . id.

θησαυρῶν, gen. pl. . . . . id.

θήσει, 3 pers. sing. fut. ind. act. (§ 28. rem. 9. a) τίθημι

θήσεις, 2 pers. sing. fut. ind. act. . . id.

θήσω, 1 pers. sing. fut. ind. act. . . id.

θήσω, 1 pers. sing. aor. 1, subj. act. . . id.

θιγγάνω], fut. θίξομαι, aor. 2, ἔθἴγον, (§ 36. rem. 2) *to touch*, Col. 2. 21; He. 12. 20; *to harm*, He. 11. 28.

θίγῃ, 3 pers. sing. aor. 2, subj . . θιγγάνω

θίγῃς, 2 pers. sing. aor. 2, subj. . . . id.

θλίβεσθαι, pres. infin. pass. . . . θλίβω

θλιβόμεθα, 1 pers. pl. pres. ind. pass. . id.

θλιβόμενοι, nom. pl. masc. part. pres. pass. id.

θλιβομένοις, dat. pl. masc. part. pres. pass. id.

θλίβουσι, dat. pl. masc. part. pres. act. . id.

θλίβω], fut. ψω, perf. pass. τέθλιμμαι, (§ 23. rem. 1. a, and rem. 7) *to squeeze, press; to press upon, encumber, throng, crowd*, Mar. 3. 9; met. *to distress, afflict*, 2 Co. 1. 6; 4. 8, et al.; pass. *to be compressed, narrow*, Mat. 7. 14. (ῑ).

θλῖψις, εως, ἡ, (§ 5. tab. E. c) pr. *pressure, compression*; met. *affliction, distress* of mind, 2 Co. 2. 4; *distressing circumstances, trial, affliction*, Mat. 24. 9, et al. L.G.

θλίβωσι, 3 pers. pl. pres. subj. act. . . θλίβω

θλίψει, dat. sing. . . . . . θλῖψις

θλίψεις, nom. pl. . . . . id.

θλίψεσι, dat. pl. . . . . . id.

θλίψεων, gen. pl. . . . . id.

θλίψεως, gen. sing. . . . . . id.

θλῖψιν, acc. sing. . . . . id.

θλῖψις, εως, ἡ, (§ 5. tab. E. c) . . . θλίβω

θνήσκω], (§ 36. rem. 4) fut. θανοῦμαι, perf. τέθνηκα, aor. 2, ἔθἄνον, *to die*; in N.T., only in the perf. and pluperf., τέθνηκα, ἐτεθνήκειν, inf. τεθνάναι, (ᾰ) part. τεθνηκώς, *to be dead*, Mat. 2. 20; Mar. 15. 44, et al.

θνητός, ή, όν, (§ 7. tab. F. a) *mortal, obnoxious to death*, Ro. 6. 12; 8. 11, 2 Co. 4. 11; τὸ θνητόν, *mortality*, 1 Co. 15. 53, 54; 2 Co. 5. 4.

θάνᾰτος, ου, ὁ, (§ 3. tab. C. a) *death, the extinction of life*, whether naturally, Lu. 2. 26; Mar. 9. 1; or violently, Mat. 10. 21; 15. 4; *imminent danger of death*, 2 Co. 4. 11, 12; 11. 23; in N.T. spiritual *death*, as opposed to ζωή in its spiritual sense, in respect of a forfeiture of salvation, Jno. 8. 51; Ro. 6. 16, et al.

θανάσῐμος, ου, ὁ, ἡ, (§ 7. rem. 2) *deadly, mortal, fatal*, Mar. 16. 18.

θανατόω, ῶ, fut. ώσω, aor. 1, ἐθανά-

[a] Ro. 11. 8.

[b] Lu. 11. 54.

τωσα, (§ 20. tab. T) *to put to death, deliver to death*, Mat. 10. 21; 26. 59; Mar. 13. 12; pass. *to be exposed to imminent danger of death*, Ro. 8. 36; in N.T. met. *to mortify, subdue*, Ro. 8. 13; pass. *to be dead to, to be rid, parted from*, as if by the intervention of death, Ro. 7. 4.

θνητά, acc. pl. neut. . . . θνητός
θνητῇ, dat. sing. fem. . . . . id.
θνητόν, nom. and acc. sing. neut. . . id.
θνητός], ή, όν, (§ 7. tab. F. a) . . θνήσκω
θνητῷ, dat. sing. neut. . . . . θνητός
θορυβάζῃ, 2 pers. sing. pres. pass.—B.C.D. Ln. Tdf. . . . . } θορυβάζομαι
τυρβάζῃ, Rec. Gr. Sch. (Lu. 10. 41)
θορυβάζομαι], v.r. . . . . θόρυβος
θορυβεῖσθε, 2 pers. pl. pres. pass. . . θορυβέω
θορυβεῖσθε, 2 pers. pl. pres. imper. pass. . id.
θορυβέω, ῶ], fut. ήσω, (§ 16. tab. P) . . θόρυβος
θόρυβον, acc. sing. . . . . id.

θόρυβος, ου, ὁ, (§ 3. tab. C. a) *an uproar, din; an outward expression of mental agitation, outcry*, Mar. 5. 38; *a tumult, commotion*, Mat. 26. 5, et al.

θορυβάζομαι, *to be troubled, disturbed*, v.r. Lu. 10. 41.

θορυβέω, ῶ, fut. ήσω, (§ 16. tab. P) intrans. *to make a din, uproar*; trans. *to disturb, throw into commotion*, Ac. 17. 5; in N.T. mid. *to manifest agitation of mind, to raise a lament*, Mat. 9. 23; Mar. 5. 39; Ac. 20. 10.

θορύβου, gen. sing. . . . . θόρυβος
θορυβούμενον, acc. s. masc. part. pres. pass. θορυβέω

θραύω], fut. αύσω, *to break, shiver*; met., perf. pass. part. τεθραυσμένος, *shattered, crushed* by cruel oppression, Lu. 4. 18.

θρέμμα], ατος, τό, (§ 4. tab. D. c) . . τρέφω
θρέμματα,[a] nom. pl. . . . . θρέμμα
θρηνέω, ῶ], fut. ήσω . . . . θρῆνος
θρηνήσετε, 2 pers. pl. fut. ind. . . . θρηνέω
θρῆνος,[b] ου, ὁ, (§ 3 tab. C. a) (θρέομαι, *to shriek*) *wailing, lamentation*.

θρηνέω, ῶ, fut. ήσω, aor. 1, ἐθρήνησα, (§ 16 tab. P) *to lament, bewail*, Mat. 11. 17; Lu. 7. 32; Jno. 16. 20.

θρησκεία, ας, ἡ, (§ 2. tab. B. b, and rem. 2) θρῆσκος
θρησκείᾳ, dat. sing. . . . . θρησκεία
θρησκείας, gen. sing. . . . . id.

θρῆσκος,[c] ου, ὁ, ἡ, *occupied with religious observances*; in N.T. *religious, devout, pious*.

θρησκεία, ας, ἡ, (§ 2. tab. B. b, and rem. 2) *religious worship*, Col. 2. 18; *religion, a religious system*, Ac. 26. 5; *religion, piety*, Ja. 1. 26, 27.

θριαμβεύοντι, dat. sing. masc. part. pres. . θριαμβεύω
θριαμβεύσας, nom. sing. masc. part. aor. 1 . id.
θριαμβεύω], fut. εύσω, (§ 13. tab. M) (θρίαμβος, *a hymn in honour of Bacchus; a triumph*) pr. *to celebrate a triumph*; trans. *to lead in triumph, celebrate a triumph over*, Col. 2. 15; in N.T. *to cause to triumph*, or, *to render conspicuous*, 2 Co. 2. 14. L.G.

θρίξ, τρῐχός, ἡ, (§ 4. rem. 2. b) *a hair*; pl. αἱ τρίχες, dat. θριξί, *the hair* of the head, Mat. 5. 36; 10. 30, et al.; of an animal, Mat. 3. 4; Mar. 1. 6.

τρίχινος, η, ον, (§ 7. tab. F. a) *of hair, made of hair*, Re. 6. 12.

θριξί, dat. pl. . . . . . θρίξ
θροεῖσθαι, pres. infin. pass. . . . θροέω
θροεῖσθε, 2 pers. pl. pres. imper. pass. . id.
θροέω, ῶ], fut. ήσω, (§ 16. tab. P) (θρόος, *an uproar*, fr. θρέομαι, *to make a clamour*) *to cry aloud*; in N.T. pass. *to be disturbed, disquieted, alarmed, terrified*, Mat. 24. 6; Mar. 13. 7; 2 Thes. 2. 2.

θρόμβοι,[d] nom. pl. . . . . . θρόμβος
θρόμβος], ου, ὁ, (§ 3. tab. C. a) *a lump*; espec. *a clot* of blood.

θρόνοι, nom. pl. . . . . . θρόνος
θρόνον, acc. sing. . . . . . id.
θρόνος, ου, ὁ, (θράω, *to set*) *a seat, a throne*, Mat. 5. 34; 19. 28; Lu. 1. 52; meton. *power, dominion*, Lu. 1. 32; He. 1. 8; *a potentate*, Col. 1. 16, et al.

θρόνου, gen. sing. . . . . . θρόνος
θρόνους, acc. pl. . . . . . id.
θρόνῳ, dat. sing. . . . . . id.
θρόνων, gen. pl. . . . . . id.
Θυάτειρα, ων, τά, (§ 3. tab. C. c) *Thyatira*, a city of Lydia.
Θυατείροις, dat. . . . . . Θυάτειρα

a Jno. 4. 12. b Mat. 2. 18. c Ja. 1. 26. d Lu. 22. 44.

Θυατείρων, gen. . . . . . . Θυάτειρα
θύγατερ, voc. sing. (§ 6. rem. 1. 2) . . θυγάτηρ
θυγατέρα, acc. sing. . . . . . . id.
θυγατέρας, acc. pl. . . . . . id.
θυγατέρες, nom. and voc. pl. . . . id.
θυγατέρων, gen. pl. . . . . id.

θυγάτηρ, τέρος, τρός, dat. τέρι, τρί, acc. τέρα, voc. θύγατερ, ἡ, (§ 6. rem. 2) *a daughter*, Mat. 9. 18; 10. 35, 37; in the vocative, an expression of affection and kindness, Mat. 9. 22; from the Heb., *one of the female posterity* of any one, Lu. 1. 5; met. *a city*, Mat. 21. 5; Jno. 12. 15; pl. *female inhabitants*, Lu. 23. 28. (ᾰ).

θυγάτριον, ου, τό, (§ 3. tab. C. c) *a little daughter, female child*, Mar. 5. 23; 7. 25.

θυγατρί, dat. sing. . . . . . θυγάτηρ
θυγάτριον, ου, τό . . . id.
θυγατρός, gen. sing. . . . id.
θύει, 3 pers. sing. pres. ind. act. . θύω
θύειν, pres. infin. act. . . . . . id.
θύελλα], ης, ἡ, (§ 2. rem. 3) (θύω, *to rush*) *a tempest, whirlwind, hurricane*.
θυέλλῃ,[a] dat. sing. . . . . θύελλα
θύεσθαι, pres. infin. pass. . . . . θύω
θύϊνον,[b] acc. sing. neut. . . . . θύϊνος
θύϊνος], η, ον, (§ 7. tab. F. a) *thyme*, of θυΐα, *thya*, an aromatic evergreen tree, arbor vitæ, resembling the cedar, and found in Libya. (ῐ).
θυμίαμα], ατος, τό, (§ 4. tab. D. c) . . θύω
θυμιάματα, nom. and acc. pl. . . θυμίαμα
θυμιάματος, gen. sing. . . . . . id.
θυμιαμάτων, gen. pl. . . . . . id.
θυμιᾶσαι,[c] aor. 1, infin. . . . . . θυμιάω
θυμιᾱτήριον,[d] ου, τό, (§ 3. tab. C. c) . θύω
θυμιάω, ῶ], fut. άσω, (§ 18. tab. R) . . id.
θυμοί, nom. pl. . . . . . . θυμός
θυμομᾰχέω, ῶ], fut. ήσω, (§ 16. tab. P) (θυμός & μάχομαι) *to wage war fiercely; to be warmly hostile to, be enraged against*. L.G.
θυμομαχῶν,[e] nom. sing. masc. part. pres. θυμομαχέω
θυμόν, acc. sing. . . . . . . θυμός
θῡμός, ου, ὁ, (§ 3. tab. C. a) (θύω, *to rush*) pr. *the soul, mind*; hence, *a strong passion or emotion of the mind; anger, wrath*, Lu. 4. 28; Ac. 19. 28, et al.; pl. *swellings of anger*, 2 Co. 12. 20; Gal. 5. 20.

θυμόω, ῶ, fut. ώσω, (§ 20. tab. T) *to provoke to anger*; pass. *to be angered, enraged*, Mat. 2. 16.

θυμοῦ, gen. sing. . . . . . θυμος
θυμόω, ῶ], fut. ώσω . . . . . id.
θύουσι, 3 pers. pl. pres. ind.—Al. Ln. Tdf. } θύω
θύει, Rec. Gr. Sch. (1 Co. 10. 20) . }

θύρα, ας, ἡ, (§ 2. tab. B. b) *a door, gate*, Mat. 6. 6; Mar. 1. 33; *an entrance*, Mat. 27. 60, et al.; in N.T. met. *an opening, occasion, opportunity*, Ac. 14. 27; 1 Co. 16. 9, et al.; meton. *a medium or means of entrance*, Jno. 10. 7, 9.

θυρεός, οῦ, ὁ, (§ 3. tab. C. a) *a stone or other material employed to close a doorway*; later, *a large oblong shield*, Ep. 6. 16.

θυρίς, ίδος, ἡ, (§ 4. rem. 2. c) *a small opening; a window*, Ac. 20. 9; 2 Co. 11. 33.

θύρᾳ, dat. sing. . . . . . . θύρα
θύραι, nom. pl. . . . . . . id.
θύραις, dat. pl. . . . . . . id.
θύραν, acc. sing. . . . . . id.
θύρας, gen. sing. or acc. pl. . . . id.
θυρεόν,[f] acc. sing. . . . . θυρεός
θυρεός], οῦ, ὁ, (§ 3. tab. C. a) . . θύρα
θυρίδος, gen. sing. . . . . . θυρίς
θυρίς], ίδος, ἡ, (§ 4. rem. 2. c) . . . θύρα
θυρῶν, gen. pl. . . . . . . id.
θυρωρός, οῦ, ὁ, ἡ, (§ 3. tab. C. a. b) (θύρα & οὖρος, *a keeper*) *a door-keeper, porter*, Mar. 13. 34; Jno. 10. 3; 18. 16, 17.
θυρωρῷ, dat. sing. masc. and fem. . . θυρωρος
θύσατε, 2 pers. pl. aor. 1, imper. act. . θύω
θύσῃ, 3 pers. sing. aor. 1, subj. act. . . id.
θυσία, ας, ἡ, (§ 2. tab. B. b, and rem. 2) . id.
θυσίᾳ, dat. sing. . . . . . . θυσία
θυσίαι, nom. pl. . . . . . . id.
θυσίαις, dat. pl. . . . . . . id.
θυσίαν, acc. sing. . . . . . id.
θυσίας, gen. sing. and acc. pl. . . . id.
θυσιαστήρια, acc. pl. . . . θυσιαστήριον
θυσιαστήριον, ου, τό, (§ 3. tab. C. c) . . θύω
θυσιαστηρίου, gen. sing. . . . θυσιαστήριον

[a] He. 12. 18. [b] Re. 18. 12. [c] Lu. 1. 9. [d] He. 9. 4. [e] Ac. 12. 20. [f] Ep. 6. 16.

θυσιαστηρίῳ, dat. sing. . . . θυσιαστήριον
θυσιῶν, gen. pl. . . . . . θυσία
θῦσον, 2 pers. sing. aor. 1, imper. act. . . θύω

θύω], fut. θύσω, perf. τέθυκα, aor. 1, ἔθυσα, perf. pass. τέθυμαι, aor. 1, ἐτύθην, *to offer; to kill in sacrifice, sacrifice, immolate,* Ac. 14. 13, 18, et al.; in N.T. *to slaughter* for food, Mat. 22. 4, et al. (ῡ in θύω, ῠ in ἐτύθην).

θυμιάω, ῶ, fut. άσω, (§ 18. tab. R) *to burn incense,* Lu. 1. 9.

θυμίᾱμα, ατος, τό, (§ 4. tab. D. c) *incense, any odoriferous substance burnt in religious worship,* Re. 5. 8; 8. 3, 4; 18. 13; or, *the act of burning incense,* Lu. 1. 10, 11.

θυμιᾱτήριον, ου, τό, (§ 3. tab. C. c) *a censer* for burning incense, He. 9. 4.

θυσία, ας, ἡ, (§ 2. tab. B. b, and rem. 2) *sacrifice, the act of sacrificing,* He. 9. 26; *the thing sacrificed, a victim,* Mat. 9. 13; 12. 7; *the flesh of victims* eaten by the sacrificers, 1 Co. 10. 18; in N.T. *an offering or service* to God, Phi. 4. 18, et al.

θυσιαστήριον, ίου, τό, (§ 3. tab. C. c) *an altar,* Mat. 5. 23, 24; Lu. 1. 11, et al.; spc. *the altar of burnt-offering,* Mat. 23. 35; Lu. 11. 51; meton. *a class of sacrifices,* He. 13. 10. LXX.

θῶ, 1 pers. sing. aor. 2, subj. act. (§ 28. tab. V) τίθημι
Θωμᾷ, dat. . . . . . Θωμᾶς
Θωμᾶ, voc. . . . . . . id.
Θωμᾶν, acc. . . . . . . id.
Θωμᾶς, ᾶ, ὁ, (§ 2. rem. 4) *Thomas,* pr. name.
θῶμεν, 1 pers. pl. aor. 2, subj. act.—B. Ln. Tdf. . . . . } τίθημι
παραβάλωμεν, Rec. Gr. Sch. (Mar. 4. 30) . . . . }
θώρακα, acc. sing. . . . . . θώραξ
θώρακας, acc. pl. . . . . id.

θώραξ], ᾶκος, ὁ, (§ 4. rem. 2. b) *a breast-plate, armour for the body,* consisting of two parts, one covering the breast and the other the back, Re. 9. 9, 17; Ep. 6. 14; 1 Thes. 5. 8.

I.

Ἰάειρος, ου, ὁ, (§ 3. tab. C. a) *Jairus,* pr. name.
ἰᾱθείς, nom. sing. masc. part. aor. 1, pass. . ἰάομαι
ἰαθέντος, gen. sing. masc. part. aor. 1 pass. id.
ἰάθη, 3 pers. sing. aor. 1, ind. pass. . . id.
ἰᾱθῇ, 3 pers. sing. aor. 1, subj. pass. . id.
ἰαθῆναι, aor. 1, infin. pass. . . . id.
ἰαθήσεται, 3 pers. sing. fut. 1, ind. pass. id.
ἰάθητε, 2 pers. pl. aor. 1, ind. pass. . id.
ἰαθῆτε, 2 pers. pl. aor. 1, subj. pass. . id.
ἰαθήτω, 3 pers. sing. aor. 1, imper. pass.—B. Tdf. . . . . } id.
ἰαθήσεται, Rec. Gr. Sch. (Lu. 7. 7) . }
Ἰακώβ, ὁ, *Jacob,* pr. name, indecl.
I. *Son of Isaac,* Mat. 1. 2, et al.
II. *Father of Joseph, Mary's husband,* Mat. 1. 15, 16.
Ἰάκωβον, acc. . . . . . . Ἰάκωβος
Ἰάκωβος, ου, ὁ, (§ 3. tab. C. a) *James,* pr. name.
I. *Son of Zebedee,* Mat. 4. 21, et al.
II. *Son of Alphæus and Mary, brother of Jude,* Mat. 10. 3, et al.
III. *James the less, brother of Jesus,* Gal. 1. 19.
Ἰακώβου, gen. . . . . . . Ἰάκωβος
Ἰακώβῳ, dat. . . . . . . id.
ἴᾱμα], ατος, τό, (§ 4. tab. D. c) . . ἰάομαι
ἰαμάτων, gen. pl. . . . . . ἴαμα
Ἰαμβρῆς,[a] οῦ, ὁ, (§ 2. tab. B. c) *Jambres,* pr. name.
Ἰαννά,[b] ὁ, *Janna,* pr. name, indecl.
Ἰαννῆς,[c] οῦ, ὁ, *Jannes,* pr. name.

ἰάομαι, ῶμαι], (§ 19. tab. S) fut. άσομαι, aor. 1, ἰᾱσάμην, perf. pass. ἴᾱμαι, aor. 1, ἰάθην, (ᾱ) *to heal, cure,* Mat. 8. 8; Lu. 9. 2; met. *to heal,* spiritually, *restore from a state of sin and condemnation,* Mat. 13. 15; He. 12. 13, et al.

ἴᾱμα, ατος, τό, (§ 4. tab. D. c) *healing, cure,* 1 Co. 12. 9, 28, 30.

ἴᾱσις, εως, ἡ, (§ 5. tab. E. c) *healing, cure,* Lu. 13. 32; Ac. 4. 22, 30.

ἰᾱτρός, οῦ, ὁ, (§ 3. tab. C. a) *a physician,* Mat. 9. 12; Mar. 2. 17; 5. 26, et al.

Ἰαρέδ,[d] ὁ, *Jared,* pr. name, indecl.
ἰάσασθαι, aor. 1, infin. mid. . . . ἰάομαι

[a] 2 Ti. 3. 8. [b] Lu. 3. 24. [c] 2 Ti. 3. 8. [d] Lu. 3. 37.

ἰάσατο, 3 pers. sing. aor. 1, ind. mid. . . ἰάομαι
ἰάσεις, acc. pl. . . . . . . ἴασις
ἰάσεως, gen. sing. . . . . . . id.
ἰάσηται, 3 pers. sing. aor. 1, subj. mid. . ἰάομαι
ἰᾶσθαι, pres. infin. . . . . . . id.
ἴασιν, acc. sing. . . . . . . ἴασις
ἴασις], εως, ἡ, (§ 5. tab. E. c) . . . ἰάομαι
ἰάσομαι, 1 pers. sing. fut. ind.—Ln. }
ἰάσωμαι, R. Gr. Sch. Tdf. (Mat. 13. 15) } id.
Ἰάσονα, acc. . . . . . . Ἰάσων
Ἰάσονος, gen. . . . . . . id.
ἰάσπιδι, dat. sing. . . . . . . ἴασπις
ἴασπις, ἴδος, ἡ, (§ 4. rem. 2. c) *jasper*, a precious stone of various colours, as purple, cerulian, green, etc., Re. 4. 3; 21. 11, 18, 19.
ἰάσωμαι, 1 pers. sing. aor. 1, subj. mid. . ἰάομαι
Ἰάσων, ονος, ὁ, (§ 4. rem. 2. e) *Jason*, pr. name.
ἰᾶται, 3 pers. sing. pres. ind. mid. . . ἰάομαι
ἴαται, 3 pers. sing. perf. ind. pass. . . id.
ἰᾶτο, 3 pers. sing. imperf. mid. . . . id.
ἰατρέ, voc. sing. . . . . . . ἰατρός
ἰατροῖς, dat. pl. . . . . . . id.
ἰᾱτρός, οῦ, ὁ, (§ 3. tab. C. a) . . . ἰάομαι
ἰατροῦ, gen. sing. . . . . . . ἰατρός
ἰατρῶν, gen. pl. . . . . . . id.
ἴδε, or ἰδέ, imperat. of εἶδον, (§ 36. rem. 1) used as an interj. *lo! behold!* Jno. 11. 36; 16. 29; 19. 4, 5, et al.
ἰδέα,[a] ας, ἡ, (§ 2. tab. B. b, and rem. 2) (ἰδεῖν, see ὁράω) *form; look, aspect.*—Rec. Gr. Sch. Ln.
εἰδέα, A. B. C. D. Tdf. (Mat. 28. 3)
ἰδεῖν, aor. 2, infin. (§ 36. rem. 1) . . ὁράω
ἴδετε, 2 pers. pl. aor. 2, imper. . . . id.
ἴδῃ, 2 pers. sing. aor. 2, subj. . . . id.
ἴδῃς, 2 pers. sing. aor. 2, subj. . . . id.
ἴδητε, 2 pers. pl. aor. 2, subj. . . . id.
ἰδίᾳ, dat. sing. fem. . . . . . ἴδιος
ἴδια, nom. and acc. pl. neut. . . . id.
ἰδίαις, dat. pl. fem. . . . . . id.
ἰδίαν, acc. sing. fem. . . . . . id.
ἰδίας, gen. sing. and acc. pl. fem. . . id.
ἴδιοι, nom. pl. masc. . . . . . id.
ἰδίοις, dat. pl. masc. and neut. . . . id.
ἴδιον, acc. sing. masc. and neut. . . . id.

ἴδιος, ία, ιον, (§ 7. rem. 1) *one's own*, Mar. 15. 20; Jno. 7. 18, et al.; *due, proper, specially assigned*, Gal. 6. 9; 1 Ti. 2. 6; 6. 15; Tit. 1. 3; also used in N.T. as a simple possessive, Ep. 5. 22, et al.; τὰ ἴδια, *one's home, household, people*, Jno. 1. 11; 16. 32, 19. 17; οἱ ἴδιοι, *members of one's own household, friends*, Jno. 1. 11; Ac. 24. 23, et al.; ἰδίᾳ, adverbially, *severally, respectively*, 1 Co. 12. 11; κατ' ἰδίαν, adv. *privately, aside, by one's self, alone*, Mat. 14. 13, 23, et al.

ἰδιώτης, ου, ὁ, (§ 2. tab. B. c) pr. *one in private life; one devoid of special learning or gifts, a plain person*, Ac. 4. 13; 2 Co. 11. 6; *ungifted*, 1 Co. 14. 16, 23, 24.

ἰδίου, gen. sing. masc. and neut. . . ἴδιος
ἰδίους, acc. pl. masc. . . . . . id.
ἰδίῳ, dat. sing. masc. and neut. . . . id.
ἰδίων, gen. pl. . . . . . . id.
ἰδιῶται, nom. pl. . . . . . ἰδιώτης
ἰδιώτης, ου, ὁ, (§ 2. tab. B. c) . . . ἴδιος
ἰδιώτου, gen. sing. . . . . . ἰδιώτης
ἰδόντες, nom. pl. masc. part. aor. 2 . . ὁράω
ἰδού, varied in accent from ἰδοῦ, imperat. of εἰδόμην, a particle serving to call attention, *lo!* Mat. 1. 23; Lu. 1. 38; Ac. 8. 36, et al. freq.
Ἰδουμαία], ας, ἡ, (§ 2. tab. B. b, and rem. 2) *Idumæa*, a country south of Judea.
Ἰδουμαίας,[b] gen. . . . . . Ἰδουμαία
ἰδοῦσα, nom. sing. fem. part. aor. 2 . . ὁράω
ἱδρώς,[c] ῶτος, ὁ, (§ 4. rem. 2. c) (ἶδος, *sweat*) *sweat.*
ἴδω, 1 pers. sing. aor. 2, subj. . . . ὁράω
ἴδωμεν, 1 pers. pl. aor. 2, subj. . . . id.
ἰδών, nom. sing. masc. part. aor. 2 . . . id.
ἴδωσι, 3 pers. pl. aor. 2. subj. . . . id.
Ἰεζαβήλ,[d] ἡ, *Jezebel*, pr. name, indecl.—Rec.
Ἰεζαβέλ, Gr. Sch. Tdf. (Re. 2. 20)
ἱερά, acc. pl. neut. . . . . . ἱερός
Ἱεραπόλει,[e] dat. . . . . . Ἱεράπολις
Ἱεράπολις], εως, ἡ, (§ 5. tab. E. c) *Hierapolis*, a city of Phrygia.
ἱερᾱτεία], ας, ἡ, (§ 2. tab. B. b, and rem. 2) ἱερός
ἱερατείαν, acc. sing. . . . . . ἱερατεία
ἱερατείας, gen. sing. . . . . . id.
ἱερατεύειν,[f] pres. infin. . . . . ἱερατεύω
ἱεράτευμα, ατος, τό, (§ 4. tab. D. c) . . ἱερός
ἱερατεύω], fut. εύσω . . . . . id.

[a] Mat. 28. 3. [b] Mar. 3. 8. [c] Lu. 22. 44. [d] Re. 2. 20. [e] Col. 4. 13. [f] Lu. 1. 8.

ἱερέα, acc. sing. . . . . . ἱερεύς
ἱερεῖ, dat. sing. . . . . . . id.
ἱερεῖς, nom. and. acc. pl. . . . . id.
Ἱερεμίαν, acc. . . . . . . Ἱερεμίας
Ἱερεμίας], ου, ὁ, (§ 2. tab. B. d) *Jeremiah*, pr. name.
Ἱερεμίου, gen. . . . . . . Ἱερεμίας
ἱερεύς, έως, ὁ, (§ 5. tab. E. d) . . ἱερός
ἱερεῦσι, dat. pl. . . . . . . ἱερεύς
ἱερέων, gen. pl. . . . . . . id.
Ἱεριχώ, ἡ, *Jericho*, indecl., a city of Palestine.
ἱερόθυτον, nom. sing. neut.—A. B. Ln. Tdf. } ἱερόθυτος
εἰδωλόθυτον, Rec. Gr. Sch. (1 Co. 10. 28) }
ἱερόθῦτος], ου, ὁ, ἡ, (§ 7. rem. 2) (ἱερός & θύω) *offered in sacrifice*. v.r.
ἱερόν, ου, τό, (§ 3. tab. C. c) . . . ἱερός
ἱεροπρεπεῖς,[a] acc. pl. fem. . . . ἱεροπρεπής
ἱεροπρεπής], έος, οῦς, ὁ, ἡ, (§ 7. tab. G. b) (ἱερός & πρέπει) *beseeming what is sacred; becoming holy persons*, Tit. 2. 3.

ἱερός], ά, όν, (§ 7. rem. 1) *hallowed; holy, divine*, 2 Ti. 3. 15; τὰ ἱερά, *sacred rites*, 1 Co. 9. 13, bis.

ἱερᾶτεία, ας, ἡ, (§ 2. tab. B. b, and rem. 2) *priesthood, sacerdotal office*, Lu. 1. 9.

ἱεράτευμα, ατος, τό, (§ 4. tab. D. c) *a priesthood*; meton. *a body of priests*, 1 Pe. 2. 5, 9.

ἱερατεύω, *to officiate as a priest, perform sacred rites*, Lu. 1. 8.

ἱερεύς, έως, ὁ, (§ 5. tab. E. d) *a priest, one who performs sacrificial rites*, Mat. 8. 4; Lu. 1. 5; Jno. 1. 19, et al.

ἱερόν, ου, τό, (§ 3. tab. C. c) *a temple*, Mat. 4. 5; Lu. 4. 9; Ac. 19. 27, et al.

ἱερωσύνη, ης, ἡ, (§ 2. tab. B. a) *priesthood, sacerdotal office*, He. 7. 11, 12, 14, 24. (ῠ).

Ἱεροσόλυμα, ης, ἡ, and ων, τά, *Jerusalem*, the Greek forms of Ἱερουσαλήμ.
Ἱεροσολυμῖται, nom. pl. . . . Ἱεροσολυμίτης
Ἱεροσολυμίτης], ου, ὁ, (§ 2. tab. B. c) *a native of Jerusalem*, Mar. 1. 5; Jno. 7. 25. (ῑτ).
Ἱεροσολυμιτῶν, gen. pl. . . . Ἱεροσολυμίτης
Ἱεροσολύμοις, dat. pl. . . . . Ἱεροσόλυμα
Ἱεροσολύμων, gen. pl. . . . . id.

ἱεροσυλεῖς,[b] 2 pers. sing. pres. ind. . ἱεροσυλέω
ἱεροσυλέω, ῶ], fut. ήσω . . . ἱερόσυλος
ἱεροσύλους,[c] acc. pl. masc. . . . . id.
ἱερόσῡλος], ου, ὁ, ἡ, (§ 7. rem. 2) (ἱερός & συλάω) *one who despoils temples, commits sacrilege*.

ἱεροσῡλέω, ῶ, fut. ήσω, (§ 16. tab. P) *to despoil temples, commit sacrilege*.

ἱεροῦ, gen. sing. . . . . . . ἱερόν
ἱερουργοῦντα,[d] acc. sing. masc. part. pres. ἱερουργέω
ἱερουργέω, ῶ], fut. ήσω, (§ 16. tab. P) (ἱερός & ἔργον) *to officiate as priest, perform sacred rites*; in N.T. *to minister* in a divine commission. L.G.
Ἱερουσαλήμ, ἡ, *Jerusalem*, pr. name, indecl.
ἱερῷ, dat. sing. . . . . . . ἱερόν
ἱερωσύνη], ης, ἡ, (§ 2. tab. B. a) . . ἱερός
ἱερωσύνην, acc. sing. . . . . ἱερωσύνη
ἱερωσύνης, gen. sing. . . . . . id.
Ἰεσσαί, ὁ, *Jesse*, pr. name, indecl.
Ἰεφθαέ,[e] ὁ, *Jephthae*, pr. name, indecl.
Ἰεχονίαν, acc. . . . . . . Ἰεχονίας
Ἰεχονίας, ου, ὁ, (§ 2, tab. B. d) *Jechonias*, pr. name.
Ἰησοῦς, οῦ, ὁ, (§ 6. rem. 3) (Heb. יְהוֹשׁוּעַ contr. יֵשׁוּעַ) *a Saviour, Jesus*, Mat. 1. 21, 25; 2. 1, et al. freq.; *Joshua*, Ac. 7. 45; He. 4. 8; *Jesus*, a Jewish Christian, Col. 4. 11.
Ἰησοῦ, gen. . . . . . . Ἰησοῦς
Ἰησοῦ, dat. . . . . . . id.
Ἰησοῦ, voc. . . . . . . id.
Ἰησοῦν, acc. . . . . . . id.
ἱκανά, acc. pl. neut. . . . . ἱκανός
ἱκαναί, nom. pl. fem. . . . . id.
ἱκαναῖς, dat. pl. fem. . . . . id.
ἱκανάς, acc. pl. fem. . . . . id.
ἱκανοί, nom. pl. masc. . . . . id.
ἱκανοῖς, dat. pl. masc. . . . . id.
ἱκανόν, acc. sing. masc. and nom. and acc. neut. id.
ἱκᾰνός, ή, όν, (§ 7. tab. F. a) (ἵκω, or, ἱκάνω, *to arrive at, reach to*) *befitting; sufficient, enough*, Lu. 22. 38; ἱκανὸν ποιεῖν τινί, *to satisfy, gratify*, Mar. 15. 15; τὸ ἱκανὸν λαμβάνειν, *to take security or bail* of any one, Ac. 17. 9; of persons, *adequate, competent, qualified*, 2 Co. 2. 16; *fit, worthy*, Mat. 3. 11; 8. 8; of number or quantity, *considerable, large, great, much*,

[a] Tit. 2. 3. [b] Ro. 2. 22. [c] Ac. 19. 37. [d] Ro. 15. 16. [e] He. 11. 32.

and pl. *many*, Mat. 28. 12; Mar. 10. 46, et al.

ἱκανότης, τητος, ἡ, (§ 4. rem. 2. c) *sufficiency, ability, fitness, qualification*, 2 Co. 3. 5.

ἱκανόω, ῶ, fut. ώσω, (§ 20. tab. T) aor. 1, ἱκάνωσα, *to make sufficient or competent, qualify*, 2 Co. 3. 6; Col. 1. 12. L.G.

ἱκανότης,[a] τητος, ἡ . . . . . ἱκανός
ἱκανόω, ῶ], fut. ώσω . . . . . id.
ἱκανοῦ, gen. sing. masc. and neut. . . id.
ἱκανούς, acc. pl. masc. . . . . . id.
ἱκανῷ, dat. sing. masc. . . . . . id.
ἱκανῶν, gen. pl. . . . . . . id.
ἱκανώσαντι, dat. sing. masc. part. aor. 1 . ἱκανόω
ἱκάνωσε, 3 pers. sing. aor. 1, ind. (§ 13. rem. 3) id.

ἱκετηρία], ας, ἡ, (§ 2. tab. B. b, and rem. 2) (fem. of ἱκετήριος, sc. ῥάβδος, fr. ἱκέτης, *suppliant*) pr. *an olive branch* borne by suppliants in their hands; *supplication*.

ἱκετηρίας,[b] acc. pl. . . . . . ἱκετηρία
ἱκμάδα,[c] acc. sing. . . . . . ἱκμάς

ἰκμάς], άδος, ἡ, (§ 4. rem. 2. c) *moisture*.

Ἰκόνιον, ου, τό, (§ 3. tab. C. c) *Iconium*, a city of Lycaonia, in Asia Minor.

Ἰκονίῳ, dat. . . . . . . Ἰκόνιον
ἱλαρόν,[d] acc. sing. masc. . . . . ἱλαρός

ἱλᾰρός], ά, όν, (§ 7. rem. 1) *cheerful, not grudging*.

ἱλαρότης, τητος, ἡ, (§ 4. rem. 2. c) *cheerfulness*. L.G.

ἱλαρότης], τητος, ἡ . . . . . ἱλαρος
ἱλαρότητι,[e] dat. sing. . . . . . ἱλαρότης
ἱλάσθητι, 2 pers. sing. aor. 1, imper. pass. ἱλάσκομαι
ἱλάσκεσθαι, pres. infin. . . . . id.

ἱλάσκομαι], fut. ἱλάσομαι, aor. 1, ἱλάσθην, *to appease, render propitious*; in N.T. *to expiate, make an atonement or expiation for*, He. 2. 17; ἱλάσθητι, *be gracious, show mercy, pardon*, Lu. 18. 13.

ἱλασμός, οῦ, ὁ, (§ 3. tab. C. a) *propitiation, expiation; one who makes expiation*, 1 Jno. 2. 2; 4. 10.

ἱλαστήριος, α, ον, (§ 7. rem. 1) *propitiatory; invested with propitiatory power*, Ro. 3. 25; in N.T. and LXX. τὸ ἱλαστήριον, *the cover of the ark of the covenant the mercy-seat*, He. 9. 5.

ἱλασμόν, acc. sing. . . . . . ἱλασμός
ἱλασμός, οῦ, ὁ, (§ 3. tab. C. a) . . ἱλάσκομαι
ἱλαστήριον, ου, τό, (§ 3. tab. C. c) . . id.

ἵλεως, ων, ὁ, ἡ, (§ 7. tab. F. b, and rem. 3) (Att. for ἵλαος) *propitious, favourable, merciful, clement*, He. 8. 12; from the Heb., ἵλεως σοι (ὁ Θεός) *God have mercy on thee, God forbid, far be it from thee*, Mat. 16. 22.

Ἰλλυρικόν], ου, τό, *Illyricum*, a country between the Adriatic and the Danube.

Ἰλλυρικοῦ,[f] gen. . . . . . Ἰλλυρικόν
ἱμάντα, acc. sing. . . . . . . ἱμάς

ἱμάς], άντος, ὁ, (§ 4. rem. d) *a strap or thong of leather*, Ac. 22. 25; *a shoe-latchet*, Mar. 1. 7; Lu. 3. 16; Jno. 1. 27.

ἱμᾶσι, dat. pl. . . . . . . ἱμάς
ἱμάτια, nom. and acc. pl. . . . . ἱμάτιον
ἱματίζω], fut. ίσω, (§ 26. rem. 1) . . id.
ἱματίοις, dat. pl. . . . . . . id.

ἱμάτιον, ου, τό, (§ 3. tab. C. c) (ἕννυμι, *to clothe*, εἷμα) *a garment; the upper garment, mantle*, Mat. 5. 40; 9. 16, 20, 21; pl. *the mantle and tunic together*, Mat. 26. 65; pl. genr. *garments, raiment*, Mat. 11. 8; 24. 18, et al.

ἱματίζω, fut. ίσω, perf. pass. ἱμάτισμαι, (§ 26. rem. 1) *to clothe*; pass. *to be clothed*, Mar. 5. 15; Lu. 8. 35. N.T.

ἱματισμός, οῦ, ὁ, (§ 3. tab. C. a) *a garment; raiment, apparel, clothing*, Lu. 7. 25; 9. 29, et al. L.G.

ἱματίου, gen. sing. . . . . . ἱμάτιον
ἱματισμένον, acc. sing. masc. part. perf. pass. ἱματίζω
ἱματισμόν, acc. sing. . . . . . ἱματισμός
ἱματισμός, οῦ, ὁ, (§ 3. tab. C. a) . . ἱμάτιον
ἱματισμοῦ, gen. sing. . . . . . ἱματισμός
ἱματισμῷ, dat. sing. . . . . . id.
ἱματίῳ, dat. sing. . . . . . . ἱμάτιον
ἱματίων, gen. pl. . . . . . . id.
ἱμειρόμενοι,[g] nom. pl. masc. part. pres. mid. ἱμείρω

ἱμείρω and ἱμείρομαι], (ἵμερος, *desire*) *to desire earnestly*; by. impl. *to have a strong affection for, love fervently*.

ἵνα, conj., *that, in order that*, Mat. 19. 13; Mar. 1. 38; Jno. 1. 22; 3. 15; 17. 1; ἵνα μή, *that not, lest*, Mat. 7. 1; in N.T. equiva-

a 2 Co. 3. 5. b He. 5. 7. c Lu. 8. 6. d 2 Co. 9. 7. e Ro. 12. 8. f Ro. 15. 19. g 1 Thes. 2. 8

lent to ὥστε, *so that, so as that,* Jno. 9. 2, et al.; also, marking a simple circumstance, *the circumstance that,* Mat. 10. 25; Jno. 4. 34; 6. 29; 1 Jno. 4. 17; 5. 3, et al.

ἱνατί, adv. (ἵνα & τί) *why is it that? wherefore? why?* Mat. 9. 4; 27. 46, et al.

Ἰόππη], ης, ἡ, (§ 2. tab. B. a) *Joppa,* a city of Palestine.

Ἰόππῃ, dat. . . . . . . Ἰόππη

Ἰόππην, acc. . . . . . . id.

Ἰόππης, gen. . . . . . . id.

Ἰορδάνῃ, dat. . . . . Ἰορδάνης

Ἰορδάνην, acc. . . . . . id.

Ἰορδάνης], ου, ὁ, (§ 2. tab. B. c) *the river Jordan.*

Ἰορδάνου, gen. . . . . . Ἰορδάνης

ἰός, οῦ, ὁ, (§ 3. tab. C. a) *a missile weapon, arrow, dart; venom, poison,* Ro. 3. 13; Ja. 3. 8; *rust,* Ja. 5. 3.

ἰοῦ, gen. sing. . . . . . ἰός

Ἰούδα, gen. and voc. (§ 2. rem. 4) . . Ἰούδας

Ἰούδᾳ, dat. . . . . id.

Ἰουδαία, ας, ἡ, (§ 2. tab. B. b, and rem. 2) Ἰουδαῖος

Ἰουδαία, nom. sing. fem. (adj.) . . id.

Ἰουδαίᾳ, dat. . . . . . . Ἰουδαία

Ἰουδαίᾳ, dat. sing. fem. (adj.) . . Ἰουδαῖος

Ἰουδαίαν, acc. . . . . . . Ἰουδαία

Ἰουδαίαν, acc. sing. fem. (adj.) . . . Ἰουδαῖος

Ἰουδαίας, gen. . . . . Ἰουδαία

Ἰουδαίας, gen. sing. fem. (adj.) . . Ἰουδαῖος

Ἰουδαΐζειν,[a] pres. infin. . . . Ἰουδαΐζω

Ἰουδαΐζω], fut. ίσω . . . . Ἰουδαῖος

Ἰουδαϊκοῖς,[b] dat. pl. masc. . . . Ἰουδαϊκός

Ἰουδαϊκός], ή, όν, (§ 7. tab. F. a) . . Ἰουδαῖος

Ἰουδαϊκῶς,[c] adv. . . . . . . id.

Ἰουδαῖοι, nom. and voc. pl. . . . id.

Ἰουδαίοις, dat. pl. . . . . . id.

Ἰουδαῖον, acc. sing. . . . . . id.

Ἰουδαῖος, ου, ὁ, (Heb. יְהוּדִי) pr. *one sprung from the tribe of Judah, or a subject of the kingdom of Judah;* in N.T. *a descendant of Jacob, a Jew,* Mat. 28. 15; Mar. 7. 3; Ac. 19. 34; Ro. 2. 28, 29, et al.

Ἰουδαία, ας, ἡ, (§ 2. tab. B. b, and rem. 2) *Judea,* Mat. 2. 1, 5, 22; 3. 1, et al.; meton. *the inhabitants of Judea,* Mat. 3. 5.

Ἰουδαῖος, α, ον, (§ 7. rem. 1) *Jewish,* Mar. 1. 5; Jno. 3. 22; Ac. 16. 1; 24. 24.

Ἰουδαΐζω, fut. ίσω, *to judaize, live like a Jew, follow the manners and customs of the Jews,* Gal. 2. 14.

Ἰουδαϊκός, ή, όν, (§ 7. tab. F. a) *Jewish, current among the Jews,* Tit. 1. 14.

Ἰουδαϊκῶς, adv. *Jewishly, in the manner of Jews,* Gal. 2. 14.

Ἰουδαϊσμός, οῦ, ὁ, (§ 3. tab. C. a) *Judaism, the character and condition of a Jew; practice of the Jewish religion,* Gal. 1. 13, 14.

Ἰουδαίου, gen. sing. . . . . Ἰουδαῖος

Ἰουδαίους, acc. pl. . . . . . id.

Ἰουδαίῳ, dat. sing. . . . . . id.

Ἰουδαίων, gen. pl. . . . . . id.

Ἰουδαϊσμός], οῦ, ὁ, (§ 3. tab. C. a) . . id.

Ἰουδαϊσμῷ, dat. sing. . . . . Ἰουδαϊσμός

Ἰούδαν, acc. . . . . . . Ἰούδας

Ἰούδας, α, ὁ, (§ 2. rem. 4) *Judas, Jude,* pr. name.

I. *Judah, son of Jacob; the tribe of Judah,* Mat. 1. 2; Lu. 1. 39, et al.

II. *Juda, son of Joseph, of the ancestry of Jesus,* Lu. 3. 30.

III. *Juda, son of Joanna, of the ancestry of Jesus,* Lu. 3. 26.

IV. *Judas, brother of James, Jude,* Lu. 6. 16, et al.; Jude 1.

V. *Judas Iscariot, son of Simon,* Mat. 10. 4; Jno. 6. 71, et al.

VI. *Judas, brother of Jesus,* Mat. 13. 55; Mar. 6. 3.

VII. *Judas of Galilee,* Ac. 5. 37.

VIII. *Judas, surnamed Barsabas,* Ac. 15. 22, et al.

IX. *Judas of Damascus,* Ac. 9. 11.

Ἰουλία], ας, ἡ, (§ 2. tab. B. b, and rem. 2) *Julia,* pr. name.

Ἰουλίαν,[d] acc. . . . . . . Ἰουλία

Ἰούλιος, ου, ὁ, (§ 3. tab. C. a) *Julius,* pr. name.

Ἰουλίῳ, dat. . . . . Ἰούλιος

Ἰουνίαν,[e] acc. . . . . . . Ἰουνίας

Ἰουνίας], ου, ὁ, (§ 2. rem. 4) *Junia,* pr. name.

Ἰοῦστος, ου, ὁ, (§ 3. tab. C. a) *Justus,* pr. name.

I. *Joseph Barsabas,* Ac. 1. 23.

II. *Justus of Corinth,* Ac. 18. 7.

III. *Jesus, called Justus,* Col. 4. 11.

Ἰούστου, gen. . . . . . . Ἰοῦστος

ἱππεῖς, acc. pl. . . . . . ἱππεύς

---

[a] Gal. 2. 14. [b] Tit. 1. 14. [c] Gal. 2. 14. [d] Ro. 16. 15. [e] Ro. 16. 7.

ἱππεύς], έως, ὁ, (§ 5. tab. E. d) . . . ἵππος
ἱππικός], ή, όν, (§ 7. tab. F. a) . . id.
ἱππικοῦ,[a] gen. sing. neut. . . . . ἱππικός
ἵπποις, dat. pl. . . . . . . ἵππος

ἵππος, ου, ὁ, (§ 3. tab. C. a) *a horse*, Ja. 3. 3; Re. 6. 2, 4, 5, 8, et al.

ἱππεύς, έως, ὁ, (§ 5. tab. E. d) *a horseman*; pl. ἱππεῖς, *horsemen, cavalry*, Ac. 23. 23, 32.

ἱππῐκός, ή, όν, (§ 7. tab. F. a) *equestrian*; τὸ ἱππικόν, *cavalry, horse*, Re. 9. 16

ἵππου, gen. sing. . . . . . . ἵππος
ἵππους, acc. pl. . . . . . id.
ἵππων, gen. pl. . . . . . id.

ἶρις, ἴρῐδος, ἡ, (§ 4. rem. 2. c) *a rainbow, iris*, Re. 4. 3; 10. 1.

ἴσα, nom. and. acc. pl. neut. . . . ἴσος
Ἰσαάκ, ὁ, *Isaac*, pr. name, indecl.
ἰσάγγελοι,[b] nom. pl. masc. . . . ἰσάγγελος
ἰσάγγελος], ου, ὁ, ἡ, (§ 7. rem. 2) (ἴσος & ἄγγελος) *equal or similar to angels*. N.T.
ἴσαι, nom. pl. fem. . . . . . ἴσος
ἴσᾱσι, 3 pers. pl. of οἶδα, (§ 33. rem. 2. and § 37. rem. 1) usually in N.T. οἴδασι, Ac. 26. 4.
Ἰσαχάρ,[c] ὁ, *Issachar*, pr. name, indecl.
ἴση, nom. sing. fem. . . . . . ἴσος
ἴσην, acc. sing. fem. . . . id.
ἴσθι, 2 pers. sing. imper. (§ 12. tab. L) . εἰμί
Ἰσκαριώτῃ, dat. . . . . . . Ἰσκαριώτης
Ἰσκαριώτην, acc. . . . . . . id.
Ἰσκαριώτης, ου, ὁ, (§ 2. tab. B. c) *Iscariot*, (man of Carioth) pr. name.
Ἰσκαριώτου, gen. . . . . . Ἰσκαριώτης
ἴσον, acc. sing. masc. . . . . . ἴσος

ἴσος, η, ον, (§ 7. tab. F. a) *equal, like*, Mat. 20. 12; Lu. 6. 34, et al.; neut. pl. ἴσα, adverbially, *on an equality*, Phi. 2. 6; met. *correspondent, consistent*, Mar. 14. 56, 59.

ἰσότης, τητος, ἡ, (§ 4. rem. 2. c) *equality, equal proportion*, 2 Co. 8. 13, 14; *fairness, equity, what is equitable*, Col. 4. 1.

ἴσως, adv. *equally; perhaps, it may be that*, Lu. 20. 13.

ἰσότης, τητος, ἡ . . . . . ἴσος
ἰσότητα, acc. sing. . . . . . ἰσότης
ἰσότητος, gen. sing. . . . . . ἰσότης
ἰσότιμον,[d] acc. sing. fem. . . . . ἰσότιμος
ἰσότῑμος], ου, ὁ, ἡ, (§ 7. rem. 2) (ἴσος & τιμή) *of equal price, equally precious or valuable*.
ἴσους, acc. pl. masc. . . . . . ἴσος
ἰσόψυχον,[e] acc. sing. masc. . . . ἰσόψυχος
ἰσόψῡχος], ου, ὁ, ἡ, (§ 7. rem. 2) (ἴσος & ψυχή) *like-minded, of the same mind and spirit*.
Ἰσραήλ, ὁ, *Israel*, pr. name, indecl.
Ἰσραηλῖται, nom. and voc. pl. . . Ἰσραηλίτης
Ἰσραηλίτης, ου, ὁ, (§ 2. tab. B. c) *an Israelite, a descendant of* Ἰσραήλ, *Israel or Jacob*, Jno. 1. 48; Ac. 2. 22, et al.
ἱστάνομεν, 1 pers. pl. pres. ind.—A. C. D. Ln. Tdf. . . . . } ἱστάνω
ἱστῶμεν, Rec. Gr. Sch. (Ro. 3. 31) . }
ἱστάνω], same signif. as ἵστημι, v.r.
ἴστε, 2 pers. pl. pres. ind. for ἴσατε, (§ 37. rem. 1) . . . . . . οἶδα

ἵστημι, and, in N.T., **ἱστάω, ῶ**], (§ 29. tab. X) fut. στήσω, aor. 1, ἔστησα, trans. *to make to stand, set, place*, Mat. 4. 5, et al.; *to set forth, appoint*, Ac. 1. 23; *to fix, appoint*, Ac. 17. 31; *to establish, confirm*, Ro. 10. 3; He. 10. 9; *to set down, impute*, Ac. 7. 60; *to weigh out, pay*, Mat. 26. 15; intrans. perf. ἕστηκα, infin. ἑστάναι, (ᾰ) part. ἑστώς, pluperf. εἱστήκειν, aor. 2, ἔστην, pass. ἵσταμαι, fut. σταθήσομαι, aor. 1, ἐστάθην, (ᾰ), *to stand*, Mat. 12. 46, et al.; *to stand fast, be firm, be permanent, endure*, Mat. 12. 25; Ep. 6. 13, et al.; *to be confirmed, proved*, Mat. 18. 16; 2 Co. 13. 1; *to stop*, Lu. 7. 14; 8. 44; Ac. 8. 38, et al.

στάσις, εως, ἡ, (§ 5. tab. E. c) *a setting; a standing; an* effective *position, an* unimpaired *standing or dignity*, He. 9. 8; *a gathered party, a group*; hence, *a tumultuous assemblage, popular outbreak*, Mar. 15. 7; Ac. 19. 40, et al.; *seditious movement*, Ac. 24. 5; *discord, dispute, dissension*, Ac. 15. 2; 23. 7, 10.

στασιαστής, οῦ, ὁ, (στάσις) *a partizan*, v.r. Mar. 15. 7.

στατήρ, ῆρος, ὁ, (§ 4. rem. 2. f)

[a] Re. 9. 16. [b] Lu. 20. 36. [c] Re. 7. 7. [d] 2 Pe. 1. 1. [e] Phi. 2. 20.

(ἵστημι, *to weigh*) pr. *a weight; a stater*, an Attic silver coin, equal in value to the Jewish shekel, or to four Attic or two Alexandrian drachms, and equivalent to about three shillings of our money, Mat. 17. 27.

στήκω, a late equivalent to ἕστηκα, *to stand*, Mar. 11. 25; met. *to stand* when under judgment, *to be approved*, Ro. 14. 4; *to stand firm, be constant, persevere*, 1 Co. 16. 13, et al.

στηρίζω, fut. ίξω, aor. 1, ἐστήριξα, (§ 26. rem. 2) *to set fast; to set* in a certain position or direction, Lu. 9. 51; met. *to render* mentally *steadfast, to settle, confirm*, Lu. 22. 32; Ro. 1. 11, et al.; perf. pass. ἐστήριγμαι, *to stand immovable*, Lu. 16. 26; met. *to be* mentally *settled*, 2 Pe. 1. 12.

στηριγμός, οῦ, ὁ, (§ 3. tab. C. a) pr. *a fixing, settling; a state of firmness, fixedness*; met. *firmness* of belief, *settled frame* of mind, 2 Pe. 3. 17.

στοά, ᾶς, ἡ, (§ 2. tab. B. b, and rem. 2) *a colonnade, piazza, cloister, covered walk supported by columns*, Jno. 5. 2; 10. 23; Ac. 3. 11; 5. 12.

ἵστησι, 3 pers. sing. pres. ind. act. . . . ἵστημι

ἱστορέω, ῶ], fut. ήσω, (§ 16. tab. P) (ἵστωρ, *knowing*) *to ascertain by inquiry and examination; to inquire of*; in N.T. *to visit* in order to become acquainted with.

ἱστορῆσαι,[a] aor. 1, infin. . . . ἱστορέω

ἱστῶμεν, 1 pers. pl. pres. ind. . . . ἱστάω

ἴσχυε, 3 pers. sing. imperf. . . . ἰσχύω

ἰσχύει, 3 pers. sing. pres. ind. . . . id.

ἰσχύειν, pres. infin. . . . id.

ἰσχύϊ, dat. sing. . . . ἰσχύς

ἰσχύν, acc. sing. . . . id.

ἴσχυον, 3 pers. pl. imperf. . . . ἰσχύω

ἰσχύοντες, nom. pl. masc. part. pres. . . id.

ἰσχύοντος, gen. sing. masc. part. pres. . . id.

ἰσχύος, gen. sing. . . . ἰσχύς

ἰσχυρά, nom. sing. fem. and acc. pl. neut. . ἰσχυρός

ἰσχυρᾷ, dat. sing. fem.—Gr. Sch. Tdf. . } id.
ἰσχύϊ, Rec. (Re. 18. 2) . . }

ἰσχυραί, nom. pl. fem. . . . id.

ἰσχυράν, acc. sing. fem. . . . id.

ἰσχυρᾶς, gen. sing. fem. . . . ἰσχυρός

ἰσχυροί, nom. pl. masc. . . . id.

ἰσχυρόν, acc. sing. masc. . . . id.

ἰσχῡρός], ά, όν, (§ 7. rem. 1) . . . ἰσχύς

ἰσχυρότεροι, nom. pl. masc. comp. (§ 8. rem. 4) ἰσχυρός

ἰσχυρότερον, nom. sing. neut. comp. . . id.

ἰσχυρότερος, nom. sing. masc. comp. . . id.

ἰσχυροῦ, gen. sing. masc. . . . id.

ἰσχυρῶν, gen. pl. . . . id.

ἰσχύς, ύος, ἡ, (§ 5. tab. E. g) *strength, might, power*, Re. 18. 2; Ep. 1. 19; *faculty, ability*, 1 Pe. 4. 11; Mar. 12. 30, 33; Lu. 10. 27.

ἰσχῡρός, ά, όν, (§ 7. rem. 1) *strong, mighty, robust*, Mat. 12. 29; Lu. 11. 21; *powerful, mighty*, 1 Co. 1. 27; 4. 10; 1 Jno. 2. 14; *strong, fortified*, Re. 18. 10; *vehement*, Mat. 14. 30; *energetic*, 2 Co. 10. 10; *sure, firm*, He. 6. 18, et al.

ἰσχύω, fut. ύσω, (§ 13. tab. M) aor. 1, ἴσχῡσα, *to be strong, be well, be in good health*, Mat. 9. 12; *to have power, be able*, Mat. 8. 28; 26. 40; *to have power or efficiency, avail, be valid*, Gal. 5. 6; He. 9. 17; *to be of service, be serviceable*, Mat. 5. 13; meton. *to prevail*, Ac. 19. 16; Re. 12. 8, et al. (ῡ).

ἰσχύσαμεν, 1 pers. pl. aor. 1, ind. . . ἰσχύω

ἴσχυσαν, 3 pers. pl. aor. 1, ind. . . . id.

ἴσχυσας, 2 pers. sing. aor. 1, ind. . . id.

ἰσχύσατε, 2 pers. pl. aor. 1, ind. . . id.

ἴσχυσε, 3 pers. sing. aor. 1, ind. . . id.

ἰσχύσουσι, 3 pers. pl. fut. ind. . . . id.

ἰσχύω], fut. ύσω . . . . ἰσχύς

ἴσως,[b] adv. . . . . ἴσος

Ἰταλία], ας, ἡ, (§ 2. tab. B. b, and rem. 2) *Italy*.

Ἰταλίαν, acc. . . . . Ἰταλία

Ἰταλίας, gen. . . . . id.

Ἰταλικῆς,[c] gen. sing. fem. . . . Ἰταλικός

Ἰταλικός], ή, όν, (§ 7. tab. F. a) *Italian*.

Ἰτουραία], ας, ἡ, (§ 2. tab. B. b, and rem. 2) *Ituræa*, a district of Palestine beyond Jordan.

Ἰτουραίας,[d] gen. . . . . Ἰτουραία

ἰχθύας, acc. pl. . . . . ἰχθύς

ἰχθύδια, acc. pl. . . . . ἰχθύδιον

ἰχθύδιον], ου, τό . . . . ἰχθύς

[a] Gal. 1. 18. [b] Lu. 20. 13. [c] Ac. 10. 1. [d] Lu. 3. 1.

ἰχθύες, nom. pl. . . . . . . ἰχθύς
ἰχθύν, acc. sing. . . . . . id.
ἰχθύος, gen. sing. . . . . . . id.
ἰχθύς], ύος, ὁ, (§ 5. tab. E. g) *a fish*, Mat. 15. 36; 17. 27; Lu. 5. 6, et al.

ἰχθύδιον, ου, τό, (§ 3. tab. C. c) dimin. of ἰχθύς, *a small fish*, Mat. 15. 34; Mar. 8. 7.

ἰχθύων, gen. pl. . . . . . . ἰχθύς
ἴχνεσι, dat. pl. . . . . . ἴχνος
ἴχνος], εος, τό, (§ 5. tab. E. b) (ἵκω) *a footstep, track*; in N.T. pl. *footsteps, line of conduct*, Ro. 4. 12; 2 Co. 12. 18; 1 Pe. 2. 21.
Ἰωάθαμ, ὁ, *Joatham*, pr. name, indecl.
Ἰωάννα, ἡ, *Joanna*, pr. name.
Ἰωαννᾶ,[a] gen. . . . . . . Ἰωαννᾶς
Ἰωαννᾶς, ᾶ, ὁ, (§ 2. rem. 4) *Joanna, Joannas*, pr. name.
Ἰωάννῃ, dat. . . . . . . Ἰωάννης
Ἰωάννην, acc. . . . . . . id.
Ἰωάννης, ου, ὁ, (§ 2. tab. B. c) *Joannes, John*, pr. name.

I. *John the Baptist*, Mat. 3. 1, et al.
II. *John, son of Zebedee, the apostle*, Mat. 4. 21, et al.
III. *John, surnamed Mark*, Ac. 12. 12, et al.
IV. *John, the high-priest*, Ac. 4. 6.

Ἰωάννου, gen. . . . . . . Ἰωάννης
Ἰώβ,[b] ὁ, *Job*, pr name, indecl.
Ἰωήλ,[c] ὁ, *Joel*, pr. name, indecl.
ἰώμενος, nom. sing. masc. part. pres. . ἰάομαι
Ἰωνᾶ, gen. . . . . Ἰωνᾶς
Ἰωνάν,[d] ὁ, *Jonan*, pr. name, indecl.
Ἰωνᾶς, ᾶ, ὁ, (§ 2. rem. 4) *Jonas*, pr. name.

I. *Jonah, the prophet*, Mat. 12. 39, et al.
II. *Jonas, father of Simon Peter*, Jno. 1. 43, et al.

Ἰωράμ, ὁ, *Joram*, pr. name, indecl.
Ἰωρείμ,[e] ὁ, *Jorim*, pr. name, indecl.
Ἰωσαφάτ, ὁ, *Josaphat*, pr. name, indecl.
Ἰωσῆ, gen.—Rec. Gr. Sch. . . . } Ἰωσῆς
Ἰωσῆτος, B. D. Ln. Tdf. (Mar. 6. 3) }
Ἰωσῆς, ῆ, ὁ, (§ 2. rem. 5) *Joses*, pr. name.

I. *Joses, son of Eliezer*, Lu. 3. 29.
II. *Joses, son of Mary, brother of Jesus*, Mat. 13. 55, et al.
III. *Joses, surnamed Barnabas*, Ac. 4. 36.

Ἰωσήφ, ὁ, *Joseph*, pr. name, indecl.

I. *Joseph, son of Jacob*, Jno. 4. 5, et al.
II. *Joseph, son of Jonan*, Lu. 3. 30.
III. *Joseph, son of Judas*, Lu. 3. 26.
IV. *Joseph, son of Mattathias*, Lu. 3. 24.
V. *Joseph, the husband of Mary*, Mat 1. 16, et al.
VI. *Joseph of Arimathea*, Mat. 27. 57, et al.
VII. *Joseph Barsabas*, Ac. 1. 23.
VII. *Joseph Barnabas*.—A. D. Ln. Tdf. Ἰωσῆς, Rec. Gr. Sch. (Ac. 4. 36)

Ιωσίαν, acc. . . . . Ἰωσίας
Ἰωσίας, ου, ὁ, (§ 2. tab. B. d) *Josias*, pr. name.
ἰῶτα,[f] indecl. τό, *iota*; in N.T. used like the Heb. יוֹד, the smallest letter in the Hebrew alphabet, as an expression for *the least or minutest part; a jot*.

K.

κἀγώ, contracted from καὶ ἐγώ, dat. κἀμοί, acc. κἀμέ, καί retaining, however, its independent force, Jno. 6. 57; 10. 15, et al.
κάδος], ου, ὁ, *a cask*, Lat. cadus, v.r.
κάδους, acc. pl.—D. . . . . } κάδος
βάτους, Rec. Gr. Sch. Tdf. (Lu. 16. 6) }
καθ' by apostrophe for κατά.
καθά,[g] adv. (καθ' ἅ) lit. *according to what; as, according as*.
καθαίρει, 3 pers. sing. pres. ind. act. . . καθαίρω
καθαιρεῖσθαι, pres. inf. pass. (§ 17. tab. Q) καθαιρέω
καθαίρεσιν, acc. sing. . . . . . καθαίρεσις
καθαίρεσις], εως, ἡ, (§ 5. tab. E. c) . . καθαιρέω
καθαιρέω, ῶ], fut. ήσω, and καθελῶ, aor. 2, καθεῖλον, (§ 36. rem. 1) (κατά & αἱρέω) *to take down*, Mat. 15. 36, 46; Lu. 23. 53; Ac. 13. 29; *to pull down, demolish*, Lu. 12. 18; *to throw or cast down, degrade*, Lu. 1. 52; *to destroy, put an end to*, Ac. 19. 27; *to overthrow, conquer*, Ac. 13. 19; *to pull down, subvert*, 2 Co. 10. 5.

καθαίρεσις, εως, ἡ, (§ 5. tab. E. c) pr. *a taking down; a pulling down, overthrow, demolition*, 2 Co. 10. 4; met. *a razing* as respects spiritual state, a counter process to religious advancement by apostolic instrumentality, 2 Co. 10. 8; 13. 10.

[a] Lu. 3. 27. [b] Ja. 5. 11. [c] Ac. 2. 16. [d] Lu. 3. 30. [e] Lu. 3. 29. [f] Mat. 5. 18. [g] Mat. 27. 10.

καθαιροῦντες, nom. pl. masc. part. pres. . καθαιρέω
καθαίρω], fut. αρῶ, (§ 27. rem. 1. c) . καθαρός
καθάπερ, adv. (καθ' ἅ περ) *even as, just as*, Ro. 4. 6, et al. (ᾰ).
καθάπτω], fut. ψω, (§ 23. rem. 1) (κατά & ἅπτω) trans. *to fasten or fit to*; in N.T. equivalent to καθάπτομαι, *to fix one's self upon, fasten upon*, Ac. 28. 3.
καθαρά, nom. sing. fem. and neut. pl. . . καθαρός
καθαρᾷ, dat. sing. fem. . . . . id.
καθαρᾶς, gen. sing. fem. . . . . id.
καθαριεῖ, 3 pers. sing. fut. Att. for καθαρίσει, (§ 35. rem. 11) . . . καθαρίζω
καθαρίζει, 3 pers. sing. pres. ind. act. . . id.
καθαρίζεσθαι, pres. infin. pass. . . id.
καθαρίζεται, 3 pers. sing. pres. ind. pass. . id.
καθαρίζετε, 2 pers. pl. pres. ind. act. . id.
καθαρίζετε, 2 pers. pl. pres. imper. act. . id.
καθαρίζον, nom. sing. neut. part. pres. act. id.
καθαρίζονται, 3 pers. pl. pres. ind. pass. . id.
καθαρίζω], fut. ίσω, (§ 26. rem. 1) . . καθαρός
καθαρίζων, nom. sing. masc. part. pres. act.—A. B. Ln. . . . . } καθαρίζω
καθαρίζον, R. Gr. Sch. Tdf. (Mar. 7. 19)
καθαρίσαι, aor. 1, infin. act. . . . id.
καθαρίσας, nom. sing. masc. part. aor. 1, act. id.
καθαρίσατε, 2 pers. pl. aor. 1, imper. act. . id.
καθαρίσῃ, 3 pers. sing. aor. 1, subj. act. . id.
καθαρίσθητι, 2 pers. sing. aor. 1, imper. pass. id.
καθαρισμόν, acc. sing. . . . καθαρισμός
καθαρισμός], οῦ, ὁ, (§ 3 tab. C. a) . . καθαρός
καθαρισμοῦ, gen. sing. . . . καθαρισμός
καθάρισον, 2 pers. sing. aor. 1, imper. act. . καθαρίζω
καθαρίσωμεν, 1 pers. pl. aor. 1, subj. act. id.
καθαροί, nom. pl. masc. . . . . καθαρός
καθαροῖς, dat. pl. masc. . . . id.
καθαρόν, acc. sing. masc. . . . id.
καθαρόν, nom. and acc. sing. neut. . . id.

καθᾰρός, ά, όν, (§ 7. rem. 1) *clean, pure, unsoiled*, Mat. 23. 26; 27. 59; met. *clean* from guilt, *guiltless, innocent*, Ac. 18. 6; 20. 26; *sincere, unfeigned, upright, virtuous, void of evil*, Mat. 5. 8; Jno. 15. 3; *clean* ceremonially, Lu. 11. 41.

καθαίρω, fut. αρῶ, perf. pass. κεκάθαρμαι, (§ 27. rem. 1. c, and rem. 3) *to cleanse* from filth; *to clear* by pruning, *prune*, Jno. 15. 2; met. *to cleanse* from sin, *make expiation*, He. 10. 2.

καθαρίζω, fut. ίσω, & ιῶ, aor. 1, ἐκαθάρισα, (§ 26. rem. 1) a later equivalent to καθαίρω, *to cleanse, render pure*, Mat. 23. 25; Lu. 11. 39; *to cleanse* from leprosy, Mat. 8. 2, 3; 10. 8; met. *to cleanse* from sin, *purify by an expiatory offering, make expiation for*, He. 9. 22, 23; 1 Jno. 1. 7; *to cleanse* from sin, *free from the influence of error and sin*, Ac. 15. 9; 2 Co. 7. 1; *to pronounce* ceremonially *clean*, Ac. 10. 15; 11. 9, et al.

καθαρισμός, οῦ, ὁ, (§ 3. tab. C. a) ceremonial *cleansing, purification*, Lu. 2. 22; Jno. 2. 6; *mode of purification*, Jno. 2. 6; 3. 35; *cleansing* of lepers, Mar. 1. 44; met. *expiation*, He. 1. 3; 2 Pe. 1. 9, et al. L.G.

καθαρότης, τητος, ἡ, (§ 4. rem. 2. c) *cleanness*; ceremonial *purity*, He. 9. 13.

καθαρότης], τητος, ἡ . . . . καθαρός
καθαρότητα,[a] acc. sing. . . . καθαρότης
καθαρῷ, dat. sing. masc. and neut. . . καθαρός
καθέδρα], ας, ἡ, (§ 2. tab. B. b) (κατά & ἕδρα) *a seat*, Mat. 21. 12; 23. 2; Mar. 11. 15.
καθέδρας, gen. sing. and acc. pl. . . καθέδρα
καθέζησθε, 2 pers. pl. pres. subj.—D. . } καθέζομαι
καθίσησθε, Rec. Sch. . . .
καθίσεσθε, Tdf. (Lu. 22. 30)
καθέζομαι], fut. καθεδοῦμαι, *to seat one's self, sit down*, Mat. 26. 55; Lu. 2. 46, et al.
καθεζόμενοι, nom. pl. masc. part. pres. . . καθέζομαι
καθεζόμενον, acc. sing. masc. part. pres. . id.
καθεζόμενος, nom. sing. masc. part. pres.—Al. Ln. Tdf. . . . } id.
καθήμενος, Rec. Gr. Sch. (Ac. 20. 9) .
καθεζομένους, acc. pl. masc. part. pres. . id.
καθεῖλε, 3 pers. sing. aor. 2, ind. act. (§ 36. rem. 1) καθαιρέω
καθεῖς, (καθ' εἷς) *one by one, one after another*, 1 Co. 14. 31; Ep. 5. 33. N.T.
καθελεῖν, aor. 2, infin. act. . . . καθαιρέω
καθελόντες, nom. pl. masc. part. aor. 2, act. . id.
καθελῶ, 1 pers. sing. fut. ind. act. . . id.
καθελών, nom. sing. masc. part. aor. 2, act. . id.
καθεξῆς, adv. (κατά & ἑξῆς) *in a continual order or series, successively, consecutively*, Lu. 1. 3; Ac. 11. 4; 18. 23; ὁ, ἡ, καθεξῆς, *suc-*

[a] He. 9. 13.

ceeding, subsequent, Lu. 8. 1; Ac. 3. 24. L.G.

καθεύδει, 3 pers. sing. pres. ind. . . . καθεύδω
καθεύδειν, pres. infin. . . . . id.
καθεύδεις, 2 pers. sing. pres. ind. . . id.
καθεύδετε, 2 pers. pl. pres. ind. and imper. id.
καθεύδῃ, 3 pers. sing. pres. subj. . . id.
καθεύδοντας, acc. pl. masc. part. pres. . . id.
καθεύδοντες, nom. pl. masc. part. pres. . id.
καθεύδουσι, 3 pers. pl. pres. ind. . . id.

καθεύδω], fut. ευδήσω, (κατά & εὕδω, *to sleep*) *to sleep, be fast asleep*, Mat. 8. 24; 9. 24, et al.; met. *to sleep* in spiritual sloth, Ep. 5. 14; 1 Thes. 5. 6; *to sleep* the sleep of death, 1 Thes. 5. 10.

καθεύδωμεν, 1 pers. pl. pres. subj. . . καθεύδω
καθεύδων, nom. sing. masc. part. pres. . id.
κάθῃ, 2 pers. sing. Att. for κάθησαι . κάθημαι
καθηγηταί, nom. pl. . . . καθηγητής

καθηγητής], οῦ, ὁ, (§ 2. tab. B. c) (καθηγέομαι, *to lead, conduct*, fr. κατά & ἡγέομαι) pr. *a guide, leader*; in N.T. *a teacher, instructor*, Mat. 23. 8, 10. L.G.

καθῆκαν, 3 pers. pl. aor. 1, ind. act. . καθίημι
καθῆκε, 3 pers. sing. (impers.) imperf.—Gr. Sch. Tdf. . . . . } καθήκω
καθῆκον, Rec. (Ac. 22. 22) . . }
καθῆκον, nom. sing. neut. (impers.) part. pres. id.
καθήκοντα, acc. pl. neut. part. pres. . . id.

καθήκω], (κατά & ἥκω) *to reach, extend to*; καθήκει, impers. *it is fitting, meet*, Ac. 22. 22; τὸ καθῆκον, *what is fit, right, duty*; τὰ μὴ καθήκοντα, by litotes for *what is abominable or detestable*, Ro. 1. 28.

κάθημαι], 2 pers. κάθησαι & κάθῃ, imperat. κάθησο & κάθου, (κατά & ἧμαι, *to sit*) *to sit, be sitting*, Mat. 9. 9; Lu. 10. 13; *to be seated*, 1 Co. 14. 30; *to dwell*, Mat. 4. 16; Lu. 1. 79; 21. 35, et al.

καθήμεναι, nom. pl. fem. part. pres. . κάθημαι
καθημένην, acc. sing. fem. part. pres. . . id.
καθημένης, gen. sing. fem. part. pres. . id.
καθήμενοι, nom. pl. masc. part. pres. . . id.
καθημένοις, dat. pl. masc. part. pres. . id.
καθήμενον, acc. sing. masc. part. pres. . . id.
καθήμενος, nom. sing. masc. part. pres. . id.
καθημένου, gen. sing. masc. part. pres. . id.
καθημένους, acc. pl. masc. part. pres. . id.
καθημένῳ, dat. sing. masc. part. pres. . . id.
καθημένων, gen. pl. part. pres. . . κάθημαι
καθημερινῇ,[a] dat. sing. fem. . . καθημερινός

καθημερινός], ή, όν, (§ 7. tab. F. a) (καθ' ἡμέραν, *daily*) *daily, day by day*. L.G.

καθήσεσθε, 2 pers. pl. fut. ind.—A. . } κάθημαι
καθίσησθε, Rec. Sch. . . }
καθίσεσθε, Tdf. (Lu. 22. 30) . }
καθῆσθαι, pres. infin. . . . . id.
κάθηται, 3 pers. sing. pres. ind. . . id.
καθήψατο, 3 pers. sing. aor. 1, mid.—C. } καθάπτω
καθῆψε, Rec. Gr. Sch. Tdf. (Ac. 28. 3) }
καθῆψε,[b] 3 pers. sing. aor. 1, ind. (§ 23. rem. 2) id.
καθιεμένην, acc. sing. fem. part. pres. pass. (§ 32. tab. C. C) . . . . καθίημι
καθιέμενον, acc. sing. neut. part. pres. pass. id.
καθίζετε, 2 pers. pl. pres. imper. . . καθίζω

καθίζω], fut. ίσω, perf. κεκάθικα, aor. 1, ἐκάθισα, (§ 26. rem. 1) trans. *to cause to sit, place*; καθίζομαι, *to be seated, sit*, Mat. 19. 28; Lu. 22. 30; *to cause to sit* as judges, *place, appoint*, 1 Co. 6. 4; intrans. *to sit, sit down*, Mat. 13. 48; 26. 36; *to remain, stay, continue*, Lu. 24. 49.

καθίημι], fut. καθήσω, aor. 1, καθῆκα, (§ 32. tab. C. C) (κατά & ἵημι) *to let down, lower*, Lu. 5. 19; Ac. 9. 25; 10. 11; 11. 5.

καθίσαι, aor. 1, infin. . . . . καθίζω
καθίσαντες, nom. pl. masc. part. aor. 1 . id.
καθίσαντος, gen. sing. masc. part. aor. 1 . id.
καθίσας, nom. sing. masc. part. aor. 1 . id.
καθίσατε, 2 pers. pl. aor. 1, imper. . . id.
καθίσει, 3 pers. sing. fut. ind. . . id.
καθίσεσθε, 2 pers. pl. fut. ind. mid. . . id.
καθίσῃ, 3 pers. sing. aor. 1, subj. . . id.
καθίσησθε, 2 pers. pl. aor. 1, subj. mid. . id.
καθίσταται, 3 pers. sing. pres. pass. . καθίστημι

καθίστημι, and, in N.T., καθιστάω, ῶ], fut. καταστήσω, aor. 1, κατέστησα, aor. 1, pass. κατεστάθην, (ᾰ), (§ 29. tabb. X. Y) (κατά & ἵστημι) *to place, set*, Ja. 3. 6; *to set, constitute, appoint*, Mat. 24. 45, 47; Lu. 12. 14; *to set down* in a place, *conduct*, Ac. 17. 15; *to make, render, or cause to be*, 2 Pe. 1. 8; pass. *to be rendered*, Ro. 5. 19.

κατάστημα, ατος, τό, (§ 4. tab. D. c) *determinate state, condition; personal appearance, mien, deportment*, Tit. 2. 3. L.G.

[a] Ac. 6. 1.

[b] Ac. 28. 3.

καθίστησι, 3 pers. sing. pres. ind. act. . καθίστημι
καθιστῶντες, nom. pl. masc. part. pres. act. (§ 31. rem. 2) . . . . καθιστάω
καθίσωμεν, 1 pers. pl. aor. 1, subj. . . καθίζω
καθίσωσι, 3 pers. pl. aor. 1, subj. . . id.
καθό, (καθ' ὅ) *as*, Ro. 8. 26; *according as, in proportion as*, 2 Co. 8. 12; 1 Pe. 4. 13.
καθόλου,[a] (καθ' ὅλου) *on the whole, in general, altogether*; and with a negative, *not at all*.
καθοπλίζω], fut. ίσω, (§ 26. rem. 1) (κατά & ὁπλίζω) *to arm completely*, Lu. 11. 21.
καθοράω, ῶ], (κατά & ὁράω) pr. *to look down upon*; in N.T. *to mark, perceive, discern*.
καθορᾶται,[b] 3 pers. sing. pres. pass. (§ 19. tab. S) καθοράω
καθότι, (καθ' ὅτι) *according as, in proportion as*, Ac. 2. 45; 4. 35; *inasmuch as*, Lu. 1. 7; 19. 9; Ac. 2. 24.
κάθου, 2 pers. sing. imper. . . . . κάθημαι
καθωπλισμένος,[c] nom. sing. m. part. perf. pass. καθοπλίζω
καθώς, (κατά & ὡς) *as, in the manner that*, Mat. 21. 6; 26. 24; *how, in what manner*, Ac. 15. 14; *according as*, Mar. 4. 33; *inasmuch as*, Jno. 17. 2; of time, *when*, Ac. 7. 17. L.G.

καί, conj. *and*, Mat. 2. 2, 3, 11; 4. 22; καὶ—καί, *both—and*; as a cumulative particle, *also, too*, Mat. 5. 39; Jno. 8. 19; 1 Co. 11. 6, et al.; emphatic, *even, also*, Mat. 10. 30; 1 Co. 2. 10, et al.; in N.T. adversative, *but*, Mat. 11. 19, et al.; also introductory of the apodosis of a sentence, Ja. 2. 4; Gal. 3. 28.

Καϊάφα, gen. . . . . . . Καϊάφας
Καϊάφαν, acc. . . . . . . id.
Καϊάφας, α, ὁ, (§ 2. rem. 4) *Caiaphas*, pr. name.
καίγε, (καί & γε) *at least, were it only*, Lu. 19. 42; *and even, yea too*, Ac. 2. 18. L.G.
καίεται, 3 pers. sing. pres. ind. pass. . . καίω
Κάϊν, ὁ, *Cain*, pr. name, indecl.
καινά, nom. and acc. pl. neut. . . καινός
καιναῖς, dat. pl. fem. . . . . id.
Καϊνάν, ὁ, Cainan, pr. name, indecl.
I. *Cainan, son of Enos*, Lu. 3. 37.
II. *Cainan, son of Arphaxad*, Lu. 3. 36.
καινή, nom. sing. fem. . . . . καινός
καινήν, acc. sing. fem. . . . . id.
καινῆς, gen. sing. fem. . . . . id.
καινόν, acc. sing. masc. . . . . καινός
καινόν, nom. and acc. sing. neut. . . id.

καινός], ή, όν, (§ 7. tab. F. a) *new, recently made*, Mat. 9. 17; Mar. 2. 22; *new* in species, character, or mode, Mat. 26. 28, 29; Mar. 14. 24, 25; Lu. 22. 20; Jno. 13.34; 2 Co. 5. 17; Gal. 6. 15; Ep. 2. 15; 4. 24; 1 Jno. 2. 7; Re. 3. 12, et al.; *novel, strange*, Mar. 1. 27; Ac. 17. 19, *new* to the possessor, Mar. 16. 17; *unheard of, unusual*, Mar. 1. 27; Ac. 17. 19; met. *renovated, better, of higher excellence*, 2 Co. 5. 17; Re. 5. 9, et al.

καινότερος, α, ον, (§ 8. rem. 4) comparat. of preced. *newer, more recent*; but used for the positive, *new, novel*, Ac. 17. 21.

καινότης, τητος, ἡ, (§ 4. rem. 2. c) *newness*, Ro. 6. 4; 7. 6.

καινότερον,[d] acc. sing. neut. . . . καινότερος
καινότερος], α, ον . . . . . καινός
καινότης], τητος, ἡ . . . . id.
καινότητι, dat. sing. . . . . καινότης
καινοῦ, gen. sing. neut. . . . καινός
καινούς, acc. pl. masc. . . . . id.
καινῷ, dat. sing. neut. . . . . id.
καιόμεναι, nom. sing. fem. part. pres. pass. . καίω
καιομένη, nom. sing. fem. part. pres. pass. id.
καιομένῃ, dat. sing. fem. part. pres. pass. . id.
καιομένην, acc. sing. fem. part. pres. pass. id.
καιόμενοι, nom. pl. masc. part. pres. pass. . id.
καιόμενον, nom. sing. neut. part. pres. pass. . id.
καιόμενος, nom. sing. masc. part. pres. pass. id.
καίουσι, 3 pers. pl. pres. ind. act. . . id.
καίπερ, (καί & περ) *though, although*; Phi. 3. 4; Re. 17. 8, et al.
καιροί, nom. pl. . . . . . καιρός
καιροῖς, dat. pl. . . . . . id
καιρόν, acc. sing. . . . . . id.

καιρός, οῦ, ὁ, (§ 3. tab. C. a) pr. *fitness, proportion, suitableness; a fitting situation, suitable place*, 1 Pe. 4. 17; *a limited period of time marked by a suitableness of circumstances, a fitting season*, 1 Co. 4. 5; 1 Ti. 2. 6; 6. 15; Tit. 1. 3; *opportunity*, Ac. 24. 25; Gal. 6. 10; He. 11. 15; *a limited*

[a] Ac. 4. 18. [b] Ro. 1. 20. [c] Lu. 11. 21. [d] Ac. 17. 21.

period of time marked by characteristic circumstances, a signal juncture, a marked season, Mat. 16. 3; Lu. 12. 56; 21. 8; 1 Pe. 1. 11, et al.; *a destined time,* Mat. 8. 29; 26. 18; Mar. 1. 15; Lu. 21. 24; 1 Thes. 5. 1, et al.; *a season* in ordinary succession, equivalent to ὥρα, Mat. 13. 30; Ac. 14. 17, et al.; in N.T. *a limited time, a short season,* Lu. 4. 13, et al., simply, *a point of time,* Mat. 11. 25; Lu. 13. 1, et al.

καιροῦ, gen. sing. . . . . . καιρός

καιρούς, acc. pl. . . . . . id.

καιρῷ, dat. sing. . . . . . id.

καιρῶν, gen. pl. . . . . . id.

Καῖσαρ], ἄρος, ὁ, (§ 4. rem. 2. f) *Cæsar,* pr. name.

Καίσαρα, acc. . . . . . Καῖσαρ

Καίσαρι, dat. . . . . . id.

Καισάρεια], ας, ἡ, (§ 2. tab. B. b, and rem. 2) *Cæsarea.*

I. *Cæsarea Philippi,* Mat. 16. 13; Mar. 8. 27.

II. *Cæsarea Augusta,* Ac. 8. 40, et al.

Καισαρείᾳ, dat. . . . . Καισάρεια

Καισάρειαν, acc. . . . . id.

Καισαρείας, gen. . . . . id.

Καίσαρος, gen. . . . . . Καῖσαρ

καίτοι,[a] (καί & enclitic τοι) *and yet, though, although.*

καίτοιγε, (καίτοι & γε) *although indeed,* Jno. 4. 2; Ac. 14. 17; 17. 27.

καίω], fut. καύσω, aor. 1, pass. ἐκαύθην, (§ 35. rem. 3) *to cause to burn, kindle, light,* Mat. 5. 15; pass. *to be kindled, burn, flame,* Lu. 12. 35; met. *to be kindled* into emotion, Lu. 24. 32; *to consume with fire,* Jno. 15. 6; 1 Co. 13. 3.

καῦμα, ατος, τό, (§ 4. tab. D. c) *heat, scorching or burning heat,* Re. 7. 16; 16. 9.

καυματίζω, fut. ίσω, (§ 26. rem. 1) *to scorch, burn,* Mat. 13. 6; Mar. 4. 6; Re. 16. 8, 9. L.G.

καῦσις, εως, ἡ, (§ 5. tab. E. c) *burning, being burned,* He. 6. 8.

καυσόομαι, οῦμαι, *to be on fire, burn intensely,* 2 Pe. 3. 10, 12. L.G.

καύσων, ωνος, ὁ, (§ 4. rem. 2. e) *fervent scorching heat; the scorching* of the sun, Mat. 20. 12; *hot weather, a hot time,* Lu. 12. 55; *the scorching wind of the East, Eurus,* Ja. 1. 11.

καυτηριάζω, fut. άσω, (§ 26. rem. 1) perf. pass. κεκαυτηρίασμαι, (καυτήριον, *an instrument for branding,* fr. καίω) *to cauterise, brand;* pass. met. *to be branded* with marks of guilt, or, *to be seared* into insensibility, 1 Ti. 4. 2.

κακά, nom. and acc. pl. neut. . . κακός

κακαί, nom. pl. fem. . . . . id.

κἀκεῖ, (by crasis for καί ἐκεῖ) *and there,* Mat. 5. 23; 10. 11; *there also,* Mar. 1. 38; *thither also,* Ac. 17. 13, et al.

κἀκεῖθεν, (by crasis for καί ἐκεῖθεν) *and thence,* Mar. 10. 1; Ac. 7. 4; 14. 26; 20. 15; 21. 1; 27. 4, 12; 28. 15; *and then, afterwards,* Ac. 13. 21.

κἀκεῖνα, nom. and acc. pl. neut. . . κἀκεῖνος

κἀκεῖνοι, nom. pl. masc. . . . . id.

κἀκείνοις, dat. pl. masc. . . . id.

κἀκεῖνον, acc. sing. masc. . . . . id.

κἀκεῖνος, είνη, εῖνο, (by crasis for καί ἐκεῖνος) *and he, she, it; and this, and that,* Mat. 15. 18; 23. 23; *he, she, it also; this also, that also,* Mat. 20. 4.

κἀκείνους, acc. pl. masc. . . . κἀκεῖνος

κακήν, acc. sing. fem. . . . . κακός

κακία, ας, ἡ, (§ 2. tab. B. b, and rem. 2) . id.

κακίᾳ, dat. sing. . . . . κακία

κακίαν, acc. sing. . . . . id.

κακίας, gen. sing. . . . . . id.

κακοήθεια], ας, ἡ, (§ 2. tab. B. b, and rem. 2) (κακός & ἦθος) *disposition for mischief, malignity.*

κακοηθείας,[b] gen. sing. . . κακοήθ

κακοί, nom. pl. masc. . . . . κακός

κακολογέω, ῶ], fut. ήσω, (§ 16. tab. P) (κακός & λέγω) *to speak evil of, revile, abuse, assail with reproaches,* Mar. 9. 39; Ac. 19. 9; *to address with offensive language, to treat with disrespect, contemn,* Mat. 15. 4; Mar. 7. 10.

κακολογῆσαι, aor. 1, infin. . . . κακολογέω

κακολογοῦντες, nom. pl. masc. part. pres. . id.

κακολογῶν, nom. sing. masc. part. pres. id.

κακόν, nom. and acc. sing. neut. . . κακός

[a] He. 4. 3.

[b] Ro. 1. 29.

κακοπαθεῖ, 3 pers. sing. pres. ind. . . κακοπαθέω
κακοπάθεια], ας, ἡ, (§ 2. tab. B. b, and rem. 2) id.
κακοπαθείας,[a] gen. sing. . . κακοπάθεια
κακοπᾰθέω, ῶ], fut. ήσω, (§ 16. tab. P) (κακός & πάσχω) *to suffer evil or afflictions*, 2 Ti. 2. 9; *to be vexed, troubled, dejected*, Ja. 5. 13; in N.T. *to show endurance in trials and afflictions*, 2 Ti. 2. 3.

κακοπάθεια, ας, ἡ, (§ 2. tab. B. b, and rem. 2) *a state of suffering, affliction, trouble;* in N.T. *endurance in affliction*, Ja. 5. 10.

κακοπάθησον, 2 pers. sing. aor. 1, imper. κακοπαθέω
κακοπαθῶ, 1 pers. sing. pres. ind. . . id.
κακοποιέω, ῶ], fut. ήσω, (§ 16. tab. P) (κακός & ποιέω) *to cause evil, injure, do harm*, Mar. 3. 4; Lu. 6. 9; *to do evil, commit sin*, 1 Pe. 3. 17.

κακοποιός, οῦ, ὁ, ἡ, (§ 7. rem. 2) *an evil-doer*, 1 Pe. 2. 12, et al.; *a malefactor, criminal*, Jno. 18. 30.

κακοποιῆσαι, aor. 1, infin. . . . κακοποιέω
κακοποιός, οῦ, ὁ, ἡ . . . . id.
κακοποιοῦντας, acc. pl. masc. part. pres. . id.
κακοποιῶν, nom. sing. masc. part. pres. . id.
κακοποιῶν, gen. pl. . . . . κακοποιός

κακός, ή, όν, (§ 7. tab. F. a) *bad, of a bad quality or disposition, worthless, corrupt, depraved*, Mat. 21. 41; 24. 48; Mar. 7. 21; *wicked, criminal, morally bad;* τὸ κακόν, *evil, wickedness, crime*, Mat. 27. 23; Ac. 23. 9; *malediction*, 1 Pe. 3. 10; *mischievous, harmful, baneful;* τὸ κακόν, *evil, mischief, harm, injury*, Tit. 1. 12; *afflictive;* τὸ κακόν, *evil, misery, affliction, suffering*, Lu. 16. 25.

κακία, ας, ἡ, (§ 2. tab. B. b, and rem. 2) *malice, malignity*, Ro. 1. 29; Ep. 4. 31; *wickedness, depravity*, Ac. 8. 22; 1 Co. 5. 8; in N.T. *evil, trouble, calamity*, Mat. 6. 34.

κακόω, ῶ, fut. ώσω, aor. 1, ἐκάκωσα, (§ 20. tab. T) *to maltreat, cause evil to, oppress*, Ac. 7. 6, 19; 12. 1; 18. 10; 1 Pe. 3. 13; in N.T. *to render ill-disposed, to embitter*, Ac. 14. 2.

κακῶς, adv, *ill, badly;* physically *ill, sick*, Mat. 4. 24; 8. 16, et al.; *grievously, vehemently*, Mat. 15. 22; *wretchedly, miserably*, Mat. 21. 41; *wickedly, reproachfully*, Ac. 23. 5; *wrongly, criminally*, Jno. 18. 23; *amiss*, Ja. 4. 3.

κάκωσις, εως, ἡ, (§ 5. tab. E. c) *ill-treatment, affliction, misery*, Ac. 7. 34.

κακοῦ, gen. sing. neut. . . . . κακός
κακοῦργοι, nom. pl. masc. . . . κακοῦργος
κακοῦργος], ου, ὁ, ἡ, (§ 7. rem. 2) (κακός & ἔργον) *an evil-doer, malefactor, criminal*, Lu. 23. 32, 33, 39; 2 Ti. 2. 9.
κακούργους, acc. pl. masc. . . . κακοῦργος
κακούργων, gen. pl. . . . id.
κακούς, acc. pl. masc. . . . . κακός
κακουχέω, ῶ], fut. ήσω, (§ 16. tab. P) (κακός & ἔχω) *to maltreat, afflict, harass;* pass. *to be afflicted, be oppressed with evils*, He. 11. 37; 13. 3.
κακουχούμενοι, nom. pl. masc. part. pres. pass. κακουχέω
κακουχουμένων, gen. pl. part. pres. pass. . id.
κακόω, ῶ], fut. ώσω, (§ 20. tab. T) . κακός
κακῶν, gen. pl. . . . . . id.
κακῶς, adv. . . . . . . id.
κακῶσαι, aor. 1, infin. act. . . κακόω
κάκωσιν,[b] acc. sing. . . . . κάκωσις
κάκωσις], εως, ἡ, (§ 5 tab. E. c) . . κακός
κακώσουσι, 3 pers. pl. fut. ind. act. . . κακόω
κακώσων, nom. sing. masc. part. fut. act. . κακόω
καλά, nom. and acc. pl. neut. . . . καλός
καλάμη], ης, ἡ, (§ 2. tab. B. a) *the stalk* of grain, *straw, stubble.* (ᾰ).
καλάμην,[c] acc. sing. . . . . καλάμη
κάλαμον, acc. sing. . . . . . κάλαμος
κάλᾰμος, ου, ὁ, (§ 3. tab. C. a) *a reed, cane*, Mat. 11. 7; 12. 20; Lu. 7. 24; *a reed* in its various appliances, as, a wand, a staff, Mat. 27. 29, 30, 48; Mar. 15. 19, 36; *a measuring-rod*, Re. 11. 1; a writer's *reed*, 3 Jno. 13.
καλάμου, gen. sing. . . . . κάλαμος
καλάμῳ, dat. sing. . . . . . id.
καλεῖ, 3 pers. sing. pres. ind. act. . . καλέω
κάλει, 2 pers. sing. pres. imper. act. . . id.
καλεῖν, pres. infin. act. . . . . id.
καλεῖσθαι, pres. inf. pass. (§ 17. tab. Q) . id.
καλεῖται, 3 pers. sing. pres. ind. pass. . id.
καλεῖτε, 2 pers. pl. pres. ind. act. . . id.

a Ja. 5. 10. b Ac. 7. 34. c 1 Co. 3. 12.

καλέσαι, aor. 1, infin. act. . . καλέω
καλέσαντα, acc. sing. masc. part. aor. 1, act. . id.
καλέσαντες, nom. pl. masc. part. aor. 1, act. id.
καλέσαντι, dat. sing. masc. part. aor. 1, act.—B. Ln. . . . . id.
Rec. Gr. Sch. Tdf. om. (Col. 1. 12)
καλέσαντος, gen. sing. masc. part. aor. 1, act. id.
καλέσας, nom. sing. masc. part. aor. 1, act. . id.
καλέσατε, 2 pers. pl. aor. 1, imper. act. . id.
καλέσεις, 2 pers. sing. fut. act. (§ 22. rem. 1) id.
καλέσητε, 2 pers. pl. aor. 1, subj. act. . . id.
κάλεσον, 2 pers. sing. aor. 1, imper. act. . id.
καλέσουσι, 3 pers. pl. fut. ind. act. . . id.
καλέσω, 1 pers. sing. fut. ind. act. . id.

καλεω, ῶ], fut. έσω, perf. κέκληκα, aor 1, ἐκάλεσα, perf. pass. κέκλημαι, aor. 1, pass. ἐκλήθην, (§ 22. rem. 1. 4) *to call, call to*, Jno. 10. 3; *to call* into one's presence, *send for* a person, Mat. 2. 7; *to summon*, Mat. 2. 15; 25. 14, et al.; *to invite*, Mat. 22. 9, et al.; *to call* to the performance of a certain thing, Mat. 9. 13; He. 11. 8, et al.; *to call* to a participation in the privileges of the Gospel, Ro. 8. 30; 9. 24; 1 Co. 1. 9; 7. 18, et al.; *to call* to an office or dignity, He. 5. 4; *to name, style*, Mat. 1. 21, et al.; pass. *to be styled, regarded*, Mat. 5. 9, 19, et al.

κλῆσις, εως, ἡ, (§ 5. tab. E. c) *a call, calling, invitation*; in N.T. *the call or invitation* to the privileges of the Gospel, Ro. 11. 29; Ep. 1. 18, et al.; *the favour and privilege of the invitation*, 2 Thes. 1. 11; 2 Pe. 1. 10; *the temporal condition in which the call found a person*, 1 Co. 1. 26; 7. 20.

κλητός, ή, όν, (§ 7. tab. F. a) *called, invited*; in N.T. *called* to privileges or functions, Mat. 20. 16; 22. 14; Ro. 1. 1, 6, 7; 1 Co. 1. 1, 2, et al.

καλῇ, dat. sing. fem. . . . καλός
καλήν, acc. sing. fem. . . . . id.
καλῆς, gen. sing. fem. . . . id.
καλλιέλαιον,[a] acc. sing. . . . καλλιέλαιος
καλλιέλαιος], ου, ὁ, ἡ, (§ 7. rem. 2) (κάλλος & ἔλαιον) pr. adj. *productive of good oil*; as subst. *a cultivated olive tree*.

κάλλῖον,[b] adv. . . . . . . καλλιων
καλλίων], ονος, ὁ, ἡ, (§ 8. rem. 2) . καλός
καλοδιδάσκαλος], ου, ὁ, ἡ, (§ 7. rem. 2) (καλός & διδάσκαλος) *teaching what is good, a teacher of good*. N.T.
καλοδιδασκάλους,[c] acc. pl. fem. . καλοδιδάσκαλος
καλοί, nom. pl. masc. . . . . καλός
καλοῖς, dat. pl. masc. and neut. . . . id.
καλόν, acc. sing. masc. and nom. and acc. neut. id.
καλοποιέω, ῶ], fut. ήσω, (§ 16. tab. P) (καλός & ποιέω) *to do well, do good*. LXX.
καλοποιοῦντες,[d] nom. pl. masc. part. pres. καλοποιέω

καλός, ή, όν, (§ 7. tab. F. a) pr. *beautiful; good, of good quality or disposition; fertile, rich*, Mat. 13. 8, 23; *useful, profitable*, Lu. 14. 34; καλόν ἐστι, *it is profitable, it is well*, Mat. 18. 8, 9; *excellent, choice, select, goodly*, Mat. 7. 17, 19; καλόν ἐστι, *it is pleasant, delightful*, Mat. 17. 4; *just, full* measure, Lu. 6. 38; *honourable, distinguished*, Ja. 2. 7; *good, possessing moral excellence, worthy, upright, virtuous*, Jno. 10. 11, 14; 1 Ti. 4. 6; τὸ καλὸν & τὸ καλὸν ἔργον, *what is good and right, a good deed, rectitude, virtue*, Mat. 5. 16; Ro. 7. 18, 21; *right, duty, propriety*, Mat. 15. 26; *benefit, favour*, Jno. 10. 32, 33, et al.

καλλίων, ονος, ὁ, ἡ, (§ 8. rem. 2) *better*; neut. κάλλῖον, as an adv. *full well*, Ac. 25. 10.

καλῶς, adv. *well, rightly, suitably, with propriety, becomingly*, 1 Co. 7. 37; 14. 17; Gal. 4. 17; 5. 7, et al.; *truly, justly, correctly*, Mar. 12. 32; Lu. 20. 39; Jno. 4. 17, et al.; *appositely*, Mat. 15. 7; Mar. 7. 6; *becomingly, honourably*, Ja. 2. 3; *well, effectually*, Mar. 7. 9, 37, et al.; καλῶς εἰπεῖν, *to speak well, praise, applaud*, Lu. 6. 26; καλῶς ἔχειν, *to be convalescent*, Mar. 16. 18; καλῶς ποιεῖν, *to do good, confer benefits*, Mat. 5. 44; 12. 12; *to do well, act virtuously*, Phi. 4. 14, et al.

καλοῦ, gen. sing. neut. . . . . . καλός
καλουμένη, nom. sing. fem. part. pres. pass. . καλέω
καλουμένῃ, dat. sing. fem. part. pres. pass. id.
καλουμένην, acc. sing. fem. part. pres. pass. id.

[a] Ro. 11. 24. [b] Ac. 25. 10. [c] Tit. 2. 3. [d] 2 Thes. 3. 13.

καλουμένης, gen. sing. fem. part. pres. pass. . καλέω
καλούμενον, acc. sing. masc. part. pres. pass. id.
καλούμενος, nom. sing. masc. part. pres. pass. id.
καλουμένου, gen. sing. masc. part. pres. pass. id.
καλοῦνται, 3 pers. pl. pres. ind. pass. . id.
καλοῦντος, gen. sing. masc. part. pres. act. . id.
καλούς, acc. pl. masc. . . . . . καλὸς
Καλοὺς Λιμένας,[a] acc. of Καλοὶ Λιμένες, *Fair Havens*, a harbour of Crete.
καλοῦσα, nom. sing. fem. part. pres. act. . καλέω
κάλυμμα, ατος, τό, (§ 4. tab. D. c) . . καλύπτω
καλύπτει, 3 pers. sing. pres. ind. act. . . id.
καλύπτεσθαι, pres. infin. pass. . . id.

καλύπτω], fut. ψω, (§ 23. rem. 1) aor. 1, ἐκάλυψα, perf. pass. κεκάλυμμαι, *to cover*, Mat. 8. 24; Lu. 8. 16; 23. 30; *to hide, conceal*, Mat. 10. 26; 2 Co. 4. 3; met. *to cover, throw a veil* of oblivion *over*, Ja. 5. 20; 1 Pe. 4. 8.

κάλυμμα, ατος, τό, (§ 4. tab. D. c) *a covering; a veil*, 2 Co. 3. 13; met. *a veil, a blind* to spiritual vision, 2 Co. 3. 14, 15, 16.

καλύψατε, 2 pers. pl. aor. 1, imper. act. . καλύπτω
καλύψει, 3 pers. sing. fut. ind. act. . . id.
καλῷ, dat. sing. neut. . . . . καλός
καλῶν, gen. pl. . . . . . . id.
καλῶν, nom. sing. masc. part. pres. act. . καλέω
καλῶς, adv. . . . . . καλός
κἀμέ, (καὶ ἐμέ) see κἀγώ.
κάμηλον, acc. sing. . . . . . κάμηλος
κάμηλος], ου, ὁ, ἡ, *a camel*, (Heb. גמל) Mat. 3. 4; 23. 24, et al.
καμήλου, gen. sing. . . . . κάμηλος
κάμητε, 2 pers. pl. aor. 2, subj. (§ 27. rem. 2. d) κάμνω
κάμινον, acc. sing. . . . . κάμινος
κάμῑνος], ου, ἡ, (§ 3. tab. C. b) *a furnace, oven, kiln*, Mat. 13. 42, 50; Re. 1. 15; 9. 2.
καμίνου, gen. sing. . . . . . κάμινος
καμίνῳ, dat. sing. . . . . . id.
καμμύω], fut. ύσω, aor. 1, ἐκάμμυσα, (§ 13. tab. M) (contr. for καταμύω, fr. κατά & μύω) *to shut, close* the eyes, Mat. 13. 15; Ac. 28. 27.
κάμνοντα, acc. sing. masc. part. pres. . . κάμνω

κάμνω], fut. καμοῦμαι, perf. κέκμηκα, aor. 2, ἔκᾰμον, (§ 27. rem. 2. d) pr. *to tire with exertion, labour to weariness; to be wearied, tired out, exhausted*, He. 12. 3; Re. 2. 3; *to labour* under disease, *be sick*, Ja. 5. 15.

κἀμοί, (καί ἐμοί) see κἀγώ.

κάμπτω, fut. ψω, (§ 23. rem. 2) aor. 1, ἔκαμψα, trans. *to bend, inflect* the knee, Ro. 11. 4; Ep. 3. 14; intrans. *to bend, bow*, Ro. 14. 11; Phi. 2. 10.

κάμψει, 3 pers. sing. fut. ind. . . κάμπτω
κάμψῃ, 3 pers. sing. aor. 1, subj. . . . id.
κἄν, (by crasis for καὶ ἐάν) *and if*, Mar. 16. 18; *also if*, Mat. 21. 21; *even if, if even, although*, Jno. 10. 38; *if so much as*, He. 12. 20; also in N.T. simply equivalent to καί as a particle of emphasis, by a pleonasm of ἄν, *at least, at all events*, Mar. 6. 56; Ac. 5. 15; 2 Co. 11. 16.
Κανᾶ, ἡ, indecl. *Cana*, a town of Galilee.
Καναναῖος, ου, ὁ, (§ 3. tab. C. a) *a Canaanite*, Al. Ln.
Κανανίτης, R. Gr. Sch. Tdf. (Mat. 10. 4)
Καναναῖον, acc.—Al. Ln. . . . } Καναναῖος
Κανανίτην, R. Gr. Sch. Tdf. (Mar. 3. 18) }
Κανανίτην, acc. . . . . . . Κανανίτης
Κανανίτης, ου, ὁ, (§ 2. tab. B. c) (Aram. קַנְאָן, from the Heb. קָנָא, *to be zealous*) *Cananite*, i.q. ζηλωτής, *zealot*, Mat. 10. 4; Mar. 3. 18; coll. Lu. 6. 15, and Ac. 1. 13.
Κανδάκη], ης, ἡ, (§ 2. tab. B. a) *Candace*, pr. name.
Κανδάκης,[b] gen. . . . . Κανδάκη
κανόνα, acc. sing. . . . . . κανών
κανόνι, dat. sing. . . . . id.
κανόνος, gen. sing. . . . . . id.
κανών], όνος, ὁ, (§ 4. rem. 2. e) (κάννα or κάνη, *a cane*) *a measure, rule*; in N.T. *prescribed range* of action or duty, 2 Co. 10. 13, 15, 16; met. *rule* of conduct or doctrine, Gal. 6. 16; Phi. 3. 16.
Καπερναούμ, ἡ, indecl. *Capernaum*, a city of Galilee.
καπηλεύοντες,[c] nom. pl. masc. part. pres. . καπηλεύω
καπηλεύω], fut. εύσω, (§ 13. tab. M) pr. *to be* κάπηλος, *a retailer, to huckster; to peddle with; to deal paltrily with*, or, *to corrupt, adulterate*.
καπνόν, acc. sing. . . . . καπνός

[a] Ac. 27. 8. [b] Ac. 8. 27. [c] 2 Co. 2. 17.

καπνός, ου, ὁ, (§ 3. tab. C. a) *smoke,* Ac. 2. 19; Re. 8. 4, et al.

καπνοῦ, gen. sing. . . . . . . καπνός

Καππαδοκία], ας, ἡ, (§ 2. tab. B. b, and rem. 2) *Cappadocia,* a district of Asia Minor.

Καππαδοκίαν, acc. . . . Καππαδοκία

Καππαδοκίας, gen. . . . . . . id.

καρδία, ας, ἡ, (§ 2. tab. B. b, and rem. 2) (κέαρ, idem) *the heart; the heart,* regarded as the seat of feeling, impulse, affection, desire, Mat. 6. 21; 22. 37; Phi. 1. 7, et al.; *the heart,* as the seat of intellect, Mat. 13. 15; Ro. 1. 21, et al.; *the heart,* as the inner and mental frame, Mat. 5. 8; Lu. 16. 15; 1 Pe. 3. 4, et al.; *the conscience,* 1 Jno. 3. 20, 21; *the heart, the inner part, middle, centre,* Mat. 12. 40, et al.

καρδίᾳ, dat. sing. . . . . . καρδία

καρδίαι, nom. pl. . . . . . . id.

καρδίαις, dat. pl. . . . . . id.

καρδίαν, acc. sing. . . . . . . id.

καρδίας, gen. sing. and acc. pl. . . id.

καρδιογνῶστα, voc. sing. (§ 2. rem. 6) καρδιογνώστης

καρδιογνώστης, ου, ὁ, (§ 2. tab. B. c) (καρδία & γινώσκω) *heart-knower, searcher of hearts,* Ac. 1. 24; 15. 8. N.T.

καρδιῶν, gen. pl. . . . . καρδία

καρπόν, acc. sing. . . . . . . καρπός

καρπός, οῦ, ὁ, (§ 3. tab. C. a) *fruit,* Mat. 3. 10; 21. 19, 34; from the Heb. καρπὸς κοιλίας, *fruit of the womb, offspring,* Lu. 1. 42; καρπὸς ὀσφύος, *fruit of the loins, offspring, posterity,* Ac. 2. 30; καρπὸς χειλέων, *fruit of the lips, praise,* He. 13. 15; met. *conduct, actions,* Mat. 3. 8; 7. 16; Ro. 6. 22, *benefit, profit, emolument,* Ro. 1. 13; 6. 21; *reward,* Phi. 4. 17, et al.

Κάρπος], ου, ὁ, *Carpus,* pr. name.

καρποῦ, gen. sing. . . . . . καρπός

καρπούς, acc. pl. . . . . . . id.

καρποφορεῖ, 3 pers. sing. pres. ind. . καρποφορέω

καρποφορέω, ῶ], fut. ήσω, aor. 1, ἐκαρποφόρησα, (§ 16. tab. P) (καρπός & φορέω, fr. φέρω) *to bear fruit, yield,* Mar. 4. 28; met. *to bring forth the fruit* of action or conduct, Mat. 13. 23; Ro. 7. 5; mid. *to expand by fruitfulness, to develope itself by success,* Col. 1. 6.

καρποφόρος, ου, ὁ, ἡ, (§ 7. rem. 2) *fruitful, adapted to bring forth fruit,* Ac. 14. 17.

καρποφορῆσαι, aor. 1, infin. . . καρποφορέω

καρποφορήσωμεν, 1 pers. pl. aor. 1, subj. . id.

καρποφορούμενον, nom. s. neut. pt. pres. mid. id.

καρποφοροῦντες, nom. pl. masc. part. pres. id.

καρποφόρος], ου, ὁ, ἡ, (§ 7. rem. 2) . id.

καρποφόρους,[a] acc. pl. masc. . . καρποφόρος

καρποφοροῦσι, 3 pers. pl. pres. ind. . καρποφορέω

Κάρπῳ,[b] dat. . . . . . Κάρπος

καρπῶν, gen. pl. . . . . . καρπός

καρτερέω, ῶ], fut. ήσω, aor. 1, ἐκαρτέρησα, (§ 16. tab P) (καρτερός, by metath. fr. κράτος) *to be stout; to endure patiently, bear up with fortitude,* He. 11. 27.

κάρφος, εος, τό, (§ 5. tab. E. b) (κάρφω, *to shrivel*) *any small dry thing,* as *chaff, stubble, splinter, mote,* etc.; Mat. 7. 3, 4, 5; Lu. 6. 41, 42.

κατ by apostrophe for κατά.

κατά, prep., with a genitive, *down from, adown,* Mat. 8. 32; *down upon, upon,* Mar. 14. 3; Ac. 27. 14; *down into;* κατὰ βάθους, *profound, deepest,* 2 Co. 8. 2; *down over, throughout* a space, Lu. 4. 14; 23. 5; *concerning,* in cases of pointed allegation, 1 Co. 15. 15; *against,* Mat. 12. 30, et al.; *by,* in oaths, Mat. 26. 63, et al.; with an acc. of place, *in the quarter of; about, near, at,* Lu. 10. 32; Ac. 2. 10; *throughout,* Lu. 8. 39; *in,* Ro. 16. 5; *among,* Ac. 21. 21; *in the presence of,* Lu. 2. 31; *in the direction of, towards,* Ac. 8. 26; Phi. 3. 14; of time, *within the range of; during, in the course of, at, about,* Ac. 12. 1; 27. 27; distributively, κατ' οἶκον, *by houses, from house to house,* Ac. 2. 46; κατὰ δύο, *two and two,* 1 Co. 14. 27; καθ' ἡμέραν, *daily,* Mat. 26. 55, et al.; trop., *according to, conformably to, in proportion to,* Mat. 9. 29; 25. 15; *after the fashion or likeness of,* He. 5. 6; *in virtue of,* Mat. 19. 3; *as respects,* Ro. 1. 3; Ac. 25. 14; He. 9. 9.

---

a Ac. 14. 17.

b 2 Ti. 4. 13.

κατάβα, 2 pers. sing. aor. 2, imper. (§ 31. rem. 1. d) Att. for κατάβηθι . . . καταβαίνω
καταβαίνει, 3 pers. sing. pres. ind. . . id.
καταβαίνειν, pres. infin. . . . id.
καταβαινέτω, 3 pers. sing. pres. imper. . id.
καταβαῖνον, nom. and acc. sing. neut. part. pres. id.
καταβαίνοντα, acc. sing. masc. part. pres. . id.
καταβαίνοντας, acc. pl. masc. part. pres. . id.
καταβαίνοντες, nom. pl. masc. part. pres. . id.
καταβαίνοντος, gen. sing. masc. part. pres. . id.
καταβαινόντων, gen. pl. masc. part. pres. . id.
καταβαίνουσα, nom. sing. fem. part. pres. . id.
καταβαίνουσαν, acc. sing. fem. part. pres. . id.
καταβαίνω], (§ 37. rem. 1) fut. βήσομαι, aor. 2, κατέβην, imper. κατάβηθι, & κατάβα, perf. καταβέβηκα, (κατά & βαίνω) *to come or go down, descend*, Mat. 8. 1; 17. 9; *to lead down*, Ac. 8. 26; *to come down, fall*, Mat. 7. 25, 27, et al.; *to be let down*, Ac. 10. 11; 11. 5.

κατάβἄσις, εως, ἡ, (§ 5. tab. E. c) *the act of descending; a way down, descent*, Lu. 19. 37.

καταβαίνων, nom. sing. masc. part. pres. . καταβαίνω
καταβαλλόμενοι, nom. pl. masc. part. pres. pass. and mid. . . . καταβάλλω
καταβάλλω], fut. βαλῶ, (§ 27. rem. 1, b) (κατά & βάλλω) *to cast down*, Re. 12. 10; *to prostrate*, 2 Co. 4. 9; mid. *to lay down, lay* a foundation, He. 6. 1.

καταβολή, ῆς, ἡ, (§ 2. tab. B. a) pr. *a casting down; laying the foundation, foundation; beginning, commencement*, Mat. 13. 35; 25. 34, et al.; *conception* in the womb, He. 11. 11.

καταβάν, acc. sing. neut. part. aor. 2 . καταβαίνω
καταβάντες, nom. pl. masc. part. aor. 2 . id.
καταβάντι, dat. sing. masc. part. aor. 2 . id.
καταβάντος, gen. sing. masc. part. aor. 2—Al. Ln. . . . . } id.
καταβάντι, Rec. Gr. Sch. Tdf. (Mat. 8. 1)
καταβαρέω, ῶ], fut. ήσω, (§ 16. tab. P) (κατά & βαρέω) pr. *to weigh down*; met. *to burden, be burdensome to*, 2 Co. 12. 16. L.G.
καταβαρυνόμενοι, nom. pl. masc. part. pres. pass.—Al. Ln. Tdf. . . . } καταβαρύνω
βεβαρημένοι, Rec. Gr. Sch. (Mar. 14. 40)
καταβαρύνω], v.r. *to weigh down, depress.*

καταβάς, nom. sing. masc. part. aor. 2 . καταβαίνω
καταβάσει,[a] dat. sing. . . . . κατάβασις
κατάβασις], εως, ἡ, (§ 5. tab. E. c) . καταβαίνω
καταβάτω, 3 pers. sing. aor. 2, imper. . . id.
καταβέβηκα, 1 pers. sing. perf. ind. . id.
καταβεβηκότες, nom. pl. masc. part. perf. id.
καταβῇ, 3 pers. sing. aor. 2, subj. . . id.
κατάβηθι, 2 pers. sing. aor. 2, imper. . . id.
καταβῆναι, aor. 2, infin. . . . id.
καταβήσεται, 3 pers. sing. fut. (§ 37. rem. 1) id.
καταβήσῃ, 2 pers. sing. fut. ind.—B. D. Ln. Tdf. . . . . } id.
καταβιβασθήσῃ, R. Gr. Sch. (Mat. 11. 23)
καταβιβάζω], fut. άσω, (§ 26. rem. 1) (κατά & βιβάζω) *to cause to descend, bring or thrust down*, Mat. 11. 23; Lu. 10. 15.
καταβιβασθήσῃ, 2 pers. sing. fut. pass. . καταβιβάζω
κατβολή], ῆς, ἡ, (§ 2. tab. B. a) . καταβάλλω
καταβολήν, acc. sing. . . . . καταβολή
καταβολῆς, gen. sing. . . . . id.
καταβραβευέτω,[b] 3 pers. sing. pres. imper. καταβραβεύω
καταβραβεύω], fut. εύσω, (§ 13. tab. M) (κατά & βραβεύω) pr. *to give an unfavourable decision as respects a prize, to disappoint of the palm*; hence, *to make a victim of practices, to overreach.*
καταγἄγεῖν, aor. 2, inf. act. (§ 13. rem. 7. d) κατάγω
κατάγῃ, 3 pers. sing. aor. 2, subj. act. id.
καταγάγῃς, 2 pers. sing. aor. 2, subj. act. . id.
καταγόντες, nom. pl. masc. part. aor. 2, act. id.
καταγἄγών, nom. sing. masc. part. aor. 2, act. id.
καταγγελεύς,[c] έως, ὁ, (§ 5. tab. E. d) . καταγγέλλω
καταγγέλλειν, pres. infin. act. . . . id.
καταγγέλλεται, 3 pers. sing. pres. ind. pass. id.
καταγγέλλετε, 2 pers. pl. pres. ind. act. . id.
καταγγέλλομεν, 1 pers. pl. pres. ind. act. . id.
καταγγέλλουσι, 3 pers. pl. pres. ind. act. . id.
καταγγέλλουσι, dat. pl. masc. part. pres. act. id.
καταγγέλλω, fut. γελῶ, (§ 27. rem. 1. b) aor. 2, pass. κατηγγέλην, (§ 27. rem. 4. a) (κατά & ἀγγέλλω) *to announce, proclaim*, Ac. 13. 38; in N.T. *to laud, celebrate*, Ro. 1. 8.

καταγγελεύς, έως, ὁ, (§ 5. tab. E. d) *one who announces* anything, *a proclaimer, publisher*, Ac. 17. 18: equivalent to κατάγγελος. N.T.

καταγγέλλων, nom. sing. masc. part. pres. καταγγέλλω

[a] Lu. 19. 37. [b] Col. 2. 18. [c] Ac. 17. 18.

καταγελάω, ῶ], fut. άσω, άσομαι, (§ 22. rem. 2) (κατά & γελάω) *to deride, jeer,* Mat. 9. 24; Mar. 5. 40; Lu. 8. 53.

καταγινώσκῃ, 3 pers. sing. pres. subj. act. καταγινώσκω

καταγινώσκω], fut. γνώσομαι, (§ 36. rem. 3) (κατά & γινώσκω) *to determine against, condemn, blame, reprehend,* Gal. 2. 11; 1 Jno. 3. 20, 21.

κατάγνυμι, or -ύω], fut. κατάξω, & κατεάξω, aor. 1, κατέαξα, aor. 2, pass. κατεάγην, (ᾱ) (§ 36. rem. 5) (κατά & ἄγνυμι, *to break*) *to break in pieces, crush, break in two,* Mat. 12. 20; Jno. 19. 31, 32, 33.

κατάγω], fut. ξω, (§ 23. rem. 1. b) aor. 2, κατήγᾰγον, (§ 13. rem. 7. d) (κατά & ἄγω) *to lead, bring, or conduct down,* Ac. 9. 30; 22. 30; 23. 15, 20, 28; *to bring* a ship *to land;* pass. κατάγομαι, aor. 1, κατήχθην, *to come to land, land, touch,* Lu. 5. 11, et al.

καταγωνίζομαι], fut. ίσομαι, aor. 1, κατηγωνισάμην, (§ 26. rem. 1) (κατά & ἀγωνίζομαι) *to subdue, vanquish, conquer,* He. 11. 33. L.G.

καταδέω], fut. ήσω, (§ 35. rem. 1) (κατά & δέω) *to bind down; to bandage* a wound, Lu. 10. 34.

κατάδηλον,[a] nom. sing. neut. . . κατάδηλος

κατάδηλος], ου, ὁ, ἡ, τό, -ον, (§ 7. rem. 2) (κατά & δῆλος) *quite manifest or evident.*

καταδικάζετε, 2 pers. pl. pres. imper. act. καταδικάζω

καταδικάζω], fut. άσω, (§ 26. rem. 1) (κατά & δικάζω) *to give judgment against, condemn,* Mat. 12. 7, 37; Lu. 6. 37; Ja. 5. 6.

καταδικασθήσῃ, 2 pers. sing. fut. pass. . καταδικάζω

καταδικασθῆτε, 2 pers. pl. aor. 1, subj. pass. id.

καταδίκη], ης, ἡ, (§ 2. tab. B. a) (κατά & δίκη) *condemnation, sentence of condemnation,* v.r. (ῐ).

καταδίκην, acc. sing.—A. B. C. Ln. Tdf. } καταδίκη
δίκην, Rec. Gr. Sch. (Ac. 25. 15) }

καταδιώκω], fut. ξω, (§ 23. rem. 1. b) (κατά & διώκω) *to follow hard upon; to track, follow perseveringly,* Mar. 1. 36.

καταδουλοῖ, 3 pers. sing. pres. ind. act. . καταδουλόω

καταδουλόω, ῶ], fut. ώσω, (§ 20. tab. T) (κατά & δουλόω) *to reduce to absolute servitude, make a slave of,* 2 Co. 11. 20; Gal. 2. 4.

καταδουλώσουσι, 3 pers. pl. fut. ind.—Al. Ln. Sch. Tdf. . . . . } καταδουλόω
καταδουλώσωνται, Rec. Gr. (Gal. 2. 4) }

καταδουλώσωνται, 3 pers. pl. aor. 1, subj. mid. id.

καταδυναστευομένους, acc. pl. masc. part. pres. pass. . . . . καταδυναστεύω

καταδυναστεύουσι, 3 pers. pl. pres. ind. act. id.

καταδυναστεύω], fut. εύσω, (§ 13. tab. M) (κατά & δυναστεύω, *to rule, reign*) *to tyrannise over, oppress,* Ac. 10. 38; Ja. 2. 6.

κατάθεμα, ατος, τό, (§ 4. tab. D. c)—Gr. Sch. Tdf. . . . . . } κατατίθημι
καταναθεμα, Rec. (Re. 22. 3). . }

καταθεματίζειν, pres. infin.—Gr. Sch. Tdf. } id.
καταναθεματίζειν, Rec (Mat. 26. 74) }

καταθεματίζω], fut. ίσω, (§ 26. rem. 1) . id.

καταθέσθαι, aor. 2, inf. mid. (§ 28. tab. W) id.

καταισχύνει, 3 pers. sing. pres. ind. act. . καταισχύνω

καταισχύνετε, 2 pers. pl. pres. ind. act. . id.

καταισχύνῃ, 3 pers. sing. pres. subj. act. . id.

καταισχυνθῇ, 3 pers. sing. aor. 1, subj. pass. id.

καταισχυνθήσεται, 3 pers. sing. fut. ind. pass. id.

καταισχυνθῶμεν, 1 pers. pl. aor. 1, subj. pass. id.

καταισχυνθῶσι, 3 pers. pl. aor. 1, subj. pass. id.

καταισχύνω], fut. υνῶ, (§ 27. rem. 1. a) (κατά & αἰσχύνω) *to shame, put to shame, put to the blush,* 1 Co. 1. 27; pass. *to be ashamed, be put to the blush,* Lu. 13. 17; *to dishonour, disgrace,* 1 Co. 11. 4, 5; from the Heb. *to frustrate, disappoint,* Ro. 5. 5; 9. 33.

κατακαήσεται, 3 pers. sing. fut. 2, pass. . κατακαίω

κατακαίεται, 3 pers. sing. pres. ind. pass. . id.

κατακαίονται, 3 pers. pl. pres. ind. pass.—D. } id.
κατακαίεται, Rec. Ln. . . }
καίεται, Tdf. (Mat. 13. 40) . }

κατακαίω], fut. καύσω, (§ 35. rem. 3) aor. 2, pass. κατεκάην, (ᾰ), (κατά & καίω) *to burn up, consume with fire,* Mat. 3. 12; 13. 30, 40, et al.

κατακαλύπτεσθαι, pres. inf. pass. . κατακαλύπτω

κατακαλυπτέσθω, 3 pers. sing. pres. imper. pass. id.

κατακαλύπτεται, 3 pers. sing. pres. ind. pass. id.

κατακαλύπτω], mid. κατακαλύπτομαι, (κατά & καλύπτω) *to veil;* mid. *to veil one's self, to be veiled or covered,* 1 Co. 11. 6, 7.

κατακαυθήσεται, 3 pers. sing. fut. ind. pass. . κατακαίω

κατακαῦσαι, aor. 1, infin. act. . . id.

[a] He. 7. 15.

κατακαύσει, 3 pers. sing. fut. ind. act. . κατακαίω
κατακαύσουσι, 3 pers. pl. fut. ind. act. . id.
κατακαυχάομαι, ῶμαι], fut. ήσομαι, (§ 19. tab. S) (κατά & καυχάομαι) *to vaunt one's self against, to glory over, to assume superiority over*, Ro. 11. 18; Ja. 2. 13; 3. 14. LXX.
κατακαυχᾶσαι, 2 pers. sing. pres. ind. κατακαυχάομαι
κατακαυχᾶσθε, 2 pers. pl. pres. imper. . id.
κατακαυχάσθω, 3 pers. sing. pres. imper.—A. κατακαυχᾶται, Rec. Gr. Sch. Tdf. (Ja. 2. 13) . . . . . id.
κατακαυχᾶται, 3 pers. sing. pres. ind. . id.
κατακαυχῶ, 2 pers. sing. pres. imper. . id.
κατάκειμαι], fut. είσομαι, (§ 33. tab. DD) (κατά & κεῖμαι) *to lie, be in a recumbent position, be laid down*, Mar. 1. 30; 2. 4; *to recline* at table, Mar. 2. 15; 14. 3, et al.
κατακείμενοι, nom. pl. masc. part. pres. . κατάκειμαι
κατακείμενον, acc. sing. masc. part. pres. . id.
κατακειμένου, gen. sing. masc. part. pres. . id.
κατακεῖσθαι, pres. infin. . . . . . id.
κατάκειται, 3 pers. sing. pres. ind.—Al. Ln. Tdf. ἀνάκειται, Rec. Gr. Sch. (Lu. 7. 37) . id.
κατακέκριται, 3 pers. sing. perf. ind. pass. κατακρίνω
κατακλάω, ῶ], fut. άσω, (§ 22. rem. 2) aor. 1, κατέκλᾰσα, (κατά & κλάω) *to break, break in pieces*, Mar. 6. 41; Lu. 9. 16.
κατακλείω], fut. είσω, (§ 22. rem. 4) (κατά & κλείω) *to close, shut fast; to shut up, confine*, Lu. 3. 20; Ac. 26. 10.
κατακληροδοτέω, ῶ], fut. ήσω, (§ 16. tab. P) (κατά, κλῆρος, & δίδωμι) *to divide out by lot, distribute by lot*, Ac. 13. 19. LXX.
κατακληρονομέω, ῶ], fut. ήσω, (§ 16. tab. P) (κατά, κλῆρος, & νέμω, *to distribute*) same as preceding, for which it is a v.r.
κατακλιθῆναι, aor. 1, inf. pass. (§ 27. rem. 3) κατακλίνω
κατακλιθῇς, 2 pers. sing. aor. 1, subj. pass. id.
κατακλίνατε, 2 pers. pl. aor. 1, imper. act. id.
κατακλίνω], fut. ινῶ, (ῑ), (§ 27. rem. 1. a) aor. 1, κατέκλῑνα, aor. 1, pass. κατεκλίθην, (ῐ), (κατά & κλίνω) *to cause to lie down, cause to recline* at table, Lu. 9. 14; mid. *to lie down, recline*, Lu. 14. 8; 24. 30.
κατακλύζω], fut. ύσω, (§ 26. rem. 1) aor. 1, pass. κατεκλύσθην, (κατά & κλύζω, *to lave, wash*) *to inundate, deluge*.

κατακλυσμός, οῦ, ὁ, (§ 3. tab. C. a) *an inundation, deluge*, Mat. 24. 38, 39, et al.

κατακλυσθείς,[a] nom. sing. masc. part. aor. 1, pass. κατακλύζω
κατακλυσμόν, acc. sing. . . . κατακλυσμός
κατακλυσμός], οῦ, ὁ, (§ 3. tab. C. a) . κατακλύζω
κατακλυσμοῦ, gen. sing. . . . κατακλυσμός
κατακολουθέω, ῶ], fut. ήσω, (§ 16. tab. P) (κατά & ἀκολουθέω) *to follow closely or earnestly*, Lu. 23. 55; Ac. 16. 17.
κατακολουθήσασα, nom. s. fem. part. aor. 1 κατακολουθέω
κατακολουθήσασαι, nom. pl. fem. part. aor. 1 id.
κατακόπτω], fut. ψω, (§ 23. rem. 1. a) (κατά & κόπτω) *to cut or dash in pieces; to mangle, wound.*
κατακόπτων,[b] nom. sing. masc. part. pres. act. κατακόπτω
κατακρημνίζω], fut. ίσω, (§ 26. rem. 1) (κατά & κρημνός, *a precipice*) *to cast down headlong, precipitate.*
κατακρημνίσαι,[c] aor. 1, infin. act. . κατακρημνίζω
κατακριθήσεται, 3 pers. sing. fut. pass. . κατακρίνω
κατακριθῆτε, 2 pers. pl. aor. 1, subj. pass. . id.
κατακριθῶμεν, 1 pers. pl. aor. 1, subj. pass. id.
κατάκρῐμα], ατος, τό, (§ 4. tab. D. c) . id.
κατακρινεῖ, 3 pers. sing. fut. ind. act. . . id.
κατακρίνεις, 2 pers. sing. pres. ind. act. . id.
κατακρινοῦσι, 3 pers. pl. fut. ind. act. . id.
κατακρίνω, (ῑ), fut. ινῶ, (§ 27. rem. 1. a) aor. 1, κατέκρῑνα, perf. pass. κατακέκρῐμαι, aor. 1, pass. κατεκρίθην, (ῐ), (κατά & κρίνω) *to give judgment against, condemn*, Mat. 27. 3; Jno. 8. 10, 11, et al.; *to condemn, to place in a guilty light* by contrast, Mat. 12. 41, 42; Lu. 11. 31, 32; He. 11. 7.

κατάκρῐμα, ατος, τό, *condemnation, condemnatory sentence*, Ro. 5. 16, 18; 8. 1. L.G.

κατάκρῐσις, εως, ἡ, (§ 5. tab. E. c) *condemnation*, 2 Co. 3. 9; *censure*, 2 Co. 7. 3. LXX.

κατακρίνων, nom. sing. masc. part. pres. act. κατακρίνω
κατακρίσεως, gen. sing. . . . κατάκρισις
κατάκρισιν, acc. sing. . . . . id.
κατάκρισις], εως, ἡ, (§ 5. tab. E. c) . . κατακρίνω
κατακυριεύοντες, nom. pl. masc. part. pres. κατακυριεύω
κατακυριεύουσι, 3 pers. pl. pres. ind. . . id.
κατακυριεύσας, nom. sing. masc. part. aor. 1 id.
κατακυριεύω], fut. εύσω, (§ 13. tab. M) (κατά & κυριεύω) *to get into one's power*; in N.T.

[a] 1 Pe. 3. 6. [b] Mar. 5. 5. [c] Lu. 4. 29.

to bring under, master, overcome, Ac. 19. 16; *to domineer over,* Mat. 20. 25, et al. L.G.

καταλαβέσθαι, aor. 2, inf. mid. (§ 36. rem. 2) καταλαμβάνω

καταλάβῃ, 3 pers. sing. aor. 2, subj. act. id.

καταλάβητε, 2 pers. pl. aor. 2, subj. act. id.

καταλαβόμενοι, nom. pl. masc. part. aor. 2, mid. id.

καταλαβόμενος, nom. s. masc. part. aor. 2, mid. id.

καταλάβω, 1 pers. sing. aor. 2, subj. act. id.

καταλαλεῖ, 3 pers. sing. pres. ind. καταλαλέω

καταλαλεῖσθε, 2 pers. pl. pres. ind. pass.—B. καταλαλοῦσιν [ὑμῶν], R. Gr. Sch. Tdf. (1 Pe. 2. 12) id.

καταλαλεῖτε, 2 pers. pl. pres. imper. id.

καταλᾰλέω, ῶ], fut. ήσω, (§ 16. tab. P) (κατά & λαλέω) *to blab out; to speak against, calumniate,* Ja. 4. 11; 1 Pe. 2. 12; 3. 16.

καταλαλιά, ᾶς, ἡ, (§ 2. tab. B. b, and rem. 2) *evil-speaking, detraction, backbiting, calumny,* 2 Co. 12. 20; 1 Pe. 2. 1. LXX.

κατάλᾰλος, ου, ὁ, ἡ, (§ 7. rem. 2) *slanderous; a detractor, calumniator,* Ro. 1. 30. N.T.

καταλαλιά], ᾶς, ἡ καταλαλέω

καταλαλιαί, nom. pl. καταλαλιά

καταλαλιάς, acc. pl. id.

κατάλαλος], ου, ὁ, ἡ καταλαλέω

καταλάλους,[a] acc. pl. masc. κατάλαλος

καταλαλοῦσι, 3 pers. pl. pres. ind. καταλαλέω

καταλαλῶν, nom. sing. masc. part. pres. id.

καταλαλῶσι, 3 pers. pl. pres. subj. id.

καταλαμβάνομαι, 1 pers. s. pres. ind. mid. καταλαμβάνω

καταλαμβάνω], fut. λήψομαι, aor. 2, κατέλᾰβον, (§ 36. rem. 2) (κατά & λαμβάνω) *to lay hold of, grasp; to obtain, attain,* Ro. 9. 30; 1 Co. 9. 24; *to seize, to take possession of,* Mar. 9. 18; *to come suddenly upon, overtake, surprise,* Jno. 12. 35; *to deprehend, detect in the act, seize,* Jno. 8. 3, 4; met. *to comprehend, apprehend,* Jno. 1. 5; mid. *to understand, perceive,* Ac. 4. 13; 10. 34, et al.

καταλέγω], fut. ξω, (§ 23. rem. 1. b) (κατά & λέγω) *to select; to reckon in a number, enter in a list or catalogue, enrol.*

καταλεγέσθω,[b] 3 pers. sing. pres. imper. pass. καταλέγω

κατάλειμμα],[c] ατος, τό, (§ 4. tab. D. c) καταλείπω

καταλείπει, 3 pers. sing. pres. ind. act. id.

καταλειπομένης, gen. sing. fem. part. pres. pass. καταλείπω

καταλείπω], fut. ψω, aor. 2, κατέλῐπον, (§ 24. rem. 9) (κατά & λείπω) *to leave behind; to leave behind* at death, Mar. 12. 19; *to relinquish, let remain,* Mar. 14. 52; *to quit, depart from, forsake,* Mat. 4. 13; 16. 4; *to neglect,* Ac. 6. 2; *to leave alone, or without assistance,* Lu. 10. 40; *to reserve,* Ro. 11. 4.

κατάλειμμα, ατος, τό, *a remnant, a small residue,* Ro. 9. 27. L.G.

κατάλοιπος, ου, ὁ, ἡ, (§ 7. rem. 2) *remaining;* οἱ κατάλοιποι, *the rest,* Ac. 15. 17.

καταλειφθῆναι, aor. 1, inf. pass. (§ 23. rem. 4) καταλείπω

καταλείψαντας, acc. pl. masc. part. aor. 1, act. id.

καταλείψει, 3 pers. sing. fut. ind. act. id.

καταλελειμμένος, nom. sing. masc. part. perf. pass. id.

καταλιθάζω], fut. άσω, (§ 26. rem. 1) (κατά & λιθάζω) *to stone, kill by stoning.* LXX.

καταλιθάσει,[d] 3 pers. sing. fut. ind. καταλιθάζω

καταλίπῃ, 3 pers. sing. aor. 2, subj. act. καταλείπω

καταλιπόντες, nom. pl. masc. part. aor. 2, act. id.

καταλιπών, nom. sing. masc. part. aor. 2, act. id

καταλλαγέντες, nom. pl. masc. pt. aor. 2, pass. καταλλάσσω

καταλλᾰγή], ῆς, ἡ, (§ 2. tab. B. a) id.

καταλλαγήν, acc. sing. καταλλαγή

καταλλαγῆς, gen. sing. id.

καταλλάγητε, 2 pers. pl. aor. 2, imper. pass. καταλλάσσω

καταλλαγήτω, 3 pers. sing. aor. 2, imper. pass. id.

καταλλάξαντος, gen. sing. masc. part. aor. 1, act. id.

καταλλάσσω], fut. άξω, (§ 26. rem. 3) aor. 2, pass. κατηλλάγην, (ᾰ), (κατά & ἀλλάσσω) *to change, exchange; to reconcile;* pass. *to be reconciled,* Ro. 5. 10; 1 Co. 7. 11; 2 Co. 5. 18, 19, 20.

καταλλᾰγή, ῆς, ἡ, (§ 2. tab. B. a) pr. *an exchange; reconciliation, restoration to favour,* Ro. 5. 11; 11. 15; 2 Co. 5. 18, 19.

καταλλάσσων, nom. sing. masc. part. pres. καταλλάσσω

κατάλοιποι,[e] nom. pl. masc. κατάλοιπος

κατάλοιπος], ου, ὁ, ἡ, (§ 7. rem. 2) καταλείπω

κατάλυε, 2 pers. sing. pres. imper. act. καταλύω

καταλυθῇ, 3 pers. sing. aor. 1, subj. pass. id.

καταλυθήσεται, 3 pers. sing. fut. ind. pass. (§ 14. tab. N) id.

κατάλῠμα], ατος, τό, (§ 4. tab. D. c) id.

[a] Ro. 1. 30. [b] 1 Ti. 5. 9. [c] Ro. 9. 27. [d] Lu. 20. 6. [e] Ac. 15. 17.

καταλυματι, dat. sing. . . . κατάλυμα
καταλῦσαι, aor. 1, infin. act. . . . καταλύω
καταλύσει, 3 pers. sing. fut. ind. act. . id.
καταλύσω, 1 pers. sing. fut. ind. act. . . id.
καταλύσωσι, 3 pers. pl. aor. 1, subj. act. . id.

καταλύω], fut. ύσω, (ῡ), aor. 1, pass. κατελύθην, (ῠ), (§ 13. tab. M. and § 14. tab. N) (κατά & λύω) *to dissolve; to destroy, demolish, overthrow, throw down*, Mat. 24. 2; 26. 61; met. *to nullify, abrogate*, Mat. 5. 17; Ac. 5. 38, 39, et al.; absol. *to unloose* harness, etc., *to halt, to stop for the night, lodge*, Lu. 9. 12. (ῡ).

κατάλῠμα, ατος, τό, (§ 4. tab. D. c) *a lodging, inn, khan*, Lu. 2. 7; *a guest-chamber, cœnaculum*, Mar. 14. 14; Lu. 22. 11.

καταλύων, nom. sing. masc. part. pres. act. . καταλύω
καταμάθετε,[a] 2 pers. pl. aor. 2, imper. . καταμανθάνω

καταμανθάνω], fut. μαθήσομαι, aor. 2, κατέμᾰθον, (§ 36. rem. 2) (κατά & μανθάνω) *to learn or observe thoroughly; to consider accurately and diligently, contemplate, mark.*

καταμαρτῠρέω, ῶ], fut. ήσω, (§ 16. tab. P) (κατά & μαρτυρέω) *to witness or testify against*, Mat. 26. 62; 27. 13, et al.

καταμαρτυροῦσι, 3 pers. pl. pres. ind. καταμαρτυρέω
καταμένοντες,[b] nom. pl. masc. part. pres. . καταμένω

καταμένω], fut. ενῶ, (§ 27. rem. 1. a) (κατά & μένω) *to remain; to abide, dwell.*

καταμόνας, adv. (κατά & μόνος) *alone, apart, in private*, Mar. 4. 10; Lu. 9. 18.

κατανάθεμα,[c] ατος, τό, (§ 4. tab. D. c) (κατά & ἀνάθεμα) *a curse, execration;* meton. *one accursed, execrable.* N.T.

καταναθεματίζω, fut. ίσω, (§ 26. rem. 1) *to curse.* N.T.

καταναθεματίζειν,[d] pres. infin. . καταναθεματίζω
καταναθεματίζω], fut. ίσω . . κατανάθεμα
καταναλίσκον,[e] nom. sing. neut. part. pres. καταναλίσκω

κατανᾱλίσκω], fut. λώσω, (§ 36. rem. 4) (κατά & ἀναλίσκω) *to consume*, as fire.

καταναρκάω, ῶ], fut. ήσω, (§ 18. tab. R) (κατά & ναρκάω, *to grow torpid*) in N.T. *to be torpid to the disadvantage of* any one, *to be a dead weight upon;* by impl. *to be troublesome, burdensome to*, in respect of maintenance, 2 Co. 11. 9; 12. 13, 14.

καταναρκήσω, 1 pers. sing. fut. ind. . καταναρκάω

κατανεύω], fut. εύσομαι, (κατά & νεύω) pr. *to nod, signify assent by a nod;* genr. *to make signs, beckon*, Lu. 5. 7.

κατανοεῖς, 2 pers. sing. pres. ind. . . κατανοέω

κατανοέω, ῶ], fut. ήσω, (§ 16. tab. P) (κατά & νοέω) *to perceive, understand, apprehend*, Lu. 20. 23; *to observe, mark, contemplate*, Lu. 12. 24, 27; *to discern, descry*, Mat. 7. 3; *to have regard to, make account of*, Ro. 4. 19.

κατανοῆσαι, aor. 1, infin. . . . κατανοέω
κατανοήσας, nom. sing. masc. part. aor. 1 . id.
κατανοήσατε, 2 pers. pl. aor. 1, imper. . id.
κατανοοῦντι, dat. sing. masc. part. pres. . id.
κατανοῶμεν, 1 pers. pl. pres. subj. . . id.

καταντάω, ῶ], fut. ήσω, (§ 18. tab. K) (κατά & ἀντάω) *to come to, arrive at*, Ac. 16. 1; 20. 15; of an epoch, *to come upon*, 1 Co. 10. 11; met. *to reach, attain to*, Ac. 26. 7, et al. L.G.

καταντῆσαι, aor. 1, infin. . . . . καταντάω
καταντήσαντες, nom. pl. masc. part. aor. 1 id.
καταντήσειν, fut. infin.—B. . . . } id.
καταντῆσαι, R. Gr. Sch. Tdf. (Ac. 26. 7) }
καταντήσω, 1 pers. sing. aor. 1, subj. . . id.
καταντήσωμεν, 1 pers. pl. aor. 1, subj. . id.
κατανύξεως,[f] gen. sing. . . . . κατάνυξις

κατάνυξις], εως, ἡ, (§ 5. tab. E. c) in N.T. *deep sleep, stupor, dulness.* LXX.

κατανύσσω], fut. ξω, aor. 2, pass. κατενύγην, (§ 26. rem. 3) (κατά & νύσσω) *to pierce through; to pierce* with compunction and pain of heart, Ac. 2. 37.

καταξιόω, ῶ], fut. ώσω, (§ 20. tab. T) (κατά & ἀξιόω) *to account worthy of*, Lu. 20. 35; 21. 36; Ac. 5. 41; 2 Thes. 1. 5.

καταξιωθέντες, nom. pl. masc. part. aor. 1, pass. (§ 21. tab. U) . . καταξιόω
καταξιωθῆναι, aor. 1, infin. pass. . . id.
καταξιωθῆτε, 2 pers. pl. aor. 1, subj. pass. id.
καταπατεῖν, pres. infin. act. . . . καταπατέω
καταπᾰτεῖσθαι, pres. infin. pass. . . id.

καταπᾰτέω, ῶ], fut. ήσω, (§ 16. tab. P) (κατά & πατέω) *to trample upon, tread down or under feet*, Mat. 5. 13; 7. 6; Lu. 8. 5; 12. 1; met. *to trample on* by indignity, *spurn*, He. 10. 29.

[a] Mat. 6. 28. [b] Ac. 1. 13. [c] Re. 22. 3. [d] Mat. 26. 74. [e] He. 12. 29. [f] Ro. 11. 8.

καταπατήσας, nom. sing. masc. part. aor. 1, act. καταπατέω
καταπατήσωσι, 3 pers. pl. aor. 1, subj. act. . id.
καταπαύσεως, gen. sing. . . . κατάπαυσις
κατάπαυσιν, acc. sing. . . . . id.
κατάπαυσις], εως, ἡ, (§ 5. tab. E. c) . καταπαύω
καταπαύω], fut. αύσω, (§ 13. tab. M) (κατά & παύω) *to cause to cease, restrain,* Ac. 14. 18; *to cause to rest, give final rest to, to settle finally,* He. 4. 8; intrans. *to rest, desist from,* He. 4. 4, 10.

κατάπαυσις, εως, ἡ, (§ 5. tab. E. c) pr. *the act of giving rest; a state of settled or final rest,* He. 3. 11, 18; 4. 3, 11, et al.; *a place of rest, place of abode, dwelling, habitation,* Ac. 7. 49.

καταπεσόντων, gen. pl. masc. part. aor. 2, (§ 37. rem. 1) . . . . καταπίπτω
καταπέτασμα, ατος, τό, (§ 4. tab. D. c) (καταπετάννυμι, *to expand*) *a veil, curtain,* Mat. 27. 51; Mar. 15. 38; Lu. 23. 45; He. 6. 19; 10. 20. LXX.
καταπετάσματος, gen. sing. . . . καταπέτασμα
καταπιεῖν, aor. 2, infin. act.—B. Ln. } καταπίνω
καταπίῃ, R. Gr. Sch. Tdf. (1 Pe. 5. 8) }
καταπίῃ, 3 pers. sing. aor. 2, subj. act. . id.
καταπίνοντες, nom. pl. masc. part. pres. act. id.
καταπίνω], fut. πίομαι, aor. 2, κατέπιον, aor. 1, pass. κατεπόθην, (§ 37. rem. 1) (κατά & πίνω) *to drink, swallow, gulp down,* Mat. 23. 24; *to swallow up, absorb,* Re. 12. 16; 2 Co. 5. 4; *to ingulf, submerge, overwhelm,* He. 11. 29; *to swallow greedily, devour,* 1 Pe. 5. 8; *to destroy, annihilate,* 1 Co. 15. 54; 2 Co. 2. 7.
καταπίπτειν, pres. infin. . . . καταπίπτω
καταπίπτω], fut. πεσοῦμαι, aor. 2, κατέπεσον, perf. πέπτωκα, (§ 37. rem. 1) (κατά & πίπτω) *to fall down, fall prostrate,* Ac. 26. 14; 28. 6.
καταπλέω], fut. εύσομαι, aor. 1, κατέπλευσα, (§ 35. rem. 1. 3) (κατά & πλέω) *to sail towards land, to come to land,* Lu. 8. 26.
καταποθῇ, 3 pers. sing. aor. 1, subj. pass. . καταπίνω
καταπονέω, ῶ], fut. ήσω, (§ 16. tab. P) (κατά & πονέω) *to exhaust by labour or suffering; to weary out,* 2 Pe. 2. 7; *to overpower, oppress,* Ac. 7. 24.
καταπονούμενον, acc. sing. masc. part. pres. pass. καταπονέω
καταπονουμένῳ, dat. sing. masc. part. pres. pass. id.
καταποντίζεσθαι, pres. infin. pass. . . καταποντίζω
καταποντίζω], fut. ίσω, (§ 26. rem. 1) (κατά & ποντίζω, *to sink,* fr. πόντος) *to sink in the sea;* pass. *to sink,* Mat. 14. 30; *to be plunged, submerged,* Mat. 18. 6.
καταποντισθῇ, 3 pers. sing. aor. 1, subj. pass. καταποντίζω
κατάρα, ας, ἡ, (§ 2. tab. B. b) (κατά & ἀρά) *a cursing, execration, imprecation,* Ja. 3. 10; from the Heb. *condemnation, doom,* Gal. 3. 10, 13; 2 Pe. 2. 14; meton. *a doomed one, one on whom condemnation falls,* Gal. 3. 13. (ᾰρ).

καταράομαι, ῶμαι, fut. άσομαι, aor. 1, κατηρᾱσάμην, (§ 19. tab. S) in N.T. perf. pass. part. κατηραμένος, *to curse, to wish evil to, imprecate evil upon,* Mat. 5. 44; Mar. 11. 21, et al.; in N.T. pass. *to be doomed,* Mat. 25. 41.

κατάραν, acc. sing. . . . . κατάρα
καταράομαι, ῶμαι], fut. άσομαι . . id.
κατάρας, gen. sing. . . . . id.
καταρᾶσθε, 2 pers. pl. pres. imper. . καταράομαι
καταργεῖ, 3 pers. sing. pres. ind. act. . καταργέω
καταργεῖται, 3 pers. sing. pres. ind. pass. . id.
καταργέω, ῶ], (§ 16. tab. P) fut. ήσω, perf. κατήργηκα, aor. 1, κατήργησα, perf. pass. κατήργημαι, aor. 1, pass. κατηργήθην, (κατά & ἀργός) *to render useless or unproductive, occupy unprofitably,* Lu. 13. 7; *to render powerless,* Ro. 6. 6; *to make empty and unmeaning,* Ro. 4. 14; *to render null, to abrogate, cancel,* Ro. 3. 3, 31; Ep. 2. 15, et al.; *to bring to an end,* 1 Co. 2. 6; 13. 8; 15. 24, 26; 2 Co. 3. 7, et al.; *to destroy, annihilate,* 2 Thes. 2. 8; He. 2. 14; *to free from, dissever from,* Ro. 7. 2, 6; Gal. 5. 4
καταργηθῇ, 3 pers. sing. aor. 1, subj. pass. . καταργέω
καταργηθήσεται, 3 pers. sing. fut. ind. pass. id.
καταργηθήσονται, 3 pers. pl. fut. ind. pass. id.
καταργῆσαι, aor. 1, infin. act. . . id.
καταργήσαντος, gen. sing. masc. part. aor. 1, act. id.
καταργήσας, nom. sing. masc. part. aor. 1, act. id.
καταργήσει, 3 pers. sing. fut. ind. act. . . id.
καταργήσῃ, 3 pers. sing. aor. 1, subj. act. . id.
καταργοῦμεν, 1 pers. pl. pres. ind. act. . id.
καταργουμένην, acc. sing. fem. part. pres. pass. id.
καταργούμενον, nom. sing. neut. part. pres. pass. id.
καταργουμένου, gen. sing. neut. part. pres. pass. id.
καταργουμένων, gen. pl. part. pres. pass. . id.
καταριθμέω, ῶ], fut. ήσω, (§ 16. tab. P) (κατά &

ἀριθμέω) *to enumerate, number with, count with,* Ac. 1. 17.

καταρτίζεσθε, 2 pers. pl. pres. imper. pass. καταρτίζω

καταρτίζετε, 2 pers. pl. pres. imper. act. id.

καταρτίζοντας, acc. pl. masc. part. pres. act. id.

καταρτίζω], fut. ίσω, aor. 1, κατήρτισα, (§ 26. rem. 1) (κατά & ἀρτίζω) *to adjust thoroughly; to knit together, unite completely,* 1 Co. 1. 10; *to frame,* He. 11. 3; *to prepare, provide,* Mat. 21. 16; He. 10. 5; *to qualify fully, to complete* in character, Lu. 6. 40; He. 13. 21; 1 Pe. 5. 10; perf. pass. κατηρτισμένος, *fit, ripe,* Ro. 9. 22; *to repair, refit,* Mat. 4. 21; Mar. 1. 19; *to supply, make good,* 1 Thes. 3. 10; *to restore* to a forfeited condition, *to reinstate,* Gal. 6. 1.

κατάρτισις, εως, ἡ, (§ 5. tab. E. c) pr. *a complete adjustment; completeness* of character, *perfection,* 2 Co. 13. 9. L.G.

καταρτισμός, οῦ, ὁ, (§ 3. tab. C. a) *a perfectly adjusted adaptation; complete qualification* for a specific purpose, Ep. 4. 12. L.G.

καταρτίσαι, aor. 1, infin. act. καταρτίζω

καταρτίσαι, 3 pers. sing. aor. 1, opt. act. id.

καταρτίσει, 3 pers. sing. fut. act.—Al. Ln. Tdf. } id.
καταρτίσαι, Rec. Gr. Sch. (1 Pe. 5. 10) }

κατάρτισιν,[a] acc. sing. κατάρτισις

κατάρτισις], εως, ἡ, (§ 5. tab. E. c) καταρτίζω

καταρτισμόν,[b] acc. sing. καταρτισμός

καταρτισμός], οῦ, ὁ, (§ 3. tab. C. a) καταρτίζω

καταρώμεθα, 1 pers. pl. pres. ind. καταράομαι

καταρωμένους, acc. pl. masc. part. pres. id.

κατασείσας, nom. sing. masc. part. aor. 1 κατασείω

κατασείω], fut. σείσω, (§ 13. tab. M) (κατά & σείω) *to shake down or violenty;* τὴν χεῖρα, or τῇ χειρί, *to wave the hand, beckon; to sign silence by waving the hand,* Ac. 12. 17, et al.

κατασκάπτω], fut. ψω, (§ 23. rem. 1. a) (κατά & σκάπτω) pr. *to dig down under, undermine;* by impl. *to overthrow, demolish, raze,* Ro. 11. 3; τὰ κατεσκαμμένα, *ruins,* Ac. 15. 16.

κατασκευάζεται, 3 pers. sing. pres. pass. κατασκευάζω

κατασκευαζομένης, gen. s. fem. part. pres. pass. id.

κατασκευάζω,], fut. άσω, (§ 26. rem. 1) (κατά & σκευάζω, fr. σκεῦος) *to prepare, put in readiness,* Mat. 11. 10; Mar. 1. 2; Lu. 1. 17; 7. 27; *to construct, form, build,* He. 3. 3, 4; 9. 2, 6; 11. 7; 1 Pe. 3. 20.

κατασκευάσας, nom. sing. masc. part. aor. 1 κατασκευάζω

κατασκευάσει, 3 pers. sing. fut. ind. id.

κατασκηνοῦν, pres. infin. κατασκηνόω

κατασκηνόω, ῶ], fut. ώσω, (§ 20. tab. T) (κατά & σκηνόω, fr. σκηνή) *to pitch one's tent;* in N.T. *to rest in* a place, *settle, abide,* Ac. 2. 26; *to haunt, roost,* Mat. 13. 32; Mar. 4. 32; Lu. 13. 19.

κατασκήνωσις, εως, ἡ, (§ 5. tab. E. c) pr. *the pitching a tent; a tent;* in N.T. *a dwelling-place; a haunt, roost,* Mat. 8. 20; Lu. 9. 58. L.G.

κατασκηνώσει, 3 pers. sing. fut. ind. κατασκηνόω

κατασκηνώσεις, acc. pl. κατασκήνωσις

κατασκήνωσις], εως, ἡ κατασκηνόω

κατασκιάζοντα,[c] nom. pl. neut. part. pres. κατασκιάζω

κατασκιάζω], fut. άσω, (§ 26. rem. 1) (κατά & σκιάζω, idem) *to overshadow.*

κατασκοπέω, ῶ], fut. κατασκέψομαι, in N.T. aor. 1, infin. κατασκοπῆσαι, (κατά & σκοπέω) *to view closely and accurately; to spy out,* Gal. 2. 4.

κατάσκοπος, ου, ὁ, (§ 3. tab. C. a) *a scout, spy,* He. 11. 31.

κατασκοπῆσαι,[d] aor. 1, infin. κατασκοπέω

κατάσκοπος], ου, ὁ id.

κατασκόπους,[e] acc. pl. κατάσκοπος

κατασοφίζομαι], fut. ίσομαι, (§ 26. rem. 1) (κατά & σοφίζω) *to exercise cleverness to the detriment of* any one, *to outwit; to make a victim of subtlety, to practise on by insidious dealing.* L.G.

κατασοφισάμενος,[f] nom. s. masc. pt. aor. 1 κατασοφίζομαι

κατασταθήσονται, 3 pers. pl. fut. ind. pass. (§ 29. rem. 6) καθίστημι

καταστείλας, nom. s. masc. part. aor. 1, act. καταστέλλω

καταστέλλω], fut. στελῶ, aor. 1, κατέστειλα, (§ 27. rem. 1, b. d) perf. pass. κατέσταλμαι, (§ 27. rem. 3) (κατά & στέλλω) *to arrange, dispose in regular order; to appease, quiet, pacify,* Ac. 19. 35, 36.

καταστολή, ῆς, ἡ, (§ 2. tab. B. a) pr. *an arranging in order; adjustment of dress;* in N.T. *apparel, dress,* 1 Ti. 2. 9.

κατάστημα], ατος, τό, (§ 4. tab. D. C) καθίστημι

[a] 2 Co. 13. 9. [b] Ep. 4. 12. [c] He. 9. 5. [d] Gal. 2. 4. [e] He. 11. 31. [f] Ac. 7. 19.

καταστήματι,[a] dat. sing. . . . . κατάστημα

καταστήσει, 3 pers. sing. fut. ind. act. . . καθίστημι

καταστήσῃς, 2 pers. sing. aor. 1, subj. act. id.

καταστήσομεν, 1 pers. pl. fut. ind. act. . id.

καταστήσω, 1 pers. sing. fut. ind. act. . id.

καταστήσωμεν, 1 pers. pl. aor. 1, subj. act. id.

καταστολή], ῆς, ἡ, (§ 2. tab. B. a) . . καταστέλλω

καταστολῇ,[b] dat. sing. . . . καταστολή

καταστρέφω], fut. ψω, (§ 23. rem. 1. a) (κατά & στρέφω) *to invert; to overturn, overthrow, throw down*, Mat. 21. 12; Mar. 11. 15.

καταστροφή, ῆς, ἡ, (§ 2. tab. B. a) *an overthrow, destruction*, 2 Pe. 2. 6; met. *overthrow* of right principle or faith, *utter detriment, perversion*, 2 Ti. 2. 14.

καταστρηνιάω], fut. άσω, (κατά & στρηνιάω, *to be headstrong, wanton*, fr. στρηνής or στρηνός, *hard, harsh*) *to be headstrong or wanton towards*. N.T.

καταστρηνιάσωσι,[c] 3 pers. pl. aor. 1, subj. καταστρηνιάω

καταστροφή], ῆς, ἡ, (§ 2. tab. B. a) . καταστρέφω

καταστροφῇ, dat. sing. . . . καταστροφή

καταστρώννυμι, or νύω], fut. καταστρώσω, aor. 1, pass. κατεστρώθην, (§ 36. rem. 5) (κατά & στρώννυμι—νύω) *to strew down, lay flat*; pass. *to be strewn, laid prostrate* in death, 1 Co. 10. 5.

κατασύρῃ,[d] 3 pers. sing. pres. subj. . κατασύρω

κατασύρω], (κατά & σύρω) *to drag down, to drag away*. (ῡ).

κατασφάξατε,[e] 2 pers. pl. aor. 1, imper. κατασφάζω

κατασφάζω, or σφάττω], fut. σφάξω, (§ 26. rem. 3) (κατά & σφάζω, or σφάττω) *to slaughter, slay*.

κατασφρᾱγίζω], fut. ίσω, perf. pass. κατεσφράγισμαι, (§ 26. rem. 1) (κατά & σφραγίζω) *to seal up*, Re. 5. 1.

κατασχέσει, dat. sing. . . . . κατάσχεσις

κατάσχεσιν, acc. sing. . . . . id.

κατάσχεσις], εως, ἡ, (§ 5. tab. E. c) . . κατέχω

κατάσχωμεν, 1 pers. pl. aor. 2, subj. (§ 36. rem. 4) . . . . . id.

κατατίθημι], fut. θήσω, aor. 1, κατέθηκα, (§ 28. tab. V) (κατά & τίθημι) *to lay down, deposit*, Mar. 15. 46; mid. *to deposit or lay up for one's self*; χάριν, or χάριτας, *to lay up a store of favour for one's self, earn a title to favour* at the hands of a person, *to curry favour with*, Ac. 24. 27; 25. 9.

κατάθεμα, ατος, τό, (§ 4. tab. D. c) *an execration, curse*; by meton. *what is worthy of execration*, i. q. κατανάθεμα, Re. 22. 3. N.T.

καταθεματίζω, fut. ίσω, (§ 26. rem. 1) *to curse*, v.r. Mat. 26. 74. N.T.

κατατομή], ῆς, ἡ, (§ 2. tab. B. a) (κατατέμνω, *to cut up*, fr. κατά & τέμνω) *concision, mutilation*.

κατατομήν,[f] acc. sing. . . . . κατατομή

κατατοξευθήσεται,[g] 3 pers. sing. fut. pass. κατατοξεύω

κατατοξεύω], fut. εύσω, (§ 13. tab. M) (κατά & τοξεύω, *to shoot with a bow*) *to shoot down* with arrows; *to transfix* with an arrow or dart.

κατατρέχω], fut. καταδραμοῦμαι, aor. 2, ἔδρᾰμον, (§ 36. rem. 1) (κατά & τρέχω) *to run down*, Ac. 21. 32.

καταυγάζω], fut. άσω, (κατά & αὐγάζω) *to shine down, or upon*. v.r.

καταυγάσαι, aor. 1, infin.—C. D. . . }
αὐγάσαι, Rec. Gr. Sch. Tdf. (2 Co. 4. 4) } καταυγάζω

κατάφαγε, 2 pers. sing. aor. 2, imper. . . κατεσθίω

καταφάγεται, 3 pers. sing. fut. ind.—Gr. Sch. Tdf. . . . . . . }
κατέφαγε, Rec. (Jno. 2. 17) . } id.

καταφάγῃ, 3 pers. sing. aor. 2, subj. . id.

καταφαγών, nom. sing. masc. part. aor. 2 . id.

καταφέρω], fut. κατοίσω, aor. 1, pass. κατηνέχθην, (§ 36. rem. 1) (κατά & φέρω) *to bear down; to overpower*, as sleep, Ac. 20. 9; καταφέρειν ψῆφον, *to give a vote or verdict*, Ac. 26. 10.

καταφερόμενος, nom. sing. masc. part. pres. pass. καταφέρω

καταφέροντες, nom. pl. masc. part. pres. act.—Al. Ln. Tdf. . . . }
φέροντες κατά—R. Gr. Sch. (Ac. 25. 7) } id.

καταφεύγω], fut. ξομαι, aor. 2, κατέφῠγον, (§ 24. rem. 9) (κατά & φεύγω) *to flee to* for refuge, Ac. 14. 6; He. 6. 18.

καταφθαρήσονται, 3 pers. pl. fut. 2, pass. καταφθείρω

καταφθείρω], fut. φθερῶ, (§ 27. rem. 1. c) fut. pass. καταφθαρήσομαι, (§ 27. rem. 4. b. c) (κατά & φθείρω) *to destroy, cause to perish*, 2 Pe. 2. 12; *to corrupt, deprave*, 2 Ti. 3. 8.

καταφῐλέω, ῶ], fut. ήσω, (§ 16. tab. P) (κατά &

[a] Tit. 2. 3. [b] 1 Ti. 2. 9. [c] 1 Ti. 5. 11. [d] Lu. 12. 58. [e] Lu. 19. 27 [f] Phi. 3. 2. [g] He. 13. 20.

φιλέω) *to kiss affectionately or with a semblance of affection, to kiss with earnest gesture*, Mat. 26. 49; Lu. 7. 38; Ac. 20. 37, et al.

καταφιλοῦσα, nom. sing. fem. part. pres. . καταφιλέω

καταφρονεῖς, 2 pers. sing. pres. ind. . καταφρονέω

καταφρονεῖτε, 2 pers. pl. pres. ind. . id.

καταφρονείτω, 3 pers. sing. pres. imper. . id.

καταφρονείτωσαν, 3 pers. pl. pres. imper. id.

καταφρονέω, ῶ], fut. ήσω, (§ 16. tab. P) (κατά & φρονέω) pr. *to think in disparagement of; to contemn, scorn, despise*, Mat. 18. 10; Ro. 2. 4; *to slight*, Mat. 6. 24; Lu. 16. 13; 1 Co. 11. 22; 1 Ti. 4. 12; 6. 2; 2 Pe. 2. 10; *to disregard*, He. 12. 2.

καταφρονητής, οῦ, ὁ, (§ 2. tab. B. c) *a contemner, despiser, scorner*, Ac. 13. 41. L.G.

καταφρονήσας, nom. sing. masc. part. aor. 1 καταφρονέω

καταφρονήσει, 3 pers. sing. fut. ind. . id.

καταφρονήσητε, 2 pers. pl. aor. 1, subj. . id.

καταφρονηταί,[a] nom. pl. . . καταφρονητής

καταφρονητής], οῦ, ὁ . . . καταφρονέω

καταφρονοῦντας, acc. pl. masc. part. pres. . id.

καταφυγόντες, nom. pl. masc. part. aor. 2 . καταφεύγω

καταχέω], fut. εύσω, (§ 35. rem. 1, 3) (κατά & χέω) *to pour down upon*, Mat. 26. 7; Mar. 14. 3.

καταχθέντες, nom. pl. masc. part. aor. 1, pass. κατάγω

καταχθόνιος], ίου, ὁ, ἡ, (§ 7. rem. 2) (κατά & χθών, *the earth*) *under the earth, subterranean, infernal.*

καταχθονίων,[b] gen. pl. . . . καταχθόνιος

καταχράομαι, ῶμαι], fut. ήσομαι, (§ 19. tab. S) (κατά & χράομαι) *to use downright; to use up, consume; to make an unrestrained use of, use eagerly*, 1 Co. 7. 31; *to use to the full, stretch to the utmost*, 1 Co. 9. 18.

καταχρήσασθαι, aor. 1, infin. . καταχράομαι

καταχρώμενοι, nom. pl. masc. part. pres. . id.

καταψύξῃ,[c] 3 pers. sing. aor. 1, subj. . καταψύχω

καταψύχω], fut. ξω, (§ 23. rem. 1. b) (κατά & ψύχω) *to cool, refresh*. (ῡ).

κατεαγῶσι, 3 pers. pl. aor. 2, subj. pass. (§ 36. rem. 5) . . . . κατάγνυμι

κατέαξαν, 3 pers. pl. aor. 1, ind. act. . id.

κατεάξει, 3 pers. sing. fut. ind act. . id.

κατέβαινε, 3 pers. sing. imperf. . . καταβαίνω

κατεβάρησα,[d] 1 pers. sing. aor. 1, ind. . καταβαρέω

κατέβη, 3 pers. s. aor. 2, ind. (§ 31. rem. 1. d) καταβαίνω

κατέβην, 1 pers. sing. aor. 2. ind. (§ 37. rem. 1) id.

κατέβησαν, 3 pers. pl. aor. 2, ind. . . id.

κατεβλήθη, 3 pers. sing. aor. 1, pass. (§ 27. rem. 3) . . . . καταβάλλω

κατεγέλων, 3 pers. pl. imperf. . . καταγελάω

κατεγνωσμένος, nom. sing. masc. part. perf. pass. (§ 36. rem. 3) . . καταγινώσκω

κατέδησε,[e] 3 pers. sing. aor. 1, ind. act. . καταδέω

κατεδικάσατε, 2 pers. pl. aor. 1, ind. . καταδικάζω

κατεδίωξαν,[f] 3 pers. pl. aor. 1, ind. . καταδιώκω

κατέδραμε,[g] 3 pers. sing. aor. 2, ind. (§ 36. rem. 1) . . . . . κατατρέχω

κατέθηκε, 3 pers. sing. aor. 1, ind. act. . κατατίθημι

κατείδωλον,[h] acc. sing. fem. . . κατείδωλος

κατείδωλος], ου, ὁ, ἡ, (§ 7. rem. 2) (κατά & εἴδωλον) *rife with idols, sunk in idolatry, grossly idolatrous.* N.T.

κατειλημμένην, acc. sing. fem. part. perf. pass. (§ 36. rem. 2) . . καταλαμβάνω

κατειληφέναι, perf. infin. act. . . . id.

κατειλήφθη, 3 pers. sing. aor. 1, ind. pass. id.

κατειργάσατο, 3 pers. sing. aor. 1, ind. (§ 13. rem. 4) . . . κατεργάζομαι

κατειργάσθαι, perf. infin.—A. B. Ln. Tdf. } id.
κατεργάσασθαι, Rec. Gr. Sch. (1 Pe. 4. 3) }

κατειργάσθη, 3 pers. sing. aor. 1, ind. pass. . id.

κατείχετο, 3 pers. sing. imperf. pass. . κατέχω

κατειχόμεθα, 1 pers. pl. imperf. pass. . . id.

κατεῖχον, 3 pers. pl. imperf. act. (§ 13. rem. 4) id.

κατεκάη, 3 pers. sing. aor. 2, pass. (§ 24. rem. 11) κατακαίω

κατέκαιον, 3 pers. pl. imperf. act. . . id.

κατέκειτο, 3 pers. sing. imperf. . . κατάκειμαι

κατέκλασε, 3 pers. sing. aor. 1, ind. (§ 22. rem. 2) κατακλάω

κατέκλεισα, 1 pers. sing. aor. 1, ind. act. . κατακλείω

κατέκλεισε, 3 pers. sing. aor. 1, ind. act. . id.

κατεκληροδότησε,[i] 3 pers. s. aor. 1, ind. κατακληροδοτέω

κατεκληρονόμησε, 3 pers. s. aor. 1, ind. —A. B. C. D. Gr. Sch. Tdf. } κατακληρονομέω
κατεκληροδότησε, Rec. (Ac. 13. 19) }

κατεκλίθη, 3 pers. sing. aor. 1, pass.—Al. Ln. Tdf. . . . . } κατακλίνω
ἀνεκλίθη, Rec. Gr. Sch. (Lu. 7. 36) }

κατεκρίθη, 3 pers. sing. aor. 1, pass. (§ 27. rem. 3) κατακρίνω

κατέκριναν, 3 pers. pl. aor. 1, ind. act. . . id.

κατέκρινε, 3 pers. sing. aor. 1, ind. act. . id.

κατέλαβε, 3 pers. sing. aor. 2, ind. act. καταλαμβάνω

---

[a] Ac. 13. 41. [b] Phi. 2. 10. [c] Lu. 16. 24. [d] 2 Co. 12. 16. [e] Lu. 10. 34. [f] Mar. 1. 36. [g] Ac. 21. 32. [h] Ac. 17. 16. [i] Ac. 13. 19.

κατελαβόμην, 1 pers. sing. aor. 2, mid.—Al. Ln. Tdf. . . . . } καταλαμβάνω
καταλαβόμενος, R. Gr. Sch. (Ac. 25. 25)

κατελείφθη, 3 pers. sing. aor. 1, pass. (§ 23 rem. 4) . . . . . καταλείπω

κατελήφθην, 1 pers. sing. aor. 1, ind. pass. (§ 36. rem. 2) . . . . . καταλαμβάνω

κατελθεῖν, aor. 2, infin. (§ 36. rem. 1) . κατέρχομαι

κατελθόντες, nom. pl. masc. part. aor. 2 . id.

κατελθόντων, gen. pl. masc. part. aor. 2 . id.

κατελθών, nom. sing. masc. part. aor. 2 . id.

κατέλιπε, 3 pers. sing. aor. 2, ind. act. (§ 24. rem. 9) . . . . . καταλείπω

κατέλιπον, 1 pers. sing. and 3 pers. pl. aor. 2, ind. act. . . . . . id.

κατέλυσα, 1 pers. sing. aor. 1, ind. act. . καταλύω

κατέναντι, adv. (κατά & ἔναντι) *over against, opposite to*, Mar. 11. 2; 12. 41; 13. 3; ὁ, ἡ, τὸ, κατέναντι, *opposite*, Lu. 19. 30; *before, in the presence of, in the sight of*, Ro. 4. 17. LXX.

κατενάρκησα, 1 pers. sing. aor. 1, ind. . καταναρκάω

κατένευσαν,[a] 3 pers. pl. aor. 1, ind. . κατανεύω

κατενεχθείς, nom. sing. masc. part. aor. 1, pass. (§ 36. rem. 1) . . . . . καταφέρω

κατενόησα, 1 pers. sing. aor. 1, ind. . κατανοέω

κατενόουν, 1 pers. sing. and 3 pers. pl. imperf. id.

κατενύγησαν,[b] 3 pers. pl. aor. 2, ind. pass. (§ 26. rem. 3) . . . . . κατανύσσω

κατενώπιον, adv. or prep. (κατά & ἐνώπιον) *in the presence of, in the sight of*, 2 Co. 2. 17; 12. 19; Ep. 1. 4. LXX.

κατεξουσιάζουσι, 3 pers. pl. pres. ind. . κατεξουσιάζω

κατεξουσιάζω], fut. άσω, (§ 26. rem. 1) (κατά & ἐξουσιάζω) *to exercise lordship over, domineer over*, Mat. 20. 25; Mar. 10. 42. N.T.

κατεπατήθη, 3 pers. sing. aor. 1, pass. (§ 17. tab. Q) . . . . . καταπατέω

κατέπαυσαν, 3 pers. pl. aor. 1, ind. act. . καταπαύω

κατέπαυσε, 3 pers. sing. aor. 1, ind. act. . id.

κατεπέστησαν,[c] 3 pers. pl. aor. 2, ind. . κατεφίστημι

κατέπιε, 3 pers. sing. aor. 2, ind. act. (§ 37. rem. 1) . . . . . . καταπίνω

κατέπλευσαν,[d] 3 pers. pl. aor. 1, ind. (§ 35. rem. 3) . . . . . καταπλέω

κατεπόθη, 3 pers. sing. aor. 1, ind. pass. (§ 37. rem. 1) . . . . . καταπίνω

κατεπόθησαν, 3 pers. pl. aor. 1, ind. pass. καταπίνω

κατεργάζεσθαι, pres. infin. . . κατεργάζομαι

κατεργάζεσθε, 2 pers. pl. pres. imper. . id.

κατεργάζεται, 3 pers. sing. pres. ind. . . id.

κατεργάζομαι, fut. άσομαι, (κατά & ἐργάζομαι) *to work out; to effect, produce, bring out as a result*, Ro. 4. 15; 5. 3; 7. 13; 2 Co. 4. 17, 7. 10; Phi. 2. 12; 1 Pe. 4. 3; Ja. 1. 3; *to work, practise, realise in practice*, Ro. 1. 27; 2. 9, et al.; *to work or mould into fitness*, 2 Co. 5. 5; *to despatch, subdue*, Ep. 6. 13.

κατεργαζομένη, nom. sing. fem. part. pres. κατεργάζομαι

κατεργαζόμενοι, nom. pl. masc. part. pres. id.

κατεργαζομένου, gen. sing. masc. part. pres. id.

κατεργασάμενοι, nom. pl. masc. part. aor. 1 id.

κατεργασάμενον, acc. sing. masc. part. aor. 1 id.

κατεργασάμενος, nom. sing. masc. part. aor. 1 id.

κατεργάσασθαι, aor. 1, infin. . . id.

κατέρχομαι], fut. ελεύσομαι, aor. 2, κατῆλθον, (§ 36. rem. 1) (κατά & ἔρχομαι) *to come or go down*, Lu. 4. 31; 9. 37; Ac. 8. 5; 9. 32, et al., *to land at, touch at*, Ac. 18. 22; 27. 5.

κατερχομένη, nom. sing. fem. part. pres. κατέρχομαι

κατέσεισε, 3 pers. sing. aor. 1, ind. act. . κατασείω

κατεσθίει, 3 pers. sing. pres. ind. act. . κατεσθίω

κατεσθίετε, 2 pers. pl. pres. ind. act. . . id.

κατεσθίοντες, nom. pl. masc. part. pres. act. id.

κατεσθίουσι, 3 pers. pl. pres. ind. act. . id.

κατεσθίω], fut. καθέδομαι, and καταφάγομαι, aor. 2, κατέφᾰγον, (§ 36. rem. 1) (κατά & ἐσθίω) *to eat up, devour*, Mat. 13. 4, et al.; *to consume*, Re. 11. 5, *to expend, squander*, Lu. 15. 30; met. *to make a prey of, plunder*, Mat. 23. 13; Mar. 12. 40; Lu. 20. 47; 2 Co. 11. 20; *to vex, injure*, Gal. 5. 15

κατεσκαμμένα, acc. pl. neut. part. perf. pass. κατασκάπτω

κατέσκαψαν, 3 pers. pl. aor. 1, ind. act. id.

κατεσκεύασε, 3 pers. sing. aor. 1, ind. act. κατασκευάζω

κατεσκευάσθη, 3 pers. sing. aor. 1, ind. pass. id.

κατεσκευασμένον, acc. s. masc. part. perf. pass. id.

κατεσκευασμένων, gen. pl. part. perf. pass. id.

κατεσκήνωσε, 3 pers. sing. aor. 1, ind. . κατασκηνόω

κατεστάθησαν, 3 pers. pl. aor. 1, pass. (§ 29. rem. 6) καθίστημι

κατεσταλμένους, acc. pl. masc. part. perf. pass. (§ 27. rem. 3) . . . . καταστέλλω

[a] Lu. 5. 7. [b] Ac. 2. 37. [c] Ac. 18. 12. [d] Lu. 8. 26.

κατέστησας, 2 pers. s. aor. 1, ind. act. ((§ 29. tab. X) καθίστημι
κατέστησε, 3 pers. pl. aor. 1, ind. act. . id.
κατέστρεψε, 3 pers. sing. aor. 1, ind. act. . καταστρέφω
κατεστρώθησαν,[a] 3 pers. pl. aor. 1. ind. pass. καταστρώννυμι
κατεσφραγισμένον,[b] acc. sing. neut. part. perf. pass. . . . . καταασφραγίζω
κατευθῦναι, aor. 1, infin. act. . . κατευθύνω
κατευθύναι, 3 pers. sing. aor. 1, opt. act. . id.
κατευθύνω], fut. υνῶ, aor. 1, ῦνα, (§ 27. rem. 1. a. f) (κατά & εὐθύνω, fr. εὐθύς, *straight*) *to make straight; to direct, guide aright*, Lu. 1. 79; 1 Thes. 3. 11; 2 Thes. 3. 5.
κατευλογέω, ῶ], fut. ήσω, (κατά & εὐλογέω) *to bless*, v.r. Mar. 10. 16.
κατέφαγε, 3 pers. sing. aor. 2, ind. . . κατεσθίω
κατέφαγον, 1 pers. sing. aor. 2, ind. . . id.
κατεφθαρμένοι, nom. pl. masc. part. perf. pass. (§ 27. rem. 3) . . . καταφθείρω
κατεφίλει, 3 pers. sing. imperf. act. . καταφιλέω
κατεφίλησε, 3 pers. sing. aor. 1, ind. act. . id.
κατεφίλουν, 3 pers. pl. imperf. act. . . id.
κατεφίστημι], intrans. aor. 2, κατεπέστην, (§ 29. tab. X) (κατά & ἐφίστημι) *to come upon suddenly, rush upon, assault*, Ac. 18. 12. N.T.
κατέφυγον, 3 pers. pl. aor. 2, ind. (§ 24. rem. 9) καταφεύγω
κατέχεε, 3 pers. sing. aor. 1, ind. (§ 36. rem. 1) καταχέω
κατέχειν, pres. infin. act. . . . κατέχω
κατέχετε, 2 pers. pl. pres. ind. and imper. act. id.
κατέχον, acc. sing. neut. part. pres. act. . id.
κατέχοντες, nom. pl. masc. part. pres. act. . id.
κατεχόντων, gen. pl. masc. part. pres. act. . id.
κατέχουσι, 3 pers. pl. pres. ind. act. . id.
κατέχω], fut. καθέξω, and κατασχήσω, imperf. κατεῖχον, aor. 2, κατέσχον, (§ 36. rem. 4) (κατά & ἔχω) *to hold down; to detain, retain*, Lu. 4. 42; Philem. 13; *to hinder, restrain*, 2 Thes. 2. 6, 7; *to hold downright, hold in a firm grasp, to have in full and secure possession*, 1 Co. 7. 30; 2 Co. 6. 10; *to come into full possession of, seize upon*, Mat. 21. 38; *to keep, retain*, 1 Thes. 5. 21; *to occupy*, Lu. 14. 9; met. *to hold fast* mentally, *retain*, Lu. 8. 15; 1 Co. 11. 2; 15. 2; *to maintain*, He. 3. 6, 14; 10. 23; intrans. a nautical term, *to land, touch*, Ac. 27. 40; pass. *to be in the grasp of, to be bound by*, Ro. 7. 6; *to be afflicted with*, Jno. 5. 4.

κατάσχεσις, εως, ἡ, (§ 5. tab. E. c) *a possession, thing possessed*, Ac. 7. 5, 45. LXX.

κατέχωμεν, 1 pers. pl. pres. subj. act. . κατέχω
κατέχων, nom. sing. masc. part. pres. act. . id.
κατήγαγον, 1 pers. sing. or 3 pers. pl. aor. 2, ind. act. (§ 13. rem. 7. d) . κατάγω
κατηγγέλη, 3 pers. sing. aor. 2, pass. (§ 27. rem. 4. a) . . καταγγέλλω
κατηγγείλαμεν, 1 pers. pl. aor. 1, ind. act. id.
κατήγγειλαν, 3 pers. pl. aor. 1, ind. act.—Gr. Sch. Tdf. . . . } id.
προκατήγγειλαν, Rec. (Ac. 3. 24) }
κατήγγελλον, 3 pers. pl. imperf. act. . id.
κατηγορεῖν, pres. infin. act. . . . κατηγορέω
κατηγορεῖσθαι, pres. infin. pass. (§ 17. tab. Q) id.
κατηγορεῖται, 3 pers. sing. pres. ind. pass. . id.
κατηγορείτωσαν, 3 pers. pl. pres. imper. act. id.
κατηγορέω, ῶ], fut. ήσω, (§ 16. tab. P) (κατά & ἀγορεύω, *to harangue*) *to speak against, accuse*, Mat. 12. 10; 27. 12; Jno. 5. 45, et al.

κατηγορία, ας, ἡ, (§ 2. tab. B. b, and rem. 2) *an accusation, crimination*, Lu. 6. 7, et al.

κατήγορος, ου, ὁ, (§ 3. tab. C. a) *an accuser*, Jno. 8. 10; Ac. 23. 30, 35; 24. 8, et al.

κατήγωρ, ορος, ὁ, (§ 4. rem. 2. f) *an accuser*, v.r. Re. 12. 10, a barbarous form for κατήγορος.

κατηγορῆσαι, aor. 1, infin. act. . . κατηγορέω
κατηγορήσω, 1 pers. sing. fut. ind. act. . id.
κατηγορήσωσι, 3 pers. pl. aor. 1, subj. act. id.
κατηγορία], ας, ἡ, (§ 2. tab. B. b, and rem. 2) id.
κατηγορίᾳ, dat. sing. . . . . κατηγορία
κατηγορίαν, acc. sing. . . . . id.
κατήγοροι, nom. pl. . . . . κατήγορος
κατηγόροις, dat. pl. . . . . id.
κατήγορος, ου, ὁ, (§ 3. tab. C. a) . . κατηγορέω
κατηγοροῦμεν, 1 pers. pl. pres. ind. act. . id
κατηγορούμενος, nom. s. masc. part. pres. pass. id.
κατηγόρουν, 3 pers. pl. imperf. act. . . id.
κατηγοροῦντες, nom. pl. masc. part. pres. act. id.
κατηγορούντων, gen. pl. masc. part. pres. act. id.
κατηγόρους, acc. pl. . . . . κατήγορος
κατηγοροῦσι, 3 pers. pl. pres. ind. act. . κατηγορέω
κατηγορῶν, nom. sing. masc. part. pres. act. . id.
κατηγωνίσαντο,[c] 3 pers. pl. aor. 1, ind. καταγωνίζομαι

[a] 1 Co. 10. 5. [b] Re. 5. 1. [c] He. 11. 33.

κατήγωρ, ορος, ὁ—A. Gr. Sch. Tdf. } κατηγορέω
κατήγορος, Rec. (Re. 12. 10) }

κατῆλθε, 3 pers. sing. aor. 2, ind. . . κατέρχομαι

κατήλθομεν, 1 pers. pl. aor. 2, ind. . . id.

κατῆλθον, 3 pers. pl. aor. 2, ind. . . id.

κατηλλάγημεν, 1 pers. pl. aor. 2, ind. pass. (§ 26. rem. 3) . . . καταλλάσσω

κατήνεγκα, 1 pers. s. aor. 1, ind. (§ 36. rem. 1) καταφέρω

κατήντηκε, 3 pers. sing. perf. ind.—B. Ln. Tdf. } καταντάω
κατήντησε, Rec. Gr. Sch. (1 Co. 10. 11) }

κατηντήσαμεν, 1 pers. pl. aor. 1, ind. . id.

κατήντησαν, 3 pers. pl. aor. 1, ind. . . id.

κατήντησε, 3 pers. sing. aor. 1, ind. . id.

κατηξιώθησαν, 3 pers. pl. aor. 1, ind. pass. (§ 21. tab. U) . . . . καταξιόω

κατηραμένοι, nom. pl. masc. part. perf. pass. καταράομαι

κατηράσω, 2 pers. s. aor. 1, ind. (§ 15. rem. 3. b) id.

κατηργήθημεν, 1 pers. pl. aor. 1, ind. pass. καταργέω

κατηργήθητε, 2 pers. pl. aor. 1, ind. pass. . id.

κατήργηκα, 1 pers. sing. perf. ind. act. . id.

κατήργηται, 3 pers. sing. perf. ind. pass. . id.

κατηριθμημένος,[a] nom. s. masc. part. perf. pass. καταριθμέω

κατηρτίσθαι, perf. infin. pass. . . . καταρτίζω

κατηρτισμένα, acc. pl. neut. part. perf. pass. id.

κατηρτισμένοι, nom. pl. masc. part. perf. pass. id.

κατηρτισμένος, nom. sing. masc. part. perf. pass. id.

κατηρτίσω, 2 pers. sing. aor. 1, ind. mid. (§ 15. rem. 3. b) . . . . id.

κατῃσχύνθην, 1 pers. sing. aor. 1, ind. pass. (§ 13. rem. 2) . . . καταισχύνω

κατῃσχύνοντο, 3 pers. pl. imperf. pass. . id.

κατηυλόγει, 3 pers. sing. imperf.—B. Tdf. } κατευλογέω
ηὐλόγει, Rec. Gr. . . . }
εὐλόγει, Ln. Sch. (Mar. 10. 16) . }

κατήφεια], ας, ἡ, (§ 2. tab. B. b, and rem. 2) (κατηφής, *having a downcast look*, κατά & φάος) *dejection, sorrow*.

κατήφειαν,[b] acc. sing. . . . . κατήφεια

κατηχέω, ῶ], fut. ήσω, (§ 16. tab. P) (κατά & ἠχέω) pr. *to sound in the ears, make the ears ring; to instruct orally, to instruct, inform*, 1 Co. 14. 19; pass. *to be taught, be instructed*, Lu. 1. 4; Ro. 2. 18; Gal. 6. 6; *to be made acquainted*, Ac. 18. 25; *to receive information, hear report*, Ac. 21. 21, 24. L.G.

κατηχήθης, 2 pers. sing. aor. 1, ind. pass. . κατηχέω

κατηχήθησαν, 3 pers. pl. aor. 1, ind. pass. . id.

κατηχημένος, nom. sing. masc. part. perf. pass. κατηχέω

κατήχηνται, 3 pers. pl. perf. ind. pass. . id.

κατηχήσω, 1 pers. sing. aor. 1, subj. act. . id.

κατήχθημεν, 1 pers. pl. aor. 1, ind. pass. (§ 23. rem. 4) . . . . κατάγω

κατηχούμενος, nom. sing. masc. part. pres. pass. κατηχέω

κατηχοῦντι, dat. sing. masc. part. pres. act. . id.

κατιόω, ῶ], fut. ώσω, (§ 20. tab. T) perf. pass. κατίωμαι, (κατά & ἰός) *to cover with rust*; pass. *to rust, become rusty or tarnished*. L.G.

κατίσχυον, 3 pers. pl. imperf. . . κατισχύω

κατισχύσουσι, 3 pers. pl. fut. ind. . . id.

κατισχύω], fut. ύσω, (§ 13. tab. M) (κατά & ἰσχύω) *to overpower*, Mat. 16. 18; absol. *to predominate, get the upper hand*, Lu. 23. 23. (ῡ).

κατίωται,[c] 3 pers. sing. perf. pass. (§ 21. tab. U) κατιόω

κατοικεῖ, 3 pers. sing. pres. ind. . . κατοικέω

κατοικεῖν, pres. infin. . . . . id.

κατοικεῖς, 2 pers. sing. pres. ind. . . id.

κατοικεῖτε, 2 pers. pl. pres. ind. . . id.

κατοικέω, ῶ], fut. ήσω, (§ 16. tab. P) (κατά & οἰκέω) trans. *to inhabit*, Ac. 1. 19, et al.; absol. *to have an abode, dwell*, Lu. 13. 4, Ac. 11. 29, et al.; *to take up or find an abode*, Ac. 7. 2, et al.; *to indwell*, Ep. 3. 17; Ja. 4. 5, et al.

κατοίκησις, εως, ἡ, (§ 5. tab. E. c) *an abode, dwelling, habitation*, Mar. 5. 3.

κατοικητήριον, ου, τό, (§ 3. tab. C. c) the same as the preceding, Ep. 2. 22; Re. 18. 2.

κατοικία, ας, ἡ, (§ 2. tab. B. b, and rem. 2) *habitation*, i.q. κατοίκησις, Ac. 17. 26. L.G.

κατοικῆσαι, aor. 1, infin. . . . κατοικέω

κατοικήσαντι, dat. sing. masc. part. aor. 1—Gr. Sch. Tdf. . . . } id.
κατοικοῦντι, Rec. Ln. (Mat. 23. 21) . }

κατοικήσας, nom. sing. masc. part. aor. 1 . id.

κατοίκησιν,[d] acc. sing. . . . . κατοίκησις

κατοίκησις], εως, ἡ, (§ 5. tab. E. c) . . κατοικέω

κατοικητήριον, ου, τό, (§ 3. tab. C. c) . id.

κατοικία], ας, ἡ, (§ 2. tab. B. b, and rem. 2) . id.

κατοικίας,[e] gen. sing. . . . . κατοικία

κατοικοῦντας, acc. pl. masc. part. pres. . . κατοικέω

κατοικοῦντες, nom. pl. masc. part. pres. . id.

κατοικοῦντι, dat. sing. masc. part. pres. . id.

κατοικούντων, gen. pl. masc. part. pres. . id.

[a] Ac. 1. 17. [b] Ja. 4. 9. [c] Ja. 5. 3. [d] Mar. 5. 3 [e] Ac. 17. 26.

κατοικοῦσι, dat. pl. masc. part. pres. . κατοικέω

κατοικῶν, nom. sing. masc. part. pres. . . id.

κατοπτριζόμενοι,[a] nom. pl. m. part. pres. mid. κατοπτρίζω

κατοπτρίζω], fut. ίσω, (§ 26. rem. 1) (κάτοπτρον, *a mirror*) *to show in a mirror; to present a clear and correct image of* a thing; mid. *to have presented in a mirror, to have a clear image presented*, or, *to reflect*. L.G.

κατόρθωμα], ατος, τό, (§ 4. tab. D. c) (κατορθόω, *to set upright, accomplish happily*, fr. κατά & ὀρθόω, *to make straight*) *anything happily and successfully accomplished; a beneficial and worthy deed*. L.G.

κατορθωμάτων,[b] gen. pl. . . . . κατόρθωμα

κάτω, adv. and prep. (κατά) *down, downwards*, Mat. 4. 6; Lu. 4. 9; *beneath, below, under*, Mat. 27. 51; Mar. 14. 66, et al.; ὁ, ἡ, τὸ, κάτω, *what is below, earthly*, Jno. 8. 23.

κατώτερος, α, ον, (comparat. from κάτω) *lower*, Ep. 4. 9.

κατωτέρω, adv. (compar. of κάτω) *lower, farther down*; of time, *under*, Mat. 2. 16.

κατῴκησε, 3 pers. sing. aor. 1, ind. (§ 13. rem. 2) κατοικέω

κατώτερα,[c] acc. pl. neut. . . . . κατώτερος

κατώτερος], α, ον, (§ 7. rem. 1) . . κάτω

κατωτέρω,[d] adv. . . . . . . id.

Καῦδα, indecl. prop. name of an island—B. Ln. Tdf.

Κλαύδην, Rec. Gr. Sch. (Ac. 27. 16).

καυθήσωμαι, 1 pers. sing. fut. subj. pass. (an unusual form) . . . καίω

καῦμα, ατος, τό, (§ 4. tab. D. c) . . id.

καυματίζω], fut. ίσω, (§ 26. rem. 1) . id.

καυματίσαι, aor. 1, infin. act. . . . καυματίζω

καῦσιν,[e] acc. sing. . . . . καῦσις

καῦσις], εως, ἡ, (§ 5. tab. E. c) . . καίω

καυσόομαι, οῦμαι], (§ 21. tab U) . . id.

καυσούμενα, nom. pl. neut. part. pres. . καυσόομαι

καυστηριάζω], v.r. same signif. as . . καυτηριάζω

καύσων, ωνος, ὁ, (§ 4. rem. 2. e) . . καίω

καύσωνα, acc. sing. . . . καύσων

καύσωνι, dat. sing. . . . . . id.

καυτηριάζω], fut. άσω, (§ 26. rem. 1) . καίω

καυχᾶσαι, 2 pers. sing. pres. ind. for καυχᾷ, a later form combining the inflexions of a contract verb and a verb in μι } καυχάομαι

καυχᾶσθαι, pres. infin. . . . . καυχάομαι

καυχᾶσθε, 2 pers. pl. pres. ind. . . id.

καυχάσθω, 3 pers. sing. pres. imper. . . id.

καυχάομαι, ῶμαι], fut. ήσομαι, aor. 1, ἐκαυχησάμην, perf. κεκαύχημαι, (§ 19. tab. S) *to glory, boast*, Ro. 2. 17. 23; ὑπέρ τινος, *to boast of* a person or thing, *to undertake a laudatory testimony to*, 2 Co. 12. 5; *to rejoice, exult*, Ro. 5. 2, 3, 11, et al.

καύχημα, ατος, τό, (§ 4. tab. D. c) *a glorying, boasting*, 1 Co. 5. 6; *a ground or matter of glorying or boasting*, Ro. 4. 2; *joy, exultation*, Phi. 1. 26; *laudatory testimony*, 1 Co. 9. 15, 16; 2 Co. 9. 3, et al.

καύχησις, εως, ἡ, (§ 5. tab. E. c) a later equivalent to καύχημαι, Ro. 3. 27; 2 Co. 7. 4, 14; 11. 10, et al.

καύχημα, ατος, τό . . . . . καυχάομαι

καυχήματος, gen. sing. . . . . καύχημα

καυχήσασθαι, aor. 1, infin. . . . καυχάομαι

καυχήσεως, gen. sing. . . . . καύχησις

καυχήσηται, 3 pers. sing. aor. 1, subj. . καυχάομαι

καύχησιν, acc. sing. . . . . καύχησις

καύχησις, εως, ἡ, (§ 5. tab. E. c) . . καυχάομαι

καυχήσομαι, 1 pers. sing. fut. ind. . id.

καυχησόμεθα, 1 pers. pl. fut. ind. . . id.

καυχήσωμαι, 1 pers. sing. aor. 1, subj. . id.

καυχήσωνται, 3 pers. pl. aor. 1, subj. . id.

καυχῶμαι, 1 pers. sing. pres. ind. . . id.

καυχώμεθα, 1 pers. pl. pres. ind. . . id.

καυχώμενοι, nom. pl. masc. part. pres. . id.

καυχώμενος, nom. sing. masc. part. pres. . id.

καυχωμένους, acc. pl. masc. part. pres. . id.

καυχῶνται, 3 pers. pl. pres. ind. . . id.

Κεγχρεαί], ῶν, αἱ, *Cenchreæ*, the port of Corinth on the Saronic Gulf.

Κεγχρεαῖς, dat. . . . . . . Κεγχρεαί

κέδρος], ου, ἡ, (§ 3. tab. C. b) *a cedar*, Jno. 18. 1, where κέδρων is a false reading for the proper name Κεδρών.

κέδρων, gen. pl.—Rec. . . . . }
Κεδρών, Gr. Sch. Tdf. . . } κέδρος
Κέδρου, D. (Jno. 18. 1) . . }

Κεδρών,[f] ὁ, *Cedron*, a mountain torrent near Jerusalem.

---

a 2 Co. 3. 18. b Ac. 24. 3. c Ep. 4. 9. d Mat. 2. 16 e He. 6. 8. f Jno. 18. 1.

κεῖμαι, fut. κείσομαι, (§ 33. tab. DD) *to lie, to be laid; to recline, to be lying, to have been laid down*, Mat. 28. 6; Lu. 2. 12, et al.; *to have been laid, placed, set*, Mat. 3. 10; Lu. 3. 9; Jno. 2. 6, et al.; *to be situated*, as a city, Mat. 5. 14; Re. 21. 16; *to be in store*, Lu. 12. 19; met. *to be constituted, established* as a law, 1 Ti. 1. 9; in N.T. of persons, *to be specially set, solemnly appointed, destined*, Lu. 2. 34; Phi. 1. 17; 1 Thes. 3. 3; *to lie* under an influence, *to be involved in*, 1 Jno. 5. 19.

κοίτη, ης, ἡ, (§ 2. tab. B. a) *a bed*, Lu. 11. 7; *the* conjugal *bed*, He. 13. 4; meton. *sexual intercourse, concubitus*; hence, *lewdness, whoredom, chambering*, Ro. 13. 13; in N.T. *conception*, Ro. 9. 10.

κοιτών, ῶνος, ὁ, (§ 4. rem. 2. e) *a bed-chamber*, Ac. 12. 20.

κείμεθα, 1 pers. pl. pres. ind. . . . κεῖμαι
κείμενα, acc. pl. neut. part. pres. . . . id.
κείμεναι, nom. pl. fem. part. pres. . . . id.
κειμένη, nom. sing. fem. part. pres. . . . id.
κειμένην, acc. sing. fem. part. pres. . . . id.
κείμενον, acc. sing. masc. and neut. part. pres. id.
κείμενος, nom. sing. masc. part. pres. . . id.
κειράμενος, nom. sing. masc. part. aor. 1, mid. (§ 27. rem. 1. d) . . . κείρω
κείραντος, gen. sing. masc. part. aor. 1, act—A. C. Tdf. . . . . } id.
κείροντος, Rec. Gr. Sch. Ln. (Ac. 8. 32) }
κείρασθαι, aor. 1, infin. mid. . . . id.
κειράσθω, 3 pers. sing. aor. 1, imper. mid. id.
κειρία], ας, ἡ, (§ 2. tab. B. b, and rem. 2) *a bandage, swath, roller*; in N.T. pl. *grave-clothes*.
κειρίαις,[a] dat. pl. . . . . κειρία
κείροντος, gen. sing. masc. part. pres. act. . κείρω

κείρω], fut. κερῶ, (§ 27. rem. 1. c) aor. 1, mid. ἐκειράμην, *to cut off* the hair, *shear, shave*, Ac. 8. 32; 18. 18; 1 Co. 11. 6, bis.

κέρμα, ατος, τό, (§ 4. tab. D. c) *something clipped small; small change, small pieces of money, coin*, Jno. 2. 15.

κερματιστής, οῦ, ὁ, (§ 2. tab. B. c) *a money changer*, Jno. 2. 14. N.T.

κεῖται, 3 pers. sing. pres. ind. . . . κεῖμαι

κεκαθαρισμένους, acc. pl. masc. part. perf. pass. —Al. Ln. Tdf. . . . } καθαρίζω
κεκαθαρμένους, Rec. Gr. Sch. (He. 10. 2) }
κεκαθαρμένους, acc. pl. masc. part. perf. pass. (§ 27. rem. 3) . . . καθαίρω
κεκάθικε, 3 pers. sing. perf. ind. . . . καθίζω
κεκαλυμμένον, nom. sing. neut. part. perf. pass. καλύπτω
κεκαυμένῳ, dat. sing. neut. part. perf. pass. καίω
κεκαυστηριασμένων, gen. pl. part. perf. p. —A. Ln. Tdf. . . } καυστηριάζω
κεκαυτηριασμένων, Rec. Gr. Sch. (1 Ti. 4. 2) . . . }
κεκαυτηριασμένων,[b] gen. pl. part. perf. pass. καυτηριάζω
κεκαύχημαι, 1 pers. sing. perf. ind. . . καυχάομαι
κεκένωται, 3 pers. sing. perf. ind. pass. (§ 21 tab. U) . . . . . . κενόω
κεκερασμένου, gen. sing. masc. part. perf. pass. (§ 36. rem. 5) . . . κεράννυμι
κεκλεισμένον, acc. sing. neut. part. perf. pass. κλείω
κεκλεισμένων, gen. pl. part. perf. pass. . id.
κέκλεισται, 3 pers. sing. perf. ind. pass. (§ 22. rem. 5, 6) . . . . . id.
κέκληκε, 3 pers. s. perf. ind. act. (§ 22. rem. 4) καλέω
κεκληκότι, dat. sing. masc. part. perf. act. . id.
κεκληκώς, nom. sing. masc. part. perf. act. id.
κεκλημένοι, nom. pl. masc. part. perf. pass. id.
κεκλημένοις, dat. pl. masc. part. perf. pass. id.
κεκλημένος, nom. sing. masc. part. perf. pass. id.
κεκλημένους, acc. pl. masc. part. perf. pass. id.
κεκλημένων, gen. pl. part. perf. pass. . id.
κεκληρονόμηκε, 3 pers. sing. perf. ind. κληρονομέω
κέκληται, 3 pers. sing. perf. ind. pass.—B. Ln. Tdf. . . . . } καλέω
ἐκλήθη, Rec. Gr. Sch. (1 Co. 7. 18) . }
κέκλικε, 3 pers. sing. perf. ind. act. (§ 13. rem. 6. c) κλίνω
κέκμηκας, 2 pers. sing. perf. ind. (§ 27. rem. 2. d) κάμνω
κεκοιμημένων, gen. pl. part. perf. pass. . κοιμάω
κεκοίμηται, 3 pers. sing. perf. ind. pass. . id.
κεκοίνωκε, 3 pers. sing. perf. ind. act. . κοινόω
κεκοινωμένους, acc. pl. masc. part. perf. pass. (§ 21. tab. U) . . . id.
κεκοινώνηκε, 3 pers. sing. perf. ind. . . κοινωνέω
κεκονιαμένε, voc. sing. masc. part. perf. pass. κονιάω
κεκονιαμένοις, dat. pl. masc. part. perf. pass. id
κεκοπίακα, 1 pers. sing. perf. ind. (§ 22. rem. 2) κοπιάω
κεκοπίακας, 2 pers. sing. perf. ind. . . id.
κεκοπιάκασι, 3 pers. pl. perf. ind. . . id.
κεκοπιάκατε, 2 pers. pl. perf. ind. . . id.

[a] Jno. 11. 44.

[b] 1 Ti. 4. 2.

κεκοπιακώς, nom. sing. masc. part. perf. . κοπιάω
κεκορεσμένοι, nom. pl. masc. part. perf. pass. (§ 36. rem. 5) . . . . κορέννυμι
κεκοσμημένην, acc. sing. fem. part. perf. pass. κοσμέω
κεκοσμημένοι, nom. pl. masc. part. perf. pass. id.
κεκοσμημένον, acc. sing. masc. part. perf. pass. id.
κεκόσμηται, 3 pers. sing. perf. ind. pass. . id.
κέκραγε, 3 pers. sing. perf. 2. ind. (§ 26. rem. 2) κράζω
κεκράξονται, 3 pers. pl. fut. 3, (§ 14. rem. 1. g) id.
κεκρατηκέναι, perf. infin. act. . . . κρατέω
κεκράτηνται, 3 pers. pl. perf. ind. pass. . id.
κέκρικα, 1 pers. sing. perf. ind. act. (§ 13. rem. 6. c) κρίνω
κεκρίκατε, 2 pers. pl. perf. ind. act. . . id.
κεκρίκει, 3 pers. sing. pluperf. act.—A. B. C. D. Gr. Tdf. . . . . } id.
ἔκρινε, Rec. Sch. (Ac. 20. 16) . }
κέκρικε, 3 pers. sing. perf. ind. act. . id.
κεκριμένα, acc. pl. neut. part. perf. pass. . id.
κέκριται, 3 pers. sing. perf. ind. pass. . id.
κεκρυμμένα, acc. pl. n. pt. pf. pass. (§ 23. r. 7) κρύπτω
κεκρυμμένον, nom. sing. neut. part. perf. pass. id.
κεκρυμμένος, nom. sing. masc. part. perf. pass. id.
κεκρυμμένου, gen. sing. neut. part. perf. pass. id.
κεκρυμμένῳ, dat. sing. masc. part. perf. pass. id.
κέκρυπται, 3 pers. sing. perf. ind. pass. id.
κεκυρωμένην, acc. sing. fem. part. perf. pass. (§ 21. tab. U) . . . . . κυρόω
κελεύεις, 2 pers. sing. pres. ind. . . κελεύω
κελεύσαντες, nom. pl. masc. part. aor. 1 . id.
κελεύσαντος, gen. sing. masc. part. aor. 1 id.
κελεύσας, nom. sing. masc. part. aor. 1 . id.
κέλευσμα], ατος, τό, (§ 4. tab. D. c) . . id.
κελεύσματι,[a] dat. sing. . . . κέλευσμα
κέλευσον, 2 pers. sing. aor. 1, imper. . . κελεύω

κελεύω], fut. εύσω, aor. 1, ἐκέλευσα, (§ 13. tab. M) (κέλω, κέλομαι, idem) *to order, command, direct, bid*, Mat. 8. 18; 14. 19, 28, et al.

κέλευσμα, ατος, τό, *a word of command; a mutual cheer;* hence, in N.T. *a loud shout, an arousing outcry*, 1 Thes. 4. 16.

κενά, acc. pl. . . . . . . κενός
κενέ, voc. sing. masc. . . . . . id.
κενή, nom. sing. fem. . . . . . id.
κενῆς, gen. sing. fem. . . . . . id.
κενοδοξία], ας, ἡ . . . . . κενόδοξος
κενοδοξίαν,[b] acc. sing. . . . . κενοδοξία
κενόδοξοι,[c] nom. pl. masc. . . . . κενόδοξος

κενόδοξος], ου, ὁ, ἡ, (§ 7. rem. 2) (κενός & δόξα) *vainglorious, desirous of vainglory.*

κενοδοξία, ας, ἡ, (§ 2. tab. B. b, and rem. 2) *empty conceit, vainglory.*

κενοῖς, dat. pl. masc. . . . . . κενός
κενόν, acc. sing. m. and nom. and acc. s. neut. id.

κενός, ή, όν, (§ 7. tab. F. a) *empty; having no thing, empty-handed*, Mar. 12. 3; met. *vain, fruitless, void of effect*, Ac. 4. 25; 1 Co. 15. 10; εἰς κενόν, *in vain, to no purpose*, 2 Co. 6. 1, et al.; *hollow, fallacious, false*, Ep. 5. 6; Col. 2. 8; *inconsiderate, foolish*, Ja. 2. 20.

κενόω, ῶ, fut. ώσω, aor. 1, ἐκένωσα, (§ 20. tab. T) *to empty, evacuate;* ἑαυτόν, *to divest one's self of one's prerogatives, abase one's self*, Phi. 2. 7; *to deprive a* thing *of its proper functions*, Ro. 4. 14; 1 Co. 1. 17; *to show to be without foundation, falsify*, 1 Co. 9. 15; 2 Co. 9. 3.

κενῶς, adv. *in vain, to no purpose, unmeaningly*, Ja. 4. 5. L.G.

κενούς, acc. pl. masc. . . . . . κενός
κενοφωνία], ας, ἡ, (§ 2. tab. B. b, and rem. 2) (κενός & φωνή) *vain, empty babbling, vain disputation, fruitless discussion*, 1 Ti. 6. 20; 2 Ti. 2. 16. N.T.
κενοφωνίας, acc. pl. . . . . . κενοφωνία
κενόω, ῶ], fut. ώσω . . . . . κενός
κέντρα, nom. and acc. pl. . . . . . κέντρον
κέντρον, ου, τό, (§ 3. tab. C. c) (κεντέω, *to prick*) *a sharp point; a sting*, Re. 9. 10; *a prick, stimulus, goad*, Ac. 9. 5; 26. 14; met. of death, *destructive power, deadly venom*, 1 Co. 15. 55, 56.
κεντυρίων, ωνος, ὁ, (§ 4. rem. 2. e) (Lat. centurio, fr. centum, *a hundred*) in its original signification, *a commander of a hundred* foot-soldiers, *a centurion*, Mar. 15. 39, 44, 45.
κεντυρίωνα, acc. sing. . . . . . κεντυρίων
κεντυρίωνος, gen. sing. . . . . . id.
κενωθῇ, 3 pers. sing. aor. 1, subj. pass. . κενόω
κενῶς,[d] adv. . . . . κενός
κενώσῃ, 3 pers. sing. aor. 1, subj. act. . κενόω
κεραία, ας, ἡ, (§ 2. tab. B. b, and rem. 2) . κέρας
κεραίαν, acc. sing. . . . . . κεραία
κεράμεύς], έως, ὁ, (§ 5. tab. E. d) . . κέραμος

[a] 1 Thes. 4. 16. [b] Phi. 2. 3. [c] Gal. 5. 26. [d] Ja. 4. 5.

κεραμέως, gen. sing. . . . κεραμεύς
κεραμικά,[a] nom. pl. neut. . . . κεραμικός
κεραμῐκός], ή, όν, (§ 7. tab. F. a) . . κέραμος
κεράμιον, ου, τό, (§ 3. tab. C. a) . . id.

κέρᾰμος], ου, ὁ, (§ 3. tab. C. a) *potter's clay; earthenware; a tile, tiling*, Lu. 5. 19.

κερᾰμεύς, έως, ὁ, *a potter*, Mat. 27. 7. 10; Ro. 9. 21.

κεραμῐκός, ή, όν, *made by a potter, earthen*, Re. 2. 7.

κεράμιον, ίου, τό, (dimin. of κέραμος) *an earthenware vessel, a pitcher, jar*, Mar. 14. 13; Lu. 22. 10.

κεράμων,[b] gen. pl. . . . . κέραμος
κεράννῡμι, or νύω], (κεράω) fut. κεράσω, aor. 1, ἐκέρᾰσα, perf. pass. κέκρᾱμαι, later κεκέρασμαι, (§ 36. rem. 5) *to mix, mingle*, drink; *to prepare* for drinking, Re. 14. 10; 18. 6, bis.

κέρας, ᾰτος, τό, (§ 5. tab. E. j) *a horn*, Re. 5. 6; 12. 3, et al.; *a horn-like projection* at the corners of an altar, Re. 9. 13; from the Heb., *a horn* as a symbol of power, Lu. 1. 69.

κεραία, ας, ἡ, (§ 2. tab. B. b, and rem. 2) pr. *a horn-like projection, a point, extremity*; in N.T. *an apex, or fine point*; as of letters, used for *the minutest part, a tittle*, Mat. 5. 18; Lu. 16. 17.

κεράτιον, ίου, τό, (§ 3. tab. C. c) (dimin. of κέρας) pr. *a little horn*; in N.T. *a pod, the pod of the carob tree, or Ceratonia siliqua* of Linnæus, a common tree in the East and the south of Europe, growing to a considerable size, and producing long slender pods, with a pulp of a sweetish taste, and several brown shining seeds like beans, sometimes eaten by the poorer people in Syria and Palestine, and commonly used for fattening swine, Lu. 15. 16.

κεράσατε, 2 pers. pl. aor. 1, imper. . . κεράννυμι
κέρατα, nom. and acc. pl. . . . κέρας
κεράτιον], ου, τό, (§ 3. tab. D. c) . . id.
κερατίων,[c] gen. pl. . . . . κεράτιον
κεράτων, gen. pl. . . . . . κέρας
κερδαίνω], fut. δανῶ, (§ 27. rem. 1. c) . κέρδος
κερδάνω, 1 pers. sing. aor. 1, subj.—Al. Ln. Tdf. . . . . } κερδαίνω
κερδήσω, Rec. Gr. Sch. (1 Co. 9. 21) }
κέρδη, nom. pl. . . . . . . κέρδος
κερδηθήσονται, 3 pers. pl. fut. ind. pass.—A. B. Ln. Tdf. . . . } κερδαίνω
κερδηθήσωνται, R. Gr. Sch. (1 Pe. 3. 1) }
κερδηθήσωνται, 3 pers. pl. fut. subj. pass. (an unusual form) . . . id.
κερδῆσαι, aor. 1, infin. act. . . . id.
κερδήσας, nom. sing. masc. part. aor. 1, act. id
κερδήσῃ, 3 pers. sing. aor. 1, subj. act. . id.
κερδήσω, 1 pers. sing. aor. 1, subj. act. . id.
κερδήσωμεν, 1 pers. pl. aor. 1, subj. act. . id

κέρδος, εος, τό, (§ 5. tab. E. b) *gain, profit*, Phi. 1. 21; 3. 7; Tit. 1. 11.

κερδαίνω, fut. ανῶ, κερδήσω & ομαι, aor. 1, ἐκέρδησα, *to gain* as a matter of profit, Mat. 25. 17, et al.; *to win, acquire possession of* Mat. 16. 26; *to profit in the avoidance of, to avoid*, Ac. 27. 21; in N.T. Χριστόν, *to win* Christ, *to become possessed of* the privileges of the Gospel, Phi. 3. 8; *to win over* from estrangement, Mat. 18. 15; *to win over* to embrace the Gospel, 1 Co. 9. 19, 20, 21, 22; 1 Pe. 3. 1; absol. *to make gain*, Ja. 4. 13.

κέρδους, gen. sing. . . . . . κέρδος
κέρμα],[d] ατος, τό, (§ 4. tab. D. c) . . κείρω
κερματιστάς,[e] acc. pl. . . . κερματιστής
κερματιστής], οῦ, ὁ, (§ 2. tab. B. c) . κείρω
κεφαλαί, nom. pl. . . . . . κεφαλή
κεφάλαιον, ου, τό, (§ 3. tab. C. c) . . id.
κεφαλαίου, gen. sing. . . . . κεφάλαιον
κεφαλαιόω, ῶ], fut. ώσω, (§ 20. tab. T) . κεφαλή
κεφαλάς, acc. pl. . . . . . id.

κεφᾰλή, ῆς, ἡ, (§ 2. tab. B. a) *the head*, Mat. 5. 36; 6. 17, et al.; *the head, top*; κεφαλὴ γωνίας, *the head of the corner, the chief corner-stone*, Mat. 21. 42; Lu. 20. 17; met. *the head, superior, chief, principal, one to whom others are subordinate*, 1 Co. 11. 3; Ep. 1. 22, et al.

κεφάλαιον, ου, τό, *a sum total; a sum of money, capital*, Ac. 22. 28; *the crowning or ultimate point* to preliminary matters, He. 8. 1.

[a] Re. 2. 27. [b] Lu. 5. 19. [c] Lu. 15. 16. [d] Jno. 2. 15. [e] Jno. 2. 14.

κεφαλαιόω, ῶ, fut. ώσω, *to sum up;* but in N.T. equiv. to κεφαλίζω, *to wound on the head,* Mar. 12. 4.

κεφαλίς, ίδος, ἡ, (§ 4. rem. 2. c) (dimin. of κεφαλή) in N.T. *a roll, volume, division* of a book, He. 10. 7.

κεφαλῇ, dat. sing. . . . . . κεφαλή
κεφαλήν, acc. sing. . . . . id.
κεφαλῆς, gen. sing. . . . . id.
κεφαλίδι,[a] dat. sing. . . . . κεφαλίς
κεφαλίς], ίδος, ἡ . . . . . κεφαλή
κεφαλῶν, gen. pl. . . . . id.
κεχάρισμαι, 1 pers. sing. perf. ind. . . χαρίζομαι
κεχάρισται, 3 pers. sing. perf. ind. . . id.
κεχαριτωμένη, nom. sing. fem. part. perf. pass. (§ 21. tab. U) . . . . χαριτόω
κέχρημαι, 1 pers. sing. perf. ind. pass.—Gr. Sch. Tdf. . . . . } χράω
ἐχρησάμην, Rec. (1 Co. 9. 15) . }
κεχρηματισμένον, nom. s. neut. part. perf. pass. χρηματίζω
κεχρηματισμένος, nom. sing. masc. part. perf. pass.—D. . . . . } id.
κεχρηματισμένον, Rec. Gr. Sch. Tdf. (Lu. 2. 26) . . . }
κεχρημάτισται, 3 pers. sing. perf. ind. pass. id.
κεχρυσωμένη, nom. sing. fem. part. perf. pass. χρυσόω
κεχωρισμένος, nom. sing. masc. part. perf. pass. χωρίζω
κημόω, ῶ], fut. ώσω, (κημός, *a curb, bridle, muzzle*) *to muzzle,* v.r.
κημώσεις, 2 pers. sing. fut. ind.—D. . } κημόω
φιμώσεις, Rec. Gr. Sch. Tdf. (1 Co. 9. 9) }
κῆνσον, acc. sing. . . . . . κῆνσος
κῆνσος], ου, ὁ, (§ 3. tab. C. a) (Lat. census) *a census, assessment, enumeration of the people and a valuation of their property;* in N.T. *tribute, tax,* Mat. 17. 25; *poll-tax,* Mat. 22. 17, 19; Mar. 12. 14.
κήνσου, gen. sing. . . . . κῆνσος
κῆπον, acc. sing. . . . . . κῆπος

κῆπος, ου, ὁ, (§ 3. tab. C. a) *a garden, any place planted with trees and herbs,* Lu. 13. 19; Jno. 18. 1, 26; 19. 41.

κήπῳ, dat. sing. . . . . . κῆπος
κηπουρός],[b] οῦ, ὁ, (κῆπος & οὖρος, *a watcher*) *a garden-keeper, gardener.*
κηρίον], ου, τό, (§ 3. tab. C. c) (κηρός, *beeswax*) *a honeycomb; a comb filled with honey.*
κηρίου,[c] gen. sing. . . . . . κηρίον
κήρυγμα], ατος, τό, (§ 4. tab. D. c) . κηρύσσω
κηρύγματι, dat. sing. . . . . κήρυγμα
κηρύγματος, gen. sing. . . . id.
κήρυκα, acc. sing. . . . . . κήρυξ
κήρυξ], ῦκος, ὁ . . . . . κηρύσσω
κηρῦξαι, aor. 1, infin. . . . . id.
κηρύξας, nom. sing. masc. part. aor. 1, act. id.
κηρύξατε, 2 pers. pl. aor. 1, imper. act. . id.
κήρυξον, 2 pers. sing. aor. 1, imper. act. . id.
κηρύξουσι, 3 pers. pl. fut. ind. act. . id.
κηρύξω, 1 pers. sing. aor. 1, subj. act. . . id.
κηρύσσει, 3 pers. sing. pres. ind. act. . id.
κηρύσσειν, pres. infin. act. . . . id.
κηρύσσεται, 3 pers. sing. pres. ind. pass. . id.
κηρύσσετε, 2 pers. pl. pres. imper. act. . id.
κηρύσσομεν, 1 pers. pl. pres. ind. act. . id.
κηρύσσοντα, acc. sing. masc. part. pres. act. . id.
κηρύσσοντας, acc. pl. masc. part. pres. act. id.
κηρύσσοντος, gen. sing. masc. part. pres. act. id.
κηρύσσουσι, 3 pers. pl. pres. ind. act. . . id.

κηρύσσω, fut. κηρύξω, aor. 1, ἐκήρυξα, (§ 26. rem. 3) *to publish, proclaim,* as a herald, 1 Co. 9. 27; *to announce openly and publicly,* Mar. 1. 4; Lu. 4. 18; *to noise abroad,* Mar. 1. 45; 7. 36; *to announce* as a matter of doctrine, *inculcate, preach,* Mat. 24. 14; Mar. 1. 38; 13. 10; Ac. 15. 21; Ro. 2. 21, et al.

κήρυγμα, ατος, τό, (§ 4. tab. D. c) *proclamation, proclaiming, public annunciation,* Mat. 12. 41; *public inculcation, preaching,* 1 Co. 2. 4; 15. 14; meton. *what is publicly inculcated, doctrine,* Ro. 16. 25, et al.

κήρυξ, ῦκος, ὁ, (§ 4. rem. 2. b) *a herald, public messenger;* in N.T. *a proclaimer, publisher, preacher,* 1 Ti. 2. 7; 2 Ti. 1. 11; 2 Pe. 2. 5.

κηρυσσων, nom. sing. masc. part. pres. act. κηρύσσω
κηρυχθείς, acc. sing. masc. part. aor. 1, pass. id.
κηρυχθέντος, gen. sing. neut. part. aor. 1, pass. id.
κηρυχθῇ, 3 pers. sing. aor. 1, subj. pass. . id.
κηρυχθῆναι, aor. 1, infin. pass. . . . id.
κηρυχθήσεται, 3 pers. sing. fut. ind. pass. . id.

κῆτος], εος, τό, (§ 5. tab. E. b) *a large fish, sea monster, whale.*

[a] He. 10. 7. [b] Jno. 20. 15. [c] Lu. 24. 42.

κήτους,[a] gen. sing. . . . . . κῆτος
Κηφᾶ, gen. . . . . Κηφᾶς
Κηφᾷ, dat. . . . . . . id.
Κηφᾶν, acc.—A. B. Ln. Sch. Tdf. . } id.
Πέτρον, Rec. Gr. (Gal. 1. 18) . }
Κηφᾶς, ᾶ, ὁ, (§ 2. rem. 4) (Aramæan, כֵּיפָא) *Cephas, Rock*, rendered into Greek by Πέτρος, Jno. 1. 43; 1 Co. 1. 12, et al.
κιβωτόν, acc. sing. . . . . . κιβωτός
κιβωτός, ου, ἡ, (§ 3. tab. C. b) *a chest, coffer; the ark* of the covenant, He. 9. 4; *the ark* of Noah, Mat. 24. 38; Lu. 17. 27, et al.
κιβωτοῦ, gen. sing. . . . . . κιβωτός

κιθάρα, ας, ἡ, (§ 2. tab. B. b) *a lyre*, 1 Co. 14. 7; Re. 5. 8; 14. 2; 15. 2. (ᾰ).

κιθαρίζω, fut. ίσω, (§ 26. rem. 1) *to play on a lyre, to harp*, 1 Co. 14. 7; Re. 14. 2.

κιθάραις, dat. pl. . . . . . κιθάρα
κιθάρας, acc. pl. . . . . . . id.
κιθαρίζω], fut. ίσω . . . . . id.
κιθαριζόμενον, nom. sing. neut. part. pres. pass. κιθαρίζω
κιθαριζόντων, gen. pl. masc. part. pres. act. id.
κιθαρῳδός], οῦ, ὁ, (§ 3. tab. C. a) (κιθάρα & ἀείδω) *one who plays on the lyre and accompanies it with his voice, a harper*, Re. 14. 2; 18. 22.
κιθαρῳδῶν, gen. pl. . . . . . κιθαρῳδός
Κιλικία], ας, ἡ, (§ 2. tab. B. b, and rem. 2) *Cilicia*, a province of Asia Minor.
Κιλικίαν, acc. . . . . . . Κιλικία
Κιλικίας, gen. . . . . . . id.
κινάμωμον,[b] or κιννάμωμον, ου, τό, (§ 3. tab. C. c) *cinnamon*, the aromatic bark of the *laurus cinnamomum*, which grows in Arabia, Syria, etc.
κινδυνεύει, 3 pers. sing. pres. ind. . . κινδυνεύω
κινδυνεύομεν, 1 pers. pl. pres. ind. . . id.
κινδυνεύω], fut. εύσω, (§ 13. tab. M) . κίνδυνος
κινδύνοις, dat. pl. . . . . . id.

κίνδῡνος, ου, ὁ, (§ 3. tab. C. a) *danger, peril*, Ro. 8. 35; 2 Co. 11. 26.

κινδυνεύω, fut. εύσω, *to be in danger or peril*, Lu. 8. 23; Ac. 19. 27, 40; 1 Co. 15. 30.

κῑνέω, ῶ], fut. ήσω, aor. 1, ἐκίνησα, (§ 16. tab. P) (κίω, *to go*) *to set a-going; to move*, Mat. 23. 4; *to excite, agitate*, Ac. 21. 30; 24. 5; *to remove*, Re. 2. 5; 6. 14; in N.T. κεφαλήν, *to shake the head* in derision, Mat. 27. 39; Mar. 15. 29; mid. *to move, possess the faculty of motion, exercise the functions of life*, Ac. 17. 28.

κίνησις, εως, ἡ, (§ 5. tab. E. c) *a moving, motion*, Jno. 5. 3.

κινῆσαι, aor. 1, infin. act. . . . κινέω
κίνησιν,[c] acc. sing. . . . . . κίνησις
κίνησις], εως, ἡ . . . . . . κινέω
κινήσω, 1 pers. sing. fut. ind. act. . . id.
κιννάμωμον, ου, τό, *cinnamon*—A. Tdf.
κινάμωμον, Rec. Gr. Sch. (Re. 18. 13).
κινούμεθα, 1 pers. pl. pres. ind. pass. . κινέω
κινοῦντα, acc. sing. masc. part. pres. act. . id.
κινοῦντες, nom. pl. masc. part. pres. act. . id.
Κίς,[d] ὁ, (Heb. קִישׁ) *Cis*, pr. name, indecl.
κίχρημι], fut. χρήσω, aor. 1, ἔχρησα, (another form of χράω) *to lend*, Lu. 11. 5.
κλάδοι, nom. pl. . . . . . . κλάδος
κλάδοις, dat. pl. . . . . . . id.
κλάδος, ου, ὁ, (§ 3. tab. C. a) . . . κλάω
κλάδους, acc. pl. . . . . . κλάδος
κλάδων, gen. pl. . . . . . . id.
κλαῖε, 2 pers. sing. pres. imper. . . κλαίω
κλαίειν, pres. infin. . . . . . id.
κλαίεις, 2 pers. sing. pres. ind. . . id
κλαίετε, 2 pers. pl. pres. ind. and imper. . id
κλαίοντας, acc. pl. masc. part. pres. . id
κλαίοντες, nom. pl. masc. part. pres. . . id.
κλαιόντων, gen. pl. masc. part. pres. . id.
κλαίουσα, nom. sing. fem. part. pres. . . id.
κλαίουσαι, nom. pl. fem. part. pres. . id.
κλαίουσαν, acc. sing. fem. part. pres. . . id.
κλαίουσι, dat. pl. masc. part. pres. . . id.
κλαίουσι, 3 pers. pl. pres. ind. . . . id.

κλαίω], fut. κλαύσομαι, in N.T. κλαύσω, (§ 35. rem. 3) aor. 1, ἔκλαυσα, intrans. *to weep, shed tears*, Mat. 26. 75; Mar. 5. 38, 39; Lu. 19. 41; 23. 28, et al.; trans. *to weep for, bewail*, Mat. 2. 18.

κλαυθμός, οῦ, ὁ, (§ 3. tab. C. a) *weeping*, Mat. 2. 18; 8. 12, et al.

κλαίων, nom. sing. masc. part. pres. . κλαιω
κλάσαι, aor. 1, infin. (§ 22. rem. 2) . . κλάω
κλάσας, nom. sing. masc. part. aor. 1 . id.

[a] Mat. 12. 40. [b] Re. 18. 13. [c] Jno. 5. 3. [d] Ac. 13. 21.

κλάσει, dat. sing. . . . . . . κλάσις

κλάσις], εως, ἡ, (§ 5. tab. E. c) . . κλάω

κλάσμα], ατος, τό, (§ 4. tab. D. c) . . id.

κλάσματα, acc. pl. . . . . . κλάσμα

κλασμάτων, gen. pl. . . . . . id.

Κλαύδη], ης, ἡ, (§ 2. tab. B. a) *Clauda*, a small island near Crete.

Κλαύδην,[a] acc. . . . . . . Κλαύδη

Κλαυδία,[b] ας, ἡ, (§ 2. tab. B. b, and rem. 2) *Claudia*, pr. name.

Κλαύδιον, acc. . . . . . . Κλαύδιος

Κλαύδιος, ου, ὁ, (§ 3. tab. C. a) *Claudius*, pr. name.

I. *The fourth Roman Emperor*, Ac. 11. 28, et al.

II. *Claudius Lysias, a Roman captain*, Ac. 23. 26.

Κλαυδίου, gen. . . . . . . Κλαύδιος

κλαυθμός, οῦ, ὁ, (§ 3. tab. C. a) . . κλαίω

κλαύσατε, 2 pers. pl. aor. 1, imper. . id.

κλαύσετε, 2 pers. pl. fut. ind. . . . id.

κλαύσῃ, 3 pers. sing. aor. 1, subj. . . id.

κλαύσονται, 3 pers. pl. fut. ind. mid. . . id.

κλαύσουσι, 3 pers. pl. fut. ind.—B. C. Sch. Tdf. . . . . . } id.
κλαύσονται, Rec. Gr. Ln. (Re. 18. 9) }

κλάω], fut. κλάσω, (§ 22. rem. 2) aor. 1, ἔκλᾰσα, *to break off*; in N.T. *to break* bread, Mat. 14. 19, et al.; with figurative reference to the violent death of Christ, 1 Co. 11. 24.

κλάδος, ου, ὁ, (§ 3. tab. C. a) *a bough, branch, shoot*, Mat. 13. 32; 21. 8, et al.; met. *a branch* of a family stock, Ro. 11. 16, 21.

κλάσις, εως, ἡ, (§ 5. tab. E. c) *a breaking, the act of breaking*, Lu. 24. 35; Ac. 2. 42.

κλάσμα, ατος, τό, (§ 4. tab. D. c) *a piece broken off, fragment*, Mat. 14. 20; 15. 37; Mar. 6. 43, et al.

κλῆμα, ατος, τό, (§ 4. tab. D. c) *a branch, shoot, twig*, esp. of the vine, Jno. 15. 2, 4, 5, 6.

κλεῖδα, acc. sing. (§ 4. rem. 4) . . . κλείς

κλεῖδας, acc. pl.—B. Ln. . . . } id.
κλεῖς, Rec. Gr. Sch. Tdf. (Mat. 16. 19) }

κλείει, 3 pers. sing. pres. ind. act. . . κλείω

κλείετε, 2 pers. pl. pres. ind. act. . . κλείω

κλεῖν, acc. sing.—Gr. Sch. Tdf. . . } κλείς
κλεῖδα, Rec. (Re. 3. 7) . . }

κλείς], δός, ἡ, (§ 4. rem. 4) . . . κλείω

κλεῖς, acc. pl. for κλεῖδας, (§ 5. rem. 8. b) κλείς

κλεῖσαι, aor. 1, infin. act. . . . κλείω

κλείσας, nom. sing. masc. part. aor. 1, act. . id.

κλείσῃ, 3 pers. sing. aor. 1, subj. act. . id.

κλεισθῶσι, 3 pers. pl. aor. 1, subj. pass. . id.

κλείω], fut. είσω, aor. 1, ἔκλεισα, perf. pass. κέκλεισμαι, aor. 1, pass. ἐκλείσθην, (§ 22. rem. 4) *to close, shut*, Mat. 6. 6; 25. 10, et al.; *to shut up* a person, Re. 20. 3; met. of the heavens, Lu. 4. 25; Re. 11. 6; κλεῖσαι τὰ σπλάγχνα, *to shut up one's bowels, to be hard-hearted, void of compassion*, 1 Jno. 3. 17; κλείειν τὴν βασιλείαν τῶν οὐρανῶν, *to endeavour to prevent entrance into the kingdom of heaven*, Mat. 23. 14.

κλείς, κλειδός, κλειδί, κλεῖδα, and κλεῖν, ἡ, pl. κλεῖδες and κλεῖς, *a key*, used in N.T. as the symbol of power, authority, etc., Mat. 16. 19; Re. 1. 18; 3. 7; 9. 1; 20. 1; met. *the key* of entrance into knowledge, Lu. 11. 52.

κλέμμα], ατος, τό, (§ 4. tab. D. c) . . κλέπτω

κλεμμάτων,[c] gen. pl. . . . . . κλέμμα

Κλεόπας,[d] α, ὁ, (§ 2. rem. 4) *Cleopas*, pr. name.

κλέος,[e] έεος, έους, τό, (§ 5. tab. E. b) pr. *rumour, report; good report, praise, credit*.

κλέπται, nom. pl. . . . . . . κλέπτης

κλέπτειν, pres. infin. . . . . . κλέπτω

κλέπτεις, 2 pers. sing. pres. ind. . . id.

κλεπτέτω, 3 pers. sing. pres. imper. . . id.

κλέπτης, ου, ὁ, (§ 2. tab. B. c) . . id.

κλέπτουσι, 3 pers. pl. pres. ind. . . id.

κλέπτω], fut. ψω, and ψομαι, (§ 23. rem. 1. a) perf. 2. κέκλοφα, (§ 25. rem. 5) aor. 1, ἔκλεψα, *to steal*, Mat. 6. 19, 20; 19. 18, et al.; *to take away stealthily, remove secretly*, Mat. 27. 64; 28. 13.

κλέμμα, ατος, τό, (§ 4. tab. D. c) *theft*, Re. 9. 21.

κλέπτης, ου, ὁ, (§ 2. tab. B. c) *a thief*, Mat. 6. 19, 20; 24. 43, et al.; trop. *a thief* by imposture, Jno. 10. 8.

[a] Ac. 27. 16. [b] 2 Ti. 4. 21. [c] Re. 9. 21. [d] Lu. 24. 18. [e] 1 Pe. 2. 20.

κλοπή, ῆς, ἡ, (§ 2. tab. B. a) *theft*, Mat. 15. 19; Mar. 7. 22.

κλέπτων, nom. sing. masc. part. pres. . . κλέπτω
κλέψεις, 2 pers. sing. fut. ind. . . . . id.
κλέψῃ, 3 pers. sing. aor. 1, subj. . . . id.
κλέψῃς, 2 pers. sing. aor. 1, subj. . . . id.
κλέψωσι, 3 pers. pl. aor. 1, subj. . . . id.
κληθείς, nom. sing. masc. part. aor. 1, pass. (§ 22. rem. 4) . . . . καλέω
κληθέν, nom. sing. neut. part. aor. 1, pass. id.
κληθέντος, gen. sing. masc. part. aor. 1, pass. id.
κληθῆναι, aor. 1, infin. pass. . . . . id.
κληθῇς, 2 pers. sing. aor. 1, subj. pass. . id.
κληθήσεται, 3 pers. sing. fut. ind. pass. . id.
κληθήσῃ, 2 pers. sing. fut. ind. pass. . . id.
κληθήσονται, 3 pers. pl. fut. ind. pass. . id.
κληθῆτε, 2 pers. pl. aor. 1, subj. pass. . . id.
κληθῶμεν, 1 pers. pl. aor. 1, subj. pass. . id.
κλῆμα], ατος, τό, (§ 4. tab. D. c) . . κλάω
κλήματα, nom. pl. . . . . . κλῆμα
Κλήμεντος,[a] gen. . . . . . . Κλήμης
Κλήμης], εντος, ὁ, (§ 4. rem. 2. d) *Clemens, Clement*, pr. name. Latin.
κλῆρον, acc. sing. . . . . . κλῆρος
κληρονομεῖ, 3 pers. sing. pres. ind. . κληρονομέω
κληρονομεῖν, pres. infin. . . . . id.
κληρονομέω, ῶ], fut. ήσω, (§ 16. tab. P) κληρονόμος
κληρονομῆσαι, aor. 1, infin. . . . κληρονομέω
κληρονομήσατε, 2 pers. pl. aor. 1, imper. . id.
κληρονομήσει, 3 pers. sing. fut. ind. . . id.
κληρονομήσῃ, 3 pers. sing. aor. 1, subj. . id.
κληρονομήσητε, 2 pers. pl. aor. 1, subj. . id.
κληρονομήσουσι, 3 pers. pl. fut. ind. . id.
κληρονομήσω, 1 pers. sing. fut. ind. . . id.
κληρονομήσω, 1 pers. sing. aor. 1, subj. . id.
κληρονομία], ας, ἡ, (§ 2. tab. B. b, and rem. 2) κληρονόμος
κληρονομίαν, acc. sing. . . . . κληρονομία
κληρονομίας, gen. sing. . . . . id.
κληρονόμοι, nom. pl. . . . . κληρονόμος
κληρονόμοις, dat. pl. . . . . . id.
κληρονόμον, acc. sing. . . . . . id.
κληρονόμος, ου, ὁ, (§ 3. tab. C. a) (κλῆρος & νέμομαι) *an heir*, Mat. 21. 38; Gal. 4. 1, et al.; *a possessor*, Ro. 4. 13; He. 11. 7; Ja. 2. 5, et al.

κληρονομέω, ῶ, fut. ήσω, (§ 16. tab. P) perf. κεκληρονόμηκα, aor. 1, ἐκληρονόμησα, pr. *to acquire by lot; to inherit, obtain by inheritance*; in N.T. *to obtain, acquire, receive possession of*, Mat. 5. 5; 19. 29, et al.; absol. *to be heir*, Gal. 4. 30.

κληρονομία, ας, ἡ, (§ 2. tab. B. b, and rem. 2) *an inheritance, patrimony*, Mat. 21. 38; Mar. 12. 7; *a possession, portion, property*, Ac. 7. 5; 20. 32, et al.; in N.T. *a share, participation* in privileges, Ac. 20. 32; Ep. 1. 14, et al.

κληρονομούντων, gen. pl. masc. part. pres. κληρονομέω
κληρονόμους, acc. pl. . . . . . κληρονόμος

κλῆρος, ου, ὁ, (§ 3 tab. C. a) *a lot, die, a thing used in determining chances*, Mat. 27. 35; Mar. 15. 24, et al.; *assignment, investiture*, Ac. 1. 17, 25; *allotment, destination*, Col. 1. 12; *a part, portion, share*, Ac. 8. 21; 26. 18; *a* constituent *portion* of the Church, 1 Pe. 5. 3.

κληρόω, ῶ, fut. ώσω, (§ 20. tab. T) *to choose by lot*; mid. κληροῦμαι, aor. 1, (pass. form) ἐκληρώθην, (§ 21. tab. U) *to obtain by lot or assignment; to obtain a portion, receive a share*, Ep. 1. 11.

κλήρου, gen. sing. . . . . . κλῆρος
κλήρους, acc. pl. . . . . . id.
κληρόω, ῶ], fut. ώσω . . . . id
κλήρων, gen. pl. . . . . . id.
κλήσει, dat. sing. . . . . . κλῆσις
κλήσεως, gen. sing. . . . . . id.
κλῆσιν, acc. sing. . . . . . id.
κλῆσις], εως, ἡ, (§ 5. tab. E. c) . . καλέω
κλητοί, nom. pl. masc. . . . . κλητός
κλητοῖς, dat. pl. masc. . . . . id.
κλητός, ή, όν, (§ 7. tab. F. a) . . . καλέω
κλίβανον, acc. sing. . . . . . κλίβανος
κλίβᾰνος], ου, ὁ, (Att. κρίβανος) (§ 3. tab. C. a) *an oven*, Mat. 6. 30; Lu. 12. 28.
κλίμα], ατος, τό, (§ 4. tab. D. c) . . κλίνω
κλίμασι, dat. pl. . . . . . κλίμα
κλίματα, acc. pl. . . . . . id
κλινάριον], ου, τό, v.r. . . . . κλίνω
κλιναρίων, gen. pl.—A. D. Ln. Tdf. } κλινάριον
κλινῶν, Rec. Gr. Sch. (Ac. 5. 15) }
κλίνας, nom. sing. masc. part. aor. 1, act. . κλίνω
κλίνειν, pres. infin. act. . . . . id.
κλίνῃ, 3 pers. sing. pres. subj. act. . . id.
κλίνη], ης, ἡ, (§ 2. tab. B. a) . . . id.

[a] Phi. 4. 3

κλίνην, acc. sing. . . . . . . κλίνη
κλίνης, gen. sing. . . . . . id.
κλινίδιον, ου, τό, (§ 3. tab. C. c) . . κλίνω
κλινιδίῳ, dat. sing. . . . . . κλινίδιον
κλινουσῶν, gen. pl. fem. part. pres. act. . κλίνω

κλίνω], fut. ινῶ, perf. κέκλἴκα, (§ 27. rem. 1. a, and rem. 2. c) aor. 1, ἔκλῖνα, pr. trans. *to cause to slope or bend; to bow down*, Lu. 24. 5; Jno. 19. 30; *to lay down* to rest, Mat. 8. 20; Lu. 9. 58; *to put to flight* troops, He. 11. 34; intrans. of the day, *to decline*, Lu. 9. 12; 24. 29.

κλίμα, ατος, τό, (§ 4. tab. D. c) pr. *a slope; a portion of the* ideal *slope* of the earth's surface; *a tract or region* of country, Ro. 15. 23; 2 Co. 11. 10; Gal. 1. 21.

κλίνη, ης, ἡ, (§ 2. tab. B. a) *a couch, bed*, Mat. 9. 2, 6; Mar. 4. 21, et al.

κλῖνίδιον, ου, τό, dimin. of κλίνη, *a small couch or bed*, Lu. 5. 19, 24.

κλινάριον, ου, τό, (§ 3. tab. C. c) *a small bed or couch*. v.r. Ac. 5. 15.

κλἴσία, ας, ἡ, (§ 2. tab. B. b, and rem. 2) pr. *a place for reclining; a tent, seat, couch*; in N.T. *a company of persons reclining* at a meal, Lu. 9. 14.

κλινῶν, gen. pl. . . . . . . κλίνη
κλισία], ας, ἡ . . . . . κλίνω
κλισίας,[a] acc. pl. . . . . κλισία
κλοπαί, nom. pl. . . . . . . κλοπή
κλοπή], ῆς, ἡ, (§ 2. tab. B. a) . . κλέπτω
κλύδων], ωνος, ὁ, (§ 4. rem. 2. e) (κλύζω, *to dash, surge, like the waves*) *a wave, billow, surge*, Lu. 8. 24; Ja. 1. 6.

κλυδωνίζομαι, *to be tossed by waves*; met. *to fluctuate* in opinion, *be agitated, tossed to and fro*, Ep. 4. 14. L.G.

κλύδωνι, dat. sing. . . . . . . κλύδων
κλυδωνίζομαι], fut. ίσομαι . . . id.
κλυδωνιζόμενοι,[b] nom. pl. masc. part. pres. κλυδωνίζομαι
κλῶμεν, 1 pers. pl. pres. ind. act. . . κλάω
κλώμενον, nom. sing. neut. part. pres. pass.—Rec. Gr. Sch. . . . . id.
A. B. C. Ln. Tdf. om. (1 Co. 11. 24)
κλῶντες, nom. pl. masc. part. pres. act. . id.
Κλωπᾶ,[c] gen. . . . . . Κλωπᾶς

Κλωπᾶς], ᾶ, ὁ, (§ 2. rem. 4) contr. for Κλεόπας, *Cleopas*, pr. name.
κνηθόμενοι,[d] nom. pl. masc. part. pres. mid. . κνήθω
κνήθω], (κνάω) fut. κνήσω, (§ 23. rem. 1. c) *to scratch; to tickle, cause titillation*; in N.T. mid. met. *to procure pleasurable excitement for, to indulge an itching*
Κνίδον,[e] acc. . . . . . Κνίδος
Κνίδος], ου, ἡ, (§ 3. tab. C. b) *Cnidus*, a city of Caria, in Asia Minor.
κοδράντην, acc. sing. . . . . κοδράντης
κοδράντης, ου, ὁ, (§ 2. tab. B. c) (Lat. *quadrans*) *a Roman brass coin*, equivalent to the *fourth part* of an *as*, or ἀσσάριον, or to δύο λεπτά, and equal to about three-fourths of a farthing, Mat. 5. 26; Mar. 12. 42. N.T.
κοιλία, ας, ἡ, (§ 2. tab. B. b, and rem. 2) (κοῖλος, *hollow*) *a cavity; the belly*, Mat. 15, 17; Mar. 7. 19; *the stomach*, Mat. 12. 40; Lu. 15. 16; *the womb*, Mat. 19. 12; Lu. 1. 15, et al.; from the Heb., *the inner self*, Jno. 7. 38.
κοιλίᾳ, dat. sing. . . . . . κοιλία
κοιλίαι, nom. pl. . . . . . id.
κοιλίαν, acc. sing. . . . . . id.
κοιλίας, gen. sing. . . . . . . id.

κοιμάω, ῶ], fut. ήσω, (§ 18. tab. R) perf. pass. κεκοίμημαι, *to lull to sleep*; pass. *to fall asleep, be asleep*, Mat. 28. 13; Lu. 22. 45; met. *to sleep* in death, Ac. 7. 60; 13. 36; et al.

κοίμησις, εως, ἡ, (§ 5. tab. E. c) *sleep*; meton. *rest, repose*, Jno. 11. 13.

κοιμηθέντας, acc. pl. masc. part. aor. 1, pass. κοιμάω
κοιμηθέντες, nom. pl. masc. part. aor. 1, pass. id.
κοιμηθῇ, 3 pers. sing. aor. 1, subj. pass. . id.
κοιμηθησόμεθα, 1 pers. pl. fut. ind. pass. . id.
κοιμήσεως,[f] gen. sing. . . . . κοίμησις
κοίμησις], εως, ἡ . . . . . κοιμάω
κοιμώμενος, nom. sing. masc. part. pres. pass. id.
κοιμωμένους, acc. pl. masc. part. pres. pass. id.
κοιμωμένων, gen. pl. part. pres. pass. . id.
κοιμῶνται, 3 pers. pl. pres. ind. pass. . . id.
κοινά, nom. and acc. pl. neut. . . κοινός
κοιναῖς, dat. pl. fem. . . . . id.
κοινήν, acc. sing. fem. . . . . id.

a Lu. 9. 14. b Ep. 4. 14. c Jno. 19. 25. d 2 Ti. 4. 3. e Ac. 27. 7. f Jno. 11. 13.

κοινῆς, gen. sing. fem. . . . . . κοινός
κοινοῖ, 3 pers. sing. pres. ind. act. . . κοινόω
κοινόν, acc. sing. masc. . . . . . κοινός
κοινόν, nom. and acc. sing. neut. . . id.

κοινός], ή, όν, (§ 7. tab. F. a) *common, belonging equally to several,* Ac. 2. 44; 4. 32; in N.T. *common, profane,* He. 10. 29; ceremonially *unclean,* Mar. 7. 2; Ac. 10. 14, et al.

κοινόω, ῶ, fut. ώσω, perf. κεκοίνωκα, aor. 1, ἐκοίνωσα, (§ 20. tab. T) *to make common;* in N.T. *to profane, desecrate,* Ac. 21. 28; *to render* ceremonially *unclean, defile, pollute,* Mat. 15. 11, 18, 20; *to pronounce unclean* ceremonially, Ac. 10. 15; 11. 9.

κοινωνός, οῦ, ὁ, ἡ, (§ 3. tab. C. a. b) *a fellow, partner,* Mat. 23. 30; Lu. 5. 10; 1 Co. 10. 18, 20; 2 Co. 8. 23; Phile. 17; He. 10. 33; *a sharer, partaker,* 2 Co. 1. 7; 1 Pe. 5. 1; 2 Pe. 1. 4.

κοινωνέω, ῶ, fut. ήσω, perf. κεκοινώνηκα, aor. 1, ἐκοινώνησα, (§ 16. tab. P) *to have in common, share,* He. 2. 14; *to be associated in, to become a sharer in,* Ro. 15. 27; 1 Pe. 4. 13; *to become implicated in, be a party to,* 1 Ti. 5. 22; 2 Jno. 11; *to associate one's self with* by sympathy and assistance, *to communicate with* in the way of aid and relief, Ro. 12. 13; Gal. 6. 6.

κοινωνία, ας, ἡ, (§ 2. tab. B. b, and rem. 2) *fellowship, partnership,* Ac. 2. 42; 2 Co. 6. 14; Gal. 2. 9; Phi. 3. 10; 1 Jno. 1. 3, et al.; *participation, communion,* 1 Co. 10. 16, et al.; *aid, relief,* He. 13. 16, et al.; *contribution in aid,* Ro. 15. 26.

κοινωνικός, ή, όν, (§ 7. tab. F. a) *social;* in N.T. *ready to communicate* in kind offices, *liberal, beneficent,* 1 Ti. 6. 18.

κοίνου, 2 pers. sing. pres. imper. act. . . κοινόω
κοινοῦν, nom. sing. neut. part. pres. act. . id.
κοινοῦντα, nom. pl. neut. part. pres. act. . id.
κοινόω, ῶ], fut. ώσω, (§ 20. tab. T) . κοινός
κοινωνεῖ, 3 pers. sing. pres. ind. . . κοινωνέω
κοινώνει, 3 pers. sing. pres. imper. . . id.
κοινωνεῖτε, 2 pers. pl pres. ind. . . . id.
κοινωνείτω, 3 pers. sing. pres. imper. . κοινωνέω
κοινωνέω, ῶ], fut. ήσω, (§ 16. tab. P) . . κοινός
κοινωνία], ας, ἡ, (§ 2. tab. B. b, and rem. 2) id.
κοινωνίᾳ, dat. sing. . . . . κοινωνία
κοινωνίαν, acc. sing. . . . . id.
κοινωνίας, gen. sing. . . . . id.
κοινωνικός], ή, όν, (§ 7. tab. F. a) . . κοινός
κοινωνικούς,[a] acc. pl. masc. . . . κοινωνικός
κοινωνοί, nom. pl. masc. . . . . κοινωνός
κοινωνόν, acc. sing. masc. . . . id.
κοινωνός], οῦ, ὁ, ἡ, (§ 3. tab. C. a. b) . . κοινός
κοινωνοῦντες, nom. pl. masc. part. pres. . κοινωνέω
κοινωνούς, acc. pl. masc. . . . . κοινωνός
κοινῶσαι, aor. 1, infin. act. . . . κοινόω
κοίταις, dat. pl. . . . . . κοίτη
κοίτη], ης, ἡ, (§ 2. tab. B. a) . . . κεῖμαι
κοίτην, acc. sing. . . . . κοίτη
κοιτῶνος,[b] gen. sing. . . κοιτών
κοιτών], ῶνος, ὁ, (§ 4. rem. 2. e) . . κεῖμαι
κοκκίνην, acc. sing. fem. . . . κόκκινος
κόκκινον, acc. sing. neut. . . . . id.
κόκκινος], η, ον, (§ 7. tab. F. a) (κόκκος, *kermes, the coccus ilicis* of Linnæus, a small insect, found on the leaves of the *quercus cocciferus, or holm oak,* which was used by the ancients, as the cochineal insect now is, for dyeing a beautiful crimson or deep scarlet colour, and supposed by them to be the *berry* of a plant or tree) *dyed with coccus, crimson, scarlet,* Mat. 27. 28; He. 9. 19; Re. 17. 3, 4; 18. 12, 16.
κοκκίνου, gen. sing. neut. . . . κόκκινος
κοκκίνῳ, dat. sing. neut. . . . . id.
κόκκον, acc. sing. . . . . κόκκος

κόκκος, ου, ὁ, (§ 3. tab. C. a) *a kernel, grain, seed,* Mat. 13. 31; 17. 20, et al.

κόκκῳ, dat. sing. . . . . . κόκκος
κολαζομένους, acc. pl. masc. part. pres. pass. κολάζω

κολάζω], fut. άσομαι & άσω, (§ 26. rem. 1) pr. *to curtail, to coerce; to chastise, punish,* Ac. 4. 21; 2 Pe. 2. 9.

κόλασις, εως, ἡ, (§ 5. tab. E. c) *chastisement, punishment,* Mat. 25. 46; *painful disquietude, torment,* 1 Jno. 4. 18.

κολακεία], ας, ἡ, (§ 2. tab. B. b. and rem. 2) (κόλαξ, *a flatterer*) *flattery, adulation, obsequiousness.*

---

[a] 1 Ti. 6. 18.

[b] Ac. 12. 20.

κολακείας,[a] gen. sing. . . . . κολακεία

κόλασιν, acc. sing. . . . . κόλασις

κόλασις], εως, ἡ, (§ 5. tab. E. c) . . κολάζω

κολάσωνται, 3 pers. pl. aor. 1, subj. mid. . id.

κολαφίζειν, pres. infin. act. . . . κολαφίζω

κολαφίζῃ, 3 pers. sing. pres. subj. act. . id.

κολαφιζόμεθα, 1 pers. pl. pres. ind. pass. . id.

κολαφιζόμενοι, nom. pl. masc. part. pres. pass. id.

κολαφίζω], fut. ίσω, (§ 26. rem. 1) (κόλαφος, *a blow with the fist*) *to beat with the fist, buffet*, Mat. 26. 67; Mar. 14. 65; met. *to maltreat, treat with contumely and ignominy*, 1 Co. 4. 11; *to punish*, 1 Pe. 2. 20; *to buffet, fret, afflict*, 2 Co. 12. 7.

κολλᾶσθαι, pres. inf. mid. (§ 19. tab. S) . κολλάω

κολλάω, ῶ], fut. ήσω, (§ 18. tab. R) *to glue or weld together*; mid. *to adhere to*, Lu. 10. 11; met. *to attach one's self to, unite with, associate with*, Lu. 15. 15; Ac. 5. 13, et al.

κολληθέντα, acc. sing. masc. part. aor. 1, pass. κολλάω

κολληθέντες, nom. pl. masc. part. aor. 1, pass. id.

κολληθήσεται, 3 pers. sing. fut. ind. pass.—Al. Ln. Sch. Tdf. . . } id.
προσκολληθήσεται, Rec. Gr. (Mat. 19. 5) . . . . }

κολλήθητι, 2 pers. sing. aor. 1, imper. pass. . id.

κολλούριον,[b] or κολλύριον, ου, τό, (§ 3. tab. C. c) (dimin. of κολλύρα, *a cake*) *collyrium. eye-salve*.

κολλυβιστής], οῦ, ὁ, (§ 2. tab. B. c) (κόλλυβος, *small coin*) *a money-changer*, Mat. 21. 12; Mar. 11. 15; Jno. 2. 15.

κολλυβιστῶν, gen. pl. . . . κολλυβιστής

κολλώμενοι, nom. pl. masc. part. pres. mid. κολλάω

κολλώμενος, nom. sing. masc. part. pres. mid. id.

κολοβόω, ῶ], fut. ώσω, (§ 20. tab. T) (κολοβός, *curtailed, mutilated*, fr. κόλος, id.) in N.T. of time, *to cut short, shorten*, Mat. 24. 22; Mar. 13. 20.

κολοβωθήσονται, 3 pers. pl. fut. ind. pass. κολοβόω

Κολοσσαί], ῶν, αἱ, (§ 2. tab. B. a) *Colosse*, a city of Phrygia.

Κολοσσαῖς,[c] dat.—Rec. Gr. Sch. } Κολοσσαί
Κολασσαῖς, A. B. C. Ln. Tdf. (Col. 1. 2) . . . . . }

κόλποις, dat. pl. . . . . . κόλπος

κόλπον, acc. sing. . . . id.

κόλπος], ου, ὁ, (§ 3. tab. C. a) *the bosom*, Lu. 16. 22. 23; Jno. 1. 18; 13. 23; *the bosom of a garment*, Lu. 6. 38; *a bay, creek, inlet*, Ac. 27. 39.

κόλπῳ, dat. sing. . . . . . κόλπος

κολυμβᾶν,[d] pres. infin. . . . κολυμβάω

κολυμβάω, ῶ], fut. ήσω, (§ 18. tab. R) *to dive*; in N.T. *to swim*.

κολυμβήθρα, ας, ἡ, (§ 2. tab. B. b) *a place where any one may swim; a pond, pool*, Jno. 5. 2, 4, 7; 9. 7. 11.

κολυμβήθρα], ας, ἡ . . . . κολυμβάω

κολυμβήθρᾳ, dat. sing. . . . κολυμβήθρα

κολυμβήθραν, acc. sing. . . . . id.

κολωνία],[e] ας, ἡ, (§ 2. tab. B. b, and rem. 2) (Lat. *colonia*) *a Roman colony*.

κομᾷ, 3 pers. sing. pres. subj. . . κομάω

κομάω, ῶ], fut. ήσω, (§ 18. tab. R) . . κόμη

κόμη, ης, ἡ, (§ 2. tab. B. a) *the hair; a head of long hair*.

κομάω, ῶ, fut. ήσω, *to have long hair, wear the hair long*, 1 Co. 11. 14, 15.

κομιεῖσθε, 2 pers. pl. fut. ind. mid. (Att. for κομίσεσθε) (§ 35. rem. 11) . } κομίζω

κομιεῖται, 3 pers. sing. fut. ind. mid. (Att. for κομίσεται) . . . } id.

κομιζόμενοι, nom. pl. masc. part. pres. mid. . id.

κομίζω], fut. ίσω & ιῶ, mid. ιοῦμαι, aor. 1, ἐκόμισα, (§ 26. rem. 1) (§ 35. rem. 11) (κομέω, *to take care of*) pr. *to take into kindly keeping, to provide for; to convey, bring*, Lu. 7. 37; mid. *to bring for one's self; to receive, obtain*, 2 Co. 5. 10; Ep. 6. 8, et al.; *to receive again, recover*, Mat. 25. 27; He. 11. 19.

κομιούμενοι, nom. pl. masc. part. fut. mid. (Att. for κομισόμενοι) . . . κομίζω

κομίσασα, nom. sing. fem. part. aor. 1, act. . id.

κομίσεται, 3 pers. sing. fut. ind. mid.—A. D. Ln. Tdf. . . . . . } id.
κομιεῖται, Rec. Gr. Sch. (Ep. 6. 8) . }

κομίσησθε, 2 pers. pl. aor. 1, subj. mid. . id.

κομίσηται, 3 pers. sing. aor. 1, subj. mid. . id.

κομψότερον,[f] adv. (compar. of κόμψως, *well, smartly*) in N.T. *in better health*.

κονιάω, ῶ], fut. άσω, (§ 18. tab. R) perf. pass.

[a] 1 Thes. 2. 5. [b] Re. 3. 18. [c] Col. 1. 2. [d] Ac. 27. 43. [e] Ac. 16. 12. [f] 1 Co. 11. 15. [g] Jno. 4. 52.

κεκονίᾶμαι, (κόνις, or κονία, *dust, lime-dust*) *to whitewash*, or, *plaster*, Mat. 23.27; Ac. 23.3.

κονιορτόν, acc. sing. . . . . . κονιορτός

κονιορτός], οῦ, ὁ, (§ 3. tab. C. a) (κόνις & ὄρνυμι, *to raise*) *dust excited; dust*, Mat. 10. 14; Lu. 9. 5; 10. 11; Ac. 13. 51; 22. 23.

κοπάζω], fut. άσω, (§ 26. rem. 1) . . κόπτω

κοπετόν,[a] acc. sing. . . . . . κοπετός

κοπετός], οῦ, ὁ, (§ 3. tab. C. a) . . κόπτω

κοπή], ῆς, ἡ, (§ 2. tab. B. a) . . . id.

κοπῆς,[b] gen. sing. . . . . . κοπή

κοπιᾷ, 3 pers. sing. pres. ind. . . . κοπιάω

κοπιάσαντες, nom. pl. masc. part. aor. 1, (§ 22. rem. 2) . . . . . id.

κοπιάτω, 3 pers. sing. pres. imper. . . id.

κοπιάω, ῶ], fut. άσω, (§ 22. rem. 2) . κόπτω

κοπιῶ, 1 pers. sing. pres. ind. . . . κοπιάω

κοπιῶμεν, 1 pers. pl. pres. ind. . . id.

κοπιῶντα, acc. sing. masc. part. pres. . . id.

κοπιῶντας, acc. pl. masc. part. pres. . id.

κοπιῶντες, nom. pl. masc. part. pres. . . id.

κοπιῶντι, dat. sing. masc. part. pres. . id.

κοπιώσας, acc. pl. fem. part. pres. . . id.

κοπιῶσι, 3 pers. pl. pres. ind.—B. Ln. } id.
κοπιᾷ, Rec. Gr. Sch. Tdf. (Mat. 6. 28) }

κόποις, dat. pl. . . . . . . κόπος

κόπον, acc. sing. . . . . . id.

κόπος], ου, ὁ, (§ 3. tab. C. a) . . κόπτω

κόπου, gen. sing. . . . . . κόπος

κόπους, acc. pl. . . . . . . id.

κοπρία], ας, ἡ, (§ 2. tab. B. b, and rem. 2) *dung, manure*, Lu. 13. 8; 14. 35.

κόπρια, acc. pl.—A. B. Gr. Sch. Tdf. } κόπριον,
κόπριον, Rec. (Lu. 13. 8) . . }

κοπρίαν, acc. sing. . . . . . κοπρία

κοπριον], ου, τό, (§ 3. tab. C. c) *dung, manure*, v.r. Lu. 13. 8. L.G.

κόπτω], fut. ψω, (§ 23. rem. 1. a) *to smite, cut; to cut off or down*, Mat. 21. 8; Mar. 11. 8; mid. *to beat one's self* in mourning, *lament, bewail*, Lu. 8. 52; 23. 27, et al.

κόπος, ου, ὁ, (§ 3. tab. C. a) *trouble, vexation, uneasiness*, Mat. 26. 10; Mar. 14. 6; *labour, wearisome labour, travail, toil*, 1 Co. 3. 8; 15. 58, et al.; meton. *he fruit or consequence of labour*, Jno. 4. 38 2 Co. 10. 15.

κοπάζω, fut. άσω, (§ 26. rem. 1) pr. *to grow weary, suffer exhaustion; to abate, be stilled*, Mat. 14. 32; Mar. 4. 39; 6. 51.

κοπιάω, ῶ, fut. άσω, (§ 22. rem. 2) perf. κεκοπίᾶκα, aor. 1, ἐκοπίᾶσα, *to be wearied or spent with labour, faint from weariness*, Mat. 11. 28; Jno. 4. 6; in N.T. *to labour hard, to toil*, Lu. 5. 5; Jno. 4. 38, et al.

κοπετός, οῦ, ὁ, (§ 3. tab. C. a) pr. *a beating* of the breast, etc., in token of grief; *a wailing, lamentation*, Ac. 8. 2.

κοπή, ῆς, ἡ, (§ 2. tab. B. a) *a stroke, smiting*; in N.T. *slaughter*, He. 7. 1.

κόπῳ, dat. sing. . . . . . . κόπος

κόπων, gen. pl. . . . . . . id.

κόρακας,[c] acc. pl. . . . . . κόραξ

κόραξ], ᾶκος, ὁ, (§ 4. rem. 2. b) *a raven, crow*.

κοράσιον, ίου, τό, (§ 3. tab. C. c) (dimin. of κόρη) *a girl, damsel, maiden*, Mat. 9. 24, 25; 14. 11, et al. (ᾰ).

κορασίῳ, dat. sing. . . . . . κοράσιον

κορβᾶν, ὁ, indecl. or κορβανᾶς, ᾶ, ὁ, (§ 2. rem. 4) (Heb. קָרְבָּן; Aram. קוּרְבָּנָא, explained in Greek by δῶρον) *corban, a gift, offering, oblation, anything consecrated to God*, Mar. 7. 11; meton. *the sacred treasury*, Mat. 27. 6.

κορβανᾶν, acc. . . . . . . κορβανᾶς

Κορέ,[d] ὁ, (Heb. קֹרַח) *Core, Korah*, pr. name, indecl.

κορέννυμι], fut. κορέσω, perf. pass. κεκόρεσμαι, (§ 36. rem. 5) *to satiate, satisfy*, Ac. 27. 38; 1 Co. 4. 8.

κορεσθέντες, nom. pl. masc. part. aor. 1, pass. κορέννυμι

Κορίνθιοι, voc. pl. masc. . . . . Κορίνθιος

Κορίνθιος], ία, ιον, (§ 7. rem. 1) *Corinthian; an inhabitant of* Κόρινθος, *Corinth*, Ac. 18. 8; 2 Co. 6. 11.

Κορινθίων, gen. pl. . . . . Κορίνθιος

Κόρινθον, acc. . . . . . . Κόρινθος

Κόρινθος], ου, ἡ, (§ 3 tab. C. b) *Corinth*, a celebrated city of Greece.

Κορίνθῳ, dat. . . . . . . Κόρινθος

Κορνήλιε, voc. . . . . . . Κορνήλιος

Κορνήλιος], ου, ὁ, *Cornelius*, a Latin pr. name.

Κορνηλίου, gen. . . . . . Κορνήλιος

Κορνηλίῳ, dat. . . . . . . id.

[a] Ac. 8. 2. [b] He. 7. 1. [c] Lu. 12. 24 [d] Jude 11.

κόρος], ου, ὁ, (§ 3. tab. C. a) (Heb. כֹּר) *a cor*, the largest Jewish measure for things dry, equal to the homer, and about fifteen bushels English, according to Josephus, (Ant. l. xv. c. 9. § 2).

κόρους,[a] acc. pl. . . . . . κόρος

κοσμεῖν, pres. infin. act. . . . . κοσμέω

κοσμεῖτε, 2 pers. pl. pres. ind. . . id.

κοσμέω, ῶ], fut. ήσω, (§ 16. tab. P) . . κόσμος

κοσμικάς, acc. pl. fem. . . . κοσμικός

κοσμικός], ή, όν, (§ 7. tab. F. a) . . κόσμος

κοσμικόν, acc. sing. neut. . . . κοσμικός

κόσμιον, acc. sing. masc. . . . . κόσμιος

κόσμιος], ου, ὁ, ἡ, (§ 7. rem. 2) . . κόσμος

κοσμίῳ, dat. sing. fem. . . . . κόσμιος

κοσμίως, adv. *decently, becomingly*.—D. } κόσμος
κοσμίῳ, Rec. Gr. Sch. Tdf. (1 Ti. 2. 9) }

κοσμοκράτορας,[b] acc. pl. . . . κοσμοκράτωρ

κοσμοκράτωρ], ορος, ὁ, (§ 4. rem. 2. f) (κόσμος & κρατέω) pr. *monarch of the world*; in N.T. *a worldly prince, a power paramount in the world* of the unbelieving and ungodly. (ᾰ) L.G.

κόσμον, acc. sing. . . . . κόσμος

κόσμος], ου, ὁ, (§ 3. tab. C. a) pr. *order, regular disposition; ornament, decoration, embellishment*, 1 Pe. 3. 3; *the world, the material universe*, Mat. 13. 35, et al.; *the world, the aggregate of sensitive existence*, 1 Co. 4. 9; *the* lower *world, the earth*, Mar. 16. 15, et al.; *the world, the aggregate of mankind*, Mat. 5. 14, et al.; *the world, the public*, Jno. 7. 4; in N.T. *the present order of things, the* secular *world*, Jno. 18. 36, et al.; *the human race* external to the Jewish nation, *the* heathen *world*, Ro. 11. 12, 15; *the world* external to the Christian body, 1 Jno. 3. 1. 13, et al.; *the world or material system* of the Mosaic covenant, Gal. 4. 3; Col. 2. 8, 20.

κοσμέω, ῶ, fut. ήσω, perf. κεκόσμηκα, aor. 1, ἐκόσμησα, (§ 16. tab. P) *to arrange, set in order; to adorn, decorate, embellish*, Mat. 12. 44; 23. 29; *to prepare, put in readiness, trim*, Mat. 25. 7; met. *to honour, dignify*, Tit. 2. 10.

κοσμῐκός, ή, όν, pr. *belonging to the universe*; in N.T. *accommodated to the present state of things, adapted to this world, worldly*, Tit. 2. 12; τὸ κοσμικόν, as a subst. *the apparatus* for the service of the tabernacle, He. 9. 1.

κόσμιος, ία, ιον, or ου, ὁ, ἡ, *decorous, well-ordered*, 1 Ti. 2. 9; 3. 2.

κοσμίως, adv. *decorously, becomingly*, v.r. 1 Ti. 2. 9.

κόσμου, gen. sing . . . . . κόσμος

κόσμῳ, dat. sing. . . . . . id.

κοσμῶσι, 3 pers. pl. pres. subj. act. . κοσμέω

Κούαρτος],[c] ου, ὁ, *Quartus*, a Latin pr. name.

κοῦμι,[d] (Aram. קוּמִי, 2 pers. sing. fem. imperat. of קוּם, *to arise*) *cumi, arise*.

κουστωδία], ας, ἡ, (§ 2. tab. B. b, and rem. 2) (Lat. *custodia*) *a watch, guard*, Mat. 27. 65, 66; 28. 11.

κουστωδίαν, acc. sing. . . . . κουστωδία

κουστωδίας, gen. sing. . . . . id.

κουφίζω], fut. ίσω, (§ 26. rem. 1) (κοῦφος, *light*) *to lighten, make light or less heavy*, Ac. 27. 38.

κόφινοι, nom. pl. . . . . κόφινος

κόφῐνος], ου, ὁ, (§ 3. tab. C. a) *a basket*, Mat. 14. 20; 16. 9; Mar. 6. 43, et al.

κοφίνους, acc. pl. . . . . κόφινος

κόψονται, 3 pers. pl. fut. ind. mid. . . κόπτω

κραβΒάτοις, dat. pl. . . . . κράββατος

κράββατον, acc. sing. . . . . id.

κράββατος], ου, ὁ, (§ 3. tab. C. a) (Lat. *grabātus*) *a couch* capable of holding one person, Mar. 2. 4, 9, 11, 12, et al. L.G.

κραββάτῳ, dat. sing. . . . . κράββατο

κραββάτων, gen. pl. . . . . id.

κράζει, 3 pers. sing. pres. ind. . . κράζω

κράζειν, pres. infin. . . . . . id.

κράζομεν, 1 pers. pl. pres. ind. . . . id.

κράζον, nom. and acc. sing. neut. part. pres. . id.

κράζοντα, nom. pl. neut. part. pres. . id.

κράζοντας, acc. pl. masc. part. pres. . . id.

κράζοντες, nom. pl. masc. part. pres. . id.

κραζόντων, gen. pl. masc. part. pres. . . id.

κράζουσι, 3 pers. pl. pres. ind.—Gr. Sch. Tdf. } id.
κράζοντες, Rec. (Re. 7. 10) . . }

κράζω], fut. κεκράξομαι, aor. ἔκρᾰγον, later fut. κράξω, aor. ἔκραξα, perf. κέκρᾱγα, with a pres. signif. (§ 26. rem. 2) *to utter*

[a] Lu. 16. 7. [b] Ep. 6. 12. [c] Ro. 16. 23. [d] Mar. 5. 41

a cry, Mat. 14. 26, et al.; *to exclaim, vociferate*, Mat. 9. 27; Jno. 1. 15, et al.; *to cry* for vengeance, Ja. 5. 4; *to cry* in supplication, Ro. 8. 15; Gal. 4. 6.

κραυγή, ῆς, ἡ, (§ 2. tab. B. a) *a cry, outcry, clamour, vociferation*, Mat. 25. 6; Ac. 23. 9; Ep. 4. 31; Re. 14. 18; *a cry* of sorrow, *wailing, lamentation*, Re. 21. 4; *a cry* for help, *earnest supplication*, He. 5. 7.

κραυγάζω, fut. άσω, aor. 1, ἐκραύγασα, (§ 26. rem. 1) *to cry out, exclaim, vociferate*, Mat. 12. 19; 15. 22, et al.

κράζων, nom. sing. masc. part. pres. . κράζω

κραιπάλη], ης, ἡ, (§ 2. tab. B. a) *debauch*, (ᾰ).

κραιπάλῃ,[a] dat. sing. . . . . κραιπάλη

κρᾱνίον], ου, τό, (§ 3. tab. C. c) (κάρα, *the head*) *a skull*, Mat. 27. 33; Mar. 15. 22; Lu 23. 33; Jno. 19. 17.

κρανίου, gen. sing. . . κρανίον

κράξαν, nom. sing. neut. part. aor. 1 . . κράζω

κράξαντες, nom. pl. masc. part. aor. 1 id.

κράξας, nom. sing. masc. part. aor. 1 . id.

κράξονται, 3 pers. pl. fut. mid.—D. . }
κεκράξονται, Rec. Gr. Sch. Tdf. (Lu. } id.
19. 40) . . . . . }

κράξουσι, 3 pers. pl. fut. ind.—B. . . }
κεκράξονται, Rec. Gr. Sch. Tdf. (Lu. } id.
19. 40) . . . . . }

κράσπεδα, acc. pl. . . . . . κράσπεδον

κράσπεδον], ου, τό, (§ 3. tab. C. c) *a margin, border*; in N.T. *a fringe, tuft, tassel*, Mat. 9. 20; 14. 36; 23. 5, et al.

κρασπέδου, gen. sing. . . . . κράσπεδον

κραταιάν,[b] acc. sing. fem. . . . κραταιός

κραταιός], ά, όν, (§ 7. rem. 1) . . . κράτος

κραταιοῦσθε, 3 pers. pl. pres. imper. pass. (§ 21. tab. U) . . . κραταιόω

κραταιόω, ῶ], fut. ώσω, (§ 20. tab. T) . κράτος

κραταιωθῆναι, aor. 1, infin. pass. . . κραταιόω

κράτει, dat. sing. . . . . . . κράτος

κράτει, 2 pers. sing. pres. imper. act. κρατέω

κρατεῖν, pres. infin. act. . . . . id.

κρατεῖς, 2 pers. sing. pres. ind. act. . . id.

κρατεῖσθαι, pres. infin. pass. (§ 17. tab. Q) . id.

κρατεῖτε, 2 pers. pl. pres. ind. and imper. act. id.

κρατέω, ῶ], fut. ήσω, (§ 16. tab. P) . κράτος

κρατῆσαι, aor. 1, infin. act. . . . κρατέω

κρατήσαντες, nom. pl. masc. part. aor. 1, act. id.

κρατήσας, nom. sing. masc. part. aor. 1, act. κρατέω

κρατήσατε, 2 pers. pl. aor. 1, imper. act. . id.

κρατήσει, 3 pers. sing. fut. ind. act. . . id.

κρατήσωσι, 3 pers. pl. aor. 1, subj. act. . id.

κρατῆτε, 2 pers. pl. pres. subj. act. . . id.

κράτιστε, voc. sing. masc. . . . κράτιστος

κράτιστος], η, ον, (§ 8. rem. 5) (superl. from κρατύς, *strong*) *strongest*; in N.T. κράτιστε, a term of respect, *most excellent, noble*, or *illustrious*, Lu. 1. 3; Ac. 23. 26; 24. 3; 26. 25.

κρατίστῳ, dat. sing. masc. . . . κράτιστος

κράτος], εος, τό,

(§ 5. tab. E. b) *strength, power, might, force*, Ac. 19. 20; Ep. 1. 19; meton. *a display of might*, Lu. 1. 51; *power, sway, dominion*, He. 2. 14; 1 Pe. 4. 11; 5. 11, et al. (ᾰ).

κραταιός, ά, όν, (§ 7. rem. 1) *strong, mighty, powerful*, 1 Pe. 5. 6.

κραταιόω, ῶ, fut. ώσω, (§ 20. tab. T) *to strengthen, render strong, corroborate, confirm*; pass. *to grow strong, acquire strength*, Lu. 1. 80; 2. 40; Ep. 3. 16; *to be firm, resolute*, 1 Co. 16. 13. L.G.

κρατέω, ῶ, fut. ήσω, perf. κεκράτηκα, aor. 1, ἐκράτησα, (§ 16. tab. P) pr. *to be strong; to be superior to* any one, *subdue, vanquish*, Ac. 2. 24; *to get into one's power, lay hold of, seize, apprehend*, Mat. 14. 3; 18. 28; 21. 46; *to gain, compass, attain*, Ac. 27. 13; in N.T. *to lay hold of, grasp, clasp*, Mat. 9. 25; Mar. 1. 31; 5. 41; *to retain, keep under reserve*, Mar. 9. 10; met. *to hold fast, observe*, Mar. 7. 3. 8; 2 Thes. 2. 15; *to hold to, adhere to*, Ac. 3. 11; Col. 2. 19; *to restrain, hinder, repress*, Lu. 24. 16; Re. 7. 1; *to retain, not to remit*, sins, Jno. 20. 23.

κρατοῦντας, acc. pl. masc. part. pres. act. . κρατέω

κρατοῦντες, nom. pl. masc. part. pres. act. . id.

κρατοῦντος, gen. sing. masc. part. pres. act. id.

κράτους, gen. sing. . . . . κράτος

κρατοῦσι, 3 pers. pl. pres. ind. act. . . κρατέω

κρατῶμεν, 1 pers. pl. pres. subj. act. . id.

κρατῶν, nom. sing. masc. part. pres. act. . id.

κραυγάζοντα, nom. pl. neut. pt. pres.—A. D. Ln. }
κράζοντα, Rec. Gr. Sch. Tdf. (Lu. 4. 41) } κραυγάζω

a Lu. 21. 34. b 1 Pe. 5. 6.

κραυγαζόντων, gen. pl. masc. part. pres. . κραυγάζω

κραυγάζω], fut. άσω, (§ 26. rem. 1) . . κράζω

κραυγάσει, 3 pers. sing. fut. ind. . . κραυγάζω

κραυγή, ῆς, ἡ, (§ 2. tab. B. a) . . . κράζω

κραυγῇ, dat. sing. . . . . . κραυγή

κραυγῆς, gen. sing. . . . . . id.

κρέα, acc. pl. . . . . . . κρέας

κρέας], ατος, ως, τό, pl. κρέατα, κρέα, (§ 5. tab. E. j) *flesh, meat,* Ro. 14. 21; 1 Co. 8. 13.

κρεῖσσον, nom. and acc. sing. neut. . . κρείσσων

κρείσσων], or κρείττων, ονος, ὁ, ἡ, τὸ, -ον, (§ 8. rem. 5) (used as the compar. of ἀγαθός) *better, more useful or profitable, more conducive to good,* 1 Co. 7. 9, 38; *superior, more excellent, of a higher nature, more valuable,* He. 1. 4; 6. 9; 7. 7, 19, 22, et al.

κρεῖττον, nom. and acc. sing. neut. . . κρείττων

κρείττονα, acc. sing. fem. and acc. pl. neut. . id.

κρείττονος, gen. sing. masc. and fem. . id.

κρείττοσι, dat. pl. fem. . . . . . id.

κρεμάμενον, acc. sing. neut. part. pres. mid. κρεμάννυμι

κρεμάμενος, nom. sing. masc. part. pres. mid. id.

κρεμάννυμι], fut. άσω, aor. 1, ἐκρέμασα, aor. 1, pass. ἐκρεμάσθην, (§ 36. rem. 5) *to hang, suspend,* Ac. 5. 30; 10. 39; pass. *to be hung, suspended,* Mat. 18. 6; Lu. 23. 39; mid. κρέμαμαι, *to hang, be suspended,* Ac. 28. 4; Gal. 3. 13, et al.; met. κρέμαμαι ἐν, *to hang upon, to be referable to* as an ultimate principle, Mat. 22. 40.

κρημνός, οῦ, ὁ, (§ 3. tab. C. a) *a hanging steep, precipice, a steep bank,* Mat. 8. 32; Mar. 5. 13; Lu. 8. 33.

κρέμανται, 3 pers. pl. pres. ind. mid. . κρεμάννυμι

κρεμάσαντες, nom. pl. masc. part. aor. 1, act. id.

κρεμασθέντων, gen. pl. masc. part. aor. 1, pass. id.

κρεμασθῇ, 3 pers. sing. aor. 1, subj. pass. . id.

κρέμαται, 3 pers. sing. pres. ind. mid.—Al. Ln. Tdf. (ὁ νόμος κρέμαται καὶ οἱ πρ.) . . . } id.
κρέμανται, Rec. Gr. Sch. (Mat. 22. 40) }

κρημνός], οῦ, ὁ, (§ 3. tab. C. a) . . . id.

κρημνοῦ, gen. sing. . . . . . κρημνός

Κρής], ητος, ὁ, (§ 4. rem. 2. c) pl. Κρῆτες, *a Cretan, an inhabitant of* Κρήτη, Ac. 2. 11; Tit. 1. 12.

Κρήσκης],[a] εντος, ὁ, (§ 4. rem. 2. d) *Crescens,* a Latin pr. name.

Κρῆτες, nom. pl. . . . . . . Κρής

Κρήτη], ης, ἡ, (§ 2. tab. B. a) *Crete,* a large island in the eastern part of the Mediterranean.

Κρήτῃ, dat. . . . . . . Κρήτη

Κρήτην, acc. . . . . . . id.

Κρήτης, gen. . . . . . . id.

κριθή], ῆς, ἡ, (§ 2. tab. B. a) *barley.*

κρίθινος, η, ον, (§ 7. tab. F. a) *made of barley,* Jno. 6. 9, 13.

κριθῆναι, aor. 1, infin. pass. . . . κρίνω

κριθῆς,[b] gen. sing. . . . . . κριθή

κριθήσεσθε, 2 pers. pl. fut. pass. (§ 27. rem. 3) κρίνω

κριθήσονται, 3 pers. pl. fut. ind. pass. . . id.

κριθῆτε, 2 pers. pl. aor. 1, subj. pass. . id.

κρίθινος], η, ον, (§ 7. tab. F. a) . . . κριθή

κριθίνους, acc. pl. masc. . . . . κρίθινος

κριθίνων, gen. pl. masc. . . . . . id.

κριθῶν, gen. pl.—A. C. Ln. Tdf. . . } κριθή
κριθῆς, Rec. Gr. Sch. (Re. 6. 6) . }

κριθῶσι, 3 pers. pl. aor. 1, subj. pass. . κρίνω

κρίμα, or κρῖμα], ατος, τό (§ 4. tab. D. c) . id.

κρίματα, nom. and acc. pl. . . . κρίμα

κρίματι, dat. sing. . . . . . id.

κρίματος, gen. sing. . . . . . id.

κρίνα, acc. pl. . . . . . . κρίνον

κρῖναι, aor. 1, infin. act. (§ 27. rem. 1. f) . κρίνω

κρίναντας, acc. pl. masc. part. aor. 1, act. . id.

κρίναντες, nom. pl. masc. part. aor. 1, act. id.

κρίναντος, gen. sing. masc. part. aor. 1, act. id.

κρίνας, nom. sing. masc. part. aor. 1, act.—Gr. Sch. Tdf. . . . } id.
κρίνων, Rec. (Re. 18. 8) . . }

κρίνατε, 2 pers. pl. aor. 1, imper. act. id.

κρίνει, 3 pers. sing. pres. ind. act. . . id.

κρινεῖ, 3 pers. sing. fut. ind. act. (§ 27. rem. 1. a) id.

κρίνειν, pres. infin. act. . . id.

κρίνεις, 2 pers. sing. pres. ind. act. . . id.

κρίνεσθαι, pres. infin. pass. . . id.

κρίνεται, 3 pers. sing. pres. ind. pass. . . id.

κρίνετε, 2 pers. pl. pres. ind. or imper. act. id

κρινέτω, 3 pers. sing. pres. imper. act. . id.

κρίνῃ, 3 pers. sing. pres. subj. act. . . id.

κρίνομαι, 1 pers. sing. pres. ind. pass. . id.

κρινόμενοι, nom. pl. masc. part. pres. pass. . id.

κρινόμενος, nom. sing. masc. part. pres. pass. id.

[a] 2 Ti. 4. 10.

[b] Re. 6. 6.

κρίνον], ου, τό, (§ 3. tab. C. c) *a lily*, Mat. 6. 28; Lu. 12. 27.

κρίνοντα, acc. sing. masc. part. pres. act. . κρίνω
κρίνοντες, nom. pl. masc. part. pres. act. id.
κρίνοντι, dat. sing. masc. part. pres. act. . id.
κρινοῦμεν, 1 pers. pl. fut. ind. act. . . id.
κρινοῦσι, 3 pers. pl. fut. ind. act. . . id.

κρίνω], fut. κρῐνῶ, aor. 1, ἔκρῑνα, perf. κέκρῐκα, perf. pass. κέκρῐμαι, aor. 1, ἐκρίθην (ῐ), pr. *to separate; to make a distinction between; to exercise judgment upon; to estimate*, Ro. 14. 5; *to judge, to assume censorial power over, to call to account*, Mat. 7. 1; Lu. 6. 37; Ro. 2. 1, 3; 14. 3, 4, 10, 13; Col. 2. 16; Ja. 4. 11, 12; *to bring under question*, Ro. 14. 22; *to judge* judicially, *to try* as a judge, Jno. 18. 31, et al.; *to bring to trial*, Ac. 13. 27; *to sentence*, Lu. 19. 22; Jno. 7. 51; *to resolve on, decree*, Ac. 16. 4; Re. 16. 5; absol. *to decide, determine, resolve*, Ac. 3. 13; 15. 19; 27. 1, et al.; *to deem*, Ac. 13. 46; *to form a judgment, pass judgment*, Jno. 8. 15, et al.; pass. *to be brought to trial*, Ac. 25. 10. 20; Ro. 3. 4, et al.; *to be brought to account, to incur arraignment, be arraigned*, 1 Co. 10. 29; mid. *to go to law, litigate*, Mat. 5. 40; in N.T. *to judge, to visit judicially*, Ac. 7. 7; 1 Co. 11. 31, 32; 1 Pe. 4. 6; *to judge, to right, to vindicate*, He. 10. 30; *to administer government over, to govern*, Mat. 19. 28; Lu. 22. 30.

κρίσις, εως, ἡ, pr. *distinction; discrimination; judgment, decision, award*, Jno. 5. 30; 7. 24; 8. 16; *a* judicial *sentence*, Jno. 3. 19; Ja. 2. 13, et al.; *an* adverse *sentence*, Mat. 23. 33; Mar. 3. 29, et al.; *judgment, judicial process, trial*, Mat. 10. 15; Jno. 5. 24; 12. 31; 16. 8, et al.; *judgment, administration of justice*, Jno. 5. 22, 27; in N.T. *a court of justice, tribunal*, Mat. 5. 21, 22; *an impeachment*, 2 Pe. 2. 11; Jude 9; from the Heb., *justice, equity*, Mat. 12. 18, 20; 23. 23; Lu. 11. 42. (ῐ).

κρίμα, or κρῖμα, ατος, τό, *judgment; a sentence, award*, Mat. 7. 2; *a* judicial *sentence*, Lu. 23. 40; 24. 20; Ro. 2. 2; 5. 16, et al.; *an* adverse *sentence*, Mat. 23. 14; Ro. 13. 2; 1 Ti. 5. 12; Ja. 3. 1; *judgment, administration of justice*, Jno. 9. 39; Ac. 24. 25, et al.; *execution of justice*, 1 Pe. 4. 17; *a lawsuit*, 1 Co. 6. 7; in N.T. *judicial visitation*, 1 Co. 11. 29; 2 Pe. 2. 3; *an* administrative *decree*, Ro. 11. 33.

κρῐτής, ου, ὁ, *a judge*, Mat. 5. 25, et al.; from the Heb., *a magistrate, ruler*, Ac. 13. 20; 24. 10.

κριτῐκός, ή, όν, (§ 7. tab. F. a) *able or quick to discern or judge*, He. 4. 12.

κριτήριον, ίου, τό, (§ 3. tab. C. c) pr. *a standard or means by which to judge, criterion; a court of justice, tribunal*, Ja. 2. 6; *a cause, controversy*, 1 Co. 6. 2, 4.

κρινῶ, 1 pers. sing. fut. ind. act. . . . κρίνω
κρίνω, 1 pers. sing. pres. subj. act. . . id.
κρίνωμεν, 1 pers. pl. pres. subj. act. . . id.
κρίνων, nom. sing. masc. part. pres. act. . id.
κρίσει, dat. sing. . . . . . κρίσις
κρίσεις, nom. pl. . . . . id.
κρίσεως, gen. sing. . . . . . id.
κρίσιν, acc. sing. . . . . id.
κρίσις], εως, ἡ, (§ 5. tab. E. c) . . . κρίνω
Κρίσπον, acc. . . . . . . Κρίσπος
Κρίσπος], ου, ὁ, (§ 3. tab. C. a) *Crispus*, a Latin pr. name.
κριταί, nom. pl. . . . . . . κριτής
κριτάς acc. pl. . . . . . . id.
κριτῇ, dat. sing. . . . . . id.
κριτήν, acc. sing. . . . . id.
κριτήρια, acc. pl. . . . . . κριτήριον
κριτήριον], ου, τό, (§ 3. tab. C. c) . . κρίνω
κριτηρίων, gen. pl. . . . . . κριτήριον
κριτής], οῦ, ὁ, (§ 2. tab. B. c) . . κρίνω
κριτικός],[a] ή, όν, (§ 7. tab. F. a) . . id.
κρούειν, pres. infin. . . . . κρούω
κρούετε, 2 pers. pl. pres. imper. . . id.
κρούοντι, dat. sing. masc. part. pres. . id.
κρούσαντος, gen. sing. masc. part. aor. 1 . id.

κρούω], fut. ούσω, (§ 13. tab. M) *to knock* at a door, Mat. 7. 7, 8; Lu. 11. 9, 10; 13. 25, et al.

κρούων, nom. sing. masc. part. pres. . κρούω
κρυβῆναι, aor. 2, infin. pass. (§ 24. rem. 8 a) κρύπτω

[a] He. 4. 12.

κρυπτά, nom. and acc. pl. neut. . . κρυπτός
κρύπτη], ης, ἡ, (§ 2. tab. B. a) . . . κρύπτω
κρύπτην, acc. sing.—Gr. Tdf. . . } κρύπτη
κρυπτόν, Rec. Sch. (Lu. 11. 33) . }
κρυπτόν, nom. and acc. sing. neut. . . κρυπτός
κρυπτός, ή, ον, (§ 7. tab. F. a) . . . κρύπτω

κρύπτω], fut. ψω, aor. 1, ἔκρυψα, (§ 23. rem. 1. a, and rem. 2) perf. pass. κέκρυμμαι, (§ 23. rem. 7. 8) aor. 2, pass. ἐκρύβην, (ῠ), (§ 24. rem. 8. a) *to hide, conceal*, Mat. 5. 14, et al.; in N.T. *to lay up in store*, Col. 3. 3; Re. 2. 17; κεκρυμμένος, *concealed, secret*, Jno. 19. 38.

κρύπτη, ης, ἡ, *a vault or closet, a cell* for stowage, v.r. Lu. 11. 33.

κρυπτός, ή, όν, (§ 7. tab. F. a) *hidden, concealed, secret, clandestine*, Mat. 6. 4, 6, 18, et al.; τὰ κρυπτά, *secrets*, Ro. 2. 16; 1 Co. 14. 25.

κρυφαῖος, α, ον, (§ 7. rem. 1) *secret, hidden*, v.r. Mat. 6. 18.

κρυφῆ, adv. *in secret, secretly, not openly*, Ep. 5. 12.

κρυπτῷ, dat sing. neut. . . . . κρυπτός
κρυσταλλίζοντι,[a] dat. sing. masc. part. pres. κρυσταλλίζω
κρυσταλλίζω], fut. ίσω . . . . κρύσταλλος
κρύσταλλον, acc. sing. . . . . . id.
κρύσταλλος], ου, ὁ, (§ 3. tab. C. a) (κρύος, *cold*), pr. *clear ice; crystal*, Re. 4. 6; 22. 1.

κρυσταλλίζω, fut. ίσω, (§ 26. rem. 1) *to be clear, brilliant like crystal*, Re. 21. 11. N.T.

κρυστάλλῳ, dat. sing. . . . . . κρύσταλλος
κρυφαῖος], α, ον . . . . . . κρύπτω
κρυφαίῳ, dat. sing. neut.—B. D. Ln. Gr. Tdf. } κρυφαῖος
κρυπτῷ, Rec. Sch. (Mat. 6. 18) . }
κρυφῆ,[b] adv. . . . . . . κρύπτω
κρύψατε, 2 pers. pl. aor. 1, imper. act. . id.

κτάομαι, ῶμαι, fut. ήσομαι, (§ 19. tab. S) *to get, procure, provide*, Mat. 10. 9; *to make gain, gain*, Lu. 18. 12; *to purchase*, Ac. 8. 20; 22. 28; *to be the cause or occasion of purchasing*, Ac. 1. 18; *to preserve, save*, Lu. 21. 19; *to get under control, to be winning the mastery over*, 1 Thes. 4. 4; perf. κέκτημαι, *to possess*.

κτῆμα, ατος, τό, (§ 4. tab. D. c) *a possession, property*, and spc. *real estate*, Mat. 19. 22 Mar. 10. 22; Ac. 2. 45; 5. 1.

κτήτωρ, ορος, ὁ, (§ 4. rem. 2. f) *a possessor, owner*, Ac. 4. 34. L.G.

κτᾶσθαι, pres. infin. . . . . . κτάομαι
κτῆμα], ατος, τό . . . . . . id.
κτήματα, acc. pl. . . . . . κτῆμα
κτήνη, acc. pl. . . . . . . κτῆνος

κτῆνος, εος, τό, (§ 5. tab. E. b) pr. *property*, generally used in the plural, τὰ κτήνη; *property* in animals; *a beast of burden*, Lu. 10. 34; Ac. 23. 24; *beasts, cattle*, 1 Co. 15. 39; Re. 18. 13.

κτηνῶν, gen. pl. . . . . . . κτῆνος
κτήσασθε, 2 pers. pl. aor. 1, imper. . κτάομαι
κτήσεσθε, 2 pers. pl. fut. ind.—A. B. Ln. Tdf. } id.
κτήσασθε, Rec. Gr. Sch. (Lu. 21. 19) }
κτήσησθε, 2 pers. pl. aor. 1, subj. . . id.
κτήτορες,[c] nom. pl. . . . . . κτήτωρ
κτήτωρ], ορος, ὁ, (§ 4. rem. 2. f) . . κτάομαι

κτίζω], fut. ίσω, aor. 1, ἔκτισα, perf. pass. ἔκτισμαι, (§ 26. rem. 1) pr. *to reduce from a state of disorder and wildness*; in N.T. *to call into being, to create*, Mar. 13. 19, et al.; *to call into individual existence, to frame*, Ep. 2. 15; *to create* spiritually, *to invest with a* spiritual *frame*, Ep. 2. 10; 4. 24.

κτίσις, εως, ἡ, (§ 5. tab. E. c) pr. *a framing, founding*; in N.T. *creation, the act of creating*, Ro. 1. 20; *creation, the material universe*, Mar. 10. 6; 13. 19; He. 9. 11; 2 Pe. 3. 4; *a created thing, a creature*, Ro. 1. 25; 8. 39; Col. 1. 15; He. 4. 13; *the* human *creation*, Mar. 16. 15; Ro. 8. 19, 20, 21, 22; Col. 1. 23; *a* spiritual *creation*, 2 Co. 5. 17; Gal. 6. 15; *an institution, ordinance*, 1 Pe. 2. 13.

κτίσμα, ατος, τό, (§ 4. tab. D. c) pr. *a thing founded*; in N.T. *a created being, creature*, 1 Ti. 4. 4; Ja. 1. 18, et al. L.G.

κτιστής, οῦ, ὁ, or κτίστης, ου, ὁ, (§ 3. tab. B. c) *a founder*; in N.T. *a creator*, 1 Pe. 4. 19. L.G.

κτίσαντα, acc. sing. masc. part. aor. 1, act. κτίζω
κτίσαντι, dat. sing. masc. part. aor. 1, act. . id.
κτίσαντος, gen. sing. masc. part. aor. 1, act. id.

[a] Re. 21. 11. [b] Ep. 5. 12. [c] Ac. 4. 34.

κτίσει, dat. sing. . . . . . κτίσις
κτίσεως, gen. sing. . . . . . id.
κτίσῃ, 3 pers. sing. aor. 1, subj. act. . κτίζω
κτισθέντα, acc. sing. masc. part. aor. 1, pass. id.
κτισθέντες, nom. pl. masc. part. aor. 1, pass. id.
κτίσις], εως, ἡ, (§ 5. tab. E. c) . . . id.
κτίσμα], ατος, τό, (§ 4. tab. D. c.) . . id.
κτισμάτων, gen. pl. . . . . . κτίσμα
κτίστῃ,[a] dat. sing. . . . . κτίστης
κτίστης], ου, ὁ, (§ 2. tab. B. c) . . κτίζω
κτῶμαι, 1 pers. sing. contr. pres. ind. . κτάομαι

κυβεία], ας, ἡ, (§ 2. tab. B. b, and rem. 2) (κυβεύω, *to play at dice*; fr. κύβος, *a cube, die*) pr. *dicing*; met. *sleight, versatile artifice*.

κυβείᾳ,[b] dat. sing. . . . . . κυβεία
κυβερνήσεις,[c] acc. pl. . . . . κυβέρνησις

κυβέρνησις], εως, ἡ, (§ 5. tab. E. c) (κυβερνάω, *to steer, direct*) *government, office of a governor or director*; meton. *a director*.

κυβερνήτης, ου, ὁ, (§ 2. tab. B. c) *a pilot, helmsman*, Ac. 27. 11; Re. 18. 17.

κυβερνήτῃ, dat. sing. . . . . κυβερνήτης
κυβερνήτης], ου, ὁ . . . . . κυβέρνησις
κυκλεύω], fut. εύσω, (§ 13. tab. M) v.r. κύκλος
κυκλόθεν, adv. . . . . . . id.

κύκλος], ου, ὁ, (§ 3 tab. C. a) *a circle*; in N.T. κύκλῳ, adverbially, *round, round about, around*, Mar. 3. 34; 6. 6, 36, et al.

κυκλεύω, fut. εύσω, aor. 1, ἐκύκλευσα, *to encircle, encompass*, v.r. Re. 20. 9.

κυκλόθεν, adv. *around, round about*, Re. 4. 3, 4, 8; 5. 11.

κυκλόω, ῶ, fut. ώσω, aor. 1, ἐκύκλωσα, (§ 20. tab. T) *to encircle, surround, encompass, come around*, Jno. 10. 24; Ac. 14. 20; spc. *to beleaguer*, Lu. 21. 20; Re. 20. 9; *to march round*, He. 11. 30.

κυκλουμένην, acc. sing. fem. part. pres. pass. (§ 21. tab. U) . . . κυκλόω
κυκλόω, ῶ], fut. ώσω, (§ 20. tab. T) . . κύκλος
κύκλῳ, dat. sing. . . . . . id.
κυκλωθέντα, nom. pl. neut. part. aor. 1, pass. κυκλόω
κυκλωσάντων, gen. pl. masc. part. aor. 1, act. id.
κύλισμα],[d] ατος, τό, (§ 4. tab. D. c) . . κυλίω
κυλίω], fut. ίσω, aor. 1, ἐκύλῐσα, (§ 13. tab. M) (a later form for κυλίνδω) *to roll*; mid. *to roll one's self, to wallow*, Mar. 9. 20. (ῑ).

κύλισμα, ατος, τό, pr. *a rolling thing*; in N.T. *a place of rolling or wallowing, wallowing-place*. L.G.

κυλλόν, acc. sing. masc. . . . κυλλός

κυλλός], ή, όν, (§ 7. tab. F. a) pr. *crooked, bent maimed, lame, crippled*, Mat. 18. 8, et al.

κυλλούς, acc. pl. masc. . . . . κυλλός

κῦμα], ατος, τό, (§ 4. tab. D. c) *a wave, surge, billow*, Mat. 8. 24; 14. 24, et al.

κύματα, nom. pl. . . . . . κῦμα
κυμάτων, gen. pl. . . . . . id.

κύμβᾰλον],[e] ου, τό, (§ 3. tab. C. c) (κύμβος, *a hollow*) *a cymbal*.

κύμῑνον,[f] ου, το, *cumin, cuminum sativum* of Linnæus, a plant, a native of Egypt and Syria, whose seeds are of an aromatic, warm, bitterish taste, with a strong but not disagreeable smell, and used by the ancients as a condiment.

κυνάρια, nom. pl. . . . . . κυνάριον
κυναρίοις, dat. pl. . . . . . id.
κυνάριον], ου, τό, (§ 3. tab. C. c) . . κύων
κύνας, acc. pl. . . . . . id.
κύνες, nom. pl. . . . . . id.
Κύπριοι, nom. pl. . . . . . Κύπριος
Κύπριος], ου, ὁ, (§ 3. tab. C. a) . . Κύπρος
Κυπρίῳ, dat. sing. . . . . . Κύπριος
Κύπρον, acc. . . . . . . Κύπρος

Κύπρος], ου, ἡ, (§ 3. tab. C. b) *Cyprus*, an island in the eastern part of the Mediterranean, Ac. 11. 19, et al.

Κύπριος, ου, ὁ, *a Cypriot, an inhabitant of Cyprus*, Ac. 4. 36; 11. 20; 21. 16.

Κύπρου, gen. . . . . . . Κύπρος

κύπτω], fut. ψω, aor. 1, ἔκυψα, (§ 23. rem. 1. a, and rem. 2) *to bend forwards, stoop down*, Mar. 1. 7; Jno. 8. 6, 8.

Κυρηναῖοι, nom. pl. . . . . Κυρηναῖος
Κυρηναῖον, acc. sing. . . . . . id.
Κυρηναῖος], ου, ὁ . . . . . Κυρήνη
Κυρηναίου, gen. sing. . . . . Κυρηναῖος
Κυρηναίων, gen. pl. . . . . . id.
Κυρήνη], ης, ἡ, (§ 2. tab. B. a) *Cyrene*, a city

[a] 1 Pe. 4. 19. [b] Ep. 4. 14. [c] 1 Co. 12. 28. [d] 2 Pe. 2. 22. [e] 1 Co. 13. 1. [f] Mat. 23. 23.

founded by a colony of Greeks, in Northern Africa.

Κυρηναῖος, ου, ὁ, (§ 3. tab. C. a) *a Cyrenian, an inhabitant of Cyrene,* Mat. 27. 32, et al.

Κυρήνην,[a] acc. . . . . . Κυρήνη

Κυρήνιος], ου, ὁ, (§ 3. tab. C. a) *Cyrenius,* (perhaps *Quirinus*) pr. name.

Κυρηνίου,[b] gen. . . . . . Κυρήνιος

κυρία], ας, ἡ, (§ 2. tab. B. b, and rem. 2) . κύριος

κυρία, voc. sing. . . . . . κυρία

κυρίᾳ, dat. sing. . . . . . id.

κυριακῇ, dat. sing. fem. . . . . κυριακός

κυριακόν, acc. sing. neut. . . id.

κυριακός], ή, όν, (§ 7. tab. F. a) . . . κύριος

κύριε, voc. sing. . . . . . id.

κυριεύει, 3 pers. sing. pres. ind. . . . κυριεύω

κυριεύομεν, 1 pers. pl. pres. ind. . . id.

κυριευόντων, gen. pl. masc. part. pres. . . id.

κυριεύουσι, 3 pers. pl. pres. ind. . . id.

κυριεύσει, 3 pers. sing. fut. ind. . . . id.

κυριεύσῃ, 3 pers. sing. aor. 1, subj. . . id.

κυριεύω], fut. εύσω, (§ 13. tab. M) . . κύριος

κύριοι, nom. and voc. pl. . . . id.

κυρίοις, dat. pl. . . . . . id.

κύριον, acc. sing. . . . . . id.

κύριος, ίου, ὁ, (§ 3. tab. C. a) *a lord, master,* Mat. 12. 8, et al.; *an owner, possessor,* Mat. 20. 8, et al.; *a potentate, sovereign,* Ac. 25. 26; *a power, deity,* 1 Co. 8. 5; *the Lord, Jehovah,* Mat. 1. 22, et al.; *the Lord* Jesus Christ, Mat. 24. 42; Mar. 16. 19; Lu. 10. 1; Jno. 4. 1; 1 Co. 4. 5, et al. freq.; κύριε, a term of respect of various force, *Sir, Lord,* Mat. 13. 27; Ac. 9. 6, et al. freq.

κυρία, ας, ἡ, (§ 2. tab. B. b, and rem. 2) *a lady,* 2 Jno. 1. 5.

κυριᾰκός, ή, ον, (§ 7. tab. F. a) *pertaining to the Lord Jesus Christ, the Lord's,* 1 Co. 11. 20; Re. 1. 10. N.T.

κυριεύω, fut. εύσω, (§ 13. tab. M) Ro. 14. 9; aor. 1, ἐκυρίευσα, *to be lord over, to be possessed of mastery over,* Ro. 6. 9, 14; 7. 1; 2 Co. 1. 24; *to exercise sway over,* Lu. 22. 25.

κυριότης, τητος, ἡ, (§ 4. rem. 2. c) *lordship; constituted authority,* Ep. 1. 21; 2 Pe. 2. 10; Jude 8; pl. *authorities, potentates* Col. 1. 16. N.T.

κυριότης], τητος, ἡ . . . . . κύριος

κυριότητα, acc. sing. . . . . κυριότης

κυριότητες, nom. pl. . . . . id.

κυριότητος, gen. sing. . . . . id.

κυρίου, gen. sing. . . . . . κύριος

κυρίῳ, dat. sing. . . . . . id.

κυρίων, gen. pl. . . . . . id.

κυρόω, ῶ], fut. ώσω, perf. κεκύρωκα, (§ 20. tab. T) (κῦρος, *authority, confirmation*) *to confirm, ratify,* Gal. 3. 15; *to assure,* 2 Co. 2. 8.

κυρῶσαι, aor. 1, infin. . . . κυρόω

κυσί, dat. pl. . . . . . κύων

κύψας, nom. sing. masc. pl. aor. 1 . . κύπτω

κύων], κυνος, ὁ, ἡ, (§ 6. rem. 4. e) *a dog,* Lu. 16. 21; 2 Pe. 2. 22; met. *a dog, a religious corrupter,* Phi. 3. 2; *miscreant,* Re. 22. 15.

κυνάριον, ίου, τό, (§ 3. tab. C. c) (dimin. of κύων) *a little dog; a cur,* Mat. 15. 26, 27; Mar. 7. 27, 28.

κῶλα,[c] nom. pl. . . . . . κῶλον

κῶλον], ου, τό, (§ 3. tab. C. c) *a member or limb of the body.*

κωλύει, 3 pers. sing. pres. ind. act. . . κωλύω

κωλύειν, pres. infin. act. . . . . id.

κωλύεσθαι, pres. infin. pass. . . . id.

κωλύετε, 2 pers. pl. pres. imper. act. . . id.

κωλυθέντες, nom. pl. masc. part. aor. 1, pass. id.

κωλύοντα, acc. sing. masc. part. pres. act. . id.

κωλυόντων, gen. pl. masc. part. pres. act. . id.

κωλῦσαι, aor. 1, infin. act. . . id.

κωλύσῃς, 2 pers. sing. aor. 1, subj. act. . id.

κωλύσητε, 2 pers. pl. aor. 1, subj. act.—D. }
κωλύετε, Rec. Gr. Sch. Tdf. (Mat. 19. 14) } id.

κωλύω], fut ύσω, aor. 1, ἐκώλῦσα, (§ 13. tab. M) aor. 1, pass. ἐκωλύθην, (ῡ), *to hinder, restrain, prevent,* Mat. 19. 14; Ac. 8. 36; Ro. 1. 13, et al. (ῡ).

κώμας, acc. pl. . . . . . κώμη

κώμη], ης, ἡ, (§ 2. tab. B. a) *a village, a country town,* Mat. 9. 35; 10. 11; Lu. 8. 1, et al.

κώμῃ, dat. sing. . . . . . κώμη

κώμην, acc. sing. . . . . . id.

[a] Ac. 2. 10. [b] Lu. 2. 2. [c] He. 3. 17.

κώμης, gen. sing. . . . . κώμη
κῶμοι, nom. pl. . . . . . κῶμος
κώμοις, dat. pl. . . . . . id.
κωμοπόλεις,[a] acc. pl. . . . . κωμόπολις
κωμόπολις], εως, ἡ, (§ 5. tab. E. c) (κώμη & πόλις) *a large village, open town.* L.G.

κῶμος], ου, ὁ, (§ 3. tab. C. a) pr. *a festive procession, a merry-making;* in N.T. *a revel, lascivious feasting,* Ro. 13. 13; Gal. 5. 21; 1 Pe. 4. 3.

Κῶ, acc. (§ 3. rem. 5).—Gr. Sch. Tdf. . } Κῶς
Κῶν, Rec. (Ac. 21. 1) . . . }
Κῶν,[b] acc. . . . . . . id.
κώνωπα,[c] acc. sing. . . . . κώνωψ

κώνωψ], ωπος, ὁ, (§ 4. rem. 2. a) *a gnat, culex,* which is found in wine when acescent.

Κῶς], ῶ, ἡ, (§ 3. tab. C. d) *Cos,* an island in the Ægean sea.
Κωσάμ],[d] ὁ, *Cosam,* pr. name, indecl.
κωφοί, nom. pl. masc. . . . . κωφός
κωφόν, acc. sing. masc. and nom. neut. . id.

κωφός, ή, όν, (§ 7. tab. F. a) pr. *blunt, dull,* as a weapon; *dull* of hearing, *deaf,* Mat. 11. 5; Mar. 7. 32, 37; Lu. 7. 22; *dumb, mute,* Mat. 9. 32, 33, et al.; meton. *making dumb, causing dumbness,* Lu. 11. 14.

κωφούς, acc. pl. masc. . . . . κωφός

Λ.

λάβε, 2 pers. sing. aor. 2, imper. act. . λαμβάνω
λαβεῖν, aor. 2, infin. act. (§ 36. rem. 2) . id.
λάβετε, 2 pers. pl. aor. 2, imper. act. . id.
λαβέτω, 3 pers. sing. aor. 2, imper. act.—Gr. Sch. Tdf. . . . . } id.
λαμβανέτω, Rec. (Re. 22. 17) . . }
λάβῃ, 3 pers. sing. aor. 2, subj. act. . . id.
λάβητε, 2 pers. pl. aor. 2, subj. act. . id.
λάβοι, 3 pers. sing. aor. 2, opt. act. . . id.
λαβόντα, acc. sing. masc. part. aor. 2, act. . id.
λαβόντας, acc. pl. masc. part. aor. 2, act. . id.
λαβόντες, nom. pl. masc. part. aor. 2, act. . id.
λαβοῦσα, nom. sing. fem. part. aor. 2, act. . id.
λαβοῦσαι, nom. pl. fem. part. aor. 2, act. . id.

λάβω, 1 pers. sing. aor. 2, subj. act. . . λαμβάνω
λάβωμεν, 1 pers. pl. aor. 2, subj. act. . id.
λαβών, nom. sing. masc. part. aor. 2, act. . id.
λάβωσι, 3 pers. pl. aor. 2, subj. act. . id.

λαγχάνω], fut. λήξομαι, perf. εἴληχα, perf. 2, λέλογχα, aor. 2, ἔλᾰχον, (§ 36. rem. 2) *to have assigned to one, to obtain, receive,* Ac. 1. 17; 2 Pe. 1. 1; *to have fall to one by lot,* Lu. 1. 9; absol. *to cast lots,* Jno. 19. 24.

Λάζαρε, voc. . . . . . . Λάζαρος
Λάζαρον, acc. . . . . . . id.
Λάζαρος], ου, ὁ, (§ 3. tab. C. a) *Lazarus,* pr. name.
λαθεῖν, aor. 2, infin. . . . . λανθάνω
λάθρα, adv. . . . . . . id.
λαίλαπος, gen. sing. . . . . λαῖλαψ

λαῖλαψ, ᾰπος, ἡ, (§ 4. rem. 2. a) *a squall of wind, a hurricane,* Mar. 4. 37, et al.

λακτίζειν, pres. infin. . . . . λακτίζω
λακτίζω], fut. ίσω, (§ 26. rem. 1) (λάξ, *with the heel*) *to kick,* Ac. 9. 5; 26. 14.
λαλεῖ, 3 pers. sing. pres. ind. act. . . λαλέω
λάλει, 2 pers. sing. pres. imper. act. . id.
λαλεῖν, pres. infin. act. . . . . id.
λαλεῖς, 2 pers. sing. pres. ind. act. . . id.
λαλεῖσθαι, pres. infin. pass. (§ 17. tab. Q) . id.
λαλεῖται, 3 pers. sing. pres. ind. mid. id.
λαλεῖτε, 2 pers. pl. pres. imper. act. . . id.
λαλείτω, 3 pers. sing. pres. imper. act . id.
λαλείτωσαν, 3 pers. pl. pres. imper. act. . id.

λαλέω, ῶ], fut. ήσω, perf. λελάληκα, aor. 1, ἐλάλησα, (§ 16. tab. P) *to make vocal utterance; to babble, to talk;* in N.T. absol. *to exercise the faculty of speech,* Mat. 9. 33, et al.; *to speak,* Mat. 10. 20, et al.; *to hold converse with, to talk with,* Mat. 12. 46; Mar. 6. 50; Re. 1. 12, et al.; *to discourse, to make an address,* Lu. 11. 37; Ac. 11. 20; 21. 39, et al.; *to make announcement, to make a declaration,* Lu. 1. 55, et al.; *to make mention,* Jno. 12. 41; Ac. 2. 31; He. 4. 8; 2 Pe. 3. 16; trans. *to speak, address, preach,* Mat. 9. 18; Jno. 3. 11; Tit. 2. 1, et al.; *to give utterance to, to utter,* Mar. 2. 7; Jno. 3. 34, et al.;

[a] Mar. 1. 38. [b] Ac. 21. 1. [c] Mat. 23. 24. [d] Lu. 3. 28.

to declare, announce, reveal, Lu. 24. 25, et al.; *to disclose,* 2 Co. 12. 4.

λαλιά, ᾶς, ἡ, (§ 2. tab. B. b, and rem. 2) *talk;* in N.T. *matter of discourse,* Jno. 4. 42; 8. 43; *language, dialect,* Mat. 26. 73; Mar. 14. 70.

λαλῇ, 3 pers. sing. pres. subj. . . λαλέω
λαληθείς, nom. sing. masc. part. aor. 1, pass. . id.
λαληθείσης, gen. sing. fem. part. aor. 1, pass. id.
λαληθέντος, gen. sing. neut. part. aor. 1, pass. id.
λαληθέντων, gen. pl. neut. part. aor. 1, pass. id.
λαληθῆναι, aor. 1, infin. pass. . . id.
λαληθήσεται, 3 pers. sing. fut. ind. pass. . id.
λαληθησομένων, gen. pl. neut. part. fut. pass. id.
λαλῆσαι, aor. 1, infin. act. . . . id.
λαλήσαντες, nom. pl. masc. part. aor. 1, act. . id.
λαλήσαντος, gen. sing. masc. part. aor. 1, act. id.
λαλήσας, nom. sing. masc. part. aor. 1, act. id.
λαλήσει, 3 pers. sing. fut. ind. act. . . id.
λαλήσετε, 2 pers. pl. fut. ind. act. . . id.
λαλήσῃ, 3 pers. sing. aor. 1, subj. act. . id.
λαλήσητε, 2 pers. pl. aor. 1, subj. act. . . id.
λαλήσομεν, 1 pers. pl. fut. ind. act. . id.
λαλήσουσι, 3 pers. pl. fut. ind. act. . . id.
λαλήσω, 1 pers. sing. fut. ind. act. . . id.
λαλήσω, 1 pers. sing. aor. 1, subj. act. . id.
λαλήσωσι, 3 pers. pl. aor. 1, subj. act. . id.
λαλιά], ᾶς, ἡ, (§ 2. tab. B. b, and rem. 2) . id.
λαλιάν, acc. sing. . . . . λαλιά
λαλοῦμεν, 1 pers. pl. pres. ind. act. . . λαλέω
λαλουμένη, nom. sing. fem. part. pres. . id.
λαλουμένοις, dat. pl. neut. part. pres. pass. . id.
λαλούμενον, acc. s. m. & nom. neut. part. pres. p. id.
λαλοῦν, nom. sing. neut. part. pres. act. . id.
λαλοῦντα, acc. sing. masc. part. pres. act. . id.
λαλοῦντας, acc. pl. masc. part. pres. act. . id.
λαλοῦντες, nom. pl. masc. part. pres. act. . id.
λαλοῦντι, dat. sing. masc. part. pres. act. . id.
λαλοῦντος, gen. sing. masc. part. pres. act. id.
λαλούντων, gen. pl. masc. part. pres. act. id.
λαλοῦσα, nom. sing. fem. part. pres. act. . id.
λαλοῦσαι, nom. pl. fem. part. pres. act. . id.
λαλοῦσαν, acc. sing. fem. part. pres. act. . id.
λαλούσης, gen. sing. fem. part. pres. act. . id.
λαλοῦσι, 3 pers. pl. pres. ind. act. . . id.
λαλῶ, 1 pers. sing. pres. ind. and subj. act. . id.
λαλῶν, nom. sing. masc. part. pres. act. . id.
λαλῶσι, 3 pers. pl. pres. subj. act. . . id.
λαμά], or λαμμᾶ, (Heb. לָמָּה) *for what? why? wherefore?* Mat. 27. 46; Mar. 15. 34.

λαμβάνει, 3 pers. sing. pres. ind. act. . λαμβάνω
λαμβάνειν, pres. infin. act. . . . id.
λαμβάνεις, 2 pers. sing. pres. ind. act. . id.
λαμβάνετε, 2 pers. pl. pres. ind. and imper. act. id.
λαμβανέτω, 3 pers. sing. pres. imper. act. . id.
λαμβάνῃ, 3 pers. sing. pres. subj. act. . id.
λαμβάνομεν, 1 pers. pl. pres. ind. act. . id.
λαμβανόμενον, nom. sing. neut. part. pres. pass. id.
λαμβανόμενος, nom. sing. masc. part. pres. pass. id.
λαμβάνοντες, nom. pl. masc. part. pres. act. id.
λαμβάνουσι, 3 pers. pl. pres. ind. act. . id.

λαμβάνω, fut. λήψομαι, perf. εἴληφα, aor. 2, ἔλᾰβον, aor. 1, pass. ἐλήφθην, (§ 36. rem. 2) *to take, take up, take in the hand,* Mat. 10. 38; 13. 31, 33, et al.; *to take on one's self, sustain,* Mat. 8. 17; *to take, seize, seize upon,* Mat. 5. 40; 21. 34; Lu. 5. 26; 1 Co. 10. 13, et al.; *to catch,* Lu. 5. 5; 2 Co. 12. 16; *to assume, put on,* Phi. 2. 7; *to make a rightful or successful assumption of,* Jno. 3. 27; *to conceive,* Ac. 28. 15; *to take* by way of provision, Mat. 16. 5; *to get, get together,* Mat. 16. 9; *to receive* as payment, Mat. 17. 24; He. 7. 8; *to take* to wife, Mar. 12. 19; *to admit, give reception to,* Jno. 6. 21; 2 Jno. 10; met. *to give* mental *reception to,* Jno. 3. 11, et al.; *to be* simply *recipient of, to receive,* Mat. 7. 8; Jno. 7. 23, 39; 19. 30; Ac. 10. 43; in N.T. λαμβάνειν πεῖραν, *to make encounter of* a matter of difficulty or trial, He. 11. 29, 36; λαμβάνειν ἀρχήν, *to begin,* He. 2. 3; λαμβάνειν συμβούλιον, *to take counsel, consult,* Mat. 12. 14; λαμβάνειν λήθην, *to forget,* 2 Pe. 1. 9; λαμβάνειν ὑπόμνησιν, *to recollect, call to mind,* 2 Ti. 1. 5; λαμβάνειν περιτομήν, *to receive circumcision, be circumcised,* Jno. 7. 23; λαμβάνειν καταλλαγήν, *to be reconciled,* Ro. 5. 11; λαμβάνειν κρίμα, *to receive condemnation or punishment, be punished,* Mar. 12. 40; from the Heb., πρόσωπον λαμβάνειν, *to accept the person* of any one, *show partiality towards,* Lu. 20. 21. (ᾰν).

λῆψις, εως, ἡ, (§ 5. tab. E. c) *a taking, receiving, receipt,* Phi. 4. 15.

λαμβάνων, nom. sing. masc. part. pres. act. λαμβάνω

Λάμεχ],[a] ὁ, *Lamech*, pr. name, indecl.
λαμμᾶ], see λαμά
λαμπάδας, acc. pl. . . . . . λαμπάς
λαμπάδες, nom. pl. . . . . id.
λαμπάδων, gen. pl. . . . . id.
λαμπάς], άδος, ἡ, (§ 4. tab. D. b) . . λάμπω
λάμπει, 3 pers. sing. pres. ind. . . id.
λαμπρά, nom. pl. neut. . . . . λαμπρός
λαμπρᾷ, dat. sing. fem. . . . id.
λαμπράν, acc. sing. fem. . . . . id.
λαμπρόν, acc. sing. masc. and neut. . id.
λαμπρός, ά, όν, (§ 7. rem. 1) . . . λάμπω
λαμπρότης], τητος, ἡ, (§ 4. rem. 2. c) . id.
λαμπρότητα,[b] acc. sing. . . . . λαμπρότης
λαμπρῶς],[c] adv. . . . . . . λάμπω

λάμπω], fut. ψω & ψομαι, aor. 1, ἔλαμψα, (§ 23. rem. 1. a, and rem. 2) *to shine, give light*, Mat. 5. 15, 16; 17. 2; Lu. 17. 24, et al.

λαμπάς, άδος, (ᾰ) ἡ, (§ 4. tab. D. b) *a light*, Ac. 20. 8; *a lamp*, Re. 4. 5; *a* portable *lamp, lantern, or flambeau*, Mat. 25. 1, 3, 4, 7, 8; Jno. 18. 3.

λαμπρός, ά, όν, (§ 7. rem. 1) *bright, resplendent*, Re. 22. 16; *clear, pellucid*, Re. 22. 1; *white, glistering*, Ac. 10. 30; Re. 15. 6; *of a bright colour, gaudy*, Lu. 23. 11; by impl. *splendid, magnificent, sumptuous*, Ja. 2. 2, 3; Re. 18. 14.

λαμπρότης, τητος, ἡ, (§ 4. rem. 2. c) *brightness, splendour*, Ac. 26. 13.

λαμπρῶς, adv. *splendidly; magnificently, sumptuously*, Lu. 16. 19.

λάμψαι, aor. 1, infin. . . . . . λάμπω
λαμψάτω, 3 pers. sing. aor. 1, imper. . id.
λάμψει, 3 pers. sing. fut. ind.—A. B. D. Ln. Tdf. } id.
λάμψαι, Rec. Gr. Sch. (2 Co. 4. 6) }
λάμψουσι, 3 pers. pl. fut. ind.—D. . . } id.
ἐκλάμψουσι, R. Gr. Sch. Tdf. (Mat. 13. 43) }
λανθάνει, 3 pers. sing. pres. ind. . . λανθάνω
λανθάνειν, pres. infin. . . . . . id.
λανθανέτω, 3 pers. sing. pres. imper. . . id.
λανθάνω], fut. λήσω, aor. 2, ἔλᾰθον, perf. λέληθα, (§ 36. rem. 2) (λήθω, obsolete) *to be unnoticed; to escape the knowledge or observation of* a person, Ac. 26. 26; 2 Pe. 3. 5, 8; absol. *to be concealed, escape detection*, Mar. 7. 24; Lu. 8. 47; with a participle of another verb, *to be unconscious* of an action while the subject or object of it, He. 13. 2. (ᾰν).

λάθρα, adv. *secretly*, Mat. 1. 19; 2. 7, et al.

λήθη, ης, ἡ, (§ 2. tab. B. a) *forgetfulness, oblivion*, 2 Pe. 1. 9.

λαξευτός], ή, όν, (§ 7. tab. F. a) (λᾶς, *a stone*, and ξέω, *to cut, hew*) *cut in stone, hewn out of stone or rock*. LXX.
λαξευτῷ,[d] dat. sing. neut. . . . λαξευτός
Λαοδίκεια], ας, ἡ, (§ 2. tab. B. b, and rem. 2) *Laodicea*, a city of Phrygia in Asia Minor.
Λαοδικείᾳ, dat. . . . . . . Λαοδίκεια
Λαοδίκειαν, acc. . . . . . id.
Λαοδικείας, gen. . . . . . . id.
Λαοδικεύς], εως, ὁ, (§ 5. tab. E. d) *a Laodicean, an inhabitant of Laodicea*, Col. 4. 16; Re. 3. 14.
Λαοδικέων, gen. pl. . . . . Λαοδικεύς
λαοί, nom. pl. . . . . . . λαός
λαοῖς, dat. pl. . . . . . . id.
λαόν, acc. sing. . . . . . . id.

λαός], οῦ, ὁ, (§ 3. tab. C. a) *a body of people; a concourse of people, a multitude*, Mat. 27. 25; Lu. 8. 47, et al.; *the common people*, Mat. 26. 5, et al.; *a people, nation*, Mat. 2. 4; Lu. 2. 32; Tit. 2. 14, et al.; ὁ λαός, *the people* of Israel, Lu. 2. 10.

λαοῦ, gen. sing. . . . . . . λαός

λάρυγξ],[e] υγγος, ὁ, (§ 4. rem. 2. b) *the throat, gullet*.

Λασαία],[f] ας, ἡ,—Rec. Gr. Sch.
Λασέα, B. Tdf.
Ἄλασσα, Ln. *Lasæa*, a maritime town in Crete.

λάσκω], fut. λᾰκήσω, aor. 1, ἐλάκησα, pr. *to emit a sound, ring*; hence, *to break with a sharp noise; to burst*, Ac. 1. 18.

λᾰτομέω, ῶ], fut. ήσω, perf. λελατόμηκα, aor. 1, ἐλατόμησα, (§ 16. tab. P) (λᾶς, *a stone*, and τέμνω) *to hew stones; to cut out of stone, hew from stone*, Mat. 27. 60; Mar. 15. 46. L.G.
λατρεία, ας, ἡ, (§ 2. tab. B. b, and rem. 2) . λατρεύω

[a] Lu. 3. 36. [b] Ac. 26. 13. [c] Lu. 16. 19. [d] Lu. 23. 53. [e] Ro. 3. 13. [f] Ac. 27. 8.

λατρείαν, acc. sing. . . . . λατρεία
λατρείας, gen. sing. and acc. pl. . . id.
λατρεύειν, pres. infin. . . . . λατρεύω
λατρευόμεν, 1 pers. pl. pres. ind. Const. } λατρεύωμεν, Rec. Gr. Sch. Tdf. (He. 12. 28) . . . . . id.
λατρεῦον, nom. sing. neut. part. pres. . id.
λατρεύοντα, acc. sing. masc. part. pres. id.
λατρεύοντας, acc. pl. masc. part. pres. . id.
λατρεύοντες, nom. pl. masc. part. pres. . id.
λατρεύουσα, nom. sing. fem. part. pres. . id.
λατρεύουσι, 3 pers. pl. pres. ind. . . id.
λατρεύσεις, 2 pers. sing. fut. ind. . . id.
λατρεύσουσι, 3 pers. pl. fut. ind. . . id.

λατρεύω, fut. εύσω, aor. 1, ἐλάτρευσα, (§ 13. tab. M) (λάτρις, *a servant*) *to be a servant, to serve*, Ac. 27. 23; *to render religious service and homage, worship*, Mat. 4. 10; Lu. 1. 74; spc. *to offer sacrifices, present offerings*, He. 8. 5; 9. 9.

λατρεία, ας, ἡ, *service, servitude; religious service, worship*, Jno. 16. 2; Ro. 9. 4; 12. 1; He. 9. 1, 6.

λατρεύωμεν, 1 pers. pl. pres. subj. . . λατρεύω
λάχανα, acc. pl. . . . . . . λάχανον

λάχανον], ου, τό, (§ 3. tab. C. c) (λαχαίνω, *to dig*) *a garden herb, vegetable*, Mat. 13. 32; Lu. 11. 42; Ro. 14. 2.

λαχάνων, gen. pl. . . . . . λάχανον
λαχοῦσι, dat. pl. masc. part. aor. 2 . . λαγχάνω
λάχωμεν, 1 pers. pl. aor. 2, subj. . . id.
λαῷ, dat. sing. . . . . . . λαός
λαῶν, gen. pl. . . . . . . id.

Λεββαῖος,[a] ου, ὁ, (§ 3. tab. C. a) *Lebbæus*, pr. name.

λέγε, 2 pers. sing. pres. imper. act. . . λέγω
λέγει, 3 pers. sing. pres. ind. act. . . id.
λέγειν, pres. infin. act. . . . id.
λέγεις, 2 pers. sing. pres. ind. act. . . id.
λέγεσθαι, pres. infin. pass. . . . id.
λέγεται, 3 pers. sing. pres. ind. pass. . . id.
λέγετε, 2 pers. pl. pres. ind. and imper. act. id.
λεγέτω, 3 pers. sing. pres. imper. act. . id.

λεγεών], ῶνος, ὁ, (§ 4. rem. 2. e) (Lat. *legio*) *a Roman legion*; in N.T. *legion* used indefinitely for a great number, Mat. 26. 53; Mar. 5. 9, 15; Lu. 8. 30.

λεγεῶνα, acc. sing. . . . . . λεγεών
λεγεῶνας, acc. pl. . . . . . λεγεών
λεγεώνων, gen. pl.—A. C. Tdf. . . } [ἢ δώδεκα] λεγεῶνας, Rec. Gr. Sch. (Mat. 26. 53) . . . id.
λέγῃ, 3 pers. sing. pres. subj. act. . . λέγω
λέγητε, 2 pers. pl. pres. subj. act. . . id.
λέγομεν, 1 pers. pl. pres. ind. act. . . id.
λεγόμενα, acc. pl. neut. part. pres. pass. . id.
λεγομένη, nom. sing. fem. part. pres. pass. . id.
λεγομένην, acc. sing. fem. part. pres. pass. id.
λεγομένης, gen. sing. fem. part. pres. pass. id.
λεγόμενοι, nom. pl. masc. part. pres. pass. . id.
λεγομένοις, dat. pl. neut. part. pres. pass. . id.
λεγόμενον, acc. sing. masc. part. pres. pass. id.
λεγόμενος, nom. sing. masc. part. pres. pass. id.
λεγομένου, gen. sing. masc. part. pres. pass. id.
λέγον, nom. sing. neut. part. pres. act. . id.
λέγοντα, acc. sing. masc. part. pres. act. . id.
λέγοντα, nom. pl. neut. part. pres. act. . id.
λέγοντας, acc. pl. masc. part. pres. act. . id.
λέγοντες, nom. pl. masc. part. pres. act. . id.
λέγοντι, dat. sing. masc. part. pres. act.—B. D. Ln. Tdf. . . . } εἰπόντι, Rec. Gr. Sch. (Mat. 12. 48) id.
λέγοντος, gen. sing. masc. and neut. pt. pres. act. id.
λεγόντων, gen. pl. masc. part. pres. act. . id.
λέγουσα, nom. sing. fem. part. pres. act. . id.
λέγουσαι, nom. pl. fem. part. pres. act. . id.
λέγουσαν, acc. sing. fem. part. pres. act. . id.
λεγούσης, gen. sing. fem. part. pres. act. . id.
λέγουσι, 3 pers. pl. pres. ind. act. . . id.
λέγουσι, dat. pl. masc. part. pres. act. . id.

λέγω, fut. ξω, (§ 23. rem. 1. b) *to lay, to arrange, to gather; to say*, Mat. 1. 20, et al. freq.; *to speak, make an address or speech*, Ac. 26. 1; *to say* mentally, in thought, Mat. 3. 9; Lu. 3. 8; *to say* in written language, Mar. 15. 28; Lu. 1. 63; Jno. 19. 37, et al.; *to say*, as distinguished from acting, Mat. 23. 3; *to mention, speak of*, Mar. 14. 71; Lu. 9. 31; Jno. 8. 27; *to tell, declare, narrate*, Mat. 21. 27; Mar. 10. 32; *to express*, He. 5. 11; *to put forth, propound*, Lu. 5. 36; 13. 6; Jno. 16. 29; *to mean, to intend to signify*, 1 Co. 1. 12; 10. 29; *to say, declare, affirm, maintain*, Mat. 3. 9; 5. 18; Mar. 12. 18; Ac. 17. 7; 26. 22; 1 Co. 1. 10, et al.; *to enjoin*, Ac.

[a] Mat. 10. 3.

15. 24; 21. 21; Ro. 2. 22; *to term, designate, call,* Mat. 19. 17; Mar. 12. 37; Lu. 20. 37; 23. 2; 1 Co. 8. 5, et al.; *to call* by a name, Mat. 2. 23, et al.; pass. *to be further named, to be surnamed,* Mat. 1. 16, et al.; *to be explained, interpreted,* Jno. 4. 25; 20. 16, 24; in N.T. σὺ λέγεις, *thou sayest,* a form of affirmative answer to a question, Mat. 27. 11; Mar. 15. 2; Jno. 18. 37.

λόγος, ου, ὁ, (§ 3. tab. C. a) *a word, a thing uttered,* Mat. 12. 32, 37; 1 Co. 14. 19; *speech, language, talk,* Mat. 22. 15; Lu. 20. 20; 2 Co. 10. 10; Ja. 3. 2; *converse,* Lu. 24. 17; mere *talk, wordy show,* 1 Co. 4. 19, 20; Col. 2. 23; 1 Jno. 3. 18; *language, mode of discourse, style of speaking,* Mat. 5. 37; 1 Co. 1. 17; 1 Thes. 2. 5; *a saying, a speech,* Mar. 7. 29; Ep. 4. 29; *an expression, form of words, formula,* Mat. 26. 44; Ro. 13. 9; Gal. 5. 14; *a saying, a thing propounded in discourse,* Mat. 7. 24; 19. 11; Jno. 4. 37; 6. 60; 1 Ti. 1. 15, et al.; *a message, announcement,* 2 Co. 5. 19; *a* prophetic *announcement,* Jno. 12. 38; *an account, statement* 1 Pe. 3. 15; *a story, report,* Mat. 28. 15; Jno. 4. 39; 21. 23; 2 Thes. 2. 2; *a written narrative, a treatise,* Ac. 1. 1; *a set discourse,* Ac. 20. 7; *doctrine,* Jno. 8. 31, 37; 2 Ti. 2. 17; *subject-matter,* Ac. 15. 6; *reckoning, account,* Mat. 12. 36; 18. 23; 25. 19; Lu. 16. 2; Ac. 19. 40; 20. 24; Ro. 9. 28; Phi. 4. 15, 17; He. 4. 13; *a plea,* Mat. 5. 32; Ac. 19. 38; *a motive,* Ac. 10. 29; *reason,* Ac. 18. 14; ὁ λόγος, *the word* of God, especially in the Gospel, Mat. 13. 21, 22; Mar. 16. 20; Lu. 1. 2; Ac. 6. 4, et al.; ὁ λόγος, *the* divine *WORD,* or *Logos,* Jno. 1. 1.

λογϊκός, ή, όν, (§ 7. tab. F. a) *pertaining to speech; pertaining to reason;* in N.T. *rational, spiritual, pertaining to the mind and soul,* Ro. 12. 1; 1 Pe. 2. 2.

λόγιον, ίου, τό, (§ 3. tab. C. c) *an oracle, a divine communication or revelation,* Ac. 7. 38; Ro. 3. 2, et al.

λόγιος, ου, ὁ, ἡ, (§ 7. rem. 2) *gifted with learning or eloquence,* Ac. 18. 24.

λογίζομαι, fut. ίσομαι, aor. 1, ἐλογισάμην, aor. 1, pass. ἐλογίσθην, fut. λογισθήσομαι, perf. λελόγισμαι, (§ 26. rem. 1) pr. *to count, calculate; to count, enumerate,* Mar. 15. 28; Lu. 22. 37; *to set down* as a matter of account, 1 Co. 13. 5, 2 Co. 3. 5; 12. 6; *to impute,* Ro. 4. 3; 2 Co. 5. 19; 2 Ti. 4. 16, et al.; *to account,* Ro. 2. 26; 8. 36; εἰς οὐδὲν λογισθῆναι, *to be set at nought, despised,* Ac. 19. 27; *to regard, deem, consider,* Ro. 6. 11; 14. 14; 1 Co. 4. 1; 2 Co. 10. 2; Phi. 3. 13; *to infer, conclude, presume,* Ro. 2. 3; 3. 28; 8. 18; 2 Co. 10. 2, 7, 11; He. 11. 19; 1 Pe. 5. 12; *to think upon, ponder,* Phi. 4. 8; absol. *to reason,* Mar. 11. 31; 1 Co. 13. 11.

λογισμός, οῦ, ὁ, (§ 3. tab. C. a) pr. *a computation, act of computing; a thought, cogitation,* Ro. 2. 15; *a conception, device,* 2 Co. 10. 5.

λογία], ας, ἡ, (§ 2. tab. B. b, & rem. 2) *a gathering, collection,* 1 Co. 16. 1, 2.

λέγω,	1 pers. sing. pres. subj. act.	λέγω
λέγωμεν,	1 pers. pl. pres. subj. act.	id.
λέγων,	nom. sing. masc. part. pres. act.	id.
λέγωσι,	3 pers. pl. pres. subj. act.	id.
λείας,[a]	acc. pl. fem.	λεῖος
λεῖμμα],[b]	ατος, τό, (§ 4. tab. D. c)	λείπω

λεῖος], εία, εῖον, (§ 7. rem. 1) *smooth, level, plain.*

λείπει,	3 pers. sing. pres. ind. act.	λείπω
λείπεται,	3 pers. sing. pres. ind. pass.	id.
λείπῃ,	3 pers. sing. pres. subj. act.	id.
λειπόμενοι,	nom. pl. masc. part. pres. pass.	id.
λείποντα,	acc. pl. neut. part. pres.	id.

λείπω], fut. ψω, (§ 23. rem. 1. a) aor. 2, ἔλῐπον, (§ 24. rem. 9) trans. *to leave, forsake;* pass. *to be left, deserted;* by impl. *to be destitute of, deficient in,* Ja. 1. 4, 5; 2. 15; intrans. *to fail, be wanting, be deficient* Lu. 18. 22, et al.

λεῖμμα, ατος, τό, pr. *a remnant;* in N.T. *a small residue,* Ro. 11. 5.

λοιπός, ή, όν, (§ 7. tab. F. a) *remaining; the rest, remainder,* Mat. 22. 6, et al.

[a] Lu. 3. 5.

[b] Ro. 11. 5.

as an adv. τοῦ λοιποῦ, *henceforth*, Gal. 6. 17; τὸ λοιπόν, or λοιπόν, *henceforwards, thenceforwards*, Mat. 26. 45; 2 Ti. 4. 8; Ac. 27. 20, et al.; *as to the rest, besides*, 1 Co. 1. 16; *finally*, Ep. 6. 10, et al.; ὃ δὲ λοιπόν, *cæterum, but, now*, 1 Co. 4. 2.

λειτουργέω, ῶ], fut. ήσω, (§ 16. tab. P) . λειτουργός

λειτουργῆσαι, aor. 1, infin. . . λειτουργέω

λειτουργία], ας, ἡ, (§ 2. tab. B. b, and rem. 2) λειτουργός

λειτουργίᾳ, dat. sing. . . . . λειτουργία

λειτουργίας, gen. sing. . . . . id.

λειτουργικά,[a] nom. pl. neut. . . . λειτουργικός

λειτουργικός], ή, όν, (§ 7. tab. F. a) . λειτουργός

λειτουργοί, nom. pl. . . . . id.

λειτουργόν, acc. sing. . . . . id.

λειτουργός], οῦ, ὁ, (§ 3. tab. C. a) (λεῖτος, *public*, & ἔργον) pr. *a person of property who performed a public duty or service to the state at his own expense*; in N.T. *a minister or servant*, Ro. 13. 6, et al.; *one who ministers relief*, Phi. 2. 25.

λειτουργέω, ῶ, fut. ήσω, perf. λελειτούργηκα, (§ 16. tab. P) pr. *to perform some public service at one's own expense*; in N.T. *to officiate* as a priest, He. 10. 11; *to minister* in the Christian Church, Ac. 13. 2; *to minister to, assist, succour*, Ro. 15. 27.

λειτουργία, ας, ἡ, (§ 2. tab. B. b, and rem. 2) pr. *a public service discharged by a citizen at his own expense*; in N.T. *a sacred ministration*, Lu. 1. 23; Phi. 2. 17; He. 8. 6; 9. 21; *a kind office, aid, relief*, 2 Co. 9. 12; Phi. 2. 30.

λειτουργϊκός, ή, όν, (§ 7. tab. F. a) *ministering; engaged in subordinate service*, He. 1. 14. LXX.

λειτουργούντων, gen. pl. masc. part. pres. λειτουργέω

λειτουργούς, acc. pl. . . . λειτουργός

λειτουργῶν, nom. sing. masc. part. pres. . λειτουργέω

λείχω], fut. ξω, *to lick*, v.r. Lu. 16. 21.

λελάληκα, 1 pers. sing. perf. ind. act. . . λαλέω

λελάληκε, 3 pers. sing. perf. ind. act. . id.

λελαλημένοις, dat. pl. neut. part. perf. pass. . id.

λελάληται, 3 pers. sing. perf. ind. pass. . id.

λελατομημένον, nom. sing. neut. part. perf. pass. λατομέω

λελουμένοι, nom. pl. masc. part. perf. pass. λούω

λελουμένος, nom. sing. masc. part. perf. pass. (§ 14. rem. 1. e) . . . λούω

λελυμένα, nom. pl. neut. part. perf. pass. . λύω

λελυμένον, nom. sing. neut. part. perf. pass. (§ 14. tab. N) . . . . id.

λελύπηκε, 3 pers. sing. perf. ind. act. . λυπέω

λέλυσαι, 2 pers. s. perf. ind. pass. (§ 14. rem. 1. e) λύω

λέντιον], ίου, τό, (§ 3. tab. C. c) (Lat. *linteum*) *a coarse cloth*, with which servants were girded, *a towel, napkin, apron*, Jno. 13. 4, 5.

λεντίῳ, dat. sing. . . λέντιον

λέοντι, dat. sing. . . . λέων

λέοντος, gen. sing. (§ 4. rem. 2. d) . . id.

λεόντων, gen. pl. . . . id.

λεπίδες,[b] nom. pl. . . . . . λεπίς

λεπίς], ίδος, ἡ, (§ 4. rem. 2. c) (λέπω, *to peel or strip off*) *a scale, shell, rind, crust, incrustation*. (ῐ).

λέπρα, ας, ἡ, (§ 2. tab. B. b) *the leprosy*, Mat. 8. 3; Mar. 1. 42; Lu. 5. 12, 13.

λεπρός, οῦ, ὁ, (§ 3. tab. C. a) *leprous; a leper*, Mat. 8. 2; 10. 8, et al.

λέπρα], ας, ἡ . . . . . . λεπίς

λέπρας, gen. sing. . . . . . λέπρα

λεπροί, nom. pl. . . . . λεπρός

λεπρός], οῦ, ὁ . . . . . λεπίς

λεπροῦ, gen. sing. . . . . λεπρός

λεπρούς, acc. pl. . . . . . . id.

λεπτά, acc. pl. . . . . . λεπτόν

λεπτόν], οῦ, τό, (§ 3. tab. C. c) (λεπτός, *thin, fine, small*) *a mite*, the smallest Jewish coin, equal to half a κοδράντης, and consequently to about three-eighths of a farthing, Mar. 12. 42, et al.

Λευΐ, ὁ, *Levi*, pr. name, indecl.

I. *Levi, son of Jacob*, He. 7. 5, et al.

II. *Levi, son of Symeon*, Lu. 3. 29.

III. *Levi, son of Melchi*, Lu. 3. 24.

Λευΐν, acc. . . . . Λευΐς

Λευΐς, ὁ, *Levi, son of Alphæus, the publican*, Mar. 2. 14, et al.

Λευΐτας, acc. pl. . . . . . Λευΐτης

Λευΐτης], ου, ὁ, (§ 2. tab. B. c) *a Levite, one of the posterity of Levi*, Lu. 10. 32; Jno. 1. 19; Ac. 4. 36. (ῑ).

Λευϊτικῆς,[c] gen. sing. fem. . . . Λευϊτικός

[a] He. 1. 14. [b] Ac. 9. 18. [c] He. 7. 11.

Λευϊτικός], ή, όν, (§ 7. tab. F. a) *Levitical, pertaining to the Levites.*

λευκά, nom. and acc. pl. neut. . . . λευκός
λευκαί, nom. pl. fem. . . . . id.
λευκαίνω], fut. ανῶ . . . . id.
λευκαῖς, dat. pl. fem.—Al. Ln. Tdf. . } id.
λευκῇ, Rec. Gr. Sch. (Ac. 1. 10) . }
λευκᾶναι, aor. 1, infin. . . . λευκαίνω
λευκάς, acc. pl. fem. . . . . λευκός
λευκή, nom. sing. fem. . . . id.
λευκῇ, dat. sing. fem. . . . . id.
λευκήν, acc. sing. fem. . . . id.
λευκοῖς, dat. pl. masc. and neut. . . id.
λευκόν, acc. sing. masc. and nom. neut. id.

λευκός], ή, όν, (§ 7. tab. F. a) pr. *light, bright; white,* Mat. 5. 36; 17. 2, et al.; *whitening, growing white,* Jno. 4. 35.

λευκαίνω, fut. ανῶ, aor. 1, ἐλεύκᾶνα, (§ 27. rem. 1. c. e) *to brighten, to make white,* Mar. 9. 3; Re. 7. 14.

λέων], οντος, ὁ, (§ 4. rem. 2. d) *a lion,* He. 11. 33; 1 Pe. 5. 8, et al.; met. *a lion, cruel adversary, tyrant,* 2 Ti. 4. 17; *a lion, a hero, deliverer,* Re. 5. 5.

λήθη], ης, ἡ, (§ 2. tab. B. a) . . . λανθάνω
λήθην,[a] acc. sing. . . . . λήθη
ληνόν, acc. sing. . . . . . ληνός

ληνός], οῦ, ὁ, ἡ, (§ 3. tab. C. a. b) pr. *a tub, trough; a wine-press,* into which grapes were cast and trodden, Re. 14. 19, 20; 19. 15; *a wine-vat,* i.q. ὑπολήνιον, the lower vat into which the juice of the trodden grapes flowed, Mat. 21. 33.

ληνοῦ, gen. sing. . . . . . ληνός

λῆρος],[b] ου, ὁ, (§ 3. tab. C. a) *idle talk; an empty tale,* Lu. 24. 11.

λῃσταί, nom. pl. . . . . . λῃστής
λῃσταῖς, dat. pl. . . . . . id.
λῃστάς, acc. pl. . . . . . id.
λῃστήν, acc. sing. . . . . . id.
λῃστής], οῦ, ὁ, (§ 2. tab. B. c) (ληΐζομαι, ληΐς, *plunder*) *a plunderer, robber, highwayman,* Mat. 21. 13; 26. 55; Mar. 11. 17; Lu. 10. 30; 2 Co. 11. 26, et al.; *a bandit, brigand,* Mat. 27. 38, 44; Mar. 15. 27; Jno. 18. 40; trop. *a robber, rapacious impostor,* Jno. 10. 1, 8.

λῃστῶν, gen. pl. . . . . . λῃστής
λήψεσθε, 2 pers. pl. fut. ind. (§ 36. rem. 2) λαμβάνω
λήψεται, 3 pers. sing. fut. ind. . . . id.
λήψεως,[c] gen. sing. . . . . λῆψις
λῆψις], εως, ἡ, (§ 5. tab. E. c) . . λαμβάνω
ληψόμεθα, 1 pers. pl. fut. ind. . . id.
λήψονται, 3 pers. pl. fut. ind. . . . id.

λίαν], adv. *much, greatly, exceedingly,* Mat. 2. 16; 4. 8; 8. 28, et al.

λίβα,[d] acc. . . . . . . λίψ
λίβανον, acc. sing. . . . . . λίβανος
λίβᾰνος], ου, ὁ, (§ 3. tab. C. a) *arbor thurifera,* the tree producing frankincense, growing in Arabia and Mount Lebanon; in N.T. *frankincense,* the transparent gum which distils from incisions in the tree, Mat. 2. 11; Re. 18. 13.

λιβανωτός, οῦ, ὁ, ἡ, *frankincense;* in N.T. *a censer,* Re. 8. 3, 5.

λιβανωτόν, acc. sing. . . . . λιβανωτός
λιβανωτός], οῦ, ὁ, ἡ, (§ 3. tab. C. a. b) . λίβανος
λιβερτῖνος], ου, ὁ, (Lat. *libertinus*) *a freed-man, one who having been a slave has obtained his freedom, or whose father was a freed-man;* in N.T. the λιβερτῖνοι probably denote Jews who had been carried captive to Rome, and subsequently manumitted.

λιβερτίνων,[e] gen. pl. . . . . λιβερτῖνος
Λιβύη], ης, ἡ, (§ 2. tab. B. a) *Libya,* a part of Africa, bordering on the West of Egypt.
Λιβύης,[f] gen. . . . . . . Λιβύη
λιθάζειν, pres. infin.—D. Sch. . . } λιθάζω
λιθοβολεῖσθαι, Rec. Gr. Tdf. (Jno. 8. 5) }
λιθάζετε, 2 pers. pl. pres. ind. act. . . id.
λιθάζομεν, 1 pers. pl. pres. ind. act. . id.
λιθάζω], fut. άσω, (§ 26. rem. 1) . . λίθος
λιθάσαι, aor. 1, infin. act. . . . λιθάζω
λιθάσαντες, nom. pl. masc. part. aor. 1, act. id.
λιθασθῶσι, 3 pers. pl. aor. 1, subj. pass. . id.
λιθάσωσι, 3 pers. pl. aor. 1, subj. act. . id.
λίθινα, acc. pl. neut. . . . . λίθινος
λίθιναι, nom. pl. fem. . . . . id.
λιθίναις, dat. pl. fem. . . . . . id.
λίθῐνος], η, ον, (§ 7. tab. F. a) . . λίθος
λιθοβολεῖσθαι, pres. infin. pass. (§ 17. tab. Q) λιθοβολέω
λιθοβολέω, ῶ], ήσω, aor. 1, ἐλιθοβόλησα, (§ 16. tab. P) (λίθος & βάλλω) *to stone, pelt*

[a] 2 Pe. 1. 9. [b] Lu. 24. 11. [c] Phi. 4. 15. [d] Ac. 27. 12. [e] Ac. 6. 9. [f] Ac. 2. 10.

with stones, in order to kill, Mat. 21. 35; 23. 37, et al.

λιθοβοληθήσεται, 3 pers. sing. fut. ind. pass. λιθοβολέω

λιθοβολήσαντες, nom. pl. masc. part. aor. 1, act. id.

λιθοβολῆσαι, aor. 1, infin. act. . . . . id.

λιθοβολοῦσα, nom. sing. fem. part. pres. act. id.

λίθοι, nom. pl. . . . . . . λίθος

λίθοις, dat. pl. . . . . . id.

λίθον, acc. sing. . . . . . . id.

λίθος], ου, ὁ, (§ 3. tab. C. a) *a stone,* Mat. 3. 9; 4. 3, 6, et al.; used figuratively, of Christ, Ep. 2. 20; 1 Pe. 2. 6, et al.; of believers, 1 Pe. 2. 5; meton. *a tablet of stone,* 2 Co. 3. 7; *a precious stone,* Re. 4. 3, et al.

λιθάζω, fut. άσω, (§ 26. rem. 1) *to stone, pelt or kill with stones,* Jno. 10. 31, 32, 33, et al.

λίθῐνος, η, ον, (§ 7. tab. F. a) *made of stone,* Jno. 2. 6, et al.

λιθόστρωτον],[a] ου, τό, (neut. of λιθόστρωτος, *paved with stone,* λίθος & στρώννυμι) *a tessellated pavement.*

λίθου, gen. sing. . . . . . . λίθος

λίθους, acc. pl. . . . . . id.

λίθῳ, dat. sing. . . . . . id.

λίθων, gen. pl. . . . . . . id.

λικμάω, ῶ], fut. ήσω, (§ 18. tab. R) pr. *to winnow grain;* in N.T. *to scatter like chaff,* Mat. 21. 44; Lu. 20. 18.

λικμήσει, 3 pers. sing. fut. ind. . . . λικμάω

λιμένα, acc. sing. . . . . . λιμήν

λιμένας, acc. pl. . . . . . . id.

λιμένος, gen. sing. . . . . . id.

λῐμήν], ένος, ὁ, (§ 4. rem. 2. e) *a port, haven, harbour,* Ac. 27. 8, 12.

λίμνη], ης, ἡ, (§ 2. tab. B. a) *a tract of standing water; a lake,* Lu. 5. 1, et al.

λίμνῃ, dat. sing. . . . . . . λίμνη

λίμνην, acc. sing. . . . . . id.

λίμνης, gen. sing. . . . . . id.

λιμοί, nom. pl. . . . . . . λιμός

λιμόν, acc. sing. . . . . . . id.

λῖμός], οῦ, ὁ, (§ 3. tab. C. a) *famine, scarcity of food, want of grain,* Mat. 24. 7; *famine, hunger, famishment,* Lu. 15. 17; Ro. 8. 35, et al.

λιμῷ, dat. sing. . . . . . . λιμός

Λῖνος,[b] ου, ὁ, *Linus,* pr. name.

λίνον, ου, τό, (§ 3. tab. C. c) *flax;* by meton *a flaxen wick,* Mat. 12. 20; *linen,* Re. 15. 6.

λιπαρά,[c] nom. pl. neut. . . . . . λιπαρός

λῐπᾰρός], ά, όν, (§ 7. rem. 1) (λίπος, *fat, fatness*) *fat; dainty, delicate, sumptuous.*

λίτρα], ας, ἡ, (§ 2 tab. B. b) *a pound, libra,* equivalent to about twelve ounces avoirdupois, Jno. 12. 3; 19. 39.

λίτραν, acc. sing. . . . . . λίτρα

λίτρας, acc. pl . . . . . . id

λίψ], λιβός, ὁ, (§ 4. rem. 2. a) pr. *the south-west wind;* meton. *the south-west quarter of the heavens,* Ac. 27. 12.

λόγια, acc. pl. . . . . . . λόγιον

λογίαι, nom. pl. . . . . . . λογία

λογίας, gen. sing. . . . . . id.

λογίζεσθαι, pres. infin. . . . . λογίζομαι

λογίζεσθε, 2 pers. pl. pres. ind.—Al. Ln. Tdf. } id.
διαλογίζεσθε, Rec. Gr. Sch. (Jno. 11. 50) }

λογίζεσθε, 2 pers. pl. pres. imper. . . id.

λογιζέσθω, 3 pers. sing. pres. imper. . . id.

λογίζεται, 3 pers. sing. pres. ind. (in both a trans. and pass. sense) . . id.

λογίζῃ, 2 pers. sing. pres. ind. . . . . id.

λογίζομαι], fut. ίσομαι, (§ 26. rem. 1) . λέγω

λογιζόμεθα, 1 pers. pl. pres. ind. . . λογίζομαι

λογιζόμενος, nom. sing. masc. part. pres. . id.

λογιζομένους, acc. pl. masc. part. pres. . id.

λογιζομένῳ, dat. sing. masc. part. pres. . id.

λογικήν, acc. sing. fem. . . . . λογικός

λογικόν, acc. sing. neut. . . . . id.

λογικός], ή, όν, (§ 7. tab. F. a) . . . λέγω

λόγιον], ίου, τό, (§ 3. tab. C. c) . . id.

λόγιος],[d] ου, ὁ, ἡ, (§ 7. rem. 2) . . . id.

λογισάμενος, nom. sing. masc. part. aor. 1 . λογίζομαι

λογίσασθαι, aor. 1, infin. . . . . id.

λογίσηται, 3 pers. sing. aor. 1, subj. . . id.

λογισθείη, 3 pers. sing. aor. 1, opt. pass. . id.

λογισθῆναι, aor. 1, infin. pass. . . . id.

λογισθήσεται, 3 pers. sing. fut. ind. pass. . id.

λογισμός], οῦ, ὁ, (§ 3. tab. C. a) . . λέγω

λογισμούς, acc. pl. . . . . . λογισμός

λογισμῶν, gen. pl. . . . . . id.

λογίων, gen. pl. . . . . . . λόγιον

a Jno. 19. 13. b 2 Ti. 4. 21. c Re. 18. 14. d Ac. 18. 24.

λόγοι, nom. pl. λόγος

λόγοις, dat. pl. id.

λογομάχει, 2 pers. sing. pres. imper.—A. C. Ln.
λογομαχεῖν, R. Gr. Sch. Tdf. (2 Ti. 2. 14) } λογομαχέω

λογομαχεῖν,[a] pres. infin. id.

λογομᾰχέω, ῶ], fut. ήσω, (§ 16. tab. P) (λόγος & μάχομαι) *to contend about words*; by impl. *to dispute about trivial things*. N.T.

λογομαχία, ας, ἡ, (§ 2. tab. B. b, and rem. 2) *contention or strife about words*; by impl. *a dispute about trivial things, unprofitable controversy*. N.T.

λογομαχία], ας, ἡ λογομαχέω

λογομαχίας,[b] acc. pl. λογομαχία

λόγον, acc. sing. λόγος

λόγος], ου, ὁ, (§ 3. tab. C. a) λέγω

λόγου, gen. sing. λόγος

λόγους, acc. pl. id.

λόγχη], ης, ἡ, (§ 2. tab. B. a) pr. *the head of a javelin; a spear, lance*, Jno. 19. 34.

λόγχῃ,[c] dat. sing. λόγχη

λόγῳ, dat. sing. λόγος

λόγων, gen. pl. id.

λοιδορεῖς, 2 pers. sing. pres. ind. λοιδορέω

λοιδορέω, ῶ], fut. ήσω, (§ 16. tab. P) λοίδορος

λοιδορία], ας, ἡ, (§ 2. tab. B. b, and rem. 2) id.

λοιδορίαν, acc. sing. λοιδορία

λοιδορίας, gen. sing. id.

λοίδοροι, nom. pl. masc. λοίδορος

λοίδορος], ου, ὁ, ἡ, *reviling, railing*; as a subst. *a reviler, railer*, 1 Co. 5. 11; 6. 10.

λοιδορέω, ῶ, fut. ήσω, (§ 16. tab. P) *to revile, rail at*, Jno. 9. 28; Ac. 23. 4, et al.

λοιδορία, ας, ἡ, (§ 2. tab. B. b, and rem. 2) *reviling, railing*, 1 Ti. 5. 14; 1 Pe. 3. 9.

λοιδορούμενοι, nom. pl. masc. part. pres. pass. (§ 17. tab. Q) λοιδορέω

λοιδορούμενος, nom. sing. masc. part. pres. pass. id.

λοιμοί, nom. pl. λοιμός

λοιμόν, acc. sing. id.

λοιμός], ου, ὁ, (§ 3. tab. C. a) *a pestilence, plague*, Mat. 24. 7; Lu. 21. 11; met. *a pest, pestilent fellow*, Ac. 24. 5.

λοιπά, nom. and acc. pl. neut. λοιπός

λοιπαί, nom. pl. fem. id.

λοιπάς, acc. pl. fem. id.

λοιποί, nom. pl. masc. λοιπός

λοιποῖς, dat. pl. masc. and neut. id.

λοιπόν, nom. and acc. sing. neut. id.

λοιπός], ή, όν, (§ 7. tab. F. a) λείπω

λοιποῦ, gen. sing. neut. λοιπός

λοιπούς, acc. pl. masc. id.

λοιπῶν, gen. pl. id

Λουκᾶς], ᾶ, ὁ, (§ 2. rem. 4) *Lucas, Luke*, pr. name.

Λούκιος], ου, ὁ, (§ 3. tab. C. a) *Lucius*, pr. name.

λουσαμένη, nom. sing. fem. part. aor. 1, mid. (§ 15. tab. O) λούω

λούσαντες, nom. pl. masc. part. aor. 1, act. id.

λούσαντι, dat. sing. masc. part. aor. 1, act. id.

λουτρόν], ου, τό, (§ 3. tab. C. c) id.

λουτροῦ, gen. sing. λουτρόν

λουτρῷ, dat. sing. id.

λούω], fut. σω, aor. 1, ἔλουσα, (§ 13. tab. M) perf. pass. λέλουμαι, pr. *to bathe the body*, as distinguished from washing only the extremities, Jno. 13. 10, *to bathe, wash*, Ac. 9. 37; 16. 33; He. 10. 23; 2 Pe. 2. 22; met. *to cleanse* from sin, Re. 1. 5.

λουτρόν, οῦ, τό, (§ 3. tab. C. c) *a bath, water for bathing; a bathing, washing, ablution*, Ep. 5. 26; Tit. 3. 5.

Λύδδα], ης, ἡ, (§ 2. rem. 3) *Lydda*, a town in Palestine.

Λύδδαν, acc. Λύδδα

Λύδδης, gen. id.

Λυδία], ας, ἡ, (§ 2. tab. B. b, and rem. 2) *Lydia*, pr. name of a woman, Ac. 16. 14, 40.

Λυδίαν, acc. Λυδία

λύει, 3 pers. sing. pres. ind. act. λύω

λύετε, 2 pers. pl. pres. ind. act. id.

λυθείσης, gen. sing. fem. part. aor. 1, pass. (§ 14. tab. N) id.

λυθῇ, 3 pers. sing. aor. 1, subj. pass. id.

λυθῆναι, aor. 1, infin. pass. id.

λυθήσεται, 3 pers. sing. fut. ind. pass. (§ 14. rem. 1. c) id.

λυθήσονται, 3 pers. pl. fut. ind. pass. id.

Λυκαονία], ας, ἡ, (§ 2. tab. B. b, and rem. 2) *Lycaonia*, a province of Asia Minor.

Λυκαονίας,[d] gen. Λυκαονία

Λυκαονιστί,[e] adv. *in the dialect of Lycaonia*.

Λυκία], ας, ἡ, (§ 2. tab. B. b, and rem. 2) *Lycia*, a province of Asia Minor

[a] 2 Ti. 2. 14. [b] 1 Ti. 6. 4. [c] Jno. 19. 34. [d] Ac. 14. 6. [e] Ac. 14. 11.

Λυκίας,[a] gen. . . . . . Λυκία
λύκοι, nom. pl. . . . . . λύκος
λύκον, acc. sing. . . . . . id.

λύκος], ου, ὁ, (§ 3. tab. C. a) *a wolf*, Mat. 10. 16; Lu. 10. 3; Jno. 10. 12; met. *a person of wolf-like character*, Mat. 7. 15; Ac. 20. 29.

λύκων, gen. pl. . . . . . λύκος
λυμαίνομαι], fut. οῦμαι, (λύμη, *outrage*) *to outrage, violently maltreat*; in N.T. *to make havock of*, Ac. 8. 3.
λυομένων, gen. pl. neut. part. pres. pass. . λύω
λύοντες, nom. pl. masc. part. pres. act. . id.
λυόντων, gen. pl. masc. part. pres. act. . id.
λύουσι, 3 pers. pl. pres. ind. act. . . id.
λύπας, acc. pl. . . . . . λύπη
λυπεῖσθαι, pres. infin. pass. (§ 17. tab. Q) λυπέω
λυπεῖται, 3 pers. sing. pres. ind. pass. . id.
λυπεῖτε, 2 pers. pl. pres. imper. act. . . id.
λυπέω, ῶ], fut. ήσω, (§ 16. tab. P) . . λύπη

λύπη], ης, ἡ, (§ 2. tab. B. a) *pain, distress*, Jno 16. 21; *grief, sorrow*, Jno. 16. 6, 20, 22, et al.; meton. *cause of grief, trouble, affliction*, 1 Pe. 2. 19.

λυπέω, ῶ, fut. ήσω, perf. λελύπηκα, aor. 1, ἐλύπησα, (§ 16. tab. P) *to occasion grief or sorrow to, to distress*, 2 Co. 2. 2, 5; 7. 8; pass. *to be grieved, pained, distressed, sorrowful*, Mat. 17. 23; 19. 22, et al.; *to aggrieve, cross, vex*, Ep. 4. 30; pass. *to feel pained*, Ro. 14. 15.

λύπῃ, dat. sing. . . . . . λύπη
λυπηθείς, nom. sing. masc. part. aor. 1, pass. —B. D. Ln. Tdf. . . . } λυπέω
ἐλυπήθη, Rec. Gr. Sch. (Mat. 14. 9)
λυπηθέντας, acc. pl. masc. part. aor. 1, pass. Const. . . . . } id.
λυπηθέντες, Rec. Gr. Sch. Tdf. (1 Pe. 1. 6)
λυπηθέντες, nom. pl. masc. part. aor. 1, pass. id.
λυπηθῆναι, aor. 1, infin. pass. . . id.
λυπηθήσεσθε, 2 pers. pl. fut. ind. pass. . id.
λυπηθῆτε, 2 pers. pl. aor. 1, subj. pass. . id.
λύπην, acc. sing. . . . . . λύπη
λύπης, gen. sing. . . . . id.
λυπῆσθε, 2 pers. pl. pres. subj. pass. . . λυπέω
λυπούμενοι, nom. pl. masc. part. pres. pass. id.
λυπούμενος, nom. sing. masc. part. pres. pass. id.
λυπῶ, 1 pers. sing. pres. ind. contr. . . id.

λῦσαι, aor. 1, infin. act. (§ 13. rem. 12) . λύω
Λυσανίας], ου, ὁ, (§ 2. tab. B. d) *Lysanias*, pr. name.
Λυσανίου,[b] gen. . . . . . Λυσανιας
λύσαντες, nom. pl. masc. part. aor. 1, act. . λύω
λύσαντι, dat. sing. masc. part. aor. 1, act.— Al. Ln. Tdf. . . . . } id.
λούσαντι, Rec. Gr. Sch. (Re. 1. 5)
λύσας, nom. sing. masc. part. aor. 1, act. . id.
λύσατε, 2 p. pl. aor. 1, imper. act. (§ 13. rem. 13) id.
λύσῃ, 3 pers. sing. aor. 1, subj. act. . . id.
λύσῃς, 2 pers. sing. aor. 1, subj. act. . id.
λύσητε, 2 pers. pl. aor. 1, subj. act. . . id.
Λυσίας], ου, ὁ, (§ 2. tab. B. d) *Lysias*, pr. name.
λύσιν,[c] acc. sing. . . . . . λύσις
λύσις], εως, ἡ, (§ 5. tab. E. c) . . . λύω
λυσιτελεῖ,[d] 3 pers. sing. pres. ind. . . λυσιτελέω
λυσιτελέω, ῶ], fut. ήσω, (§ 16. tab. P) (λύω, *to pay*, & τέλος, *an impost*) pr. *to compensate for incurred expense*; by impl. *to be advantageous to, to profit, advantage*; impers. Lu. 17. 2.
λῦσον, 2 pers. sing. aor. 1, imper. act. . . λύω
Λύστρα], ας, ἡ, and Λύστρα], ων, τά, (§ 2. tab. B. b; § 3. tab. C. c) *Lystra*, a city of Lycaonia, in Asia Minor.
Λύστραν, acc. . . . . . Λύστρα
Λύστροις, dat. pl. neut. . . . . id.
λύσω, 1 pers. sing. aor. 1, subj. act. . λύω
λύτρον, ου, τό, (§ 3. tab. C. c) . . . id.
λυτρόω, ῶ], fut. ώσω, (§ 20. tab. T) . id.
λυτροῦσθαι, pres. infin. mid. (§ 21. tab. U) . λυτρόω
λυτρώσηται, 3 pers. sing. aor. 1, subj. mid. id
λύτρωσιν, acc. sing. . . . . λύτρωσις
λύτρωσις], εως, ἡ, (§ 5. tab. E. c) . . λύω
λυτρωτήν,[e] acc. sing. . . . . λυτρωτής
λυτρωτής], οῦ, ὁ, (§ 2. tab. B. c) . . λύω
λυχνία, ας, ἡ, (§ 2. tab. B. b, and rem. 2) . λύχνος
λυχνίαι, nom. pl. . . . . . λυχνία
λυχνίαν, acc. sing. . . . . id.
λυχνίας, gen. sing. and acc. pl. . . . id.
λυχνιῶν, gen. pl. . . . . id.
λύχνοι, nom. pl. . . . . . λύχνος
λύχνον, acc. sing. . . . . . id.

λύχνος], ου, ὁ, (§ 6. rem. 7) *a light, lamp, candle*, etc., Mat. 5. 15; Mar. 4. 21, et al.; met *a lamp*, as a figure of a distinguished teacher, Jno. 5. 35.

[a] Ac. 27. 5. [b] Lu. 3. 1. [c] 1 Co. 7. 27. [d] Lu. 17. 2. [e] Ac. 7. 35.

λυχνία, ας, ἡ, (§ 2. tab. B. b, and rem. 2) *a candlestick, lampstand*, Mat. 5. 15, et al.; met. *a candlestick*, as a figure of a Christian church, Re. 1. 12, 13, 20; of a teacher or prophet, Re. 11. 4. L.G.

λύχνου, gen. sing. . . . . . . λύχνος

λύχνῳ, dat. sing. . . . . . id.

λύω], fut. λύσω, perf. λέλῠκα, aor. 1, ἔλῡσα, (§ 13. tab. M) perf. pass. λέλῠμαι, aor. 1, pass. ἐλύθην, (ῠ), (§ 14. tab. N) *to loosen, unbind, unfasten*, Mar. 1. 7, et al.; *to loose, untie*, Mat. 21. 2; Jno. 11. 44; *to disengage*, 1 Co. 7. 27; *to set free, set at liberty, deliver*, Lu. 13. 16; *to break*, Ac. 27. 41; Re. 5. 2, 5; *to break up, dismiss*, Ac. 13. 43; *to destroy, demolish*, Jno. 2. 19; Ep. 2. 14; met. *to infringe*, Mat. 5. 19; Jno. 5. 18; 7. 23; *to make void, nullify*, Jno. 10. 35; in N.T. *to declare free*, of privileges, or, in respect of lawfulness, Mat. 16. 19, et al.

λύσις, εως, ἡ, (§ 5. tab. E. c) *a loosing*; in N.T. *a release* from the marriage bond, *a divorce*, 1 Co. 7. 27.

λύτρον, ου, τό, (§ 3. tab. C. c) (λύω, in the sense of *to pay quittance*) pr. *price paid; a ransom*, Mat. 20. 28; Mar. 10. 45.

λυτρόω, ῶ, fut. ώσω, (§ 20. tab. T) *to release for a ransom*; mid. *to ransom, redeem, deliver, liberate*, Lu. 24. 21; Tit. 2. 14; 1 Pe. 1. 18.

λύτρωσις, εως, ἡ, (§ 5. tab. E. c) *redemption*, He. 9. 12; *liberation, deliverance*, Lu. 1. 68; 2. 38. L.G.

λυτρωτής, οῦ, ὁ, (§ 2. tab. B. c) *a redeemer; a deliverer*, Ac. 7. 35. LXX.

Λωΐδι,[a] dat. . . . . Λωΐς

Λωΐς], ΐδος, ἡ, (§ 4. rem. 2. c) *Lois*, pr. name of a woman.

Λώτ], ὁ, *Lot*, pr. name, indecl.

M.

Μαάθ],[b] ὁ, *Maath*, pr. name, indecl.

Μαγαδάν], indecl.—B. D. Ln.

Μαγδαλά, Rec. Gr. Sch. Tdf. (Mat. 15. 39)

Μαγδαλά], ἡ, indecl. *Magdala*, a town of Judea.

Μαγδαληνή], ῆς, ἡ, (§ 2. tab. B. a) *Magdalene*, pr. name, (*of Magdala*).

Μαγδαληνῇ, dat. . . . . . Μαγδαληνή

μαγεία], ας, ἡ, (§ 2. tab. B. b, and rem. 2) . μάγος

μαγείαις,[c] dat. pl. . . . . . μαγεία

μαγεύω], fut. εύσω, (§ 13. tab. M) . . μάγος

μαγεύων,[d] nom. sing. masc. part. pres. . μαγεύω

μάγοι, nom. pl. . . . . . . μάγος

μάγον, acc. sing. . . . . . id.

μάγος], ου, ὁ, (§ 3. tab. C. a) (Pers. *mogh*, Heb. מָג, akin to μέγας, *magnus*) *a magus, sage of the magian religion, magian*, Mat. 2. 1, 7, 16; *a magician, sorcerer*, Ac. 13. 6, 8.

μαγεία, ας, ἡ, pr. *the system of the magians; magic*, Ac. 8. 11.

μαγεύω, fut. εύσω, (§ 13. tab. M) *to be a magian; to use magical arts, practise magic, sorcery*, etc. Ac. 8. 9.

μάγους, acc. pl. . . . . . . μάγος

Μαγώγ],[e] ὁ, *Magog*, pr. name, indecl.

μάγων, gen. pl. . . . . . . μάγος

Μαδιάμ],[f] indeclin. *Madian*, a district of Arabia Petræa.

μαζοῖς, dat. pl.—A. Ln. Tdf. . . . } μαζός
μαστοῖς, Rec. Gr. Sch. (Re. 1. 13) }

μαζός], οῦ, ὁ, v.r. equivalent to μαστός.

μαθεῖν, aor. 2, infin. (§ 36. rem. 2) . . μανθάνω

μάθετε, 2 pers. pl. aor. 2, imper. . . id.

μαθηταί, nom. pl. . . . . . . μαθητής

μαθηταῖς, dat. pl. . . . . . id.

μαθητάς, acc. pl. . . . . . . id.

μάθητε, 2 pers. pl. aor. 2, subj. . . μανθάνω

μαθητευθείς, nom. sing. masc. part. aor. 1, pass. μαθητεύω

μαθητεύσαντες, nom. pl. masc. part. aor. 1, act. id.

μαθητεύσατε, 2 pers. pl. aor. 1, imper. act. . id.

μαθητεύω], fut. εύσω, (§ 13. tab. M) . μανθάνω

μαθητῇ, dat. sing. . . . . . . μαθητής

μαθητήν, acc. sing. . . . . . id.

μαθητής], οῦ, ὁ, (§ 2. tab. c) . . . μανθάνω

μαθητοῦ, gen. sing. . . . . . μαθητής

μαθήτρια],[g] ας, ἡ, (§ 2. tab. B. b, and rem. 2) μανθάνω

μαθητῶν, gen. pl. . . . . . . μαθητής

Μαθουσάλα],[h] ὁ, *Mathusala*, pr. name, indecl.

μαθών, nom. sing. masc. part. aor. 2 . μανθάνω

Μαϊνάν],[i] ὁ, *Mainan*, pr. name, indecl.—R. Gr. Sch.

Μεννᾶ, Ln. Tdf.

μαίνεσθε, 2 pers. pl. pres. ind. . . . μαίνομαι

a 2 Ti. 1. 5. b Lu. 3. 26. c Ac. 8. 11. d Ac. 8. 9. e Re. 20. 8. f Ac. 7. 29. g Ac. 9. 36. h Lu. 3. 37. i Lu. 3. 31.

μαίνεται, 3 pers. sing. pres. ind. . . μαίνομαι
μαίνῃ, 2 pers. sing. pres. ind. . . . id.

μαίνομαι], fut. μανήσομαι and μανοῦμαι, perf. μέμηνα, (§ 25. rem. 5) *to be disordered in mind, mad*, Jno. 10. 29, et al.

μανία, ας, ἡ, (§ 2. tab. B. b, and rem. 2) *madness, insanity*, Ac. 26. 24.

μακαρία, nom. sing. fem. . . . μακάριος
μακάριαι, nom. pl. fem. . . . . id.
μακαρίαν, acc. sing. fem. . . . id.
μακαρίζομεν, 1 pers. pl. pres. ind. . . μακαρίζω
μακαρίζω], fut. ίσω, (§ 26. rem. 1) . μακάριος
μακάριοι, nom. pl. masc. . . . . id.
μακάριον, acc. sing. masc. and nom. neut. id.

μακάριος], ία, ιον, (§ 7. rem. 1) (μάκαρ, idem) *happy, blessed*, Mat. 5. 3, 4, 5, 7; Lu. 1. 45, et al.

μακαρίζω, fut. ίσω, Att. ιῶ, *to pronounce happy, felicitate*, Lu. 1. 48; Ja. 5. 11.

μακαρισμός, οῦ, ὁ, (§ 3. tab. C. a) *a calling happy, the act of pronouncing happy, felicitation*, Ro. 4. 6, 9; *self-congratulation*, Gal. 4. 15.

μακαρίου, gen. sing. masc. . . . μακάριος
μακαριοῦσι, 3 pers. pl. fut. Att. (§ 35. rem. 11) μακαρίζω
μακαρισμόν, acc. sing. . . . . μακαρισμός
μακαρισμός], οῦ, ὁ, (§ 3. tab. C. a) . μακάριος
μακαριωτέρα, nom. sing. fem. compar. (§ 8. rem. 4) . . . . . id.
Μακεδόνας, acc. pl. . . . . Μακεδών
Μακεδόνες, nom. pl. . . . . id.

Μακεδονία], ας, ἡ, (§ 2. tab. B. b, and rem. 2) *Macedonia*.

Μακεδονίᾳ, dat. . . . . Μακεδονία
Μακεδονίαν, acc. . . . . id.
Μακεδονίας, gen. . . . . id.
Μακεδόνος, gen. sing. . . . . Μακεδών
Μακεδόσι, dat. pl. . . . . id.

Μακεδών], όνος, ὁ, (§ 4. rem. 2. e) *a native of Macedonia*, Ac. 16. 9, et al.

μάκελλον], ου, τό, (§ 3. tab. C. c) (Lat. *macĕllum*) *a place where all kinds of provisions are exposed to sale, provision mart, shambles*.

μακέλλῳ,[a] dat. sing. . . . . μάκελλον
μακρά, acc. pl. neut. . . . . μακρός
μακράν, acc. sing. fem. . . . . μακρός
μακράν, adv. . . . . . μῆκος
μακρόθεν, adv. . . . . . id.
μακροθυμεῖ, 3 pers. sing. pres. ind. . μακροθυμέω
μακροθυμεῖτε, 2 pers. pl. pres. imper. . . id.

μακροθῠμέω, ῶ], fut. ήσω, (§ 16. tab. P) (μακρόθυμος, μακρός & θυμός) *to be slow towards, be long-enduring; to exercise patience, be long-suffering, clement, or indulgent, to forbear*, Mat. 18. 26, 29; 1 Co. 13. 4; 1 Thes. 5. 14; 2 Pe. 3. 9; *to have patience, endure patiently, wait with patient expectation*, He. 6. 15; Ja. 5. 7, 8; *to bear long* with entreaties for deliverance and avengement, Lu. 18. 7.

μακροθυμία, ας, ἡ, (§ 2. tab. B. b, and rem. 2) *patience; patient enduring of evil, fortitude*, Col. 1. 11; *slowness of avenging injuries, long-suffering, forbearance, clemency*, Ro. 2. 4; 9. 22; 2 Co. 6. 6; *patient expectation*, He. 6. 12, et al.

μακροθύμως, adv. *patiently, with indulgence*, Ac. 26. 3. (ῡ).

μακροθυμήσας, nom. sing. masc. part. aor. 1 μακροθυμέω
μακροθυμήσατε, 2 pers. pl. aor. 1, imper. . id.
μακροθύμησον, 2 pers. sing. aor. 1, imper. id.
μακροθυμία], ας, ἡ, (§ 2. tab. B. b, and rem. 2) id.
μακροθυμίᾳ, dat. sing. . . . . μακροθυμία
μακροθυμίαν, acc. sing. . . . . id.
μακροθυμίας, gen. sing. . . . . id.
μακροθυμῶν, nom. sing. masc. part. pres. μακροθυμέω
μακροθύμως,[b] adv. . . . . . id.
μακρός], ά, όν, (§ 7. rem. 1) . . . μῆκος

μακροχρόνιος],[c] ου, ὁ, ἡ, (§ 7. rem. 2) (μακρός & χρόνος) *of long duration; long-lived*, Ep. 6. 3. L.G.

μαλακά, acc. pl. neut. . . . . μαλακός
μαλακία], ας, ἡ, (§ 2. tab. B. b, and rem. 2) id.
μαλακίαν, acc. sing. . . . . μαλακία
μαλακοί, nom. pl. masc. . . . . μαλακός
μαλακοῖς, dat. pl. neut. . . . . id.

μαλᾰκός], ή, όν, (§ 7. tab. F. a) *soft; soft to the touch, delicate*, Mat. 11. 8; Lu. 7. 25; met. *cinædus, an instrument of unnatural lust, effeminate*, 1 Co. 6. 9.

μαλακία, ας, ἡ, *softness; languor, indisposition, weakness, infirmity of body*, Mat. 4. 23, et al.

[a] 1 Co. 10. 25. [b] Ac. 26. 3. [c] Ep. 6. 3.

Μαλελεήλ],[a] ὁ, *Maleleel*, pr. name, indecl.

μάλιστα], adv. (superlat. of μάλα, *very, much*) *most, most of all, chiefly, especially*, Ac. 20. 38; 25. 26, et al.

μᾶλλον], adv. (comparative of μάλα), *more, to a greater extent, in a higher degree*, Mat. 18. 13; 27. 24; Jno. 5. 18; 1 Co. 14. 18, et al.; *rather, in preference*, Mat. 10. 6; Ep. 4. 28, et al.; used in a periphrasis for the comparative, Ac. 20. 35, et al.; as an intensive with a comparative term, Mat. 6. 26; Mar. 7. 36; 2 Co. 7. 13; Phi. 1. 23; μᾶλλον δέ, *yea rather*, or, *more properly speaking*, Ro. 8. 34; Gal. 4. 9; Ep. 5. 11.

Μάλχος],[b] ου, ὁ, (§ 3. tab. C. a) *Malchus*, pr. name.

μάμμῃ,[c] dat. sing. . . . . . μάμμη

μάμμη, and μάμμα], ης, ἡ, (§ 2. tab. B. a, and rem. 3) *a mother; later, a grandmother.*

μαμμωνᾶ, gen. . . . . . μαμμωνᾶς

μαμμωνᾷ, dat. . . . . . id.

μαμμωνᾶς, or μαμωνᾶς], ᾶ, ὁ, (§ 2. rem. 4) (Aram. מָמוֹנָא) *wealth, riches*, Lu. 16. 9, 11; personified, like the Greek Πλοῦτος, *Mammon*, Mat. 6. 24; Lu. 16. 13.

Μαναήν],[d] ὁ, *Manaen*, pr. name, indecl.

Μανασσῆ, acc. . . . . . Μανασσῆς

Μανασσῆ, indecl. and Μανασσῆς, acc. ῆ] (§ 2. rem. 5) *Manasses*, pr. name.

I. *The tribe of Manasseh*, Re. 7. 6.

II. *Manasseh, king of Judah*, Mat. 1. 10.

μανθανέτω, 3 pers. sing. pres. imper. . . μανθάνω

μανθανέτωσαν, 3 pers. pl. pres. imper. . id.

μανθάνοντα, acc. pl. neut. part. pres. . . id.

μανθάνουσι, 3 pers. pl. pres. ind. . . id.

μανθάνω], fut. μαθήσομαι, aor. 2, ἔμᾰθον, perf. μεμάθηκα, (§ 36. rem. 2) *to learn, be taught*, Mat. 9. 13; 11. 29; 24. 32; *to learn* by practice or experience, *acquire a custom or habit*, Phi. 4. 11; 1 Ti. 5. 4, 13; *to ascertain, be informed*, Ac. 23. 27, et al. *to understand, comprehend*, Re. 14. 3. (ᾰ).

μαθητής, οῦ, ὁ, (§ 2. tab. B. c) *a disciple*, Mat. 10. 24, 42, et al.

μαθήτρια, ας, ἡ, (§ 2. tab. B. b, and rem. 2) *a female disciple; a female Christian*, Ac. 9. 36.

μαθητεύω, fut. εύσω, aor. 1, ἐμαθήτευσα, (§ 13. tab. M) intrans. *to be a disciple, follow as a disciple*, Mat. 27. 57; in N.T. trans. *to make a disciple of, to train in discipleship*, Mat. 28. 19; Ac. 14. 21; pass. *to be trained, disciplined, instructed*, Mat. 13. 52. L.G.

μανθάνωσι, 3 pers. pl. pres. subj. . . μανθάνω

μανία], ας, ἡ, (§ 2. tab. B. b, and rem. 2) μαίνομαι

μανίαν,[e] acc. sing. . . . . . μανία

μάννα], τό, indecl. (Heb. מָן, Exod. 16. 15) *manna*, the miraculous food of the Israelites while in the desert, Jno. 6. 31, 49, 58, et al.

μαντεύομαι], fut. εύσομαι, (μάντις, *a soothsayer diviner*) *to utter oracles, to divine.*

μαντευομένη, nom. sing. fem. part. pres. μαντεύομαι

μαρὰν ἀθά],[f] (Chald. מָרַנָא אֲתָה) i.q. κύριος ἔρχεται, *the Lord cometh, or will come* to judgment.—Rec. Gr. Sch.

μαραναθά, Ln. Tdf.

μαραίνω], fut. ανῶ, aor. 1, pass. ἐμαράνθην, (§ 27. rem. 1. c, and rem. 3) *to quench, cause to decay, fade, or wither*; pass. *to wither, waste away*; met. *to fade away, disappear, perish*, Ja. 1. 11.

μαρανθήσεται,[g] 3 pers. sing. fut. ind. pass. . μαραίνω

μαργαρῖται, nom. pl. . . . . μαργαρίτης

μαργαρίταις, dat. pl. . . . . id.

μαργαρίτην, acc. sing. . . . . id.

μαργαρίτης], ου, ὁ, (§ 2. tab. B. c) (μάργαρον, idem) *a pearl*, Mat. 7. 6; 13. 45, 46, et al. (ῑ).

μαργαρίτου, gen. sing. . . . . μαργαρίτης

Μάρθα], ας, ἡ, *Martha*, pr. name.

Μάρθαν, acc. . . . . . Μάρθα

Μάρθας, gen. . . . . . id.

Μαρία], (or Μαριάμ, indecl.) *Mary* pr. name.

I. *The mother of Jesus*, Mat. 1. 16, et al.

II. *Mary, wife of Clopas, mother of James*, Mar. 15. 40; Jno. 19. 25, et al.

III. *Mary Magdalene*, Mat. 27. 56, et al.

IV. *Mary, sister of Martha and Lazarus*, Lu. 10. 39; Jno. 11. 1, et al.

V. *Mary, mother of John surnamed Mark*, Ac. 12. 12.

VI. *Mary, a Christian at Rome*, Ro. 16. 6.

---

[a] Lu. 3. 37. [b] Jno. 18. 10. [c] 2 Ti. 1. 5. [d] Ac. 13. 1. [e] Ac. 26. 24. [f] 1 Co. 16. 22. [g] Ja. 1. 11.

Μαρίᾳ, dat. . . . . Μαρία
Μαριάμ, the indeclinable form of . . id.
Μαρίαν, acc. . . . . id.
Μαρίας, gen. . . . . . id.
Μάρκον, acc. . . . . . Μάρκος
Μάρκος], ου, ὁ, *Marcus, Mark,* pr. name.
Μάρκου, gen. . . . . . . Μάρκος
μάρμᾰρος], ου, ὁ, (§ 3. tab. C. a) (μαρμαίρω, *to glisten, shine*) *a white glistening stone; marble.*
μαρμάρου,[a] gen. sing. . . . . μάρμαρος
μάρτυρα, acc. sing. . . . . μάρτυς
μάρτυρας, acc. pl. . . . . . id.
μαρτυρεῖ, 3 pers. sing. pres. ind. . . μαρτυρέω
μαρτυρεῖν, pres. infin. . . . . id.
μαρτυρεῖς, 2 pers. sing. pres. ind. . id.
μαρτυρεῖτε, 2 pers. pl. pres. ind. . . id.
μάρτυρες, nom. pl. . . . . μάρτυς
μαρτυρέω], ῶ, fut. ήσω, (§ 16. tab. P) . . id.
μαρτυρηθέντες, nom. pl. masc. part. aor. 1, pass. (§ 17. tab. Q) . . μαρτυρέω
μαρτυρῆσαι, aor. 1, infin. . . . . id.
μαρτυρήσαντος, gen. sing. masc. part. aor. 1 id.
μαρτυρήσας, nom. sing. masc. part. aor. 1 . id.
μαρτυρήσει, 3 pers. sing. fut. ind. . . id.
μαρτυρήσῃ, 3 pers. sing. aor. 1, subj. . id.
μαρτύρησον, 2 pers. sing. aor. 1, imper. . id.
μαρτυρήσω, 1 pers. sing. aor. 1, subj. . id.
μαρτυρία], ας, ἡ, (§ 2. tab. B. b, and rem. 2) . μάρτυς
μαρτυρίαι, nom. pl. . . . . μαρτυρία
μαρτυρίαν, acc. sing. . . . . id.
μαρτυρίας, gen. sing. . . . . id.
μαρτύριον], ου, τό, (§ 3. tab. C. c) . . μάρτυς
μαρτυρίου, gen. sing. . . . . μαρτύριον
μαρτύρομαι], (§ 37. rem. 1) . . . μάρτυς
μαρτυρόμενος, nom. sing. masc. part. pres.—A. B. Ln. Tdf. . . . } μαρτύρομαι
μαρτυρούμενος, R. Gr. Sch. (Ac. 26. 22) }
μάρτυρος, gen. sing. . . . . μάρτυς
μαρτυροῦμεν, 1 pers. pl. pres. ind. . . μαρτυρέω
μαρτυρουμένη, nom. sing. fem. part. pres. pass. id.
μαρτυρούμενοι, nom. pl. masc. part. pres. mid. id.
μαρτυρούμενος, nom. sing. masc. part. pres. pass. and mid. . . . . id.
μαρτυρουμένους, acc. pl. masc. part. pres. pass. and mid. . . . . id.
μαρτυροῦν, nom. sing. neut. part. pres. . id.
μαρτυροῦντες, nom. pl. masc. part. pres. . id.
μαρτυροῦντι, dat. sing. masc. part. pres. . μαρτυρέω
μαρτυροῦντος, gen. sing. masc. part. pres. . id.
μαρτυρούντων, gen. pl. masc. part. pres. . id.
μαρτυροῦσαι, nom. pl. fem. part. pres. . id.
μαρτυρούσης, gen. sing. fem. part. pres. . id
μαρτυροῦσι, 3 pers. pl. pres. ind. . . id.
μαρτυρῶ, 1 pers. sing. pres. ind. and subj. . id.
μαρτυρῶν, nom. sing. masc. part. pres. . id.
μαρτύρων, gen. pl. . . . . . μάρτυς

μάρτυς, ῠρος, ὁ, ἡ, *a* judicial *witness, deponent,* Mat. 18. 16; He. 10. 28, et al.; generally, *a witness* to a circumstance, Lu. 24. 48; Ac. 10. 41, et al.; in N.T. *a witness, a testifier* of a doctrine, Re. 1. 5; 3. 14; 11. 3; *a martyr,* Ac. 22. 20; Re. 2. 13.

μαρτῠρέω, ῶ, fut. ήσω, perf. μεμαρτύρηκα, aor. 1, ἐμαρτύρησα, (§ 16. tab. P) trans. *to testify, depose,* Jno. 3. 11, 32; 1 Jno. 1. 2; Re. 1. 2; 22. 20; absol. *to give evidence,* Jno. 18. 23; *to bear testimony, testify,* Lu. 4. 22; Jno. 1. 7, 8, et al.; *to bear testimony* in confirmation, Ac. 14. 3; *to declare* distinctly and formally, Jno. 4. 44; pass. *to be the subject of testimony, to obtain attestation* to character, Ac. 6. 3; 10. 22; 1 Ti. 5. 10; He. 11. 2, 4; mid. equivalent to μαρτύρομαι, *to make a solemn appeal,* Ac. 26. 22; 1 Thes. 2. 12.

μαρτυρία, ας, ἡ, (§ 2. tab. B. b, and rem. 2) judicial *evidence,* Mar. 14. 55, 56, 59; Lu. 22. 71; *testimony* in general, Tit. 1. 13; 1 Jno. 5. 9; *testimony, declaration* in a matter of fact or doctrine, Jno. 1. 19; 3. 11; Ac. 22. 18, et al.; *attestation* to character, Jno. 5. 34, 36, et al.; *reputation,* 1 Ti. 3. 7.

μαρτύριον, ίου, τό, (§ 3. tab. C. c) *testimony, evidence,* 2 Co. 1. 12; Ja. 5. 3; *testification,* Ac. 4. 33; in N.T. *testimony, mode of solemn declaration or testification,* Mat. 8. 4; Lu. 9. 5, et al.; *testimony, matter of solemn declaration,* 1 Co. 1. 6; 2. 1; 1 Ti. 2. 6; σκηνὴ τοῦ μαρτυρίου, a title of the Mosaic tabernacle, Ac. 7. 44; Re. 15. 5.

[a] Re. 18. 12.

μαρτυρομαι, *to call to witness;* intrans. *to make a solemn affirmation or declaration, asseverate,* Ac. 20. 26; Gal. 5. 3; *to make a solemn appeal,* Ep. 4. 17.

μάρτυσι, dat. pl. (§ 4. rem. 3. a) . . μάρτυς

μασσάομαι, ῶμαι], rather μασάομαι, fut. ήσομαι, (§ 19. tab. S) *to chew, masticate;* in N.T. *to gnaw,* Re. 16. 10.

μάστιγας, acc. pl. . . . . . μάστιξ

μαστιγοῖ, 3 pers. sing. pres. ind. . . μαστιγόω

μάστιγος, gen. sing. . . . . μάστιξ

μαστιγόω, ῶ], fut. ώσω, (§ 20. tab. T) . id.

μαστίγων, gen. pl. . . . . . id.

μαστιγῶσαι, aor. 1, infin. . . . μαστιγόω

μαστιγώσαντες, nom. pl. masc. part. aor. 1 id.

μαστιγώσετε, 2 pers. pl. fut. ind. . . id.

μαστιγώσουσι, 3 pers. pl. fut. ind. . . id.

μαστίζειν,[a] pres. infin. . . . . μαστίζω

μαστίζω], fut. ίξω . . . . μάστιξ

μάστιξ], ῖγος, ἡ, (§ 4. rem. 2. b) *a scourge, whip,* Ac. 22. 24; He. 11. 36; met. *a scourge* of disease, Mar. 3. 10; 5. 29, 34; Lu. 7. 21.

μαστιγόω, ῶ, fut. ώσω, aor. 1, ἐμαστίγωσα, (§ 20. tab. T) *to scourge,* Mat. 10. 17; 20. 19, et al.; met. *to chastise,* He. 12. 6.

μαστίζω, fut. ίξω, (§ 26. rem. 2) *to scourge,* Ac. 22. 25. (Poet. and L.G.)

μάστιξι, dat. pl. . . . . . μάστιξ

μαστοί, nom. pl. . . . . μαστός

μαστοῖς, dat. pl. . . . . . id.

μαστός], οῦ, ὁ, (§ 3. tab. C. a) (a collateral form of μαζός) *the breast, pap,* Lu. 11. 27, et al.

ματαία, nom. sing. fem. . . . μάταιος

ματαίας, gen. sing. fem. . . . . id.

μάταιοι, nom. pl. masc. . . . id.

ματαιολογία], ας, ἡ . . . ματαιολόγος

ματαιολογίαν,[b] acc. sing. . . . ματαιολογία

ματαιολόγοι,[c] nom. pl. masc. . . ματαιολόγος

ματαιολόγος], ου, ὁ, ἡ, (§ 7. rem. 2) (μάταιος & λέγω) *a vain talker, given to vain talking or trivial disputation.*

ματαιολογία, ας, ἡ, (§ 2. tab. B. b, and rem. 2) *vain talking, idle disputation.* L.G.

μάταιος], αία, αιον, & ὁ, ἡ . . . μάτην

ματαιότης], τητος, ἡ, (§ 4. rem. 2. c) . id.

ματαιότητι, dat. sing. . . . . ματαιότης

ματαιότητος, gen. sing. . . . id.

ματαιόω, ῶ], fut. ώσω, (§ 20. tab. T) . id.

ματαίων, gen. pl. . . . . μάταιος

μάτην, adv. *in vain, fruitlessly, without profit,* Mat. 15. 9; Mar. 7. 7.

μάταιος, αία, αιον, & ου, ὁ, ἡ, (§ 7. rem. 1 and 2) *vain, ineffective, bootless,* 1 Co. 3. 20; *groundless, deceptive, fallacious,* 1 Co. 15. 17; *useless, fruitless, unprofitable,* Tit. 3. 9; Ja. 1. 26; from the Heb., *erroneous* in principle, *corrupt, perverted,* 1 Pe. 1. 18; τὰ μάταια, *superstition, idolatry,* Ac. 14. 15.

ματαιότης, τητος, ἡ, (§ 4. rem. 2. c) *vanity, folly;* from the Heb., religious *error,* Ep. 4. 17; 2 Pe. 2. 18; *false religion,* Ro. 8. 20. LXX.

ματαιόω, ῶ, fut. ώσω, (§ 20. tab. T) *to make vain;* from the Heb., pass. *to fall into religious error, to be perverted,* Ro. 1. 21. LXX.

Ματθαῖον, acc. . . . . . Ματθαῖος

Ματθαῖος], ου, ὁ, *Matthew,* pr. name.

Ματθάν], ὁ, *Matthan,* pr. name, indecl.

Ματθάτ], ὁ, *Matthat,* pr. name, indecl.

Ματθίαν, acc. . . . . . Ματθίας

Ματθίας], ου, ὁ, (§ 2. tab. B. d) *Matthias,* pr. name.

Ματταθά],[d] ὁ, *Mattatha,* pr. name, indecl.

Ματταθίας], ου, ὁ, (§ 2. tab. B. d) *Mattathias,* pr. name.

Ματταθίου, gen. . . . . . Ματταθίας

μάχαι, nom. pl. . . . . . μάχη

μάχαιρα], ας, ἡ, (§ 2. tab. B. b) *a large knife, poniard; a sword,* Mat. 26. 47, 51, et al.; *the sword* of the executioner, Ac. 12. 2; Ro. 8. 35; He. 11. 37; hence, φορεῖν μάχαιραν, *to bear the sword, to have the power of life and death,* Ro. 13. 4; meton. *war,* Mat. 10. 34.

μαχαίρᾳ, dat. sing. . . . . μάχαιρα

μάχαιραι, nom. pl. . . . . . id.

μαχαίρας, gen. sing. . . . . μάχαιρα

μαχαίρῃ, dat. sing.—A. B. C. Ln. . . } id.
μαχαίρᾳ, Rec. Gr. Sch. Tdf. (Mat. 26. 52) }

a Ac. 22. 25. b 1 Ti. 1. 6. c Tit. 1. 10. d Lu. 3. 31.

μαχαιρῶν, gen. pl. . . . . . . μάχαιρα
μάχας, acc. pl. . . . . . . μάχη
μάχεσθαι, pres. infin. . . . . μάχομαι
μάχεσθε, 2 pers. pl. pres. ind. . . id.
μάχη], ης, ἡ, (§ 2. tab. B. a) . . id.

μάχομαι], fut. οῦμαι, or έσομαι, (§ 35. rem. 5) *to fight; to quarrel*, Ac. 7. 26; *to contend, dispute*, Jno. 6. 52, et al.

μάχη, ης, ἡ, (§ 2. tab. B. a) *a fight, battle, conflict*; in N.T. *contention, dispute, strife, controversy*, 2 Co. 7. 5; 2 Ti. 2. 23, et al.

μαχομένοις, dat. pl. masc. part. pres. . μάχομαι
μέ, acc. sing. (§ 11. tab. K. a) . . . ἐγώ
μέγα, nom. and acc. sing. neut. . . μέγας
μεγάλα, nom. and acc. pl. neut. . . id.
μεγάλαι, nom. pl. fem. . . . id.
μεγάλαις, dat. pl. fem. . . . . id.
μεγάλας, acc. pl. fem. . . . . id.
μεγαλαυχεῖ,[a] 3 pers. sing. pres. ind.—Rec. Gr. Sch. Tdf. } μεγαλαυχέω
μεγάλα αὐχεῖ, Ln. . . . }
μεγαλαυχέω, ῶ], fut. ήσω, (μέγας & αὐχέω, *to boast*) *to boast, vaunt; to cause a great stir*, Ja. 3. 5.
μεγαλεῖα, acc. pl. neut. . . . . μεγαλεῖος
μεγαλεῖος], εία, ειον, (§ 7. rem. 1) . μέγας
μεγαλειότης], τητος, ἡ, (§ 4. rem. 2. c) . id.
μεγαλειότητα, acc. sing. . . . μεγαλειότης
μεγαλειότητι, dat. sing. . . . . id.
μεγαλειότητος, gen. sing. . . . id.
μεγάλη, nom. sing. fem. . . . . μέγας
μεγάλῃ, dat. sing. fem. . . . id.
μεγάλην, acc. sing. fem. . . . id.
μεγάλης, gen. sing. fem. . . . id.
μεγάλοι, nom. pl. masc. . . . . id.
μεγάλοις, dat. pl. masc. . . . id.
μεγαλοπρεπής], έος, οῦς, ὁ, ἡ, (§ 7. tab. G. b) (μέγας & πρέπω) pr. *becoming a great man; magnificent, glorious, most splendid.*
μεγαλοπρεποῦς,[b] gen. sing. . . μεγαλοπρεπής
μεγάλου, gen. sing. masc. . . . μέγας
μεγάλους, acc. pl. masc. . . . . id.
μεγαλύνει, 3 pers. sing. pres. ind. act. . μεγαλύνω
μεγαλύνω], fut. υνῶ, (§ 27. rem. 1. a) . . μέγας
μεγαλυνθῆναι, aor. 1, infin. pass. . . μεγαλύνω
μεγαλυνθήσεται, 3 pers. sing. fut. ind. pass. . id.

μεγαλυνόντων, gen. pl. masc. part. pres. act. μεγαλύνω
μεγαλύνουσι, 3 pers. pl. pres. ind. act. . id.
μεγάλῳ, dat. sing. masc. . . . . μέγας
μεγάλων, gen. pl. . . . . . id.
μεγάλως,[c] adv. . . . . . . id.
μεγαλωσύνη], ης, ἡ, (§ 2. tab. B. a) . id.
μεγαλωσύνης, gen. sing. . . . μεγαλωσύνη
μέγαν, acc. sing. masc. . . . . μέγας

μέγας], μεγάλη (ᾰ), μέγα, (§ 7. rem. 8. b) compar. μείζων, superl. μέγιστος, *great, large in size*, Mat. 27. 60; Mar. 4. 32, et al.; *great, much, numerous*, Mar. 5. 11; He. 11. 26; *great, grown up, adult*, He. 11. 24; *great, vehement, intense*, Mat. 2. 10; 28. 8; *great, sumptuous*, Lu. 5. 29; *great, important, weighty, of moment*, 1 Co. 9. 11; 13. 13; *great, splendid, magnificent*, Re. 15. 3; *extraordinary, wonderful*, 2 Co. 11. 15; *great, solemn*, Jno. 7. 37; 19. 31; *great* in rank, *noble*, Re. 11. 18; 13. 16; *great* in dignity, *distinguished, eminent, illustrious, powerful*, Mat. 5. 19; 18. 1, 4, et al.; *great, arrogant, boastful*, Re. 13. 5.

μεγαλεῖος, εία, εῖον, (§ 7. rem. 1) *magnificent, splendid*; τὰ μεγαλεῖα, *great things, wonderful works*, Lu. 1. 49; Ac. 2. 11.

μεγαλειότης, τητος, ἡ, (§ 4. rem. 2. c) *majesty, magnificence, glory*, Lu. 9. 43; Ac. 19. 27; 2 Pe. 1. 16. LXX.

μεγαλύνω, fut. υνῶ, aor. 1, ἐμεγάλῡνα, (§ 27. rem. 1. a. f) *to enlarge, amplify*, Mat. 23. 5; *to manifest in an extraordinary degree*, Lu. 1. 58; *to magnify, exalt, extol*, Lu. 1. 46; Ac. 5. 13, et al. (ῡ).

μεγάλως, adv. *greatly, very much, vehemently*, Phi. 4. 10. (ᾰ).

μεγαλωσύνη, ης, ἡ, (§ 2. tab. B. a) *greatness, majesty*, He. 1. 3; 8. 1; ascribed *majesty*, Jude 25. LXX.

μέγεθος, εος, ους, τό, (§ 5. tab. E. b) *greatness, vastness*, Ep. 1. 19.

μεγιστᾶνες, ων, οἱ, (§ 4. rem. 2. e) *great men, lords, chiefs, nobles, princes*, Mar. 6. 21; Re. 6. 15; 18. 23. L.G.

μέγεθος],[d] εος, ους, τό, (§ 5. tab. E. b) . μέγας
μέγιστα,[e] nom. pl. neut. superl. (§ 8. rem. 2) id.

[a] Ja. 3. 5. [b] 2 Pe. 1. 17. [c] Phi. 4. 10. [d] Ep. 1. 19. [e] 2 Pe. 1. 4.

μεγιστᾶνες], ων, οἱ, (§ 4. rem. 2. e) . μέγας
μεγιστᾶσι, dat. . . . . . μεγιστᾶνες
μέγιστος], η, ον, (§ 7. tab. F. a) *greatest; pre-eminent*, 2 Pe. 1. 4.
μεθ', by apostrophe for μετά.
μέθαι, nom. pl. . . . . . μέθη
μέθαις, dat. pl. . . . . . id.
μεθερμηνεύεται, 3 pers. sing. pres. ind. pass. μεθερμηνεύω
μεθερμηνευόμενον, nom. s. neut. part. pres. pass. id.
μεθερμηνεύω], fut. εύσω, (§ 13. tab. M) (μετά & ἑρμηνεύω) *to translate, interpret*, Mat. 1. 23; Mar. 5. 41, et al. L.G.
μέθη], ης, ἡ, (§ 2. tab. B. a) . . . μεθύω
μέθῃ, dat. sing. . . . . . μέθη
μεθιστάναι, pres. infin. act.—B. D. Ln. Tdf. } μεθίστημι
μεθιστάνειν, Rec. Gr. Sch. (1 Co. 13. 2) }
μεθιστάνειν, pres. infin. act. . . . μεθιστάνω
μεθίστημι, or μεθιστάνω (ᾰ)], fut. μεταστήσω, (§ 29. tab. X) aor. 1, μετέστησα, (μετά & ἵστημι) *to cause a change of position; to remove, transport*, 1 Co. 13. 2; *to transfer*, Col. 1. 13; met. *to cause to change sides*; by impl. *to pervert, mislead*, Ac. 19. 26; *to remove* from office, *dismiss, discard*, Lu. 16. 4; Ac. 13. 22.
μεθοδεία], ας, ἡ, (§ 2. tab. B. b, and rem. 2) (μεθοδεύω, *to trace, investigate; to handle methodically; to handle cunningly*; from μέθοδος, μετά & ὁδός) *artifice, wile*, Ep. 4. 14; 6. 11. N.T.
μεθοδείαν, acc. sing. . . . . . μεθοδεία
μεθοδείας, acc. pl. . . . . . id.
μεθόρια,[a] acc. pl. . . . . μεθόριον
μεθόριον], ου, τό, (§ 3. tab. C. c) (neut. from μεθόριος, *interjacent*, μετά & ὅρος) *confine, border*, Mar. 7. 24.
μεθύει, 3 pers. sing. pres. ind. . . μεθύω
μεθυόντων, gen. pl. masc. part. pres. . . id.
μεθύουσαν, acc. sing. fem. part. pres. . id.
μεθύουσι, 3 pers. pl. pres. ind. . . id.
μεθυσθῶσι, 3 pers. pl. aor. 1, subj. pass. . μεθύσκω
μεθύσκεσθαι, pres. infin. pass. . . . id.
μεθύσκεσθε, 2 pers. pl. pres. imper. pass. . id.
μεθυσκόμενοι, nom. pl. masc. part. pres. pass. id.
μεθύσκω], fut. ύσω, (§ 36. rem. 3) . . μεθύω
μέθυσοι, nom. pl. masc. . . . μέθυσος
μέθυσος, ου, ὁ, ἡ, (§ 7. rem. 2) . . . μεθύω
μεθύω], fut. ύσω, (§ 13. tab. M) (μέθυ, *strong drink*) *to be intoxicated, be drunk*, Mat. 24. 49, et al. (ῡ).

μέθη, ης, ἡ, (§ 2. tab. B. a) *strong drink; drunkenness*, Lu. 21. 34; *a debauch in drinking*, Ro. 13. 13; Gal. 5. 21.

μεθύσκω, fut. ύσω, aor. 1, pass. ἐμεθύσθην, *to inebriate, make drunk*; pass. *to be intoxicated, to be drunk*, Lu. 12. 45; 1 Thes. 5. 7, et al.; *to drink freely*, Jno. 2. 10.

μέθυσος, ου, ὁ, ἡ, (§ 7. rem. 2) *drunken; a drunkard*, 1 Co. 5. 11; 6. 10.

μεῖζον,[b] adv. *to a greater degree* . . μέγας
μεῖζον, nom. and acc. sing. neut. compar. . id.
μείζονα, acc. sing. fem. and neut. pl. compar. id.
μείζονας, acc. pl. fem. compar. . . id.
μείζονες, nom. pl. masc. compar. (§ 8. rem. 3) id.
μείζονος, gen. sing. compar. masc. and fem. . id.
μειζοτέραν,[c] acc. sing. fem. . . . μειζότερος
μειζότερος], α, ον, (§ 8. rem. 2) *greater*, a comparative formed of μείζων.
μείζω, acc. sing. fem. and acc. pl. neut. compar. μέγας
μείζων], ονος, ὁ, ἡ, τό, -ον, (§ 8. rem. 3) *greater*, comparat. of μέγας.
μεῖναι, aor. 1, infin. (§ 27. rem. 1. d) . . μένω
μείναντες, nom. pl. masc. part. aor. 1 . id.
μείνατε, 2 pers. pl. aor. 1, imper. . . id.
μείνῃ, 3 pers. sing. aor. 1, subj. . . μένω
μείνητε, 2 pers. pl. aor. 1, subj. . . id.
μεῖνον, 2 pers. sing. aor. 1, imper. . . id.
μείνωσι, 3 pers. pl. aor. 1, subj. . . . id.
μέλαιναν, acc. sing. fem. . . . μέλας
μέλαν], ἄνος, τό, (neut. fr. μέλας) *ink*, 2 Co. 3. 3; 2 Jno. 12; 3 Jno. 13.
μέλανι, dat. sing. neut. . . . μέλας
μέλανος, gen. sing. neut. . . . . id.

μέλας], αινα, αν, (§ 7. tab. H. a) *black*, Mat. 5. 36; Re. 6. 5, 12.

Μελεᾶ,[d] gen. . . . . . Μελεᾶς
Μελεᾶς], ᾶ, ὁ, (§ 2. rem. 4) *Meleas*, pr. name.

μέλει], fut. μελήσει, imperf. ἔμελε, imperat. μελέτω, impers. verb, *there is a care, it concerns*, Mat. 22. 16; Ac. 18. 17; 1 Co. 9. 9, et al.

μελετάω, ῶ, fut. ήσω, (§ 18. tab. R) aor. 1, ἐμελέτησα, *to care for; to bestow careful thought upon, to give painful at-*

[a] Mar. 7. 24. [b] Mat. 20. 31. [c] 3 Jno. 4. [d] Lu. 3. 31.

tention to, be earnest in, 1 Ti. 4. 15; *to devise,* Ac. 4. 25; absol. *to study beforehand, premeditate,* Mar. 13. 11.

μέλεσι, dat. pl. . . . . . μέλος

μελέτα, 2 pers. sing. pres. imper. . . μελετάω

μελετᾶτε, 2 pers. pl. pres. imper. . . id.

μελετάω, ῶ], fut. ήσω . . . . μέλει

μελέτω, 3 pers. sing. pres. imper. . . id.

μέλη, nom. and acc. pl. . . . μέλος

μέλι], ιτος, τό, (§ 5. rem. 4) *honey,* Mat. 3. 4; Mar. 1. 6; Re. 10. 9, 10.

μελίσσιος, ίου, ὁ, ἡ, (§ 7. rem. 2) (μέλισσα, *a bee,* μέλι) *of bees, made by bees,* Lu. 24. 42.

μελισσίου,[a] gen. sing. neut. . . . μελίσσιος

Μελίτη],[b] ης, ἡ, (§ 2. tab. B. a) *Melita,* an island in the Mediterranean.

μέλλει, 3 pers. sing. pres. ind. . . μέλλω

μέλλειν, pres. infin. . . . . id.

μέλλεις, 2 pers. sing. pres. ind. . . id.

μέλλετε, 2 pers. pl. pres. ind. . . . id.

μέλλῃ, 3 pers. sing. pres. subj. . . id.

μελλήσετε, 2 pers. pl. fut. ind. (§ 35. rem. 5) id.

μελλήσω, 1 pers. sing. fut. ind.—Al. Ln. Tdf. } id.
οὐκ ἀμελήσω, Rec. Gr. Sch. (2 Pe. 1. 12) }

μέλλομεν, 1 pers. pl. pres. ind. . . . id.

μέλλον, acc. sing. neut. part. pres. . . id.

μέλλοντα, acc. sing. masc. part. pres. . id.

μέλλοντα, nom. and acc. pl. neut. part. pres. id.

μέλλοντας, acc. pl. masc. part. pres. . id.

μέλλοντες, nom. pl. masc. part. pres. . . id.

μέλλοντι, dat. sing. masc. part. pres. . id.

μέλλοντος, gen. sing. masc. and neut. part. pres. id.

μελλόντων, gen. pl. masc. and neut. part. pres. id.

μέλλουσαν, acc. sing. fem. part. pres. . . id.

μελλούσης, gen. sing. fem. part. pres. . id.

μέλλουσι, 3 pers. pl. pres. ind. . . . id.

μέλλω], fut. ήσω, (§ 35. rem. 5) imperf. ἔμελλον, Att. ἤμελλον, *to be about to, be on the point of,* Mat. 2. 13; Jno. 4. 47; it serves to express in general a settled futurity, Mat. 11. 14; Lu. 9. 31; Jno. 11. 51, et al.; *to intend,* Lu. 10. 1, et al.; particip. μέλλων, ουσα, ον, *future* as distinguished from past and present, Mat. 12. 32; Lu. 13; 9, et al.; *to be always, as it were, about to do, to delay, linger,* Ac. 22. 16

μέλλων, nom. sing. masc. part. pres. μέλλω

μέλος], εος, ους, τό, (§ 5. tab. E. b) *a member, limb, any part of the body,* Mat. 5. 29, 30; Ro. 12. 4: 1 Co. 6. 15; 12. 12, et al.

μέλους, gen. sing.—A. C. Tdf. . . } μέλος
μέρους, Rec. Gr. Sch. Ln. (Ep. 4. 16) }

Μελχί], ὁ, *Melchi,* pr. name, indecl.

Μελχισεδέκ], ὁ, *Melchisedec,* pr. name, indecl.

μελῶν, gen. pl. . . . . . id.

μεμαθηκώς, nom. sing. masc. part. perf. (§ 36. rem. 2) . . . . μανθάνω

μεμαρτύρηκα, 1 pers. sing. perf. ind. act. . μαρτυρέω

μεμαρτύρηκας, 2 pers. sing. perf. ind. act. id.

μεμαρτύρηκε, 3 pers. sing. perf. ind. act. . id.

μεμαρτύρηται, 3 pers. sing. perf. ind. pass. id

μεμβράνα], ης, ἡ, (§ 2. rem. 3) (Lat. *membrana*) *parchment, vellum.* (ᾰ).

μεμβράνας,[c] acc. pl. . . . μεμβράνα

μεμενήκεισαν, 3 pers. pl. pluperf. for ἐμεμενήκεισαν, (§ 27. rem. 2. d) . μένω

μεμέρισται, 3 pers. sing. perf. ind. pass. . μερίζω

μεμεστωμένοι,[d] nom. pl. masc. part. perf. pass. (§ 21. tab. U) . . . μεστόω

μεμιαμμένοις, dat. pl. masc. part. perf. pass. } μιαίνω
A. D. Ln. . . . }
μεμιασμένοις, R. Gr. Sch. Tdf. (Tit. 1. 15) }

μεμίανται, 3 pers. sing. perf. ind. pass. . id.

μεμιασμένοις, dat. pl. masc. part. perf. pass. (§ 27. rem. 3) . . . . id.

μεμιγμένην, acc. sing. fem. part. perf. pass. (§ 36. rem. 5) . . . μίγνυμι

μεμιγμένον, acc. sing. neut. part. perf. pass. . id.

μεμισήκασι, 3 pers. pl. perf. ind. act. . μισέω

μεμίσηκε, 3 pers. sing. perf. ind. act. . . id.

μεμισημένου, gen. sing. neut. part. perf. pass. (§ 17. tab. Q) . . . id.

μεμνημένος, nom. sing. masc. part. perf. pass. (§ 22. rem. 5) . . . μιμνήσκω

μέμνησθε, 2 pers. pl. perf. ind. (§ 36. rem. 3) id.

μεμνηστευμένῃ, dat. sing. fem. part. perf. pass. μνηστεύω

μεμνηστευμένην, acc. sing. fem. part. perf. pass. id.

μεμονωμένη,[e] nom. sing. fem. part. perf. pass. (§ 21. tab. U) . . . μονόω

μεμύημαι,[f] 1 pers. s. perf. ind. pass. (§ 38. rem. 2) μυέω

μέμφεται, 3 pers. sing. pres. ind. . . μέμφομαι

a Lu. 24. 42. b Ac. 28. 1. c 2 Ti. 4. 13. d Ac. 2. 13. e 1 Ti. 5. 5 f Phi. 4. 12.

μέμφομαι], fut. ψομαι, (§ 23. rem. 1. a) aor. 1, ἐμεμψάμην, *to find fault with, blame, censure; to intimate dissatisfaction with,* He. 8. 8; absol. *to find fault,* Ro. 9. 19.

μομφή, ῆς, ἡ, (§ 2. tab. B. a) *a complaint, cause or ground of complaint,* Col. 3. 13.

μεμφόμενος, nom. sing. masc. part. pres. . . μέμφομαι

μεμψίμοιροι,[a] nom. pl. masc. . . . μεμψίμοιρος

μεμψίμοιρος] ου, ὁ, ἡ, (§ 7. rem. 2) (μέμψις, *a finding fault,* fr. μέμφομαι, & μοῖρα, *a portion, lot*) *finding fault or being discontented with one's lot, querulous; a discontented, querulous person, a repiner,* Jude 16.

μέν], a particle serving to indicate that the term or clause with which it is used stands distinguished from another, usually in the sequel, and then mostly with δέ correspondent, Mat. 3. 11; 9. 39; Ac. 1. 1; ὁ μὲν—ὁ δὲ, *this—that, the one—the other,* Phi. 1. 16. 17; *one—another,* οἱ μὲν—οἱ δὲ, *some—others,* Mat. 22. 5; ὃς μὲν—ὃς δὲ, *one—another,* pl. *some—others,* Mat. 13. 8; 21. 35; ἄλλος μὲν—ἄλλος δὲ, *one—another,* 1 Co. 15. 39; ὧδε μὲν—ἐκεῖ δὲ, *here—there,* He. 7. 8; τοῦτο μὲν—τοῦτο δὲ, *partly—partly,* He. 10. 33, et al. freq.

μένε, 2 pers. sing. pres. imper. . . . μένω

μένει, 3 pers. sing. pres. ind. . . . . id.

μενεῖ, 3 pers. sing. fut. ind.—Gr. Sch. Tdf. } id.
μένει, Rec. (1 Cor. 3. 14) . . }

μένειν, pres. infin. . . . . . . id.

μένεις, 2 pers. sing. pres. ind. . . . id.

μενεῖτε, 2 pers. pl. fut. ind. . . . . id.

μένετε, 2 pers. pl. pres. imper. . . . id.

μενέτω, 3 pers. sing. pres. imper. . . . id.

μένῃ, 3 pers. sing. pres. subj. . . . . id.

μένομεν, 1 pers. pl. pres. ind. . . . . id.

μένον, nom. and acc. sing. neut. part. pres. id.

μένοντα, acc. sing. masc. part. pres. . . id.

μένοντος, gen. sing. masc. part. pres. . . id.

μενοῦνγε], (μέν, οὖν, γε) a combination of particles serving to take up what has just preceded, with either addition or abatement, like the Latin *imo; yea indeed, yea truly, yea rather,* Lu. 11. 28; Ro. 9. 20; 10. 18, Phi. 3. 8. N.T.

μένουσαν, acc. sing. fem. part. pres. . . μένω

μένουσι, 3 pers. pl. pres. ind. . . . id.

μέντοι, conj. (μέν & τοι) *truly, certainly, sure,* Jude 8; *nevertheless, however,* Jno. 4. 27, et al.

μένω], fut. μενῶ, perf. μεμένηκα, (§ 27. rem. 1. a, and rem. 2. d) aor. 1, ἔμεινα, (§ 27. rem. 1. d) *to stay,* Mat. 26. 38; Ac. 27. 31; *to continue,* 1 Co. 7. 11; 2 Ti. 2. 13; *to dwell, lodge, sojourn,* Jno. 1. 39; Ac. 9. 43, et al.; *to remain,* Jno. 9. 41; *to rest, settle,* Jno. 1. 32, 33; 3. 36; *to last, endure,* Mat. 11. 23; Jno. 6. 27; 1 Co. 3. 14; *to survive,* 1 Co. 15. 6; *to be existent,* 1 Co. 13. 13; *to continue unchanged,* Ro. 9. 11; *to be permanent,* Jno. 15. 16; 2 Co. 3. 11; He. 10. 34; 13. 14; 1 Pe. 1. 23; *to persevere, be constant, be steadfast,* 1 Ti. 2. 15; 2 Ti. 3. 14; *to abide, to be in close and settled union,* Jno. 6. 56; 14. 10; 15. 4, et al.; *to indwell,* Jno. 5. 38; 1 Jno. 2. 14; trans. *to wait for,* Ac. 20. 5, 23.

μονή, ῆς, ἡ, (§ 2. tab. B. a) *a stay in any place; an abode, dwelling, mansion,* Jno. 14. 2, 23.

μενῶ, 1 pers. sing. fut. ind. (§ 27 rem. 1. a) μένω

μένων, nom. sing. masc. part. pres. . . id.

μέρη, acc. pl. . . . . . . μέρος

μέρει, dat. sing. . . . . . . id.

μερίδα, acc. sing. . . . . μερίς

μερίδος, gen. sing. . . . . id.

μερίζω], fut. ίσω, (§ 26. rem. 1) . . μερος

μέριμνα], ης, ἡ, (§ 2. rem. 3) (μερίζειν τὸν νοῦν, *dividing the mind*) *care,* Mat. 13. 22; Lu. 8. 14, et al.; *anxious interest,* 2 Co. 11. 28.

μεριμνάω, ῶ, fut. ήσω, (§ 18. tab. R) aor. 1, ἐμερίμνησα, *to be anxious, or solicitous,* Phi. 4. 6; *to expend careful thought,* Mat. 6. 27; *to concern one's self,* Mat. 6. 25, et al.; *to have the thoughts occupied with,* 1 Co. 7. 32, 33, 34; *to feel an interest in,* Phi. 2. 20.

μεριμνᾷ, 3 pers. sing. pres. ind. . . . μεριμνάω

μέριμναι, nom. pl. . . . . . μέριμνα

μερίμναις, dat. pl. . . . . . . id.

[a] Jude 16.

μέριμναν, acc. sing. . . . . . μέριμνα
μεριμνᾷς, 2 pers. sing. pres. ind. . . μεριμνάω
μεριμνᾶτε, 2 pers. pl. pres. ind. and imper. id.
μεριμνάω, ῶ], fut. ήσω, (§ 18. tab. R.) . μέριμνα
μεριμνήσει, 3 pers. sing. fut. ind. . . μεριμνάω
μεριμνήσητε, 2 pers. pl. aor. 1, subj. . id.
μεριμνῶν, nom. sing. masc. part. pres. . id.
μεριμνῶσι, 3 pers. pl. pres. subj. . . id.
μερίς], ίδος, ἡ, (§ 4. rem. 2. c) . . . μέρος
μερίσασθαι, aor. 1, infin. mid. . . μερίζω
μερισθεῖσα, nom. sing. fem. part. aor. 1, pass. id.
μερισθῇ, 3 pers. sing. aor. 1, subj. pass. (§ 26. rem. 1) . . . . . . id.
μερισμοῖς, dat. pl. . . . . . μερισμός
μερισμός], οῦ, ὁ, (§ 3. tab. C. a) . . μέρος
μερισμοῦ, gen. sing. . . . . . μερισμός
μεριστήν,[a] acc. sing. . . . . μεριστής
μεριστής], οῦ, ὁ, (§ 2. tab. B. c) . . μέρος
μέρος], εος, ους, τό, (§ 5. tab. E. b) *a part, portion, division,* of a whole, Lu. 11. 36; 15. 12; Ac. 5. 2; Eph. 4. 16, et al.; *a piece, fragment,* Lu. 24. 42; Jno. 19. 23; *a party, faction,* Ac. 23. 9; allotted *portion, lot, destiny,* Mat. 24. 51; Lu. 12. 46; *a calling, craft,* Ac. 19. 27; *a* partner's *portion, partnership, fellowship,* Jno. 13. 8, pl. μέρη, *a* local *quarter, district, region,* Mat. 2. 22; 16. 13; Ac. 19. 1; Eph. 4. 9, et al.; *side* of a ship, Jno. 21. 6; ἐν μέρει, *in respect, on the score,* 2 Co. 3. 10; 9. 3; Col. 2. 16; 1 Pe. 4. 16; μέρος τι, *partly, in some part,* 1 Co. 11. 18; ἀνὰ μέρος, *alternately, one after another,* 1 Co. 14. 27; ἀπὸ μέρους, *partly, in some part or measure,* 2 Co. 1. 14; ἐκ μέρους, *individually,* 1 Co. 12. 27; *partly, imperfectly,* 1 Co. 13. 9; κατὰ μέρος, *particularly, in detail,* He. 9. 5.

μερίς, ίδος, (ῐ), ἡ, (§ 4. rem. 2. c) *a part; a division* of a country, *district, region, tract,* Ac. 16. 12; *a portion,* Lu. 10. 42; *an* allotted *portion,* Col. 1. 12; *a portion* in common, *share,* Ac. 8. 21; 2 Co. 6. 15.

μερίζω, fut. ίσω, (§ 26. rem. 1) *to divide; to divide out, distribute,* Mar. 6. 41; *to assign, bestow,* Ro. 12. 3; 1 Co. 7. 17; 2 Co. 10. 13; He. 7. 2; mid. *to share,* Lu. 12. 13; pass. *to be subdivided, to admit distinctions,* 1 Co. 1. 13; *to be severed* by discord, *be at variance,* Mat. 12. 25, et al.; *to differ,* 1 Co. 7. 34.

μερισμός, οῦ, ὁ, (§ 3. tab. C. a) *a dividing, act of dividing,* He. 4. 12; *distribution, gifts distributed,* He. 2. 4.

μεριστής, οῦ, ὁ, (§ 2. tab. B. c) *a divider; an apportioner, arbitrator,* Lu. 12. 14. N.T.

μέρους, gen. sing. . . . . . μέρος
μεσημβρία], ας, ἡ, (§ 2. tab. B. b, and rem. 2) (μέσος & ἡμέρα) *mid-day, noon,* Ac. 22. 6; meton. *the south,* Ac. 8. 26.
μεσημβρίαν, acc. sing. . . . . μεσημβρία
μέσης, gen. sing. fem. . . . . . μέσος
μεσιτεύω], fut. εύσω, (§ 13. tab. M) . . id.
μεσίτῃ, dat. sing. . . . . . μεσίτης
μεσίτης], ου, ὁ, (§ 2. tab. B. c) . . . μέσος
μεσίτου, gen. sing. . . . . . μεσίτης
μέσον, acc. sing. masc. . . . . μέσος
μέσον, nom. and acc. sing. neut. . . id.
μεσονύκτιον], ίου, τό, (§ 3. tab. C. c) (μέσος & νύξ) *midnight,* Lu. 11. 5, et al.
μεσονυκτίου, gen. sing. . . . μεσονυκτίον
Μεσοποταμία], ας, ἡ, (§ 2. tab. B. b, and rem. 2) (μέσος & ποταμός) *Mesopotamia,* the country lying between the rivers Tigris and Euphrates.
Μεσοποταμίᾳ, dat. . . . . Μεσοποταμία
Μεσοποταμίαν, acc. . . . . . id.

μέσος], η, ον, (§ 7. tab. F. a) *mid, middle,* Mat. 25. 6; Ac. 26. 13; τὸ μέσον, *the middle, the midst,* Mat. 14. 24; ἀνὰ μέσον, *in the midst;* from the Heb., *in, among,* Mat. 13. 25; *between,* 1 Co. 6. 5; διὰ μέσου, *through the midst of,* Lu. 4. 30; εἰς τὸ μέσον, *into, or in the midst,* Mar. 3. 3; Lu. 6. 8; ἐκ μέσου, *from the midst, out of the way,* Col. 2. 14; 2 Thes. 2. 7; from the Heb., *from, from among,* Mat. 13. 49; ἐν τῷ μέσῳ, *in the midst,* Mat. 10. 16; *in the midst, in public, publicly,* Mat. 14. 6; ἐν μέσῳ, *in the midst of, among,* Mat. 18. 20; κατὰ μέσον τῆς νυκτός, *about midnight,* Ac. 27. 27.

μεσίτης, ου, ὁ, (§ 2. tab. B. c) *one that acts between two parties; a mediator,*

[a] Lu. 12. 14.

one who interposes to reconcile two adverse parties, 1 Ti. 2. 5; an internuncius, one who is the medium of communication between two parties, a mid-party, Gal. 3. 19, 20; He. 8. 6, et al. (ῑ). L.G.

μεσῑτεύω, fut. εύσω, (§ 13. tab. M) aor. 1, ἐμεσίτευσα, to perform offices between two parties; to intervene, interpose, He. 6. 17. L.G.

μεσόω, ῶ, fut. ώσω, (§ 20. tab. T) to be in the middle or midst; to be advanced midway, Jno. 7. 14.

μεσότοιχον],[a] ου, τό, (§ 3. tab. C. c) (μέσος & τοῖχος) a middle wall; a partition wall, a barrier, Ep. 2. 14. N.T.

μεσου, gen. sing. neut. . . . . μέσος

μεσουράνημα], ατος, τό, (§ 4. tab. D. c) (μέσος & οὐρανός) the mid-heaven, mid-air, Re. 8. 13, et al. L.G.

μεσουρανήματι, dat. sing. . . . . μεσουράνημα

μεσούσης,[b] gen. sing. fem. part. pres. . . μεσόω

μεσόω, ῶ], fut. ώσω, (§ 20. tab. T) . . μέσος

Μεσσίαν, acc. . . . . . . Μεσσίας

Μεσσίας], ου, ὁ, (§ 2. tab. B. d) (Heb. מָשִׁיחַ, from מָשַׁח, to anoint) the Messiah, the Anointed One, i.q. ὁ Χριστός, Jno. 1. 42; 4. 25.

μεστή, nom. sing. fem. . . . . . μεστός

μεστοί, nom. pl. masc. . . . . . id.

μεστόν, nom. and acc. sing. neut. . . . id.

μεστός], ή, όν, (§ 7. tab. F. a) full, full of, filled with, Jno. 19. 29, et al.; replete, Ro. 1. 29; 15. 14, et al.

μεστόω, ῶ, fut. ώσω, (§ 20. tab. T) to fill; pass. to be filled, be full, Ac. 2. 13.

μεστούς, acc. pl. masc. . . . . . μεστός

μεστόω, ῶ], fut. ώσω . . . . . id.

μέσῳ, dat. sing. neut. . . . . . μέσος

μετ', by apostrophe for μετά.

μετά], prep., with a genitive, with, together with, Mat. 16. 27; 12. 41; 26. 55; with, on the same side or party with, in aid of, Mat. 12. 30; 20. 20; with, by means of, Ac. 13. 17; with, of conflict, Re. 11. 7; with, among, Lu. 24. 5; with, to, towards, Lu. 1. 58, 72; with an accusative, after, of place, behind, He. 9. 3; of time, after, Mat. 17. 1; 24. 29; followed by an infin. with the neut. article, after, after that, Mat. 26. 32; Lu. 22. 20.

μετάβα, 2 pers. sing. aor. 2, imper.—B. Ln. }
μετάβηθι, Rec. Gr. Sch. Tdf. (Mat. 17. 20) } μεταβαίνω

μεταβαίνετε, 2 pers. pl. pres. imper. . . id.

μεταβαίνω], fut. βήσομαι, (§ 37. rem. 1) perf. μεταβέβηκα, aor. 2, μετέβην (μετά & βαίνω) to go or pass from one place to another, Jno. 5. 24; to pass away, be removed, Mat. 17. 20; to go away, depart, Mat. 8. 34, et al.

μεταβαλλόμενοι,[c] nom. pl. m. part. pres. mid. μεταβάλλω

μεταβάλλω], (μετά & βάλλω) to change; mid. to change one's mind.

μεταβάς, nom. sing. masc. part. aor. 2 . μεταβαίνω

μεταβεβήκαμεν, 1 pers. pl. perf. ind. . . id.

μεταβέβηκε, 3 pers. sing. perf. ind. . . id.

μεταβῇ, 3 pers. sing. aor. 2, subj. . . id.

μετάβηθι, 2 pers. sing. aor. 2, imper. . id.

μεταβήσεται, 3 pers. sing. fut. ind. . . id.

μετάγεται, 3 pers. sing. pres. ind. pass. . μετάγω

μετάγομεν, 1 pers. pl. pres. ind. act. . . id.

μετάγω], fut. ξω, (§ 23. rem. 1. b) (μετά & ἄγω) to lead or move from one place to another; to change direction, to turn about, Ja. 3. 3, 4. (ᾰ).

μεταδιδόναι, pres. infin. act. . . . μεταδίδωμι

μεταδιδούς, nom. sing. masc. part. pres. act. . id.

μεταδίδωμι], fut. δώσω, (§ 30. tab. Z) (μετά & δίδωμι) to give a part, to share, Lu. 3. 11; to impart, bestow, Ro. 1. 11; 12. 8, et al.

μεταδότω, 3 pers. sing. aor. 2, imper. act. μεταδίδωμι

μεταδοῦναι, aor. 2, infin. act. . . . id.

μεταδῶ, 1 pers. sing. aor. 2, subj. act. . . id.

μεταθέσεως, gen. sing. . . . . μετάθεσις

μετάθεσιν, acc. sing. . . . . . id.

μετάθεσις], εως, ἡ, (§ 5. tab. E. c) . . μετατίθημι

μεταίρω], fut. αρῶ, aor. 1, μετῆρα, (§ 27. rem. 1. c. e) (μετά & αἴρω) to remove, transfer; in N.T. intrans. to go away, depart, Mat. 13. 53; 19. 1.

μετακάλεσαι, 2 pers. sing. aor. 1, imper. mid. μετακαλέω

μετακαλέσομαι, 1 pers. sing. fut. ind. mid. . id.

μετακαλέω, ῶ], fut. έσω, (§ 22. rem. 1) (μετά & καλέω) to call from one place into another;

[a] Ep. 2. 14. [b] Jno. 7. 14. [c] Ac. 28. 6.

mid. *to call or send for, invite to come to one's self,* Ac. 7. 14, et al.

μετακινέω, ῶ], fut. ήσω, (§ 16. tab. P) (μετά & κινέω) *to move away, remove;* pass. met. *to stir away from, to swerve,* Col. 1. 23.

μετακινούμενοι,[a] nom. pl. masc. part. pres. pass. μετακινέω

μεταλαβεῖν, aor. 2, infin. . . . μεταλαμβάνω

μεταλαβών, nom. sing. masc. part. aor. 2 . id.

μεταλαμβάνει, 3 pers. sing. pres. ind. . id.

μεταλαμβάνειν, pres. infin. . . . id.

μεταλαμβάνω], fut. λήψομαι, (§ 36. rem. 2) aor. 2, μετέλᾰβον, (μετά & λαμβάνω) *to partake of, share in,* Ac. 2. 46; 2 Ti. 2. 6, et al.; *to get, obtain, find,* Ac. 24. 25. (ᾰ).

μετάληψις, εως, ἡ, (§ 5. tab. E. c) *a partaking of, a being partaken of.*

μετάληψιν,[b] acc. sing. . . . . μετάληψις

μετάληψις], εως, ἡ . . . . μεταλαμβάνω

μεταλλάσσω, or ττω], fut. ξω, (§ 26. rem. 3) (μετά & ἀλλάσσω) *to exchange, change for or into, transmute,* Ro. 1. 25, 26.

μεταμεληθείς, nom. sing. m. part. aor. 1, pass. μεταμέλομαι

μεταμεληθήσεται, 3 pers. sing. fut. ind. . id.

μεταμέλομαι], fut. (pass. form) ηθήσομαι, aor. 1, (pass. form) μετεμελήθην, (§ 35. rem. 5) (μετά & μέλομαι) *to change one's judgment on past points of conduct; to change one's mind and purpose,* He. 7. 21; *to repent, regret,* Mat. 21. 29, 32; 27. 3; 2 Co. 7. 8.

μεταμορφόω, ῶ], fut. ώσω, (§ 20. tab. T) (μετά & μορφόω) *to change the external form, transfigure;* mid. *to change one's form, be transfigured,* Mat. 17. 2; Mar. 9. 2; *to undergo a* spiritual *transformation,* Ro. 12. 2; 2 Co. 3. 18.

μεταμορφούμεθα, 1 pers. pl. pres. ind. pass. (§ 21. tab. U) . . . μεταμορφόω

μεταμορφοῦσθαι, pres. infin. pass.—A. B. D. Ln. Tdf. . . . . } id.
μεταμορφοῦσθε, R. Gr. Sch. (Ro. 12. 2) }

μεταμορφοῦσθε, 2 pers. pl. pres. imper. pass. id.

μετανοεῖν, pres. infin. . . . . μετανοέω

μετανοεῖτε, 2 pers. pl. pres. imper. . . id.

μετανοέω, ῶ], fut. ήσω, (§ 16. tab. P) μετά & νοέω) *to undergo a change in frame of mind and feeling, to repent,* Lu. 17. 3, 4, et al.; *to make a change of principle and practice, to reform,* Mat. 3. 2, et al.

μετάνοια, ας, ἡ, (§ 2. tab. B. b, and rem. 2) *a change of mode of thought and feeling, repentance,* Mat. 3. 8; Ac. 20. 21; 2 Ti. 2. 25, et al.; practical *reformation,* Lu. 15. 7, et al.; *reversal* of the past, He 12. 17.

[οὐ θέλει], μετανοῆσαι, aor. 1, infin.—Gr. Sch. Tdf. . . . . } μετανοέω
[οὐ], μετένοησεν, Rec. (Re. 2. 21) . }

μετανοησάντων, gen. pl. masc. part. aor. 1 . id.

μετανοήσατε, 2 pers. pl. aor. 1, imper. . id.

μετανοήσῃ, 3 pers. sing. aor. 1, subj. . . id

μετανοήσῃς, 2 pers. sing. aor. 1, subj. . id.

μετανοήσητε, 2 pers. pl. aor. 1, subj.—A. D. Ln. Tdf. . . . . } id.
μετανοῆτε, Rec. Gr. Sch. (Lu. 13. 5) . }

μετανόησον, 2 pers. sing. aor. 1, imper. . id.

μετανοήσουσι, 3 pers. pl. fut. ind. . . id.

μετανοήσωσι, 3 pers. pl. aor. 1, subj. . . id.

μετανοῆτε, 2 pers. pl. pres. subj. . . id.

μετάνοια], ας, ἡ, (§ 2. tab. B. b, and rem. 2 . id.

μετάνοιαν, acc. sing. . . . . μετάνοια

μετανοίας, gen. sing. . . . . id.

μετανοοῦντι, dat. sing. masc. part. pres. . μετανοέω

μετανοῶ, 1 pers. sing. pres. ind. . . . id.

μεταξύ], adv. (μετά) *between,* Mat. 23. 35; Lu. 11. 51; 16. 26; Ac. 15. 9; ἐν τῷ μεταξύ, scil. χρόνῳ, *in the meantime, meanwhile,* Jno. 4. 31; in N.T. ὁ μεταξύ, *following, succeeding,* Ac. 13. 42.

μεταπεμπόμενος, nom. s. masc. part. pres. mid. μεταπέμπω

μεταπέμπω], fut. ψω, (§ 23. rem. 1. a) (μετά & πέμπω) *to send after;* mid. *to send after or for* any one, *invite to come to one's self,* Ac. 10. 5, et al.

μεταπεμφθείς, nom. s. masc. part. aor. 1, pass. μεταπέμπω

μετάπεμψαι, 2 pers. sing. aor. 1, imper. mid. id.

μεταπεμψάμενος, nom. sing. masc. part. aor. 1, mid.—B. . . . . } id.
προσκαλεσάμενος, Rec. Gr. Sch. Tdf. (Ac. 20. 1) . . . }

μεταπέμψασθαι, aor. 1, infin. mid. . . id.

μεταπέμψηται, 3 pers. sing. aor. 1, subj. mid. id.

μεταστᾰθῶ, 1 pers. sing. aor. 1, subj. pass. (§ 29. rem. 6) . . . . μεθίστημι

μεταστήσας, nom. sing. masc. part. aor. 1, act. (§ 29. tab. X) . . . id.

μεταστραφήσεται, 3 pers. s. fut. 2, ind. pass. μεταστρέφω

[a] Col. 1. 23. [b] 1 Ti. 4. 3.

μεταστραφήτω, 3 pers. sing. aor. 2, imper. pass. μεταστρέφω

μεταστρέφω], fut. ψω, (§ 23. rem. 1. a) aor. 2, pass. μετεστράφην, (§ 24. rem. 10) (μετά & στρέφω) *to turn about; convert* into something else, *change*, Ac. 2. 20; Ja. 4. 9; by impl. *to pervert*, Gal. 1. 7.

μεταστρέψαι, aor. 1, infin. act. . . μεταστρέφω

μετασχηματίζεται, 3 pers. s. pres. ind. pass. μετασχηματίζω

μετασχηματιζόμενοι, nom. pl. m. part. pres. mid. id.

μετασχηματίζονται, 3 pers. pl. pres. ind. pass. id.

μετασχηματίζω], fut. ίσω, (§ 26. rem. 1) aor. 1, μετεσχημάτισα, (μετά & σχηματίζω, *to fashion*, σχῆμα) *to remodel, transfigure*, Phi. 3. 21; mid. *to transform one's self*, 2 Co. 11. 13, 14, 15; *to make an* imaginary *transference* of circumstances from the parties really concerned in them to others, *to transfer* an imagination, 1 Co. 4. 6.

μετασχηματίσει, 3 pers. sing. fut. ind. . μετασχηματίζω

μετατιθεμένης, gen. sing. fem. part. pres. pass. μετατίθημι

μετατιθέντες, nom. pl. masc. part. pres. act. . id.

μετατίθεσθε, 2 pers. pl. pres. ind. pass. . id.

μετατίθημι], fut. θήσω, (§ 28. tab. V) aor. 1, μετέθηκα, aor. 1, pass. μετετέθην, (μετά & τίθημι) *to transport*, Ac. 7. 16; *to transfer*, He. 7. 12; *to translate* out of the world, He. 11. 5; met. *to transfer* to other purposes, *to pervert*, Jude 4; mid *to transfer one's self, to change over* Gal. 1. 6.

μετάθεσις, εως, ἡ, (§ 5. tab. E. c) *a removal, translation*, He. 11. 5; *a transmutation, change* by the abolition of one thing, and the substitution of another, He. 7. 12.

μετέβη, 3 pers. sing. aor. 2, ind. (§ 37. rem. 1) μεταβαίνω

μετέθηκε, 3 pers. sing. aor. 1, ind. act. . μετατίθημι

μετεκαλέσατο, 3 pers. sing. aor. 1, ind. mid. (§ 22. rem. 1) . . . μετακαλέω

μετελάμβανον, 3 pers. pl. imperf. act. . μεταλαμβάνω

μετεμελήθητε, 2 pers. pl. aor. 1, ind. pass. μεταμέλομαι

μετεμελόμην, 1 pers. sing. imperf. . . id.

μετεμορφώθη, 3 pers. sing. aor. 1, ind. pass. μεταμορφόω

μετενόησαν, 3 pers. pl. aor. 1, ind. . . μετανοέω

μετενόησε, 3 pers. sing. aor. 1, ind. . . id.

μετέπειτα],[a] adv. (μετά & ἔπειτα) *afterwards*, He. 12. 17.

μετεπέμψασθε, 2 pers. pl. aor. 1, ind. mid. . μεταπέμπω

μετεπέμψατο, 3 pers. sing. aor. 1, ind. mid. μεταπέμπω

μετέστησε, 3 pers. sing. aor. 1, ind. act. . μεθίστημι

μετέσχε, 3 pers. sing. aor. 2, ind. . . μετέχω

μετέσχηκε, 3 pers. sing. perf. ind. . . id.

μετεσχημάτισα, 1 pers. s. aor. 1, ind. act. μετασχηματίζω

μετετέθη, 3 pers. sing. aor. 1, ind. pass. (§ 28. rem. 10) . . . . . μετατίθημι

μετετέθησαν, 3 pers. pl. aor. 1, ind. pass. . id.

μετέχειν, pres. infin. . . . . μετέχω

μετέχομεν, 1 pers. pl. pres. ind. . id.

μετέχουσι, 3 pers. pl. pres. ind. . . . id.

μετέχω], fut. μεθέξω, (§ 35. rem. 4) perf. μετέσχηκα, aor. 2, μετέσχον, (§ 36. rem. 4) (μετά & ἔχω) *to share in, partake*, 1 Co. 9. 10, 12; 10. 17, 21, et al.; *to be a member of*, He. 7. 13.

μετοχή, ῆς, ἡ, (§ 2. tab. B. a) *a sharing, partaking; communion, fellowship*, 2 Co. 6. 14.

μέτοχος, ου, ὁ, (§ 3. tab. C. a) *a partaker*, He. 3. 1, 14; 12. 8; *an associate, partner, fellow*, Lu. 5. 7; He. 1. 9.

μετέχων, nom. sing. masc. part. pres. . μετέχω

μετεωρίζεσθε,[b] 2 pers. pl. pres. imper. pass. . μετεωρίζω

μετεωρίζω], fut. ίσω, (§ 26. rem. 1) (μετέωρος, *raised from the ground*) *to raise aloft*; met. *to unsettle in mind*; pass. *to be excited with anxiety, be in anxious suspense*, Lu. 12. 29.

μετήλλαξαν, 3 pers. pl. aor. 1, ind. act. . μεταλλάσσω

μετῆρε, 3 pers. sing. aor. 1, ind. act. (§ 27. rem. 1. e) . . . . μεταίρω

μετοικεσία], ας, ἡ, (§ 2. tab. B. b, and rem. 2) (μετοικέω, *to change one's abode*, μετά & οἰκέω) *change of abode or country, migration*, Mat. 1. 11, 12, 17. L.G.

μετοικεσίαν, acc. sing. . . . μετοικεσια

μετοικεσίας, gen. sing. . . . . id.

μετοικίζω], fut. ίσω, (§ 26. rem. 1) (μετά & οἰκίζω, *to fix in a habitation*) *to cause to change abode, cause to emigrate*, Ac. 7. 4.

μετοικιῶ, 1 pers. sing. fut. ind. act. Att. (§ 35. rem. 11) . . . . μετοικίζω

μετοχή],[c] ῆς, ἡ, (§ 2. tab. B. a) . . . μετέχω

μέτοχοι, nom. pl. . . . . μέτοχος

μετόχοις, dat. pl. . . . . . id.

μέτοχος], ου, ὁ . . . . . μετέχω

μετόχους, acc. pl. . . . . . μέτοχος

a He. 12. 17. b Lu. 12. 29. c 2 Co. 6. 14.

μετρεῖτε, 2 pers. pl. pres. ind. act. . . μετρέω

μετρέω, ῶ], fut. ήσω, (§ 16. tab. P) . . μέτρον

μετρηθήσεται, 3 pers. sing. fut. ind. pass. . μετρέω

μετρήσῃ, 3 pers. sing. aor. 1, subj. act. . id.

μετρήσῃς, 2 pers. sing. aor. 1, subj. act. . id.

μέτρησον, 2 pers. sing. aor. 1, imper. act. . id.

μετρητάς,[a] acc. pl. . . . . μετρητής

μετρητής], οῦ, ὁ, (§ 2. tab. B. c) . . μέτρον

μετριοπαθεῖν,[b] pres. infin. . . . μετριοπαθέω

μετριοπᾰθέω, ῶ], fut. ήσω, (§ 16. tab. P) (μέτριος & πάθος) *to moderate one's passions; to be gentle, compassionate*, He. 5. 2. L.G.

μετρίως], adv. . . . . . μέτρον

μέτρον], ου, τό, (§ 3. tab. C. c) *measure*, Mat. 7. 2; Mar. 4. 24; Lu. 6. 38; Re. 21. 17, et al.; *measure, standard*, Ep. 4. 13; *extent, compass*, 2 Co. 10. 13; allotted *measure, specific portion*, Ro. 12. 3; Ep. 4. 7, 16; ἐκ μέτρου, *by measure, with definite limitation*, Jno. 3. 34.

μετρέω, ῶ, fut. ήσω, (§ 16. tab. P) aor. 1, ἐμέτρησα, *to mete, measure*, Mat. 7. 2; Re. 11. 1, 2, et al.; met. *to estimate*, 2 Co. 10. 12.

μετρητής, οῦ, ὁ, (§ 2. tab. B. c) pr. *a measurer*; also, *metretes*, Lat. *metreta*, equivalent to the attic ἀμφορεύς, i.e. three-fourths of the Attic μέδιμνος, or Hebrew בַּת, and therefore equal to about nine gallons, Jno. 2. 6.

μετρίως, adv. *moderately; slightly*; οὐ μετρίως, *no little, not a little, much, greatly*, Ac. 20. 12.

μέτρου, gen. sing. . . . . . μέτρον

μετροῦντες, nom. pl. masc. part. pres. act. . μετρέω

μέτρῳ, dat. sing. . . . . μέτρον

μετῴκισε, 3 pers. sing. aor. 1, ind. act. (§ 13. rem. 2) . . . . . μετοικίζω

μέτωπον], ου, τό, (§ 3. tab. C. c) (μετά & ὤψ) *forehead, front*, Re. 7. 3; 9. 4, et al.

μετώπου, gen. sing. . . . . μέτωπον

μετώπων, gen. pl. . . . . . id.

μέχρι], and μέχρις before a vowel, adv., of place, *unto, even to*, Ro. 15. 19; of time, *until, till*, Mat. 11. 23; 13. 30, et al.

μή], a particle of negation, *not*; for the particulars of its usage, especially as distinguished from that of οὐ, see the grammars; as a conjunction, *lest, that not*, Mat. 5. 29, 30; 18. 10; 24. 6; Mar. 13. 36; μή, or μήτι, or μήποτε, prefixed to an interrogative clause, is a mark of tone, since it expresses an intimation either of the reality of the matters respecting which the question is asked, Mat. 12. 23, et al.; or the contrary, Jno. 4. 12, et al.

μήγε], a strengthened form for μή, (μή & γε) Mat. 6. 1; 9. 17, et al.

μηδαμῶς], adv. (μηδαμός, i.q. μηδείς) *by no means*, Ac. 10. 14; 11. 8.

μηδέ], conj. *neither*, and repeated, *neither—nor*, Mat. 6. 25; 7. 6; 10. 9, 10; *not even, not so much as*, Mar. 2. 2, et al.

μηδείς], μηδεμίᾰ, μηδέν, (§ 10. rem. 6. c) (μηδέ, εἷς) *not one, none, no one*, Mat. 8. 4, et al.

μηδεμίαν, acc. sing. fem. . . . μηδείς

μηδέν, nom. and acc. sing. neut. . . id.

μηδένα, acc. sing. masc. . . . id.

μηδενί, dat. sing. masc. and neut. . . id.

μηδενός, gen. sing. neut. . . . id.

μηδέποτε],[c] adv. (μηδέ & ποτε) *not at any time, never*.

μηδέπω,[d] adv. (μηδέ & πω) *not yet, not as yet*.

Μῆδοι,[e] nom. pl. . . . . . Μῆδος

Μῆδος], ου, ὁ, (§ 3. tab. C. a) *a Mede, a native of Media* in Asia.

μηκέτι], adv. (μή & ἔτι) *no more, no longer*, Mar. 1. 45; 2. 2, et al.

μῆκος], εος, ους, τό, (§ 5. tab. E. b) *length*, Ep. 3. 18; Re. 21. 16.

μηκύνω, fut. υνῶ, (§ 27. rem. 1. a) *to lengthen, prolong*; mid. *to grow up*, as plants, Mar. 4. 27.

μακράν, adv. (acc. fem. of μακρός) *far, far off, at a distance, far distant*, Mat. 8. 30; Mar. 12. 34, et al.; met. οἱ μακράν, *remote, alien*, Ep. 2. 13, 17; so οἱ εἰς μακράν, Ac. 2. 39.

μακρόθεν, adv. *far off, at a distance, from afar, from a distance*, Mar. 3. 8; 11. 13; preceded by ἀπό, in the same sense, Mat. 26. 58.

μακρός, ά, όν, (§ 7. rem. 1) *long*; of

a Jno. 2. 6. b He. 5. 2. c 2 Ti. 3. 7. d He. 11. 7. e Ac. 2. 9.

space, *far, distant, remote,* Lu. 15. 13; 19. 12; of time, *of long duration; prolix,* Mat. 23. 13; Mar. 12. 40; Lu. 20. 47.

μηκύνηται,[a] 3 pers. sing. pres. subj. pass. . μηκύνω

μηκύνω], fut. υνῶ, (§ 27. rem. 1. a) . μῆκος

μηλωταῖς,[b] dat. pl. . . . . . μηλωτή

μηλωτή], ῆς, ἡ, (§ 2. tab. B. a) (μῆλον, *a sheep*) *a sheepskin.*

μήν],[c] a particle occurring in the N.T. only in the combination ἦ μήν. See ἦ.

μήν], μηνός, ὁ, (§ 4. rem. 2. e) *a month,* Lu. 1. 24, 26, 36, 56, et al.; in N.T. *the new moon, the day of the new moon,* Gal. 4. 10.

μῆνα, acc. sing. . . . . . . μήν

μῆνας, acc. pl. . . . . . . id.

μηνί, dat. sing. . . . . . . id.

μηνυθείσης, gen. sing. fem. part. aor. 1, pass. (§ 14. tab. N) . . . . μηνύω

μηνύσαντα, acc. sing. masc. part. aor. 1, act. id.

μηνύσῃ, 3 pers. sing. aor. 1, subj. act. . id.

μηνύω], fut. ύσω, (§ 13. tab. M) perf. μεμήνυκα, aor. 1, ἐμήνῡσα, *to disclose* what is secret, Jno. 11. 57; Ac. 23. 30; 1 Co. 10. 28; *to declare, indicate,* Lu. 20. 37.

μήποτε], (μή & ποτε) has the same significations and usage as μή; which see; He. 9. 17; Mat. 4. 6; 13. 15; also, *whether,* Lu. 3. 15.

μήπου], adv. *lest perhaps.*—B. C. Tdf.
μήπω, A. Ln.
μήπως, Rec. Gr. Sch. (Ac. 27. 29.)

μήπω], adv. (μή & πω) *not yet, not as yet,* Ro. 9. 11; He. 9. 8.

μήπως], conj. (μή & πως) *lest in any way or means, that in no way,* Ac. 27. 29; Ro. 11. 21; 1 Co. 8. 9; 9. 27, et al.; *whether perhaps,* 1 Thes. 3. 5.

μηρόν,[d] acc. sing. . . . . . . μηρός

μηρός], οῦ, ὁ, (§ 3. tab. C. a) *the thigh,* Re. 19. 16.

μήτε], conj. (μή & τε) *neither;* μήτε—μήτε, or μὴ—μήτε, or μηδὲ—μητέ, *neither—nor,* Mat. 5. 34, 35, 36; Ac. 23. 8; 2 Thes. 2. 2; in N.T. also equivalent to μηδὲ, *not even, not so much as,* Mar. 3. 20.

μητέρα, acc. sing. . . . . . μήτηρ

μητέρας, acc. pl. . . . . . . id.

μήτηρ], τέρος, τρός, ἡ, (§ 6. rem. 2) *a mother,* Mat. 1. 18; 12. 49, 50, et al. freq.; *a parent* city, Gal. 4. 26; Re. 17. 5.

μήτρα, ας, ἡ, (§ 2. tab. B b) *the womb,* Lu. 2. 23; Ro. 4. 19.

μήτι], (μή & τι) has the same use as μή in the form εἰ μήτι, Lu. 9. 13, et al.; also when prefixed to an interrogative clause, Mat. 7. 16; Jno. 4. 29. See μή.

μήτιγε, (μήτι & γε) strengthened for μήτι, *surely then, much more then,* 1 Co. 6. 3.

μητραλῴαις,[e] dat. pl. . . . . μητραλῴης

μητραλῴης, or λῴας], ου, ὁ, (§ 2. rem. 4) (μήτηρ & ἀλοιάω, poet. for ἀλοάω, *to smite*) *a striker of his mother, matricide,* 1 Ti. 1. 9.

μήτραν, acc. sing. . . . . . μήτρα

μήτρας, gen. sing. . . . . . id.

μητρί, dat. sing. . . . . . . μήτηρ

μητρός, gen. sing. . . . . . id.

μία, nom. sing. fem. (§ 9. tab. I. a) . . εἷς

μιᾷ, dat. sing. fem. . . . . . id.

μιαίνουσι, 3 pers. pl. pres. ind. act. . . μιαίνω

μιαίνω], fut. ανῶ, (§ 27. rem. 1. c) aor. 1, ἐμίηνα & ἐμίᾱνα, (§ 27. rem. 1. e) perf. μεμίαγκα, perf. pass. μεμίασμαι, aor. 1, pass. ἐμιάνθην, (§ 27. rem. 3) pr. *to tinge, dye, stain; to pollute, defile,* ceremonially, Jno. 18. 28; *to corrupt, deprave,* Tit. 1. 15; He. 12. 15; Jude 8.

μίασμα, ατος, τό, (§ 4. tab. D. c) *pollution,* moral *defilement,* 2 Pe. 2. 20.

μιασμός, οῦ, ὁ, (§ 3. tab. C. a) *pollution, defiling,* 2 Pe. 2. 10. L.G.

μίαν, acc. sing. fem. . . . . . εἷς

μιανθῶσι, 3 pers. pl. aor. 1, subj. pass. . μιαίνω

μιᾶς, gen. sing. fem. . . . . . εἷς

μίασμα], ατος, τό, (§ 4. tab. D. c) . . μιαίνω

μιάσματα,[f] acc. pl. . . . . . μίασμα

μιασμός], οῦ, ὁ, (§ 3. tab. C. a) . . . μιαίνω

μιασμοῦ,[g] gen. sing. . . . . . μιασμός

μίγμα],[h] ατος, τό, (§ 4. tab. D. c) . . μίγνυμι

μίγνυμι], fut. μίξω, (§ 36. rem. 5) aor. 1, ἔμιξα, perf. pass. μέμιγμαι, *to mix, mingle,* Mat. 27. 34; Lu. 13. 1; Re. 8. 7.

μίγμα, ατος, τό, (or μῖγμα) (§ 4. tab. D. c) *a mixture,* Jno. 19. 39.

---

[a] Mar. 4. 27. [b] He. 11. 37. [c] He. 6. 14. [d] Re. 19. 16. [e] 1 Ti. 1. 9. [f] 2 Pe. 2. 20. [g] 2 Pe. 2. 10. [h] Jno. 19. 39.

μικρά, nom. sing. fem. . . . μικρός
μικράν, acc. sing. fem. . . . . id.
μικροί, nom. pl. masc. . . . . id.
μικροῖς, dat. pl. masc. . . . . id.
μικρόν, acc. sing. masc. and nom. neut. . id.

μῑκρός, ά, όν, (§ 7. rem. 1) *little, small* in size, quantity, etc., Mat. 13. 32; *small, little* in age, *young, not adult,* Mar. 15. 40; *little, short* in time, Jno. 7. 33; μικρόν, sc. χρόνον, *a little while, a short time,* Jno. 13. 33; μετὰ μικρόν, *after a little while, a little while afterwards,* Mat. 26. 73; *little* in number, Lu. 12. 32; *small, little* in dignity, *low, humble,* Mat. 10. 42; 11. 11; μικρόν, as an adv., *little, a little,* Mat. 26. 39, et al.

μικρότερον, nom. sing. neut. compar. . . μικρός
μικρότερος, nom. sing. masc. comp. (§ 8. rem. 5) id.
μικροῦ, gen. sing. masc. . . . . id.
μικρούς, acc. pl. masc. . . . . id.
μικρῷ, dat. sing. masc. . . . . id.
μικρῶν, gen. pl. . . . . . id.
Μίλητον, acc. . . . . . Μίλητος
Μίλητος], ου, ἡ, (§ 3. tab. C. b) *Miletus,* a celebrated city of Caria.
Μιλήτου, gen. . . . . . Μίλητος
Μιλήτῳ, dat. . . . . . id.
μίλιον],[a] ίου, τό, (§ 3. tab. C. c) (Lat. *miliarium*) *a Roman mile,* which contained *mille passuum,* 1000 paces, or 8 stadia, i.e. about 1680 English yards. L.G.
μιμεῖσθαι, pres. infin. . . . . μιμέομαι
μιμεῖσθε, 2 pers. pl. pres. imper. . . id.
μῑμέομαι, οῦμαι], fut. ήσομαι, (§ 17. tab. Q) (μῖμος, *an imitator*) *to imitate, follow* as an example, *strive to resemble,* 2 Thes. 3. 7, 9; He. 13. 7; 3 Jno. 11.

μιμητής, οῦ, ὁ, (§ 2. tab. B. c) *an imitator, follower,* 1 Co. 4. 16; Ep. 5. 1, et al.

μιμηταί, nom. pl. . . . . . μιμητής
μιμητής], οῦ, ὁ . . . . . μιμέομαι
μιμνήσκεσθε, 2 pers. pl. pres. imper. mid. . μιμνήσκω
μιμνήσκῃ, 2 pers. sing. pres. ind. mid. . id.
μιμνήσκω], *to remind;* mid. μιμνήσκομαι, aor. 1, (pass. form) ἐμνήσθην, fut. μνησθήσομαι, perf. μέμνημαι, with pres. signif. (§ 36. rem. 3) *to remember, recollect, call to mind,* Mat. 26. 75; Lu. 1. 54, 72; 16. 25; in N.T., in a passive sense, *to be called to mind, be borne in mind,* Ac. 10. 31; Re. 16. 19, et al.

μνεία, ας, ἡ, (§ 2. tab. B. b, and rem. 2) *remembrance, recollection,* Phi. 1. 3; 1 Thes. 3. 6; 2 Ti. 1. 3; *mention;* μνείαν ποιεῖσθαι, *to make mention,* Ro. 1. 9; Ep. 1. 16; 1 Thes. 1. 2; Phile. 4.

μνῆμα, ατος, τό, (§ 4. tab. D. c) pr. *a memorial, monument; a tomb, sepulchre,* Mar. 5. 5, et al.

μνημεῖον, ου, τό, (§ 3. tab. C. c) the same as μνῆμα, Mat. 8. 28; 23. 29, et al.

μνήμη, ης, ἡ, (§ 2. tab. B. a) *remembrance, recollection, mention;* μνήμην ποιεῖσθαι, *to make mention,* 2 Pe. 1. 15.

μνημονεύω, fut. εύσω, (§ 13. tab. M) aor. 1, ἐμνημόνευσα, *to remember, recollect, call to mind,* Mat. 16. 9; Lu. 17. 32; Ac. 20. 31, et al.; *to be mindful of, to fix the thoughts upon,* He. 11. 15; *to make mention, mention, speak of,* He. 11. 22

μνημόσυνον, ου, τό, (§ 3. tab. C. c) *a record, memorial,* Ac. 10. 4; honourable *remembrance,* Mat. 26. 13; Mar. 14. 9.

μιμοῦ, 2 pers. sing. pres. imper. . . . μιμέομαι
μισεῖ, 3 pers. sing. pres. ind. act. . . μισέω
μισεῖν, pres. infin. act. . . . . . id.
μισεῖς, 2 pers. sing. pres. ind. act. . . id.
μῑσέω], ῶ, fut. ήσω, (§ 16. tab. P) perf. μεμίσηκα, aor. 1, ἐμίσησα, (μῖσος, *hatred*) *to hate, regard with ill-will,* Mat. 5. 43, 44; 10. 22; *to detest, abhor,* Jno. 3. 20; Ro. 7. 15, in N.T. *to regard with less affection, love less, esteem less,* Mat. 6. 24; Lu. 14. 26.
μισῇ, 3 pers. sing. pres. subj. act. . . μισέω
μισήσει, 3 pers. sing. fut. ind. act. . . id.
μισήσεις, 2 pers. sing. fut. ind. act. . . id.
μισήσουσι, 3 pers. pl. fut. ind. act. . id.
μισήσωσι, 3 pers. pl. aor. 1, subj. act. . id.
μισθαποδοσία], ας, ἡ, (§ 2. tab. B. b, and rem. 2) (μισθός, ἀποδίδωμι) pr. *the discharge of wages; requital; reward,* He. 10. 35; 11. 26; *punishment,* He. 2. 2.
μισθαποδοσίαν, acc. sing. . . . μισθαποδοσία

[a] Mat. 5. 41.

μισθαποδότης],[a] ου, ὁ, (§ 2. tab. B. c) (μισθός, ἀποδίδωμι) *a bestower of remuneration; recompenser, rewarder*. N.T.

μίσθιοι, nom. pl. masc. . . . . μίσθιος

μίσθιος], ίου, ὁ, ἡ . . . . μισθός

μισθίων, gen. pl. . . . . μίσθιος

μισθόν, acc. sing. . . . . μισθός

μισθός], οῦ, ὁ, (§ 3. tab. C. a) *hire, wages*, Mat. 20. 8; Ja. 5. 4, et al.; *reward*, Mat. 5. 12, 46; 6. 1, 2, 5, 16, et al.; *punishment*, 2 Pe. 2. 13, et al.

μίσθιος, ία, ιον, (§ 7. rem. 1) *hired; as a subst., a hired servant, hireling*, Lu. 15. 17, 19. L.G.

μισθόω, ῶ, fut. ώσω, (§ 20. tab. T) *to hire out, let out to hire*; mid. *to hire*, Mat. 20. 1, 7.

μίσθωμα, ατος, τό, (§ 4. tab. D. c) *hire, rent*; in N.T. *a hired dwelling*, Ac. 28. 30.

μισθωτός, οῦ, ὁ, (§ 3. tab. C. a) *a hireling*, Mar. 1. 20; Jno. 10. 12, 13.

μισθοῦ, gen. sing. . . . . μισθός

μισθόω, ῶ], fut. ώσω, (§ 20. tab T) . id.

μίσθωμα], ατος, τό . . . . id.

μισθώματι,[b] dat. sing. . . . μίσθωμα

μισθώσασθαι, aor. 1, infin. mid. . . μισθόω

μισθωτός], οῦ, ὁ, (§ 3. tab. C. a) . μισθός

μισθωτῶν, gen. pl. . . . . μισθωτός

μισούμενοι, nom. pl. masc. part. pres. pass. μισέω

μισοῦντας, acc. pl. masc. part. pres. act. . id.

μισοῦντες, nom. pl. masc. part. pres. act. . id.

μισούντων, gen. pl. masc. part. pres. act. . id.

μισοῦσι, dat. pl. masc. part. pres. act. . id.

μισῶ, 1 pers. sing. pres. ind. act. . . id.

μισῶν, nom. sing. masc. part. pres. act. . id.

Μιτυλήνη], ης, ἡ, (§ 2. tab. B. a) *Mitylene*, the capital city of Lesbos, in the Ægean sea.

Μιτυλήνην,[c] acc. . . . . . Μιτυλήνη

Μιχαήλ], ὁ, *Michael, the archangel*, indecl.

μνάα μνᾶ, άας, ᾶς, ἡ, (§ 2. rem. 5) Lat. *mina; a weight*, equivalent to 100 drachmæ; also *a sum*, equivalent to 100 drachmæ and the sixtieth part of a talent, worth about four pounds sterling, Lu. 19. 13, et al.

μνᾶν, acc. sing. contr. . . . . μνάα

μνάομαι, ῶμαι], (§ 36. rem. 3) see μιμνήσκω.

μνᾶς, acc. pl. contr. . . . . . μνάα

Μνάσων], ωνος, ὁ, (§ 4. rem. 2. e) *Mnason*, pr. name.

Μνάσωνι,[d] dat. . . . . Μνάσων

μνεία], ας, ἡ, (§ 2. tab. B. b, and rem 2) . μιμνήσκω

μνείᾳ, dat. sing. . . . . . μνεία

μνείαν, acc. sing. . . . . . id.

μνῆμα], ατος, τό, (§ 4. tab. D. c) . . μιμνήσκω

μνήμασι, dat. pl. . . . . . μνῆμα

μνήματα, acc. pl. . . . . . id.

μνήματι, dat. sing. . . . . . id.

μνημεῖα, nom. and acc. pl. . . . μνημεῖον

μνημείοις, dat. pl. . . . . . id.

μνημεῖον], ου, τό, (§ 3. tab. C. c) . . μιμνήσκω

μνημείου, gen. sing. . . . . μνημεῖον

μνημείῳ, dat. sing. . . . . id.

μνημείων, gen. pl. . . . . . id.

μνήμη], ης, ἡ, (§ 2. tab. B. a) . . μιμνήσκω

μνήμην,[e] acc. sing. . . . . . μνήμη

μνημόνευε, 2 pers. sing. pres. imper. . μνημονεύω

μνημονεύει, 3 pers. sing. pres. ind. . . id.

μνημονεύειν, pres. infin. . . . . id.

μνημονεύετε, 2 pers. pl. pres. ind. and imper. . id.

μνημονεύητε, 2 pers. pl. pres. subj. . . id.

μνημονεύοντες, nom. pl. masc. part. pres. . id.

μνημονεύω], fut. εύσω, (§ 13. tab. M) . μιμνήσκω

μνημονεύωμεν, 1 pers. pl. pres. subj. . μνημονεύω

μνημόσυνον], ου, τό, (§ 3. tab. C. c) . μιμνήσκω

μνησθῆναι, aor. 1, infin. pass. . . . id.

μνησθῇς, 2 pers. sing. aor. 1, subj. pass. . id.

μνήσθητε, 2 pers. pl. aor. 1, imper. pass. id.

μνήσθητι, 2 pers. sing. aor. 1, imper. pass. . id.

μνησθῶ, 1 pers. sing. aor. 1, subj. pass. . id.

μνηστευθείσης, gen. sing. fem. part. aor. 1, pass. μνηστεύω

μνηστεύω], fut. εύσω, (§ 13. tab. M) aor. 1, pass. ἐμνηστεύθην, *to ask in marriage; to betroth*; pass. *to be betrothed, affianced*, Mat. 1. 18; Lu. 1. 27; 2. 5.

μογιλάλον,[f] acc. sing. masc. . . . μογιλάλος

μογιλάλος], ου, ὁ, ἡ, (§ 7. rem. 2) (μόγις & λαλέω) *having an impediment in one's speech, speaking with difficulty, a stammerer*. (ᾰ). LXX.

μόγις],[g] adv. (μόγος, *labour, toil*) *with difficulty, scarcely, hardly*.

μόδιον, acc. sing. . . . . . μόδιος

μόδιος], ου, ὁ, (§ 3. tab. C. a) (Lat. *modius*) *a modius*, a Roman measure for things dry, containing 16 sextarii, and equivalent to

[a] He. 11. 6. [b] Ac. 28. 30. [c] Ac. 20. 14. [d] Ac. 21. 16. [e] 2 Pe. 1. 15. [f] Mar. 7. 32. [g] Lu. 9. 39.

about *a peck;* in N.T. *a corn measure,* Mat. 5. 15; Mar. 4. 21; Lu. 11. 33.

μοί, dat. sing. (§ 11. tab. K. a) . . ἐγώ

μοιχαλίδα, acc. sing. . . . . μοιχαλίς

μοιχαλίδες, voc. pl. . . . . id.

μοιχαλίδι, dat. sing. . . . . id.

μοιχαλίδος, gen. sing. . . . . id.

μοιχαλίς], ίδος, ἡ, (§ 4. rem. 2. c) . . μοιχός

μοιχάομαι, ῶμαι], fut. ήσομαι . . id.

μοιχᾶσθαι, pres. infin. . . . . μοιχάομαι

μοιχᾶται, 3 pers. sing. pres. ind. . . id.

μοιχεία], ας, ἡ, (§ 2. tab. B. b, and rem. 2) . μοιχός

μοιχείᾳ, dat. sing. . . . . μοιχεία

μοιχεῖαι, nom. pl. . . . . . id.

μοιχεύει, 3 pers. sing. pres. ind. . . μοιχεύω

μοιχεύειν, pres. infin. . . . . id.

μοιχεύεις, 2 pers. sing. pres. ind. . . id.

μοιχευθῆναι, aor. 1, infin. pass.—B. D. Ln. } id.
μοιχᾶσθαι, R. Gr. Sch. Tdf. (Mat. 5. 32) }

μοιχευομένη, nom. sing. fem. part. pres. mid. . id.

μοιχεύοντας, acc. pl. masc. part. pres. . id.

μοιχεύσεις, 2 pers. sing. fut. ind. . . id.

μοιχεύσῃς, 2 pers. sing. aor. 1, subj. . id.

μοιχεύω], fut. εύσω, (§ 13. tab. M) . . μοιχός

μοιχοί, nom. and voc. pl. . . . . id.

μοιχός], οῦ, ὁ, (§ 3. tab. C. a) *an adulterer,* Lu. 18. 11; 1 Co. 6. 9; He. 13. 4; Ja. 4. 4.

μοιχᾰλίς, ίδος, ἡ, (§ 4. rem. 2. c) (equivalent to μοιχάς, fem. of μοιχός) *an adulteress,* Ro. 7. 3; Ja. 4. 4; by meton. *an adulterous mien, lustful significance,* 2 Pe. 2. 14; from the Heb., spiritually *adulterous, faithless, ungodly,* Mat. 12. 39; 16. 4; Mar. 8. 38. L.G.

μοιχάομαι, ῶμαι, fut. ήσομαι, (§ 19. tab. S) (mid. of μοιχάω, *to defile a married woman) to commit or be guilty of adultery,* Mat. 5. 32, et al.

μοιχεία, ας, ἡ, (§ 2. tab. B. b, and rem. 2) *adultery,* Mat. 15. 19; Mar. 7. 21, et al.

μοιχεύω, fut. εύσω, (§ 13. tab. M) aor. 1, ἐμοίχευσα, trans. *to commit adultery with, debauch,* Mat. 5. 28; absol. and mid. *to commit adultery,* Mat. 5. 27; Jno. 8. 4, et al.; *to commit* spiritual *adultery, be guilty of idolatry,* Re. 2. 22.

μοιχούς, acc. pl. . . . . . μοιχός

μόλις], adv. (μόλος, *labour*) *with difficulty, scarcely, hardly,* Ac. 14. 18; 27. 7, 8, 16; Ro. 5. 7; 1 Pe. 4. 18.

Μολόχ],[a] ὁ, *Moloch,* pr. name, indecl.

μολύνεται, 3 pers. sing. pres. ind. pass. . μολύνω

μολύνω], fut. υνῶ, (§ 27. rem. 1. a) aor. 1, ἐμόλυνα, perf. pass. μεμόλυσμαι, aor. 1, ἐμολύνθην, (§ 27. rem. 3) pr. *to stain, sully; to defile, contaminate* morally, 1 Co. 8. 7; Re. 14. 4; *to soil,* Re. 3. 4.

μολυσμός, οῦ, ὁ, (§ 3. tab. C. a) *pollution,* 2 Co. 7. 1. L.G.

μολυσμοῦ,[b] gen. sing. . . . . μολυσμός

μομφή], ῆς, ἡ, (§ 2. tab. B. a) . . μέμφομαι

μομφήν,[c] acc. sing. . . . . μομφή

μόνα, acc. pl. neut. . . . . μόνος

μοναί, nom. pl. . . . . μονή

μονή], ῆς, ἡ, (§ 2. tab. B. a) . . μένω

μονήν, acc. sing. . . . . . μονή

μόνην, acc. sing. fem. . . . . μόνος

μονογενῆ, acc. sing. masc. . . μονογενής

μονογενής], έος, οῦς, ὁ, ἡ, (§ 7. tab. G. b) (μόνος & γένος) *only-begotten, only-born,* Lu. 7. 12; 8. 42; 9. 38; He. 11. 17; *only-begotten* in respect of peculiar generation, Jno. 1. 14, 18; 3. 16, 18; 1 Jno. 4. 9.

μονογενοῦς, gen. sing. masc. . . . μονογενής

μόνοι, nom. pl. masc. . . . . μόνος

μόνοις, dat. pl. masc. . . . . id.

μόνον, acc. sing. masc. . . . . id.

μόνον], adv. . . . . . μόνος

μόνος], η, ον, (§ 7. tab. F. a) *without accompaniment, alone,* Mat. 14. 23; 18. 15; Lu. 10. 40, et al.; *singly existent, sole, only,* Jno. 17. 3, et al.; *lone, solitary,* Jno. 8. 29; 16. 32; *alone* in respect of restriction, *only,* Mat. 4. 4; 12. 4, et al.; *alone* in respect of circumstances, *only,* Lu. 24. 18; *not multiplied by reproduction, lone, barren,* Jno. 12. 24.

μόνον, adv. *only,* Mat. 5. 47; 8. 8; οὐ μόνον—ἀλλὰ καὶ, *not only—but also,* Mat. 21. 21; Jno. 5. 18; μὴ μόνον—ἀλλὰ, *not only—but,* Phi. 2. 12, et al.

μονόω, ῶ, fut. ώσω, (§ 20. tab. T) perf. pass. μεμόνωμαι, *to leave alone;* pass. *to be left alone, be lone,* 1 Ti. 5. 5.

---

[a] Ac. 7. 43. [b] 2 Co. 7. 1. [c] Col. 3. 13.

μόνου, gen. sing. masc. . . μόνος
μόνους, acc. pl. masc. . . . . . id.
μονόφθαλμον, acc. sing. masc. . . μονόφθαλμος
μονόφθαλμος], ου, ὁ, ἡ, (§ 7. rem. 2) (μόνος & ὀφθαλμός) *one-eyed; deprived of an eye*, Mat. 18. 9; Mar. 9. 47.
μονόω, ῶ], fut. ώσω, (§ 20. tab. T) . . μόνος
μόνῳ, dat. sing. masc. . . . . . id.

μορφή], ῆς, ἡ, (§ 2. tab. B. a) *form*, Mar. 16. 12; Phi. 2. 6, 7.

μορφόω, ῶ, fut. ώσω, (§ 20. tab. T) aor. 1, pass. ἐμορφώθην, *to give shape to, mould, fashion*, Gal. 4. 19.

μόρφωσις, εως, ἡ, (§ 5. tab. E. c) pr. *a shaping, moulding*; in N.T. *external form, appearance*, 2 Ti. 3. 5; a settled *form*, prescribed *system*, Ro. 2. 20.

μορφῇ, dat. sing. . . . . . μορφή
μορφήν, acc. sing. . . . . . id.
μορφόω, ῶ], fut. ώσω . . . id.
μορφωθῇ,[a] 3 pers. sing. aor. 1, subj. pass. (§ 21. tab. U) . . . . . μορφόω
μόρφωσιν, acc. sing. . . . . . μόρφωσις
μόρφωσις], εως, ἡ, (§ 5. tab. E. c) . μορφή
μόσχον, acc. sing. . . . . . μόσχος
μοσχοποιέω, ῶ], fut. ήσω, (§ 16. tab. P) aor. 1, ἐμοσχοποίησα, (μόσχος & ποιέω) *to form an image of a calf*, Ac. 7. 41. N.T.

μόσχος], ου, ὁ, ἡ, (§ 3. tab. C. a) pr. *a tender branch, shoot; a young animal; a calf, young bullock*, Lu. 15. 23, 27, 30; He. 12. 19; Re. 4. 7.

μόσχῳ, dat. sing. . . . . . μόσχος
μόσχων, gen. pl. . . . . . . id.
μοῦ, gen. sing. (§ 11. tab. K. a) . . ἐγώ
μουσικός], ή, όν, or οῦ, ὁ, ἡ, (μοῦσα, *a muse, song, music*) pr. *devoted to the arts of the Muses; a musician*; in N.T., perhaps, *a singer*, Re. 18. 22.
μουσικῶν,[b] gen. pl. . . . . . μουσικός
μόχθον, acc. sing. . . . . . μόχθος
μόχθος], ου, ὁ, (§ 3. tab. C. a) *wearisome labour, toil, travail*, 2 Co. 11. 27; 1 Thes. 2. 9; 2 Thes. 3. 8.
μόχθῳ, dat. sing. . . . . . . μόχθος

μυελός], οῦ, ὁ, (§ 3. tab. C. a) *marrow*, He. 4. 12.

μυελῶν,[c] gen. pl. . . . . . μυελός
μυέω, ῶ], fut. ήσω, (§ 16. tab. P) perf. pass. μεμύημαι, (μύω, *to shut the mouth*) *to initiate, instruct* in the sacred mysteries; in N.T. pass. *to be disciplined* in a practical lesson, *to learn* a lesson, Phi. 4. 12.

μυστήριον, ίου, τό, (§ 3. tab. C. c) (μύστης, *an initiated person*, μυέω) *a matter to the knowledge of which initiation is necessary; a secret* which would remain such but for revelation, Mat. 3. 11; Ro. 11. 25; Col. 1. 26, et al.; *a concealed power or principle*, 2 Thes. 2. 7; *a hidden meaning* of a symbol, Re. 1. 20; 17. 7.

μύθοις, dat. pl. . . . . . . μῦθος

μῦθος], ου, ὁ, (§ 3. tab. C. a) *a word, speech, a tale; a fable, figment*, 1 Ti. 1. 4, et al.

μύθους, acc. pl. . . . . . . μῦθος

μυκάομαι, ῶμαι], (§ 19. tab. S) *to low, bellow*, as a bull; also, *to roar*, as a lion.

μυκᾶται,[d] 3 pers. sing. pres. ind. . . μυκάομαι
μυκτηρίζεται,[e] 3 pers. sing. pres. ind. pass. μυκτηρίζω
μυκτηρίζω], fut. ίσω, (§ 26. rem. 1) (μυκτήρ, *the nose*) *to contract the nose in contempt and derision, toss up the nose; to mock, deride*, Gal. 6. 7.
μυλικός],[f] ή, όν, (§ 7. tab. F. a) (μύλη, *a mill*) *of a mill, belonging to a mill*.
μύλον, acc. sing. . . . . . μύλος
μύλος], ου, ὁ, (§ 3. tab. C. a) *a millstone*, Mat. 18. 6, et al.
μύλου, gen. sing. . . . . . . μύλος
μύλῳ, dat. sing.—B. Ln. . . . } id.
μύλωνι, Rec. Gr. Sch. Tdf. (Mat. 24. 41) }
μύλων], ωνος, ὁ, (§ 4. rem. 2. e) *a mill-house*, a place where the grinding of corn was performed.
μύλωνι,[g] dat. sing. . . . . . μύλων
Μύρα],[h] ων, τά, *Myra*, a city of Lycia.—Rec. Gr. Sch.
Μύῤῥα, B. Ln. Tdf.
μύρα, acc. pl. . . . . . . μύρον
μυριάδας, acc. pl. . . . . . μυριάς
μυριάδες, nom. pl. . . . . . . id.
μυριάδων, gen. pl. . . . . . id.
μυριάς], άδος (ᾰ), ἡ, (§ 4. tab. D. b) (μυρίος, *innumerable*) *a myriad, ten thousand*, Ac.

[a] Gal. 4. 19. [b] Re. 18. 22. [c] He. 4. 12. [d] Re. 10. 3. [e] Gal. 6. 7. [f] Mar. 9. 42. [g] Mat. 24. 41. [h] Ac. 27. 5.

19. 19; indefinitely, *a vast multitude*, Lu. 12. 1; Ac. 21. 20, et al.

μυριάσι, dat. pl. . . . . . μυριάς

μυρίζω], fut. ίσω, (§ 26. rem. 1) . . μύρον

μυρίοι], αι, α, (§ 9. tab. I. d) (μυρίος, *innumerable*) indefinitely, *a great number*, 1 Co. 4. 15; 14. 19; specifically, μύριοι, *a myriad, ten thousand*, Mat. 18. 24.

μυριους, acc. pl. masc. . . . μυρίοι

μυρίσαι,[a] aor. 1, infin. . . . . μυρίζω

μυρίων, gen. pl. . . . . μυρίοι

μύρον], ου, τό, (§ 3. tab. C. c) pr. *aromatic juice which distils from trees; ointment, unguent*, usually perfumed, Mat. 26. 7, 12; Mar. 14. 3, 4, et al.

μυρίζω, fut. ίσω, (§ 26. rem. 1) *to anoint*, Mar. 14. 8.

Μυσία], ας, ἡ, (§ 2. tab. B. b, and rem. 2) *Mysia*, a province of Asia Minor.

Μυσίαν, acc. . . . . . Μυσία

μυστήρια, acc. pl. . . . . μυστήριον

μυστήριον], ου, τό, (§ 3. tab. C. c) . . μυέω

μυστηρίου, gen. sing. . . . . μυστήριον

μυστηρίῳ, dat. sing. . . . . id.

μυστηρίων, gen. pl. . . . . id.

μυωπάζω], fut. άσω, (§ 26. rem. 1) (μύω, *to shut, close*, & ὤψ) pr. *to close the eyes, contract the eyelids, wink; to be near-sighted, dim-sighted, purblind*, 2 Pe. 1. 9.

μυωπάζων,[b] nom. sing. masc. part. pres. . μυωπάζω

μώλωπι,[c] dat. sing. . . . . μώλωψ

μώλωψ], ωπος, ὁ, (§ 4. rem. 2. a) *the mark of a blow; a stripe, a wound*, 1 Pe. 2. 24.

μωμεομαι, οῦμαι], fut. ήσομαι, (§ 17. tab. Q) μῶμος

μωμηθῇ, 3 pers. sing. aor. 1, subj. pass. . μωμέομαι

μωμήσηται, 3 pers. sing. aor. 1, subj. mid. id.

μῶμοι,[d] nom. pl. . . . . μῶμος

μῶμος], ου, ὁ, (§ 3. tab. C. a) *blame, ridicule; a disgrace* to society, *a stain*, 2 Pe. 2. 13.

μωμέομαι, οῦμαι, or μωμάομαι, ῶμαι], fut. ήσομαι, aor. 1, pass. ἐμωμήθην, *to find fault with, censure, blame*, 2 Co. 8. 20; passively, 2 Co. 6. 3.

μωρά, acc. pl. neut. . . . . μωρός

μωραί, nom. pl. fem. . . . . id.

μωραίνω], fut. ανῶ, (§ 27. rem. 1. c) . . id.

μωρανθῇ, 3 pers. sing. aor. 1, subj. pass. . μωραίνω

μωράς, acc. pl. fem. . . . . μωρός

μωρέ, voc. sing. masc. . . . . id.

μωρία], ας, ἡ, (§ 2. tab. B. b, and rem. 2) . . μωρός

μωρίαν, acc. sing. . . . . μωρία

μωρίας, gen. sing. . . . . id.

μωροί, nom. and voc. pl. masc. . . μωρός

μωρολογία],[e] ας, ἡ, (§ 2. tab. B. b, and rem. 2) (μωρός & λόγος) *foolish talk*.

μωρόν, nom. sing. neut. . . . . μωρός

μωρός], ά, όν, (§ 7. rem. 1) pr. *dull; foolish*, Mat. 7. 26; 23. 17, 19; 2 Ti. 2. 23, et al.; from the Heb., *a fool* in senseless wickedness, Mat. 5. 22.

μωραίνω, fut. ανῶ, (§ 27. rem. 1. c) aor. 1, ἐμώρᾱνα, *to be foolish, to play the fool*; in N.T. trans. *to make foolish, convict of folly*, 1 Co. 1. 20; pass. *to be convicted of folly, to incur the character of folly*, Ro. 1. 22; *to be rendered insipid*, Mat. 5. 13; Lu. 14. 34.

μωρία, ας, ἡ, (§ 2. tab. B. b, and rem. 2) *foolishness*, 1 Co. 1. 18, 21, 23, et al.

μωρῷ, dat. sing. masc. . . . . μωρός

Μωσέα, acc. . . . . . Μωσῆς

Μωσεῖ, dat. . . . . id.

Μωσέως, gen. . . . . . id.

Μωσῇ, dat. . . . . . id.

Μωσῆν, acc. . . . . . id.

Μωσῆς, or Μωϋσῆς, έως, ὁ, *Moses*, pr. name.

Μωϋσέα, acc. . . . . Μωϋσῆς

Μωϋσεῖ, dat. . . . . . id.

Μωϋσέως, gen. . . . . . id.

Μωϋσῆν, acc. . . . . id.

N.

Ναασσών, ὁ, *Naasson*, pr. name, indecl.

Ναγγαί,[f] ὁ, *Naggai, Nagge*, pr. name, indecl.

Ναζαρέθ, or Ναζαρέτ, ἡ, *Nazareth*, a city of Galilee, indecl.

Ναζαρηνέ, voc. sing. . . . . Ναζαρηνός

Ναζαρηνόν, acc. sing. . . . . id.

Ναζαρηνός, οῦ, ὁ, *an inhabitant of Nazareth*, B. Ln. Tdf. (Mar. 10. 47.)

Ναζωραῖος, Rec. Gr. Sch.

Ναζαρηνοῦ, gen. sing. . . . Ναζαρηνός

[a] Mar. 14. 8. [b] 2 Pe. 1. 9. [c] 1 Pe. 2. 24. [d] 2 Pe. 2. 13. [e] Ep. 5. 4. [f] Lu. 3. 25.

Ναζωραῖον, acc. sing. . . . . Ναζωραῖος

Ναζωραῖος, οῦ, ὁ, (§ 3. tab. C. a) *a Nazarite; an inhabitant of Nazareth.*

Ναζωραίου, gen. sing. . . . . Ναζωραῖος

Ναζωραίων, gen. pl. . . . . id.

Ναθάν,[a] ὁ, *Nathan*, pr. name, indecl.

Ναθαναήλ, ὁ, *Nathanael*, pr. name, indecl.

ναί, a particle, used to strengthen an affirmation, *verily*, Re. 22. 20; to make an affirmation, or express an assent, *yea, yes*, Mat. 5. 37; Ac. 5. 8, et al.

Ναΐν,[b] ἡ, *Nain*, a town of Palestine, indecl.

ναοῖς, dat. pl. . . . . ναός

ναόν, acc. sing. . . . . id.

ναός], οῦ, ὁ, (§ 3. tab. C. a) (ναίω, *to dwell*) pr. *a dwelling; the dwelling* of a deity, *a temple*, Mat. 26. 61; Ac. 7. 48, et al.; used figuratively of individuals, Jno. 2. 19; 1 Co. 3. 16, et al.; spc. *the cell of a temple;* hence, *the Holy Place* of the Temple of Jerusalem, Mat. 23. 35; Lu. 1. 9, et al.; *a model of a temple, a shrine*, Ac. 19. 24.

ναοῦ, gen. sing. . . . . ναός

Ναούμ,[c] ὁ, *Naum*, pr. name, indecl.

ναούς, acc. pl. . . . . id.

νάρδος], ου, ἡ, (§ 3. tab. C. b) (Heb. נֵרְדְּ, *spikenard, andropogon nardus* of Linn., a species of aromatic plant with grassy leaves and a fibrous root, of which the best and strongest grows in India; in N.T. *oil of spikenard*, an oil extracted from the plant, which was highly prized and used as an ointment either pure or mixed with other substances, Mar. 14. 3; Jno. 12. 3.

νάρδου, gen. . . . . νάρδος

Νάρκισσος], ου, ὁ, *Narcissus*, pr. name.

Ναρκίσσου,[d] gen. . . . . Νάρκισσος

ναυᾱγέω, ῶ], fut. ήσω, aor. 1, ἐναυάγησα, (§ 16. tab. P) (ναῦς & ἄγνυμι, *to break*) *to make shipwreck, be shipwrecked*, 2 Co. 11. 25; Re. 18. 17.

ναύκληρος], ου, ὁ, (§ 3. tab. C. a) (ναῦς & κλῆρος) *the master or owner of a ship.*

ναυκλήρῳ,[e] dat. sing. . . . . ναύκληρος

ναῦν,[f] acc. sing. . . . . ναῦς

ναῦς], νεώς, ἡ, (§ 6. rem. 4. g) (νέω, *to swim*) *a ship, vessel.*

> **ναύτης, ου, ὁ,** (§ 2. tab. B. c) *a shipman, sailor, seaman*, Ac. 27. 27, 30; Re. 18. 17.

ναῦται, nom. pl. . . . . ναύτης

ναύτης], ου, ὁ . . . . ναῦς

ναυτῶν, gen. pl. . . . . ναύτης

Ναχώρ,[g] ὁ, *Nachor*, pr. name, indecl.

ναῷ, dat. sing. . . . . ναος

νεανίαν, acc. sing. . . . . νεανίας

νεανίας], ου, ὁ, (§ 2. tab. B. d) . . . νέος

νεανίου, gen. sing. . . . . νεανίας

νεανίσκε, voc. sing. . . . . νεανίσκος

νεανίσκοι, nom. and voc. pl. . . . id.

νεανίσκον, acc. sing. . . . . id.

νεανίσκος], ου, ὁ, (§ 3. tab. C. a) . . νέος

Νεάπολιν,[h] acc. . . . . Νεάπολις

Νεάπολις], εως, ἡ, (§ 5. tab. E. c) *Neapolis*, a city of Thrace on the Strymonic gulf.

νέας, gen. sing. and acc. pl. fem. . . νέος

Νεεμάν,[i] ὁ, *Neeman, Naaman*, pr. name, indecl.

νεκρά, nom. sing. fem. . . . . νεκρός

νεκράν, acc. sing. fem. . . . . id.

νεκροί, nom. pl. masc. . . . . id.

νεκροῖς, dat. pl. masc. . . . . id.

νεκρόν, nom. sing. neut. and acc. masc. . id.

νεκρός], ά, όν, (§ 7. rem. 1) (νέκυς, *a dead body*) *dead, without life*, Mat. 11. 5; 22. 31; met. νεκρός τινι, *dead to a thing, no longer devoted to, or under the influence of a thing*, Ro. 6. 11; *dead* in respect of fruitlessness, Ja. 2. 17, 20, 26; morally or spiritually *dead*, Ro. 6. 13; Ep. 5. 14; *dead* in alienation from God, Ep. 2. 1, 5; Col. 2. 13; *obnoxious to death, mortal*, Ro. 8. 10; *causing death and misery, fatal, having a destructive power*, He. 6. 1; 9. 14, et al.

> **νεκρόω, ῶ,** fut. ώσω aor. 1, ἐνέκρωσα, (§ 20. tab. T) pr. *to put to death, kill;* in N.T. met. *to deaden, mortify*, Col. 3. 5; pass. *to be rendered impotent, effete*, Ro. 4. 19; He. 11. 12. L.G.

> **νέκρωσις, εως, ἡ,** (§ 5. tab. E. c) pr. *a putting to death; dying, abandonment to death*, 2 Co. 4. 10; *deadness, impotency*, Ro. 4. 19. L.G.

νεκροῦ, gen. sing. masc. . . . . νεκρός

νεκρούς, acc. pl. masc. . . . . νεκρός

[a] Lu. 3. 31. [b] Lu. 7. 11. [c] Lu. 3. 25. [d] Ro. 16. 11. [e] Ac. 27. 11. [f] Ac. 27. 41. [g] Lu. 3. 34. [h] Ac. 16. 11. [i] Lu. 4. 27.

νεκρόω, ῶ], fut. ώσω, (§ 20. tab. T) . νεκρός
νεκρῶν, gen. pl. . . . . id.
νεκρώσατε, 2 pers. pl. aor. 1, imper. . νεκρόω
νέκρωσιν, acc. sing. . . . . νέκρωσις
νέκρωσις], εως, ἡ, (§ 5. tab. E. c) . . νεκρός
νενεκρωμένον, acc. sing. neut. part. perf. pass. (§ 21. tab. U) . . . . νεκρόω
νενεκρωμένου, gen. sing. masc. part. perf. pass. id.
νενίκηκα, 1 pers. sing. perf. ind. act. . νικάω
νενικήκατε, 2 pers. pl. perf. ind. act. . . id.
νενομοθέτηται, 3 pers. sing. perf. ind. pass. νομοθετέω
νενομοθέτητο, 3 pers. sing. pluperf. pass. for ἐνενομοθέτητο, (§ 14. rem. 1. f) id.
νέον, acc. sing. masc. and nom. neut. . νέος

νέος], α, ον, (§ 7. rem. 1) *recent, new, fresh*, Mat. 9. 17; 1 Co. 5. 7; Col. 3. 10, He. 12. 24; *young, youthful*, Tit. 2. 4, et al.

νεᾶνίας, ου, ὁ, (§ 2. tab. B. d) (νεάν, idem, from νέος) *a young man, youth*, Ac. 20. 9; 23. 17, 18, 22; used of *one who is in the prime and vigour of life*, Ac. 7. 58.

νεᾶνίσκος, ου, ὁ, (§ 3. tab. C. a) *a young man, youth*, Mar. 14. 51; 16. 5, et al.; used of *one in the prime of life*, Mat. 19. 20, 22; νεανίσκοι, *soldiers*, Mar. 14. 51.

νεοσσός, οῦ, ὁ, (§ 3. tab. C. a) *the young of birds, a young bird, youngling, chick*, Lu. 2. 24.

νοσσιά, ᾶς, ἡ, (§ 2. tab. B. b, and rem. 2) (contr. for νεοσσιά, from νεοσσός) *a brood* of young birds, Lu. 13. 34.

νοσσίον, ου, τό, (§ 3. tab. C. c) contr. for νεοσσίον) *the young of birds, a chick*; pl. *a brood* of young birds, Mat. 23. 37.

νοσσός, οῦ, ὁ, (contr. for νεοσσός) *a young bird*, v.r. Lu. 2. 24.

νεότης, τητος, ἡ, (§ 4. rem. 2. c) *youth*, Mat. 19. 20; Ac. 26. 4, et al.

νεώτερος, α, ον, (§ 7. rem. 1) (compar. of νέος) *younger, more youthful*, Lu. 15. 12, 13, et al.

νεωτερῐκός, ή, όν, (§ 7. tab. F. a) *juvenile, natural to youth, youthful*, 2 Ti 2. 22. L.G.

νεοσσός], οῦ, ὁ . . . . . . νέος
νεοσσούς,[a] acc. pl. . . . . . νεοσσός
νεότης], τητος, ἡ . . . . . . νέος
νεότητος, gen. sing. . . . . νεότης
νεόφυτον,[b] acc. sing. masc. . . . νεόφυτος
νεόφῠτος], ου, ὁ, ἡ, (§ 7. rem. 2) (νέος & φύω) *newly or recently planted*; met. *a neophyte, one newly implanted* into the Christian Church, *a new convert*, 1 Ti. 3. 6. LXX.
νεύει, 3 pers. sing. pres. ind. . . . νεύω
νεύσαντος, gen. sing. masc. part. aor. 1 . id

νεύω], fut. νεύσω, aor. 1, ἔνευσα, (§ 13. tab. M) *to nod; to intimate by a nod or significant gesture*, Jno. 13. 24; Ac. 24. 10.

νυστάζω, fut. σω & ξω, (§ 26. rem. 2) *to nod; to nod in sleep; to sink into a sleep*, Mat. 25. 5; *to slumber* in inactivity, 2 Pe. 2. 3.

νεφέλαι, nom. pl. . . . . . νεφέλη
νεφέλαις, dat. pl. . . . . . id.
νεφέλη], ης, ἡ, (§ 2. tab. B. a) *a cloud*, Mat. 17. 5; 24. 30; 26. 64, et al.
νεφέλῃ, dat. sing. . . . . . νεφέλη
νεφέλην, acc. sing. . . . . . id.
νεφέλης, gen. sing. . . . . . id.
νεφελῶν, gen. pl. . . . . . . id.
Νεφθαλείμ, ὁ, *Nephthalim*, pr. name, indecl.
νέφος],[c] εος, τό, (§ 5. tab. E. b) *a cloud*; trop. *a cloud, a throng* of persons, He. 12. 1.

νεφρός], οῦ, ὁ, (§ 3. tab. C. a) *a kidney*; pl. νεφροί, *the kidneys, reins*; from the Heb., *the reins* regarded as a seat of desire and affection, Re. 2. 23.

νεφρούς,[d] acc. pl. . . . . . νεφρός
νεωκόρον,[e] acc. sing. fem. . . . . νεωκόρος
νεωκόρος], ου, ὁ, ἡ, (§ 7. rem. 2) (ναός, Att. νεώς, & κορέω, *to sweep clean*) pr. *one who sweeps or cleanses a temple*; generally, *one who has the charge of a temple, æditiuus*; in N.T. *a devotee* city, as having specially dedicated a temple to some deity.
νεωτέρας, acc. pl. fem. . . . . νεώτερος
νεωτερικάς,[f] acc. pl. fem. . . . . νεωτερικός
νεωτερικός], ή, όν, (§ 7. tab. F. a) . . νέος
νεώτεροι, nom. pl. masc. . . . . νεώτερος
νεώτερος, α, ον, (§ 7. rem. 1) . . . νέος
νεωτέρους, acc. pl. masc. . . . . νεώτερος

[a] Lu. 2. 24. [b] 1 Ti. 3. 6. [c] He. 12. 1. [d] Re. 2. 23. [e] Ac. 19. 35. [f] 2 Ti. 2. 22.

νή,[a] a particle used in affirmative oaths, *by*.
νήθει, 3 pers. sing. pres. ind. . . . νήθω
νήθουσι, 3 pers. pl. pres. ind.—B. Ln. } id.
νήθει, Rec. Gr. Sch. Tdf. (Mat. 6. 28) }
νήθω], fut. νήσω, (§ 23. rem. 1. c) (νέω, idem) *to spin*, Mat. 6. 28; Lu. 12. 27.
νηπιάζετε,[b] 2 pers. pl. pres. imper. . . νηπιάζω
νηπιάζω], fut. άσω . . . . . . νήπιος
νήπιοι, nom. pl. . . . . . id.
νηπίοις, dat. pl. . . . . . . id.
νήπιος], ίου, ὁ, (§ 3. tab. C. a) (νή & ἔπος) pr. *not speaking, infans; an infant, babe, child*, Mat. 21. 16; 1 Co. 13. 11; *one below the age of manhood, a minor*, Gal. 4. 1; met. *a babe* in knowledge, *unlearned, simple*, Mat. 11. 25; Ro. 2. 20.

νηπιάζω, fut. άσω, (§ 26. rem. 1) *to be childlike*, 1 Co. 14. 20.

νηπίου, gen. sing. . . . . . νήπιος
νηπίων, gen. pl. . . . . . id.
Νηρέα,[c] acc. . . . . . . Νηρεύς
Νηρεύς], έως, ὁ, (§ 5. tab. E. d) *Nereus*, pr. name.
Νηρί,[d] ὁ, *Neri*, pr. name, indecl.
νησίον,[e] ου, τό . . . . . νῆσος
νῆσον, acc. sing. . . . . . id.
νῆσος], ου, ἡ, (§ 3. tab. C. b) (νέω, *to swim*) *an island*, Ac. 13. 6; 27. 26, et al.

νησίον, ου, τό, (§ 3. tab. C. c) *a small island*, Ac. 27. 16.

νήσου, gen. sing. . . . . . . νῆσος
νηστείᾳ, dat. sing. . . . . . νηστεία
νηστεία], ας, ἡ, (§ 2. tab. B. b, and rem. 2) νῆστις
νηστείαις, dat. pl. . . . . νηστεία
νηστείαν, acc. sing. . . . . id.
νήστεις, acc. pl. masc. . . . . . νῆστις
νηστειῶν, gen. pl. . . . . . νηστεία
νηστεύειν, pres. infin. . . . . . νηστεύω
νηστεύητε, 2 pers. pl. pres. subj. . . . id.
νηστεύομεν, 1 pers. pl. pres. ind. . . . id.
νηστεύοντες, nom. pl. masc. part. pres. . id.
νηστευόντων, gen. pl. masc. part. pres. . id.
νηστεύουσι, 3 pers. pl. pers. ind. . . id.
νηστεύσαντες, nom. pl. masc. part. aor. 1 . id.
νηστεύσας, nom. sing. masc. part. aor. 1 . id.
νηστεύσουσι, 3 pers. pl. fut. ind. . . . id.
νηστεύω, fut. εύσω, (§ 13. tab. M) . . νῆστις
νηστεύων, nom. sing. masc. part. pres. . . νηστεύω
νῆστις], ιος, εως, (§ 5. tab. E. c) and ιδος, ὁ, ἡ, (§ 4. rem. 2. c) (νή & ἐσθίω) *fasting*, Mat 15. 32; Mar. 8. 3.

νηστεία, ας, ἡ, *fasting, want of food*, 2 Co. 6. 5; 11. 27; *a fast*, religious *abstinence from food*, Mat. 17. 21; Lu. 2. 37, et al.; spc. *the annual public fast of the Jews, the great day of atonement*, occurring in the month Tisri, corresponding to the new moon of October, Ac. 27. 9.

νηστεύω, fut. εύσω, aor. 1, ἐνήστευσα, (§ 13. tab. M) *to fast*, Mat. 4. 2; 6. 16, 17, 18; 9. 15, et al.

νήσῳ, dat. sing. . . . . . . νῆσος
νηφάλιον, acc. sing. masc.—Gr. Sch. Tdf. } νηφάλιος
νηφάλεον, Rec. (1 Ti. 3. 2) . . }
νηφάλιος], ου, ὁ, ἡ . . . . . νήφω
νηφαλίους, acc. pl. masc.—Gr. Sch. Tdf. } νηφάλιος
νηφαλέους, Rec. (1 Ti. 3. 11) . }
νῆφε, 2 pers. sing. pres. imper. . . νήφω
νήφοντες, nom. pl. masc. part. pres. . . id.

νήφω], fut. ψω, (§ 23. rem. 1. a) aor. 1, ἔνηψα, *to be sober, not intoxicated*; in N.T. met. *to be vigilant, circumspect*, 1 Thes. 5. 6, 8, et al.

νηφάλιος, (and later νηφάλεος) ίου, ὁ, ἡ, (§ 7. rem. 2) *sober, temperate, abstinent in respect to wine*, etc.; in N.T. met. *vigilant, circumspect*, 1 Ti. 3. 2, 11; Tit. 2. 2.

νήφωμεν, 1 pers. pl. pres. subj. . . νήφω
νήψατε, 2 pers. pl. aor. 1, imper. . . id.
Νίγερ,[f] ὁ, *Niger*, pr. name, probably not declined.
νικᾷ, 3 pers. sing. pres. ind. . . . νικάω
νίκα, 2 pers. sing. pres. imper. . . . id.
Νικάνορα,[g] acc. . . . . . Νικάνωρ
Νικάνωρ], ορος, ὁ, (§ 4. rem. 2. f) *Nicanor*, pr. name.
νικάω, ῶ], fut. ήσω . . . . . νίκη

νίκη],[h] ης, ἡ, (§ 2. tab. B. a) *victory*; meton. *a victorious principle*, 1 Jno. 5. 4.

νικάω, ῶ, fut. ήσω, perf. νενίκηκα, aor. 1, ἐνίκησα, (§ 18. tab. R) *to conquer, overcome, vanquish, subdue*, Lu. 11. 22; Jno. 16. 33; absol. *to overcome, prevail*, Re. 5. 5; *to come off superior* in a judicial cause, Ro. 3. 4.

νῖκος, εος, το, (§ 5. tab. E. b) (a later

[a] 1 Co. 15. 31. [b] 1 Co. 14. 20. [c] Ro. 16. 15. [d] Lu. 3. 27. [e] Ac. 27. 16. [f] Ac. 13. 1. [g] Ac. 6. 5. [h] 1 Jno. 5. 4.

equivalent to νίκη) *victory*, Mat. 12. 20; 1 Co. 15. 54, 55, 57.

νικῆσαι, aor. 1, infin. . . . . . νικάω

νικήσασα, nom. sing. fem. part. aor. 1. . id.

νικήσει, 3 pers. sing. fut. ind. . . . id.

νικήσῃ, 3 pers. sing. aor. 1, subj. . . . id.

νικήσῃς, 2 pers. sing. aor. 1, subj. . . . id.

Νικόδημος], ου, ὁ, (§ 3. tab. C. a) *Nicodemus*, pr. name.

Νικολαΐτης], ου, ὁ, (§ 2. tab. B. c) *a Nicolaitan*, or follower of Nicolaus, an heresiarch of the Apostolic age, Re. 2. 6, 15. (ῑ).

Νικολαϊτῶν, gen. pl. . . . . Νικολαΐτης

Νικόλαον,[a] acc. . . . . . . Νικόλαος

Νικόλᾱος], ου, ὁ, (§ 3. tab. C. a) *Nicolaus*, pr. name.

Νικόπολιν,[b] acc. . . . . . . Νικόπολις

Νικόπολις], εως, ἡ, (§ 5. tab. E. c) *Nicopolis*, a city of Macedonia.

νῖκος], εος, ους, τό, (§ 5. tab. E. b) . . νίκη

νικῶ, 2 pers. sing. pres. imper. pass. . . νικάω

νικῶν, nom. sing. masc. part. pres. . . id.

νικῶντας, acc. pl. masc. part. pres. . . id.

νικῶντι, dat. sing. masc. part. pres. . . id.

Νινευΐ,[c] ἡ, *Nineveh*, the capital of Assyria, indecl.

Νινευῖται, nom. pl. . . . . . Νινευΐτης

Νινευΐταις, dat. pl. . . . . . id.

Νινευΐτης], ου, ὁ, (§ 2. tab. B. c) *a Ninevite, an inhabitant of Nineveh*. (ῑ).

νίπτειν, pres. infin. . . . . . νίπτω

νίπτεις, 2 pers. sing. pres. ind. . . . id.

νιπτήρ], ῆρος, ὁ, (§ 4. rem. 2. f) . . id.

νιπτῆρα,[d] acc. sing. . . . . . νιπτήρ

νίπτω], fut. ψω, (§ 23. rem. 1. a) aor. 1, ἔνιψα, (a form of later use for νίζω) *to wash*; spc. *to wash* some part of the person, as distinguished from λούω, Mat. 6. 17; Jno. 13. 8, et al.

νιπτήρ, ῆρος, ὁ, (§ 4. rem. 2. f.) *a basin* for washing some part of the person. N.T.

νίπτονται, 3 pers. pl. pres. ind. mid. . . νίπτω

νίψαι, 2 pers. sing. aor. 1, imper. mid. . id.

νιψάμενος, nom. sing. masc. part. aor. 1, mid. id.

νίψασθαι, aor. 1, infin. mid. . . . id.

νίψῃς, 2 pers. sing. aor. 1, subj. act. . id.

νίψω, 1 pers. sing. aor. 1, subj. act. . . id.

νίψωνται, 3 pers. pl. aor. 1, subj. mid. . id.

νόει, 2 pers. sing. pres. imper. . . . . νοέω

νοεῖτε, 2 pers. pl. pres. ind. . . . id.

νοείτω, 3 pers. sing. pres. imper. . . id.

νοέω, ῶ], fut. ήσω, (§ 16. tab. P) . . νοῦς

νόημα], ατος, τό, (§ 4. tab. D. c) . . id.

νοήματα, nom. and acc. pl. . . . νόημα

νοῆσαι, aor. 1, infin. . . . . . νοέω

νοήσωσι, 3 pers. pl. aor. 1, subj. . . id.

νόθοι,[e] nom. pl. masc. . . . . . νόθος

νόθος], ου, ὁ, ἡ, *spurious, bastard*.

νοΐ, dat. sing. (§ 6. rem. 4. h) . . νοῦς

νομή], ῆς, ἡ, (§ 2. tab. B. a) (νέμω, *to feed*) *pasture, pasturage*, Jno. 10. 9; ἔχειν νομήν, *to eat its way, spread corrosion*, 2 Ti. 2. 17.

νομήν, acc. sing. . . . . . . νομή

νομίζει, 3 pers. sing. pres. ind. . . νομίζω

νομίζειν, pres. infin. . . . . . id.

νομίζοντες, nom. pl. masc. part. pres.—B. Ln. Tdf. . . . . . } id.
νομίσαντες, Rec. Gr. Sch. (Ac. 14. 19) }

νομιζόντων, gen. pl. masc. part. pres. . . id.

νομίζω], fut. ίσω, (§ 26. rem. 1) . . νόμος

νομίζων, nom. sing. masc. part. pres. . . νομίζω

νομικάς, acc. pl. fem. . . . . . νομικός

νομικοί, nom. pl. masc. . . . . id.

νομικοῖς, dat. pl. masc. . . . . id.

νομικόν, acc. sing. masc. . . . . id.

νομικός], ή, όν, (§ 7. tab. F. a) . . νόμος

νομικούς, acc. pl. masc. . . . . νομικός

νομικῶν, gen. pl. . . . . . id.

νομιμῶς], adv. . . . . . . νόμος

νομίσαντες, nom. pl. masc. part. aor. 1 . νομίζω

νομίσητε, 2 pers. pl. aor. 1, subj. . . id.

νόμισμα],[f] ατος, τό, (§ 4. tab. D. c). . νόμος

νομοδιδάσκαλοι, nom. pl. . . νομοδιδάσκαλος

νομοδιδάσκᾰλος], ου, ὁ, (§ 3. tab. C. a) (νόμος & διδάσκαλος) *a teacher and interpreter of the* Mosaic *law*, Lu. 5. 17, et al. N.T.

νομοθεσία],[g] ας, ἡ . . . . . νομοθέτης

νομοθετεῶ, ῶ], fut. ήσω . . . . id.

νομοθέτης],[h] ου, ὁ, (§ 2. tab. B. c) (νόμος & τίθημι) *a legislator, lawgiver*.

νομοθετέω, ῶ, fut. ήσω, (§ 16. tab. P) *to impose a law, give laws*; in N.T. pass. *to have a law imposed on one's self, receive a law*, He. 7. 11; *to be enacted, constituted*, He. 8. 6.

[a] Ac. 6. 5. [b] Tit. 3. 12. [c] Lu. 11. 32. [d] Jno. 13. 5. [e] He. 12. 8. [f] Mat. 22. 19. [g] Ro. 9. 4. [h] Jas. 4. 12.

νομοθεσία, ας, ἡ, (§ 2. tab. B. b, and rem. 2) *legislation; ἡ νομοθεσία, the gift of the* Divine *law*, or *the* Mosaic *law* itself, Ro. 9. 4.

νόμον, acc. sing. . . . . . νόμος

νόμος], ου, ὁ, (§ 3. tab. C. a) (νέμω, *to dispense, distribute*) *a law*, Ro. 4. 15; 1 Ti. 1. 9; *the* Mosaic *law*, Mat. 5. 17, et al. freq.; *the Old Testament Scripture*, Jno. 10. 34; *a legal tie*, Ro. 7. 2, 3; *a law, a rule, standard*, Ro. 3. 27; *a rule* of life and conduct, Gal. 6. 2; Ja. 1. 25.

νομίζω, fut. ίσω, perf. νενόμικα, aor. 1, ἐνόμισα, (§ 26. rem. 1) *to own as settled and established; to deem*, 1 Co. 7. 26; 1 Ti. 6. 5; *to suppose, presume*, Mat. 5. 17; 20. 10; Lu. 2. 44, et al.; pass. *to be usual, customary*, Ac. 16. 13.

νομῐκός, ή, όν, (§ 7. tab. F. a) *pertaining to law; relating to the* Mosaic *law*, Tit. 3. 9; as a subst., *one skilled in law, a jurist, lawyer*, Tit. 3. 13; spc. *an interpreter and teacher of the* Mosaic *law*, Mat. 22. 35, et al.

νομῐμῶς, adv. *lawfully, agreeably to law or custom, rightfully*, 1 Ti. 1. 8; 2 Ti. 2. 5.

νόμισμα, ατος, τό, (§ 4. tab. D. c) pr. *a thing sanctioned by law or custom; lawful money, coin*, Mat. 22. 19.

νόμου, gen. sing. . . . . . νόμος

νόμους, acc. pl. . . . . . id.

νόμῳ, dat. sing. . . . . . id.

νοός, gen. sing. (§ 6. rem. 4. h) . . νοῦς

νοοῦμεν, 1 pers. pl. pres. ind. act. . . νοέω

νοούμενα, nom. pl. neut. part. pres. pass. . id.

νοοῦντες, nom. pl. masc. part. pres. act. . id.

νοσέω, ῶ], fut. ήσω, (§ 16. tab. P) . . νόσος

νόσημα], ατος, τό, (§ 4. tab. D. c) . . id.

νοσήματι,[a] dat. sing. . . . . νόσημα

νόσοις, dat. pl. . . . . . νόσος

νόσον, acc. sing. . . . . . id.

νόσος], ου, ἡ, (§ 3. tab. C. b) *a disease, sickness, distemper*, Mat. 4. 23, 24; 8. 17; 9. 35, et al.

νοσέω, ῶ, fut. ήσω, (§ 16. tab. P) *to be sick*; met. *to have a diseased appetite or craving for* a thing, *have an excessive and vicious fondness for* a thing, *to dote*, 1 Ti. 6. 4.

νόσημα, ατος, τό, (§ 4. tab. D. c) *disease, sickness*, Jno. 5. 4.

νόσους, acc. pl. . . . . . νόσος

νοσσιά], ᾶς, ἡ, (§ 2. tab. B. b, and rem. 2) νέος

νοσσία,[b] acc. pl. . . . . νοσσίον

νοσσιάν,[c] acc. sing. . . . . νοσσιά

νοσσίον], ου, τό, (§ 3. tab. C. c) . . νέος

νοσσός], οῦ, ὁ, (§ 3. tab. C. a) . . . id.

νοσσούς, acc. pl.—Const. Tdf. . . } νοσσός
νεοσσούς, Rec. Gr. Sch. Ln. (Lu. 2. 24) }

νοσφιζομένους, acc. pl. masc. part. pr. mid . νοσφίζω

νοσφίζω], fut. ίσω, (§ 26. rem. 1) (νόσφι, *apart, separate*) *to deprive, rob*; mid. *to appropriate; to make secret reservation*, Ac. 5. 2, 3; *to purloin*, Tit. 2. 10.

νοσφίσασθαι, aor. 1, infin. mid. . . νοσφίζω

νόσων, gen. pl. . . . . . νόσος

νοσῶν,[d] nom. sing. masc. part. pres. . νοσέω

νότον, acc. . . . . . . νότος

νότος], ου, ὁ, (§ 3. tab. C. a) *the south wind*, Lu. 12. 55, Ac. 27. 13; meton. *the south, the southern quarter of the heavens*, Mat. 12. 42; Lu. 11. 31; 13. 29; Re. 21. 13.

νότου, gen. . . . . . . νότος

νουθεσία], ας, ἡ . . . . . νουθετέω

νουθεσίᾳ, dat. sing. . . . . νουθεσία

νουθεσίαν, acc. sing. . . . . id.

νουθετεῖν, pres. infin. . . . . νουθετέω

νουθετεῖτε, 2 pers. pl. pres. imper. . . id.

νουθετέω, ῶ], fut. ήσω, (§ 16. tab. P) (νοῦς & τίθημι) pr. *to put in mind; to admonish, warn*, Ac. 20. 31; Ro. 15. 14, et al.

νουθεσία, ας, ἡ, (§ 2. tab. B. b, and rem. 2) *warning, admonition*, 1 Co. 10. 11; Ep. 6. 4; Tit. 3. 10.

νουθετοῦντας, acc. pl. masc. part. pres. . νουθετέω

νουθετοῦντες, nom. pl. masc. part. pres. . id.

νουθετῶ, 1 pers. sing. pres. ind. . . id.

νουθετῶν, nom. sing. masc. part. pres. . id.

νουμηνία], ας, ἡ, (§ 2. tab. B. b, and rem. 2) (contr. for νεομηνία, νέος & μήν) *the new moon*.

νουμηνίας,[e] gen. sing.—Rec. Gr. Sch. Tdf. . } νουμηνια
νεομηνίας, Ln. (Col. 2. 16) . . }

νοῦν, acc. sing. . . . . . νοῦς

νουνεχῶς],[f] adv. (νουνεχής, νοῦς & ἔχω) *understandingly, sensibly, discreetly*.

---

[a] Jno. 5. 4. [b] Mat. 23. 37. [c] Lu. 13. 34. [d] 1 Ti. 6. 4. [e] Col. 2. 16. [f] Mar. 12. 34.

νοῦς, νοῦ, and in N.T. νοός, dat. νοΐ, ὁ, (contr. for νόος) (§ 3. rem. 3. and § 6. rem. 4. h) *the mind, intellect*, 1 Co. 14. 15, 19; *understanding, intelligent faculty*, Lu. 24. 45; *intellect, judgment*, Ro. 7. 23, 25; *opinion, sentiment*, Ro. 14. 5; 1 Co. 1. 10; *mind, thought, conception*, Ro. 11. 34; 1 Co. 2. 16; Phi. 4. 7; *settled state of mind*, 2 Thes. 2. 2; *frame of mind*, Ro. 1. 28; 12. 2; Col. 2. 18; Eph. 4. 23; 1 Ti. 6. 5; 2 Ti. 3. 8; Tit. 1. 15.

νοέω, ῶ, fut. ήσω, aor. 1, ἐνόησα, (§ 16. tab. P) *to perceive, observe; to mark* attentively, Mat. 24. 15; Mar. 13. 14; 2 Ti. 2. 7; *to understand, comprehend*, Mat. 15. 17, et al.; *to conceive*, Eph. 3. 20.

νόημα, ατος, τό, (§ 4. tab. D. c) *the mind, the understanding, intellect*, 2 Co. 3. 14; 4. 4; *the heart, soul, affections, feelings, disposition*, 2 Co. 11. 3; *a conception of the mind, thought, purpose, device*, 2 Co. 2. 11; 10. 5.

νύκτα, acc. sing. . . . . . . νύξ
νύκτας, acc. pl. . . . . . . id.
νυκτί, dat. sing. . . . . . id.
νυκτός, gen. sing. . . . . . id.
Νυμφᾶν,[a] acc. . . . . . Νυμφᾶς
Νυμφᾶς], ᾶ, ὁ, (§ 2. rem. 4) *Nymphas*, pr. name.

νύμφη], ης, ἡ, (§ 2. tab. B. a) *a bride*, Jno. 3. 29; Re. 18. 23; 21. 2, 9; 22. 17; opposed to πενθερά, *a daughter-in-law*, Mat. 10. 35; Lu. 12. 53.

νυμφίος, ου, ὁ, (§ 3. tab. C. a) *a bridegroom*, Mat. 9. 15; 25. 1, 5, 6, 10, et al.

νυμφών, ῶνος, ὁ, (§ 4. rem. 2. e) *a bridal-chamber*; in N.T. υἱοὶ τοῦ νυμφῶνος, *sons of the bridal-chamber, the bridegroom's attendant friends, bridemen*, perhaps the same as the Greek παρανύμφιοι, Mat. 9. 15; Mar. 2. 19; Lu. 5. 34. L.G.

νύμφην, acc. sing. . . . . . . νύμφη
νύμφης, gen. sing. . . . . . id.
νυμφίον, acc. sing. . . . . . . νυμφίος
νυμφίος], ου, ὁ . . . . . νύμφη
νυμφίου, gen. sing. . . . . . . νυμφίος
νυμφών, ῶνος, ὁ.—B. . . . . . } νύμφη
γάμος, Rec. Gr. Sch. Tdf. (Mat. 22. 10) }

νυμφῶνος, gen. sing. . . . . . νυμφών

νῦν], and νυνί, adv. *now, at the present time*, Mar. 10. 30; Lu. 6. 21, et al. freq.; *just now*, Jno. 11. 8, et al.; *forthwith*, Jno. 12. 31; καὶ νῦν, *even now, as matters stand*, Jno. 11. 22; *now*, expressive of a marked tone of address, Ac. 7. 34; 13. 11; Ja. 4. 13; 5. 1; τὸ νῦν, *the present time*, Lu. 1. 48, et al.; τανῦν, or τὰ νῦν, *now*, Ac. 4. 29, et al.

νύξ], νυκτός, ἡ, (§ 4. rem. 2. b) *night*, Mat. 2. 14; 28. 13; Jno. 3. 2; met. spiritual *night*, moral *darkness*, Ro. 13. 12; 1 Thes. 5. 5.

νύσσω, or ττω], fut. ξω, aor. 1, ἔνυξα, (§ 26. rem. 3) *to prick, pierce*, Jno. 19. 34.

νυστάζει, 3 pers. sing. pres. ind. . . . νυστάζω
νυστάζω], fut. σω & ξω, (§ 26. rem. 2) . νεύω
νυστάξει, 3 pers. sing. fut. ind.—Const. } νυστάζω
νυστάζει, Rec. Gr. Sch. Tdf. (2 Pe. 2. 3) }
νυχθήμερον],[b] ου, τό, (§ 3. tab. C. c) (νύξ & ἡμέρα) *a day and night, twenty-four hours*. L.G.
Νῶε, ὁ, *Noe, Noah*, pr. name, indecl.
νωθροί, nom. pl. masc. . . . . . νωθρός
νωθρός], ά, όν, (§ 7. rem. 1) *slow, sluggish; untoward*, He. 5. 11; 6. 12.
νῶτον,[c] acc. sing. . . . . . νῶτος

νῶτος], ου, ὁ, (§ 3. tab. C. a) *the back* of men or animals.

Ξ.

ξέναις, dat. pl. fem. . . . . . ξένος
ξενία], ας, ἡ, (§ 2. tab. B. b, and rem. 2) . id.
ξενίαν, acc. sing. . . . . . ξενία
ξενίζεσθε, 2 pers. pl. pres. imper. pass. . ξενίζω
ξενίζεται, 3 pers. sing. pres. ind. pass. . . id.
ξενίζοντα, acc. pl. neut. part. pres. . . id.
ξενίζονται, 3 pers. pl. pres. ind. pass. . . id.
ξενίζω], fut. ίσω, (§ 26. rem. 1) . . ξένος
ξενίσαντες, nom. pl. masc. part. aor. 1, act. . ξενίζω
ξενισθῶμεν, 1 pers. pl. aor. 1, subj. pass. . id.
ξενοδοχέω, ῶ], fut. ήσω, (§ 16. tab. P) (ξενοδόχος, ξένος & δέχομαι) *to receive and entertain strangers, exercise hospitality*, 1 Ti. 5. 10.

[a] Col. 4. 15. [b] 2 Co. 11. 25. [c] Ro. 11. 10.

ξένοι, nom. pl. masc. . . . . . ξένος
ξένοις, dat. pl. masc. . . . . id.
ξένον, acc. sing. masc. . . . . . id.

ξένος], η, ον, adj. *strange, foreign; alien*, Ep. 2. 12, 19; *strange, unexpected, surprising*, 1 Pe. 4. 12, *novel*, He. 13. 9; subst. *a stranger*, Mat. 25. 35, et al.; *a host*, Ro. 16. 23.

ξενία, ας, ἡ, (§ 2. tab. B. b, and rem. 2) pr. *state of being a guest;* then, *the reception of a guest or stranger, hospitality;* in N.T. *a lodging*, Ac. 28. 23; Phile. 22.

ξενίζω, fut. ίσω, aor. 1, ἐξένισα, (§ 26. rem. 1) *to receive as a guest, entertain*, Ac. 10. 23; 28. 7; He. 13. 2; pass. *to be entertained as a guest, to lodge or reside with*, Ac. 10. 6, 18, 32; 21. 16; *to strike with a feeling of strangeness, to surprise;* pass. or mid. *to be struck with surprise, be staggered, be amazed*, 1 Pe. 4. 4, 12; intrans. *to be strange;* ξενίζοντα, *strange matters, novelties*, Ac. 17. 20.

ξένου, gen. sing. neut. . . . . . ξένος
ξένους, acc. pl. masc. . . . . . id.
ξένων, gen. pl. . . . . . . id.

ξέστης], ου, ὁ, (§ 2. tab. B. c) (Lat. *sextus* or *sextarius*) *a sextarius*, a Roman measure, containing about one pint English; in N.T. used for *a small vessel, cup, pot*, Mar. 7. 4, 8.

ξεστῶν, gen. pl. . . . . . . ξέστης
ξηρά, nom. sing. fem. . . . . . ξηρός
ξηραίνεται, 3 pers. sing. pres. ind. pass. . ξηραίνω
ξηραίνω], fut. ανῶ, (§ 27. rem. 1. c) . ξηρός
ξηράν, acc. sing. fem. . . . . . id.
ξηρᾶς, gen. sing. fem. . . . . . id.

ξηρός], ά, όν, (§ 7. rem. 1) *dry, withered*, Lu. 23. 31; ἡ ξηρά, sc. γῆ, *the dry land, land*, Mat. 23. 15; He. 11. 29; of parts of the body, *withered, tabid*, Mat. 12. 10.

ξηραίνω, fut. ανῶ, aor. 1, ἐξήρᾱνα, (§ 27. rem. 1. c. e) perf. pass. ἐξήραμμαι, aor. 1, pass. ἐξηράνθην, (§ 27. rem. 3) *to dry up, parch*, Ja. 1. 11; pass. *to be parched*, Mat. 13. 6, et al.; *to be ripened* as corn, Re. 14. 15; *to be withered, to wither*, Mar. 11. 20; of parts of the body, *to be withered*, Mar. 3. 1, 3; *to pine*, Mar. 9. 18.

ξηρῷ, dat. sing. neut. . . . . . ξηρός
ξηρῶν, gen. pl. . . . . . . id.
ξύλα, acc. pl. . . . . . . ξύλον
ξύλινα, nom. and acc. pl. neut. . . ξύλινος
ξύλῐνος], η, ον, (§ 7. tab. F. a) . . . ξύλον

ξύλον], ου, τό, (§ 3. tab. C. c) *wood, timber*, 1 Co. 3. 12; Re. 18. 12; *stocks*, Ac. 16. 24; *a club*, Mat. 26. 47, 55; *a post, cross, gibbet*, Ac. 5. 30; 10. 39; 13. 29; *a tree*, Lu. 23. 31; Re. 2. 7.

ξύλινος, ίνη, ινον, *wooden, of wood, made of wood*, 2 Ti. 2. 20; Re. 9. 20.

ξύλου, gen. sing. . . . . . . ξύλον
ξύλῳ, dat. sing. . . . . . . id.
ξύλων, gen. pl. . . . . . . id.
ξυρᾶσθαι, pres. infin. pass. (§ 19. tab. S) . ξυράω
ξυράω, ῶ], fut. ήσω, aor. 1, ἐξύρησα, (§ 18. tab. R) perf. pass. ἐξύρημαι, (ξυρόν, *a razor*) *to cut off the hair, shear, shave*, Ac. 21. 24; 1 Co. 11. 5, 6.
ξυρήσωνται, 3 pers. pl. aor. 1, subj. mid. . ξυραω

O.

ὁ, ἡ, τό, (§ 1. tab. A, and remarks) the prepositive article, answering, to a considerable extent, to the English definite article: but, for the principle and facts of its usage, see the grammars; ὁ μὲν—ὁ δέ, *the one—the other*, Phi. 1. 16, 17; He. 7. 5, 6, 20, 21, 23, 24; pl. *some—others*, Mat. 13. 23; 22. 5, 6; ὁ δέ, *but he*, Mat. 4. 4; 12. 48; οἱ δέ, *but others*, Mat. 28. 17, et al.; used, in a poetic quotation, for a personal pronoun, Ac. 17. 28.

ὅ, nom. and acc. sing. neut. (§ 10. tab. J. g) . ὅς
ὀγδόῃ, dat. sing. fem. . . . . . ὄγδοος
ὀγδοήκοντα], οἱ, αἱ, τά . . . . . ὀκτώ
ὄγδοον, acc. sing. masc. . . . . ὄγδοος
ὄγδοος], η, ον, (§ 7. tab. F. a) . . . ὀκτώ
ὄγκον,[a] acc. sing. . . . . . ὄγκος

ὄγκος], ου, ὁ, (§ 3. tab. C. a) pr. *bulk, weight; a burden, impediment*, He. 12. 1.

[a] He. 12. 1.

ὅδε], ἥδε, τόδε, (§ 10. tab. J. a, and rem. 1) demon. pron. (ὁ, ἡ, τό & δέ) *this, that, he, she, it*, Lu. 10. 39; 16. 25; Ac. 15. 23, et al.

ὧδε, adv. *thus; here, in this place*, Mat. 12. 6, 41; ὧδε ἢ ὧδε, *here or there*, Mat. 24. 23; τὰ ὧδε, *the state of things here*, Col. 4. 9; met. *herein, in this thing*, Re. 13. 10, 18; *hither, to this place*, Mat. 8. 29; 14. 18, et al.

ὁδεύω], fut. εύσω . . . . . . ὁδός

ὁδεύων,[a] nom. sing. masc. part. pres. . . ὁδεύω

ὁδηγεῖν, pres. infin. . . . . . . ὁδηγέω

ὁδηγέω, ῶ], fut. ήσω, (§ 16. tab. P) . ὁδηγός

ὁδηγῇ, 3 pers. sing. pres. subj. . . . ὁδηγέω

ὁδηγήσει, 3 pers. sing. fut. ind. . . id.

ὁδηγήσῃ, 3 pers. sing. aor. 1, subj. . . id.

ὁδηγοί, nom. and voc. pl. . . . ὁδηγός

ὁδηγόν, acc. sing. . . . . . . id.

ὁδηγός], ου, ὁ, (§ 3. tab. C. a) (ὁδός & ἡγέομαι) *a guide, leader*, Ac. 1. 16; met. *an instructor, teacher*, Mat. 15. 14; 23. 16, 24; Ro. 2. 19.

ὁδηγέω, ῶ, fut. ήσω, (§ 16. tab. P) *to lead, guide*, Mat. 15. 14; Lu. 6. 39; Re. 7. 17; met. *to instruct, teach*, Jno. 16. 13; Ac. 8. 31.

ὁδηγοῦ, gen. sing. . . . . . ὁδηγός

ὁδοί, nom. pl. . . . . . . ὁδός

ὁδοιπορέω, ῶ], fut. ήσω, (ὁδός & πόρος) *to journey, travel*, Ac. 10. 9.

ὁδοιπορία, ας, ἡ, (§ 2. tab. B. b, and rem. 2) *a journey, journeying, travel*, Jno. 4. 6; 2 Co. 11. 26.

ὁδοιπορία], ας, ἡ . . . . . ὁδοιπορέω

ὁδοιπορίαις, dat. pl. . . . . . ὁδοιπορία

ὁδοιπορίας, gen. sing. . . . . . id.

ὁδοιπορούντων,[b] gen. pl. masc. part. pres. . ὁδοιπορέω

ὁδοῖς, dat. pl. . . . . . . ὁδός

ὁδόν, acc. sing. . . . . . . id.

ὀδόντα, acc. sing. . . . . . ὀδούς

ὀδόντας, acc. pl. . . . . . . id.

ὀδόντες, nom. pl. . . . . . id.

ὀδόντος, gen. sing. . . . . . . id.

ὀδόντων, gen. pl. . . . . . . id.

ὁδοποιεῖν, pres. infin.—B. Ln. Tdf. ὁδὸν ποιεῖν, Rec. Gr. Sch. (Mar. 2. 23) } ὁδοποιέω

ὁδοποιέω, ῶ], fut. ήσω, (§ 16. tab. P) (ὁδός & ποιέω) *to journey*, v.r. Mar. 2. 23.

ὁδός], οῦ, ἡ, (§ 3. tab. C. b) *a way, road*, Mat. 2. 12; 7. 13, 14; 8. 28; 22. 9, 10; *means access, approach, entrance*, Jno. 14. 6; He. 9.8; *direction, quarter, region*, Mat. 4. 15; 10. 5; *the act of journeying, a journey, way, course*, Mat. 10. 10; Mar. 2. 23; 1 Thes. 3. 11, et al.; *a journey*, as regards extent, Ac. 1. 12; met. *a way*, systematic *course* of pursuit, Lu. 1. 79; Ac. 2. 28; 16. 17; *a way*, systematic *course* of action or conduct, Mat. 21. 32; Ro. 11. 33; 1 Co. 4. 17, et al.; *a way, system of doctrine*, Ac. 18. 26: ἡ ὁδός, *the way* of the Christian faith, Ac. 19. 9, 23; 24. 22.

ὁδεύω, fut. εύσω, (§ 13 tab. M) *to journey, travel*, Lu. 10. 33.

ὁδοῦ, gen. sing. . . . . ὁδός

ὁδούς, acc. pl. . . . . id.

ὀδούς], ὀδόντος, ὁ, (§ 4. rem. 2. d) *a tooth*, Mat. 5. 38; 8. 12, et al.

ὀδύναις, dat. pl. . . . . ὀδύνη

ὀδυνᾶσαι, 2 p. s. pres. ind. pass. for ὀδυνᾷ, an impure form combining the terminations of a contract verb and a verb in μι ὀδυνάω

ὀδυνάω, ῶ], fut. ήσω, (§ 18. tab. R) . . ὀδύνη

ὀδύνη], ης, ἡ, (§ 2. tab. B. a) *pain* of body or mind; *sorrow, grief*, Ro. 9. 2; 1 Ti. 6. 10. (ῠ).

ὀδυνάω, ῶ, *to pain* either bodily or mentally; pass. *to be in an agony, be tormented*, Lu. 2. 48; 16. 24, 25; *to be distressed, grieved*, Ac. 20. 38.

ὠδίς, and in N.T. ὠδίν, ῖνος, ἡ, *the throe* of a woman in travail, *a birth-pang*, 1 Thes. 5. 3; pl. met. *birth-throes, preliminary troubles* to the development of a catastrophe, Mat. 24. 8; Mar. 13. 9; from the Heb., *a stringent band, a snare, noose*, Ac. 2. 24.

ὠδίνω, fut. ϊνῶ, (§ 27. rem. 1. a) *to be in travail*, Gal. 4. 27; Re. 12. 2; met. *to travail with, to make effort to bring to spiritual birth*, Gal. 4. 19. (ῑ).

ὀδυνῶμαι, 1 pers. sing. pres. ind. pass. . ὀδυνάω

ὀδυνώμενοι, nom. pl. masc. part. pres. pass. . id.

ὀδυρμόν, acc. sing. . . . . ὀδυρμός

[a] Lu. 10. 33. [b] Ac. 10. 9.

ὀδυρμός], οῦ, ὁ, (§ 3. tab. C. a) (ὀδύρομαι, *to lament, bewail*) *bitter lamentation, wailing*, Mat. 2. 18; meton. *sorrow, mourning*, 2 Co. 7. 7.

ὀδῷ, dat. sing. . . . . . . ὁδός
ὀδῶν, gen. pl. . . . . . . id.
ὄζει,[a] 3 pers. sing. pres. ind. . . . ὄζω
Ὀζίαν, acc. . . . . . . Ὀζίας
Ὀζίας], ου, ὁ, (§ 2. tab. B. d) *Ozias*, pr. name.

ὄζω], fut. ὀζήσω & ὀζέσω, (§ 35. rem. 5) *to smell, emit an odour; to have an offensive smell, stink*, Jno. 11. 39.

ὀσμή, ῆς, ἡ, (§ 2. tab. B. a) *smell, odour; fragrant odour*, Jno. 12. 3; Ep. 5. 2; Phi. 4. 18; met. 2 Co. 2. 14, 16.

ὅθεν], adv. *whence*, Mat. 12. 44; Ac. 14. 26; *from the place where*, Mat. 25. 24, 26; *whence, from which circumstance*, 1 Jno. 2. 18; *wherefore, whereupon*, Mat. 14. 7.

ὀθόνη], ης, ἡ, (§ 2. tab. B. a) pr. *fine linen; a linen cloth; a sheet*, Ac. 10. 11; 11. 5.

ὀθόνιον, ου, τό, (§ 3. tab. C. c) *a linen cloth*; in N.T. *a swath, bandage* for a corpse, Lu. 24. 12, et al.

ὀθόνην, acc. sing. . . . . . . ὀθόνη
ὀθόνια, acc. pl. . . . . . . ὀθόνιον
ὀθονίοις, dat. pl. . . . . . . id.
ὀθόνιον], ου, τό . . . . . . ὀθόνη
ὀθονίων, gen. pl. . . . . . . ὀθόνιον
οἵ, nom. pl. masc. (§ 10. tab. J. g) . . ὅς
οἵα, nom. sing. fem. (§ 10. rem. 7) . . οἷος
οἷα, nom. and acc. pl. neut. . . . . id.

οἶδα, (§ 37. rem. 1) 2 perf. from obsol. εἴδω, with the sense of the present, (§ 38. rem. 2) pluperf. ᾔδειν, imper. ἴσθι, subj. εἰδῶ, opt. εἰδείην, infin. εἰδέναι, part. εἰδώς, fut εἴσομαι & εἰδήσω, *to know*, Mat. 6. 8, et al.; *to know how*, Mat. 7. 11, et al.; from the Heb., *to regard with favour*, 1 Thes. 5. 12.

οιδαμεν, 1 pers. pl. . . . . . οἶδα
οἶδας, 2 pers. sing. . . . . . id.
οἴδασι, 3 pers. pl. . . . . . id.
οἴδατε, 2 pers. pl. . . . . . id.
οἶδε, 3 pers. sing. . . . . . . id.
οἰέσθω, 3 pers. sing. pres. imper. . . . οἴομαι
οἰκεῖ, 3 pers. sing. pres. ind. . . . . οἰκέω

οἰκεῖν, pres. infin. . . . . οἰκέω
οἰκεῖοι, nom. pl. masc. . . . . οἰκεῖος
οἰκεῖος], εία, εῖον, (§ 7. rem. 1) . . οἶκος
οἰκείους, acc. pl. masc. . . . . οἰκεῖος
οἰκείων, gen. pl. . . . . . . id.
οἰκέται, nom. pl. . . . . . οἰκέτης
οἰκετεία], ας, ἡ, v.r. . . . . . οἶκος
οἰκετείας, gen. sing.—B. Ln. Tdf. . . } οἰκετεία
θεραπείας, Rec. Gr. Sch. (Mat. 24. 45) }
οἰκέτην, acc. sing. . . . . . οἰκέτης
οἰκέτης], ου, ὁ, (§ 2. tab. B. c) . . . οἶκος
οἰκετῶν, gen. pl. . . . . . οἰκέτης
οἰκέω, ῶ], fut. ήσω, (§ 16. tab. P) . . οἶκος
οἴκημα], ατος, τό, (§ 4. tab. D. c) . . id.
οἰκήματι,[b] dat. sing. . . . . . οἴκημα
οἰκητήριον], ου, τό, (§ 3. tab. C. c) . . οἶκος
οἰκία], ας, ἡ, (§ 2. tab. B. b, and rem. 2) . id.
οἰκίᾳ, dat. sing. . . . . . . οἰκία
οἰκιακοί, nom. pl. . . . . . οἰκιακός
οἰκιακός], οῦ, ὁ, (§ 3. tab. C. a) . . οἶκος
οἰκιακούς, acc. pl. . . . . . οἰκιακός
οἰκίαν, acc. sing. . . . . . οικία
οἰκίας, gen. sing. and acc. pl. . . . id.
οἰκιῶν, gen. pl. . . . . . . id.
οἰκοδεσποτεῖν,[c] pres. infin. . . . οἰκοδεσποτέω
οἰκοδεσποτέω, ῶ], fut. ήσω . . . οἰκοδεσπότης
οἰκοδεσπότῃ, dat. sing. . . . . . id.
οἰκοδεσπότην, acc. sing. . . . . id.

οἰκοδεσποτης], ου, ὁ, (§ 2. tab. B. c) (οἶκος & δεσπότης) *the master or head of a house or family*, Mat. 10. 25; 13. 27, 52, et al.

οἰκοδεσποτέω, ῶ, fut. ήσω, (§ 16. tab. P) pr. *to be master of a household; to occupy one's self in the management of a household*, 1 Ti. 5. 14. L.G.

οἰκοδεσπότου, gen. sing. . . . . οἰκοδεσπότης
οἰκοδομαί, nom. pl. . . . . . οἰκοδομη
οἰκοδομάς, acc. pl. . . . . . id.
οἰκοδομεῖ, 3 pers. sing. pres. ind. act. . οἰκοδομέω
οἰκοδομεῖν, pres. infin. act. . . . . id.
οἰκοδομεῖσθε, 2 pers. pl. pres. ind. or imper. p. id.
οἰκοδομεῖται, 3 pers. sing. pres. ind. pass. . id.
οἰκοδομεῖτε, 2 pers. pl. pres. ind. and imper. act. id.
οἰκοδομέω], ῶ, fut. ήσω . . . . οἰκοδόμος
οἰκοδομή], ῆς, ἡ, (§ 2. tab. B. a) . . id.
οἰκοδομηθήσεται, 3 pers. sing. fut. ind. pass. . οἰκοδομεω
οἰκοδομήν, acc. sing. . . . . . οἰκοδομη
οἰκοδομῆς, gen. sing. . . . . . id.

[a] Jno. 11. 39. [b] Ac. 12. 7. [c] 1 Ti. 5. 14.

οἰκοδομῆσαι, aor. 1, infin. act. . . . οἰκοδομέω
οἰκοδομήσαντι, dat. sing. masc. part. aor. 1 . id.
οἰκοδομήσετε, 2 pers. pl. fut. ind. act. . id.
οἰκοδομήσω, 1 pers. sing. fut. ind. act. . id.
οἰκοδομία], ας, ἡ, (§ 2. tab. B. b, and rem. 2) οἰκοδόμος
οἰκοδομίαν,[a] acc. sing.—Rec. . . . } οἰκοδομία
οἰκονομίαν, Gr. Sch. Tdf. (1 Ti. 1. 4) }
οἰκοδόμος], ου, ὁ, (§ 3. tab. C. a) (οἶκος & δέμω, *to construct*) *a builder, architect*, v.r. Ac. 4. 11.

οἰκοδομέω, ῶ, fut. ήσω, (§ 16. tab. P) aor. 1, ᾠκοδόμησα, (§ 13. rem. 2) perf. pass. ᾠκοδόμημαι, *to build a house; to build*, Mat. 7. 24, et al.; *to repair, embellish, and amplify* a building, Mat. 23. 29, et al.; *to construct, establish*, Mat. 16. 18; met. *to contribute to advancement* in religious knowledge, *to edify*, 1 Co. 14. 4, 17; *to advance* a person's spiritual condition, *to edify*, 1 Co. 8. 1, et al.; pass. *to make* spiritual *advancement, be edified*, Ac. 9. 31; *to advance* in presumption, *be emboldened*, 1 Co. 8. 10.

οἰκοδομή, ῆς, ἡ, (§ 2. tab. B. a) pr. *the act of building; a building, structure*, Mat. 24. 1, et al.; in N.T. *a* spiritual *structure*, as instanced in the Christian body, 1 Co. 3. 9; Ep. 2. 21; religious *advancement, edification*, Ro. 14. 19; 1 Co. 14. 3. et al. L.G.

οἰκοδομία, ας, ἡ, (§ 2. tab. B. b, and rem. 2) pr. *a building of a house;* met. spiritual *advancement, edification*, v. r. 1 Ti. 1. 4.

οἰκοδομούμεναι, nom. pl. fem. part. pres. pass. οἰκοδομέω
οἰκοδομοῦντες, nom. pl. masc. part. pres. act. id.
οἰκοδομοῦντι, dat. sing. masc. part. pres. act. id.
οἰκοδομούντων, gen. pl. masc. part. pres. act. id.
οἰκοδομῶ, 1 pers. sing. pres. ind. and subj. id.
οἰκοδομῶν, nom. sing. masc. part. pres. act. . id.
οἰκοδόμων, gen. pl.—Al. Ln. Tdf. . . } οἰκοδόμος
οἰκοδομούντων, Rec. Gr. Sch. (Ac. 4. 11) }
οἴκοις, dat. pl. . . . . . οἶκος
οἶκον, acc. sing. . . . . . id.
οἰκονομεῖν,[b] pres. infin. . . . . οἰκονομέω
οἰκονομέω, ῶ], fut. ήσω . . . οἰκονόμος
οἰκονομία, ας, ἡ.—Gr. Sch. Tdf. . } id.
κοινωνία, Rec. (Eph. 3. 9) . . }

οἰκονομίαν, acc. sing. . . . οἰκονομία
οἰκονομίας, gen. sing. . . . . id.
οἰκονόμοι, nom. pl. . . . . οἰκονόμος
οἰκονόμοις, dat. pl. . . . . id.
οἰκονόμον, acc. sing. . . . . id.
οἰκονόμος], ου, ὁ, (§ 3. tab. C. a) (οἶκος & νέμω, *to administer*) *the manager of a household; a steward*, Lu. 12. 42; 16. 1, 3, 8; 1 Co. 4. 2; *a manager, trustee*, Gal. 4. 2; *a* public *steward, treasurer*, Ro. 16. 23; *a* spiritual *steward, the holder of a commission* in the service of the Gospel, 1 Co. 4. 1; Tit. 1. 7; 1 Pe. 4. 10.

οἰκονομέω, ῶ, fut. ήσω, (§ 16. tab. P) *to manage a household; to manage the affairs* of any one, *be steward*, Lu. 16. 2.

οἰκονομία, ας, ἡ, (§ 2. tab. B. b, and rem. 2) pr. *the management of a household; a stewardship*, Lu. 16. 2, 3, 4; in N.T. *an* apostolic *stewardship, a* ministerial *commission* in the publication and furtherance of the Gospel, 1 Co. 9. 17; Ep. 1. 10; 3. 2; Col. 1. 25; or, *an arranged plan, a scheme*, Ep. 1. 10; *a due discharge of a commission*, 1 Ti. 1. 4.

οἰκονόμους, acc. pl. . . . . . οἰκονόμος

οἶκος], ου, ὁ, (§ 3. tab. C. a) *a house, dwelling*, Mat. 9. 6, 7; Mar. 2. 1, 11; 3. 20, et al.; *place of abode, seat, site*, Mat. 23. 38; Lu. 13. 35; met. *a* spiritual *house or structure*, 1 Pe. 2. 5; meton. *a household, family*, Lu. 10. 5; 11. 17; *a* spiritual *household*, 1 Ti. 3. 15; He. 3. 6; *family, lineage*, Lu. 1. 27, 69; 2. 4; from the Heb., *a people, nation*, Mat. 10. 6; 15. 24.

οἰκεῖος, εία, εῖον, (§ 7. rem. 1) *belonging to a house, domestic;* pl. *members of a family, immediate kin*, 1 Ti. 5. 8; *members of a* spiritual *family*, Eph. 2. 19; *members of a* spiritual *brotherhood*, Gal. 6. 10.

οἰκέτης, ου, ὁ, (§ 2. tab. B. c) pr. *an inmate of a house; a domestic servant, household slave*, Lu. 16. 13; Ac. 10. 7; Ro. 14. 4; 1 Pe. 2. 18.

οἰκετεία, ας, ἡ, (§ 2. tab. B. b, and rem. 2) *the members, or arrangements, of a household*, v.r. Mat. 24. 45.

[a] 1 Ti. 1. 4. [b] Lu. 16. 2.

οἰκέω, ῶ, fut. ήσω, (§ 16. tab. P) *to dwell in, inhabit,* 1 Ti. 6. 16; intrans. *to dwell, live; to cohabit,* 1 Co. 7. 12, 13; *to be indwelling, indwell,* Ro. 7. 17, 18, 20; 8. 9, 11; 1 Co. 3. 16.

οἰκουμένη, ης, ἡ, (pr. fem. part. pass. of οἰκέω) scil. γῆ, *the habitable earth, world,* Mat. 24. 14; Ro. 10. 18; He. 1. 6, et al.; used, however, with various restrictions of meaning, according to the context, Lu. 2. 1; Ac. 17. 6, et al.; meton. *the inhabitants of the earth, the whole human race, mankind,* Ac. 17. 31; 19. 27, Re. 3. 10.

οἴκημα, ατος, τό, (§ 4. tab. D. c) *a dwelling;* used in various conventional senses, and among them, *a prison, cell,* Ac. 12. 7.

οἰκητήριον, ου, τό, (§ 3. tab. C. c) *a habitation, dwelling, an abode,* Jude 6; trop. *the* personal *abode* of the soul, 2 Co. 5. 2.

οἰκία, ας, ἡ, (§ 2. tab. B. b, and rem. 2) *a house, dwelling, an abode,* Mat. 2. 11; 7. 24, 27, et al.; trop. *the* bodily *abode* of the soul, 2 Co. 5. 1; meton. *a household, family,* Mat. 10. 13; 12. 25; meton. *goods, property, means,* Mat. 23. 13, et al.

οἰκιᾰκός, οῦ, ὁ, (§ 3. tab. C. a) *belonging to a house;* pl. *the members of a household or family, kindred,* Mat. 10. 25, 36. L.G.

οικου, gen. sing. . . . . . . οἶκος

οἰκουμένη], ης, ἡ . . . . . id.

οἰκουμένῃ, dat. sing. . . . . οἰκουμένη

οἰκουμένην, acc. sing. . . . . id.

οἰκουμένης, gen. sing. . . . . id.

οἰκουργός], οῦ, ὁ, ἡ, (οἶκος & ἔργον) *one who is occupied in domestic affairs* v.r. Tit. 2. 5. N.T.

οἰκουργούς, acc. pl. fem.—Al. Ln. Tdf. } οἰκουργός
οἰκουρούς, Rec. Gr. Sch. (Tit. 2. 5) }

οἰκουρός], οῦ, ὁ, ἡ, (§ 7. rem. 2) (οἶκος & οὖρος, *a watcher*) pr. *a keeper or guard of a house; a home-keeper, stay-at-home, domestic,* Tit. 2. 5.

οἰκουρούς,[a] acc. pl. fem. . . . . οἰκουρός

οἴκους, acc. pl. . . . . . . οἶκος

οἰκοῦσα, nom. sing. fem. part. pres. . . οἰκέω

οἰκτειρήσω, 1 pers. sing. fut. ind. . . οἰκτείρω

οἰκτείρω], later fut. ήσω, (οἶκτος, *compassion*) *to compassionate, have compassion on, exercise grace or favour towards,* Ro. 9. 15.

οἰκτιρμός, οῦ, ὁ, (§ 3. tab. C. a) *compassion; kindness,* in relieving sorrow and want, Phi. 2. 1; Col. 3. 12; *favour, grace, mercy,* Ro. 12. 1; 2 Co. 1. 3.

οἰκτίρμων, ονος, ὁ, ἡ, (§ 7. tab. G. a) *compassionate, merciful,* Lu. 6. 36; Ja. 5. 11.

οἰκτείρω, 1 pers. sing. pres. subj. . . οἰκτείρω

οἰκτιρμοί, nom. pl. . . . . . οἰκτιρμός

οἰκτίρμονες, nom. pl. masc. . . . οἰκτίρμων

οἰκτιρμός], οῦ, ὁ, (§ 3. tab. C. a) . . οἰκτείρω

οἰκτιρμοῦ, gen. sing.—Gr. Sch. Tdf. . } οἰκτιρμός
οἰκτιρμῶν, Rec. (Col. 3. 12) . . }

οἰκτιρμῶν, gen. pl. . . . . . . id.

οἰκτίρμων], ονος, ὁ, ἡ . . . . . οἰκτείρω

οἴκῳ, dat. sing. . . . . . . οἶκος

οἴκων, gen. pl. . . . . . . id.

οἰκῶν, nom. sing. masc. part. pres. . . οἰκέω

οἶμαι, 1 pers. sing. pres. ind. (by sync.) . οἴομαι

οἶνον, acc. sing. . . . . . . οἶνος

οἰνοπότης], ου, ὁ, ἡ, (§ 2. tab. B. c) (οἶνος & πότης, πίνω) *wine-drinking;* in a bad sense, *a wine-bibber, tippler,* Mat. 11. 19; Lu. 7. 34.

οἶνος], ου, ὁ, (§ 3. tab. C. a) *wine,* Mat. 9. 17; Mar. 2. 22, et al.; meton. *the vine and its clusters,* Re. 6. 6; met. οἶνος, *a potion,* οἶνος τοῦ θυμοῦ, *a furious potion,* Re. 14. 8, 10; 16. 19; 17. 2; 18. 3.

οἴνου, gen. sing. . . . . . . οἶνος

οἰνοφλῠγία], ας, ἡ, (§ 2. tab. B. b, and rem. 2) (οἰνόφλυξ, οἶνος & φλύω, *to bubble over, overflow*) *a debauch with wine, drunkenness.*

οἰνοφλυγίαις,[b] dat. pl. . . . . οἰνοφλυγία

οἴνῳ, dat. sing. . . . . . . οἶνος

οἴομαι], syncop. οἶμαι, fut. οἰήσομαι, (§ 37. rem. 1) *to think, suppose, imagine, presume,* Jno. 21. 25; Phi. 1. 16; Ja. 1. 7.

οἰόμενοι, nom. pl. masc. part. pres. . . οἴομαι

οἷοι, nom. pl. masc. . . . . . οἷος

[a] Tit. 2. 5.

[b] 1 Pe. 4. 3.

οἷον, acc. sing. masc. and nom. neut. . . οἷος

οἷος], οἵα, οἷον, (§ 10. rem. 7) relat. pron., correlative to ποῖος & τοῖος, *what, of what kind or sort, as*, Mat. 24. 21; Mar. 9. 3, et al.; οὐχ οἷον, *not so as, not as implying*, Ro. 9. 6.

οἵου, gen. sing. neut. . . . . . οἷος

οἵους, acc. pl. masc. . . . id.

οἷς, dat. pl. masc. and neut. . ὅς

οἴσει, 3 pers. sing. fut. ind. (§ 36. rem. 1) φέρω

οἴσουσι, 3 pers. pl. fut. ind. . . . id.

οἵτινες, nom. pl. masc. . . . . ὅστις

οἵῳ, dat. sing. neut. οἵῳ δηποτοῦν.—Al. Ln. ᾧ δήποτε, Rec. Gr. Sch. Tdf. om. (Jno. 5. 4) } οἷος

ὀκνέω, ῶ], fut. ήσω, aor. 1, ὤκνησα, (§ 16. tab. P) (ὄκνος, *backwardness, slowness*) *to be slow, loth; to delay, hesitate*, Ac. 9. 38.

ὀκνηρός, ά, όν, (§ 7. rem. 1) *slow; slothful, indolent, idle*, Mat. 25. 26; Ro. 12. 11; *tedious, troublesome*, Phi. 3. 1.

ὀκνηρέ, voc. sing. masc. . . . . ὀκνηρός

ὀκνηροί, nom. pl. masc. . . . id.

ὀκνηρόν, nom. sing. neut. . . . id.

ὀκνηρός], ά, όν . . . . . ὀκνέω

ὀκνῆσαι,[a] aor. 1, infin. . . . . id.

ὀκταήμερος],[b] ου, ὁ, ἡ, (§ 7. rem. 2) (ὀκτώ & ἡμέρα) *on the eighth day*. N.T.

ὀκτώ], οἱ, αἱ, τά, *eight*, Lu. 2. 21; 9. 28, et al.

ὀγδοήκοντα, οἱ, αἱ, τά, indecl. *eighty*, Lu. 2. 37; 16. 7.

ὄγδοος, η, ον, *the eighth*, Lu. 1. 59; Ac. 7. 8, et al.

ὀλέθριον, acc. sing. fem.—A. Ln. ὄλεθρον, Rec. Gr. Sch. Tdf. (2 Thes. 1. 9) } ὀλέθριος

ὀλέθριος], ου, ὁ, ἡ . . . . ὄλεθρος

ὄλεθρον, acc. sing. . . . . . id.

ὄλεθρος], ου, ὁ, (§ 3. tab. C. a) (ὄλλυμι, *to destroy*) *perdition, destruction*, 1 Co. 5. 5, et al.

ὀλέθριος, ίου, ὁ, ἡ, (§ 7. rem. 2) *destructive, fatal*, v.r. 2 Thes. 1. 9.

ὀλοθρεύω, fut. εύσω, (§ 13. tab. M) *to destroy, cause to perish*, He. 11. 28. LXX.

ὀλοθρευτής, οῦ, ὁ, (§ 2. tab. B. c) *a destroyer*, 1 Co. 10. 10.

ὅλη, nom. sing. fem. . . . . ὅλος

ὅλῃ, dat. sing. fem. . . . . . id.

ὅλην, acc. sing. fem. . . . . . ὅλος

ὅλης, gen. sing. fem. . . . id.

ὀλίγα, acc. pl. neut. . . . ὀλίγος

ὀλίγαι, nom. pl. fem. . . . . id.

ὀλίγας, acc. pl. fem. . . . . id.

ὀλίγην, acc. sing. fem. . . id.

ὀλίγης, gen. sing. fem. . . . id.

ὀλίγοι, nom. pl. masc. . . id.

ὀλίγοις, dat. pl. masc. . . id.

ὀλίγον, acc. sing. masc. and nom. neut. . id.

ὀλίγον, adv. . . . . id.

ὀλιγόπιστε, voc. sing. masc. . . ὀλιγόπιστος

ὀλιγοπιστία], ας, ἡ, v.r. . . . id.

ὀλιγοπιστίαν, acc. sing.—B. Ln. ἀπιστίαν, Rec. Gr. Sch. Tdf. (Mat. 17. 20) } ὀλιγοπιστία

ὀλιγόπιστοι, voc. pl. masc. . . ὀλιγόπιστος

ὀλιγόπιστος], ου, ὁ, ἡ, (§ 7. rem. 2) (ὀλίγος & πίστις) *scant of faith, of little faith, one whose faith is small and weak*, Mat. 6. 30; 8. 26, et al.

ὀλιγοπιστία, ας, ἡ, *littleness or imperfectness of faith*, v.r. Mat. 17. 20.

ὀλίγος], η, ον, (§ 7. tab. F. a) *little, small*, in number, etc.; pl. *few*, Mat. 7. 14; 9. 37; 20. 16; Lu. 13. 23; δι' ὀλίγων, sc. λόγων, *in a few words, briefly*, 1 Pe. 5. 12; *little* in time, *short, brief*, Ac. 14. 28; Re. 12. 12; πρὸς ὀλίγον, sc. χρόνον, *for a short time, for a little while*, Ja. 4. 14; *little, small, light*, etc., in magnitude, amount, etc., Lu. 7. 47; Ac. 12. 18; 15. 2.; ἐν ὀλίγῳ, *concisely, briefly*, Ep. 3. 3; *almost*, Ac. 26. 28, 29. (ῐ).

ὀλίγον, adv. (pr. neut. of ὀλίγος) *a little*, Mar. 1. 19; 6. 31, et al.

ὀλίγως, adv. *little, scarcely*, v.r. 2 Pe. 2. 18.

ὀλίγου, gen. sing. masc. . . . . ὀλίγος

ὀλιγόψῡχος], ου, ὁ, ἡ, (§ 7. rem. 2) (ὀλίγος & ψυχή) *faint-hearted, desponding*. L.G.

ὀλιγοψύχους,[c] acc. pl. masc. . . . ὀλιγόψυχος

ὀλίγῳ, dat. sing. masc. and neut. . . ὀλίγος

ὀλίγων, gen. pl. . . . . . id.

ὀλιγώρει,[d] 2 pers. sing. pres. imper. . . ὀλιγωρέω

ὀλιγωρέω, ῶ], fut. ήσω, (§ 16. tab. P) (ὀλίγος & ὥρα, *care*) *to neglect, regard slightly, make light of, despise, contemn*.

[a] Ac. 9. 38. [b] Phi. 3. 5. [c] 1 Thes. 5. 14. [d] He. 12. 5.

ὀλίγως, adv.—Gr. Sch. Tdf. . . . } ὀλίγος
ὄντως, Rec. (2 Pe. 2. 18) . . }

ὀλοθρευτής], οῦ, ὁ, (§ 2. tab. B. c) . ὄλεθρος

ὀλοθρευτοῦ,[a] gen. sing. . . . ὀλοθρευτής

ὀλοθρεύω], fut. εύσω . . . . ὄλεθρος

ὀλοθρεύων,[b] nom. sing. masc. part. pres.— Rec. Gr. Sch. . . . } ὀλοθρεύω
ὀλεθρεύων, A. D. Ln. Tdf. . . }

ὁλοκαύτωμα], ατος, τό, (§ 4. tab. D. c) (ὁλοκαυτόω, *to offer a whole burnt-offering*, ὁλόκαυτος, ὅλος & καίω) *a holocaust, whole burnt-offering*, Mar. 12. 33; He. 10. 6, 8. LXX.

ὁλοκαυτώματα, acc. pl. . . . ὁλοκαύτωμα

ὁλοκαυτωμάτων, gen. pl. . . . id.

ὁλοκληρία], ας, ἡ . . . . ὁλόκληρος

ὁλοκληρίαν,[c] acc. sing. . . . ὁλοκληρία

ὁλόκληροι, nom. pl. masc. . . ὁλόκληρος

ὁλόκληρον, nom. sing. neut. . . . id.

ὁλόκληρος], ου, ὁ, ἡ, (§ 7. rem. 2) (ὅλος & κλῆρος) *whole, having all its parts, sound, perfect, complete in every part*; in N.T. *the whole*, 1 Thes. 5. 23; morally, *perfect, faultless, blameless*, Ja. 1. 4.

ὁλοκληρία, ας, ἡ, (§ 2. tab. B. b, and rem. 2) *perfect soundness*, Ac. 3. 16. LXX.

ὀλολύζοντες,[d] nom. pl. masc. part. pres. . ὀλολύζω

ὀλολύζω], fut. ξω, aor. 1, ὠλόλυξα, (§ 26. rem. 2) pr. *to cry aloud in invocation; to howl, utter cries of distress, lament, bewail*, Ja. 5. 1.

ὅλον, acc. sing. masc. . . . . ὅλος

ὅλον, nom. and acc. sing. neut. . . . id.

ὅλος], η, ον, (§ 7. tab. F. a) *all, whole, entire*, Mat. 1. 22; 4. 23, 24, et al. freq.

ὅλως, adv. *wholly, altogether; actually, really*, 1 Co. 5. 1; 6. 7; 15. 29; with a negative, *at all*, Mat. 5. 34.

ὁλοτελεῖς,[e] acc. pl. masc. . . . ὁλοτελής

ὁλοτελής], έος, ὁ, ἡ, (§ 7. tab. G. b) (ὅλος & τέλος) *complete; all, the whole*, 1 Thes. 5. 23.

ὅλου, gen. sing. masc. and neut. . . ὅλος

ὅλους, acc. pl. masc. . . . . id.

Ὀλυμπᾶν,[f] acc. . . . . . Ὀλυμπᾶς

Ὀλυμπᾶς], ᾶ, ὁ, (§ 2. rem. 4) *Olympas*, pr. name.

ὄλυνθος], ου, ὁ, (§ 3. tab. C. a) *an unripe or unseasonable fig*, such as, shaded by the foliage, do not ripen at the usual season, but hang on the trees during winter.

ὀλύνθους,[g] acc. pl. . . . . ὄλυνθος

ὅλῳ, dat. sing. masc. and neut. . . . ὅλος

ὅλως, adv. . . . . . id.

ὄμβρος],[h] ου, ὁ, (§ 3. tab. C. a) (Lat. *imber*) *rain, a storm of rain*.

ὁμείρομαι], *to desire earnestly, have a strong affection for*, v.r. 1 Thes. 2. 8.

ὁμειρόμενοι, nom. pl. masc. part. pres.— Gr. Sch. Tdf. . . . } ὁμείρομαι
ἱμειρόμενοι, Rec. (1 Thes. 2. 8) . }

ὁμιλεῖν, pres. infin. . . . . ὁμιλέω

ὁμιλέω, ῶ], fut. ήσω . . . . ὅμιλος

ὁμιλήσας, nom. sing. masc. part. aor. 1 . ὁμιλέω

ὁμιλία], ας, ἡ . . . . . ὅμιλος

ὁμιλίαι,[i] nom. pl. . . . . . ὁμιλία

ὅμῑλος,[k] ου, ὁ, (§ 3. tab. C. a) (ὁμοῦ & ἴλη, *a band*) *a multitude, company, crowd*.

ὁμῑλέω, ῶ, fut. ήσω, (§ 16. tab. P) *to be in company with, associate with; to converse with, talk with*, Lu. 24. 14, 15; Ac. 20. 11; 24. 26.

ὁμιλία, ας, ἡ, (§ 2. tab. B. b, and rem. 2) *intercourse, communication, converse*, 1 Co. 15. 33.

ὁμίχλαι, nom. pl.—Gr. Sch. Tdf. . } ὁμίχλη
νεφέλαι, Rec. (2 Pe. 2. 17) . }

ὁμίχλη], ης, ἡ, (§ 2. tab. B. a) *a mist, fog, a cloud*, v.r. 2 Pe. 2. 17.

ὄμμα], ατος, τό, (§ 4. tab. D. c) *the eye*.

ὄμματα,[l] acc. pl. . . . . . ὄμμα

ὀμμάτων, gen. pl.—Al. Ln. . . . } id.
ὀφθαλμῶν, R. Gr. Sch. Tdf. (Mat. 20. 34) }

ὀμνύει, 3 pers. sing. pres. ind. . . . ὀμνύω

ὀμνύειν, pres. infin. . . . . id.

ὀμνύετε, 2 pers. pl. pres. imper. . . id.

ὀμνύναι, pres. infin.—Gr. Tdf. . . } id.
ὀμνύειν, Rec. Sch. (Mar. 14. 71) }

ὀμνυουσι, 3 pers. pl. pres. ind. . . . id.

ὀμνύω, or ὄμνῡμι], fut. ὀμοῦμαι, perf. ὀμώμοκα, aor. 1, ὤμοσα, (§ 36. rem. 5) *to swear*, Mat. 5. 34, et al.; *to promise with an oath*, Mar. 6. 23; Ac. 2. 30; 7. 17, et al. (ῠ).

---

a 1 Co. 10. 10. b He. 11. 28. c Ac. 3. 16. d Ja. 5. 1. e 1 Thes. 5. 23. f Ro. 16. 15. g Re. 6. 13. h Lu. 12. 54.
i 1 Co. 15. 33. k Re. 18. 17. l Mar. 8. 33.

ὁμοθυμᾰδόν], adv. (ὁμοῦ & θυμός) *with one mind, with one accord, unanimously*, Ac. 1. 14; Ro. 15. 6; *together, at once, at the same time*, Ac. 2. 1, 46; 4. 24, et al.

ὁμοία, nom. sing. fem. . . . . ὅμοιος
ὅμοια, nom. and acc. pl. neut. . . . id.
ὁμοιάζει,[a] 3 pers. sing. pres. ind. . . ὁμοιάζω
ὁμοιάζετε, 2 pers. pl. pres. ind.—B. Ln. παρομοιάζετε, Rec. Gr. Sch. Tdf. (Mat. 23. 27) . . . . id.
ὁμοιάζω], fut. άσω . . . . ὅμοιος
ὅμοιαι, nom. pl. fem. . . . . id.
ὁμοίας, acc. pl. fem. . . . . id.
ὅμοιοι, nom. pl. masc. . . . . id.
ὅμοιον, acc. sing. masc. and nom. and acc. neut. id.
ὁμοιοπαθεῖς, nom. pl. masc. . . . ὁμοιοπαθής
ὁμοιοπᾰθής], έος, οῦς, ὁ, ἡ, (§ 7. tab. G. b) (ὅμοιος & πάθος) *being affected in the same way* as another, *subject to the same incidents, of like infirmities, obnoxious to the same frailties and evils*, Ac. 14. 15; Ja. 5. 17.

ὅμοιος], οία, οιον, (§ 7. rem. 1) (ὁμός, *like*) *like, similar, resembling*, Mat. 11. 16; 13. 31, 33, 44, 45, 47, 52; Jno. 8. 55, et al. freq.; *like, of similar drift and force*, Mat. 22. 39; Mar. 12. 31.

ὁμοιάζω, fut. άσω, (§ 26. rem. 1) *to be like, resemble*, Mar. 14. 70. N.T.

ὁμοιότης, τητος, ἡ, (§ 4. rem. 2. c) *likeness, similitude*, He. 4. 15; 7. 15.

ὁμοιόω, ῶ, fut. ώσω, aor. 1, ὡμοίωσα, (§ 20. tab. T) *to make like, cause to be like or resemble, assimilate*; pass. *to be made like, become like, resemble*, Mat. 6. 8; 13. 24; 18. 23; *to liken, compare*, Mat. 7. 24, 26; 11. 16, et al.

ὁμοίωμα, ατος, τό, (§ 4. tab. D. c) pr. *that which is conformed or assimilated; form, shape, figure*, Re. 9. 7; *likeness, resemblance, similitude*, Ro. 1. 23; 5. 14; 6. 5; 8. 3; Phi. 2. 7.

ὁμοίως, adv. *likewise, in a similar manner*, Mat. 22. 26; 27. 41; Mar. 4. 16, et al.

ὁμοίωσις, εως, ἡ, (§ 5. tab. E. c) pr. *assimilation; likeness, resemblance*, Ja. 3. 9.

ὁμοιότης], τητος, ἡ, (§ 4. rem. 2. c) . . ὅμοιος

ὁμοιότητα, acc. sing. . . . . . ὁμοιότης
ὁμοιόω, ῶ], fut. ώσω, (§ 20. tab. T) . . ὅμοιος
ὁμοιωθέντες, nom. pl. masc. part. aor. 1, pass. (§ 21. tab. U) . . . ὁμοιόω
ὁμοιωθῆναι, aor. 1, infin. pass. . . . id.
ὁμοιωθήσεται, 3 pers. sing. fut. ind. pass. . id.
ὁμοιωθῆτε, 2 pers. pl. aor. 1, subj. pass. . id.
ὁμοίωμα], ατος, τό, (§ 4. tab. D. c) . ὅμοιος
ὁμοιώματα, nom. pl. . . . . ὁμοίωμα
ὁμοιώματι, dat. sing. . . . . id.
ὁμοίως, adv. . . . . . . ὅμοιος
ὁμοίωσιν,[b] acc. sing. . . . . ὁμοίωσις
ὁμοίωσις], εως, ἡ, (§ 5. tab. E. c) . . ὅμοιος
ὁμοιώσω, 1 pers. sing. fut. ind. act. . . ὁμοιόω
ὁμοιώσωμεν, 1 pers. pl. aor. 1, subj. act. . id.
ὁμολογεῖ, 3 pers. sing. pres. ind. act. . ὁμολογέω
ὁμολογεῖται, 3 pers. sing. pres. ind. pass. . id.
ὁμολογέω], ῶ, fut. ήσω, aor. 1, ὡμολόγησα, (§ 16. tab. P) (ὁμός, *like*, and λόγος) *to speak in accordance, adopt the same terms of language; to engage, promise*, Mat. 14. 7; *to admit, avow frankly*, Jno. 1. 20; Ac. 24. 14; *to confess*, 1 Jno. 1. 9; *to profess, confess*, Jno. 9. 22; 12. 42; Ac. 23. 8, et al.; *to avouch, declare openly and solemnly*, Mat. 7. 23; in N.T. ὁμολογεῖν ἐν, *to accord belief*, Mat. 10. 32; Lu. 12. 8; *to accord approbation*, Lu. 12. 8; from the Heb., *to accord praise*, He. 13. 15.

ὁμολογία, ας, ἡ, (§ 2. tab. B. b, and rem. 2) *assent, consent; profession*, 2 Co. 9. 13; 1 Ti. 6. 12, 13; He. 3. 1; 4. 14; 10. 23.

ὁμολογουμένως, adv. (ὁμολογούμενος, pass. pres. part. of ὁμολογέω) *confessedly, avowedly, without controversy*, 1 Ti. 3. 16.

ὁμολογήσαντες, nom. pl. masc. part. aor. 1 ὁμολογέω
ὁμολογήσει, 3 pers. sing. fut. ind. act. . id.
ὁμολογήσῃ, 3 pers. sing. aor. 1, subj. act. . id.
ὁμολογήσῃς, 2 pers. sing. aor. 1, subj. act. id.
ὁμολογήσω, 1 pers. sing. fut. ind. act. . id.
ὁμολογία], ας, ἡ, (§ 2. tab. B. b, and rem. 2) id.
ὁμολογίαν, acc. sing. . . . . ὁμολογία
ὁμολογίας, gen. sing. . . . . id.
ὁμολογουμένως,[c] adv. . . . . ὁμολογέω
ὁμολογοῦντες, nom. pl. masc. part. pres. act. id.

[a] Mar. 14. 70. [b] Ja. 3. 9. [c] 1 Ti. 3. 16.

ὁμολογούντων, gen. pl. masc. part. pres. act. — ὁμολογέω
ὁμολογοῦσι, 3 pers. pl. pres. ind. act. — id.
ὁμολογῶ, 1 pers. sing. pres. ind. act. — id.
ὁμολογῶμεν, 1 pers. pl. pres. subj. act. — id.
ὁμολογῶν, nom. sing. masc. part. pres. act. — id.
ὀμόσαι, aor. 1, infin. (§ 36. rem. 5) — ὀμνύω
ὀμόσας, nom. sing. masc. part. aor. 1 — id.
ὀμόσῃ, 3 pers. sing. aor. 1, subj. — id.
ὀμόσῃς, 2 pers. sing. aor. 1, subj. — id.
ὁμότεχνον,[a] acc. sing. masc. — ὁμότεχνος
ὁμότεχνος], ου, ὁ, ἡ, (§ 7. rem. 2) (ὁμός, *the same*, and τέχνη) *of the same trade or occupation.*
ὁμοῦ], adv. (ὁμός) *together; in the same place*, Jno. 21. 2; *together at the same time*, Jno. 4. 36; 20. 4.
ὁμόφρονες,[b] nom. pl. masc. — ὁμόφρων
ὁμόφρων], ονος, ὁ, ἡ, (§ 7. tab. G. a) (ὁμός & φρήν) *of like mind, of the same mind, like-minded.*
ὅμως], conj. (ὁμός) *yet, nevertheless*; with μέντοι, *but nevertheless, but for all that*, Jno. 12. 42; *even, though it be but*, 1 Co. 14. 7; Gal. 3. 15.
ὅν, acc. sing. masc. (§ 10. tab. J. g) — ὅς
ὀναίμην,[c] 1 pers. sing. aor. 2, opt. mid. (§ 37. rem. 1) — ὀνίνημι

ὄναρ], τό, indecl. (§ 6. rem. 5) *a dream*, Mat. 1. 20; 2. 12, 13, 19, 22; 27. 19.

ὀνάριον],[d] ίου, τό, (§ 3. tab. C. c) — ὄνος
ὀνειδίζειν, pres. infin. act. — ὀνειδίζω
ὀνειδίζεσθε, 2 pers. pl. pres. ind. pass. — id.
ὀνειδιζόμεθα, 1 pers. pl. pres. ind. pass. — id.
ὀνειδίζοντος, gen. sing. masc. part. pres. act. — id.
ὀνειδιζόντων, gen. pl. masc. part. pres. act. — id.
ὀνειδίζω], fut. ίσω, (§ 26. rem. 1) — ὄνειδος
ὀνειδισμοί, nom. pl. — ὀνειδισμός
ὀνειδισμοῖς, dat. pl. — id.
ὀνειδισμόν, acc. sing. — id.
ὀνειδισμός], οῦ, ὁ, (§ 3. tab. C. a) — ὄνειδος
ὀνειδίσωσι, 3 pers. pl. aor. 1, subj. — ὀνειδίζω

ὄνειδος],[e] εος, τό, (§ 5. tab. E. b) pr. *fame, report, character*; usually, *reproach, disgrace.*

ὀνειδίζω, fut. ίσω, aor. 1, ὠνείδισα, (§ 26. rem. 1) *to censure, inveigh against*, Mat. 11. 20; Mar. 16. 14; *to upbraid*, Ja. 1. 5; *to revile, insult with opprobrious language*, Mat. 5. 11, et al.

ὀνειδισμός, οῦ, ὁ, (§ 3. tab. C. a) *censure*, 1 Ti. 3. 7; *reproach, reviling, contumely*, Ro. 15. 3, et al. L.G.

Ὀνήσιμον, acc. — Ὀνήσιμος
Ὀνήσιμος], ου, ὁ, (§ 3. tab. C. a) *Onesimus*, pr. name.
Ὀνησίμῳ, dat. — Ὀνήσιμος
Ὀνησίφορος], ου, ὁ, *Onesiphorus*, pr. name.
Ὀνησιφόρου, gen. — Ὀνησίφορος
ὀνικός], ή, όν, (§ 7. tab. F. a) — ὄνος
ὀνίνημι], fut. ὀνήσω, *to help, profit, benefit*; mid. ὀνίναμαι, aor. 2, ὠνήμην & ὠνάμην, opt. ὀναίμην, *to receive profit, pleasure*, etc.; with a gen., *to have joy of*, Phile. 20.

ὄνομα], ατος, τό, (§ 4. tab. D. c) *a name*; *the proper name* of a person, etc., Mat. 1. 23, 25; 10. 2; 27. 32, et al.; *a mere name or reputation*, Re. 3. 1; in N.T. *a name* as the representative of a person, Mat. 6. 9; Lu. 6. 22; 11. 2; *the name* of the author of a commission, delegated authority, or religious profession, Mat. 7. 22; 10. 22; 12. 21; 18. 5, 20; 19. 29; 21. 9; 28. 19; Ac. 3. 16; 4. 7, 12, et al.; εἰς ὄνομα, ἐν ὀνόματι, *on the score of being* possessor of a certain character, Mat. 10. 41, 42; Mar. 9. 41.

ὀνομάζω, fut. άσω, (§ 26. rem. 1) *to name*, Lu. 6. 14; *to style, entitle*, Lu. 6. 13; 1 Co. 5. 11; *to make mention of*, 1 Co. 5. 1; Ep. 5. 3; *to make known*, Ro. 15. 20; *to pronounce* in exorcism, Ac. 19. 13; in N.T. *to profess*, 2 Ti. 2. 19.

ὀνομάζειν, pres. infin. act. — ὀνομάζω
ὀνομαζέσθω, 3 pers. sing. pres. imper. pass. — id.
ὀνομάζεται, 3 pers. sing. pres. ind. pass. — id.
ὀνομαζόμενος, nom. sing. masc. part. pres. pass. — id.
ὀνομαζομένου, gen. sing. neut. part. pres. pass. — id.
ὀνομάζω], fut. άσω, (§ 26. rem. 1) — ὄνομα
ὀνομάζων, nom. sing. masc. part. pres. act. — ὀνομάζω
ὀνόματα, nom. and acc. pl. — ὄνομα
ὀνόματι, dat. sing. — id.
ὀνόματος, gen. sing. — id.
ὀνομάτων, gen. pl. — id.
ὄνον, acc. sing. — ὄνος

[a] Ac. 18. 3. [b] 1 Pe. 3. 8. [c] Phile. 20. [d] Jno. 12. 14. [e] Lu. 1. 25.

ὄνος], ου, ὁ, ἡ, (§ 3. tab. C. a. b) *an ass*, male or female, Mat. 21. 2, 5, 7, et al.

ὀνάριον, ίου, τό, (§ 3. tab. C. c) (dimin. of ὄνος) *a young ass, an ass's colt*, Jno. 12. 14.

ὀνῐκός, ή, όν, (§ 7. tab. F. a) *pertaining to an ass*; μύλος ὀνικός, *a millstone turned by an ass, a large*, or, *an upper, millstone*, Mat. 18. 6; Lu. 17. 2. N.T.

ὄνου, gen. sing. . . . . . . ὄνος

ὅνπερ,[a] acc. sing. masc. . . . . ὅσπερ

ὄντα, acc. sing. masc. and nom. or acc. neut. pl. part. pres. (§ 12. tab. L) . εἰμί

ὄντας, acc. pl. masc. part. pres. . . . id.

ὄντες, nom. pl. masc. part. pres. . . id.

ὄντι, dat. sing. masc. part. pres. . . . id.

ὄντος, gen. sing. masc. and neut. part. pres. id.

ὄντων, gen. pl. masc. and neut. part. pres. . id.

ὄντως], adv. . . . . id.

ὀξεῖα, nom. sing. fem. . . . . ὀξύς

ὀξεῖαν, acc. sing. fem. . . . . id.

ὀξεῖς, nom. pl. masc. . . . . id.

ὄξος], εος, τό, (§ 5. tab. E. b) . . . id.

ὄξους, gen. sing. . . . . . . ὄξος

ὀξύ, acc. sing. neut. . . . . ὀξύς

ὀξύς], εῖα, ύ, (§ 7. tab. H. g) *sharp, keen*, Re. 1. 16; 2. 12; 14. 14, 17, 18; 19. 15; *swift, nimble*, Ro. 3. 15.

ὄξος, εος, τό, (§ 5. tab. E. b) *vinegar; a wine of sharp flavour, posca*, which was an ordinary beverage, and was often mixed with bitter herbs, etc., and thus given to the condemned criminals in order to stupify them, and lessen their sufferings, Mat. 27. 34, 48; Mar. 15. 36; Lu. 23. 36; Jno. 19. 29, 30.

ὀπαῖς, dat. pl. . . . . . . ὀπή

ὀπή], ῆς, ἡ, (§ 2. tab. B. a) *a hole; a hole, vent, opening*, Ja. 3. 11; *a hole, cavern*, He. 11. 38.

ὀπῆς, gen. sing. . . . . . . ὀπή

ὄπισθεν], adv. of place, *from behind, behind, after, at the back of*, Mat. 9. 20; 15. 23, et al.

ὀπίσω], adv. *behind, after, at one's back*, Mat. 4. 10; Lu. 7. 38; Re. 1. 10; τὰ ὀπίσω, *the things which are behind*, Phi. 3. 14; ὀπίσω and εἰς τὰ ὀπίσω, *back, backwards*, Mat 24. 18; Mar. 13. 16; Lu. 9. 62.

ὅπλα, nom. and acc. pl. . ὅπλον

ὁπλίζω], fut. ίσω, (§ 26. rem. 1) . . id.

ὁπλίσασθε,[b] 2 pers. pl. aor. 1, imper. mid. . ὁπλίζω

ὅπλον], ου, τό, (§ 3. tab. C. c) *an implement*, Ro. 6. 13; pl. τὰ ὅπλα, *arms, armour, weapons*, whether offensive or defensive, Jno. 18. 3; Ro. 13. 12; 2 Co. 6. 7; 10. 4.

ὁπλίζω, fut. ίσω, (§ 26. rem. 1) *to arm, equip*; mid. *to arm one's self, equip one's self*, 1 Pe. 4. 1.

ὅπλων, gen. pl. . . . . . ὅπλον

ὁποίαν, acc. sing. fem. . . . . ὁποῖος

ὁποῖοι, nom. pl. masc. . . . . id.

ὁποῖον, nom. sing. neut. . . . . id.

ὁποῖος], οία, οῖον, (§ 10. rem. 7. a) *what, of what sort or manner*, 1 Co. 3. 13; Gal. 2. 6; 1 Thes. 1. 9; Ja. 1. 24; after τοιοῦτος, *as*, Ac. 26. 29.

ὁπότε],[c] adv. *when*.

ὅπου], adv. *where, in which place, in what place*, Mat. 6. 19, 20, 21; Re. 2. 13; *whither, to what place*, Jno. 8. 21; 14. 4; ὅπου ἄν, or ἐάν, *wherever, in whatever place*, Mat. 24. 28; *whithersoever*, Mat. 8. 19; Ja. 3. 4; met. *where, in which thing, state*, etc., Col. 3. 11; *whereas*, 1 Co. 3. 3; 2 Pe. 2. 11.

ὀπτάνομαι], *to be seen, appear*, Ac. 1. 3.

ὀπτανόμενος,[d] nom. sing. masc. part. pres. . ὀπτάνομαι

ὀπτασία], ας, ἡ, (§ 2. tab. B. b, and rem. 2) (ὀπτάζω, equiv. to ὁράω) *a vision, apparition*, Lu. 1. 22; 24. 23; Ac. 26. 19; 2 Co. 12. 1. L.G.

ὀπτασίᾳ, dat. sing. . . . . ὀπτασία

ὀπτασίαν, acc. sing. . . . . id.

ὀπτασίας, acc. pl. . . . . id.

ὀπτός], ή, όν, (§ 7. tab. F. a) (ὀπτάω, *to roast*) *dressed by fire, roasted, broiled*, etc.

ὀπτοῦ,[e] gen. sing. masc. . . . . ὀπτός

ὀπώρα],[f] ας, ἡ, (§ 2. tab. B. b) *autumn; the fruit season*; meton. *fruits*, Re. 18. 14.

ὅπως], adv. *how, in what way or manner, by what means*, Mat. 22. 15; Lu. 24. 20; conj. *that, in order that*, and ὅπως μή, *that*

[a] Mar. 15. 6. [b] 1 Pe. 4. 1. [c] Lu. 6. 3. [d] Ac. 1. 3. [e] Lu. 24. 42. [f] Re. 18. 14.

not, lest, Mat. 6. 2, 4, 5, 16, 18; Ac. 9. 2, et al. freq.

ὁρᾷ, 3 pers. sing. pres. ind. act. . . ὁράω

ὅρα, 2 pers. sing. pres. imper. act. . . id.

ὅραμα], ατος, τό, (§ 4. tab. D. c) . . id.

ὁράματι, dat. sing. . . . . . ὅραμα

ὁράματος, gen. sing. . . . . id.

ὁράσει, dat. sing. . . . . . ὅρασις

ὁράσεις, acc. pl. . . . . . id.

ὅρασις], εως, ἡ, (§ 5. tab. E. c) . . . ὁράω

ὁρατά,[a] nom. pl. neut. . . . . ὁρατός

ὁρᾶτε, 2 pers. pl. pres. ind. and imper. . . ὁράω

ὁρατός], ή, όν, (§ 7. tab. F. a) . . id.

ὁράω], ῶ, fut. ὄψομαι, rarely aor. 1, ὠψάμην, imperf. ἑώρων, perf. ἑώρᾱκα, aor. 2, εἶδον, aor. 1, pass. ὤφθην, fut. ὀφθήσομαι, (§ 36. rem. 1) *to see, behold,* Mat. 2. 2, et al. freq.; *to look,* Jno. 19. 37; *to visit,* Jno. 16. 22; He. 13. 23; *to mark, observe,* Ac. 8. 23; Ja. 2. 24; *to be admitted to witness,* Lu. 17. 22; Jno. 3. 36; Col. 2. 18; with Θεόν, *to be admitted into the more immediate presence of God,* Mat. 5. 8; He. 12. 14; *to attain to a true knowledge of God,* 3 Jno. 11; *to see to a thing,* Mat. 27. 4; Ac. 18. 15; ὅρα, *see, take care,* Mat. 8. 4; He. 8. 5, et al.; pass. *to appear,* Lu. 1. 11; Ac. 2. 3, et al.; *to reveal one's self,* Ac. 26. 16; *to present one's self,* Ac. 7. 26.

ὅρᾱμα, ατος, τό, (§ 4. tab. D. c) *a thing seen, sight, appearance,* Ac. 7. 31; *a vision,* Mat. 17. 9; Ac. 9. 10, 12, et al.

ὅρᾱσις, εως, ἡ, (§ 5. tab. E. c) *seeing, sight; appearance, aspect,* Re. 4. 3; *a vision,* Ac. 2. 17; Re. 9. 17.

ὁρᾱτός, ή, όν, (§ 7. tab. F. a) *visible,* Col. 1. 16.

ὀφθαλμός, οῦ, ὁ, (§ 3. tab. C. a) (ὄψομαι, ὤφθην) *an eye,* Mat. 5. 29, 38; 6. 23; 7. 3, 4, 5, et al.; ὀφθαλμὸς πονηρός, *an evil eye, an envious eye, envy,* Mat. 20. 15; Mar. 7. 22; met. *the* intellectual *eye,* Mat. 13. 15; Mar. 8. 18; Jno. 12. 40; Ac. 26. 18.

ὄψις, εως, ἡ, (§ 5. tab. E. c) *a sight; the face, visage, countenance,* Jno. 11. 44; Re. 1. 16; *external appearance,* Jno. 7. 24.

ὀργή], ῆς, ἡ, (§ 2. tab. B. a) pr. *mental bent, impulse; anger, indignation, wrath,* Ep. 4. 31; Col. 3. 8, μετ' ὀργῆς, *indignantly,* Mar. 3. 5; *vengeance, punishment,* Mat. 3. 7; Lu. 3. 7; 21. 23; Ro. 13. 4, 5, et al.

ὀργίζω, fut. ίσω & ιῶ, (§ 35. rem. 11) aor. 1, pass. ὠργίσθην, *to provoke to anger, irritate;* pass. *to be angry, indignant, enraged,* Mat. 5. 22; 18. 34, et al.

ὀργίλος, η, ον, (§ 7. tab. F. a) *prone to anger, irascible, passionate,* Tit. 1. 7. (ῐ).

ὀργῇ, dat. sing. . . . . . . ὀργή

ὀργήν, acc. sing. . . . . . id.

ὀργῆς, gen. sing. . . . . . . id.

ὀργίζεσθε, 2 pers. pl. pres. imper. pass. . ὀργίζω

ὀργιζόμενος, nom. sing. masc. part. pres. pass. id.

ὀργίζω], fut. ίσω, (§ 26. rem. 1) . . ὀργή

ὀργίλον,[b] acc. sing. masc. . . . ὀργίλος

ὀργίλος], η, ον, (§ 7. tab. F. a) . . . ὀργή

ὀργισθείς, nom. sing. masc. part. aor. 1, pass. ὀργίζω

ὀργυιά], ᾶς, ἡ, (§ 2. tab. B. b, and rem. 2) ὀρέγω

ὀργυιάς, acc. pl. . . . . . ὀργυιά

ὀρέγεται, 3 pers. sing. pres. ind. mid. . . ὀρέγω

ὀρεγόμενοι, nom. pl. masc. part. pres. mid. id.

ὀρέγονται, 3 pers. pl. pres. ind. mid. . id.

ὀρέγω], fut. ξω, (§ 23. rem. 1. b) *to extend, stretch out;* mid. *to stretch one's self out, to reach forward to;* met. *to desire earnestly, long after,* 1 Ti. 3. 1; He. 11. 16; by impl. *to indulge in, be devoted to,* 1 Ti. 6. 10.

ὀργυιά, ᾶς, ἡ, *the space measured by the arms outstretched; a fathom,* Ac. 27. 28, bis.

ὄρεξις, εως, ἡ, (§ 5. tab. E. c) *desire, longing; lust, concupiscence,* Ro. 1. 27.

ὄρει, dat. sing. . . . . . . ὄρος

ὀρεινῇ, dat. sing. fem. . . . . ὀρεινός

ὀρεινήν, acc. sing. fem. . . . . id.

ὀρεινός], ή, όν, (§ 7. tab. F. a) . . ὄρος

ὀρέξει,[c] dat. sing. . . . . . ὄρεξις

ὄρεξις], εως, ἡ, (§ 5. tab. E. c) . . ὀρέγω

ὄρεσι, dat. pl. . . . . . . ὄρος

ὀρέων, gen. pl. . . . . . id.

[a] Col. 1. 16. [b] Tit. 1. 7. [c] Ro. 1. 27.

ὄρη, nom. and acc. pl. . . . . . ὄρος
ὀρθάς, acc. pl. fem. . . . . . ὀρθός
ὀρθοποδέω, ῶ], fut. ήσω, (§ 16. tab. P) (ὀρθός & πούς) *to walk in a straight course; to be straightforward* in moral conduct, Gal. 2. 14. N.T.
ὀρθοποδοῦσι,[a] 3 pers. pl. pres. ind. . . ὀρθοποδέω
ὀρθός], ή, όν, (§ 7. tab. F. a) (ὄρω, *to raise up*) *erect, upright*, Ac. 14. 10; *plain, level, straight*, He. 12. 13.

ὀρθῶς, adv. *straightly; rightly, correctly*, Mar. 7. 35; Lu. 7. 43, et al.

ὀρθοτομέω, ῶ], fut. ήσω, (§ 16. tab. P) (ὀρθός & τέμνω) *to cut straight; to direct aright; to set forth truthfully, without perversion or distortion*, 2 Ti. 2. 15. LXX.
ὀρθοτομοῦντα,[b] acc. sing. masc. part. pres. . ὀρθοτομέω
ὄρθριαι,[c] nom. pl. fem. . . . . ὄρθριος
ὀρθρίζω], fut. ίσω, (§ 26. rem. 1) . . ὄρθρος
ὀρθριναί, nom. pl. fem.—Al. Ln. Tdf. } ὀρθρινός
ὄρθριαι, Rec. Gr. Sch. (Lu. 24. 22) }
ὀρθρινός],[d] ή, όν, (§ 7. tab. F. a) . . ὄρθρος
ὄρθριος], α, όν, (§ 7. rem. 1) . . . id.
ὄρθρον, acc. sing. . . . . . . id.

ὄρθρος], ου, ὁ, (§ 3. tab. C. a) *the dawn; the morning*, Jno. 8. 2; Ac. 5. 21; ὄρθρος βαθύς, *the first streak of dawn, the early dawn*, Lu. 24. 1.

ὀρθρίζω, fut. ίσω, (§ 26. rem. 1) *to rise early in the morning; to come with the dawn*, Lu. 21. 38. LXX.

ὀρθρινός, ή, όν, (§ 7. tab. F. a) *of or belonging to the morning, morning*, Re. 22. 16; (usually ῐ), a later form for ὄρθριος.

ὄρθριος, ία, ιον, (§ 7. rem. 1) *at daybreak, early*, Lu. 24. 22.

ὄρθρου, gen. sing. . . . . . ὄρθρος
ὀρθῶς], adv. . . . . ὀρθός
ὅρια, acc. pl. . . . . . . ὅριον
ὁρίζει, 3 pers. sing. pres. ind. act. . . . ὁρίζω
ὁρίζω], fut. ίσω, (§ 26. rem. 1) aor. 1, pass. ὡρίσθην, perf. ὥρισμαι, (ὅρος, *a bound, limit*) *to set bounds to, to bound; to restrict*, He. 4. 7; *to settle, appoint definitively*, Ac. 17. 26; *to fix determinately*, Ac. 2. 23; *to decree, destine*, Lu. 22. 22; *to constitute, appoint*, Ac. 10. 42; 17. 31; *to characterise with precision, to set forth distinctively*, Ro. 1. 4; absol. *to resolve*, Ac. 11. 29.
ὁρίοις, dat. pl. . . . . . . ὅριον
ὅριον], ου, τό, (§ 3. tab. C. c) (ὅρος) *a limit, bound, border of a territory or country*; pl. τὰ ὅρια, *region, territory, district*, Mat. 2. 16; 4. 13; 8. 34, et al.
ὁρίσας, nom. sing. masc. part. aor. 1, act. . ὁρίζω
ὁρισθέντος, gen. sing. masc. part. aor. 1, pass. id.
ὁρίων, gen. pl. . . . . . . ὅριον
ὁρκίζομεν, 1 pers. pl. pres. ind. . . . ὁρκίζω
ὁρκίζω], fut. ίσω . . . . . . ὅρκος
ὅρκον, acc. sing. . . . . . . id.

ὅρκος], ου, ὁ, (§ 3. tab. C. a) *an oath*, Mat. 14. 7, 9; 26. 72, et al.; meton. *that which is solemnly promised, a vow*, Mat. 5. 33.

ὁρκίζω, fut. ίσω, (§ 26. rem. 1) *to put to an oath; to obtest, adjure, conjure*, Mar. 5. 7; Ac. 19. 13.

ὅρκου, gen. sing. . . . . . . ὅρκος
ὅρκους, acc. pl. . . . . . . id.
ὅρκῳ, dat. sing. . . . . . . id.
ὁρκωμοσία], ας, ἡ, (§ 2. tab. B. b, and rem. 2) (ὅρκος & ὄμνυμι) *the act of taking an oath; an oath*, He. 7. 20, 21, 28. LXX.
ὁρκωμοσίας, gen. sing. . . . . ὁρκωμοσία
ὁρμάω, ῶ], fut. ήσω, (§ 18. tab. R) . . ὁρμή
ὁρμή], ῆς, ἡ, (§ 2. tab. B. a) (ὄρω, ὄρνυμι, *to put in motion*) *impetus, impulse; assault, violent attempt*, Ac. 14. 5; met. *impulse of mind, purpose, will*, Ja. 3. 4.

ὁρμάω, ῶ, fut. ήσω, aor. 1, ὥρμησα, (§ 18. tab. R) pr. trans. *to put in motion, incite*; intrans. *to rush*, Mat. 8. 32; Mar. 5. 13; Lu. 8. 33, et al.

ὅρμημα, ατος, τό, (§ 4. tab. D. c) *violent or impetuous motion; violence*, Re. 18. 21.

ὅρμημα], ατος, τό . . . . ὁρμή
ὁρμήματι,[e] dat. sing. . . . . ὅρμημα
ὄρνεα, nom. pl. . . . . . ὄρνεον
ὀρνέοις, dat. pl. . . . . . . id.
ὄρνεον], ου, τό, (§ 3. tab. C. c) . . . ὄρνις
ὀρνέου, gen. sing. . . . . . ὄρνεον

ὄρνις], ῑθος, ὁ, ἡ, (§ 4. rem. 4) *a bird, fowl; the* domestic *hen*, Mat. 23. 37; Lu. 13. 34.

---

[a] Gal. 2. 14. [b] 2 Ti. 2. 15. [c] Lu. 24. 22. [d] Re. 22. 16. [e] Re. 18. 21.

ὄρνεον, ου, τό, (§ 3. tab. C. c) *a bird, fowl,* Re. 18. 2; 19. 17, 21.

ὁροθεσία], ας, ἡ, (§ 2. tab. B. b, and rem. 2) (ὅρος, *a bound, limit,* and τίθημι) pr. *the act of fixing boundaries; a bound set, certain bound, fixed limit,* Ac. 17. 26. N.T.

ὁροθεσίας,[a] acc. pl. . . . . . ὁροθεσία

ὄρος], εος, τό, (§ 5. tab. E. b) *a mountain, hill,* Mat. 5. 1, 14; 8. 1; 17. 20, et al.

ὀρεινός, ή, όν, (§ 7. tab. F. a) *mountainous, hilly,* Lu. 1. 39, 65.

ὄρους, gen. sing. . . . . . . ὄρος

ὀρύσσω, or ττω], fut. ξω, aor. 1, ὤρυξα, (§ 26. rem. 2) *to dig, excavate,* Mat. 21. 33; 25. 18; Mar. 12. 1.

ὀρφᾰνός], ή, όν, or οῦ, ὁ, ἡ, *bereaved* of parents, *orphan,* Ja. 1. 27; *bereaved, desolate,* Jno. 14. 18.

ὀρφανούς, acc. pl. masc. . . . . ὀρφανός

ὀρχέομαι, οῦμαι], fut. ήσομαι, (§ 17. tab. Q) aor. 1, ὠρχησάμην, *to dance,* Mat. 11. 17, et al.

ὀρχησαμένης, gen. sing. fem. part. aor. 1 . ὀρχέομαι

ὁρῶ, 1 pers. sing. pres. ind. . . . . ὁράω

ὁρῶμεν, 1 pers. pl. pres. ind. . . . . id.

ὁρῶν, nom. sing. masc. part. pres. . . . id.

ὁρῶντες, nom. pl. masc. part. pres. . . id.

ὁρῶσαι, nom. pl. fem. part. pres. . . . id.

ὅς, ἥ, ὅ], (§ 10. tab. J. g) rel. pron. *who, which, qui, quæ, quod,* Mat. 1. 16, 23, 25, et al.; in N.T. interrog. ἐφ᾽ ὅ, *wherefore, why,* Mat. 26. 50; in N.T. ὃς μὲν—ὃς δὲ, for ὁ μὲν—ὁ δὲ, Mat. 21. 35; 2 Co. 2. 16, et al.

ὡς, adv. *as,* correlatively, Mar. 4. 26; Jno. 7. 46; Ro. 5. 15, et al.; *as, like as,* Mat. 10. 16; Ep. 5. 8, et al.; *according as,* Gal. 6. 10, et al.; *as, as it were,* Re. 8. 8, et al.; *as,* Lu. 16. 1; Ac. 3. 12, et al.; before numerals, *about,* Mar. 5. 13, et al.; conj. *that,* Ac. 10. 28, et al.; *how,* Ro. 11. 2, et al.; *when,* Mat. 28. 9; Phi. 2. 23; as an exclamatory particle, *how,* Ro. 10. 15; equivalent to ὥστε, *accordingly,* He. 3. 11; also, *on condition that, provided that,* Ac. 20. 24; ὡς εἰπεῖν, *so to speak* He. 7. 9.

ὅσα, nom. and acc. pl. neut. . . . ὅσος

ὅσαι, nom. pl. fem. . . . . . id

ὁσάκις], adv. . . . . . . id.

ὅσας, acc. pl. fem. . . . . . id.

ὅσια, acc. pl. neut. . . . . . ὅσιος

ὅσιον, acc. sing. masc. . . . . . id.

ὅσιος], ία, ιον, (§ 7. rem. 1) pr. *sanctioned by the supreme law of God, and nature; pious, devout,* Tit. 1. 8; *pure,* 1 Ti. 2. 8; supremely *holy,* Ac. 2. 27; 13. 35; He. 7. 26; Re. 15. 4; 16. 5; τὰ ὅσια, *pledged bounties, mercies,* Ac. 13. 34.

ὁσιότης, τητος, ἡ, (§ 4. rem. 2. c) *piety, sacred observance of all duties towards God, holiness,* Lu. 1. 75; Ep. 5. 24.

ὁσίως, adv. *piously, holily,* 1 Thes. 2. 10.

ὁσιότης], τήτος, ἡ . . . . . . ὅσιος

ὁσιότητι, dat. sing. . . . . . ὁσιότης

ὁσίους, acc. pl. masc. . . . . . ὅσιος

ὁσίως],[b] adv. . . . . . . id.

ὀσμή], ῆς, ἡ, (§ 2. tab. B. a) . . . ὄζω

ὀσμήν, acc. sing. . . . . . ὀσμή

ὀσμῆς, gen. sing. . . . . . id.

ὅσοι, nom. pl. masc. . . . . . ὅσος

ὅσον, acc. sing. masc. and nom. and acc. neut. id.

ὅσος], η, ον, (§ 10. rem. 7. b) a correlative to τόσος, τοσοῦτος, etc., *as great, as much,* Mar. 7. 36; Jno. 6. 11; He. 1. 4; 8. 6; 10. 25; ἐφ᾽ ὅσον χρόνον, *for how long a time, while, as long as,* Ro. 7. 1; so, ἐφ᾽ ὅσον, sc. χρόνον, Mat. 9. 15; ὅσον χρόνον, *how long,* Mar. 2. 19; neut. ὅσον repeated, ὅσον ὅσον, used to give intensity to other qualifying words, e.g. μικρόν, *the very least, a very very little while,* He. 10. 37; ἐφ᾽ ὅσον, *in as much as,* Mat. 25. 40, 45; καθ᾽ ὅσον, *by how much, so far as,* He. 3. 3; or, *in as much as, as, so,* He. 7. 20; 9. 27; pl. ὅσα, *so far as, as much as,* Re. 1. 2; 18. 7; *how great, how much, how many, what,* Mar. 3. 8; 5. 19, 20; *how many soever, as many as, all who,* 2 Co. 1. 20; Phi. 3. 15; 1 Ti. 6. 1; ὅσος ἄν, or ἐάν, *whoever, whatsoever,* Mat. 7. 12; 18. 18.

---

[a] Ac. 17. 26.

[b] 1 Thes. 2. 10.

ὁσάκις, adv. *as often as*, 1 Co. 11. 25, 26; Re. 11. 6. (ᾰ).

ὅσους, acc. pl. masc. . . . . . ὅσος

ὅσπερ], ἥπερ, ὅπερ, (ὅς & περ) an emphatic form of the relative, Mar. 15. 6.

ὀστέα, acc. pl. . . . . . . ὀστέον

ὀστέον, οῦν], έου, οῦ, τό, (§ 3. rem. 3) *a bone*, Mat. 23. 27; Lu. 24. 39, et al.

ὀστέων, gen. pl. . . . . . . ὀστέον

ὀστοῦν, nom. sing. contr. . . . . id.

ὅστις], ἥτις, ὅ τι, gen. οὗτινος, ἧστινος, οὗτινος, & ὅτου, (§ 10. tab. J. h) (ὅς & τις) relat. pron. *whoever, whatever; whosoever, whatsoever*, Mat. 5. 39, 41; 13. 12; 18. 4; its use in place of the simple relative is also required in various cases, which may be learnt from the grammars; ἕως ὅτου, sc. χρόνου, *until*, Lu. 13. 8; *while*, Mat. 5. 25.

ὅτι, conj. *that*, Mat. 2. 16, 22, 23; 6. 5, 16; often used pleonastically in reciting another's words, Mat. 9. 18; Lu. 19. 42; Ac. 5. 23; as a causal particle, *for that, for, because*, Mat. 2. 18; 5. 3, 4, 5; 13. 13; *because, seeing that, since*, Lu. 23. 40; Ac. 1. 17.

ὀστράκινα, nom. pl. neut. . . . ὀστράκινος

ὀστρακίνοις, dat. pl. neut. . . . . id.

ὀστράκῐνος], η, ον, (§ 7. tab. F. a) (ὄστρᾰκον, *an earthen vessel*) *earthen, of earthenware*, 2 Co. 4. 7; 2 Ti. 2. 20. L.G.

ὄσφρησις],[a] εως, ἡ, (§ 5. tab. E. c) (ὀσφραίνομαι, *to smell*) *smell, the sense of smelling*.

ὀσφύας, acc. pl. . . . . . . ὀσφύς

ὀσφύες, nom. pl. . . . . . id.

ὀσφύϊ, dat. sing. . . . . . id.

ὀσφύν, acc. sing. . . . . . id.

ὀσφύος, gen. sing. . . . . . . id.

ὀσφῦς], ύος, ἡ, (§ 5. tab. E. g) pl. αἱ ὀσφύες, *the loins*, Mat. 3. 4; Mar. 1. 6, et al.

ὅσῳ, dat. sing. neut. . . . . . ὅσος

ὅσων, gen. pl. . . . . . . id.

ὅταν], conj. (ὅτε & ἄν) *when, whenever*, Mat. 5. 11; 6. 2; Mar. 3. 11; Re. 4. 9, et al. freq.; in N.T. *in case of, on occasion of*, Jno. 9. 5; 1 Co. 15. 27; He. 1. 6.

ὅτε], adv. *when, at the time that, at what time*, Mat. 7. 28; 9. 25; Lu. 13. 35, et al. freq.

ὅ τι, acc. sing. neut. . . . . . ὅστις

ὅτι], conj. . . . . id.

ὅτου, gen. sing. neut. Att. for οὗτινος . id.

οὗ, gen. sing. masc. or neut. . . . ὅς

οὗ], adv. (pr. gen. of ὅς) *where, in what place*, Mat. 2. 9; 18. 20; *whither, to what place*, Lu. 10. 1; 22. 10; 24. 28; οὗ ἐὰν, *whithersoever*, 1 Co. 16. 6.

οὐ before a consonant, **οὐκ** before a vowel with a lenis, and **οὐχ** with an aspirate], adv. of negation, *not, no*, Mat. 5. 37; 12. 43; 23. 37; the peculiarities of its usage, and as distinct from μή, may be learnt from the grammars.

οὐχί, adv. *not*, Jno. 13. 10, 11; when followed by ἀλλά, *nay, not so, by no means*, Lu. 1. 60; 12. 51; used also in negative interrogations, Mat. 5. 46, 47, 6. 25.

οὐά],[b] interj. (Lat. *vah*) expressive of insult and derision, *ah! aha!*

οὐαί], interj. (Lat. *væ*) *wo! alas!* Mat. 11. 21; 18. 7; 23. 13, 14, 15, 16, et al.; ἡ οὐαί, subst., *a woe, calamity*, Re. 9. 12; 11. 14.

οὐδαμῶς],[c] adv. (οὐδαμός, *no one, ne unus quidem*) *by no means*.

οὐδέ], adv. (οὐ & δέ) *neither, nor, and not, also not*, Mat. 5. 15; 6. 15, 20, 26, 28; when single, *not even*, Mat. 6. 29; 8. 10.

οὐδείς], οὐδεμία, οὐδέν, (§ 10. rem. 6. c) (οὐδέ & εἷς) *not one, no one, none, nothing*, Mat. 5. 13; 6. 24; 19. 17; met. οὐδέν, *nothing, of no account, naught*, Jno. 8. 54; Ac. 21. 24.

οὐδεμία, nom. sing. fem. . . . . οὐδείς

οὐδεμίαν, acc. sing. fem. . . . . id.

οὐδέν, nom. and acc. sing. neut. . . id.

οὐδένα, acc. sing. masc. . . . . id.

οὐδενί, dat. sing. neut. . . . . id.

οὐδενός, gen. sing. masc. and neut. . . id.

οὐδέποτε], adv. (οὐδέ & πότε) *never*, Mat. 7. 23; 21. 16, 42, et al. freq.

οὐδέπω], adv. (οὐδέ & πω) *not yet, never yet, never*, Lu. 23. 53; Jno. 7. 39, et al.

[a] 1 Co. 12. 17. [b] Mar. 15. 29. [c] Mat. 2. 6.

οὐθείς], οὐθέν, later forms for οὐδείς, οὐδέν, v.r. 1 Co. 13. 2; 2 Co. 11. 8.

οὐθέν, nom. sing. neut.—A. C. Ln. Tdf. } οὐθείς
οὐδέν, Rec. Gr. Sch. (1 Co. 13. 2) }

οὐθενός, gen. sing. masc.—B. Ln. Tdf. } id.
οὐδενός, Rec. Gr. Sch. (2 Co. 11. 8) }

οὐκ, see οὐ.

οὐκέτι], adv. (οὐκ & ἔτι) *no longer, no more,* Mat. 22. 46, et al.

οὐκοῦν],[a] *then, therefore;* used interrogatively, Jno. 18. 37.

οὖν], a particle expressing either simple sequence or consequence; *then, now then,* Mat. 13. 18; Jno. 19. 29, et al.; *then, thereupon,* Lu. 15. 28; Jno. 6. 14, et al.; *therefore, consequently,* Mat. 5. 48; Mar. 10. 9, et al.; it also serves to mark the resumption of discourse after an interruption by a parenthesis, 1 Co. 8. 4, et al.

οὔπω], adv. (οὐ & πω) *not yet,* Mat. 15. 17; 16. 9; 24. 6; Jno. 2. 4, et al.

οὐρά], ᾶς, ἡ, (§ 2. tab. B. b) *a tail,* Re. 9. 10, 19; 12. 4.

οὐραί, nom. pl. . . . . . . οὐρά
οὐραῖς, dat. pl. . . . . . . id.
οὐρανέ, voc. sing. . . . . . οὐρανός
οὐράνιος], ία, ιον, or ίου, ὁ, ἡ . . . id.
οὐρανίου, gen. sing. fem. . . . . οὐράνιος
οὐρανίῳ, dat. sing. fem. . . . . id.
οὐρανόθεν], adv. . . . . . . οὐρανός
οὐρανοί, nom. pl. . . . . . id.
οὐρανοῖς, dat. pl. . . . . . id.
οὐρανόν, acc. sing. . . . . . id.

οὐρᾰνός], οῦ, ὁ, (§ 3. tab. C. a) and pl. οὐρανοί, ῶν, οἱ, *heaven, the heavens, the visible heavens and all their phenomena,* Mat. 5. 18; 16. 1; 24. 29, et al. freq.; *the air, atmosphere,* in which the clouds and tempests gather, the birds fly, etc., Mat. 6. 26; 16. 2, 3, et al.; *heaven* as the peculiar seat and abode of God, of angels, of glorified spirits, etc., Mat. 5. 34, 45, 48; 6. 1, 9, 10; 12. 50; Jno. 3. 13, 31; 6. 32, 38, 41, 42, 50, 51, 58; in N.T. *heaven* as a term expressive of the Divine Being, His administration, etc., Mat. 19. 14; 21. 25; Lu. 20. 4, 5; Jno. 3. 27.

οὐράνιος, ία, ιον, or ίου, ὁ, ἡ, *heavenly, celestial,* Mat. 6. 14, 26, 32; 15. 13, et al.

οὐρανόθεν, adv. *from heaven,* Ac. 14. 17; 26. 13.

οὐρανοῦ, gen. sing. . . . . οὐρανός
οὐρανούς, acc. pl. . . . . . id.
οὐρανῷ, dat. sing. . . . . . id.
οὐρανῶν, gen. pl. . . . . . id.
οὐράς, acc. pl. . . . . . οὐρά
Οὐρβανόν,[b] acc. . . . . . Οὐρβανός

Οὐρβᾶνός], οῦ, ὁ, (§ 3. tab. C. a) *Urbanus, Urban,* pr. name.

Οὐρίας], ου, ὁ, (§ 2. tab. B. d) *Urias, Uriah,* pr. name.

Οὐρίου,[c] gen. . . . . . . Οὐρίας
οὕς, acc. pl. masc. . . . . . ὅς

οὖς], ὠτός, τό, (§ 4. rem. 3. b) *the ear,* Mat. 10. 27; Mar. 7. 33; Lu. 22. 50; Ac. 7. 57, et al.

ὠτάριον, ου, τό, (dimin. of ὠτίον) *an ear,* v.r. Mat. 14. 47.

ὠτίον, ου, τό, in N.T. simply equivalent to οὖς, *an ear,* Mat. 26. 51; Mar. 14. 47; Lu. 22. 51; Jno. 18. 10, 26.

οὖσα, nom. sing. fem. part. pres. (§ 12. tab. L) εἰμί
οὖσαι, nom. pl. fem. part. pres. . . id.
οὖσαν, acc. sing. fem. part. pres. . . id.
οὔσῃ, dat. sing. fem. part. pres. . . id.
οὔσης, gen. sing. fem. part. pres. . . id.
οὖσι, dat. pl. masc. part. pres. . . id.
οὐσία], ας, ἡ, (§ 2. tab. B. b, and rem. 2) . id.
οὐσίαν, acc. sing. . . . . . οὐσία
οὐσίας, gen. sing. . . . . . id.
οὐσῶν, gen. pl. fem. part. pres. . . εἰμί

οὔτε], conj. (οὐ & τε) *neither, nor,* Lu. 20. 36; οὔτε—οὔτε, or οὐδὲ—οὔτε, *neither—nor,* Lu. 20. 35; Gal. 1. 12; in N.T. also used singly in the sense of οὐδέ, *not even,* Mar. 5. 3; Lu. 12. 26; 1 Co. 3. 2.

οὗτοι, nom. pl. masc. . . . . . οὗτος

οὗτος], αὕτη, τοῦτο, (§ 10. tab. J. c, and rem. 3) demons. pron. *this, this* person or thing, Mat. 3. 3, 9, 17; 8. 9; 10. 2; 24. 34, et al. freq.; used by way of contempt, *this fellow,* Mat. 13. 55; 27. 47; αὐτὸ τοῦτο, *this very thing, this same thing,* 2 Co. 2. 3; 7. 11; εἰς αὐτὸ τοῦτο, and

[a] Jno. 18. 37. [b] Ro. 16. 9. [c] Mat. 1. 6.

elliptically, αὐτὸ τοῦτο, *for this same purpose, on this account*, Ep. 6. 18, 22; 2 Pe. 1. 5; καὶ οὗτος, *and moreover*, Lu. 7. 12; 16. 1; 20. 30; καὶ τοῦτο, *and that too*, 1 Co. 6. 6, 8; τοῦτο μὲν—τοῦτο δὲ, *partly—partly*, He. 10. 33.

οὕτως & οὕτω before a consonant, adv. *thus, in this way*, Mat. 1. 18; 2. 5; 5. 16, et al. freq.; ὃς μὲν οὕτως, ὃς δὲ οὕτως, *one so, and another so, one in one way, and another in another*, 1 Co. 7. 7; *so*, Mat. 7. 12; 12. 40; 24. 27, 37, et al. freq.; *thus, under such circumstances*, Ac. 20. 11; *in such a condition*, viz., one previously mentioned, Ac. 27. 17; 1 Co. 7. 26, 40; and, perhaps, Jno. 4. 6; *in an ordinary way, at ease*, like Lat. *sic*, perhaps, Jno. 4. 6.

οὐχ, see οὐ.

οὐχί], adv. . . . . . . οὐ

ὀφειλάς, acc. pl. . . . . . ὀφειλή

ὀφείλει, 3 pers. sing. pres. ind. . . ὀφείλω

ὀφείλεις, 2 pers. sing. pres. ind. . . . id.

ὀφειλέται, nom. pl. . . . . ὀφειλέτης

ὀφειλέταις, dat. pl. . . . . . id.

ὀφείλετε, 2 pers. pl. pres. ind. and imper. . ὀφείλω

ὀφειλέτης], ου, ὁ, (§ 2. tab. B. c) . . id.

ὀφειλή], ῆς, ἡ, (§ 2. tab. B. a) . . id.

ὀφείλημα], ατος, τό, (§ 4. tab. D. c) . id.

ὀφειλήματα, acc. pl. . . . . ὀφείλημα

ὀφειλήν, acc. sing. . . . . . ὀφειλή

ὀφείλομεν, 1 pers. pl. pres. ind. . . ὀφείλω

ὀφειλομένην, acc. sing. fem. part. pres. pass. . id.

ὀφειλόμενον, acc. sing. neut. part. pres. pass. id.

ὀφείλοντες, nom. pl. masc. part. pres. . id.

ὀφείλοντι, dat. sing. masc. part. pres. . . id.

ὀφείλουσι, 3 pers. pl. pres. ind. . id.

ὀφείλω], fut. ήσω, (§ 35. rem. 5) aor. 2, ὤφελον, *to owe, be indebted*, Mat. 18. 28, 30, 34; *to incur a bond, to be bound to make discharge*, Mat. 23. 16, 18; *to be bound or obliged* by what is due or fitting or consequently necessary, Lu. 17. 10; Jno. 13. 14, et al.; *to incur desert, to deserve*, Jno. 19. 7; *to be due or fitting*, 1 Co. 7. 3, 36; from the Aram. *to be delinquent*, Lu. 11. 4.

ὀφειλέτης, ου, ὁ, (§ 2. tab. B. c) *a debtor, one who owes*, Mat. 18. 24; met. *one who is in any way bound, or under obligation* to perform any duty, Ro. 1. 14; 8. 12; 15. 27; Gal. 5. 3; in N.T. *one who fails in duty, a delinquent, offender*, Mat. 6. 12; *a sinner*, Lu. 13. 4, cf. v. 2.

ὀφειλή, ῆς, ἡ, (§ 2. tab. B. a) *a debt*, Mat. 18. 32; met. *a duty, due*, Ro. 13. 7; 1 Co. 7. 3.

ὀφείλημα, ατος, τό, (§ 4. tab. D. c) *a debt; a due*, Ro. 4. 4; in N.T. *a delinquency, offence, fault, sin*, Mat. 6 12, cf. v. 14.

ὄφελον, (pr. aor. 2, of ὀφείλω) used later and in N.T. as an interj., *O that! would that!* 1 Co. 4. 8; Gal. 5. 12, et al.

ὄφεις, nom., acc., and voc. pl. . . . ὄφις

ὄφελον, ... ὀφείλω

ὄφελος], τό, only in the nom. (§ 6. rem. 5) (ὀφέλλω, *to further, augment*) *profit, utility, advantage*, 1 Co. 15. 32, et al.

ὠφελέω, ῶ, fut. ήσω, aor. 1, ὠφέλησα, (§ 16. tab. P) *to help, profit, benefit*, Mat. 27. 24; Mar. 7. 11; Ro. 2. 25, et al.

ὠφέλεια, ας, ἡ, (§ 2. tab. B. b, and rem. 2) *help; profit, gain, advantage, benefit*, Ro. 3. 1; Jude 16.

ὠφέλῐμος, ου, ὁ, ἡ, τό, -ον, (§ 7. rem. 2) *profitable, useful, beneficial; serviceable*, 1 Ti. 4. 8, bis.; 2 Ti. 3. 16; Tit. 3. 8.

ὄφεσι, dat. pl. . . . . . ὄφις

ὄφεων, gen. pl. . . . . . id.

ὄφεως, gen. sing. . . . . . id.

ὀφθαλμοδουλεία], ας, ἡ, (§ 2. tab. B. b, and rem. 2) (ὀφθαλμός & δουλεία) *eye-service, service rendered only while under inspection*, Ep. 6. 6; Col. 3. 22. N.T.

ὀφθαλμοδουλείᾳ, dat. sing.—Al. Ln. Sch. } ὀφθαλμοδουλεία
ὀφθαλμοδουλείαις, Rec. Gr. Tdf. (Col. 3. 22) . . . }

ὀφθαλμοδουλείαις, dat. pl. . . . . id.

ὀφθαλμοδουλείαν, acc. sing. . . . id.

ὀφθαλμοί, nom. pl. . . . . ὀφθαλμός

ὀφθαλμοῖς, dat. pl. . . . . id.

ὀφθαλμόν, acc. sing. . . . . id.

ὀφθαλμός], οῦ, ὁ, (§ 3. tab. C. a) . . ὁράω

ὀφθαλμοῦ, gen. sing. . . . . ὀφθαλμός

ὀφθαλμούς, acc. pl. . . . . id.

ὀφθαλμῷ, dat. sing. . . . id.

ὀφθαλμῶν, gen. pl. . . . . . ὀφθαλμός
ὀφθείς, nom. sing. masc. part. aor. 1, pass. (§ 36. rem. 1) . . . . ὁράω
ὀφθέντες, nom. pl. masc. part. aor. 1, pass. id.
ὀφθέντος, gen. sing. masc. part. aor. 1, pass. id.
ὀφθήσεται, 3 pers. sing. fut. pass. . . id.
ὀφθήσομαι, 1 pers. sing. fut. pass. . . id.
ὄφιν, acc. sing. . . . . . . ὄφις

ὄφις], εως, ὁ, (§ 5. tab. E. c) *a serpent*, Mat. 7. 10; 10. 16; *an* artificial *serpent*, Jno. 3. 14; used of *the devil or Satan*, Re. 12. 9, 14, 15; 20. 2; met. *a man of serpentine character*, Mat. 23. 33.

ὀφρύος,[a] gen. sing. . . . . . . ὀφρύς

ὀφρύς], ύος, ἡ, (§ 5. tab. E. g) *a brow, eyebrow; the brow* of a mountain, *edge* of a precipice, Lu. 4. 29.

ὀχλέω, ῶ], fut. ήσω, (§ 16. tab. P) . . ὄχλος
ὄχλοι, nom. pl. . . . . . . id.
ὄχλοις, dat. pl. . . . . . . id.
ὄχλον, acc. sing. . . . . . id.
ὀχλοποιέω, ῶ], fut. ήσω, (§ 16. tab. P) (ὄχλος & ποιέω) *to collect a mob, create a tumult*. N.T.
ὀχλοποιήσαντες,[b] nom. pl. masc. part. aor. 1 ὀχλοποιέω

ὄχλος], ου, ὁ, (§ 3. tab. C. a) *a crowd, a confused multitude of people*, Mat. 4. 25; 5. 1; 7. 28; spc. *the common people*, Jno. 7. 49; *a multitude, great number*, Lu. 5. 29; 6. 17; Ac. 1. 15; by impl. *tumult, uproar*, Lu. 22. 6; Ac. 24. 18.

ὀχλέω, ῶ, fut. ήσω, (§ 16. tab. P) pr. *to mob; to vex, trouble*, Lu. 6. 18; Ac. 5. 16.

ὄχλου, gen. sing. . . . . . ὄχλος
ὀχλούμενοι, nom. pl. masc. part. pres. pass. . ὀχλέω
ὀχλουμένους, acc. pl. masc. part. pres. pass. id.
ὄχλους, acc. pl. . . . . . . ὄχλος
ὄχλῳ, dat. sing. . . . . . . id.
ὄχλων, gen. pl. . . . . . . id.
ὀχύρωμα], ατος, τό, (§ 4. tab. D. c) (ὀχυρόω, *to fortify*, ὀχυρός, *firm, strong*) *a stronghold*; met. *an* opposing *bulwark* of error or vice, 2 Co. 10. 4. LXX.
ὀχυρωμάτων,[c] gen. pl. . . . . ὀχύρωμα
ὀψάρια, acc. pl. . . . . . . ὀψάριον

ὀψάριον], ίου, τό, (§ 3. tab. C. c) (dimin. of ὄψον, *cooked provision as distinguished from bread; a dainty dish; fish*) *a little fish*, Jno. 6. 9, 11; 21. 9, 10, 13.
ὀψαρίων, gen. pl. . . . . . . ὀψάριον

ὀψέ], adv. *late*; put for *the first watch, at evening*, Mar. 11. 19; 13. 35; ὀψὲ σαββάτων, *after the close of the Sabbath*, Mat. 28. 1.

ὄψῐμος, ου, ὁ, ἡ, (§ 7. rem. 2) *late; latter*, Ja. 5. 7; poetic and later prose for

ὄψιος, ία, ιον, (§ 7. rem. 1) *late*, Mar. 11. 11; ἡ ὀψία, sc. ὥρα, *evening*, two of which were reckoned by the Hebrews; one, from the ninth hour until sunset, Mat. 8. 16; 14. 15, et al.; and the other, from sunset until dark, Mat. 14. 23; 16. 2, et al.

ὄψει, 2 pers. sing. fut. ind. Att. (§ 35. rem. 11) ὁράω
ὄψεσθε, 2 pers. pl. fut. ind. . . . id.
ὄψεται, 3 pers. sing. fut. ind. . . . id.
ὄψῃ, 2 pers. sing. fut. ind.—A. B. C. Ln. Sch. Tdf. . . . . } id.
ὄψει, Rec. Gr. (Mat. 27. 4) . }
ὄψησθε, 2 pers. pl. aor. 1, subj. . . id.
ὀψία, nom. sing. fem. . . . . ὄψιος
ὀψίας, gen. sing. fem. . . . . id.
ὄψιμον,[d] acc. sing. masc. . . . . ὄψιμος
ὄψιμος], ου, ὁ, ἡ . . . . . ὀψέ
ὄψιν, acc. sing. . . . . . . ὄψις
ὄψιος], ία, ιον, (§ 7. rem. 2) . . . ὀψέ
ὄψις], εως, ἡ, (§ 5. tab. E. c) . . . ὁράω
ὄψομαι, 1 pers. sing. fut. ind. (§ 36. rem. 1) id.
ὀψόμεθα, 1 pers. pl. fut. ind. . . . id.
ὄψονται, 3 pers. pl. fut. ind. . . . id.
ὀψώνια, nom. pl. . . . . . . ὀψώνιον
ὀψώνιον], ίου, τό, (§ 3. tab. C. c) (ὄψον, *cooked provisions*, etc.), *provisions; a stipend or pay* of soldiers, Lu. 3. 14; 1 Co. 9. 7; *wages* of any kind, 2 Co. 11. 8; due *wages, a* stated *recompense*, Ro. 6. 23. L.G.
ὀψωνίοις, dat. pl. . . . . . ὀψώνιον

Π.

παγίδα, acc. sing. . . . . . . παγίς
παγιδεύσωσι,[e] 3 pers. pl. aor. 1, subj. . παγιδεύω
παγιδεύω], fut. εύσω, (§ 13. tab. M) . . πήγνυμι
παγίδος, gen. sing. . . . . . παγίς

[a] Lu. 4. 29. [b] Ac. 17. 5. [c] 2 Co. 10. 4. [d] Ja. 5. 7. [e] Mat. 22. 15.

πα̣γίς], ίδος, ἡ, (§ 4. rem. 2. c) . . . πήγνυμι
πάγον, acc. sing. . . . . . . πάγος
πάγος], ου, ὁ, (§ 3. tab. C. a) . . . πήγνυμι
πάγου, gen. sing. . . . . . πάγος
πάθει, dat. sing. . . . . . πάθος
παθεῖν, aor. 2, infin. (§ 36. rem. 4) . . πάσχω
πάθη, acc. pl. . . . . . . πάθος
πάθῃ, 3 pers. sing. aor. 2, subj. . . πάσχω
πάθημα], ατος, τό, (§ 4. tab. D. c) . . id.
παθήμασι, dat. pl. . . . . . πάθημα
παθήματα, nom. and acc. pl. . . . id.
παθημάτων, gen. pl. . . . . id.
παθητός],[a] ή, όν, (§ 7. tab. F. a) . . πάσχω
παθόντας, acc. pl. m. part. aor. 2, (§ 36. rem. 4) id.
παθόντος, gen. sing. masc. part. aor. 2 . id.
πάθος], εος, τό, (§ 5. tab. E. b) . . . id.
παθοῦσα, nom. sing. fem. part. aor. 2 . id.
παθών, nom. sing. masc. part. aor. 2 . . id.
παῖδα, acc. sing. . . . . . . παῖς
παιδαγωγόν, acc. sing. . . . παιδαγωγός
παιδαγωγός], οῦ, ὁ, (§ 3. tab. C. a) (παῖς & ἀγωγός, ἄγω) *a pedagogue, child-tender*, a person, usually a slave or freedman, to whom the care of the boys of a family was committed, whose duty it was to attend them at their play, lead them to and from the public school, and exercise a constant superintendence over their conduct and safety; in N.T. an ordinary *director or minister* contrasted with an Apostle, as a pedagogue occupies an inferior position to a parent, 1 Co. 4. 15; a term applied to the Mosaic law, as dealing with men as in a state of mere childhood and tutelage, Gal. 3. 24, 25.
παιδαγωγούς, acc. pl. . . . . . παιδαγωγός
παιδαρίοις, dat. pl. . . . . . παιδάριον
παιδάριον], ίου, τό, (§ 3. tab. C. c) . . παῖς
παῖδας, acc. pl. . . . . . . id.
παιδεία], ας, ἡ, (§ 2. tab. B. b, and rem. 2) id.
παιδείᾳ, dat. sing. . . . . . παιδεία
παιδείαν, acc. sing. . . . . . id.
παιδείας, gen. sing. . . . . . id.
παιδεύει, 3 pers. sing. pres. ind. act. . παιδεύω
παιδευθῶσι, 3 pers. pl. aor. 1, subj. pass. (§ 14. rem. 3. b) . . . . id.
παιδευόμεθα, 1 pers. pl. pres. ind. pass. . id.
παιδευόμενοι, nom. pl. masc. part. pres. pass. . id.
παιδεύοντα, acc. sing. masc. part. pres. act. παιδεύω
παιδεύουσα, nom. sing. fem. part. pres. act. id.
παιδεύσας, nom. sing. masc. part. aor. 1, act. id.
παιδευτάς, acc. pl. . . . . . παιδευτής
παιδευτήν, acc. sing. . . . . . id.
παιδευτής], οῦ, ὁ, (§ 2. tab. B. c) . . παῖς
παιδεύω], fut. εύσω, (§ 13. tab. M) . . id.
παιδία, nom., acc., and voc. pl. . . παιδίον
παιδιόθεν],[b] adv.—Rec. Gr. Sch. . . } παῖς
ἐκ παιδιόθεν, B. C. Ln. Tdf. (Mar. 9. 21) }
παιδίοις, dat. pl. . . . . . . παιδίον
παιδίον], ου, τό, (§ 3. tab. C. c) . . . παῖς
παιδίου, gen. sing. . . . . . παιδίον
παιδίσκας, acc. pl. . . . . . . παιδίσκη
παιδίσκη], ης, ἡ, (§ 2. tab. B. a) . . παῖς
παιδίσκην, acc. sing. . . . . . παιδίσκη
παιδίσκης, gen. sing. . . . . . id.
παιδισκῶν, gen. pl. . . . . . . id.
παιδίων, gen. pl. . . . . . παιδίον
παιδός, gen. sing. . . . . παῖς
παίδων, gen. pl. . . . . . id.
παίζειν,[c] pres. infin. . . . . . παίζω
παίζω], fut. παίξομαι, (§ 26. rem. 2) . παῖς

παῖς], παιδός, ὁ, ἡ, (§ 4. rem. 2. c) *a child* in relation to parents, of either sex, Jno. 4. 51, et al.; *a child* in respect of age, either male or female, and of all ages from infancy up to manhood, *a boy, youth, girl, maiden*, Mat. 2. 16; 17. 18; Lu. 2. 43; 8. 54; *a servant, slave*, Mat. 8. 6, 8, 13, cf. v. 9; Lu. 7. 7, cf. v. 3. 10; *an attendant, minister*, Mat. 14. 2; Lu. 1. 69; Ac. 4. 25; also, Lu. 1. 54; or, perhaps, *a child* in respect of fatherly regard.

παιδάριον, ίου, τό, (§ 3. tab. C. c) (dimin. of παῖς) *a little boy, child; a boy, lad*, Mat. 11. 16; Jno. 6. 9.

παιδεία, ας, ἡ, (§ 2. tab. B. b, and rem. 2) (παιδεύω) *education, training up, nurture* of children, Ep. 6. 4; *instruction, discipline*, 2 Ti. 3. 16; in N.T. *correction, chastisement*, He. 12. 5, 7, 8, 11.

παιδευτής, οῦ, ὁ, (§ 2. tab. B. c) *a preceptor, instructor, teacher*, pr. of boys; genr. Ro. 2. 20; in N.T. *a chastiser*, He. 12. 9.

παιδεύω, fut. εύσω, (§ 13. tab. M)

[a] Ac. 26. 23. [b] Mar. 9. 21. [c] 1 Co. 10. 7.

aor. 1, ἐπαίδευσα, *to educate, instruct* children, Ac. 7. 22; 22. 3; genr. παιδεύομαι, *to be taught, learn*, 1 Ti. 1. 20; *to admonish, instruct by admonition*, 2 Ti. 2. 25; Tit. 2. 12; in N.T. *to chastise, chasten*, 1 Co. 11. 32; 2 Co. 6. 9; He. 12. 6, 7, 10; Re. 3. 19; of criminals, *to scourge*, Lu. 23. 16, 22.

παιδιόθεν, adv. *from childhood, from a child*, Mar. 9. 21. N.T.

παιδίον, ου, τό, (§ 2. tab. C. c) (dimin. of παῖς) *an infant, babe*, Mat. 2. 8, et al.; but usually in N.T. as equiv. to παῖς, Mat. 14. 21; Mar. 7. 28, et al. freq.; pl. voc. used by way of endearment, *my dear children*, 1 Jno. 2. 18, et al.; also as a term of familiar address, *children, my lads*, Jno. 21. 5.

παιδίσκη, ης, ἡ, (§ 2. tab. B. a) (fem. dimin. of παῖς) *a girl, damsel, maiden; a female slave or servant*, Mat. 26. 69; Mar. 14. 66, 69, et al.

παίζω, fut. παίξομαι, (§ 26. rem. 2) *to play in the manner of children; to sport, to practise the festive gestures* of idolatrous worship, 1 Co. 10. 7.

παίσας, nom. sing. masc. part. aor. 1 . . . παίω

παίσῃ, 3 pers. sing. aor. 1, subj. . . . id.

παισί, dat. pl. (§ 4. rem. 3. b) . . . παῖς

παίω], fut. παίσω, perf. πέπαικα, aor. 1, ἔπαισα, (§ 13. tab. M) *to strike, smite*, with the fist, Mat. 26. 68; Lu. 22. 64; with a sword, Mar. 14. 47; Jno. 18. 10; *to strike* as a scorpion, *to sting*, Re. 9. 5.

πάλαι], adv. *of old, long ago*, Mat. 11. 21; Lu. 10. 13; He. 1. 1; Jude 4; οἱ πάλαι, *old, former*, 2 Pe. 1. 9; *some time since, already*, Mar. 15. 44.

παλαιός, ά, όν, (§ 7. rem. 1) *old, not new or recent*, Mat. 9. 16, 17; 13. 52; Lu. 5. 36, et al.

παλαιότης, τητος, ἡ, (§ 4. rem. 2. c) *oldness, antiquatedness, obsoleteness*, Ro 7. 6.

παλαιόω, ῶ, fut. ώσω, perf. πεπαλαίωκα, (§ 20. tab. T) *to make old*; pass. *to grow old, to become worn or effete*, Lu. 12. 33; He. 1. 11; met. *to treat as antiquated, to abrogate, supersede*, He. 8. 13.

παλαιά, nom. sing. fem. and acc. pl. neut. . παλαιός

παλαιᾷ, dat. sing. fem. . . . id.

παλαιάν, acc. sing. fem. . . . . id.

παλαιᾶς, gen. sing. fem. . . . id.

παλαιόν, acc. sing. masc. and neut. . . id.

παλαιός], ά, όν, (§ 7. rem. 1) . . πάλαι

παλαιότης], τητος, ἡ, (§ 4. rem. 2. c) . . id.

παλαιότητι,[a] dat. sing. . . . . παλαιότης

παλαιοῦ, gen. sing. neut. . . . . παλαιός

παλαιούμενα, acc. pl. neut. part. pres. pass. παλαιόω

παλαιούμενον, nom. sing. neut. part. pres. pass. (§ 21. tab. U) . . . id.

παλαιούς, acc. pl. masc. . . . . παλαιός

παλαιόω, ῶ], fut. ώσω, (§ 20. tab. T) . πάλαι

παλαιῷ, dat. sing. neut. . . . . παλαιός

παλαιωθήσονται, 3 pers. pl. fut. pass. . παλαιόω

πάλη],[b] ης, ἡ, (§ 2. tab. B. a) (πάλλω, *to swing round, sway backward and forward*) *wrestling; struggle, contest*, Ep. 6. 12.

παλιγγενεσία], ας, ἡ, (§ 2. tab. B. b, and rem. 2) (πάλιν & γένεσις) *a new birth; regeneration, renovation*, Mat. 19. 28; Tit. 3. 5. L.G.

παλιγγενεσίᾳ, dat. sing. . . παλιγγενεσία

παλιγγενεσίας, gen. sing. . . id.

πάλιν], adv. pr. *back; again, back again*, Jno. 10. 17; Ac. 10. 16; 11. 10, et al.; *again* by repetition, Mat. 26. 43, et al.; *again* in continuation, *further*, Mat. 5. 33; 13. 44, 45, 47; 18. 19; *again, on the other hand*, 1 Jno. 2. 8, et al.

παμπληθεί],[c] adv. (πᾶς & πλῆθος) *the whole multitude together, all at once*.

παμπόλλου,[d] gen. sing masc.—Rec. Gr. Sch. } πάμπολυς
πάλιν πολλοῦ, B. D. Ln. Tdf. (Mar. 8. 1) }

πάμπολυς], παμπόλλη, πάμπολυ, (§ 7. rem. 8. a) (πᾶς & πολύς) *very many, very great, vast*

Παμφυλία], ας, ἡ, (§ 2. tab. B. b, and rem. 2) *Pamphylia*, a country of Asia Minor.

Παμφυλίαν, acc. . . . . . Παμφυλία

Παμφυλίας, gen. . . . . . id.

πᾶν, nom. and acc. sing. neut. . . πᾶς

πανδοχεῖ,[e] dat. sing. . . . . πανδοχεύς

πανδοχεῖον],[f] ου, τό, (§ 3. tab. C. c) . id.

πανδοχεύς], έως, ὁ, (§ 5. tab. E. d) (a later form

[a] Ro. 7. 6. [b] Ep. 6. 12. [c] Lu. 23. 18. [d] Mar. 8. 1. [e] Lu. 10. 35. [f] Lu. 10. 34.

for πανδοκεύς, πᾶς & δέχομαι) *the keeper of a public inn or caravanserai, a host.*

πανδοχεῖον, ου, τό, *a public inn, place where travellers may lodge,* called in the East by the name of *menzil, khan, caravanserai.*

πανηγύρει,[a] dat. sing. . . . . . πανήγυρις

πανήγυρις], εως, ἡ, (§ 5. tab. E. c) (πᾶς & ἄγυρις, *an assembly*) pr. *an assembly of an entire people; a solemn gathering at a festival; a festive convocation,* He. 12. 23.

πανοικί],[b] adv. (πᾶς & οἶκος) *with one's whole household or family.*

πανοπλία], ας, ἡ, (§ 2. tab. B. b, and rem. 2) (πᾶς & ὅπλον) *panoply, complete armour, a complete suit of armour,* both offensive and defensive, as the shield, sword, spear, helmet, breastplate, etc., Lu. 11. 22; Ep. 6. 11, 13.

πανοπλίαν, acc. sing. . . . . . πανοπλία

πανουργία], ας, ἡ, (§ 2. tab. B. b, and rem. 2) πανοῦργος

πανουργίᾳ, dat. sing. . . . . πανουργία

πανουργίαν, acc. sing. . . . . . id.

πανοῦργος],[c] ου, ὁ, ἡ, (§ 7. rem. 2) (πᾶς & ἔργον) pr. *ready to do anything;* hence, *crafty, cunning, artful, wily.*

πανουργία, ας, ἡ, *knavery, craft, cunning,* Lu. 20. 23; 1 Co. 3. 19, et al.

πάντα, acc. sing. masc. and nom. and acc. pl. neut. πᾶς

πάντας, acc. pl. masc. . . . . . id.

πανταχῇ], adv.—Al. Ln. Tdf. . . . } id.
πανταχοῦ, Rec. Gr. Sch. (Ac. 21. 28) }

πανταχόθεν], adv. . . . . . id.

πανταχοῦ], adv. . . . . . . id.

παντελές, acc. sing. neut. . . . . παντελής

παντελής], έος, ὁ, ἡ, (§ 7. tab. G. b) (πᾶς & τέλος) *perfect, complete;* εἰς τὸ παντελές, adverbially, *throughout, through all time, ever,* He. 7. 25; with a negative, *at all,* Lu. 13. 11.

πάντες, nom. pl. masc. . . . . πᾶς

πάντῃ],[d] adv. . . . . . . id.

παντί, dat. sing. masc. and neut. . . . id.

πάντοθεν], adv. . . . . . . id.

παντοκράτορος, gen. sing. . . . παντοκράτωρ

παντοκράτωρ], ορος, ὁ, (§ 4. rem. 2. f) (πᾶς & κράτος) *almighty, omnipotent,* 2 Co. 6. 18; Re. 1. 8; 4. 8, et al. (ᾰ). L.G.

παντός, gen. sing. masc. and neut. . . . πᾶς

πάντοτε], adv. . . . . . . id.

πάντων, gen. pl. masc. and neut. . . . id.

πάντως], adv. . . . . . . id.

παρ' by apostrophe for παρά.

παρά], prep., with a genitive, *from,* indicating source or origin, Mat. 2. 4, 7; Mar. 8. 11; Lu. 2. 1, et al.; οἱ παρ' αὐτοῦ, *his relatives or kinsmen,* Mar. 3. 21; τὰ παρ' αὐτῆς πάντα, *all her substance, property,* etc., Mar. 5. 26; with a dative, *with, by, nigh to, in, among,* etc., Mat. 6. 1; 19. 26; 21. 25; 22. 25; παρ' ἑαυτῷ, *at home,* 1 Co. 16. 2; *in the sight of, in the judgment or estimation of,* 1 Co. 3. 19; 2 Pe. 2. 11; 3. 8; with an accusative, motion, *by, near to, along,* Mat. 4. 18; motion, *towards, to, at,* Mat. 15. 30; Mar. 2. 13; motion terminating in rest, *at, by, near, by the side of,* Mar. 4. 1, 4; Lu. 5. 1; 8. 5; *in deviation from, in violation of, inconsistently with,* Ac. 18. 13; Ro. 1. 26; 11. 24; *above, more than,* Lu. 13. 2, 4; Ro. 1. 25; after comparatives, Lu. 3. 13; 1 Co. 3. 11; *except, save,* 2 Co. 11. 24; *beyond, past,* He. 11. 11; *in respect of, on the score of,* 1 Co. 12. 15, 16.

παραβαίνετε, 2 pers. pl. pres. ind. . . . παραβαίνω

παραβαίνουσι, 3 pers. pl. pres. ind. . . . id.

παραβαίνω], fut. βήσομαι, aor. 2, παρέβην, (§ 37. rem. 1) (παρά & βαίνω) pr. *to step by the side of; to deviate;* met. *to transgress, violate,* Mat. 15. 2, 3; 2 Jno. 9; *to incur forfeiture,* Ac. 1. 25.

παράβᾰσις, εως, ἡ, (§ 5. tab. E. c) *a stepping by the side, deviation; a transgression, violation of law,* Ro. 2. 23; 4. 15, et al.

παραβάτης, ου, ὁ, (§ 2. tab. B. c) *a transgressor, violator of law,* Ro. 2. 25, 27; Gal. 2. 18; Ja. 2. 9, 11. (ᾰ).

παραβαίνων, nom. sing. masc. part. pres. . παραβαίνω

παραβάλλω], fut. βαλῶ, (§ 27. rem. 1. b) (παρά & βάλλω) *to cast or throw by the side of;* met. *to compare,* Mar. 4. 30; absol., a nautical term, *to bring-to, land,* Ac. 20. 15.

παραβολή, ῆς, ἡ, (§ 2. tab. B. a) a

[a] He. 12. 23. [b] Ac. 16. 34. [c] 2 Co. 12. 16. [d] Ac. 24. 3.

placing one thing by the side of another; a comparing; a parallel case cited in illustration; a comparison, simile, similitude, Mar. 4. 30; He. 11. 19; *a parable,* a short relation under which something else is figured, or in which that which is fictitious is employed to represent that which is real, Mat. 13. 3, 10, 13, 18, 24, 31, 33, 34, 36, 53; 21. 33, 45; 22. 1; 24. 32, et al.; in N.T. *a type, pattern, emblem,* He. 9. 9; *a sentiment, grave and sententious precept, maxim,* Lu. 14. 7; *an obscure and enigmatical saying, anything expressed in remote and ambiguous terms,* Mat. 13. 35; Mar. 7. 17; *a proverb, adage,* Lu. 4. 23.

παραβάλωμεν, 1 pers. pl. aor. 2, subj. . παραβάλλω

παραβάσει, dat. sing. . . . . παράβασις

παραβάσεων, gen. pl. . . . . id.

παραβασέως, gen. sing. . . . id.

παράβασις], εως, ἡ, (§ 5. tab. E. c) . παραβαίνω

παραβάται, nom. pl. . . . παραβάτης

παραβάτην, acc. sing. . . . . id.

παραβάτης], ου, ὁ, (§ 2. tab. B. c) . . παραβαίνω

παραβιάζομαι], fut. άσομαι, (§ 26. rem. 1) (παρά & βιάζω) *to force; to constrain, press* with urgent entreaties, Lu. 24. 29; Ac. 16. 15. L.G.

παραβολαῖς, dat. pl. . . . . παραβολή

παραβολάς, acc. pl. . . . . id.

παραβολεύομαι], fut. εύσομαι, (παράβολος, *risking, venturesome*) *to stake or risk one's self,* v.r. Phi. 2. 30. N.T.

παραβολευσάμενος, nom. sing. masc. part. aor. 1.—Gr. Sch. Tdf. παραβουλευσάμενος, R. (Phi. 2. 30) } παραβολεύομαι

παραβολή], ῆς, ἡ, (§ 2. tab. B. a) . παραβάλλω

παραβολῇ, dat. sing. . . . . παραβολή

παραβολήν, acc. sing. . . . . id.

παραβολῆς, gen. sing. . . . . id.

παραβουλεύομαι], fut. ευσομαι, (§ 15. tab. O) παρά & βουλεύω) *to be reckless, regardless,* Phi. 2. 30. N.T.

παραβουλευσάμενος,[a] nom. sing. masc. part. aor. 1 . . . . παραβουλεύομαι

παραγ, είλαντες, nom. pl. masc. part. aor. 1, (§ 27. rem. 1. d) . . παραγγέλλω

παραγγείλα, nom. sing. masc. part. aor. 1 id.

παραγγείλῃς, 2 pers. sing. aor. 1, subj. παραγγέλλω

παραγγελία], ας, ἡ, (§ 2. tab. B. b, and rem. 2) id.

παραγγελίᾳ, dat. sing. . . . παραγγελία

παραγγελίαν, acc. sing. . . . . id.

παραγγελίας, gen. sing. and acc. pl. . id.

παράγγελλε, 2 pers. sing. pres. imper. . παραγγέλλω

παραγγέλλει, 3 pers. sing. pres. ind. . id.

παραγγέλλειν, pres. infin. . . . id.

παραγγέλλομεν, 1 pers. pl. pres. ind. . id

παραγγέλλω], fut. ελῶ, (§ 27. rem. 1. b) (παρά & ἀγγέλλω) *to announce, notify; to command, direct, charge,* Mat. 10. 5; Mar. 6. 8; 8. 6; Lu. 9. 21, et al.; *to charge, obtest, entreat solemnly,* 1 Ti. 6. 13.

παραγγελία, ας, ἡ, (§ 2. tab. B. b, and rem. 2) *a command, order, charge,* Ac. 5. 28; *direction, precept,* 1 Thes. 4. 2, et al.

παραγγέλλων, nom. sing. masc. part. pres. παραγγέλλω

παράγει, 3 pers. sing. pres. ind. . . . παράγω

παραγενόμενοι, nom. pl. masc. part. aor. 2, (§ 37. rem. 1) . . . παραγίνομαι

παραγενόμενον, acc. sing. masc. part. aor. 2 . id.

παραγενόμενος, nom. sing. masc. part. aor. 2 id.

παραγενομένου, gen. sing. masc. part. aor. 2 id.

παραγενομένους, acc. pl. masc. part. aor. 2 id.

παραγένωμαι, 1 pers. sing. aor. 2, subj. . id.

παραγένωνται, 3 pers. pl. aor. 2, subj. . id.

παράγεται, 3 pers. sing. pres. ind. pass. . παράγω

παραγίνεται, 3 pers. sing. pres. ind. . παραγίνομαι

παραγίνομαι], fut. γενήσομαι, aor. 2, παρεγενόμην, (§ 37. rem. 1) (παρά & γίνομαι) *to be by the side of; to come, approach, arrive,* Mat. 2. 1; 3. 13; Mar. 14. 43; Lu. 7. 4, et al.; seq. ἐπί, *to come upon* in order to seize, Lu. 22. 52; *to come forth in public, make appearance,* Mat. 3. 1; He. 9. 11.

παράγοντα, acc. sing. masc. part. pres. . παράγω

παράγοντι, dat. sing. masc. part. pres. . id.

παράγω], fut. άξω, (§ 23. rem. 1. b) (παρά & ἄγω) *to lead beside;* intrans. *to pass along or by,* Mat. 20. 30; Jno. 9. 1; *to pass on,* Mat. 9. 9, 27; intrans. and mid. *to pass away, be in a state of transition,* 1 Co. 7. 31; 1 Jno. 2. 8, 17. (ᾰ).

παράγων, nom. sing. masc. part. pres. . . παράγω

παραδεδομένοι, nom. pl. masc. part. perf. pass. παραδίδωμι

[a] Phi. 2. 30.

παραδέδοται, 3 pers. sing. perf. pass. (§ 30. rem. 4) . . . . παραδίδωμι

παραδεδώκεισαν, 3 pers. pl. pluperf. act. (§ 13. rem. 8. f) . . . . id.

παραδεδωκόσι, dat. pl. masc. part. perf. act. (§ 30. tab. Z) . . . . id.

παραδειγματιζόντας, acc. pl. masc. part. pres. act. . . . . παραδειγματίζω

παραδειγματίζω], fut. ίσω, (§ 26. rem. 1) (παράδειγμα, *an example*) *to make an example of; to expose to ignominy and shame*, Mat. 1. 19; He. 6. 6. L.G.

παραδειγματίσαι, aor. 1, infin. act. . παραδειγματίζω

παράδεισον, acc. sing. . . . . παράδεισος

παράδεισος], ου, ὁ, (§ 3. tab. C. a) (*of Oriental origin*; in the Heb. פַּרְדֵּס) *a park, a forest where wild beasts were kept for hunting; a pleasure-park, a garden of trees of various kinds*; used in the LXX. for *the Garden of Eden*; in N.T. the celestial *paradise*, Lu. 23. 43; 2 Co. 12. 4; Re. 2. 7.

παραδείσῳ, dat. sing. . . . . παράδεισος

παραδέξονται, 3 pers. pl. fut. ind. . . παραδέχομαι

παραδέχεσθαι, pres. infin. . . . . id.

παραδέχεται, 3 pers. sing. pres. ind. . id.

παραδέχομαι], fut. ξομαι, (§ 23. rem. 1. b) (παρά & δέχομαι) *to accept, receive*; met. *to receive, admit, yield assent to*, Mar. 4. 20; Ac. 16. 21; 22. 18; 1 Ti. 5. 19; in N.T. *to receive or embrace with favour, approve, love*, He. 12. 6.

παραδέχονται, 3 pers. pl. pres. ind. . παραδέχομαι

παραδέχου, 2 pers. sing. pres. imper. . id.

παραδιατριβαί,[a] nom. pl. . . . παραδιατριβή

παραδιατρῐβή], ῆς, ἡ, (§ 2. tab. B. a) (παρά & διατριβή, *waste of time, delay*) *useless disputation*.

παραδιδοῖ, 3 pers. sing. pres. subj.—Ln. Tdf. (§ 30. rem. 5) . . . } παραδίδωμι
παραδῷ, Rec. Gr. Sch. (1 Co. 15. 24) }

παραδιδόμεθα, 1 pers. pl. pres. ind. pass. (§ 30 tab. A. A) . . . . id.

παραδιδόναι, pres. infin. act. . . . id.

παραδιδόντα, acc. sing. masc. part. pres. act. id.

παραδιδόντες, nom. pl. masc. part. pres. act. id.

παραδιδόντος, gen. sing. masc. part. pres. act. id.

παραδίδοσθαι, pres. infin. pass. . . id.

παραδίδοται, 3 pers. sing. pres. ind. pass. . παραδίδωμι

παραδιδούς, nom. sing. masc. part. pres. act. id.

παραδιδῷ, 3 pers. sing. pres. subj.—A. B. D. } id.
παραδῷ, Rec. Gr. Sch. (1 Co. 15. 24) }

παραδίδωμι], fut. δώσω, (§ 30. tab. Z) (παρά & δίδωμι) *to give over, hand over, deliver up*, Mat. 4. 12; 5. 25; 10. 4, 17, et al.; *to commit, intrust*, Mat. 11. 27; 25. 14, et al.; *to commit, commend*, Ac. 14. 26; 15. 40; *to yield up*, Jno. 19. 30; 1 Co. 15. 24; *to abandon*, Ac. 7. 42; Ep. 4. 19, *to stake, hazard*, Ac. 15. 26; *to deliver* as a matter of injunction, instruction, etc., Mar. 7. 13; Lu. 1. 2; Ac. 6. 14, et al.; absol. *to render a yield, to be matured*, Mar. 4. 29.

παράδοσις, εως, ἡ, (§ 5. tab. E. c) *delivery, handing over, transmission*; in N.T. *what is transmitted* in the way of teaching, *precept, doctrine*, 1 Co. 11. 2; 2 Thes. 2. 15; 3. 6; *tradition, traditionary law*, handed down from age to age, Mat. 15, 2, 3, 6, et al.

παραδίδως, 2 pers. sing. pres. ind. act. . παραδίδωμι

παραδιδῶσι, 3 pers. pl. pres. subj. act. . . id.

παραδοθείς, nom. sing. masc. part. aor. 1, pass. (§ 30. rem. 4) . . . id

παραδοθείσῃ, dat. sing. fem. part. aor. 1, pass. id.

παραδοθείσης, gen. sing. fem. part. aor. 1, pass. id.

παραδοθῆναι, aor. 1, infin. pass. . . . id.

παραδοθήσεσθε, 2 pers. pl. fut. ind. pass. . id.

παραδοθήσεται, 3 pers. sing. fut. ind. pass. . id.

παραδοθῶ, 1 pers. sing. aor. 1, subj. pass. . id

παραδοῖ, 3 pers. sing. aor. 2, subj. (§ 30. rem. 5).—B. D. Ln. Tdf. . } id
παραδῷ, Rec. Gr. Sch. (Mar. 4. 29) . }

παραδόντος, gen. sing. masc. part. aor. 2, act. id.

παράδοξα,[b] acc. pl. neut. . . . παράδοξος

παράδοξος], ου, ὁ, ἡ, (§ 7. rem. 2) (παρὰ δόξαν, *beside expectation*) *unexpected; strange, wonderful, astonishing*, Lu. 5. 26.

παραδόσει, dat. sing. . . . . παράδοσις

παραδόσεις, acc. pl. . . . . id.

παραδόσεων, gen. pl. . . . . id.

παράδοσιν, acc. sing. . . . id.

παράδοσις], εως, ἡ, (§ 5. tab. E. c) . παραδίδωμι

παραδοῦναι, aor. 2, infin. act. (§ 30. rem. 1) id.

παραδούς, nom. sing. masc. part. aor. 2, act. id.

[a] 1 Ti. 6. 5.

[b] Lu. 5. 26.

παραδῶ, 1 pers. sing. aor. 2, subj. act. . παραδίδωμι
παραδῷ, 3 pers. sing. aor. 2, subj. act. . . id.
παραδώσει, 3 pers. sing. fut. ind. act. . id.
παραδῶσι, 3 p. pl. aor. 2, subj. act.—B. Ln. Tdf. παραδιδῶσι, Rec. Gr. Sch. (Mat. 10. 19) } id.
παραδώσουσι, 3 pers. pl. fut. ind. act. . . id.
παραδώσω, 1 pers. sing. fut. ind. act. . id.
παραδώσων, nom. sing. masc. part. fut. act. . id.
παραζηλοῦμεν, 1 pers. pl. pres. ind. . παραζηλόω
παραζηλόω, ῶ], fut. ώσω, (§ 20. tab. T) (παρά & ζηλόω) *to provoke to jealousy,* Ro. 10. 19; *to excite to emulation,* Ro. 11. 11, 14; *to provoke to indignation,* 1 Co. 10. 22. LXX.
παραζηλῶσαι, aor. 1, infin. . . . παραζηλόω
παραζηλώσω, 1 pers. sing. fut. ind. . . id.
παραζηλώσω, 1 pers. sing. aor. 1, subj. . id.
παραθαλασσίαν,[a] acc. sing. fem. . παραθαλάσσιος
παραθαλάσσιος], ία, ιον, (§ 7. rem. 1) (παρά & θάλασσα) *by the sea-side, situated on the sea-coast, maritime.*
παραθεῖναι, aor. 2, infin. act. (§ 28. tab. V) παρατίθημι
παραθεωρέω, ῶ], fut. ήσω, (§ 16. tab. P) (παρά & θεωρέω) *to look at things placed side by side,* as in comparison, *to compare in thus looking, to regard less in comparison, overlook, neglect,* Ac. 6. 1.
παραθήκη], ης, ἡ, (§ 2. tab. B. a) . . παρατίθημι
παραθήκην, acc. sing. . . . . . παραθήκη
παραθήσομαι, 1 pers. sing. fut. ind. mid. (§ 28. tab. W) . . . . παρατίθημι
παραθήσω, 1 pers. sing. fut. ind. act. . id.
παράθου, 2 pers. sing. aor. 2, imper. mid. (§ 28. rem. 8. d) . . . id.
παραθῶσι, 3 pers. pl. aor. 2, subj. act. . id.
παραινέω], ῶ, fut. έσω, (§ 22. rem. 1) (παρά & αἰνέω) *to advise, exhort,* Ac. 27. 9, 22.
παραινῶ, 1 pers. sing. pres. ind. . . . παραινέω
παραιτεῖσθαι, pres. infin. . . . παραιτέομαι
παραιτέομαι], οῦμαι, fut. ήσομαι, (§ 17. tab. Q) (παρά & αἰτέω) *to entreat; to beg off, excuse one's self,* Lu. 14. 18, 19; *to deprecate, entreat against,* Ac. 25. 11; He. 12. 19; *to decline receiving, refuse, reject,* 1 Ti. 4. 7; 5. 11; Tit. 3. 10; He. 12. 25; *to decline, avoid, shun,* 2 Ti. 2. 23.
παραιτησάμενοι, nom. pl. masc. part. aor. 1 παραιτέομαι
παραιτήσησθε, 2 pers. pl. aor. 1, subj. id.
παραιτοῦ, 2 pers. sing. pres. imper. . . id.

παραιτοῦμαι, 1 pers. sing. pres. ind. . παραιτέομαι
παρακαθέζομαι], aor. 1, (pass. form) καθέσθην, (παρά & καθέζομαι) *to sit down by,* v.r. Lu. 10. 39.
παρακαθεσθεῖσα, nom. sing. fem. part. aor. 1.—A. B. C. Tdf. . παρακαθίσασα, Rec. Gr. Sch. (Lu. 10. 39) . . . } παρακαθέζομαι
παρακαθίζω], fut. ίσω, (§ 26. rem. 1) (παρά & καθίζω) *to set beside;* intrans. *to sit by the side of, sit near,* Lu. 10. 39.
παρακαθίσασα,[b] nom. sing. fem. part. aor. 1 παρακαθίζω
παρακάλει, 2 pers. sing. pres. imper. act. . παρακαλέω
παρακαλεῖν, pres. infin. act. . . . id.
παρακαλεῖσθε, 2 pers. pl. pres. imper. pass. id
παρακαλεῖται, 3 pers. sing. pres. ind. pass. . id.
παρακαλεῖτε, 2 pers. pl. pres. imper. act. . id.
παρακαλέσαι, aor. 1, infin. act. . . . id.
παρακαλέσαι, 3 pers. sing. aor. 1, optat. act. id.
παρακαλέσας, nom. sing. masc. part. aor. 1, act. id.
παρακαλέσῃ, 3 pers. sing. aor. 1, subj. act. id.
παρακάλεσον, 2 pers. sing. aor. 1, imper. act. id.
παρακᾰλέω], ῶ, fut. έσω, (§ 22. rem. 1) (παρά & καλέω) *to call for, invite to come, send for,* Ac. 28. 20; *to call upon, exhort, admonish, persuade,* Lu. 3. 18; Ac. 2. 40; 11. 23; *to beg, beseech, entreat, implore,* Mat. 8. 5, 31; 18. 29; Mar. 1. 40; *to animate, encourage, comfort, console,* Mat. 2. 18; 5. 4; 2 Co. 1. 4, 6; pass. *to be cheered, comforted,* Lu. 16. 25; Ac. 20. 12; 2 Co. 7. 13, et al.

παράκλησις, εως, ἡ, (§ 5. tab. E. c) *a calling upon, exhortation, incitement, persuasion,* Ro. 12. 8; 1 Co. 14. 3; *hortatory instruction,* Ac. 13. 15; 15. 31; *entreaty, importunity, earnest supplication,* 2 Co. 8. 4; *solace, consolation,* Lu. 2. 25; Ro. 15. 4, 5; 2 Co. 1. 3, 4, 5, 6, 7; *cheering and supporting influence,* Ac. 9. 31; *joy, gladness, rejoicing,* 2 Co. 7. 13; *cheer, joy, enjoyment,* Lu. 6. 24.

παράκλητος, ου, ὁ, (§ 3. tab. C. a) *one called or sent for to assist another; an advocate, one who pleads the cause of another,* 1 Jno. 2. 1; genr. *one present to render various beneficial service,* and thus *the Paraclete,* whose influence and opera-

[a] Mat. 4. 13.
[b] Lu. 10. 39.

tion were to compensate for the departure of Christ himself, Jno. 14. 16, 26; 15. 26; 16. 7.

παρακαλούμεθα, 1 pers. pl. pres. ind. pass. παρακαλέω
παρακαλοῦμεν, 1 pers. pl. pres. ind. act. id.
παρακαλοῦντες, nom. pl. masc. part. pres. act. id.
παρακαλοῦντος, gen. sing. masc. part. pres. act. id.
παρακαλοῦσι, 3 pers. pl. pres. ind. act. id.

παρακαλύπτω], fut. ψω, (§ 23. rem. 1. a) (παρά & καλύπτω) *to cover over, veil;* met. pass. *to be veiled* from comprehension, Lu. 9. 45.

παρακαλῶ, 1 pers. sing. pres. ind. παρακαλέω
παρακαλῶν, nom. sing. masc. part. pres. act. id.
παρακαλῶνται, 3 pers. pl. pres. subj. pass. id.

παρακαταθήκη], ης, ἡ, (§ 2. tab. B. a) (παρακατατίθημι, *to lay down by, deposit*) *a deposit, a thing committed to one's charge, a trust,* 1 Ti. 6. 20; 2 Ti. 1. 14.

παρακαταθήκην, acc. sing. παρακαταθήκη

παράκειμαι], (§ 33. tab. D.D) (παρά & κεῖμαι) *to lie near, be adjacent;* met. *to be at hand, be present,* Ro. 7. 18, 21.

παράκειται, 3 pers. sing. pres. ind. παράκειμαι
παρακεκαλυμμένον,[a] nom. sing. neut. part. perf. pass. παρακαλύπτω
παρακεκλήμεθα, 1 pers. pl. perf. ind. pass. (§ 22. rem. 4) παρακαλέω
παρακεχειμακότι, dat. sing. masc. part. perf. παραχειμάζω
παρακληθῆναι, aor. 1, infin. pass. παρακαλέω
παρακληθήσονται, 3 pers. pl. fut. ind. pass. id.
παρακληθῶσι, 3 pers. pl. aor. 1, subj. pass. id.
παρακλήσει, dat. sing. παράκλησις
παρακλήσεως, gen. sing. id.
παράκλησιν, acc. sing. id.
παράκλησις], εως, ἡ, (§ 5. tab. E. c) παρακαλέω
παράκλητον, acc. sing. παράκλητος
παράκλητος], ου, ὁ, (§ 3. tab. C. a) παρακαλέω
παρακοή], ῆς, ἡ, (§ 2. tab. B. a) παρακούω
παρακοήν, acc. sing. παρακοή
παρακοῆς, gen. sing. id.

παρακολουθέω, ῶ], fut. ήσω, (§ 11. tab. P.) (παρά & ἀκολουθέω) *to follow or accompany closely; to accompany, attend, characterise,* Mar. 16. 17; *to follow* with the thoughts, *trace,* Lu. 1. 3; *to conform to,* 1 Ti. 4. 6; 2 Ti. 3. 10.

παρακολουθήσει, 3 pers. sing. fut. ind. παρακολουθέω
παρακούσῃ, 3 pers. sing. aor. 1, subj. παρακούω

παρακούω], fut. ούσομαι, (παρά & ἀκούω) *to hear amiss, to fail to listen, neglect to obey, disregard,* Mat. 18. 17, bis.

παρακοή, ῆς, ἡ, (§ 2. tab. B. a) *an erroneous or imperfect hearing; disobedience,* Ro. 5. 19; *a deviation from obedience,* 2 Co. 10. 6; He. 2. 2.

παρακύπτω], fut. ψω, (§ 23. rem. 1. a) (παρά & κύπτω) *to stoop beside; to stoop down* in order to take a view, Lu. 24. 12; Jno. 20. 5, 11; *to bestow a close and attentive look, to look intently, to penetrate,* Ja. 1. 25; 1 Pe. 1. 12.

παρακύψαι, aor. 1, infin. παρακύπτω
παρακύψας, nom. sing. masc. part. aor. 1 id.
παράλαβε, 2 pers. sing. aor. 2, imper. παραλαμβάνω
παραλαβεῖν, aor. 2, infin. act. id.
παραλαβόντα, acc. sing. masc. part. aor. 2, act. id.
παραλαβόντες, nom. pl. masc. part. aor. 2, act. id.
παραλαβών, nom. sing. masc. part. aor. 2, act. id.
παραλαμβάνει, 3 pers. sing. pres. ind. act. id.
παραλαμβάνεται, 3 pers. sing. pres. ind. pass. id.
παραλαμβάνοντες, nom. pl. masc. part. pres. act. id.
παραλαμβάνουσι, 3 pers. pl. pres. ind. act. id.

παραλαμβάνω], fut. λήψομαι, (§ 36. rem. 2) aor. 2, παρέλᾰβον, (παρά & λαμβάνω) pr. *to take to one's side; to take, receive to one's self,* Mat. 1. 20; Jno. 14. 3; *to take* with one's self, Mat. 2. 13, 14, 20, 21; 4. 5, 8; *to receive* in charge or possession, Col. 4. 17; He. 12. 28; *to receive* as a matter of instruction, Mar. 7. 4; 1 Co. 11. 23; 15. 3; *to receive, admit, acknowledge,* Jno. 1. 11; 1 Co. 15. 1; Col. 2. 6; pass. *to be carried off,* Mat. 24. 40, 41; Lu. 17. 34, 35, 36.

παραλέγομαι], (παρά & λέγω, *to gather*) *to gather* a course *along; to sail by, coast along,* Ac. 27. 8, 13.

παραλεγόμενοι, nom. pl. masc. part. pres. παραλέγομαι
παραλελυμένα, acc. pl. neut. part. perf. pass. παραλύω
παραλελυμένοι, nom. pl. masc. part. perf. pass. id.
παραλελυμένῳ, dat. sing. masc. part. perf. pass. id.
παραληφθήσεται, 3 pers. sing. fut. ind. pass. (§ 36. rem. 2) παραλαμβάνω
παραλήψομαι, 1 pers. sing. fut. ind. id.

παράλιος], ίου, ὁ, ἡ, (§ 7. rem. 2) (παρά & ἅλς) *adjacent to the sea, maritime;* ἡ παράλιος, sc. χώρα, *the sea-coast,* Lu. 6. 17.

παραλίου,[b] gen. sing. fem. παράλιος

[a] Lu. 9. 45. [b] Lu. 6. 17.

παραλλᾰγή], [a] ῆς, ἡ, (§ 2. tab. B. a) (παραλλάσσω, *to interchange*) *a shifting, mutation, change.*
παραλογίζηται, 3 pers. sing. pres. subj. παραλογίζομαι
παραλογίζομαι], fut. ίσομαι, (§ 26. rem. 1) (παρά & λογίζομαι) *to misreckon, make a false reckoning; to impose upon, deceive, delude, circumvent*, Col. 2. 4; Ja. 1. 22.
παραλογιζόμενοι, nom. pl. masc. part. pres. παραλογίζομαι
παραλυτικόν, acc. sing. masc. . . . παραλυτικός
παραλυτικός], ή, όν . . . . . παραλύω
παραλυτικούς, acc. pl. masc. . . . παραλυτικός
παραλυτικῷ, dat. sing. masc. . . . . id.
παραλύω], fut. ύσω, (§ 13. tab. M) (παρά & λύω) *to unloose from proper fixity or consistency of substance; to enervate or paralyse* the body or limbs; pass. *to be enervated or enfeebled*, He. 12. 12; pass. perf. part. παραλελυμένος, *paralytic*, Lu. 5. 18, 24, et al.

παραλυτῐκός, ή, όν, (§ 7. tab. F. a) *paralytic, palsied*, Mat. 4. 24; 8. 6; 9. 2, 6, et al.

παραμείνας, nom. sing. masc. part. aor. 1 παραμένω
παραμένειν, pres. infin. . . . . id.
παραμένω], fut. μενῶ, aor. 1, παρέμεινα, (§ 27. rem. 1. a. d) *to stay beside; to continue, stay, abide*, 1 Co. 16. 6; He. 7. 23; met. *to remain constant in, persevere in*, Ja. 1. 25.
παραμενῶ, 1 pers. sing. fut. ind. . . . παραμένω
παραμυθεῖσθε, 2 pers. pl. pres. imper. παραμυθέομαι
παραμυθέομαι, οῦμαι], fut. ήσομαι, (§ 17. tab. Q) (παρά & μυθέομαι, *to speak*, from μῦθος) *to exercise a gentle influence by words; to soothe, comfort, console*, Jno. 11. 19, 31; 1 Thes. 5. 14; *to cheer, exhort*, 1 Thes. 2. 11.

παραμυθία, ας, ἡ, (§ 2. tab. B. b, and rem. 2) *comfort, encouragement*, 1 Co. 14. 3.

παραμύθιον, ίου, τό, (§ 3. tab. C. c) *gentle cheering, encouragement*, Phi. 2. 1.

παραμυθήσωνται, 3 pers. pl. aor. 1, subj. παραμυθέομαι
παραμυθία], ας, ἡ . . . . . id.
παραμυθίαν, [b] acc. sing. . . . . παραμυθία
παραμύθιον], [c] ίου, τό . . . . παραμυθέομαι
παραμυθούμενοι, nom. pl. masc. part. pres. id.
παρανομέω, ῶ], fut. ήσω, (§ 16. tab. P) (παρά & νόμος) *to violate or transgress the law*, Ac. 23. 3.

παρανομία, ας, ἡ, (§ 2. tab. B. b, and rem. 2) *violation of the law, transgression*, 2 Pe. 2. 16.

παρανομία], ας, ἡ . . . . . παρανομέω
παρανομίας, [d] gen. sing. . . . . παρανομία
παρανομῶν, [e] nom. sing. masc. part. pres. παρανομέω
παραπεσόντας, [f] acc. pl. masc. part. aor. 2, (§ 37. rem. 1) . . . . παραπίπτω
παραπικραίνω], fut. ανῶ, aor. 1, παρεπίκρᾶνα, (§ 27. rem. 1. c. e) (παρά & πικραίνω) pr. *to incite to bitter feelings; to provoke;* absol. *to act provokingly, be refractory*, He. 3. 16. LXX.

παραπικρασμός, οῦ, ὁ, (§ 3. tab. C. a) *exacerbation, exasperation, provocation; contumacy, rebellion*, He. 3. 8, 15. LXX.

παραπικρασμός], οῦ, ὁ . . . . παραπικραίνω
παραπικρασμῷ, dat. sing. . . . παραπικρασμός
παραπίπτω], fut. πεσοῦμαι, aor. 2, παρέπεσον, (§ 37. rem. 1) (παρά & πίπτω) pr. *to fall by the side of;* met. *to fall off or away from, make defection from*, He. 6. 6.

παράπτωμα, ατος, τό, (§ 4. tab. D. c) pr. *a stumbling aside, a false step;* in N.T. *a trespass, fault, offence, transgression*, Mat. 6. 14, 15; Mar. 11. 25, 26; Ro. 4. 25, et al.; *a fall, defalcation* in faith, Ro. 11. 11, 12. L.G.

παραπλεῦσαι, [g] aor. 1, infin. . . . . παραπλέω
παραπλέω], fut. εύσομαι, (§ 35. rem. 1. 3) (παρά & πλέω) *to sail by or past* a place.
παραπλήσιον, [h] adv. . . . . παραπλήσιος
παραπλήσιος] ου, ὁ, ἡ, τό,—ον, (§ 7. rem. 2) (παρά & πλησίος, *near*) pr. *near alongside;* met. *like, similar;* neut. παραπλήσιον, adverbially, *near to, with a near approach to*, Phi. 2. 27.

παραπλησίως, adv. *like, in the same or like manner*, He. 2. 14.

παραπλησίως, [i] adv. . . . . . παραπλήσιος
παραπορεύεσθαι, pres. infin. . . . παραπορεύομαι
παραπορεύομαι], fut. εύσομαι, (§ 14. tab. N) παρά & πορεύομαι) *to pass by the side of; to pass along*, Mat. 27. 39; Mar. 11. 20; 15. 29, et al.
παραπορευόμενοι, nom. pl. masc. part. pres. παραπορεύομαι
παράπτωμα], ατος, τό, (§ 4. tab. D. c) . παραπίπτω
παραπτώμασι, dat. pl. . . . . παράπτωμα

[a] Ja. 1. 17. [b] 1 Co. 14. 3. [c] Phi. 2. 1. [d] 2 Pe. 2. 16. [e] Ac. 23. 3. [f] He. 6. 6. [g] Ac 20. 16. [h] Phi. 2. 27. [i] He. 2. 14.

παραπτώματα, acc. pl. . . . . παράπτωμα
παραπτώματι, dat. sing. . . . id.
παραπτώματος, gen. sing. . . . id.
παραπτωμάτων, gen. pl. . . . id.

παραῤῥέω], fut. ῥεύσομαι, aor. 2, παρεῤῥύην, (§ 36. rem. 1) (παρά & ῥέω) *to flow beside; to glide aside from; to fall off* from profession, *decline* from steadfastness, *make forfeit* of faith, He. 2. 1.

παραῤῥυῶμεν,[a] 1 pers. pl. aor. 2, subj. . παραῤῥέω

παράσημον], ου, τό, (§ 3. tab. C. c) (παρά & σῆμα) *a distinguishing mark*; *an ensign or device* of a ship.

παρασήμῳ,[b] dat. sing. . . . . παράσημον
παρασκευαζόντων, gen. pl. masc. part. pres. παρασκευάζω

παρασκευάζω], fut. άσω, (§ 26. rem. 1) (παρά & σκευάζω, *to equip*) *to prepare, make ready*, 2 Co. 9. 2, 3; mid. *to prepare one's self, put one's self in readiness*, Ac. 10. 10; 1 Co. 14. 8.

παρασκευή, ῆς, ἡ, (§ 2. tab. B. a) *a getting ready, preparation*; in N.T. *preparation* for a feast, *day of preparation*, Mat. 27. 62; Mar. 15. 42, et al.

παρασκευάσεται, 3 pers. sing. fut. mid. . παρασκευάζω
παρασκευή], ῆς, ἡ . . . . . id.
παρασκευήν, acc. sing. . . . . παρασκευή
παρασκευῆς, gen. sing.—B. Ln. Tdf. . } id.
παρασκευή, Rec. Gr. Sch. (Lu. 23. 54) }
παραστῆναι, aor. 2, infin. (§ 29. tab. X) . παρίστημι
παραστῆσαι, aor. 1, infin. . . . id.
παραστήσατε, 2 pers. pl. aor. 1, imper. . id.
παραστήσει, 3 pers. sing. fut. ind. . . id.
παραστήσῃ, 3 pers. sing. aor. 1, subj. . id.
παραστησόμεθα, 1 pers. pl. fut. ind. mid. (§ 29. tab. Y) . . . . id.
παραστήσωμεν, 1 pers. pl. aor. 1, subj. . id.
παραστῆτε, 2 pers. pl. aor. 2, subj. . . id.
παρασχών, nom. sing. masc. part. aor. 2 . παρέχω
παρατεθῆναι, aor. 1, infin. pass.—A. Ln. }
παραθεῖναι, Rec. Gr. Sch. . . } παρατίθημι
παρατιθέναι, Tdf. (Mar. 8. 7) . }

παρατείνω], (παρά & τείνω) *to extend, stretch out; to prolong, continue*, Ac. 20. 7.

παρατηρεῖσθε, 2 pers. pl. pres. mid. . . παρατηρέω

παρατηρέω, ῶ], fut. ήσω, (§ 16. tab. P) (παρά & τηρέω) *to watch narrowly*, Ac. 9. 24; *to observe or watch insidiously*, Mar. 3. 2; Lu. 6. 7; 14. 1; 20. 20; *to observe scrupulously* Gal. 4. 10.

παρατήρησις, εως, ἡ, (§ 5. tab. E. c) *careful watching, intent observation*, Lu. 17. 20. L.G.

παρατηρήσαντες, nom. pl. masc. part. aor. 1 παρατηρέω
παρατηρήσεως,[c] gen. sing. . . . παρατήρησις
παρατήρησις], εως, ἡ . . . . παρατηρέω
παρατηρούμενοι, nom. pl. masc. part. pres. mid. id.
παρατίθεμαι, 1 pers. sing. pres. ind. mid. (§ 28. tab. W) . . . παρατίθημι
παρατιθέμενα, acc. pl. neut. part. pres. pass. . id.
παρατιθέμενον, acc. sing. neut. part. pres. pass. id.
παρατιθέμενος, nom. sing. masc. part. pres. mid. id.
παρατιθέναι, pres. infin. act. . . . id.
παρατιθέσθωσαν, 3 pers. pl. pres. imper. pass. id.

παρατίθημι], fut. παραθήσω, (§ 28. tab. V) παρά & τίθημι) *to place by the side of, or near; to set before*, Mar. 6. 41; 8. 6, 7; Lu. 9. 16; met. *to set or lay before, propound*, Mat. 13. 24, 31; *to inculcate*, Ac. 17. 3; *to deposit, commit to the charge of, intrust*, Lu. 12. 48; 23. 46; *to commend*, Ac. 14. 23.

παραθήκη, ης, ἡ, (§ 2. tab. B. a) *a deposit, a thing committed to one's charge, a trust*, 2 Ti. 1. 12; v.r. 1 Ti. 6. 20; 2 Ti. 1. 14.

παρατιθῶσι, 3 pers. pl. pres. subj.—B. C. Tdf. } παρατίθημι
παραθῶσι, Rec. Gr. Ln. Sch. (Mar. 8. 6) }
παρατυγχάνοντας,[d] acc. pl. masc. part. pres. παρατυγχάνω

παρατυγχάνω], fut. τεύξομαι, aor. 2, παρέτυχον, (§ 36. rem. 2) (παρά & τυγχάνω) *to happen, to chance upon, chance to meet*.

παραυτίκα],[e] adv. (παρά & αὐτίκα) *instantly, immediately*; ὁ, ἡ, τὸ, παραυτίκα, *momentary, transient*, 2 Co. 4. 17. (ῐ).

παραφέρεσθε, 2 pers. pl. pres. imper. pass.— Gr. Sch. Tdf. . . . } παραφέρω
περιφέρεσθε, Rec. (He. 13. 9) . . }
παραφερόμεναι, nom. pl. fem. part. pres. pass. —Gr. Sch. Tdf. . . . . } id.
περιφερόμεναι, Rec. (Jude 12) . . }

παραφέρω], fut. παροίσω, aor. 2, παρήνεγκον, (§ 36. rem. 1) (παρά & φέρω) *to carry past; to cause to pass away*, Mar. 14. 36; Lu. 22. 42; pass. *to be swept along*, v.r. Jude 12; *to be led away, misled, seduced*, v.r. He. 13. 9.

a He. 2. 1. b Ac. 28. 11. c Lu. 17. 20. d Ac. 17. 17. e 2 Co. 4. 17.

παραφρονέω, ῶ], fut. ήσω, (§ 16. tab. P) (παρά & φρονέω) *to be beside one's wits;* παραφρονῶν, *in foolish style,* 2 Co. 11. 23.

παραφρονία, ας, ἡ, (§ 2. tab. B. b, and rem. 2) *madness, folly,* 2 Pe. 2. 16. N.T.

παραφρονία], ας, ἡ . . . παραφρονέω
παραφρονίαν,[a] acc. sing. . . . παραφρονία
παραφρονῶν,[b] nom. sing. masc. part. pres. παραφρονέω

παραχειμάζω], (παρά & χειμάζω) *to winter, spend the winter,* Ac. 27. 12; 28. 11; 1 Co. 16. 6; Tit. 3. 12.

παραχειμασία, ας, ἡ, (§ 2. tab. B. b, and rem. 2) *a wintering* in a place, Ac. 27. 12. L.G.

παραχειμάσαι, aor. 1, infin. . . . παραχειμάζω
παραχειμασία], ας, ἡ . . . . id.
παραχειμασίαν,[c] acc. sing. . . . παραχειμασία
παραχειμάσω, 1 pers. sing. fut. ind. . παραχειμάζω

παραχρῆμα], adv. (παρά & χρῆμα) *forthwith, immediately,* Mat. 21. 19, 20; Lu. 1. 64, et al.

παρδάλει,[d] dat. sing. . . . . πάρδαλις

πάρδᾰλις], εως, ἡ, (§ 5. tab. E. c) (equiv. to πάρδος) *a leopard, or panther.*

παρεβάλομεν, 1 pers. pl. aor. 2, ind. act. (§ 27. rem. 2. d) . . παραβάλλω
παρέβη, 3 pers. sing. aor. 2, ind. (§ 37. rem. 1) παραβαίνω
παρεβιάσαντο, 3 pers. pl. aor. 1, ind. . παραβιάζομαι
παρεβιάσατο, 3 pers. sing. aor. 1, ind. . . id.
παρεγένετο, 3 pers. sing. aor. 2, ind. (§ 37. rem. 1) . . . . παραγίνομαι
παρεγενόμην, 1 pers. sing. aor. 2, ind. . id.
παρεγένοντο, 3 pers. pl. aor. 2, ind. . id.
παρεγίνοντο, 3 pers. pl. imperf. . . . id.
παρεδέχθησαν, 3 pers. pl. aor. 1, ind. pass. B. Ln. Tdf. . . . } παραδέχομαι
ἀπεδέχθησαν, Rec. Gr. Sch. (Ac. 15. 4)
παρεδίδοτο, 3 pers. sing. imperf. pass. (§ 30. tab. A. A) . . . παραδίδωμι
παρεδίδου, 3 pers. s. imperf. act. (§ 31. rem. 2) id
παρεδίδουν, 3 pers. pl. imperf. act. . . id.
παρεδόθη, 3 pers. sing. aor. 1, pass. (§ 30. rem. 4) id.
παρεδόθην, 1 pers. sing. aor. 1, ind. pass. . id.
παρεδόθητε, 2 pers. pl. aor. 1, ind. pass. . id.
παρέδοσαν, 3 pers. pl. aor. 2, ind. act. . . id.
παρεδρεύοντες, nom. pl. masc. part. pres.—Al. Ln. Tdf. . . . . } παρεδρεύω
προσεδρεύοντες, R. Gr. Sch. (1 Co. 9. 13)

παρεδρεύω], fut. εύσω, (§ 13. tab. M) (πάρεδρος, *one who sits by,* παρά & ἕδρα) *to sit near; to attend, serve,* v.r. 1 Co. 9. 13.

παρέδωκα, 1 pers. sing. aor. 1, ind. act. (§ 28. rem. 9. b. c) . . . παραδίδωμι
παρεδώκαμεν, 1 pers. pl. aor. 1, ind. act. id.
παρέδωκαν, 3 pers. pl. aor. 1, ind. act. . . id.
παρέδωκας, 2 pers. sing. aor. 1, ind. act. . id.
παρεδώκατε, 2 pers. pl. aor. 1, ind. act. . id.
παρέδωκε, 3 pers. sing. aor. 1, ind. act. . id.
παρέθεντο, 3 pers. pl. aor. 2, ind. mid. (§ 28. tab. W) . . . . . παρατίθημι
παρεθεωροῦντο,[e] 3 pers. pl. imperf. pass. . παραθεωρέω
παρέθηκαν, 3 pers. pl. aor. 1, ind. act. . . παρατίθημι
παρέθηκε, 3 pers. sing. aor. 1, ind. act. . id.
πάρει, 2 pers. sing. pres. ind. . . . πάρειμι
παρειμένας,[f] acc. pl. fem. part. perf. pass. . παρίημι

πάρειμι], (§ 12. tab. L) (παρά & εἰμί) *to be beside, to be present,* Lu. 13. 1, et al.; *to be come,* Mat. 26. 50; Jno. 7. 6; 11. 28; Col. 1. 6, et al.; *to be in possession,* He. 13. 5; 2 Pe. 1. 9, 12; part. παρών, οῦσα, όν, *present,* 1 Co. 5. 3; τὸ παρόν, *the present time, the present,* He. 12. 11.

παρουσία, ας, ἡ, (§ 2. tab. B. b, and rem. 2) *presence,* 2 Co. 10. 10; Phi. 2. 12; *a coming, arrival, advent,* Phi. 1. 26; Mat. 24. 3, 27, 37, 39; 1 Co. 15. 23, et al.

παρεῖναι, pres. infin. . . . πάρειμι

παρεισάγω], fut. άξω, (§ 23. rem. 1. b) (παρά & εἰσάγω) *to introduce stealthily,* 2 Pe. 2. 1.

παρείσακτος, ου, ὁ, ἡ, (§ 7. rem. 2) *clandestinely introduced, brought in stealthily,* Gal. 2. 4. N.T.

παρείσακτος], ου, ὁ, ἡ . . . . παρεισάγω
παρεισάκτους,[g] acc. pl. masc. . . παρείσακτος
παρεισάξουσι,[h] 3 pers. pl. fut. ind. . . παρεισάγω

παρεισδύω, or δύνω], fut. δύσω, aor. 1, παρεισέδῡσα, (παρά & εἰσδύω) *to enter privily, creep in stealthily, steal in.*

παρεισέδυσαν,[i] 3 pers. pl. aor. 1, ind. . . παρεισδύω
παρεισενέγκαντες,[k] nom. pl. masc. part. aor. 1, (§ 36. rem. 1) . . . παρεισφέρω

παρεισέρχομαι], aor. 2, παρεισῆλθον, (§ 36. rem. 1) (παρά & εἰσέρχομαι) *to supervene,* Ro. 5. 20; *to steal in,* Gal. 2. 4.

παρεισῆλθε, 3 pers. sing. aor. 2, ind. . παρεισέρχομαι

---

[a] 2 Pe. 2. 16. [b] 2 Co. 11. 23. [c] Ac. 27. 12. [d] Re. 13. 2. [e] Ac. 6. 1. [f] He. 12. 12. [g] Gal. 2. 4. [h] 2 Pe. 2. 1. [i] Jude 4. [k] 2 Pe. 1. 5.

παρεισῆλθον, 3 pers. pl. aor. 2, ind. . . παρεισέρχομαι
πάρεισι, 3 pers. pl. pres. ind. . . . πάρειμι
παρειστήκεισαν, 3 pers. pl. pluperf. (§ 29. rem. 4) . . . . παρίστημι
παρεισφέρω], fut. παρεισοίσω, aor. 1, παρεισήνεγκα, (§ 36. rem. 1) (παρά & εἰσφέρω) *to bring in beside; to bring into play, superinduce, exhibit in addition*, 2 Pe. 1. 5.
παρεῖχε, 3 pers. sing. imperf. (§ 13. rem. 4) . παρέχω
παρείχετο, 3 pers. sing. imperf. mid. . id.
παρεῖχον, 3 pers. pl. imperf. act. . . id.
παρεκάλει, 3 pers. sing. imperf. act. . παρακαλέω
παρεκάλεσα, 1 pers. sing. aor. 1, ind. (§ 22. rem. 1) . . . . . id.
παρεκάλεσαν, 3 pers. pl. aor. 1, ind. act. . id.
παρεκάλεσας, 2 pers. sing. aor. 1, ind. act. . id.
παρεκάλεσε, 3 pers. sing. aor. 1, ind. act. . id.
παρεκαλοῦμεν, 1 pers. pl. imperf. act. . . id.
παρεκάλουν, 3 pers. pl. imperf. act. . id.
παρεκλήθη, 3 pers. sing. aor. 1, ind. pass. (§ 22. rem. 4) . . . . . id.
παρεκλήθημεν, 1 pers. pl. aor. 1, ind. pass. id.
παρεκλήθησαν, 3 pers. pl. aor. 1, ind. pass. id.
παρεκτός], adv. (παρά & ἐκτός) *without, on the outside; except*, Mat. 5. 32; Ac. 26. 29; τὰ παρεκτός, *other matters*, 2 Co. 11. 28. LXX.
παρέκυψε, 3 pers. sing. aor. 1, ind. . . παρακύπτω
παρέλαβε, 3 pers. sing. aor. 2, ind. act. (§ 36. rem. 2) . . . . παραλαμβάνω
παρέλαβες, 2 pers. sing. aor. 2, ind. act. . id.
παρελάβετε, 2 pers. pl. aor. 2, ind. act. . id.
παρέλαβον, 1 pers. sing. and 3 pers. pl. aor. 2, ind. act. . . . . . id.
παρελάβοσαν, 3 pers. pl. aor. 2, ind. act. (§ 35. rem. 13).—A. Gr. Tdf. } id.
παρέλαβον, Sch. . . . }
παρέλαβε, Rec. (2 Thes. 3. 6) . }
παρελέγοντο, 3 pers. pl. imperf. . . παραλέγομαι
παρελεύσεται, 3 pers. sing. fut. ind. (§ 36. rem. 1) . . . . παρέρχομαι
παρελεύσονται, 3 pers. pl. fut. ind. . . id.
παρεληλυθέναι, perf. 2, infin. . . id.
παρεληλυθώς, nom. sing. masc. part. perf. 2 . id.
παρελθάτω, 3 pers. sing. aor. 1, imper. (§ 35. rem. 12).—A. C. D. Ln. Tdf. . } id.
παρελθέτω, Rec. Gr. Sch. (Mat. 26. 39) }
παρελθεῖν, aor. 2, infin. . . . id.
παρελθέτω, 3 pers. sing. aor. 2, imper. . . παρέρχομαι
παρέλθῃ, 3 pers. sing. aor. 2, subj. . . id.
παρελθόντες, nom. pl. masc. part. aor. 2 . id.
παρελθών, nom. sing. masc. part. aor. 2 . id.
παρέλθωσι, 3 pers. pl. aor. 2, subj. . . id.
παρεμβολάς, acc. pl. . . . . . παρεμβολή
παρεμβολή], ῆς, ἡ, (§ 2. tab. B. a) (παρεμβάλλω, *to interpose or insert*, παρά & ἐμβάλλω) *an insertion besides*; later, *a marshalling* of an army; *an array* of battle, *army*, He. 11. 34; *a camp*, He. 13. 11, 13; Re. 20. 9; *a standing camp, fortress, citadel, castle*, Ac. 21. 34, 37; 22. 24; 23. 10, 16, 32.
παρεμβολήν, acc. sing. . . . . παρεμβολή
παρεμβολῆς, gen. sing. . . . . id.
παρένεγκε, 2 pers. sing. aor. 2, imper. (§ 36. rem. 1) . . . . . παραφέρω
παρενεγκεῖν, aor. 2, infin. . . . . id.
παρενοχλεῖν,[a] pres. infin. . . . παρενοχλέω
παρενοχλέω, ῶ], fut. ήσω, (§ 16. tab. P) (παρά & ἐνοχλέω) *to superadd molestation; to trouble, harass*, Ac. 15. 19.
παρέξει, 3 pers. sing. fut. ind. . . παρέχω
παρέξῃ, 3 pers. sing. aor. 1, subj.—Al. Ln. Tdf. } id.
παρέξει, Rec. Gr. Sch. (Lu. 7. 4) . }
παρεπίδημοι, nom. pl. masc. . . . παρεπίδημος
παρεπιδήμοις, dat. pl. masc. . . . id.
παρεπίδημος], ου, ὁ, ἡ, (§ 7. rem. 2) (παρά & ἐπίδημος) *residing in a country not one's own, a sojourner, stranger*, He. 11. 13; 1 Pe. 1. 1; 2. 11. L.G.
παρεπιδήμους, acc. pl. masc. . . . παρεπίδημος
παρεπίκραναν,[b] 3 pers. pl. aor. 1, ind. (§ 27. rem. 1. e) . . . παραπικραίνω
παρεπορεύοντο, 3 pers. pl. imperf. . παραπορεύομαι
παρέρχεσθε, 2 pers. pl. pres. ind. . παρέρχομαι
παρέρχεται, 3 pers. sing. pres. ind. . . id.
παρέρχομαι], fut. παρελεύσομαι, aor. 2, παρῆλθον, (§ 36. rem. 1) (παρά & ἔρχομαι) *to pass beside, pass along, pass by*, Mat. 8. 28; Mar. 6. 48; *to pass, elapse*, as time, Mat. 14. 15; Ac. 27. 9; *to pass away, be removed*, Mat. 26. 39, 42; Mar. 14. 35; met. *to pass away, disappear, vanish, perish*, Mat. 5. 18; 24. 34, 35; *to become vain, be rendered void*, Mat. 5. 18; Mar. 13. 31; trans. *to pass by, disregard, neglect*, Lu.

[a] Ac. 15. 19.
[b] He. 3. 16.

11. 42; 15. 29; *to come to the side of, come to,* Lu. 12. 37; 17. 7.

πάρεσιν, acc. sing. . . . . . . πάρεσις

πάρεσις], εως, ἡ, (§ 5. tab. E. c) . . παρίημι

παρεσκευασμένοι, nom. pl. masc. part. perf. pass. (§ 26. rem. 1) . . παρασκευάζω

παρεσκεύασται, 3 pers. sing. perf. ind. pass. id.

πάρεσμεν, 1 pers. pl. pres. ind. . . . πάρειμι

παρέσται, 3 pers. sing. fut. ind. . . } id.
καὶ παρέσται, Gr. Sch. Tdf. . .
καίπερ ἐστίν, Rec. (Re. 17. 8)

πάρεστε, 2 pers. pl. pres. ind. . . id.

παρέστη, 3 pers. sing. aor. 2, ind. (§ 29. tab. X) παρίστημι

παρέστηκε, 3 pers. sing. perf. ind. . . id.

παρεστηκόσι, dat. pl. masc. part. perf. . . id.

παρεστηκότων, gen. pl. masc. part. perf. . id.

παρεστηκώς, nom. sing. masc. part. perf. . id.

παρέστησαν, 3 pers. pl. aor. 1, ind. . id.

παρεστήσατε, 2 pers. pl. aor. 1, ind. . id.

παρέστησε, 3 pers. sing. aor. 1, ind. . id.

πάρεστι, 3 pers. sing. pres. ind. . . . πάρειμι

παρεστῶσι, dat. pl. masc. part. perf. (§ 35. rem. 8) παρίστημι

παρεστῶτα, acc. sing. masc. part. perf. contr. id.

παρεστῶτες, nom. pl. masc. part. perf. contr. id.

παρεστώτων, gen. pl. masc. part. perf.—B. D. Tdf. . . . . } id.
παρεστηκότων, Rec. Gr. Sch. Ln. (Mar. 15. 35) . . . .

παρέσχον, 3 pers. pl. aor. 2, ind. (§ 36. rem. 4) παρέχω

παρέτεινε,[a] 3 pers. sing. imperf. . . παρατείνω

παρετήρουν, 3 pers. pl. imperf. act. . . παρατηρέω

παρετηροῦντο, 3 pers. pl. imperf. mid—A. C. D. Ln. Tdf. . . . . } id.
παρετήρουν, Rec. Gr. Sch. (Mar. 3. 2)

πάρεχε, 2 pers. sing. pres. imper. act. . . παρέχω

παρέχειν, pres. infin. act. . . . id.

παρέχεσθε, 2 pers. pl. pres. imper. mid. . id.

παρέχετε, 2 pers. pl. pres. ind. act. . . id.

παρεχέτω, 3 pers. sing. pres. imper. act. . id.

παρεχόμενος, nom. sing. masc. part. pres. mid. id.

παρέχοντι, dat. sing. masc. part. pres. act. . id.

παρέχουσι, 3 pers. pl. pres. ind. act. . . id.

παρέχω], fut. ἕξω, aor. 2, παρέσχον, (§ 36. rem. 4) (παρά & ἔχω) *to hold beside; to hold out to, offer, present,* Lu. 6. 29; *to confer, render,* Lu. 7. 4; Ac. 22. 2; 28. 2; Col. 4. 1; *to afford, furnish,* Ac. 16. 16; 17. 31; 19. 24; 1 Ti. 6. 17; *to exhibit,* Tit. 2. 7; *to be the cause of, occasion,* Mat. 26. 10; Mar. 14. 6; Lu. 11. 7, et al.

παρηγγείλαμεν, 1 pers. pl. aor. 1, ind. (§ 27. rem. 1. d) . . . . παραγγέλλω

παρήγγειλαν, 3 pers. pl. aor. 1, ind. . . id.

παρήγγειλε, 3 pers. sing. aor. 1, ind. . id.

παρηγγέλλομεν, 1 pers. pl. imperf. . . id.

παρῆγε, 3 pers. sing. imperf. . . . παράγω

παρηγορία],[b] ας, ἡ, (§ 2. tab. B. b, and rem. 2) (παρηγορέω, *to exhort; to console*) *exhortation; comfort, solace, consolation.*

παρηκολούθηκας, 2 pers. sing. perf. ind. παρακολουθέω

παρηκολουθηκότι, dat. sing. masc. part. perf. id.

παρηκολούθησας, 2 pers. sing. aor. 1.—A. C. Ln. Tdf. . . . . } id.
παρηκολούθηκας, Rec. Gr. Sch. (2 Ti. 3. 10) . . . .

παρῆλθε, 3 pers. sing. aor. 2, ind. . . παρέρχομαι

παρῆλθον, 1 pers. sing. aor. 2, ind. . . id.

παρῄνει, 3 pers. sing. imperf. (§ 13. rem. 2) παραινέω

παρῆσαν, 3 pers. pl. imperf. . . . πάρειμι

παρῃτημένον, acc. sing. masc. part. perf. pass. (§ 13. rem. 2) . . . παραιτέομαι

παρῃτήσαντο, 3 pers. pl. aor. 1, ind. . . id.

παρθενία], ας, ἡ, (§ 2. tab. B. b, and rem. 2) παρθένος

παρθενίας,[c] gen. sing. . . . . παρθενία

παρθένοι, nom. pl. . . . . . παρθένος

παρθένοις, dat. pl. . . . . . id.

παρθένον, acc. sing. . . . . . id.

παρθένος, ου, ἡ, (§ 3. tab. C. b) *a virgin, maid,* Mat. 1. 23; 25. 1, 7, 11; Ac. 21. 9, et al.; in N.T. also masc., *chaste,* Re. 14. 4.

παρθενία, ας, ἡ, *virginity,* Lu. 2. 36.

παρθένου, gen. sing. . . . . παρθένος

παρθένων, gen. pl. . . . . . id.

Πάρθοι,[d] nom. pl. . . . . Πάρθος

Πάρθος], ου, ὁ, (§ 3. tab. C. a) *a Parthian, a native of Parthia in central Asia.*

παρίημι], fut. παρήσω, (§ 32. tab. C. C) (παρά & ἵημι) *to let pass beside, let fall beside; to relax;* pass. perf. part. παρειμένος, *hanging down helplessly, unstrung, feeble,* He. 12. 12.

πάρεσις, εως, ἡ, (§ 5. tab. E. c) *a letting pass; a passing over,* Ro. 3. 25.

παριστάνετε, 2 pers. pl. pres. ind. and imper. παριστάνω

[a] Ac. 20. 7. [b] Col. 4. 11. [c] Lu. 2. 36. [d] Ac. 2. 9.

παρίστημι, and later also παριστάνω], fut. παραστήσω, (§ 29. tab. X) (παρά & ἵστημι) trans. *to place beside; to have in readiness, provide*, Ac. 23. 24; *to range beside, to place at the disposal of*, Mat. 26. 53; Ac. 9. 41; *to present* to God, *dedicate, consecrate, devote*, Lu. 2. 22; Ro. 6. 13, 19; *to prove, demonstrate, show*, Ac. 1. 3; 24. 13; *to commend, recommend*, 1 Co. 8. 8; intrans. perf. παρέστηκα, part. παρεστώς, pluperf. παρειστήκειν, aor. 2, παρέστην, and mid., *to stand by or before*, Ac. 27. 24; Ro. 14. 10; *to stand by, to be present*, Mar. 14. 47, 69, 70; *to stand in attendance, attend*, Lu. 1. 19; 19. 24; of time, *to be present, have come*, Mar. 4. 29; *to stand by* in aid, *assist, support*, Ro. 16. 2.

παρίστησι, 3 pers. sing. pres. ind. . . . παρίστημι

Παρμενᾶν,[a] acc. . . . . . Παρμενᾶς

Παρμενᾶς], ᾶ, ὁ, (§ 2. rem. 4) *Parmenas*, pr. name.

πάροδος], ου, ἡ, (§ 3. tab. C. b) (παρά & ὁδός) *a way by; a passing by*; ἐν παρόδῳ, *in passing, by the way*, 1 Co. 16. 7.

παρόδῳ,[b] dat. sing. . . . . . πάροδος

παροικεῖς, 2 pers. sing. pres. ind. . . . παροικέω

παροικέω, ῶ], fut. ήσω, (§ 16. tab. P) . πάροικος

παροικία], ας, ἡ, (§ 2. tab. B. b, and rem. 2) . id.

παροικίᾳ, dat. sing. . . . . παροικία

παροικίας, gen. sing. . . . . id.

πάροικοι, nom. pl. masc. . . . . πάροικος

πάροικον, nom. sing. neut. . . . . id.

πάροικος], ου, ὁ, ἡ, (§ 7. rem. 2) (παρά & οἶκος) *a neighbour*; later, *a sojourner, temporary resident, stranger*, Ac. 7. 6, 29; Ep. 2. 19; 1 Pe. 2. 11.

παροικέω, ῶ, fut. ήσω, (§ 16. tab. P) *to dwell beside*; later, *to reside in a place as a stranger, sojourn, be a stranger or sojourner*, Lu. 24. 18; He. 11. 9.

παροικία, ας, ἡ, (§ 2. tab. B. b, and rem. 2) *a sojourning, temporary residence in a foreign land*, Ac. 13. 17; 1 Pe. 1. 17. LXX.

παροίκους, acc. pl. masc. . . . πάροικος

παροιμία], ας, ἡ, (§ 2. tab. B. b, and rem. 2) (πάροιμος, *by the road, trite*, παρά & οἶμος) *a by word, proverb, adage*, 2 Pe. 2. 22; in N.T. *an obscure saying, enigma*, Jno. 16. 25, 29; *a parable, similitude, figurative discourse*, Jno. 10. 6.

παροιμίαις, dat. pl. . . . . παροιμία

παροιμίαν, acc. sing. . . . . id.

παροιμίας, gen. sing. . . . . id.

πάροινον, acc. sing. masc. . . . πάροινος

πάροινος], ου, ὁ, ἡ, (§ 7. rem. 2) (παρά & οἶνος) pr. *pertaining to wine; given to wine, prone to intemperance, drunken*; hence, *quarrelsome, insolent, overbearing*, 1 Ti. 3. 3; Tit. 1. 7.

παροίχομαι], fut. οιχήσομαι, perf. ᾤχημαι, (§ 13. rem. 2) (παρά & οἴχομαι, *to depart*) *to have gone by*; perf. part. παρῳχημένος, *by-gone*, Ac. 14. 16.

παρόμοια, acc. pl. neut. . . . . παρόμοιος

παρομοιάζετε,[c] 2 pers. pl. pres. ind. . παρομοιάζω

παρομοιάζω], fut. άσω . . . . παρόμοιος

παρόμοιος], οία, οιον, (§ 7. rem. 1) (παρά & ὅμοιος) *nearly resembling, similar, like*, Mar. 7. 8, 13.

παρομοιάζω, fut. άσω, (§ 26. rem. 1) *to be like, to resemble*, Mat. 23. 27. N.T.

παρόν, acc. sing. neut. part. pres. . . πάρειμι

παρόντα, nom. pl. neut. part. pres.—A. Ln. } id.
ὑπάρχοντα, Rec. Gr. Sch. Tdf. (2 Pe. 1. 8) }

παρόντες, nom. pl. masc. part. pres. . . id.

παρόντος, gen. sing. neut. part. pres. . id.

παροξύνεται, 3 pers. sing. pres. pass. . . παροξύνω

παροξύνω], fut. υνῶ, (§ 27. rem. 1 a) (παρά & ὀξύνω, *to sharpen*, from ὀξύς) *to sharpen*; met. *to incite, stir up*, Ac. 17. 16; *to irritate, provoke*, 1 Co. 13. 5.

παροξυσμός, οῦ, ὁ, (§ 3. tab. C. a) *an inciting, incitement*, He. 10. 24; *a sharp fit of anger, sharp contention, angry dispute*, Ac. 15. 39.

παροξυσμόν, acc. sing. . . . παροξυσμός

παροξυσμός], οῦ, ὁ . . . . . παροξύνω

παροργίζετε, 2 pers. pl. pres. imper. . παροργίζω

παροργίζω], fut. ίσω, (§ 26. rem. 1) (παρά & ὀργίζω) *to provoke to anger, irritate, exasperate*, Ro. 10. 19; Ep. 6. 4. LXX.

παροργισμός, οῦ, ὁ, (§ 3. tab. C. a) *provocation to anger; anger excited, indignation, wrath*, Ep. 4. 26. LXX.

παροργισμός], οῦ, ὁ . . . . . παροργίζω

[a] Ac. 6. 5. [b] 1 Co. 16. 7. [c] Mat. 23. 27.

παροργισμῷ,[a] dat. sing. . . . . παροργισμός

παροργιῶ, 1 pers. sing. fut. ind. Att. (§ 35. rem. 11) . . . . . παροργίζω

παροτρύνω], fut. υνῶ, (§ 27. rem. 1. a) (παρά & ὀτρύνω, *to excite*) *to stir up, incite, instigate*, Ac. 13. 50.

παρούσῃ, dat. sing. fem. part. pres. . πάρειμι

παρουσία], ας, ἡ, (§ 2. tab. B. b, and rem. 2) id.

παρουσίᾳ, dat. sing. . . . . παρουσία

παρουσίαν, acc. sing. . . . . id.

παρουσίας, gen. sing. . . . . id.

παροῦσι, dat. pl. neut. part. pres. . . πάρειμι

παροψίδος, gen. sing. . . . . παροψίς

παροψίς], ίδος (ῐ), ἡ, (§ 4. rem. 2. c) (παρά & ὄψον) pr. *a dainty side-dish*; meton. *a plate, platter*, Mat. 23. 25, 26.

παῤῥησία], ας, ἡ, (§ 2. tab. B. b, and rem. 2) (ῥῆσις, *a speech*) *freedom in speaking, boldness of speech*, Ac. 4. 13; παῤῥησίᾳ, as an adv. *freely, boldly*, Jno. 7. 13, 26; so μετὰ παῤῥησίας, Ac. 2. 29; 4. 29, 31; *licence, authority*, Phile. 8; *confidence, assurance*, 2 Co. 7. 4; Ep. 3. 12; He. 3. 6; 10. 19; *openness, frankness*, 2 Co. 3. 12; παῤῥησίᾳ, and ἐν παῤῥησίᾳ, adverbially, *openly, plainly, perspicuously, unambiguously*, Mar. 8. 32; Jno. 10. 24; *publicly, before all*, Jno. 7. 4.

παῤῥησιάζομαι, fut. άσομαι, (§ 26. rem. 1) *to speak plainly, freely, boldly, and confidently*, Ac. 13. 46; 14. 3, et al.

παῤῥησιάζεσθαι, pres. infin. . . παῤῥησιάζομαι

παῤῥησιάζομαι], fut. άσομαι . . παῤῥησία

παῤῥησιαζόμενοι, nom. pl. m. part. pres. παῤῥησιάζομαι

παῤῥησιαζόμενος, nom. sing. masc. part. pres. id.

παῤῥησίαν, acc. sing. . . . . παῤῥησία

παῤῥησίας, gen. sing. . . . . id.

παῤῥησιασάμενοι, nom. pl. m. part. aor. 1 παῤῥησιάζομαι

παῤῥησιάσωμαι, 1 pers. sing. aor. 1, subj. id.

παρῴκησε, 3 pers. sing. aor. 1 (§ 13. rem. 2) παροικέω

παρών, nom. sing. masc. part. pres. . . πάρειμι

παρωξύνετο, 3 pers. sing. imperf. pass. . παροξύνω

παρώτρυναν,[b] 3 pers. pl. aor. 1, ind. . παροτρύνω

παρῳχημέναις,[c] dat. pl. fem. part. perf. pass. (§ 13. rem. 2) . . . παροίχομαι

πᾶς, πᾶσα, πᾶν], gen. παντός, πάσης, παντός, (§ 7. tab. H. b) *all*; in the sing. *all, the whole*, usually when the substantive has the article, Mat. 6. 29; 8. 32; Ac. 19. 26, et al.; *every*, only with an anarthrous subst., Mat. 3. 10; 4. 4, et al.; plur. *all*, Mat. 1. 17, et al. freq.; πάντα, *in all respects*, Ac. 20. 35; 1 Co. 9. 25; 10. 33; 11. 2; by a Hebraism, a negative with πᾶς is sometimes equivalent to οὐδείς or μηδείς, Mat. 24. 22; Lu. 1. 37; Ac. 10. 14; Ro. 3. 20; 1 Co. 1. 29; Eph. 4. 29, et al.

πανταχῆ, adv. *everywhere*, v. r. Ac. 21. 28.

πανταχόθεν, adv. *from all parts, from every quarter*, Mar. 1. 45.

πανταχοῦ, adv. *in all places, everywhere*, Mar. 16. 20; Lu. 9. 6, et al.

πάντῃ, adv. *everywhere; in every way, in every instance*, Ac. 24. 3.

πάντοθεν, adv. (πᾶς & θεν) *from every place, from all parts*, Jno. 18. 20; *on all sides, on every side, round about*, Lu. 19. 43; He. 9. 4.

πάντοτε, adv. *always, at all times, ever*, Mat. 26. 11; Mar. 14. 7; Lu. 15. 31; 18. 1, et al. L.G.

πάντως, adv. *wholly, altogether; at any rate, by all means*, 1 Co. 9. 22; by impl. *surely, assuredly, certainly*, Lu. 4. 23; Ac. 18. 21; 21. 22; 28. 4; 1 Co. 9. 10; οὐ πάντως, *in nowise, not in the least*, Ro. 3. 9; 1 Co. 5. 10; 16. 12.

πᾶσα, nom. sing. fem. . . . . πᾶς

πᾶσαι, nom. pl. fem. . . . . id.

πάσαις, dat. pl. fem. . . . . id.

πᾶσαν, acc. sing. fem. . . . id.

πάσας, acc. pl. fem. . . . . id.

πάσῃ, dat. sing. fem. . . . . id.

πάσης, gen. sing. fem. . . . . id.

πᾶσι, dat. pl. masc. and neut. . . id.

πάσχα], τό, indecl. (Heb. פֶּסַח, Aram. פַּסְחָא, fr. פָּסַח, *to pass over*) *the passover, the paschal lamb*, Mat. 26. 17; Mar. 14. 12; met. used of Christ, the true *paschal lamb*, 1 Co. 5. 7; *the feast of the passover, the day on which the paschal lamb was slain and eaten*, the 14th of Nisan, Mat. 26. 18; Mar. 14. 1; He. 11. 28; more genr. *the whole paschal festival*, including the seven days of *the*

[a] Ep. 4. 26. [b] Ac. 13. 50. [c] Ac. 14. 16.

feast of unleavened bread, Mat. 26. 2; Lu. 2. 41; Jno. 2. 13, et al.

πάσχει, 3 pers. sing. pres. ind. . . . . πάσχω
πάσχειν, pres. infin. . . . . . . id.
πάσχετε, 2 pers. pl. pres. ind. . . . . id.
πασχέτω, 3 pers. sing. pres. imper. . . . id.
πάσχοιτε, 2 pers. pl. pres. optat. . . . id.
πάσχομεν, 1 pers. pl. pres. ind. . . . id.
πάσχοντες, nom. pl. masc. part. pres. . . id.

πάσχω], fut. πείσομαι, aor. 2, ἔπăθον, perf. πέπονθα, (§ 36. rem. 4) *to be affected by* a thing, whether good or bad, *to suffer, endure* evil, Mat. 16. 21; 17. 12, 15; 27. 19; absol. *to suffer* death, Lu. 22. 15; 24. 26, et al.

πάθημα, ατος, τό, (§ 4. tab. D. c) *what is suffered; suffering, affliction*, Ro. 8. 18; 2 Co. 1. 5, 6, 7; Phi. 3. 10, et al.; *emotion, passion*, Ro. 7. 5; Gal. 5. 24.

παθητός, οῦ, ὁ, ἡ, (§ 7. rem. 2) *passible, capable of suffering, liable to suffer*; in N.T. *destined to suffer*, Ac. 26. 23.

πάθος, εος, τό, (§ 5. tab. E. b) *suffering; an affection, passion*, Ro. 1. 26, et al.

πάσχων, nom. sing. masc. part. pres. . . πάσχω
πασῶν, gen. pl. fem. . . . . . πᾶς
πατάξαι, aor. 1, infin. . . . . . πατάσσω
πατάξας, nom. sing. masc. part. aor. 1 . . id.
πατάξῃ, 3 pers. sing. aor. 1, subj.—Gr. Sch. Tdf. . . . . . . } id.
πατάσσῃ, Rec. (Re. 19. 15) . . }
πατάξομεν, 1 pers. pl. fut. ind. . . . id.
πατάξω, 1 pers. sing. fut. ind. . . . . id.

Πάτăρα],[a] ων, τά, (§ 3. tab. C. c) *Patara*, a city on the sea-coast of Lycia, in Asia Minor.

πατάσσῃ, 3 pers. sing. aor. 1, subj. . . πατάσσω

πατάσσω], fut. άξω, aor. 1, ἐπάταξα, (§ 26. rem. 3) *to strike, beat upon; to smite, wound*, Mat. 26. 51; Lu. 22. 49. 50; by impl. *to kill, slay*, Mat. 26. 31; Mar. 14. 27; Ac. 7. 24; *to strike gently*, Ac. 12. 7; from the Heb., *to smite* with disease, plagues, etc., Ac. 12. 23; Re. 11. 6; 19. 15.

πατεῖ, 3 pers. sing. pres. ind. act. . . . πατέω
πατεῖν, pres. infin. act. . . . . id.
πάτερ, voc. sing. (§ 6. rem. 1) . . . . πατήρ
πατέρα, acc. sing. . . . . . . πατήρ
πατέρας, acc. pl. . . . . . . id.
πατέρες, nom. and voc. pl. . . . . id.
πατέρων, gen. pl. . . . . . . id.

πατέω, ῶ], fut. ήσω, (§ 16. tab. P) (πάτος, *a path*) intrans. *to tread*, Lu. 10. 19; trans. *to tread* the winepress, Re. 14. 20; 19. 15; *to trample*, Lu. 21. 24; Re. 11. 2.

πατήρ], τέρος, τρός, ὁ, (§ 6. rem. 1) *a father*, Mat. 2. 22; 4. 21, 22; spc. used of God, as the *Father* of man by creation, preservation, etc., Mat. 5. 16, 45, 48; and peculiarly as the *Father* of our Lord Jesus Christ, Mat. 7. 21; 2 Co. 1. 3; *the founder of a race, remote progenitor, forefather, ancestor*, Mat. 3. 9; 23. 30, 32; *an elder, senior, father* in age, 1 Jno. 2. 13, 14; *a* spiritual *father*, 1 Co. 4. 15; *father* by origination, Jno. 8. 44; He. 12. 9; used as an appellation of honour, Mat. 23. 9; Ac. 7. 2.

πατριά, ᾶς, ἡ, (§ 2. tab. B. b, and rem. 2) *descent, lineage; a family, tribe, race*, Lu. 2. 4; Ac. 3. 25; Eph. 3. 15.

πατρĭκός, ή, όν, (§ 7. tab. F. a) *from fathers or ancestors, ancestral, paternal*, Gal. 1. 14.

πατρίς, ίδος (ĭ), ἡ, (§ 4. rem. 2. c) *one's native place, country, or city*, Mat. 13. 54, 57; Mar. 6. 1, 4; Lu. 4. 23, 24; Jno. 4. 44; *a* heavenly *country*, He. 11. 14.

πατρῷος, α, ον, (§ 7. rem. 1) *received from one's ancestors, paternal, ancestral*, Ac. 22. 3; 24. 14; 28. 17.

πατήσουσι, 3 pers. pl. fut. ind. act. . . πατέω

Πάτμος], ου, ἡ, (§ 3. tab. C. b) *Patmos*, an island in the Ægean sea.

Πάτμῳ,[b] dat. . . . . . . Πάτμος
πατουμένη, nom. sing. fem. part. pres. pass. (§ 17. tab. Q) . . . . . πατέω
πατραλῴαις,[c] dat. pl.—Rec. Gr. Sch. . } πατραλῴας
πατρολῴαις, Al. Ln. Tdf. (1 Ti. 1. 9) }

πατραλῴας, or λῴης], ου, ὁ, (§ 2. tab. B. c, and rem. 4) (πατήρ & ἀλοάω or ἀλοιάω, *to smite*) *a striker of his father; a parricide*, 1 Ti. 1. 9.

πατράσι, dat. pl. . . . . . πατήρ

[a] Ac. 21. 1. [b] Re. 1. 9. [c] 1 Ti. 1. 9.

πατρί, dat. sing. . . . . . . πατήρ
πατριά], ᾶς, ἡ, (§ 2. tab. B. b, and rem. 2) id.
πατριαί, nom. pl. . . . . . πατριά
πατριάρχαι, nom. pl. . . . . πατριάρχης
πατριάρχας, acc. pl. . . . . . id.
πατριάρχης], ου, ὁ, (§ 2. tab. B. c, and rem. 4) (πατριά & ἀρχή) *a patriarch, head or founder of a family*, Ac. 2. 29; 7. 8, 9; He. 7. 4. LXX.
πατριάρχου, gen. sing. . . . . πατριάρχης
πατριᾶς, gen. sing. . . . . πατριά
πατρίδα, acc. sing. . . . . . . πατρίς
πατρίδι, dat. sing. . . . . id.
πατρικός], ή, όν, (§ 7. tab. F. a) . . πατήρ
πατρικῶν,[a] gen. pl. . . . πατρικός
πατρίς], ίδος, ἡ, (§ 4. rem. 2. c) . . πατήρ
Πατρόβαν,[b] acc. . . . . . Πατρόβας
Πατρόβας], α, ὁ, (§ 2. rem. 4) *Patrobas*, pr. name.
πατροπαράδοτος], ου, ὁ, ἡ, (§ 7. rem. 2) (πατήρ & παραδοτός, fr. παραδίδωμι) *handed down or received by tradition from one's fathers or ancestors*. L.G.
πατροπαραδότου,[c] gen. sing. fem. . πατροπαράδοτος
πατρός, gen. sing. . . . . . πατήρ
πατρῴοις, dat. pl. neut. . . . . . πατρῷος
πατρῷος], α, ον, (§ 7. rem. 1) . . πατήρ
πατρῴου, gen. sing. masc. . . . . πατρῷος
πατρῴῳ, dat. sing. masc. . . . . id.
παύεται, 3 pers. sing. pres. ind. mid. . παύω
Παῦλε, voc. . . . . . . Παῦλος
Παῦλον, acc. . . . . id.
Παῦλος], ου, ὁ, (§ 3. tab. C. a) *Paulus, Paul*, pr. name.

I. *Paul, the Apostle*, Ac. 13. 9, et al. freq.

II. *Sergius Paulus, the deputy or pro-consul of Cyprus*, Ac. 13. 7.

Παύλου, gen. . . . . . . Παῦλος
Παύλῳ, dat. . . . . id.
παύομαι, 1 pers. sing. pres. ind. mid. . . παύω
παυόμεθα, 1 pers. pl. pres. ind. mid. . id.
παύσασθαι, aor. 1, infin. mid. . . . id.
παυσάτω, 3 pers. sing. aor. 1, ind. act. . id.
παύσῃ, 2 pers. sing. fut. ind. mid. . . id.
παύσονται, 3 pers. pl. fut. ind. mid. . id.

παύω], fut. παύσω, (§ 13. tab. M) *to cause to pause or cease, restrain, prohibit*, 1 Pe. 3. 10; mid., perf. (pass. form) πέπαυμαι, *to cease, stop, leave off, desist, refrain*, Lu. 5. 4; 8. 24, et al.

Πάφος], ου, ἡ, (§ 3. tab. C. b) *Paphos*, the chief city in the island of Cyprus.
Πάφου, gen. . . . . . . Πάφος
παχύνω], fut. υνῶ, aor. 1. pass. ἐπαχύνθην, (§ 27. rem. 1. a, and rem. 3) (παχύς, *fat, gross*) *to fatten, make gross*; met. pass. *to be rendered gross, dull, unfeeling*, Mat. 13. 15; Ac. 28. 27.
πέδαις, dat. pl. . . . . . . πέδη
πέδας, acc. pl. . . . . . . id.
πέδη], ης, ἡ, (§ 2. tab. B. a) (πέζα, *the foot*) *a fetter*, Mar. 5. 4; Lu. 8. 29.
πεδινός], ή, όν, (§ 7. tab. F. a) (πεδίον, *a plain*, πέδον, *the ground*) *level, flat*.
πεδινοῦ,[d] gen. sing. masc. . . . . πεδινός
πεζεύειν,[e] pres. infin. . . . . πεζεύω
πεζεύω], fut. εύσω, (§ 13. tab. M) (πέζα, *the foot*) pr. *to travel on foot; to travel by land*, Ac. 20. 13.
πεζῇ], adv. (pr. dat. fem. of πεζός, ή, όν, *pedestrian*, fr. πέζα) *on foot*, or, *by land*, Mat. 14. 13; Mar. 6. 33.
πειθαρχεῖν, pres. infin. . . . . πειθαρχέω
πειθαρχέω, ῶ], fut. ήσω, (§ 16. tab. P) (πείθομαι & ἀρχή) *to obey* one *in authority*, Ac. 5. 29, 32; Tit. 3. 1; genr. *to obey, follow, or conform to advice*, Ac. 27. 21.
πειθαρχήσαντας, acc. pl. masc. part. aor. 1 πειθαρχέω
πειθαρχοῦσι, dat. pl. masc. part. pres. . id.
πείθεις, 2 pers. sing. pres. ind. act. . . πείθω
πείθεσθαι, pres. infin. mid. . . . id.
πείθεσθε, 2 pers. pl. pres. imper. mid. . id.
πειθοῖ, dat. sing. in some copies and ancient versions . . . }
πειθοῖς, R. Gr. Sch. Ln. Tdf. (1 Co. 2. 4) } id.
πειθοῖς,[f] dat. pl. masc. . . . πειθός
πείθομαι, 1 pers. sing. pres. ind. mid. . . πείθω
πειθόμεθα, 1 pers. pl. pres. ind. mid.—Al. Ln. Tdf. . . . . }
πεποίθαμεν, Rec. Gr. Sch. (He. 13. 18) } id.
πείθομεν, 1 pers. pl. pres. ind. act. . . id.
πειθομένοις, dat. pl. masc. part. pres. mid. id.
πειθομένου, gen. sing. masc. part. pres. mid. id.
πειθός], ή, όν, (§ 7. tab. F. a) . . id.
πειθώ], όος, οῦς, ἡ, (§ 5. tab. E. h) *Suada, the goddess of persuasion; persuasiveness*, v.r. 1 Co. 2. 4.

[a] Gal. 1. 14. [b] Ro. 16. 14. [c] 1 Pe. 1. 18. [d] Lu. 6. 17. [e] Ac. 20. 13. [f] 1 Co. 2. 4.

πείθω], fut. πείσω, perf. πέπεικα, (§ 23. rem. 1. c, and rem. 6) aor. 1, ἔπεισα, perf. pass. πέπεισμαι, aor. 1, pass. ἐπείσθην, (§ 23. rem. 4. 7) *to persuade, seek to persuade, endeavour to convince,* Ac. 18. 4; 19. 8, 26; 28. 23; *to persuade, influence by persuasion,* Mat. 27. 20; Ac. 13. 43; 26. 28; *to incite, instigate,* Ac. 14. 19; *to appease, render tranquil, to quiet,* 1 Jno. 3. 19; *to strive to conciliate, aspire to the favour of,* Gal. 1. 10; *to pacify, conciliate, win over,* Mat. 28. 14; Ac. 12. 20; pass. and mid. *to be persuaded of, be confident of,* Lu. 20. 6; Ro. 8. 38; He. 6. 9; *to suffer one's self to be persuaded, yield to persuasion, to be induced,* Ac. 21. 14; *to be convinced, to believe, yield belief,* Lu. 16. 31; Ac. 17. 4; *to assent, listen to, obey, follow,* Ac. 5. 36, 37, 40; perf. 2, πέποιθα, (§ 25. rem. 5) *to be assured, be confident,* 2 Co. 2. 3; Phi. 1. 6; He. 13. 18; *to confide in, trust, rely on, place hope and confidence in,* Mat. 27. 43; Mar. 10. 24; Ro. 2. 19.

πειθός, ή, όν, (§ 7. tab. F. a) *persuasive,* 1 Co. 2. 4. N.T.

πεισμονή, ῆς, ἡ, (§ 2. tab. B. a) *a yielding to persuasion, assent,* Gal. 5. 8. N.T.

πεποίθησις, εως, ἡ, (§ 5. tab. E. c) (πέποιθα, perf. 2 of πείθω) *trust, confidence, reliance,* 2 Co. 1. 15, et al. LXX.

πίστις, εως, ἡ, (§ 5. tab. E. c) (πείθομαι) *faith, belief, firm persuasion,* 2 Co. 5. 7; He. 11. 1; *assurance, firm conviction,* Ro. 14. 23; *ground of belief, guarantee, assurance,* Ac. 17. 31; *good faith, honesty, integrity,* Mat. 23. 23; Gal. 5. 22; Tit. 2. 10; *faithfulness, truthfulness,* Ro. 3. 3; in N.T. *faith* in God and Christ, Mat. 8. 10; Ac. 3. 16, et al. freq.; ἡ πίστις, *the* matter of Gospel *faith,* Ac. 6. 7; Jude 3, et al.

πιστεύω, fut. εύσω, perf. πεπίστευκα, (§ 13. tab. M) *to believe, give credit to,* Mar. 1. 15; 16. 13; Lu. 24. 25; intrans. *to believe, have a mental persuasion,* Mat. 8. 13; 9. 28; Ja. 2. 19; *to believe, be of opinion,* Ro. 14. 2; in N.T. πιστεύειν ἐν, εἰς, ἐπί, *to believe in or on,* Mat. 18. 6; 27. 42; Jno. 3. 15, 16, 18; absol. *to believe, be a believer* in the religion of Christ, Ac. 2. 44; 4. 4, 32; 13. 48; trans. *to intrust, commit to the charge or power of* Lu. 16. 11; Jno. 2. 24; pass. *to be intrusted with,* Ro. 3. 2; 1 Co. 9. 17.

πιστός, ή, όν, (§ 7. tab. F. a) *faithful, true, trusty,* Mat. 24. 45; 25. 21, 23; Lu. 12. 42; 2 Ti. 2. 2; *put in trust,* 1 Co. 7. 25; *true, veracious,* Re. 1. 5; 2. 13; *credible, sure, certain, indubitable,* Ac. 13. 34; 1 Ti. 1. 15; *believing, yielding belief and confidence,* Jno. 20. 27; Gal. 3. 9; spc. *a* Christian *believer,* Ac. 10. 45; 16. 1, 15; 2 Co. 6. 15; πιστόν, *in a true-hearted manner right-mindedly,* 3 Jno. 5.

πιστόω, ῶ, fut. ώσω, (§ 20. tab. T) *to make trustworthy;* pass. *to be assured, feel sure belief,* 2 Ti. 3. 14.

πείθων,	nom. sing. masc. part. pres. act.	πείθω
πεινᾷ,	3 pers. sing. pres. ind. and subj.	πεινάω
πεινᾶν,	pres. infin.	id.
πεινάσετε,	2 pers. pl. fut. ind.	id.
πεινάσῃ,	3 pers. sing. aor. 1, subj.	id
πεινάσουσι,	3 pers. pl. fut. ind.	id.

πεινάω, ῶ], fut. άσω, (§ 22. rem. 2) and ήσω, aor. 1, ἐπείνᾱσα, (πεῖνα, *hunger*) *to hunger, be hungry,* Mat. 4. 2; Mar. 11. 12; *to be exposed to hunger, be famished,* 1 Co. 4. 11; Phi. 4. 12; met. *to hunger after desire earnestly, long for,* Mat. 5. 6.

πεινῶμεν,	1 pers. pl. pres. ind.	πεινάω
πεινῶντα,	acc. sing. masc. part. pres.	id.
πεινῶντας,	acc. pl. masc. part. pres.	id.
πεινῶντες,	nom. pl. masc. part. pres	id.

πεῖρα], ας, ἡ, (§ 2. tab. B. b) *a trial, attempt, endeavour;* λαμβάνειν πεῖραν, *to attempt,* He. 11. 29; also, *to experience,* He. 11. 36.

πειράζω, fut. άσω, (§ 26. rem. 1) aor. 1, ἐπείρᾰσα, perf. pass. πεπείρασμαι, aor. 1, pass. ἐπειράσθην, *to make proof or trial of, put to the proof,* whether with good or mischievous intent, Mat. 16. 1; 22. 35, et al.; absol. *to attempt, essay,* Ac. 16. 7; 24. 6; in N.T. *to tempt,* Mat. 4. 1, et al.; *to try, subject to trial,* 1 Co. 10. 13, et al.

πειρασμός, οῦ, ὁ, (§ 3. tab. C. a) *a putting to the proof, proof, trial,* 1 Pe. 4. 12; He. 3. 8; direct *temptation* to sin, Lu. 4. 13; *trial, temptation,* Mat.

6. 13; 26. 41; 1 Co 10. 13, et al.; *trial, calamity, affliction*, Lu. 22. 28, et al. LXX.

πειράομαι, ῶμαι, fut. άσομαι, (§ 19. tab. S) (i.q. Att. πειράω) *to try, attempt, essay, endeavour*, Ac. 9. 26; 26. 21.

πειράζει, 3 pers. sing. pres. ind. act. . . πειράζω
πειράζεται, 3 pers. sing. pres. ind. pass. . id.
πειράζετε, 2 pers. pl. pres. ind. and imper. act. id.
πειράζῃ, 3 pers. sing. pres. subj. act. . . id.
πειράζομαι, 1 pers. sing. pres. ind. pass. . id.
πειραζομένοις, dat. pl. masc. part. pres. pass. . id.
πειραζόμενος, nom. sing. masc. part. pres. pass. id.
πειράζοντες, nom. pl. masc. part. pres. act. id.
πειράζω], fut. άσω, (§ 26. rem. 1) . . πεῖρα
πειράζων, nom. sing. masc. part. pres. act. . πειράζω
πεῖραν, acc. sing. . . . . . πεῖρα
πειράομαι, ῶμαι], fut. άσομαι . . . id.
πειράσαι, aor. 1, infin. act. . . . πειράζω
πειρασθείς, nom. sing. masc. part. aor. 1, pass. id.
πειρασθῆναι, aor. 1, infin. pass. . . . id.
πειρασθῇς, 2 pers. sing. aor. 1, subj. pass. . id.
πειρασθῆτε, 2 pers. pl. aor. 1, subj. pass. . id.
πειρασμοῖς, dat. pl. . . . . πειρασμός
πειρασμόν, acc. sing. . . . . . id.
πειρασμός], οῦ, ὁ, (§ 3. tab. C. a) . . πεῖρα
πειρασμοῦ, gen. sing. . . . . πειρασμός
πειρασμῷ, dat. sing. . . . . . id.
πειρασμῶν, gen. pl. . . . . . id.
πείσαντες, nom. pl. masc. part. aor. 1, act. . πείθω
πείσας, nom. sing. masc. part. aor. 1, act. . id.
πεισθέντες, nom. pl. masc. part. aor. 1, pass. id.
πεισθῇς, 2 pers. sing. aor. 1, subj. pass. . id.
πεισθήσονται, 3 pers. pl. fut. ind. pass. . id.
πεισμονή],[a] ῆς, ἡ, (§ 2. tab. B. a) . . id.
πείσομεν, 1 pers. pl. fut. ind. act. . . id.
πελάγει, dat. sing. . . . . . πέλαγος
πέλᾰγος], εος, τό, (§ 5. tab. E. b) *the deep, the open sea*, Mat. 18.6; *a sea*, contradistinguished from the sea in general, and named from an adjacent country, Ac. 27. 5.
πελεκίζω], fut. ίσω, (§ 26. rem. 1) (πέλεκυς, *an axe*) *to strike or cut with an axe; to behead*, Re. 20. 4.
πέμπειν, pres. infin. act. . . . . πέμπω
πεμπομένοις, dat. pl. masc. part. pres. pass. id.
πέμποντα, acc. sing. masc. part. pres. act. . id.
πέμπτην, acc. sing. fem. . . . . πέμπτος
πέμπτος], η, ον, (§ 7. tab. F. a) . . πέντε

πέμπω, fut. ψω, aor. 1, ἔπεμψα, aor. 1, pass. ἐπέμφθην (§ 23. rem. 1. a, and rem. 2. 4) *to send, to despatch on any message, embassy, business*, etc., Mat. 2. 8; 11. 2; 14. 10; *to transmit*, Ac. 11. 29; Re. 1. 11; *to dismiss, permit to go*, Mar. 5. 12; *to send in or among*, 2 Thes. 2. 11; *to thrust in, or put forth*, Re. 14. 15, 18.

πεμφθέντες, nom. pl. masc. part. aor. 1, pass. πέμπω
πέμψαι, aor. 1, infin. act. . . . . id.
πέμψαντα, acc. sing. masc. part. aor. 1, act. id.
πέμψαντες, nom. pl. masc. part. aor. 1, act. id.
πέμψαντι, dat. sing. masc. part. aor. 1, act. id.
πέμψαντος, gen. sing. masc. part. aor. 1, act. id.
πέμψας, nom. sing. masc. part. aor. 1, act. . id.
πέμψασι, dat. pl. masc. part. aor. 1, act. . id.
πέμψει, 3 pers. sing. fut. ind. act. . . id.
πέμψῃς, 2 pers. sing. aor. 1, subj. act. . . id.
πέμψον, 2 pers. sing. aor. 1, imper. act. . id.
πέμψουσι, 3 pers. pl. fut. ind. act. . . id.
πέμψω, 1 pers. sing. fut. ind. act. . id.
πέμψω, 1 pers. sing. aor. 1, subj. act. . . id.
πένησι,[b] dat. pl. masc. . . . . πένης
πένης], ητος, ὁ, ἡ, (§ 4. rem. 2. c) (πένομαι, *to labour* for one's bread) pr. *one who labours for his bread; poor, needy*, 2 Co. 9. 9.

πενιχρός, ά, όν, (§ 7. rem. 1) *poor, needy*, Lu. 21. 2.

πενθεῖν, pres. infin. . . . . . πενθέω
πενθερά], ᾶς, ἡ, (§ 2. tab. B. b) . . πενθερός
πενθεράν, acc. sing. . . . . . πενθερά
πενθερᾶς, gen. sing. . . . . . id.

πενθερός],[c] οῦ, ὁ, (§ 3. tab. C. a) *a father-in-law.*

πενθερά, ᾶς, ἡ, *a mother-in-law*, Mat. 8. 14; 10. 35; Mar. 1. 30; Lu. 4. 38; 12. 53.

πενθέω, ῶ], fut. ήσω, (§ 16. tab. P) . . πένθος
πενθήσατε, 2 pers. pl. aor. 1, imper. . πενθέω
πενθήσετε, 2 pers. pl. fut. ind. . . . id.
πενθήσω, 1 pers. sing. aor. 1, subj. . . id

πένθος], εος, τό, (§ 5. tab. E. b) *mourning, sorrow, sadness, grief*, Ja. 4. 9, et al.

πενθέω, ῶ, fut. ήσω, aor. 1, ἐπένθησα, (§ 16. tab. P) trans. *to lament over*, 2 Co. 12. 21; absol. *to lament, be sad, mourn*, Mat. 5. 4; 9. 15; Mar. 16. 10,

[a] Gal. 5. 8. [b] 2 Co. 9. 9. [c] Jno. 18. 13.

et al.; mid. *to bewail one's self, to feel compunction*, 1 Co. 5. 2.

πενθοῦντες, nom. pl. masc. part. pres. . . πενθέω
πενθοῦσι, dat. pl. masc. part. pres. . . id.
πενθοῦσι, 3 pers. pl. pres. ind. . . . id.
πενιχράν,[a] acc. sing. fem. . . . πενιχρός
πενιχρός], ά, όν, (§ 7. rem. 1) . . . πένης
πεντάκις],[b] adv. . . . . . πέντε
πεντακισχίλιοι], αι, α, (πέντε & χίλιοι) *five times one thousand, five thousand*, Mat. 14. 21; 16. 9, et al.
πεντακισχιλίους, acc. pl. masc. . . πεντακισχίλιοι
πεντακισχιλίων, gen. pl. . . . id.
πεντακόσια, acc. pl. neut. . . πεντακόσιοι
πεντακόσιοι], αι, α . . . . πέντε
πεντακοσίοις, dat. pl. masc. . . πεντακόσιοι

πέντε], οἱ, αἱ, τά, indecl. *five*, Mat. 14. 17, 19; 16. 9, et al.

πέμπτος, η, ον, (§ 7. tab. F. a) *fifth*, Re. 6. 9; 9. 1; 16. 10; 21. 20.

πεντάκις, adverb, *five times*, 2 Co. 11. 24. (ᾰ).

πεντακόσιοι, αι, α, *five hundred*, Lu. 7. 41; 1 Co. 15. 6.

πεντήκοντα, οἱ, αἱ, τά, indecl. *fifty*, Mar. 6. 40; Lu. 7. 41, et al.

πεντηκοστή, ῆς, ἡ, (§ 2. tab. B. a) (fem. of πεντηκοστός, *fiftieth*) *Pentecost*, or *the Feast of Weeks*; one of the three great Jewish festivals, so called because it was celebrated on the *fiftieth* day, reckoning from the second day of the feast of unleavened bread, *i.e.* from the 16th day of Nisan, Ac. 2. 1; 20. 16; 1 Co. 16. 8.

πεντεκαιδέκᾰτος], η, ον, (§ 7. tab. F. a) (πέντε, καί, and δέκα) *fifteenth*.
πεντεκαιδεκάτῳ, dat. sing. neut. . πεντεκαιδέκατος
πεντήκοντα], οἱ, αἱ, τά . . . . πέντε
πεντηκοστή], ῆς, ἡ . . . . id.
πεντηκοστῆς, gen. sing. . . . πεντηκοστή
πεπαιδευμένος, nom. sing. masc. part. perf. pass. παιδεύω
πεπαλαίωκε, 3 pers. sing. perf. ind. act. (§ 13. rem. 5. a) . . . . παλαιόω
πέπαυται, 3 pers. s. perf. ind. pass. (§ 22. rem. 5) παύω
πεπειρᾱμένον, acc. sing. masc. part. perf. pass. —B. C. Tdf. . . . } πειράομαι
πεπειρασμένον, Rec. Gr. Sch. (He. 4. 15) } πειράομαι
πεπειρασμένον, acc. sing. masc. part. perf. pass. πειράζω
πέπεισμαι, 1 pers. sing. perf. ind. pass. . πείθω
πεπείσμεθα, 1 pers. pl. perf. ind. pass. . . id.
πεπεισμένος, nom. sing. masc. part. perf. pass. id.
πεπελεκισμένων,[c] gen. pl. part. perf. pass. . πελεκίζω
πεπιεσμένον, acc. sing. neut. part. perf. pass. . πιέζω
πεπίστευκα, 1 pers. sing. perf. ind. . . πιστεύω
πεπιστεύκαμεν, 1 pers. pl. perf. ind. . . id.
πεπίστευκας, 2 pers. sing. perf. ind. . id.
πεπιστεύκατε, 2 pers. pl. perf. ind. . . id.
πεπίστευκε, 3 pers. sing. perf. ind. . . id.
πεπιστεύκεισαν, 3 pers. pl. plup. (§ 13. rem. 8. f) id.
πεπιστευκόσι, dat. pl. masc. part. perf. . id.
πεπιστευκότας, acc. pl. masc. part. perf. . id.
πεπιστευκότες, nom. pl. masc. part. perf. . id.
πεπιστευκότων, gen. pl. masc. part. perf. . id.
πεπιστευκώς, nom. s. m. part. perf. (§ 13. rem. 13) id.
πεπίστευμαι, 1 pers. sing. perf. ind. pass. . id.
πεπλανημένοις, dat. pl. masc. part. perf. pass. πλανάω
πεπλάνησθε, 2 pers. pl. perf. pass. (§ 19. tab. S) id.
πεπλάτυνται, 3 pers. sing. perf. ind. pass. (§ 27. rem. 2. a) . . . . πλατύνω
πεπληροφορημένοι, nom. pl. masc. part. perf. pass.—A. C. D. Ln. Tdf. . . } πληροφορέω
πεπληρωμένοι, Rec. Gr. Sch. (Col. 4. 12) } πληροφορέω
πεπληροφορημένων, gen. pl. part. perf. pass. . id.
πεπληρώκατε, 2 pers. pl. perf. ind. act. . πληρόω
πεπλήρωκε, 3 pers. sing. perf. ind. act. . id.
πεπληρωκέναι, perf. infin. act. . . id.
πεπλήρωμαι, 1 pers. sing. perf. ind. pass. . id.
πεπληρωμένα, acc. pl. neut. part. perf. pass. id.
πεπληρωμένη, nom. sing. fem. part. perf. pass. id.
πεπληρωμένην, acc. sing. fem. part. perf. pass. id.
πεπληρωμένοι, nom. pl. masc. part. perf. pass. id.
πεπληρωμένους, acc. pl. masc. part. perf. pass. id.
πεπλήρωται, 3 pers. sing. perf. ind. pass. . id.
πεπλούτηκα, 1 pers. sing. perf. ind. act. . πλουτέω
πεποίηκα, 1 pers. sing. perf. ind. act. . ποιέω
πεποιήκαμεν, 1 pers. pl. perf. ind. act. . . id.
πεποίηκε, 3 pers. sing. perf. ind. act. . id.
πεποιήκεισαν, 3 p. pl. pluperf. act. (§ 13. rem. 8. f) id.
πεποιηκέναι, perf. infin. act. . . . id.
πεποιηκόσι, dat. pl. masc. part. perf. act. . id.
πεποιηκότες, nom. pl. masc. part. perf. act. . id.
πεποιηκότος, gen. sing. masc. part. perf. act. id.
πεποιηκώς, nom. sing. masc. part. perf. act. id.
πεποιημένων, gen. pl. part. perf. pass. . . id.
πέποιθα, 1 pers. sing. perf. 2, (§ 25. rem. 4. 5) πείθω

[a] Lu. 21. 2. [b] 2 Co. 11. 24. [c] Re. 20. 4

πεποίθαμεν, 1 pers. pl. perf. 2, ind. . . . πείθω
πέποιθας, 2 pers. sing. perf. 2, ind. . . . id.
πέποιθε, 3 pers. sing. perf. 2, ind. . . . id.
πεποιθέναι, perf. 2, infin. . . . . id.
πεποιθήσει, dat. sing. . . . . πεποίθησις
πεποίθησιν, acc. sing. . . . . id.
πεποίθησις], εως, ἡ, (§ 5. tab. E. c) . πείθω
πεποιθότας, acc. pl. masc. part. perf. 2 . . id.
πεποιθότες, nom. pl. masc. part. perf. 2 . id.
πεποιθώς, nom. sing. masc. part. perf. 2 . id.
πεπολίτευμαι, 1 pers. sing. perf. ind. pass. (§ 14. tab. N) . . . . πολιτεύω
πεπόνθασι, 3 pers. pl. perf. 2, ind. (§ 36. rem. 4) πάσχω
πέπονθε, 3 pers. sing. perf. 2, ind. . . id.
πεπορευμένους, acc. pl. masc. part. perf. . πορεύομαι
πεπότικε, 3 pers. sing. perf. ind. act. . . ποτίζω
πεπραγμένον, nom. sing. neut. part. perf. pass. πράσσω
πέπρακε, 3 pers. sing. perf. ind. act. . πιπράσκω
πεπραμένος, nom. sing. masc. part. perf. pass. (§ 36. rem. 3) . . . . id.
πέπραχα, 1 pers. sing. perf. ind. act. . πράσσω
πεπραχέναι, perf. infin. act. . . . . id.
πέπτωκαν, 3 pers. pl. perf. ind. (§ 35. rem. 13) A. C. Ln. . . . . } πίπτω
πέπωκε, Rec. Gr. Sch. Tdf. (Re. 18. 3)
πέπτωκας, 2 pers. sing. perf. ind.—Gr. Sch. Tdf. } id.
ἐκπέπτωκας, Rec. (Re. 2. 5) .
πεπτωκότα, acc. sing. masc. part. perf. (§ 13. rem. 6. c) . . . . id.
πεπτωκυῖαν, acc. sing. fem. part. perf. (§ 37. rem. 1) . . . . . id.
πεπυρωμένα, acc. pl. neut. part. perf. pass. . πυρόω
πεπυρωμένης, gen. sing. fem. part. p. pass.— A. C. Ln. . . . . } id.
πεπυρωμένοι, R. Gr. Sch. Tdf. (Re. 1. 15)
πεπυρωμένοι, nom. pl. masc. part. perf. pass. . id.
πεπυρωμένον, acc. sing. neut. part. perf. pass. id
πέπωκε, 3 pers. sing. perf. ind. act. (§ 37. rem. 1) πίνω
πεπώρωκε, 3 pers. sing. perf. ind. act. . πωρόω
πεπωρωμένη, nom. sing. fem. part. perf. pass. . id.
πεπωρωμένην, acc. sing. fem. part. perf. pass. id.

περ], enclitic particle, serving to add force to the word to which it is subjoined.

πέρᾱν], adv. *across, beyond, over, on the other side*, Mat. 4. 15, 25; 19. 1; Jno. 6. 1, 17; ὁ, ἡ, τό, πέραν, *farther, on the farther side*, and τὸ πέραν, *the farther side, the other side*, Mat. 8. 18, 28; 14. 22, et al.

περαιτέρω], adv. compar. of πέραν.—B. Ln. Tdf.
περὶ ἑτέρων, Rec. Gr. Sch. (Ac. 19. 39).

πέρας], ατος, τό, (§ 4. rem. 2. c) *an extremity, end*, Mat. 12. 42, Lu. 11. 31; Ro. 10. 18; *an end, conclusion, termination*, He. 6. 16.

πέρυσι, adv. *last year, a year ago*, 2 Co. 8. 10; 9. 2.

πέρατα, acc. pl. . . . . . . πέρας
περάτων, gen. pl. . . . . . . id.
Πέργαμον, acc. . . . . . . Πέργαμος
Πέργᾰμος], ου, ἡ, (§ 3. tab. C. b) *Pergamus*, a city of Mysia, in Asia Minor.
Περγάμῳ, dat. . . . . . . Πέργαμος
Πέργη], ης, ἡ, (§ 2. tab. B. a) *Perga*, the chief city of Pamphylia, in Asia Minor.
Πέργῃ, dat. . . . . . . Πέργη
Πέργην, acc. . . . . id.
Πέργης, gen. . . . . id.

περί], prep., with a genitive, pr. of place, *about, around; about, concerning, respecting*, Mat. 2. 8; 11. 10; 22. 31; Jno. 8. 18; Ro. 8. 3, et al. freq.; with an accusative, of place, *about, around, round about*, Mat. 3. 4; Mar. 3. 34; Lu. 13. 8; οἱ περί τινα, *the companions* of a person, Lu. 22. 49; *a person and his companions*, Ac. 13. 13; simply *a person*, Jno. 11. 19; τὰ περί τινα, *the condition, circumstances of* any one, Phi. 2. 23; of time, *about*, Mat. 20. 3, 5, 6, 9; *about, concerning, respecting, touching*, Lu. 10. 40; 1 Ti. 1. 19; 6. 21; Tit. 2. 7, et al.

πέριξ, adv. *round about*; ὁ, ἡ, τό, πέριξ, *circumjacent, neighbouring*, Ac. 5. 16.

περισσός, ή, όν, (§ 7. tab. F. a) *over and above*, Mat. 5. 37; *superfluous*, 2 Co. 9. 1; *extraordinary*, Mat. 5. 47; comparat. *more, greater*, Mat. 11. 9; 23. 14, et al.; *excessive*, 2 Co. 2. 7; adverbially, περισσόν, *in full abundance*, Jno. 10. 10; περισσότερον, and ἐκ περισσοῦ, *exceedingly, vehemently*, Mar. 6. 51; 7. 36; 1 Co. 15. 10; Ep. 3. 20, et al.; τὸ περισσόν, *pre-eminence, advantage*, Ro. 3. 1.

περισσῶς, adv. *much, abundantly, vehemently*, Ac. 26. 11; *more, more abundantly*, Mat. 27. 23; Mar. 10. 26.

περισσοτέρως, adv. *more, more abundantly, more earnestly, more vehemently*,

Mar. 15. 14; 2 Co. 7. 13, et al.; *exceedingly*, Gal. 1. 14.

περισσεύω, fut. εύσω, (§ 13. tab. M) *to be over and above, to be superfluous*, Mat. 14. 20; Mar. 12. 44; Lu. 21. 4, et al.; *to exist in full quantity, to abound, be abundant*, Ro. 5. 15; 2 Co. 1. 5; *to increase, be augmented*, Ac. 16. 5; *to be advanced, be rendered more prominent*, Ro. 3. 7; of persons, *to be abundantly gifted, richly furnished, abound*, Lu. 15. 17; Ro. 15. 13; 1 Co. 14. 12; 2 Co. 8. 7, et al.; *to be possessed of a full sufficiency*, Phi. 4. 12, 18; *to abound* in performance, 1 Co. 15. 58; *to be a gainer*, 1 Co. 8. 8; in N.T. trans. *to cause to be abundant*, 2 Co. 4. 15; 9. 8; Ep. 1. 8; *to cause to be abundantly furnished, cause to abound*, 1 Thes. 3. 12; pass. *to be gifted with abundance*, Mat. 13. 12; 25. 29.

περίσσευμα, ατος, τό, (§ 4. tab. D. c) *more than enough, residue over and above*, Mar. 8. 8; *abundance, exuberance*, Mat. 12. 34; Lu. 6. 45; *superabundance, affluence*, 2 Co. 8. 13, 14. L.G.

περισσεία, ας, ἡ, (§ 2. tab. B. b, and rem. 2) *superabundance*, Ro. 5. 17; 2 Co. 8. 2; 10. 15; Ja. 1. 21. LXX.

περιάγειν, pres. infin. (§ 34. rem. 1. b) . . . περιάγω
περιάγετε, 2 pers. pl. pres. ind. . . . id.
περιάγω], fut. άξω, (περί & ἄγω) *to lead around, carry about* in one's company, 1 Co. 9. 5; *to traverse*, Mat. 4. 23; 9. 35; 23. 15; Mar. 6. 6; absol. *to go up and down*, Ac. 13. 11. (ᾰ).
περιάγων, nom. sing. masc. part. pres. . . περιάγω
περιαιρεῖται, 3 pers. sing. pres. ind. pass. . περιαιρέω
περιαιρέω, ῶ], fut. ήσω, aor. 2, περιεῖλον, (§ 36. rem. 1) (περί & αἱρέω) *to take off, lift off, remove*, 2 Co. 3. 16; *to cast off*, Ac. 27. 40; met. *to cut off* hope, Ac. 27. 20; met. *to take away* sin, *remove the guilt* of sin, *make expiation for* sin, He. 10. 11.
περιαστράπτω], fut. ψω, (§ 23. rem. 1. a) (περί & ἀστράπτω) *to lighten around, shine like lightning around*, Ac. 9. 3; 22. 6.
περιαστράψαι, aor. 1, infin. . . . περιαστράπτω

περιβαλεῖται, 3 pers. sing. fut. ind. mid. (§ 24. rem. 4) . . . . . περιβάλλω
περιβάλῃ, 2 pers. sing. aor. 2, subj. mid. . id.
περιβάληται, 3 pers. sing. aor. 2, subj. mid. id.
περιβάλλω], fut. βαλῶ, aor. 2, περιέβᾰλον, perf. pass. περιβέβλημαι, (§ 27. rem. 1. b, and rem. 3) (περί & βάλλω) *to cast around; to clothe*, Mat. 25. 36, 38, 43; mid. *to clothe one's self, to be clothed*, Mat. 6. 29, 31; Lu. 23. 11; Jno. 19. 2; Ac. 12. 8; Re. 4. 4, et al.; *to cast around* a city, *to draw* a line of circumvallation, Lu. 19. 43.

περιβόλαιον, ου, τό, (§ 3. tab. C. c) *that which is thrown around* any one, *clothing, covering, vesture; a cloak, mantle*, He. 1. 12; *a covering*, 1 Co. 11. 15.

περιβαλοῦ, 2 pers. sing. aor. 2, imper. mid. περιβάλλω
περιβαλοῦσι, 3 pers. pl. fut. ind. act. id.
περιβαλώμεθα, 1 pers. pl. aor. 2, subj. mid. id.
περιβαλών, nom. sing. masc. part. aor. 2, act. id.
περιβεβλημένη, nom. sing. fem. part. perf. pass. id.
περιβεβλημένοι, nom. pl. masc. part. perf. pass. id.
περιβεβλημένον, acc. sing. masc. part. perf. pass. id.
περιβεβλημένος, nom. sing. masc. part. perf. pass. id.
περιβεβλημένους, acc. pl. masc. part. perf. pass. id.
περιβλέπομαι], fut. ψομαι, (§ 23. rem. 1. a) (i.q. περιβλέπω, from περί & βλέπω) trans. *to look round upon*, Mar. 3. 5, 34; 11. 11; Lu. 6. 10; absol. *to look around*, Mar. 5. 32; 9. 8; 10. 23.
περιβλεψάμενοι, nom. pl. masc. part. aor. 1 περιβλέπομαι
περιβλεψάμενος, nom. sing. masc. part. aor. 1 id.
περιβόλαιον], ου, τό, (§ 3. tab. C. c) . . περιβάλλω
περιβολαίου, gen. sing. . . . περιβόλαιον
περιδέω], fut. ήσω, perf. pass. δέδεμαι, (§ 37. rem. 1) (περί & δέω) *to bind round about*; pass. *to be bound around, be bound up*, Jno. 11. 44.
περιδραμόντες,[a] nom. pl. masc. part. aor. 2 (§ 36. rem. 1) . . . . περιτρέχω
περιεβάλετε, 2 pers. pl. aor. 2, ind. act. (§ 34. rem. 1. b) . . . . περιβάλλω
περιεβάλετο, 3 pers. sing. aor. 2, ind. mid. . id.
περιεβάλομεν, 1 pers. pl. aor. 2, ind. act. . id.
περιέβαλον, 3 pers. pl. aor. 2, ind. act. . id.
περιεβλέπετο, 3 pers. sing. imperf. . περιβλέπομαι
περιεδέδετο,[b] 3 pers. sing. pluperf. pass. . περιδέω

[a] Mar. 6. 55.

[b] Jno. 11. 44.

περιεζωσμέναι, nom. pl. fem. part. perf. pass. (§ 26. rem 5) . . . . περιζώννυμι
περιεζωσμένοι, nom. pl. masc. part. perf. pass. id.
περιεζωσμένον, acc. sing. masc. part. perf. pass. id.
περιέθηκαν, 3 pers. pl. aor. 1, ind. act. . περιτίθημι
περιέθηκε, 3 pers. sing. aor. 1, ind. act. . id.
περιέκρυβε,[a] 3 pers. sing. aor. 2, ind. (§ 24. rem. 8. a) . . . περικρύπτω
περιέλαμψε, 3 pers. sing. aor. 1, ind. . περιλάμπω
περιελεῖν, aor. 2, infin. act. (§ 36. rem. 1) . περιαιρέω
περιελθόντες, nom. pl. masc. part. aor. 2 περιέρχομαι
περιελόντες, nom. pl. masc. part. aor. 2, act. περιαιρέω
περιεπάτει, 3 pers. sing. imperf. . . περιπατέω
περιεπάτεις, 2 pers. sing. imperf. . . id.
περιεπατήσαμεν, 1 pers. pl. aor. 1, ind. . id.
περιεπατήσατε, 2 pers. pl. aor. 1, ind. . id.
περιεπάτησε, 3 pers. sing. aor. 1, ind. . id.
περιεπάτουν, 3 pers. pl. imperf. . . . id.
περιέπειραν,[b] 3 pers. pl. aor. 1, ind. . περιπείρω
περιεπεπατήκει, 3 pers. sing. pluperf. . . περιπατέω
περιέπεσε, 3 pers. sing. aor. 2, ind. (§ 37. rem. 1) . . . . περιπίπτω
περιεποιήσατο, 3 pers. sing. aor. 1, ind. mid. περιποιέω
περίεργα, acc. pl. neut. . . . . περίεργος
περιεργαζομένους,[c] acc. pl. masc. part. pres. περιεργάζομαι
περιεργάζομαι], fut. άσομαι, (περί, intensive, & ἐργάζομαι) *to do a thing with excessive or superfluous care; to be a busy-body*, 2 Thes. 3. 11.
περίεργοι, nom. pl. masc. . . . περίεργος
περίεργος], ου, ὁ, ἡ, (§ 7. rem. 2) (περί & ἔργον) *over careful; officious, a busy-body*, 1 Ti. 5. 13; in N.T. περίεργα, *magic arts, sorcery*, Ac. 19. 19.
περιέρχομαι], aor. 2. περιῆλθον, (§ 36. rem. 1) (περί & ἔρχομαι) *to go about, wander about, rove*, Ac. 19. 13; He. 11. 37; *to go about, visit* from house to house, 1 Ti. 5. 13; *to take a circuitous course*, Ac. 28. 13.
περιερχόμεναι, nom. pl. fem. part. pres. . περιέρχομαι
περιερχομένων, gen. pl. part. pres. . . id.
περιεσπᾶτο,[d] 3 pers. sing. imperf. pass. (§ 19. tab. S) . . . . περισπάω
περιέστησαν, 3 pers. pl. aor. 2, ind. . περιΐστημι
περιεστῶτα, acc. sing. masc. part. perf. contr. (§ 35. rem. 8) . . . id.
περιέσχε, 3 pers. sing. aor. 2, ind. . . περιέχω
περιέτεμε, 3 pers. sing. aor. 2, ind. act. . περιτέμνω

περιετμήθητε, 2 pers. pl. aor. 1, ind. pass. (§ 27. rem. 3) . . . περιτέμνω
περιέχει, 3 pers. sing. pres. ind. . . . περιέχω
περιέχουσαν, acc. sing. fem. part. pres. . id.
περιέχω], fut. περιέξω, aor. 2, περιέσχον, (§ 36. rem. 4) (περί & ἔχω) *to encompass, enclose; to embrace, contain*, as a writing, Ac. 23. 25; met. *to encompass, seize on* the mind, Lu. 5. 9; περιέχει, impers. *it is contained, it is among the contents* of a writing, 1 Pe. 2. 6.

περιοχή, ῆς, ἡ, (§ 2. tab. B. a) *a compass, circumference, contents; a section, a portion* of Scripture, Ac. 8. 32.

περιζώννυμι, and νύω], fut. ζώσω, perf. pass. περιέζωσμαι, (§ 36. rem. 5) (περί & ζώννυμι) *to bind around with a girdle, gird*; in N.T. mid. *to gird one's self* in preparation for bodily motion and exertion, Lu. 12. 37; 17. 8, et al.; *to wear a girdle*, Re. 1. 13; 15. 6.
περίζωσαι, 2 pers. sing. aor. 1, imper. mid. περιζώννυμι
περιζωσάμενοι, nom. pl. masc. part. aor. 1, mid. id.
περιζωσάμενος, nom. sing. masc. part. aor. 1, mid. id.
περιζώσεται, 3 pers. sing. fut. ind. mid. . id.
περιῆγε, 3 pers. sing. imperf. . . . περιάγω
περιῆλθον, 3 pers. pl. aor. 2. ind. . περιέρχομαι
περιῃρεῖτο, 3 pers. s. imperf. pass. (§ 13. rem. 2) περιαιρέω
περιήστραψε, 3 pers. sing. aor. 1, ind. περιαστράπτω
περιθείς, nom. sing. masc. part. aor. 2, act. περιτίθημι
περιθέντες, nom. pl. masc. part. aor. 2, act. . id.
περιθέσεως,[e] gen. sing. . . . περίθεσις
περίθεσις], εως, ἡ, (§ 5. tab. E. c) . περιτίθημι
περιΐστασο, 2 pers. sing. pres. imper. mid. (§ 29. tab. Y) . . . . περιΐστημι
περιΐστημι], fut. περιστήσω, (§ 29. tab. X) περί & ἵστημι) *to place around*; intrans. aor. 2, περιέστην, perf. part. περιεστώς, *to stand around*, Jno. 11. 42; Ac. 25. 7; mid. *to keep aloof from, avoid, shun*, 2 Ti. 2. 16; Tit. 3. 9.
περικάθαρμα], ατος, τό, (§ 4. tab. D. c) (περικαθαίρω, *to cleanse, purify*, fr. περί & καθαίρω) pr. *offscouring, filth*; met. *refuse, outcast*. LXX.
περικαθάρματα,[f] nom. pl. . . περικάθαρμα
περικαθίζω], fut ίσω, (περί & καθίζω) *to sit around*, v.r. Lu. 22. 55.

[a] Lu. 1. 24. [b] 1 Ti. 6. 10. [c] 2 Thes. 3. 11. [d] Lu. 10. 40. [e] 1 Pe. 3. 3. [f] 1 Co. 4. 13.

περικαθισάντων, gen. pl. masc. part. aor. 1—D. Ln. } περικαθίζω
συγκαθισάντων, Rec. Gr. Sch.
καθισάντων, Tdf. (Lu. 22. 55)

περικαλύπτειν, pres. infin. act. . . . περικαλύπτω

περικαλύπτω], fut. ψω, (§ 23. rem. 1. a) (περί & καλύπτω) *to cover round about, cover over; to cover* the face, Mar. 14. 65; *to blindfold*, Lu. 22. 64; pass. *to be overlaid*, He. 9. 4.

περικαλύψαντες, nom. pl. masc. part. aor. 1 περικαλύπτω

περίκειμαι], fut. κείσομαι, (§ 33. tab. D.D) (περί & κεῖμαι) *to lie around, be circumjacent; to environ*, He. 12. 1; *to be hung around*, Mar. 9. 42; Lu. 17. 2; *to have around one's self, to wear*, Ac. 28. 20; *to be beset*, He. 5. 2.

περικείμενον, acc. sing. neut. part. pres. . περίκειμαι

περίκειται, 3 pers. sing. pres. ind. . . id.

περικεκαλυμμένην, acc. sing. fem. part. perf. pass. . . . . . περικαλύπτω

περικεφαλαία], ας, ἡ, (fem. of περικεφάλαιος, περί & κεφαλή) *a helmet*, Ep. 6. 17; 1 Thes. 5. 8. L.G.

περικεφαλαίαν, acc. sing. . . . περικεφαλαία

περικρατεῖς,[a] nom. pl. masc. . . περικρατής

περικρᾰτής], έος, ὁ, ἡ, (§ 7. tab. G. b) (περί & κρατέω) *overpowering*; περικρατὴς γενέσθαι, *to become master of, to secure*, Ac. 27. 16. L.G.

περικρύπτω], fut. ψω, (§ 23. rem. 1. a) aor. 2, περιέκρῠβον, (περί & κρύπτω) *to conceal by envelopment; to conceal* in retirement, Lu. 1. 24. L.G.

περικυκλώσουσι,[b] 3 pers. pl. fut. ind. . περικυκλόω

περικυκλόω, ῶ], fut. ώσω, (§ 20. tab. T) (περί & κυκλόω) *to encircle, surround*.

περιλάμπω], fut. ψω, (§ 23. rem. 1. a) (περί & λάμπω) *to shine around*, Lu. 2. 9; Ac. 26. 13. L.G.

περιλάμψαν, acc. sing. neut. part. aor. 1 . περιλάμπω

περιλειπόμενοι, nom. pl. masc. part. pres. pass. . . . . . περιλείπω

περιλείπω], fut. ψω, (§ 23. rem. 1. a) (περί & λείπω) *to leave remaining*; pass. *to remain, survive*, 1 Thes. 4. 15, 17.

περίλυπον, acc. sing. masc. . . . περίλυπος

περίλῠπος], ου, ὁ, ἡ, (§ 7. rem. 2) (περί & λύπη) *greatly grieved, exceedingly sorrowful*, Mat. 26. 38, Mar. 6. 26; 14. 34, et al.

περιμένειν,[c] pres. infin. . . . περιμένω

περιμένω], fut. ενῶ, (§ 27. rem. 1. a) (περί & μένω) *to await, wait for*.

πέριξ],[d] adv. . . . . . περί

περιοικέω, ῶ], fut. ήσω . . . . περίοικος

περίοικοι,[e] nom. pl. masc. . . . id.

περίοικος], ου, ὁ, ἡ, (§ 7. rem. 2) (περί & οἶκος) *one who dwells in the vicinity, a neighbour*.

περιοικέω, ῶ, fut. ήσω, (§ 16. tab. P) *to dwell around, or in the vicinity; to be a neighbour*, Lu. 1. 65.

περιοικοῦντας,[f] acc. pl. masc. part. pres. . περιοικέω

περιούσιον,[g] acc. sing. masc. . . . περιούσιος

περιούσιος], ου, ὁ, ἡ, (§ 7. rem. 2) (περιουσία, *abundance, wealth*, fr. περίειμι, to superabound) *superabundant; peculiar, special*, Tit. 2. 14. LXX.

περιοχή],[h] ῆς, ἡ, (§ 2. tab. B a) . . περιέχω

περιπατεῖ, 3 pers. sing. pres. ind. . . περιπατέω

περιπάτει, 2 pers. sing. pres. imper. . . id.

περιπατεῖν, pres. infin. . . . . id.

περιπατεῖς, 2 pers. sing. pres. ind. . . id.

περιπατεῖτε, 2 pers. pl. pres. ind. and imper. id.

περιπατείτω, 3 pers. sing. pres. imper. . id.

περιπᾰτέω, ῶ], fut. ήσω, (§ 16. tab. P) (περί & πατέω) *to walk, walk about*, Mat. 9. 5; 11. 5; 14. 25, 26, 29, et al.; *to rove, roam*, 1 Pe. 5. 8; with μετά, *to accompany, follow, have intercourse with*, Jno. 6. 66; Re. 3. 4; *to walk, frequent* a locality, Jno. 7. 1; 11. 54; from the Heb., *to maintain a* certain *walk* of life and conduct, Ro. 6. 4; 8. 1, et al.

περιπατῇ, 3 pers. sing. pres. subj. . . περιπατέω

περιπατῆσαι, aor. 1, infin. . . . id.

περιπατήσαντες, nom. pl. masc. part. aor. 1 . id

περιπατήσει, 3 pers. sing. fut. ind. . id

περιπατήσουσι, 3 pers. pl. fut. ind. . . id.

περιπατήσωμεν, 1 pers. pl. aor. 1, subj. . id.

περιπατῆτε, 2 pers. pl. pres. subj. . . id.

περιπατοῦμεν, 1 pers. pl. pres. ind. . id.

περιπατοῦντα, acc. sing. masc. part. pres. . id.

περιπατοῦντας, acc. pl. masc. part. pres. . id.

περιπατοῦντες, nom. pl. masc. part. pres. . id.

περιπατοῦντι, dat. sing. masc. part. pres. . id.

περιπατοῦντος, gen. sing. masc. part. pres. . id.

[a] Ac. 27. 16. [b] Lu. 19. 43. [c] Ac. 1. 4. [d] Ac. 5. 16. [e] Lu. 1. 58. [f] Lu. 1. 65. [g] Tit. 2. 14. [h] Ac. 8. 32.

περιπατοῦσι, dat. pl. masc. part. pres. . περιπατέω

περιπατοῦσι, 3 pers. pl. pres. ind. . . id.

περιπατῶμεν, 1 pers. pl. pres. subj. id.

περιπατῶν, nom. sing. masc. part. pres. . id.

περιπείρω], fut. περῶ, aor. 1, περιέπειρα, (§ 27. rem. 1. d) (περί & πείρω) *to put on a spit, transfix;* met. *to pierce, wound deeply,* 1 Ti. 6. 10.

περιπεπατήκει, 3 pers. sing. pluperf.—Gr. Sch. } περιπατέω
περιεπεπατήκει, Rec. . . . }
περιεπάτησεν, Tdf. (Ac. 14. 8) }

περιπέσητε, 2 pers. pl. aor. 2, subj. . . περιπίπτω

περιπεσόντες, nom. pl. masc. part. aor. 2 . id.

περιπίπτω], fut. πεσοῦμαι, aor. 2, περιέπεσον, (§ 37. rem. 1) (περί & πίπτω) *to fall around or upon, to fall in with,* Lu. 10. 30; *to fall into, light upon,* Ac. 27. 41; *to be involved in,* Ja. 1. 2.

περιποιέω, ῶ], fut. ήσω, (§ 16. tab. P) (περί & ποιέω) *to cause to remain over and above, to reserve, save;* mid. *to acquire, gain, earn,* 1 Ti. 3. 13; *to purchase,* Ac. 20. 28.

περιποίησις, εως, ἡ, (§ 5. tab. E. c) *a laying up, keeping; an acquiring or obtaining, acquisition,* 1 Thes. 5. 9; 2 Thes. 2. 14; *a saving, preservation,* He. 10. 39; *a peculiar possession, specialty,* Ep. 1. 14; 1 Pe. 2. 9.

περιποιήσασθαι, aor. 1, infin. mid.—B. Tdf. } περιποιέω
σῶσαι, Rec. Gr. Sch. (Lu. 17. 33) . }

περιποιήσεως, gen. sing. . . περιποίησις

περιποίησιν, acc. sing. . . . . id.

περιποίησις], εως, ἡ, (§ 5. tab. E. c) . . περιποιέω

περιποιοῦνται, 3 pers. pl. pres. ind. mid. . id.

περιῤῥήξαντες,[a] nom. pl. masc. part. aor. 1 περιῤῥήγνυμι

περιῤῥήγνυμι], fut. ῥήξω, (§ 36. rem. 5) (περί & ῥήγνυμι) *to break or tear all round; to strip off,* Ac. 16. 22.

περισπάω, ῶ], fut. άσω, (§ 22. rem. 2) (περί & σπάω) *to draw off from around; to wheel about; to distract;* pass. *to be distracted, over-busied,* Lu. 10. 40.

περισσεία], ας, ἡ, (§ 2. tab. B. b, and rem. 2) περί

περισσείαν, acc. sing. . . . . . περισσεία

περισσεύει, 3 pers. sing. pres. ind. . . περισσεύω

περισσεύειν, pres. infin. . . . . id.

περισσεύετε, 2 pers. pl. pres. ind. . id.

περισσευθήσεται, 3 pers. sing. fut. ind. pass. (§ 14. tab. N) . . . περισσεύω

περισσεύῃ, 3 pers. sing. pres. subj. . . id.

περισσεύητε, 2 pers. pl. pres. subj. . . id.

περίσσευμα], ατος, τό, (§ 4. tab. D. c) . περί

περισσεύματα, acc. pl. . . . . περίσσευμα

περισσεύματος, gen. sing. . . . id.

περισσεύομεν, 1 pers. pl. pres. ind. . . περισσεύω

περισσεῦον, acc. sing. neut. part. pres. . id.

περισσεύονται, 3 pers. pl. pres. ind. mid.—A. B. Tdf. . . . . } id.
περισσεύουσι, Rec. Gr. Sch. Ln. (Lu. 15. 17) . . . . . }

περισσεύοντες, nom. pl. masc. part. pres. . id.

περισσεύοντος, gen. sing. neut. part. pres. id.

περισσεύουσα, nom. sing. fem. part. pres. id.

περισσεύουσι, 3 pers. pl. pres. ind. . id.

περισσεύσαι, 3 pers. sing. aor. 1, optat. . id.

περισσεῦσαι, aor. 1, infin. . . . . id.

περισσεῦσαν, nom. sing. neut. part. aor. 1 . id.

περισσεύσαντα, acc. pl. neut. part. aor. 1 id.

περισσεύσῃ, 3 pers. sing. aor. 1, subj. . id.

περισσεύω], fut. εύσω, (§ 13. tab. M) . . περί

περισσόν, nom. and acc. sing. neut. . περισσός

περισσός], ή, όν, (§ 7. tab. F. a) . . περί

περισσοτέρᾳ, dat. sing. fem. compar. (§ 8. rem. 4) . . . . . περισσός

περισσοτέραν, acc. sing. fem. compar. . . id.

περισσότερον, acc. sing. masc. compar. . id.

περισσότερον, nom. and acc. sing. neut. compar. id.

περισσοτέρως], adv. . . . . . περί

περισσοῦ, gen. sing. neut. . . . . περισσός

περισσῶς], adv. . . . . . . περί

περιστερά], ᾶς, ἡ, (§ 2. tab. B. b) *a dove, pigeon,* Mat. 3. 16; 10. 16, et al.

περιστεραί, nom. pl. . . . . . περιστερά

περιστεράν, acc. sing. . . . . id.

περιστεράς, acc. pl. . . . . id.

περιστερῶν, gen. pl. . . . . id.

περιτεμεῖν, aor. 2, infin. act. . . . περιτέμνω

περιτέμνειν, pres. infin. act. . . . id.

περιτέμνεσθαι, pres. infin. pass. . . id.

περιτεμνέσθω, 3 pers. sing. pres. imper. pass. id.

περιτέμνετε, 2 pers. pl. pres. ind. act. . . id.

περιτέμνησθε, 2 pers. pl. pres. subj. pass. . id.

περιτεμνόμενοι, nom. pl. masc. part. pres. pass. id.

περιτεμνομένῳ, dat. sing. masc. part. pres. pass. id.

περιτέμνω], fut. τεμῶ, (§ 27. rem. 1. b) perf. pass.

[a] Ac. 16. 22.

περιτέτμημαι, aor. 2, περιέτεμον, (§ 27. rem. 4. b) (περί & τέμνω) *to cut around; to circumcise, remove the prepuce*, Lu. 1. 59; 2. 21, et al.; met. Col. 2. 11; mid. *to submit to circumcision*, Ac. 15. 1, et al.

περιτομή, ῆς, ἡ, (§ 2. tab. B. a) *circumcision, the act or custom of circumcision*, Jno. 7. 22, 23; Ac. 7. 8; *the state of being circumcised, the being circumcised*, Ro. 2. 25, 26, 27; 4. 10; meton. *the circumcision, those who are circumcised*, Ro. 3. 30; 4. 9; met. spiritual *circumcision* of the heart and affections, Ro. 2. 29; Col. 2. 11; meton. *persons* spiritually *circumcised*, Phi. 3. 3. LXX.

περιτετμημένοι, nom. pl. masc. part. perf. pass.—B. Sch. Ln. Tdf. } περιτέμνω
περιτεμνόμενοι, Rec. Gr. (Gal. 6. 13)

περιτετμημένος, nom. sing. masc. part. perf. pass. id.

περιτιθέᾱσι, 3 pers. sing. pres. ind. act. Att. for περιτιθεῖσι, (§ 28. rem. 6) περιτίθημι

περιτίθεμεν, 1 pers. pl. pres. ind. act. id.

περιτίθημι], fut. περιθήσω, aor. 1, περιέθηκα, aor. 2, περιέθην, (§ 28. tab. V) (περί & τίθημι) *to place around, put about or around*, Mat. 21. 33; 27. 28, et al.; met. *to attach, bestow*, 1 Co. 12. 23.

περίθεσις, εως, ἡ, (§ 5. tab. E. c) *a putting on, wearing* of dress, etc., 1 Pe. 3. 3. N.T.

περιτμηθῆναι, aor. 1, infin. pass. περιτέμνω

περιτμηθῆτε, 2 pers. pl. aor. 1, subj. pass.—Al. Ln. Tdf. } id.
περιτέμνησθε, Rec. Gr. Sch. (Ac. 15. 1)

περιτομή], ῆς, ἡ, (§ 2. tab. B. a) id.

περιτομῇ, dat. sing. περιτομή

περιτομήν, acc. sing. id.

περιτομῆς, gen. sing. id.

περιτρέπει,[a] 3 pers. sing. pres. ind. περιτρέπω

περιτρέπω], fut. ψω, (§ 23. rem. 1. a) (περί & τρέπω) *to turn about; to bring round* into any state, Ac. 26. 24.

περιτρέχω], aor. 2, περιέδρᾰμον, (§ 36. rem. 1) (περί & τρέχω) *to run about, run up and down*, Mar. 6. 55.

περιφέρειν, pres. infin. act. περιφέρω

περιφέρεσθε, 2 pers. pl. pres. imper. pass. id.

περιφερόμεναι, nom. pl. fem. part. pres. pass. id.

περιφερόμενοι, nom. pl. masc. part. pres. pass. περιφέρω

περιφέροντες, nom. pl. masc. part. pres. act. id.

περιφέρω], fut. περιοίσω, aor. 1, περιήνεγκα, aor. 2, περιήνεγκον, (§ 36. rem. 1) (περί & φέρω) *to bear or carry about*, Mar. 6. 55; 2 Co. 4. 10; pass. *to be borne about hither and thither, to be whirled about, driven to and fro*, Ep. 4. 14; He. 13. 9; Jude 12.

περιφρονείτω,[b] 3 pers. sing. pres. imper. περιφρονέω

περιφρονέω, ῶ], fut. ήσω, (§ 16. tab. P) (περί & φρήν) *to contemplate, reflect on; to despise, disregard*, Tit. 2. 15.

περίχωρον, acc. sing. fem. περίχωρος

περίχωρος], ου, ὁ, ἡ, (§ 7. rem. 2) (περί & χώρα) *circumjacent*; ἡ περίχωρος, sc. γῆ, *an adjacent or circumjacent region, country round about*, Mat. 14. 35; Mar. 1. 28; meton. *inhabitants of the region round about*, Mat. 3. 5. L.G.

περιχώρου, gen. sing. fem. περίχωρος

περιχώρῳ, dat. sing. fem. id.

περίψημα],[c] ατος, τό, (§ 4. tab. D. c) (περιψάω, *to wipe on every side*) *filth which is wiped off; offscouring*; met. 1 Co. 4. 13. N.T.

περπερεύεται,[d] 3 pers. sing. pres. ind. περπερεύομαι

περπερεύομαι], fut. εύσομαι, (πέρπερος, *braggart*) *to vaunt one's self*. L.G.

Περσίδα,[e] acc. Περσίς

Περσίς], ίδος (ῐ), ἡ, (§ 4. rem. 2. c) *Persis*, pr. name.

πέρῡσι], adv. πέρας

πεσεῖν, aor. 2, infin. (§ 37. rem. 1) πίπτω

πεσεῖται, 3 pers. sing. fut. ind. id.

πέσετε, 2 pers. pl. aor. 2, imper. id.

πέσῃ, 3 pers. sing. aor. 2, subj. id.

πέσητε, 2 pers. pl. aor. 2, subj. id.

πεσόν, nom. sing. neut. part. aor. 2 id.

πεσόντα, acc. sing. masc. part. aor. 2 id.

πεσόντας, acc. pl. masc. part. aor. 2 id.

πεσόντες, nom. pl. masc. part. aor. 2 id.

πεσοῦνται, 3 pers. pl. fut. ind. id.

πεσών, nom. sing. masc. part. aor. 2 id.

πέσωσι, 3 pers. pl. aor. 2, subj. id.

πετάομαι, ῶμαι] πέτομαι

πετεινά, nom. and acc. pl. πετεινόν

πετεινόν], οῦ, τό, (§ 3. tab. C. c) πέτομαι

πετεινῶν, gen. pl. πετεινόν

πέτηται,[f] 3 pers. sing. pres. subj. πέτομαι

πέτομαι], fut. πετήσομαι & πτήσομαι, *to fly*.

[a] Ac. 26. 24. [b] Tit. 2. 15. [c] 1 Co. 4. 13. [d] 1 Co. 13. 4. [e] Ro. 16. 12. [f] Re. 12. 14.

πετάομαι, ῶμαι, a later form for πέτομαι, Re. 4. 7; 14. 6; 19. 17.

πετεινόν, οῦ, τό, (neut. of πετεινός, ή, ον, *winged*, *flying*, fr. πέτομαι) *a bird*, *fowl*, Mat. 6. 26; 8. 20, et al.

πτηνόν, οῦ, τό, (pr. neut. of πτηνός, ή, όν, *winged*, fr. πέτομαι) *a bird*, *fowl*, 1 Co. 15. 39.

πετομένοις, dat. pl. neut. part. pres.—Gr. Sch. Tdf. . . . . . } πέτομαι
πετωμένοις, Rec. (Re. 19. 17) . }

πετόμενον, acc. sing. masc. part. pres.—Gr. Sch. Tdf. . . . . . } id.
πετώμενον, Rec. (Re. 14. 6) . }

πετομένου, gen. sing. masc. part. pres.—Gr. Sch. Tdf. . . . . } id.
πετωμένου, Rec. (Re. 8. 13) . }

πετομένῳ, dat. sing. masc. part. pres.—Gr. Sch. Tdf. . . . . . } id.
πετωμένῳ, Rec. (Re. 4. 7) . . }

πέτρα], ας, ἡ, (§ 2. tab. B. b) *a rock*, Mat. 7. 24, 25, et al.; met. Ro. 9. 33; 1 Pe. 2. 8; *crags*, *clefts*, Re. 6. 15, 16; *stony ground*, Lu. 8. 6, 13.

Πέτρος, ου, ὁ, (§ 3. tab. C. a) *a stone*; in N.T. the Greek rendering of the surname Cephas, given to the Apostle Simon, and having, therefore, the same sense as πέτρα, *Peter*, Mat. 4. 18; 8. 14, et al.

πετρώδης, εος, ους, ὁ, ἡ, το, -ες, (§ 7. tab. G. b) *like rock*; *stony*, *rocky*, Mat. 13. 5, 20; Mar. 4. 5, 16.

πέτρᾳ, dat. sing. . . . . . πέτρα
πέτραι, nom. pl. . . . . . . id.
πέτραις, dat. pl. . . . . . . id.
πέτραν, acc. sing. . . . . . . id.
πέτρας, gen. sing. and acc. pl. . . . id.
Πέτρε, voc. . . . . Πέτρος
Πέτρον, acc. . . . . id.
Πέτρος], ου, ὁ . . . . . . πέτρα
Πέτρου, gen. . . . . . . Πέτρος
Πέτρῳ, dat. . . . . id.
πετρῶδες, acc. sing. neut. . . . . πετρώδης
πετρώδη, acc. pl. neut. . . . . . id.
πετρώδης], εος, ους, ὁ, ἡ . . . . πέτρα
πετωμένοις, dat. pl. neut. part. pres. . . πετάομαι

πετώμενον, acc. sing. masc. part. pres. . πετάομαι
πετωμένου, gen. sing. masc. part. pres. . id.
πετωμένῳ, dat. sing. masc. part. pres. . id.
πεφανερώμεθα, 1 pers. pl. perf. ind. pass. (§ 21. tab. U) . . . . . φανερόω
πεφανερῶσθαι, perf. infin. pass. . . id.
πεφανέρωται, 3 pers. sing. perf. ind. pass. . id.
πεφιλήκατε, 2 pers. pl. perf. ind. act. (§ 16. rem. 5) . . . . . φιλέω
πεφίμωσο, 2 pers. sing. perf. imper. pass. . φιμόω
πεφορτισμένοι, nom. pl. masc. part. perf. pass. φορτίζω
πεφυσιωμένοι, nom. pl. masc. part. perf. pass. φυσιόω
πεφυσιωμένων, gen. pl. part. perf. pass. . id.
πεφυτευμένην, acc. sing. fem. part. perf. pass. φυτεύω
πεφωτισμένους, acc. pl. masc. part. perf. pass. (§ 26. rem. 1) . . . . . φωτίζω
πηγαί, nom. pl. . . . . . . πηγή

πήγᾰνον],[a] ου, τό, (§ 3. tab. C. c) *rue*, a plant, *ruta graveolens* of Linn.

πηγάς, acc. pl. . . . . πηγη

πηγή], ῆς, ἡ, (§ 2. tab. B. a) *a source*, *spring*, *fountain*, Ja. 3. 11, 12; *a well*, Jno. 4. 6; *an issue*, *flux*, *flow*, Mar. 5. 29; met. Jno. 4. 14.

πηγῇ, dat. sing. . . . . . πηγή
πηγῆς, gen. sing. . . . . . id.

πήγνυμι, and **πηγνύω**], fut. ξω, aor. 1, ἔπηξα, (§ 36. rem. 5) *to fasten*; *to pitch* a tent, He. 8. 2.

παγίς, ίδος, ἡ (ῐ), (§ 4. rem. 2. c) *a snare*, *trap*, *gin*, Lu. 21. 35; met. *artifice*, *stratagem*, *device*, *wile*, 1 Ti. 3. 7; 6. 9; 2 Ti. 2. 26; met. *a trap* of ruin, Ro. 11. 9.

παγιδεύω, fut. εύσω, (§ 13. tab. M) *to ensnare*, *entrap*, *entangle*, Mat. 22. 15.

πάγος, ου, ὁ, (§ 3. tab. C. a) *a hill*; Ἄρειος πάγος, *Areopagus*, *the hill of Mars*, at Athens, Ac. 17. 19, 22.

πηδάλιον], ίου, τό, (§ 3. tab. C. c) (πηδόν, *the blade of an oar*) *a rudder*, Ac. 27. 40; Ja. 3. 4.

πηδαλίου, gen. sing. . . . . πηδάλιον
πηδαλίων, gen. pl. . . . . . id.
πηλίκοις, dat. pl. neut. . . . . πηλίκος
πηλίκος], η, ον, (§ 10. rem. 7. c) *how large*, Gal. 6. 11; *how great* in dignity, He. 7. 4. (ῐ).

[a] Lu. 11. 42.

πηλόν, acc. sing. . . . . . . πηλός

πηλός], οῦ, ὁ, (§ 3. tab. C. a) *moist earth, mud, slime,* Jno. 9. 6, 11, 14, 15; *clay,* potter's *clay,* Ro. 9. 21.

πηλοῦ, gen. sing. . . . . . πηλός

πήρα], ας, ἡ, (§ 2. tab. B. b) *a leather bag or sack* for provisions, *scrip, wallet,* Mat. 10. 10; Mar. 6. 8, et al.

πήραν, acc. sing. . . . . . . πήρα

πήρας, gen. sing. . . . . . . id.

πῆχυν, acc. sing. (§ 5. rem. 5) . . . . πῆχυς

πῆχυς], εως, ὁ, (§ 5. tab. E. c) pr. *cubitus, the fore-arm;* hence, *a cubit,* a measure of length, equal to the distance from the elbow to the extremity of the little finger, usually considered as equivalent to a foot and a half, or 17 inches and a half, Jno. 21. 8; Re. 21. 17; met. of time, *a span,* Mat. 6. 27; Lu. 12. 25.

πηχῶν, gen. pl. . . . . . . πῆχυς

πιάζω], (a later form for πιέζω, derived from the Doric) fut. άσω, aor. 1, ἐπίασα, (§ 26. rem. 1) *to press;* in N.T. *to take or lay hold of,* Ac. 3. 7; *to take, catch* fish, etc., Jno. 21. 3, 10; Re. 19. 20; *to take, seize, apprehend, arrest,* Jno. 7. 30, 32, 44, et al.

πιάσαι, aor. 1, infin. act. . . . . . πιάζω

πιάσας, nom. sing. masc. part. aor. 1, act. id.

πιάσωσι, 3 pers. pl. aor. 1, subj. act. . id.

πίε, 2 pers. sing. aor. 2, imper. (§ 37. rem. 1) πίνω

πιέζω], fut. έσω, perf. pass. πεπίεσμαι, (§ 26. rem. 1) *to press, to press or squeeze down, make compact by pressure,* Lu. 6. 38.

πιεῖν, aor. 2, infin act. . . . . . πίνω

πίεσαι, 2 pers. sing. fut. ind. (§ 37. rem. 1) id.

πίεσθε, 2 pers. pl. fut. ind. . . . . id.

πίεται, 3 pers. sing. fut. ind. . . . . id.

πίετε, 2 pers. pl. aor. 2, imper. . . . id.

πίῃ, 3 pers. sing. aor. 2, subj. . . . id.

πίητε, 2 pers. pl. aor. 2, subj. . . . id.

πιθανολογία], ας, ἡ, (§ 2. tab. B. b, and rem. 2) (πιθανός, *persuasive,* πείθω & λόγος) *persuasive speech, plausible discourse.*

πιθανολογίᾳ,[a] dat. sing. . . . . πιθανολογία

πικραίνεσθε, 2 pers. pl. pres. imper. pass. . πικραίνω

πικραίνω], fut. ανῶ, (§ 27. rem. 1. c) . . πικρός

πικρανεῖ, 3 pers. sing. fut. ind. act. . πικραίνω

πικρία], ας, ἡ, (§ 2. tab. B. b, and rem. 2) . πικρός

πικρίας, gen. sing. . . . . . πικρία

πικρόν, acc. sing. masc. and neut. . . πικρός

πικρός], ά, όν, (§ 7. rem. 1) *bitter,* Ja. 3. 11; met. *bitter, harsh,* Ja. 3. 14.

πικραίνω, fut. ανῶ, *to embitter, render bitter,* Re. 10. 9; pass. *to be embittered, be made bitter,* Re. 8. 11; 10. 10; met. pass. *to be embittered, to grow angry, harsh,* Col. 3. 19.

πικρία, ας, ἡ, *bitterness,* Ac. 8. 23; He. 12. 15; met. *bitterness* of spirit and language, *harshness,* Ro. 3. 14; Ep. 4. 31.

πικρῶς, adv. *bitterly,* Mat. 26. 75; Lu. 22. 62.

πικρῶς], adv. . . . . πικρός

Πιλάτον, acc. . . . . . . Πιλάτος

Πιλάτος], ου, ὁ, (§ 3. tab. C. a) *Pilate,* pr. name.

Πιλάτῳ, dat. . . . . . . Πιλάτος

πίμπλημι, or πλήθω], fut. πλήσω, aor. 1, pass. ἐπλήσθην, (§ 23. rem. 1. c, and rem. 4) *to fill,* Mat. 27. 48, et al.; pass. *to be filled* mentally, *be under full influence,* Lu. 1. 15; 4. 28, et al.; *to be fulfilled,* v.r. Lu. 21. 22; of stated time, *to be brought to a close, arrive at its close,* Lu. 1. 23, 57; 2. 6, 21, 22.

πλῆθος, εος, τό, (§ 5. tab. E. c) *fulness, amplitude, magnitude; a multitude, a great number,* Lu. 1. 10; 2. 13; 5. 6; *a multitude, a crowd, throng,* Mar. 3. 7, 8; Lu. 6. 17, et al.

πληθύνω, fut. υνῶ, aor. 1, ἐπλήθυνα, aor. 1, pass. ἐπληθύνθην, (§ 27. rem. 1. a. f, and rem. 3) trans. *to multiply, cause to increase, augment,* 2 Co. 9. 10; He. 6. 14; pass. *to be multiplied, increase, be accumulated,* Mat. 24. 12; Ac. 6. 7; 7. 17, et al.; intrans. *to multiply, increase, be augmented,* Ac. 6. 1.

πλησμονή, ῆς, ἡ, (§ 2. tab. B. a) *a filling up;* met. *gratification, satisfaction,* Col. 2. 23.

πίμπρασθαι,[b] pres. infin. pass. . . πίμπρημι

πίμπρημι], fut. πρήσω, *to set on fire, burn,*

[a] Col. 2. 4.

[b] Ac. 28. 6.

inflame; in N.T. pass. *to swell from inflammation*, Ac. 28. 6.

πίνακι, dat. sing. . . . . . . πίναξ

πινακίδιον],[a] ίου, τό . . . . . id.

πίνακος, gen. sing. . . . . . . id.

πίναξ], ἄκος, ὁ, (§ 4. rem. 2. b) pr. *a board or plank*; in N.T. *a plate, platter, dish* on which food was served, Mar. 14. 8, 11, et al.

πινακίδιον, ίου, τό, (§ 3. tab. C. c) *a small tablet* for writing.

πίνει, 3 pers. sing. pres. ind. . . . . πίνω

πίνειν, pres. infin. . . . . . . id.

πίνετε, 2 pers. pl. pres. ind. . . . . id.

πινέτω, 3 pers. sing. pres. imper. . . . id.

πίνῃ, 3 pers. sing. pres. subj. . . . . id.

πίνητε, 2 pers. pl. pres. subj. . . . . id.

πίνοντες, nom. pl. masc. part. pres. . . . id.

πίνουσι, 3 pers. pl. pres. ind. . . . . id.

πίνω], fut. πίομαι & πιοῦμαι, aor. 2, ἔπῐον, perf. πέπωκα, (§ 37. rem. 1) *to drink*, Mat. 6. 25, 31; 26. 27, 29, et al. freq.; trop. of the earth, *to drink in, imbibe*, He. 6. 7.

πόμα, ατος, τό, (§ 4. tab. D. c) (πέπομαι, perf. pass. of πίνω) *drink*, 1 Co. 10. 4; He. 9. 10.

πόσις, εως, ἡ, (§ 5. tab. E. c) *drinking; drink, beverage*, Jno. 6. 55; Ro. 14. 17; Col. 2. 16.

ποτήριον, ίου, τό, (§ 3. tab. C. c) (ποτήρ, πότος, πίνω) *a vessel for drinking, cup*, Mat. 10. 42; 23. 25, 26; meton. *the contents of a cup, liquor contained in a cup*, Lu. 22. 20; 1 Co. 10. 16; from the Heb., *the cup or potion* of what God's administration deals out, Mat. 20. 22, 23; Re. 14. 10, et al.

ποτίζω, fut. ίσω, Att. ιῶ, perf. πεπότικα, aor. 1, ἐπότισα, (§ 26. rem. 1) *to cause to drink, give drink to*, Mat. 10. 42, et al.; met. 1 Co. 3. 2; Re. 14. 8; *to water, irrigate*, met. 1 Co. 3. 6, 7, 8.

πότος, ου, ὁ, (§ 3. tab. C. a) *a drinking; a drinking together, drinking-bout, compotation*, 1 Pe. 4. 3.

πίνω, 1 pers. sing. pres. subj. . . . . πίνω

πίνων, nom. sing. masc. part. pres. . . . πίνω

πιότης], τητος, ἡ, (§ 4. rem. 2. c) (πίων, *fat*) *fatness, richness*.

πιότητος,[b] gen. sing. . . . . . πιότης

πιοῦσα, nom. sing. fem. part. aor. 2 . . . πίνω

πιπρασκομένων, gen. pl. part. pres. pass. . . πιπράσκω

πιπράσκω], perf. πέπρᾱκα, perf. pass. πέπρᾱμαι, aor. 1, ἐπράθην, (§ 36. rem. 3) (redupl. from περάω, *to bring from a distance to sell*) *to sell*, Mat. 13. 46; 18. 25, et al.; met. with ὑπό, pass. *to be sold under, to be a slave to, be devoted to*, Ro. 7. 14.

πίπτει, 3 pers. sing. pres. ind. . . . . πίπτω

πίπτοντες, nom. pl. masc. part. pres.—Al. Ln. } id.
ἐκπίπτοντες, R. Gr. Sch. Tdf. (Mar. 13. 25) }

πιπτόντων, gen. pl. neut. part. pres. . . . id.

πίπτω], fut. πεσοῦμαι, perf. πέπτωκα, aor. 2, ἔπεσον, and, in N.T., aor. 1, ἔπεσα, (§ 37. rem. 1) *to fall*, Mat. 15. 27; Lu. 10. 18; *to fall, fall prostrate, fall down*, Mat. 17. 6; 18. 29; Lu. 17. 16; *to fall down* dead, Lu. 21. 24; *to fall, fall in ruins*, Mat. 7. 25, 27; Lu. 11. 17; met. *to fall, come by chance*, as a lot, Ac. 1. 26; *to fall, to fail, become null and void, fall to the ground*, Lu. 16. 17; *to fall* into a worse state, Re. 2. 5; *to come to ruin*, Ro. 11. 11; He. 4. 11; *to fall* into sin, Ro. 11. 22; 1 Co. 10. 2; *to fall* in judgment, by condemnation, Re. 14. 8; *to fall* upon, *seize*, Re. 11. 11; *to light* upon, Re. 7. 16; *to fall* under, *incur*, Ja. 5. 12.

πτῶμα, ατος, τό, (§ 4. tab. D. c) *a fall; a dead body, carcase, corpse*, Mat. 24. 28; Mar. 6. 29; Re. 11. 8, 9.

πτῶσις, εως, ἡ, (§ 5. tab. E. c) *a fall, crash, ruin*, Mat. 7. 27; met. *downfall, ruin*, Lu. 2. 34.

Πισιδία], ας, ἡ, (§ 2. tab. B. b, and rem. 2) *Pisidia*, a country of Asia Minor.

Πισιδίαν, acc. . . . . . . Πισιδία

Πισιδίας, gen. . . . . . . id.

πιστά, acc. pl. neut. . . . . . πιστός

πιστάς, acc. pl. fem. . . . . . id.

πιστέ, voc. sing. masc. . . . . . id.

πίστει, dat. sing. . . . . . πίστις

[a] Lu. 1. 63.

[b] Ro. 11. 17.

πίστευε, 2 pers. sing. pres. imper. . . . πιστεύω

πιστεύει, 3 pers. sing. pres. ind. . . id.

πιστεύειν, pres. infin. . . . . id.

πιστεύεις, 2 pers. sing. pres. ind. . . id.

πιστεύεται, 3 pers. sing. pres. ind. pass. . id.

πιστεύετε, 2 pers. pl. pres. ind. and imper. . id.

πιστεύητε, 2 pers. pl. pres. subj. . . id.

πιστευθῆναι, aor. 1, infin. pass. . . id.

πιστεύομεν, 1 pers. pl. pres. ind. . . id.

πιστεύοντα, acc. sing. masc. part. pres. . id.

πιστεύοντας, acc. pl. masc. part. pres. . . id.

πιστεύοντες, nom. pl. masc. part. pres. . id.

πιστεύοντι, dat. sing. masc. part. pres. . . id.

πιστευόντων, gen. pl. masc. part. pres. . id.

πιστεύουσι, dat. pl. masc. part. pres. . . id.

πιστεύουσι, 3 pers. pl. pres. ind. . . id.

πιστεῦσαι, aor. 1, infin. . . . . id.

πιστεύσαντας, acc. pl. masc. part. aor. 1 . id.

πιστεύσαντες, nom. pl. masc. part. aor. 1 . id.

πιστευσάντων, gen. pl. masc. part. aor. 1 . id.

πιστεύσας, nom. sing masc. part. aor. 1 . id.

πιστεύσασα, nom. sing. fem. part. aor. 1 . id.

πιστεύσασι, dat. pl. masc. part. aor. 1, (§ 4. rem. 3. c) . . . . id.

πιστεύσατε, 2 pers. pl. aor. 1, imper. . id.

πιστεύσει, 3 pers. sing. fut. ind. . . id.

πιστεύσετε, 2 pers. pl. fut. ind. . . id.

πιστεύσῃ, 3 pers. sing. aor. 1, subj. . . id.

πιστεύσῃς, 2 pers. sing. aor. 1, subj. . . id.

πιστεύσητε, 2 pers. pl. aor. 1, subj. . . id.

πιστεύσομεν, 1 pers. pl. fut. ind. . . id.

πίστευσον, 2 pers. sing. aor. 1, imper. . . id.

πιστευσόντων, gen. pl. masc. part. fut. . id.

πιστεύσουσι, 3 pers. pl. fut. ind. . . id.

πιστεύσω, 1 pers. sing. fut. ind. . . id.

πιστεύσω, 1 pers. sing. aor. 1, subj. . . id.

πιστεύσωμεν, 1 pers. pl. aor. 1, subj. . id.

πιστεύσωσι, 3 pers. pl. aor. 1, subj. . . id.

πιστεύω], fut. εύσω, (§ 13. tab. M) . . πείθω

πιστεύων, nom. sing. masc. part. pres. . . πιστεύω

πίστεως, gen. sing. . . . . πίστις

πιστή, nom. sing. fem. . . . . πιστός

πιστήν, acc. sing. fem. . . id.

πιστῆς, gen. sing. fem. . . . . id.

πιστικῆς, gen. sing. fem. . . . πιστικός

πιστῐκός], ή, όν, (§ 7. tab. F. a) (πιστός) *genuine, unadulterated*, or, (πίνω) *liquid*, Mar. 14. 3; Jno. 12. 3. N.T.

πίστιν, acc. sing. . . . . . πίστις

πίστις], εως, ἡ, (§ 5. tab. E. c) . . πείθω

πιστοί, nom. pl. masc. . . . . πιστός

πιστοῖς, dat. pl. masc. . . . . id.

πιστόν, acc. sing. masc. and nom. and acc. s. neut. id.

πιστός], ή, όν, (§ 7. tab. F. a) . . . πείθω

πιστοῦ, gen. sing. masc. . . . πιστός

πιστούς, acc. sing. masc. . . . . id.

πιστόω, ῶ], fut. ώσω, (§ 20. tab. T) . . πείθω

πιστῷ, dat. sing. masc. . . . πιστός

πιστῶν, gen. pl. . . . . id.

πίω, 1 pers. sing. aor. 2, subj. (§ 37. rem. 1) πίνω

πίωμεν, 1 pers. pl. aor. 2, subj. act. . . id.

πιών, nom. sing. masc. part. aor. 2, act. . id.

πίωσι, 3 pers. pl. aor. 2, subj. act. . . id.

πλάκες, nom. pl. . . . . πλάξ

πλανᾷ, 3 pers. sing. pres. ind. act. . . πλανάω

πλανᾷ, 3 pers. sing. pres. subj. act.—Gr. Sch. } πλανήσῃ, Rec. Tdf. (Re. 20. 3) . } id.

πλανᾶσθαι, pres. infin. pass. (§ 19. tab. S) id.

πλανᾶσθε, 2 pers. pl. pres. ind. and imper. id.

πλανάτω, 3 pers. sing. pres. imper. act. . id.

πλανάω, ῶ], fut. ήσω, (§ 18. tab. R) . . πλάνη

πλάνη], ης, ἡ, (§ 2. tab. B. a) *a wandering; deceit, deception, delusion, imposture, fraud*, Mat. 27. 64; 1 Thes. 2. 3; *seduction, deceiving*, Ep. 4. 14; 2 Thes. 2. 11; 1 Jno. 4. 6; *error, false opinion*, 2 Pe. 3. 17; *wandering* from the path of truth and virtue, *perverseness, wickedness, sin*, Ro. 1. 27; Ja. 5. 20; 2 Pe. 2. 18; Jude 11.

πλανάω, ῶ, fut. ήσω, aor. 1, ἐπλάνησα, (§ 18. tab. R) *to lead astray, cause to wander*; pass. *to go astray, wander about, stray*, Mat. 18. 12, 13; 1 Pe. 2. 25; met. *to mislead, deceive*, Mat. 24. 4, 5, 11, 24; pass. *to be deceived, err, mistake*, Mat. 22. 29; *to seduce, delude*, Jno. 7. 12, pass. *to be seduced* or *wander* from the path of virtue, *to sin, transgress*, Tit. 3. 3; He. 5. 2; Ja. 5. 19, et al.

πλανήτης, ου, ὁ, (§ 2. tab. B. c) *a rover, roving, a wanderer, wandering*; ἀστὴρ πλανήτης, *a wandering star*, Jude 13.

πλάνος, η, ον, and ος, ον, *a wanderer, vagabond*; also act. *deceiving, seducing; a deceiver, impostor*, Mat. 27. 63; 2 Co. 6. 8; 1 Ti. 4. 1; 2 Jno. 7.

πλάνῃ, dat. sing. . . . . . πλάνη

πλανηθῇ, 3 pers. sing. aor. 1, subj. pass. . πλανάω

πλανηθῆναι, aor. 1, infin. pass.—D. }
πλανῆσαι, Rec. Gr. Sch. Tdf. (Mat. 24. 24) } πλανάω
πλανηθῆτε, 2 pers. pl. aor. 1, subj. pass. . id.
πλάνης, gen. sing. . . . . . πλάνη
πλανῆσαι, aor. 1, infin. act. . . . πλανάω
πλανήσῃ, 3 pers. sing. aor. 1, subj. act. id.
πλανήσουσι, 3 pers. pl. fut. ind. act. . id.
πλανῆται,[a] nom. pl. . . . . πλανήτης
πλανήτης], ου, ὁ . . . πλάνη
πλάνοι, nom. pl. masc. . . . . πλάνος
πλάνοις, dat. pl. neut. . . . id.
πλάνος], η, ον, and ος, ον . . . πλάνη
πλανῶμεν, 1 pers. pl. pres. ind. act. . πλανάω
πλανώμενα, nom. pl. neut. part. pres. pass. . id.
πλανώμενοι, nom. pl. masc. part. pres. pass. id.
πλανωμένοις, dat. pl. masc. part. pres. pass. id.
πλανώμενον, acc. sing. neut. part. pres. pass. id.
πλανῶν, nom. sing. masc. part. pres. act. . id.
πλανῶνται, 3 pers. pl. pres. ind. pass. . id.
πλανῶντες, nom. pl. masc. part. pres. act. id.
πλανώντων, gen. pl. masc. part. pres. act. . id.

πλάξ], ακός, ἡ, (§ 4. rem. 2. b) *a flat broad surface; a table, tablet,* 2 Co. 3. 3; He. 9. 4.

πλαξί, dat. pl. (§ 4. rem. 3. a) . . . πλάξ
πλάσαντι, dat. sing. masc. part. aor. 1, act. πλάσσω
πλάσμα],[b] ατος, το . . . . id.

πλάσσω, or **ττω**], future πλάσω, aor. 1, ἔπλασα, aor. 1, pass. ἐπλάσθην, (§ 26. rem. 3) *to form, fashion, mould,* Ro. 9. 20; 1 Ti. 2. 13.

πλάσμα, ατος, τό, (§ 4. tab. D. c) *a thing formed or fashioned;* spc. *a potter's vessel,* Ro. 9. 20.

πλαστός, ή, όν, (§ 7. tab. F. a) *formed, fashioned, moulded;* met. *fabricated, counterfeit, delusive,* 2 Pe. 2. 3.

πλαστοῖς,[c] dat. pl. masc. . . . . πλαστός
πλαστός], ή, όν . . . . πλάσσω
πλατεῖα,[d] nom. sing. fem. . . . πλατύς
πλατεῖα], ας, ἡ . . . . . id.
πλατείαις, dat. pl. . . . . . πλατεῖα
πλατείας, gen. sing. and acc. pl. . . id.
πλατειῶν, gen. pl. . . . . . id.
πλάτος], εος, τό, (§ 5. tab. E. b) . . πλατύς
πλατύνθητε, 2 pers. pl. aor. 1, imper. pass. . πλατύνω
πλατύνουσι, 3 pers. pl. pres. ind. act. . πλατύνω
πλατύνω], fut. υνῶ . . . . πλατύς

πλατύς], εῖα, ύ, (§ 7. tab. H. g) *broad, wide,* Mat. 7. 13.

πλατεῖα, ας, ἡ, (§ 2. tab. B. b, and rem. 2) (pr. fem. of πλατύς) *a street, broad way,* Mat. 6. 5; 12. 19; Lu. 10. 10, et al.

πλάτος, εος, τό, (§ 5. tab. E. b) *breadth,* Eph. 3. 18; Re. 20. 9; 21. 16, bis.

πλατύνω, fut. υνῶ, perf. pass. πεπλάτυμαι, aor. 1, pass. ἐπλατύνθην, (§ 27. rem. 2. a) *to make broad, widen, enlarge,* Mat. 23. 5; pass. met. of the heart, from the Heb., *to be expanded* with kindly and genial feelings, 2 Co. 6. 11, 13.

πλέγμα], ατος, τό, (§ 4. tab. D. c) . πλέκω
πλέγμασι,[e] dat. pl. . . . . πλέγμα
πλεῖν, pres. infin. . . . . πλέω
πλεῖον, nom. and acc. sing. neut. . . πλείων
πλείονα, acc. sing. masc. and fem. and acc. pl. neut. . . . . . id.
πλείονας, acc. pl. masc. . . . . id.
πλείονες, nom. pl. masc. . . . id.
πλείονος, gen. sing. fem. . . . . id.
πλειόνων, gen. pl. . . . . id.
πλείοσι, dat. pl. masc. . . . . id.
πλείους, nom. pl. masc. and fem. (§ 8. rem. 3) id.
πλείους, acc. pl. fem. . . . . id.
πλεῖσται, nom. pl. fem. . . . . πλεῖστος
πλεῖστον, nom. sing. neut. . . . id.
πλεῖστος], η, ον, (§ 8. rem. 2) . . . πολύς
πλείω, acc. pl. neut.—B. D. Ln. . . }
πλείους, R. Gr. Sch. Tdf. (Mat. 26. 53) } πλείων
πλείων], ονος, ὁ, ἡ, (§ 8. rem. 2) . . πολύς

πλέκω], fut. ξω, (§ 23. rem. 1. b) *to interweave, weave, braid, plait,* Mar. 15. 17; Jno. 19. 2.

πλέγμα, ατος, τό, (§ 4. tab. D. c) *anything plaited or intertwined; a braid* of hair, 1 Ti. 2. 9.

πλέξαντες, nom. pl. masc. part. aor. 1, act. πλέκω
πλέον, acc. sing. neut. . . . πλείων
πλέον, acc. sing. neut. part. pres. . . πλέω
πλεονάζει, 3 pers. sing. pres. ind. . πλεονάζω
πλεονάζοντα, acc. sing. masc. and nom. pl. neut. part. pres. . . . id.

[a] Jude 13. [b] Ro. 9. 20. [c] 2 Pe. 2. 3. [d] Mat. 7. 13. [e] 1 Ti. 2. 9.

πλεονάζω], fut. άσω, (§ 26. rem. 1) . πολύς
πλεονάσαι, 3 pers. sing. aor. 1, optat. . . πλεονάζω
πλεονάσασα, nom. sing. fem. part. aor. 1 . id.
πλεονάσῃ, 3 pers. sing. aor. 1, subj. . . id.
πλεονέκται, nom. pl. . . . . πλεονέκτης
πλεονέκταις, dat. pl. . . . id.
πλεονεκτεῖν, pres. infin. . . . πλεονεκτέω
πλεονεκτέω, ῶ], fut. ήσω, (§ 16. tab. P) (πλείων, πλέον, & ἔχω) *to have more* than another; *to take advantage of; to overreach, make gain of*, 2 Co. 7. 2; 12. 17, 18; *to wrong*, 1 Thes. 4. 6; *to get the better, or an advantage of*, 2 Co. 2. 11.

πλεονέκτης, ου, ὁ, (§ 2. tab. B. c) *one who has or claims to have more than his share; a covetous, avaricious person, one who defrauds for the sake of gain*, 1 Co. 5. 10, 11; 6. 10; Ep. 5. 5.

πλεονεξία, ας, ἡ, (§ 2. tab. B. b, and rem. 2) *some advantage which one possesses over another; an inordinate desire of riches, covetousness*, Lu. 12. 15, et al.; *grasping, overreaching, extortion*, Ro. 1. 29; 1 Thes. 2. 5, et al.; *a gift exacted by importunity and conferred with grudging, a hard-wrung gift*, 2 Co. 9. 5; *a scheme of extortion*, Mar. 7. 22.

πλεονεκτηθῶμεν, 1 pers. pl. aor. 1, subj. pass. (§ 17. tab. Q) . . . πλεονεκτέω
πλεονέκτης], ου, ὁ . . . . . id.
πλεονεξία], ας, ἡ . . . . . id.
πλεονεξίᾳ, dat. sing. . . . . πλεονεξία
πλεονεξίαι, nom. pl. . . . . id.
πλεονεξίαις, dat. pl. . . . . id.
πλεονεξίαν, acc. sing. . . . . id.
πλεονεξίας, gen. sing. . . . . id.
πλέοντας, acc. pl. masc. part. pres. . . πλέω
πλεόντων, gen. pl. masc. part. pres. . id.

πλευρά], ᾶς, ἡ, (§ 2. tab. B. b) pr. *a rib; the side* of the body, Jno. 19. 34; 20. 20, 25, 27; Ac. 12. 7.

πλευράν, acc. sing. . . . . . πλευρά

πλέω], fut. πλεύσομαι & πλευσοῦμαι, (§ 35. rem. 1, 3) aor. 1, ἔπλευσα, perf. πέπλευκα, *to sail*, Lu. 8. 23; Ac. 21. 3; 27. 2, 6, 24.

πλοῖον, ου, τό, (§ 3. tab. C. c) *a vessel, ship, bark*, whether large or small, Mat. 4. 21, 22; Ac. 21. 2, 3, et al.

πλοιάριον, ου, τό, (dimin. of πλοῖον) *a small vessel, boat*, Mar. 3. 9, et al.

πλόος, οῦς, όου, οῦ, and later, πλοῦς, πλοός, ὁ, (§ 3. rem. 3) *sailing, navigation, voyage*, Ac. 21. 7; 27. 9, 10.

πλέων, nom. sing. masc. part. pres. . ⎫
ὁ ἐπὶ τόπον πλέων, Gr. Sch. Tdf. ⎬ πλέω
ἐπὶ τῶν πλοίων ὁ ὅμιλος, Rec. (Re. 18. 17) . . . ⎭

πληγαί, nom. pl. . . . . . πληγή
πληγαῖς, dat. pl. . . . . . id.
πληγάς, acc. pl. . . . . . id.
πληγή], ῆς, ἡ, (§ 2. tab. B. a) . . . πλήσσω
πληγῇ, dat. sing. . . . . . πληγή
πληγήν, acc. sing. . . . . . id.
πληγῆς, gen. sing. . . . . . id.
πληγῶν, gen. pl. . . . . . id.
πλήθει, dat. sing. . . . . . πλῆθος
πλήθη, nom. pl. . . . . . id.
πλῆθος], εος, τό, (§ 5. tab. E. b) . . πίμπλημι
πλήθους, gen. sing. . . . . . πλῆθος
πληθύναι, 3 pers. sing. aor. 1, opt. act. . πληθύνω
πληθυνεῖ, 3 pers. sing. fut. ind. act.—Gr. Sch. Tdf. . . . . ⎫
πληθύναι, Rec. (2 Co. 9. 10) . . ⎭ id.
πληθυνθείη, 3 pers. sing. aor. 1, opt. pass. . id
πληθυνθῆναι, aor. 1, infin. pass. . . . id.
πληθυνόντων, gen. pl. masc. part. pres. act. . id.
πληθύνω], fut. υνῶ, (§ 27. rem. 1. a) . πίμπλημι
πληθυνῶ, 1 pers. sing. fut. ind. act. . . πληθύνω
πληθύνων, nom. sing. masc. part. pres. act. id.
πλήθω, see πίμπλημι.
πλήκτην, acc. sing. . . . . . πλήκτης
πλήκτης], ου, ὁ, (§ 2. tab. B. c) . . πλήσσω
πλήμμυρα], ας, ἡ, (§ 2. tab. B. b) (πλήμμη, *the flow of the sea*, πλήθω) *the flood-tide; a flood, inundation*, Lu. 6. 48.

πλημμύρας,[a] gen. sing. . . . . πλήμμυρα
πλήν], adv. . . . . . . πολύς
πλήρεις, nom. and acc. pl. masc. . . πλήρης
πλήρη, acc. sing. masc. . . . . id
πλήρης], εος, ους, ὁ, ἡ, (§ 7. rem. 5. a) (πλέος, *full*) *full, filled*, Mat. 14. 20; 15. 37; *full* of disease, Lu. 5. 12; met. *full of, abounding in, wholly occupied with, completely under the influence of, or affected by*, Lu.

a Lu. 6. 48.

4. 1; Jno. 1. 14; Ac. 9. 36, et al.; *full, complete, perfect*, Mar. 4. 28.

πληρόω, ῶ, fut. ώσω, perf. πεπλήρωκα, aor. 1, ἐπλήρωσα, (§ 20. tab. T) *to fill, make full, fill up*, Mat. 13. 48; 23. 32; Lu. 3. 5; *to fill up* a deficiency, Phi. 4. 18, 19, *to pervade*, Jno. 12. 3; Ac. 2. 2; *to pervade* with an influence, *to influence fully, possess fully*, Jno. 16. 6; Ac. 2. 28; 5. 3; Ro. 1. 29; Ep. 5. 18, et al.; *to complete, perfect*, Jno. 3. 29; Ep. 3. 19, et al.; *to bring to an end*, Lu. 7. 1; *to perform fully, discharge*, Mat. 3. 15; Ac. 12. 25; 13. 25; 14. 26; Ro. 13. 8; Col. 4. 17; *to consummate*, Mat. 5. 17; *to realise, accomplish, fulfil*, Lu. 1. 20; 9. 31; Ac. 3. 18· 13. 27; from the Heb., *to set forth fully*, Ro. 15. 19; Col. 1. 25; pass. of time, *to be fulfilled, come to an end, be fully arrived*, Mar. 1. 15; Lu. 21. 24; Jno. 7. 8, et al.; of prophecy, *to receive fulfilment*, Mat. 1. 22, et al. freq.

πλήρωμα, ατος, τό, (§ 4. tab. D. c) *that which fills up; full measure, entire contents*, Mar. 8. 20; 1 Co. 10. 26, 28; *complement, full extent, full number*, Gal. 4. 4; Ep. 1. 10; *that which fills up a deficiency, a supplement, a patch*, Mat. 9. 16; *fulness, abundance*, Jno. 1. 16; *full measure*, Ro. 15. 29; *a fulfilling, perfect performance*, Ro. 13. 10; *complete attainment* of entire belief, *full acceptance*, Ro. 11. 12; *full development, plenitude*, Ep. 1. 23; 3. 19; 4. 13; Col. 1. 19; 2. 9.

πληροῖς, 2 pers. sing. pres. subj. act. . . . πληρόω
πληρούμενον, nom. sing. neut. part. pres. pass. . . id.
πληρουμένου, gen. sing. masc. part. pres. (transitive) . . . . . id.
πληροῦν, pres. infin. act. . . . . id.
πληροῦσθε, 2 pers. pl. pres. imper. pass. (§ 21. tab. U) . . . . . . id.
πληροῦται, 3 pers. sing. pres. ind. pass. . . id.
πληροφορείσθω, 3 pers. sing. pres. imper. pass. . . . . . πληροφορέω

πληροφορέω, ῶ], fut. ήσω, aor. 1, ἐπληροφόρησα, (§ 16. tab. P) (πλήρης & φορέω) *to bring full measure, to give in full; to carry out fully, to discharge completely*, 2 Ti. 4. 5, 17; pass. of things, *to be fully established* as a matter of certainty, Lu. 1. 1; of persons, *to be fully convinced, assured*, Ro. 4. 21

πληροφορία, ας, ἡ, (§ 2. tab. B. b, and rem. 2) *full conviction, firm persuasion, assurance*, 1 Thes. 1. 5; Col. 2. 2, et al. N.T.

πληροφορηθείς, nom. sing. masc. part. aor. 1, pass. (§ 17. tab. Q) . . πληροφορέω
πληροφορηθῇ, 3 pers. sing. aor. 1, subj. pass. . id.
πληροφόρησον, 2 pers. sing. aor. 1, imper. act. . id.
πληροφορία], ας, ἡ . . . . . id.
πληροφορίᾳ, dat. sing. . . . . πληροφορία
πληροφορίαν, acc. sing. . . . . id.
πληροφορίας, gen. sing. . . . . . id.
πληρόω, ῶ], fut. ώσω, (§ 20. tab. T) . . πλήρης
πληρωθείσης, gen. sing. fem. part. aor. 1, pass. πληρόω
πληρωθέντων, gen. pl. neut. part. aor. 1, pass. id.
πληρωθῇ, 3 pers. sing. aor. 1, subj. pass. . id.
πληρωθῆναι, aor. 1, infin. pass. . . . id.
πληρωθήσεται, 3 pers. sing. fut. ind. pass. . id.
πληρωθήσονται, 3 pers. pl. fut. ind. pass. . id.
πληρωθῆτε, 2 pers. pl. aor. 1, subj. pass. . id.
πληρωθῶ, 1 pers. sing. aor. 1, subj. pass. . id.
πληρωθῶσι, 3 pers. pl. aor. 1, subj. pass. . id.
πλήρωμα], ατος, τό, (§ 4. tab. D. c) . . πλήρης
πληρώματα, acc. pl. . . . . . πλήρωμα
πληρώματι, dat. sing. . . . . id.
πληρώματος, gen. sing. . . . . id.
πληρώσαι, 3 pers. sing. aor. 1, optat. act. . πληρόω
πληρῶσαι, aor. 1, infin. act. . . . . id.
πληρώσαντες, nom. pl. masc. part. aor. 1, act. id.
πληρώσατε, 2 pers. pl. aor. 1, imper. act. . id.
πληρώσει, 3 pers. sing. fut. ind. act. . . id.
πληρώσεις, 2 pers. sing. fut. ind. act. . . id.
πληρώσετε, 2 pers. pl. fut. ind. act.—B. πληρώσατε, Rec. Gr. Sch. Tdf. (Mat. 23. 32) . . . . . } id.
πληρώσῃ, 3 pers. sing. aor. 1, subj. act. . id.
πληρώσονται, 3 pers. pl. fut. ind. mid. . id.
πληρώσωσι, 3 pers. pl. aor. 1, subj.—Gr. Sch. πληρώσονται, Rec. . . . πληρωθῶσι, Tdf. (Re. 6. 11) . } id.
πλήσαντες, nom. pl. masc. part. aor. 1, act. πίμπλημι
πλήσας, nom. sing. masc. part. aor. 1, act. . id.
πλησθείς, nom. sing. masc. part. aor. 1, pass. id.
πλησθῆναι, aor. 1, infin. pass.—Gr. Sch. Tdf. πληρωθῆναι, Rec. (Lu. 21. 22) . } id.
πλησθῇς, 2 pers. sing. aor. 1, subj. pass. . id.
πλησθήσεται, 3 pers. sing. fut. ind. pass. id.

πλησίον], adv. (πέλας, idem) *near, near by*, Jno. 4. 5; ὁ πλησίον, *a neighbour*, Mat. 19. 19; Ro. 15. 2, et al.; *a* friendly *neighbour*, Mat. 5. 43.

πλησμονή], ῆς, ἡ, (§ 2. tab. B. a) . . πίμπλημι

πλησμονήν,[a] acc. sing. . . πλησμονή

πλήσσω], fut. ξω, aor. 2, pass. ἐπλήγην, (§ 24. rem. 9) *to strike, smite*; from the Heb., *to smite, to plague, blast*, Re. 8. 12.

πληγή, ῆς ἡ, (§ 2. tab. B. a) *a blow, stroke, stripe*, Lu. 10. 30; 12. 48; meton. *a wound*, Ac. 16. 33; Re. 13. 3, 12, 14; from the Heb., *a plague, affliction, calamity*, Re. 9. 20; 11. 6.

πλήκτης, ου, ὁ, (§ 2. tab. B. c) *a striker, one apt to strike; a quarrelsome, violent person*, 1 Ti. 3. 3, Tit. 1. 7.

πλοῖα, nom. and acc. pl. . . . . πλοῖον

πλοιάρια, nom. pl. . . . . πλοιάριον

πλοιάριον], ου, τό, (§ 3. tab. C. c) . . πλέω

πλοιαρίῳ, dat. sing. . . . πλοιάριον

πλοῖον], ου, τό, (§ 3. tab. C. c) . . . πλέω

πλοίου, gen. sing. . . . . πλοῖον

πλοίῳ, dat. sing. . . . . . id.

πλοίων, gen. pl. . . . . . id.

πλόος, οῦς], όου, οῦ, ὁ, (§ 3. rem. 3) . . πλέω

πλοός, gen. sing. . . . πλόος, πλοῦς

πλοῦν, acc. sing. . . . . . id.

πλούσιοι, nom. pl. masc. . . πλούσιος

πλουσίοις, dat. pl. masc. . . . . id.

πλούσιον, acc. sing. masc. . . id.

πλούσιος], α, ον, (§ 7. rem. 1) . . . πλοῦτος

πλουσίου, gen. sing. masc. . . . πλούσιος

πλουσίους, acc. pl. masc. . . . . id.

πλουσίως], adv. . . . . πλοῦτος

πλουτεῖν, pres. infin. . . . . πλουτέω

πλουτέω, ῶ], fut. ήσω, (§ 16. tab. P) . πλοῦτος

πλουτήσαντες, nom. pl. masc. part. aor. 1 . πλουτέω

πλουτήσῃς, 2 pers. sing. aor. 1, subj. . id.

πλουτήσητε, 2 pers. pl. aor. 1, subj. . . id.

πλουτιζόμενοι, nom. pl. masc. part. pres. pass. πλουτίζω

πλουτίζοντες, nom. pl. masc. part. pres. act. id.

πλουτίζω], fut. ίσω, (§ 26. rem. 1) . . πλοῦτος

πλοῦτον, acc. sing. . . . . . . id.

πλοῦτος], ου, ὁ, (§ 3. tab. C. a) [τὸ πλοῦτος, Al. Ln. Tdf. Ep. 1. 7; 2. 7, et al.] *riches, wealth, opulence*, Mat. 13. 22; Lu. 8. 14; in N.T., πλοῦτος τοῦ Θεοῦ, or Χριστοῦ, *those rich benefits, those abundant blessings which flow from God or Christ*, Ep. 3. 8; Phi. 4. 19; meton. *richness, abundance, copiousness*, Ro. 2. 4; 11. 33; 2 Co. 8. 2; meton. *a* spiritual *enriching*, Ro. 11. 12.

πλούσιος, α, ον, (§ 7. rem. 1) *rich, opulent, wealthy*; and pl. οἱ πλούσιοι, *the rich*, Mat. 19. 23, 24; 27. 57, et al.; met. *rich, abounding in, distinguished for*, Ep. 2. 4; Ja. 2. 5; Re. 2. 9; 3. 17; *rich* in glory, dignity, bliss, etc., 2 Co. 8. 9.

πλουσίως, adv. *richly, largely, abundantly*, Col. 3. 16, et al.

πλουτέω, ῶ, fut. ήσω, perf. πεπλούτηκα, aor. 1, ἐπλούτησα, (§ 16. tab. P) *to be or become rich*, Lu. 1. 25; 1 Ti. 6. 9; trop. Lu. 12. 21; met. *to abound in, be abundantly furnished with*, 1 Ti. 6. 18; *to be* spiritually *enriched*, 2 Co. 8. 9, et al.

πλουτίζω, fut. ίσω, aor. 1, ἐπλούτισα, (§ 26. rem. 1) *to make rich, enrich*; met. *to enrich* spiritually, 1 Co. 1. 5; 2 Co. 6. 10; 9. 11.

πλούτου, gen. sing. . . . . πλοῦτος

πλουτοῦντας, acc. pl. masc. part. pres. . . πλουτέω

πλουτῶν, nom. sing. masc. part. pres. . id.

πλύνοντες, nom. pl. masc. part. pres. . } πλύνω
πλύνοντες τὰς στολὰς αὐτῶν.—A. Ln. Tdf. . . . . }
ποιοῦντες τὰς ἐντολὰς αὐτοῦ, Rec. Gr. Sch. (Re. 22. 14) . }

πλύνω], fut. υνῶ, aor. 1, ἔπλῦνα, (§ 27. rem. 1. a. f) *to wash* garments, Re. 14. 7.

πνέῃ, 3 pers. sing. pres. subj. . . . πνέω

πνεῖ, 3 pers. sing. pres. ind. (§ 35. rem. 1) . id.

πνέοντα, acc. sing. masc. part. pres. . . id.

πνέοντος, gen. sing. masc. part. pres. . id.

πνεούσῃ, dat. sing. fem. part. pres. . . id.

πνεῦμα], ατος, το, (§ 4. tab. D. c) . . id.

πνευμασι, dat. pl. . . . . . . πνεῦμα

πνεύματα, nom. and acc. pl. . . . id.

[a] Col. 2. 23

πνεύματι, dat. sing . . . . πνεῦμα
πνευματικά, acc. pl. neut. . . . πνευματικός
πνευματικαῖς, dat. pl. fem. . . . id.
πνευματικάς, acc. pl. fem. . . . id.
πνευματικῇ, dat. sing. fem. . . . id.
πνευματικῆς, gen. sing. fem. . . . id.
πνευματικοί, nom. pl. masc. . . . id.
πνευματικόν, nom. and acc. sing. neut. . id.
πνευματικός], ή, όν, (§ 7. tab. F. a) . πνέω
πνευματικῶν, gen. pl. . . . . πνευματικός
πνευματικῶς], adv. . . . . . πνέω
πνεύματος, gen. sing. . . . . πνεῦμα
πνευμάτων, gen. pl. . . . . . id.

πνέω], fut. πνεύσω, (§ 35. rem. 3) later, πνεύσομαι & πνευσοῦμαι, aor. 1, ἔπνευσα, *to breathe; to blow,* as the wind, Mat. 7. 25, 27, et al.

πνεῦμα, ατος, τό, (§ 4. tab. D. c) *wind, air in motion,* Jno. 3. 8; *breath,* 2 Thes. 2. 8; the substance *spirit,* Jno. 3. 6; *a spirit, spiritual being,* Jno. 4. 24; Ac. 23. 8, 9; He. 1. 14; *a* bodiless *spirit, spectre,* Lu. 24. 37; *a* foul *spirit,* δαιμόνιον, Mat. 8. 16; Lu. 10. 20; *spirit,* as a vital principle, Jno. 6. 63; 1 Co. 15. 45; *the* human *spirit, the soul,* Mat. 26. 41; 27. 50; Ac. 7. 59; 1 Co. 7. 34; Ja. 2. 26; *the spirit* as the seat of thought and feeling, *the mind,* Mar. 8. 12; Ac. 19. 21, et al.; *spirit, mental frame,* 1 Co. 4. 21; 1 Pe. 3. 4; *a* characteristic *spirit, an influential principle,* Lu. 9. 55; 1 Co. 2. 12; 2 Ti. 1. 7; *a pervading influence,* Ro. 11. 8; *spirit, frame of mind,* as distinguished from outward circumstances and actions, Mat. 5. 3; *spirit* as distinguished from outward show and form, Jno. 4. 23; *spirit, a* divinely-bestowed *spiritual frame,* characteristic of true believers, Ro. 8. 4; Jude 19; *spirit,* latent *spiritual import, spiritual significance,* as distinguished from the mere letter, Ro. 2. 29; 7. 6; 2 Co. 3. 6, 17; *spirit,* as a term for a process superior to a merely natural or carnal course of things, by the operation of the Divine Spirit, Ro. 8. 4; Gal. 4. 29; *a spiritual dispensation,* or, *a* sealing energy of the Holy *Spirit,* He. 9. 14; THE HOLY SPIRIT, Mat. 3. 16, 12. 31; Jno. 1. 32, 33, et al.; *a gift of the Holy Spirit,* Jno. 7. 39; Ac. 19. 2; 1 Co. 14. 12, et al.; *an operation or influence of the Holy Spirit,* 1 Co. 12. 3, et al.; *a spiritual influence, an inspiration,* Mat. 22. 43; Lu. 2. 27; Ep. 1. 17; *a professedly divine communication,* or, *a professed possessor of a spiritual communication,* 1 Co. 12. 10; 2 Thes. 2. 2; 1 Jno. 4. 1, 2, 3.

πνευματικός, ή, όν, (§ 7. tab. F. a) *spiritual, pertaining to the soul,* as distinguished from what concerns the body, Ro. 15. 27; 1 Co. 9. 11; *spiritual, pertaining to the nature of spirits,* 1 Co. 15. 44; τὰ πνευματικὰ τῆς πονηρίας, i. q. τὰ πνεύματα τὰ πονηρά, *evil spirits,* Ep. 6. 12; *spiritual, pertaining or relating to the influences of the Holy Spirit,* of things, Ro. 1. 11; 7. 14, et al.; τὰ πνευματικά, *spiritual gifts,* 1 Co. 12. 1; 14. 1; *superior in process to the natural course of things, miraculous,* 1 Co. 10. 3; of persons, *gifted with a spiritual frame of mind, spiritually affected,* 1 Co. 2. 13, 15; *endowed with spiritual gifts, inspired,* 1 Co. 14. 37.

πνευματικῶς, adv. *spiritually, through spiritual views and affections,* 1 Co. 2. 14; *spiritually, in a spiritual sense, allegorically,* Re. 11. 8.

πνοή, ῆς, ἡ, (§ 2. tab. B. a) *breath, respiration,* Ac. 17. 25; *a wind, a blast of wind, breeze,* Ac. 2. 2.

πνίγω], fut. ξω, ξομαι, and ξοῦμαι, aor. 1, ἔπνιξα, (§ 23. rem. 1. b, and rem. 2) *to stifle, suffocate, choke,* Mar. 5. 13; *to seize by the throat,* Mat. 18. 28. (ῑ).

πνικτός, ή, όν, (§ 7. tab. F. a) *strangled, suffocated;* in N.T., τὸ πνικτόν, *the flesh of animals killed by strangulation or suffocation,* Ac. 15. 20, 29; 21. 25.

πνικτόν, acc. sing. neut. . . . . πνικτος
πνικτός], ή, όν . . . . . . πνίγω
πνικτοῦ, gen. sing. neut. . . . . πνικτός
πνοή], ῆς, ἡ, (§ 2. tab. B. a) . . . πνέω
πνοήν, acc. sing. . . . . . πνοή
πνοῆς, gen. sing. . . . . . id.
πόδα, acc. sing. (§ 4. rem. 2. c) . . πούς
πόδας, acc. pl. . . . . . . id.
πόδες, nom. pl. . . . . . . id

ποδήρη,[a] acc. sing. masc. . . . . . ποδήρης

ποδήρης], εος, ους, ὁ, ἡ, (§ 7. tab. G. b) (πούς & ἄρω, *to fit*) *reaching to the feet*; as a sub. sc. ἐσθής, *a long, flowing robe reaching down to the feet*, Re. 1. 13.

ποδός, gen. sing. . . . . . πούς

ποδῶν, gen. pl. . . . . . id.

πόθεν], adv. *whence? whence*, used of place, etc., Mat. 15. 33; met. of a state of dignity, Re. 2. 5; used of origin, Mat. 21. 25; of cause, source, author, etc., Mat. 13. 27, 54, 56; Lu. 1. 43; *how? in what way?* Mar. 8. 4; 12. 37.

ποία, nom. sing. fem. . . . . . ποῖος

ποῖα, acc. pl. neut. . . . . . id.

ποίᾳ, dat. sing. fem. . . . . . id.

ποίαν, acc. sing. fem. . . . . . id.

ποίας, gen. sing. and acc. pl. fem. . . . id.

ποίει, 2 pers. sing. pres. imper. act. . . ποιέω

ποιεῖ, 3 pers. sing. pres. ind. act. . . id.

ποιεῖν, pres. infin. act. . . . . . id

ποιεῖς, 2 pers. sing. pres. ind. act. . . id.

ποιεῖσθαι, pres. infin. mid. . . . id.

ποιεῖσθε, 2 pers. pl. pres. imper. mid. . . id.

ποιεῖται, 3 pers. sing. pres. ind. mid. . . id.

ποιεῖτε, 2 pers. pl. pres. ind. and imper. act. id.

ποιείτω, 3 pers. sing. pres. imper. act. . . id.

ποιέω], ῶ, fut. ήσω, perf. πεποίηκα, aor. 1, ἐποίησα, (§ 16. tab. P) *to make, form, construct*, Mat. 17. 4; Mar. 9. 5; Jno. 2. 15; of God, *to create*, Mat. 19. 4; Ac. 4. 24; *to make, prepare* a feast, etc., Mat. 22. 2; Mar. 6. 21; met. *to make, establish, ratify*, a covenant, He. 8. 9; *to make, assume, consider, regard*, Mat. 12. 33; *to make, effect, bring to pass, cause to take place, do, accomplish*, Mat. 7. 22; 21. 21; Mar. 3. 8; 6. 5; 7. 37; met. *to perfect, accomplish, fulfil, put in execution* a purpose, promise, etc., Lu. 16. 4; 19. 48; *to cause, make*, Mat. 5. 32; Jno. 11. 37; Ac. 24. 12; *to make* gain, *gain, acquire*, Mat. 25. 16; Lu. 19. 18; *to get, procure*, Lu. 12. 33; *to make, to cause to be or become* a thing, Mat. 21. 13; 23. 15; *to use, treat*, Lu. 15. 19; *to make, constitute, appoint* to some office, Mat. 4. 19; Mar. 3. 14; *to make, declare to be*, 1 Jno. 1. 10; 5. 10; *to do, to perform, execute, practise, act*, Mat. 5. 46, 47; 6. 2, 3; *to commit* evil, Mat. 13. 41; 27. 23; *to be devoted to, follow, practise*, Jno. 3. 21; 5. 29; Ro. 3. 12; *to do, execute, fulfil, keep, observe, obey*, precepts, etc., Mat. 1. 24; 5. 19; 7. 21, 24, 26; *to bring* evil *upon, inflict*, Ac. 9. 13; *to keep, celebrate* a festival, Mat. 26. 18; *to institute the celebration of* a festival, He. 11. 28; ποιεῖν τινα ἔξω, *to cause to leave* a place, i.q. ἔξω ἄγειν, *to lead or conduct out*, Ac. 5. 34; *to pass, spend* time, *continue for* a time, Mat. 20. 12; Ac. 15. 33; 18. 23; Ja. 4. 13; *to bear*, as trees, *yield, produce*, Mat. 3. 8, 10; 7. 17, 18, 19; with a substantive or adjective it forms a periphrasis for the verb corresponding to the noun or adjective, e.g. δῆλον ποιεῖν, i.q. δηλοῦν, *to make manifest, betray*, Mat. 26. 73; ἐκδίκησιν π., i.q. ἐκδικεῖν, *to vindicate, avenge*, Lu. 18. 7, 8; ἔκθετον π., i.q. ἐκτιθέναι, *to expose* infants, Ac. 7. 19; ἐνέδραν π., i.q. ἐνεδρεύειν, *to lie in wait*, Ac. 25. 3; ἐξουσίαν π., i.q. ἐξουσιάζειν, *to exercise power or authority*, Re. 13. 12; κρίσιν π., i.q. κρίνειν, *to judge, act as judge*, Jno. 5. 27; λύτρωσιν π., i.q. λυτροῦν, *to deliver, set free*, Lu. 1. 68; μονὴν π., i.q. μένειν, *to remain, dwell*, Jno. 14. 23; πόλεμον π., i.q. πολεμεῖν, *to make or wage war, fight*, Re. 11. 7; συμβούλιον π., i.q. συμβουλεύεσθαι, *to consult together, deliberate*, Mar. 3. 6; συνωμοσίαν π., i.q. συνομνύναι, and συστροφὴν π., i.q. συστρέφεσθαι, *to conspire together, form a conspiracy*, Ac. 23. 12, 13; φανερὸν π., i.q. φανεροῦν, *to make known, betray*, Mat. 12. 16; ἀναβολὴν ποιεῖσθαι, i.q. ἀναβάλλεσθαι, *to delay, procrastinate*, Ac. 25. 17; βέβαιον π., i.q. βεβαιοῦν, *to confirm, render firm and sure*, 2 Pe. 1. 10; δεήσεις π., i.q. δεῖσθαι, *to pray, offer prayer*, Lu. 5. 33; ἐκβολὴν π., i.q. ἐκβάλλειν, *to cast out, throw overboard*, Ac. 27. 18; κα-

[a] Re. 1. 13.

θαρισμὸν π., i.q. καθαρίζειν, *to cleanse* from sin, He. 1. 3; κοινωνίαν π., i.q. κοινωνεῖν, *to communicate in liberality, bestow alms,* Ro. 15. 26; κοπετὸν π., i.q. κόπτεσθαι, *to lament, bewail,* Ac. 8. 2; λόγον π., *to regard, make account of,* Ac. 20. 24; μνείαν π., i.q. μνησθῆναι, *to call to mind,* Ro. 1. 9; μνήμην π., *to remember, retain in memory,* 2 Pe. 1. 15; πορείαν π., i.q. πορεύεσθαι, *to go, journey, travel,* Lu. 13. 22; πρόνοιαν π., i.q. προνοεῖσθαι, *to take care of, provide for,* Ro. 13. 14; σπουδὴν π., i.q. σπουδάζειν, *to act with diligence and earnestness,* Jude 3.

ποίημα, ατος, τό, (§ 4. tab. D. c) *that which is made or done; a work, workmanship, creation,* Ro. 1. 20; met. Ep. 2. 10.

ποίησις, εως, ἡ, (§ 5. tab. E. c) *a making; an acting, doing, performance; observance* of a law, Ja. 1. 25.

ποιητής, οῦ, ὁ, (§ 2. tab. B. c) *a maker; the maker or author* of a song or poem, *a poet,* Ac. 17. 28; *a doer; a performer* of the enactments of a law, Ro. 2. 13, et al.

ποιῇ, 3 pers. sing. pres. subj. act. . . . ποιέω
ποίημα], ατος, τό . . . . . id.
ποιήμασι, dat. pl. . . . . . . ποίημα
ποιῇς, 2 pers. sing. pres. subj. act. . . . ποιέω
ποιῆσαι, aor. 1, infin. act. . . . . id.
ποιήσαιεν, 3 pers. pl. aor. 1, opt. act.—B. Ln. Tdf. . . . . . } id.
ποιήσειαν, Rec. Gr. Sch. (Lu. 6. 11) }
ποιησάμενος, nom. sing. masc. part. aor. 1, mid. id.
ποιήσαντες, nom. pl. masc. part. aor. 1, act. . id.
ποιήσαντι, dat. sing. masc. part. aor. 1, act. id.
ποιήσας, nom. sing. masc. part. aor. 1, act. . id.
ποιήσασαν, acc. sing. fem. part. aor. 1, act. id.
ποιήσασθαι, aor. 1, infin. mid. . . . id.
ποιήσατε, 2 pers. pl. aor. 1, imper. act. . id.
ποιησάτω, 3 pers. sing. aor. 1, imper. act. id.
ποιήσει, 3 pers. sing. fut. ind. act. . . . ποιέω
ποιήσει,[a] dat. sing. . . . . . . ποίησις
ποιήσειαν, 3 pers. pl. aor. 1 (Æolic) act. (§ 13. rem. 11. b. note) . . . . ποιέω
ποιήσεις, 2 pers. sing. fut. ind. act. . . . id.
ποιήσετε, 2 pers. pl. fut. ind. act. . . . id.
ποιήσῃ, 3 pers. sing. aor. 1, subj. act. . . ποιέω
ποιήσῃς, 2 pers. sing. aor. 1, subj. act. . id.
ποίησις], εως, ἡ, (§ 5. tab. E. c) . . id.
ποιήσομεν, 1 pers. pl. fut. ind. act. . id.
ποίησον, 2 pers. sing. aor. 1, imper. act. . id.
ποιήσουσι, 3 pers. pl. fut. ind. act. . id.
ποιήσω, 1 pers. sing. fut. ind. act. . . id.
ποιήσω, 1 pers. sing. aor. 1, subj. act. . id.
ποιήσωμεν, 1 pers. pl. aor. 1, subj. act. . id.
ποιήσων, nom. sing. masc. part. fut. act. . id.
ποιήσωσι, 3 pers. pl. aor. 1, subj. act. . id.
ποιηταί, nom. pl. . . . . . ποιητής
ποιῆτε, 2 pers. pl. pres. subj. act. . . ποιέω
ποιητής], οῦ, ὁ, (§ 2. tab. B. c) . id.
ποιητῶν, gen. pl. . . . . . ποιητής
ποικίλαις, dat. pl. fem. . . . ποικίλος
ποικίλης, gen. sing. fem. . . . . id.
ποικίλοις, dat. pl. masc. . . . . id.

ποικίλος], η, ον, (§ 7. tab. F. a) *of various colours, variegated, chequered; various, diverse, manifold,* Mat. 4. 24, et al. (ĭ).

ποίμαινε, 2 pers. sing. pres. imper. . . ποιμαίνω
ποιμαίνει, 3 pers. sing. pres. ind. . . id.
ποιμαίνειν, pres. infin. . . . . . id.
ποιμαίνοντα, acc. sing. masc. part. pres. . id.
ποιμαίνοντες, nom. pl. masc. part. pres. . id.
ποιμαίνω], fut. ανῶ . . . . ποιμήν
ποιμανεῖ, 3 pers. sing. fut. ind. . . . ποιμαίνω
ποιμάνατε, 2 pers. pl. aor. 1, imper. . id.
ποιμένα, acc. sing. . . . . . ποιμήν
ποιμένας, acc. pl. . . . . . id.
ποιμένες, nom. pl. . . . . . . id.
ποιμένων, gen. pl. . . . . . id.

ποιμήν], ένος, ὁ, (§ 4. rem. 2. e) *one who tends flocks or herds, a shepherd, herdsman,* Mat. 9. 36; 25. 32; met. *a pastor, superintendent, guardian,* Jno. 10. 11, 14, 16, et al.

ποιμαίνω, fut. ανῶ, aor. 1. ἐποίμᾱνα, (§ 27. rem. 1. c. e) *to feed, pasture, tend a flock,* Lu. 17. 7; 1 Co. 9. 7; trop. *to feed* with selfish indulgence, *to pamper,* Jude 12; met. *to tend, direct, superintend,* Mat. 2. 6; Jno. 21. 16, et al.; *to rule,* Re. 2. 27.

ποίμνη, ης, ἡ, (§ 2. tab. B. a) *a flock* of sheep, Lu. 2. 8; 1 Co. 9. 7; meton. *a flock* of disciples, Mat. 26. 31; Jno. 10. 16.

[a] Ja. 1. 25.

πoίμνιον, ου, τό, (§ 3. tab. C. c) (contr. for ποιμένιον, *a flock*) *a flock*; met. *a flock* of Christian disciples, Lu. 12. 32; Ac. 20. 28, 29; 1 Pe. 5. 2, 3.

ποίμνη], ης, ἡ . . . . . ποιμήν
ποίμνην, acc. sing. . . . . . ποίμνη
ποίμνης, gen. sing . . . . . id.
ποίμνιον], ου, τό . . . . . ποιμήν
ποιμνίου, gen. sing. . . . . . ποίμνιον
ποιμνίῳ, dat. sing. . . . . . id.
ποῖον, acc. sing. masc. and nom. and acc. neut. ποῖος
ποῖος], οία, οῖον, (§ 10. rem. 7. a) *of what kind, sort, or species*, Jno. 12. 33; 21. 19; *what? which?* Mat. 19. 18; 21. 23, 24, 27, et al.
ποίου, gen. sing. masc. . . . . . ποῖος
ποιοῦμαι, 1 pers. sing. pres. ind. mid. (§ 17. tab. Q) . . . . . ποιέω
ποιοῦμεν, 1 pers. pl. pres. ind. act. . . id.
ποιούμενοι, nom. pl. masc. part. pres. mid. id.
ποιούμενος, nom. sing. masc. part. pres. mid. id.
ποιοῦν, nom. sing. neut. part. pres. act. . id.
ποιοῦντα, acc. sing. masc. part. pres. act. . id.
ποιοῦντα, nom. pl. neut. part. pres. act. . id.
ποιοῦνται, 3 pers. pl. pres. ind. mid. . . id.
ποιοῦντας, acc. pl. masc. part. pres. act. . id.
ποιοῦντες, nom. pl. masc. part. pres. act. . id.
ποιοῦντι, dat. sing. masc. and neut. part. pres. act. id.
ποιοῦντος, gen. sing. masc. part. pres. act. . id.
ποιοῦσι, 3 pers. pl. pres. ind. act. . . id.
ποιοῦσι, dat. pl. masc. part. pres. act. . id.
ποίῳ, dat. sing. masc. and neut. . . . ποῖος
ποιῶ, 1 pers. sing. pres. ind. and subj. act. ποιέω
ποιῶμεν, 1 pers. pl. pres. subj. act. . id.
ποιῶν, nom. sing. masc. part. pres. act. . id.
ποιῶσι, 3 pers. pl. pres. subj. act. . . id.
πόλει, dat. sing. . . . . . πόλις
πόλεις, nom. and acc. pl. . . . id.
πολεμεῖ, 3 pers. sing. pres. ind. . . . πολεμέω
πολεμεῖτε, 2 pers. pl. pres. ind. . . id.
πολεμέω, ῶ], fut. ήσω, (§ 16. tab. P) . . πόλεμος
πολεμῆσαι, aor. 1, infin. . . . . πολεμέω
πολεμήσουσι, 3 pers. pl. fut. ind. . . id.
πολεμήσω, 1 pers. sing. fut. ind. . . id.
πόλεμοι, nom. pl. . . . . . . πόλεμος
πόλεμον, acc. sing. . . . . . . πόλεμος

πόλεμος], ου, ὁ, (§ 3. tab. C. a) *war*, Mat. 24. 6; Mar. 13. 7; *battle, engagement, combat*, 1 Co. 14. 8; He. 11. 34; *battling, strife*, Ja. 4. 1, et al.

πολεμέω, ῶ, fut. ήσω, aor. 1, ἐπολέμησα (§ 16. tab. P) *to make or wage war, fight*, Re. 2. 16; 12. 7, et al.; *to battle, quarrel*, Ja. 4. 2.

πολέμους, acc. pl. . . . . . . πόλεμος
πολέμῳ, dat. sing. . . . . . id.
πολέμων, gen. pl. . . . . . id.
πόλεσι, dat. pl. . . . . . πόλις
πόλεων, gen. pl. . . . . . id
πόλεως, gen. sing. . . . . . id.
πόλιν, acc. sing. . . . . . . id.

πόλις], εως, ἡ, (§ 5. tab. E. c) *a city, an enclosed and walled town*, Mat. 10. 5, 11; 11. 1; meton. *the inhabitants of a city*, Mat. 8. 34; 10. 15; with a gen. of person, or a personal pronoun, *the city* of any one, *the city* of one's birth or residence, Mat. 9. 1; Lu. 2. 4, 11; ἡ πόλις, *the city*, κατ' ἐξοχήν, *Jerusalem*, Mat. 21. 18; 28. 11; met. *a place of permanent residence, abode, home*, He. 11. 10, 16; 13. 14.

πολίτης, ου, ὁ, (§ 2. tab. B. c) *a citizen*, Lu. 15. 15; 19. 14; Ac. 21. 39. (ῑ).

πολιτεύω, fut. εύσω, (§ 13. tab. M) intrans. *to be a citizen*; trans. *to govern a city or state, administer the affairs of a state*; pass. *to be governed*; in N.T. *to order one's life and conduct, converse, live*, in a certain manner as to habits and principles, Ac. 23. 1; Phi. 1. 27.

πολίτευμα, ατος, τό, (§ 4. tab. D. c) *the administration of a commonwealth*; in N.T. equivalent to πολιτεία, *a community, commonwealth*, Phi. 3. 20.

πολιτεία, ας, ἡ, (§ 2. tab. B. b, and rem. 2) *the state of being a citizen; citizenship, the right or privilege of being a citizen, freedom of a city or state*, Ac. 22. 28; *a commonwealth, community*, Ep. 2. 12.

πολῖται, nom. pl. . . . . . πολίτης
πολιτάρχας, acc. pl. . . . . . πολιτάρχης
πολῑτάρχης], ου, ὁ, (§ 2. tab. B. c) (πόλις & ἄρχω) *a ruler or prefect of a city, city magistrate*, Ac. 17. 6, 8. N.T.
πολιτεία], ας, ἡ . . . . . . πόλις
πολιτείαν, acc. sing. . . . . . πολιτεία

πολιτείας, gen. sing. . . . . . πολιτεία
πολιτεύεσθε, 2 pers. pl. pres. imper. mid. . πολιτεύω
πολίτευμα],[a] ατος, τό . . . . πόλις
πολιτεύω], fut. εύσω, (§ 13. tab. M) . . id.
πολίτην, acc. sing.—Gr. Sch. Tdf. . . } πολίτης
πλησίον, Rec. (He. 8. 11) . . }
πολίτης], ου, ὁ, (§ 2. tab. B. c) . . πόλις
πολιτῶν, gen. pl. . . . . . πολίτης
πολλά, nom. and acc. pl. neut . . πολύς
πολλά, neut. pl. adverbially . . id.
πολλαί, nom. pl. fem. . . . . id.
πολλαῖς, dat. pl. fem. . . . . id.
πολλάκις], adv. . . . . . id.
πολλαπλασίονα, acc. pl. neut. . . πολλαπλασίων
πολλαπλἄσίων], ονος, ὁ, ἡ, τό, -ον . πολύς
πολλάς, acc. pl. fem. . . . . id.
πολλή, nom. sing. fem. . . . id.
πολλῇ, dat. sing. fem. . . . . id.
πολλήν, acc. sing. fem. . . . id.
πολλῆς, gen. sing. fem. . . . . id.
πολλοί, nom. pl. masc. . . . id.
πολλοῖς, dat. pl. masc. and neut. . . id.
πολλοῦ, gen. sing. masc. and neut. . . id.
πολλούς, acc. pl. masc. . . . . id.
πολλῷ, dat. sing. masc. and neut. . . id.
πολλῶν, gen. pl. . . . . . id.
πολύ, neut. sing. adverbially . . . id.
πολύ, nom. and acc. sing. neut. . . . id.

πολυεύσπλαγχνος], ου, ὁ, ἡ, (πολύς, εὖ, & σπλάγχνον) *very merciful, very compassionate*, v.r. Ja. 5. 11. N.T.

πολυλογία], ας, ἡ, (§ 2. tab. B. b, and rem. 2) (πολύς & λόγος), *wordiness, loquacity.*

πολυλογίᾳ,[b] dat. sing. . . . . πολυλογία

πολυμερῶς],[c] adv. (πολυμερής, *consisting of many parts*, πολύς & μέρος) *in many parts or parcels.*

πολυποίκἴλος],[d] ου, ὁ, ἡ, (§ 7. rem. 2) (πολύς & ποικίλος) *exceedingly various, multifarious, multiform, manifold;* by impl. *immense, infinite*, Ep. 3. 10.

πολύς], πολλή, πολύ, gen. πολλοῦ, πολλῆς, πολλοῦ, (§ 7. rem. 8. a) *great* in magnitude or quantity, *much, large*, Mat. 13. 5; Jno. 3. 23; 15. 8; pl. *many*, Mat. 3. 7; in time, *long*, Mat. 25. 19; Mar. 6. 35; Jno. 5. 6; οἱ πολλοί, *the many, the mass*, Ro. 5. 15; 12. 5; 1 Co. 10. 33; τὸ πολύ, *much*, 2 Co. 8. 15; πολύ, as an adv. *much, greatly*, Mar. 12. 27; Lu. 7. 47; of time, ἐπὶ πολύ, *a long time*, Ac. 28. 6; μετ' οὐ πολύ, *not long after*, Ac. 27. 14; followed by a compar. *much*, 2 Co. 8. 22; πολλῷ, *much, by much*, Mat. 6. 30; Mar. 10. 48; τὰ πολλά, as an adv. *most frequently, generally*, Ro. 15. 22; πολλά, as an adv. *much, greatly, vehemently*, Mar. 1. 45; 3. 12; of time, *many times, frequently, often*, Mat. 9. 14.

πολλάκις, adv. *many times, often, frequently*, Mat. 17. 15; Mar. 5. 4; 9. 22, et al. (ᾰ).

πολλαπλασίων, ονος, ὁ, ἡ, τό, -ον, (§ 7. tab. G. a) (a later equivalent to πολλαπλάσιος, from πολύς) *manifold, many times more*, Lu. 18. 30.

πλείων, ονος, ὁ, ἡ, τό, -ον, & πλέον, (§ 8. rem. 2) (compar. of πολύς) *more* in number, Mat. 21. 36; 26. 53; *more* in quantity, Mar. 12. 43; Lu. 21. 3; οἱ πλείονες, or πλείους, *the greater part, the majority*, Ac. 19. 32; 27. 12; *the more*, 1 Co. 9. 19; 2 Co. 4. 15; neut. πλεῖον, as an adv. *more*, Lu. 7. 42; ἐπὶ πλεῖον, *more*, of time, *longer, further*, Ac. 24. 4; of space, *more widely*, Ac. 4. 17; 2 Ti. 2. 16; 3. 9; for the posit. *much*, of time, *long*, Ac. 20. 9; *more, higher, greater, more excellent, of higher value*, Mat. 5. 20; 6. 25.

πλεῖστος, η, ον, (§ 8. rem. 2) *most; very great*, Mat. 11. 20; 21. 8; τὸ πλεῖστον, as an adv. *at most*, 1 Co. 14. 27; superlat. of πολύς.

πλήν, adv. (πλέον) *besides, except*, Mar. 12. 32; Ac. 8. 1; 20. 23; as a conj. *but, however, nevertheless*, Mat. 18. 7; Lu. 19. 27; Ep. 5. 33, et al.; equivalent to ἀλλά, Lu. 6. 35; 12. 31; Ac. 27. 22.

πλεονάζω, fut. άσω, aor. 1, ἐπλεόνασα, (§ 26. rem. 1) (πλείων, πλέον) *to be more than enough; to have more than enough, to have in abundance*, 2 Co. 8. 15; *to abound, be abundant*, 2 Thes. 1. 3; 2 Pe. 1. 8; *to increase, be augmented*, Ro. 5. 20;

a Ph. 3. 20. b Mat. 6. 7. c He. 1. 1. d Ep. 3. 10.

to come into wider action, be more widely spread, Ro. 6. 1; 2 Co. 4. 15; in N.T. trans. *to cause to abound or increase, to augment,* 1 Thes. 3. 12.

πολύσπλαγχνος],[a] ου, ὁ, ἡ, (§ 7. rem. 2) (πολύς & σπλάγχνον) *very merciful, very compassionate.* N.T.

πολυτελεῖ, dat. sing. masc. . . . . πολυτελής

πολυτελές, nom. sing. neut. . . . . id.

πολυτελής], έος, οῦς, ὁ, ἡ, (§ 7. tab. G. b) (πολύς & τέλος) *expensive, costly,* Mar. 14. 3; 1 Ti. 2. 9; *of great value, very precious,* 1 Pe. 3. 4.

πολυτελοῦς, gen. sing. fem. . . . . πολυτελής

πολύτιμον, acc. sing. masc. . . . . πολύτιμος

πολύτῖμος], ου, ὁ, ἡ, (§ 7. rem. 2) (πολύς & τιμή) *of great price, costly, precious,* Mat. 13. 46; Jno. 12. 3.

πολυτιμότερον, nom. sing. neut. compar.—Gr. Sch. Tdf. . . . }
πολὺ τιμιώτερον, Rec. (1 Pe. 1. 7) } πολύτιμος

πολυτίμου, gen. sing. fem. . . . . id.

πολυτρόπως],[b] adv. (πολύτροπος, *manifold, various,* πολύς & τρόπος) *in many ways, in various modes.*

πόμα], ατος, τό, (§ 4. tab. D. c) . . πίνω

πόμασι, dat. pl. . . . . . πόμα

πονηρά, nom. s. fem. and nom. and acc. pl. neut. πονηρός

πονηρᾷ, dat. sing. fem. . . . . id.

πονηραί, nom. pl. fem. . . . . id.

πονηρᾶς, gen. sing. fem. . . . . id.

πονηρέ, voc. sing. masc. . . . . id.

πονηρία], ας, ἡ, (§ 2. tab. B. b, and rem. 2) πόνος

πονηρίᾳ, dat. sing. . . . . . πονηρία

πονηρίαι, nom. pl. . . . . . id.

πονηρίαν, acc. sing. . . . . . id.

πονηρίας, gen. sing. . . . . . id.

πονηριῶν, gen. pl. . . . . . id.

πονηροί, nom. pl. masc. . . . . πονηρός

πονηροῖς, dat. pl. masc. and neut. . . id.

πονηρόν, acc. sing. masc. and nom. and acc. neut. id.

πονηρός], ά, όν, (§ 7. rem. 1) . . . πόνος

πονηρότερα, acc. pl. neut. compar. . . πονηρός

πονηροῦ, gen. sing. masc. . . . . id.

πονηρῷ, dat. sing. masc. and neut. . . id.

πονηρῶν, gen. pl. . . . . . id.

πόνον, acc. sing.—Gr. Sch. Tdf. . . }
ζῆλον, Rec. (Col. 4. 13) . . } πόνος

πόνος], ου, ὁ, (§ 3. tab. C. a) (πένομαι) *labour, travail; pain, misery, anguish,* Re. 16. 10, 11; 21. 4.

πονηρία, ας, ἡ, pr. *badness, bad condition;* in N.T. *evil disposition* of mind, *wickedness, mischief, malignity,* Mat. 22. 18, et al.; pl. πονηρίαι, *wicked deeds, villanies,* Mar. 7. 23; Ac. 3. 26.

πονηρός, ά, όν, *bad, unsound,* Mat. 6. 23; 7. 17, 18; *evil, afflictive,* Ep. 5. 16; 6. 13; Re. 16. 2; *evil, wrongful, malignant, malevolent,* Mat. 5. 11, 39; Ac. 28. 21; *evil, wicked, impious,* and τὸ πονηρόν, *evil, wrong, wickedness,* Mat. 5. 37, 45; 9. 4; *slothful, inactive,* Mat. 25. 26; Lu. 19. 22; ὁ πονηρός, *the evil one, the devil,* Mat. 13. 19, 38; Jno. 17. 15; *evil* eye, i.q. φθονερός, *envious,* Mat. 20. 15; Mar. 7. 22; impl. *covetous, niggardly,* Mat. 7. 11.

πόνου, gen. sing. . . . . πόνος

Ποντικόν,[c] acc. sing. masc. . . . Ποντικός

Ποντῐκός], ή, όν, *belonging to, or an inhabitant of,* Πόντος.

Πόντιος], ου, ὁ, (§ 3. tab. C. a) *Pontius,* pr. name.

Ποντίου, gen. . . . . . . Πόντιος

Ποντίῳ, dat. . . . . . . id.

Πόντον, acc. . . . . . . Πόντος

Πόντος], ου, ὁ, *Pontus,* a country of Asia Minor.

Πόντου, gen. . . . . . . Πόντος

πόνων, gen. pl. . . . . . πόνος

Πόπλιος], ου, ὁ, (§ 3. tab. C. a) *Publius,* pr. name.

Ποπλίου, gen. . . . . . . Πόπλιος

Ποπλίῳ, dat. . . . . . . id.

πορεία], ας, ἡ . . . . πορεύομαι

πορείαις, dat. pl. . . . . . πορεία

πορείαν, acc. sing. . . . . . id.

πορεύεσθαι, pres. infin. . . . . πορεύομαι

πορεύεσθε, 2 pers. pl. pres. imper. . . id.

πορεύεται, 3 pers. sing. pres. ind. . . id.

πορευθείς, nom. sing. masc. part. aor. 1 . id.

πορευθεῖσα, nom. sing. fem. part. aor. 1 id.

πορευθεῖσαι, nom. pl. fem. part. aor. 1 id.

πορευθέντα, acc. sing. masc. part. aor. 1 . id.

πορευθέντες, nom. pl. masc. part. aor. 1 . id.

πορευθέντι, dat. sing. masc. part. aor. 1—A. B. Tdf. . . . . }
πορευθέντα, Rec. Gr. Sch. (Ac. 27. 3) } id.

[a] Ja. 5. 11. [b] He. 1. 1. [c] Ac. 18. 2.

πορευθῇ, 3 pers. sing. aor. 1, subj. . πορεύομαι
πορευθῆναι, aor. 1, infin. . . . id.
πορευθῆτε, 2 pers. pl. aor. 1, subj. . . id.
πορεύθητι, 2 pers. sing. aor. 1, imper. . id.
πορευθῶ, 1 pers. sing. aor. 1, subj. . . id.
πορευθῶσι, 3 pers. pl. aor. 1, subj. . . id.
πορεύομαι, fut. εύσομαι, aor. 1, (pass. form) ἐπορεύθην, (§ 14. tab. N) (mid. of πορεύω, *to convey, transport,* from πόρος) *to go, pass from one place to another,* Mat. 17. 27; 18. 12; *to go away, depart,* Mat. 24. 1; 25. 41; Jno. 14. 2, 3; trop. *to go away, depart,* from life, *to die,* Lu. 22. 22; *to go, pass on one's way, journey, travel,* Mat. 2. 8, 9; Lu. 1. 39; 2. 41; πορεύομαι ὀπίσω, *to go after, to become a follower or partisan,* Lu. 21. 8; or, *to pursue after, be devoted to,* 2 Pe. 2. 10; from the Heb., *to go or proceed* in any way or course of life, *live* in any manner, Lu. 1. 6; 8. 14; Ac. 9. 31.

πορεία, ας, ἡ, (§ 2. tab. B. b, and rem. 2) *a going, progress; a journey, travel,* Lu. 13. 22; from the Heb., *way* of life, *business, occupation,* Ja. 1. 11.

πορευόμεναι, nom. pl. fem. part. pres. . πορεύομαι
πορευόμενοι, nom. pl. masc. part. pres. . id.
πορευομένοις, dat. pl. masc. part. pres. id.
πορευόμενον, acc. sing. masc. and nom. neut. part. pres. . . . . id.
πορευομένου, gen. sing. masc. part. pres. . id.
πορευομένους, acc. pl. masc. part. pres. . id.
πορευομένῳ, dat. sing. masc. part. pres. . id.
πορευομένων, gen. pl. part. pres. . . id.
πορεύου, 2 pers. sing. pres. imper. . . id.
πορεύσεται, 3 pers. sing. fut. ind. . . id.
πορεύσῃ, 2 pers. sing. fut. ind. . . . id.
πορεύσομαι, 1 pers. sing. fut. ind. . . id.
πορευσόμεθα, 1 pers. pl. fut. ind.—Rec. / πορευσώμεθα, Gr. Sch. Tdf. (Ja. 4. 13) } id.
πορεύσονται, 3 pers. pl. fut. ind. . . id.
πορευσώμεθα, 1 pers. pl. aor. 1, subj. . id.
πορεύωμαι, 1 pers. sing. pres. subj. . . id.
πορθέω, ῶ], fut. ήσω, (§ 16. tab. P) (a collateral form of πέρθω) *to lay waste, destroy;* impl. *to harass, ravage,* Ac. 9. 21; Gal. 1. 13, 23.
πορθήσας, nom. sing. masc. part. aor. 1 . πορθέω

πορισμόν, acc. sing. . . . . πορισμός
πορισμός], ου, ὁ, (§ 3. tab. C. a) (πορίζομαι, *to furnish to one's self, acquire, gain,* mid. of πορίζω, *to furnish, supply*) *a providing, procuring;* meton. *source of gain,* 1 Ti. 6. 5, 6. L.G.
Πόρκιον,[a] acc. . . . . . Πόρκιος
Πόρκιος], ου, ὁ, *Porcius,* pr. name.
πόρναι, nom. pl. . . . . . πόρνη
πορνεία], ας, ἡ, (§ 2. tab. B. b, and rem. 2) id.
πορνείᾳ, dat. sing. . . . . πορνεία
πορνεῖαι, nom. pl. . . . . . id.
πορνείαν, acc. sing. . . . . id.
πορνείας, gen. sing. and acc. pl. . id.
πορνεῦσαι, aor. 1, infin. . . . πορνεύω
πορνεύσαντες, nom. pl. masc. part. aor. 1 . id.
πορνεύω], fut. εύσω . . . . πόρνη
πορνεύων, nom. sing. masc. part pres. . . πορνεύω
πορνεύωμεν, 1 pers. pl. pres. subj. . id.
πόρνη], ης, ἡ, (§ 2. tab. B. a) (περνάω, or πέρνημι, *to sell*) *a prostitute, a whore, harlot, an unchaste female,* Mat. 21. 31, 32; from the Heb., *an idolatress,* Re. 17. 1, 5, 15.

πορνεία, ας, ἡ, (§ 2. tab. B. b, and rem. 2) *fornication, whoredom,* Mat. 15. 19; Mar. 7. 21; Ac. 15. 20, 29; *concubinage,* Jno. 8. 41; *adultery,* Mat. 5. 32; 19. 9; *incest,* 1 Co. 5. 1; *lewdness, uncleanness,* genr., Ro. 1. 29; from the Heb., put symbolically for *idolatry,* Re. 2. 21; 14. 8.

πορνεύω, fut. εύσω, aor. 1, ἐπόρνευσα, (§ 13. tab. M) *to commit fornication or whoredom,* 1 Co. 6. 18; 10. 8; Re. 2. 14, 20; from the Heb., *to commit* spiritual *fornication, practise idolatry,* Re. 17. 2; 18. 3. 9.

πόρνος, ου, ὁ, (§ 3. tab. C. a) *a catamite;* in N.T. *a fornicator, impure person,* 1 Co. 5. 9, 10, 11; 6. 9, et al.

πόρνῃ, dat. sing. . . . . . πόρνη
πόρνην, acc. sing. . . . . . id.
πόρνης, gen. sing. . . . . . id.
πόρνοι, nom. pl. . . . . . πόρνος
πόρνοις, dat. pl. . . . . . id.
πόρνος], ου, ὁ . . . . . πόρνη
πόρνους, acc. pl. . . . . . πόρνος
πορνῶν, gen. pl. . . . . . πόρνη
πόῤῥω], adv. . . . . . . πρό

[a] Ac. 24. 27.

πόῤῥωθεν], adv. . . . . . . πρό
πορῥώτερον], adv.—A B. Ln. Tdf. . } id.
πορῥωτέρω, Rec. Gr. Sch. (Lu. 24. 28) }
πορῥωτέρω], adv. . . . . . . id.

πορφύρα], ας, ἡ, (§ 2. tab. B. b) *purpura, murex*, a species of shell-fish that yielded the purple dye, highly esteemed by the ancients, its tint being a bright crimson; in N.T. *a purple garment, robe of purple*, Lu. 16. 19; Re. 17. 4; 18. 12, et al. (ῠ).

πορφύρεος, οῦς, έα, ᾶ, εον, οῦν, (§ 7. rem. 5. c) *purple, crimson*, Jno. 19. 2, 5, col.; Mat. 27. 28, 31, et al.

πορφυρᾳ, dat. sing. . . . . . πορφύρα
πορφύραν, acc. sing. . . . . . id.
πορφύρας, gen. sing. . . . . . id.
πορφύρεος οῦς], έα, ᾶ, εον, οῦν . . . id.
πορφυρόπωλις],[a] εως, ἡ, (§ 5. tab. E. c) (fem. of πορφυροπώλης, πορφύρα & πωλέω) *a female seller of purple cloths*.
πορφυροῦν, acc. sing. neut. . . . πορφύρεος
πόσα, acc. pl. neut. . . . . . πόσος
πόσαι, nom. pl. fem. . . . . . id.
ποσάκις], adv. . . . . . . id.
πόσας, acc. pl. fem. . . . . . id.
πόσει, dat. sing. . . . . . . πόσις
πόσην, acc. sing. fem. . . . . . πόσος
ποσί, dat. pl. (§ 4. rem. 3. b) . . . πούς
πόσις], εως, ἡ, (§ 5. tab. E. c) . . . πίνω
πόσοι, nom. pl. masc. . . . . . πόσος
πόσον, nom. and acc. sing. neut. . . . id.
πόσος], η, ον, (§ 10. rem. 7. b) interrog. to ὅσος & τόσος, *how great? how much?* Mat. 6. 23; Lu. 16. 5, 7; 2 Co. 7. 11; πόσῳ, adverbially before a comparative, *how much? by how much?* Mat. 7. 11; 10. 25; He. 10. 29; of time, *how long?* Mar. 9. 21; of number, pl. *how many?* Mat. 15. 34; 16. 9, 10, et al.

ποσάκις, adv. *how many times? how often?* Mat. 18. 21; 23. 37; Lu. 13. 34. (ᾰ).

πόσους, acc. pl. masc. . . . . . πόσος
πόσῳ, dat. sing. neut. . . . . . id.
πόσων, gen. pl. . . . . . . id.
ποταμοί, nom. pl. . . . . . . ποταμός
ποταμόν, acc. sing. . . . . . . id.

ποταμός], οῦ, ὁ, (§ 3. tab. C. a) *a river, stream*, Mar. 1. 5; Ac. 16. 13; met. and allegor. Jno. 7. 38; Re. 22. 1, 2; *a flood, winter torrent*, for χείμαῤῥος ποταμός, Mat. 7. 25, 27.

ποταμοῦ, gen. sing. . . . . . ποταμός
ποταμούς, acc. pl. . . . . . . id.
ποταμοφόρητον,[b] acc. sing. fem. . ποταμοφόρητος
ποταμοφόρητος], ου, ὁ, ἡ, (§ 7. rem. 2) (ποταμός & φορητός, from φορέω) *borne along or carried away by a flood or torrent*. N.T.
ποταμῷ, dat. sing. . . . . . . ποταμός
ποταμῶν, gen. pl. . . . . . . id.
ποταπαί, nom. pl. fem. . . . . . ποταπός
ποταπή, nom. sing. fem. . . . . id.
ποταπήν, acc. sing. fem. . . . . . id.
ποταποί, nom. pl. masc. . . . . id.
ποτᾰπός], ή, όν, (§ 7. tab. F. a) a later form of ποδαπός, *of what country?* in N.T. equivalent to ποῖος, *what? of what manner? of what kind or sort?* Lu. 1. 29; 7. 37; denoting admiration, *what? what kind of? how great?* Mat. 8. 27; Mar. 13. 1, et al.
ποταπούς, acc. pl. masc. . . . . . ποταπός
πότε], interrog. particle, *when? at what time?* Mat. 24. 3; 25. 37, 38, 39, 44; ἕως πότε, *till when? how long?* Mat. 17. 17, et al.
ποτέ], an enclitic particle of time, *once, some time or other*, either past or future; *formerly*, Jno. 9. 13; *at length*, Lu. 22. 32; *at any time, ever*, Ep. 5. 29; He. 2. 1; intensive after interrogatives, *ever*, 1 Co. 9. 7; He. 1. 5, et al.
πότερον],[c] adv. . . . . . . πότερος
πότερος], α, ον, *which of the two? whether?* πότερον, adverbially, *whether?* Jno. 7. 17.
ποτήριον], ίου, τό, (§ 3. tab. C. c) . . πίνω
ποτηρίου, gen. sing. . . . . . ποτήριον
ποτηρίῳ, dat. sing. . . . . . . id.
ποτηρίων, gen. pl. . . . . . . id.
πότιζε, 2 pers. sing. pres. imper. . . . ποτίζω
ποτίζει, 3 pers. sing. pres. ind. . . . id.
ποτίζω], fut. ίσω, (§ 26. rem. 1) . . πίνω
ποτίζων, nom. sing. masc. part. pres. . ποτίζω
Ποτίολοι], ων, οἱ, *Puteoli*, a town of Italy.
Ποτιόλους,[d] acc. . . . . . . Ποτίολοι
ποτίσῃ, 3 pers. sing. aor. 1, subj. . . ποτίζω
πότοις,[e] dat. pl. . . . . . . πότος

[a] Ac. 16. 14. [b] Re. 12. 15. [c] Jno. 7. 17. [d] Ac. 28. 13. [e] 1 Pe. 4. 3.

πότος], ου, ὁ, (§ 3. tab. C. a) . . πίνω

που], an enclitic indefinite particle, *somewhere, in a certain place,* He. 2. 6; 4. 4; with numerals, *thereabout,* Ro. 4. 19.

ποῦ], an interrog. particle, of place, *where? in what place?;* direct, Mat. 2. 2; Lu. 8. 25; Jno. 1. 39; indirect, Mat. 2. 4; Jno. 1. 40; *whither,* Jno. 3. 8; 7. 35; 13. 36.

Πούδης],[a] εντος, ὁ, (§ 4. rem. 2. d) *Pudens,* pr. name. Latin.

πούς], ποδός, ὁ, (§ 4. rem. 2. c) *the foot,* Mat. 4. 6; 5. 35; 7. 6; 22. 44; 28. 9; Lu. 1. 79; Ac. 5. 9; Ro. 3. 15, et al.

πρᾶγμα, ατος, τό, (§ 4. tab. D. c) . . πράσσω

πραγματεία], ας, ἡ . . . . . id.

πραγματείαις,[b] dat. pl. . . πραγματεία

πραγματεύομαι], fut. εύσομαι . . πράσσω

πραγματεύσασθε,[c] 2 pers. pl. aor. 1, imper. πραγματεύομαι

πράγματι, dat. sing. . . . . . πρᾶγμα

πράγματος, gen. sing. . . . . . id.

πραγμάτων, gen. pl. . . . . . id.

πραεῖς, nom. pl. masc. (§ 7. rem. 9) . πραΰς

πραέος, gen. sing. neut. . . . . . id.

πραθέν, nom. sing. neut. part. aor. 1, pass. . πιπράσκω

πραθῆναι, aor. 1, infin. pass. . . . id.

πραιτώριον], ίου, τό, (§ 3. tab. C. c) (Lat. *prætorium,* from *prætor*) when used in reference to a camp, *the tent of the general or commander-in-chief;* hence, in reference to a province, *the palace in which the governor of the province resided,* Mat. 27. 27; Mar. 15. 16; Ac. 23. 35, et al.; *the camp occupied by the prætorian cohorts at Rome, the prætorian camp,* or, *the Roman emperor's palace,* Phi. 1. 13.

πραιτωρίῳ, dat. sing. . . . . πραιτώριον

πράκτορι, dat. sing. . . . . . πράκτωρ

πράκτωρ], ορος, ὁ, (§ 4. rem. 2. f) . . πράσσω

πρᾶξαι, aor. 1, infin. act. . . . . id.

πράξαντες, nom. pl. masc. part. aor. 1, act. . id.

πραξάντων, gen. pl. masc. part. aor. 1, act. . id.

πράξας, nom. sing. masc. part. aor. 1, act.—A. C.
ποιήσας, Rec. Gr. Sch. Tdf. (1 Co. 5. 2) } id.

πράξατε, 2 pers. pl. aor. 1, imper. act.—C. D.
πράξετε, Rec. Gr. Sch. Tdf. (Ac. 15. 29) } id.

πράξει, dat. sing. . . . . . . πρᾶξις

πράξεις, acc. pl. . . . . . . id.

πράξεσι, dat. pl. . . . . . πρᾶξις

πράξετε, 2 pers. pl. fut. ind. act. . . πράσσω

πράξῃς, 2 pers. sing. aor. 1, subj. act. . . id.

πρᾶξιν, acc. sing. . . . . . πρᾶξις

πρᾶξις], εως, ἡ, (§ 5. tab. E. c) . . . πράσσω

πρᾶος],[d] εῖα, ον, (§ 7. rem. 9) *mild; gentle, kind.* —Gr. Sch.

πρᾷος, Rec.

πραΰς, Tdf. (Mat. 11. 29).

πραότης, τητος, ἡ, (§ 4. rem. 2. c) *meekness, forbearance,* 1 Co. 4. 21; Gal. 5. 23; *gentleness, kindness, benevolence,* 2 Co. 10. 1, et al.

πραότης], τητος, ἡ . . . . . πρᾶος

πραότητα, acc. sing. . . . . πραότης

πραότητι, dat. sing. . . . . . id.

πραότητος, gen. sing. . . . . . id.

πρασιά], ᾶς, ἡ, (§ 2. tab. B. b, and rem. 2) *a small area or bed in a garden;* trop. *a company of persons disposed in squares;* from the Heb., πρασιαὶ πρασιαί, *by areas, by squares,* like beds in a garden, Mar. 6. 40.

πρασιαί, nom. pl. . . . . . πρασιά

πράσσει, 3 pers. sing. pres. ind. act. . . πράσσω

πράσσειν, pres. infin. act. . . . . id.

πράσσεις, 2 pers. sing. pres. ind. act. . . id.

πράσσετε, 2 pers. pl. pres. imper. act. . id.

πράσσῃς, 2 pers. sing. pres. subj. act. . . id.

πράσσοντας, acc. pl. masc. part. pres. act. . id.

πράσσοντες, nom. pl. masc. part. pres. act. . id.

πράσσοντι, dat. sing. masc. part. pres. act. . id.

πράσσουσι, dat. pl. masc. part. pres. act. . id.

πράσσω, or ττω], fut. ξω, perf. πέπρᾱχα, aor. 1, ἔπραξα, (§ 26. rem. 3) *to do, execute, perform, practise, act, transact,* and of evil, *to commit,* Lu. 22. 23; 23. 15; Jno. 3. 20; Ac. 26. 9, 20, 26, 31, et al.; *to fulfil, obey, observe* a law, Ro. 2. 25; *to do to* any one, Ac. 16. 28; 5. 35; *to occupy one's self with, be engaged in, busy one's self about,* Ac. 19. 19; 1 Thes. 4. 11; absol. *to fare,* Ac. 15. 29; Ep. 6. 21; *to exact, require, collect* tribute, money lent, etc., Lu. 3. 13; 19. 23.

πρᾶγμα, ατος, τό, (§ 4. tab. D. c) *a thing done, fact, deed, work, transaction,* Lu. 1. 1; Ja. 3. 16; *a matter, affair,*

a 2 Ti. 4. 21. b 2 Ti. 2. 4. c Lu. 19. 13. d Mat. 11. 29.

Mat. 18. 19; Ro. 16. 2; *a matter* of dispute, 1 Co. 6. 1; *a thing*, genr., He. 10. 1; 11. 1; τὸ πρᾶγμα, an euphemism for *profligacy*, perhaps, 1 Thes. 4. 6.

πραγματεία, ας, ἡ, (§ 2. tab. B. b, and rem. 2) *an application to a matter of business*; in N.T. *business, affair, transaction*, 2 Ti. 2. 4.

πραγματεύομαι, fut. εύσομαι, (§ 15. tab. O) *to be occupied with or employed in any business, do business; to trade, traffic* Lu. 19. 13.

πράκτωρ, ορος, ὁ, (§ 4. rem. 2. f) *an exactor of dues or penalties; an officer* who enforced payment of debts by imprisonment, Lu. 12. 58.

πρᾶξις, εως, ἡ, (§ 5. tab. E. c) *operation, business, office*, Ro. 12. 4; πρᾶξις, and πράξεις, *actions, mode of acting, ways, deeds, practice, behaviour*, Mat. 16. 27; Lu. 23. 51, et al.

πράσσων, nom. sing. masc. part. pres. act. . . πράσσω
πράττειν, pres. infin. act. . . . . id.
πράττουσι, 3 pers. pl. pres. ind. act. . id.
πραϋπάθεια], ας, ἡ, (§ 2. tab. B. b, and rem. 2) (πραΰς & πάθος, from πάσχω) *meekness, gentleness of mind, kindness*, v.r. 1 Ti. 6. 11. L.G.
πραϋπάθειαν, acc. sing.—A. Ln. Sch. Tdf. } πραϋπάθεια
πραότητα, Rec. Gr. (1 Ti. 6. 11) . }
πραΰς], εῖα, ύ, έος, οῦς, είας, έος, οῦς, (§ 7. rem. 9) i.q. πρᾶος, *meek, gentle, kind, forgiving*, Mat. 5. 5; *mild, benevolent, humane*, Mat. 21. 5; 1 Pe. 3. 4.

πραΰτης, τητος, ἡ, (§ 4. rem. 2. c) i.q. πραότης, *meekness, mildness, forbearance*, 1 Pe. 3. 15; *gentleness, kindness*, Ja. 1. 21; 3. 13. LXX.

πραΰτης], τητος, ἡ.—A. B. C. Ln. Tdf. } πραΰς
πραότης, Rec. Gr. Sch. (Gal. 5. 23) }
πραΰτητα, acc. sing.—Ln. Tdf. } πραΰτης
πραότητα, Rec. Gr. Sch. (Col. 3. 12) . }
πραΰτητι, dat. sing. . . . . . id.
πραΰτητος, gen. sing. . . . . . id.

πρέπει], impers. verb, *it becomes, it is fitting, it is proper, it is right*, etc., and part. πρέπον, *becoming, suitable, decorous*, etc., Mat. 3. 15; 1 Co. 11. 13; Ep. 5. 3; 1 Ti. 2. 10, et al.

πρέπον, nom. sing. neut. part. . . . πρέπει
πρεσβεία], ας, ἡ . . . . . . πρεσβεύω
πρεσβείαν, acc. sing. . . . . πρεσβεία
πρεσβεύομεν, 1 pers. plur. pres. ind. . πρεσβεύω
πρεσβεύω], fut. εύσω, (§ 13. tab. M) (πρέσβυς, *an old man, an ambassador*) *to be elder; to be an ambassador, perform the duties of an ambassador*, 2 Co. 5. 20; Ep. 6. 20.

πρεσβεία, ας, ἡ, (§ 2. tab. B. b, and rem. 2) *eldership, seniority; an embassy, legation; a body of ambassadors, legates*, Lu. 14. 32; 19. 14.

πρεσβύτας, acc. pl. . . . πρεσβύτης
πρεσβυτέρας, acc. pl. fem. . . . πρεσβύτερος
πρεσβυτέριον], ου, τό . . . . id.
πρεσβυτερίου, gen. sing. . . . πρεσβυτέριον
πρεσβύτεροι, nom. and voc. pl. masc. . πρεσβύτερος
πρεσβυτέροις, dat. pl. masc. . . . id.
πρεσβύτερος], τέρα, τερον, (§ 7. rem. 1) (comp. of πρέσβυς) *elder, senior; older, more advanced in years*, Lu. 15. 25; Jno. 8. 9; Ac. 2. 17; *an elder* in respect of age, *person advanced in years*, 1 Ti. 5. 1, 2; pl. spc. *ancients, ancestors, fathers*, Mat. 15. 2; He. 11. 2; as an appellation of dignity, *an elder*, local *dignitary*, Lu. 7. 3; *an elder, member of the Jewish Sanhedrin*, Mat. 16. 21; 21. 23; 26. 3, 47, 57, 59; *an elder or presbyter* of the Christian church, Ac. 11. 30; 14. 23, et al. freq.

πρεσβυτέριον, ίου, τό, (§ 3. tab. C. c) *a body of old men, an assembly of elders; the Jewish Sanhedrin*, Lu. 22. 66; Ac. 22. 5; *a body of elders* in the Christian church, *a presbytery*, 1 Ti. 4. 14. N.T.

πρεσβύτης, ου, ὁ, (§ 2. tab. C. c) *an old man, aged person*, Lu. 1. 18; Tit. 2. 2; Phile. 9. (ῡ).

πρεσβῦτις, ιδος, ἡ, (§ 4. rem. 2. c) *an aged woman*, Tit. 2. 3.

πρεσβυτέρου, gen. sing. masc. . . πρεσβύτερος
πρεσβυτέρους, acc. pl. masc. . . . id.
πρεσβυτέρῳ, dat. sing. masc. . . . id.
πρεσβυτέρων, gen. pl. . . . . id.
πρεσβύτης], ου, ὁ . . . . . id.
πρεσβῦτις], ιδος, ἡ . . . . . id.
πρεσβύτιδας,[a] acc. pl. . . . . πρεσβῦτις

[a] Tit. 2. 3.

πρηνής],[a] έος, οῦς, ὁ, ἡ, (§ 7. tab. G. b) *prone, headforemost; πρηνὴς γενόμενος, falling headlong*, Ac. 1. 18.

πρίζω, or **πρίω**], aor. 1, pass. ἐπρίσθην, (§ 26. rem. 1) *to saw, saw asunder*, He. 11. 37.

πρίν], adv. *before*, of time, Mat. 26. 34, 75; Mar. 14. 72; πρὶν ἤ, *sooner than, before*, Mat. 1. 18; Lu. 2. 26, et al.

Πρίσκα], ης, ἡ, *Prisca*, pr. name.—B. Ln.

Πρίσκιλλα, Rec. Gr. Sch. Tdf. (1 Co. 16. 19).

Πρίσκαν, acc. . . . . . . Πρίσκα

Πρίσκιλλα], ης, ἡ, (§ 2. rem. 3) *Priscilla*, pr. name.

Πρίσκιλλαν, acc. . . . . . Πρίσκιλλα

πρό], prep. with a gen., *before*, of place, *in front of, in advance of*, Mat. 11. 10; Lu. 1. 76; Ac. 5. 23; *before*, of time, Mat. 5. 12; Lu. 11. 38; before an infin. with the gen. of the article, *before, before that*, Mat. 6. 8; Lu. 2. 21; *before, above, in preference*, Ja. 5. 12; 1 Pe. 4. 8.

πόῤῥω, adv. (a later form of πρόσω, from πρό) *forward, in advance, far advanced; far, far off, at a distance*, Mat. 15. 8; Mar. 7. 6.

πόῤῥωθεν, adv. *from a distance, from afar*, He. 11. 13; *at a distance, far, far off*, Lu. 17. 12.

ποῤῥώτερον, adv. *farther*, v.r. Lu. 24. 28.

ποῤῥωτέρω, adv. (compar. of πόῤῥω) *farther, beyond*, Lu. 24. 28.

πρότερον, adv. *before, first*, Jno. 7. 51; 2 Co. 1. 15; ὁ, ἡ, πρότερον, *former*, He. 10. 32, et al.; pr. neut. of

πρότερος, α, ον, (§ 7. rem. 1) (comp. of πρό) *former, prior*, Ep. 4. 22; τὸ πρότερον, as an adv. *before, formerly*, Jno. 6. 62, et al.

πρῷρα, ας, ἡ, (§ 2. tab. B. b) *the forepart of a vessel, prow*, Ac. 27. 30, 41.

πρῶτον, adv. *first* in time, *in the first place*, Mar. 4. 28; 16. 9; τὸ πρῶτον, *at the first, formerly*, Jno. 12. 16; 19. 39; *first* in dignity, importance, etc., *before all things*, Mat. 6. 33; Lu. 12. 1: pr. neut. of

πρῶτος, η, ον, (superl. of πρό, as if contr. from πρότατος) *first* in time, order, etc., Mat. 10. 2; 26. 17; *first* in dignity, importance, etc., *chief, principal, most important*, Mar. 6. 21; Lu. 19. 47; Ac. 13. 50; 16. 12; as an equivalent to the compar. πρότερος, *prior*, Jno. 1. 15, 30; 15. 18; Mat. 27. 64; adverbially, *first*, Jno. 1. 42; 5. 4; 8. 7.

πρωτεύω, fut. εύσω, (§ 13. tab. M) *to be first, to hold the first rank or highest dignity, have the pre-eminence, be chief*, Col. 1. 18.

προαγᾰγών, nom. sing. masc. part. aor. 2, (§ 13. rem. 7. d) . . . προάγω

προάγει, 3 pers. sing. pres. ind. . . . id.

προάγειν, pres. infin. . . . . . id.

προάγοντες, nom. pl. masc. part. pres. . . id.

προάγουσαι, nom. pl. fem. part. pres. . id.

προαγούσας, acc. pl. fem. part. pres. . . id.

προαγούσης, gen. sing. fem. part. pres. . id.

προάγουσι, 3 pers. pl. pres. ind. . . id.

προάγω], fut. άξω, (§ 23. rem. 1. b) aor. 2, προήγᾰγον, (πρό & ἄγω) *to lead, bring, or conduct forth, produce*, Ac. 12. 6; 16. 30; 25. 26; intrans. *to go before, to go first*, Mat. 2. 9; 21. 9; Mar. 6. 45; 1 Ti. 5. 24; part. προάγων, ουσα, ον, *preceding, previous, antecedent*, 1 Ti. 1. 18; He. 7. 18; hence, in N.T., trans. *to precede*, Mat. 14. 22, et al.; *to be in advance of*, Mat. 21. 31. (ᾰ).

προάγων, nom. sing. masc. part. pres. . προάγω

προαιρεῖται,[b] 3 pers. sing. pres. ind. . προαιρέομαι

προαιρέομαι, οῦμαι], fut. ήσομαι, (§ 17. tab. Q) πρό & αἱρέω) *to prefer, choose*; met. *to purpose, intend considerately*, 2 Co. 9. 7.

προαιτιάομαι, ῶμαι], fut. άσομαι, (πρό & αἰτιάομαι, from αἰτία) pr. *to charge beforehand; to convict beforehand*, Ro. 3. 9, since the charges in the case in question were drawn from Scripture. N.T.

προακούω], (πρό & ἀκούω) *to hear beforehand*, aor. 1, προήκουσα, *to have heard of previously, or already*, Col. 1. 5.

προαμαρτάνω], (πρό & ἁμαρτάνω) *to sin before*; perf. προημάρτηκα, *to have already sinned, have sinned heretofore*, 2 Co. 12. 21; 13. 2. N.T.

προάξω, 1 pers. sing. fut. ind. . . προάγω

[a] Ac. 1. 18.

[b] 2 Co. 9. 7.

προαύλιον],[a] ίου, τό, (§ 3. tab. C. c) (πρό & αὐλή) *the exterior court* before an edifice, Mar. 14. 68, col.; Mat. 26. 71.

προβαίνω], fut. βήσομαι, aor. 2, προὔβην, part. προβάς, (§ 37. rem. 1) (πρό & βαίνω) *to go forward, advance,* Mat. 4. 21; Mar. 1. 19; *to advance* in life, Lu. 1. 7, 18; 2. 36.

προβαλλόντων, gen. pl. masc. part. pres. . προβάλλω

προβάλλω], fut. βαλῶ, aor. 2, προὔβᾰλον, (§ 34. rem. 1. b) (πρό & βάλλω) *to cast before, project; to put or urge forward,* Ac. 19. 33; *to put forth,* as a tree its blossoms, etc., Lu. 21. 30.

προβαλόντων, gen. pl. masc. part. aor. 2.—A. B. Tdf. . . . . } προβάλλω
προβαλλόντων, Rec. Gr. Sch. Ln. (Ac. 19. 33) . . . . } προβάλλω

προβάλωσι, 3 pers. pl. aor. 2, subj. . . id.

προβάς, nom. sing. masc. part. aor. 2 . . προβαίνω

πρόβατα, nom. and acc. pl. . . . πρόβατον

προβατικῇ,[b] dat. sing. fem. . . . προβατικός

προβατικός], ή, όν . . . . πρόβατον

πρόβᾰτον], ου, τό, (§ 3. tab. C. c) *a sheep,* Mat. 7. 15; 9. 36; 10. 16; met. Mat. 10. 6; 15. 24, et al.

προβατῐκός, ή, όν, (§ 7. tab. F. a) *belonging or pertaining to sheep;* ἡ προβατικὴ (πύλη), *the sheep-gate,* Jno. 5. 2.

προβάτου, gen. sing. . . . . πρόβατον

προβάτων, gen. pl. . . . . id.

προβεβηκότες, nom. pl. masc. part. perf. . προβαίνω

προβεβηκυῖα, nom. sing. fem. part. perf. . id.

προβιβάζω], fut. άσω, (§ 26. rem. 1) (πρό & βιβάζω) *to cause* any one *to advance, to lead forward; to advance, push forward,* Ac. 19. 33; met. *to incite, instigate,* Mat. 14. 8.

προβιβασθεῖσα, nom. s. fem. part. aor. 1, pass. προβιβάζω

προβλέπω], fut. ψω, (§ 23. rem. 1. a) (πρό & βλέπω) *to foresee;* mid. *to provide beforehand,* He. 11. 40. LXX.

προβλεψαμένου,[c] gen. sing. m. part. aor. 1, mid. προβλέπω

προγεγονότων,[d] gen. pl. neut. part. perf. . προγίνομαι

προγεγραμμένοι, nom. pl. masc. part. perf. pass. (§ 23. rem. 7) . . προγράφω

προγίνομαι], perf. προγέγονα, (§ 37. rem. 1) (πρό & γίνομαι) *to be or happen before, be previously done or committed;* προγεγονώς, *bygone, previous,* Ro. 3. 25.

πρόγονος, ου, ὁ, (§ 3. tab. C. a) *born earlier, elder; a progenitor,* pl. *progenitors; parents,* 1 Ti. 5. 4; *forefathers, ancestors,* 2 Ti. 1. 3.

προγινώσκοντες, nom. pl. masc. part. pres. προγινώσκω

προγινώσκω], fut. γνώσομαι, aor. 2, προέγνων, perf. pass. προέγνωσμαι, (§ 36. rem. 3) (πρό & γινώσκω) *to know beforehand, to be previously acquainted with,* Ac. 26. 5; 2 Pe. 3. 17; *to determine on beforehand, to fore-ordain,* 1 Pe. 1. 20; in N.T., from the Heb., *to foreknow, to appoint as the subjects of future privileges,* Ro. 8. 29; 11. 2.

πρόγνωσις, εως, ἡ, (§ 5. tab. E. c) *foreknowledge, prescience;* in N.T. *previous determination, purpose,* Ac. 2. 23; 1 Pe. 1. 2.

προγνώσει, dat. sing. . . . . πρόγνωσις

πρόγνωσιν, acc. sing. . . . . id.

πρόγνωσις], εως, ἡ . . . . προγινώσκω

προγόνοις, dat. pl. . . . . πρόγονος

πρόγονος], ου, ὁ . . . . προγίνομαι

προγόνων, gen. pl. . . . . πρόγονος

προγράφω], fut. ψω, perf. pass. προγέγραμμαι, (§ 23. rem. 6, 7) aor. 2, pass. προεγράφην, (ᾰ) (πρό & γράφω) *to write before or aforetime,* Ro. 15. 4; Ep. 3. 3; *to make a subject of public notice; to set forth unreservedly and distinctly,* Gal. 3. 1; *to designate clearly,* Jude 4.

πρόδηλα, nom. pl. neut. . . . . πρόδηλος

πρόδηλοι, nom. pl. fem. . . . id.

πρόδηλον, nom. sing. neut. . . . id.

πρόδηλος], ου, ὁ, ἡ, τό, -ον, (§ 7. rem. 2) (πρό & δῆλος) *previously manifest, before known; plainly manifest, very clear, prominently conspicuous,* 1 Ti. 5. 24, 25; He. 7. 14.

προδίδωμι], fut. δώσω, (§ 30. tab. Z) (πρό & δίδωμι) *to give before, precede in giving;* Ro. 11. 35; *to give up, abandon, betray.*

προδότης, ου, ὁ, (§ 2. tab. B. c) *a betrayer, traitor,* Lu. 6. 16; Ac. 7. 52; 2 Ti. 3. 4.

προδόται, nom. pl. . . . . προδότης

[a] Mar. 14. 68. [b] Jno. 5. 2. [c] He. 11. 40. [d] Ro. 3. 25.

προδότης], ου, ὁ . . . . προδίδωμι
προδραμών, nom. sing. masc. part. aor. 2 . προτρέχω
πρόδρομος],[a] ου, ὁ, ἡ . . . . id.
προεβίβασαν, 3 pers. pl. aor. 1, ind. . προβιβάζω
προέγνω, 3 pers. sing. aor. 1, ind. (§ 36. rem. 3) προγινώσκω
προεγνωσμένου, gen. sing. masc. part. perf. pass. id.
προεγράφη, 3 pers. sing. aor. 2, ind. pass. (§ 24. rem. 6) . . . . . προγράφω
προέγραψα, 1 pers. sing. aor. 1, ind. act. . id.
προέδραμε, 3 pers. sing. aor. 2, ind. (§ 36. rem. 1) προτρέχω
προέδωκε,[b] 3 pers. sing. aor. 1, ind. act. . προδίδωμι
προεθέμην, 1 pers. sing. aor. 2, ind. mid. (§ 28. tab. W) . . . προτίθημι
προέθετο, 3 pers. sing. aor. 2, ind. mid. . id.
προεῖδον], part. προϊδών, aor. 2 of προοράω: which see.
προείπαμεν, 1 pers. pl. aor. 1, ind. . προλέγω
προεῖπε, 3 pers. sing. aor. 2, ind. (§ 35. rem. 7) id.
προείπομεν, 1 pers. pl. aor. 2, ind.—A. Gr. Sch. } id.
προείπαμεν, B. D. Rec. Tdf. (1 Thes. 4. 6) }
προεῖπον, 1 pers. sing. aor. 2, ind . . id.
προείρηκα, 1 pers. sing. perf. ind. (§ 36. rem. 1) id.
προειρήκαμεν, 1 pers. pl. perf. ind. . . id.
προείρηκε, 3 pers. sing. perf. ind. . . id.
προειρηκέναι, perf. infin. . . . id.
προειρημένων, gen. pl. part. perf. pass. . id.
προείρηται, 3 pers. sing. perf. ind. pass.—A. C. D. Ln. Tdf. . . . } id.
εἴρηται, Rec. Gr. Sch. (He. 4. 7) . }
προέκοπτε, 3 pers. sing. imperf. . . προκόπτω
προέκοπτον, 1 pers. sing. imperf. . . id.
προέκοψε, 3 pers. sing. aor. 1, ind. . . id.
προέλαβε, 3 pers. sing. aor. 2, ind. act. (§ 36. rem. 2) . . . . προλαμβάνω
προελέγομεν, 1 pers. pl. imperf. . . προλέγω
προελεύσεται, 3 pers. sing. fut. ind. (§ 36. rem. 1) προέρχομαι
προελθόντες, nom. pl. masc. part. aor. 2 . id.
προελθών, nom. sing. masc. part. aor. 2 . id.
προέλθωσι, 3 pers. pl. aor. 2, subj. . . id.
προελπίζω], fut. ίσω, (§ 26. rem. 1) (πρό & ἐλπίζω) *to repose hope and confidence* in a person or thing *beforehand*, Ep. 1. 12.
προενάρχομαι], fut. ξομαι, (§ 23. rem. 1. b) (πρό & ἐνάρχομαι) *to begin before* a particular time, 2 Co. 8. 6, 10. N.T.
προενήρξασθε, 2 pers. pl. aor. 1, ind. . προενάρχομαι
προενήρξατο, 3 pers. sing. aor. 1, ind. . . id.
προεπαγγέλλομαι], aor. 1, προεπηγγειλάμην, (§ 27. rem. 1. d) (πρό & ἐπαγγέλλομαι) *to promise beforehand, or aforetime*, Ro. 1. 2. L.G.
προέπεμπον, 3 pers. pl. imperf. act. . . προπέμπω
προεπηγγείλατο,[c] 3 pers. s. aor. 1, ind. προεπαγγέλλομαι
προεπηγγελμένην, acc. sing. fem. part. perf. pass.—Al. Tdf. . . . } id.
προκατηγγελμένην, Rec. Gr. Sch. (2 Co. 9. 5) . . . . . }
προέρχομαι], fut. προελεύσομαι, aor. 2, προῆλθον, (§ 36. rem. 1) (πρό & ἔρχομαι) *to go forwards, advance, proceed*, Mat. 26. 39; Mar. 14. 35; Ac. 12. 10; *to precede, go before* any one, Lu. 22. 47; *to precede* in time, *be a forerunner or precursor*, Lu. 1. 17; *to outgo, outstrip in going*, Mar. 6. 33; *to travel in advance of* any one, *precede*, Ac. 20. 5, 13; 2 Co. 9. 5.
προεστῶτες, nom. pl. masc. part. perf. (§ 35. rem. 8) . . . . . προΐστημι
προέτειναν, 3 p. pl. aor. 1, ind.—Gr. Sch. Tdf. } προτείνω
προέτεινεν, Rec. (Ac. 22. 25) . . }
προέτεινε,[d] 3 pers. sing. aor. 1, ind. (§ 27. rem. 1. d) id.
προετοιμάζω], fut. άζω, (§ 26. rem. 1) (πρό & ἑτοιμάζω) *to prepare beforehand*; in N.T. *to appoint beforehand*, Ro. 9. 23; Ep. 2. 10.
προευαγγελίζομαι], fut. ίσομαι, *to announce joyful tidings beforehand*. L.G.
προευηγγελίσατο,[e] 3 pers. sing. aor. 1, ind. (§ 23. rem. 5) . . προευαγγελίζομαι
προεφήτευον, 3 pers. pl. imperf. (§ 34. rem. 2) προφητεύω
προεφητεύσαμεν, 1 pers. pl. aor. 1, ind. . id.
προεφήτευσαν, 3 pers. pl. aor. 1, ind. . . id.
προεφήτευσε, 3 pers. sing. aor. 1, ind. . id.
προέφθασε, 3 pers. sing. aor. 1, ind. (§ 37. rem. 1) προφθάνω
προεχειρίσατο, 3 pers. sing. aor. 1, ind. προχειρίζομαι
προεχόμεθα,[f] 1 pers. pl. pres. ind. mid. . προέχω
προέχω], fut. ξω, (πρό & ἔχω) *to have or hold before*; intrans. and mid. *to excel, surpass, have advantage or pre-eminence*.
προεωρακότες, nom. pl. m. part. perf. (§ 36. rem. 1) προοράω
προήγαγον, 1 pers. sing. aor. 2, (§ 13. rem. 7. d) προάγω
προῆγε, 3 pers. sing. imperf. act. . . . id.
προηγέομαι, οῦμαι], fut. ήσομαι, (§ 17. tab. Q) (πρό & ἡγέομαι) *to go before, precede, lead onward*; met. *to endeavour to take the lead of, vie with*, or, *to give precedence to, to prefer*, Ro. 12. 10.

[a] He. 6. 20. [b] Ro. 11. 35. [c] Ro. 1. 2. [d] Ac. 22. 25. [e] Gal. 3. 8. [f] Ro. 3. 9.

προηγούμενοι,[a] nom. pl. masc. part. pres. . προηγέομαι
προηκούσατε,[b] 2 pers. pl. aor. 1, ind. . . προακούω
προῆλθον, 3 pers. pl. aor. 2, ind. . . προέρχομαι
προηλπικότας,[c] acc. pl. masc. part. perf. . προελπίζω
προημαρτηκόσι, dat. pl. masc. part. perf. . προαμαρτάνω
προημαρτηκότων, gen. pl. masc. part. perf. . id.
προῄρηται, 3 pers. sing. perf. ind. pass.—B. C. Ln. Tdf. . . . . προαιρέομαι
προαιρεῖται, Rec. Gr. Sch. (2 Co. 9. 7) προαιρέομαι
προήρχετο, 3 pers. sing. imperf. . . . προέρχομαι
προῃτιασάμεθα,[d] 1 pers. pl. aor. 1, ind. (§ 13. rem. 2) . . . . προαιτιάομαι
προητοίμασε, 3 pers. sing. aor. 1, ind. . προετοιμάζω
προθέσει, dat. sing. . . . . . πρόθεσις
προθέσεως, gen. sing. . . . . . id.
πρόθεσιν, acc. sing. . . . . . . id.
πρόθεσις], εως, ἡ, (§ 5. tab. E. c) . . προτίθημι
προθεσμία], ας, ἡ, (§ 2. tab. B. b, and rem. 2) (pr. fem. of προθέσμιος, *before appointed*, πρό & θεσμός) sc. ἡμέρα, *a time before appointed, set or appointed time.*
προθεσμίας,[e] gen. sing. . . . . προθεσμία
προθυμία], ας, ἡ . . . . . . πρόθυμος
προθυμίαν, acc. sing. . . . . . προθυμία
προθυμίας, gen. sing. . . . . . id.
πρόθυμον, nom. sing. neut. . . . . πρόθυμος
πρόθῡμος], ου, ὁ, ἡ, (§ 7. rem. 2) (πρό & θυμός) *ready in mind, prepared, prompt, willing*, Mat. 26. 41; Mar. 14. 38; τὸ πρόθυμον, i.q. ἡ προθυμία, *readiness, alacrity of mind*, Ro. 1. 15.

προθυμία, ας, ἡ, (§ 2. tab. B. b, and rem. 2) *promptness, readiness, alacrity of mind, willingness*, Ac. 17. 11; 2 Co. 8. 11, 12, 19; 9. 2.

προθύμως, adv. *promptly, with alacrity, readily, willingly, heartily, cheerfully*, 1 Pe. 5. 2.

προθύμως],[f] adv. . . . . . πρόθυμος
προϊδοῦσα, nom. sing. fem. part. aor. 2, (§ 36. rem. 1) . . . . . προοράω
προϊδών, nom. sing. masc. part. aor. 2 . id.
προϊστάμενοι, nom. pl. masc. part. pres. mid. προΐστημι
προϊστάμενον, acc. sing. masc. part. pres. mid. id.
προϊστάμενος, nom. sing. masc. part. pres. mid. id.
προισταμένους, acc. pl. masc. part. pres. mid. id.
προΐστασθαι, pres. infin. mid. (§ 29. tab. Y) . id.
προΐστημι], fut. προστήσω, (§ 29. tab. X) (πρό & ἵστημι) *to set before*; met. *to set over, appoint with authority*; intrans. aor. 2, προὔστην, perf. προέστηκα, part. προεστώς, and mid. προΐσταμαι, *to preside, govern, superintend*, Ro. 12. 8; 1 Thes. 5. 12; 1 Ti. 3. 4, 5, 12; 5. 17; mid. *to undertake resolutely, to practise diligently, to maintain the practice of*, Tit. 3. 8, 14.

προστάτις, ιδος, ἡ, (§ 4. rem. 2. c) (fem. of προστάτης, *one who stands in front or before; a leader; a protector, champion, patron*, from προΐστημι) *a patroness, protectress*, Ro. 16. 2. (ᾰ).

προκαλούμενοι,[g] nom. pl. masc. part. pres. προκαλέομαι
προκαλέομαι, οῦμαι], fut. έσομαι, (§ 17. tab. Q, and § 22. rem. 1) (προκαλέω, *to call forth, invite to stand forth*, from πρό & καλέω) *to call out, challenge to fight; to provoke, irritate with feelings of ungenerous rivalry*, Gal. 5. 26.
προκαταγγείλαντας, acc. pl. masc. part. aor. 1, act. (§ 27. rem. 1. d) . προκαταγγέλλω
προκαταγγέλλω], fut. γελῶ, (§ 27. rem. 1. b) (πρό & καταγγέλλω) *to declare or announce beforehand, foretel, predict*, Ac. 3. 18, 24; 7. 52; 2 Co. 9. 5. L.G.
προκαταρτίζω], fut. ίσω, (§ 26. rem. 1) (πρό & καταρτίζω) *to make ready, prepare, or complete beforehand.*
προκαταρτίσωσι, 3 pers. pl. aor. 1, subj. προκαταρτίζω
προκατήγγειλαν, 3 pers. pl. aor. 1, ind. προκαταγγέλλω
προκατήγγειλε, 3 pers. sing. aor. 1, ind. act. . id.
προκατηγγελμένην, acc. sing. fem. part. perf. pass. . . . . . . id.
πρόκειμαι], fut. είσομαι, (§ 33. tab. DD) (πρό & κεῖμαι) *to lie or be placed before*; met. *to be proposed or set before*, as a duty, example, reward, etc., He. 6. 18; 12. 1, 2; Jude 7; *to be at hand, be present*, 2 Co. 8. 12.
προκειμένης, gen. sing. fem. part. pres. . πρόκειμαι
προκείμενον, acc. sing. masc. part. pres. . id.
πρόκεινται, 3 pers. pl. pres. ind. . . id.
πρόκειται, 3 pers. sing. pres. ind. . . id.
προκεκηρυγμένον, acc. sing. masc. part. perf. pass. . . . . . προκηρύσσω
προκεκυρωμένην,[h] acc. sing. fem. part. perf. pass. . . . . . προκυρόω

[a] Ro. 12. 10. [b] Col. 1. 5. [c] Ep. 1. 12. [d] Ro. 3. 9. [e] Gal. 4. 2. [f] 1 Pe. 5. 2. [g] Gal. 5. 26. [h] Gal. 3. 17.

προκεχειρισμένον, acc. sing. masc. part. perf. pass.—Gr. Sch. Tdf. } προχειρίζομαι
προκεκηρυγμένον, Rec. (Ac. 3. 20) }

προκεχειροτονημένοις,[a] dat. pl. masc. part. perf. pass. . . . προχειροτονέω

προκηρύξαντος, gen. sing. masc. part. aor. 1 προκηρύσσω

προκηρύσσω], fut. ξω, (§ 26. rem. 3) (πρό & κηρύσσω) *to announce publicly*; in N.T. *to announce before*, Ac. 3. 20; 13. 24.

προκοπή], ῆς, ἡ . . . . . προκόπτω

προκοπήν, acc. sing. . . . . προκοπή

προκόπτω], fut. ψω, (§ 23. rem. 1. a) (πρό & κόπτω) pr. *to cut* a passage *forward; to advance, make progress; to advance*, as time, *to be far spent*, Ro. 13. 12; met. *to advance* in wisdom, age, or stature, Lu. 2. 52; seq. ἐν, *to make progress or proficiency in*, Gal. 1. 14; πρ. ἐπὶ πλεῖον, *to proceed or advance further*, 2 Ti. 2. 16; 3. 9; πρ. ἐπὶ τὸ χεῖρον, *to grow worse and worse*, 2 Ti. 3. 13.

προκοπή, ῆς, ἡ, (§ 2. tab. B. a) *advance upon a way*; met. *progress, advancement, furtherance*, Phi. 1. 12; 1 Ti. 4. 15.

προκόψουσι, 3 pers. pl. fut. ind. . . προκόπτω

πρόκριμα], ατος, τό, (§ 4. tab. D. c) (προκρίνω, *to prejudge, prefer*) *previous judgment, prejudice, prepossession*, or, *preference, partiality*. N.T.

προκρίματος,[b] gen. sing. . . . . πρόκριμα

προκυρόω, ῶ], fut. ώσω, (§ 20. tab. T) (πρό & κυρόω) *to sanction and establish previously, ratify and confirm before*, Gal. 3. 17. N.T.

προλαμβάνει, 3 pers. sing. pres. ind. . προλαμβάνω

προλαμβάνω], fut. λήψομαι, aor. 2, προὔλἄβον, (§ 36. rem. 2) (πρό & λαμβάνω) *to take before* another, 1 Co. 11. 21; trop. *to anticipate, do beforehand*, Mar. 14. 8; *to take by surprise*; pass. *be taken unexpectedly, be overtaken, be taken by surprise*, Gal. 6. 1.

προλέγω], fut. ξω, aor. 1, προεῖπα, aor. 2, προεῖπον, perf. προείρηκα, (§ 36. rem. 1) (πρό & λέγω) *to tell beforehand, to foretel*, Mat. 24. 25; Ac. 1. 16; Ro. 9. 29; 2 Co. 13. 2; Gal. 5. 21; 1 Thes. 3. 4, et al.

προληφθῇ, 3 pers. sing. aor. 1, subj. pass. προλαμβάνω

προμαρτύρομαι], (πρό & μαρτύρομαι) pr. *to witness or testify beforehand; to declare beforehand, predict*, 1 Pe. 1. 11. N.T.

προμαρτυρόμενον,[c] nom. sing. neut. part. pres. . . . . προμαρτύρομαι

προμελετᾶν,[d] pres. infin. . . . προμελετάω

προμελετάω, ῶ], fut. ήσω, (§ 18. tab. R) (πρό & μελετάω) *to practise beforehand; to premeditate*, Lu. 21. 14.

προμεριμνᾶτε,[e] 2 pers. pl. pres. imper. . προμεριμνάω

προμεριμνάω, ῶ], fut. ήσω, (§ 18. tab. R) (πρό & μεριμνάω), *to be anxious or solicitous beforehand, to ponder beforehand*. N.T.

προνοέω, ῶ], fut. ήσω, (§ 16. tab. P) (πρό & νοέω) *to perceive beforehand, foresee; to provide for*, 1 Ti. 5. 8; mid. *to provide for one's self*; by impl. *to apply one's self to* a thing, *practise, strive to exhibit*, Ro. 12. 17; 2 Co. 8. 21.

πρόνοια, ας, ἡ, (§ 2. tab. B. b, and rem. 2) *forethought; providence, provident care*, Ac. 24. 3; *provision*, Ro. 13. 14.

πρόνοια], ας, ἡ . . . . . . προνοέω

πρόνοιαν, acc. sing. . . . . πρόνοια

προνοίας, gen. sing. . . . . id.

προνοεῖ, 3 pers. sing. pres. ind. . . προνοέω

προνοοῦμεν, 1 pers. pl. pres. ind.—B. D. Ln. Sch. Tdf. . . . . } id.
προνοούμενοι, Rec. Gr. (2 Co. 8. 21) }

προνοούμενοι, nom. pl. masc. part. pres. mid. id.

προοράω, ῶ], fut. προόψομαι, perf. προεώρᾶκα, aor. 2, προεῖδον, (§ 36. rem. 1) (πρό & ὁράω) *to foresee*, Ac. 2. 31; Gal. 3. 8; *to see before*, Ac. 21. 29; in N.T. *to have vividly present to the mind, to be mindful of*, Ac. 2. 25.

προορίζω], fut. ίσω, (§ 26. rem. 1) (πρό & ὁρίζω) *to limit or mark out beforehand; to design definitely beforehand, ordain beforehand, predestine*, Ac. 4. 28; Ro. 8. 29, 30, et al.

προορίσας, nom. sing. masc. part. aor. 1, act. προορίζω

προορισθέντες, nom. pl. masc. part. aor. 1, pass. id.

προπαθόντες,[f] nom. pl. masc. part. aor. 2 . προπάσχω

προπάσχω], (πρό & πάσχω) aor. 2, προέπᾰθον, (§ 36. rem. 4) *to experience previously*, of ill treatment, 1 Thes. 2. 2.

---

[a] Ac. 10. 41. [b] 1 Ti. 5. 21. [c] 1 Pe. 1. 11. [d] Lu. 21. 14. [e] Mar. 13. 11. [f] 1 Thes. 2. 2.

προπάτορα, acc. sing.—A. B. C. Ln. Tdf. } προπάτωρ
πατέρα, Rec. Gr. Sch. (Ro. 4. 1) }

προπάτωρ], ορος, ὁ, (§ 4. rem. 2. f) (πρό & πατήρ) *a grandfather; a progenitor, or ancestor*, v.r. Ro. 4. 1.

προπεμπόντων, gen. pl. masc. part. pres. act. προπέμπω

προπέμπω], fut. ψω, (§ 23. rem. 1. a) (πρό & πέμπω) *to send on before; to accompany or attend out of respect, escort, accompany for a certain distance on setting out on a journey*, Ac. 15. 3; 20. 38; 21. 5, et al.; *to furnish with things necessary for a journey*, Tit. 3. 13; 3 Jno. 6.

προπεμφθέντες, nom. pl. masc. part. aor. 1, pass. προπέμπω

προπεμφθῆναι, aor. 1, infin. pass. . . id.

προπέμψας, nom. sing. masc. part. aor. 1, act. id.

προπέμψατε, 2 pers. pl. aor. 1, imper. act. id.

πρόπεμψον, 2 pers. sing. aor. 1, imper. act. . id.

προπετεῖς, nom. pl. masc. . . . προπετής

προπετές, acc. sing. neut. . . . . id.

προπετής], έος, οῦς, ὁ, ἡ, τό, -ές, (§ 7. tab. G. b) (πρό & πίπτω) *falling forwards*; meton. *precipitate, rash*, Ac. 19. 36; 2 Ti. 3. 4.

προπορεύομαι], fut. εύσομαι, (§ 14. tab. N) (προ & πορεύομαι) *to precede, go before*, Ac. 7. 40; Lu. 1. 76.

προπορεύσῃ, 2 pers. sing. fut. ind. . προπορεύομαι

προπορεύσονται, 3 pers. pl. fut. ind. act. . id.

πρός], prep., with a genitive, *from*; met. *for the benefit of*, Ac. 27. 34; with a dative, *near, by, at, by the side of, in the vicinity of*, Mar. 5. 11; Lu. 19. 37; with an accusative, used of the place to which anything tends, *to, unto, towards*, Mat. 2. 12; 3. 5, 13; *at, close upon*, Mat. 3. 10; Mar. 5. 22; *near to, in the vicinity of*, Mar. 6. 45; after verbs of speaking, praying, answering to a charge, etc., *to*, Mat. 3. 15; 27. 14; of place where, *with, in, among, by, at*, etc., Mat. 26. 55; Mar. 11. 4; Lu. 1. 80; of time, *for, during*, Lu. 8. 13; 1 Co. 7. 5; *near, towards*, Lu. 24. 29; of the end, object, purpose for which an action is exerted, or to which any quality, etc., has reference, *to*, Jno. 4. 35; Ac. 3. 10; 27. 12; before an infin. with τό, *in order to, that, in order that*, Mat. 6. 1; 13. 30; 26. 12; *so as to, so that*, Mat. 5. 28; of the relation which any action, state, quality, etc., bears to any person or thing, *in relation to, of, concerning, in respect to, with reference to*, Mat. 19. 8; Lu. 12. 41; 18. 1; 20. 19; *as it respects, as it concerns, with relation to*, Mat. 27. 4; Jno. 21. 22, 23; *according to, in conformity with*, Lu. 12. 47; 2 Co. 5. 10; *in comparison with*, Ro. 8. 18; *in attention to*, Ep. 3. 4; of the actions, dispositions, etc., exhibited with respect to any one, whether friendly, *towards*, Gal. 6. 10; Ep. 6. 9; or unfriendly, *with, against*, Lu. 23. 12; Ac. 23. 30; after verbs signifying to converse, dispute, make a covenant, etc., *with*, Lu. 24. 14; Ac. 2. 7; 3. 25.

προσάββᾰτον],[a] ου, τό, (§ 3. tab. C. c) (πρό & σάββατον) *the day before the sabbath, sabbath-eve*. LXX.

προσάγαγε, 2 pers. sing. aor. 2, imper. act. (§ 13. rem. 7. d) . . . προσάγω

προσαγάγῃ, 3 pers. sing. aor. 2, subj. act. . id.

προσαγαγόντες, nom. pl. masc. part. aor. 2, act. id.

προσάγειν, pres. infin. act. . . . id.

προσαγορευθείς,[b] nom. sing. masc. part. aor. 1, pass. . . . . . προσαγορεύω

προσαγορεύω], fut. εύσω, (§ 13. tab. M) (πρός & ἀγορεύω, *to speak*) *to speak to, accost, to name, denominate; to nominate, declare*, He. 5. 10.

προσάγω], fut. ξω, aor. 2, προσήγᾰγον, (§ 13. rem. 7. d) *to lead or conduct to, bring*, Lu. 9. 41; Ac. 16. 20; *to conduct to the presence of, to procure access for*, 1 Pe. 3. 18; *to bring near; to near*, in a nautical sense, Ac. 27. 27. (ᾰ).

προσαγωγή, ῆς, ἡ, (§ 2. tab. B. a) *approach; access, admission*, to the presence of any one, Ro. 5. 2; Ep. 2. 18.

προσαγωγή], ῆς, ἡ . . . . . προσάγω

προσαγωγήν, acc. sing. . προσαγωγή

προσαιτέω, ῶ], fut ήσω, (§ 16. tab P) (πρός & αἰτέω) *to ask for in addition; to ask earnestly, beg; to beg* alms, Mar. 10. 46; Lu. 18. 35; Jno. 9. 8.

προσαίτης, ου, ὁ, (§ 2. tab. B. c) *a beggar, mendicant*, v.r. Jno. 9. 8. N.T.

[a] Mar. 15. 42.

[b] He. 5. 10.

προσαίτης, ου, ὁ, Gr. Sch. Tdf. } προσαιτέω
τυφλός, Rec. (Jno. 9. 8) }
προσαιτῶν, nom. sing. masc. part. pres. . id.
προσαναβαίνω], fut. βήσομαι, aor. 2, προσανέβην, (§ 37. rem. 1) (πρός & ἀναβαίνω) *to go up further*, Lu. 14. 10.
προσανάβηθι,[a] 2 pers. sing. aor. 2, imper. προσαναβαίνω
προσανᾱλίσκω], fut. λώσω, (§ 36. rem. 4) (πρός & ἀναλίσκω) *to consume besides; to expend* on a definite object, Lu. 8. 43.
προσαναλώσασα,[b] nom. s. fem. part. aor. 1 προσαναλίσκω
προσαναπληροῦσα, nom. sing. fem. part. pres. act. . . . . . προσαναπληρόω
προσαναπληρόω, ῶ], fut. ώσω, (§ 20. tab. T) (πρός & ἀναπληρόω) *to fill up by addition; to supply* deficiencies, 2 Co. 9. 12; 11. 9.
προσανατίθημι], (§ 28. tab. V) (πρός & ἀνατίθημι) *to lay upon over and above;* mid. *to put one's self in free communication with, to confer with,* Gal. 1. 16; *to confer upon, to propound as a matter of consideration,* Gal. 2. 6.
προσανεθέμην, 1 pers. sing. aor. 2, ind. mid. (§ 28. tab. W) . . προσανατίθημι
προσανέθεντο, 3 pers. pl. aor. 2, ind. mid. . id.
προσανεπλήρωσαν, 3 pers. pl. aor. 1, ind. προσαναπληρόω
προσανέχειν, pres. infin.—B. Ln. } προσανέχω
προσάγειν, R. Gr. Sch. Tdf. (Ac. 27. 27) }
προσανέχω], (πρός & ἀνέχω) *to draw near to, be close to,* v.r. Ac. 27. 27.
προσαπειλέω, ῶ], fut. ήσω, (§ 16. tab. P) (πρός & ἀπειλέω) *to threaten in addition, utter additional threats.*
προσαπειλησάμενοι,[c] nom. pl. masc. part. aor. 1, mid. (§ 17. tab. Q) . . προσαπειλέω
προσδαπανάω, ῶ], fut. ήσω, (§ 18. tab. R) (πρός & δαπανάω) *to spend besides, expend over and above.* L.G.
προσδαπανήσῃς,[d] 2 pers. sing. aor. 1, subj. προσδαπανάω
προσδεξάμενοι, nom. pl. masc. part. aor. 1 προσδέχομαι
προσδέξησθε, 2 pers. pl. aor. 1, subj. . id.
προσδέομαι], fut. δεήσομαι, (§ 37. rem. 1) (πρός & δέομαι) *to want besides or in addition.*
προσδεόμενος,[e] nom. sing. masc. part. pres. προσδέομαι
προσδέχεσθε, 2 pers. pl. pres. imper. προσδέχομαι
προσδέχεται, 3 pers. sing. pres. ind. . . id.
προσδέχομαι], fut. δέξομαι, (§ 23. rem. 1. b) (πρός & δέχομαι) *to receive, accept to receive, admit, grant access to,* Lu. 15. 2; *to receive, admit, accept,* and with οὐ, *to reject,* He. 11. 35; *to submit to,* He. 10. 34; *to receive kindly,* as a guest, *entertain,* Ro. 16. 2; *to receive admit,* as a hope, Ac. 24. 15; *to look or wait for, expect, await,* Mar. 15. 43; Lu. 2. 25, et al.
προσδεχόμενοι, nom. pl. masc. part. pres προσδέχομαι
προσδεχομένοις, dat. pl. masc. part. pres. . id.
προσδεχόμενος, nom. sing. masc. part. pres. id.
προσδέχονται, 3 pers. pl. pres. ind. . id.
προσδοκᾷ, 3 pers. sing. pres. ind. . . προσδοκάω
προσδοκάω, ῶ], fut. ήσω, (§ 18. tab. R) *to look for, be expectant of,* Mat. 11. 3; Lu. 7. 19, 20; Ac. 3. 5; 2 Pe. 3. 12, 13, 14; *to expect,* Ac. 28. 6; *to wait for,* Lu. 1. 21; 8. 40; Ac. 10. 24; 27. 33; absol. *to think, anticipate,* Mat. 24. 50; Lu. 12. 46.

προσδοκία, ας, ἡ, (§ 2. tab. B. b, and rem. 2) *a looking for, expectation, anticipation,* Lu. 21. 26; meton. *expectation, what is expected or anticipated,* Ac. 12. 11.

προσδοκία], ας, ἡ . . . . . προσδοκάω
προσδοκίας, gen. sing. . . . . προσδοκία
προσδοκῶμεν, 1 pers. sing. pres. ind. . προσδοκάω
προσδοκῶν, nom. sing. masc. part. pres . id.
προσδοκῶντας, acc. pl. masc. part. pres. id.
προσδοκῶντες, nom. pl. masc. part. pres. . id.
προσδοκῶντος, gen. sing. masc. part. pres. id.
προσδοκώντων, gen. pl. masc. part. pres . id.
προσδραμών, nom. sing. masc. part. aor. 2 (§ 36. rem. 1) . . . . προστρέχω
προσεάω, ῶ], fut. άσω, (§ 22. rem. 2) (πρός & ἐάω) *to permit an approach,* Ac. 27. 7. N.T.
προσεγγίζω], fut. ίσω, (§ 26. rem. 1) (πρός & ἐγγίζω) *to approach, come near.* L.G.
προσεγγίσαι,[f] aor. 1, infin. . . προσεγγίζω
προσεδέξασθε, 2 pers. pl. aor. 1, ind. . προσδέχομαι
προσεδέχετο, 3 pers. sing. imperf. . . id.
προσεδόκων, 3 pers. pl. imperf. . . προσδοκάω
προσεδρεύοντες,[g] nom. pl. masc. part. pres. προσεδρεύω
προσεδρεύω], fut. εύσω, (§ 13. tab. M) (πρός & ἕδρα) *to sit near;* met. *to wait or attend upon, have charge of,* 1 Co. 9. 13.
προσέθετο, 3 pers. sing. aor. 2, ind. mid. προστίθημι
προσέθηκε, 3 pers. sing. aor. 1, ind. act. . id.

a Lu. 14. 10. b Lu. 8. 43. c Ac. 4. 21. d Lu. 10. 35. e Ac. 17. 25. f Mar. 2. 4. g 1 Co. 9. 13.

προσειργάσατο,[a] 3 pers. sing. aor. 1, ind. (§ 13. rem. 4) . . προσεργάζομαι
προσεῖχον, 3 pers. pl. imperf. . . . προσέχω
προσεκληρώθησαν,[b] 3 pers. pl. aor. 1, ind. pass. (§ 21. tab. U) . . προσκληρόω
προσεκλίθη, 3 pers. sing. aor. 1, pass.—B. C. Ln. Tdf. . . . . } προσκλίνω
προσεκολλήθη, Rec. Gr. Sch. (Ac. 5. 36) }
προσεκολλήθη, 3 pers. sing. aor. 1, ind. pass. (§ 19. tab. S) . . . προσκολλάω
προσέκοψαν, 3 pers. pl. aor. 1, ind. . προσκόπτω
προσεκύλισε, 3 pers. sing. aor. 1, ind. . προσκυλίω
προσεκύνει, 3 pers. sing. imperf. . προσκυνέω
προσεκύνησαν, 3 pers. pl. aor. 1, ind. . id.
προσεκύνησε, 3 pers. sing. aor. 1, ind. . . id.
προσεκύνουν, 3 pers. pl. imperf. . . id.
προσελάβετο, 3 pers. sing. aor. 2, ind. mid. (§ 36. rem. 2) . . . προσλαμβάνω
προσελάβοντο, 3 pers. pl. aor. 2, ind. mid. . id.
προσεληλύθατε, 2 pers. pl. perf. 2 (§ 36. rem. 1) . . . . . προσέρχομαι
πρόσελθε, 2 pers. sing. aor. 2, imper. . . id.
προσελθόντες, nom. pl. masc. part. aor. 2 . id.
προσελθόντων, gen. pl. masc. part. aor. 2 . id.
προσελθοῦσα, nom. sing. fem. part. aor. 2 id.
προσελθοῦσαι, nom. pl. fem. part. aor. 2 . id.
προσελθών, nom. sing. masc. part. aor. 2 . id.
προσενέγκας, nom. sing. masc. part. aor. 1, act. (§ 36. rem. 1) . . . προσφέρω
προσένεγκε, 2 pers. sing. aor. 2, imper. act. . id.
προσενέγκῃ, 3 pers. sing. aor. 1, subj. act. id.
προσενεχθείς, nom. sing. masc. part. aor. 1, pass. id.
προσενεχθῇ, 3 pers. sing. aor. 1, subj. pass. id.
προσενήνοχε, Att. for προσήνοχε, 3 pers. sing. perf. 2. (§ 36. rem. 1) . . id.
προσέπεσαν, 3 pers. pl. aor. 1, ind.—B. C. Ln. Tdf. . . . . . } προσπίπτω
προσέπεσον, Rec. Gr. Sch. (Mat. 7. 25) }
προσέπεσε, 3 pers. sing. aor. 2, ind. (§ 37. rem. 1) id.
προσέπεσον, 3 pers. pl. aor. 2, ind. . . id.
προσέπιπτε, 3 pers. sing. imperf. . . id.
προσέπιπτον, 3 pers. pl. imperf.—A. C. D. Ln. Tdf. . . . . . } id.
προσέπιπτεν, Rec. Gr. Sch. (Mar. 3. 11) }
προσεποιεῖτο,[c] 3 pers. sing. imperf. mid. . προσποιέω
προσεποιήσατο, 3 pers. sing. aor. 1, ind. mid.—A. B. D. Ln. Tdf. . . } id.
προσεποιεῖτο, Rec. Gr. Sch. (Lu. 24. 28) }

προσεργάζομαι], fut. άσομαι, (πρός & ἐργάζομαι) pr. *to work in addition; to gain in addition* in trade, Lu. 19. 16.

προσέῤῥηξε, 3 pers. sing. aor. 1, ind. (§ 36. rem. 5) . . . . προσρήγνυμι
προσέρχεσθαι, pres. infin. . . προσέρχομαι
προσέρχεται, 3 pers. sing. pres. ind. . id.

προσέρχομαι], fut. ελεύσομαι, aor. 2, προσῆλθον, perf. προσελήλυθα, (§ 36. rem. 1) (πρός & ἔρχομαι) *to come or go to* any one, *approach*, Mat. 4. 3, 11; 5. 1; 8. 19, 25, et al. freq.; trop. *to come or go to, approach, draw near*, spiritually, He. 7. 25; 11. 6; 4. 16; 1 Pe. 2. 4; met. *to assent to, accede to, concur in*, 1 Ti. 6. 3.

προσήλυτος, ου, ὁ, ἡ, (§ 3. tab. C. a. b) pr. *a new comer, a stranger*; in N.T. *a proselyte, convert from paganism to Judaism*, Mat. 23. 15; Ac. 2. 10; 6. 5; 13. 43. LXX.

προσερχόμενοι, nom. pl. masc. part. pres. προσέρχομαι
προσερχόμενον, acc. sing. masc. part. pres. . id.
προσερχομένου, gen. sing. masc. part. pres. id.
προσερχομένους, acc. pl. masc. part. pres. id.
προσέρχονται, 3 pers. pl. pres. ind. . id.
προσερχώμεθα, 1 pers. pl. pres. subj. . . id.
προσέσχε, 3 pers. sing. aor. 2.—A. C. Tdf. } προσέχω
προσέσχηκε, Rec. Gr. Ln. Sch. (He. 7. 13) }
προσέσχηκε, 3 pers. sing. perf. ind. (§ 36. rem. 4) id.
προσέταξε, 3 pers. sing. aor. 1, ind. act. . προστάσσω
προσετέθη, 3 pers. sing. aor. 1, ind. pass. (§ 28. rem. 10) . . . . . προστίθημι
προσετέθησαν, 3 pers. pl. aor. 1, ind. pass. . id.
προσετίθει, 3 pers. sing. imperf. act. (§ 31. rem. 2) id.
προσετίθεντο, 3 pers. pl. imperf. pass (§ 28, tab. W) . . . . . id.
πρόσευξαι, 2 pers. sing. aor. 1, imper. . προσεύχομαι
προσευξάμενοι, nom. pl. masc. part. aor. 1 id.
προσευξάμενος, nom. sing. masc. part. aor. 1 id
προσεύξασθαι, aor. 1, infin. . . id.
προσευξάσθωσαν, 3 pers. pl. aor. 1, imper. id.
προσεύξηται, 3 pers. sing. aor. 1, subj. . id.
προσεύξομαι, 1 pers. sing. fut. ind. . . id.
προσευξόμεθα, 1 pers. pl. fut. ind. Const. } id.
προσευξώμεθα, Rec. Gr. Sch. Tdf. (Ro. 8. 26) . . . . . }
προσευξώμεθα, 1 pers. pl. pres. subj. . . id.
προσευχαί, nom. pl. . . . . . προσευχή

[a] Lu. 19. 16. [b] Ac. 17. 4. [c] Lu. 24. 28.

προσευχαῖς, dat. pl. . . . . προσευχή
προσευχάς, acc. pl. . . . id.
προσεύχεσθαι, pres. infin. . . προσεύχομαι
προσεύχεσθε, 2 pers. pl. pres. imper. id.
προσευχέσθω, 3 pers. sing. pres. imper. id.
προσεύχεται, 3 pers. sing. pres. ind. . id.
προσεύχῃ, 2 pers. sing. pres. subj. . . id.
προσευχή], ῆς, ἡ, (§ 2. tab. B. a) . . id.
προσευχῇ, dat. sing. . . . . προσευχή
προσευχήν, acc sing. . . . . id.
προσευχῆς, gen. sing. . . . . id.
προσεύχησθε, 2 pers. pl. pres. subj. . προσεύχομαι
προσεύχομαι, fut. εὔξομαι, imperf. προσηυχόμην, aor. 1, προσηυξάμην, (§ 13. rem. 3) *to pray, offer prayer,* Mat. 5. 44; 6. 5, 6, et al.

προσευχή, ῆς, ἡ, (§ 2. tab. B. a) *prayer,* Mat. 17. 21; 21. 13, 22; Lu. 6. 12; Ac. 1. 14, et al.; meton. *a place where prayer is offered, an oratory,* perhaps, Ac. 16. 13, 16. LXX.

προσευχόμεθα, 1 pers. pl. pres. ind. . προσεύχομαι
προσευχομένη, nom. sing. fem. part. pres. . id.
προσευχόμενοι, nom. pl. masc. part. pres. id.
προσευχόμενον, acc. sing. masc. and nom. neut. part. pres. . . . . id.
προσευχόμενος, nom. sing. masc. part. pres. . id.
προσευχομένου, gen. sing. masc. part. pres. id.
προσεύχονται, 3 pers. pl. pres. ind. . id.
προσεύχωμαι, 1 pers. sing. pres. subj. . . id.
προσευχῶν, gen. pl. . . . . προσευχή
προσέφερε, 3 pers. sing. imperf. act. . . προσφέρω
προσέφερον, 3 pers. pl. imperf. act. . id.
προσεφώνει, 3 pers. sing. imperf. . προσφωνέω
προσεφώνησε, 3 pers. sing. aor. 1, ind. . id.
πρόσεχε, 2 pers. sing. pres. imper. . . προσέχω
προσέχειν, pres. infin. . . . . id.
προσέχετε, 2 pers. pl. pres. imper. . . id.
προσέχοντας, acc. pl. masc. part. pres. . id.
προσέχοντες, nom. pl. masc. part. pres. . id.
προσέχω], fut. ξω, (§ 36. rem 4) (πρός & ἔχω) *to have in addition; to hold to, bring near;* absol. *to apply* the mind *to* a thing, *to give heed to, attend to, observe, consider,* Ac. 5. 35; He. 2. 1; 2 Pe. 1. 19; *to take care of, provide for,* Ac. 20. 28; when followed by ἀπό, μή, or μήποτε, *to beware of, take heed of, guard against,* Mat. 6. 1; 7. 15; *to assent to, yield credence to, follow, adhere or be attached to,* Ac. 8. 6, 10, 11; 16. 14; *to give one's self up to, be addicted to, engage in, be occupied with,* 1 Ti. 1. 4; 3. 8, et al.

προσεῶντος,[a] gen. sing. masc. part. pres. . προσεάω
προσῆλθαν, 3 pers. pl. aor. 1 (§ 35. rem. 12) —LXX. . . . . } προσέρχομαι
προσῆλθον, Rec. Gr. Sch. Tdf. (Mat. 13. 36) . . . . }
προσῆλθε, 3 pers. sing. aor. 2, ind. . id.
προσῆλθον, 3 pers. pl. aor. 2, ind. . . id.
προσηλόω, ῶ], fut. ώσω, (§ 20. tab. T) (πρός & ἧλος) *to nail to, affix with nails,* Col. 2. 14.
προσήλυτοι, nom. pl. masc. . . προσήλυτος
προσήλυτον, acc. sing. masc. . . id.
προσήλυτος], ου, ὁ, ἡ . . . προσέρχομαι
προσηλύτων, gen. pl. . . . . προσήλυτος
προσηλώσας,[b] nom. sing. masc. part. aor. 1 προσηλόω
προσήνεγκα, 1 pers. sing. aor. 1, ind. act. (§ 36. rem. 1) . . . . προσφέρω
προσήνεγκαν, 3 pers. pl. aor. 1, ind. act. . id.
προσηνέγκατε, 2 pers. pl. aor. 1, ind. act. . id.
προσήνεγκε, 3 pers. sing. aor. 1, ind. act. . id.
προσηνέχθη, 3 pers. sing. aor. 1, ind. pass. . id.
προσήρχοντο, 3 pers. pl. imperf. . . προσέρχομαι
προσηυξάμεθα, 1 pers. pl. aor. 1, ind. . προσεύχομαι
προσηύξαντο, 3 pers. pl. aor. 1, ind. (§ 13. rem. 3) . . . . id.
προσηύξατο, 3 pers. sing. aor. 1, ind. . id.
προσηύχετο, 3 pers. sing. imperf. . . id.
προσθεῖναι, aor. 2, infin. act. (§ 28. tab. V) προστίθημι
προσθείς, nom. sing. masc. part. aor. 2, act. id.
προσθές, 2 pers. sing. aor. 2, imper. act. (§ 38. rem. 7) . . . . id.
πρόσκαιρα, nom. pl. neut. . . πρόσκαιρος
πρόσκαιροι, nom. pl. masc. . . . id.
πρόσκαιρον, acc. sing. fem. . . . id.
πρόσκαιρος], ου, ὁ, ἡ, τό, -ον, (§ 7. rem. 2) (πρός & καιρός) *opportune;* in N.T. *continuing for a limited time, temporary, transient,* Mat. 13. 21; Mar. 4. 17; 2 Co. 4. 18; He. 11. 25. L.G.
προσκαλεῖται, 3 pers. sing. pres. ind. . προσκαλέομαι
προσκαλέομαι, οῦμαι], fut. έσομαι, (§ 22. rem. 1) perf. (pass. form) προσκέκλημαι, (mid. of προσκαλέω, *to call to, summon, invite,* from

[a] Ac. 27. 7.

[b] Col. 2. 14.

πρός & καλέω) *to call to one's self, summon*, Mat. 10. 1; 15. 10, 32; 18. 2, et al.; *to invite*, Ac. 2. 39; *to call* to the performance of a thing, *appoint*, Ac. 13. 2; 16. 10.

προσκαλεσάμενοι, nom. pl. m. part. aor. 1 προσκαλέομαι

προσκαλεσάμενος, nom. sing. masc. part. aor. 1 id.

προσκαλεσάσθω, 3 pers. sing. aor. 1, imper. id.

προσκαλέσηται, 3 pers. sing. aor. 1, subj. . id.

προσκαρτερεῖτε, 2 pers. pl. pres. imper. προσκαρτερέω

προσκαρτερέω, ῶ], fut. ήσω, (§ 16. tab. P) (πρός & καρτερέω) *to persist in adherence to* a thing; *to be intently engaged in, attend constantly to*, Ac. 1. 14; 2. 42; Ro. 13. 6, et al.; *to remain constantly in* a place, Ac. 2. 46; *to constantly attend upon, continue near to, be at hand*, Mar. 3. 9; Ac. 8. 13; 10. 7.

προσκαρτέρησις, εως, ἡ, (§ 5. tab. E. c) *perseverance, unremitting continuance in* a thing, Ep. 6. 18. N.T.

προσκαρτερῇ, 3 pers. sing. pres. subj. . προσκαρτερέω

προσκαρτερήσει,[a] dat. sing. . . προσκαρτέρησις

προσκαρτέρησις], εως, ἡ . . . προσκαρτερέω

προσκαρτερήσομεν, 1 pers. pl. fut. ind. . id.

προσκαρτεροῦντες, nom. pl. masc. part. pres. id.

προσκαρτερούντων, gen. pl. masc. part. pres. id.

προσκαρτερῶν, nom. sing. masc. part. pres. id.

προσκέκλημαι, 1 pers. sing. perf. ind. (§ 22. rem. 4) . . . . προσκαλέομαι

προσκέκληται, 3 pers. sing. perf. ind. . . id.

προσκεφάλαιον],[b] ου, τό, (§ 3. tab. C. c) (πρός & κεφαλή) pr. *a cushion for the head, pillow*; also, *a boat-cushion*, Mar. 4. 38.

προσκληρόω, ῶ], fut. ώσω, (§ 20. tab. T) (πρός & κληρόω) pr. *to assign by lot*; in N.T., mid., aor. 1, (pass. form) προσεκληρώθην, *to adjoin one's self to, associate with, follow as a disciple*, Ac. 17. 4.

πρόσκλησιν, acc. sing.—A. D. Ln. . } πρόσκλησις
πρόσκλισιν, R. Gr. Sch. Tdf. (1 Ti. 5. 21) }

πρόσκλησις], εως, ἡ, (§ 5. tab. E. c) (πρός & καλέω) *advocacy*, or, perhaps, *partiality*, v.r. 1 Ti. 5. 21.

προσκλίνω], fut. ινῶ, (πρός & κλίνω) pr. *to make to lean upon or against* a thing; met., mid., aor. 1, (pass. form) προσεκλίθην, (ῐ) *to join one's self to, follow as an adherent*, v.r. Ac. 5. 36.

πρόσκλῐσις, εως, ἡ, (§ 5. tab. E. c) pr. *a leaning upon or towards* a thing; met. *a leaning towards* any one, *inclination* of mind *towards, partiality*, 1 Ti. 5. 21. L.G.

πρόσκλισιν,[c] acc. sing. . . . . πρόσκλισις

πρόσκλισις], εως, ἡ . . . . προσκλίνω

προσκολλάω, ῶ], fut. ήσω, (§ 18. tab. R) (πρός & κολλάω) pr. *to glue to*; in N.T., mid., aor. 1, (pass. form) προσεκολλήθη, fut. προσκολληθήσομαι, *to join one's self to* any one, *follow as an adherent*, Ac. 5. 36; *to cleave closely to*, Mat. 19. 5; Mar. 10. 7; Ep. 5. 31.

προσκολληθήσεται, 3 pers. s. fut. ind. pass. προσκολλάω

πρόσκομμα], ατος, τό . . . . προσκόπτω

προσκόμματος, gen. sing. . . . πρόσκομμα

προσκοπή], ῆ, ἡ . . . . . προσκόπτω

προσκοπήν,[d] acc. sing. . . . προσκοπή

προσκόπτει, 3 pers. sing. pres. ind. . . προσκόπτω

προσκόπτουσι, 3 pers. pl. pres. ind. . id.

προσκόπτω], fut. ψω, (§ 23. rem. 1. a) (πρός & κόπτω) *to dash against, to beat upon*, Mat. 7. 27; *to strike* the foot *against*, Mat. 4. 6; Lu. 4. 11; *to stumble*, Jno. 11. 9, 10, met. *to stumble at, to take offence at*, Ro. 9. 32; 14. 21; 1 Pe. 2. 8.

πρόσκομμα, ατος, τό, (§ 4. tab. D. c) *a stumbling*, Ro. 9. 32, 33; 1 Pe. 2. 8, met. *a stumbling-block, an occasion of sinning, means of inducing to sin*, Ro. 14. 13; 1 Co. 8. 9; met. *a* moral *stumbling, a shock* to the moral or religious sense, a moral *embarrassment*, Ro. 14. 20. L.G.

προσκοπή, ῆς, ἡ, (§ 2. tab. B. a) pr. *a stumbling; offence*; in N.T. *an offence, shock, ground of exception*, 2 Co. 6. 3.

προσκόψῃς, 2 pers. sing. aor. 1, subj. . . προσκόπτω

προσκυλίσας, nom. sing. masc. part. aor. 1 προσκυλίω

προσκυλίω, or προσκυλίνδω], fut. ίσω, (§ 13. tab. M) (πρός & κυλίω) *to roll to or against*, Mat. 27. 60; Mar. 15. 46. (ῑ).

προσκυνεῖ, 3 pers. sing. pres. ind. . . προσκυνέω

προσκυνεῖν, pres. infin. . . . . . id.

προσκυνεῖτε, 2 pers. pl. pres. ind. . . id.

προσκυνέω, ῶ], fut. ήσομαι & ήσω, aor. 1, προσεκύνησα, (§ 16. tab. P) (πρός & κυνέω,

[a] Ep. 6. 18. [b] Mar. 4. 38. [c] 1 Ti. 5. 21. [d] 2 Co. 6. 3.

to kiss) *to do reverence or homage by kissing the hand*; in N.T. *to do reverence or homage by prostration*, Mat. 2. 2, 8, 11; 20. 20; Lu. 4. 7; 24. 52; *to pay* divine *homage, worship, adore*, Mat. 4. 10; Jno. 4. 20, 21; He. 1. 6, et al.; *to bow one's self in adoration*, He. 11. 21.

προσκυνητής, οῦ, ὁ, (§ 2. tab. B. c) *a worshipper*, Jno. 4. 23. N.T.

προσκυνῆσαι, aor. 1, infin. . . . προσκυνέω
προσκυνήσαντες, nom. pl. masc. part. aor. 1 id.
προσκυνήσατε, 2 pers. pl. aor. 1, imper. . id.
προσκυνησάτωσαν, 3 pers. pl. aor. 1, imper. . id.
προσκυνήσει, 3 pers. sing. fut. ind. . . id.
προσκυνήσεις, 2 pers. sing. fut. ind. . . id.
προσκυνήσετε, 2 pers. pl. fut. ind. . . id.
προσκυνήσῃς, 2 pers. sing. aor. 1, subj. . id.
προσκύνησον, 2 pers. sing. aor. 1, imper. . id.
προσκυνήσουσι, 3 pers. pl. fut. ind. . . id.
προσκυνήσω, 1 pers. sing. fut. ind. . . id.
προσκυνήσων, nom. sing. masc. part. fut. . id.
προσκυνήσωσι, 3 pers. pl. aor. 1, subj. . id.
προσκυνηταί,[a] nom. pl. . . . προσκυνητής
προσκυνητής], οῦ, ὁ . . . . προσκυνέω
προσκυνοῦμεν, 1 pers. pl. pres. ind. . . id.
προσκυνοῦντας, acc. pl. masc. part. pres. . id.
προσκυνοῦντες, nom. pl. masc. part. pres. . id.
προσκυνοῦσα, nom. sing. fem. part. pres. . id.
προσκυνοῦσι, 3 pers. pl. pres. ind.—Rec. } id.
προσκυνήσουσι, Gr. Sch. Tdf. (Re. 4. 10) }
προσλάβεῖν, aor. 2, infin. (§ 36. rem. 2) προσλαμβάνω
προσλαβόμενοι, nom. pl. m. part. aor. 2, mid. id.
προσλαβόμενος, nom. s. masc. part. aor. 2, mid. id.
προσλάβοῦ, 2 pers. sing. aor. 2, imper. mid. . id.

προσλάλέω, ῶ], fut. ήσω, (§ 16. tab. P) (πρός & λαλέω) *to speak to, converse with*, Ac. 13. 43; 28. 20. L.G.

προσλαλῆσαι, aor. 1, infin. . . . προσλαλέω
προσλαλοῦντες, nom. pl. masc. part. pres. . id.
προσλαμβάνεσθε, 2 p. pl. pres. imper. mid. προσλαμβάνω

προσλαμβάνω], (§ 36. rem. 2) *to take besides*; mid. προσλαμβάνομαι, fut. λήψομαι, aor. 2, προσελάβόμην, *to take to one's self, assume, take as a companion or associate*, Ac. 17. 5; 18. 26; *to take*, as food, Ac. 27. 33, 34, 36; *to receive kindly or hospitably, admit to one's society and friendship, treat with kindness*, Ac. 28. 2; Ro. 14. 1, 3; 15. 7; Phile. 12. 17; *to take or draw to one's self* as a preliminary to an address of admonition, Mat. 16. 22; Mar. 8. 32.

πρόσληψις, εως, ἡ, (§ 5. tab. E. c) *an assuming*; *a receiving, reception*, Ro. 11. 15.

πρόσληψις],[b] εως, ἡ . . . . προσλαμβάνω
προσμεῖναι, aor. 1, infin. (§ 27. rem. 1. d) . προσμένω
προσμείνας, nom. sing. masc. part. aor. 1 . id.
προσμένει, 3 pers. sing. pres. ind. . . id.
προσμένειν, pres. infin. . . . id.
προσμένουσι, 3 pers. pl. pres. ind. . . id.

προσμένω], fut. μενῶ, (§ 27. rem. 1. a) (πρός & μένω) *to continue, remain, stay* in a place, 1 Ti. 1. 3; *to remain or continue with* any one, Mat. 15. 32; Mar. 8. 2; Ac. 18. 18; *to adhere to*, Ac. 11. 23; met. *to remain constant in, persevere in*, Ac. 13. 43; 1 Ti. 5. 5.

προσορμίζω], fut. ίσω, (§ 26. rem. 1) (πρός & ὁρμίζω, from ὅρμος, *a station for ships*) *to bring a ship to its station or to land*; mid. *to come to the land*, Mar. 6. 53.

προσοφείλεις,[c] 2 pers. sing. pres. ind. . προσοφείλω

προσοφείλω], fut. ήσω, (§ 35. rem. 5) (πρός & ὀφείλω) *to owe besides or in addition*, Phile. 19.

προσοχθίζω], fut. ίσω, (§ 26. rem. 1) (πρός & ὀχθίζω, *to be vexed, offended*) *to be vexed or angry at*, He. 3. 10. LXX.

πρόσπεινος],[d] ου, ὁ, ἡ, (§ 7. rem. 2) (πρός & πεῖνα) *very hungry*. N.T.

προσπεσοῦσα, nom. sing. fem. part. aor. 2 . προσπίπτω
προσπήξαντες,[e] nom. pl. masc. part. aor. 1 προσπήγνυμι

προσπήγνυμι], fut. πήξω, (§ 36. rem. 5) (πρός & πήγνυμι) *to fix to, affix to*.

προσπίπτω], fut. πεσοῦμαι, aor. 2, προσέπεσον, (§ 37. rem. 1) (πρός & πίπτω) *to fall or impinge upon or against* a thing; *to fall down to* any one, Mar. 3. 11; 7. 25, et al.; *to rush violently upon, beat against*, Mat. 7. 25.

προσποιέω, ῶ], fut. ήσω, (§ 16. tab. P) πρός & ποιέω) *to add or attach*; mid. *to attach to one's self*; *to claim or arrogate to one's self*; *to assume the appearance of, make a show of, pretend*, Lu. 24. 28.

προσπορεύομαι], fut. εύσομαι, (§ 14. tab. N)

[a] Jno. 4. 23. [b] Ro. 11. 15. [c] Phile. 19. [d] Ac. 10. 10. [e] Ac. 2. 23.

(πρός & πορεύομαι) *to go or come to* any one. L.G.

προσπορεύονται,[a] 3 pers. pl. pres. ind. προσπορεύομαι

προσρήγνυμι], fut. ρήξω, (§ 36. rem. 5) (πρός & ῥήγνυμι) *to break or burst upon, dash against,* Lu. 6. 48, 49. N.T.

προστάσσω, or ττω], fut. ξω, (§ 26. rem. 3) (πρός & τάσσω) pr. *to place or station at or against; to enjoin, command, direct,* Mat. 1. 24; 8. 4; 21. 6; Mar. 1. 44, et al.; *to assign, constitute, appoint,* Ac. 17. 26.

προστάτις], ιδος, ἡ, (§ 4. rem. 2. c) . προΐστημι

προστεθῆναι, aor. 1, infin. pass. (§ 28. rem. 10) προστίθημι

προστεθήσεται, 3 pers. sing. fut. ind. pass. . id.

προστεταγμένα, acc. pl. neut. part. perf. pass. προστάσσω

προστεταγμένους, acc. pl. masc. part. perf. pass. id.

προστῆναι, aor. 2, infin. (§ 29. tab. X) . προΐστημι

προστίθημι], fut. θήσω, aor. 1, pass. προσετέθην, (§ 28. tab. V, and rem. 10) (πρός & τίθημι) *to put to or near; to lay with or by the side of,* Ac. 13. 36; *to add, superadd, adjoin,* Mat. 6. 27, 33; Lu. 3. 20; Ac. 2. 41, et al.; from the Heb., προστίθεμαι, before an infinitive, and the part. προσθείς, before a finite verb, denote *continuation,* or *repetition,* Lu. 19. 11; 20. 11, 12; Ac. 12. 3.

προστρέχοντες, nom. pl. masc. part. pres. . προστρέχω

προστρέχω], aor. 2, προσέδρᾰμον, (§ 36. rem. 1) (πρός & τρέχω) *to run to,* or *up,* Mar. 9. 15; 10. 17; Ac. 8. 30.

προσφάγιον],[b] ου, τό, (§ 3. tab. C. c) (πρός & φαγεῖν) *what is eaten besides;* hence, genr. *victuals, food.* N.T.

πρόσφατον,[c] acc. sing. fem. . . . πρόσφατος

πρόσφᾰτος], ου, ὁ, ἡ, (§ 7. rem. 2) (πρός & πέφαμαι, from φάω, *to slay*) pr. *recently killed;* hence, genr. *recent, new, newly or lately made.*

προσφάτως, adv. *newly, recently, lately,* Ac. 18. 2.

προσφάτως],[d] adv. . . . . . πρόσφατος

πρόσφερε, 2 pers. sing. pres. imper. act. προσφέρω

προσφέρει, 3 pers. sing. pres. ind. act. . . id.

προσφέρειν, pres. infin. act. . id.

προσφέρεται, 3 pers. sing. pres. ind. pass. . id.

προσφέρῃ, 3 pers. sing. pres. subj. act. id.

προσφέρῃς, 2 pers. sing. pres. subj. act. . id.

προσφερόμεναι, nom. pl. fem. part. pres. pass. προσφέρω

προσφέρονται, 3 pers. pl. pres. ind. pass. . id.

προσφέροντες, nom. pl. masc. part. pres. act. . id.

προσφερόντων, gen. pl. masc. part. pres. act. id.

προσφέρουσι, dat. pl. masc. part. pres. act. . id.

προσφέρουσι, 3 pers. pl. pres. ind. act. . id.

προσφέρω], fut. προσοίσω, aor. 1, προσήνεγκα, aor. 2, προσήνεγκον, (§ 36. rem. 1) (πρός & φέρω) *to bear or bring to,* Mat. 4. 24; 25. 20; *to bring to or before* magistrates, Lu. 12. 11; 23. 14; *to bring near to, apply to,* Jno. 19. 29; *to offer, tender, proffer,* as money, Ac. 8. 18; *to offer, present,* as gifts, oblations, etc., Mat. 2. 11; 5. 23; He. 5. 7; *to offer* in sacrifice, Mar. 1. 44; Lu. 5. 14; *to offer up* any one as a sacrifice to God, He. 9. 25, 28; 11. 17, et al.; mid. *to bear one's self towards, behave or conduct one's self towards, to deal with, treat* any one, He. 12. 7.

προσφορά, ᾶς, ἡ, (§ 2. tab. B. b) pr. *a bringing to;* in N.T. *an offering, an act of offering up or sacrificing,* He. 10. 10; trop. Ro. 15. 16; *an offering, oblation, a thing offered,* Ep. 5. 2; He. 10. 5, 8; *a sacrifice, victim offered,* Ac. 21. 26; 24. 17.

προσφέρων, nom. sing. masc. part. pres. act. προσφέρω

προσφέρωσι, 3 pers. pl. pres. subj. act. . id.

προσφιλῆ,[e] nom. pl. neut. . . προσφιλής

προσφῐλής], έος, οῦς, ὁ, ἡ, (§ 7. tab. G. b) (πρός & φίλος) *friendly, amicable, grateful, acceptable.*

προσφορά], ᾶς, ἡ . . . . προσφέρω

προσφορᾷ, dat. sing. . . . . προσφορά

προσφοράν, acc. sing. . . . . id.

προσφορᾶς, gen. sing. . . . . id.

προσφοράς, acc. pl. . . . . id.

προσφωνέω, ῶ], fut. ήσω, (§ 16. tab. P) (πρός & φωνέω) *to speak to, address,* Mat. 11. 16, Lu. 7. 32; 13. 12, et al.; *to address, harangue,* Ac. 22. 2; *to call* to one's self, Lu. 6. 13.

προσφωνοῦντα, nom. pl. neut. part. pres. } προσφωνέω
ἃ προσφωνοῦντα τοῖς ἑτέροις λέγουσιν,—B. C. D. Ln. Tdf. .
καὶ προσφωνοῦσι τοῖς ἑταίροις αὐτῶν, etc., Rec. Gr. Sch. (Mat. 11. 16) . . . .

[a] Mar. 10. 35. [b] Jno. 21. 5. [c] He. 10. 20. [d] Ac. 18. 2. [e] Phi. 4. 8.

προσφωνοῦσι, dat. pl. masc. part. pres. προσφωνέω

πρόσχυσιν,[a] acc. sing. . . . . πρόσχυσις

πρόσχῠσις], εως, ἡ, (§ 5. tab. E. c) (προσχέω, *to pour out upon, besprinkle,* from πρός & χέω) *an effusion, sprinkling.* L.G.

προσψαύετε,[b] 2 pers. pl. pres. ind. . . προσψαύω

προσψαύω], fut. αύσω, (§ 13. tab. M) (πρός & ψαύω, *to touch*) *to touch upon, touch lightly.*

πρόσωπα, nom. and acc. pl. . . . προσωπον

προσωποληπτεῖτε,[c] 2 pers. pl. pres. ind. προσωποληπτέω

προσωποληπτέω, ῶ], fut. ήσω . . προσωπολήπτης

προσωπολήπτης], ου, ὁ, (§ 2. tab. B. c) (πρόσωπον & λαμβάνω) *a respecter of persons.* N.T.

προσωποληπτέω, ῶ, fut. ήσω, (§ 16. tab. P) *to accept or respect the person* of any one, *to pay regard to external appearance, condition, circumstances,* etc., *to show partiality to,* Ja. 2. 9. N.T.

προσωποληψία, ας, ἡ, (§ 2. tab. B. b, and rem. 2) *respect of persons, partiality,* Ro. 2. 11, et al. N.T.

προσωποληψία], ας, ἡ . . προσωπολήπτης

προσωποληψίαις, dat. pl. . . προσωποληψία

πρόσωπον], ου, τό, (§ 3. tab. C. c) (πρός & ὤψ) *the face, countenance, visage,* Mat. 6. 16, 17; 17. 2, 6; according to late usage, *a person, individual,* 2 Co. 1. 11; hence, *personal presence,* 1 Thes. 2. 17; from the Heb., πρόσωπον πρὸς πρόσωπον, *face to face, clearly, perfectly,* 1 Co. 13. 12; *face, surface, external form, figure, appearance,* Mat. 16. 3; Lu. 12. 56; *external circumstances, or condition* of any one, Mat. 22. 16; Mar. 12. 14; πρόσωπον λαμβάνειν, *to have respect to the external circumstances* of any one, Lu. 20. 21; Gal. 2. 6; ἐν προσώπῳ, *in presence of,* 2 Co. 2. 10; ἀπὸ προσώπου, *from the presence of, from,* Ac. 3. 19; also, *from before,* Ac. 7. 45; εἰς πρόσωπον, & κατὰ πρόσωπον, *in the presence of, before,* Ac. 3. 13; 2 Co. 8. 24; also, *openly,* Gal. 2. 11; κατὰ πρόσωπον ἔχειν, *to have before one's face, to have* any one *present,* Ac. 25. 16; ἀπὸ προσώπου, *from,* Re. 12. 14; πρὸ προσώπου, *before,* Ac. 13. 24.

προσώπου, gen. sing. . . . . . πρόσωπον

προσώπῳ, dat. sing. . . . . id.

προσώπων, gen. pl. . . . . id.

προσωρμίσθησαν,[d] 3 pers. pl. aor. 1, ind. pass. (§ 26. rem. 1) . . . προσορμίζω

προσώχθισα, 1 pers. sing. aor. 1, ind. . προσοχθίζω

προσώχθισε, 3 pers. sing. aor. 1, ind. . . id.

προτάσσω, or ττω], fut. ξω, (§ 26. rem. 3) (πρό & τάσσω) *to place or arrange in front; to assign beforehand, foreordain,* Ac. 17. 26.

προτείνω], fut. ενῶ, (§ 27. rem. 1. c) (πρό & τείνω) *to extend before; to stretch out,* Ac. 22. 25.

προτέραν, acc. sing. fem. . . . πρότερος

πρότερον, neut. sing. adverbially . . . id.

πρότερος], α, ον, (§ 8. rem. 6) . . πρό

προτεταγμένους,[e] acc. pl. masc. part. perf. pass.—Rec. . . . . } προτάσσω
προστεταγμένους, Gr. Sch. Tdf. (Ac. 17. 26) . . . . }

προτίθημι], fut. προθήσω, (§ 28. tab. V) (πρό & τίθημι) *to place before; to set forth, propose publicly,* Ro. 3. 25; mid. προτίθεμαι, *to purpose, determine, design beforehand,* Ro. 1. 13; Ep. 1. 9.

πρόθεσις, εως, ἡ, (§ 5. tab. E. c) *a setting forth or before;* οἱ ἄρτοι τῆς προθέσεως, & ἡ πρόθεσις τῶν ἄρτων, *the shewbread,* the twelve loaves of bread, corresponding to the twelve tribes, which were *set out* in two rows upon the golden table in the sanctuary, Mat. 12. 4; Mar. 2. 26; Lu. 6. 4; He. 9. 2; *predetermination, purpose,* Ac. 11. 23; 27. 13; Ro. 8. 28; 2 Ti. 3. 10, et al.

προτρέπω], fut. ψω, (§ 23. rem. 1. a) (πρό & τρέπω) *to turn forwards; to impel; to excite, urge, exhort,* Ac. 18. 27.

προτρεψάμενοι,[f] nom. pl. masc. part. aor. 1, masc. προτρέπω

προτρέχω], aor. 2, προῦδρᾰμον, (§ 36. rem. 1) (πρό & τρέχω) *to run before, or in advance,* Lu. 19. 4; Jno. 20. 4.

πρόδρομος, ου, ὁ, ἡ, (δραμεῖν) *a precursor, forerunner, one who advances to explore and prepare the way,* He. 6. 20.

προϋπάρχω], fut. ξω, (§ 23. rem. 1. b) (πρό & ὑπάρχω) imperf. προϋπῆρχον, *to be before, or formerly,* Lu. 23. 12; Ac. 8. 9.

προϋπῆρχε, 3 pers. sing. imperf. . προυπάρχω

[a] He. 11. 28. [b] Lu. 11. 46. [c] Ja. 2. 9. [d] Mar. 6. 53. [e] Ac. 17. 26. [f] Ac. 18. 27

προϋπῆρχον, 3 pers. pl. imperf. . . . προυπάρχω
προφάσει, dat. sing. . . . . . πρόφασις
πρόφασιν, acc. sing. . . . . . id.
πρόφᾰσις], εως, ἡ, (§ 5. tab. E. c) (πρό & φαίνω) pr. *that which appears in front, that which is put forward to hide the true state of things; a fair show or pretext*, Ac. 27. 30; *a specious cloak*, Mat. 23. 13; 1 Thes. 2. 5; *an excuse*, Jno. 15. 22.
προφέρει, 3 pers. sing. pres. ind. . . . προφέρω
προφέρω], fut. προοίσω, (§ 36. rem. 1) (πρό & φέρω) *to bring before, present; to bring forth or out, produce*, Lu. 6. 45, bis.
προφῆται, nom. pl. . . . . . προφήτης
ποφήταις, dat. pl. . . . . . id.
προφήτας, acc. pl. . . . . . id.
προφητεία], ας, ἡ . . . . . id.
προφητείᾳ, dat. sing. . . . . . προφητεία
προφητεῖαι, nom. pl. . . . . . id.
προφητείαν, acc. sing. . . . . . id.
προφητείας, gen. sing. and acc. pl. . . . id.
προφητεύειν, pres. infin. . . . . προφητεύω
προφητεύητε, 2 pers. pl. pres. subj. . . . id.
προφητεύομεν, 1 pers. pl. pres. ind. . . id.
προφητεύουσα, nom. sing. fem. part. pres. . id.
προφητεύουσαι, nom. pl. fem. part. pres. . id.
προφητεῦσαι, aor. 1, infin. . . . id.
προφητεύσαντες, nom. pl. masc. part. aor. 1 id.
προφήτευσον, 2 pers. sing. aor. 1, imper. . id.
προφητεύσουσι, 3 pers. pl. fut. ind. . . id.
προφητεύω], fut. εύσω . . . . προφήτης
προφητεύων, nom. sing. masc. part. pres. προφητεύω
προφητεύωσι, 3 pers. pl. pres. subj. . . id.
προφήτην, acc. sing. . . . . . προφήτης
προφήτης], ου, ὁ, (§ 2. tab. B. c) (πρό & φημί) pr. *a spokesman for* another; spc. *a spokesman or interpreter* for a deity; *a prophet, seer*, Tit. 1. 12; in N.T. *a prophet, a divinely-commissioned and inspired person*, Mat. 14. 5; Lu. 7. 16, 39; Jno. 9. 17. et al.; *a prophet* in the Christian church, *a person gifted for the exposition of divine truth*, 1 Co. 12. 28, 29, et al.; *a prophet, a foreteller of the future*, Mat. 1. 22, et al. freq.; οἱ προφῆται, *the prophetic scriptures of the Old Testament*, Lu. 16. 29, et al.

προφητεύω, fut. εύσω, aor. 1, προεφήτευσα, (§ 13. tab. M) *to exercise the function of a* προφήτης; *to prophesy, to foretel the future*, Mat. 11. 13; *to divine*, Mat. 26. 68; Mar. 14. 65; Lu. 22. 64; *to prophesy, to set forth matter of divine teaching by special faculty*, 1 Co. 13. 9; 14. 1, et al.

προφητεία, ας, ἡ, (§ 2. tab. B. b, and rem. 2) *prophecy, a prediction of future events*, Mat. 13. 14; 2 Pe. 1. 20, 21; *prophecy, a gifted faculty of setting forth and enforcing revealed truth*, 1 Co. 12. 10; 13. 2, et al.; *prophecy, matter of divine teaching set forth by special gift*, 1 Ti. 1. 18.

προφητῐκός, ή, όν, (§ 7. tab. F. a) *prophetic, uttered by prophets*, Ro. 16. 26; 2 Pe. 1. 19. L.G.

προφῆτις, ῐδος, ἡ, (§ 4. rem. 2. c) *a prophetess, a divinely-gifted female teacher*, Lu. 2. 36; Re. 2. 20.

προφητικόν, acc. sing. masc. . . . προφητικός
προφητικός], ή, όν . . . . . προφήτης
προφητικῶν, gen. pl. . . . . . προφητικός
προφῆτιν, acc. sing. . . . . . προφῆτις
προφῆτις], ιδος, ἡ . . . . . προφήτης
προφήτου, gen. sing. . . . . . id.
προφητῶν, gen. pl. . . . . . id.
προφθάνω], fut. άσω, & ήσομαι, aor. 1, προέφθᾰσα, (§ 37. rem. 1) (πρό & φθάνω) *to outstrip, anticipate; to anticipate* any one in doing or saying a thing, *be beforehand with*, Mat. 17. 25.
προχειρίζομαι], fut. ίσομαι, (§ 26. rem. 1) (πρό & χείρ) *to take into the hand, to make ready for use or action; to constitute, destine*, Ac. 22. 14; 26. 16.
προχειρίσασθαι, aor. 1, infin. . . . προχειρίζομαι
προχειροτονέω, ῶ], fut. ήσω, (§ 16. tab. P) (πρό & χειροτονέω) pr. *to elect before; to foreappoint*, Ac. 10. 41.
Πρόχορον,[a] acc. . . . . . Πρόχορος
Πρόχορος], ου, ὁ, (§ 3. tab. C. a) *Prochorus*, pr. name.
προώρισε, 3 pers. sing. aor. 1, ind. . . . προορίζω
προωρώμην, 1 pers. sing. imperf. mid. . προοράω
πρύμνα], ης, ἡ, (§ 2. rem. 3) (πρυμνός, *last, hindmost*) *the hinder part of a vessel, stern*, Mar. 4. 38, et al.

[a] Ac. 6. 5.

πρύμνῃ, dat. sing. . . . . . πρύμνα

πρύμνης, gen. sing. . . . . . id.

πρωΐ], adv. *in the morning, early*, Mat. 16. 3; 20. 1; Mar. 15. 1; Ac. 28. 23, et al.; *the morning watch*, which ushers in the dawn, Mar. 13. 35.

πρωΐα, ας, ἡ, (pr. fem. of πρώϊος, α, ον, *in the morning, early*) sc. ὥρα, *morning, the morning hour*, Mat. 21. 18; 27. 1; Jno. 18. 28; 21. 4.

πρώϊμος, η, ον, (§ 7. tab. F. a) *early*, Ja. 5. 7.

πρωϊνός, ή, όν, (a later form of πρώϊος) *belonging to the morning, morning*, Re. 2. 28; 22. 16.

πρωΐα], ας, ἡ· . . . . . πρωΐ

πρωΐας, gen. sing. . . . . . πρωΐα

πρώϊμον,[a] acc. sing. masc. . . . . πρώϊμος

πρώϊμος], η, ον . . . . . . πρωΐ

πρωϊνόν, acc. sing. masc. . . . . πρωϊνός

πρωϊνός], ή, όν . . . . . . πρωΐ

πρῷρα], ας, ἡ, (§ 2. tab. B. b) . . πρό

πρῴρας, gen. sing. . . . . . πρῷρα

πρῶτα, nom. and acc. pl. neut. . . . πρῶτος

πρωτεύω], fut. εύσω (§ 13. tab. M) . . πρό

πρωτεύων,[b] nom. sing. masc. part. pres. . πρωτεύω

πρώτη, nom. sing. fem. . . . . . πρῶτος

πρώτῃ, dat. sing. fem. . . . . . id.

πρώτην, acc. sing. fem. . . . . . id.

πρώτης, gen. sing. fem. . . . . . id.

πρῶτοι, nom. pl. masc. . . . . . id.

πρώτοις, dat. pl. masc. and neut. . . . id.

πρωτοκαθεδρία], ας, ἡ, (§ 2. tab. B. b, and rem. 2) (πρῶτος & καθέδρα) *the first or uppermost seat, the most honourable seat*, Mat. 23. 6; Mar. 12. 39; Lu. 11. 43; 20. 46. N.T.

πρωτοκαθεδρίαν, acc. sing. . . . πρωτοκαθεδρία

πρωτοκαθεδρίας, acc. pl. . . . . id.

πρωτοκλισία], ας, ἡ, (§ 2. tab. B. b, and rem. 2) (πρῶτος & κλισία) *the first place of reclining* at table, *the most honourable place at table*, Mat. 23. 6; Mar. 12. 39; Lu. 14. 7, 8; 20. 46. N.T.

πρωτοκλισίαν, acc. sing. . . . πρωτοκλισία

πρωτοκλισίας, acc. pl. . . . . id.

πρῶτον, acc. sing. masc. and nom. and acc. neut. πρῶτος

πρῶτον], adv. . . . . πρό

πρῶτος], η, ον, (§ 8. rem. 6) . . . . id.

πρωτοστάτην,[c] acc. sing. . . . . πρωτοστάτης

πρωτοστάτης], ου, ὁ, (§ 2. tab. B. c) (πρῶτος & ἵστημι) pr. *one stationed in the first rank* of an army; *a leader; a chief, ringleader* Ac. 24. 5. (ᾰ).

πρωτότοκα, acc. pl. neut. . . . . πρωτότοκος

πρωτοτόκια],[d] ων, τά . . . . . id.

πρωτότοκον, acc. sing. masc. . . . . id.

πρωτότοκος], ου, ὁ, ἡ, τό, -ον, (§ 7. rem. 2) (πρῶτος & τίκτω) *first-born*, Mat. 1. 25; Lu. 2. 7; He. 11. 28; in N.T. *prior in generation*, Col. 1. 15; *a first-born* head of a spiritual family, Ro. 8. 29; He. 1. 6; *first-born*, as possessed of the peculiar privilege of spiritual generation, He. 12. 23.

πρωτοτόκια, ων, τα, (§ 3. tab. C. c) *the rights of primogeniture, birthright*, He. 12. 16. LXX.

πρωτοτόκων, gen. pl. . . . . . πρωτότοκος

πρώτου, gen. sing. masc. and neut. . . πρῶτος

πρώτους, acc. pl. masc. . . . . id.

πρώτῳ, dat. sing. masc. . . . . id.

πρώτων, gen. pl. . . . . . . id.

πταίει, 3 pers. sing. pres. ind. . . . πταίω

πταίομεν, 1 pers. pl. pres. ind. . . . id.

πταίσει, 3 pers. sing. fut. ind. . . . id.

πταίσῃ, 3 pers. sing. aor. 1, subj.—Al. Ln. Tdf. } id.
πταίσει, Rec. Gr. Sch. (Ja. 2. 10) . }

πταίσητε, 2 pers. pl. aor. 1, subj. . . . id.

πταίω], fut. αίσω, aor. 1, ἔπταισα, (§ 13. tab. M) *to cause to stumble*; intrans. *to stumble, stagger, fall; to make a false step*; met. *to err, offend, transgress*, Ro. 11. 11; Ja. 2. 10; 3. 2, bis; met. *to fail* of an object, 2 Pe. 1. 10.

πτέρνα], ης, ἡ, (§ 2. rem. 3) *the heel*.

πτέρναν,[e] acc. sing. . . . . . πτέρνα

πτέρυγας, acc. pl. . . . . . . πτέρυξ

πτέρυγες, nom. pl. . . . . . id.

πτερύγιον], ου, τό . . . . . . id.

πτερύγων, gen. pl. . . . . . id.

πτέρυξ], υγος, ἡ, (§ 4. rem. 2. b) (πτέρον, id.) *a wing, pinion*, Mat. 23. 37; Lu. 13. 34, et al.

πτερύγιον, ου, τό, (§ 3. tab. C. c) a

---

[a] Ja. 5. 7. [b] Col. 1. 18. [c] Ac. 24. 5. [d] He. 12. 16. [e] Jno. 13. 18.

little wing; the extremity, the extreme point of a thing; a pinnacle, or apex of a building, Mat. 4. 5; Lu. 4. 9.

πτηνόν], οῦ, τό . . . . . . πέτομαι

πτηνῶν,[a] gen. pl. . . . . πτηνόν

πτοέω, ῶ], fut. ήσω, (§ 16. tab. P) aor. 1, pass. ἐπτοήθην, to terrify, affright; pass. to be terrified, be in consternation, Lu. 21. 9; 24. 37.

πτόησις, εως, ἡ, (§ 5. tab. E. c) consternation, dismay, 1 Pe. 3. 6.

πτοηθέντες, nom. pl. masc. part. aor. 1, pass. (§ 17. tab. Q) . . . . πτοέω

πτοηθῆτε, 2 pers. pl. aor. 1, subj. pass. . id.

πτόησιν,[b] acc. sing. . . . . . πτόησις

πτόησις], εως, ἡ . . . . . πτοέω

Πτολεμαΐδα,[c] acc. . . . . Πτολεμαΐς

Πτολεμαΐς], ΐδος, ἡ, (§ 4. rem. 2. c) Ptolemais, a city on the sea-coast of Galilee: the modern Acre.

πτύξας,[d] nom. sing. masc. part. aor. 1 . πτύσσω

πτύον], ου, τό, (§ 3. tab. C. c) . πτύω

πτυρόμενοι,[e] nom. pl. masc. part. pres. pass. πτύρω

πτύρω], to scare, terrify; pass. to be terrified, be in consternation.

πτύσας, nom. sing. masc. part. aor. 1 . πτύω

πτύσμα], ατος, τό . . . . . id.

πτύσματος,[f] gen. sing. . . . . πτύσμα

πτύσσω], fut. ξω, aor. 1, ἔπτυξα, (§ 26. rem. 3) to fold; to roll up a scroll, Lu. 4. 20.

πτύω], fut. ύσω, aor. 1, ἔπτυσα, (§ 13. tab. M) to spit, spit out, Mar. 7. 33; 8. 23; Jno. 9. 6.

πτύον, ου, τό, (§ 3. tab. C. c) a fan, winnowing-shovel, Mat. 3. 12; Lu. 3. 17.

πτύσμα, ατος, τό, (§ 4. tab. D. c) spittle, saliva, Jno. 9. 6.

πτῶμα], ατος, τό . . . . . πίπτω

πτώματα, acc. pl. . . . . πτῶμα

πτῶσιν, acc. sing. . . . . . πτῶσις

πτῶσις], εως, ἡ, (§ 5. tab. E. c) . . πίπτω

πτωχά, acc. pl. neut. . . . . πτωχός

πτωχεία], ας, ἡ . . . . . id.

πτωχείᾳ, dat. sing. . . . . . πτωχεία

πτωχείαν, acc. sing. . . . . id.

πτωχεύω], fut. εύσω, (§ 13. tab. M) . . πτωχός

πτωχῇ, nom. sing. fem. . . . . id.

πτωχοί, nom. pl. masc. . . . . id.

πτωχοῖς, dat. pl. masc. . . . . id.

πτωχόν, acc. sing. masc. . . . id.

πτωχός], ή, όν, reduced to beggary, mendicant; poor, indigent, Mat. 19. 21; 26. 9, 11, et al.; met. spiritually poor, Re. 3. 17; by impl. a person of low condition, Mat. 11. 5; Lu. 4. 18; 7. 22; met. beggarly, sorry, Gal. 4. 9; met. lowly, Mat. 5. 3; Lu. 6. 20.

πτωχεία, ας, ἡ, (§ 2. tab. B. b, and rem. 2) begging; beggary; poverty, 2 Co. 8. 2, 9; Re. 2. 9.

πτωχεύω, fut. εύσω, to be a beggar; to be or become poor, be in poverty, 2 Co. 8. 9.

πτωχούς, acc. pl. masc. . . . πτωχός

πτωχῷ, dat. sing. masc. . . . . id.

πτωχῶν, gen. pl. . . . . id.

πυγμή], ῆς, ἡ, (§ 2. tab. B. a) (πύξ) the fist; πυγμῇ, together with the fore-arm, or, with care, carefully.

πυγμῇ,[g] dat. sing. . . . . . πυγμή

πυθέσθαι, aor. 2, infin. mid. (§ 36. rem. 2) πυνθάνομαι

πυθόμενος, nom. sing. masc. part. aor. 2, mid. id.

Πύθων], ωνος, ὁ, (§ 4. rem. 2. e) Python, the name of the mythological serpent slain by Apollo, thence named the Pythian; later, equivalent to ἐγγαστρίμαντις, a soothsaying ventriloquist; πνεῦμα πύθωνος, i.q. δαιμόνιον μαντικόν, a soothsaying demon, Ac. 16. 16

πύθωνα, acc. sing.—Al. Ln. Tdf. . . } πύθων
πύθωνος, Rec. Gr. Sch. (Ac. 16. 16) }

πύθωνος,[h] gen. sing. . . . . id.

πυκνά, pl. neut. adverbially . . . πυκνός

πυκνάς, acc. pl. fem. . . . . id.

πυκνός], ή, όν, (§ 7. tab. F. a) dense, thick; frequent, 1 Ti. 5. 23; πυκνά, as an adverb, frequently, often, Lu. 5. 33; so the compar. πυκνότερον, very frequently, Ac. 24. 26.

πυκνότερον, neut. compar. adverbially . πυκνός

πυκτεύω],[i] fut. εύσω, (§ 13. tab. M) (πύκτης, a boxer, from πύξ) to box, fight as a pugilist.

[a] 1 Co. 15. 39. [b] 1 Pe. 3. 6. [c] Ac. 21. 7. [d] Lu. 4. 20. [e] Phi. 1. 28. [f] Jno. 9. 6. [g] Mar. 7. 3. [h] Ac. 16. 16. [i] 1 Co. 9. 26.

πύλη], ης, ἡ, (§ 2. tab. B. a) *a gate*, Mat. 7. 13, 14; Lu. 7. 12; Ac. 12. 10, et al.; πύλαι ᾅδου, *the gates of hades, the nether world and its powers, the powers of destruction, dissolution*, Mat. 16. 18.

πυλών, ῶνος, ὁ, (§ 4. rem. 2. e) *a gateway, vestibule*, Mat. 26. 71; Lu. 16. 20; *a gate*, Ac. 14. 13; Re. 21. 12, 13, 15, 21, 25, et al. L.G.

πύλῃ, dat. sing. . . . . πύλη
πύλην, acc. sing. . . . . id.
πύλης, gen. sing. . . . . . . id.
πυλών], ῶνος, ὁ . . . . . id.
πυλῶνα, acc. sing. . . . . . πυλών
πυλῶνας, acc. pl. . . . . . id.
πυλῶνες, nom. pl. . . . . . id.
πυλῶνος, gen. sing. . . . . . id.
πυλώνων, gen. pl. . . . . . id.
πυλῶσι, dat. pl. . . . . . . id.
πυνθάνεσθαι, pres. infin. . . . . πυνθάνομαι
πυνθάνομαι], fut. πεύσομαι, aor. 2, ἐπυθόμην, (§ 36. rem. 2) *to ask, inquire*, Mat. 2. 4; Lu. 15. 26, et al.; *to investigate, examine* judicially, Ac. 23. 20; *to ascertain by inquiry, understand*, Ac. 23. 34.

πῦρ], πυρός, τό, (§ 4. rem. 2. f) *fire*, Mat. 3. 10; 7. 19; 13. 40, et al. freq.; πυρός, used by Hebraism with the force of an adjective, *fiery, fierce*, He. 10. 27; *fire* used figuratively to express various circumstances of severe trial, Lu. 12. 49; 1 Co. 3. 13; Jude 23.

πυρά, ᾶς, ἡ, (§ 2. tab. B. b) *a fire, heap of combustibles*, Ac. 28. 2, 3.

πυρετός, οῦ, ὁ, (§ 3. tab. C. a) *scorching and noxious heat*; *a fever*, Mat. 8. 15; Mar. 1. 31, et al.

πυρέσσω, or ττω, fut. ξω, (§ 26. rem. 3) *to be feverish, be sick of a fever*, Mat. 8. 14; Mar. 1. 30.

πύρϊνος, η, ον, (§ 7. tab. F. a) pr. *of fire, fiery, burning; shining, glittering*, Re. 9. 17.

πυρόω, ῶ, fut. ώσω, (§ 20. tab. T) *to set on fire, burn*; pass. *to be kindled, be on fire, burn, flame*, Ep. 6. 16; 2 Pe. 3. 12; Re. 1. 15; met. *to fire* with distressful feelings, 2 Co. 11. 29; of lust, *to be inflamed, burn*, 1 Co. 7. 9; *to be tried with fire*, as metals, Re. 3. 18.

πύρωσις, εως, ἡ, (§ 5. tab. E. c) *a burning, conflagration*, Re. 18. 9, 18; met. *a fiery test* of trying circumstances, 1 Pe. 4. 12.

πυῤῥός, ά, όν, (§ 7. rem. 1) *of the colour of fire, fiery-red*, Re. 6. 4; 12. 3.

πυῤῥάζω, fut. άσω, (§ 26. rem. 1) *to be fiery-red*, Mat. 16. 2, 3. N.T.

πυρά], ᾶς, ἡ . . . . . . πῦρ
πυράν, acc. sing. . . . . . . πυρά
πύργον, acc. sing. . . . . . πύργος

πύργος], ου, ὁ, (§ 3. tab. C. a) *a tower*, Mat. 21. 33; Mar. 12. 1; Lu. 13. 4; genr. *a castle, palace*, Lu. 14. 28.

πυρέσσουσα, nom. sing. fem. part. pres. . πυρέσσω
πυρέσσουσαν, acc. sing. fem. part. pres. . id.
πυρέσσω, or ττω], fut. ξω . . . . πῦρ
πυρετοῖς, dat. pl. . . . . . πυρετός
πυρετός], οῦ, ὁ . . . . . . πῦρ
πυρετῷ, dat. sing. . . . . . πυρετός
πυρί, dat. sing. . . . . . . πῦρ
πύρινος], η, ον . . . . . . id.
πυρίνους,[a] acc. pl. masc. . . . . πύρινος
πυρός, gen. sing. (§ 4. rem. 2. f) . . πῦρ
πυροῦμαι, 1 pers. sing. pres. ind. pass. (§ 21. tab. U) . . . . . . πυρόω
πυρούμενοι, nom. pl. masc. part. pres. pass. id.
πυροῦσθαι, pres. infin. pass. . . . id.
πυρόω, ῶ], fut. ώσω . . . . . πῦρ
πυῤῥάζει, 3 pers. sing. pres. ind. . . πυῤῥάζω
πυῤῥάζω], fut. άσω . . . . . . πῦρ
πυῤῥός, ά, όν . . . . . . id.
Πύῤῥος], ου, ὁ, (§ 3. tab. C. a) *Pyrrhus*, pr. name.
Πύῤῥου, gen.—A. D. Gr. Sch. Tdf. } Πύῤῥος
Rec. om. (Ac. 20. 4) . . . }
πυρώσει, dat. sing. . . . . . . πύρωσις
πυρώσεως, gen. sing. . . . . . id.
πύρωσις], εως, ἡ . . . . . . πῦρ
πω], an enclitic particle, *yet*; see in μήπω, μηδέπω, οὔπω, οὐδέπω, πώποτε.
πωλεῖ, 3 pers. sing. pres. ind. act. . . πωλέω
πωλεῖται, 3 pers. sing. pres. ind. pass. (§ 17. tab. Q) id.

πωλέω, ῶ], fut. ήσω, (§ 16. tab. P) *to sell*, Mat. 10. 29; 13. 44, et al.

[a] Re. 9. 17.

πωλῆσαι, aor. 1, infin. act. . . . . πωλέω
πωλήσας, nom. sing. masc. part. aor. 1, act. id.
πωλήσατε, 2 pers. pl. aor. 1, imper. act. . id.
πωλησάτω, 3 pers. sing. aor. 1, imper. act. . id.
πωλήσει, 3 pers. sing. fut. ind. act.—Const. **πωλησάτω**, R. Gr. Sch. Tdf. (Lu. 22. 36) id.
πώλησον, 2 pers. sing. aor. 1, imper. act. . id.
πῶλον, acc. sing. . . . . . . πῶλος

πῶλος], ου, ὁ, (§ 3. tab. C. a) *a youngling; a foal or colt*, Mat. 21. 2, 5, 7; Mar. 11. 2, et al.

πωλούμενον, acc. sing. neut. part. pres. pass. πωλέω
πωλοῦντας, acc. pl. masc. part. pres. act. . id.
πωλοῦντες, nom. pl. masc. part. pres act. . id.
πωλούντων, gen. pl. masc. part. pres. act. . id.
πωλοῦσι, dat. pl. masc. part. pres. act. . id.
πώποτε], adv. (πω & πότε) *ever yet, ever, at any time*, Lu. 19. 30; Jno. 1. 18, et al.
πωρόω, ῶ], fut. ώσω, (§ 20. tab. T) (πῶρος, *a stony concretion*) *to petrify; to harden*; in N.T. *to harden* the feelings, Jno. 12. 40; pass. *to become callous, unimpressible*, Mar. 6. 52; 8. 17; Ro. 11. 7; 2 Co. 3. 14.

πώρωσις, εως, ἡ, (§ 5. tab. E. c) *a hardening*; met. *hardness* of heart, *callousness, insensibility*, Mar. 3. 5, Ro. 11. 25; Ep. 4. 18.

πωρώσει, dat. sing. . . . . . πώρωσις
πώρωσιν, acc. sing. . . . . . . id.
πώρωσις], εως, ἡ · . . . . . πωρόω
πως], an enclitic particle, *in any way, by any means*; see εἴπως, μήπως.
πῶς], adv. *how? in what manner? by what means?* Mat. 7. 4; 22. 12; Jno. 6. 52; used in interrogations which imply a negative, Mat. 12. 26, 29, 34; 22. 45; 23. 33; Ac. 8. 31; put concisely for *how is it that? how does it come to pass that?* Mat. 16. 11; 22. 43; Mar. 4. 40; Jno. 7. 15; with an indirect interrogation, *how, in what manner*, Mat. 6. 28; 10. 19; Mar. 11. 18; put for τί, *what?* Lu. 10. 26; put for ὡς, as a particle of exclamation, *how, how much, how greatly*, Mar. 10. 23, 24.

P.

Ῥαάβ, ἡ, *Rahab*, pr. name, indecl.
Ῥαββί, ὁ, indecl. (later Heb. רַבִּי, from רַב, which was deemed less honourable) *Rabbi, my master, teacher, doctor*, Mat. 23. 7, 8; 26. 25, 49, et al.
Ῥαββονί, or **Ῥαββουνί**, (later Heb. רַבָּן, Aram. with suffix, רַבּוֹנִי) *Rabboni, my master*, the highest title of honour in the Jewish schools, Mar. 10. 51; Jno. 20. 16.
Ῥαββουνί, same signif. as **Ῥαββονί**.
ῥαβδίζειν, pres. infin. act. . . . . ῥαβδίζω
ῥαβδίζω], fut. ίσω . . . . . ῥάβδος
ῥάβδον, acc. sing. . . . . . . id.

ῥάβδος], ου, ἡ, (§ 3. tab. C. b) *a rod, wand*, He. 9. 4; Re. 11. 1; *a rod* of correction, 1 Co. 4. 21; *a staff*, Mat. 10. 10; He. 11. 21; *a sceptre*, He. 1. 8; Re. 2. 27.

ῥαβδίζω, fut. ίσω, (§ 26. rem. 1) aor. 1, ἐῤῥάβδισα, aor. 1, pass. ἐῤῥαβδίσθην, *to beat with rods*, Ac. 16. 22; 2 Co. 11. 25.

ῥάβδου, gen. sing. . . . . . ῥάβδος
ῥάβδους, acc. pl. . . . . . . id.
ῥαβδοῦχοι, nom. pl. . . . . . ῥαβδοῦχος
ῥαβδοῦχος], ου, ὁ, (§ 3. tab. C. a) (ῥάβδος & ἔχω) *the bearer of a wand* of office; *a lictor, serjeant*, a public servant who bore a bundle of rods before the magistrates as insignia of their office, and carried into execution the sentences they pronounced, Ac. 16. 35, 38.

ῥαβδούχους, acc. pl. . . . . ῥαβδοῦχος
ῥάβδῳ, dat. sing. . . . . . ῥάβδος
Ῥαγαῦ,[a] ὁ, *Ragau*, pr. name, indecl.
ῥᾳδιούργημα],[b] ατος, τό, (§ 4. tab. D. c) (ῥᾳδιουργέω, *to do easily, to act recklessly*; ῥᾴδιος, *easy*, and ἔργον,) pr. *anything done lightly, levity; reckless conduct, crime*. L.G.
ῥᾳδιουργία], ας, ἡ, (§ 2. tab. B. b, and rem. 2) (from same) *facility of doing* anything; *levity in doing; recklessness, profligacy, wickedness*, Ac. 13. 10.
ῥᾳδιουργίας,[c] gen. sing. . . . . ῥᾳδιουργία
ῥακά],[d] *Raca*, an Aramæan term of bitter contempt, *worthless fellow*.
ῥάκος], εος, τό, (§ 5. tab. E. b) . . ῥήγνυ
ῥάκους, gen. sing. . . . . . . ῥάκος
Ῥαμᾶ], ἡ, indecl. *Rama*, a city of Judæa.

[a] Lu. 3. 35. [b] Ac. 18. 14. [c] Ac. 13. 10. [d] Mat. 5. 22.

ῥαντίζουσα, nom. sing. fem. part. pres. act. ῥαντίζω

ῥαντίζω], fut. ίσω, (§ 26. rem. 1) aor. 1, ἐῤῥάντισα, perf. pass. ἐῤῥάντισμαι, (ῥαίνω, idem) *to sprinkle, besprinkle*, He. 9. 13, 19, 21; met. and by impl. *to cleanse by sprinkling, purify, free from pollution*, He. 10. 22. L.G.

ῥαντισμός, οῦ, ὁ, (§ 3. tab. C. a) pr. *a sprinkling*; met. *a cleansing, purification, lustration*, He. 12. 24; 1 Pe. 1. 2. LXX.

ῥαντισμόν, acc. sing. . . . . ῥαντισμός

ῥαντισμός], οῦ, ὁ . . . . . ῥαντίζω

ῥαντισμοῦ, gen. sing. . . . . ῥαντισμός

ῥαπίζω], fut. ίσω, aor. 1, ἐῤῥάπισα, (§ 26. rem. 1) (ῥαπίς, *a rod*) *to beat with rods; to strike with the palm of the hand, cuff, slap*, Mat. 5. 39; 26. 67.

ῥάπισμα, ατος, τό, (§ 4. tab. D. c) *a blow with the palm of the hand, cuff, slap*, Mar. 14. 65; Jno. 18. 22; 19. 3. L.G.

ῥαπίσει, 2 pers. sing. fut. ind. act. . . ῥαπίζω

ῥάπισμα], ατος, τό . . . . . id.

ῥαπίσμασι, dat. pl. . . . . . ῥάπισμα

ῥαπίσματα, acc. pl. . . . . . id.

ῥαφίδος, gen. sing. . . . . . ῥαφίς

ῥαφίς], ίδος, (ῐ) ἡ, (§ 4. rem. 2. c) (ῥάπτω, *to sew, sew together*) *a needle*, Mat. 19. 24; Mar. 10. 25; Lu. 18. 25.

Ῥαχάβ],[a] ἡ, *Rachab*, pr. name, indecl.

Ῥαχήλ],[b] ἡ, *Rachel*, pr. name, indecl.

Ῥεβέκκα],[c] ας, ἡ, *Rebecca*, pr. name.

ῥέδα, or ῥέδη], ης, ἡ, (§ 2. tab. B. a) (Lat. *rheda*) *a carriage with four wheels* for travelling, *a chariot*.

ῥεδῶν,[d] gen. pl. . . . . . ῥέδα

Ῥεμφάν,[e] or Ῥεφάν], ὁ, indecl. the name of an idol, Ac. 7. 43. The original passage, Amos 5. 26, has כִּיּוּן; the Sept. Ῥαιφάν, the Egyptian name for the planet Saturn.

ῥεύσουσι,[f] 3 pers. pl. fut. ind. . . . ῥέω

Ῥεφάν, ὁ—C. Ln. Tdf.

Ῥεμφάν, Rec. Gr. Sch. (Ac. 7. 43).

ῥέω], fut. ῥεύσω, ῥεύσομαι, (§ 35. rem. 3) aor. 1, ἔῤῥευσα, *to flow*.

ῥύσις, εως, ἡ, (§ 5. tab. E. c) *a flowing; a morbid flux*, Mar. 5. 25; Lu. 8. 43, 44

ῥέω], an obsolete form, whence perf. εἴρηκα, perf. pass. εἴρημαι, aor. 1, pass. ἐῤῥήθην, & ἐῤῥέθην, part. ῥηθείς, (§ 36. rem. 1) *to say, speak*, Mat. 1. 22; 2 Co. 12. 9; Re. 7. 14, et al.; *to speak of*, Mat. 3. 3; *to direct, command, prescribe*, Mat. 5. 21, et al.; *to address* one *as* anything, *to call, name*, Jno. 15. 15, et al.

ῥῆμα, ατος, τό, (§ 4. tab. D. c) *that which is spoken; declaration, saying, speech, word*, Mat. 12. 36; 26. 75; Mar. 9. 32; 14. 72; *a command, mandate, direction*, Lu. 3. 2; 5. 5; *a promise*, Lu. 1. 38; 2. 29; *a prediction, prophecy*, 2 Pe. 3. 2; *a doctrine* of God or Christ, Jno. 3. 34; 5. 47; 6. 63, 68; Ac. 5. 20; *an accusation, charge, crimination*, Mat. 5. 11; 27. 14; from the Heb., *a thing*, Mat. 4. 4; Lu. 4. 4; *a matter, affair, transaction, business*, Mat. 18. 16; Lu. 1. 65; 2 Co. 13. 1, et al.

ῥήτωρ, ορος, ὁ, (§ 4. rem. 2. f) *an orator, advocate*, Ac. 24. 1.

ῥητῶς, adv. (ῥητός, ῥέω) *in express words, expressly*, 1 Ti. 4. 1. L.G.

Ῥήγιον],[g] ου, τό, (§ 3. tab. C. c) *Rhegium*, a city at the south-western extremity of Italy.

ῥῆγμα],[h] ατος, τό . . . . . ῥήγνυμι

ῥήγνυμι, or ῥήσσω], fut. ξω, aor. 1, ἔῤῥηξα, (§ 36. rem. 5) *to rend, shatter; to break or burst in pieces*, Mat. 9. 17; Mar. 2. 22; Lu. 5. 37, et al.; *to rend, lacerate*, Mat. 7. 6; *to cast or dash* upon the ground, *convulse*, Mar. 9. 18; Lu. 9. 42; absol. *to break forth* into exclamation, Gal. 4. 27.

ῥῆγμα, ατος, τό, (§ 4. tab. D. c) *a rent; a crash, ruin*, Lu. 6. 49.

ῥήγνυνται, 3 pers. pl. pres. ind. pass. . . ῥήγνυμι

ῥηθείς, part. of ἐῤῥήθην, aor. 1, pass. used in connection with λέγω, φημί, and εἰπεῖν. See ῥέω.

ῥηθέν, nom. and acc. sing. neut. part. aor. 1, pass. ῥέω

ῥῆμα], ατος, τό . . . . . . id.

ῥήμασι, dat. pl. . . . . . ῥῆμα

ῥήματα, nom. and acc. pl. . . . . id.

[a] Mat. 1. 5. [b] Mat. 2. 18. [c] Ro. 9. 10. [d] Re. 18. 13. [e] Ac. 7. 43. [f] Jno. 7. 38. [g] Ac. 28. 13. [h] Lu. 6. 49.

ῥήματι, dat. sing. . . . . . . ῥῆμα
ῥήματος, gen. sing. . . . . . id.
ῥημάτων, gen. pl. . . . . . . id.
ῥήξει, 3 pers. sing. fut. ind. act. . . ῥήγνυμι
ῥῆξον, 2 pers. sing. aor. 1, imper. . . id.
ῥήξωσι, 3 pers. pl. aor. 1, subj. act. . id.
Ῥησά],[a] ὁ, *Rhesa*, pr. name, indecl.
ῥήσσει, 3 pers. sing. pres. ind. act. . . ῥήσσω
ῥήσσω], see ῥήγνυμι.
ῥήτορος,[b] gen. sing. . . . . . ῥήτωρ
ῥήτωρ], ορος, ὁ . . . . . . ῥέω
ῥητῶς],[c] adv. . . . . id.

ῥίζα], ης, ἡ, (§ 2. rem. 3) *a root* of a tree, Mat. 3. 10; 13. 6; met. ἔχειν ῥίζαν, or ἔχειν ῥίζαν ἐν ἑαυτῷ, *to be rooted* in faith, Mat. 13. 21; Mar. 4. 17; Lu. 8. 13; met. *cause, source, origin*, 1 Ti. 6. 10; He. 12. 15; by synecd. *the trunk, stock* of a tree, met. Ro. 11. 16, 17, 18; met. *offspring, progeny, a descendant*, Ro. 15. 12; Re. 5. 5; 22. 16.

ῥιζόω, ῶ, fut. ώσω, (§ 20. tab. T) *to root, cause to take root*; pass. part. perf. ἐῤῥιζωμένος, *firmly rooted, strengthened with roots*; met. *firm, constant, firmly fixed*, Ep. 3. 18; Col. 2. 7.

ῥίζαν, acc. sing. . . . ῥίζα
ῥίζης, gen. sing. . . id.
ῥιζόω, ῶ], fut. ώσω . . . id.
ῥιζῶν, gen. pl. . . . . . id.
ῥιπή], ῆς, ἡ . . . . . . ῥίπτω
ῥιπῇ,[d] dat. sing. . . . . . . ῥιπή
ῥιπιζομένῳ,[e] dat. sing. masc. part. pres. pass. ῥιπίζω
ῥιπίζω], fut. ίσω . . . . . ῥίπτω
ῥιπτέω, ῶ], frequentative . . . id.
ῥιπτούντων,[f] gen. pl. masc. part. pres. . . ῥιπτέω

ῥίπτω], fut. ψω, aor. 1, ἔῤῥιψα, (§ 23. rem. 1. a, and rem. 2) perf. pass. ἔῤῥιμμαι, (§ 23. rem. 7) *to hurl, throw, cast; to throw or cast down*, Mat. 27. 5; Lu. 4. 35; 17. 2; *to throw or cast* out, Ac. 27. 19, 29; *to lay down, set down*, Mat. 15. 30; pass. *to be dispersed, scattered*, Mat. 9. 36.

ῥιπτέω, ῶ, *to toss repeatedly, toss up* with violent gesture, Ac. 22. 23.

ῥιπή, ῆς, ἡ, (§ 2. tab. B. a) pr. *a rapid sweep, jerk; a wink, twinkling* of the eye, 1 Co. 15. 52.

ῥιπίζω, fut. ίσω, (§ 26. rem. 1) (ῥιπίς, *a fan or bellows*, from ῥίπτω) *to fan, blow, ventilate; to toss, agitate*, e.g. the ocean by the wind, Ja. 1. 6.

ῥῖψαν, nom. sing. neut. part. aor. 1, act. . ῥίπτω
ῥίψαντες, nom. pl. masc. part. aor. 1, act. id
ῥίψας, nom. sing. masc. part. aor. 1, act. . id.
Ῥοβοάμ], ὁ, *Roboam*, pr. name, indecl.
Ῥόδη],[g] ης, ἡ, *Rhoda*, pr. name.
Ῥόδον,[h] acc. . . . . Ῥόδος
Ῥόδος], ου, ἡ, (§ 3. tab. C. a) *Rhodes*, an island in the Mediterranean, south of Caria.
ῥοιζηδόν],[i] adv. (ῥοῖζος, *a whizzing, a rushing noise*) *with a noise, with a crash*, etc. L.G

ῥομφαία], ας, ἡ, (§ 2. tab. B. b, and rem. 2) pr. *a* Thracian *broad-sword, a sword*, Re. 1. 16; 2. 12; by meton. *war*, Re. 6. 8; met. *a thrill of anguish*, Lu. 2. 35.

ῥομφαίᾳ, dat. sing. . . . . ῥομφαία
ῥομφαίαν, acc. sing. . . . . id.
Ῥουβήν],[k] ὁ, *Reuben*, pr. name, indecl.
Ῥούθ],[l] ἡ, *Ruth*, pr. name, indecl.
Ῥοῦφον, acc. . . . . . Ῥοῦφος
Ῥοῦφος], ου, ὁ, (§ 3. tab. C. a) *Rufus*, pr. name.
Ῥούφου, gen. . . . . . . Ῥοῦφος
ῥύεσθαι, pres. infin. . . . . ῥύομαι
ῥύεται, 3 pers. sing. pres. ind. . . . id.
ῥύμαις, dat. pl. . . . . . . ῥύμη
ῥύμας, acc. pl. . . . . . . id.
ῥύμη], ης, ἡ, (§ 2. tab. B. a) (ῥύω, *to draw*) pr. *a rush or sweep* of a body in motion; *a street*, Ac. 9. 11; 12. 10; *a narrow street, lane, alley*, as distinguished from πλατεῖα, Mat. 6. 2; Lu. 14. 21.
ῥύμην, acc. sing. . . . . . ῥύμη
ῥύομαι], fut. ῥύσομαι, aor. 1, ἐῤῥυσάμην, (§ 14. tab. N) *to drag* out of danger, *to rescue, save*, Mat. 6. 13; 27. 43; later also pass. aor. 1, ἐῤῥύσθην, *to be rescued, delivered*, Lu. 1. 74; Ro. 15. 31; 2 Thes. 3. 2; 2 Ti. 4. 17.
ῥυόμενον, acc. sing. masc. part. pres. . . ῥύομαι
ῥυόμενος, nom. sing. masc. part. pres. . id.

---

[a] Lu. 3. 27. [b] Ac. 24. 1. [c] 1 Ti. 4. 1. [d] 1 Co. 15. 52. [e] Ja. 1. 6. [f] Ac. 22. 23. [g] Ac. 12. 13. [h] Ac. 21. 1. [i] 2 Pe. 3. 10. [k] Re. 7. 5. [l] Mat. 1. 5.

ῥυπαρᾷ, dat. sing. fem. . . . . . ῥυπαρός
ῥυπαρευθήτω, 3 pers. sing. aor. 1, imper. pass.—Gr. Sch. Tdf. . . } ῥυπαρεύομαι
ῥυπωσάτω, Rec. (Re. 22. 11) . }
ῥυπαρεύομαι], fut. εύσομαι, v.r. . . ῥύπος
ῥυπαρία], ας, ἡ . . . . . . id.
ῥυπαρίαν,[a] acc. sing. . . . ῥυπαρία
ῥυπαρός], ά, όν . . . . . ῥύπος

ῥύπος], ου, ὁ, (§ 3. tab. C. a) *filth, squalor,* 1 Pe. 3. 21.

ῥυπόω, ῶ, fut. ώσω, (§ 20. tab. T) *to be filthy;* met. *to be* morally *polluted,* Re. 22. 11, bis.

ῥυπᾰρός, ά, όν, (§ 7. rem. 1) *filthy, squalid, sordid, dirty,* Ja. 2. 2; met. *defiled, polluted,* v.r. Re. 22. 11.

ῥυπαρία, ας, ἡ, (§ 2. tab. B. b, and rem. 2) *filth;* met. moral *filthiness, uncleanness, pollution,* Ja. 1. 21.

ῥυπαρεύομαι, (ῥυπαρός) *to be filthy, squalid;* met. *to be polluted,* v.r. Re. 22. 11. N.T.

ῥύπου,[b] gen. sing. . . . . ῥύπος
ῥυπόω, ῶ], fut. ώσω . . . . . id.
ῥυπῶν, nom. sing. masc. part. pres. . . ῥυπόω
ῥυπωσάτω, 3 pers. sing. aor. 1, imper. . . id.
ῥῦσαι, 2 pers. sing. aor. 1, imper. . . ῥύομαι
ῥυσάσθω, 3 pers. sing. aor. 1, imper. . . id.
ῥύσει, dat. sing. . . . . . . ῥύσις
ῥύσεται, 3 pers. sing. fut. ind. . . . ῥύομαι
ῥυσθέντας, acc. pl. masc. part. aor. 1, pass. id.
ῥυσθῶ, 1 pers. sing. aor. 1, subj. pass. . id.
ῥυσθῶμεν, 1 pers. pl. aor. 1, subj. pass. . id.
ῥύσις], εως, ἡ, (§ 5. tab. E. c) . . ῥέω
ῥυτίδα,[c] acc. sing. . . . . . ῥυτίς
ῥυτίς], ίδος, (ῐ) ἡ, (§ 4. rem. 2. c) (ῥύω, *to draw*) *a wrinkle;* met. *a* disfiguring *wrinkle, flaw, blemish,* Ep. 5. 27.

Ῥωμαϊκοῖς,[d] dat. pl. neut. . . . Ῥωμαϊκός
Ῥωμαϊκός], ή, όν . . . . . Ῥώμη
Ῥωμαῖοι, nom. pl. . . . . . Ῥωμαῖος
Ῥωμαῖον, acc. sing. . . . . . id.
Ῥωμαῖος], ου, ὁ . . . Ῥώμη
Ῥωμαίους, acc. pl. . . . . . Ῥωμαῖος
Ῥωμαϊστί],[e] adv. . . . . . Ῥώμη
Ῥωμαίων, gen. pl. . . . . . Ῥωμαῖος
Ῥώμη], ης, ἡ, (§ 2. tab. B. a) *Rome.*

Ῥωμαϊκός, ή, όν, (§ 7. tab. F. a) *Roman, Latin,* Lu. 23. 38.

Ῥωμαῖος, ου, ὁ, (§ 3. tab. C. a) *a Roman, Roman citizen,* Jno. 11. 48; Ac. 2. 10; 16. 21, et al.

Ῥωμαϊστί, adv. *in the Roman language, in Latin,* Jno. 19. 20.

Ῥώμῃ, dat. . . . . Ῥώμη
Ῥώμην, acc. . . . . id.
Ῥώμης, gen. . . . . id.

ῥώννυμι, or **νύω**], fut. ῥώσω, (§ 36. rem. 5) *to strengthen, render firm;* pass. perf. ἔῤῥωμαι, *to be well, enjoy firm health;* imperative ἔῤῥωσο, ἔῤῥωσθε, at the end of letters, like the Lat. *vale, farewell,* Ac. 15. 29; 23. 30.

Σ.

σά, nom. and acc. pl. neut. . . . . σός
σαβαχθανί, (Aram. שְׁבַקְתַּנִי, from שְׁבַק, *to leave, forsake*) *sabacthani, thou hast forsaken me;* interrogatively, *hast thou forsaken me?* (with λαμᾶ, *why,* preceding), Mat. 27. 46; Mar. 15. 34.
σαβαώθ, (Heb. צְבָאוֹת, pl. of צָבָא) *hosts, armies,* Ro. 9. 29; Ja. 5. 4.
σάββασι, dat. pl. (§ 6. rem. 8) . . . σάββατον
σάββατα, acc. pl. . . . . . . id.
σαββατισμός],[f] οῦ, ὁ . . . . . id.
σάββᾰτον], ου, τό, (§ 3. tab. C. c) (Heb. שַׁבָּת) pr. *cessation from labour, rest; the* Jewish *sabbath,* both in the sing. and pl., Mat. 12. 2, 5, 8; 28. 1; Lu. 4. 16; *a week,* sing. and pl., Mat. 28. 1; Mar. 16. 9, et al.; pl. *sabbaths, or times of sacred rest,* Col. 2. 16.

σαββατισμός, οῦ, ὁ, (§ 3. tab. C. a) (σαββατίζω, i.q. Heb. שָׁבַת, whence it is formed, *to cease or rest from labour,* and thus *keep sabbath*) pr. *a keeping of a sabbath; a state of rest, a sabbath-state,* He. 4. 9.

σαββάτου, gen. sing. . . . . . σάββατον
σαββάτῳ, dat. sing. . . . . . id.
σαββάτων, gen. pl. . . . . . id.
σαγήνη], ης, ἡ, (§ 2. tab. B. a) (σαγή, from σάττω, *to load*) *a large net, drag.* L.G.

[a] Ja. 1. 21. [b] 1 Pe. 3. 21. [c] Ep. 5. 27. [d] Lu. 23. 38. [e] Jno. 19. 20. [f] He. 4. 9.

σαγήνῃ,[a] dat. sing. . . . . . σαγήνη

Σαδδουκαῖοι, nom. pl. . . . . Σαδδουκαῖος

Σαδδουκαῖος], ου, ὁ, (§ 3. tab. C. a) *a Sadducee, one belonging to the sect of the Sadducees,* which, according to the Talmudists, was founded by one צָדוֹק, *Sadoc,* about three centuries before the Christian era: they were directly opposed in sentiments to the Pharisees, Mat. 3. 7; 16. 1, 6, 11, 12; 22. 23, 34, et al.

Σαδδουκαίους, acc. pl. . . . . . Σαδδουκαῖος

Σαδδουκαίων, gen. pl. . . . . . id.

Σαδώκ], ὁ, *Sadoc,* pr. name, indecl.

σαίνεσθαι,[b] pres. infin. pass. . . . . σαίνω

σαίνω], fut. σανῶ, aor. 1, ἔσηνα & ἔσᾱνα, (§ 27. rem. 1. c. e) pr. *to wag* the tail; *to fawn, flatter, cajole;* pass. *to be cajoled; to be wrought upon, to be perturbed,* 1 Thes. 3. 3.

σάκκος], ου, ὁ, (§ 3. tab. C. a) (Heb. שַׂק) *sackcloth,* a species of very coarse black cloth made of hair, Re. 6. 12; a mourning garment of *sackcloth,* Mat. 11. 21; Lu. 10. 13; Re. 11. 3.

σάκκους, acc. pl. . . . . . σάκκος

σακκῳ, dat. sing. . . . . . id.

Σαλά],[c] ὁ, *Sala,* pr. name, indecl.

Σαλαθιήλ], ὁ, *Salathiel,* pr. name, indecl.

Σαλαμῖνι,[d] dat. . . . . . . Σαλαμίς

Σαλαμίς], ῖνος, ἡ, (§ 4. rem. 2. e) *Salamis,* a city in the island of Cyprus.

Σαλείμ],[e] indecl. *Salim,* pr. name of a place.

σαλευθῆναι, aor. 1, infin. pass. (§ 14. tab. N) σαλεύω

σαλευθήσονται, 3 pers. pl. fut. ind. pass. . id.

σαλευθῶ, 1 pers. sing. aor. 1, subj. pass. . id.

σαλευόμενα, nom. pl. neut. part. pres. pass. id.

σαλευόμενον, acc. sing. masc. part. pres. pass. id.

σαλευομένων, gen. pl. part. pres. pass. . id.

σαλεύοντες, nom. pl. masc. part. pres. act. . id.

σαλεῦσαι, aor. 1, infin. act. . . . . id.

σαλεύω], fut. εύσω . . . . . . σάλος

Σαλήμ], ἡ, *Salem,* pr. name, indecl.

Σαλμών], ὁ, *Salmon,* pr. name, indecl.

Σαλμώνη], ης, ἡ, (§ 2. tab. B. a) *Salmone,* a promontory, the eastern extremity of Crete.

Σαλμώνην,[f] acc. . . . . . . Σαλμώνη

σάλος], ου, ὁ, (§ 3. tab. C. a) *agitation, tossing, rolling,* spc. of the sea, Lu. 21. 25

σαλεύω, fut. εύσω, aor. 1, ἐσάλευσα, (§ 13. tab. M) *to make to rock, to shake,* Mat. 11. 7; 24. 29; Lu. 6. 48; Ac. 4. 31, et al.; met. *to stir up, excite* the people, Ac. 17. 13; *to agitate, disturb* mentally, Ac. 2. 25; 2 Thes. 2. 2; pass. impl. *to totter, be ready to fall, be near to ruin,* met. He. 12. 27.

σάλου,[g] gen. sing. . . . . . . σάλος

σάλπιγγα, acc. sing. . . . . . σάλπιγξ

σάλπιγγας, acc. pl. . . . . . id.

σάλπιγγες, nom. pl. . . . . . id.

σάλπιγγι, dat. sing. . . . . . id.

σάλπιγγος, gen. sing. . . . . . id.

σάλπιγξ], ιγγος, ἡ, (§ 4. rem. 2. b) *a trumpet,* Mat. 24. 31; 1 Thes. 4. 16, et al.

σαλπίζω, fut. ίγξω, and later, ίσω, (§ 26. rem. 2) aor. 1, ἐσάλπιγξα & ἐσάλπῐσα, *to sound a trumpet,* Re. 8. 6, 7, 8, 10, 12, 13, et al.

σαλπιστής, οῦ, ὁ, (§ 2. tab. B. c) *a trumpeter,* Re. 18. 22. L G.

σαλπίζειν, pres. infin. . . . . . σαλπίζω

σαλπίζω], fut. ίγξω and ίσω . . . . σάλπιγξ

σαλπίσει, 3 pers. sing. fut. ind. . . . σαλπίζω

σαλπίσῃς, 2 pers. sing. aor. 1, subj. . . id.

σαλπίσωσι, 3 pers. pl. aor. 1, subj. . . id.

σαλπιστής], οῦ, ὁ . . . . . σάλπιγξ

σαλπιστῶν,[h] gen. pl. . . . . . σαλπιστής

Σαλώμη], ης, ἡ, *Salome,* pr. name.

Σαμάρεια], ας, ἡ, (§ 2. tab. B. b, and rem. 2) *Samaria,* the city and region so called.

Σαμαρείτης, ου, ὁ, (§ 2. tab. B. c) *a Samaritan, an inhabitant of the city or region of* Σαμάρεια, *Samaria,* applied by the Jews as a term of reproach and contempt, Mat. 10. 5; Jno. 4. 9; 8. 48, et al.

Σαμαρεῖτις, ιδος, ἡ, (§ 4. rem. 2. c) *a Samaritan woman,* Jno. 4. 9, bis.

Σαμαρείᾳ, dat. . . . . . . Σαμαρεια

Σαμάρειαν, acc. . . . . . . id.

Σαμαρείας, gen. . . . . . . id.

Σαμαρεῖται, nom. pl. . . . . . Σαμαρείτης

Σαμαρείταις, dat. pl. . . . . . id.

Σαμαρείτης], ου, ὁ . . . . . . Σαμάρεια

Σαμαρείτιδος, gen. sing. . . . . Σαμαρεῖτις

---

a Mat. 13. 47. b 1 Thes. 3. 3. c Lu. 3. 35. d Ac. 13. 5. e Jno. 3. 23. f Ac. 27. 7. g Lu. 21. 25. h Re. 18. 22.

Σαμαρεῖτις], ιδος, ἡ . . . . . Σαμάρεια
Σαμαρειτῶν, gen. pl. . . . . . Σαμαρείτης
Σαμοθρᾴκη], ης, ἡ, (§ 2. tab. B. a) *Samothrace*, an island in the northern part of the Ægean sea.
Σαμοθρᾴκην,[a] acc. . . . . . . Σαμοθρᾴκη
Σάμον,[b] acc. . . . . . . Σάμος
Σάμος], ου, ἡ, (§ 3. tab. C. b) *Samos*, a celebrated island in the Ægean sea.
Σαμουήλ], ὁ, *Samuel*, pr. name, indecl.
Σαμψών], ὁ,[c] *Samson*, pr. name, indecl.
σανδάλια, acc. pl. . . . . . . σανδάλιον
σανδάλιον], ου, τό, (§ 3. tab. C. c) (pr. dimin. of σάνδαλον) *a sandal*, a sole of wood or hide, covering the bottom of the foot, and bound on with leathern thongs, Mar. 6. 9; Ac. 12. 8.

σανίς], ίδος, (ῐ) ἡ, (§ 4. rem. 2. c) *a board, plank.*
σανίσι,[d] dat. pl. . . . . . . σανίς
Σαούλ], ὁ, *Saul*, pr. name, indecl.
I. *Saul, king of Israel*, Ac. 13. 21.
II. *The Apostle Paul*, Ac. 9. 4, et al.
σαπρά, acc. pl. neut. . . . . . σαπρός
σαπρόν, acc. sing. masc. and nom. and acc. neut. id.
σαπρός], ά, όν, (§ 7. rem. 1) . . . σήπω
Σαπφείρη], ης, ἡ, *Sapphira*, pr. name.
Σαπφείρῃ,[e] dat. . . . . . . Σαπφείρη
σάπφειρος],[f] ου, ἡ, (§ 3. tab. C. b) (Heb. סַפִּיר) *a sapphire*, a precious stone of a blue colour in various shades, next in hardness and value to the diamond.

σαργάνη], ης, ἡ, (§ 2. tab. B. a) *twisted or plaited work; a network of cords like a basket, basket of ropes*, etc., 2 Co. 11. 33. (ᾰ).
σαργάνῃ,[g] dat. sing. . . . . σαργάνη
Σάρδεις], εων, αἱ, (§ 5. tab. E. c) *Sardis*, the chief city of Lydia.
Σάρδεις, acc. . . . . . . Σάρδεις
Σάρδεσι, dat. . . . . . . id.
σάρδῐνος], ου, ὁ, (§ 3. tab. C. a) *a sardine*, a precious stone of a blood-red colour.
σαρδίνῳ,[h] dat. sing.—Rec. . . . } σάρδινος
σαρδίῳ, Gr. Sch Tdf. (Re. 4. 3) . }
σάρδιον, ου, τό, but, in the common text of Re. 21. 20, σάρδιος, *a carnelian.*

σάρδιος,[i] ου, ὁ, Rec. Gr. Sch.
σάρδιον, A. Ln. Tdf. (Re. 21. 20)
σαρδόνυξ,[k] υχος, ἡ, (§ 4. rem. 2. b) (σάρδιον & ὄνυξ) *sardonyx*, a gem exhibiting the colour of the carnelian and the white of the calcedony, intermingled in alternate layers.
Σάρεπτα], τά, *Sarepta*, a city of Phœnicia, between Tyre and Sidon.
σάρκα, acc. sing. . . . . . . σάρξ
σάρκας, acc. pl. . . . . . id.
σαρκί, dat. sing . . . . . id.
σαρκικά, nom. and acc. pl. neut . . σαρκικός
σαρκικῇ, dat. sing. fem. . . . . id.
σαρκικῆς, gen. sing. fem. . . . id.
σαρκικοί, nom. pl. masc. . . . . id.
σαρκικοῖς, dat. pl. masc. and neut. . . id.
σαρκικός], ή, όν . . . . . . σάρξ
σαρκικῶν, gen. pl. . . . . . σαρκικός
σαρκός, gen. sing. . . . . . σάρξ
σαρκίναις,[l] dat. pl. fem. . . . σάρκινος
σαρκίνης, gen. sing. fem.—A. B. C. D. Gr. Ln. Tdf. . . . . } id.
σαρκικῆς, Rec. Sch. (He. 7. 16) . }
σαρκίνοις, dat. pl. masc.—A. B. C. D. Gr. Ln. Tdf. . . . . } id.
σαρκικοῖς, Rec. Sch. (1 Co. 3. 1) . }
σάρκινος, η, ον.—A. B. C. D. Gr. Sch. Tdf. } σάρξ
σαρκικός, Rec. (Ro. 7. 14) . }
σαρκῶν, gen. pl. . . . . . . id.

σάρξ], σαρκός, ἡ, (§ 4. rem. 2. b) *flesh*, Lu. 24. 39; Jno. 3. 6, et al.; *the* human *body*, 2 Co. 7. 5; *flesh, human nature, human frame*, Jno. 1. 13, 14; 1 Pe. 4. 1; 1 Jno. 4. 2, et al.; *kindred*, Ro. 11. 14; *consanguinity, lineage*, Ro. 1. 3; 9. 3, et al.; *flesh, humanity, human beings*, Mat. 24. 22; Lu. 3. 6; Jno. 17. 2, et al.; *the circumstances of the body, material condition*, 1 Co. 5. 5; 7. 28; Phile. 16, et al.; *flesh, mere humanity, human fashion*, 1 Co. 1. 26; 2 Co. 1. 17; *flesh* as the seat of passion and frailty, Ro. 8. 1, 3, 5, et al.; *carnality*, Gal. 5. 24; *materiality, material circumstance*, as opposed to the spiritual, Phi. 3. 3, 4; Col. 2. 18;

[a] Ac. 16. 11. [b] Ac. 20. 15. [c] He. 11. 32. [d] Ac. 27. 44. [e] Ac. 5. 1. [f] Re. 21. 19. [g] 2 Co. 11. 33. [h] Re. 4. 3. [i] Re. 21. 20. [k] Re. 21. 20. [l] 2 Co. 3. 3.

a material system or mode, Gal. 3. 3; He. 9. 10.

σαρκϊκός, ή, όν, (§ 7. tab. F. a) *fleshly; pertaining to the body, corporeal, physical,* Ro. 15. 27; 1 Co. 9. 11; *carnal, pertaining to the flesh,* 1 Pe. 2. 11; *carnal, subject to the propensity of the flesh,* Ro. 7. 14; *carnal, low in spiritual knowledge and frame,* 1 Co. 3. 1, 3; *carnal, human* as opposed to divine, 2 Co. 1. 12; 10. 4; *carnal, earthly,* He. 7. 16. L.G.

σάρκϊνος, η, ον, (§ 7. tab. F. a) *of flesh, fleshy,* 2 Co. 3. 3.

σαροῖ, 3 pers. sing. pres. ind. act. . . . σαρόω

Σαρούχ],[a] ὁ, *Saruch,* pr. name, indecl.—Rec. **Σερούχ,** Gr. Sch. Tdf. (Lu. 3. 35.)

σαρόω, ῶ], fut. ώσω, (§ 20. tab. T) perf. pass. σεσάρωμαι, (i. q. σαίρω) *to sweep, to cleanse with a broom,* Mat. 12. 44; Lu. 11. 25; 15. 8.

Σάῤῥα], ας, ἡ, *Sara, Sarah,* pr. name.

Σάῤῥᾳ, dat. . . . . . . Σάῤῥα

Σάῤῥας, gen. . . . . . . id.

Σαρών], ῶνος, ὁ, (§ 4. rem. 2. e) *Saron,* a level tract of Palestine, between Cæsarea and Joppa.

Σαρῶνα,[b] acc. . . . . . . Σαρών

σάτα, acc. pl. . . . . . . σάτον

Σατᾶν],[c] ὁ, *Satan,* indecl.

Σατανᾶ, gen. and voc. . . . . Σατανᾶς

Σατανᾷ, dat. . . . . . . id.

Σατανᾶν, acc. . . . . . . id.

Σατανᾶς, ᾶ, ὁ, (§ 2. rem. 4) and once, 2 Co. 12. 7, Σατᾶν, ὁ, indecl. (Heb. שָׂטָן) *an adversary, opponent, enemy,* perhaps, Mat. 16. 23; Mar. 8. 33; Lu. 4. 8; elsewhere, *Satan, the devil,* Mat. 4. 10; Mar. 1. 13, et al.

σάτον], ου, τό, (§ 3. tab. C. c) (Heb. סְאָה, Chald. סָאתָא) *a satum or seah,* a Hebrew measure for things dry, containing, as Josephus testifies, (Ant. l. ix. c. 4. § 5) an Italian modius and a half, or 24 sextarii, and therefore equivalent to somewhat less than three gallons English, Mat. 13. 33; Lu. 13. 21. N.T.

Σαῦλον, acc. . . . . . . Σαῦλος

Σαῦλος], ου, ὁ, *Saul,* the Hebrew name of the Apostle Paul, Σαούλ with a Greek termination.

Σαύλου, gen. . . . . . . Σαῦλος

Σαύλῳ, dat. . . . . . . id.

σβέννυμι], fut. σβέσω, aor. 1, ἔσβεσα, (§ 36. rem. 5) *to extinguish, quench,* Mat. 12. 20; 25. 8; Mar. 9. 44, 46, 48, et al.; met. *to quench, damp, hinder, thwart,* 1 Thes. 5. 19.

σβέννυνται, 3 pers. pl. pres. ind. pass. . σβέννυμι

σβέννυται, 3 pers. sing. pres. ind. pass. . id.

σβέννυτε, 2 pers. pl. pres. imper. act. . id.

σβέσαι, aor. 1, infin. act. . . . . id.

σβέσει, 3 pers. sing. fut. ind. act. . . id.

σέ, (and σε, enclitic) acc. sing. . . . σύ

σεαυτόν, acc. sing. masc. . . . . σεαυτοῦ

σεαυτοῦ, ῆς, οῦ, (§ 11. tab. K. d) reflexive pronoun, *of thyself,* and dat. σεαυτῷ, ῇ, ῷ, *to thyself,* etc., Mat. 4. 6; 8. 4; 19. 19, et al.

σεαυτῷ, dat. sing. masc. . . . . σεαυτοῦ

σεβάζομαι], fut. άσομαι . . . . σέβομαι

σέβασμα], ατος, τό . . . . . id.

σεβάσματα, acc. pl. . . . . . σέβασμα

σεβαστῆς, gen. sing. fem. . . . σεβαστός

σεβαστόν, acc. sing. masc. . . . id.

σεβαστός], ή, όν . . . . . σέβομαι

σεβαστοῦ, gen. sing. masc. . . . σεβαστός

σέβεσθαι, pres. infin. . . . . σέβομαι

σέβεται, 3 pers. sing. pres. ind. . . . id.

σέβομαι], *to stand in awe; to venerate, reverence, worship, adore,* Mat. 15. 9; Ac. 19. 27, et al.; part. σεβόμενος, η, ον, *worshipping, devout, pious,* a term applied to proselytes to Judaism, Ac. 13. 43, et al.

σεβάζομαι, fut. άσομαι, aor. 1, ἐσεβάσθην, (§ 26. rem. 1) (σέβας, *adoration,* from σέβομαι) *to feel dread of* a thing; *to venerate, adore, worship,* Ro. 1. 25.

σέβασμα, ατος, τό, (§ 4. tab. D. c) *an object of religious veneration and worship,* Ac. 17. 23; 2 Thes. 2. 4. L.G.

σεβαστός, ή, όν, (§ 7. tab. F. a) pr. *venerable, august;* ὁ Σεβαστός, i.q. Lat. *Augustus,* Ac. 25. 21, 25; *Augustan,* or, *Sebastan,* named from the city Sebaste, Ac. 27. 1.

σεμνός, ή, όν, (§ 7. tab. F. a) *august, venerable; honourable, reputable,* Phi. 4. 8;

[a] Lu. 3. 35. [b] Ac. 9. 35. [c] 2 Co. 12. 7.

grave, serious, dignified, 1 Ti. 3. 8, 11; Tit. 2. 2.

σεμνότης, τητος, η, (§ 4. rem. 2. c) pr. majesty; gravity, dignity, dignified seriousness, 2 Ti. 2. 2; 3. 4.

σεβομένας, acc. pl. fem. part. pres. . σέβομαι
σεβομένη, nom. sing. fem. part. pres. . . id.
σεβομένοις, dat. pl. masc. part. pres. . id.
σεβομένου, gen. sing. masc. part. pres. . id.
σεβομένων, gen. pl. part. pres. . . id.
σέβονται, 3 pers. pl. pres. ind. . . . id.
σειομένη, nom. sing. fem. part. pres. pass. σείω

σειρά], ᾶς, ἡ, (§ 2. tab. B. b) a cord, rope, band; in N.T. a chain, 2 Pe. 2. 4.

σειραῖς,[a] dat. pl. . . . . σειρά
σειροῖς, dat. pl.—A. B. Ln. . . } σειρός
σειραῖς, Rec. Gr. Sch. Tdf. (2 Pe. 2. 4) } σειρός
σειρός], οῦ, ὁ, a pitfall, a den or cave, v.r.
σεισμοί, nom. pl. . . . . . σεισμός
σεισμόν, acc. sing. . . . . id.
σεισμός], οῦ, ὁ, (§ 3. tab. C. a) . . . σείω
σεισμῷ, dat. sing. . . . . σεισμός

σείω], fut. σείσω, aor. 1, ἔσεισα, (§ 13. tab. M) to shake, agitate, He. 12. 26; Re. 6. 13; pass. to quake, Mat. 27. 51; 28. 4; met. to put in commotion, agitate, Mat. 21. 10.

σεισμός, οῦ, ὁ, pr. a shaking, agitation, concussion; an earthquake, Mat. 24. 7, 27. 54, et al.; a tempest, Mat. 8. 24.

Σεκοῦνδος],[b] ου, ὁ, Secundus, pr. name.
Σελεύκεια], ας, ἡ, (§ 2. tab. B. b, and rem. 2) Seleucia, a city of Syria, west of Antioch, on the Orontes.
Σελεύκειαν,[c] acc. . . . . . Σελεύκεια
σελήνη], ης, ἡ, (§ 2. tab. B. a) the moon, Mat. 24. 29; Mar. 13. 24, et al.

σεληνιάζομαι, fut. άσομαι, (§ 26. rem. 1) to be lunatic, Mat. 4. 24; 17. 15. L.G.

σελήνῃ, dat. sing. . . . σελήνη
σελήνης, gen. sing. . . . . . id.
σεληνιάζεται, 3 pers. sing. pres. ind. . σεληνιάζομαι
σεληνιάζομαι], fut. άσομαι . . . σελήνη
σεληνιαζομένους, acc. pl. masc. part. pres. σεληνιάζομαι
Σεμεΐ],[d] ὁ, Semei, pr. name, indecl.
σεμίδαλιν,[e] acc. sing. . . . . σεμίδαλις
σεμίδαλις], εως, ἡ, (§ 5. tab. E. c) the finest flour.
σεμνά, nom. pl. neut. . . . σεμνός
σεμνάς, acc. pl. fem. . . . . . σεμνός
σεμνός], ή, όν . . . . . σέβομαι
σεμνότης], τητος, ἡ . . . id.
σεμνότητα, acc. sing. . . . . σεμνότης
σεμνότητι, dat. sing. . . . . id.
σεμνότητος, gen. sing. . . . . id.
σεμνούς, acc. pl. masc. . . . σεμνός
Σέργιος], ου, ὁ, (§ 3. tab. C. a) Sergius, pr. name.
Σεργίῳ,[f] dat. . . . . . Σέργιος
σεσαλευμένον, acc. sing. neut. part. perf. pass. σαλεύω
σεσαρωμένον, acc. sing. masc. part. perf. pass. (§ 21. tab. U) . . . . σαρόω
σέσηπε,[g] 3 pers. sing. perf. 2, ind. (§ 25. rem. 1) σήπω
σεσιγημένου, gen. sing. neut. part. perf. pass. σιγάω
σεσοφισμένοις, dat. pl. masc. part. perf. pass. σοφίζω
σέσωκε, 3 pers. sing. perf. ind. act. . σώζω
σεσωρευμένα, acc. pl. neut. part. perf. pass. . σωρεύω
σεσωσμένοι, nom. pl. masc. part. perf. pass. σώζω
σέσωσται, 3 pers. sing. perf. ind. pass. (§ 37. rem. 1) . . . . id.
σῇ, dat. sing. fem. . . . . . σός
Σήθ],[h] ὁ, Seth, pr. name, indecl.
Σήμ],[i] ὁ, Sem, Shem, pr. name, indecl.
σημαίνω], fut. ανῶ, aor. 1, ἐσήμηνα and ἐσήμᾱνα, (§ 27. rem. 1. c. e) (σῆμα, a sign, mark) to indicate by a sign, to signal; to indicate, intimate, Jno. 12. 33; to make known, communicate, Ac. 11. 28; Re. 1. 1; to specify, Ac. 25. 27.
σημαίνων, nom. sing. masc. part. pres. . σημαίνω
σημᾶναι, aor. 1, infin. . . . . id.
σημεῖα, nom. and acc. pl. . . . σημεῖον
σημείοις, dat. pl. . . . . . id.
σημεῖον], ου, τό, (§ 3. tab. C. c) (σῆμα) a sign, a mark, token, by which anything is known or distinguished, Mat. 16. 3; 24. 3; 2 Thes. 3. 17; a token, pledge, assurance, Lu. 2. 12; a proof, evidence, convincing token, Mat. 12. 38; 16. 1; Jno. 2. 18; in N.T. a sign, wonder, remarkable event, wonderful appearance, extraordinary phenomenon, 1 Co. 14. 22; Re. 12. 1, 3; 15. 1; a portent, prodigy, Mat. 24. 30; Ac. 2. 19; a wonderful work, miraculous operation, miracle, Mat. 24. 24; Mar. 16, 17, 20; meton. a sign, a signal character, Lu. 2. 34.

σημειόω, ῶ, fut. ώσω, (§ 20. tab. T)

[a] 2 Pe. 2. 4. [b] Ac. 20. 4. [c] Ac. 13. 4. [d] Lu. 3. 26. [e] Re. 18. 13. [f] Ac. 13. 7. [g] Ja. 5. 2. [h] Lu. 3. 38. [i] Lu. 3. 36.

to mark, inscribe marks upon; mid. to mark for one's self, note, 2 Thes. 3. 14.

σημειοῦσθε,[a] 2 pers. pl. pres. imper. mid. . σημειόω

σημειόω, ῶ], fut. ώσω . . . . . σημεῖον

σημείων, gen. pl. . . . . . id.

σήμερον], adv. to-day, this day, Mat. 6. 11, 30; 16. 3; 21. 28; now, at present, He. 13. 8; 2 Co. 3. 15; ἡ σήμερον, sc. ἡμέρα, sometimes expressed, this day, the present day, Ac. 20. 26; ἕως or ἄχρι τῆς σήμερον, until this day, until our times, Mat. 11. 23; 27. 8, et al. freq.

σήν, acc. sing. fem. . . . . . σός

σήπω], to cause to putrify, make rotten; mid. σήπομαι, perf. 2, σέσηπα, (§ 25. rem. 1) to putrify, rot, be corrupted or rotten, Ja. 5. 2.

σαπρός, ά, όν, (§ 7. rem. 1) pr. rotten, putrid; hence, bad, of a bad quality, Mat. 7. 17, 18; 12. 33; Lu. 6. 43; refuse, Mat. 13. 48; met. corrupt, depraved, vicious, foul, impure, Ep. 4. 29.

σηρῐκός], ή, όν, (§ 7. tab. F. a) (σήρ, a silkworm) silk, of silk, silken; τὸ σηρικόν, silken stuff, silk, Re. 18. 12. L.G.

σηρικοῦ,[b] gen. sing. neut. . . . . σηρικός

σής], σεός, and σητός, ὁ, (§ 4. rem. 2. c) a moth, Mat. 6. 19, 20; Lu. 12. 33.

σῆς, gen. sing. fem. . . . . . σός

σητόβρωτα,[c] nom. pl. neut. . . . . σητόβρωτος

σητόβρωτος], ου, ὁ, ἡ, (§ 7. rem. 2) (σής & βιβρώσκω) moth-eaten. LXX.

σθενόω, ῶ], fut. ώσω, aor. 1, ἐσθένωσα, (§ 20. tab. T) (σθένος, strength) to strengthen, impart strength. N.T.

σθενώσαι,[d] 3 pers. sing. aor. 1, optat. . σθενόω

σθενώσει, 3 pers. sing. fut. ind.—Gr. Sch. Tdf. } id.
σθενώσαι, Rec. (1 Pe. 5. 10) . }

σιαγόνα, acc. sing. . . . . . σιαγών

σιᾱγών], όνος, ἡ, (§ 4. rem. 2. e) the jaw-bone, in N.T. the cheek, Mat. 5. 39; Lu. 6. 29.

σιγᾶν, pres. infin. . . . . . σιγάω

σιγάτω, 3 pers. sing. pres. imper. . . id.

σιγάτωσαν, 3 pers. pl. pres. imper. . . id.

σιγάω, ῶ], fut. ήσω . . . . . σιγή

σῑγή], ῆς, ἡ, (§ 2. tab. B. a) silence, Ac. 21. 40; Re. 8. 1

σιγάω, ῶ, fut. ήσω, (§ 18. tab. R) perf. pass. σεσίγημαι, to be silent, keep silence, Lu. 9. 36; 20. 26, et al.; trans. to keep in silence, not to reveal, to conceal; pass. to be concealed, not to be revealed, Ro. 16. 25.

σιγῆς, gen. sing. . . . . . σιγή

σιγῆσαι, aor. 1, infin. . . . . σιγάω

σιγήσῃ, 3 pers. sing. aor. 1, subj.—B. D. Ln. Tdf. . . . . } id.
σιωπήσῃ, Rec. Gr. Sch. (Lu. 18. 39) }

σιδηρᾷ, dat. sing. fem. . . . . σιδήρεος

σιδηρᾶν, acc. sing. fem. . . . . id.

σιδήρεος, οῦς], εα, ᾶ, εον, οῦν . . σίδηρος

σίδηρος], ου, ὁ, (§ 3. tab. C. a) iron.

σιδήρεος, οῦς, εα, ᾶ, εον, οῦν, (§ 7. rem. 5. c) made of iron, Ac. 12. 10; Re. 2. 27; 9. 9; 12. 5; 19. 15.

σιδήρου,[e] gen. sing. . . . . σίδηρος

σιδηροῦς, acc. pl. masc. . . . . σιδήρεος

Σιδών], ῶνος, ἡ, (§ 4. rem. 2. e) Sidon, a celebrated city of Phœnicia

Σιδῶνα, acc. . . . . . . Σιδών

Σιδῶνι, dat. . . . . . . id.

Σιδωνία], ας, ἡ, (sc. χώρα) the country or district of Sidon. v.r.

Σιδωνίας, gen. sing.—Al. Ln. Tdf. } Σιδωνία
Σιδῶνος, Rec. Gr. Sch. (Lu. 4. 26) }

Σιδωνίοις,[f] dat. pl. . . . . Σιδώνιος

Σιδώνιος], ου, ὁ, a Sidonian, an inhabitant of Σιδών, Sidon.

Σιδῶνος, gen. . . . . . Σιδών

σικάριος], ου, ὁ, (§ 3. tab. C. a) (Lat. sicarius, from sica, a dagger, poniard) an assassin, bandit, robber.

σικαρίων,[g] gen. pl. . . . . σικάριος

σίκερα],[h] τό, indecl. (Heb. שֵׁכָר) strong or inebriating drink. LXX.

Σίλᾳ, dat. . . . . . Σίλας

Σίλαν, acc. . . . . . id.

Σίλας], ᾶ, ὁ, (§ 2. rem. 4) Silas, pr. name, in Luke, Ac. 15. 22, et al.; Σιλουανός in Paul, 2 Co. 1. 19, et al.; and Peter, 1 Pe. 5. 12.

Σιλουανός], οῦ, ὁ, (§ 3. tab. C. a) Silvanus, pr. name.

[a] 2 Thes. 3. 14. [b] Re. 18. 12. [c] Ja. 5. 2. [d] 1 Pe. 5. 10. [e] Re. 18. 12. [f] Ac. 12. 20. [g] Ac. 21. 38. [h] Lu. 1. 15.

Σιλουανοῦ, gen. . . . . . Σιλουανός

Σιλωάμ], ὁ, indecl. *Siloam*, a pool or fountain near Jerusalem.

σιμικίνθια,[a] acc. pl. . . . . . σιμικίνθιον

σιμικίνθιον], ου, τό, (§ 3. tab. C. c) (Lat. *semicinctium*, from *semi*, *half*, and *cingo, to gird*) *an apron*.

Σίμων], ωνος, ὁ, (§ 4. rem. 2. e) *Simon*, pr. name.

I. *Simon Peter*, Mat. 4. 18, et al. freq.

II. *Simon*, (*the Cananite*), *Zelotes*, Mat. 10. 4; Ac. 1. 13, et al.

III. *Simon, brother of Jesus*, Mat. 13. 55; Mar. 6. 3.

IV. *Simon, the leper*, Mat. 26. 6; Mar. 14. 3.

V. *Simon, the Pharisee*, Lu. 7. 40, et al.

VI. *Simon of Cyrene*, Mat. 27. 32, et al.

VII. *Simon, father of Judas Iscariot*, Jno. 6. 71, et al.

VIII. *Simon, the sorcerer*, Ac. 8. 9, et al.

IX. *Simon, the tanner, of Joppa*, Ac. 9. 43; 10. 6, et al.

Σίμων, voc. . . . . . . Σίμων

Σίμωνα, acc. . . . . . . id.

Σίμωνι, dat. . . . . . . id.

Σίμωνος, gen. . . . . . . id.

Σινᾶ], τό, indecl. *Mount Sina, Sinai*, in Arabia.

σινάπεως, gen. sing. . . . . σίναπι

σίναπι], εως, τό, (§ 5. rem. 4) *mustard*; in N.T. probably the shrub, not the herb, *Khardal, Salvadora Persica L.*, the fruit of which possesses the pungency of mustard, Mat. 13. 31; 17. 20, et al.

σινδόνα, acc. sing. . . . . . σινδών

σινδόνι, dat. sing. . . . . . id.

σινδών], όνος, ἡ, (§ 4. rem. 2. e) *sindon*; pr. *fine Indian cloth*; *fine linen*; in N.T. *a linen garment, an upper garment or wrapper of fine linen*, worn in summer by night, and used to envelope dead bodies, Mat. 27. 59; Mar. 14. 51, 52; 15. 46; Lu. 23. 53.

σινιάζω], fut. άσω, (§ 26. rem. 1) (σινίον, *a sieve*) *to sift*; met. *to sift* by trials and temptation. L.G.

σινιάσαι,[b] aor. 1, infin. . . . . . σινιάζω

σιτευτόν, acc. sing. masc. . . . . . σιτευτός

σιτευτός], ή, όν . . . . . . σῖτος

σιτία, acc. pl.—Al. Ln. Tdf. } σιτίον

σῖτα, Rec. Gr. Sch. (Ac. 7. 12) } σιτίον

σιτίον], ου, τό, v.r. . . . . . σῖτος

σιτιστά,[c] nom. pl. neut. . . . . σιτιστός

σιτιστός], ή, όν . . . . . . σῖτος

σῖτα, acc. pl. (§ 6. rem. 7) . . . . id.

σιτομέτριον],[d] ου, τό, (§ 3. tab. C. c) (σῖτος & μετρέω) *a certain measure of grain* distributed for food at set times to the slaves of a family, *a ration*. L.G.

σῖτον, acc. sing. . . . . . . σῖτος

σῖτος], ου, ὁ.—B. D. Ln. Tdf.

σῖτον, Rec. Gr. Sch. (Mar. 4. 28), *corn, grain, wheat*, Mat. 3. 12; 13. 25, 29, 30, Mar. 4. 28, et al.; pl. σῖτα, *bread, food*, Ac. 7. 12.

σιτευτός, ή, όν, (§ 7. tab. F. a) (σιτεύω, *to feed or fatten*, σῖτος) *fed, fatted*, Lu. 15. 23, 27, 30.

σιτίον, ου, τό, (§ 3. tab. C. c) *provision of corn, food*, v.r. Ac. 7. 12.

σιτιστός, ή, όν, (σιτίζω, *to fatten*, from σῖτος) *fatted, a fatling*, Mat. 22. 4.

σίτου, gen. sing. . . . . . . σῖτος

Σιχάρ,[e] ἡ, indecl. *Sichar*, a city of Samaria.

Σιών, ὁ, or τό, indecl. *Mount Sion*.

σιώπα, 2 pers. sing. pres. imper. . . σιωπάω

σιωπάω, ῶ], fut. ήσω, aor. 1, ἐσιώπησα, (§ 18. tab. R) *to be silent, keep silence, hold one's peace*, Mat. 20. 31; 26. 63, et al.; σιωπῶν, *silent, dumb*, Lu. 1. 20; met. *to be silent, still, hushed, calm*, as the sea, Mar. 4. 39.

σιωπήσῃ, 3 pers. sing. aor. 1, subj. . . σιωπάω

σιωπήσῃς, 2 pers. sing. aor. 1, subj. . . id.

σιωπήσωσι, 3 pers. pl. aor. 1, subj. . id.

σιωπῶν, nom. sing. masc. part. pres. . . id.

σκάνδαλα, acc. pl. . . . . . σκάνδαλον

σκανδαλίζει, 3 pers. sing. pres. ind. act. . σκανδαλίζω

σκανδαλίζεται, 3 pers. sing. pres. ind. pass. id.

σκανδαλίζῃ, 3 pers. sing. pres. subj. act. . id.

σκανδαλίζονται, 3 pers. pl. pres. ind. pass. . id.

σκανδαλίζω], fut. ίσω . . . . . σκάνδαλον

σκανδαλίσῃ, 3 pers. sing. aor. 1, subj. act. . σκανδαλίζω

σκανδαλισθῇ, 3 pers. sing. aor. 1, subj. pass. id.

σκανδαλισθήσεσθε, 2 pers. pl. fut. ind. pass. id.

a Ac. 19. 12. b Lu. 22. 31. c Mat. 22. 4. d Lu. 12. 42. e Jno. 4. 5.

σκανδαλισθήσομαι, 1 pers. sing. fut. ind. pass. σκανδαλίζω
σκανδαλισθήσονται, 3 pers. pl. fut. ind. pass. id.
σκανδαλισθῆτε, 2 pers. pl. aor. 1, subj. pass. id.
σκανδαλίσω, 1 pers. sing. aor. 1, subj. act. id.
σκανδαλίσωμεν, 1 pers. pl. aor. 1, subj. act. id.

σκάνδἄλον], ου, τό, (§ 3. tab. C. c) (a later equivalent to σκανδάληθρον) pr. *a trap-spring; also genr. a stumbling-block, anything against which one stumbles, an impediment;* met. *a cause of ruin, destruction, misery,* etc., Ro. 9. 33; 11. 9; *a cause or occasion of sinning,* Mat. 18. 7, ter; Lu. 17. 1; *scandal, offence, cause of indignation,* 1 Co. 1. 23; Gal. 5. 11.

σκανδαλίζω, fut. ίσω, aor. 1, ἐσκανδάλισα, (§ 26. rem. 1) pr. *to cause to stumble;* met. *to offend, vex,* Mat. 17. 27; *to offend, shock, excite feelings of repugnance,* Jno. 6. 61; 1 Co. 8. 13; pass. *to be offended, shocked, pained,* Mat. 15. 12; Ro. 14. 21; 2 Co. 11. 29; σκανδαλίζεσθαι ἔν τινι, *to be affected with scruples or repugnance towards any one* as respects his claims or pretensions, Mat. 11. 6; 13. 57, et al.; met. *to cause to stumble* morally, *to cause to falter or err,* Mat. 5. 29; 18. 6, et al.; pass. *to falter, fall away,* Mat. 13. 21, et al. LXX.

σκανδάλου, gen. sing. σκάνδαλον
σκανδάλων, gen. pl. id.
σκάπτειν, pres. infin. σκάπτω

σκάπτω], fut. ψω, aor. 1, ἔσκαψα, (§ 23 rem. 1. a, and rem. 2) *to dig, excavate,* Lu. 6. 48; 13. 8; 16. 3.

σκάφη, ης, ἡ, (§ 2. tab. B. a) pr. *anything excavated or hollowed; a boat, skiff,* Ac. 27. 16, 30, 32.

σκάφη], ης, ἡ σκάπτω
σκάφην, acc. sing. σκάφη
σκάφης, gen. sing. id.
σκάψω, 1 pers. sing. aor. 1, subj. σκάπτω
σκέλη, nom. and acc. pl. σκέλος

σκέλος], εος, τό, pl. τὰ σκέλη, (§ 5. tab. E. b) *the leg,* Jno. 19. 31, 32, 33.

σκέπασμα], ατος, τό, (§ 4. tab. D. c) (σκεπάζω, *to cover*) *covering; clothing, raiment,* 1 Ti. 6. 8.

σκεπάσματα,[a] acc. pl. σκέπασμα
Σκευᾶ,[b] gen. Σκευᾶς
Σκευᾶς], ᾶ, ὁ, (§ 2. rem. 4) *Sceva,* pr. name.
σκεύει, dat. sing. σκεῦος
σκεύεσι, dat. pl. id.
σκεύη, nom. and acc. pl. id.
σκευή], ῆς, ἡ id.
σκευήν,[c] acc. sing. σκευή

σκεῦος, εος, τό, (§ 5. tab. E. b) *a vessel, utensil* for containing anything, Mar. 11. 16; Lu. 8. 16; Ro. 9. 21; *any utensil, instrument;* σκεύη, *household stuff, furniture, goods,* etc., Mat. 12. 29; Mar. 3. 27, et al.; *the mast of a ship,* or, *the sail,* Ac. 27. 17; met. *an instrument, means, organ, minister,* Ac. 9. 15; σκεύη ὀργῆς and σκεύη ἐλέους, *vessels of wrath,* or, *of mercy, persons visited by punishment,* or, *the divine favour,* Ro. 9. 22, 23, *the vessel or frame* of the human individual, 1 Thes. 4. 4 1 Pe. 3. 7.

σκευή, ῆς, ἡ, (§ 2. tab. B. a) *apparatus; tackle,* Ac. 27. 19.

σκηναῖς, dat. pl. σκηνή
σκηνάς, acc. pl. id.
σκήνει, dat. sing. σκῆνος

σκηνή], ῆς, ἡ, (§ 2. tab. B. a) *a tent, tabernacle;* genr. *any temporary dwelling; a tent, booth,* Mat. 17. 4; He. 11. 9; *the tabernacle* of the covenant, He. 8. 5; 9. 1, 21; 13. 10; allegor. *the* celestial or true *tabernacle,* He. 8. 2; 9. 11; *a division or compartment of the tabernacle,* He. 9. 2, 3, 6; a small portable *tent or shrine,* Ac. 7. 43; *an abode or seat* of a lineage, Ac. 15. 16; *a mansion, habitation, abode, dwelling,* Lu. 16. 9; Re. 13. 6.

σκῆνος, εος, τό, (§ 5. tab. E. b) (equivalent to σκηνή) *a tent, tabernacle;* met. *the* corporeal *tabernacle,* 2 Co. 5. 1, 4.

σκηνόω, ῶ, fut. ώσω, aor. 1, ἐσκήνωσα, (§ 20. tab. T) *to pitch tent, encamp; to tabernacle, dwell in a tent; to dwell, have one's abode,* Jno. 1. 14; Re. 7. 15; 12. 12; 13. 6; 21. 3.

σκήνωμα, ατος, τό, (§ 4. tab. D. c) *a habitation, abode, dwelling,* Ac. 7. 46;

[a] 1 Ti. 6. 8. [b] Ac. 19. 14. [c] Ac. 27. 19.

the corporeal *tabernacle* of the soul, 2 Pe. 1. 13, 14.

σκηνῇ, dat. sing. . . . . . . σκηνή

σκηνήν, acc. sing. . . . . . id.

σκηνῆς, gen. sing. . . . . . id.

σκηνοπηγία],[a] ας, ἡ, (§ 2. tab. B. b, and rem. 2) (σκῆνος & πήγνυμι) pr. *a pitching of tents or booths*; hence, *the feast of tabernacles or booths*, instituted in memory of the forty years' wandering of the Israelites in the desert, and as a season of gratitude for the ingathering of harvest, celebrated during eight days, commencing on the 15th of Tisri.

σκηνοποιοί,[b] nom. pl. . . . . σκηνοποιός

σκηνοποιός], οῦ, ὁ, (σκηνή & ποιέω) *a tent-maker*. N.T.

σκῆνος], εος, τό . . . . . . σκηνή

σκηνοῦντας, acc. pl. masc. part. pres. . σκηνόω

σκηνοῦντες, nom. pl. masc. part. pres. . . id.

σκήνους, gen. sing. . . . . . σκῆνος

σκηνόω, ῶ], fut. ώσω . . . . . σκηνή

σκήνωμα], ατος, τό . . . . . id.

σκηνώματι, dat. sing. . . . . σκήνωμα

σκηνώματος, gen. sing. . . . . id.

σκηνώσει, 3 pers. sing. fut. ind. . . . σκηνόω

σκιά], ᾶς, ἡ, (§ 2. tab. B. b, and rem. 2) *a shade, shadow*, Mar. 4. 32; Ac. 5. 15; met. *a shadow, a shadowing forth, adumbration*, in distinction from ἡ εἰκών, the perfect image or delineation, and τὸ σῶμα, the reality, Col. 2. 17; He. 8. 5; 10. 1; *gloom*; σκιὰ θανάτου, *death-shade, the thickest darkness*, Mat. 4. 16; Lu. 1. 79.

σκιᾷ, dat. sing. . . . . . σκιά

σκιάν, acc. sing. . . . . . . id.

σκιρτάω, ῶ], fut. ήσω, aor. 1, ἐσκίρτησα, (§ 18. tab. R) *to leap*, Lu. 1. 41, 44; *to leap, skip, bound* for joy, Lu. 6. 23.

σκιρτήσατε, 2 pers. pl. aor. 1, imper. . σκιρτάω

σκληροκαρδία], ας, ἡ, (§ 2. tab. B. b, and rem. 2) (σκληρός & καρδία) *hardness of heart, obduracy, obstinacy, perverseness*, Mat. 19. 8; Mar. 10. 5; 16. 14. LXX.

σκληροκαρδίαν, acc. sing. . . . σκληροκαρδία

σκληρόν, nom. sing. neut. . . . σκληρός

σκληρός], ά, όν, (§ 7. rem. 1) *dry, hard*; met. *harsh, severe, stern*, Mat. 25. 24; *vehement, violent, fierce*, Ja. 3. 4; *grievous, painful*, Ac 9. 5; 26. 14; *grating* to the mind, *repulsive, offensive*, Jno. 6. 60; *stubborn, contumacious*, Jude 15.

σκληρότης, τητος, ἡ, (§ 4. rem. 2. c) *hardness*; met. σκληρότης τῆς καρδίας, *hardness of heart, obduracy, obstinacy, perverseness*, Ro. 2. 5.

σκληρύνω, fut. υνῶ, aor. 1, ἐσκλήρυνα, (§ 27. rem. 1. a. f) *to harden*; met. *to harden* morally, *to make stubborn*, He. 3. 8, 15; 4. 7; as a negation of ἐλεεῖν, *to leave to stubbornness and contumacy*, Ro. 9. 18; mid. and pass. *to put on a stubborn frame, become obdurate*, Ac. 19. 9; He. 3. 13.

σκληρότης], τητος, ἡ . . . . σκληρός

σκληρότητα,[c] acc. sing. . . . σκληρότης

σκληροτράχηλοι,[d] voc. pl. masc. . σκληροτράχηλος

σκληροτράχηλος], ου, ὁ, ἡ, (§ 7. rem. 2) (σκληρός & τράχηλος) *stiff-necked, obstinate, refractory*. LXX.

σκληρύνει, 3 pers. sing. pres. ind. act. σκληρύνω

σκληρύνητε, 2 pers. pl. pres. subj. act. . id.

σκληρυνθῇ, 3 pers. sing. aor. 1, subj. pass. id.

σκληρύνω], fut. υνῶ . . . . . σκληρός

σκληρῶν, gen. pl. . . . . . id.

σκολιά, nom. pl. neut. . . . . . σκολιός

σκολιᾶς, gen. sing. fem. . . . . id.

σκολιοῖς, dat. pl. masc. . . . . id.

σκολιός], ά, όν, (§ 7. rem. 1) *crooked, tortuous*, Lu. 3. 5; met. *perverse, wicked*, Ac. 2. 40; Phi. 2. 15; *crooked, peevish, morose*, 1 Pe. 2. 18.

σκόλοψ],[e] οπος, ὁ, (§ 4. rem. 2. a) *anything pointed*; met. *a thorn, a plague*, 2 Co. 12. 7.

σκόπει, 2 pers. sing. pres. imper. . . σκοπέω

σκοπεῖν, pres. infin. . . . . . id.

σκοπεῖτε, 2 pers. pl. pres. imper. . . id.

σκοπέω, ῶ], fut. ήσω . . . . . σκοπός

σκοπόν,[f] acc. sing. . . . . . . id.

σκοπός], οῦ, ὁ, (§ 3. tab. C. a) (σκέπτομαι, *to look around, survey*) *a watcher*; also, *a distant object on which the eye is kept fixed*; *a mark, goal*, Phi. 3. 14.

σκοπέω, ῶ, fut. ήσω, (§ 16. tab. P) *to*

[a] Jno. 7. 2. [b] Ac. 18. 3. [c] Ro. 2. 5. [d] Ac. 7. 51. [e] 2 Co. 12. 7. [f] Phi. 3. 14.

view attentively, watch, reconnoitre; to see, observe, take care, beware, Lu. 11. 35; Gal. 6. 1; *to regard, have respect to,* 2 Co. 4. 18; Phi. 2. 4 *to mark, note,* Ro. 16. 17; Phi. 3. 17.

σκοποῦντες, nom. pl. masc. part. pres.—Gr. Sch. Tdf. } σκοπέω
σκοπεῖτε, Rec. (Phi. 2. 4) }

σκοπούντων, gen. pl. masc. part. pres. — id.

σκοπῶν, nom. sing. masc. part. pres. — id.

σκορπίζει, 3 pers. sing. pres. ind. act. — σκορπίζω

σκορπίζω], fut. ίσω, aor. 1, ἐσκόρπισα, (§ 26. rem. 1) *to disperse, scatter,* Jno. 10. 12; 16. 32; *to dissipate, waste,* Mat. 12. 30; Lu. 11. 23; *to scatter abroad* one's gifts, *give liberally,* 2 Co. 9. 9.

σκορπίοι, nom. pl. — σκορπίος

σκορπίοις, dat. pl. — id.

σκορπίον, acc. sing. — id.

σκορπίος], ου, ὁ, (§ 3. tab. C. a) *a scorpion, scorpio Afer* of Linn., a large insect, sometimes several inches in length, shaped somewhat like a crab, and furnished with a tail terminating in a sting, whence it emits a dangerous poison, Lu. 10. 19; 11. 12, et al.

σκορπιου, gen. sing. — σκορπίος

σκορπισθῆτε, 2 pers. pl. aor. 1, subj. pass. — σκορπίζω

σκορπίων, gen. pl. — σκορπίος

σκότει, dat. sing. — σκότος

σκοτεινόν, nom. and acc. sing. neut. — σκοτεινός

σκοτεινός], ή, όν — σκότος

σκοτία], ας, ἡ — id.

σκοτίᾳ, dat. sing. — σκοτία

σκοτίας, gen. sing. — id.

σκοτίζω], fut. ίσω — σκότος

σκοτισθῇ, 3 pers. sing. aor. 1, subj. pass. — σκοτίζω

σκοτισθήσεται, 3 pers. sing. fut. ind. pass. — id.

σκοτισθήτωσαν, 3 pers. pl. aor. 1, imper. pass. — id.

σκότος], εος, τό, (§ 5. tab. E. b) but, according to ordinary Greek usage, ου, ὁ, He. 12. 18, *darkness,* Mat. 27. 45; Ac. 2. 20; *gloom* of punishment and misery, Mat. 8. 12; 2 Pe. 2. 17; met. moral or spiritual *darkness,* Mat. 4. 16; Jno. 3. 19; Ep. 5. 11; *a realm of* moral *darkness,* Ep. 5. 8; 6. 12.

σκοτεινός, ή, όν, (§ 7. tab. F. a) *dark, darkling* Mat. 6. 23; Lu. 11. 34, 36.

σκοτία, ας, ἡ, (§ 2. tab. B. b, and rem. 2) *darkness,* Jno. 6. 17; 20. 1; *privacy,* Mat. 10. 27; Lu. 12. 3; met. moral or spiritual *darkness,* Jno. 1. 5, bis; 8. 12; 12. 35, 46, et al.

σκοτίζω, fut. ίσω, (§ 26. rem. 1) *to darken, shroud in darkness;* pass. *to be darkened, obscured,* Mat. 24. 29; Lu. 23. 45; met. *to be shrouded in* moral *darkness, to be benighted,* Ro. 1. 21, et al. L.G.

σκοτόω, ῶ, fut. ώσω, (§ 20. tab. T) *to darken, shroud in darkness,* Re. 16. 10.

σκοτους, gen. sing. — σκότος

σκοτόω, ῶ], fut. ώσω — id.

σκότῳ,[a] dat. sing. (masc.) — id.

σκύβαλα,[b] acc. pl. — σκύβαλον

σκύβᾰλον], ου, τό, (§ 3. tab. C. c) *offal, dung, sweepings, refuse.*

Σκύθης, ου, ὁ, (§ 2. tab. B. c) *a Scythian, a native of Scythia,* the modern Mongolia and Tartary.

σκυθρωποί, nom. pl. masc. — σκυθρωπός

σκυθρωπός], οῦ, ὁ, ἡ, and ή, όν, (σκυθρός, *stern, gloomy,* and ὤψ) *of a stern, morose, sour, gloomy, or dejected countenance,* Mat. 6. 16; Lu. 24. 17.

σκῦλα,[c] acc. pl. — σκῦλον

σκύλλε, 2 pers. sing. pres. imper. act. — σκύλλω

σκύλλεις, 2 pers. sing. pres. ind. act. — id.

σκύλλου, 2 pers. sing. pres. imper. pass. — id.

σκύλλω], fut. υλῶ, perf. pass. ἔσκυλμαι, (§ 27. rem. 1. b, and rem. 3) *to flay, lacerate;* met. *to vex, trouble, annoy,* Mar. 5. 35; Lu. 7. 6; 8. 49; pass. met. ἐσκυλμένοι, *jaded, in sorry plight,* v.r. Mat. 9. 36.

σκῦλον, ου, τό, (§ 3. tab. C. c) *spoils stripped off an enemy;* σκῦλα, *spoil, plunder, booty,* Lu. 11. 22.

σκῦλον], ου, τό — σκύλλω

σκωληκόβρωτος,[d] ου, ὁ, ἡ, (σκώληξ & βιβρώσκω) *eaten of worms, consumed by worms.*

σκώληξ], ηκος, ὁ, (§ 4. rem. 2. b) *a worm;* met. *gnawing anguish,* Mar. 9. 44, 46, 48.

σμαράγδῐνος], η, ον, (§ 7. tab. F. a) — σμάραγδος

σμαραγδίνῳ,[e] dat. sing. masc. — σμαράγδινος

[a] He. 12. 18. [b] Phi. 3. 8. [c] Lu. 11. 22. [d] Ac. 12. 23. [e] Re. 4. 3.

σμάραγδος],[a] ου, ὁ, (§ 3. tab. C. a) *smaragdus, the emerald*, a gem of a pure green colour; but under this name the ancients probably comprised all stones of a fine green colour.

σμαράγδινος, ίνη, ινον, *of smaragdus or emerald*, Re. 4. 3. N.T.

Σμύρνα], ης, ἡ, (§ 2. rem. 3) *Smyrna*, a maritime city of Ionia, in Asia Minor.

Σμυρναῖος, ου, ὁ, *a Smyrnean, an inhabitant of Smyrna*, Re. 1. 11; 2. 8.

σμύρνα], ης, ἡ, (Heb. מוֹר) *myrrh*, an aromatic bitter resin, or gum, issuing by incision, and sometimes spontaneously, from the trunk and larger branches of a small thorny tree growing in Egypt, Arabia, and Abyssinia, much used by the ancients in unguents, Mat. 2. 11; Jno. 19. 39.

σμυρνίζω, fut. ίσω, (§ 26. rem. 1) *to mingle or impregnate with myrrh*, Mar. 15. 23. N.T.

Σμυρναῖος], ου, ὁ . . . . Σμύρνα
Σμυρναίων,[b] gen. pl. . . . . Σμυρναῖος
Σμύρναν, acc. . . . . . Σμύρνα
σμύρναν, acc. sing. . . . . . σμύρνα
Σμύρνῃ, dat.—Gr. Sch. Tdf. τῆς ἐν Σμύρνῃ ἐκκλησίας . . . . } τῆς ἐκκλησίας Σμυρναίων, Rec. (Re. 2. 8) Σμύρνα
σμύρνης, gen. sing. . . . . σμύρνα
σμυρνίζω], fut. ίσω . . . . . id.
Σόδομα], ων, τά, (§ 3. tab. C. c) *Sodom*, one of the four cities of the vale of Siddim, now covered by the Dead sea.
Σοδόμοις, dat. . . . . . Σόδομα
Σοδόμων, gen. . . . . . id.
σοί, dat. sing. (§ 11. tab. K. b) . . . σύ
σοι, (enclitic) dat. sing. . . . . id.
σοί, nom. pl. masc. . . . . . σός
Σολομών], ῶντος, ὁ, (§ 4. rem. 2. d) *Solomon*, pr. name.
Σολομῶντα, acc.—Rec. . . . } Σολομῶνα, Gr. Sch. Tdf. (passim) . } Σολομών
Σολομῶντος, gen.—Rec. . . . } Σολομῶνος, Gr. Sch. Tdf. (passim) } id.
σόν, nom. and acc. sing. neut. . . . σός

σορός], οῦ, ἡ, (§ 3. tab. C. b) *a coffer; an urn for receiving the ashes of the dead; a coffin*; in N.T. *a bier*, Lu. 7. 14.

σοροῦ,[c] gen. sing. . . . . . σορός

σός], σή, σόν, (§ 11. rem. 4) . . . σύ
σοῦ, gen. sing. . . . . . id.
σου, (enclitic) dat. sing. . . . . id.
σουδάρια, acc. pl. . . . . . σουδάριον
σουδάριον], ου, τό, (§ 3. tab. C. c) (Lat. *sudarium*) *a handkerchief, napkin*, etc., Lu. 19. 20; Jno. 11. 44, et al.
σουδαρίῳ, dat. sing. . . . . σουδάριον
σούς, acc. pl. masc. . . . . σός
Σουσάννα],[d] ης, ἡ, (§ 2. rem. 3) *Susanna*, pr. name.
σοφία], ας, ἡ . . . . . . σοφός
σοφίᾳ, dat. sing. . . . . . σοφία
σοφίαν, acc. sing. . . . . . id.
σοφίας, gen. sing. . . . . . id.
σοφίζω], fut. ίσω . . . . . σοφός
σοφίσαι, aor. 1, infin. act. . . . σοφίζω
σοφοί, nom. pl. masc. . . . . σοφός
σοφοῖς, dat. pl. masc. . . . . id.

σοφός], ή, όν, (§ 7. tab. F. a) *wise* generally, 1 Co. 1. 25; *shrewd, sagacious, clever*, Ro. 16. 19; 1 Co. 3. 10; 6. 5; *learned, intelligent*, Mat. 11. 25; Ro. 1. 14, 22; 1 Co. 1. 19, 20, 26, 27; 3. 18; in N.T. divinely *instructed*, Mat. 23. 34; *furnished with* Christian *wisdom*, spiritually *enlightened* Ja. 3. 13; *all-wise*, Ro. 16. 27; 1 Ti. 1. 17; Jude 25.

σοφία, ας, ἡ, (§ 2. tab. B. b, and rem. 2) *wisdom* in general, *knowledge*, Mat. 12. 42; Lu. 2. 40, 52; 11. 31; Ac. 7. 10; *ability*, Lu. 21. 15; Ac. 6. 3, 10; practical *wisdom, prudence*, Col. 4. 5; *learning, science*, Mat. 13. 54; Mar. 6. 2; Ac. 7. 22; scientific *skill*, 1 Co. 1. 17; 2. 1; professed *wisdom*, human *philosophy*, 1 Co. 1. 19, 20, 22; 2. 4, 5, 6, et al.; superior *knowledge and enlightenment*, Col. 2. 23; in N.T. divine *wisdom*, Ro. 11. 33; Ep. 3. 10; Col. 2. 3; revealed *wisdom*, Mat. 11. 19; Lu. 11. 49; 1 Co. 1. 24, 30; 2. 7; Christian *enlightenment*, 1 Co. 12. 8; Ep. 1. 8, 17; Col. 1. 9, 28; 3. 16; Ja. 1. 5; 3. 13.

σοφίζω, fut. ίσω, aor. 1, ἐσόφισα, (§ 26. rem. 1) *to make wise, enlighten*, 2 Ti. 3. 15; mid. *to invent skilfully, devise artfully*, pass. 2 Pe. 1. 16.

---

[a] Re. 21. 19. [b] Re. 2. 8. [c] Lu. 7. 14. [d] Lu. 8. 3.

σοφούς, acc. pl. masc. . . . . σοφός
σοφῷ, dat. sing. masc. . . . . id.
σοφῶν, gen. pl. . . . . . id.
σοφώτερον, nom. s. neut. compar. (§ 8. rem. 1. 4) id.
Σπανία], ας, ἡ, (§ 2. tab. B. b, and rem. 2) *Spain.*
Σπανίαν, acc. . . . . . Σπανία
σπαράξαν, nom. sing. neut. part. aor. 1 . σπαράσσω
σπαράξας, nom. sing. masc. part. aor. 1—B. C. D. Ln. . . . } id.
σπαράξαν, Rec. Gr. Sch. Tdf. (Mar. 9. 26)
σπαράσσει, 3 pers. sing. pres. ind. . . id.
σπαράσσω], fut. ξω . . . . . σπάω
σπαργανόω, ῶ], fut. ώσω, (§ 20. tab. T) (σπάργανον, *a bandage; swaddling-cloth*) *to swathe, wrap in swaddling-cloths*, Lu. 2. 7, 12.
σπαρείς, nom. sing. masc. part. aor. 2, pass. (§ 27. rem. 4. a. b) . . σπείρω
σπαρέντες, nom. pl. masc. part. aor. 2, pass. . id.
σπαρῇ, 3 pers. sing. aor. 2, subj. pass. . id.
σπασάμενος, nom. sing. masc. part. aor. 1, mid. σπάω
σπαταλάω, ῶ], fut. ήσω, (§ 18. tab. R) (σπατάλη, *riot, luxury*) *to live luxuriously, voluptuously, wantonly*, 1 Ti. 5. 6; Ja. 5. 5. L.G.
σπαταλῶσα, nom. sing. fem. part. pres. . σπαταλάω

σπάω, ῶ],

fut. άσω, (§ 22. rem. 2) perf. ἔσπακα, aor. 1, mid. ἐσπασάμην, *to draw, pull; to draw* a sword, Mar. 14. 47; Ac. 16. 27.

σπαράσσω, or ττω, fut. ξω, aor. 1, ἐσπάραξα, (§ 26. rem. 3) pr. *to tear, lacerate;* by impl. *to agitate greatly, convulse, distort by convulsions*, Mar. 1. 26; 9. 20, 26; Lu. 9. 39.

σπεῖρα],

ας, or ης, ἡ, (§ 2. rem. 2) *anything twisted or wreathed, a cord, coil, band,* etc.; *a band of soldiers, company, troop;* used for a Roman *maniple*, or, *cohort*, Mat. 27. 27; Ac. 10. 1; *the* temple *guard*, Jno. 18. 3, 12.

σπεῖραι, aor. 1, infin. act. . . . σπείρω
σπεῖραν, acc. sing. . . . . . σπεῖρα
σπείραντι, dat. sing. masc. part. aor. 1.—B. Ln. Tdf. . . . . } σπείρω
σπείροντι, Rec. Gr. Sch. (Mat. 13. 24)
σπείραντος, gen. sing. masc. part. aor. 1—B. Ln. . . . . } σπείρω
σπείροντος, R. Gr. Sch. Tdf. (Mat. 13. 18)
σπείρας, nom. sing. masc. part. aor. 1, act. . id.
σπείρει, 3 pers. sing. pres. ind. act. . . id.
σπείρειν, pres. infin. act. . . . . id.
σπείρεις, 2 pers. sing. pres. ind. act. . id.
σπείρεται, 3 pers. sing. pres. ind. pass. . id.
σπείρῃ, 3 pers. sing. pres. subj. act. . id.
σπείρης, gen. sing. (§ 2. rem. 2) . . σπεῖρα
σπειρόμενοι, nom. pl. masc. part. pres. pass. σπείρω
σπείροντι, dat. sing. masc. part. pres. act. id.
σπείροντος, gen. sing. masc. part. pres. act. id.
σπείρουσι, 3 pers. pl. pres. ind. act. . id.

σπείρω],

fut. σπερῶ, aor. 1, ἔσπειρα, (§ 27. rem. 1. c. d) perf. 2. ἔσπορα, aor. 2, pass. ἐσπάρην, (§ 27. rem. 5, and 4. a) *to sow* seed, Mat. 6. 26; 13. 3, 4, 18, 24, 25, 27, 31, 37, 39; in N.T. used with variety of metaphors, Mat. 13. 19; 25. 24; 1 Co. 9. 11; 2 Co. 9. 6; Gal. 6. 7, et al.

σπέρμα, ατος, τό, (§ 4. tab. D. c) *seed*, Mat. 13. 24, 27, 37, 38; *semen virile*, He. 11. 11; *offspring, progeny, posterity*, Mat. 22. 24, 25; Jno. 7. 42; *a seed* of future generations, Ro. 9. 29; in N.T. met. *a seed or principle* of spiritual life, 1 Jno. 3. 9.

σπορά, ᾶς, ἡ, (§ 2. tab. B. b) *a sowing; seed sown;* met. generative *seed, generation*, 1 Pe. 1. 23.

σπόριμος, ου, ὁ, ἡ, (§ 7. rem. 2) *sown, fit to be sown;* in N.T. τὰ σπόριμα, *fields which are sown, fields of grain, cornfields*, Mat. 12. 1; Mar. 2. 23; Lu. 6. 1.

σπόρος, ου, ὁ, (§ 3. tab. C. a) *a sowing;* in N.T. *seed, that which is sown*, Mar. 4. 26, 27; Lu. 8. 5, 11; met. *the seed sown* in almsgiving, 2 Co. 9. 10.

σπείρων, nom. sing. masc. part. pres. act. . σπείρω
σπεκουλάτωρ], ορος, ὁ, (§ 4. rem. 2. f) (Lat. *speculator*) *a sentinel, life-guardsman*, a kind of soldiers who formed the body-guard of princes, etc., one of whose duties was to put criminals to death, Mar. 6. 27.
σπεκουλάτωρα,[a] acc. sing. . . . σπεκουλάτωρ
σπένδομαι, 1 pers. sing. pres. ind. pass. . σπένδω

[a] Mar. 6. 27.

σπένδω], fut. σπείσω, (§ 37. rem. 1) *to pour out a libation or drink-offering*; in N.T. mid. *to make a libation of one's self* by expending energy and life in the service of the Gospel, Phi. 2. 17; pass. *to be in the act of being sacrificed* in the cause of the Gospel, 2 Ti. 4. 6.

σπέρμα], ατος, τό . . . . σπείρω

σπέρμασι, dat. pl. . . . . . σπέρμα

σπέρματι, dat. sing. . . . . id.

σπέρματος, gen. sing. . . . . id.

σπερμάτων, gen. pl. . . . . id.

σπερμολόγος],[a] ου, ὁ, (§ 3. tab. C. a) (σπέρμα & λέγω, *to pick*) pr. *seed-picking, one who picks up and retails scraps of information; a babbler*, Ac. 17. 18.

σπεύδοντας, acc. pl. masc. part. pres. . . σπεύδω

σπεύδω], fut. σπεύσω, aor. 1, ἔσπευσα, (§ 23. rem. 1. c, and rem. 2) trans. *to urge on, impel, quicken; to quicken* in idea, *to be eager for the arrival of*, 2 Pe. 3. 12; intrans. *to hasten, make haste*, Ac. 20. 16; 22. 18; the part. has the force of an adverb, *quickly, hastily*, Lu. 2. 16; 19. 5, 6.

σπουδή, ῆς, ἡ, (§ 2. tab. B. a) *haste*; μετὰ σπουδῆς, *with haste, hastily, quickly*, Mar. 6. 25; Lu. 1. 39; *earnestness, earnest application, diligence*, Ro. 12. 8, 11; 2 Co. 7. 11, 12, et al.

σπουδάζω, fut. άσω & άσομαι, (§ 26. rem. 1) perf. ἐσπούδακα, aor. 1, ἐσπούδασα, *to hasten; to be in earnest about, be bent upon*, Gal. 2. 10; *to endeavour earnestly, strive*, Ep. 4. 3, et al.

σπουδαῖος, α, ον, (§ 7. rem. 1) *earnest, eager, forward*, 2 Co. 8. 17, 22; comparat. neut. σπουδαιότερον, as an adv. *earnestly, sedulously*, 2 Ti. 1. 17.

σπουδαίως, adv. *earnestly, eagerly, diligently*, Lu. 7. 4; Tit. 3. 13; compar. σπουδαιοτέρως, *more earnestly*, Phi. 2. 28.

σπεύσαντες, nom. pl. masc. part. aor. 1 . σπεύδω

σπεύσας, nom. sing. masc. part. aor. 1 . id.

σπεῦσον, 2 pers. sing. aor. 1, imper. . id.

σπήλαια, acc. pl. . . . . . σπήλαιον

σπηλαίοις, dat. pl. . . . . id.

σπήλαιον], ου, τό, (§ 3. tab. C. c) (σπέος, *a cavern*) *a cave, cavern den*, Mat. 21. 13, et al

σπιλάδες,[b] nom. pl. . . . . σπιλάς

σπιλάς], άδος, (ᾰ) ἡ, (§ 4. rem. 2. c) *a sharply-cleft portion of rock*; in N.T. *a flaw, stigma*, Jude 12.

σπῖλοι, nom. pl. . . . . σπῖλος

σπῖλον, acc. sing. . . . . . id.

σπῖλος, and **σπίλος**], ου, ὁ, (§ 3. tab. C. a) *a spot, stain, blot; a* moral *blot*, Ep. 5. 27; 2 Pe. 2. 13. L.G.

σπιλόω, ῶ, fut. ώσω, (§ 20. tab. T) *to spot, soil; to contaminate, defile*, Ja. 3. 6; Jude 23. L.G.

σπιλοῦσα, nom. sing. fem. part. pres. act. σπιλόω

σπιλόω, ῶ], fut. ώσω . . . . σπῖλος

σπλάγχνα, nom. and acc. pl. . . σπλάγχνον

σπλαγχνίζομαι], fut. ίσομαι . . . id.

σπλαγχνισθείς, nom. s. masc. part. aor. 1 σπλαγχνίζομαι

σπλάγχνοις, dat. pl. . . . σπλάγχνον

σπλάγχνον], ου, τό, (§ 3. tab. C. c) but usually, and in N.T. only in pl. τὰ σπλάγχνα, ων, *the chief intestines, viscera; the entrails, bowels*, Ac. 1. 18; met. *the heart, the affections of the heart, the tender affections*, Lu. 1. 78; 2 Co. 6. 12; Phi. 1. 8, et al.; meton. *a cherished one, dear as one's self*, Phile. 12.

σπλαγχνίζομαι, fut. ίσομαι, aor. 1, ἐσπλαγχνίσθην, (§ 26. rem. 1) *to be moved with pity or compassion*, Mat. 9. 36; 14. 14; 20. 34; Lu. 7. 13, et al.; *to compassionate*, Mat. 18. 27. N.T.

σπόγγον, acc. sing. . . . . σπόγγος

σπόγγος], ου, ὁ, (§ 3. tab. C. a) *a sponge*, Mat. 27. 48; Mar. 15. 36; Jno. 19. 29.

σποδός], οῦ, ἡ, (§ 3. tab. C. b) *ashes*, Mat. 11. 21, et al.

σποδῷ, dat. sing. . . . . σποδός

σπορά], ᾶς, ἡ, (§ 2. tab. B. b) . . . σπείρω

σπορᾶς,[c] gen. sing. . . . . σπορά

σπόριμος], ου, ὁ, ἡ . . . . σπείρω

σποριμων, gen. pl. . . . . σπόριμος

σπόρον, acc. sing. . . . . σπόρος

σπόρος], ου, ὁ . . . . . σπείρω

σπουδάζοντες, nom. pl. masc. part. pres. . σπουδάζω

[a] Ac. 17. 18. [b] Jude 12. [c] 1 Pe. 1. 23.

σπουδάζω], fut. άσω . . . . . σπεύδω
σπουδαῖον, acc. sing. masc. . . . σπουδαῖος
σπουδαῖος], α, ον . . . . . σπεύδω
σπουδαιότερον, acc. sing. masc. compar. (§ 8. rem. 4) . . . . . σπουδαῖος
σπουδαιότερον, neut. compar. adverbially . id.
σπουδαιότερος, nom. sing. masc. compar. . id.
σπουδαιοτέρως, adv. comparat. of . . σπουδαίως
σπουδαίως], adv. . . . . . σπεύδω
σπουδάσατε, 2 pers. pl. aor. 1, imper. . id.
σπούδασον, 2 pers. sing. aor. 1, imper. . id.
σπουδάσω, 1 pers. sing. fut. ind. . . id.
σπουδάσωμεν, 1 pers. pl. aor. 1, subj. . id.
σπουδῇ, dat. sing. . . . . σπουδή
σπουδή], ῆς, ἡ . . . . . σπεύδω
σπουδήν, acc. sing. . . . . σπουδή
σπουδῆς, gen. sing. . . . . . id.
σπυρίδας, acc. pl. . . . . . σπυρίς
σπυρίδι, dat. sing. . . . . . id.
σπυρίδων, gen. pl. . . . . id.

σπυρίς], ίδος, (ῐ) ἡ, (§ 4. rem. 2. c) *a basket, hand-basket* for provisions, Mat. 15. 37; 16. 10; Mar. 8. 8, 20; Ac. 9. 25.

στάδιον], ου, τό, pl. στάδια and στάδιοι, pr. *a fixed standard of measure; a stadium*, the eighth part of a Roman mile, and nearly equal to a furlong, containing 201·45 yards, Lu. 24. 13, et al.; *a race-course, a race*, 1 Co. 9. 24.

σταδίους, acc. pl. masc. . . . . . στάδιον
σταδίῳ, dat. sing. . . . . . id.
σταδίων, gen. pl. . . . . . . id.
σταθείς, nom. sing. masc. part. aor. 1, pass. (§ 29. rem. 6) . . . . ἵστημι
σταθέντα, acc. sing. masc. part. aor. 1, pass. . id.
σταθέντες, nom. pl. masc. part. aor. 1, pass. id.
σταθῇ, 3 pers. sing. aor. 1, subj. pass. . id.
σταθῆναι, aor. 1, infin. pass. . . . . id.
σταθήσεσθε, 2 pers. pl. fut. ind. pass. . id.
σταθήσεται, 3 pers. sing. fut. ind. pass. . id.

στάμνος],[a] ου, ὁ, ἡ, *a wine-jar; a pot, jar, urn, vase.*

στάντος, gen. sing. masc. part. aor. 2 . ἵστημι
στάς, nom. sing. masc. part. aor. 2 (§ 29. tab. X) id.
στᾶσα, nom. sing. fem. part. aor. 2 . . id.
στάσει, dat. sing. . . . . . στάσις
στάσεις, acc. pl.—Al. Ln. Tdf. . . } στάσις
στάσιν, Rec. Gr. Sch. (Ac. 24. 5) }
στάσεως, gen. sing. . . . . . id.
στασιαστής], οῦ, ὁ, (§ 2. tab. B. c) v.r. . ἵστημι
στασιαστῶν, gen. pl.—C. D. Ln. Tdf. . } στασιαστής
συστασιαστῶν, Rec. Gr. Sch. (Mar. 15. 7) }
στάσιν, acc. sing. . . . . . στάσις
στάσις], εως, ἡ, (§ 5. tab. E. c) . ἵστημι
στατήρ], ῆρος, ὁ, (§ 4. rem. 2. f) . . id.
στατῆρα,[b] acc. sing. . . . . στατήρ
σταυρόν, acc. sing. . . . . . σταυρός

σταυρός], οῦ, ὁ, (§ 3. tab. C. a) *a stake; a cross*, Mat. 27. 32, 40, 42; Phi. 2. 8; by impl. *the punishment of the cross, crucifixion*, Ep. 2. 16; He. 12. 2; meton. *the crucifixion* of Christ in respect of its import, *the doctrine of the cross*, 1 Co. 17, 18; Gal. 5. 11; 6. 12, 14; met. in the phrases αἴρειν, or βαστάζειν, or λαμβάνειν τὸν σταυρὸν αὐτοῦ, *to take up, or bear one's cross, to be ready to encounter any extremity*, Mat. 10. 38; 16. 24, et al.

σταυρόω, ῶ, fut. ώσω, (§ 20. tab. T) aor. 1, ἐσταύρωσα, perf. pass. ἐσταύρωμαι, *to fix stakes; later, to crucify, affix to the cross*, Mat. 20. 19; 23. 34; met. *to crucify, to mortify, to deaden, to make a sacrifice of*, Gal. 5. 24; pass. *to be cut off* from a thing, as by a violent death, *to become dead to*, Gal. 6. 14.

σταυροῦ, gen. sing. . . . . σταυρός
σταυροῦνται, 3 pers. pl. pres. ind. pass. . σταυρόω
σταυροῦσι, 3 pers. pl. pres. ind. act. . . id.
σταυρόω, ῶ], fut. ώσω . . . σταυρός
σταυρῷ, dat. sing. . . . . . id.
σταυρωθῇ, 3 pers. sing. aor. 1, subj. pass. . σταυρόω
σταυρωθῆναι, aor. 1, infin. pass. . . . id.
σταυρωθήτω, 3 pers. sing. aor. 1, imper. pass. id.
σταυρῶσαι, aor. 1, infin. act. . . . id.
σταυρώσαντες, nom. pl. masc. part. aor. 1, act. id.
σταυρώσατε, 2 pers. pl. aor. 1, imper. act. . id.
σταυρώσετε, 2 pers. pl. fut. ind. act. . id.
σταύρωσον, 2 pers. sing. aor. 1, imper. act. . id.
σταυρώσω, 1 pers. sing. fut. ind. act. . id.
σταυρώσωσι, 3 pers. pl. aor. 1, subj. act. . id.
σταφυλαί, nom. pl. . . . . . σταφυλή

[a] He. 9. 4.

[b] Mat. 17. 27.

σταφυλάς, acc. pl.—B. Ln. } σταφυλή
σταφυλήν, Rec. Gr. Sch. Tdf. (Mat. 7. 16) } σταφυλή

σταφυλή], ῆς, ἡ, (§ 2. tab. B. a) (σταφίς, *a raisin*) *a cluster or bunch of grapes*, Mat. 7. 16; Lu. 6. 44; Re. 14. 18.

σταφυλήν, acc. sing. . . . . . σταφυλή
στάχυας, acc. pl. . . . . . στάχυς
στάχυϊ, dat. sing. . . . . . id.
στάχυν, acc. sing. . . . . . id.
Στάχυν,[a] acc. . . . . . Στάχυς
Στάχυς], υος, ὁ, *Stachys*, pr. name.

στάχυς], υος, ὁ, (§ 5. tab. E. g) *an ear of corn*, Mat. 12. 1; Mar. 2. 23; 4. 28; Lu. 6. 1.

στέγει, 3 pers. sing. pres. ind. . . . στέγω
στέγη], ης, ἡ . . . . . . id.
στέγην, acc. sing. . . . . . στέγη
στέγομεν, 1 pers. pl. pres. ind. . . . στέγω
στέγοντες, nom. pl. masc. part. pres. . . id.

στέγω], fut. ξω, (§ 23. rem. 1. b) *to cover; to hold off, to hold in;* hence, *to hold out against, to endure patiently*, 1 Co. 9. 12; 13. 7; absol. *to contain one's self*, 1 Thes. 3. 1, 5.

στέγη, ης, ἡ, (§ 2. tab. B. a) *a roof, flat roof* of a house, Mat. 8. 8; Mar. 2. 4; Lu. 7. 6.

στέγων, nom. sing. masc. part. pres. . . στέγω
στεῖρα, nom. and voc. sing. fem. . . . στεῖρος
στείρᾳ, dat. sing. fem. . . . . . id
στεῖραι, nom. pl. fem. . . . . . id.

στεῖρος], α, ον, (§ 7. rem. 1) *sterile; barren, not bearing children*, Lu. 1. 7, 36; 23. 29; Gal. 4. 27.

στέλλεσθαι, pres. infin. mid. . . . . στέλλω
στελλόμενοι, nom. pl. masc. part. pres. mid. . id.

στέλλω], fut. στελῶ, perf. ἔσταλκα, (§ 27. rem. 1. b, and rem. 2. b) aor. 1, ἔστειλα, (§ 27. rem. 1. d) pr. *to place in set order, to arrange; to equip; to despatch; to stow; to contract;* mid. *to contract one's self, to shrink; to withdraw from, avoid, shun*, 2 Co. 8. 20; 2 Thes. 3. 6.

στολή, ῆς, ἡ, (§ 2. tab. B. a) *equipment; dress; a long garment, flowing robe,* worn by priests, kings, and persons of distinction, Mark 12. 38; 16. 5, et al.

στέμμα], ατος, τό, (§ 4. tab. D. c) (στέφω, *to encircle*) *a crown; a fillet, wreath*, Ac. 14. 13.

στέμματα,[b] acc. pl. . . . . . στέμμα
στεναγμοῖς, dat. pl. . . . . . στεναγμός
στεναγμός], οῦ, ὁ . . . . . στενάζω
στεναγμοῦ, gen. sing. . . . . στεναγμός
στενάζετε, 2 pers. pl. pres. imper. . . στενάζω
στενάζομεν, 1 pers. pl. pres. ind. . . id.
στενάζοντες, nom. pl. masc. part. pres. . id.
στενάζω], fut. άξω, aor. 1, ἐστέναξα, (§ 26. rem. 2) *to groan, sigh*, Ro. 8. 23; 2 Co. 5. 2, 4; He. 13. 17; *to sigh* inwardly, Mar. 7. 34; *to give vent to querulous or censorious feelings*, Ja. 5. 9.

στεναγμός, οῦ, ὁ, (§ 3. tab. C. a) *a sighing, groaning, groan*, Ac. 7. 34; an inward *sighing, aspiration*, Ro. 8. 26.

στενή, nom. sing. fem. . . . . . στενός
στενῆς, gen. sing. fem. . . . . . id.

στενός], ή, όν, (§ 7. tab. F. a) *narrow, strait*, Mat. 7. 13, 14; Lu. 13. 24.

στενοχωρεῖσθε, 2 pers. pl. pres. ind. pass. στενοχωρέω
στενοχωρέω, ῶ], fut. ήσω, (§ 16. tab. P) (στενός & χώρα) *to crowd together into a narrow place, straiten;* pass. met. *to be in straits, to be cooped up, to be cramped* from action, 2 Co. 4. 8; *to be cramped* in feeling, 2 Co. 6. 12.

στενοχωρία, ας, ἡ, (§ 2. tab. B. b, and rem. 2) pr. *narrowness of place, a narrow place;* met. *straits, distress, anguish*, Ro. 2. 9; 8. 35; 2 Co. 6. 4; 12. 10.

στενοχωρούμενοι, nom. pl. masc. part. pr. pass. στενοχωρέω
στενοχωρία], ας, ἡ . . . . . id.
στενοχωρίαις, dat. pl. . . . . στενοχωρία
στερεά, nom. sing. fem. . . . . στερεός
στερεᾶς, gen. sing. fem. . . . . id.
στερεοί, nom. pl. masc. . . . . id.
στερεός], ά, όν, (§ 7. rem. 1) (perhaps kindred with ἵστημι) *stiff, hard;* of food, *solid*, as opposed to what is liquid and light, He. 5. 12; *firm, steadfast*, 2 Ti. 2. 19; 1 Pe. 5. 9.

στερεόω, ῶ, fut. ώσω, aor. 1, ἐστερ-

---

[a] Ro. 16. 9.

[b] Ac. 14. 13.

έωσα, (§ 20. tab. T) *to render firm; to strengthen,* Ac. 3. 7, 16; *to settle,* Ac. 16. 5.

στερέωμα, ατος, τό, (§ 4. tab. D. c) pr. *what is solid and firm;* met. *firmness, steadfastness, constancy,* Col. 2. 5.

στερεόω, ῶ], fut. ώσω . . . . . στερεός

στερέωμα],[a] ατος, τό . . . . . id.

Στεφανᾶ, gen. . . . . . . Στεφανᾶς

Στεφανᾶς], ᾶ, ὁ, (§ 2. rem 4) *Stephanas,* pr. name.

στέφανοι, nom. pl. . . . . . στέφανος

στέφανον, acc. sing. . . . . . id.

Στέφανον, acc. . . . . . . Στέφανος

Στέφανος], ου, ὁ, *Stephanus, Stephen,* pr. name.

στέφανος], ου, ὁ, (§ 3. tab. C. a) (στέφω, *to encircle*) *that which forms an encirclement; a crown,* Mat. 27. 29; Re. 4. 4, 10; *a chaplet, wreath,* conferred on a victor in the public games, 1 Co. 9. 25; met. *a crown, reward, prize,* 2 Ti. 4. 8; Ja. 1. 12; *a crown, ornament, honour, glory,* Phi. 4. 1, et al.

στεφανόω, ῶ, fut. ώσω, aor. 1, ἐστεφάνωσα, (§ 20. tab. T) *to encompass; to crown; to crown* as victor in the games, 2 Ti. 2. 5; met. *to crown, adorn, decorate,* He. 2. 7, 9.

Στεφάνου, gen. . . . . . . Στέφανος

στεφάνους, acc. pl. . . . . . στέφανος

στεφανοῦται, 3 pers. sing. pres. ind. pass. (§ 21. tab. U) . . . . . στεφανόω

στεφανόω, ῶ], fut. ώσω . . . . στέφανος

Στεφάνῳ, dat. . . . . . . Στέφανος

στήθη, acc. pl. . . . . . . στῆθος

στῆθι, 2 pers. sing. aor. 2, imper. (§ 29. rem. 2) ἵστημι

στῆθος], εος, το, and pl. τὰ στήθη, (§ 5. tab. E. b) *the breast,* Lu. 18. 13; 23. 48; Jno. 13. 25, et al.

στήκει, 3 pers. sing. pres. ind. . . . . στήκω

στήκετε, 2 pers. pl. pres. ind. and imper. . id.

στήκητε, 2 pers. pl. pres. subj. . . . . id.

στήκω], a late equivalent to ἕστηκα . ἵστημι

στῆναι, aor. 2, infin. (§ 29. tab. X) . . id.

στηριγμός], οῦ, ὁ, (§ 3. tab. C. a) . . id.

στηριγμοῦ,[b] gen. sing. . . . . . στηριγμός

στηρίζω], fut. ίξω, (§ 26. rem. 2) . . ἵστημι

στηρίζων, nom. sing. m. part. pres.—B. Ln. Tdf. }
ἐπιστηρίζων, Rec. Gr. Sch. (Ac. 18. 23) } στηρίζω

στηρίξαι, aor. 1, infin. act. . . . . στηρίζω

στηρίξαι, 3 pers. sing. aor. 1, optat. act. . id.

στηρίξατε, 2 pers. pl. aor. 1, imper. act. . id.

στήριξον, 2 pers. sing. aor. 1, imper. act. . id.

στηρίξει, 3 pers. sing. fut. ind. act. . . id.

στήρισον, 2 pers. sing. aor. 1, imper. act.—A. B. D. Ln. Tdf. . . . }
στήριξον, Rec. Gr. Sch. (Lu. 22. 32) } id.

στηριχθῆναι, aor. 1, infin. pass. . . . id.

στῆσαι, aor. 1, infin. act. . . . . ἵστημι

στήσαντες, nom. pl. masc. part. aor. 1, act. . id.

στήσει, 3 pers. sing. fut. ind. act. . . id.

στήσῃ, 3 pers. sing. aor. 1, subj. act. . . id.

στήσῃς, 2 pers. sing. aor. 1, subj. act. . id.

στήσητε, 2 pers. pl. aor. 1, subj. act.—D. Tdf. }
τηρήσητε, Rec. Gr. Sch. Ln. (Mar. 7. 9) } id.

στήσονται, 3 pers. pl. fut. ind. mid. . . id.

στῆτε, 2 pers. pl. aor. 2, imper. and subj. (§ 29. rem. 3) . . . . . id.

στιβάδας, acc. pl.—B. D. Ln. Tdf. . }
στοιβάδας, Rec. Gr. Sch. (Mar. 11. 8) } στιβάς

στιβάς], άδος, (ᾰ) ἡ, v.r. same signif. as . στοιβάς

στίγμα], ατος, τό, (§ 4. tab. D. c) (στίζω, *to prick; to burn in marks, brand*) *a brand-mark.*

στίγματα,[c] acc. pl. . . . . . . στίγμα

στιγμή], ῆς, ἡ, (§ 2. tab. B. a) (στίζω) pr. *a point;* met. *a point* of time, *moment, instant.*

στιγμῇ,[d] dat. sing. . . . . . στιγμή

στίλβοντα,[e] nom. pl. neut. part. pres. . . στίλβω

στίλβω], fut. στίλψω, (§ 23. rem. 1. a) *to shine, glisten.*

στοά], ᾶς, ἡ, (§ 2. tab. B. b, and rem. 2) . ἵστημι

στοᾷ, dat. sing. . . . . . . στοά

στοάς, acc. pl. . . . . . . id.

στοιβάδας,[f] acc. pl. . . . . . στοιβάς

στοιβάς], άδος, (ᾰ) ἡ, (§ 4. rem. 2. c) (στείβω, *to tread*) *a stuffing of leaves, boughs,* etc.; meton. *a bough, branch.* N.T.

στοιχεῖα, nom. and acc. pl. . . . . στοιχεῖον

στοιχεῖν, pres. infin. . . . . . στοιχέω

στοιχεῖον], ου, τό, (§ 3. tab. C. c) (dim. of στοῖχος, *a row, a straight rod or rule,* from στείχω, *to go in a straight line*) *an element; an element* of the natural universe, 2 Pe. 3. 10, 12; *an element or rudiment* of any intellectual or religious system, Gal. 4. 3, 9; Col. 2. 8, 20; He. 5. 12.

[a] Col. 2. 5. [b] 2 Pe. 3. 17. [c] Gal. 6. 17. [d] Lu. 4. 5. [e] Mar. 9. 3. [f] Mar. 11. 8.

στοιχεῖς, 2 pers. sing. pres. ind. . . στοιχέω

στοιχείων, gen. pl. . . . . . στοιχεῖον

στοιχέω, ῶ], fut. ήσω, (§ 16. tab. P) (στοῖχος, *a row*) pr. *to advance in a line;* met. *to frame one's conduct* by a certain rule, Ac. 21. 24; Ro. 4. 12; Gal. 5. 25; 6. 16; Phi. 3. 16.

στοιχήσουσι, 3 pers. pl. fut. ind. . . στοιχέω

στοιχοῦσι, dat. pl. masc. part. pres. . . id.

στοιχοῦσι, 3 pers. pl. pres. ind.—A. C. D. Tdf. } id.
στοιχήσουσι, R. Gr. Sch. Ln. (Gal. 6. 16) }

στοιχῶμεν, 1 pers. pl. pres. subj. . . id.

στολαί, nom. pl. . . . . . στολή

στολαῖς, dat. pl. . . . . id.

στολάς, acc. pl. . . . . . id.

στολή], ῆς, ἡ.—Gr. Sch. Tdf. . . } στέλλω
στολαί, Rec. (Re. 6. 11) . . }

στολήν, acc. sing. . . . . . στολή

στόμα], ατος, τό, (§ 4. tab. D. c) *the mouth*, Mat. 12. 34; 15. 11, 17, 18; 21. 16, et al.; *speech, words*, Mat. 18. 16; 2 Co. 13. 1; *command of speech, facility of language*, Lu. 21. 15; from the Heb., ἀνοίγειν τὸ στόμα, *to make utterance, to speak*, Mat. 5. 2; 13. 35, et al.; also, used of the earth, *to rend, yawn*, Re. 12. 16; στόμα πρὸς στόμα λαλεῖν, *to speak mouth to mouth, face to face*, 2 Jno. 12; 3 Jno. 14; *the edge or point* of a weapon, Lu. 21. 24; He. 11. 34.

στόμᾰχος, ου, ὁ, (§ 3. tab. C. a) pr. *the gullet* leading to the stomach; hence, later, *the stomach* itself, 1 Ti. 5. 23.

στόματα, acc. pl. . . . . . στόμα

στόματι, dat. sing. . . . . . id.

στόματος, gen. sing. . . . . . id.

στομάτων, gen. pl. . . . . . id.

στόμαχον,[a] acc. sing. . . . . στόμαχος

στόμαχος], ου, ὁ . . . . . στόμα

στρατεία], ας, ἡ . . . . . στρατεύω

στρατείαν, acc. sing. . . . . στρατεία

στρατείας, gen. sing. . . . . . id.

στρατεύεται, 3 pers. sing. pres. ind. mid. (§ 15. tab. O) . . . . . στρατεύω

στρατεύῃ, 2 pers. sing. pres. subj. mid. . id.

στράτευμα], ατος, τό . . . . . id.

στρατεύμασι, dat. pl. . . . . . στράτευμα

στρατεύματα, nom. and acc. pl. . . στράτευμα

στρατεύματι, dat. sing. . . . . id.

στρατεύματος, gen. sing. . . . . id.

στρατευμάτων, gen. pl. . . . . . id.

στρατευόμεθα, 1 pers. pl. pres. ind. mid. . στρατεύω

στρατευόμενοι, nom. pl. masc. part. pres. mid. id.

στρατευόμενος, nom. sing. masc. part. pres. mid. id.

στρατευομένων, gen. pl. part. pres. mid. . id.

στρατεύονται, 3 pers. pl. pres. ind. mid. . id.

στρατεύω], fut. εύσω, (§ 13. tab. M) and mid. στρατεύομαι, (στρατός, *an army*) *to perform military duty, serve as a soldier*, Lu. 3. 14; 1 Co. 9. 7; 2 Ti. 2. 4; *to battle*, Ja. 4. 1; 1 Pe. 2. 11; *to be* spiritually *militant*, 2 Co. 10. 3; 1 Ti. 1. 18.

στρατεία, ας, ἡ, (§ 2. tab. B. b, and rem. 2) *a military expedition, campaign;* and genr. *military service, warfare;* met. *the* Christian *warfare*, 2 Co. 10. 4; 1 Ti. 1. 18.

στράτευμα, ατος, τό, (§ 4. tab. D. c) *an army*, Mat. 22. 7, et al.; *an armed force, corps*, Ac. 23. 10, 27; *troops, guards*, Lu. 23. 11.

στρατηγοί, nom. pl. . . . . . στρατηγός

στρατηγοῖς, dat. pl. . . . . . id.

στρατηγός], οῦ, ὁ, (§ 3. tab. C. c) (στρατός & ἄγω) *a leader or commander of an army, general;* a Roman *prætor, provincial magistrate*, Ac. 16. 20, 22, 35, 36, 38; στρατηγὸς τοῦ ἱεροῦ, *the captain or prefect of the temple*, the chief of the Levites who kept guard in and around the temple, Lu. 22. 4, 52; Ac. 4. 1; 5. 24, 26.

στρατηγούς, acc. pl. . . . . . στρατηγός

στρατιά], ᾶς, ἡ, (§ 2. tab. B. b, and rem. 2) (στρατός) *an army, host;* from the Heb., στρατιὰ οὐράνιος, or τοῦ οὐρανοῦ, *the heavenly host, the host of heaven, the hosts of angels*, Lu. 2. 13; *the stars*, Ac. 7. 42.

στρατιώτης, ου, ὁ, (§ 2. tab. B. c) *a soldier*, Mat. 8. 9; 27. 27, et al.; met. *a soldier* of Christ, 2 Ti. 2. 3.

στρατιᾷ, dat. sing. . . . . . στρατιά

στρατιᾶς, gen. sing. . . . . . id.

στρατιῶται, nom. pl. . . . . . στρατιώτης

στρατιώταις, dat. pl. . . . . . id.

στρατιώτας, acc. pl. . . . . . id.

[a] 1 Ti. 5. 23.

στρατιώτῃ, dat. sing. . . . . στρατιώτης
στρατιώτην, acc. sing. . . . . id.
στρατιώτης], ου, ὁ . . . . στρατιά
στρατιωτῶν, gen. pl. . . . . στρατιώτης
στρατολογέω, ῶ], fut. ήσω, (§ 16. tab. P) (στρατός & λέγω) *to collect or levy an army, enlist troops.* L.G.
στρατολογήσαντι,[a] dat. sing. masc. part. aor. 1 στρατολογέω
στρατοπεδάρχῃ,[b] dat. sing. . . . στρατοπεδάρχης
στρατοπεδάρχης], ου, ὁ, (§ 2. tab. B. c) (στρατόπεδον & ἄρχω) *a commandant of a camp; a legionary tribune;* perhaps, *the prefect of the prætorian camp,* Ac. 28. 16. L.G.
στρατόπεδον], ου, τό, (§ 3. tab. C. c) (στρατός & πέδον, *ground, plain*) pr. *the site of an encampment; an encampment;* meton. *an army,* Lu. 21. 20.
στρατοπέδων,[c] gen. pl. . . . στρατόπεδον
στραφείς, nom. sing. masc. part. aor. 2, pass. (§ 24. rem. 10) . . . στρέφω
στραφεῖσα, nom. sing. fem. part. aor. 2, pass. id.
στραφέντες, nom. pl. masc. part. aor. 2, pass. id.
στραφῆτε, 2 pers pl. aor. 2, subj. pass. . id.
στραφῶσι, 3 pers. pl. aor. 2, subj. pass.—B. Ln. Tdf. . . . . } id.
ἐπιστραφῶσι, R. Gr. Sch. (Jno. 12. 40)
στρεβλοῦσι,[d] 3 pers. pl. pres. ind. . . στρεβλόω
στρεβλόω, ῶ], fut. ώσω, (§ 20. tab. T) (στρεβλή, *a windlass, a wrench, instrument of torture, rack*) pr. *to distort* the limbs *on a rack;* met. *to wrench, distort, pervert.*
στρέφειν, pres. infin. act. . . . . στρέφω
στρεφόμεθα, 1 pers. pl. pres. ind. mid. . id.

στρέφω], fut. ψω, aor. 1, ἔστρεψα, (§ 23. rem. 1. a, and rem. 2) aor. 2, pass. ἐστράφην, (ἄ) (§ 24. rem. 10) *to twist; to turn,* Mat. 5. 39; *to make a change* of substance, *to change,* Re. 11. 6; absol. *to change or turn* one's course of dealing, Ac. 7. 42, mid. *to turn one's self about,* Mat. 16. 23; Lu. 7. 9, et al.; *to turn back,* Ac. 7. 39; *to change one's direction, to turn* elsewhere, Ac. 13. 46; *to change one's course of principle and conduct, to be converted,* Mat. 18. 3.
στρέψον, 2 pers. sing. aor. 1, imper. act. . στρέφω
στρηνιάσαντες, nom. pl. masc. part. aor. 1 . στρηνιάω
στρηνιάω, ῶ], fut. άσω . . . . στρῆνος
στρῆνος], εος, τό, (§ 5. tab. E. b) (στρηνής, *strong, hard*) *headstrong pride; wantonness, luxury, voluptuousness,* Re. 18. 3.

στρηνιάω, ῶ, fut. άσω, (§ 22. rem. 2) *to be wanton, to revel, riot,* Re. 18. 7, 9.
στρήνους,[e] gen. sing. . . στρῆνος
στρουθία, nom. pl. . . . . . στρουθίον
στρουθίον], ίου, τό, (§ 3. tab. C. c) (dimin. of στρουθός) *any small bird,* spc. *a sparrow,* Mat. 10. 29, 31; Lu. 12. 6, 7.
στρουθίων, gen. pl. . . . . στρουθίον
στρώννυμι, or στρωννύω], fut. στρώσω, aor. 1, ἔστρωσα, perf. pass. ἔστρωμαι, (§ 36. rem. 5) (by metath. for στορέννυμι) *to spread, to strew,* Mat. 21. 8; Mar. 11. 8; *to spread* a couch, Ac. 9. 34; used of a supper-chamber, pass. *to have the couches spread, to be prepared, furnished,* Mar. 14. 15; Lu. 22. 12.
στρῶσον, 2 pers. sing. aor. 1, imper. . . στρώννυμι
στυγητοί,[f] nom. pl. masc. . . . . στυγητός
στυγητός], ή, όν, and ός, όν, (στυγέω, *to hate*) *hateful, odious, detested.*
στυγνάζω], fut. άσω, aor. 1, ἐστύγνασα, (§ 26. rem. 1) (στυγνός, *gloomy*) *to put on a gloomy and downcast look,* Mar. 10. 22; of the sky, *to lower,* Mat. 16. 3. LXX.
στυγνάζων, nom. sing. masc. part. pres. . στυγνάζω
στυγνάσας, nom. sing. masc. part. aor. 1 . id.
στῦλοι, nom. pl. . . . . στῦλος
στῦλον, acc. sing. . . . . . id.

στῦλος], ου, ὁ, (§ 3. tab. C. a) *a pillar, column,* Re. 10. 1; used of persons of authority, influence, etc., *a support or pillar* of the Church, Gal. 2. 9; Re. 3. 12; *a support* of true doctrine, 1 Ti. 3. 15.
Στωϊκός], ή, όν, (§ 7. tab. F. a) *stoic, belonging to the sect of the Stoics,* founded by Zeno, and deriving their name from the *portico,* στοά, where he taught.
Στωϊκῶν,[g] gen. pl. . . . . Στωϊκός

σύ], gen. σοῦ, dat. σοί, acc. σέ, and enclitic σου, σοι, σε, pl. ὑμεῖς, (§ 11. tab. K. b) pron. 2. pers. *thou,* Mat. 1. 20; 2. 6, et al. freq.

σός, σή, σόν, (§ 11. rem. 4) *thine,* Mat.

---

a 2 Ti. 2. 4. b Ac. 28. 16. c Lu. 21. 20. d 2 Pe. 3. 16. e Re. 18. 3. f Tit. 3. 3. g Ac. 17. 18.

7. 3. 22, et al.; οἱ σοί, *thy kindred, friends,* etc., Mar. 5. 19; τὸ σόν and τὰ σά, *what is thine, thy property, goods,* etc., Mat. 20. 14; 25. 25; Lu. 6. 30.

συγγένεια], ας, ἡ . . . . . συγγενής

συγγενείᾳ, dat. sing. . . . . συγγένεια

συγγένειαν, acc. sing. . . . . id.

συγγενείας, gen. sing. . . . . id.

συγγενεῖς, nom. and acc. pl. masc. . συγγενής

συγγενέσι, dat. pl. masc. . . . id.

συγγενῆ, acc. sing. masc. . . . . id.

συγγενής], έος, οῦς, ὁ, ἡ, (§ 7. tab. G. b) (σύν & γένος) *kindred, akin;* as a subst. *a kinsman or kinswoman, relative,* Mar. 6. 4; Lu. 1. 36, 58, et al.; *one* nationally *akin, a fellow-countryman,* Ro. 9. 3.

συγγένεια, ας, ἡ, (§ 2. tab. B. b, and rem. 2) *kindred; kinsfolk, kinsmen, relatives,* Lu. 1. 61; Ac. 7. 3, 14.

συγγενῶν, gen. pl. . . . συγγενής

συγγνώμη], ης, ἡ, (§ 2. tab. B. a) (συγγινώσκω, *to agree in judgment with*) *pardon; concession, leave, permission,* 1 Co. 7. 6.

συγγνώμην,[a] acc. sing. . . . . συγγνώμη

συγκάθημαι], (σύν & κάθημαι) *to sit in company with,* Mar. 14. 54; Ac. 26. 30.

συγκαθήμενοι, nom. pl. masc. part. pres. . συγκάθημαι

συγκαθήμενος, nom. sing. masc. part. pres. . id.

συγκαθίζω], fut. ίσω, (§ 26. rem. 1) (σύν & καθίζω) trans. *to cause to sit with, seat in company with,* Ep. 2. 6; intrans. *to sit in company with; to sit down together,* Ac. 22. 55.

συγκαθισάντων, gen. pl. masc. part. aor. 1 συγκαθίζω

συγκακοπαθέω, ῶ], fut. ήσω, (§ 16. tab. P) (σύν & κακοπαθέω) *to suffer evils along with* any one; *to be enduringly adherent,* 2 Ti. 1. 8. N.T.

συγκακοπάθησον,[b] 2 pers. s. aor. 1, imper. συγκακοπαθέω

συγκακουχεῖσθαι,[c] pres. infin. . συγκακουχέομαι

συγκακουχέομαι, οῦμαι], (σύν & κακουχέω) *to encounter adversity along with* any one. N.T.

συγκαλεῖ, 3 pers. sing. pres. ind. act. . . συγκαλέω

συγκαλεῖται, 3 pers. sing. pres. ind. mid. . id.

συγκαλεσάμενος, nom. sing. masc. part. aor. 1, mid. . . . . . id.

συγκαλέσασθαι, aor. 1, infin. mid. . . id.

συγκᾰλέω, ῶ,], fut. έσω, (§ 22. rem. 1) (σύν & καλέω) *to call together, convoke,* Mar. 15. 16; mid. *to call around one's self,* Lu. 9. 1, et al.

συγκαλοῦσι, 3 pers. pl. pres. ind. act. . . συγκαλέω

συγκαλύπτω], fut. ψω, perf. pass. συγκεκάλυμμαι, (§ 23. rem. 1. a, and rem. 7) (σύν & καλύπτω) *to cover altogether, to cover up;* met. *to conceal,* Lu. 12. 2.

συγκάμπτω], fut. ψω, (§ 23. rem. 1. a) (σύν & κάμπτω) *to bend or bow together; to bow down* the back of any one afflictively, Ro. 11. 10.

σύγκαμψον,[d] 2 pers. sing. aor. 1, imper. . συγκάμπτω

συγκαταβαίνω], fut. βήσομαι, (§ 37. rem. 1) (σύν & καταβαίνω) *to go down with* any one.

συγκαταβάντες,[e] nom. pl. masc. part. aor. 2 συγκαταβαίνω

συγκατάθεσις],[f] εως, ἡ . . συγκατατίθημι

συγκατατεθειμένος,[g] nom. sing. masc. part. perf. pass. (with mid. force) . . id.

συγκατατιθέμενος, nom. sing. masc. part. pres. mid.—C. D. . . . . } id.
συγκατατεθειμένος, Rec. Gr. Sch. Tdf. (Lu. 23. 51) . . . }

συγκατατίθημι], (σύν & κατατίθημι) *to set down together with;* mid. *to assent, accord.*

συγκατάθεσις, εως, ἡ, (§ 5. tab. E. c) *assent;* in N.T. *accord, alliance,* 2 Co. 6. 16. L.G.

συγκαταψηφίζω], fut. ίσω, (§ 26. rem. 1) (σύν, καταψηφίζω, ψῆφος) *to count, number with.* N.T.

συγκατεψηφίσθη,[h] 3 pers. sing. aor. 1, ind. pass. . . . . . συγκαταψηφίζω

συγκεκαλυμμένον,[i] nom. sing. neut. part. perf. pass. . . . . . συγκαλύπτω

συγκεκερασμένους, acc. pl. masc. part. perf. pass.—A. B. C. D. Ln. Tdf. } συγκεράννυμι
συγκεκραμένος, Rec. Gr. Sch. (He. 4. 2) . . . . }

συγκεκλεισμένοι, nom. pl. masc. part. p. pass. συγκλείω

συγκεκραμένος, nom. s. masc. part. perf. pass. συγκεράννυμι

συγκεράννυμι, or νύω], fut. κεράσω, aor. 1, συνεκέρᾰσα, perf. συγκέκρᾱμαι, (§ 36. rem. 5) (σύν & κεράννυμι) *to mix with, mingle together, commingle; to blend,* 1 Co. 12. 24; pass. *to be attempered, combined,* He. 4. 2.

---

[a] 1 Co. 7. 6. [b] 2 Ti. 1. 8. [c] He. 11. 25. [d] Ro. 11. 10. [e] Ac. 25. 5. [f] 2 Co. 6. 16. [g] Lu. 23. 51. [h] Ac. 1. 26. [i] Lu. 12. 2.

συγκεχυμένη, nom. sing. fem. part. perf. pass. συγχέω
συγκέχυται, 3 pers. sing. perf. ind. pass. . id.
συγκῑνέω, ῶ], fut. ήσω, (§ 16. tab. P) (σύν & κινέω) *to move together, commove, put in commotion; to excite*, Ac. 6. 12.
συγκλειόμενοι, nom. pl. masc. part. pres. pass. A. D. Ln. Sch. Tdf. . . } συγκλείω
συγκεκλεισμένοι, Rec. Gr. (Gal. 3. 23)
συγκλείω], fut. είσω, (§ 22. rem. 4) (σύν & κλείω) *to shut up together, to hem in; to enclose*, Lu. 5. 6; met. *to band* under a sweeping sentence, Ro. 11. 32; Gal. 3. 22; pass. *to be banded* under a bar of disability, Gal. 3. 23.
συγκληρονόμα, acc. pl. neut. . συγκληρονόμος
συγκληρονόμοι, nom. pl. masc. . . . id.
συγκληρονόμοις, dat. pl. masc. . . id.
συγκληρονόμος], ου, ὁ, ἡ, (§ 7. rem. 2) (σύν & κληρονόμος) pr. *a coheir*, Ro. 8. 17; *a fellow-participant*, Ep. 3. 6; He. 11. 9; 1 Pe. 3. 7. N.T.
συγκληρονόμων, gen. pl. . . συγκληρονόμος
συγκοινωνεῖτε, 2 pers. pl. pres. imper. . συγκοινωνέω
συγκοινωνέω, ῶ], fut. ήσω . . συγκοινωνός
συγκοινωνήσαντες, nom. pl. masc. part. aor. 1 συγκοινωνέω
συγκοινωνήσητε, 2 pers. pl. aor. 1, subj. . id.
συγκοινωνός], οῦ, ὁ, ἡ, (σύν & κοινωνός) *one who partakes jointly; a coparticipant*, Ro. 11. 17; *a copartner* in service, *fellow*, 1 Co. 9. 23; Phi. 1. 7; *a sharer*, Re. 1. 9. N.T.

συγκοινωνέω, ῶ, fut. ήσω, (§ 16. tab. P) *to be a joint partaker, participate with* a person; in N.T. *to mix one's self up* in a thing, *to involve one's self, be an accomplice in*, Ep. 5. 11; Re. 18. 4; *to sympathise actively in, to relieve*, Phi. 4. 14.

συγκοινωνούς, acc. pl. masc. . . συγκοιμωνός
συγκομίζω], fut. ίσω, (§ 26. rem. 1) (σύν & κομίζω) *to bring together, collect; to prepare for burial, take charge of the funeral* of any one, *bury*, Ac. 8. 2.
συγκρῖναι, aor. 1, infin. . . . συγκρίνω
συγκρίνοντες, nom. pl. masc. part. pres. . id.
συγκρίνω], fut. ινῶ, (§ 27. rem. 1. a) (σύν & κρίνω) *to combine, compound; to compare, to estimate by comparing with* something else, or, *to match*, 2 Co. 10. 12, bis; *to explain, to illustrate*, or, *to suit*, 1 Co. 2. 13
συγκύπτουσα,[a] nom. sing. fem. part. pres. συγκύπτω
συγκύπτω], fut. ψω, (§ 23. rem. 1. a) (σύν & κύπτω) *to bend or bow together; to be bowed together, bent double.*
συγκυρία], ας, ἡ, (§ 2. tab. B. b, and rem. 2) (συγκυρέω, *to happen together*, σύν & κυρέω, *to happen*) *concurrence, coincidence, chance, accident*; κατὰ συγκυρίαν, *by chance, accidentally*, Lu. 10. 31.
συγκυρίαν,[b] acc. sing. . . . . συγκυρία
συγχαίρει, 2 pers. sing. pres. ind. . . συγχαίρω
συγχαίρετε, 2 pers. pl. pres. imper. . id.
συγχαίρω], aor. 2, συνεχάρην, (§ 27. rem. 4. b) (σύν & χαίρω) *to rejoice with* any one, *sympathise in joy*, Lu. 15. 6, 9; Phi. 2. 17, 18; met. 1 Co. 12. 26; *to sympathise in the advancement of*, 1 Co. 13. 6.
συγχάρητε, 2 pers. pl. aor. 2, imper. . . συγχαίρω
συγχέω, and later, ύνω], imperf. συνέχεον & συνέχῠνον, perf. pass. συγκέχῠμαι, aor. 1, pass. συνεχύθην, (ῠ) (§ 35. rem. 1. and § 36. rem. 1) (σύν & χέω) *to pour together, mingle by pouring together*; hence, *to confound, perplex, amaze*, Ac. 2. 6; *to confound* in dispute, Ac. 9. 22; *to throw into confusion, fill with uproar*, Ac. 19. 32; 21. 27, 31.

σύγχῠσις, εως, ἡ, (§ 5. tab. E. c) pr. *a pouring together*; hence, *confusion, commotion, tumult, uproar*, Ac. 19. 29.

συγχράομαι, ῶμαι], fut. ήσομαι, (§ 18. tab. R) (σύν & χράομαι) *to use at the same time with another, use in common; to have social intercourse with, associate with.* L.G.
συγχρῶνται, 3 pers. pl. pres. ind. . συγχράομαι
συγχύνεται, 3 pers. sing. pres. ind. pass.— A. B. D. Ln. Tdf. . . . } συγχύνω
συγκέχυται, Rec. Gr. Sch. (Ac. 21. 31)
συγχύνω], see συγχέω.
συγχύσεως,[c] gen. sing. . . . . σύγχυσις
σύγχυσις], εως, ἡ . . . . συγχέω
συζάω, ῶ], fut. ήσω, (§ 25. rem. 2) (σύν & ζάω) *to live with; to continue in life with* any one, 2 Co. 7. 3; *to co-exist in life with* another, Ro. 6. 8; 2 Ti. 2. 11.
συζεύγνυμι], fut. ζεύξω, aor. 1, συνέζευξα, (§ 31. tab. B. B) (σύν & ζεύγνυμι, *to yoke*) *to*

[a] Lu. 13. 11. [b] Lu. 10. 31. [c] Ac. 19. 29.

yoke together; trop. *to conjoin, join together, unite*, Mat. 19. 6; Mar. 10. 9.

σύζυγος, ου, ὁ, ἡ, (§ 7. rem. 2) *a yoke-fellow; an associate, fellow-labourer, coadjutor*, Phi. 4. 3.

συζῆν, pres. infin. . . . . . } συζάω
συνζῆν, Ln. (and so generally) . }

συζήσομεν, 1 pers. pl. fut. ind. . . . id.

συζητεῖν, pres. infin. . . . . . συζητέω

συζητεῖτε, 2 pers. pl. pres. ind. . . . id.

συζητέω, ῶ], fut. ήσω, (§ 16. tab. P) (σύν & ζητέω) *to seek, ask, or inquire with* another; *to deliberate, debate*, Mar. 1. 27; 9. 10; *to hold discourse with, argue, reason*, Mar. 8. 11; 12. 28; Ac. 6. 9; *to question, dispute, cavil*, Mar. 9. 14, 16, et al.

συζήτησις, εως, ἡ, (§ 5. tab. E. c) *mutual discussion, debate, disputation*, Ac. 15. 2, 7; 28. 29. L.G.

συζητητής, οῦ, ὁ, (§ 2. tab. B. c) *a disputant, controversial reasoner, sophist*, 1 Co. 1. 20. N.T.

συζητήσεως, gen. sing. . . . . . συζήτησις

συζήτησιν, acc. sing. . . . . . id.

συζήτησις], εως, ἡ . . . . . συζητέω

συζητητής],[a] οῦ, ὁ . . . . . id.

συζητοῦντας, acc. pl. masc. part. pres. . . id.

συζητοῦντες, nom. pl. masc. part. pres. . . id.

συζητούντων, gen. pl. masc. part. pres. . . id.

σύζυγε,[b] voc. sing. masc. . . . . . σύζυγος

σύζυγος], ου, ὁ, ἡ . . . . . συζεύγνυμι

συζωοποιέω, ῶ], fut. ήσω, (§ 16. tab. P) (σύν & ζωοποιέω) *to quicken together with another; to make a sharer in the quickening of another*, Ep. 2. 5; Col. 2. 13. N.T.

σῦκα, acc. pl. . . . . . . σῦκον

συκάμινος], ου, ἡ, and ὁ, *a sycamine-tree*, i. q. συκομοραία, q.v.

συκαμίνῳ,[c] dat. sing. . . . . . συκάμινος

συκῆ], ῆς, ἡ, (§ 2. tab. B. a) contr. for συκέα, *a fig-tree, ficus carica* of Linn., Mat. 21. 19, et al.

συκῇ, dat. sing. . . . . . . συκῆ

συκῆν, acc. sing. . . . . . . id.

συκῆς, gen. sing. . . . . . . id.

συκομοραία, or συκομορέα], ας, ἡ, (§ 2. tab. B. b, and rem. 2) (σῦκον & μόρον, *a mulberry*) equivalent to συκόμορος, *the fig-mulberry, ficus sycamorus* of Linn., a tree whose leaves resemble those of the mulberry, and its fruit that of the fig-tree. N.T.

συκομορέαν,[d] acc. sing.—Rec. Gr. . . } συκομορέα
συκομωρέαν, B. D. Ln. Tdf. . . }
συκομωραίαν, Sch. . . }

σῦκον], ου, τό, (§ 3. tab. C. c) *a fig*, Mat. 7. 16, et al.

συκοφαντέω, ῶ], fut. ήσω, (§ 16. tab. P) (συκοφάντης, pr. among the Athenians, *an informer against those who exported figs contrary to law*, σῦκον, φαίνω) *to inform against; to accuse falsely*; by impl. *to wrong by false accusations or insidious arts; to extort* money *by false informations*, Lu. 3. 14; 19. 8.

συκοφαντήσητε, 2 pers. pl. aor. 1, subj. . συκοφαντέω

σύκων, gen. pl. . . . . . . σῦκον

συλαγωγέω, ῶ], fut. ήσω, (§ 16. tab. P) (σύλη, or σῦλον, and ἄγω) *to carry off as a prey or booty*; met. *to make victims of imposture*, Col. 2. 8. L.G.

συλαγωγῶν,[e] nom. sing. masc. part. pres. . συλαγωγέω

συλάω, ῶ], fut. ήσω, aor. 1, ἐσύλησα, (§ 18. tab. R) (σύλη, or σῦλον, *the right of seizing the goods of a merchant in payment*) *to strip, rob; to rob, encroach upon*, 2 Co. 11. 8.

συλλαβεῖν, aor. 2, infin. act. . . . . συλλαμβάνω

συλλαβέσθαι, aor. 2, infin. mid. . . . . id.

συλλαβόμενοι, nom. pl. masc. part. aor. 2, mid. . id.

συλλαβόντες, nom. pl. masc. part. aor. 2, act. . id.

συλλαβοῦσα, nom. sing. fem. part. aor. 2, act. . id.

συλλαβοῦσι, dat. pl. masc. part. aor. 2, act. . id.

συλλαλήσας, nom. sing. masc. part. aor. 1 . συλλαλέω

συλλαλοῦντες, nom. pl. masc. part. pres. . . id.

συλλᾰλέω, ῶ], fut. ήσω, (§ 16. tab. P) (σύν & λαλέω) *to talk, converse, or confer with*, Mat. 17. 3; Mar. 9. 4, et al. L.G.

συλλαμβάνου, 2 pers. sing. pres. imper. mid. συλλαμβάνω

συλλαμβάνω], fut. λήψομαι, aor. 2, συνέλᾰβον, perf. συνείληφα, aor. 1, pass. συνελήφθην, (§ 36. rem. 2) (σύν & λαμβάνω) *to catch up; to seize, apprehend*, Mat. 26. 55; Ac. 1. 16, et al.; *to catch*, as prey, Lu. 5. 9; *to conceive, become preg-*

[a] 1 Co. 1. 20. [b] Phi. 4. 3. [c] Lu. 17. 6. [d] Lu. 19. 3. [e] Col. 2. 8.

nant, Lu. 1. 24, 31, 36; 2. 21; met. Ja. 1. 15; mid. *to help, aid, assist*, Lu. 5. 7; Phi 4. 3.

συλλέγεται, 3 pers. sing. pres. ind. pass. . συλλέγω

συλλέγοντες, nom. pl. masc. part. pres. act. . id.

συλλέγουσι, 3 pers. pl. pres. ind. act. . id.

συλλέγω], fut. ξω, (§ 23. rem. 1. b) (σύν & λέγω) *to collect, gather*, Mat. 7 16; 13. 28, et al.

συλλέξατε, 2 pers. pl. aor. 1, imper. act. . συλλέγω

συλλέξουσι, 3 pers. pl. fut. ind. act. . id.

συλλέξωμεν, 1 pers. pl. aor. 1, subj. act. . id.

συλλήψῃ, 2 pers. sing. fut. ind. mid. . συλλαμβάνω

συλληφθέντα, acc. sing. masc. part. aor. 1, pass. id.

συλληφθῆναι, aor. 1, infin. pass. . . id.

συλλογίζομαι], fut. ίσομαι, (§ 26. rem. 1) (σύν & λογίζομαι) *to reckon up together; to consider, deliberate, reason*, Lu. 20. 5.

συλλυπέομαι, οῦμαι], (§ 17. tab. Q) (σύν & λυπέομαι) *to be grieved together with; to be grieved*, Mar. 3. 5.

συλλυπούμενος,[a] nom. sing. masc. part. pres. συλλυπέομαι

συμβαίνειν, pres. infin. . . . . συμβαίνω

συμβαίνοντος, gen. sing. neut. part. pres. . id.

συμβαίνω], fut. βήσομαι, aor. 2, συνέβην, (§ 37. rem. 1) (σύν & βαίνω) *to stand with the feet near together; to step or come together; to happen, befall, fall out*, Mar. 10. 32, et al.

συμβἄλεῖν, aor. 2, infin. . . συμβάλλω

συμβάλλουσα, nom. sing. fem. part. pres. . id.

συμβάλλω], fut. βαλῶ, (§ 27. rem. 2. d) (σύν & βάλλω) pr. *to throw together*; absol. *to meet and join*, Ac. 20. 14; *to meet* in war, *to encounter, engage with*, Lu. 14. 31; *to encounter* in discourse or dispute, Ac. 17. 18; *to consult together*, Ac. 4. 15; mid. *to contribute, be of service to, to aid*, Ac. 18. 27; συμβάλλειν ἐν τῇ καρδίᾳ, *to revolve in mind, ponder upon*, Lu. 2. 19

συμβάντων, gen. pl. masc. part. aor. 2 . συμβαίνω

συμβασιλεύσομεν, 1 pers. pl. fut. ind. συμβασιλεύω

συμβασιλεύσωμεν, 1 pers. pl. aor. 1, subj. . id.

συμβασιλεύω], fut. εύσω, (§ 13. tab. M) (σύν & βασιλεύω) *to reign with*; met. *to enjoy honour and felicity with*, 1 Co. 4. 8; 2 Ti. 2. 12. L.G.

συμβέβηκε, 3 pers. sing. perf. ind. (§ 37. rem. 1) συμβαίνω

συμβεβηκότι, dat. sing. neut. part. perf. . συμβαίνω

συμβεβηκότων, gen. pl. neut. part. perf. . id.

συμβιβαζόμενον, nom. s. neut. part. pres. pass. συμβιβάζω

συμβιβάζοντες, nom. pl. masc. part. pres. act. id.

συμβιβάζω], fut. άσω, (§ 26. rem. 1) (σύν & βιβάζω) pr. *to cause to come together; to unite, knit together*, Ep. 4. 16; Col. 2. 2, 19; *to infer, conclude*, Ac. 16. 10; by impl. *to prove, demonstrate*, Ac. 9. 22; in N.T. *to teach, instruct*, 1 Co. 2. 16.

συμβιβάζων, nom. sing. masc. part. pres. act. συμβιβάζω

συμβιβάσει, 3 pers. sing. fut. ind. act. . id.

συμβιβασθέντες, nom. pl. masc. part. aor. 1, pass.—Gr. Sch. Tdf. . . } id.
συμβιβασθέντων, Rec. (Col. 2. 2) . }

συμβιβασθέντων, gen. pl. m. part. aor. 1, pass. id.

συμβουλεύσας, nom. sing. masc. part. aor. 1 συμβουλεύω

συμβουλεύω], fut. εύσω, (§ 13. tab. M) (σύν & βουλεύω) *to counsel, advise, exhort*, Jno. 18. 14; Re. 3. 18; mid. *to consult together, plot*, Mat. 26. 4, et al.

συμβούλιον], ίου, τό . . . . σύμβουλος

συμβουλίου, gen. sing. . . . συμβούλιον

σύμβουλος],[b] ου, ὁ, (§ 3. tab. C. a) (σύν & βουλή) *a counsellor; one who shares one's counsel*, Ro. 11. 34.

συμβούλιον, ίου, τό, (§ 3. tab. C. c) *counsel, consultation, mutual consultation*, Mat. 12. 14; 22. 15, et al.; *a council counsellors*, Ac. 25. 12. N.T.

Συμεών], ὁ, *Symeon, Simeon*, pr. name, indecl.

I. *Simeon, son of Juda*, Lu. 3. 30.

II. *Simeon, son of Jacob*, Re. 7. 7.

III. *Simeon, a prophet of Jerusalem*, Lu. 2. 25, 34.

IV. *Simeon, or Simon Peter*, Ac. 15. 14; 2 Pe. 1. 1.

V. *Simeon, called Niger*, Ac. 13. 1.

συμμαθηταῖς,[c] dat. pl. . . . συμμαθητής

συμμαθητής], οῦ, ὁ, (§ 2. tab. B. c) (σύν & μαθητής) *a fellow-disciple*.

συμμαρτυρεῖ, 3 pers. sing. pres. ind. . συμμαρτυρέω

συμμαρτῠρέω, ῶ], fut. ήσω, (§ 16. tab. P) (σύν & μαρτυρέω) *to testify or bear witness together with* another, *add testimony*, Ro. 2. 15; 8. 16; 9. 1.

συμμαρτυροῦμαι, 1 pers. sing. pres. ind. mid. συμμαρτυρέω

συμμαρτυρούσης, gen. sing. fem. part. pres. id.

---

[a] Mar. 3. 5. [b] Ro. 11. 34. [c] Jno. 11. 16.

συμμερίζομαι], fut. ίσομαι, (§ 26. rem. 1) (σύν & μερίζω) *to divide with* another so as to receive a part to one's self, *share with, partake with.* N.T.

συμμερίζονται,[a] 3 pers. pl. pres. ind. . συμμερίζομαι

συμμέτοχα, acc. pl. neut. . . . συμμέτοχος

συμμέτοχοι, nom. pl. masc. . . . id.

συμμέτοχος], ου, ὁ, ἡ, (§ 7. rem. 2) (σύν & μέτοχος) *a partaker with* any one, *a joint partaker,* Ep. 3. 6; 5. 7. L.G.

συμμιμηταί,[b] nom. pl. . . . . συμμιμητής

συμμιμητής], οῦ, ὁ, (§ 2. tab. B. c) (σύν & μιμέομαι) *an imitator together with* any one, *a joint-imitator.*

συμμορφιζόμενος, nom. sing. masc. part. pres. pass.—A. B. D. Ln. Tdf. . } συμμορφίζω
συμμορφούμενος, R. Gr. Sch. (Phi. 3. 10) }

συμμορφίζω], fut. ίσω, (§ 26. rem. 1) (σύν & μορφίζω) equivalent to συμμορφόω; which see: v.r. Phi. 3. 10.

σύμμορφον, acc. sing. neut. . . . σύμμορφος

σύμμορφος], ου, ὁ, ἡ, (§ 7. rem. 2) (σύν & μορφή) *of like form, assimilated, conformed,* Ro. 8. 29; Phi. 3. 21. N.T.

συμμορφούμενος,[c] nom. sing. masc. part. pres. pass. . . . . . συμμορφόω

συμμόρφους, acc. pl. masc. . . . σύμμορφος

συμμορφόω, ῶ], fut. ώσω, (§ 20. tab. T) (σύν & μορφόω) *to conform to.* N.T.

συμπαθεῖς,[d] nom. pl. masc. . . . συμπαθής

συμπαθέω, ῶ], fut. ήσω . . . συμπάσχω

συμπᾰθής], έος, οῦς, ὁ, ἡ . . . . id.

συμπαθῆσαι, aor. 1, infin. . . . συμπαθέω

συμπαραγενόμενοι, nom. pl. m. part. aor. 2 συμπαραγίνομαι

συμπαραγίνομαι], aor. 2, συμπαρεγενόμην, (§ 37. rem. 1) (σύν & παραγίνομαι) *to be present together with; to come together, convene,* Lu. 23. 48; *to stand by or support* one judicially, *adesse,* 2 Ti. 4. 16.

συμπαρακαλέω, ῶ], fut. έσω, (§ 22. rem. 1) (σύν & παρακαλέω) *to invite, exhort* along with others; *to animate* in company with others; pass. *to share in mutual encouragement.*

συμπαρακληθῆναι,[e] aor. 1, infin. pass. . συμπαρακαλέω

συμπαραλαβεῖν, aor. 2, infin. . συμπαραλαμβάνω

συμπαραλαβόντες, nom. pl. masc. part. aor. 2 id.

συμπαραλαβών, nom. sing. masc. part. aor. 2 id.

συμπαραλαμβάνειν, pres. infin.—B. Ln. Tdf. . . . } συμπαραλαμβάνω
συμπαραλαβεῖν, Rec. Gr. Sch. (Ac. 15. 38) . . }

συμπαραλαμβάνω], aor. 2, συμπαρέλᾰβον, (§ 36. rem. 2) (σύν & παραλαμβάνω) *to take along with, take as a companion,* Ac. 12. 25; 15. 37, 38; Gal. 1. 2.

συμπαραμένω], fut. μενῶ, (§ 27. rem. 1. a) σύν & παραμένω) *to remain or continue with or among.*

συμπαραμενῶ,[f] 1 pers. sing. fut. ind. . συμπαραμένω

συμπαρεγένετο, 3 pers. sing. aor. 2, ind. συμπαραγίνομαι

συμπάρειμι], (σύν & πάρειμι) *to be present with* any one.

συμπαρόντες,[g] nom. pl. masc. part. pres. . συμπάρειμι

συμπάσχει, 3 pers. sing. pres. ind. . . συμπάσχω

συμπάσχομεν, 1 pers. pl. pres. ind. . . id.

συμπάσχω], fut. πείσομαι, (§ 36. rem. 4) (σύν & πάσχω), *to suffer with, sympathise,* 1 Co. 12. 26; *to suffer as* another, *endure corresponding sufferings,* Ro. 8. 17.

συμπαθής, έος, οῦς, ὁ, ἡ, (§ 7. tab. G. b) (σύν & πάθος, πάσχω) *sympathising, compassionate,* 1 Pe. 3. 8.

συμπᾰθέω, ῶ, fut. ήσω, (§ 16. tab. P) *to sympathise with,* He. 4. 15; *to compassionate,* He. 10. 34.

συμπέμπω], fut. ψω, (§ 23. rem. 1. a) (σύν & πέμπω) *to send with* any one, 2 Co. 8. 18, 22.

συμπεριλᾰβών,[h] nom. sing. m. part. aor. 2 συμπεριλαμβάνω

συμπεριλαμβάνω], fut. λήψομαι, (§ 36. rem. 2) (σύν & περιλαμβάνω) *to embrace together; to embrace,* Ac. 20. 10.

συμπίνω], fut. πίομαι and πιοῦμαι, aor. 2, συνέπῐον, (§ 37. rem. 1) (σύν & πίνω) *to drink with* any one, Ac. 10. 41. (ῑ).

συμπόσιον, ίου, τό, (§ 3. tab. C. c) *a drinking together; a feast, banquet; a festive company;* in N.T., pl. συμπόσια, *mess-parties,* Mar. 6. 39.

συμπίπτω], aor. 2, συνέπεσον, (§ 37. rem. 1) (σύν & πίπτω) *to fall together; to fall in ruins,* v.r. Lu. 6. 49.

συμπληρόω, ῶ], fut. ώσω, (§ 20. tab. T) (σύν & πληρόω *to fill, fill up, fill full,* Lu. 8. 23; pass., of time, *to be completed, have fully come,* Lu. 9. 51; Ac. 2. 1.

[a] 1 Co. 9. 13. [b] Phi. 3. 17. [c] Phi. 3. 10. [d] 1 Pe. 3. 8. [e] Ro. 1. 12. [f] Phi. 1. 25. [g] Ac. 25. 24. [h] Ac. 20. 10.

συμπληροῦσθαι, pres. infin. pass. . . συμπληρόω

συμπνίγει, 3 pers. sing. pres. ind. act. . . συμπνίγω

συμπνίγονται, 3 pers. pl. pres. ind. pass. . id.

συμπνίγουσι, 3 pers. pl. pres. ind. act. . id.

συμπνίγω], fut. ιξοῦμαι, (§ 23. rem. 1. b) (σύν & πνίγω) *to throttle, choke;* trop. *to choke* the growth or increase of seed or plants, Mat. 13. 22; Mar. 4. 7, 19; Lu. 8. 14; *to press upon, crowd, throng,* Lu. 8. 42. (ῑ).

συμπολῖται,[a] nom. pl. . . . . συμπολίτης

συμπολίτης], ου, ὁ, (§ 2. tab. B. c) (σύν & πολίτης) *a fellow-citizen,* met. Ep. 2. 19. (ῑ).

συμπορεύομαι], fut. εύσομαι, (§ 14. tab. N) (σύν & πορεύομαι) *to go with, accompany,* Lu. 7. 11; 14. 25; 24. 15; *to come together, assemble,* Mar. 10. 1.

συμπορεύονται, 3 pers. pl. pres. ind. . συμπορεύομαι

συμπόσια, acc. pl. . . . συμπόσιον

συμπόσιον], ίου, τό, (§ 3. tab. C. c) . . συμπίνω

συμπρεσβύτερος],[b] ου, ὁ, (§ 3. tab. C. a) (σύν & πρεσβύτερος) *a fellow-elder, fellow-presbyter.* N.T.

συμφέρει, 3 pers. sing. pres. ind. . . συμφέρω

συμφέρον, acc. sing. neut. part. pres. . . id.

συμφερόντων, gen. pl. neut. part. pres. . id.

συμφέρω], fut. συνοίσω, aor. 1, συνήνεγκα, aor. 2, συνήνεγκον, (§ 36. rem. 1) (σύν & φέρω) *to bring together, collect,* Ac. 19. 19; absol. *to conduce to, be for the benefit of any one, be profitable, advantageous, expedient,* 1 Co. 6. 12; *to suit best, be appropriate,* 2 Co. 8. 10; particip. neut. **τὸ συμφέρον,** *good, benefit, profit, advantage,* Ac. 20. 20; 1 Co. 7. 35; impers. **συμφέρει,** *it is profitable, advantageous, expedient,* Mat. 5. 29, 30; 19. 10, et al.

σύμφορος, ου, ὁ, ἡ, (§ 7. rem. 2) *profitable, expedient,* v.r. 1 Co. 7. 35; 10. 33.

σύμφημι],[c] (§ 33. tab. DD, and rem. 1) (σύν & φημί) pr. *to affirm with; to assent.*

σύμφορον, acc. sing. neut.—A. C. Ln. Tdf. } σύμφορος
συμφέρον, Rec. Gr. Sch. (1 Co. 10. 33) }

σύμφορος], ου, ὁ, ἡ, v.r. . . . . συμφέρω

συμφυλέτης], ου, ὁ, (§ 2. tab. B. c) (σύν & φυλή) pr. *one of the same tribe; a fellow-citizen, fellow-countryman.*

συμφυλετῶν,[d] gen. pl. . . . . συμφυλέτης

συμφυεῖσαι,[e] nom. pl. fem. part. aor. 2, pass. . συμφύω

σύμφυτοι,[f] nom. pl. masc. . . . σύμφυτος

σύμφῠτος], ου, ὁ, ἡ, (§ 7. rem. 2) (σύν & φύω) pr. *planted together, grown together;* in N.T. met. *grown together, closely entwined or united with,* Ro. 6. 5.

συμφύω], fut. φύσω, aor. 2, pass. συνεφύην, (§ 24. rem. 11) (σύν & φύω) *to make to grow together;* pass. *to grow or spring up with,* Lu. 8. 7.

συμφωνεῖ, 3 pers. sing. pres. ind. . . συμφωνέω

συμφωνέω, ῶ], fut. ήσω . . . σύμφωνος

συμφωνήσας, nom. sing. masc. part. aor. 1 . συμφωνέω

συμφωνήσει, 3 pers. sing. fut. ind.—A. B. C. D. Ln. Tdf. . . . . } id.
συμφωνεῖ, Rec. Gr. Sch. (Lu. 5. 36) }

συμφώνησις],[g] εως, ἡ . . . . σύμφωνος

συμφωνήσωσι, 3 pers. pl. aor. 1, subj. . συμφωνέω

συμφωνία], ας, ἡ . . . . . σύμφωνος

συμφωνίας,[h] gen. sing. . . . συμφωνία

σύμφωνος], ου, ὁ, ἡ, (§ 7. rem. 2) (σύν & φωνή) *agreeing in sound;* met. *accordant, harmonious, agreeing,* and neut. τὸ σύμφωνον, *accord, agreement,* 1 Co. 7. 5.

συμφωνέω, ῶ, fut. ήσω, (§ 16. tab. P) *to sound together, to be in unison, be in accord;* trop. *to agree with, accord with* in purport, Ac. 15. 15; *to harmonise with, be congruous, suit with,* Lu. 5. 36; *to agree with, make an agreement,* Mat. 18. 19; 20. 2, 13; Ac. 5. 9.

συμφώνησις, εως, ἡ, (§ 5. tab. E. c) *unison, accord; agreement, concord,* 2 Co. 6. 15. N.T.

συμφωνία, ας, ἡ, (§ 2. tab. B. b, and rem. 2) *symphony, harmony of sounds concert of instruments, music,* Lu. 15. 25.

συμφώνου,[i] gen. sing. neut. . . . σύμφωνος

συμφωνοῦσι, 3 pers. pl. pres. ind. . . συμφωνέω

συμψηφίζω], fut. ίσω, (§ 26. rem. 1) (σύν & ψηφίζω, ψῆφος) *to calculate together, compute, reckon up,* Ac. 19. 19.

σύμψυχοι,[k] nom. pl. masc. . . . σύμψυχος

σύμψῡχος], ου, ὁ, ἡ, (§ 7. rem. 2) (σύν & ψυχή) *united in mind, at unity.* N.T.

σύν], prep. governing a dat., *with, together with,* Mat. 25. 27; 26. 35; 27. 38; *attendant*

[a] Ep. 2. 19. [b] 1 Pe. 5. 1. [c] Ro. 7. 16. [d] 1 Thes. 2. 14. [e] Lu. 8. 7. [f] Ro. 6. 5. [g] 2 Co. 6. 15. [h] Lu. 15. 25. [i] 1 Co. 7. 5. [k] Phi. 2. 2.

on, 1 Co. 15. 10; *besides*, Lu. 24. 21; *with, with the assistance of*, 1 Co. 5. 4; *with, in the same manner as*, Gal. 3. 9; εἶναι σύν τινι, *to be with any one, to be in company with, accompany*, Lu. 2. 13; 8. 38; *to be on the side of, be a partisan of any one*, Ac. 4. 13; 14. 4; οἱ σύν τινι, *those with any one, the companions of any one*, Mar. 2. 26; Ac. 22. 9; *the colleagues, associates of any one*, Ac. 5. 17, 21.

συναγαγεῖν, aor. 2, infin. act. (§ 13. rem. 7. d) συνάγω
συναγάγετε, 2 pers. pl. aor. 2, imper. act. id.
συναγάγη, 3 pers. sing. aor. 2, subj. act. id.
συναγαγόντες, nom. pl. masc. part. aor. 2, act. id.
συναγαγούσῃ, dat. sing. fem. part. aor. 2, act. id.
συναγαγών, nom. sing. masc. part. aor. 2, act. id.
συνάγει, 3 pers. sing. pres. ind. act. id.
συνάγεσθε, 2 pers. pl. pres. imper. pass. id.
συνάγεται, 3 pers. sing. pres. ind. pass.—B. C. Tdf. }
συνήχθη, Rec. Gr. Sch. Ln. (Mar. 4. 1) } id.
συνάγονται, 3 pers. pl. pres. ind. pass. id.
συνάγουσι, 3 pers. pl. pres. ind. act.

συνάγω], fut. άξω, aor. 2, συνήγᾰγον, (§ 13. rem. 7. d) perf. pass. συνῆγμαι, aor. 1, pass. συνήχθην, (§ 23. rem. 7, and 4) fut. pass. συναχθήσομαι, (§ 23. rem. 3. b) (σύν & ἄγω) *to bring together, collect, gather*, as grain, fruits, etc., Mat. 3. 12; 6. 26; 13. 30, 47; *to collect* an assembly, *convoke*; pass. *to convene, come together, meet*, Mat. 2. 4; 13. 2; 18. 20; 22. 10; in N.T. *to receive with kindness and hospitality, to entertain*, Mat. 25. 35, 38, 43, et al. (ᾰ).

συναγωγή, ῆς, ἡ, (§ 2. tab. B. a) *a collecting, gathering; a Christian assembly or congregation*, Ja. 2. 2; *the congregation* of a synagogue, Ac. 9. 2, et al.; hence, the place itself, *a synagogue*, Lu. 7. 5, et al.

συναγωγάς, acc. pl. συναγωγή
συναγωγαῖς, dat. pl. id.
συναγωγή], ῆς, ἡ συνάγω
συναγωγῇ, dat. sing. συναγωγή
συναγωγήν, acc. sing. id.
συναγωγῆς, gen. sing. id.
συναγωγῶν, gen. pl. id.
συναγών, nom. sing. masc. part. pres. act. συνάγω

συναγωνίζομαι], fut. ίσομαι, (§ 26. rem. 1) (σύν & ἀγωνίζομαι) *to combat in company with* any one; *to exert one's strength with, to be earnest in aiding*, Ro. 15. 30.

συναγωνίσασθαι, aor. 1, infin. συναγωνίζομαι

συναθλέω, ῶ], fut. ήσω, (§ 16. tab. P) (σύν & ἀθλέω) pr. *to contend on the side of* any one; in N.T. *to co-operate vigorously with* a person, Phi. 4. 3; *to make effort in the cause of, in support of* a thing, Phi. 1. 27. L.G.

συναθλοῦντες, nom. pl. masc. part. pres. συναθλέω

συναθροίζω], fut. οίσω, (§ 26. rem. 1) (σύν & ἀθροίζω, *to gather*, ἀθρόος) *to gather; to bring together, convoke*, Ac. 19. 25; pass. *to come together, convene*, Lu. 24. 23; Ac. 12. 12.

συναθροίσας, nom. sing. masc. part. aor. 1 συναθροίζω
συναίρει, 3 pers. sing. pres. ind. συναίρω
συναίρειν, pres. infin. id.

συναίρω], fut. αρῶ, (§ 27. rem. 1. c) (σύν & αἴρω) *to take up* a thing *with* any one; in N.T. συναίρειν λόγον, *to adjust accounts, reckon* in order to payment, Mat. 18. 23, 24; 25. 19.

συναιχμάλωτος], ου, ὁ, ἡ, (σύν & αἰχμάλωτος) *a fellow-captive*, Ro. 16. 7; Col. 4. 10; Phi. 23. N.T.

συναιχμαλώτους, acc. pl. masc. συναιχμάλωτος

συνακολουθέω, ῶ], fut. ήσω, (§ 16. tab. P) (σύν & ἀκολουθέω) *to follow in company with, accompany*, Mar. 5. 37; Lu. 23. 49.

συνακολουθῆσαι, aor. 1, infin. συνακολουθέω
συνακολουθήσασαι, nom. pl. fem. part. aor. 1 id.

συνᾱλίζω], fut. ίσω, (§ 26. rem. 1) (σύν & ἁλίζω, *to collect*) *to cause to come together, collect, assemble, congregate*; mid. *to convene to one's self*.

συναλιζόμενος,[a] nom. s. masc. part. pres. mid. συναλίζω

συναλλάσσω], (σύν & ἀλλάσσω) *to negotiate or bargain with* any one; *to reconcile*, v.r Ac. 7. 26.

συναναβαίνω], fut. βήσομαι, aor. 2, συνανέβην, (§ 37. rem. 1) (σύν & ἀναβαίνω) *to go up, ascend with* any one, Mar. 15. 41; Ac. 13. 31.

συναναβᾶσαι, nom. pl. fem. part. aor. 2 συναναβαίνω
συναναβᾶσι, dat. pl. masc. part. aor. 2 id.

[a] Ac. 1. 4.

συνανάκειμαι], fut. είσομαι) (§ 33. tab. DD) (σύν & ἀνάκειμαι) *to recline with* any one at table, Mat. 9. 10; 14. 9, et al. N.T.

συνανακείμενοι, nom. pl. masc. part. pres. . συνανάκειμαι

συνανακειμένοις, dat. pl. masc. part. pres. . id.

συνανακειμένους, acc. pl. masc. part. pres. . id.

συνανακειμένων, gen. pl. part. pres. . . id.

συναναμίγνυμι], (σύν & ἀναμίγνυμι, *to mix, mingle*) *to mix together with, commingle*; mid. met. *to mingle one's self with, to associate with, have familiar intercourse with*, 1 Co. 5. 9, 11; 2 Thes. 3. 14. L.G.

συναναμίγνυσθαι, pres. infin. mid. . συναναμίγνυμι

συναναμίγνυσθε, 2 pers. pl. pres. imper. mid. id.

συναναπαύομαι], fut. αύσομαι, (§ 14. tab. N) (σύν & ἀναπαύομαι) *to experience refreshment in company with* any one. L.G.

συναναπαύσωμαι,[a] 1 pers. sing. aor. 1, subj. συναναπαύομαι

συνανέκειντο, 3 pers. pl. imperf. . συνανάκειμαι

συναντάω, ῶ], fut. ήσω, (§ 18. tab. R) (σύν & ἀντάω, ἀντί) *to meet with, fall in with, encounter, to meet*, Lu. 9. 37; 22. 10; Ac. 10. 25; He. 7 1, 10; *to occur, happen to, befall*, Ac. 20. 22.

συνάντησις, εως, ἡ, (§ 5. tab. E. c) *a meeting*, Mat. 8. 34.

συναντήσας, nom. sing. masc. part. aor. 1 . συναντάω

συναντήσει, 3 pers. sing. fut. ind. . : id.

συνάντησιν,[b] acc. sing. . . . . συνάντησις

συνάντησις], εως, ἡ . . . . συναντάω

συναντήσοντα, acc. pl. neut. part. fut. . id.

συναντιλάβηται, 3 pers. s. aor. 2, subj. συναντιλαμβάνομαι

συναντιλαμβάνεται, 3 pers. sing. pres. ind. . id.

συναντιλαμβάνομαι], fut. λήψομαι, (§ 36. rem. 2) (συν & ἀντιλαμβάνομαι) pr. *to take hold of with* any one; *to support, help, aid*, Lu. 10. 40; Ro. 8. 26. L.G.

συνάξει, 3 pers. sing. fut. ind. act. . . συνάγω

συνάξω, 1 pers. sing. fut. ind. act. . . id.

συναπάγω], fut. άξω, (§ 23. rem. 1. b) (σύν & ἀπάγω) *to lead or conduct away with; to seduce*; pass. *to be led away, carried astray*, Gal. 2. 13; 2 Pe. 3. 17; mid. *to conform one's self willingly to* certain circumstances, Ro. 12. 16.

συναπαγόμενοι, nom. pl. masc. part. pres. mid. συναπάγω

συναπαχθέντες, nom. pl. masc. part. aor. 1, pass. id.

συναπεθάνομεν, 1 pers. pl. aor. 2, ind. συναποθνήσκω

συναπέστειλα,[c] 1 pers. sing. aor. 1, ind. συναποστέλλω

συναπήχθη, 3 pers. sing. aor. 1, ind. pass. συναπάγω

συναποθανεῖν, aor. 2, infin. . . συναποθνήσκω

συναποθνήσκω], aor. 2, συναπέθανον, (§ 36. rem. 4) σύν & ἀποθνήσκω) *to die together with* any one, Mar. 14. 31; 2 Co. 7. 3; met. *to die with*, in respect of a spiritual likeness, 2 Ti. 2. 11.

συναπόλλυμι], aor. 2, mid. συναπωλόμην, (§ 36. rem. 5) (σύν & ἀπόλλυμι) *to destroy together with* others; mid. *to perish or be destroyed with* others, He. 11. 31.

συναποστέλλω], fut. στελῶ, aor. 1, συναπέστειλα, (§ 27. rem. 1. b. d) (σύν & ἀποστέλλω) *to send forth together with* any one, 2 Co. 12. 18.

συναπώλετο,[d] 3 pers. sing. aor. 2, ind. mid. συναπόλλυμι

συνᾶραι, aor. 1, infin. (§ 27. rem. 1. f) . συναίρω

συναρμολογέω, ῶ], fut. ήσω, (§ 16. tab. P) (σύν & ἁρμολογέω, from ἁρμός, *a joint*, & λόγος) *to join together fitly, fit or frame together, compact*, Ep. 2. 21; 4. 16. N.T.

συναρμολογουμένη, nom. sing. fem. part. pres. pass. (§ 17. tab. Q) . συναρμολογέω

συναρμολογούμενον, nom. sing. neut. part. pres. pass. . . . . id.

συναρπάζω], fut. άσω, (§ 26. rem. 1) (σύν & ἁρπάζω) *to snatch up, clutch; to seize and carry off suddenly*, Ac. 6. 12; *to seize with force and violence*, Lu. 8. 29; pass. of a ship, *to be caught and swept on* by the wind, Ac. 27. 15.

συναρπάσαντες, nom. pl. masc. part. aor. 1, act. συναρπάζω

συναρπασθέντος, gen. s. neut. part. aor. 1, pass. id.

συναυξάνεσθαι,[e] pres. infin. . . συναυξάνομαι

συναυξάνομαι], fut. ήσομαι, (§ 35. rem. 5) (σύν & αὐξάνω) *to grow together* in company.

συναχθέντες, nom. pl. masc. part. aor. 1, pass συνάγω

συναχθέντων, gen. pl. masc. part. aor. 1, pass. id.

συναχθῆναι, aor. 1, infin. pass. (§ 23. rem. 4) id.

συναχθήσεται, 3 pers. sing. fut. ind. pass. id.

συναχθήσονται, 3 pers. pl. fut. ind. pass. . id.

συνάχθητε, 2 pers. pl. aor. 1, imper. pass.—Gr. Sch. Tdf. . . . } id.
συνάγεσθε, Rec. (Re. 19. 17) .

συνδεδεμένοι,[f] nom. pl. masc. part. perf. pass. συνδέω

σύνδεσμον, acc. sing. . . . . σύνδεσμος

σύνδεσμος], ου, ὁ . . . . . συνδέω

[a] Ro. 15. 32. [b] Mat. 8. 34. [c] 2 Co. 12. 18. [d] He. 11. 31. [e] Mat. 13. 30. [f] He. 13. 3.

συνδέσμῳ, dat. sing. . . . . . σύνδεσμος
συνδέσμων, gen. pl. . . . . . id.
συνδέω], fut. δήσω, (§ 37. rem. 1) (σύν & δέω) *to bind together*; in N.T. pass. *to be in bonds together*, He. 13. 3.

σύνδεσμος, ου, ὁ, (§ 3. tab. C. a) *that which binds together*; *a ligature*, Col. 2. 19; *a band* of union, Ep. 4. 3; Col. 3. 14; *a bundle*, or, *bond*, Ac. 8. 23.

συνδοξάζω], fut. άσω, (§ 26. rem. 1) (σύν & δοξάζω) in N.T. *to glorify together with*, *to exalt to a state of dignity and happiness in company with*, *to make to partake in the glorification* of another.

συνδοξασθῶμεν,[a] 1 pers. pl. aor. 1, subj. pass. συνδοξάζω
σύνδουλοι, nom. pl. . . . . . σύνδουλος
σύνδουλον, acc. sing. . . . . . id.
σύνδουλος], ου, ὁ, (§ 3. tab. C. a) (σύν & δοῦλος) *a fellow-slave*, *fellow-servant*, Mat. 24. 49, et al.; *a fellow-minister* of Christ, Col. 1. 7, et al.

συνδούλου, gen. sing. . . . . . σύνδουλος
συνδούλους, acc. pl. . . . . . id.
συνδούλων, gen. pl. . . . . . id.
συνδρομή],[b] ῆς, ἡ, (§ 2. tab. B. a) . . συντρέχω
συνέβαινον, 3 pers. pl. imperf. . . συμβαίνω
συνέβαλε, 3 pers. sing. aor. 2, ind. (§ 27. rem. 2. d) . . . . . συμβάλλω
συνεβάλετο, 3 pers. sing. aor. 2, ind. mid. . id.
συνέβαλλον, 3 pers. pl. imperf. act. . id.
συνέβαλον, 3 pers. pl. aor. 2, ind. act. . id.
συνέβη, 3 pers. sing. aor. 2, ind. (§ 37. rem. 1) συμβαίνω
συνεβίβασαν, 3 pers. pl. aor. 1, ind.—A. B. Ln. Tdf. . . . . . } συμβιβάζω
προεβίβασαν, Rec. Gr. Sch. (Ac. 19. 33) }
συνεβουλεύσαντο, 3 pers. pl. aor. 1, ind. mid. συμβουλεύω
συνεγείρω], fut. γερῶ, (§ 37. rem. 1) (σύν & ἐγείρω) *to raise up with* any one; *to raise up with* Christ by spiritual resemblance of His resurrection, Ep. 2. 6; Col. 2. 12; 3. 1. L.G.

συνέδραμε, 3 pers. sing. aor. 2, ind. . . συντρέχω
συνέδραμον, 3 pers. pl. aor. 2, ind. . id.
συνέδρια, acc. pl. . . . . . . συνέδριον
συνέδριον], ίου, τό, (§ 3. tab. C. c) (σύν & ἕδρα) pr. *a sitting together*, *assembly*, etc.; in N.T. *the Sanhedrin*, the supreme council of the Jewish nation, Mat. 5. 22; 26. 59; meton. *the Sanhedrin*, as including the members and place of meeting, Lu. 22. 66; Ac. 4. 15, et al.; genr. *a judicial council*, *tribunal*, Mat. 10. 17; Mar. 13. 9.

συνεδρίου, gen. sing. . . . . . συνέδριον
συνεδρίῳ, dat. sing. . . . . . id.
συνέζευξε, 3 pers. sing. aor. 1, ind. . συζεύγνυμι
συνεζήτει, 3 pers. sing. imperf. (§ 34. rem. 1. c) . συζητέω
συνεζωοποίησε, 3 pers. sing. aor. 1, ind. . συζωοποιέω
συνέθλιβον, 3 pers. pl. imperf. . . . συνθλίβω
συνέθεντο, 3 pers. pl. aor. 2. ind. mid . συντίθημι
συνειδήσει, dat. sing. . . . . συνείδησις
συνειδήσεσι, dat. pl. . . . . . id.
συνειδήσεως, gen. sing. . . . . . id.
συνείδησιν, acc. sing. . . . . . id.
συνείδησις], εως, ἡ . . . . . . σύνοιδα
συνεῖδον], aor. 2 of συνοράω, pt. συνϊδών, (§ 36. rem. 1) *to see under one range of view*; *to take a deliberate glance* of a state of matters, Ac. 12. 12; 14. 6.

συνειδυίας, gen. sing. fem. part. . . σύνοιδα
συνειδώς, see σύνοιδα.
συνειληφυῖα, nom. sing. fem. part. perf. act. (§ 36. rem. 2) . . . . συλλαμβάνω
σύνειμι], fut. συνέσομαι, (§ 12. tab. L) (σύν & εἰμί) *to be with*, *be in company with*, Lu. 9. 18; Ac. 22. 11.

σύνειμι], part. συνιών, (§ 33. rem. 4) (σύν & εἶμι) *to come together*, *assemble*, Lu. 8. 4.

συνείπετο,[c] 3 pers. sing. imperf. (§ 13. rem. 4) συνέπομαι
συνεισέρχομαι], aor. 2, συνεισῆλθον, (§ 36. rem. 1) (σύν & εἰσέρχομαι) *to enter with* any one, Jno. 18. 15; *to embark with*, Jno. 6. 22.

συνεισῆλθε, 3 pers. sing. aor. 2, ind. . συνεισέρχομαι
συνείχετο, 3 pers. sing. imperf. pass. . συνέχω
συνείχοντο, 3 pers. pl. imperf. pass. . . id.
συνεκάθισε, 3 pers. sing. aor. 1, ind. (§ 34. rem. 1. c) . . . . . συγκαθίζω
συνεκάλεσαν, 3 pers. pl. aor. 1, ind. act. . . συγκαλέω
συνέκδημος], ου, ὁ, ἡ, (§ 7. rem. 2) (σύν & ἔκδημος, *a traveller to foreign countries*) *one who accompanies* another *to foreign countries*, *fellow-traveller*, Ac. 19. 29; 2 Co. 8. 19. L.G.

συνεκδήμους, acc. pl. masc. . . . συνέκδημος
συνεκέρασε, 3 pers. sing. aor. 1, ind. act. συγκεράννυμι
συνεκίνησαν,[d] 3 pers. pl. aor. 1, ind. act. . συγκινέω

[a] Ro. 8. 17. [b] Ac. 21. 30. [c] Ac. 20. 4. [d] Ac. 6. 12.

συνέκλεισαν, 3 pers. pl. aor. 1, ind. act. . συγκλείω
συνέκλεισε, 3 pers. sing. aor. 1, ind. act. . id.
συνεκλεκτή,[a] nom. sing. fem. . . συνεκλεκτός
συνεκλεκτός], ή, όν, (§ 7. tab. F. a) (σύν & ἐκλεκτός) *chosen along with* others, *elected* to Gospel privileges *along with*, 1 Pe. 5. 13. N.T.
συνεκόμισαν,[b] 3 pers. pl. aor. 1, ind. . συγκομίζω
συνέλαβε, 3 pers. sing. aor. 2, ind. act. . συλλαμβάνω
συνέλαβον, 3 pers. pl. aor. 2, ind. act. . id.
συνελάλησε, 3 pers. sing. aor. 1, ind. . συλλαλέω
συνελάλουν, 3 pers. pl. imperf. . . . id.
συνελαύνω], fut. ελάσω, aor. 1, συνήλᾰσα, (§ 36. rem. 2) (σύν & ἐλαύνω) pr. *to drive together; to urge to meet*; in N.T. *to urge* to union, Ac. 7. 26.
συνέλεξαν, 3 pers. pl. aor. 1, ind. act. . συλλέγω
συνεληλυθυῖαι, nom. pl. fem. part. perf. συνέρχομαι
συνεληλύθεισαν, 3 pers. pl. pluperf. . . id.
συνεληλυθότας, acc. pl. masc. part. perf. . id.
συνελθεῖν, aor. 2, infin. . . . . id.
συνέλθῃ, 3 pers. sing. aor. 2, subj. . . id.
συνελθόντα, acc. sing. masc. part. aor. 2 . id.
συνελθόντας, acc. pl. masc. part. aor. 2 . id.
συνελθόντες, nom. pl. masc. part. aor. 2 . id.
συνελθόντων, gen. pl. masc. part. aor. 2 id.
συνελθούσαις, dat. pl. fem. part. aor. 2 . id.
συνελογίσαντο,[c] 3 pers. pl. aor. 1, ind. συλλογίζομαι
συνενέγκαντες, nom. pl. masc. part. aor. 1 συμφέρω
συνέξουσι, 3 pers. pl. fut. ind. . . συνέχω
συνεπαθήσατε, 2 pers. pl. aor. 1, ind. . . συμπαθέω
συνεπέθεντο, 3 pers. pl. aor. 2, ind.—Gr. Sch. Tdf. . . } συνεπιτίθεμαι
συνέθεντο, Rec. (Ac. 24. 9) . }
συνεπέμψαμεν, 1 pers. pl. aor. 1, ind. act. συμπέμπω
συνέπεσε, 3 pers. sing. aor. 2, ind.—D. Tdf. } συμπίπτω
ἔπεσε, Rec. Gr. Sch. Ln. (Lu. 6. 49) }
συνεπέστη,[d] 3 pers. sing. aor. 2, ind. . συνεφίστημι
συνεπιμαρτυρέω, ῶ], fut. ήσω, (§ 16. tab. P) (σύν & ἐπιμαρτυρέω) *to join in according attestation; to support by attestation, to confirm, sanction.*
συνεπιμαρτυροῦντος,[e] gen. sing. masc. part. pres. . . . . . συνεπιμαρτυρέω
συνεπίομεν, 1 pers. pl. aor. 2, ind. . . συμπίνω
συνεπιτίθεμαι], (σύν & ἐπιτίθημι) *to set upon along with, assail at the same time; to unite in impeaching*, v.r. Ac. 24. 9.

συνεπληροῦντο, 3 pers. pl. imperf. pass. . συμπληρόω
συνέπνιγον, 3 pers. pl. imperf. act. . συμπνίγω
συνέπνιξαν, 3 pers. pl. aor. 1, ind. act. . id.
συνέπομαι], imperf. συνειπόμην, (§ 13. rem. 4) (σύν & ἕπομαι, *to follow*) *to follow with, attend, accompany*, Ac. 20. 4.
συνεπορεύετο, 3 pers. sing. imperf. . συμπορεύομαι
συνεπορεύοντο, 3 pers. pl. imperf. . . id.
συνεργεῖ, 3 pers. sing. pres. ind. . . . συνεργέω
συνεργέω, ῶ], fut. ήσω . . . συνεργός
συνεργοί, nom. pl. masc. . . . . id.
συνεργόν, acc. sing. masc. . . . id
συνεργός], οῦ, ὁ, ἡ, (σύν & ἔργον) *a fellow-labourer, associate, coadjutor*, Ro. 16. 3, 9, 21; 2 Co. 1. 24, et al.

συνεργέω, ῶ, fut. ήσω, (§ 16. tab. P) *to work together with, to co-operate*, etc., 1 Co. 16. 16; 2 Co. 6. 1; *to assist, afford aid to*, Mar. 16. 20; *to be a motive principle*, Ja. 2. 22; absol. *to conspire actively* to a result, Ro. 8. 28.

συνεργοῦντες, nom. pl. masc. part. pres. . συνεργέω
συνεργοῦντι, dat. sing. masc. part. pres. . id.
συνεργοῦντος, gen. sing. masc. part. pres. . id.
συνεργούς, acc. pl. masc. . . . συνεργός
συνεργῷ, dat. sing. masc. . . . . id.
συνεργῶν, gen. pl. . . . . . id.
συνέρχεσθε, 2 pers. pl. pres. ind. and imper. συνέρχομαι
συνέρχεται, 3 pers. sing. pres. ind. . . id.
συνέρχησθε, 2 pers. pl. pres. subj. . . id.
συνέρχομαι], aor. 2, συνῆλθον, (§ 36. rem. 1) (σύν & ἔρχομαι) *to come together; to assemble*, Mar. 3. 20; 6. 33; 14. 53; *to cohabit* matrimonially, Mat. 1. 13; 1 Co. 7. 5; *to go or come with* any one, *to accompany*, Lu. 23. 55; Ac. 9. 39; *to company with, associate with*, Ac. 1. 21, et al.
συνερχόμενοι, nom. pl. masc. part. pres. συνέρχομαι
συνερχομένων, gen. pl. part. pres. . . id.
συνέρχονται, 3 pers. pl. pres. ind. . . id.
συνέσει, dat. sing. . . . . σύνεσις
συνέσεως, gen. sing. . . . . id.
συνεσθίει, 3 pers. sing. pres. ind. . . συνεσθίω
συνεσθίειν, pres. infin. . . . . id.
συνεσθίω], aor. 2, συνέφᾰγον, (§ 36. rem. 1) (σύν & ἐσθίω) *to eat with*, 1 Co. 5. 11; by impl. *to associate with, live on familiar terms with*, Lu. 15. 2; Gal. 2. 12.

[a] 1 Pe. 5. 13 [b] Ac. 8. 2. [c] Lu. 20. 5. [d] Ac. 16. 22. [e] He. 2. 4.

σύνεσιν, acc. sing. . . . . σύνεσις
σύνεσις], εως, ἡ, (§ 5. tab. E. c) . . . συνίημι
συνεσπάραξε,[a] 3 pers. sing. aor. 1, ind. . συσπαράσσω
συνεσταλμένος, nom. s. masc. part. perf. pass. συστέλλω
συνεσταυρώθη, 3 pers. sing. aor. 1, ind. pass. (§ 21. tab. U) . . . συσταυρόω
συνεσταύρωμαι, 1 pers. sing. perf. ind. pass. . id.
συνεσταυρωμένοι, nom. pl. m. part. perf. pass. id.
συνέστειλαν, 3 pers. pl. aor. 1, ind. act. (§ 27. rem. 1. d) . . . . . συστέλλω
συνέστηκε, 3 pers. s. perf. ind. (§ 29. tab. X) συνίστημι
συνεστήσατε, 2 pers. pl. aor. 1, ind. . . id.
συνεστῶσα, nom. sing. fem. part. perf. (§ 35. rem. 8) . . . . . id.
συνεστῶτας, acc. pl. masc. part. perf. . . id.
συνέσχον, 3 pers. pl. aor. 2, ind. (§ 36. rem. 4) συνέχω
συνέταξε, 3 pers. sing. aor. 1, ind. act. . συντάσσω
συνετάφημεν, 1 pers. pl. aor. 2, ind. pass. (§ 24. rem. 8. b) . . . συνθάπτω
σύνετε, 2 pers. pl. aor. 2, imper.—B. Ln. Tdf. } συνίημι
συνίετε, Rec. Gr. Sch. (Mar. 7. 14) . }
συνετέθειντο, 3 pers. pl. pluperf. pass. (§ 28. rem. 10) . . . . . συντίθημι
συνετέλεσε, 3 pers. sing. aor. 1, ind. act. . συντελέω
συνετήρει, 3 pers. sing. imperf. act. . . συντηρέω
συνετός], ή, όν, (§ 7. tab. F. a) . . συνίημι
συνετῷ, dat. sing. masc. . . . . συνετός
συνετῶν, gen. pl. . . . . . id.
συνευδοκεῖ, 3 pers. sing. pres. ind. . συνευδοκέω
συνευδοκεῖτε, 2 pers. pl. pres. ind. . . id.
συνευδοκέω, ῶ], fut. ήσω, (§ 16. tab. P) (σύν & εὐδοκέω) *to approve with* another; *to accord with in principle*, Ro. 1. 32; *to stamp approval*, Lu. 11. 48; Ac. 8. 1; 22. 20; *to be willing, agreeable*, 1 Co. 7. 12, 13.
συνευδοκοῦσι, 3 pers. pl. pres. ind. . συνευδοκέω
συνευδοκῶν, nom. sing. masc. part. pres. . id.
συνευωχέομαι, οῦμαι], fut. ήσομαι, (§ 17. tab. Q) (σύν & εὐωχέομαι, *to feast, banquet*) *to feast together with*, 2 Pe. 2. 13; Jude 12.
συνευωχούμενοι, nom. pl. masc. part. pres. συνευωχέομαι
συνέφαγες, 2 pers. sing. aor. 2, ind. . . συνεσθίω
συνεφάγομεν, 1 pers. pl. aor. 2, ind. . id.
συνεφίστημι], (§ 29. tab. X) (σύν & ἐφίστημι) *to set together upon*; intrans. aor. 2, συνεπέστην, *to assail together*, Ac. 16. 22.
συνεφωνήθη, 3 pers. sing. aor. 1, ind. pass. συμφωνέω
συνεφώνησας, 2 pers. sing. aor. 1, ind. act. . id.

συνέχαιρον, 3 pers. pl. imperf. . συγχαίρω
συνέχεον, 3 pers. pl. imperf. (§ 35. rem. 1, συγχέω
συνέχει, 3 pers. sing. pres. ind. act. . . συνέχω
συνέχομαι, 1 pers. sing. pres. ind. pass. . id.
συνεχομένη, nom. sing. fem. part. pres. pass. id.
συνεχόμενον, acc. sing. masc. part. pres. pass. id.
συνεχομένους, acc. pl. masc. part. pres. pass. id.
συνέχοντες, nom. pl. masc. part. pres. act. . id.
συνέχουσι, 3 pers. pl. pres. ind. act. . id.
συνεχύθη, 3 pers. sing. aor. 1, ind. pass. . συγχέω
συνέχυνε, 3 pers. sing. imperf. act. . . συγχύνω
συνέχω], fut. ἕξω, (§ 36. rem. 4) (σύν & ἔχω) pr. *to hold together; to confine, shut up close*; τὰ ὦτα, *to stop the ears*, Ac. 7. 57; *to confine, straiten*, as a besieged city, Lu. 19. 43; *to hold, hold fast, have the custody of* any one, Lu. 22. 63; *to hem in, urge, press upon*, Lu. 8. 45; *to exercise a constraining influence on*, 2 Co. 5. 14; pass. *to be seized with, be affected with*, as fear, disease, etc., Mat. 4. 24; Lu. 4. 38, et al.; *to be in a state of* mental *constriction, to be hard pressed* by urgency of circumstances, Lu. 12. 50; Ac. 18. 5; Phi. 1. 23.

συνοχή, ῆς, ἡ, (§ 2. tab. B. a) pr. *a being held together; compression*; in N.T. met. *distress of mind, anxiety*, Lu. 21. 25; 2 Co. 2. 4.

συνεψήφισαν,[b] 3 pers. pl. aor. 1, ind. . συμψηφίζω
συνήγαγε, 3 pers. sing. aor. 2, ind. act. (§ 13. rem. 7. d) . . . . συνάγω
συνηγάγετε, 2 pers. pl. aor. 2, ind. act. . id.
συνηγάγομεν, 1 pers. pl. aor. 2, ind. act. . id.
συνήγαγον, 3 pers. pl. aor. 2, ind. act. . id.
συνήγειρε, 3 pers. sing. aor. 1, ind. act. . συνεγείρω
συνηγέρθητε, 2 pers. pl. aor. 1, ind. pass. . id.
συνηγμένα, acc. pl. neut. part. perf. pass. . συνάγω
συνηγμένοι, nom. pl. masc. part. perf. pass. . id
συνηγμένων, gen. pl. part. perf. pass. . id.
συνήδομαι],[c] fut. συνησθήσομαι, (σύν & ἥδομαι, *to be pleased, delighted*) *to be pleased along with* others; *to congratulate*; *to delight in, approve cordially*, Ro. 7. 22.
συνήθεια], ας, ἡ, (§ 2. tab. B. b, and rem. 2) (συνήθης, *accustomed, familiar, customary*, fr. σύν & ἦθος) *intercourse; use, custom; an established custom, practice*, Jno. 18. 39; 1 Co. 11. 16.

[a] Lu. 9. 42. [b] Ac. 19. 19. [c] Ro. 7. 22.

συνηθείᾳ, dat. sing.—A. B. Ln. Tdf. . } συνήθεια
συνειδήσει, Rec. Gr. Sch. (1 Co. 8. 7) }

συνήθειαν, acc. sing. . . . . id.

συνήθλησαν, 3 pers. pl. aor. 1, ind. . . συναθλέω

συνηθροισμένοι, nom. pl. m. part. perf. pass. συναθροίζω

συνηθροισμένους, acc. pl. m. part. perf. pass. id.

συνῆκαν, 3 pers. pl. aor. 1, ind. (§ 32. tab. C.C) συνίημι

συνήκατε, 2 pers. pl. aor. 1, ind. . . id.

συνήλασε,[a] 3 pers. sing. aor. 1, ind. . . συνελαύνω

συνῆλθε, 3 pers. sing. aor. 2, ind. . . συνέρχομαι

συνῆλθον, 3 pers. pl. aor. 2, ind. (§ 36. rem. 1) id.

συνηλικιώτας,[b] acc. pl. . . . συνηλικιώτης

συνηλικιώτης], ου, ὁ, (§ 2. tab. B. c) (σύν & ἡλικιώτης, idem, from ἡλικία) *one of the same age, an equal in age.* L.G.

συνήλλασσε, 3 pers. sing. imperf. act.— B. C. D. Ln. . . . } συναλλάσσω
συνήλασε, R. Gr. Sch. Tdf. (Ac. 7. 26) }

συνήντησε, 3 pers. sing. aor. 1, ind. . συναντάω

συνήργει, 3 pers. sing. imperf. . . . συνεργέω

συνήρπασαν, 3 pers. pl. aor. 1, ind. act. . συναρπάζω

συνηρπάκει, 3 pers. sing. pluperf. act. . . id.

συνήρχετο, 3 pers. sing. imperf. . . συνέρχομαι

συνήρχοντο, 3 pers. pl. imperf. . . . id.

συνῆσαν, 3 pers. pl. imperf. (§ 12. tab. L) σύνειμι

συνήσθιε, 3 pers. sing. imperf. . . συνεσθίω

συνήσουσι, 3 pers. pl. fut. ind. . . . συνίημι

συνῆτε, 2 pers. pl. aor. 2, subj. (§ 32. tab. C.C) id.

συνήχθη, 3 pers. sing. aor. 1, ind. pass. . συνάγω

συνήχθησαν, 3 pers. pl. aor. 1, ind. pass. . id.

συνθάπτω], fut. ψω, aor. 2, pass. συνετάφην, (§ 24. rem. 8. b) (σύν & θάπτω) *to bury with;* pass. in N.T. *to be buried with* Christ symbolically, Ro. 6. 4; Col. 2. 12.

συνθλασθήσεται, 3 pers. sing. fut. ind. pass. συνθλάω

συνθλάω, ῶ], fut. άσω, fut. pass. συνθλασθήσομαί, (§ 22. rem. 2. 4) (σύν & θλάω, *to break*) *to crush together; to break in pieces, shatter,* Mat. 21. 44; Lu. 20. 18.

συνθλίβοντα, acc. sing. masc. part. pres. . συνθλίβω

συνθλίβω], fut. ψω, (§ 23. rem. 1. a) (σύν & θλίβω) *to press together; to press upon, crowd, throng,* Mar. 5. 24, 31. (ῑ).

συνθρύπτοντες,[c] nom. pl. masc. part. pres. συνθρύπτω

συνθρύπτω], fut. ψω, (§ 23. rem. 1. a) (σύν & θρύπτω) *to crush to pieces;* met. *to break* the heart of any one, *to make to quail,* N.T.

συνιᾶσι, 3 pers. pl. pres. ind. (§ 28. rem. 6) —B. Ln. . . . . . } συνίημι
συνιοῦσι, R. Gr. Sch. Tdf. om. (2 Co. 10. 12) . . . . . }

συνιδόντες, nom. pl. masc. part (§ 36. rem. 1) συνεῖδον

συνιδών, nom. sing. masc. part. . . id.

συνιείς, nom. sing. masc. part. pres.—B. D. Ln. } συνίημι
συνιῶν, R. Gr. Sch. Tdf. (Mat. 13. 23) }

συνιέναι, pres. infin. . . . . id.

συνιέντες, nom. pl. masc. part. pres. . id.

συνιέντος, gen. sing. masc. part. pres. . . id.

συνίετε, 2 pers. pl. pres. ind. and imper. . id.

συνίημι], fut. συνήσω, and ἥσομαι, aor. 1, συνῆκα, aor. 2, subj. συνῶ, and in N.T. 3 pers. pl. pres. συνιοῦσι, (as if from συνιέω), part. συνιῶν & συνιών, (§ 32. tab. C.C) (σύν & ἵημι, *to send*) pr. *to send together;* met. *to understand, comprehend thoroughly,* Mat. 13. 51; Lu. 2. 50; 18. 34; 24. 45; *to perceive clearly,* Mat. 16. 12; 17. 13; Ac. 7. 25; Ro. 15. 21; Ep. 5. 17, absol. *to be well-judging, sensible,* 2 Co. 10. 12; *to be* spiritually *intelligent,* Mat. 13. 13, 14, 15; Ac. 28. 26, 27, et al.; *to be* religiously *wise,* Ro. 3. 11.

σύνεσις, εως, ἡ, (§ 5. tab. E. c) pr. *a sending together, a junction,* as of streams; met. *understanding, intelligence, discernment, sagaciousness,* Lu. 2. 47; 1 Co. 1. 19, et al.; meton. *the understanding, intellect, mind,* Mar. 12. 33.

συνετός, ή, όν, (§ 7. tab. F. a) *intelligent, discerning, sagacious, wise, prudent,* Mat. 11. 25; Lu. 20. 21, et al.

συνιόντος,[d] gen. s. masc. part. pres. (§ 33. rem. 4) σύνειμι

συνιοῦσι, 3 pers. pl. pres. ind. (of συνιέω) συνίημι

συνιστᾶν, pres. infin. (of συνιστάω)—B. Ln. } συνίστημι
συνιστάνειν, Rec. Gr. Sch. Tdf. (2 Co. 3. 1) }

συνιστάνειν, pres. infin. (of συνιστάνω) . id.

συνιστάνομεν, 1 pers. pl. pres. ind. (of συνιστάνω) . . . . . . id.

συνιστανόντων, gen. pl. masc. part. pres. (of συνιστάνω) . . . . . id.

συνιστάντες, nom. pl. masc. part. pres.—C. Ln. Tdf. . . . . } id.
συνιστῶντες, Rec. Gr. Sch. (2 Co. 4. 2) }

συνιστάνω, 1 pers. sing. pres. ind.—Gr. Sch. Tdf. } id.
συνίστημι, Rec. (Gal. 2. 18) . . }

[a] Ac. 7. 26. [b] Gal. 1. 14. [c] Ac. 21. 13. [d] Lu. 8. 4.

συνιστάνων, nom. sing. masc. part. pres.—B. D. Ln. Tdf. } συνίστημι

συνιστῶν, Rec. Gr. Sch. (2 Co. 10. 18) }

συνίστασθαι, pres. infin. pass. (§ 29. tab. Y) . id.

συνίστημι, and later, **συνιστάω**, and **συνιστάνω**], fut. συστήσω, (§ 29. tab. X) (σύν & ἵστημι) *to place together; to recommend to favourable attention*, Ro. 16. 1; 2 Co. 3. 1; 10. 18, et al.; *to place in a striking point of view, to evince*, Ro. 3. 5; 5. 8; Gal. 2. 18; intrans. perf. συνέστηκα, part. συνεστώς, *to stand beside*, Lu. 9. 32; *to have been permanently framed*, Col. 1. 17; *to possess consistence*, 2 Pe. 3. 5.

συστατικός, ή, όν, (§ 7. tab. F. a) *commendatory, recommendatory*, 2 Co. 3. 1, bis. L.G.

συνίστησι, 3 pers. sing. pres. ind. . . συνίστημι

συνιστῶν, nom. s. masc. pt. pres. (of συνιστάω) id.

συνιστῶντες, nom. pl. masc. part. pres. (of συνιστάω) . . . . . id.

συνιῶν, nom. sing. masc. part. pres. (of συνιέω) συνίημι

συνιῶσι, 3 pers. pl. pres. subj. . . . id.

συνοδεύοντες,[a] nom. pl. masc. part. pres. . . συνοδεύω

συνοδεύω], fut. εύσω, (§ 13. tab. M) (σύν & ὁδεύω) *to journey or travel with, accompany on a journey*. L.G.

συνοδία], ας, ἡ, (§ 2. tab. B. b, and rem. 2) (σύν & ὁδός) pr. *a journeying together*; meton. *a company of fellow-travellers, caravan*, Lu. 2. 44. L.G.

συνοδίᾳ,[b] dat. sing. . . . . . συνοδία

σύνοιδα], a perf. with the sense of a present, part. συνειδώς, (§ 37. rem. 1) *to share in the knowledge of* a thing; *to be privy to*, Ac. 5. 2; *to be conscious*; ουδὲν σύνοιδα, *to have a clear conscience*, 1 Co. 4. 4.

συνείδησις, εως, ἡ, (§ 5. tab. E. c) (συνειδέναι) *consciousness*, He. 10. 2; *a present idea, persisting notion, impression of reality*, 1 Co. 8. 7; 1 Pe. 2. 19; *conscience*, as an inward moral impression of one's actions and principles, Jno. 8. 9; Ac. 23. 1; 24. 16; Ro. 9. 1; 2 Co. 1. 12, et al.; *conscience*, as the inward faculty of moral judgment, Ro. 2. 15; 13. 5; 1 Co. 8. 7, 10, 12; 10. 25, 27, 28, 29; 2 Co. 4. 2; 5. 11, et al.; *conscience*, as the inward moral and spiritual frame, Tit. 1. 15; He. 9. 14.

συνοικέω, ῶ], fut. ήσω, (§ 16. tab. P) (σύν & οἰκέω) *to dwell with; to live or cohabit with*, 1 Pe. 3. 7.

συνοικοδομεῖσθε,[c] 2 pers. pl. pres. ind. pass. (§ 17. tab. Q) . . συνοικοδομέω

συνοικοδομέω, ῶ], (§ 16. tab. P) (σύν & οἰκοδομέω) *to build in company with* any one; pass. *to be built in along with, form a constituent part of a structure*. L.G.

συνοικοῦντες,[d] nom. pl. masc. part. pres. . συνοικέω

συνομιλέω, ῶ], fut. ήσω, (§ 16. tab. P) (σύν & ὁμιλέω) pr. *to be in company with; to talk or converse with*, Ac. 10. 27. N.T.

συνομιλῶν,[e] nom. sing. masc. part. pres. . συνομιλέω

συνομορέω, ῶ], fut. ήσω, (§ 16. tab. P) (σύν & ὁμορέω, *to border upon*, from ὁμός & ὅρος) *to be contiguous, adjoin*. N.T.

συνομοροῦσα,[f] nom. sing. fem. part. pres. . συνομορέω

συνόντων, gen. pl. masc. part. pres. . σύνειμι

συνοχή], ῆς, ἡ . . . . . . συνέχω

συνοχῆς gen. sing. . . . . . συνοχή

συντάσσω, or **ττω**], fut. ξω, (§ 26. rem. 3) (σύν & τάσσω) pr. *to arrange or place in order together*; in N.T. *to order, charge, direct*, Mat. 26. 19; 27. 10.

συνταφέντες, nom. pl. masc. part. aor. 2, pass. (§ 24. rem. 8. b) . . . . . συνθάπτω

συντέλεια], ας, ἡ . . . . . συντελέω

συντελείᾳ, dat. sing. . . . . . συντέλεια

συντελείας, gen. sing. . . . . . id.

συντελεῖσθαι, pres. infin. pass. (§ 17. tab. Q) συντελέω

συντελεσθεισῶν, gen. pl. fem. part. aor. 1, pass. id.

συντελέσας, nom. sing. masc. part. aor. 1, act. id.

συντελέσω, 1 pers. sing. fut. ind. act. . . id.

συντελέω, ῶ], fut. έσω, (§ 22. rem. 1) (σύν & τελέω) pr. *to bring to an end altogether; to finish, end*, Mat. 7. 28; *to consummate*, Ro. 9. 28; *to ratify* a covenant, He. 8. 8; pass. *to be terminated*, Lu. 4. 2; Ac. 21. 27; *to be fully realised*, Mar. 13. 4.

συντέλεια, ας, ἡ, (§ 2. tab. B. b, and rem. 2) *a complete combination; a completion, consummation, end*, Mat. 13. 39, 40, 49; 24. 3; 21. 20; He. 9. 26.

συντελῶν, nom. sing. masc. part. pres. act. συντελέω

συντέμνω], fut. τεμῶ, perf. τέτμηκα, (§ 27. rem. 2. d) perf. pass. τέτμημαι, (σύν &

[a] Ac. 9. 7. [b] Lu. 2. 44. [c] Ep. 2. 22. [d] 1 Pe. 3. 7. [e] Ac. 10. 27. [f] Ac. 18. 7.

τέμνω) pr. *to cut short, contract by cutting off*; met. *to execute speedily*, or from the Heb., *to determine, decide, decree*, Ro. 9. 28, bis.

συντόμως, adv. *concisely, briefly*, Ac. 24. 4.

συντέμνων, nom. sing. masc. part. pres. act. — συντέμνω

συντετμημένον, acc. sing. masc. part. perf. pass. (§ 27. rem. 3) — id.

συντετριμμένον, acc. sing. masc. part. perf. pass. (§ 23. rem. 7. 8) — συντρίβω

συντετριμμένους, acc. pl. masc. part. perf. pass. — id.

συντετρίφθαι, perf. infin. pass. — id.

συντηρέω, ῶ], fut. ήσω, (§ 16. tab. P) (σύν & τηρέω) *to keep safe and sound*, Mat. 9. 17; Lu. 5. 38; *to observe strictly*, or, *to secure from harm, protect*, Mar. 6. 20; *to preserve in memory, keep carefully in mind*, Lu. 2. 19. L.G.

συντηροῦνται, 3 pers. pl. pres. ind. pass. (§ 17. tab. Q) — συντηρέω

συντίθημι], (§ 28. tab. V) (σύν & τίθημι) *to place together*; mid. aor. 2, συνεθέμην, perf. συντέθειμαι, (§ 28. tab. W, and rem. 10) *to agree together, come to a mutual understanding*, Jno. 9. 22; Ac. 23. 20; *to bargain, to pledge one's self*, Lu. 22. 5; *to second* a statement, Ac. 24. 9.

συντόμως],[a] adv. — συντέμνω

συντρεχόντων, gen. pl. masc. part. pres. — συντρέχω

συντρέχω], aor. 2, συνέδρᾰμον, (§ 36. rem. 1) (σύν & τρέχω) *to run together, flock together*, Mar. 6. 33; Ac. 3. 11; *to run in company with* others, met. 1 Pe. 4. 4.

συνδρομή, ῆς, ἡ, (§ 2. tab. B. a) (συνέδραμον) *a running together, concourse*, Ac. 21. 30.

συντρίβεται, 3 pers. sing. pres. ind. pass. — συντρίβω

συντριβήσεται, 3 pers. sing. fut. 2, ind. pass. (§ 24. rem. 3) — id.

συντρῖβον, nom. sing. neut. part. pres. act. — id.

συντρίβω], fut. ψω, perf. pass. συντέτριμμαι, (§ 23. rem. 1. a, and rem. 7) fut. pass. συντρῐβήσομαι, (σύν & τρίβω) *to rub together*; *to shiver*, Mar. 14. 3; Re. 2. 27; *to break, break in pieces*, Mar. 5. 4; Jno. 19. 36; *to break down, crush, bruise*, Mat. 12. 20; met. *to break the power of* any one, *deprive of strength, debilitate*, Lu. 9. 39; Ro. 16. 20; pass. *to be broken* in heart, *be contrite*, Lu. 4. 18. (ῑ).

σύντριμμα, ατος, τό, (§ 4. tab. D. c) *a breaking, bruising*; in N.T. *destruction, ruin*, Ro. 3. 16.

σύντριμμα],[b] ατος, τό — συντρίβω

συντρίψασα, nom. sing. fem. part. aor. 1, act. — id.

συντρίψει, 3 pers. sing. fut. ind. act. — id.

σύντροφος],[c] ου, ὁ, (§ 3. tab. C. a) (συντρέφω, *to nurse, bring up together*, σύν & τρέφω) *nursed with* another; *one brought up or educated with* another, Ac. 13. 1.

συντυγχάνω], aor. 2, συνέτῠχον, (§ 36. rem. 2) (σύν & τυγχάνω) *to meet or fall in with*; in N.T. *to get to, approach*, Lu. 8. 19.

συντυχεῖν,[d] aor. 2, infin. — συντυγχάνω

Συντύχη], ης, ἡ, (§ 2. tab. B. a) *Syntyche*, pr. name.

Συντύχην,[e] acc. — Συντύχη

συνυπεκρίθησαν,[f] 3 pers. pl. aor. 1, ind. (§ 27. rem. 3) — συνυποκρίνομαι

συνυποκρίνομαι], (σύν & ὑποκρίνομαι) aor. 1, (pass. form) συνυπεκρίθην, *to dissemble, feign with, or in the same manner as* another. L.G.

συνυπουργέω, ῶ], fut. ήσω, (§ 16. tab. P) (σύν & ὑπουργέω, *to render service*, from ὑπό & ἔργον) *to aid along with* another, *help together*. L.G.

συνυπουργούντων,[g] gen. pl. masc. part. pres. — συνυπουργέω

συνωδίνει,[h] 3 pers. sing. pres. ind. — συνωδίνω

συνωδίνω], fut. ινῶ, (§ 27. rem. 1. a) (σύν & ὠδίνω, *to be in birth-pangs*) pr. *to travail at the same time with*; trop. *to be altogether in throes*, Ro. 8. 22. (ῑ).

συνωμοσία], ας, ἡ, (§ 2. tab. B. b, and rem. 2) (συνόμνυμι, *to swear together*, from σύν & ὄμνυμι) *a banding by oath*; *a combination, conspiracy*.

συνωμοσίαν,[i] acc. sing. — συνωμοσία

συνῶσι, 3 pers. pl. aor. 2, subj.—Gr. Tdf. } συνίημι
συνιῶσι, Rec. Sch. (Mat. 13. 15) }

Συρακοῦσαι], ῶν, αἱ, *Syracuse*, a celebrated city of Sicily.

Συρακούσας,[k] acc. — Συρακοῦσαι

σύρει, 3 pers. sing. pres. ind. — σύρω

Συρία], ας, ἡ, (§ 2. tab. B. b, and rem. 2) *Syria*, an extensive country of Asia.

[a] Ac. 24. 4. [b] Ro. 3. 16. [c] Ac. 13. 1. [d] Lu. 8. 19. [e] Phi. 4. 2. [f] Ga. 2. 13. [g] 2 Co. 1. 11. [h] Ro. 8. 22. [i] Ac. 23. 13. [k] Ac. 28. 12.

Συρίαν, acc. . . . . . . Συρία
Συρίας, gen. . . . . id.
σύροντες, nom. sing. masc. part. pres. . σύρω
Σύρος],[a] ου, ὁ, *a Syrian.*
Συροφοινίκισσα,[b] or Συροφοίνισσα], ης, ἡ, (§ 2. rem. 3) *a Syrophenician woman*, Phenicia being included in Syria.
σύρτιν,[c] acc. sing. . . . . . . σύρτις
σύρτις], εως, ἡ . . . . . . σύρω

σύρω], *to draw, drag*, Jno. 21. 8; Re. 12. 4; *to force away, hale* before magistrates, etc., Ac. 8. 3; 14. 19; 17. 6. (ῡ).

σύρτις, εως, ἡ, (§ 5. tab. E. c) *a shoal, sand-bank, a place dangerous on account of shoals*, two of which were particularly famous on the northern coast of Africa, one lying near Carthage, and the other, *the syrtis major*, lying between Cyrene and Leptis, which is probably referred to in Ac. 27. 17.

σύρων, nom. sing. masc. part. pres. . . σύρω
συσπαράσσω, or ττω], fut. ξω, (§ 26. rem. 3) (σύν & σπαράσσω) *to tear to pieces; to convulse altogether*, Lu. 9. 42. N.T.
σύσσημον],[d] ου, τό, (§ 3. tab. C. c) (σύν & σῆμα) *a concerted signal.*
σύσσωμα,[e] acc. pl. neut.—Rec. Gr. Sch. Tdf. } σύσσωμος
σύνσωμα, Ln. . . . . . }
σύσσωμος], ου, ὁ, ἡ, τό, -ον, (§ 7. rem. 2) (σύν & σῶμα) *united in the same body*; met. pl. *joint members* in a spiritual body, Ep. 3. 6. N.T.
συστασιαστής], οῦ, ὁ, (§ 2. tab. B. c) (συστασιάζω, *to join in a sedition with*, from σύν & στάσις) *an accomplice in sedition, associate in insurrection.* L.G.
συστασιαστῶν,[f] gen. pl. . . . συστασιαστής
συστατικός], ή, όν, (§ 7. tab. F. a) . συνίστημι
συστατικῶν, gen. pl. . . . . . συστατικός
συσταυρόω, ῶ], fut. ώσω, perf. pass. συνεσταύρωμαι, aor. 1, pass. συνεσταυρώθην, (§ 21. tab. U) (σύν & σταυρόω) *to crucify with* another, Mat. 27. 44; Mar. 15. 32; Jno. 19. 32; pass. met. *to be crucified with* another in a spiritual resemblance, Ro. 6. 6; Gal. 2. 20. N.T.

συσταυρωθέντες, nom. pl. masc. part. aor. 1, p. συσταυρόω
συσταυρωθέντος, gen. sing. masc. part. aor. 1, pass. . . . . . . id.
συστέλλω], fut. ελῶ, aor. 1, συνέστειλα, (§ 27. rem. 1. b. d) perf. pass. συνέσταλμαι, (§ 27. rem. 3) (σύν & στέλλω) *to draw together, contract, straiten; to enwrap*; hence, i.q. περιστέλλω, *to lay out, prepare for burial*, Ac. 5. 6; pass. *to be shortened*, or, *to be environed with trials*, 1 Co. 7. 29.
συστενάζει,[g] 3 pers. sing. pres. ind. . . συστενάζω
συστενάζω], fut. ξω, (§ 26. rem. 2) (σύν & στενάζω) *to groan altogether.*
συστοιχεῖ,[h] 3 pers. sing. pres. ind. . . συστοιχέω
συστοιχέω, ῶ], fut. ήσω, (§ 16. tab. P) (σύν & στοιχέω) pr. *to be in the same row with*; met. *to correspond to*, Gal. 4. 25.
συστρατιώτῃ, dat. sing. . . . συστρατιώτης
συστρατιώτην, acc. sing. . . . . id.
συστρατιώτης], ου, ὁ, (§ 2. tab. B. c) (σύν & στρατιώτης) *a fellow-soldier*; met. *a fellow-soldier, co-militant*, in the service of Christ, Phi. 2. 25; Phile. 2.
συστρεφομένων, gen. pl. part. pres. mid.—B. Ln. . . . . . } συστρέφω
ἀναστρεφομένων, Rec. Gr. Sch. Tdf. (Mat. 17. 22) . . . }
συστρέφω], fut. ψω, (§ 23. rem. 1. a) (σύν & στρέφω) *to turn or roll together; to collect, gather.*

συστροφή, ῆς, ἡ, (§ 2. tab. B. a) *a gathering, concourse, tumultuous assembly*, Ac. 19. 40; *a combination, conspiracy*, Ac. 23. 12.

συστρέψαντος,[i] gen. sing. masc. part. aor. 1 συστρέφω
συστροφή], ῆς, ἡ . . . . . . id.
συστροφήν, acc. sing. . . . . συστροφή
συστροφῆς, gen. sing. . . . . . id.
συσχηματίζεσθαι, pres. infin. mid.—A. B. D. Ln. Tdf. . . } συσχηματίζω
συσχηματίζεσθε, Rec. Gr. Sch. (Ro. 12. 2) . . . . }
συσχηματιζόμενοι, nom. pl. masc. part. pres. mid. . . . . . . id.
συσχηματίζω], (σύν & σχηματίζω, *to form*, from σχῆμα) *to fashion in accordance with;*

[a] Lu. 4. 27. [b] Mar. 7. 26. [c] Ac. 27. 17. [d] Mar. 14. 44. [e] Ep. 3. 6. [f] Mar. 15. 7. [g] Ro. 8. 22. [h] Gal. 4. 25. [i] Ac. 28. 3.

mid. *to conform or assimilate one's self to*, met. Ro. 12. 2; 1 Pe. 1. 14

Συχάρ],[a] ἡ, indecl. *Sychar*, a city of Samaria.

Συχέμ],[b] ἡ, indecl. *Sychem*, a city of Samaria.

Συχέμ],[c] ὁ, indecl. *Sychem*, proper name.

σφαγή], ῆς, ἡ . . . . σφάζω, σφάττω

σφαγήν, acc. sing. . . . . σφαγή

σφαγῆς, gen. sing. . . . . id.

σφάγια,[d] acc. pl. . . . . σφάγιον

σφάγιον], ου, τό . . . σφάζω, σφάττω

σφάζω, or Att. **σφάττω**], fut. ξω, aor. 1, ἔσφαξα, aor. 2, pass. ἐσφάγην, (ᾰ), (§ 26. rem. 3) perf. pass. ἔσφαγμαι, *to slaughter, kill, slay;* pr. used of animals killed in sacrifice, etc., Re. 5. 6, 9, 12; 13. 8; of persons, etc., 1 Jno. 3. 12; Re. 6. 4, 9; 18. 24; *to wound mortally*, Re. 13. 3.

σφαγή, ῆς, ἡ, (§ 2. tab. B. a) *slaughter*, Ac. 8. 32; Ro. 8. 36; Ja. 5. 5.

σφάγιον, ου, τό, (§ 3. tab. C. c) *a victim* slaughtered in sacrifice, Ac. 7. 42.

σφάξωσι, 3 pers. pl. aor. 1, subj. act. σφάζω, σφάττω

σφόδρα], adv. (pr. neut. pl. of σφοδρός, *vehement, violent, strong*) *much, greatly, exceedingly*, Mat. 2. 10; 17. 6, et al.

σφοδρῶς],[e] adv. (from σφοδρός) *exceedingly, vehemently*.

σφραγῖδα, acc. sing. . . . . σφραγίς

σφραγῖδας, acc. pl. . . . id.

σφραγίδων, gen. pl. . . . id.

σφραγίζω], fut. ίσω . . . . id.

σφρᾱγίς], ῖδος, ἡ, (§ 4. rem. 2. c) *a seal, a signet ring*, Re. 7. 2; *an inscription on a seal, motto*, 2 Ti. 2. 19; *a seal, the impression of a seal*, Re. 5. 1, et al.; *a seal, a distinctive mark*, Re. 9. 4; *a seal, a token, proof*, 1 Co. 9. 2; *a token* of guarantee, Ro. 4. 11.

σφραγίζω, fut. ίσω, aor. 1, ἐσφράγισα, perf. pass. ἐσφράγισμαι, aor. 1, pass. ἐσφραγίσθην, (§ 26. rem. 1) *to seal, stamp with a seal*, Mat. 27. 66; *to seal up, to close up, conceal*, Re. 10. 4; 22. 10; *to set a mark upon, distinguish by a mark*, Re. 7. 3, 8; *to seal, to mark distinctively* as invested with a certain character, Jno. 6. 27; mid. *to set one's own mark upon, seal as one's own, to impress with a mark of acceptance*, 2 Co. 1. 22; *to obtain a quittance of, to deliver over safely* to any one, Ro. 15. 28; absol. *to set to one's seal, to make a solemn declaration*, Jno. 3. 33.

σφραγισάμενος, nom. sing. m. part. aor. 1, mid. σφραγίζω

σφραγίσαντες, nom. pl. masc. part. aor. 1, act. id.

σφραγίσῃς, 2 pers. sing. aor. 1, subj. act. . id.

σφραγῖσι, dat. pl. . . . . σφραγίς

σφράγισον, 2 pers. sing. aor. 1, imper. act. . σφραγίζω

σφραγίσωμεν, 1 pers. pl. aor. 1, subj. act. . id.

σφυρά,[f] nom. pl. . . . . . σφυρόν

σφυρόν], οῦ, τό, (§ 3. tab. C. c) *the ankle;* pl. τὰ σφυρά, *the ankle bones, malleoli*, Ac. 3. 7.

σχεδόν], adv. (ἔχω, σχεῖν) pr. *near*, of place; hence, *nearly, almost*, Ac. 13. 44; 19. 26; He. 9. 22.

σχῆμα], ατος, τό, (§ 4. tab. D. c) (σχεῖν) *fashion, form; fashion, external show*, 1 Co. 7. 31; *guise, appearance*, Phi. 2. 8.

σχήματι, dat. sing. . . . . σχῆμα

σχίζει, 3 pers. sing. pres. ind. act. . . σχίζω

σχιζομένους, acc. pl. masc. part. pres. mid. id.

σχίζω], fut. ίσω, aor. 1, ἔσχισα, aor. 1, pass. ἐσχίσθην, (§ 26. rem. 1) *to split*, Mat. 27. 51; *to rend, tear asunder*, Mat. 27. 51; Lu. 5. 36, et al.; mid. *to open or unfold* with a chasm, Mar. 1. 10; pass. met. *to be divided* into parties or factions, Ac. 14. 4; 23. 7.

σχίσμα, ατος, τό, (§ 4. tab. D. c) *a rent*, Mat. 9. 16; Mar. 2. 21, met. *a division* into parties, *schism*, Jno. 7. 43; 9. 16, et al.

σχίσας, nom. sing. masc. part. aor. 1, act.—B. D. Tdf. . . . . } σχίζω
Rec. Gr. Sch. Ln. om. (Lu. 5. 36) .

σχίσει, 3 pers. sing. fut. ind. act.—B. C. D. Ln. Tdf. . . . . } id.
σχίζει, Rec. Gr. Sch. (Lu. 5. 36) .

σχίσμα], ατος, τό . . . . id.

σχίσματα, nom. and acc. pl. . . . σχίσμα

σχίσωμεν, 1 pers. pl. aor. 1, subj. act. . σχίζω

σχοινία, acc. pl. . . . . . σχοινίον

[a] Jno. 4. 5 [b] Ac. 7. 16. [c] Ac. 7. 16. [d] Ac. 7. 42. [e] Ac. 27. 18. [f] Ac. 3. 7.

σχοινίον], ου, τό, (§ 3. tab. C. c) (σχοῖνος, *a rush*) pr. *a cord made of rushes*; genr. *a rope, cord*, Jno. 2. 15; Ac. 27. 32.

σχοινίων, gen. pl. . . . . . σχοινίον

σχολάζητε, 2 pers. pl. pres. subj. . . σχολάζω

σχολάζοντα, acc. sing. masc. part. pres. . id.

σχολάζω], fut. άσω . . . . . σχολή

σχολάσητε, 2 p. pl. aor. 1, subj.—Gr. Sch. Tdf. }
σχολάζητε, Rec. (1 Co. 7. 5) . . } σχολάζω

σχολή], ῆς, ἡ, (§ 2. tab. B. a) *freedom from occupation*; later, *ease, leisure*; *a school*, Ac. 19. 9.

σχολάζω, fut. άσω, (§ 26. rem. 1) *to be unemployed, to be at leisure*; *to be at leisure* for a thing, *to devote one's self entirely* to a thing, 1 Co. 7. 5; *to be unoccupied, empty*, Mat. 12. 44.

σχολῇ,[a] dat. sing. . . . . . σχολή

σχῶ, 1 pers. sing. aor. 2, subj. (§ 36. rem. 4) ἔχω

σχῶμεν, 1 pers. pl. aor. 2, subj.—Al. Ln. Tdf. }
κατάσχωμεν, Rec. Gr. Sch. (Mat. 21. 38) } id.

σῷ, dat. sing. masc. and neut. (§ 11. rem. 4) σός

σώζειν, pres. infin. act. . . . . σώζω

σώζεσθαι, pres. infin. pass. . . . id.

σώζεσθε, 2 pers. pl. pres. ind. pass. . . id.

σώζεται, 3 pers. sing. pres. ind. pass. . . id.

σώζετε, 2 pers. pl. pres. imper. act. . . id.

σωζόμενοι, nom. pl. masc. part. pres. pass. . id.

σωζομένοις, dat. pl. masc. part. pres. pass. id.

σωζομένους, acc. pl. masc. part. pres. pass. id.

σωζομένων, gen. pl. part. pres. pass. . id.

σώζω], fut. σώσω, perf. σέσωκα, aor. 1, ἔσωσα, aor. 1, pass. ἐσώθην, perf. pass. σέσωσμαι, (§ 37. rem. 1) *to save, rescue*; *to preserve safe and unharmed*, Mat. 8. 25; 10. 22; 24. 22; 27. 40, 42, 49; 1 Ti. 2. 15; σώζειν εἰς, *to bring safely to*, 2 Ti. 4. 18; *to cure, heal, restore to health*, Mat. 9. 21, 22, Mar. 5. 23, 28, 34; 6. 56, et al.; *to save, preserve* from being lost, Mat. 16. 25, Mar. 3. 4; 8. 35; σώζειν ἀπό, *to deliver from, set free from*, Mat. 1. 21; Jno. 12. 27; Ac. 2. 40; in N.T. *to rescue* from unbelief, *convert*, Ro. 11. 14; 1 Co. 1. 21; 7. 16; *to bring within the pale of saving privilege*, Tit. 3. 5; 1 Pe. 3. 21; [or, as others, *to save*, in the fullest force of the term: see the context of these two passages]; *to save* from final ruin, 1 Ti. 1. 15; pass. *to be brought within the pale of saving privilege*, Ac. 2. 47; Ep. 2. 5, 8; [or, acc. to others, *to be* actually *saved*]; *to be in the way of salvation*, 1 Co. 15. 2; 2 Co. 2. 15; [compare, however, with this last passage, Lu. 13. 23; Ac. 2. 47].

σωτήρ, ῆρος, ὁ, (§ 4. rem. 2. f) *a saviour, preserver, deliverer*, Lu. 1. 47; 2. 11; Ac. 5. 31, et al.

σωτηρία, ας, ἡ, (§ 2. tab. B. b, and rem. 2) *a saving, preservation*, Ac. 27. 34; He. 11. 7; *deliverance*, Lu. 1. 69, 71; Ac. 7. 25; *salvation*, spiritual and eternal, Lu. 1. 77; 19. 9; Ac. 4. 12; Re. 7. 10; *a being placed in a condition of salvation* by an embracing of the Gospel, Ro. 10. 1, 10; 2 Ti. 3. 15; *means* or *opportunity of salvation*, Ac. 13. 26; Ro. 11. 11; He. 2. 3, et al.; ἡ σωτηρία, *the* promised *deliverance* by the Messiah, Jno. 4. 22.

σωτήριος, ου, ὁ, ἡ, (§ 7. rem. 2) *imparting salvation, saving*, Tit. 2. 11; neut. τὸ σωτήριον, equivalent to σωτηρία, Lu. 2. 30; 3. 6; Ac. 28. 28; Ep. 6. 17.

σωθῇ, 3 pers. sing. aor. 1, subj. pass. . . σώζω

σωθῆναι, aor. 1, infin. pass. . . . id.

σωθήσεται, 3 pers. sing. fut. ind. pass. . . id.

σωθήσῃ, 2 pers. sing. fut. ind. pass. . id.

σωθήσομαι, 1 pers. pl. fut. ind. pass. . . id.

σωθησόμεθα, 1 pers. pl. fut. ind. pass. . id.

σώθητε, 2 pers. pl. aor. 1, imper. pass. . . id.

σωθῆτε, 2 pers. pl. aor. 1, subj. pass. . id.

σωθῶ, 1 pers. sing. aor. 1, subj. pass. . . id.

σωθῶσι, 3 pers. pl. aor. 1, subj. pass. . id.

σῶμα], ατος, τό, (§ 4. tab. D. c) *the body* of an animal; *a* living *body*, Mat. 5. 29, 30; 6. 22, 23, 25; Ja. 3. 3; *a person, individual*, 1 Co. 6. 16; *a* dead *body, corpse, carcase*, Mat. 14. 12; 27. 52, 58; He. 13. 11; *the* human *body* considered as the seat and occasion of moral imperfection, as inducing to sin through its appetites and passions, Ro. 7. 24; 8. 13; genr. *a body, a material substance*, 1 Co.

[a] Ac. 19. 9.

15. 37, 38, 40; *the substance, reality,* as opposed to ἡ σκιά, Col. 2. 17; in N.T. met. *the* aggregate *body* of believers, *the body* of the Church, Ro. 12. 5; Col. 1. 18, et al.

σωματἴκός, ή, όν, (§ 7. tab. F. a) *bodily, of or belonging to the body,* 1 Ti. 4. 8; *corporeal, material,* Lu. 3. 22.

σωματἴκῶς, adv. *bodily, in a bodily frame,* Col. 2. 9.

σώματα, nom. and acc. pl. . . . . σῶμα
σώματι, dat. sing. . . . . . id.
σωματική, nom. sing. fem. . . . . σωματικός
σωματικός], ή, όν . . . . . σῶμα
σωματικῷ, dat. sing. neut. . . . σωματικός
σωματικῶς],[a] adv. . . . . . σῶμα
σώματος, gen. sing. . . . . id.
σωμάτων, gen. pl. . . . . . id.
Σώπατρος],[b] ου, ὁ, (§ 3. tab. C. a) *Sopater,* pr. name.
σωρεύσεις, 2 pers. sing. fut. ind. act. . . σωρεύω
σωρεύω], fut. εύσω, (§ 13. tab. M) (σωρός, *a heap*) *to heap or pile up,* Ro. 12. 20; met. pass. *to be laden* with sins, 2 Ti. 3. 6.
σῶσαι, aor. 1, infin. act. . . . . σώζω
σώσαντος, gen. sing. masc. part. aor. 1, act . id.
σώσας, nom. sing. masc. part. aor. 1, act. . id.
σωσάτω, 3 pers. sing. aor. 1, imper. act. . id.
σώσει, 3 pers. sing. fut. ind. act. . . id.
σώσεις, 2 pers. sing. fut. ind. act. . . id.
Σωσθένην, acc. . . . . Σωσθένης
Σωσθένης], ου, ὁ, (§ 2. tab. B. c) *Sosthenes,* pr. name.
Σωσίπατρος],[c] ου, ὁ, *Sosipater,* pr. name.
σῶσον, 2 pers. sing. aor. 1, imper. act. . . σώζω
σώσω, 1 pers. sing. aor. 1, subj. act. . id.
σώσων, nom. sing. masc. part. fut. act. . . id.
σωτήρ], ῆρος, ὁ, (§ 4. rem. 2. f) . . id.
σωτῆρα, acc. sing. . . . . . σωτήρ
σωτῆρι, dat. sing. . . . . . id.
σωτηρία], ας, ἡ . . . . . σώζω
σωτηρίαν, acc. sing. . . . . σωτηρία
σωτηρίας, gen. sing. . . . . . id.
σωτήριον, nom. and acc. sing. neut. . . σωτήριος
σωτήριος], ου, ὁ, ἡ . . . . . σώζω
σωτηρίου, gen. sing. neut. . . . . σωτήριος
σωτῆρος, gen. sing. . . . . . σωτήρ
σώφρονα, acc. sing. masc. . . . . σώφρων
σώφρονας, acc. pl. masc. and fem. . . id.
σωφρονεῖν, pres. infin. . . . . . σωφρονέω
σωφρονέω, ῶ], fut. ήσω . . . . . σώφρων
σωφρονήσατε, 2 pers. pl. aor 1, imper. . σωφρονέω
σωφρονίζω], fut. ίσω . . . . . σώφρων
σωφρονίζωσι,[d] 3 pers. pl. pres. subj. . σωφρονίζω
σωφρονισμός], οῦ, ὁ . . . . . σώφρων
σωφρονισμοῦ,[e] gen. sing. . . . σωφρονισμός
σωφρονοῦμεν, 1 pers. pl. pres. ind. . . σωφρονέω
σωφρονοῦντα, acc. sing. masc. part. pres. . id.
σωφρόνως],[f] adv. . . . . . . σώφρων
σωφροσύνη], ης, ἡ . . . . . . id.
σωφροσύνης, gen. sing. . . . . σωφροσύνη
σώφρων], ονος, ὁ, ἡ, (§ 7. tab. G. a, and rem. 4) (σῶς, *sound,* and φρήν) *of a sound mind, sane; staid, temperate, discreet,* 1 Ti. 3. 2; Tit. 1. 8; 2. 2; *modest, chaste,* Tit. 2. 5.

σωφρονέω, ῶ, fut. ήσω, aor. 1, ἐσωφρόνησα, (§ 16. tab. P) *to be of a sound mind, be in one's right mind, be sane,* Mar. 5. 15; *to be calm,* 2 Co. 5. 13; *to be sober-minded, sedate, staid,* Tit. 2. 6; 1 Pe. 4. 7; *to be of a modest, humble mind,* Ro. 12. 3.

σωφρονίζω, fut. ίσω, (§ 26. rem. 1) pr. *to render* any one σώφρων, *to restore to a right mind; to make sober-minded, to steady* by exhortation and guidance, Tit. 2. 4.

σωφρονισμός, οῦ, ὁ, (§ 3. tab. C. a) *a rendering sound-minded; calm vigour of mind,* 2 Ti. 1. 7.

σωφρόνως, adv. *in the manner of a person in his right mind; soberly, staidly, temperately,* Tit. 2. 12.

σωφροσύνη, ης, ἡ, (§ 2. tab. B. a) *sanity, soundness of mind, a sane mind,* Ac. 26. 25; female *modesty,* 1 Ti. 2. 9, 15.

T.

ταβέρνη], ης, ἡ, (Lat. *taberna*) *a tavern, inn.* See Τρεῖς Ταβέρναι.
Ταβιθά], ἡ, (Aram. טְבִיתָא) i.q. Δορκάς, *an antelope, Tabitha,* pr. name, Ac. 9. 36, 40.
τάγμα], ατος, τό . . . . . . τάσσω
τάγματι,[g] dat. sing. . . . . . τάγμα
τάδε, acc. pl. neut. . . . . . ὅδε, ἥδε, τόδε
τακήσεται, 3 pers. sing. fut. 2, ind. pass.—C. Ln. (§ 24. rem. 9) . . . } τήκω
τήκεται, Rec. Gr. Sch. Tdf. (2 Pe. 3. 12) }

[a] Col. 2. 9. [b] Ac. 20. 4. [c] Ro. 16. 21 [d] Tit. 2. 4 [e] 2 Ti. 1. 7 [f] Tit. 2. 12. [g] 1 Co. 15. 23.

ταĸτῇ,[a] dat. sing. fem. . . . . ταĸτός

ταĸτός], ή, όν . . . . . τάσσω

ταλαιπωρήσατε,[b] 2 pers. pl. aor. 1, imper. ταλαιπωρέω

ταλαιπωρέω, ῶ], fut. ήσω . . . ταλαίπωρος

ταλαιπωρία], ας, ή . . . . . id.

ταλαιπωρίαις, dat. pl. . . . . ταλαιπωρία

ταλαίπωρος], ου, ὁ, ἡ, (§ 7. rem. 2) pr. *enduring severe effort and hardship*; hence, *wretched, miserable, afflicted*, Ro. 7. 24; Re. 3. 17.

ταλαιπωρέω, ῶ, fut. ήσω, perf. τεταλαιπώρηκα, (§ 16. tab. P) *to endure severe labour and hardship; to be harassed; to suffer compunction*, Ja. 4. 9.

ταλαιπωρία, ας, ἡ, (§ 2. tab. B. b, and rem. 2) *toil, difficulty, hardship; calamity, misery, distress*, Ro. 3. 16; Ja. 5. 1.

τάλαντα, acc. pl. . . . . . τάλαντον

ταλαντιαία,[c] nom. sing. fem. . . . ταλαντιαῖος

ταλαντιαῖος], αία, αῖον . . . τάλαντον

τάλαντον], ου, τό, (§ 3. tab. C. c) (ταλάω, *to sustain*) *the scale of a balance; a talent*, which as a weight was among the Jews equivalent to 3000 shekels, i.e. as usually estimated, 114 lbs. 15 dwts. Troy; while the Attic talent, on the usual estimate, was only equal to 56 lbs. 11 oz. Troy; and as a denomination of money, it was equal among the former to 342*l*. 3*s*. 9*d*., or, if reckoned of gold, 5475*l*., and among the latter to 198*l*. 15*s*., or 225*l*., or 243*l*. 15*s*. sterling, according to various estimates, Mat. 18. 24; 25. 15, 16, 20, 24, 25, 28.

ταλαντιαῖος, αία, αῖον, (§ 7. rem. 1) *of a talent weight, weighing a talent*, Re. 16. 21.

ταλάντων, gen. pl. . . . . . τάλαντον

ταλιθά],[d] (Aram. טְלִיתָא) *talitha*, i.q. ĸοράσιον, *a damsel, maiden*.

ταμείοις, dat. pl. . . . . . ταμεῖον

ταμεῖον], ου, τό, equivalent to ταμιεῖον, (ταμιεύω, to be ταμίας, *manager, storekeeper*) *a storehouse, granary, barn*, Lu. 12. 24; *a chamber, closet, place of retirement and privacy*, Mat. 6. 6; 24. 26; Lu. 12. 3.

τανῦν], i.e. τά νῦν, q.v.

ταξάμενοι, nom. pl. masc. part. aor. 1, mid. . τάσσω

τάξει, dat. sing. . . . . . τάξις

τάξιν, acc. sing. . . . . . id.

τάξις], εως, ή . . . . . . τάσσω

ταπεινοῖς, dat. pl. masc. . . . . ταπεινός

ταπεινός, ή, όν, (§ 7. tab. F. a) *low* in situation; of condition, *humble, poor, mean, depressed*, Lu. 1. 52; 2 Co. 7. 6; Ja. 1. 9; met. of the mind, *humble, lowly, modest*, Mat. 11. 29; Ro. 12. 16, et al.

ταπεινόω, ῶ, fut. ώσω, aor. 1, ἐταπείνωσα, (§ 20. tab. T) *to bring low, depress, level*, Lu. 3. 5; met. *to humble, abase*, Phi. 2. 8; mid. *to descend to, or live in, a humble condition*, 2 Co. 11. 7; Phi. 4. 12; *to humble, depress the pride of*, any one, Mat. 18. 4; mid. *to humble one's self, exhibit humility and contrition*, Ja. 4. 10; *to humble* with respect to hopes and expectations, *to depress* with disappointment, 2 Co. 12. 21.

ταπείνωσις, εως, ἡ, (§ 5. tab. E. c) *depression; meanness, low estate, abject condition*, Lu. 1. 48; Ac. 8. 33; Phi. 3. 21; Ja. 1. 10.

ταπεινούς, acc. pl. masc. . . . . ταπεινός

ταπεινοῦσθαι, pres. infin. pass. . . . ταπεινόω

ταπεινόφρονες, nom. pl. masc.—Gr. Sch. Tdf. } ταπεινόφρων
φιλόφρονες, Rec. (1 Pe. 3. 8) . }

ταπεινοφροσύνη], ης, ή . . . . id.

ταπεινοφροσύνῃ, dat. sing. . . ταπεινοφροσύνη

ταπεινοφροσύνην, acc. sing. . . . . id.

ταπεινοφροσύνης, gen. sing. . . . . id.

ταπεινόφρων], ονος, ὁ, ἡ, (§ 7. tab. G. a) (ταπεινός & φρήν) *humble-minded*, v.r. 1 Pe. 3. 8. L.G.

ταπεινοφροσύνη, ης, ἡ, (§ 2. tab. B. a) *lowliness or humility of mind and deportment, modesty*, Ac. 20. 19; Ep. 4. 2; Phi. 2. 3, et al. N.T.

ταπεινόω, ῶ], fut. ώσω . . . . ταπεινός

ταπεινωθήσεται, 3 pers. sing. fut. ind. pass. (§ 21. tab. U) . . . . ταπεινόω

ταπεινώθητε, 2 pers. pl. aor. 1, imper. pass. id.

ταπεινῶν, nom. sing. masc. part. pres. act. . id.

ταπεινώσει, 3 pers. sing. fut. ind. act. . . id.

ταπεινώσει, dat. sing. . . . . ταπείνωσις

ταπεινώσεως, gen. sing. . . . . d.

ταπεινώσῃ, 3 pers. sing. aor. 1, subj. act. . ταπεινόω

ταπείνωσιν, acc. sing. . . . . ταπείνωσις

[a] Ac. 12. 21. [b] Ja. 4. 9. [c] Re. 16. 21. [d] Mar. 5. 41.

ταπείνωσις], εως, ἡ . . . . . ταπεινός

ταρασσέσθω, 3 pers. sing. pres. imper. pass. . ταράσσω

ταράσσοντες, nom. pl. masc. part. pres. act. id.

ταράσσω, or ττω], fut. ξω, aor. 1, ἐτάραξα, perf. pass. τετάραγμαι, aor. 1, pass. ἐταράχθην, (§ 26. rem. 3) *to agitate, trouble*, as water, Jno. 5. 4, 7; met. *to agitate, trouble* the mind; with fear, *to terrify, put in consternation*, Mat. 2. 3; 14. 26; with grief, etc., *to disquiet, affect with grief, anxiety*, etc., Jno. 12. 27; 13. 21; with doubt, etc., *to unsettle, perplex*, Ac. 15. 24; Gal. 1. 7, et al.

ταρᾰχή, ῆς, ἡ, (§ 2. tab. B. a) *agitation, troubling*, of water, Jno. 5. 4; met. *commotion, tumult*, Mat. 13. 8.

τάρᾰχος, ου, ὁ, (§ 3. tab. C. a) *agitation, commotion; perturbation, consternation, terror*, Ac. 12. 18; *excitement, tumult, public contention*, Ac. 19. 23.

ταράσσων, nom. sing. masc. part. pres. act. ταράσσω

ταραχαί, nom. pl. . . . . ταραχή

ταραχή], ῆς, ἡ . . . . ταράσσω

ταραχήν, acc. sing. . . . ταραχή

ταραχθῇ, 3 pers. sing. aor. 1, subj. pass. . ταράσσω

ταραχθῆτε, 2 pers. pl. aor. 1, subj. pass. . id.

τάραχος], ου, ὁ . . . . . . id.

Ταρσέα, acc. sing. . . . . . Ταρσεύς

Ταρσεύς], έως, ὁ, (§ 5. tab. E. d) *of, or a native of* Ταρσός, *Tarsus*, the metropolis of Cilicia, Ac. 9. 11; 21. 39.

Ταρσόν, acc. . . . . . . Ταρσός

Ταρσός], οῦ, ἡ, *Tarsus*, the chief city of Cilicia, and birth-place of the Apostle Paul.

Ταρσῷ, dat. . . . . . . Ταρσός

ταρταρόω, ῶ], fut. ώσω, (§ 20. tab. T) (Τάρταρος, *Tartarus*, which in the mythology of the ancients was that part of Hades, where the wicked were confined and tormented) *to cast or thrust down to Tartarus or Gehenna*. N.T.

ταρταρώσας,[a] nom. sing. masc. part. aor. 1 . ταρταρόω

τασσόμενος, nom. sing. masc. part. pres. pass. τάσσω

τάσσω, or ττω], fut. ξω, aor. 1, ἔταξα, perf. pass. τέταγμαι, (§ 26. rem. 3) *to arrange; to set, appoint*, in a certain station, Lu. 7. 8; Ro. 13. 1; *to set, devote*, to a pursuit, 1 Co. 16. 15; *to dispose, frame*, for an object, Ac. 13. 48; *to arrange, appoint*, place or time, Mat. 28. 16; Ac. 28. 23; *to allot, assign*, Ac. 22. 10; *to settle, decide*, Ac. 15. 2.

τάγμα, ατος, τό, (§ 4. tab. D. c) pr. *anything placed in order*; in N.T. *order* of succession, 1 Co. 15. 23.

τακτός, ή, όν, (§ 7. tab. F. a) pr. *arranged; fixed, appointed, set*, Ac. 12. 21.

τάξις, εως, ἡ, (§ 5. tab. E. c) *order, regular disposition, arrangement; order, series, succession*, Lu. 1. 8; *an order, distinctive class*, as of priests, He. 5. 6; 7. 11; *order, good order*, 1 Co. 14. 40; *orderliness, well-regulated conduct*, Col. 2. 5.

ταῦροι, nom. pl. . . . . . ταῦρος

ταῦρος], ου, ὁ, (§ 3. tab. C. a) *a bull, beeve*, Mat. 22. 4, et al.

ταύρους, acc. pl. . . . . . . ταῦρος

ταύρων, gen. pl. . . . . . id.

ταὐτά, by crasis for τὰ αὐτά, *the same things*, 1 Thes. 2. 14; κατὰ ταὐτά, *after the same manner, thus, so*, Lu. 6. 23, 26; 17. 30.

ταῦτα, nom. and acc. pl. neut. . . . οὗτος

ταύταις, dat. pl. fem. . . . . id.

ταύτας, acc. pl. fem. . . . . id.

ταύτῃ, dat. sing. fem. . . . . id.

ταύτην, acc. sing. fem. . . . . id.

ταύτης, gen. sing. fem. . . . . id.

ταφή], ῆς, ἡ, (§ 2. tab. B. a) . . . θάπτω

ταφήν,[b] acc. sing. . . . . ταφή

τάφοις, dat. pl. . . . . . τάφος

τάφον, acc. sing. . . . . id.

τάφος], ου, ὁ, (§ 3. tab. C. a) . . θάπτω

τάφου, gen. sing. . . . . . τάφος

τάφους, acc. pl. . . . . . id.

τάχα], adv. . . . . . . ταχύς

τάχει, dat. sing. . . . . . τάχος

ταχέως], adv. . . . . . . ταχύς

ταχινή, nom. sing. fem. . . . . ταχινός

ταχινήν, acc. sing. fem. . . . . id.

ταχινός], ή, όν . . . . . ταχύς

τάχιον], adv. comparat. . . . . id.

τάχιστα],[c] adv. superlat. . . . . id.

τάχος], εος, τό . . . . . . id.

[a] 2 Pe. 2. 4. [b] Mat. 27. 7. [c] Ac. 17. 15.

ταχύ], adv. . . . . ταχύς

ταχύς],[a] εῖα, ύ, (§ 7. tab. H. g) *swift, fleet, quick*; met. *ready, prompt*, Ja. 1. 19.

τάχα, adv. pr. *quickly, soon; perhaps, possibly*, Ro. 5. 7; Phile. 15.

ταχέως, adv. *quickly, speedily; soon, shortly*, 1 Co. 4. 19; Gal. 1. 6; *hastily*, Lu. 14. 21; 16. 6, et al.; *with inconsiderate haste*, 1 Ti. 5. 22.

ταχῐνός, ή, όν, (§ 7. tab. F. a) *swift, speedy*, 2 Pe. 2. 1; *near at hand, impending*, 2 Pe. 1. 14.

τάχιον, adv. (pr. neut. of ταχίων, comparat. of ταχύς) *more swiftly, more quickly, more speedily*, Jno. 20. 4; He. 13. 19; *quickly, speedily*, Jno. 13. 27, et al.

τάχιστα, adv. (pr. neut. of the superlat. of ταχύς) (§ 8. rem. 5) *most quickly, most speedily, very quickly*; ὡς τάχιστα, *as soon as possible*, Ac. 17. 15.

τάχος, εος, τό, (§ 5. tab. E. b) *swiftness, speed, quickness, celerity*; ἐν τάχει, *with speed, quickly, speedily; soon, shortly*, Lu. 18. 8; Ac. 25. 4; *hastily, immediately*, Ac. 12. 7, et al.

ταχύ, adv. *quickly, speedily, hastily*, Mat. 28. 7, 8; *soon, shortly, immediately*, Mat. 5. 25; *suddenly*, Re. 2. 5, 16; 3. 11, et al.; *easily, readily*, Mar. 9. 39; pr. neut. of ταχύς.

τέ], a combinatory enclitic particle; serving either as a lightly-appending link, Ac. 1. 15, *and*, Ac. 2. 3; or as an inclusive prefix, Lu. 12. 45; *both*, Lu. 24. 20; Ac. 26. 16, et al.

τεθέᾱμαι, 1 pers. sing. perf. ind. (§ 22. rem. 2) θεάομαι

τεθεάμεθα, 1 pers. pl. perf. ind. . . . id.

τεθέᾱται, 3 pers. sing. perf. ind. . . . id.

τέθεικα, 1 pers. sing. perf. ind. act. (§ 28. rem. 9. d) τίθημι

τεθείκατε, 2 pers. pl. perf. ind. act. . . . id.

τεθεικώς, nom. sing. masc. part. perf. act. . id.

τέθειται, 3 pers. sing. perf. ind. pass.—Al. Ln. Tdf. . . . . . } id.
τίθεται, Rec. Gr. Sch. (Mar. 15. 47) }

τεθεμελιωμένοι, nom. pl. masc. part. perf. pass. θεμελιόω

τεθεμελίωτο, 3 pers. sing. pluperf. pass. (for ἐτεθεμελίωτο) (§ 13. rem. 8. f) . id.

τεθεραπευμέναι, nom. pl. fem. part. perf. pass. θεραπεύω

τεθεραπευμένον, acc. sing. masc. part. perf. pass. id.

τεθεραπευμένῳ, dat. sing. masc. part. perf. pass. id.

τεθῇ, 3 pers. sing. aor. 1, subj. pass. (§ 28. rem. 10) τίθημι

τεθῆναι, aor. 1, infin. pass. . . . . id.

τεθησαυρισμένοι, nom. pl. masc. part. perf. pass. θησαυρίζω

τεθλιμμένη, nom. sing. fem. part. perf. pass. . θλίβω

τεθνάναι, (ᾰ) perf. 2, infin. (§ 35. rem. 8) . θνήσκω

τεθνήκασι, 3 pers. pl. perf. ind. . . . . id.

τέθνηκε, 3 pers. sing. perf. ind. (§ 38. rem. 2) id.

τεθνηκέναι, perf. infin.—Al. Ln. Tdf. . } id.
τεθνάναι, Rec. Gr. Sch. (Ac. 14. 19) }

τεθνηκότα, acc. sing. masc. part. perf. . . id.

τεθνηκότος, gen. sing. masc. part. perf. . id.

τεθνηκώς, nom. sing. masc. part. perf. (§ 36. rem. 4) . . . . . . id.

τεθραμμένος, nom. sing. masc. part. perf. pass. (§ 35. rem. 9) . . . . τρέφω

τεθραυσμένους,[b] acc. pl. masc. part. perf. pass. θραύω

τεθυμένα, nom. pl. neut. part. perf. pass. . θύω

τεθῶσι, 3 pers. pl. aor. 1, subj. pass. (§ 28. rem. 10) τίθημι

τείχη, nom. pl. . . . . . . τεῖχος

τεῖχος], εος, τό, (§ 5. tab. E. b) *a wall* of a city, Ac. 9. 25, et al.

τεκεῖν, aor. 2, infin. (§ 37. rem. 1) . . τίκτω

τέκῃ, 3 pers. sing. aor. 2, subj. . . . id.

τεκμηρίοις,[c] dat. pl. . . . . . τεκμήριον

τεκμήριον], ίου, τό, (§ 3. tab. C. c) (τέκμαρ, *a fixed mark*) *a sign, indubitable token, clear proof*.

τέκνα, nom., acc., and voc. pl. . . . τέκνον

τεκνία, voc. pl. . . . . . . τεκνίον

τεκνίον], ίου, τό . . . . . . τίκτω

τεκνογονεῖν,[d] pres. infin. . . . . τεκνογονέω

τεκνογονέω, ῶ], fut. ήσω, (§ 16. tab. P) (τέκνον & γίγνομαι) *to bear children; to rear a family*, 1 Ti. 5. 14. L.G.

τεκνογονία, ας, ἡ, (§ 2. tab. B. b, and rem. 2) *the bearing of children, the rearing of a family*. N.T.

τεκνογονία], ας, ἡ . . . . . τεκνογονέω

τεκνογονίας,[e] gen. sing. . . . . τεκνογονία

τέκνοις, dat. pl. . . . . . . τέκνον

τέκνον], ου, τό . . . . . . τίκτω

τεκνοτροφέω, ῶ], fut. ήσω, (§ 16. tab. P) (τέκνον & τρέφω) *to rear a family*, 1 Ti. 5. 10.

τέκνου, gen. sing. . . . . . τέκνον

---

[a] Ja. 1. 19. [b] Lu. 4. 18. [c] Ac. 1. 3. [d] 1 Ti. 5. 14. [e] 1 Ti. 2. 15.

τέκνῳ, dat. sing. . . . . . . τέκνον
τέκνων, gen. pl. . . . . . . id.
τέκτονος, gen. sing. . . . . . τέκτων

τέκτων], ονος, ὁ, (§ 4. rem. 2. e) *an artisan*; and spc. *one who works in wood, a carpenter*, Mat. 13. 55; Mar. 6. 3.

τελεῖ, 3 pers. sing. pres. ind. act. . . . τελέω
τελεία, nom. sing. fem. . . . . τέλειος
τέλειοι, nom. pl. masc. . . . . id.
τελείοις, dat. pl. masc. . . . . . id.
τέλειον, acc. sing. masc. and nom. neut. . . id.
τέλειος], εία, ειον . . . . . . τέλος
τελειοτέρας, gen. sing. fem. compar. (§ 8. rem. 4) τέλειος
τελειότης], τητος, ἡ . . . . . τέλος
τελειότητα, acc. sing. . . . . . τελειότης
τελειότητος, gen. sing. . . . . . id.
τελειοῦμαι, 1 pers. sing. pres. ind. pass. (§ 21. tab. U) . . . . . . τελειόω
τελειοῦται, 3 pers. sing. pres. ind. pass. . id.
τελειόω, ῶ], fut. ώσω . . . . . . τέλος
τελεῖται, 3 pers. sing. pres. ind. pass.—Al. Ln. Tdf. . . . . } τελέω
τελειοῦται, Rec. Gr. Sch. (2 Co. 12. 9) }
τελεῖτε, 2 pers. pl. pres. ind. act. . . . id.
τελειωθείς, nom. sing. masc. part. aor. 1, pass. τελειόω
τελειωθῇ, 3 pers. sing. aor. 1, subj. pass. . id.
τελειωθῶσι, 3 pers. pl. aor. 1, subj. pass. . id.
τελείων, gen. pl. . . . . . . τέλειος
τελείως],[a] adv. . . . . . . τέλος
τελειῶσαι, aor. 1, infin. act. . . . . τελειόω
τελειωσάντων, gen. pl. masc. part. aor. 1, act. id.
τελειώσας, nom. sing. masc. part. aor. 1, act. —A. B. C. Ln. Tdf. . . . } τελειόω
ἐτελείωσα, Rec. Gr. Sch. (Jno. 17. 4) }
τελείωσις], εως, ἡ . . . . . τέλος
τελειώσω, 1 pers. sing. aor. 1, subj. act. . τελειόω
τελειωτήν,[b] acc. sing. . . . . τελειωτής
τελειωτής], οῦ, ὁ . . . . . . τέλος
τελέσητε, 2 pers. pl. aor. 1, subj. act. . τελέω
τελεσθῇ, 3 pers. sing. aor. 1, subj. pass. . id.
τελεσθῆναι, aor. 1, infin. pass. . . . id.
τελεσθήσεται, 3 pers. sing. fut. ind. pass. . id.
τελεσθήσονται, 3 pers. pl. fut. ind. pass.—Gr. Sch. Tdf. . . . . } id.
τελεσθῇ, Rec. (Re. 17. 17) . }
τελεσθῶσι, 3 pers. pl. aor. 1, subj. pass. . id.
τελεσφορέω, ῶ], fut. ήσω, (§ 16. tab. P) (τελεσφόρος, from τέλος & φέρω) *to bring to maturity*, as fruits, etc.; met. Lu. 8. 14.

τελεσφοροῦσι,[c] 3 pers. pl. pres. ind. . τελεσφορέω
τελέσωσι, 3 pers. pl. aor. 1, subj. act. . τελέω
τελευτᾷ, 3 pers. sing. pres. ind. . . τελευτάω
τελευτᾶν, pres. infin. . . . . . id.
τελευτάτω, 3 pers. sing. pres. imper. . id.
τελευτάω, ῶ], fut. ήσω . . . . . τέλος
τελευτή], ῆς, ἡ . . . . . . id.
τελευτῆς,[d] gen. sing. . . . . . τελευτή
τελευτήσαντος, gen. sing. masc. part. aor. 1 τελευτάω
τελευτῶν, nom. sing. masc. part. pres. . id.
τελέω, ῶ], fut. έσω . . . . . . τέλος
τέλη, nom. and acc. pl. . . . . id.

τέλος], εος, τό, (§ 5. tab. E. b) *an end attained, consummation; an end, closing act*, Mat. 24. 6, 14; 1 Co. 15. 24, et al.; *full performance, perfect discharge*, Ro. 10. 4; *fulfilment, realisation*, Lu. 22. 37; *final dealing*, developed *issue*, Ja. 5. 11; *issue, final stage*, 1 Co. 10. 11; *issue, result*, Mat. 26. 58; Ro. 6. 21, 22; 1 Pe. 1. 9; antitypical *issue*, 2 Co. 3. 13; practical *issue*, 1 Ti. 1. 5; *ultimate destiny*, Phi. 3. 19; He. 6. 8; 1 Pe. 4. 17; *an impost, due*, Mat. 17. 25; Ro. 13. 7; εἰς τέλος, *to the full*, 1 Thes. 2. 16; εἰς τέλος, *continually*, Lu. 18. 5; εἰς τέλος, μέχρι, ἄχρι τέλους, *throughout*, Mat. 10. 22; Mar. 13. 13; Jno. 13. 1; He. 3. 6, 14, 6. 11; Re. 2. 26.

τέλειος, εία, ειον, (§ 7. rem. 1) *brought to completion; fully accomplished, fully developed*, Ja. 1. 4; *fully realised, thorough*, 1 Jno. 4. 18; *complete, entire*, as opposed to what is partial and limited, 1 Co. 13. 10; *full grown, of ripe age*, 1 Co. 14. 20; Ep. 4. 13; He. 5. 14; *fully accomplished* in Christian enlightenment, 1 Co. 2. 6; Phi. 3. 15; Col. 1. 28; *perfect* in some point of character, *without shortcoming* in respect of a certain standard, Mat. 5. 48; 19. 21; Col. 4. 12; Ja. 1. 4; 3. 2; *perfect, consummate*, Ro. 12. 2; Ja. 1. 17, 25; compar. *of higher excellence and efficiency*, He. 9. 11.

τελειότης, τητος, ἡ, (§ 4. rem. 2. c)

[a] 1 Pe. 1. 13. [b] He. 12. 2. [c] Lu. 8. 14. [d] Mat. 2. 15.

completeness, perfectness, Col. 3. 14; *ripeness* of knowledge or practice, He. 6. 1. L.G.

τελειόω, ῶ, fut. ώσω, perf. τετελείωκα, aor. 1, ἐτελείωσα, (§ 20. tab. T) *to execute fully, discharge,* Jno. 4. 34; 5. 36; 17. 4; *to reach the end of, run through, finish,* Lu. 2. 43; Ac. 20. 24; *to consummate, place in a condition of finality,* He. 7. 19; *to perfect* a person, *advance* a person *to final completeness* of character, He. 2. 10; 5. 9; 7. 28; *to perfect* a person, *advance* a person *to a completeness* of its kind, which needs no further provision, He. 9. 9; 10. 1, 14; pass. *to receive fulfilment,* Jno. 19. 28; *to be brought to the goal, to reach the end of one's course,* Lu. 13. 32; Phi. 3. 12; He. 11. 40; 12. 23; *to be fully developed,* 2 Co. 12. 9; Ja. 2. 22; 1 Jno. 2. 5; 4. 12, 17; *to be completely organised, to be closely embodied,* Jno. 17. 23.

τελείως, adv. *perfectly,* 1 Pe. 1. 13.

τελείωσις, εως, ἡ, (§ 5. tab. E. c) *a completing; a fulfilment, an accomplishment* of predictions, promises, etc.; Lu. 1. 45; *finality* of function, *completeness* of operation and effect, He. 7. 11.

τελειωτής, οῦ, ὁ, (§ 2. tab. B. c) *a finisher, one who completes and perfects* a thing; *one who brings through to final attainment,* He. 12. 2; cf. ch. 2. 10.

τελευτή, ῆς, ἡ, (§ 2. tab. B. a) *a finishing, end;* hence, *end* of life, *death, decease,* Mat. 2. 15.

τελευτάω, ῶ, fut. ήσω, perf. τετελεύτηκα, aor. 1, ἐτελεύτησα, (§ 18. tab. R) *to end, finish, complete;* absol. *to end* one's life, *to die,* Mat. 2. 19; 15. 4; 22. 25, et al.

τελέω, ῶ, fut. έσω, (§ 22. rem. 1) perf. τετέλεκα, aor. 1, ἐτέλεσα, *to finish, complete, conclude,* an operation, Mat. 11. 1; 13. 53; 19. 1, et al.; *to finish* a circuit, Mat. 10. 23; *to fulfil, to carry out into full operation,* Ro. 2. 27; Gal. 5. 16; Ja. 2. 8; *to pay* dues, Mat. 17. 24, et al.; pass. *to be fulfilled, realised,* Lu. 12. 50; 18. 31, et al.; of time, *to be ended, elapse,* Ro. 15. 8; 20. 3, 5, 7.

τέλους, gen. sing. . . . . . . τέλος

τελοῦσα, nom. sing. fem. part. pres. act. . τελέω

τελῶναι, nom. pl. . . . . . τελώνης

τελώνην, acc. sing. . . . . . . id.

τελώνης], ου, ὁ, (§ 2. tab. B. c) (τέλος & ὠνέομαι) *one who farms the public revenues;* in N.T. *a publican, collector of imposts, tax-gatherer,* Mat. 5. 46; 9. 10, 11; 10. 3 et al.

τελώνιον, ίου, τό, (§ 3. tab. C. c) *a custom-house, toll-house; collector's office,* Mat. 9. 9; Mar. 2. 14; Lu. 5. 27.

τελώνιον], ίου, τό . . . . . τελώνης

τελωνῶν, gen. pl. . . . . . . id.

τέξεται, 3 pers. sing. fut. ind. (§ 37. rem. 1) τίκτω

τέξῃ, 2 pers. sing. fut. ind. . . . . id.

τέρας], ᾰτος, τό, (§ 4. rem. 2. c) *a prodigy, portent,* Ac. 2. 19; *a signal act, wonder, miracle,* Jno. 4. 48; Ac. 2. 43, et al.

τέρασι, dat. pl. . . . . . . τέρας

τέρατα, nom. and acc. pl. . . . . id.

τεράτων, gen. pl. . . . . . . id.

Τέρτιος],[a] ου, ὁ, *Tertius,* pr. name.

Τέρτυλλος], ου, ὁ, *Tertullus,* pr. name

Τερτύλλου, gen. . . . . . Τέρτυλλος

τέσσαρα, nom. and acc. pl. neut. . . τέσσαρες

τεσσαράκοντα], οἱ, αἱ, τά . . . . id.

τεσσαρακονταετῆ, acc. sing. masc. τεσσαρακονταετής

τεσσαρακονταετής], έος, οῦς, ὁ, ἡ, (§ 7. tab. G. b) (τεσσαράκοντα & ἔτος) *of forty years,* Ac. 7. 23; 13. 18.

τέσσαρας, acc. pl. masc. and fem. . . τέσσαρες

τέσσᾰρες], Att. τέτταρες, ων, οἱ, αἱ, neut. τέσσαρα, Att. τέτταρα, (§ 9. tab. I. d) *four,* Mat. 24. 31; Mar. 2. 3, et al.

τεσσαράκοντα, οἱ, αἱ, τά, *forty,* Mat. 4. 2, et al.

τέταρτος, η, ον, (§ 7. tab. F. a) *fourth,* Mat. 14. 25, et al.

τεταρταῖος, αία, αῖον, (§ 7. rem. 1) *on the fourth day,* Jno. 11. 39.

τετράδιον, ίου, τό, (§ 3. tab. C. c) (dimin. of τετράς) *a set of four, quaternion; a detachment of four* men, Ac. 12. 4. L.G.

τετρακόσιοι, αι, α, *four hundred,* Ac. 5. 36, et al.

[a] Ro. 16. 22.

τετραπλόος, οῦς, όη, ῆ, όον, οῦν, (§ 7. rem. 5. b) (τετράς) *quadruple, fourfold,* Lu. 19. 8.

τεσσαρεσκαιδεκάτη, nom. sing. fem. . . . τεσσαρεσκαιδέκατος

τεσσαρεσκαιδεκάτην, acc. sing. fem. . . . id.

τεσσαρεσκαιδέκᾰτος], η, ον, (τέσσαρες, καί, & δέκατος) *the fourteenth,* Ac. 27. 27, 33.

τέσσαρσι, dat. pl. . . . . . τέσσαρες

τεσσάρων, gen. pl. . . . . . id.

τεταγμέναι, nom. pl. fem. part. perf. pass. . τάσσω

τεταγμένοι, nom. pl. masc. part. perf. pass. . id.

τέτακται, 3 pers. sing. perf. ind. pass. (§ 26. rem. 3) . . . . . id.

τεταραγμένοι, nom. pl. masc. part. perf. pass. ταράσσω

τετάρακται, 3 pers. sing. perf. ind. pass. . id.

τεταρταῖος],[a] α, ον . . . . τέσσαρες

τετάρτῃ, dat. sing. fem. . . . . τέταρτος

τετάρτην, acc. sing. fem. . . . . id.

τετάρτης, gen. sing. fem. . . . . id.

τέταρτον, nom. and acc. sing. neut. . . id.

τέταρτος], η, ον . . . . . τέσσαρες

τετάρτου, gen. sing. neut. . . . τέταρτος

τετελείωκε, 3 pers. sing. perf. ind. act. . τελειόω

τετελείωμαι, 1 pers. sing. perf. ind. pass. (§ 21. tab. U) . . . . . id.

τετελειωμένη, nom. sing. fem. part. perf. pass. id.

τετελειωμένοι, nom. pl. masc. part. perf. pass. id.

τετελειωμένον, acc. sing. masc. part. perf. pass. id.

τετελειωμένων, gen. pl. part. perf. pass. . id.

τετελείωται, 3 pers. sing. perf. ind. pass. . id.

τετέλεκα, 1 pers. sing. perf. ind. act. . . τελέω

τετέλεσται, 3 pers. sing. perf. ind. pass. (§ 22. rem. 5. 6) . . . . . id.

τετελευτηκότος, gen. sing. masc. part. perf.—Al. Ln. Tdf. . . . . } τελευτάω
τεθνηκότος, Rec. Gr. Sch. (Jno. 11. 39) }

τέτευχε, 3 pers. sing. perf. ind. (§ 36. rem. 2) τυγχάνω

τετήρηκα, 1 pers. sing. perf. ind. act. . τηρέω

τετήρηκαν, 3 pers. pl. perf. ind. act. contr. (§ 35. rem. 13).—B. D. Ln. Tdf. } id.
τετηρήκασι, Rec. Gr. Sch. (Jno. 17. 6) }

τετήρηκας, 2 pers. sing. perf. ind. act. . . id.

τετηρήκασι, 3 pers. pl. perf. ind. act. . id.

τετήρηκε, 3 pers. sing. perf. ind. act. . . id.

τετηρημένην, acc. sing. fem. part. perf. pass. (§ 17. tab. Q) . . . id.

τετηρημένοις, dat. pl. masc. . . . . id.

τετηρημένους, acc. pl. masc. part. perf. pass. id.

τετήρηται, 3 pers. sing. perf. ind. pass. . τηρέω

τετιμημένου, gen. sing. masc. part. perf. pass. (§ 19. tab. S) . . . . τιμάω

τετράγωνος],[b] ου, ὁ, ἡ, (§ 7. rem. 2) (τέσσαρες and γωνία) *four-angled, quadrangular, square.*

τετραδίοις,[c] dat. pl. . . . . . τετράδιον

τετράδιον], ίου, τό . . . . . τέσσαρες

τετρακισχίλιοι], αι, α, (τετράκις, *four times,* and χίλιοι) *four thousand,* Mat. 15. 38, et al.

τετρακισχιλίους, acc. pl. masc. . τετρακισχίλιοι

τετρακισχιλίων, gen. pl. . . . . . id.

τετρακόσια, acc. pl. neut. . . . τετρακόσιοι

τετρακόσιοι], αι, α . . . . . τέσσαρες

τετρακοσίοις, dat. pl. neut. . . . τετρακόσιοι

τετρακοσίων, gen. pl. . . . . . id.

τετράμηνον,[d] nom. sing. neut.—Rec. . } τετράμηνον
τετράμηνος, Gr. Sch. Tdf. (Jno. 4. 35) }

τετράμηνος], ου, ὁ, ἡ, τό, -ον, (§ 7. rem. 2) (τέσσαρες & μήν) *of four months, four months in duration.*

τετραπλόος, οῦς], όη, ῆ, όον, ουν . . τέσσαρες

τετραπλοῦν,[e] acc. sing. neut. . . . τετραπλόος

τετράποδα, nom. and acc. pl. neut. . . τετράπους

τετραπόδων, gen. pl. . . . . . id.

τετράπους], οδος, ὁ, ἡ, τό, -ουν, (§ 4. rem. 2. c) (τέσσαρες & πούς) *four-footed;* pl. τὰ τετράποδα, sc. ζῶα, *quadrupeds,* Ac. 10. 12; 11. 6; Ro. 1. 23.

τετραρχέω, ῶ], fut. ήσω . . . . τετράρχης

τετράρχης], ου, ὁ, (§ 2. tab. B. c) (τετράς & ἄρχω) *a tetrarch;* pr. one of a sovereign body of four; in N.T., according to later usage, a provincial sovereign under the Roman emperor, Mat. 14. 1; Lu. 3. 19; 9. 7; Ac. 13. 1.

τετραρχέω, ῶ, fut. ήσω, (§ 16. tab. P) *to be tetrarch, rule as tetrarch,* Lu. 3. 1, ter. L.G.

τετράρχου, gen. sing. . . . . . τετράρχης

τετραρχοῦντος, gen. sing. masc. part. pres. . τετραρχέω

τετραυματισμένους, acc. pl. masc. part. perf. pass. . . . . . . τραυματίζω

τετραχηλισμένα,[f] nom. pl. neut. part. perf. p. τραχηλίζω

τετύφλωκε, 3 pers. sing. perf. ind. act. . τυφλόω

τετυφωμένοι, nom. pl. masc. part. perf. pass. τυφόω

τετύφωται, 3 pers. sing. perf. ind. pass. (§ 21. tab. U) . . . . . id.

---

[a] Jno. 11. 39. [b] Re. 21. 16. [c] Ac. 12. 4. [d] Jno. 4. 35. [e] Lu. 19. 8. [f] He. 4. 13.

τέτυχε, 3 pers. sing. perf. 2, ind.—A. D. Ln. Tdf. } τυγχάνω
τέτευχε, Rec. Gr. Sch. (Heb. 8. 6) }

τεφρόω, ῶ], fut. ώσω, (§ 20. tab. T) (τέφρα, *ashes*) *to reduce to ashes, to consume, destroy.*

τεφρώσας,[a] nom. sing. masc. part. aor. 1, act. . . τεφρόω

τεχθείς, nom. sing. masc. part. aor. 1, pass. (§ 37. rem. 1) . . . . τίκτω

τέχνη], ης, ἡ, (§ 2. tab. B. a) *art, skill,* Ac. 17. 29; *an art, trade, craft,* Ac. 18. 3; Re. 18. 22.

τεχνίτης, ου, ὁ, (§ 2. tab. B. c) *an artisan, artificer; workman, mechanic,* Ac. 19. 24, 38; Re. 18. 22; *an architect, builder,* He. 11. 10. (ῑ).

τέχνῃ, dat. sing.—A. B. Ln. Tdf. } τέχνη
τέχνην, Rec. Gr. Sch. (Ac. 18. 3) }

τέχνην, acc. sing. . . . . . id.

τέχνης, gen. sing. . . . . . id.

τεχνῖται, nom. pl. . . . . . τεχνίτης

τεχνίταις, dat. pl. . . . . . id.

τεχνίτης], ου, ὁ . . . . . τέχνη

τῇδε, dat. sing. fem. (§ 10. tab. J. a) . . ὅδε

τήκεται,[b] 3 pers. sing. pres. ind. pass. . . τήκω

τήκω], fut. ξω, (§ 23. rem. 1. b) *to dissolve, render liquid;* pass. *to be liquefied, melt.*

τηλαυγῶς],[c] adv. (τηλαυγής, *widely resplendent,* from τῆλε, *afar,* & αὐγή) *clearly, plainly, distinctly.*

τηλικαῦτα, nom. pl. neut. . . . . τηλικοῦτος

τηλικαύτης, gen. sing. fem. . . . . id.

τηλικοῦτος], αὐτη, οῦτο, (§ 10. rem. 7. 8) (τηλίκος, *so great*) *so great,* 2 Co. 1. 10; He. 2. 3; Ja. 3. 4; Re. 16. 18.

τηλικούτου, gen. sing. masc. . . . . τηλικοῦτος

τήνδε, acc. sing. fem. . . . . . ὅδε

τηρεῖ, 3 pers. sing. pres. ind. act. . . . τηρέω

τήρει, 2 pers. sing. pres. imper. act. . . . id.

τηρεῖν, pres. infin. act. . . . . . id.

τηρεῖσθαι, pres. infin. pass. (§ 17. tab. Q) . . id.

τηρεῖτε, 2 pers. pl. pres. imper. act. . . . id.

τηρέω], ῶ, fut. ήσω, perf. τετήρηκα, aor. 1, ἐτήρησα, (§ 16. tab. P) (τηρός, *watching, watchful*) *to keep watch upon, guard,* Mat. 27. 36, 54; 28. 4; Ac. 12. 6; *to watch over* protectively, *guard,* 1 Jno. 5. 18; Re. 16. 15; *to mark attentively, to heed,* Re. 1. 3; *to observe* practically, *keep strictly,* Mat. 19. 17 23. 3; 28. 20; Mar. 7. 9; Jno. 8. 51, et al.; *to preserve, shield,* Jno. 17. 15; *to store up, reserve,* Jno. 2. 10; 12. 7; 1 Pe. 1. 4; 2 Pe. 2. 4, 9, 17, et al.; *to keep in custody,* Ac. 12. 5; 16. 23, et al.; *to maintain,* Ep. 4. 3; 2 Ti. 4. 7; *to keep* in a condition, Jno. 17. 11, 12; 1 Co. 7. 37; 2 Co. 11. 9; 1 Ti. 5. 22; Ja. 1. 27.

τήρησις, εως, ἡ, (§ 5. tab. E. c) *a keeping, custody;* meton. *a place of custody, prison, ward,* Ac. 4. 3; met. practical *observance, strict performance,* 1 Co. 7. 19.

τηρῇ, 3 pers. sing. pres. subj. act. . . . τηρέω

τηρηθείη, 3 pers. sing. aor. 1, opt. pass. . . id.

τηρηθῆναι, aor. 1, infin. pass. . . . id.

τηρῆσαι, aor. 1, infin. act. . . . . id.

τηρήσαντας, acc. pl. masc. part. aor. 1, act. . id.

τηρήσει, dat. sing. . . . . . τήρησις

τηρήσει, 3 pers. sing. fut. ind. act. . . . τηρέω

τηρήσῃ, 3 pers. sing. aor. 1, subj. act. . . id.

τηρήσῃς, 2 pers. sing. aor. 1, subj. act. . . id.

τηρήσητε, 2 pers. pl. aor. 1, subj. act. . . id.

τήρησιν, acc. sing. . . . . . τήρησις

τήρησις], εως, ἡ . . . . . τηρέω

τήρησον, 2 pers. sing. aor. 1, imper. act. . . id.

τηρήσουσι, 3 pers. pl. fut. ind. act. . . . id.

τηρήσω, 1 pers. sing. fut. ind. act. . . . id.

τηροῦμεν, 1 pers. pl. pres. ind. act. . . . id

τηρούμενοι, nom. pl. masc. part. pres. pass. . id

τηρουμένους, acc. pl. masc. part. pres. pass.—B. C. Gr. Sch. Tdf. } id.
τετηρημένους, Rec. (2 Pe. 2. 4) }

τηροῦντες, nom. pl. masc. part. pres. act. . . id.

τηρούντων, gen. pl. masc. part. pres. act. . . id.

τηρῶ, 1 pers. sing. pres. ind. act. . . . id.

τηρῶμεν, 1 pers. pl. pres. subj. act. . . . id.

τηρῶν, nom. sing. masc. part. pres. act. . . id.

τι, nom. and acc. sing. neut. (§ 10. rem. 4) indef. τις

τί, nom. and acc. sing. neut. (§ 10. tab. J. f) interrog. . . . . . . τίς

Τιβεριάδος, gen. . . . . . Τιβεριάς

Τιβεριάς], άδος, (ᾰ) ἡ, (§ 4. rem. 2. c) *Tiberias,* a city of Galilee, built by Herod Antipas, and named in honour of Tiberius.

Τιβέριος], ου, ὁ (§ 3. tab. C. a) *Tiberius,* the third Roman emperor.

---

[a] 2 Pe. 2. 6. [b] 2 Pe. 3. 12. [c] Mar. 8. 25.

Τιβερίου,* gen. . . . . . Τιβέριος

τιθέασι, 3 pers. pl. (for τιθεῖσι) (§ 28. rem. 6) . . . . . τίθημι

τιθείς, nom. sing. masc. part. pres. act. . id.

τιθέναι, pres. infin. act. . . . id.

τιθέντες, nom. pl. masc. part. pres. act. . id.

τίθεται, 3 pers. sing. pres. ind. pass. (§ 28. rem. 8. a) . . . . . id.

τιθέτω, 3 pers. sing. pres. imper. act. . . id.

τίθημι], fut. θήσω, aor. 1, ἔθηκα, perf. τέθεικα, aor. 2, ἔθην, aor. 2, mid. ἐθέμην, (§ 28. tabb. V. W) aor. 1, pass. ἐτέθην, perf. pass. τέθειμαι, pluperf. ἐτεθείμην, (§ 28. rem. 10) *to place, set, lay*, Mat. 5. 15; Mar. 6. 56; Lu. 6. 48, et al.; *to produce* at table, Jno. 2. 10; *to deposit, lay*, Mat. 27. 60; Lu. 23. 53; Ac. 3. 2; *to lay down*, Lu. 19. 21, 22; Jno. 10. 11, 15, 17, 18; 1 Jno. 3. 16, et al.; *to lay aside, put off*, Jno. 13. 4; *to allocate, assign*, Mat. 24. 51; Lu. 12. 46, *to set, constitute, appoint*, Jno. 15. 16; Ac. 13. 47; He. 1. 2; *to render, make*, Mat. 22. 44; Ro. 4. 17; 1 Co. 9. 18; mid. *to put* in custody, Mat. 14. 3; Ac. 4. 3; *to reserve*, Ac. 1. 7; *to commit* as a matter of charge, 2 C· 3. 19; *to set*, with design, in a certain arrangement or position, Ac. 20. 28; 1 Co. 12. 18, 28; 1 Thes. 5. 9; 1 Ti. 1. 12; pass. 1 Ti. 2. 7; 2 Ti. 1. 11; 1 Pe. 2. 8; τιθέναι τὰ γόνατα, *to kneel down*, Mar. 15. 19; Lu. 22. 41; Ac. 7. 60; 9. 40; 20. 36; 21. 5; τίθεσθαι ἐν τῇ καρδίᾳ, *to lay to heart, ponder*, Lu. 1. 66; also, εἰς τὰς καρδίας, Lu. 21. 14; τίθεσθαι ἐν τῇ καρδίᾳ, *to design, resolve*, Ac. 5. 4; also, ἐν πνεύματι, Ac. 19. 21; also, βουλήν, Ac. 27. 12; τίθεσθαι εἰς τὰ ὦτα, *to give attentive audience to, to listen to retentively*, Lu. 9. 44.

θεμέλιος, ίου, ὁ, (pr. an adj. from θέμα, τίθημι) and θεμέλιον, ου, τό, *a foundation*, Lu. 6. 48, 49; He. 11. 10; met. *a foundation* laid in elementary instruction, He. 6. 1; *a foundation* of a superstructure of faith, doctrine, or hope, 1 Co. 3. 10, 11, 12; Ep. 2. 20; 1 Ti. 6. 19; *a foundation* laid in a commencement of preaching the Gospel, Ro. 15. 20

θεμελιόω, ῶ, fut. ώσω, perf. τεθεμελίωκα, aor. 1, ἐθεμελίωσα, (§ 20. tab. T) *to found, lay the foundation of*, Mat. 7. 25; Lu. 6. 48; He. 1. 10; met. *to ground, establish, render firm and unwavering*, Ep. 3. 17; Col. 1. 23; 1 Pe. 5. 10.

θήκη, ης, ἡ, (§ 2. tab. B. a) *a repository, receptacle; a case, sheath, scabbard*, Jno. 18. 11.

τίθησι, 3 pers. sing. pres. ind. act. . τίθημι

τίκτει, 3 pers. sing. pres. ind. act. . . τίκτω

τίκτῃ, 3 pers. sing. pres. subj. act. . . id.

τίκτουσα, nom. sing. fem. part. pres. act. . id.

τίκτω], fut. τέξω & τέξομαι, aor. 2, ἔτεκον, perf. τέτοκα, aor. 1, pass. ἐτέχθην, (§ 37. rem. 1) *to bear, bring forth* children, Mat. 1. 21, 23, et al.; trop. *to bear, produce*, as the earth, *yield*, He. 6. 7; met. *to give, birth to*, Ja. 1. 15.

τέκνον, ου, τό, (§. 3. tab. C. c) *a child, a son or daughter*, Mat. 2. 18; Lu. 1. 7, et al.; pl. *descendants, posterity*, Mat. 3. 9; Ac. 2. 39; *child, son*, as a term of endearment, Mat. 9. 2; Mar. 2. 5; 10. 24; pl. *children, inhabitants, people*, of a city, Mat. 23. 37; Lu. 19. 44; from the Heb., met. *a child or son* in virtue of disciple ship, 1 Co. 4. 17; 1 Ti. 1. 2; 2 Ti. 1. 2; Tit. 1. 4; Phile. 10; 3 Jno. 4; *a child* in virtue of gracious acceptance, Jno. 1. 12; 11. 52; Ro. 8. 16, 21; 1 Jno. 3. 1; *a child* in virtue of spiritual conformity, Jno. 8. 39; Phi. 2. 15; 1 Jno. 3. 10; *a child of, one characterised by*, some condition or quality, Mat. 11. 19; Ep. 2. 3; 5. 8; 1 Pe. 1. 14; 2 Pe. 2. 14.

τεκνίον, ου, τό, (dimin. of τέκνον) *a little child*; τεκνία, an endearing compellation, *my dear children*, Jno. 13. 33; Gal. 4. 19; 1 Jno. 2. 1, et al.

τόκος, ου, ὁ, (§ 3. tab. C. a) *a bringing forth; offspring*; met. *produce* of money lent, *interest, usury*, Mat. 25. 27; Lu. 19. 23.

τίλλειν, pres. infin. . . . . . . τίλλω

τίλλοντες, nom. pl. masc. part. pres. . id.

* Lu. 3. 1.

τίλλω], fut. τιλῶ, (§ 27. rem. 1. b) *to pull, pluck off*, Mat. 12. 1; Mar. 2. 33; Lu. 6. 1.

τίμα, 2 pers. sing. pres. imper. act. . . τιμάω

τιμᾷ, 3 pers. sing. pres. ind. act. . . . id.

Τίμαιος], ου, ὁ, *Timæus*, pr. name.

Τιμαίου,[a] gen. . . . . . . Τίμαιος

τιμαῖς, dat. pl. . . . . . . τιμή

τιμάς, acc. pl. . . . . . . id.

τιμᾶτε, 2 pers. pl. pres. imper. act. . . τιμάω

τιμάω, ῶ], fut. ήσω . . . . . τιμή

τῑμή], ῆς, ἡ, (§ 2. tab. B. a) (τίω, *to price*) *a pricing, estimate of worth; price, value*, Mat. 27. 9; *price* paid, Mat. 27. 6; meton. *a thing of price*, and collectively, *precious things*, Re. 21. 24, 26; *preciousness*, 1 Pe. 2. 7; substantial *value*, real *worth*, Col. 2. 23; *careful regard, honour, state of honour, dignity*, Ro. 9. 21; He. 5. 4; *honour* conferred, *observance, veneration*, Ro. 2. 7, 10; 12. 10; *mark of favour and consideration*, Ac. 28. 10.

τῑμάω, ῶ, fut. ήσω, aor. 1, ἐτίμησα, (§ 18. tab. R) *to estimate in respect of worth; to hold in estimation, respect, honour, reverence*, Mat. 15. 4, 5, 8; 19. 19; Mar. 7. 10, et al.; *to honour* with reverent service, Jno. 5. 23, quater; 8. 49; *to treat with honour, manifest consideration towards*, Ac. 28. 10; *to treat graciously, visit with marks of favour*, Jno. 12. 26; mid. *to price*, Mat. 27. 9.

τίμιος, α, ον, (§ 7. rem. 1) *precious, costly, of great price*, 1 Co. 3. 12; Re. 18. 12; *precious, dear, valuable*, Ac. 20. 24; 1 Pe. 1. 7, 19; *honoured, esteemed, respected*, Ac. 5. 34; He. 13. 4.

τιμιότης, τητος, ἡ, (§ 4. rem. 2. c) *preciousness, costliness; meton. precious things, valuable merchandise*, Re. 18. 19. N.T.

τιμῇ, dat. sing. . . . . . . τιμή

τιμήν, acc. sing. . . . . . . id.

τιμῆς, gen. sing. . . . . . . id.

τιμήσατε, 2 pers. pl. aor. 1, imper. act. . τιμάω

τιμήσει, 3 pers. sing. fut. ind. act. . . . id.

τιμήσῃ, 3 pers. sing. aor. 1, subj. act. . . id.

τίμια, nom. pl. neut. . . . . . τίμιος

τιμίαν acc. sing. fem. . . . . . id.

τίμιον, acc. sing. masc. . . . . . τίμιος

τίμιος], α, ον . . . . . . τιμή

τιμιότης], τητος, ἡ . . . . . id.

τιμιότητος,[b] gen. sing. . . . . . τιμιότης

τιμίου, gen. sing. masc. . . . . . τίμιος

τιμίους, acc. pl. masc. . . . . . id.

τιμίῳ, dat. sing. masc. and neut. . . . id.

τιμιωτάτου, gen. sing. neut. superlative (§ 8. rem. 4) . . . . . id.

τιμιωτάτῳ, dat. sing. masc. superl. . . . id.

τιμιώτερον, nom. sing. neut. compar. . . . id.

Τιμόθεε, voc. . . . . . . Τιμόθεος

Τιμόθεον, acc. . . . . . . id.

Τιμόθεος], ου, ὁ, (§ 3. tab. C. a) *Timotheus, Timothy*, pr. name.

Τιμοθέου, gen. . . . . . . Τιμόθεος

Τιμοθέῳ, dat. . . . . . . id.

τιμῶ, 1 pers. sing. pres. ind. act. . . . τιμάω

τιμῶν, nom. sing. masc. part. pres. act. . . id.

Τίμων], ωνος, ὁ, (§ 4. rem. 2. e) *Timon*, pr. name.

Τίμωνα,[c] acc. . . . . . . Τίμων

τιμωρέω, ῶ], fut. ήσω, (§ 16. tab. P) aor. 1, pass. ἐτιμωρήθην, (τιμωρός, *an aider, an avenger*, from τιμή & αἴρω) *to succour, to avenge*, any one; in N.T. *to punish*, Ac. 22. 5; 26. 11.

τιμωρία], ας, ἡ, (§ 2. tab. B. b, and rem. 2) *punishment*, He. 10. 29.

τιμωρηθῶσι, 3 pers. pl. aor. 1, subj. pass. (§ 17. tab. Q) . . . . . τιμωρέω

τιμωρία], ας, ἡ . . . . . . id.

τιμωρίας,[d] gen. sing. . . . . . τιμωρία

τιμωρῶν, nom. sing. masc. part. pres. act. . τιμωρέω

τιμῶσι, 3 pers. pl. pres. ind. and subj. act. . τιμάω

τινά, acc. sing. masc. and nom. and acc. pl. neut. indef. . . . . . τις

τίνα, acc. sing. masc. and nom. pl. neut. interrog. τίς

τινάς acc. pl. masc. indef. . . . . . τις

τίνας, acc. pl. fem. interrog. . . . . τίς

τινές, nom. pl. masc. indef. . . . . . τις

τίνες, nom. pl. masc. interrog. . . . . τίς

τινί, dat. sing. indef. . . . . . τις

τίνι, dat. sing. interrog. . . . . . τίς

τινός, gen. sing. indef. . . . . . τις

τίνος, gen. sing. interrog. . . . . . τίς

τίνω], fut. τίσω, (§ 27. rem. 1. a, and note) *to pay; to pay a penalty, incur punishment*, 2 Thes. 1. 9.

---

[a] Mar. 10. 46. [b] Re. 18. 19. [c] Ac. 6. 5. [d] He. 10. 29.

τινῶν, gen. pl. indef. . . . . . τις

τίνων, gen. pl. interrog. . . . . τίς

τις], ὁ, ἡ, τό, -τι, gen. τινός, (§ 10. tab. J. e) indef. pron., *a certain one, some one,* Mat. 12. 47, et al.; pl. *some, certain, several,* Lu. 8. 2; Ac. 9. 19; 2 Pe. 3. 16, et al.; *one, a person,* Mat. 12. 29; Lu. 14. 8; Jno. 6. 50, et al.; combined with the name of an individual, *one,* Mar. 15. 21, et al.; *as it were, in a manner, a kind of,* He. 10. 27; Ja. 1. 18; *any* whatever, Mat. 8. 28; Lu. 11. 36; Ro. 8. 39, et al.; τις, *somebody* of consequence, Ac. 5. 36; τι, *something* of consequence, Gal. 2. 6; 6. 3; τι, *anything* at all, *anything* worth account, 1 Co. 3. 7; 10. 19; τι, *at all,* Phi. 3. 15; Phile. 18.

τίς], τί, τίνος, (§ 10. tab. J. f) interrog. pron., strictly of direct inquiry, *who? what?* Mat. 3. 7; 5. 13; 19. 27; equivalent to πότερος, *whether? which* of two things? Mat. 9. 5; Mar. 2. 9; Phi. 1. 22; neut. τι, *why? wherefore?* Mat. 8. 26; 9. 11, 14; τί ὅτι, *why is it that?* Mar. 2. 16; Jno. 14. 22; neut. τί, *what?* as an empathatic interrogative, Ac. 26. 8; τί, *how very!* v.r. Mat. 7. 14; in indirect question, Mat. 10. 11; 12. 3, et al.

τισί, dat. pl. indef. . . . . . τις

τίσι, dat. pl. interrog. . . . . . τίς

τίσουσι,[a] 3 pers. pl. fut. ind. . . . . τίνω

τίτλον, acc. sing. . . . . . τίτλος

τίτλος], ου, ὁ, (§ 3. tab. C. a) (Lat. *titulus*) *an inscribed roll, superscription,* Jno. 19. 19, 20.

Τίτον, acc. . . . . . . Τίτος

Τίτος], ου, ὁ, *Titus,* pr. name.

Τίτου, gen. . . . . . Τίτος

Τίτῳ, dat. . . . . . . id.

τοιᾶσδε,[b] gen. sing. fem. . . . . τοιόσδε

τοιαῦτα, acc. pl. neut. . . . . . τοιοῦτος

τοιαῦται, nom. pl. fem. . . . id.

τοιαύταις, dat. pl. fem. . . . . id.

τοιαύτας, acc. pl. fem. . . . . . id.

τοιαύτη, nom. sing. fem. . . . . . id.

τοιαύτην, acc. sing. fem. . . . . id.

τοιγαροῦν], (τοι, γάρ, and οὖν) a doubly strengthened form of the particle τοι, *well then, so then, wherefore,* 1 Thes. 4. 8; He. 12. 1.

τοίνυν], a strengthening of the particle τοι, by the enclitic νυν, *well then, therefore now, therefore,* Lu. 20. 25; 1 Co. 9. 26, et al.

τοιόσδε], τοιάδε, τοιόνδε, (§ 10. rem. 8) a more pointedly demonstrative form of τοῖος, *such as this; such as follows,* 2 Pe. 1. 17.

τοιοῦτοι, nom. pl. masc. . . . . . τοιοῦτος

τοιούτοις, dat. pl. masc. and neut. . . . id.

τοιοῦτον, acc. sing. masc. and neut. . . . id.

τοιοῦτος], τοιαύτη, τοιοῦτο, and τοιοῦτον, (§ 10. rem. 7. a) a lengthened and more demonstrative form of τοῖος, *such, such like, of this kind or sort,* Mat. 18. 5; 19. 14; *such, so great,* Mat. 9. 8; Mar. 6. 2; ὁ τοιοῦτος, *such a fellow,* Ac. 22. 22; also, *the one alluded to,* 1 Co. 1. 5; 2 Co. 2. 6, 7; 12. 2, 3, 5.

τοιούτου, gen. sing. masc. . . . . τοιοῦτος

τοιούτους, acc. pl. masc. . . . . . id.

τοιούτῳ, dat. sing. masc. . . . . id.

τοιούτων, gen. pl. . . . . . . id.

τοῖχε,[c] voc. sing. . . . . . τοῖχος

τοῖχος], ου, ὁ, (§ 3. tab. C. a) *a wall* of a building, as distinct from a city wall or fortification (τεῖχος), Ac. 23. 3.

τόκος], ου, ὁ, (§ 3. tab. C. a) . . . . τίκτω

τόκῳ, dat. sing. . . . . . . τόκος

τολμᾷ, 3 pers. sing. pres. ind. and subj. . τολμάω

τολμᾶν, pres. infin. . . . . . id.

τολμάω, ῶ], fut. ήσω, aor. 1, ἐτόλμησα, (§ 18. tab. R) *to assume resolution* to do a thing, Mar. 15. 43; Ro. 5. 7; Phi. 1. 14; *to make up the mind,* 2 Co. 10. 12; *to dare,* Ac. 5. 13; 7. 32; *to presume,* Mat. 22. 46; Mar. 12. 34; Lu. 20. 40; Jno. 21. 12; Ro. 15. 18; Jude 9; *to have the face,* 1 Co. 6. 1; absol. *to assume a bold bearing,* 2 Co. 10. 2; 11. 21.

τολμηρότερος, α, ον, (§ 7. rem. 1) compar. of τολμηρός, *bold,* from τολμάω) *bolder;* neut. τολμηρότερον, as an adv., *more boldly, with more confidence, more freely,* Ro. 15. 15.

τολμητής, οῦ, ὁ, (§ 2. tab. B. c) *one who is bold;* in a bad sense, *a presumptuous, audacious person,* 2 Pe. 2. 10.

τολμηρότερον],[d] adv. . . . . . τολμαω

τολμηροτέρως], adv. *more boldly.*—A. B. Ln.
τολμηρότερον, R. Gr. Sch. Tdf. (Ro. 15. 15) } id.

[a] 2 Thes. 1. 9. [b] 2 Pe. 1. 17. [c] Ac. 23. 3. [d] Ro. 15. 15.

τολμῆσαι, aor. 1, infin. . . . . τολμάω
τολμήσας, nom. sing. masc. part. aor. 1 . id.
τολμήσω, 1 pers. sing. fut. ind. . . id.
τολμηταί,[a] nom. pl. . . . . τολμητής
τολμητής], οῦ, ὁ . . . . τολμάω
τολμῶ, 1 pers. sing. pres. ind. . . . id.
τολμῶμεν, 1 pers. pl. pres. ind. . . id.
τομώτερος],[b] α, ον, (§ 7. rem. 1) (compar. of τομός, *cutting, sharp, keen,* from τέμνω, *to cut*) *keener, sharper.*

τόξον],[c] ου, τό, (§ 3. tab. C. c) *a bow.*

τοπάζιον],[d] ου, τό, *a topaz,* a gem of a yellowish colour, different from the modern topaz. L.G.

τόποις, dat. pl. . . . . . τόπος
τόπον, acc. sing. . . . . . id.

τόπος], ου, ὁ, (§ 3. tab. C. a) *a place, locality,* Mat. 12. 43; Lu. 6. 17, et al.; *a* limited *spot or ground,* Mat. 24. 15; 27. 33; Jno. 4. 20; Ac. 6. 13, et al.; *a* precise *spot or situation,* Mat. 28. 6; Mar. 16. 6; Lu. 14. 9, et al.; *a dwelling place, abode, mansion, dwelling, seat,* Jno. 14. 2, 3; Ac. 4. 31; *a place* of ordinary deposit, Mat. 26. 52; *a place, passage* in a book, Lu. 4. 17; *place* occupied, *room, space,* Lu. 2. 7; 14. 9, 22; *place, opportunity,* Ac. 25. 16; He. 12. 17; *place, condition, position,* 1 Co. 14. 16.

τόπου, gen. sing. . . . . τόπος
τόπους, acc. pl. . . . . . id.
τόπῳ, dat. sing. . . . . . id.
τόπων, gen. pl. . . . . . id.
τοσαῦτα, nom. and acc. pl. neut. . . τοσοῦτος
τοσαύτην, acc. sing. fem. . . . id.
τοσοῦτο, acc. sing. neut.—Al. Ln. Tdf. . } id.
τοσοῦτον, Rec. Gr. Sch. (He. 7. 22) . }
τοσοῦτοι, nom. pl. masc. . . . . id.
τοσοῦτον, acc. sing. masc. and neut. (§ 10. rem. 8) . . . . . id.
τοσοῦτος], τοσαύτη, τοσοῦτο, and τοσοῦτον, (§ 10. rem. 7. b) a lengthened and more demonstrative form of τόσος, *so great, so much,* Mat. 8. 10; 15. 33; *so long,* of time, Jno. 14. 9; pl. *so many,* Mat. 15. 33, et al.

τοσούτου, gen. sing. neut. . . . τοσοῦτος
τοσούτους, acc. pl. masc. . . . . id.
τοσούτῳ, dat. sing. neut. . . . τοσοῦτος
τοσούτων, gen. pl. . . . . . id.
τότε], adv. of time, *then, at that time,* Mat. 2. 17; 3. 5; 11. 20; *then, thereupon,* Mat. 12. 29; 13. 26; 25. 31; ἀπὸ τότε, *from that time,* Mat. 4. 17; 16. 21; ὁ τότε, *which then was,* 2 Pe. 3. 6.
τοὐναντίον], (by crasis for τὸ ἐναντίον) *that which is opposite;* as an adv., *on the contrary, on the other hand,* 2 Co. 2. 7; Gal. 2. 7; 1 Pe. 3. 9.
τοὔνομα],[e] (by crasis for τὸ ὄνομα) *the name;* in the acc. *by name,* Mat. 27. 57.
τουτέστι], (by crasis for τοῦτ' ἔστι) *that is, which signifies, which implies,* Ac. 1. 19; 19. 4, et al.

τοῦτο, nom. and acc. sing. neut. (§ 10. tab. J. c) οὗτος
τούτοις, dat. pl. masc. and neut. . . id.
τοῦτον, acc. sing. masc. . . . id.
τούτου, gen. sing. masc. and neut. . id.
τούτους, acc. pl. masc. . . . . id.
τούτῳ, dat. sing. masc. and neut. . . id.
τούτων, gen. pl. . . . . . id.
τράγος], ου, ὁ, (§ 3. tab. C. a) *a he-goat,* He. 9. 12, 13, 19; 10. 4.
τράγων, gen. pl. . . . . . τράγος
τράπεζα], ης, ἡ, (§ 2. rem. 3) (τετράς, *four,* and πέζα, *a foot*) *a table, an eating-table,* Mat. 15. 27; Mar. 7. 28; He. 9. 2; by impl. *a meal, feast,* Ro. 11. 9; 1 Co. 10. 21, *a table or counter* of a money-changer, Mat. 21. 12; *a bank,* Lu. 19. 23; by impl. pl. *money matters,* Ac. 6. 2.

τραπεζίτης, ου, ὁ, (§ 2. tab. B. c) *a money-changer, broker, banker,* who exchanges or loans money for a premium, Mat. 25. 27. (ῑ).

τραπέζαις, dat. pl. . . . . τράπεζα
τράπεζαν, acc. sing. . . . . id.
τραπέζας, acc. pl. . . . . id.
τραπέζης, gen. sing. . . . . id.
τραπεζίταις,[f] dat. pl. . . . . τραπεζίτης
τραπεζίτης, ου, ὁ . . . . . τράπεζα
τραῦμα], ατος, τό, (§ 4. tab. D. c) (τιτρώσκω, *to wound*) *a wound,* Lu. 10. 34.

[a] 2 Pe. 2. 10. [b] He. 4. 12. [c] Re. 6. 2. [d] Re. 21. 20. [e] Mat. 27. 57. [f] Mat. 25. 27.

τραυματίζω, fut. ίσω, aor. 1, ἐτραυμάτισα, (§ 26. rem. 1) *to wound*, Lu. 20. 12; Ac. 19. 16.

τραύματα,[a] acc. pl. . . . . . τραῦμα
τραυματίζω], fut. ίσω . . . . . id.
τραυματίσαντες, nom. pl. masc. part. aor. 1 τραυματίζω
τραχεῖαι, nom. pl. fem. . . . . τραχύς
τραχεῖς, acc. pl. masc. . . . . . id.
τραχηλίζω], fut. ίσω . . . . . τράχηλος
τράχηλον, acc. sing. . . . . . id.

τράχηλος], ου, ὁ, (§ 3. tab. C. a) *the neck*, Mat. 18. 6, et al.; ἐπιθεῖναι ζυγὸν ἐπὶ τὸν τράχηλον, *to put a yoke upon the neck* of any one, met. *to bind to a burdensome observance*, Ac. 15. 10; ὑποτιθέναι τὸν τράχηλον, *to lay down one's neck* under the axe of the executioner, *to imperil one's life*, Ro. 16. 4.

τραχηλίζω, fut. ίσω, perf. pass. τετραχήλισμαι, (§ 26. rem. 1) pr. *to gripe the neck; to bend the neck back*, so as to make bare or expose the throat, as in slaughtering animals, etc.; met. *to lay bare to view*, He. 4. 13.

τρᾰχύς], εῖα, ύ, (§ 7. tab. H. g) *rough, rugged, uneven*, Lu. 3. 5; εἰς τραχεῖς τόπους, *on a rocky shore*, Ac. 27. 29.

Τραχωνίτιδος,[b] gen. . . . . . Τραχωνῖτις
Τραχωνῖτις], ῐδος, ἡ, (§ 4. rem. 2. c) *Trachonitis*, part of the tetrarchy of Herod Antipas, the north-easternmost habitable district east of the Jordan.

Τρεῖς Ταβέρναι', *the Three Taverns*, the name of a small place on the Appian road, according to Antonius, 33 Roman miles from Rome, Ac. 28. 15.

τρεῖς], οἱ, αἱ, τά, τρία, (§ 9. tab. I. c) *three*, Mat. 12. 40, et al.

τριάκοντα, οἱ, αἱ, τά, *thirty*, Mat. 13. 8, 23, et al.

τριακόσιοι, αι, α, *three hundred*, Mar. 14. 5; Jno. 12. 5.

τρίς, adv. *three times, thrice*, Mat. 26. 34, 75, et al.; ἐπὶ τρίς, *to the extent of thrice, as many as three times*, Ac. 10. 16; 11. 10.

τρίτος, η, ον, (§ 7. tab. F. a) *third*, Mat. 20. 3; 27. 64; ἐκ τρίτου, *the third time, for the third time*, Mat. 26. 44; τὸ τρίτον, sc. μέρος, *the third part*, Re. 8. 7, 12; τρίτον & τὸ τρίτον, as an adv. *the third time, for the third time*, Mar. 14. 21; Lu. 23. 22.

τρεῖς, nom. and acc. masc. and fem. . . τρεῖς
τρέμουσα, nom. sing. fem. part. pres. . τρέμω
τρέμουσι, 3 pers. pl. pres. ind. . . . id

τρέμω], (τρέω, idem) *to tremble, be agitated from fear*, Mar. 5. 33; Lu. 8. 47; Ac. 9. 6; by impl. *to fear, be afraid*, 2 Pe. 2. 10.

τρόμος, ου, ὁ, (§ 3. tab. C. a) pr. *a trembling, quaking; trembling* from fear, *fear, terror, agitation of mind*, Mar. 16. 8; *anxious diffidence*, under solemn responsibility, 1 Co. 2. 3; *reverence, veneration, awe*, 2 Co. 7. 15; Ep. 6. 5; Phi. 2. 12.

τρέμων, nom. sing. masc. part. pres. . τρέμω
τρέφει, 3 pers. sing. pres. ind. act. . τρέφω
τρέφεσθαι, pres. infin. pass. . . . id.
τρέφεται, 3 pers. sing. pres. ind. pass. . id.

τρέφω], fut. θρέψω, (§ 35. rem. 4) aor. 1, ἔθρεψα, perf. pass. τέθραμμαι, (§ 35. rem. 9) *to thicken; to nourish; to feed, support, cherish, provide for*, Mat. 6. 26; 25. 37, et al.; *to bring up, rear, educate*, Lu. 4. 16; *to gorge, pamper*, Ja. 5. 5.

θρέμμα, ατος, τό, (§ 4. tab. D. c) *that which is reared*; pl. *cattle*, Jno. 4. 12.

τροφή, ῆς, ἡ, (§ 2. tab. B. a) *nutriment, nourishment, food*, Mat. 3. 4, et al.; *provision, victual*, Mat. 24. 45; *sustenance, maintenance*, Mat. 10. 10; met. *nutriment* of the mind, He. 5. 12, 14.

τροφός, οῦ, ἡ, (§ 3. tab. C. b) *a nurse*, 1 Thes. 2. 7.

τρέφωσι, 3 pers. pl. pres. subj. act. . . τρέφω
τρέχει, 3 pers. sing. pres. ind. . . . τρέχω
τρέχετε, 2 pers. pl. pres. imper. . . id.
τρέχῃ, 3 pers. sing. pres. subj. . . . id.
τρέχοντες, nom. pl. masc. part. pres. . id.
τρέχοντος, gen. sing. masc. part. pres. . id.
τρεχόντων, gen. pl. masc. part. pres. . id.

[a] Lu. 10. 34.
[b] Lu. 3. 1.

τρέχουσι, 3 pers. pl. pres. ind. . . . τρέχω

τρέχω], fut. θρέξομαι, & δραμοῦμαι, aor. 2, ἔδρᾰμον, (§ 36. rem. 1) *to run*, Mat. 27. 48; 28. 8, et al.; *to run* a race, 1 Co. 9. 24; met. 1 Co. 9. 24, 26; He. 12. 1; in N.T. *to run* a certain course of conduct, Gal. 5. 7; *to run* a course of exertion, Ro. 9. 16; Gal. 2. 2; Phi. 2. 16; *to run, to progress freely, to advance rapidly*, 2 Thes. 3. 1.

δρόμος, ου, ὁ, (§ 3. tab. C. a) (δέδρομα) *a course, race, race-course*; met. *course* of life or ministry, *career*, Ac. 13. 25; 20. 24; 2 Ti. 4. 7.

τροχός, οῦ, ὁ, (§ 3. tab. C. a) pr. *a runner; anything orbicular, a wheel; drift, course*, with which signification the word is usually written τρόχος, Ja. 3. 6.

τροχιά, ᾶς, ἡ, (§ 2. tab. B. b, and rem. 2) *a wheel-track; a track, way, path*, met. He. 12. 13.

τρέχω, 1 pers. sing. pres. subj. . . . τρέχω

τρέχωμεν, 1 pers. pl. pres. subj. . . . id.

τρῆμα], ατος, τό, (τιτράω, or τίτρημι, *to bore*, perf. pass. τέτρημαι) *an aperture*, v.r. Lu. 18. 25.

τρήματος [βελόνης], gen. sing.—B.D.Ln.Tdf. τρυμαλιᾶς [ῥαφίδος], Rec. Gr. Sch. (Lu. 18. 25) . . . τρῆμα

τρία, nom. and acc. neut. . . . τρεῖς

τριάκοντα], οἱ, αἱ, τά . . . id.

τριακόσιοι], αι, α . . . id.

τριακοσίων, gen. pl. . . . τριακόσιοι

τρίβολος], ου, ὁ, (§ 3. tab. C. a) (τρεῖς & βέλος) pr. *three-pronged*; as a subst. *a caltrop*; a plant, *land caltrop, a thorn*, Mat. 7. 16; He. 6. 8.

τριβόλους, acc. pl. . . . τρίβολος

τριβόλων, gen. pl. . . . id.

τρίβος], ου, ἡ, (§ 3. tab. C. b) (τρίβω, *to rub, wear*) *a beaten track; a road, highway*, Mat. 3. 3; Mar. 1. 3; Lu. 3. 4.

τρίβους, acc. pl. . . . τρίβος

τριετία], ας, ἡ, (§ 2. tab. B. b, and rem. 2) (τρεῖς & ἔτος) *the space of three years*.

τριετίαν,[a] acc. sing. . . . τριετία

τρίζει,[b] 3 pers. sing. pres. ind. . . . τρίζω

τρίζω], fut. ίσω, (§ 26. rem. 1) *to creak, to utter a creaking, stridulous, grating sound; to gnash grind* the teeth, Mar. 9. 18.

τρίμηνον],[c] ου, τό, (τρεῖς & μήν) *the space of three months*.

τρίς], adv. . . . τρεῖς

τρισί, dat. pl. . . . id.

τρίστεγον], ου, τό, (§ 3. tab. C. c) (neut. of τρίστεγος, *having three stories*, from τρεῖς & στέγη) *the third floor, third story*. L.G.

τριστέγου,[d] gen. sing. . . . τρίστεγον

τρισχίλιαι,[e] nom. pl. fem. . . . τρισχίλιοι

τρισχίλιοι], αι, α, (τρεῖς & χίλιοι) *three thousand*.

τρίτη, nom. sing. fem. . . . τρίτος

τρίτῃ, dat. sing. fem. . . . id.

τρίτην, acc. sing. fem. . . . id.

τρίτης, gen. sing. fem. . . . id.

τρίτον, acc. sing. masc. and nom. neut. . . . id.

τρίτον, τό, used substantively, Re. 8. 7, 8, 9, 10, 11, 12, et al.

τρίτον, and τὸ τρίτον, adverbially . . . id.

τρίτος], η, ον, (§ 7. tab. F. a) . . . τρεῖς

τρίτου, gen. sing. masc. and neut. . . . τρίτος

τρίχα, acc. sing. (§ 4. rem. 2. note) . . . θρίξ

τρίχας, acc. pl. . . . id.

τρίχες, nom. pl. . . . id.

τρίχινος],[f] η, ον, (§ 7. tab. F. a) . . . id.

τριχῶν, gen. pl. . . . id.

τριῶν, gen. pl. . . . τρεῖς

Τριῶν Ταβερνῶν,[g] gen. . . . Τρεῖς Ταβέρναι

τρόμος], ου, ὁ, (§ 3. tab. C. a) . . . τρέμω

τρόμου, gen. sing. . . . τρόμος

τρόμῳ, dat. sing. . . . id.

τροπή], ῆς, ἡ, (§ 2. tab. B. a) (τρέπω, *to turn*) *a turning round; a turning back, change, mutation*, Ja. 1. 17.

τροπῆς,[h] gen. sing. . . . τροπή

τρόπον, acc. sing. . . . τρόπος

τρόπος], ου, ὁ, (§ 3. tab. C. a) (τρέπω, *to turn*) *a turn; mode, manner, way*, Jude 7; ὃν τρόπον, & καθ' ὃν τρόπον, *in which manner, as, even as*, Mat. 23. 37; Ac. 15. 11, et al.; κατὰ μηδένα τρόπον, *in no way, by no means*, 2 Thes. 2. 3; ἐν παντὶ τρόπῳ, & παντὶ τρόπῳ, *in every way, by every means*, Phi. 1. 18; 2 Thes. 3. 16; *turn* of mind or action, *habit, disposition*, He. 13. 5.

[a] Ac. 20. 31. [b] Mar 9. 18. [c] He. 11. 23. [d] Ac. 20. 9. [e] Ac. 2. 41. [f] Re. 6. 13. [g] Ac. 28. 15. [h] Ja. 1. 17.

τροποφορέω, ῶ], fut. ήσω, aor. 1, ἐτροποφόρησα, (§ 16. tab. P) (τρόπος & φορέω) *to bear with the disposition, manners, and conduct of* anv one, Ac. 13. 18. L.G.

τρόπῳ, dat. sing. . . . . . τρόπος

τροφάς, acc. pl. . . . . . τροφή

τροφή], ῆς, ἡ, (§ 2. tab. B. a) . . . τρέφω

τροφήν, acc. sing. . . . . . τροφή

τροφῆς, gen. sing. . . . id.

Τρόφιμον, acc. . . . . . Τρόφιμος

Τρόφῐμος], ου, ὁ, (§ 3. tab. C. a) *Trophimus*, pr. name.

τροφός],[a] οῦ, ἡ, (§ 3. tab. C. b) . . τρέφω

τροφοφορέω, ῶ], fut. ήσω, (§ 16. tab. P) (τροφός & φορέω), *to sustain, provide for, cherish,* v.r. Ac. 13. 8. LXX.

τροχιά] ᾶς, ἡ, (§ 2. tab. B. b, and rem. 2) . τρέχω

τροχιάς,[b] acc. pl. . . . . τροχιά

τροχόν,[c] acc. sing. . . . . . τροχός

τροχός], οῦ, ὁ . . . . . . τρέχω

τρυβλίον], ίου, τό, (§ 3. tab. C. c) *a bowl, dish,* Mat. 26. 23; Mar. 14. 20.

τρυβλίῳ, dat. sing. . . . . . τρυβλίον

τρυγάω, ῶ], fut. ήσω, aor. 1, ἐτρύγησα, (§ 18. tab. R) (τρύγη, *ripe fruits*) *to harvest, gather,* fruits, and spc. grapes, Lu. 6. 44; Re. 14. 18, 19.

τρύγησον, 2 pers. sing. aor. 1, imper. . τρυγάω

τρυγόνων,[d] gen. pl. . . . . . τρυγών

τρυγών], όνος, ἡ, (§ 4. rem. 2. e) (τρύζω, *to murmur*) *a turtle-dove.*

τρυγῶσι, 3 pers. pl. pres. ind. . . τρυγάω

τρυμαλιά], ᾶς, ἡ, (§ 2. tab. B. b, and rem. 2) (τρύμη, from τρύω, *to rub, wear*) *a hole, perforation; eye* of a needle, Mar. 10. 25; Lu. 18. 25.

τρυμαλιᾶς, gen. sing. . . . . τρυμαλιά

τρύπημα], ατος, τό, (§ 4. tab. D. c) (τρυπάω, τρύπη, *a hole,* from τρύω) *a hole; eye* of a needle, Mat. 19. 24

τρυπήματος,[e] gen. sing. . . . τρύπημα

Τρύφαινα], ης, ἡ, (§ 2. rem. 3) *Tryphæna*, pr. name.

Τρύφαιναν,[f] acc. . . . . . Τρύφαινα

τρυφάω, ῶ], fut. ήσω . . . . τρυφή

τρυφή], ῆς, ἡ, (§ 2. tab. B. a) (θρύπτω, *to break small, to enfeeble, enervate*) *delicate living, luxury,* Lu. 7. 25; 2 Pe. 2. 13.

τρυφάω, ῶ, fut. ήσω, aor. 1, ἐτρύφησα, (§ 18. tab. R) *to live delicately and luxuriously,* Ja. 5. 5.

τρυφῇ, dat. sing. . . . . τρυφή

τρυφήν, acc. sing. . . . . . id.

Τρυφῶσα], ης, ἡ, (§ 2. rem. 3) *Tryphosa*, pr. name.

Τρυφῶσαν,[g] acc. . . . . Τρυφῶσα

Τρωάδα, acc. . . . . . . Τρωάς

Τρωάδι, dat. . . . . . . id.

Τρωάδος, gen. . . . . . id.

Τρωάς], άδος, (ᾰ) ἡ, (§ 4. rem. 2. c) *Troas*, a city on the coast of Phrygia, near the site of ancient Troy.

τρώγοντες, nom. pl. masc. part. pres. . τρώγω

Τρωγύλλιον], ου, τό, (§ 3. tab. C. c) *Trogyllium*, a town and promontory on the western coast of Ionia, opposite Samos.

Τρωγυλλίῳ,[h] dat. . . . . Τρωγύλλιον

τρώγω], fut. τρώξομαι, aor. 2, ἔτρᾰγον, (§ 36. rem. 1) pr. *to crunch; to eat,* Mat. 24. 38; from the Heb., ἄρτον τρώγειν, *to take food, partake of a meal,* Jno. 13. 18.

τρώγων, nom. sing. masc. part. pres. . . τρώγω

τυγχάνοντα, acc. sing. masc. part. pres. . τυγχάνω

τυγχάνοντες, nom. pl. masc. part. pres. . id.

τυγχάνω], fut. τεύξομαι, perf. τετύχηκα & τέτευχα, aor. 2, ἔτῠχον, (§ 36. rem. 2) *to hit* an object; *to attain to, to obtain, acquire, enjoy,* Lu. 20. 35; Ac. 24. 3, et al.; intrans. *to happen, fall out, chance;* part. τυχών, οὖσα, όν, *common, ordinary,* Ac. 19. 11; 28. 2; neut. τυχόν, as an adv., *it may be, perchance, perhaps,* 1 Co. 16. 6; εἰ τύχοι, *if it so happen, as the case may be,* 1 Co. 14. 10; 15. 37; *to be* in a certain condition, Lu. 10. 30.

τυμπανίζω], fut. ίσω, aor. 1, pass. ἐτυμπανίσθην, (§ 26. rem. 1) (τύμπανον, *a drum*) pr. *to beat a drum; to drum upon;* in N.T. *to bastinade, beat to death with rods and clubs,* He. 11. 35.

τυπικῶς, adv.—A. B. C. Ln. Tdf. . . } τύπτω
τύποι, Rec. Gr. Sch. (1 Co. 10. 11) . }

τύποι, nom. pl. . . . . τύπος

τύπον, acc. sing. . . . . . . id.

τύπος], ου, ὁ . . . . . . τύπτω

τύπους, acc. pl. . . . . . . τύπος

[a] 1 Thes. 2. 7. [b] He. 12. 13. [c] Ja. 3. 6. [d] Lu. 2. 24. [e] Mat. 19. 24. [f] Ro. 16. 12. [g] Ro. 16. 12. [h] Ac. 20. 15.

τύπτειν, pres. infin. act. . . . . τύπτω
τύπτεσθαι, pres. infin. pass. . . . . id.
τύπτοντες, nom. pl. masc. part. pres. act. . id.
τύπτοντι, dat. sing. masc. part. pres. act. . id.

τύπτω], fut. ψω, (§ 23. rem. 2) aor. 1, ἔτυψα, *to beat, strike, smite*, Mat. 24. 49; 27. 30, et al.; *to beat* the breast, as expressive of grief or strong emotion, Lu. 18. 13; 23. 48; in N.T. met. *to wound or shock* the conscience of any one, 1 Co. 8. 12; from the Heb., *to smite* with evil, *punish*, Ac. 23. 3.

τύπος, ου, ὁ, (§ 3. tab. C. a) pr. *a blow; an impress; a print, mark*, of a wound inflicted, Jno. 20. 25; *a delineation; an image, statue*, Ac. 7. 43; *a formula, scheme*, Ro. 6. 17; *form, purport*, Ac. 23. 25; *a figure, counterpart*, 1 Co. 10. 6; *an* anticipative *figure, type*, Ro. 5. 14; 1 Co. 10. 11; *a model pattern*, Ac. 7. 44; He. 8. 5; *a* moral *pattern*, Phi. 3. 17; 1 Thes. 1. 7; 2 Thes. 3. 9; 1 Ti. 4. 12; 1 Pe. 5. 3.

τυπικῶς, adv. *figuratively, typically*, v.r. 1 Co. 10. 11.

Τύραννος], ου, ὁ, (§ 3. tab. C. a) *Tyrannus*, pr. name.
Τυράννου,[a] gen. . . . . . . Τύραννος
τυρβάζω], fut. άσω, (§ 26. rem. 1) (τύρβη, *tumult*) *to stir up, render turbid; to throw into a state of perturbation, disquiet*; mid. *to trouble one's self, be troubled, be disquieted*, Lu. 10. 41.
τυρβάζῃ,[b] 2 pers. sing. pres. ind. mid. . . τυρβάζω
Τυρίοις,[c] dat. pl. masc. . . . . Τύριος
Τύριος], ου, ὁ, ἡ, *a Tyrian, an inhabitant* of Τύρος, *Tyre*.
Τύρον, acc. . . . . Τύρος
Τύρος], ου, ἡ, (§ 3. tab. C. b) *Tyrus, Tyre*, a celebrated and wealthy commercial city of Phœnicia.
Τύρου, gen. . . . . . . Τύρος
Τύρῳ, dat. . . . . id.
τυφλέ, voc. sing. masc. . . . . τυφλός
τυφλοί, nom. and voc. pl. masc. . . . id.
τυφλοῖς, dat. pl. masc. . . . . id.
τυφλόν, acc. sing. masc. . . . . . id.

τυφλός], ή, όν, (§ 7. tab. F. a) *blind*, Mat. 9. 27, 28; 11. 5; 12. 22; met. mentally *blind*, Mat. 15. 14; 23. 16, et al.

τυφλόω, ῶ, fut. ώσω, perf. τετύφλωκα, (§ 20. tab. T) *to blind, render blind*; met. Jno. 12. 40; 1 Jno. 2. 11; 2 Co. 4. 4.

τυφλοῦ, gen. sing. masc. . . . . τυφλός
τυφλούς, acc. pl. masc. . . . . . id.
τυφλόω, ῶ], fut. ώσω . . . . . id.
τυφλῷ, dat. sing. masc. . . . . . id.
τυφλῶν, gen. pl. . . . . . id.
τυφόμενον,[d] acc. sing. neut. part. pres. pass. . τύφω
τυφόω, ῶ], fut. ώσω . . . . . id.

τύφω], fut. θύψω, (§ 35. rem. 4) *to raise a smoke*; pass. *to emit smoke, smoke, smoulder*, Mat. 12. 20.

τυφόω, ῶ, fut. ώσω, perf. pass. τετύφωμαι, (§ 21. tab. U) (τῦφος, *smoke*, from τύφω) *to besmoke*; met. *to possess with the fumes* of conceit; pass. *to be demented with conceit, puffed up*, 1 Ti. 3. 6; 6. 4; 2 Ti. 3. 4.

τυφωθείς, nom. sing. masc. part. aor. 1, pass. τυφόω
τυφωνικός],[e] ή, όν, (§ 7. tab. F. a) (τυφῶν, *typhon, a hurricane*) *stormy, tempestuous*.
τυχεῖν, aor. 2, infin. (§ 36. rem. 2) . . τυγχάνω
Τύχικον, acc. . . . . . . Τύχικος
Τύχικος], ου, ὁ, *Tychicus*, pr. name.
τύχοι, 3 pers. sing. aor. 2, opt. . . . τυγχάνω
τυχόν, aor. 2, part. neut. adverbially . id.
τυχοῦσαν, acc. sing. fem. part. aor. 2 . . id.
τυχούσας, acc. pl. fem. part. aor. 2 . id.
τύχωσι, 3 pers. pl. aor. 2, subj. . . . id.
τυχών, nom. sing. masc. part. aor. 2 . id.
τῳ, dat. sing. indef. for τινί, (§ 10. rem. 4. note) ὡσπερεί τῳ ἐκτρώματι, Knappe.

ὡσπερεὶ τῷ ἐκτρ.—Rec. Gr. Sch. Tdf. (1 Co. 15. 8).

Υ.

ὑακίνθινος], η, ον . . . . . . ὑάκινθος
ὑακινθίνους,[f] acc. pl. masc. . . . ὑακίνθινος
ὑάκινθος],[g] ου, ἡ, (§ 3. tab. C. a) *a hyacinth*, a gem resembling the colour of the *hyacinth flower*.

[a] Ac. 19. 9. [b] Lu. 10. 41. [c] Ac. 12. 20. [d] Mat. 12. 20. [e] Ac. 27. 14. [f] Re. 9. 17. [g] Re. 21. 20.

ὑακίνθῐνος, η, ον, (§ 7. tab. F. a) *hyacinthine, resembling the hyacinth in colour*, Re. 9. 17.

ὑαλίνη, nom. sing. fem. . . . . ὑάλινος
ὑαλίνην, acc. sing. fem. . . . . id.
ὑάλινος], η, ον . . . . . ὕαλος

ὕᾰλος], ου, ὁ, (§ 3. tab. C. a) *a transparent stone, crystal; also, glass*, Re. 21. 18, 21.

ὑάλῐνος, η, ον, (§ 7. tab. F. a) *made of glass; glassy, translucent*, Re. 4. 6; 15. 2.

ὑάλῳ, dat. sing. . . . . . ὕαλος
ὕβρεσι, dat. pl. . . . . . ὕβρις
ὕβρεως, gen. sing. . . . . . id.
ὑβρίζεις, 2 pers. sing. pres. ind. act. . ὑβρίζω
ὑβρίζω], fut. ίσω . . . . . ὕβρις
ὕβριν acc. sing. . . . . . id.

ὕβρις], εως, ἡ, (§ 5. tab. E. c) *violent wantonness, insolence; contumelious treatment, outrage*, 2 Co. 12. 10; *damage* by sea, Ac. 17. 10.

ὑβρίζω, fut. ίσω, aor. 1, ὕβρισα, (§ 13. rem. 3) *to run riot*; trans. *to outrage*, Mat. 22. 6; Lu. 11. 45, et al.

ὑβριστής, οῦ, ὁ, (§ 2. tab. B. c) *an overbearing, wantonly violent person*, Ro. 1. 30; 1 Ti. 1. 13.

ὑβρίσαι, aor. 1, infin. act. . . . ὑβρίζω
ὕβρισαν, 3 pers. pl. aor. 1, ind. act. . id.
ὑβρισθέντες, nom. pl. masc. part. aor. 1, pass. id.
ὑβρισθήσεται, 3 pers. sing. fut. ind. pass. . id.
ὑβριστάς, acc. pl. . . . . ὑβριστής
ὑβριστήν, acc. sing. . . . . id.
ὑβριστής], οῦ, ὁ . . . . ὕβρις
ὑγιαίνειν, pres. infin. . . . . ὑγιαίνω
ὑγιαίνοντα, acc. sing. masc. part. pres. . id.
ὑγιαίνοντας, acc. pl. masc. part. pres. . . id.
ὑγιαίνοντες, nom. pl. masc. part. pres. . id.
ὑγιαινόντων, gen. pl. masc. part. pres. . id.
ὑγιαινούσῃ, dat. sing. fem. part. pres. . id.
ὑγιαινούσης, gen. sing. fem. part. pres. id.
ὑγιαίνουσι, dat. pl. masc. part. pres. . id.
ὑγιαίνω], fut. ανῶ . . . . . ὑγιής
ὑγιαίνωσι, 3 pers. pl. pres. subj. . . ὑγιαίνω
ὑγιεῖς, acc. pl. masc. . . . . ὑγιής
ὑγιῆ, acc. sing. masc. . . . . id.

ὑγιής], έος, οῦς, ὁ, ἡ, τό, -ές, (§ 7. tab. G. b) *hale, sound, in health*, Mat. 12. 13; 15. 31, et al.; met. of doctrine, *sound, pure, wholesome*, Tit. 2. 8.

ὑγιαίνω, fut. ανῶ, (§ 27. rem. 1. c) *to be hale, sound, in health*, Lu. 5. 31; 7. 10; *to be safe and sound*, Lu. 15. 27; met. *to be healthful or sound* in faith, doctrine, etc., Tit. 1. 13; 2. 2; part. ὑγιαίνων, ουσα, ον, *sound, pure, uncorrupted*, 1 Ti. 1. 10, et al.

ὑγρός], ά, όν, (§ 7. rem. 1) (ὕω, *to wet*) pr. *wet, moist, humid*; used of a tree, *full of sap, fresh, green*, Lu. 23. 31.

ὑγρῷ, dat. sing. neut. . . . . ὑγρός
ὕδασι, dat. pl. (§ 4. rem. 3. b) . . ὕδωρ
ὕδατα, nom. and acc. pl. . . . . id.
ὕδατι, dat. sing. . . . . . id.
ὕδατος, gen. sing. . . . . . id.
ὑδάτων, gen. pl. . . . . . id.
ὑδρία], ας, ἡ . . . . . . id.
ὑδρίαι, nom. pl. . . . . . ὑδρία
ὑδρίαν, acc. sing. . . . . . id.
ὑδρίας, acc. pl. . . . . . id.
ὑδροπότει,[a] 2 pers. sing. pres. imper. . . ὑδροποτέω
ὑδροποτέω, ῶ], fut. ήσω, (§ 16. tab. P) (ὑδροπότης, ὕδωρ & πίνω) *to be a water-drinker.*
ὑδρωπῐκός],[b] ή, όν, (§ 7. tab. F. a) (ὕδρωψ, *the dropsy*, from ὕδωρ) *dropsical.*

ὕδωρ], ᾰτος, τό, (§ 4. rem. 2. c) *water*, Mat. 3. 11, 16; 14. 28, 29; 17. 15; Jno. 5. 3, 4. 7; *watery fluid*, Jno. 19. 34; ὕδωρ ζῶν, *living water, fresh flowing water*, Jno. 4. 11; met. of spiritual refreshment, Jno. 4. 10; 7. 38.

ὑδρία, ας, η, (§ 2. tab. B. b, and rem. 2) *a water-pot, pitcher*, Jno. 2. 6, 7; *a bucket, pail*, Jno. 4. 28.

ὑετόν, acc. sing. . . . . . ὑετός
ὑετός], οῦ, ὁ, (§ 3. tab. C. a) (ὕω, *to rain*) *rain*, Ac. 14. 17, et al.

ὑετούς, acc. pl. . . . . . ὑετός
υἱέ, voc. sing. . . . . . υἱός
υἱοθεσία], ας, ἡ, (§ 2. tab. B. b, and rem. 2) (υἱός & τίθημι) *adoption, a placing in the condition of a son*, Ro. 8. 15, 23; 9. 4; Gal. 4. 5; Ep. 1. 5. N.T.

a 1 Ti. 5. 23. b Lu. 14. 2.

υἱοθεσίαν, acc. sing. . . . . . υἱοθεσία
υἱοθεσίας, gen. sing. . . . . . id.
υἱοί, nom. and voc. pl. . . . . . υἱός
υἱοῖς, dat. pl. . . . . . . id.
υἱόν, acc. sing. . . . . . . id.

υἱός], οῦ, ὁ, (§ 3. tab. C. a) *a son*, Mat. 1. 21, 25; 7. 9; 13. 55, et al. freq.; *a* legitimate *son*, He. 12. 8; *a son* artificially constituted, Ac. 7. 21; He. 11. 24; *a descendant*, Mat. 1. 1, 20; Mar. 12. 35, et al.; in N.T. *the young* of an animal, Mat. 21. 5; *a* spiritual *son* in respect of conversion or discipleship, 1 Pe. 5. 13; from the Heb., *a disciple*, perhaps, Mat. 12. 27; *a son* as implying connexion in respect of membership, service, resemblance, manifestation, destiny, etc., Mat. 8. 12; 9. 15; 13. 38; 23. 15; Mar. 2. 19; 3. 17; Lu. 5. 34; 10. 6; 16. 8; 20. 34, 36; Jno. 17. 12; Ac. 2. 25; 4. 36; 13. 10; Ep. 2. 2; 5. 6; Col. 3. 6; 1 Thes. 5. 5; 2 Thes. 2. 3; υἱὸς Θεοῦ, κ.τ.λ., *son of God* in respect of divinity, Mat. 4. 3, 6; 14. 33; Ro. 1. 4, et al.; also, in respect of privilege and character, Mat. 5. 9, 45; Lu. 6. 35; Ro. 8. 14, 19; 9. 26; Gal. 3. 26; ὁ υἱὸς τοῦ Θεοῦ, κ.τ.λ., a title of the Messiah, Mat. 26. 63; Mar. 3. 11; 14. 61; Jno. 1. 34, 50; 20. 31, et al.; υἱὸς ἀνθρώπου, *a son of man, a man*, Mar. 3. 28; Ep. 3. 5; He. 2. 6; ὁ υἱὸς τοῦ ἀνθρώπου, a title of the Messiah, Mat. 8. 20, et al. freq.; as also, ὁ υἱὸς Δαβίδ, Mat. 12. 23, et al.

υἱοῦ, gen. sing. . . . . . . υἱός
υἱούς, acc. pl. . . . . . . id.
υἱῷ, dat. sing. . . . . . . id.
υἱῶν, gen. pl. . . . . . . id.

ὕλη], ης, ἡ, (§ 2. tab. B. a) *wood, a forest*; in N.T. *firewood, a mass of fuel*, Ja. 3. 5.

ὕλην,[a] acc. sing. . . . . . ὕλη
ὑμᾶς, acc. pl. (§ 11. tab. K. b) . . . σύ
ὑμεῖς, nom. pl. . . . . . . id.

Ὑμέναιος], ου, ὁ, (§ 3. tab. C. a) *Hymenæus*, pr. name.

ὑμετέρα, nom. sing. fem. . . . . ὑμέτερος
ὑμετέρᾳ, dat. sing. fem. . . . . . id.
ὑμετέραν, acc. sing. fem. . . . . ὑμέτερος
ὑμετέρας, gen. sing. fem. . . . . . id.
ὑμέτερον, acc. sing. masc. and neut. . . id.

ὑμέτερος], α, ον, (§ 11. rem. 4) possess. pron. (ὑμεῖς) *your, yours*, Lu. 6. 20; Jno. 7. 6; 15. 20, et al.

ὑμετέρῳ, dat. sing. masc. and neut. . . ὑμέτερος
ὑμῖν, dat. pl. . . . . σύ
ὑμνέω, ῶ], fut. ήσω . . . . . ὕμνος
ὑμνήσαντες, nom. pl. masc. part. aor. 1 . ὑμνέω
ὑμνήσω, 1 pers. sing. fut. ind. . . . id.
ὕμνοις, dat. pl. . . . . . . ὕμνος

ὕμνος], ου, ὁ, (§ 3. tab. C. a) *a song; a hymn, song of praise* to God, Ep. 5. 19; Col. 3. 16.

ὑμνέω, ῶ, fut. ήσω, aor. 1, ὕμνησα, (§ 16. tab. P) *to hymn, praise, celebrate or worship with hymns*, Ac. 16. 25; absol. *to sing a hymn*, Mat. 26. 30; Mar. 14. 26.

ὕμνουν, 3 pers. pl. imperf. . . . . ὑμνέω
ὑμῶν, gen. pl. . . . . σύ
ὑπ', by apostrophe for ὑπό.
ὕπαγε, 2 pers. sing. pres. imper. . . ὑπάγω
ὑπάγει, 3 pers. sing. pres. ind. . . . id.
ὑπάγειν, pres. infin. . . . . . id.
ὑπάγεις, 2 pers. sing. pres. ind. . . . id.
ὑπάγετε, 2 pers. pl. pres. imper. . . . id.
ὑπάγῃ, 3 pers. sing. pres. subj. . . . id.
ὑπάγητε, 2 pers. pl. pres. subj. . . . id.
ὑπάγοντας, acc. pl. masc. part. pres. . . id
ὑπάγοντες, nom. pl. masc. part. pres. . . id.

ὑπάγω], fut. ξω, (§ 23. rem. 1. b) (ὑπό & ἄγω) *to lead or bring under; to lead or bring from under; to draw on or away*; in N.T. intrans. *to go away, depart*, Mat. 8. 4, 13; 9. 6; ὕπαγε ὀπίσω μου, *get behind me! away! begone!* Mat. 4. 10; 16. 23; *to go*, Mat. 5. 41; Lu. 12. 58, et al.; *to depart* life, Mat. 26. 24.

ὑπακοή], ῆς, ἡ . . . . . . ὑπακούω
ὑπακοῇ, dat. sing. . . . . . ὑπακοή
ὑπακοήν, acc. sing. . . . . . id.
ὑπακοῆς, gen. sing. . . . . . id.
ὑπακούει, 3 pers. sing. pres. ind. . . ὑπακούω
ὑπακούειν, pres. infin. . . . . . id.
ὑπακούετε, 2 pers. pl. pres. ind. and imper. . id.
ὑπακούουσι, 3 pers. pl. pres. ind. . . . id.
ὑπακούουσι, dat. pl. masc. part. pres. . . id.

[a] Ja. 3. 5.

ὑπακοῦσαι, aor. 1, infin. . . . ὑπακούω

ὑπακούω], fut. ούσομαι, (ὑπό & ἀκούω) *to give ear, hearken; to listen*, Ac. 12. 13; *to obey*, Mat. 8. 27; Mar. 1. 27, et al.; in N.T. *to render submissive acceptance*, Ac. 6. 7; Ro. 6. 17; 2 Thes. 1. 8; He. 5. 9; absol. *to be submissive*, Phi. 2. 12.

ὑπακοή, ῆς, ἡ, (§ 2. tab. B. a) *a hearkening to; obedience*, Ro. 5. 19; 6. 16; 1 Pe. 1. 14; *submissiveness*, Ro. 16. 19; 2 Co. 7. 15; *submission*, Ro. 1. 5; 15. 18; 16. 26; 2 Co. 10. 5; He. 5. 8; 1 Pe. 1. 2, 22; *compliance*, Phile. 21. LXX.

ὑπήκοος, ου, ὁ, ἡ, (§ 7. rem. 2) *giving ear; obedient, submissive*, Ac. 7. 39; 2 Co. 2. 9; Phi. 2. 8.

ὕπανδρος],[a] ου, ἡ, (ὑπό & ἀνήρ) *bound to a man, married*. L.G.

ὑπαντάω, ῶ], fut. ήσω, (§ 18. tab. R) (ὑπό & ἀντάω) *to meet*, Mat. 8. 28; Lu. 8. 27; Jno. 11. 20, 30; 12. 18.

ὑπάντησις, εως, ἡ, (§ 5. tab. E. c) *a meeting, act of meeting*, Jno. 12. 13. L.G.

ὑπαντῆσαι, aor. 1, infin.—A. B. D. Ln. Tdf. } ὑπαντάω
ἀπαντῆσαι, Rec. Gr. Sch. (Lu. 14. 31) }

ὑπάντησιν,[b] acc. sing. . . . . ὑπάντησις

ὑπάντησις], εως, ἡ . . . . ὑπαντάω

ὑπάρξεις, acc. pl. . . . . . ὕπαρξις

ὕπαρξιν, acc. sing. . . . . id.

ὕπαρξις], εως, ἡ . . . . . ὑπάρχω

ὑπάρχει, 3 pers. sing. pres. ind. . . . id.

ὑπάρχειν, pres. infin. . . . . id.

ὑπάρχοντα, acc. sing. masc. part. pres. . id.

ὑπάρχοντα, nom. and acc. pl. neut. part. pres. id.

ὑπάρχοντας, acc. pl. masc. part. pres. . . id.

ὑπάρχοντες, nom. pl. masc. part. pres. . id.

ὑπάρχοντος, gen. sing. masc. & neut. part. pres. id.

ὑπαρχόντων, gen. pl. neut. part. pres. . . id.

ὑπαρχούσης, gen. sing. fem. part. pres. . id.

ὑπάρχουσι, 3 pers. pl. pres. ind. . . . id.

ὑπάρχουσι, dat. pl. neut. part. pres. . id.

ὑπάρχω], fut. ξω, (§ 23. rem. 1. b) (ὑπό & ἄρχω) *to begin; to come into existence; to exist; to be, subsist*, Ac. 19. 40; 28. 18; *to be in possession, to belong*, Ac. 3. 6; 4. 37; part. neut. pl. τὰ ὑπάρχοντα, *goods, possessions, property*, Mat. 19. 21; Lu. 8. 3; *to be*, Lu. 7. 25; 8. 41, et al.

ὕπαρξις, εως, ἡ, (§ 5. tab. E. c) *goods possessed, substance, property*, Ac. 2. 45; He. 10. 34. L.G.

ὑπάρχων, nom. sing. masc. part. pres. . . ὑπάρχω

ὑπάρχωσι, 3 pers. pl. pres. subj. . . id.

ὑπέβαλον,[c] 3 p. pl. aor. 2, ind. act. (§ 27. rem. 2. d) ὑποβάλλω

ὑπέδειξα, 1 pers. sing. aor. 1, ind. . . ὑποδείκνυμι

ὑπέδειξε, 3 pers. sing. aor. 1, ind. . . id.

ὑπεδέξατο, 3 pers. sing. aor. 1, ind. . . ὑποδέχομαι

ὑπέθηκαν, 3 p. pl. aor. 1, ind. act. (§ 28. tab. V) ὑποτίθημι

ὑπείκετε,[d] 2 pers. pl. pres. imper. . . ὑπείκω

ὑπείκω], fut. ξω, (§ 23. rem. 1. b) (ὑπό & εἴκω) *to yield, give way*; absol. *to be submissive*, He. 13. 17.

ὑπέλαβε, 3 pers. sing. aor. 2, ind. act. (§ 24. rem. 9) . . . . ὑπολαμβάνω

ὑπελείφθην,[e] 1 pers. sing. aor. 1, ind. pass. (§ 23. rem. 4) . . . . ὑπολείπω

ὑπεμείνατε, 2 pers. pl. aor. 1, ind. . . ὑπομένω

ὑπέμεινε, 3 pers. sing. aor. 1, ind. (§ 27. rem. 1. d) id.

ὑπέμενον, 3 pers. pl. imperf. . . . id.

ὑπεμνήσθη, 3 pers. s. aor. 1, ind. (§ 22. rem. 5) ὑπομιμνήσκω

ὑπεναντίον, nom. sing. neut. . . . ὑπεναντίος

ὑπεναντίος], ία, ίον, (§ 7. rem. 1) (ὑπό & ἐναντίος) *over against; contrary, adverse*; ὁ ὑπεναντίος, *an opponent, adversary*, He. 10. 27; *untoward, inimical*, Col. 2. 14.

ὑπεναντίους, acc. pl. masc. . . . ὑπεναντίος

ὑπενεγκεῖν, aor. 2, infin. (§ 36. rem. 1) . ὑποφέρω

ὑπενόουν, 1 pers. sing. and 3 pers. pl. imperf. ὑπονοέω

ὑπεπλεύσαμεν, 1 pers. pl. aor. 1, (§ 35. rem. 3) ὑποπλέω

ὑπέρ], prep. with a genitive, *above, over*; met. *in behalf of*, Mat. 5. 44; Mar. 9. 40; Jno. 17. 19, et al.; *instead of* beneficially, Phile. 13; *in maintenance of*, Ro. 15. 8; *for the furtherance of*, Jno. 11. 4; 2 Co. 1. 6, 8, et al.; *for the realisation of*, Phi. 2. 13; equivalent to περί, *about, concerning*, with the further signification of interest or concern in the subject, Ac. 5. 41; Ro. 9. 27; 2 Co. 5. 12; 8. 23; 2 Thes. 2. 1, et al.; with an acc. *over, beyond*; met. *beyond, more than*, Mat. 10. 37; 2 Co. 1. 8, et al.; used after comparative terms, Lu. 16. 8; 2 Co. 12. 13; He. 4. 12; in N.T. as an adv., *in a higher degree, in fuller measure*, 2 Co. 11. 23.

---

[a] Ro. 7. 2. [b] Jno. 12. 13. [c] Ac. 6. 11. [d] He. 13. 17. [e] Ro. 11. 3.

ὑπεραιρόμενος, nom. sing. m. part. pres. pass. ὑπεραίρω

ὑπεραίρω], (ὑπέρ & αἴρω) *to raise or lift up above or over*; mid. *to lift up one's self*; met. *to be over-elated*, 2 Co. 12. 7; *to bear one's self arrogantly, to rear a haughty front*, 2 Thes. 2. 4.

ὑπεραίρωμαι, 1 pers. sing. pres. subj. pass. . ὑπεραίρω

ὑπέρακμος],[a] ου, ὁ, ἡ, (§ 7. rem. 2) (ὑπέρ & ἀκμή, *a point, prime*) *past the bloom of life*. N.T.

ὑπεράνω], adv. (ὑπέρ & ἄνω) *above, over, far above*; of place, Ep. 4. 10; He. 9. 5; of rank, dignity, etc., Ep. 1. 21. L.G. (ᾰ).

ὑπεραυξάνει,[b] 3 pers. sing. pres. ind. ὑπεραυξάνω

ὑπεραυξάνω], fut. ξήσω, (§ 35. rem. 5) (ὑπέρ & αὐξάνω) *to increase exceedingly*. (ᾰ).

ὑπερβαίνειν,[c] pres. infin. . . . . ὑπερβαίνω

ὑπερβαίνω], fut. βήσομαι, (§ 37. rem. 1) (ὑπέρ & βαίνω) *to overstep; to wrong, aggrieve*, 1 Thes. 4. 6.

ὑπερβάλλον, nom. sing. neut. part. pres. . ὑπερβάλλω

ὑπερβάλλοντα, acc. sing. masc. part. pres. . id.

ὑπερβαλλόντως],[d] adv. . . . . id.

ὑπερβάλλουσαν, acc. sing. fem. part. pres. . id.

ὑπερβαλλούσης, gen. sing. fem. part. pres. id.

ὑπερβάλλω], fut. βαλῶ, (§ 27. rem. 1. b) (ὑπέρ & βάλλω) pr. *to cast or throw over or beyond, to overshoot*; met. *to surpass, excel*; part. ὑπερβάλλων, ουσα, ον, *surpassing*, 2 Co. 3. 10; 9. 14, et al.

ὑπερβαλλόντως, adv. *exceedingly, above measure*, 2 Co. 11. 23.

ὑπερβολή, ῆς, ἡ, (§ 2. tab. B. a) pr. *a throwing beyond, an overshooting; extraordinary amount or character, transcendancy*, 2 Co. 12. 7; 4. 7; καθ' ὑπερβολήν, adverbially, *exceedingly, extremely*, Ro. 7. 13; 2 Co. 1. 8, et al.

ὑπερβολή], ῆς, ἡ . . . . ὑπερβάλλω

ὑπερβολῇ, dat. sing. . . . . ὑπερβολή

ὑπερβολήν, acc. sing. . . . . id.

ὑπερεῖδον], aor. 2, of ὑπεροράω, (§ 36. rem. 1) *to look over or above* a thing; met. *to overlook, disregard; to bear with*, Ac. 17. 30.

ὑπερέκεινα],[e] adv. (ὑπέρ, ἐκεῖνα) *beyond*. N.T.

ὑπερεκπερισσοῦ], adv. (ὑπέρ, ἐκ, περισσοῦ) *in over abundance; beyond all measure, superabundantly*, Ep. 3. 20; 1 Thes. 3. 10; 5. 13. LXX.

ὑπερεκπερισσῶς, adv.—B. Ln. Tdf.

ὑπὲρ ἐκ περισσοῦ, Rec. Sch.

ὑπερεκπερισσοῦ, Gr. (1 Thes. 5. 13).

ὑπερεκτείνομεν,[f] 1 pers. pl. pres. ind. . ὑπερεκτείνω

ὑπερεκτείνω], fut. τενῶ, (§ 27. rem. 1. c) (ὑπέρ & ἐκτείνω) *to over-extend, over-stretch*. L.G.

ὑπερεκχυνόμενον,[g] acc. sing. neut. part. pres. pass. . . . . ὑπερεκχύνω

ὑπερεκχύνω], (ὑπέρ & ἐκχύνω) *to pour out above measure or in excess*; pass. *to run over, overflow*. L.G.

ὑπερεντυγχάνει,[h] 3 pers. sing. pres. ind. ὑπερεντυγχάνω

ὑπερεντυγχάνω], (ὑπέρ & ἐντυγχάνω) *to intercede for*. (ᾰ) N.T.

ὑπερεπερίσσευσε, 3 pers. sing. aor. 1, ind. ὑπερπερισσεύω

ὑπερεπλεόνασε,[i] 3 pers. sing. aor. 1, ind. ὑπερπλεονάζω

ὑπερέχον, acc. sing. neut. part. pres. . . ὑπερέχω

ὑπερέχοντας, acc. pl. masc. part. pres. id.

ὑπερέχοντι, dat. sing. masc. part. pres. . id.

ὑπερέχουσα, nom. sing. fem. part. pres. id.

ὑπερεχούσαις, dat. pl. fem. part. pres. . . id.

ὑπερέχω], fut. ξω, (ὑπέρ & ἔχω) *to hold above*, intrans. *to stand out above, to overtop*· met. *to surpass, excel*, Phi. 2. 3; 4. 7; τὸ ὑπερέχον, *excellence, pre-eminence*, Phi. 3. 8; *to be higher, superior*, Ro. 13. 1; 1 Pe. 2. 13.

ὑπεροχή, ῆς, ἡ, (§ 2. tab. B. a) *prominence*; met. *excellence, rare quality*, 1 Co. 2. 1; *eminent station, authority*, 1 Ti. 2. 2.

ὑπερηφανία],[k] ας, ἡ . . . . ὑπερήφανος

ὑπερήφανοι, nom. pl. masc. . . . . id.

ὑπερηφάνοις, dat. pl. masc. . . . . id.

ὑπερήφᾰνος], ου, ὁ, ἡ, (§ 7. rem. 2) (ὑπέρ & φαίνω) pr. *conspicuous above, supereminent*; met. *assuming, haughty, arrogant*, Lu. 1. 51; Ro. 1. 30; 2 Ti. 3. 2; Ja. 4. 6, 1 Pe. 5. 5.

ὑπερηφανία, ας, ἡ, (§ 2. tab. B. b, and rem. 2) *haughtiness, arrogance*, Mar. 7. 22.

ὑπερηφάνους, acc. pl. masc. . ὑπερήφανος

ὑπεριδών,[l] nom. sing. masc. part. . . ὑπερεῖδον

ὑπερλίαν], adv. (ὑπέρ & λίαν) *in the highest degree*,

---

[a] 1 Co. 7. 36. [b] 2 Thes. 1. 3. [c] 1 Thes. 4. 6. [d] 2 Co. 11. 23. [e] 2 Co. 10. 16. [f] 2 Co. 10. 14. [g] Lu. 6. 38. [h] Ro. 8. 26. [i] 1 Ti. 1. 14. [k] Mar. 7. 22. [l] Ac. 17. 30.

pre-eminently, especially, superlatively, 2 Co. 11. 5; 12. 11. N.T.

ὑπερλίαν, Gr. Tdf
ὑπὲρ λίαν, Rec. Sch.

ὑπερνικάω, ῶ], fut. ήσω, (§ 18. tab. R) (ὑπέρ & νικάω) *to overpower in victory; to be abundantly victorious, prevail mightily,* Ro. 8. 37. L.G.

ὑπερνικῶμεν,[a] 1 pers. pl. pres. ind. . . ὑπερνικάω

ὑπέρογκα, acc. pl. neut. . . . . ὑπέρογκος

ὑπέρογκος], ου, ὁ, ἡ, (§ 7. rem. 2) (ὑπέρ & ὄγκος) pr. *over-swollen, overgrown;* of language, *swelling, pompous, boastful,* 2 Pe. 2. 18; Jude 16.

ὑπεροχή], ῆς, ἡ . . . . ὑπερέχω

ὑπεροχῇ, dat. sing. . . . . ὑπεροχή

ὑπεροχήν, acc. sing. . . . . id.

ὑπερπερισσεύω], fut. εύσω, (§ 13. tab. M) (ὑπέρ & περισσεύω) *to superabound; to abound still more,* Ro. 5. 20; mid. *to be abundantly filled, overflow,* 2 Co. 7. 4. N.T.

ὑπερπερισσεύομαι, 1 pers. s. pres. ind. mid. ὑπερπερισσεύω

ὑπερπερισσῶς],[b] adv. (ὑπέρ & περισσῶς) *superabundantly, most vehemently, above all measure.* N.T.

ὑπερπλεονάζω], fut. άσω, (§ 26. rem. 1) (ὑπέρ & πλεονάζω) *to superabound, be in exceeding abundance, over-exceed,* 1 Ti. 1. 14. N.T.

ὑπερυψόω, ῶ], fut. ώσω, (§ 20. tab. T) (ὑπέρ & ὑψόω) *to exalt supremely.* LXX.

ὑπερύψωσε,[c] 3 pers. sing. aor. 1, ind. ὑπερυψόω

ὑπερφρονεῖν,[d] pres. infin. . . . ὑπερφρονέω

ὑπερφρονέω, ῶ], fut. ήσω, (§ 16. tab. P) (ὑπέρ & φρονέω) *to overween, have lofty thoughts, be elated.*

ὑπερῷον], ου, τό, (§ 3. tab. C. c) (pr. neut. of ὑπερῷος, *upper,* from ὑπέρ) *the upper part of a house, upper room, or chamber,* Ac. 1. 13; 9. 37, 39; 20. 8.

ὑπερῴῳ, dat. sing. . . . . ὑπερῷον

ὑπεστειλάμην, 1 pers. sing. aor. 1, ind. mid. (§ 27. rem. 1. d) . . . ὑποστέλλω

ὑπέστελλε, 3 pers. sing. imperf. act. . id.

ὑπέστρεφον, 3 pers. pl. imperf. . . ὑποστρέφω

ὑπέστρεψα, 1 pers. sing. aor. 1, ind. . id.

ὑπέστρεψαν, 3 pers. pl. aor. 1, ind. . . id.

ὑπέστρεψε, 3 pers. sing. aor. 1, ind. . id.

ὑπεστρώννυον,[e] 3 pers. pl. imperf. . ὑποστρώννυμι

ὑπετάγη, 3 pers. sing. aor. 2, ind. pass. (§ 26. rem. 3) . . . . ὑποτάσσω

ὑπετάγησαν, 3 pers. pl. aor. 2, ind. pass. . id.

ὑπέταξας, 2 pers. sing. aor. 1, ind. act. . id.

ὑπέταξε, 3 pers. sing. aor. 1, ind. act. . . id.

ὑπέχουσαι,[f] nom. pl. fem. part. pres. . ὑπέχω

ὑπέχω], fut. ὑφέξω, (§ 36. rem. 4) (ὑπό & ἔχω) pr. *to hold under; to render, undergo, suffer,* Jude 7.

ὑπεχώρησε, 3 pers. sing. aor. 1, ind. . ὑποχωρέω

ὑπῆγον, 3 pers. pl. imperf. act. . . . ὑπάγω

ὑπήκοοι, nom. pl. masc. . . . ὑπήκοος

ὑπήκοος], ου, ὁ, ἡ . . . . . ὑπακούω

ὑπήκουον, 3 pers. pl. imperf. . . . id.

ὑπήκουσαν, 3 pers. pl. aor. 1, ind. . . id.

ὑπηκούσατε, 2 pers. pl. aor. 1, ind. . . id.

ὑπήκουσε, 3 pers. sing. aor. 1, ind. . . id.

ὑπήνεγκα, 1 pers. sing. aor. 1, ind. (§36. rem. 1) ὑποφέρω

ὑπήντησαν, 3 pers. pl. aor. 1, ind. . . ὑπαντάω

ὑπήντησε, 3 pers. sing. aor. 1, ind. . id.

ὑπηρέται, nom. pl. . . . . ὑπηρέτης

ὑπηρέταις, dat. pl. . . . . . id.

ὑπηρέτας, acc. pl. . . . . . id.

ὑπηρετεῖν, pres. infin. . . . . ὑπηρετέω

ὑπηρετέω, ῶ], fut. ήσω . . . . ὑπηρέτης

ὑπηρέτῃ, dat. sing. . . . . . id.

ὑπηρέτην, acc. sing. . . . . id.

ὑπηρέτης], ου, ὁ, (§ 2. tab. B. c) (ὑπό & ἐρέτης, *a rower*) pr. *an under-rower, a rower, one of a ship's crew; a minister, attendant, servant; an attendant* on a magistrate, *a lictor, apparitor, officer,* Mat. 5. 25; *an attendant or officer* of the Sanhedrin, Mat. 26. 58; *an attendant, or servant* of a synagogue, Lu. 4. 20; *a minister, attendant, assistant* in any work, Lu. 1. 2; Jno. 18. 36, et al.

ὑπηρετέω, ῶ, fut. ήσω, aor. 1, ὑπηρέτησα, *to subserve,* Ac. 13. 36; *to relieve, supply,* Ac. 20. 34; *to render kind offices,* Ac. 24. 23.

ὑπηρέτησαν, 3 pers. pl. aor. 1, ind. . ὑπηρετέω

ὑπηρετήσας, nom. sing. masc. part. aor. 1 . id.

ὑπηρετῶν, gen. pl. . . . . . ὑπηρέτης

ὑπῆρχε, 3 pers. sing. imperf. . . . ὑπάρχω

ὑπῆρχον, 3 pers. pl. imperf. . . . id.

ὕπνος], ου, ὁ, (§ 3. tab. C. a) *sleep,* Mat. 1. 24,

[a] Ro. 8. 37. [b] Mar. 7. 37. [c] Phi. 2. 9. [d] Ro. 12. 3. [e] Lu. 19. 36. [f] Jude 7.

et al.; met. spiritual *sleep*, religious *slumber*, Ro. 13. 11.

ὕπνου, gen. sing. . . . . . ὕπνος

ὕπνῳ, dat. sing. . . . . . id.

ὑπό], prep., with a genitive, pr. *under*; hence used to express influence, causation, agency; *by*, Mat. 1. 22, et al. freq.; *by the agency of, at the hands of*, 2 Co. 11. 24; He. 12. 3; with acc., *under*, with the idea of motion associated, Mat. 5. 15, et al.; *under*, Jno. 1. 49; 1 Co. 10. 1; *under* subjection to, Ro. 6. 14; 1 Ti. 6. 1, et al.; of time, *at, about*, Ac. 5. 21.

ὑποβάλλω], fut. βαλῶ, aor. 1, ὑπέβᾰλον, (§ 27. rem. 2. d) (ὑπό & βάλλω) *to cast under*; met. *to suggest, instigate*; *to suborn*, Ac. 6. 11.

ὑπογραμμόν,[a] acc. sing. . . . ὑπογραμμός

ὑπογραμμός], οῦ, ὁ, (§ 3. tab. C. a) (ὑπογράφω) pr. *a copy to write after*; met. *an example for imitation, pattern*, 1 Pe. 2. 21. L.G.

ὑποδέδεκται, 3 pers. sing. perf. ind. (§ 23. rem. 7) . . . . . ὑποδέχομαι

ὑποδεδεμένους, acc. pl. masc. part. perf. pass. ὑποδέω

ὑπόδειγμα], ατος, τό . . . ὑποδείκνυμι

ὑποδείγματα, acc. pl. . . . . ὑπόδειγμα

ὑποδείγματι, dat. sing. . . . . . id.

ὑποδείκνυμι], fut. δείξω, (§ 31. tab. BB) (ὑπό & δείκνυμι) *to indicate*, Ac. 20. 35; *to intimate, suggest*, Mat. 3. 7; Lu. 3. 7; 6. 47; 12. 5; Ac. 9. 16.

ὑπόδειγμα, ατος, τό, (§ 4. tab. D. c) *a token, intimation*; *an example*, proposed for imitation or admonition, Jno. 13. 15; He. 4. 11; Ja. 5. 10; 2 Pe. 2. 6; *a copy*, He. 8. 5; 9. 23.

ὑποδείξω, 1 pers. sing. fut. ind. . . ὑποδείκνυμι

ὑποδεξαμένη, nom. sing. fem. part. aor. 1 ὑποδέχομαι

ὑποδέχομαι], fut. δέξομαι, perf. ὑποδέδεγμαι, (§ 23. rem. 7) (ὑπό & δέχομαι) *to give reception to*; *to receive as a guest, entertain*, Lu. 10. 38; 19. 6; Ac. 17. 7; Ja. 2. 25.

ὑποδέω], fut. ήσω, perf. pass. ὑποδέδεμαι, (§ 37. rem. 1) (ὑπό & δέω) *to bind under*; mid. *to bind under one's self, put on one's own feet*, Ac. 12. 8; *to shoe*, Ep. 6. 15; pass. *to be shod*, Mar. 6. 9.

ὑπόδημα, ατος, τό, (§ 4. tab. D. c) *anything bound under*; *a sandal*, Mat. 3. 11; 10. 10, et al.

ὑπόδημα], ατος, τό . . . . . ὑποδέω

ὑποδήματα, acc. pl. . . . . ὑπόδημα

ὑποδήματος, gen. sing. . . . . id.

ὑποδημάτων, gen. pl. . . . . id.

ὑπόδησαι, 2 pers. sing. aor. 1, imper. mid. . ὑποδέω

ὑποδησάμενοι, nom. pl. masc. part. aor 1, mid. id.

ὑπόδῐκος],[b] ου, ὁ, ἡ, (§ 7. rem. 2) (ὑπό & δίκη) *under a legal process*; also, *under a judicial sentence*; *under verdict* to an opposed party in a suit, *liable to penalty, convict*, Ro. 3. 19.

ὑποδραμόντες,[c] nom. pl. masc. part. aor. 2, (§ 36. rem. 1) . . . . ὑποτρέχω

ὑποζύγιον], ίου, τό, (§ 3. tab. C. c) (pr. neut. of ὑποζύγιος, *under a yoke*, from ὑπό & ζυγόν) *an animal subject to the yoke, a beast of draught or burden*; in N.T. spc. *an ass*, Mat. 21. 5; 2 Pe. 2. 16.

ὑποζυγίου, gen. sing. . . . . ὑποζύγιον

ὑποζώννυμι], fut. ζώσω, (ὑπό & ζώννυμι) *to gird under*, of persons; *to undergird* a ship with cables, chains, etc.

ὑποζώννυντες,[d] nom. pl. masc. part. pres. . ὑποζώννυμι

ὑποκάτω], adv. (ὑπό & κάτω) *under, beneath, underneath*, Mar. 6. 11; 7. 28, et al.; met. He. 2. 8. (ᾰ).

ὑποκρίνομαι], fut. οῦμαι, (ὑπό & κρίνω) *to answer, respond*; *to act a part* upon the stage; hence, *to assume a counterfeit character*; *to pretend, feign*, Lu. 20. 20.

ὑπόκρῐσις, εως, ἡ, (§ 5. tab. E. c) *a response, answer*; *histrionic personification, acting*; *hypocrisy, simulation*, Mat. 23. 28; Mar. 12. 15, et al.

ὑποκρῐτής, οῦ, ὁ, (§ 2. tab. B. c) *the giver of an answer or response*; *a stage-player, actor*; in N.T. *a* moral or religious *counterfeit, a hypocrite*, Mat. 6. 2, 5, 16; 7. 5, et al.

ὑποκρινομένους,[e] acc. pl. masc. part. pres. ὑποκρίνομαι

ὑποκρίσει, dat. sing. . . . . ὑπόκρισις

ὑποκρίσεις, acc. pl. . . . . id.

ὑποκρίσεως, gen. sing. . . . . id.

ὑπόκρισιν, acc. sing. . . . . id.

ὑπόκρισις], εως, ἡ . . . . ὑποκρίνομαι

---

a 1 Pe. 2. 21. b Ro. 3. 19 c Ac. 27. 16. d Ac. 27. 17. e Lu. 20. 20.

ὑποκριτά, voc. sing. . . . . ὑποκριτής

ὑποκριταί, nom. and voc. pl. . . . id.

ὑποκριτής], οῦ, ὁ . . . . ὑποκρίνομαι

ὑποκριτῶν, gen. pl. . . . . ὑποκριτής

ὑπολαβών, nom. sing. masc. part. aor. 2 . ὑπολαμβάνω

ὑπολαμβάνειν, pres. infin.—Al. Ln. Tdf. } ἀπολαμβάνειν, Rec. Gr. Sch. (3 Jno. 8) } id.

ὑπολαμβάνετε, 2 pers. pl. pres. ind. . . id.

ὑπολαμβάνω], fut. λήψομαι, aor. 2, ὑπέλᾰβον, (§ 36. rem. 2) (ὑπό & λαμβάνω) *to take up*, by placing one's self underneath what is taken up; *to catch away, withdraw*, Ac. 1. 9; *to take up* discourse by continuation; hence, *to answer*, Lu. 10. 30; *to take up* a notion, *to think, suppose*, Lu. 7. 43; Ac. 2. 15.

ὑπόλειμμα, ατος, τό,—A. B. Ln. Tdf. } κατάλειμμα, Rec. Gr. Sch. (Ro. 9. 27) } ὑπολείπω

ὑπολείπω], fut. ψω, (§ 23. rem. 1. a) (ὑπό & λείπω) *to leave remaining, leave behind*; pass. *to be left surviving*, Ro. 11. 3.

ὑπόλειμμα, ατος, τό, (§ 4. tab. D. c) *a remnant*, v.r. Ro. 9. 27.

ὑπολήνιον],[a] ου, τό, (§ 3. tab. C. c) (ὑπό & ληνός) *a vat*, placed under the press, ληνός, to receive the juice. LXX.

ὑπολιμπάνω], (ὑπό & λιμπάνω, *to leave*) equivalent to ὑπολείπω, *to leave behind*. (ᾰ).

ὑπολιμπάνων,[b] nom. sing. masc. part. pres. **ὑπολιμπάνω**

ὑπομείναντας, acc. pl. masc. part. aor. 1.—A. Ln. Tdf. . . . . . } ὑπομένοντας, Rec. Gr. Sch. (Ja. 5. 11) } **ὑπομένω**

ὑπομείνας, nom. sing. masc. part. aor. 1 . id.

ὑπομεμενηκότα, acc. s. m. part. perf. (§ 27. rem. 2. d) id.

ὑπομένει, 3 pers. sing. pres. ind. . . . id.

ὑπομενεῖτε, 2 pers. pl. fut. ind. . . id.

ὑπομένετε, 2 pers. pl. pres. ind. . . id.

ὑπομένομεν, 1 pers. pl. pres. ind. . . id.

ὑπομένοντας, acc. pl. masc. part. pres. . id.

ὑπομένοντες, nom. pl. masc. part. pres. . id.

ὑπομένω], fut. νῶ, (§ 27. rem. 1. a) aor. 1, ὑπέμεινα, (ὑπό & μένω) intrans. *to remain or stay behind*, when others have departed, Lu. 2. 43; trans. *to bear up under, endure, suffer patiently*, 1 Co. 13. 7; He. 10. 32; absol. *to continue firm, hold out, remain constant, persevere*, Mat. 10. 22; 24. 13, et al.

ὑπομονή, ῆς, ἡ, (§ 2. tab. B. a) *patient endurance*, 2 Co. 12. 12; Col. 1. 11, et al.; *patient awaiting*, Lu. 21. 19; *a patient frame of mind, patience*, Ro. 5. 3, 4; 15. 4, 5; Ja. 1. 3, et al.; *perseverance*, Ro. 2. 7; *endurance* in adherence to an object, 1 Thes. 1. 3; 2 Thes. 3. 5; Re. 1. 9; ἐν ὑπομονῇ & δι' ὑπομονῆς, *constantly, perseveringly*, Lu. 8. 15; Ro. 8. 25; He. 12. 1; *an enduring* of affliction, etc., *the act of suffering, undergoing*, etc., 2 Co. 1. 6; 6. 4.

ὑπομιμνήσκειν, pres. infin. . . . ὑπομιμνήσκω

ὑπομίμνησκε, 2 pers. sing. pres. imper. . id

ὑπομιμνήσκω], fut. ὑπομνήσω, (§ 36. rem. 4) (ὑπό & μιμνήσκω) *to put in mind, remind*, Jno. 14. 26; Tit. 3. 1; 2 Pe. 1. 12; Jude 5; *to suggest recollection of, remind others of*, 2 Ti. 2. 14; 3 Jno. 10; mid. ὑπομιμνήσκομαι, aor. 1, (pass. form) ὑπεμνήσθην, *to call to mind, recollect, remember*, Lu. 22. 61.

ὑπόμνησις, εως, ἡ, (§ 5. tab. E. c) *a putting in mind, act of reminding*, 2 Pe. 1. 13; 3. 1; *remembrance, recollection*, 2 Ti. 1. 5.

ὑπομνῆσαι, aor. 1, infin. act. . . ὑπομιμνήσκω

ὑπομνήσει, 3 pers. sing. fut. ind. act. . . id.

ὑπομνήσει, dat. sing. . . . . ὑπόμνησις

ὑπόμνησιν, acc. sing. . . . . id.

ὑπόμνησις], εως, ἡ . . . . ὑπομιμνήσκω

ὑπομνήσω, 1 pers. sing. fut. ind. act. . . id.

ὑπομονή], ῆς, ἡ . . . . . ὑπομένω

ὑπομονῇ, dat. sing. . . . . ὑπομονη

ὑπομονήν, acc. sing. . . . . id.

ὑπομονῆς, gen. sing. . . . . id.

ὑπονοεῖτε, 2 pers. pl. pres. ind. . . ὑπονοέω

ὑπονοέω, ῶ], fut. ήσω, § 16. tab. P) (ὑπό & νοέω) *to suspect; to suppose, deem*, Ac. 13. 25; 25. 18; 27. 27.

ὑπόνοια, ας, ἡ, (§ 2. tab. B. b, and rem. 2) *suspicion, surmise*, 1 Ti. 6. 4.

ὑπόνοια], ας, ἡ . . . . . ὑπονοέω

ὑπόνοιαι,[c] nom. pl. . . . . ὑπόνοια

ὑποπλέω], fut. εύσομαι, (§ 35. rem. 3) (ὑπό & πλέω) *to sail under; to sail under* the lee, or, *to the south of*, an island. etc., Ac. 27. 4, 7. L.G.

ὑποπνευσάντος,[d] gen. sing. masc. part. aor. 1 ὑποπνέω

[a] Mar. 12. 1. [b] 1 Pe. 2. 21. [c] 1 Ti. 6. 4. [d] Ac 27. 13.

ὑποπνέω], fut. εύσω, (§ 35. rem. 1, 3) (ὑπό & πνέω) *to blow gently*, as the wind. N.T.

ὑποπόδιον], ίου, τό, (§ 3. tab. C. c) (ὑπό & πούς) *a footstool*, Mat. 5. 35; Ja. 2. 3, et al. L.G.

ὑποστάσει, dat. sing. . . . . ὑπόστασις

ὑποστάσεως, gen. sing. . . . id.

ὑπόστασις], εως, ἡ, (§ 5. tab. E. c) (ὑφίσταμαι, *to stand under*, ὑπό & ἵστημι) pr. *a standing under; a taking* of a thing *upon one's self; an assumed position, an assumption* of a specific character, 2 Co. 11. 17; *an engagement undertaken* with regard to the conduct either of others, *a vouching*, 2 Co. 9. 4; or of one's self, *a pledged profession*, He. 3. 14; *an assured impression, a mental realising*, He. 11. 1; *a substructure, basis; subsistence, essence*, He. 1. 3.

ὑποστείληται, 3 pers. sing. aor. 1, subj. mid. ὑποστέλλω

ὑποστέλλω], fut. στελῶ, aor. 1. ὑπέστειλα, (§ 27. rem. 1. b. d) (ὑπό & στέλλω) pr. *to let down, to stow away; to draw back, withdraw*, Gal. 2. 12; mid. *to shrink back, quail, recoil*, He. 10. 38; *to keep back, suppress, conceal*, Ac. 20. 20, 27.

ὑποστολή, ῆς, ἡ, (§ 2. tab. B. a) *a shrinking back*, He. 10. 39. L.G.

ὑποστολή], ῆς, ἡ . . . . ὑποστέλλω

ὑποστολῆς,[a] gen. sing. . . . . ὑποστολή

ὑπόστρεφε, 2 pers. sing. pres. imper. . ὑποστρέφω

ὑποστρέφειν, pres. infin. . . . id.

ὑποστρέφοντι, dat. sing. masc. part. pres. . id.

ὑποστρέφω], fut. ψω, (§ 23. rem. 1. a) (ὑπό & στρέφω) *to turn back, return*, Mar. 14. 40; Lu. 1. 56; 2. 39, 43, 45, et al.

ὑποστρέφων, nom. sing. masc. part. pres. . ὑποστρέφω

ὑποστρέψαι, aor. 1, infin. . . . id.

ὑποστρέψαντες, nom. pl. masc. part. aor. 1 id.

ὑποστρέψαντι, dat. sing. masc. part. aor. 1 id.

ὑποστρέψας, nom. sing. masc. part. aor. 1 id.

ὑποστρέψασαι, nom. pl. fem. part. aor. 1 id.

ὑποστρέψω, 1 pers. sing. fut. ind. . . id.

ὑποστρώννυμι, or ννύω], fut. στρώσω, (§ 36. rem. 5) (ὑπό & στρώννυμι) *to strow under, spread underneath*, Lu. 19. 36.

ὑποταγέντων, gen. pl. masc. part. aor. 2, pass. ὑποτάσσω

ὑποταγῇ, 3 pers. s. aor. 2, subj. pass. (§ 26. rem. 3) id.

ὑποταγή], ῆς, ἡ . . . . . id.

ὑποταγῇ, dat. sing. . . . . ὑποταγή

ὑποταγήσεται, 3 pers. sing. fut. 2, ind. pass. ὑποτάσσω

ὑποταγησόμεθα, 1 pers. pl. fut. 2, ind. pass. id.

ὑποτάγητε, 2 pers. pl. aor. 2, imper. pass. . id.

ὑποτάξαι, aor. 1, infin. act. . . . id.

ὑποτάξαντα, acc. sing. masc. part. aor. 1, act. id.

ὑποτάξαντι, dat. sing. masc. part. aor. 1, act. id.

ὑποτάξαντος, gen. sing. masc. part. aor. 1, act. id.

ὑποτάσσεσθαι, pres. infin. mid. . . id.

ὑποτάσσεσθε, 2 pers. pl. pres. imper. mid. . id.

ὑποτασσέσθω, 3 pers. sing. pres. imper. mid. id.

ὑποτασσέσθωσαν, 3 pers. pl. pres. imper. mid.—A. B. Ln. Tdf. . . } id.
ὑποτάσσεσθαι, R. Gr. Sch. (1 Co. 14. 34)

ὑποτάσσεται, 3 pers. sing. pres. ind. mid. . id.

ὑποτάσσησθε, 2 pers. pl. pres. subj. mid. . id.

ὑποτασσόμεναι, nom. pl. fem. part. pres. mid. id.

ὑποτασσομένας, acc. pl. fem. part. pres. mid. id.

ὑποτασσόμενοι, nom. pl. masc. part. pres. mid. id.

ὑποτασσόμενος, nom. sing. masc. part. pres. mid. id.

ὑποτάσσω, or ττω], fut. ξω, (§ 26. rem. 3) (ὑπό & τάσσω) *to place or arrange under; to subordinate*, 1 Co. 15. 27; *to bring under influence*, Ro. 8. 20; pass. *to be subordinated*, 1 Co. 14. 32, et al.; *to be brought under a state or influence*, Ro. 8. 20; mid. *to submit one's self, render obedience, be submissive*, Lu. 2. 51; 10. 17, et al.

ὑποτᾰγή, ῆς, ἡ, (§ 2. tab. B. a) *subordination*, 1 Ti. 3. 4; *submissiveness*, 2 Co. 9. 13; Gal. 2. 5; 1 Ti. 2. 11. N.T.

ὑποτεταγμένα, acc. pl. neut. part. perf. pass. ὑποτάσσω

ὑποτέτακται, 3 pers. sing. perf. ind. pass. . id.

ὑποτιθέμενος, nom. sing. masc. part. pres. mid. ὑποτίθημι

ὑποτίθημι], fut. ὑποθήσω, (§ 28. tab. V) (ὑπό & τίθημι) *to place under; to lay down* the neck beneath the sword of the executioner, *to set on imminent risk*, Ro. 16. 4; mid. *to suggest, recommend to attention*, 1 Ti. 4. 6.

ὑποτρέχω], aor. 2, ὑπέδρᾰμον, (§ 36. rem. 1) (ὑπό & τρέχω) *to run under*; as a nautical term, *to sail under* the lee of, Ac. 27. 16.

ὑποτύπωσιν, acc. sing. . . . ὑποτύπωσις

ὑποτύπωσις], εως, ἡ, (§ 5. tab. E. c) (ὑποτυπόω, *to sketch*, from ὑπό & τυπόω) *a sketch, delineation; a form, formula, presentment, sample*, 2 Ti. 1. 13; *a pattern, a model representation*, 1 Ti. 1. 16.

[a] He. 10. 39.

ὑποφέρει, 3 pers. sing. pres. ind. . . ὑποφέρω

ὑποφέρω], aor. 1, ὑπήνεγκα, aor. 2, ὑπήνεγκον, (§ 36. rem. 1) (ὑπό & φέρω) *to bear under; to bear up under, support, sustain,* 1 Co. 10. 13; *to endure patiently,* 1 Pe. 2. 19; *to undergo,* 2 Ti. 3. 11.

ὑποχωρέω, ῶ], fut. ήσω, (§ 16. tab. P) (ὑπό & χωρέω) *to withdraw, retire,* Lu. 5. 16; 9. 10.

ὑποχωρῶν, nom. sing. masc. part. pres. . ὑποχωρέω

ὑπωπιάζῃ, 3 pers. sing. pres. subj. . . ὑπωπιάζω

ὑπωπιάζω], fut. άσω, (§ 26. rem. 1) (ὑπώπιον, *the part of the face below the eyes,* from ὑπό & ὤψ) pr. *to strike one upon the parts beneath the eye; to beat black and blue;* hence, *to discipline by hardship, coerce,* 1 Co. 9. 27; met. *to weary* by continual importunities, *pester,* Lu. 18. 5.

ὗς],[a] ὑός, ὁ, ἡ, (§ 5. tab. E. g) *a nog, swine, boar or sow.*

ὕσσωπος], ου, ὁ, ἡ, (Heb. אֵזוֹב) *hyssop,* in N.T., however, not the plant usually so named, but probably the caper plant; *a bunch of hyssop,* He. 9. 19; *a hyssop stalk,* Jno. 19. 29. L.G.

ὑσσώπου, gen. sing. . . . . . ὕσσωπος

ὑσσώπῳ, dat. sing. . . . . . id.

ὑστερεῖ, 3 pers. sing. pres. ind. . . . ὑστερέω

ὑστερεῖσθαι, pres. infin. mid. and pass. . id.

ὑστερέω], ῶ, fut. ήσω . . . . ὕστερος

ὑστερηθείς, nom. sing. masc. part. aor. 1, pass. ὑστερέω

ὑστερηκέναι, perf. infin. . . . . id.

ὑστέρημα], ατος, τό . . . . . ὕστερος

ὑστερήματα, acc. pl. . . . . . ὑστέρημα

ὑστερήματος, gen. sing. . . . . id.

ὑστέρησα, 1 pers. sing. aor. 1, ind. . ὑστερέω

ὑστερήσαντος, gen. sing. masc. part. aor. 1 . id.

ὑστερήσατε, 2 pers. pl. aor. 1, ind. . . id.

ὑστερήσεως, gen. sing. . . . ὑστέρησις

ὑστέρησιν, acc. sing. . . . . id.

ὑστέρησις], εως, ἡ . . . . . ὕστερος

ὑστέροις,[b] dat. pl. masc. . . . . id.

ὕστερον], adv. . . . . . . id.

ὕστερος], α, ον, (§ 7. rem. 1) *posterior* in place or time; *subsequent,* 1 Ti. 4. 1.

ὕστερον, adv. *after, afterwards,* Mat. 4. 2; 22. 27, et al.; pr. neut. of ὕστερος.

ὑστερέω, ῶ, fut. ήσω, aor. 1, ὑστέρησα, perf. ὑστέρηκα, (§ 16. tab. P) *to be behind* in place or time, *to be in the rear; to fall short of, be inferior to,* 2 Co. 11. 5; 12. 11; *to fail of, fail to attain,* He. 4. 1; *to be in want of, lack,* Lu. 22. 35; *to be wanting,* Mar. 10. 21; absol. *to be defective, in default,* Mat. 19. 20; 1 Co. 12. 24; *to run short,* Jno. 2. 3; mid. *to come short of* a privilege or standard, *to miss,* Ro. 3. 23; absol. *to come short, be below standard,* 1 Co. 1. 7; *to come short* of sufficiency, *to be in need, want,* Lu. 15. 14; 2 Co. 11. 8; Phi. 4. 12; He. 11. 37; *to be a loser, suffer detriment,* 1 Co. 8. 8; in N.T. ὑστερεῖν ἀπό, *to be backwards with respect to, to slight,* He. 12. 15.

ὑστέρημα, ατος, τό, (§ 4. tab. D. c) *a shortcoming, defect;* personal *shortcoming,* 1 Co. 16. 17; Phi. 2. 30; Col. 1. 24; 1 Thes. 3. 10; *want, need, poverty, penury,* Lu. 21. 4; 2 Co. 8. 13, 14, et al. LXX.

ὑστέρησις, εως, ἡ, (§ 5. tab. E. c) *want, need,* Mar. 12. 44; Phi. 4. 11. N.T.

ὕστερος,—B. Ln. Tdf.
πρῶτος, Rec. Gr. Sch. (Mat. 21. 31).

ὑστερούμεθα, 1 pers. pl. pres. ind. mid. . ὑστερέω

ὑστερούμενοι, nom. pl. masc. part. pres. mid. id.

ὑστερουμένῳ, dat. sing. m. part. pres. mid.—A. B. C. Ln. . . . } id.
ὑστεροῦντι, R. Gr. Sch. Tdf. (1 Co. 12. 24) }

ὑστεροῦνται, 3 pers. pl. pres. ind. mid. . . id.

ὑστεροῦντι, dat. sing. masc. part. pres. . id.

ὑστερῶ, 1 pers. sing. pres. ind. contr. . . id.

ὑστερῶν, nom. sing. masc. part. pres. . id.

ὑφ' by apostrophe for ὑπό before an aspirate.

ὑφαντός],[c] ή, όν, (§ 7. tab. F. a) (ὑφαίνω, *to weave*) *woven.*

ὕψει, dat. sing. . . . . . ὕψος

ὑψηλά, acc. pl. neut. . . . . ὑψηλός

ὑψηλοῖς, dat. pl. neut. . . . id.

ὑψηλόν, nom. and acc. sing. neut. . . id.

ὑψηλός], ή, όν . . . . . . ὕψος

ὑψηλότερος, nom. sing. masc. compar. . ὑψηλός

ὑψηλοῦ, gen. sing. masc. . . . . id.

[a] 2 Pe. 2. 22. [b] 1 Ti. 4. 1. [c] Jno. 19. 23.

ὑψηλοφρόνει, 2 pers. sing. pres. imper.—Rec. Gr. Sch. Tdf. } ὑψηλοφρονέω
ὑψηλὰ φρόνει,—B. Ln. (Ro. 11. 20)

ὑψηλοφρονεῖν, pres. infin. . . . . id.

ὑψηλοφρονέω, ῶ], fut. ήσω, (§ 16. tab. P) (ὑψηλός & φρονέω) *to have lofty thoughts, be proud, overweening, haughty*, Ro. 11. 20; 1 Ti. 6. 17. N.T.

ὑψίστοις, dat. pl. neut. . . ὕψιστος

ὕψιστος], η, ον . . . . . ὕψος

ὑψίστου, gen. sing. masc. . . . ὕψιστος

ὕψος], εος, τό, (§ 5. tab. E. b) *height*, Ep. 3. 18; Re. 21. 16; met. *exaltation, dignity, eminence*, Ja. 1. 9; from the Heb., *the height* of heaven, Lu. 1. 78; 24. 49; Ep. 4. 8.

ὑψηλός, ή, όν, (§ 7. tab. F. a) *high, lofty, elevated*, Mat. 4. 8; 17. 1, et al.; τὰ ὑψηλά, *the highest* heaven, He. 1. 3; *upraised*, Ac. 13. 17; met. *highly esteemed*, Lu. 16. 15; φρονεῖν τὰ ὑψηλά, *to have lofty thoughts, be proud, overween*, Ro. 12. 16.

ὕψιστος, η, ον, (§ 7. tab. F. a) *highest loftiest, most elevated*; τὰ ὕψιστα, from the Heb., *the highest* heaven, Mat. 21. 9; Mar. 11. 10; met. ὁ ὕψιστος, *the Most High*, Mar. 5. 7, et al.; superlative of ὕψος.

ὑψόω, ῶ, fut. ώσω, aor. 1, ὕψωσα, *to raise aloft, lift up*, Jno. 3. 14; 8. 28; met. *to elevate* in condition, *uplift, exalt*, Mat. 11. 23; 23. 12; Lu. 1. 52.

ὕψωμα, ατος, τό, (§ 4. tab. D. c) *height*, Ro. 8. 39; *a towering* of self-conceit, *presumption*, 2 Co. 10. 5. L.G.

ὕψους, gen. sing. . . . . ὕψος

ὑψόω, ῶ], fut. ώσω, (§ 20. tab. T) . . id.

ὑψωθείς, nom. sing. masc. part. aor. 1. pass. (§ 21. tab. U) . . . . ὑψόω

ὑψωθεῖσα, nom. sing. fem. part. aor. 1, pass. id.

ὑψωθῆναι, aor. 1, infin. pass. . . . id.

ὑψώθης, 2 pers. sing. aor. 1, ind. pass.—Const. Tdf. . . . . } id.
ὑψωθεῖσα, Rec. Gr. Sch. . .
μὴ . . . . . . ὑψωθήσῃ; Al. Ln. (Mat. 11. 23) . . .

ὑψωθήσεται, 3 pers. sing. fut. ind. pass. . id.

ὑψωθήσῃ, 2 pers. sing. fut. ind. pass. . } ὑψόω
μὴ . . . . . . ὑψωθήσῃ;—B. D. Ln. Tdf.
ἡ ὑψωθεῖσα, Rec. Gr. Sch. (Lu. 10. 15). . . . .

ὑψωθῆτε, 2 pers. pl. aor. 1, subj. pass. . id.

ὑψωθῶ, 1 pers. sing. aor. 1, subj. pass. . id.

ὕψωμα], ατος, τό . . . . . ὕψος

ὑψῶν, nom. sing. masc. part. pres. act. . ὑψόω

ὕψωσε, 3 pers. sing. aor. 1, ind. act. . . id.

ὑψώσει, 3 pers. sing. fut. ind. act. . . id.

ὑψώσῃ, 3 pers. sing. aor. 1, subj. act. . . id.

ὑψώσητε, 2 pers. pl. aor. 1, subj. act. . id.

Φ.

φάγε, 3 pers. sing. aor. 2, imper. . . ἐσθίω

φαγεῖν, aor. 2, infin. . . . . id.

φάγεσαι, 2 pers. sing. fut. ind. (§ 35. rem. 6, and § 36. rem. 1) . . id.

φάγεται, 3 pers. sing. fut. ind. id.

φάγετε, 2 pers. pl. aor. 2, imper. id.

φάγῃ, 3 pers. sing. aor. 2, subj. id.

φάγῃς, 2 pers. sing. aor. 2, subj. id.

φάγητε, 2 pers. pl. aor. 2, subj. id.

φάγοι, 3 pers. sing. aor. 2, optat. id.

φάγονται, 3 pers. pl. fut. 2, ind. . . id.

φαγόντες, nom. pl. masc. part. aor. 2 . . id.

φάγομαι], see ἐσθίω.

φάγος], ου, ὁ, (§ 3. tab. C. a) *a glutton*, Mat. 11. 19, Lu. 7. 34. N.T.

φάγω, 1 pers. sing. aor. 2, subj. . . ἐσθίω

φάγωμεν, 1 pers. pl. aor. 2, subj. . . id.

φάγωσι, 3 pers. pl. aor. 2, subj. . . id.

φαιλόνην,[a] acc. sing. . . . . φαιλόνης

φαιλόνης, or φελόνης], ου, ὁ, (by metath. for φαινόλης, Lat. *pænula*) *a thick cloak* for travelling, with a hood.

φαίνει, 3 pers. sing. pres. ind. . . φαίνω

φαίνεσθε, 2 pers. pl. pres. ind. mid. . . id.

φαίνεται, 3 pers. sing. pres. ind. mid. . id.

φαίνῃ, 3 pers. sing. pres. subj. . . . id.

φαινομένη, nom. sing. fem. part. pres. mid. id.

φαινομένου, gen. sing. masc. part. pres. mid. id.

φαινομένων, gen. pl. part. pres. mid. . id.

φαίνονται, 3 pers. pl. pres. ind. mid. . . id.

φαίνοντι, dat. sing. masc. part. pres. id.

φαίνω], fut. φανῶ, perf. πέφαγκα, (§ 27.

[a] 2 Ti. 4. 13.

rem. 1. c. and rem. 2. a) aor. 2, pass. ἐφάνην, (ᾰ) (§ 27. rem. 4. b.) *to cause to appear, bring to light*; absol. *to shine*, Jno. 1. 5; 5. 35; 2 Pe. 1. 19; 1 Jno. 2. 8; Re. 1. 16; 8. 12; 21. 23; mid. or pass. *to be seen, appear, be visible*, Mat. 1. 20; 2. 7, 13, 19, et al.; τὰ φαινόμενα, *things visible, things obvious to the senses*, He. 11. 3; φαίνομαι, *to appear, seem, be in appearance*, Mat. 23. 27; Lu. 24. 11; *to appear* in thought, *seem* in idea, *be a notion*, Mar. 14. 64, et al.

φανερός, ά, όν, (§ 7. rem. 1) *apparent, conspicuous, manifest, clear, known, well-known*, Mar. 4. 22; 6. 14; Gal. 5. 19, et al.; ἐν φανερῷ, *openly*, Mat. 6. 4, 6; also, *in outward guise, externally*, Ro. 2. 28.

φανερόω, ῶ, fut. ώσω, aor. 1, ἐφανέρωσα, (§ 20. tab. T) perf. pass. πεφανέρωμαι, (§ 21. tab. U) *to bring to light, to set in a clear light; to manifest, display*, Jno. 2. 11; 7. 4; 9. 3, et al.; *to evince*, Ro. 1. 19; 2 Co. 7. 12; *to declare, make known*, Jno. 17. 6; *to disclose*, Mar. 4. 22; 1 Co. 4. 5; Col. 4. 4; *to reveal*, Ro. 3. 21; 16. 26; Col. 1. 26, et al.; *to present to view*, Jno. 21. 1, 14; pass. *to make an appearance*, Mar. 16. 12, 14; spc. of Christ, *to be* personally *manifested*, Jno. 1. 31; Col. 3. 4; 1 Pe. 1. 20; 5. 4; 1 Jno. 3. 5, et al.; *to be laid bare, appear in true character*, 2 Cor. 5. 10, 11.

φανερῶς, adv. *manifestly; clearly, plainly, distinctly*, Ac. 10. 3; *openly, publicly*, Mar. 1. 45; Jno. 7. 10.

φανέρωσις, εως, ἡ, (§ 5. tab. E. c) *an evidencing, clear display*, 2 Co. 4. 2; *an* outward *evidencing* of a latent principle, active *exhibition*, 1 Co. 12. 7. N.T.

φᾱνός, οῦ, ὁ, (§ 3. tab. C. a) *a torch, lantern, light*, Jno. 18. 3.

φαντάζω, fut. άσω, (§ 26. rem. 1) *to render visible, cause to appear*; pass. *to appear, be seen*; τὸ φανταζόμενον, *the sight, spectacle*, He. 12. 21.

φαντασία, ας, ἡ, (§ 2. tab. B. b, and rem. 2) pr. *a rendering visible; a display; pomp, parade*, Ac. 25. 23.

φάντασμα, ατος, τό, (§ 4. tab. D. c) *a phantom, spectre*, Mat. 14. 26; Mar. 6. 49.

φαίνων,	nom. sing. masc. part. pres.	φαίνω
φαίνωσι,	3 pers. pl. pres. subj.	id.
Φαλέκ], [a]	ὁ, *Phalec*, pr. name, indecl.	
φανεῖται,	3 pers. sing. fut. ind. mid.	φαίνω
φανερά,	nom. pl. neut.	φανερός
φανεροί,	nom. pl. masc.	id.
φανερόν,	acc. sing. masc. and nom. and acc. neut.	id.
φανερός],	ά, όν	φαίνω
φανερούμενοι,	nom. pl. masc. part. pres. pass.	φανερόω
φανερούμενον,	nom. sing. neut. part. pres. pass.	id.
φανεροῦντι,	dat. sing. masc. part. pres. act.	id.
φανερούς,	acc. pl. masc.	φανερός
φανεροῦται,	3 pers. sing. pres. ind. pass.	φανερόω
φανερόω, ῶ],	fut. ώσω	φαίνω
φανερῷ,	dat. sing. neut.	φανερός
φανερωθεῖσαν,	acc. sing. fem. part. aor. 1, pass.	φανερόω
φανερωθέντες,	nom. pl. masc. part. aor. 1, pass.	id.
φανερωθέντος,	gen. sing. masc. part. aor. 1, pass.	id.
φανερωθῇ,	3 pers. sing. aor. 1, subj. pass.	id.
φανερωθῆναι,	aor. 1, infin. pass.	id.
φανερωθήσεσθε,	2 pers. pl. fut. ind. pass.	id.
φανερωθῶσι,	3 pers. pl. aor. 1, subj. pass.	id.
φανερῶς],	adv.	φαίνω
φανερώσαντες,	nom. pl. m. part. aor. 1, act. —B. Ln. Tdf.	φανερόω
φανερωθέντες,	R. Gr. Sch. (2 Co. 11. 6)	
φανερώσει,	3 pers. sing. fut. ind. act.	id.
φανερώσει,	dat. sing.	φανέρωσις
φανέρωσις],	εως, ἡ	φαίνω
φανέρωσον,	2 pers. sing. aor. 1, imper. act.	φανερόω
φανερώσω,	1 pers. sing. aor. 1, subj. act.	id.
φανῇ,	3 pers. sing. aor. 2, subj. pass.	φαίνω
φανῇς,	2 pers. sing. aor. 2, subj. pass.	id.
φανήσεται,	3 p. s. fut. 2, ind. pass. (§ 27. rem. 4. c)	id.
φανός],	οῦ, ὁ	id.
Φανουήλ], [b]	ὁ, *Phanuel*, pr. name, indecl.	
φανταζόμενον, [c]	nom. sing. neut. part. pres. pass.	φαντάζω
φαντάζω],	fut. άσω	φαίνω
φαντασία],	ας, ἡ	id.
φαντασίας, [d]	gen. sing.	φαντασία
φάντασμα],	ατος, τό	φαίνω
φανῶμεν,	1 pers. pl. aor. 2, subj. pass.	id.
φανῶν, [e]	gen. pl.	φανός
φανῶσι,	3 pers. pl. aor. 2, subj. pass.	φαίνω

φάραγξ], [f] αγγος, ἡ, (§ 4. rem. 2. b) *a cleft, ravine, dell.*

[a] Lu. 3. 35. [b] Lu. 2. 36. [c] He. 12. 21. [d] Ac. 25. 23. [e] Jno. 18. 3. [f] Lu. 3. 5.

Φαραώ], ὁ, *Pharaoh*, pr. name, indecl.
Φαρές], ὁ, *Phares*, pr. name, indecl.
Φαρισαῖε, voc. sing. . . . . . Φαρισαῖος
Φαρισαῖοι, nom. and voc. pl. . . . id.
Φαρισαίοις, dat. pl. . . . . . id.
Φαρισαῖος], ου, ὁ, (§ 3. tab. C. a) *a Pharisee, a follower of the sect of the Pharisees*, a numerous and powerful sect of the Jews, distinguished for their ceremonial observances, and apparent sanctity of life, and for being rigid interpreters of the Mosaic law; but who not unfrequently violated its spirit by their traditional interpretations and precepts, to which they ascribed nearly an equal authority with the Old Testament Scriptures, Mat. 5. 20; 12. 2; 23. 14, et al.
Φαρισαίου, gen. sing. . . . . . Φαρισαῖος
Φαρισαίους, acc. pl. . . . . . id.
Φαρισαίων, gen. pl. . . . . . id.
φαρμακεία], ας, ἡ, (§ 2. tab. B. b, and rem. 2) (φάρμακον, *a drug*) *employment of drugs* for any purpose; *sorcery, magic, enchantment*, Gal. 5. 20; Re. 9. 21; 18. 23.

φαρμᾰκεύς, έως, ὁ, (§ 5. tab. E. d) pr. *one who deals in drugs; an enchanter, magician, sorcerer*, Ac. 21. 8.

φαρμᾰκός, οῦ, ὁ, (§ 3. tab. C. a) *a sorcerer*, Re. 21. 8; 22. 15.

φαρμακείᾳ, dat. sing. . . . . . φαρμακεία
φαρκακειῶν, gen. pl. . . . . . id.
φαρμακεύς], έως, ὁ . . . . . id.
φαρμακεῦσι,[a] dat. pl. . . . . φαρμακεύς
φαρμακοί,[b] nom. pl. . . . . . φαρμακός
φαρμακοῖς, dat. pl.—Gr. Sch. Tdf. }
φαρμακεῦσι, Rec. (Re. 21. 8) . . } id.
φαρμακός], οῦ, ὁ . . . . . . φαρμακεία
φασί, 3 pers. pl. pres. ind. (§ 33. rem. 1) . φημί
φάσις],[c] εως, ἡ . . . . . . id.
φάσκοντας, acc. pl. masc. part. pres. . φάσκω
φάσκοντες, nom. pl. masc. part. pres. . . id.
φάσκω], equivalent to φημί, imperf. ἔφασκον, *to assert, affirm*, Ac. 24. 9; 25. 19; Ro. 1. 22; Re. 2. 2.
φάτνη], ης, ἡ, (§ 2. tab. B. a) *a manger, crib*, Lu. 2. 7, 12, 16; 13. 15.
φάτνῃ, dat. sing. . . . . . φάτνη
φάτνης, gen. sing. . . . . . . id.

φαῦλα, acc. pl. neut. . . . . . φαῦλος
φαῦλον, nom. and acc. sing. neut. . . id.
φαῦλος], η, ον, (§ 7. tab. F. a) *sorry, vile, refuse; evil, wicked*, Jno. 3. 20; 5. 29; Tit. 2. 8; Ja. 3. 16.
φέγγος], εος, τό, (§ 5. tab. E. b) *light, splendour*, Mat. 24. 29; Mar. 13. 24; Lu. 11. 33.
φείδομαι], fut. φείσομαι, (§ 23. rem. 1. c) *to spare, be thrifty of; to spare, be tender of*, Ro. 8. 32; *to spare*, in respect of hard dealing, Ac. 20. 29; Ro. 11. 21; 1 Co. 7. 28; 2 Co. 1. 23; 13. 2; 2 Pe. 2. 4, 5; absol. *to forbear, abstain*, 2 Co. 12. 6.

φειδομένως, adv. *sparingly, parsimoniously*, 2 Co. 9. 6, bis. L.G.

φειδόμενοι, nom. pl. masc. part. pres. . φείδομαι
φειδόμενος, nom. sing. masc. pl. pres. . . id.
φειδομένως], adv. . . . . . id.
φείσεται, 3 pers. sing. fut. ind.—Gr. Sch. Tdf. }
φείσηται, Rec. (Ro. 11. 21) . } id.
φείσηται, 3 pers. sing. aor. 1, subj. . . id.
φείσομαι, 1 pers. sing. fut. ind. . . . id.
φελόνην, acc. sing.—Gr. Sch. Tdf. . }
φαιλόνην, Rec. (2 Ti. 4. 13) . } φελόνης
φελόνης], see φαιλόνης.
φέρε, 2 pers. sing. pres. imper. act. . . φέρω
φέρει, 3 pers. sing. pres. ind. act. . . id.
φέρειν, pres. infin. act. . . . . id.
φέρεσθαι, pres. infin. pass. . . . id.
φέρετε, 2 pers. pl. pres. ind. and imper. act. id.
φέρῃ, 3 pers. sing. pres. subj. act. . . id.
φέρητε, 2 pers. pl. pres. subj. act. . . id.
φερομένην, acc. sing. fem. part. pres. pass id.
φερομένης, gen. sing. fem. part. pres. mid. . id.
φερόμενοι, nom. pl. masc. part. pres. pass. . id.
φέρον, nom. sing. neut. part. pres. act. . id.
φέροντες, nom. pl. masc. part. pres. act. . id.
φέρουσαι, nom. pl. fem. part. pres. act. . id.
φέρουσαν, acc. sing. fem. part. pres. act. . id.
φέρουσι, 3 pers. pl. pres. ind. act. . . id.
φέρω], fut. οἴσω, aor. 1, ἤνεγκα, aor. 2, ἤνεγκον, aor. 1, pass. ἠνέχθην, (§ 36. rem. 1) *to bear, carry*, Mar. 2. 3, et al.; *to bring*, Mat. 14. 11, 18, et al.; *to conduct*, Mat. 17. 17; Jno. 21. 18, et al.; *to bear, endure*, Ro. 9. 22; He. 12. 20; 13. 13; *to up-*

[a] Re. 21. 8. [b] Re. 22. 15. [c] Ac. 21. 31.

hold, maintain, conserve, He. 1. 3; *to bear, bring forth, produce*, Mar. 4. 8; Jno. 12. 24; 15. 2, et al.; *to bring forward, advance, allege*, Jno. 18. 29; Ac. 25. 7; 2 Pe. 2. 11; *to offer, ascribe*, Re. 21. 24, 26; absol. used of a gate, *to lead*, Ac. 12. 10; pass. *to be brought* within reach, *offered*, 1 Pe. 1. 13; *to be brought in, to enter*, He. 9. 16; *to be under a moving influence, to be moved, be instinct*, 2 Pe. 1. 21; mid. *to rush, sweep*, Ac. 2. 2; *to proceed, come forth, have utterance*, 2 Pe. 1. 17, 18, 21; *to proceed, make progress*, He. 6. 1; used of a ship, *to drive* before the wind, Ac. 27. 15, 17.

φορέω, ῶ, fut. ήσω & έσω (§ 22. rem. 1) aor. 1, ἐφόρεσα, *to bear; to wear*, Mat. 11. 8; 1 Co. 15. 49, et al.

φόρος, ου, ὁ, (§ 3. tab. C. a) *tribute, tax*, strictly such as is laid on dependent and subject people, Lu. 20. 22; 23. 2; Ro. 13. 6, 7.

φορτίζω, fut. ίσω, perf. pass. πεφόρτισμαι, (§ 26. rem. 1) (φόρτος, *a load*) *to load, lade, burden*; met. Mat. 11. 28; Lu. 11. 46.

φορτίον, ου, τό, (§ 3. tab. C. c) *a load, burden*; of a ship, *freight, cargo*, v.r. Ac. 27. 10; met. *a burden* of imposed precepts, etc., Mat. 11. 30; 23. 4; Lu. 11. 46, bis; of faults, sins, etc., Gal. 6. 5.

φόρτος, ου, ὁ, (§ 3. tab. C. a) *a load, burden; freight, cargo*, Ac. 27. 10.

φερώμεθα, 1 pers. pl. pres. subj. mid. . . φέρω

φέρων, nom. sing. masc. part. pres. act. . id.

φεῦγε, 2 pers. sing. pres. imper. . . . φεύγω

φεύγει, 3 pers. sing. pres. ind. . . id.

φεύγετε, 2 pers. pl. pres. imper. . . . id.

φευγέτωσαν, 3 pers. pl. pres. imper. . id.

φεύγω], fut. ξομαι, aor. 2, ἔφυγον, (§ 24. rem. 9) absol. *to flee, take to flight*, Mat. 2. 13; 8. 33, et al., *to shrink, stand fearfully aloof*, 1 Co. 10. 14; *to make escape*, Mat. 23. 33; trans. *to shun*, 1 Co. 6. 18; 1 Ti. 6. 11; 2 Ti. 2. 22; *to escape*, He. 11. 34.

φυγή, ῆς, ἡ, (§ 2. tab. B. a) *a fleeing, flight*, Mat. 24. 20; Mar. 13. 18.

φεύξεται, 3 pers. sing. fut. ind. . . . φεύγω

ξονται, 3 pers. pl. fut. ind. . . id.

Φήλικα, acc. . . . . . . Φῆλιξ

Φήλικι, dat. . . . . id.

Φήλικος, gen. . . . . . Φῆλιξ

Φῆλιξ], ῖκος, ὁ, (§ 4. rem. 2. b) *Felix*, pr. name.

φήμη], ης, ἡ . . . . . φημί

φημί], fut. φήσω, imperf. ἔφην, (§ 33. tab. DD) (φάω) *to utter, tell forth; to say, speak*, Mat. 8. 8; 14. 8; 26. 34, 61; *to say, allege, affirm*, Ro. 3. 8, et al.

φάσις, εως, ἡ, (§ 5. tab. E. c) *report, information*, Ac. 21. 31.

φήμη, ης, ἡ, (§ 2. tab. B. a) pr. *a celestial or oracular utterance; an utterance; fame, rumour, report*, Mat. 9. 26; Lu. 4. 14.

φησί, 3 pers. sing. pres. ind. (§ 33. rem. 1) . φημί

Φῆστε, voc. . . . . . Φῆστος

Φῆστον, acc. . . . . . . id.

Φῆστος], ου, ὁ, (§ 3. tab. C. a) *Festus*, pr. name.

Φήστου, gen. . . . . . Φῆστος

Φήστῳ, dat. . . . . . . id.

φθάνω], fut. φθήσομαι & φθάσω, aor. 1, ἔφθᾰσα, aor. 2, ἔφθην, (§ 37. rem. 1) *to be before-hand with; to outstrip, precede*, 1 Thes. 4. 15; absol. *to advance, make progress*, 2 Co. 10. 14; Phi. 3. 16; *to come up* with, *come upon, be close at hand*, Mat. 12. 28; 1 Thes. 2. 16; *to attain* an object of pursuit, Ro. 9. 31.

φθαρῇ, 3 pers. sing. aor. 2, subj. pass. . φθείρω

φθαρήσονται, 3 pers. pl. fut. 2, ind. pass.—καὶ φθαρήσονται, Al. Ln. Tdf. . καταφθαρήσονται, Rec. Gr. Sch. (2 Pe. 2. 12) . . . . . } id.

φθαρτῆς, gen. sing. fem. . . . . φθαρτός

φθαρτοῖς, dat. pl. neut. . . . . id.

φθαρτόν, acc. sing. masc., and nom. and acc. neut. id.

φθαρτός], ή, όν . . . . . φθείρω

φθαρτοῦ, gen. sing. masc. . . . φθαρτός

φθάσωμεν, 1 pers. pl. aor. 1, subj. . . φθάνω

φθέγγεσθαι, pres. infin. . . . φθέγγομαι

φθεγγόμενοι, nom. pl. masc. part. pres. . id.

φθέγγομαι], fut. γξομαι, aor. 1, ἐφθεγξάμην, (§ 23. rem. 5) *to emit a sound; to speak*, Ac. 4. 18; 2 Pe. 2. 16, 18

φθόγγος, ου, ὁ, (§ 3. tab. C. a) *a vocal sound*, Ro. 10. 18; 1 Co. 14. 7.

φθεγξάμενον, nom. sing. neut. part. aor. 1 . φθέγγομαι

φθείρει, 3 pers. sing. pres. ind. act. . . φθείρω

φθειρόμενον, acc. sing. masc. part. pres. pass. φθείρω
φθείρονται, 3 pers. pl. pres. ind. pass. id.
φθείρουσι, 3 pers. pl. pres. ind. act. id.
φθείρω], fut. φθερῶ, perf. ἔφθαρκα, (§ 27. rem. 1. c, and rem. 2. b) aor. 1, ἔφθειρα, aor. 1, pass. ἐφθάρην, (§ 27. rem. 1. d, and rem. 4. a) (φθέω, idem) *to spoil, ruin*, 1 Co. 3. 17; 2 Co. 7. 2; *to corrupt*, morally *deprave* 1 Co. 15. 33; 2 Co. 11. 3, et al.

φθαρτός, ή, όν, (§ 7. tab. F. a) *corruptible, perishable*, Ro. 1. 23; 1 Co. 9. 25, et al.

φθορά, ᾶς, ἡ, (§ 2. tab. B. b) *corruption, decay, ruin, corruptibility, mortality*, Ro. 8. 21; 1 Co. 15. 42; meton. *corruptible, perishable substance*, 1 Co. 15. 50; *killing, slaughter*, 2 Pe. 2. 12; spiritual *ruin*, Gal. 6. 8; Col. 2. 22; met. moral *corruption, depravity*, 2 Pe. 1. 4; 2. 12, 19.

φθερεῖ, 3 pers. sing. fut. ind. act. φθείρω
φθινοπωρινά,[a] nom. pl. neut. φθινοπωρινός
φθινοπωρῐνός], ή, όν, (§ 7. tab. F. a) (φθινόπωρον, *the latter part of autumn*, from φθίνω, *to wane*, and ὀπώρα) *autumnal, sere, bare*.
φθόγγοις, dat. pl. φθόγγος
φθόγγος], ου, ὁ φθέγγομαι
φθονεῖτε, 2 pers. pl. pres. ind.—Eras. Schm. } φθονέω
φονεύετε, Rec. Gr. Sch. Tdf. (Ja. 4. 2) }
φθονέω, ῶ], fut. ήσω φθόνος
φθόνοι, nom. pl. id.
φθόνον, acc. sing. id.

φθόνος], ου, ὁ, (§ 3. tab. C. a) *envy, jealousy, spite*, Mat. 27. 18; Mar. 15. 10, et al.

φθονέω, ῶ, fut. ήσω, aor. 1, ἐφθόνησα, (§ 16. tab. P) *to envy*, Gal. 5. 26.

φθόνου, gen. sing. φθόνος
φθονοῦντες,[b] nom. pl. masc. part. pres. φθονέω
φθόνους, acc. pl. φθόνος
φθόνῳ, dat. sing. id.
φθορά], ᾶς, ἡ φθείρω
φθορᾷ, dat. sing. φθορά
φθοράν, acc. sing. id.
φθορᾶς, gen. sing. id.
φιάλας, acc. pl. φιάλη

φιάλη], ης, ἡ, (§ 2. tab. B. a) *a bowl, shallow cup, patera*, Re. 5. 8; 15. 7; 16. 1, 2, 3, 4, et al. (ᾰ).

φιλάγαθον,[c] acc. sing. masc. φιλάγαθος
φιλάγᾰθος], ου, ὁ, ἡ, (§ 7. rem. 2) (φίλος & ἀγαθός) *a lover of goodness*, or, *of the good, a fosterer of virtue*.
Φιλαδέλφεια], ας, ἡ, (§ 2. tab. B. b, and rem. 2) *Philadelphia*, a city of Lydia, near Mount Tmolus.
Φιλαδελφείᾳ, dat. Φιλαδέλφεια
Φιλαδέλφειαν, acc. id.
φιλαδελφία], ας, ἡ φιλάδελφος
φιλαδελφίᾳ, dat. sing. φιλαδελφία
φιλαδελφίαν, acc. sing. id.
φιλαδελφίας, gen. sing. id.
φιλάδελφοι,[d] nom. pl. masc. φιλάδελφος
φιλάδελφος], ου, ὁ, ἡ, (§ 7. rem. 2) (φίλος & ἀδελφός) *brother-loving*; in N.T. *loving the members of the* Christian *brotherhood*, 1 Pe. 3. 8.

φιλαδελφία, ας, ἡ, (§ 2. tab. B. b, and rem. 2) *brotherly love*; in N.T. *love of the* Christian *brotherhood*, Ro. 12. 10; 1 Thes. 4. 9, et al. L.G.

φίλανδρος], ου, ἡ, (φίλος & ἀνήρ) *husband-loving; conjugal*.
φιλάνδρους,[e] acc. pl. φίλανδρος
φιλανθρωπία], ας, ἡ, (§ 2. tab. B. b, and rem. 2) (φιλάνθρωπος, *loving mankind, humane*, from φίλος & ἄνθρωπος) *philanthropy, love of mankind*, Tit. 3. 4; *benevolence, humanity*, Ac. 28. 2.

φιλανθρώπως, adv. *humanely, benevolently, kindly*, Ac. 27. 3.

φιλανθρωπίαν, acc. sing. φιλανθρωπία
φιλανθρώπως], adv. id.
φιλαργυρία],[f] ας, ἡ φιλάργυρος
φιλάργυροι, nom. pl. masc. id.
φιλάργῠρος], ου, ὁ, ἡ, (§ 7. rem. 2) (φίλος & ἄργυρος) *money-loving, covetous*, Lu. 16. 14; 2 Ti. 3. 2.

φιλαργυρία, ας, ἡ, (§ 2. tab. B. b, and rem. 2) *love of money, covetousness*, 1 Ti. 6. 10.

φίλας, acc. pl. (pr. fem. of φίλος) φίλη
φίλαυτοι,[g] nom. pl. masc. φίλαυτος
φίλαυτος] ου, ὁ, ἡ, (§ 7. rem. 2) (φίλος & αὐτός) *self-loving; selfish*, 2 Ti. 3. 2.
φίλε, voc. sing. masc. φίλος
φιλεῖ, 3 pers. sing. pres. ind. φιλέω

[a] Jude 12. [b] Gal. 5. 26. [c] Tit. 1. 8. [d] 1 Pe. 3. 8. [e] Tit. 2. 4. [f] 1 Ti. 6. 10. [g] 2 Ti. 3. 2.

φιλεῖς, 2 pers. sing. pres. ind. . . . . φιλέω

φιλέω, ῶ], fut. ήσω . . . . . φίλος

φίλη], ης, ἡ . . . . id.

φιλήδονοι,[a] nom. pl. masc. . . . . φιλήδονος

φιλήδονος], ου, ὁ, ἡ, (§ 7. rem. 2) (φίλος & ἡδονή) *pleasure-loving; a lover of pleasure*, 2 Ti. 3. 4.

φίλημα], ατος, τό . . . . . . φίλος

φιλήματι, dat. sing. . . . . . φίλημα

Φιλήμονι,[b] dat. . . . . . . Φιλήμων

Φιλήμων], ονος, ὁ, (§ 4. rem. 2. e) *Philemon*, pr. name.

φιλῆσαι, aor. 1, infin. . . . . . φιλέω

φιλήσω, 1 pers. sing. aor. 1, subj. . . . id.

Φίλητος],[c] ου, ὁ, *Philetus*, pr. name.

φιλία],[d] ας, ἡ . . . . . . φίλος

Φίλιππε, voc. . . . . . . Φίλιππος

Φιλιππήσιοι,[e] voc. pl. . . . . . Φιλιππήσιος

Φιλιππήσιος], ου, ὁ, *a Philippian, a citizen of Φίλιπποι, Philippi*.

Φίλιπποι], ων, οἱ, *Philippi*, a considerable city of Macedonia, east of Amphipolis.

Φιλίπποις, dat. . . . . . . Φίλιπποι

Φίλιππον, acc. . . . . . . Φίλιππος

Φίλιππος], ου, ὁ, (§ 3. tab. C. a) *Philip*, pr. name.
I. *Philip, the Apostle*, Mat. 10. 3, et al.
II. *Philip, the Evangelist*, Ac. 6. 5, et al.
III. *Philip, son of Herod the Great and Mariamne*, Mat. 14. 3, et al.
IV. *Philip, son of Herod the Great and Cleopatra*, Mat. 16. 13; Lu. 3. 1.

Φιλίππου, gen. . . . . . . Φίλιππος

Φιλίππους, acc. . . . . . . Φίλιπποι

Φιλίππῳ, dat. . . . . . . Φίλιππος

Φιλίππων, gen. . . . . . . Φίλιπποι

φιλόθεοι,[f] nom. pl. masc. . . . . φιλόθεος

φιλόθεος], ου, ὁ, ἡ, (§ 7. rem. 2) (φίλος & θεός) *God-loving, pious; a lover of God*, 2 Ti. 3. 4.

φίλοι, nom. pl. . . . . . . φίλος

φίλοις, dat. pl. . . . . . . id.

Φιλόλογον,[g] acc. . . . . . . Φιλόλογος

Φιλόλογος], ου, ὁ, *Philologus*, pr. name.

φίλον, acc. sing. . . . . . . φίλος

φιλονεικία],[h] ας, ἡ . . . . . φιλόνεικος

φιλόνεικος],[i] ου, ὁ, ἡ, (§ 7. rem. 2) (φίλος & νεῖκος, *contention*) *fond of contention; contentious, disputatious*, 1 Co. 11. 16.

φιλονεικία, ας, ἡ, (§ 2. tab. B. b, and rem. 2) *a love of contention; rivalry, contention*, Lu. 22. 24.

φιλοξενία], ας, ἡ . . . . . . φιλόξενος

φιλοξενίαν, acc. sing. . . . . . φιλοξενία

φιλοξενίας, gen. sing. . . . . . id.

φιλόξενοι, nom. pl. masc. . . . . φιλόξενος

φιλόξενον, acc. sing. masc. . . . . id.

φιλόξενος], ου, ὁ, ἡ, (§ 7. rem. 2) (φίλος & ξένος) *kind to strangers, hospitable*, 1 Ti. 3. 2; Tit. 1. 8; 1 Pe. 4. 9.

φιλοξενία, ας, ἡ, (§ 2. tab. B. b, and rem. 2) *kindness to strangers, hospitality*, Ro. 12. 13; He. 13. 2.

φιλοπρωτεύω], (φίλος & πρωτεύω) *to love or desire to be first or chief, affect pre-eminence*. N.T.

φιλοπρωτεύων,[k] nom. sing. masc. part. pres. φιλοπρωτεύω

φίλος], ου, ὁ, *loved, dear*; as a subst., *a friend*, Lu. 7. 6; 11. 5, 6, 8, et al.; *a congenial associate*, Mat. 11. 19; Lu. 7. 34; Ja. 4. 4; used as a word of courteous compellation, Lu. 14. 10.

φιλέω, ῶ, fut. ήσω, aor. 1, ἐφίλησα, (§ 16. tab. P) pr. *to manifest some act or token of kindness or affection; to kiss*, Mat. 26. 48; Mar. 14. 44; Lu. 22. 47; *to love, regard with affection, have affection for*, Mat. 10. 37; Jno. 5. 20; *to like, be fond of, delight in* a thing, Mat. 23. 6; Re. 22. 15; *to cherish inordinately, set store by*, Jno. 12. 25; followed by an infin. *to be wont*, Mat. 6. 5.

φίλη, ης, ἡ, (§ 2. tab. B. a) *a female friend*, Lu. 15. 9.

φίλημα, ατος, τό, (§ 4. tab. D. c) *a kiss*, Lu. 7. 45; 22. 48; Ro. 16. 16, et al.

φιλία, ας, ἡ, (§ 2. tab. B. b, and rem. 2) *affection, fondness, love*, Ja. 4. 4.

φιλοσοφία], ας, ἡ . . . . . φιλόσοφος

φιλοσοφίας,[l] gen. sing. . . . . . φιλοσοφία

φιλόσοφος], ου, ὁ, (§ 3. tab. C. a) (φίλος & σοφία) pr. *a lover of science*, a systematic *philosopher*, Ac. 17. 18.

φιλοσοφία, ας, ἡ, (§ 2. tab. B. b, and rem. 2) *a love of science*; systematic

[a] 2 Ti. 3. 4. [b] Phile. 1. [c] 2 Ti. 2. 17. [d] Ja. 4. 4. [e] Phi. 4. 15. [f] 2 Ti. 3. 4. [g] Ro. 16. 15. [h] Lu. 22. 24. [i] 1 Co. 11. 16. [k] 3 Jno. 9. [l] Col. 2. 8

philosophy; in N.T. *the philosophy* of the Jewish gnosis, Col. 2. 8.

φιλοσόφων,[a] gen. pl. . . . . φιλόσοφος

φιλόστοργοι,[b] nom. pl. masc. . . φιλόστοργος

φιλόστοργος], ου, ὁ, ἡ, (§ 7. rem. 2) (φίλος & στοργή, *natural affection*) *tenderly affectionate.*

φιλότεκνος], ου, ὁ, ἡ, (φίλος & τέκνον) *loving one's children, duly parental.*

φιλοτέκνους,[c] acc. pl. fem. . . . φιλότεκνος

φιλοτιμεῖσθαι, pres. infin. . . . φιλοτιμέομαι

φιλοτιμέομαι, οῦμαι], fut. ήσομαι, (§ 17. tab. Q) (φιλότιμος, *studious of honour or distinction*, φίλος & τιμή) pr. *to be ambitious of honour*; by impl. *to exert one's self* to accomplish a thing, *use one's utmost efforts, endeavour earnestly*, Ro. 15. 20; 2 Co. 5. 9; 1 Thes. 4. 11.

φιλοτιμοῦμαι, 1 pers. sing. pres. ind.—B. Ln.
φιλοτιμούμενον, Rec. Gr. Sch. Tdf. (Ro. 15. 20) } φιλοτιμέομαι

φιλοτιμούμεθα, 1 pers. pl. pres. ind. . id.

φιλοτιμούμενον, acc. sing. masc. part. pres. . id.

φιλοῦντας, acc. pl. masc. part. pres. . . id.

φιλούντων, gen. pl. masc. part. pres. . . id.

φίλους, acc. pl. . . . . . . φίλος

φιλοῦσι, 3 pers. pl. pres. ind. . . . φιλέω

φιλόφρονες,[d] nom. pl. masc. . . . φιλόφρων

φιλοφρόνως],[e] adv. . . . . . . id.

φιλόφρων], ονος, ὁ, ἡ, (§ 7. tab. G. a) (φίλος & φρήν) *kindly-minded, benign, courteous.*

φιλοφρόνως, adv. *with kindly feeling or manner, courteously.*

φιλῶ, 1 pers. sing. pres. ind. and subj. . φιλέω

φιλῶν, nom. sing. masc. part. pres. . . id.

φίλων, gen. pl. . . . . . . φίλος

φιμοῦν, pres. infin. act. . . . . φιμόω

φῑμόω, ῶ], fut. ώσω, aor. 1, ἐφίμωσα, perf. pass. πεφίμωμαι, aor. 1, pass. ἐφιμώθην, (§ 20. tab. T, & § 21. tab. U) (φιμός, *a muzzle*) *to muzzle*, 1 Co. 9. 9; 1 Ti. 5. 18; met. and by impl. *to silence, put to silence*; pass. *to be silent, speechless*, Mat. 22. 12, 34; Mar. 1. 25, et al.; trop. pass. *to be hushed*, as winds and waves, Mar. 4. 39.

φιμώθητι, 2 pers. sing. aor. 1, imper. pass. φιμόω

φιμώσεις, 2 pers. sing. fut. ind. act. . id.

Φλέγοντα,[f] acc. . . . . . . Φλέγων

Φλέγων], οντος, ὁ, (§ 4. rem. 2. d) *Phlegon*, pr. name.

φλογά, acc. sing. . . . . φλόξ

φλογί, dat. sing. . . . . . . id.

φλογιζομένη, nom. sing. fem. part. pres. pass. φλογίζω

φλογίζουσα, nom. sing. fem. part. pres. act. id.

φλογίζω], fut. ίσω . . . . . φλόξ

φλογός, gen. sing. . . . . . . id.

φλόξ], φλογός, ἡ, (§ 4. rem. 2. b) (φλέγω, *to burn, blaze*) *a flame*, Lu. 16. 24; Ac. 7. 30, et al.

φλογίζω, fut. ίσω, (§ 26. rem. 1) *to set in a flame, kindle, inflame*, Ja. 3. 6, bis.

φλυᾱρέω, ῶ], fut. ήσω . . . . . φλύᾱρος

φλύαροι,[g] nom. pl. fem. . . . . . id.

φλύᾱρος], ου, ὁ, ἡ, (φλύω, *to boil over, bubble*; met. *to babble*) *a prater, tattler.*

φλυᾱρέω, ῶ, fut. ήσω, (§ 16. tab. P) *to talk folly*; in N.T. trans. *to prate about or against* any one, 3 Jno. 10.

φλυαρῶν,[h] nom. sing. masc. part. pres. . φλυαρέω

φοβεῖσθαι, pres. infin. mid. (§ 17. tab. Q) . φοβέω

φοβεῖσθε, 2 pers. pl. pres. imper. mid. . id.

φοβερά, nom. sing. fem. . . . . φοβερός

φοβερόν, nom. sing. neut. . . . . id.

φοβερός], ά, όν . . . . . φόβος

φοβέω, ῶ], fut. ήσω . . . . . id.

φοβῇ, 2 pers. sing. pres. ind. mid. . . φοβέω

φοβηθείς, nom. s. masc. part. aor. 1, pass. (mid.) id.

φοβηθεῖσα, nom. sing. fem. part. aor. 1, mid. id.

φοβηθέντες, nom. pl. masc. part. aor. 1, mid. id.

φοβηθῇ, 3 pers. sing. aor. 1, subj. mid. . id.

φοβηθῇς, 2 pers. sing. aor. 1, subj. mid. . id.

φοβηθήσομαι, 1 pers. sing. fut. ind. mid. . id.

φοβηθῆτε, 2 pers. pl. aor. 1, subj. mid. . id.

φοβήθητε, 2 pers. pl. aor. 1, imper. mid. . id.

φοβηθῶμεν, 1 pers. pl. aor. 1, subj. mid. . id.

φοβῆται, 3 pers. sing. pres. subj. mid. . id.

φόβητρα,[i] nom. pl. . . . . . φόβητρον

φόβητρον], ου, τό . . . . φόβος

φόβοι, nom. pl. . . . . . id.

φόβον, acc. sing. . . . . . id.

φόβος], ου, ὁ, (§ 3. tab. C. a) (φέβομαι, *to be affrighted, to flee*) *fear, terror, affright*, Mat. 14. 26; Lu. 1. 12; *astonishment, amazement*, Mat. 28. 8; Mar. 4. 41;

a Ac. 17. 18. b Ro. 12. 10. c Tit. 2. 4. d 1 Pe. 3. 8. e Ac. 28. 7. f Ro. 16. 14. g 1 Ti. 5. 13. h 3 Jno. 10. i Lu. 21. 11.

trembling solicitude, 1 Co. 2. 3; 2 Co. 7. 15; meton. *a terror, an object or cause of terror*, Ro. 13. 3. *reverential fear, awe*, Ac. 9. 31; Ro. 3. 18; *respect, deference*, Ro. 13. 7; 1 Pe. 2. 18.

φοβέω, ῶ, fut. ήσω, (§ 16. tab. P) *to terrify, frighten*; mid., aor. 1, (pass. form) ἐφοβήθην, fut. φοβηθήσομαι, *to fear, dread*, Mat. 10. 26; 14. 5, et al.; *to fear reverentially, to reverence*, Mar. 6. 20; Lu. 1. 50; Ac. 10. 2; Ep. 5. 33; Re. 11. 18, et al.; *to be afraid* to do a thing, Mat. 2. 22; Mar. 9. 32, et al.; *to be reluctant, to scruple*, Mat. 1. 20; *to fear, be apprehensive*, Ac. 27. 17; 2 Co. 11. 3; 12. 20; *to be fearfully anxious*, He. 4. 1; absol. *to be fearful, afraid, alarmed*, Mat. 14. 27; 17. 6, 7; Mar. 16. 8, et al.; *to be fearfully impressed*, Ro. 11. 20.

φοβερός, ά, όν, (§ 7. rem. 1) *fearful; terrible*, He. 10. 27, 31; 12. 21.

φόβητρον, ου, τό, (§ 3. tab. C. c) *something which inspires terror; terrific prodigy or portent*, Lu. 21. 11.

φόβου, gen. sing. . . . . . . φόβος

φοβοῦ, 2 pers. sing. pres. imper. mid. . φοβέω

φοβοῦμαι, 1 pers. sing. pres. ind. mid. . . id.

φοβούμεθα, 1 pers. pl. pres. ind. mid. . id.

φοβούμεναι, nom. pl. fem. part. pres. mid. . id.

φοβούμενοι, nom. pl. masc. part. pres. mid. id.

φοβουμένοις, dat. pl. masc. part. pres. mid. id.

φοβούμενος, nom. sing. masc. part. pres. mid. id.

φόβῳ, dat. sing. . . . . . . φόβος

Φοίβη], ης, ἡ, (§ 2. tab. B. a) *Phœbe*, pr. name.

Φοίβην,[a] acc. . . . . . . Φοίβη

Φοίνικα,[b] acc. . . . . . Φοῖνιξ

φοίνικες, nom. pl. . . . . . . φοίνιξ

Φοινίκη], ης, ἡ, *Phœnice, Phœnicia*, a country on the east of the Mediterranean, between Palestine and Syria, anciently celebrated for commerce.

Φοινίκην, acc. . . . . . . Φοινίκη

Φοινίκης, gen. . . . . id.

φοινίκων, gen. pl. . . . . . . φοίνιξ

φοίνιξ], ῖκος, ὁ, (§ 4. rem. 2. b) *the palm-tree, the date-palm, phœnix dactylifera* of Linn., Jno. 12. 13; Re. 7. 9.

Φοῖνιξ], ικος, ὁ, *Phœnix, Phenice*, a city, with a harbour, on the south-east coast of Crete.

φονέα, acc. sing. . . . . . . φονεύς

φονεῖς, nom. and acc. pl. . . . . id.

φονεύεις, 2 pers. sing. pres. ind.—A. Ln. Tdf. } φονεύω
φονεύσεις, Rec. Gr. Sch. (Ja. 2. 11) }

φονεύετε, 2 pers. pl. pres. ind. . . id.

φονεύς], έως, ὁ . . . . . . φόνος

φονευσάντων, gen. pl. masc. part. aor. 1 . φονεύω

φονεύσεις, 2 pers. sing. fut. ind. . . . id.

φονεύσῃ, 3 pers. sing. aor. 1, subj. . . id.

φονεύσῃς, 2 pers. sing. aor. 1, subj. . . id.

φονεῦσι, dat. pl. . . . . . φονεύς

φονεύω], fut. εύσω . . . . . φόνος

φόνοι, nom. pl. . . . . . . id.

φόνον, acc. sing. . . . . . . id.

φόνος], ου, ὁ, (§ 3. tab. C. a) *a killing, slaughter, murder*, Mat. 15. 19; Mar. 7. 21; 15. 7, et al.

φονεύς, έως, ὁ, (§ 5. tab. E. d) *a homicide, murderer*, Mat. 22. 7; Ac. 3. 14, et al.

φονεύω, fut. εύσω, aor. 1, ἐφόνευσα, (§ 13. tab. M) *to put to death, kill, slay*, Mat. 23. 31, 35, et al.; absol. *to commit murder*, Mat. 5. 21, et al.

φόνου, gen. sing. . . . . . . φόνος

φόνῳ, dat. sing. . . . . . . id.

φόνων, gen. pl. . . . . . . id.

φορεῖ, 3 pers. sing. pres. ind. . . . φορέω

φορέσομεν, 1 pers. pl. fut. ind. . . . id.

φορέσωμεν, 1 pers. pl. aor. 1, subj.—Al. Ln. Tdf. } id.
φορέσομεν, Rec. Gr. Sch. (1 Co. 15. 49) }

φορέω, ῶ], fut. ήσω and έσω . . . . φέρω

φόρον], ου, τό, (Lat. *forum*) *a forum, market-place*; Φόρον Ἀππίου, *Forum Appii*, the name of a small town on the Appian way, according to Antoninus, forty-three Roman miles from Rome, or about forty English miles, Ac. 28. 15.

φόρον, acc. sing. . . . . . . φόρος

φόρος], ου, ὁ . . . . . . φέρω

φόρου,[c] gen. sing. . . . . . φόρον

φοροῦντα, acc. sing. masc. part. pres. . . φορέω

φοροῦντες, nom. pl. masc. part. pres. . id.

φόρους, acc. pl. . . . . . . φόρος

φορτία, acc. pl. . . . . . . φορτίον

φορτίζετε, 2 pers. pl. pres. ind. act. . . φορτίζω

[a] Ro. 16. 1. [b] Ac. 27. 12. [c] Ac. 28. 15.

φορτίζω], fut. ίσω . . . . . φέρω
φορτίοις, dat. pl. . . . . . φορτίον
φορτίον], ου, τό . . . . . φέρω
φορτίου, gen. sing.—Gr. Sch. Tdf. } φορτίον
φόρτου, Rec. (Ac. 27. 10)
φόρτος], ου, ὁ . . . . . φέρω
φόρτου,[a] gen. sing. . . . . φόρτος
φορῶν, nom. sing. masc. part. pres. . . φορέω
Φορτουνάτος, or Φουρτουνάτος], ου, ὁ, *Fortunatus*, pr. name.
Φορτουνάτου,[b] gen.—A. C. D. Ln. Tdf. } Φορτουνάτος
Φουρτουνάτου, R. Gr. Sch. (1 Co. 16. 17)
φραγέλλιον],[c] ίου, τό, (§ 3. tab. C. c) (Lat. *flagellum*) *a whip, scourge.* N.T.

φραγελλόω, ῶ, fut. ώσω, (§ 20. tab. T) *to scourge,* Mat. 27. 26; Mar. 15. 15. N.T.

φραγελλόω, ῶ], fut. ώσω . . . φραγέλλιον
φραγελλώσας, nom. sing. masc. part. aor. 1 φραγελλόω
φραγῇ, 3 pers. sing. aor. 2, subj. pass. . φράσσω
φραγήσεται, 3 pers. sing. fut. 2, ind. pass. . id.
φραγμόν, acc. sing. . . . . φραγμός
φραγμός], οῦ, ὁ . . . . . φράσσω
φραγμοῦ, gen. sing. . . . . φραγμός
φραγμούς, acc. pl. . . . . . id.

φράζω], fut. άσω, aor. 1, ἔφρασα, (§ 26. rem. 1) pr. *to propound in distinct terms, to tell;* in N.T. *to explain, interpret, expound,* Mat. 13. 36; 15. 15.

φράσον, 2 pers. sing. aor. 1, imper. . φράζω

φράσσω, or ττω], fut. ξω, aor. 1, ἔφραξα, (§ 26. rem. 3) *to fence in;* by impl. *to obstruct, stop, close up,* He. 11. 33; met. *to silence, put to silence,* Ro. 3. 19; 2 Co. 11. 10.

φραγμός, οῦ, ὁ, (§ 3. tab. C. a) *a fence, hedge; a hedgeside path,* Mat. 21. 33; Mar. 12. 1; Lu. 14. 23; met. *a parting fence,* Ep. 2. 14.

φρέαρ], φρέᾰτος, τό, (§ 4. rem. 2. c) *a well, cistern,* Lu. 14. 5; Jno. 4. 11, 12; *a pit* Re. 9. 1, 2.

φρέατος, gen. sing. . . . . . φρέαρ
φρεναπατᾷ,[d] 3 pers. sing. pres. ind. . . φρεναπατάω
φρεναπάται,[e] nom. pl. . . . φρεναπάτης

φρεναπατάω, ῶ], fut. ήσω, (§ 18. tab. R) (φρήν & ἀπατάω) *to deceive the mind; to deceive, impose on,* Gal. 6. 3. N.T.

φρεναπάτης, ου, ὁ, (§ 2. tab. B. c) *a deceiver, seducer.* (ᾰ). N.T.

φρεναπάτης], ου, ὁ . . . . . φρεναπατάω
φρεσί, dat. pl. . . . . . φρήν

φρήν], ενός, ἡ, (§ 4. rem. 2. e) pr. *the diaphragm, midriff; the mind, intellect,* 1 Co. 14. 20, bis.

φρονέω, ῶ, fut. ήσω, aor. 1, ἐφρόνησα, (§ 16. tab. P) *to think, to mind; to be of opinion,* Ac. 28. 22; Phi. 1. 7; *to take thought, be considerate,* Phi. 4. 10; *to entertain sentiments or inclinations* of a specific kind, *to be minded,* Ro. 12. 16; 15. 5; 1 Co. 13. 11; 2 Co. 13. 11; Gal. 5. 10; Phi. 2. 2; 3. 16; 4. 2; *to be in a* certain *frame of mind,* Ro. 12. 3; Phi. 2. 5; *to ween, entertain conceit,* 1 Co. 4. 6; *to heed, pay regard to,* Ro. 14. 6; *to incline to, be set upon, mind,* Mat. 16. 23; Mar. 8. 33; Ro. 8. 5; Phi. 3. 15, 19; Col. 3. 2.

φρόνημα, ατος, τό, (§ 4. tab. D. c) *frame of thought, will, mind,* Ro. 8. 6, 7, 27.

φρόνησις, εως, ἡ, (§ 5. tab. E. c) *a thoughtful frame, sense, rightmindedness,* Lu. 1. 17; *intelligence,* Ep. 1. 8.

φρόνῐμος, η, ον, (§ 7. tab. F. a) *considerate, thoughtful, prudent, discreet,* Mat. 7. 24; 10. 16; 24. 45, et al.; *sagacious, wise,* Ro. 11. 25; 12. 16; 1 Co. 4. 10; 10. 15; 2 Co. 11. 19.

φρονίμως, adv. *considerately, providently,* Lu. 16. 8. (ῐ).

φροντίζω, fut. ίσω, perf. πεφρόντικα, aor. 1, ἐφρόντισα, (§ 26. rem. 1) (φροντίς, *thought, care,* from φρονέω) *to be considerate, be careful,* Tit. 3. 8.

φρίσσουσι,[f] 3 pers. pl. pres. ind. . . φρίσσω
φρίσσω, or ττω], fut. ξω, perf. πέφρῑκα, aor. 1, ἔφριξα, (§ 26. rem. 3) *to be ruffled, to bristle; to shiver, shudder* from fear, Ja. 2. 19.

φρονεῖ, 3 pers. sing. pres. ind. . . . φρονέω

[a] Ac. 27. 10. [b] 1 Co. 16. 17. [c] Jno. 2. 15. [d] Gal. 6. 3. [e] Tit. 1. 10. [f] Ja. 2. 19.

φρόνει, 2 pers. sing. pres. imper. } φρονέω
ὑψηλὰ φρόνει,—B. Ln. (Ro. 11. 20)
ὑψηλοφρόνει, Rec. Gr. Sch. Tdf.
φρονεῖν, pres. infin. . . . . id.
φρονεῖς, 2 pers. sing. pres. ind. . . id.
φρονείσθω, 3 pers. sing. pres. imper. pass. . id.
φρονεῖτε, 2 pers. pl. pres. ind. and imper. id.
φρονέω, ῶ], fut. ήσω . . . . φρήν
φρόνημα], ατος, τό . . . . . id.
φρονήσει, dat. sing. . . . . φρόνησις
φρονήσετε, 2 pers. pl. fut. ind. . . . φρονέω
φρόνησις], εως, ἡ . . . . φρήν
φρονῆτε, 2 pers. pl. pres. subj. . . φρονέω
φρόνιμοι, nom. pl. masc. . . . φρόνιμος
φρονίμοις, dat. pl. masc. . . . . id.
φρόνιμος], η, ον . . . . . φρήν
φρονίμῳ, dat. sing. masc. . . . . φρόνιμος
φρονίμως],[a] adv. . . . . φρήν
φρονιμώτεροι, nom. pl. masc. compar. (§ 8. rem. 4) . . . . . φρόνιμος
φρονοῦντες, nom. pl. masc. part. pres. . φρονέω
φρονοῦσι, 3 pers. pl. pres. ind. . . . id.
φροντίζω], fut. ίσω . . . . φρήν
φροντίζωσι,[b] 3 pers. pl. pres. subj. . . φροντίζω
φρονῶμεν, 1 pers. pl. pres. subj. . . φρονέω
φρονῶν, nom. sing. masc. part. pres. . . id
φρουρέω, ῶ], fut. ήσω, (§ 16. tab. P) (φρουρός, *a watcher, guard*) *to keep watch*; trans. *to guard, watch*, with a military guard, 2 Co. 11. 32; *to keep* in a condition of restraint, Gal. 3. 23; *to keep* in a state of settlement or security, Phi. 4. 7; 1 Pe. 1. 5.
φρουρησει, 3 pers. sing. fut. ind. . . . φρουρέω
φρουρουμένους, acc. pl. masc. part. pres. pass. (§ 17. tab. Q) . . . . id.

φρυάσσω], fut. ξω, aor. 1, ἐφρύαξα, (§ 26. rem. 3) in classical usage φρυάσσομαι, pr. *to snort, neigh, stamp*, etc., as a high-spirited horse; hence, *to be noisy, fierce, insolent, and tumultuous, to rage, tumultuate*, Ac. 4. 25. LXX.
φρύγᾰνον], ου, τό, (§ 3. tab. C. c) (φρύγω, or φρύσσω, *to parch*) *a dry twig, branch*, etc., *faggot*.
φρυγάνων,[c] gen. pl. . . . . . φρύγανον
Φρυγία], ας, ἡ, (§ 2. tab. B. b, and rem. 2) *Phrygia*, an inland province of Asia Minor.

Φρυγίαν, acc. . . . . . Φρυγία
φυγεῖν, aor. 2, infin. (§ 24. rem. 9) . . φεύγω
Φύγελλος],[d] ου, ὁ, *Phygellus*, pr. name.—Rec. Gr. Sch.
Φύγελος, C. D. Ln. Tdf. (2 Ti. 1. 15)
φυγή], ῆς, ἡ, (§ 2. tab. B. a) . . . φεύγω
φύγητε, 2 pers. pl. aor. 2, subj. . . id.
φυέν, nom. sing. neut. part. aor. 2, pass. (§ 24. rem. 11) . . . . . . φύω
φυλαί, nom. pl. . . . . . φυλή
φυλαῖς, dat. pl. . . . . . id.
φύλακας, acc. pl. . . . . . φύλαξ
φυλακάς, acc. pl. . . . . . φυλακή
φυλακαῖς, dat. pl. . . . . . id.
φύλακες, nom. pl. . . . . . φύλαξ
φυλᾰκή], ῆς, ἡ . . . . . φυλάσσω
φυλακῇ, dat. sing. . . . . . φυλακή
φυλακήν, acc. sing. . . . . . id.
φυλακῆς, gen. sing. . . . . . id.
φυλακίζω], fut. ίσω . . . . φυλάσσω
φυλακίζων,[e] nom. sing. masc. part. pres. . φυλακίζω
φυλακτήρια,[f] acc. pl. . . . . φυλακτήριον
φυλακτήριον], ου, τό . . . . φυλάσσω
φύλαξ], ακος, ὁ . . . . . . id.
φυλάξαι, aor. 1, infin. act. . . . id.
φυλάξατε, 2 pers. pl. aor. 1, imper. act. . id.
φυλάξει, 3 pers. sing. fut. ind. act. . . id.
φυλάξῃ, 3 pers. sing. aor. 1, subj.—A. B. Ln. Tdf. . . . . } id.
πιστεύσῃ, Rec. Gr. Sch. (Jno. 12. 47)
φυλάξῃς, 2 pers. sing. aor. 1, subj. act. . id.
φύλαξον, 2 pers. sing. aor. 1, imper. act. . id.
φυλάς, acc. pl. . . . . . . φυλή
φυλάσσειν, pres. infin. act. . . . φυλάσσω
φυλάσσεσθαι, pres. infin. mid. . . . id.
φυλάσσεσθε, 2 pers. pl. pres. imper. mid. . id.
φυλάσσῃ, 3 pers. sing. pres. subj. act. . id.
φυλασσόμενος, nom. sing. masc. part. pres. mid. id.
φυλάσσοντες, nom. pl. masc. part. pres. act. id.
φυλάσσοντι, dat. sing. masc. part. pres. act. id.
φυλάσσου, 2 pers. sing. pres. imper. mid. . id.
φυλάσσουσι, 3 pers. pl. pres. ind. act. . id.

φυλάσσω, or ττω], fut. ξω, aor. 1, ἐφύλαξα, (§ 26. rem. 3) *to be on watch, keep* watch, Lu. 2. 8; *to have in keeping*, Ac. 22. 20; *to have in custody*, Ac. 28. 16; *to keep* under restraint, *confine*, Lu. 8. 29;

[a] Lu. 16. 8. [b] Tit. 3. 8. [c] Ac. 28. 3. [d] 2 Ti. 1. 15. [e] Ac. 22. 19. [f] Mat. 23. 5.

Ac. 12. 4; 23. 35; *to guard, defend*, Lu. 11. 21; *to keep safe, preserve*, Jno. 12. 25; 17. 12; 2 Thes. 3. 3; 2 Pe. 2. 5; Jude 24; *to keep* in abstinence, *debar*, Ac. 21. 25; 1 Jno. 5. 21; *to observe* a matter of injunction or duty, Mat. 19. 20; Mar. 10. 20; Lu. 11. 28; 18. 21; Ac. 7. 53; 16. 4; 21. 24, et al.; mid. *to be on one's guard, beware*, Lu. 12. 15; 2 Ti. 4. 15; 2 Pe. 3. 17.

φυλᾰκή, ῆς, ἡ, (§ 2. tab. B. a) *a keeping watch, ward, guard*, Lu. 2. 8; *a place of watch, haunt*, Re. 18. 2; *a watch, guard, body of guards*, Ac. 12. 10; *ward, custody, imprisonment*, 2 Co. 6. 5; 11. 23; He. 11. 36; *durance*, 1 Pe. 3. 19; *a place of custody, prison*, Mat. 14. 10; 25. 39, 44; *a watch or division*, of the night, which in the time of our Saviour was divided into four watches of three hours each, called ὀψέ, μεσονύκτιον, ἀλεκτοροφωνία, & πρωΐα, or πρωΐ, Mat. 14. 25; 24. 43; Mar. 6. 48; Lu. 12. 38, bis.

φυλακίζω, fut. ίσω, (§ 26. rem. 1) *to deliver into custody, put in prison, imprison*, Ac. 22. 19. LXX.

φυλακτήριον, ίου, τό, (§ 3. tab. C. c) *the station of a guard or watch; a preservative, safeguard*; hence, *a phylactery or amulet*, worn about the person; from which circumstance the word is used in the N.T. as a term for the Jewish *Tephillin* or *prayer-fillets*, which took their rise from the injunction in Deut. 6. 8; 11. 18; Mat. 23. 5.

φύλαξ, ᾰκος, ὁ, (§ 4. rem. 2. b) *a watchman, guard, sentinel*, Ac. 5. 23; 12. 6. 19.

φυλάσσων, nom. sing. masc. part. pres. act. . . φυλάσσω
φυλή], ῆς, ἡ . . . . φύω
φυλήν, acc. sing. . . . . . φυλή
φυλῆς, gen. sing. . . . . . . id.
φύλλα, nom. and acc. pl. . . . . φύλλον

φύλλον], ου, τό, (§ 3. tab. C. c) *a leaf*, Mat. 21. 19, et al.

φυλῶν, gen. pl. . . . . . φυλή
φύουσα, nom. sing. fem. part. pres. . . φύω
φύρᾱμα], ατος, τό, (§ 4. tab. D. c) (φυράω, *to mix, mingle by kneading*, etc.) *that which is mingled and reduced to a uniform consistence by kneading, beating, treading*, etc.; *a mass* of potter's clay, Ro. 9. 21; of dough, 1 Co. 5. 6; Gal. 5. 9; met. Ro. 11. 16, 1 Co. 5. 7.

φυράματος, gen. sing. . . . . . φύραμα
φύσει, dat. sing. . . . . . . φύσις
φύσεως, gen. sing. . . . . . id.
φυσικά, nom. pl. neut. . . . . φυσικός
φυσικήν, acc. sing. fem. . . . . . id.
φυσικός], ή, όν . . . . . . φύω
φυσικῶς],[a] adv. . . . . . . id.
φύσιν, acc. sing. . . . . . . φύσις
φυσιοῖ, 3 pers. sing. pres. ind. act. . . φυσιόω
φυσιούμενος, nom. sing. masc. part. pres. pass. id.
φυσιοῦσθε, an irreg. form for φυσιῶσθε, 2 pers. pl. pres. subj. pass. (§ 21. tab. U) id.
φυσιοῦται, 3 pers. sing. pres. ind. pass. . id.

φυσιόω, ῶ], fut. ώσω, (§ 20. tab. T) perf. pass πεφυσίωμαι, used in N.T. as an equivalent to φυσάω, *to inflate, puff up*; met. *to inflate* with pride and vanity, 1 Co. 8. 1; pass. *to be inflated* with pride, *to be proud, vain, arrogant*, 1 Co. 4. 6, 19; 5. 2; 8. 1; 13. 4, et al.

φυσίωσις, εως, ἡ, (§ 5. tab. E. c) pr. *inflation*; met. *inflation* of mind, *pride*, 2 Co. 12. 20. N.T.

φύσις], εως, ἡ . . . . . . φύω
φυσιώσεις,[b] nom. pl. . . . . φυσίωσις
φυσίωσις], εως, ἡ . . . . . φυσιόω
φυτεία],[c] ας, ἡ . . . . . . φύω
φυτεύει, 3 pers. sing. pres. ind. act. . . φυτεύω
φυτεύθητι, 2 pers. sing. aor. 1, imper. pass. id.
φυτεύω], fut. εύσω . . . . . φύω
φυτεύων, nom. sing. masc. part. pres. act. . φυτεύω

φύω], fut. φύσω, perf. πέφῡκα, (§ 13. tab. M) aor. 2, pass. ἐφύην, (§ 24. rem. 11) *to generate, produce*; pass. *to be generated, produced*; of plants, *to germinate, sprout*, Lu. 8. 6; intrans. *to germinate, spring or grow up*, He. 12. 15.

φυλή, ῆς, ἡ, (§ 2. tab. B. a) *a tribe*, Mat. 19. 28; 24. 30; Lu. 2. 36; *a people, nation*, Re. 1. 7; 5. 9, et al.

φύσις, εως, ἡ, (§ 5. tab. E. c) *essence*,

[a] Jude 10. [b] 2 Co. 12. 20. [c] Mat. 15. 13.

Gal. 4. 8; *native condition, birth*, Ro. 2. 27; 11. 21, 24; Gal. 2. 15; Ep. 2. 3; *native species, kind*, Ja. 3. 7; *nature, natural frame*, 2 Pe. 1. 4; *nature, native instinct*, Ro. 2. 14; 1 Co. 11. 14; *nature, prescribed course of nature*, Ro. 1. 26.

φυσῐκός, ή, όν, (§ 7. tab. F. a) *natural, agreeable to nature*, Ro. 1. 26, 27; *following the instinct of nature*, as animals, 2 Pe. 2. 12.

φυσῐκῶς, adv. *naturally, by natural instinct*, Jude 10.

φυτεύω, fut. εύσω, aor. 1, ἐφύτευσα, (§ 13. tab. M) (φυτόν, *a plant*, from φύω) *to plant, set*, Mat. 21. 33; Lu. 13. 6, et al.; met. Mat. 15. 13; *to plant* the Gospel, 1 Co. 3. 6, 7, 8.

φυτεία, ας, ἡ, (§ 2. tab. B. b, and rem. 2) *plantation, the act of planting; a plant*, met. Mat. 15. 13.

φωλεός], οῦ, ὁ, (§ 3. tab. C. a) *a den, lair, burrow*, Mat. 8. 20; Lu. 9. 58.

φωλεούς, acc. pl. . . . . . φωλεός

φωναί, nom. pl. . . . . . . φωνή

φωναῖς, dat. pl. . . . . . . id.

φωνάς, acc. pl. . . . . . . id.

φωνεῖ, 3 pers. sing. pres. ind. . . φωνέω

φώνει, 2 pers. sing. pres. imper. . . . id.

φωνεῖτε, 2 pers. pl. pres. ind. . . id.

φωνέω, ῶ], fut. ήσω . . . . φωνή

φωνή], ῆς, ἡ, (§ 2. tab. B. a) *a sound*, Mat. 24. 31; Jno. 3. 8; Re. 4. 5; 8. 5; *a cry*, Mat. 2. 18; *an* articulate *sound, voice*, Mat. 3. 3, 17; 17. 5; 27. 46, 50; *voice, speech, discourse*, Jno. 10. 16, 27; Ac. 7. 31; 12. 22; 13. 27; He. 3. 7. 15; *tone* of address, Gal. 4. 20; *language, tongue, dialect*, 1 Co. 14. 10.

φωνέω, ῶ, fut. ήσω, aor. 1, ἐφώνησα, (§ 16. tab. P) *to sound, utter a sound*; of the cock, *to crow*, Mat. 26. 34, 74, 75; *to call, or cry out, exclaim*, Lu. 8. 8, 54; 16. 24; 23. 46; *to call to*, Mat. 27. 47; Mar. 3. 31, et al.; *to call, entitle*, Jno. 13. 13; *to call, summon*, Mat. 20. 32, et al.; *to invite* to a feast, Lu. 14. 12.

φωνῇ, dat. sing. . . . . . φωνή

φωνηθῆναι, aor. 1, infin. pass. . . φωνέω

φωνήν, acc. sing. . . . . . φωνή

φωνῆς, gen. sing. . . . . . id.

φωνῆσαι, aor. 1, infin. . . . . φωνέω

φωνήσαντες, nom. pl. masc. part. aor. 1 . id.

φωνήσας, nom. sing. masc. part. aor. 1 . id.

φωνήσατε, 2 pers. pl. aor. 1, imper. . } id.
φωνήσατε αὐτόν,—B. C. Tdf. .
αὐτὸν φωνηθῆναι, Rec. Gr. Sch.
(Mar. 10. 49) .

φωνήσει, 3 pers. sing. fut. ind. . . . id.

φώνησον, 2 pers. sing. aor. 1, imper. . id.

φωνοῦντες, nom. pl. masc. part. pres. . . id.

φωνοῦσι, 3 pers. pl. pres. ind. . . id.

φωνῶν, gen. pl. . . . . . . φωνή

φῶς], φωτός, τό, (§ 4. rem. 2. c) (contr. for φάος) *light*, Mat. 17. 2; 2 Co. 4. 6; *daylight, broad day*, Mat. 10. 27; Lu. 12. 3; *radiance, blaze of light*, Mat. 4. 16; Ac. 9. 3; 12. 7, et al.; *an instrument or means of light, a light*, Mat. 6. 23; Ac. 16. 29; *a fire*, Mar. 14. 54; Lu. 22. 56; from the Heb., *the light* of God's presence, 2 Co. 11. 14; 1 Ti. 6. 16; met. *the light* of Divine truth, spiritual *illumination*, Lu. 16. 8; Jno. 3. 19; Ro. 13. 12; Ep. 5. 8; 1 Pe. 2. 9; 1 Jno. 1. 7; 2. 8, 9, 10, et al.; *a source or dispenser of* spiritual *light*, Mat. 5. 14; Jno. 1. 4, 5, 7, 8, 9; 8. 12; 9. 5, et al.; pure *radiance*, perfect *brightness*, 1 Jno. 1. 5.

φωστήρ, ῆρος, ὁ, (§ 4. rem. 2. f) *a cause of light, illuminator; a light, luminary*, Phi. 2. 15; *radiance*, or, *luminary*, Re. 21. 11.

φωτεινός, ή, όν, (§ 7. tab. F. a) *radiant, lustrous*, Mat. 17. 5; *enlightened, illuminated*, Mat. 6. 22; Lu. 11. 34, 36, bis.

φωτίζω, fut. ίσω, aor. 1, ἐφώτισα, (§ 26. rem. 1) *to light, give light to, illuminate, shine upon*, Lu. 11. 36; Re. 18. 1; met. *to enlighten* spiritually, Jno. 1. 9; Ep. 1. 18; 3. 9; He. 6. 4: 10. 32; *to reveal, to bring to light, make known*, 1 Co. 4. 5; 2 Ti. 1. 10.

φωτισμός, οῦ, ὁ, (§ 3. tab. C. a) *illumination: a shining forth, effulgence*, 2 Co. 4. 4, 6 LXX.

φωστήρ], ῆρος, ὁ . . . . . φῶς

φωστῆρες, nom. pl. . . . . . φωστήρ

φωσφόρος],[a] ου, ὁ, ἡ (φῶς & φέρω) *light-bringing*; sc. ἀστήρ, *Lucifer, the morning star*, met. 2 Pe. 1. 19.

φῶτα, acc. pl. . . . . . . φῶς
φωτεινή, nom. sing. fem. . . . . φωτεινός
φωτεινόν, nom. sing. neut. . . . . id.
φωτεινός], ή, όν . . . . . . φῶς
φωτί, dat. sing. . . . . . . id.
φωτιεῖ, 3 pers. sing. fut. Att. (§ 35. rem. 11) φωτιεῖ ἐπ αὐτους,—Gr. Sch. (Re. 22. 5) . . . . . φωτίζει αὐτούς, Rec. . . . φωτισει, Tdf. . . . } φωτίζω
φωτίζει, 3 pers. sing. pres. ind. act. . . id.
φωτίζῃ, 3 pers. sing. pres. subj. act. . . id.
φωτίζω], fut. ίσω . . . . . . φῶς
φωτίσαι, aor. 1, infin. act. . . . . φωτίζω
φωτίσαντος, gen. sing. masc. part. aor. 1, act. id.
φωτίσει, 3 pers. sing. fut. ind. act. . . id.
φωτισθέντας, acc. pl. masc. part. aor. 1, pass. id.
φωτισθέντες, nom. pl. masc. part. aor. 1, pass. id.
φωτισμόν, acc. sing. . . . . . φωτισμός
φωτισμός], οῦ, ὁ . . . . . . φῶς
φωτός, gen. sing. . . . . . id.
φώτων, gen. pl. . . . . . id.

X.

χαῖρε, 2 pers. sing. pres. imper. . . . χαίρω
χαίρει, 3 pers. sing. pres. ind. . . . . id.
χαίρειν, pres. infin. . . . . . id.
χαίρετε, 2 pers. pl. pres. imper. . . . id.
χαίρῃ, 3 pers. sing. pres. subj. . . . id.
χαίρομεν, 1 pers. pl. pres. ind. . . . . id.
χαίροντες, nom. pl. masc. part. pres. . . id.
χαιρόντων, gen. pl. masc. part. pres. . . id.
χαίρουσι, 3 pers. pl. pres. ind.—Gr. Sch. Tdf. χαροῦσι, Rec. (Re. 11. 10) . } id.

χαίρω], fut. χαιρήσω, and, later, χαρήσομαι, aor. 2, ἐχάρην, (ᾰ) (§ 27. rem. 4. b) *to rejoice, be glad, be joyful, be full of joy*, Mat. 2. 10; 5. 12; 18. 13; Mar. 14. 11; Ro. 12. 12; 2 Co. 2. 3; imperat. χαῖρε, χαίρετε, a term of salutation, *hail!* Mat. 26. 49; λέγω χαίρειν, *to greet*, 2 Jno. 10. 11; infin. χαίρειν, an epistolary formula, *health!* Ac. 15. 23.

χαρά, ᾶς, ἡ, (§ 2. tab. B. b) *joy, gladness, rejoicing*, Mat. 2. 10; 13. 20, 44; 28. 8, et al.; meton. *joy, cause of joy, occasion of rejoicing*, Lu. 2. 10; Phi. 4. 1; 1 Thes. 2. 19, 20; *bliss*, Mat. 25. 21, 23.

χάρις, ἴτος, ἡ, (§ 4. rem. 2. c) *pleasing show, charm; beauty, gracefulness; a pleasing circumstance, matter of approval*, 1 Pe. 2. 19, 20; *kindly bearing, graciousness*, Lu. 4. 22; *a beneficial opportunity, benefit*, 2 Co. 1. 15; Ep. 4. 29; *a charitable act, generous gift*, 1 Co. 16. 3, 2 Co. 8. 4, 6, et al.; *an act of favour*, Ac. 25. 3; *favour, acceptance*, Lu. 1. 30, 52; Ac. 2. 47; 7. 10, 46; *free favour, free gift, grace*, Jno. 1. 14, 16, 17; Ro. 4. 4, 16; 11. 5, 6; Ep. 2. 5, 8; 1 Pe. 3. 7; *free favour* specially manifested by God towards man in the Gospel scheme, *grace*, Ac. 15. 11; Ro. 3. 24, 5. 15, 17, 20, 21; 6. 1; 2 Co. 4. 15, et al.; *a gracious provision, gracious scheme, grace*, Ro. 6. 14, 15; He. 2. 9; 12. 28; 13. 9; *gracious dealing* from God, *grace*, Ac. 14. 26; 15. 40; Ro. 1. 7; 1 Co. 1. 4; 15. 10; Gal. 1. 15, et al.; *a commission graciously devolved* by God upon a human agent, Ro. 1. 5; 12. 3; 15. 15; 1 Co. 3. 10; 2 Co. 1. 12; Gal. 2. 9; Ep. 3. 8; *grace, graciously bestowed* divine *endowment or influence*, Lu. 2. 40; Ac. 4. 33; 11. 23; Ro. 12. 6; 2 Co. 12. 9, et al.; *grace, a graciously vouchsafed* spiritual *position*, Ac. 11. 43; Ro. 5. 2; Gal. 5. 4; 2 Pe. 3. 18; *an emotion correspondent to what is pleasing or kindly; sense of obligation*, Lu. 17. 9; *a grateful frame of mind*, 1 Co. 10. 30; *thanks*, Lu. 6. 32, 33, 34; Ro. 6. 17; 1 Co. 15. 57, et al.; χάριν or χάριτας καταθέσθαι, *to oblige, gratify*, Ac. 24. 27; 25. 9.

χάριν, used as a particle governing the genitive case, *on account of*, Lu. 7. 47; Ep. 3. 1, 14; 1 Jno. 3. 12; *for the sake of, in order to*, Gal. 3. 19; Tit. 1. 5. 11; Jude 16; *on the score of*, 1 Ti. 5. 14; from the accus. of χάρις.

χαρίζομαι, fut. ίσομαι, aor. 1, ἐχαρισάμην, fut. pass. χαρισθήσομαι,

[a] 2 Pe. 1. 19.

aor. 1, ἐχαρίσθην, (§ 26. rem. 1) *to gratify; to bestow* in kindness, *grant* as a free favour, Lu. 7. 21; Ro. 8. 32; *to grant the deliverance* of a person in favour to the desire of others, Ac. 3. 14; 27. 24; Phile. 22; *to sacrifice* a person to the demands of enemies, Ac. 25. 11; *to remit, forgive,* Lu. 7. 42; 2 Co. 2. 7, 10.

χάρισμα, ατος, τό, (§ 4. tab. D. c) *a free favour, free gift,* Ro. 5. 15, 16; 6. 23; 2 Co. 1. 11, et al.; *benefit,* Ro. 1. 11; a divinely-conferred *endowment,* 1 Co. 12. 4, 9, 28, 30, 31, et al.

χαριτόω, ῶ, fut. ώσω, perf. pass. κεχαρίτωμαι, (§ 21. tab. U) *to favour, visit with favour, to make an object of favour, to gift;* pass. *to be visited with free favour, be an object of gracious visitation,* Lu. 1. 28. L.G.

χαίρωμεν, 1 pers. pl. pres. subj. . . . χαίρω
χαίρων, nom. sing. masc. part. pres. . . id.

χάλαζα], ης, ἡ, (§ 2. rem. 3) *hail,* Re. 8. 7; 11. 19; 16. 21, bis.

χαλάζης, gen. sing. . . . . . χάλαζα
χαλάσαντες, nom. pl. masc. part. aor. 1, act. . χαλάω
χαλασάντων, gen. pl. masc. part. aor. 1, act. id.
χαλάσατε, 2 pers. pl. aor. 1, imper. act. . id.
χαλάσω, 1 pers. sing. fut. ind. act. . . id.

χαλάω, ῶ], fut. άσω, (ᾰ) (§ 22. rem. 2) aor. 1, ἐχάλᾰσα, *to slacken; to let down, lower,* Mar. 2. 4; Lu. 5. 4, et al.

Χαλδαῖος], ου, ὁ, *a Chaldean, a native of Chaldea,* a country of central Asia, which seems to have included Mesopotamia.

Χαλδαίων,[a] gen. pl. . . . . . Χαλδαῖος
χαλεποί, nom. pl. masc. . . . χαλεπός
χαλεπός], ή, όν, (§ 7. tab. F. a) *hard, rugged; furious, ferocious,* Mat. 8. 28; *trying,* 2 Ti. 3. 1.

χαλῐναγωγέω, ῶ], fut. ήσω, (§ 16. tab. P) (χαλινός & ἄγω) pr. *to guide with a bridle;* met. *to bridle, control, sway,* Ja. 1. 26; 3. 2. L.G

χαλιναγωγῆσαι, aor. 1, infin. . . χαλιναγωγέω
χαλιναγωγῶν, nom. sing. masc. part. pres. . id.

χαλῑνός], οῦ, ὁ, (§ 3. tab. C. a) *a bridle, bit, curb,* Ja. 3. 2; Re. 14. 20.

χαλινούς, acc. pl. . . . . . χαλινός
χαλινῶν, gen. pl. . . . . . id.
χαλκᾶ,[b] acc. pl. neut. . . . . χάλκεος
χάλκεος], έα, and έη, εον . . . . χαλκός
χαλκεύς],[c] εως, ὁ . . . . . id.
χαλκηδών],[d] όνος, ὁ, (§ 4. rem. 2. e) *chalcedony,* the name of a gem, generally of a whitish, bluish, or gray colour, susceptible of a high and beautiful polish, and of which there are several varieties, as the onyx, modern carnelian, etc.

χαλκίον], ου, τό . . . . . χαλκός
χαλκίων,[e] gen. pl. . . . . χαλκίον
χαλκολίβανον], ου, τό, (§ 3. tab. C. c) *orichalcum, fine bronze,* a factitious metal of which there were several varieties, the white being of the highest repute, or, *deep-tinted frankincense,* Re. 1. 15; 2. 18 N.T.

χαλκολιβάνῳ, dat. sing. . . . χαλκολίβανον
χαλκόν, acc. sing. . . . . . χαλκός

χαλκός], οῦ, ὁ, (§ 3. tab. C. a) *copper,* also, *bronze,* Re. 18. 12; *a brazen musical instrument,* 1 Co. 13. 1; *copper money,* Mat. 10. 9; *money* in general, Mar. 6. 8; 12. 41.

χάλκεος, έα, and έη, εον, contr. οῦς, ῆ, οῦν, (§ 7. rem. 5. b) *brazen,* Re. 9. 20.

χαλκεύς, έως, ὁ, (§ 5. tab. E. d) pr. *a coppersmith;* hence, genr. *a worker in metals, smith,* 2 Ti. 4. 14.

χαλκίον, ου, τό, (§ 3. tab. C. c) *a vessel, copper, brazen utensil,* Mar. 7. 4.

χαλκοῦ, gen. sing. . . . . . . χαλκός
χαλῶσι, 3 pers. pl. pres. ind. . . . χαλάω

χαμαί], adv. *on the ground, to the earth,* Jno. 9. 6; 18. 6.

Χαναάν], ὁ, indecl. *Canaan,* the ancient name of Palestine.

Χαναναία,[f] nom. sing. fem. . . . Χαναναῖος
Χαναναῖος], αία, αῖον, (§ 7. rem. 1) *Cananitish.*
χαρά], ᾶς, ἡ . . . . . . χαίρω
χαρᾷ, dat. sing. . . . . . . χαρά
χάραγμα], ατος, τό, (§ 4. tab. D. c) (χαράσσω *to*

[a] Ac. 7. 4. [b] Re. 9. 20. [c] 2 Ti. 4. 14. [d] Re. 21. 19. [e] Mar. 7. 4. [f] Mat. 15. 22.

notch, *engrave*) *an imprinted mark*, Re. 13. 16, et al.; *sculpture*, Ac. 17. 29.

χαρακτήρ, ῆρος, ὁ, (§ 4. rem. 2. f) *a graver, graving-tool; an engraven or impressed device; an impress, exact expression*, He. 1. 3.

χάραξ, ἄκος, ὁ, ἡ, (§ 4. rem. 2. b) *a stake; a pale; a* military *palisade, rampart*, formed from the earth thrown out of the ditch, and stuck with sharp stakes or palisades, Lu. 19. 43.

χαράγματι, dat. sing. . . . . χάραγμα
χαράγματος, gen. sing. . . . . id.
χάρακα,[a] acc. sing. . . . . χάραξ
χαρακτήρ],[b] ῆρος, ὁ . . . . χάραγμα
χάραξ], ακος, ὁ, ἡ . . . . id.
χαράν, acc. sing. . . . . χαρά
χαρᾶς, gen. sing. . . . . id.
χαρῆναι, aor. 2, infin. pass. . . . χαίρω
χαρήσεται, 3 pers. sing. fut. 2, ind. pass. . id.
χαρήσομαι, 1 pers. sing. fut. 2, ind. pass. . id.
χαρήσονται, 3 pers. pl. fut. 2, ind. pass. . id.
χάρητε, 2 pers. pl. aor. 2, imper. pass.—Gr. Sch. Tdf. . . . } id.
χαίρετε, Rec. (Lu. 6. 23) . . }
χαρῆτε, 2 pers. pl. aor. 2, subj. pass. . . id.
χαρίζεσθαι, pres. infin. . . . . χαρίζομαι
χαρίζεσθε, 2 pers. pl. pres. ind. . . . id.
χαρίζομαι], fut. ίσομαι . . . χαίρω
χαριζόμενοι, nom. pl. masc. part. pres. . χαρίζομαι
χάριν, acc. sing. (§ 4. rem. 4) . . χάρις
χάριν, adv. . . . . . . χαίρω
χάρις], ιτος, ἡ . . . . . id.
χαρισάμενος, nom. sing. masc. part. aor. 1 . χαρίζομαι
χαρίσασθαι, aor. 1, infin. . . . id.
χαρίσασθε, 2 pers. pl. aor. 1, imper. . . id.
χαρίσεται, 3 pers. sing. fut. ind. . . id.
χαρισθέντα, acc. pl. neut. part. aor. 1, pass. . id.
χαρισθῆναι, aor. 1, infin. pass. . . id.
χαρισθήσομαι, 1 pers. sing. fut. ind. pass. . id.
χάρισμα], ατος, τό . . . . χαίρω
χαρίσματα, nom. and acc. pl. . . . χάρισμα
χαρίσματι, dat. sing. . . . id.
χαρίσματος, gen. sing. . . . . id.
χαρισμάτων, gen. pl. . . . . id.
χάριτα, acc. sing.—A. B. C. Ln. Tdf. . } χάρις
χάριτας, Rec. Gr. Sch. (Ac. 27. 27) . }
χάριτας, acc. pl. . . . . . id.
χάριτι, dat. sing. . . . . χάρις
χάριτος, gen. sing. . . . . id.
χαριτόω, ῶ], fut. ώσω . . . χαίρω
χαροῦσι, 3 pers. pl. fut. ind. . . . id.
Χαῤῥάν], ἡ, indecl. *Charran*, a city in the northern part of Mesopotamia.
χάρτης], ου, ὁ, (§ 2. rem. 4) *paper*.
χάρτου,[c] gen. sing. . . . . χάρτης
χάσμα],[d] ατος, τό, (§ 4. tab. D. c) (χαίνω, *to gape, yawn*) *a chasm, gulf*.
χείλεσι, dat. pl. . . . . χεῖλος
χειλέων, gen. pl. . . . . id.
χείλη, acc. pl. . . . . . id.

χεῖλος], εος, τό, (§ 5. tab. E. b) *a lip*, and pl. τὰ χείλη, *the lips*, Mat. 15. 8; Ro. 3. 13, et al.; trop. χεῖλος τῆς θαλάσσης, *the sea-shore*, He. 11. 12; meton. *language, dialect*, 1 Co. 14. 21.

χειμαζομένων,[e] gen. pl. masc. part. pres. pass. χειμάζω
χειμάζω], fut. άσω, (§ 26. rem. 1) (χεῖμα, *a storm*) *to excite a tempest, toss with a tempest;* pass. *to be storm-tossed*, Ac. 27. 18.
χείμαῤῥος], ου, ὁ, (§ 3. tab. C. a) (χεῖμα & ῥέω) *winter-flowing;* as a subst. *a stream which flows in winter*, but is dry in summer, *a brook*, Jno. 18. 1.
χειμάῤῥου,[f] gen. sing. . . . . χείμαῤῥος
χειμών], ῶνος, ὁ, (§ 4. rem. 2. e) (χεῖμα) *stormy weather*, Mat. 16. 3; *a storm, tempest*, Ac. 27. 20; *winter*, Mat. 24. 20, et al.
χειμῶνος, gen. sing. . . . . χειμών

χείρ], χειρός, ἡ, (§ 6. rem. 4. f) *a hand*, Mat. 3. 12; 4. 6; 8. 15, et al. freq.; from the Heb., χεὶρ Κυρίου, a special *operation of God*, Ac. 11. 21; 13. 3; ἐν χειρί, *by agency*, Ac. 7. 35; Gal. 3. 19.

χεῖρα, acc. sing. . . . . . χείρ
χειραγωγέω, ῶ], fut. ήσω, (§ 16. tab. P) *to lead by the hand*, Ac. 9. 8; 22. 11. L.G.
χειραγωγός], οῦ, ὁ, (§ 3. tab. C. a) (χείρ & ἀγωγός, *a leader*) *one who leads another by the hand*, Ac. 13. 11.
χειραγωγούμενος, nom. sing. masc. part. pres. pass. (§ 17. tab. Q) . . χειραγωγέω
χειραγωγοῦντες, nom. pl. masc. part. pres. act. id.
χειραγωγούς,[g] acc. pl. . . . . χειραγωγός
χεῖρας, acc. pl. . . . . . χείρ

[a] Lu. 19. 43. [b] He. 1. 3. [c] 2 Jno. 12. [d] Lu. 16. 26. [e] Ac. 27. 18. [f] Jno. 18. 1. [g] Ac. 13. 11.

χεῖρες, nom. pl. . . . . . . χείρ
χειρί, dat. sing. . . . id.
χειρόγρᾰφον],[a] ου, τό, (§ 3. tab. C. c) (χείρ & γράφω) *handwriting; a written form, literal instrument*, as distinguished from a spiritual dispensation, Col. 2. 14.
χεῖρον, nom. and acc. sing. neut. . . χείρων
χείρονα, nom. pl. neut. . . . . id.
χείρονος, gen. sing. fem. . . . id.
χειροποίητα, acc. pl. neut. . . χειροποίητος
χειροποιήτοις, dat. pl. . . . . . id.
χειροποίητον, acc. sing. masc. . . id.
χειροποίητος], ου, ὁ, ἡ, (§ 7. rem. 2) (χείρ & ποιητός, *made*, from ποιέω) *made by hand, artificial, material*, Mar. 14. 58; Ac. 7. 48, et al.
χειροποιήτου, gen. sing. fem. . . . χειροποίητος
χειρός, gen. sing. . . . . . χείρ
χειροτονέω, ῶ], fut. ήσω, (§ 16. tab. P) (χείρ & τείνω) *to stretch out the hand; to constitute by voting; to appoint, constitute*, Ac. 14. 23; 2 Co. 8. 19.
χειροτονηθείς, nom. sing. masc. part. aor. 1, pass. (§ 17. tab. Q) . . χειροτονέω
χειροτονήσαντες, nom. pl. masc. part. aor. 1, act. id.
χειρῶν, gen. pl. . . . . . χείρ
χείρων], ονος, ὁ, ἡ, (§ 8. rem. 5) (irregular comparat. of κακός) *worse*, Mat. 9. 16; 1 Ti. 5. 8; *more severe*, Jno. 5. 14; He. 10. 29.
Χερουβείν, B. Ln.
Χερουβίμ, Rec. Gr. Sch. Tdf. (He. 9. 5).
Χερουβίμ],[b] (Heb. כְּרוּבִים) *cherubim*, the emblematic figures, representing cherubim, on the ark.
χερσί, dat. pl. (§ 6. rem. 4. f) . . χείρ
χήρα], ας, ἡ, (§ 2. tab. B. b) (pr. fem. of χῆρος, *bereft*) *a widow*, Mat. 23. 14; Lu. 4. 26, et al.
χῆραι, nom. pl. . . . . . χήρα
χήραις, dat. pl. . . . . . id.
χήραν, acc. sing. . . . . . id.
χήρας, acc. pl. . . . . . id.
χηρῶν, gen. pl. . . . . . id.
χθές], adv. *yesterday*, Jno. 4. 52; Ac. 7. 28; He. 13. 8.
χίλια, nom. and acc. pl. neut. . . . χίλιοι
χιλιάδες, nom. pl. . . . . . χιλιάς
χιλιάδων, gen. pl. . . . . . id.
χιλίαρχοι, nom. pl. . . . . . χιλίαρχος
χιλιάρχοις, dat. pl. . . . χιλίαρχος
χιλίαρχον, acc. sing. . . . . id.
χῑλίαρχος], ου, ὁ, (§ 3. tab. C. a) (χίλιοι & ἄρχω) *a chiliarch, commander of a thousand men*; hence, genr. *a commander, military chief*, Mar. 6. 21; Re. 6. 15; 19. 18; spc. *a legionary tribune*, Ac. 21. 31, 32, 33, 37, et al.; *the prefect* of the temple, Jno. 18. 12.
χιλιάρχῳ, dat. sing. . . . . . χιλίαρχος
χιλιάρχων, gen. pl. . . . . . id.
χιλιάς], άδος, ἡ . . . . . χίλιοι
χιλίας, acc. pl. fem. . . . . id.
χιλιάσι, dat. pl. . . . . χιλιάς

χίλιοι], αι, α, *a thousand*, 2 Pe. 3. 8; Re. 11. 3, et al.

χιλιάς, άδος, (ᾰ) ἡ, (§ 4. rem. 2. c) the number *one thousand, a thousand*, Lu. 14. 31; Ac. 4. 4, et al.

χιλίων, gen. pl. . . . . . χίλιοι
Χίος], ου, ἡ, (§ 3. tab. C. b) *Chios*, an island near the coast of Asia Minor, in the Ægean sea, between Samos and Lesbos.
Χίου,[c] gen. . . . . . . Χίος

χιτών], ῶνος, ὁ, (§ 4. rem. 2. e) *a tunic, vest*, the inner garment which fitted close to the body, having armholes, and sometimes sleeves, and reaching below the knees, Mat. 5. 40; 10. 10; pl. χιτῶνες, *clothes, garments* in general, Mar. 14. 63.

χιτῶνα, acc. sing. . . . . . χιτών
χιτῶνας, acc. pl. . . . . . id.

χιών], όνος, ἡ, (§ 4. rem. 2. e) *snow*, Mat. 28. 3; Mar. 9. 3; Re. 1. 14.

χλαμύδα, acc. sing. . . . . χλαμύς

χλαμύς], ύδος, (ῠ) ἡ, (§ 4. rem. 2. e) *chlamys*, a species of *cloak*; a Roman military commander's *cloak, paludamentum*, Mat. 27. 28, 31.

χλευάζοντες, nom. pl. masc. part. pres. . χλευάζω
χλευάζω], fut. άσω, aor. 1, ἐχλεύασα, (§ 26. rem. 1) (χλεύη, *jest*) *to jeer, scoff*, Ac. 2. 13; 17. 32.
χλιᾰρός],[d] ά, όν, (§ 7. rem. 1) (χλίω, *to become warm*) *warm, tepid; lukewarm*, Re. 3. 16.
Χλόη], ης, ἡ, (§ 2. tab. B. a) *Chloe*, pr. name.

[a] Col. 2. 14. [b] He. 9. 5. [c] Ac. 20. 15. [d] Re. 3. 16.

Χλόης,[a] gen. . . . . Χλόη
χλωρόν, acc. sing. neut. . . . . χλωρός
χλωρός], ά, όν, (§ 7. rem. 1) (χλόη, *the first tender shoot of vegetation*) *pale green; green, verdant*, Mar. 6. 39; Re. 8. 7; 9. 4; *pale, sallow*, Re. 6. 8.
χλωρῷ, dat. sing. masc. . . . . . χλωρός
χξς', *six hundred and sixty-six*, the number denoted by these letters: viz., χ' = 600, ξ' = 60, ς' = 6, Re. 13. 18.
χοϊκοί, nom. pl. masc. . . . . . χοϊκός
χοϊκός], ή, όν . . . . χόος, χοῦς
χοϊκοῦ, gen. sing. masc. . . . . χοϊκός
χοίνικες, nom. pl. . . . . . . χοῖνιξ

χοῖνιξ], ικος, ἡ, (§ 4. rem. 2. b) *a chœnix*, an Attic measure for things dry, being the 48th part of a medimnus, consequently equal to the 8th part of the Roman modius, and nearly equivalent to about one quart, being considered a sufficient daily allowance for the sustenance of one man, Re. 6. 6, bis.

χοῖροι, nom. pl. . . . . χοῖρος

χοῖρος], ου, ὁ, ἡ, pr. *a young swine; a swine, hog, or sow*, Mat. 8. 30, 31, 32, et al.

χοίρους, acc. pl. . . . . . . χοῖρος
χοίρων, gen. pl. . . . . . . id.
χολᾶτε,[b] 2 pers. pl. pres. ind. . . . . χολάω
χολάω, ῶ], fut. άσω . . . . . . χολή

χολή], ῆς, ἡ, (§ 2. tab. B. a) *the bile, gall*; in N.T. *a bitter ingredient, as wormwood*, Mat. 27. 34; χολὴ πικρίας, *intense bitterness*, met. *thorough disaffection* to divine truth, *utter estrangement*, Ac. 8. 23.

χολάω, ῶ, (χολή, considered as the seat or cause of anger and of melancholy) pr. *to be melancholy*; used later as an equivalent to χολοῦμαι, *to be angry, incensed*, Jno. 7. 23.

χολήν, acc. sing. . . . . . . χολή
χολῆς, gen. sing. . . . . . . id.
χόος, χοῦς], gen. χοός, dat. χοΐ, acc. χοῦν, (§ 3. rem. 3) (χέω, *to pour*) *earth dug out and heaped up; loose earth, dirt, dust*, Mar. 6. 11; Re. 18. 19.

χοϊκός, ή, όν, (§ 7. tab. F. a) *of earth, earthy*, 1 Co. 15. 47, 48, 49. N.T.

Χοραζίν], ἡ, indecl. *Chorazin*, a town of Galilee, probably near Bethsaida and Capernaum.
χορηγεῖ, 3 pers. sing. pres. ind. . . . χορηγέω
χορηγέω, ῶ], fut. ήσω, (§ 16. tab. P) (χορός & ἡγέομαι) *to lead a chorus*; at Athens, *to defray the cost of a chorus*; hence, *to supply funds*; *to supply, furnish*, 2 Co. 9. 10; 1 Pe. 4. 11.
χορηγήσαι, 3 pers. sing. aor. 1, optat. . . χορηγέω
χορηγήσει, 3 pers. sing. fut. ind.—Gr. Sch. Tdf. } id.
χορηγήσαι, Rec. (2 Co. 9. 10) }

χορός], οῦ, ὁ, (§ 3. tab. C. a) *dancing* with music, Lu. 15. 25.

χορτάζεσθαι, pres. infin. pass. . . . χορτάζω
χορτάζεσθε, 2 pers. pl. pres. imper. pass. . . id.
χορτάζω], fut. άσω . . . . . χόρτος
χορτάσαι, aor. 1, infin. act. . . . χορτάζω
χορτασθῆναι, aor. 1, infin. pass. . . . id.
χορτασθήσεσθε, 2 pers. pl. fut. ind. pass. . id.
χορτασθήσονται, 3 pers. pl. fut. ind. pass. . id.
χόρτασμα], ατος, τό . . . . . χόρτος
χορτάσματα,[c] acc. pl. . . . . . χόρτασμα
χόρτον, acc. sing. . . . . . . χόρτος

χόρτος], ου, ὁ, (§ 3. tab. C. a) *an inclosure; pasture-ground; fodder* for beasts; in N.T. *herbage, verdure*, Mat. 6. 30; 14. 19, et al.; *a plant* of corn, Mat. 13. 26; Mar. 4. 28.

χορτάζω, fut. άσω, aor. 1, ἐχόρτασα, (§ 26. rem. 1) pr. *to feed or fill with grass, herbage*, etc., *to fatten*; used of animals of prey, *to satiate, gorge*, Re. 19. 21; of persons, *to satisfy with food*, Mat. 14. 20; 15. 33, 37; met. *to satisfy* the desire of any one, Mat. 5. 6, et al.

χόρτασμα, ατος, τό, (§ 4. tab. D. c) *pasture, provender* for cattle; *food, provision, sustenance*, for men, Ac. 7. 11. L.G.

χόρτου, gen. sing. . . . . . . χόρτος
χόρτους, acc. pl. . . . . . . id.
χόρτῳ, dat. sing. . . . . . . id.
χορῶν,[d] gen. pl. . . . . . . χορός
Χουζᾶ,[e] gen. . . . . Χουζᾶς
Χουζᾶς], ᾶ, ὁ, (§ 2. rem. 4) *Chuzas, Chuza*, pr. name.
χοῦν, acc. sing. . . . . . . χόος, χοῦς
χράομαι, ῶμαι], fut. χρήσομαι, (§ 35. rem. 2) to

[a] 1 Co. 1. 11. [b] Jno. 7. 23. [c] Ac. 7. 11. [d] Lu. 15. 25. [e] Lu. 8. 3.

use, make use of, employ, Ac. 27. 17; 1 Co. 7. 31, et al.; *to avail one's self of,* 1 Co. 7. 21; 9. 12, 15; *to use, to treat, behave towards,* Ac. 27. 3; 2 Co. 13. 10.

χρεία, ας, ἡ, (§ 2. tab. B. b, and rem. 2) *use; need, necessity, requisiteness,* Ep. 4. 29; He. 7. 11; personal *need, an* individual *want,* Ac. 20. 34; Ro. 12. 13; Phi. 2. 25; 4. 16, 19; χρείαν ἔχω, *to need, require, want,* Mat. 6. 8; 14. 16; Mar. 2. 25; Jno. 2. 25; ἐστὶ χρεία, *there is need,* Lu. 10. 42; τὰ πρὸς τὴν χρείαν, *necessary things,* Ac. 28. 10, et al.; *a necessary business, affair,* Ac. 6. 3.

χρήζω, (χρεία) *to need, want, desire,* Mat. 6. 32; Lu. 11. 8; 12. 30; Ro. 16. 2; 2 Co. 3. 1.

χρῆμα, ατος, τό, (§ 4. tab. D. c) *anything useful, or needful;* plur. *wealth, riches,* Mar. 10. 23, 24; Lu. 18. 24; *money,* Ac. 8. 18, 20; 24. 26; sing. *price,* Ac. 4. 37.

χρηματίζω, fut. ίσω, aor. 1, ἐχρημάτισα, (§ 26. rem. 1) *to have dealings, transact business; to negotiate; to give answer on deliberation;* in N.T. *to utter a divine communication,* He. 12. 25; pass. *to be divinely instructed, receive a revelation or warning from God,* Mat. 2. 12, 22; Lu. 2. 26; Ac. 10. 22; He. 8. 5; 11. 7; intrans. *to receive an appellation, be styled,* Ac. 11. 26; Ro. 7. 3.

χρηματισμός, οῦ, ὁ, (§ 3. tab. C. a) in N.T. *a response from God, a divine communication, oracle,* Ro. 11. 4.

χρῆσις, εως, ἡ, (§ 5. tab. E. c) *use, employment; manner of using,* Ro. 1. 26, 27.

χρήσιμος, η, ον, and ὁ, ἡ, τό, -ον, *useful, profitable,* 2 Ti. 2. 14.

χρηστός, ή, όν, (§ 7. tab. F. a) *useful, profitable; good, agreeable,* Lu. 5. 39; *easy,* as a yoke, Mat. 11. 30; *gentle, benign, kind, obliging, gracious,* Lu. 6. 35; Ep. 4. 32; Ro. 2. 4; 1 Pe. 2. 3; *good* in character, disposition, etc., *virtuous,* 1 Co. 15. 33.

χρηστεύομαι, fut. εύσομαι, (§ 14. tab. N) *to be gentle, benign, kind,* 1 Co. 13. 4. N.T.

χρηστότης, τητος, ἡ, (§ 4. rem. 2. c) pr *utility; goodness, kindness, gentleness,* Ro. 2. 4; 11. 22, et al.; *kindness* shown, *beneficence,* Ep. 2. 7; *goodness, virtue,* Ro. 3. 12.

χρεία], ας, ἡ	χράομαι
χρείαις, dat. pl.	χρεία
χρείαν, acc. sing.	id.
χρείας, gen. sing. and acc. pl.	id.
χρεωφειλέται, nom. pl.—R. Gr. Sch. Tdf. / χρεοφειλέται, Ln. (Lu. 7. 41)	χρεωφειλέτης
χρεωφειλέτης], ου, ὁ, (§ 2. tab. B. c) (χρέος, *a debt,* & ὀφειλέτης) *one who owes a debt, a debtor,* Lu. 7. 41; 16. 5. L.G.	
χρεωφειλετῶν, gen. pl.—R. Gr. Sch. Tdf. / χρεοφειλετῶν, A. D. Ln. (Lu. 16. 5)	χρεωφειλέτης
χρή],[a] imperson. verb, *there is need or occasion, it is necessary, it is requisite; it behoves, it becometh, it is proper,* Ja. 3. 10.	
χρῄζει, 3 pers. sing. pres. ind.	χρήζω
χρῄζετε, 2 pers. pl. pres. ind.	id.
χρῄζῃ, 3 pers. sing. pres. subj.	id.
χρῄζομεν, 1 pers. pl. pres. ind.	id.
χρήζω], (χρεία)	χράομαι
χρῆμα], ατος, τό	id.
χρήμασι, dat. pl.	χρῆμα
χρήματα, nom. and acc. pl.	id.
χρηματίζοντα, acc. sing. masc. part. pres.	χρηματίζω
χρηματίζω], fut. ίσω	χράομαι
χρηματίσαι, aor. 1, infin.	χρηματίζω
χρηματίσει, 3 pers. sing. fut. ind.	id.
χρηματισθείς nom. sing. masc. part. aor. 1, pass.	id.
χρηματισθέντες, nom. pl. masc. part. aor. 1, pass.	id.
χρηματισμός],[b] οῦ, ὁ	χράομαι
χρημάτων, gen. pl.	χρῆμα
χρῆσαι, 2 pers. sing. aor. 1, imper.	χράομαι
χρησάμενος, nom. sing. masc. part. aor. 1	id.
χρήσηται, 3 pers. sing. aor. 1, subj.—A. Ln. Tdf. / χρῆται, Rec. Gr. Sch. (1 Ti. 1. 8)	id.
χρῆσθ', (for χρηστά) acc. pl. neut.—Rec. / χρηστά, Gr. Sch. Tdf. (1 Co. 15. 33)	χρηστός
χρήσιμον,[c] acc. sing. neut.	χρήσιμος
χρήσιμος], η, ον, or ὁ, ἡ, τό, -ον	χράομαι
χρῆσιν, acc. sing.	χρῆσις
χρῆσις], εως, ἡ	χράομαι
χρῆσον,[d] 2 pers. sing. aor. 1, imper.	κίχρημι
χρηστεύεται,[e] 3 pers. sing. pres. ind.	χρηστεύομαι
χρηστεύομαι], fut. εύσομαι	χράομαι

[a] Ja. 3. 10. [b] Ro. 11. 4. [c] 2 Ti. 2. 14. [d] Lu. 11. 5. [e] 1 Co. 13. 4.

χρηστοί, nom. pl. masc. . . . χρηστός

χρηστολογία], ας, ἡ, (§ 2. tab. B. b, and rem. 2) (χρηστός & λόγος) *bland address, fair speaking*. N.T.

χρηστολογίας,[a] gen. sing. . . χρηστολογία

χρηστόν, nom. sing. neut. . . . χρηστός

χρηστός], ή, όν . . . . . χράομαι

χρηστότερος, nom. sing. masc. compar. (§ 8. rem. 4) . . . . χρηστός

χρηστότης], τητος, ἡ . . . . χράομαι

χρηστότητα, acc. sing. . . . χρηστότης

χρηστότητι, dat. sing. . . . . id.

χρηστότητος, gen. sing. . . . id.

χρήσωμαι, 1 pers. sing. aor. 1, subj. . . χράομαι

χρῆται, 3 pers. sing. pres. subj. (§ 35. rem. 2) id.

χρίσας, nom. sing. masc. part. aor. 1 . χρίω

χρῖσμα], ατος, τό . . . . . id.

Χριστέ, voc. . . . . . Χριστός

Χριστιανόν, acc. sing. . . Χριστιανός

Χριστιανός], οῦ, ὁ . . . . χρίω

Χριστιανούς, acc. pl. . . . Χριστιανός

Χριστόν, acc. . . . . . Χριστός

Χριστός], οῦ, ὁ . . . . . χρίω

Χριστοῦ, gen. . . . . . Χριστός

Χριστῷ, dat. . . . . . . id.

χρίω], fut. ίσω, aor. 1, ἔχρισα, (§ 22. rem. 4) *to anoint*; in N.T. *to anoint*, by way of instituting to a dignity, function, or privilege, Lu. 4. 18; Ac. 4. 27; 10. 38; 2 Co. 1. 21; He. 1. 9.

χρῖσμα, ατος, τό, (§ 4. tab. D. c) pr. *anything which is applied by smearing; ointment, unguent*; in N.T. *an anointing, unction*, in the reception of spiritual privileges, 1 Jno. 2. 20, 27, bis.

χριστός, οῦ, ὁ, (§ 3. tab. C. a) pr. *anointed*; ὁ Χριστός, *the Christ, the Anointed One*, i.q. Μεσσίας, *the Messiah*, Mat. 1. 16, 17; Jno. 1. 20, 25, 42, et al. freq.; meton. *Christ, the word or doctrine of Christ*, 2 Co. 1. 19, 21; Ep. 4. 20; *Christ, a* truly *Christian frame* of doctrine and affection, Ro. 8. 10; Gal. 4. 19; *Christ, the Church of Christ*, 1 Co. 12. 12; *Christ the* distinctive *privileges of the Gospel of Christ*, Gal. 3. 27; Phi. 3. 8; He. 3. 14.

Χριστιανός, οῦ, ὁ, *a Christian, follower of Christ*, Ac. 11. 26; 26. 28; 1 Pe. 4. 16.

χρονιεῖ, 3 pers. sing. fut. Att. (§ 35. rem. 11) . χρονίζω

χρονίζει, 3 pers. sing. pres. ind. . . id.

χρονίζειν, pres. infin. . . . . . id.

χρονίζοντος, gen. sing. masc. part. pres. . id.

χρονίζω], fut. ίσω . . . . . χρόνος

χρόνοις, dat. pl. . . . . . id.

χρόνον, acc. sing. . . . . . id.

χρόνος], ου, ὁ, (§ 3. tab. C. a) *time*, whether in respect of duration or a definite point of its lapse, Mat. 2. 7; 25. 19, et al. freq.; *an epoch, era*, marked *duration*, Ac. 1. 7; 1 Thes. 5. 1.

χρονίζω, fut. ίσω, Att. ιῶ, aor. 1, ἐχρόνισα, (§ 26. rem. 1) *to while, spend time; to linger, delay, be long*, Mat. 24. 48; 25. 5; Lu. 1. 21; 12. 45; He. 10. 37.

χρονοτρῐβέω, ῶ], fut. ήσω, (§ 16. tab. P) (χρόνος & τρίβω) *to spend time, while away time, linger, delay*.

χρονοτριβῆσαι,[b] aor. 1, infin. . . χρονοτριβέω

χρόνου, gen. sing. . . . . . χρόνος

χρόνους, acc. pl. . . . . . id.

χρόνῳ, dat. sing. . . . . . id.

χρόνων, gen. pl. . . . . . id.

χρυσᾶ, nom. and acc. pl. neut. . . χρύσεος

χρυσᾶς, acc. pl. fem. . . . . id.

χρύσεος], η, ον, and οῦς, ῆ, οῦν . . χρυσός

χρυσῆ, nom. sing. fem. . . . . χρύσεος

χρυσῆν, acc. sing. fem. . . . . id.

χρυσίον], ίου, τό . . . . . χρυσός

χρυσίου, gen. sing. . . . . χρυσίον

χρυσίῳ, dat. sing. . . . . . id.

χρυσίων, gen. pl. . . . . . id.

χρυσοδακτύλιος],[c] ου, ὁ, ἡ, (§ 7. rem. 2) (χρυσός & δακτύλιος) *having rings of gold on the fingers*. N.T

χρυσοῖ, nom. pl. masc.—Gr. Sch. . } χρύσεος
ὅμοιοι χρυσῷ, Rec. B. C. Ln. Tdf. (Re. 9. 7) . . . . }

χρυσόλῐθος],[d] ου, ἡ, (χρυσός & λίθος) *chrysolite*, a name applied by the ancients to all gems of a gold colour; spc. the modern *topaz*, Re. 21. 20.

χρυσόν, acc. sing. . . . χρυσός

χρυσόπρᾰσος],[e] ου, ὁ, (§ 3. tab. C. a) (χρυσός &

[a] Ro. 16. 18. [b] Ac. 20. 16. [c] Ja. 2. 2. [d] Re. 21. 20. [e] Re. 21. 20.

πράσον, *a leek*) *a chrysoprase*, a species of gem of a golden green colour like that of a leek.

χρυσός], οῦ, ὁ, (§ 3. tab. C. a) *gold*, Mat. 2. 11; 23. 16, 17; meton. *gold ornaments*, 1 Ti. 2. 9; *gold coin, money*, Mat. 10. 9, et al.

χρύσεος, η, ον, contr. οῦς, ῆ, οῦν, (§ 7. rem. 5. b) *golden, of gold*, 2 Ti. 2. 20; He. 9. 4, et al.

χρυσίον, ίου, τό, (§ 3. tab. C. c) (dim. from χρυσός) *gold*, He. 9. 4; 1 Pe. 1. 7; Re. 21. 18, 21; spc. *gold when coined or manufactured; golden ornaments*, 1 Pe. 3. 3; *gold coin, money*, Ac. 3. 6; 20. 33; 1 Pe. 1. 18.

χρυσόω, ῶ, fut. ώσω, perf. pass. κεχρύσωμαι, (§ 21. tab. U) *to gild, overlay with gold, adorn or deck with gold*, Re. 17. 4; 18. 6.

χρυσοῦ, gen. sing. . . . . . . χρυσός
χρυσοῦ, gen. sing. neut. . . . . . χρύσεος
χρυσοῦν, acc. sing. masc. and neut. . . . id.
χρυσοῦς, acc. pl. masc. . . . . id.
χρυσόω, ῶ], fut. ώσω . . . . χρυσός
χρυσῷ, dat. sing. . . . . . . id.
χρυσῶν, gen. pl. . . . . . . χρύσεος
χρῶ, 2 pers. sing. pres. imper. . . . χράομαι
χρώμεθα, 1 pers. pl. pres. ind. . . . . id.
χρώμενοι, nom. pl. masc. part. pres. . . . id.

χρώς], χρωτός, ὁ, (§ 4. rem. 2. c) *the skin; the body*, Ac. 19. 12.

χρωτός,[a] gen. sing. . . . . . χρώς
χωλοί, nom. pl. masc. . . . . . χωλός
χωλόν, acc. sing. masc. and nom. neut. . . id

χωλός], ή, όν, (§ 7. tab. F. a) *crippled in the feet, limping, halting, lame*, Mat. 11. 5; 15. 30, 31, et al.; met. *limping, weak*, spiritually, He. 12. 13; *maimed, deprived of a foot*, for ἀναπηρός, Mar. 9. 45.

χωλοῦ, gen. sing. masc. . . . . . χωλός
χωλούς, acc. pl. masc. . . . . . id.
χωλῶν, gen. pl. . . . . id.

χώρα], ας, ἡ, (§ 2. tab. B. b) (χῶρος, id.) *space, room; a country, region, tract, province*, Mar. 5. 10; Lu. 2. 8; *a district, territory, environs*, Mat. 8. 28; meton. *the inhabitants of a country, region*, etc., Mar. 1. 5; Ac. 12. 20; *the country*, as opposed to the city or town, Lu. 21. 21; *a field, farm*, Lu. 12. 16; Jno. 4. 35.

χωρέω, ῶ, fut. ήσω, aor. 1, ἐχώρησα, (§ 16. tab. P) *to make room*, either by motion or capacity; *to move, pass*, Mat. 15. 17; *to proceed, go on*, 2 Pe. 3. 9; *to progress, make way*, Jno. 8. 37; trans. *to hold* as contents, *contain, afford room for*, Mar. 2. 2; Jno. 2. 6; 21. 25; met. *to give* mental *admittance to, to yield accordance*, Mat. 19. 11, 12; *to admit* to approbation and esteem, *to regard cordially*, 2 Co. 7. 2.

χωρίον, ου, τό, (§ 3. tab. C. c) (pr. dimin. of χῶρος) *a place, spot*; Mat. 26. 36; Mar. 14. 32; *a field, farm, estate, domain*, Jno. 4. 5; Ac. 1. 18, et al.

χώρᾳ, dat. sing. . . . . . . χώρα
χώραις, dat. pl. . . . . . . id.
χώραν, acc. sing. . . . . . . id.
χώρας, gen. sing. and acc. pl. . . . id.
χωρεῖ, 3 pers. sing. pres. ind. . . . χωρέω
χωρεῖν, pres. infin. . . . . . . id.
χωρείτω, 3 pers. sing. pres. imper. . . id.
χωρέω, ῶ], fut. ήσω . . . . . χώρα
χωρῆσαι, aor. 1, infin. . . . . . χωρέω
χωρήσατε, 2 pers. pl. aor. 1, imper. . . id.
χωρία, nom. pl. . . . . . . χωρίον
χωρίζεσθαι, pres. infin. mid. . . . χωρίζω
χωριζέσθω, 3 pers. sing. pres. imper. mid. id.
χωρίζεται, 3 pers. sing. pres. ind. mid. . id.
χωριζέτω, 3 pers. sing. pres. ind. act. . . id.
χωρίζω], fut. ίσω . . . . . χωρίς
χωρίον], ου, τό . . . . . χώρα
χωρίου, gen. sing. . . . . . χωρίον

χωρίς], adv. *apart*, Jno. 20. 7, *apart from, parted from*, Jno. 15. 5; Ja. 2. 18, 20, 26; *alien from*, Ep. 2. 12; *apart from, on a distinct footing from*, 1 Co. 11. 11; *apart from, distinct from, without the intervention of*, Ro. 3. 21, 28; 4. 6; *apart from* the company of, *independently of*, 1 Co. 4. 8; He. 11. 40; *without* the presence of, He. 9. 28; *without* the agency of, Jno. 1. 3; Ro. 10. 14; *without* the employment of, Mat. 13. 34; Mar. 4. 34; He.

[a] Ac. 19. 12.

7. 20, 21; 9. 7, 18, 22; *without*, Lu. 6. 49; Phi. 2. 14; 1 Ti. 2. 8; 5. 21; Phile. 14; He. 10. 28; 11. 6; 12. 8, 14; *clear from*, He. 7. 7; *irrespectively of*, Ro. 7. 8, 9; *without reckoning, besides*, Mat. 14. 21; 15. 38; 2 Co. 11. 28; *with the exception of*, He. 4. 15.

χωρίζω, fut. ίσω, aor. 1, ἐχώρισα, (§ 26. rem. 1) *to sunder, sever, disunite*, Mat. 19. 6; Ro. 8. 35, 39; mid. aor. 1, (pass. form) ἐχωρίσθην, perf. κεχώρισμαι, *to dissociate one's self, to part*, 1 Co. 7. 10, 11, 15; *to withdraw, depart*, Ac. 1. 4; 18. 1, 2; Phile. 15; *to be aloof*, He. 7. 26.

χωρίσαι, aor. 1, infin. act. . . . χωρίζω
χωρίσει, 3 pers. sing. fut. ind. act. . . id.
χωρισθείς, nom. sing. masc. part. aor. 1, pass. (mid. signif.) . . . id.
χωρισθῇ, 3 pers. sing. aor. 1, subj. pass. (mid. signif.) . . . . id.
χωρισθῆναι, aor. 1, infin. pass. (mid. signif.) id.
χωρίων, gen. pl. . . . . . χωρίον
χῶρον,[a] acc. sing. . . . . . χῶρος
χῶρος], ου, ὁ, (§ 3. tab. C. a) *Corus, or Caurus, the north-west wind*; meton. *the north-west* quarter of the heavens, Ac. 27. 12.
χωροῦσαι, nom. pl. fem. part. pres. . χωρέω
χωροῦσι, 3 pers. pl. pres. ind. . . id.

Ψ.

ψαλλέτω, 3 pers. sing. pres. imper. . . ψάλλω
ψάλλοντες, nom. pl. masc. part. pres. . . id.
ψάλλω], fut. ψαλῶ, aor. 1, ἔψηλα, (§ 27. rem. 1. b, e) (ψάω, *to touch*) *to move by a touch, to twitch; to touch, strike* the strings or chords of an instrument; absol. *to play on a stringed instrument; to sing to music*; in N.T. *to sing praises*, Ro. 15. 9; 1 Co. 14. 15; Ep. 5. 19; Ja. 5. 13.

ψαλμός, οῦ, ὁ, (§ 3. tab. C. a) *impulse, touch*, of the chords of a stringed instrument; in N.T. *a sacred song, psalm*, 1 Co. 14. 26; Ep. 5. 19, et al.

ψηλαφάω, ῶ, fut. ήσω, aor. 1, ἐψηλάφησα, (§ 18. tab. R) *to feel, handle* Lu. 24. 39; *to feel or grope for or after*, as persons in the dark, Ac. 17. 27.

ψαλμοῖς, dat. pl. . . . . . ψαλμός
ψαλμόν, acc. sing. . . . . . id.
ψαλμός], οῦ, ὁ . . . . . ψάλλω
ψαλμῷ, dat. sing. . . . . . ψαλμός
ψαλμῶν, gen. pl. . . . . . id.
ψαλῶ, 1 pers. sing. fut. ind. . . . ψάλλω
ψευδαδέλφοις, dat. pl. . . . . ψευδάδελφος
ψευδάδελφος], ου, ὁ, (§ 3. tab. C. a) (ψευδής & ἀδελφός) *a false brother, a pretended Christian*, 2 Co. 11. 26; Gal. 2. 4. N.T.
ψευδαδέλφους, acc. pl. . . . ψευδάδελφος
ψευδαπόστολοι,[b] nom. pl. . . ψευδαπόστολος
ψευδαπόστολος], ου, ὁ, (ψευδής & ἀπόστολος) *a false apostle, pretended minister of Christ*. N.T.
ψεύδει, dat. sing. . . . . . ψεῦδος
ψευδεῖς, acc. pl. masc. . . . . ψευδής
ψεύδεσθε, 2 pers. pl. pres. imper. mid. . ψεύδω
ψευδέσι, dat. pl. . . . . . ψευδής
ψευδής], έος, οῦς, ὁ, ἡ . . . . ψεύδω
ψευδοδιδάσκαλοι,[c] nom. pl. . . ψευδοδιδάσκαλος
ψευδοδιδάσκᾰλος], ου, ὁ, (ψευδής & διδάσκαλος) *a false teacher, one who inculcates false doctrines*. N.T.
ψευδολόγος], ου, ὁ, ἡ, (§ 7. rem. 2) (ψευδής & λέγω) *false-speaking*.
ψευδολόγων,[d] gen. pl. . . . ψευδολόγος
ψεύδομαι, 1 pers. sing. pres. ind. mid. . ψεύδω
ψευδομάρτυρ], ῠρος, ὁ, (§ 4. rem. 2. f) (ψευδής & μάρτυς) *a false witness*, Mat. 26. 60, bis.; 1 Co. 15. 15.

ψευδομαρτῠρέω, ῶ, fut. ήσω, (§ 16. tab. P) *to bear false witness, give false testimony*, Mat. 19. 18; Mar. 14. 56, 57, et al.

ψευδομαρτυρία, ας, ἡ, (§ 2. tab. B. b, and rem. 2) *false witness, false testimony*, Mat. 15. 19; 26. 59.

ψευδομάρτυρες, nom. pl. . . . ψευδομάρτυρ
ψευδομαρτυρέω, ῶ], fut. ήσω . . id.
ψευδομαρτυρήσεις, 2 pers. sing. fut. ind. ψευδομαρτυρέω
ψευδομαρτυρήσῃς, 2 pers. sing. aor. 1, subj. . id.
ψευδομαρτυρία], ας, ἡ . . . . ψευδομάρτυρ
ψευδομαρτυρίαι, nom. pl. . . . ψευδομαρτυρία
ψευδομαρτυρίαν, acc. sing. . . . id.
ψευδομαρτύρων, gen. pl. . . . ψευδομάρτυρ
ψευδόμεθα, 1 pers. pl. pres. ind. mid. . . ψεύδω
ψευδόμενοι, nom. pl. masc. part. pres. mid. id.
ψεύδονται, 3 pers. pl. pres. ind. mid. id.

[a] Ac. 27. 12 [b] 2 Co. 11. 13. [c] 2 Pe. 2. 1. [d] 1 Ti. 4. 2.

ψευδοπροφῆται, nom. pl. . . ψευδοπροφήτης
ψευδοπροφήταις, dat. pl. . . . . id.
ψευδοπροφήτην, acc. sing. . . . id.
ψευδοπροφήτης], ου, ὁ, (§ 2. tab. B. c) (ψευδής & προφήτης) *a false prophet, one who falsely claims to speak by divine inspiration*, whether as a foreteller of future events, or as a teacher of doctrines, Mat. 7. 15; 24. 24, et al.
ψευδοπροφήτου, gen. sing. . . ψευδοπροφήτης
ψευδοπροφητῶν, gen. pl. . . . id.
ψεῦδος], εος, ους, τό . . . . ψεύδω
ψεύδους, gen. sing. . . . . ψεῦδος
ψευδόχριστοι, nom. pl. . . . ψευδόχριστος
ψευδόχριστος], ου, ὁ, (§ 3. tab. C. a) (ψευδής & χριστός) *a false Christ, pretended Messiah*, Mat. 24. 24; Mar. 13. 22. N.T.

ψεύδω], fut. ψεύσω, (§ 23. rem. 1. c) *to deceive*; mid. *to speak falsely or deceitfully, utter falsehood, lie*, Mat. 5. 11; Ro. 9. 1, et al.; trans. *to deceive, or attempt to deceive, by a lie*, Ac. 5. 3.

ψευδής, έος, οῦς, ὁ, ἡ, (§ 7. tab. G. b) *false, lying*, Ac. 6. 13; Re. 2. 2; in N.T. pl. *maintainers of* religious *falsehood, corrupters of the truth* of God, Re. 21. 8.

ψεῦδος, εος, τό, (§ 5. tab. E. b) *falsehood*, Jno. 8. 44; Ep. 4. 25; 2 Thes. 2. 9, 11; 1 Jno. 2. 27; in N.T. religious *falsehood, perversion* of religious truth, *false religion*, Ro. 1. 25; *the practices of false religion*, Re. 21. 27; 22. 15.

ψεῦσμα, ατος, τό, (§ 4. tab. D. c) *a falsehood, lie*; in N.T. *delinquency*, Ro. 3. 7.

ψεύστης, ου, ὁ, (§ 2. tab. B. c) *one who utters a falsehood, a liar*, Jno. 8. 44, 55, et al.; in N.T. *a delinquent*, Ro. 3. 4.

ψευδώνυμος], ου, ὁ, ἡ, (§ 7. rem. 2) (ψευδής & ὄνομα) *falsely named, falsely called*.
ψευδωνύμου,[a] gen. sing. fem. . . . ψευδώνυμος
ψεύσασθαι, aor. 1, infin. masc. . . . ψεύδω
ψεῦσμα], ατος, τό . . . . id.
ψεύσματι,[b] dat. sing . . . ψεῦσμα
ψεῦσται, nom. pl. . . . . ψεύστης
ψεύσταις, dat. pl. . . . . id.
ψεύστην, acc. sing. . . . . id.
ψεύστης], ου, ὁ . . . . . ψεύδω

ψηλαφάω, ῶ], fut. ήσω . . . ψάλλω
ψηλαφήσατε, 2 pers. pl. aor. 1, imper. . ψηλαφάω
ψηλαφήσειαν, 3 p. pl. aor. Æol. (§ 13. rem. 11. note) id.
ψηλαφωμένῳ, dat. sing. neut. part. pres. pass. id.
ψηφίζει, 3 pers. sing. pres. ind. . . . ψηφίζω
ψηφίζω], fut. ίσω . . . . ψῆφος
ψηφισάτω, 3 pers. sing. aor. 1, imper. . . ψηφίζω
ψῆφον, acc. sing. . . . . ψῆφος

ψῆφος], ου, ἡ, (§ 3. tab. C. b) *a small stone, pebble*; *a pebble* variously employed, especially in a ballot; hence, *a vote, suffrage*, Ac. 26. 10; *a pebble or stone*, probably given as a token, Re. 2. 17, bis.

ψηφίζω, fut. ίσω, (§ 26. rem. 1) *to reckon by means of pebbles, compute by counters*; hence genr. *to compute, reckon, calculate*, Lu. 14. 28; Re. 13. 18.

ψιθυρισμοί,[c] nom. pl. . . . ψιθυρισμός
ψιθυρισμός], οῦ, ὁ, (ψιθυρίζω, *to whisper*) *a whispering*; *a* calumnious *whispering, detraction*, 2 Co. 12. 20. L.G.
ψιθυριστάς,[d] acc. pl. . . . . ψιθυριστής
ψιθυριστής], οῦ, ὁ, (§ 2. tab. B. c) (ψιθυρίζω) *a whisperer*; *a* calumnious *whisperer, detractor*, Ro. 1. 30.
ψιχίον], ίου, τό, (§ 3. tab. C. c) (dimin. of ψίξ, *a fragment, morsel*) *a morsel, crumb, bit*, Mat. 15. 27; Mar. 7. 28; Lu. 16. 21. N.T.
ψιχίων, gen. pl. . . . . . ψιχίον
ψυγήσεται,[e] 3 pers. sing. fut. 2. ind. pass (§ 24. rem. 8 c) . . . ψύχω
ψυχαί, nom. pl. . . . . ψυχή
ψυχαῖς, dat. pl. . . . . id.
ψυχάς, acc. pl. . . . . id.
ψύχει, dat. sing. . . . . ψῦχος
ψυχή], ῆς, ἡ . . . . ψύχω
ψυχή, voc. sing. . . . . ψυχή
ψυχῇ, dat. sing. . . . . id.
ψυχήν, acc. sing. . . . . id.
ψυχῆς, gen. sing. . . . . id.
ψυχική, nom. sing. fem. . . . ψυχικός
ψυχικοί, nom. pl. masc. . . . id.
ψυχικόν, nom. sing. neut. . . . id.
ψυχικός], ή, όν . . . . . ψύχω
ψῦχος], εος, τό . . . . id.
ψυχρός], ά, όν . . . . . id.
ψυχροῦ, gen. sing. neut. . . . ψυχρός

---

[a] 1 Ti. 6. 20. [b] Ro. 3. 7. [c] 2 Co. 12. 20. [d] Ro. 1. 30 [e] Mat. 24. 12.

ψύχω], fut. ξω, aor. 2, pass. ἐψύγην, fut. 2, ψυγήσομαι, (§ 24. rem. 8. c) *to breathe; to cool;* pass. *to be cooled;* met. of affection, Mat. 24. 12.

ψυχή, ῆς, ἡ, (§ 2. tab. B. a) *breath; the principle of animal life; the life,* Mat. 2. 20; 6. 25; Mar. 3. 4; Lu. 21. 19; Jno. 10. 11, et al.; *an inanimate being,* 1 Co. 15. 45; *a* human *individual, soul,* Ac. 2. 41; 3. 23; 7. 14; 27. 37; Ro. 13. 1; 1 Pe. 3. 20; *the* immaterial *soul,* Mat. 10. 28; 1 Pe. 1. 9; 2. 11, 25; 4. 19, et al.; *the soul* as the seat of religious and moral sentiment, Mat. 11. 29; Ac. 14. 2, 22; 15. 24; Ep. 6. 6, et al.; *the soul,* as a seat of feeling, Mat. 12. 18; 26. 38, et al.; *the soul, the* inner *self,* Lu. 12. 19.

ψυχϊκός ή, όν, (§ 7. tab. F. a) *pertaining to the life or the soul;* in N.T. *animal,* as distinguished from spiritual subsistence, 1 Co. 15. 44, 46; *occupied with mere animal things, animal, sensual,* 1 Co. 2. 14; Ja. 3. 15; Jude 19.

ψῦχος, εος, τό, (§ 5. tab. E. b) *cold,* Jno. 18. 18; Ac. 28. 2; 2 Co. 11. 27.

ψυχρός, ά, όν, (§ 7. rem. 1) *cool, cold,* Mat. 10. 42; met. Re. 3. 15, 16.

ψυχῶν, gen. pl. . . . . . . ψυχή
ψώμιζε, 2 pers. sing. pres. imper. . . ψωμίζω

ψωμίζω], fut. ίσω, (§ 26. rem. 1) (ψωμός, *a bit, morsel*) pr. *to feed by morsels;* hence, genr. *to feed, supply with food,* Ro. 12. 20; *to bestow in supplying food,* 1 Co. 13. 3.

ψωμίον], ου, τό, (§ 3. tab. C. c) (dimin. of ψωμός, from ψάω, *to break into bits*) *a bit, morsel, mouthful,* Jno. 13. 26, 27, 30.

ψωμίσω, 1 pers. sing. aor. 1, subj.—Gr. Sch. Tdf. } ψωμίζω
ψωμίζω, Rec. (1 Co. 13. 3) }
ψώχοντες,[a] nom. pl. masc. part. pres. . ψώχω

ψώχω], fut. ξω, (§ 23. rem. 1. b) (ψάω) *to rub in pieces,* as the ears of grain.

Ω.

Ω, ω, *Omega,* the last letter of the Greek alphabet, hence met. τὸ Ω, *the last,* Re. 1. 8, 11; 21. 6; 22. 13.

ὦ, interject. *O!* Mat. 15. 28; 17. 17, et al.

ὦ, 1 pers. sing. pres. subj. . . . . . εἰμί
ᾧ, dat. sing. masc. or neut. . . . . ὅς

Ὠβήδ], ὁ, *Obed,* pr. name, indecl.—R. Gr. Sch. Ἰωβής, A. B. C. Ln. Tdf.

ᾠδαῖς, dat. pl. . . . . . . ᾠδή
ὧδε], adv. . . . . ὅδε

ᾠδή], ῆς, ἡ, (§ 2. tab. B. a) (contr. for ἀοιδή, from ἀείδω) *an ode, song, hymn,* Ep. 5. 19; Col. 3. 16; Re. 5. 9; 14. 3; 15. 3.

ᾠδήν, acc. sing. . . . . . . ᾠδή
ὠδίς], ῖνος, (in N.T. ὠδίν) ἡ . . . ὀδύνη
ὠδῖνας, acc. pl. . . . . . . ὠδίν
ὠδίνουσα, nom. sing. fem. part. pres. . . ὠδίνω
ὠδίνω], fut. ινῶ . . . . . . ὀδύνη
ὠδίνων, gen. pl. . . . . . . ὠδίν
ᾠκοδομήθη, 3 pers. s. aor. 1, ind. pass. (§ 13. rem. 2) οἰκοδομέω
ᾠκοδόμησε, 3 pers. sing. aor. 1, ind. act. . id.
ᾠκοδόμητο, 3 pers. sing. pluperf. pass. . id.
ᾠκοδόμουν, 3 pers. pl. imperf. act. . . id.
ὦμεν, 1 pers. pl. pres. subj. . . . εἰμί
ὡμίλει, 3 pers. sing. imperf. (§ 13. rem. 2) . ὁμιλέω
ὡμίλουν, 3 pers. pl. imperf. . . . id.
ὡμοιώθη, 3 pers. sing. aor. 1, ind. pass. . ὁμοιόω
ὡμοιώθημεν, 1 pers. pl. aor. 1, ind. pass. . id.
ὡμολόγησας, 2 pers. sing. aor. 1, ind. . . ὁμολογέω
ὡμολόγησε, 3 pers. sing. aor. 1, ind. . id.
ὡμολόγουν, 3 pers. pl. imperf. . . . id.

ὦμος], ου, ὁ, (§ 3. tab. C. a) *the shoulder,* Mat. 23. 4; Lu. 15. 5.

ὤμοσα, 1 pers. sing. aor. 1, ind. . . ὄμνυμι
ὤμοσε, 3 pers. sing. aor. 1, ind. . . . id.
ὤμους, acc. pl. . . . . . . ὦμος
ὤν, nom. sing. masc. part. pres. . . . εἰμί
ὧν, gen. pl. . . . . ὅς
ὠνείδιζον, 3 pers. pl. imperf. . . . ὀνειδίζω
ὠνείδισε, 3 pers. sing. aor. 1, ind. . . id.

ὠνέομαι, οῦμαι], fut. ήσομαι, aor. 1, ὠνησάμην, (§ 17. tab. Q) *to buy, purchase.*

ὠνήσατο,[b] 3 pers. sing. aor. 1, ind. . . ὠνέομαι
ὠνόμασε, 3 pers. sing. aor. 1, ind. act. . ὀνομάζω
ὠνομάσθη, 3 pers. sing. aor. 1, ind. pass. . id.

ᾠόν],[c] οῦ, τό, (§ 3. tab. C. c) *an egg.*

ὥρα], ας, ἡ, (§ 2. tab. B. b) *a limited portion of time,* marked out by part of a settled routine

[a] Lu. 6. 1. [b] Ac. 7. 16. [c] Lu. 11. 12.

or train of circumstances; *a season of the year; time of day*, Mat. 14. 15; Mar. 6. 35; 11. 11; *an hour*, Mat. 20. 3; Jno. 11. 9, et al.; in N.T. *an eventful season*, 1 Jno. 2. 18, bis.; Re. 3. 10; 14. 7; *due time*, Jno. 16. 21; Ro. 13. 11; *a destined period, hour*, Mat. 26. 45; Mar. 14. 35; Jno. 2. 4; 7. 30, et al.; *a short period*, Mat. 26. 40; Jno. 5. 35; 2 Co. 7. 8; Gal. 2. 5; 1 Thes. 2. 17; Phile. 15; *a point of time, time*, Mat. 8. 13; 24. 42; Lu. 2. 38, et al.

ὡραῖος, α, ον, (§ 7. rem. 1) *timely, seasonable; in prime, blooming;* in N.T. *beautiful*, Mat. 23. 27; Ac. 3. 2, 10; Ro. 10. 15.

ὥρᾳ, dat. sing. . . . . . . ὥρα

ὧραι, nom. pl. . . . . . . id.

ὡραίᾳ, dat. sing. fem. . . . . ὡραῖος

ὡραίαν, acc. sing. fem. . . . . id.

ὡραῖοι, nom. pl. masc. . . . . id.

ὡραῖος], α, ον . . . . . ὥρα

ὥραν, acc. sing. . . . . . id.

ὥρας, gen. sing. and acc. pl. . . . id.

ὠργίσθη, 3 pers. sing. aor. 1, ind. pass. . ὀργίζω

ὠργίσθησαν, 3 pers. pl. aor. 1, ind. pass. . id.

ὤρθριζε,[a] 3 pers. sing. imperf. . . . ὀρθρίζω

ὥρισαν, 3 pers. pl. aor. 1, ind. act. . . ὁρίζω

ὥρισε, 3 pers. sing. aor. 1, ind. act. . . id.

ὡρισμένῃ, dat. sing. fem. part. perf. pass. . id.

ὡρισμένον, acc. sing. neut. part. perf. pass . id.

ὡρισμένος, nom. sing. masc. part. perf. pass. id.

ὥρμησαν, 3 pers. pl. aor. 1, ind. . . ὁρμάω

ὥρμησε, 3 pers. sing. aor. 1, ind. . . id.

ὤρυξε, 3 pers. sing. aor. 1, ind. act. . ὀρύσσω

ὠρύομαι], fut. ύσομαι, (§ 14. tab. N) *to howl; to roar*, as a lion, 1 Pe. 5. 8.

ὠρυόμενος,[b] nom. sing. masc. part. pres. . ὠρύομαι

ὠρχήσασθε, 2 pers. pl. aor. 1, ind. . . ὀρχέομαι

ὠρχήσατο, 3 pers. sing. aor. 1, ind. . . id.

ὡρῶν, gen. pl. . . . . . ὥρα

ὡς], adv. and conj. . . . . . ὅς

ὡσαννά], (Heb. הוֹשִׁיעָה־נָּא) *hosanna! save now, succour now*, Mat. 21. 9, 15, et al.

ὡσαύτως], adv. (ὡς & αὔτως, αὐτός) *just so, in just the same way or manner, likewise*, Mat. 20. 5; 21. 30, et al.

ὡσεί], adv. (ὡς & εἰ) *as if; as it were, as, like*, Mat 3. 16; 9. 36, et al.; with terms of number or quantity, *about*, Mat. 14. 21; Lu. 1. 56; 22. 41, 59.

Ὡσηέ],[c] ὁ, *Osee, Hosea*, pr. name, indecl.

ὦσι, 3 pers. pl. pres. subj. . . . . εἰμί

ὠσί, dat. pl. (§ 4. rem. 3. b) . . . οὖς

ὥσπερ], adv. (ὡς & περ) *just as, as, like as*, Mat. 6. 2; 24. 38; 1 Thes. 5. 3, et al.

ὡσπερεί],[d] adv. (ὥσφερ & εἰ) *just as if; as it were*, 1 Co. 15. 8.

ὥστε], conj. (ὡς & τε) *so that, so as that, so as to*, Mat. 8. 24; Mar. 2. 12; Ac. 14. 1; Gal. 2. 13; as an illative particle, *therefore, consequently*, Mat. 12. 12; 23. 31, et al.; in N.T. as a particle of design, *in order that, in order to*, Lu. 9. 52.

ὦτα, nom. and acc. pl. . . . οὖς

ὠτάριον, ου, τό,—B. D. Ln. Tdf. . . } id.
ὠτίον, Rec. Gr. Sch. Mar. 14. 47. . }

ὠτίον], ου, τό . . . . . . id.

ὠτίου, gen. sing. . . . . . . ὠτίον

ὤφειλε, 3 pers. sing. imperf. . . . ὀφείλω

ὠφείλομεν, 1 pers. pl. imperf. . . . id.

ὤφειλον, 1 pers. sing. imperf. . . . id.

ὠφελεῖ, 3 pers. sing. pres. ind. act. . . ὠφελέω

ὠφέλεια], ας, ἡ . . . . . . ὄφελος

ὠφελείας, gen. sing. . . . . ὠφέλεια

ὠφελεῖται, 3 pers. sing. pres. ind. pass. . ὠφελέω

ὠφελεῖτε, 2 pers. pl. pres. ind. act. . . id.

ὠφελέω, ῶ], fut. ήσω . . . . . ὄφελος

ὠφεληθεῖσα, nom. sing. fem. part. aor. 1, pass. . . . . . . ὠφελέω

ὠφεληθῇς, 2 pers. sing. aor. 1, subj. pass. id.

ὠφελήθησαν, 3 pers. pl. aor. 1, ind. pass. . id.

ὠφεληθήσεται, 3 pers. sing. fut. ind. pass.—B. Ln. Tdf. . . . . } id.
ὠφελεῖται, Rec. Gr. Sch. (Mat. 16. 26) }

ὠφελήσει, 3 pers. sing. fut. ind. act. . . id.

ὠφέλησε, 3 pers. sing. aor. 1, ind. act. . id.

ὠφελήσω, 1 pers. sing. fut. ind. act. . . id.

ὠφέλιμα, nom. pl. neut. . . . ὠφέλιμος

ὠφέλιμος], ου, ὁ, ἡ . . . . . ὄφελος

ὠφελοῦμαι, 1 pers. sing. pres. ind. pass. . ὠφελέω

ὤφθη, 3 pers. sing. aor. 1, ind. pass. . . ὁράω

ὤφθην, 1 pers. sing. aor. 1, ind. pass. (§ 36. rem. 1) . . . . id.

ὤφθησαν, 3 pers. pl. aor. 1, ind. pass. . . id.

---

[a] Lu. 31. 38. [b] 1 Pe. 5. 8. [c] Ro. 9. 25. [d] 1 Co. 15. 8.